# Cadence
## A Study of Closure in Tonal Music

William E. Caplin

OXFORD
UNIVERSITY PRESS

# OXFORD
UNIVERSITY PRESS

Oxford University Press is a department of the University of Oxford. It furthers
the University's objective of excellence in research, scholarship, and education
by publishing worldwide. Oxford is a registered trade mark of Oxford University
Press in the UK and certain other countries.

Published in the United States of America by Oxford University Press
198 Madison Avenue, New York, NY 10016, United States of America.

© Oxford University Press 2024

All rights reserved. No part of this publication may be reproduced, stored in
a retrieval system, or transmitted, in any form or by any means, without the
prior permission in writing of Oxford University Press, or as expressly permitted
by law, by license, or under terms agreed with the appropriate reproduction
rights organization. Inquiries concerning reproduction outside the scope of the
above should be sent to the Rights Department, Oxford University Press, at the
address above.

You must not circulate this work in any other form
and you must impose this same condition on any acquirer.

CIP data is on file at the Library of Congress

ISBN 978-0-19-778216-3 (pbk.)
ISBN 978-0-19-005644-5 (hbk.)

DOI: 10.1093/oso/9780190056445.001.0001

Paperback printed by Sheridan Books, Inc., United States of America
Hardback printed by Bridgeport National Bindery, Inc., United States of America

# Cadence

*For my sister, Wendy Ann Caplin*

# Contents

*Preface xiii*
*Acknowledgments xvii*
*Guide to the Analytical Annotations xix*

1. Ideas of Closure   1

    1.1. Closure in Literature   2
    1.2. Closure in Music   4
       *1.2.1. Leonard Meyer   4*
       *1.2.2. Kofi Agawu   6*
       *1.2.3. Robert Hatten   6*
       *1.2.4. Patrick McCreless   7*
       *1.2.5. Mark Anson-Cartwright   8*

## PART I.   THE CLASSICAL CADENCE   11

2. General Concepts of the Classical Cadence   13

    2.1. Traditional Notions of Cadence   14
    2.2. Cadence as Formal Closure   15
       *2.2.1. Formal Units Closed by Cadence; Cadence and Phrase   16*
       *2.2.2. Cadence and Higher-Level Formal Units   17*
    2.3. Cadence as Harmony; Harmony as Cadence   20
       *2.3.1. Progression Types   21*
          *2.3.1.1. Prolongational Progressions   22*
          *2.3.1.2. Sequential Progressions   22*
          *2.3.1.3. Cadential Progressions   22*

2.3.2. Ambiguity of Progression Types  24
2.4. Bass-Line Melody and Cadence  25
2.5. Cadential Arrival versus Cadential Function  31
2.6. Cadential Function versus Cadential Content  33
2.7. Limited Cadential Scope  36
2.8. Cadential Function versus Postcadential Function  38
    2.8.1. Theoretical Background  38
    2.8.2. Postcadential Function as "Confirmation"  40
    2.8.3. Hepokoski and Darcy's Critique  41
    2.8.4. Two "Registers" of Closure  43
    2.8.5. Consecutive (Repeated) PACs  44
2.9. "End" versus "Stop"  46
2.10. Cadence as Punctuation  48
2.11. Cadential Strength—Syntactical versus Rhetorical  50

# 3. Basic Cadence Types: Morphology and Function  55

3.1. Perfect Authentic Cadence  56
    3.1.1. Morphology—Harmonic Content  56
        3.1.1.1. Stages of the Cadence Schema  56
        3.1.1.2. Stage 1—Initial Tonic  57
        3.1.1.3. Stage 2—Pre-dominant  58
        3.1.1.4. Stage 3—Dominant  59
        3.1.1.5. Stage 4—Final Tonic  60
        3.1.1.6. Complete versus Incomplete Cadential Progressions  60
        3.1.1.7. Boundaries of the Cadential Progression  60
    3.1.2. Morphology—Melodic Content  62
        3.1.2.1. Basic Patterns  63
        3.1.2.2. Varied Patterns  69
        3.1.2.3. Combined Patterns  70
        3.1.2.4. Additional Patterns  75
    3.1.3. Function  79
        3.1.3.1. Standard Functions of the PAC  79
        3.1.3.2. Exceptional Situations  80

3.2. Imperfect Authentic Cadence  82
    3.2.1. Morphology  83
        3.2.1.1. Basic Tenor Stream ($\hat{8}/\hat{6}/\hat{5}/\hat{3}$); Varied ($\hat{5}/\hat{6}/\hat{5}/\hat{3}$)  83
        3.2.1.2. Prinner Cadence  85
        3.2.1.3. Other Patterns; Melodic Diversion  86
        3.2.1.4. Combined Patterns  88
        3.2.1.5. Ending on $\hat{5}$?  90
    3.2.2. Function  93
        3.2.2.1. Independent IAC  93
        3.2.2.2. Way-Station IAC  94
        3.2.2.3. Additional Functions of the IAC  96
3.3. Half Cadence  101
    3.3.1. General Conditions for Half Cadence  102
    3.3.2. Morphology—Harmonic Content  103
        3.3.2.1. Stage 1—Initial Tonic  104
        3.3.2.2. Stage 2—Pre-dominant  104
        3.3.2.3. Stage 3—Dominant  104
    3.3.3. Morphology—Melodic Content  105
        3.3.3.1. Simple (I–V) HC  106
        3.3.3.2. Converging HC  106
        3.3.3.3. Expanding HC  112
        3.3.3.4. Miscellaneous Issues  114
    3.3.4. Function  116
        3.3.4.1. Levels of Phrase Functionality  116
        3.3.4.2. Levels of Thematic Functionality  118
        3.3.4.3. Some Functional Generalizations  120
    3.3.5. Special Cases  121
        3.3.5.1. Reinterpreted HC  121
        3.3.5.2. Reopened HC  124
3.4. Additional Aspects of the Basic Cadence Types  129
    3.4.1. Meter  129
        3.4.1.1. A Ratio Model of Metrical Strength  130
        3.4.1.2. Metrically Weaker Cadences  132
        3.4.1.3. Hypermetrical Considerations  137

- 3.4.1.4. Metrical Weighting—Syntactical or Rhetorical? 138
- 3.4.2. Texture 139
  - 3.4.2.1. Textural Types 139
  - 3.4.2.2. Texture and Cadence 139
  - 3.4.2.3. Covered Cadence 140
- 3.5. Other Cadence Types 142
  - 3.5.1. "Contrapuntal Cadence"; Prolongational Closure 142
  - 3.5.2. "Plagal Cadence" 146

# 4. Cadential Deviations 150
- 4.1. Deceptive Cadence 151
  - 4.1.1. Morphology 153
  - 4.1.2. Function 157
    - 4.1.2.1. Way-Station Deceptive Cadence, Replacing a PAC 158
    - 4.1.2.2. Way-Station Deceptive Cadence, Replacing an IAC 160
    - 4.1.2.3. Way-Station Deceptive Cadence, Denied 162
    - 4.1.2.4. Independent Deceptive Cadence 164
    - 4.1.2.5. Noncadential Uses of a Deceptive Cadential Progression 167
    - 4.1.2.6. Deceptive Resolution of a Noncadential Dominant 169
    - 4.1.2.7. Elided Deceptive Cadence 169
- 4.2. Evaded Cadence 169
  - 4.2.1. Morphology 170
    - 4.2.1.1. Harmonic Content 170
    - 4.2.1.2. Melodic Content 174
  - 4.2.2. Function 175
    - 4.2.2.1. Way Station 175
    - 4.2.2.2. One-More-Time Technique 176
    - 4.2.2.3. New Material 177
- 4.3. Abandoned Cadence 178
  - 4.3.1. Cadential Dominant Undermined by Inversion 179
  - 4.3.2. Cadential Dominant Replaced by Inverted Dominant 182
    - 4.3.2.1. Replaced by $V_2^4$ 182
    - 4.3.2.2. Replaced by $V_5^6$ 183
  - 4.3.3. Cadential Dominant Replaced by Nondominant Harmony 183
  - 4.3.4. Prolongational versus Cadential; Harmonic Expansion 185
  - 4.3.5. Cadential Abandonment and Harmonic Reduction 186
- 4.4. Dominant Arrival 187
  - 4.4.1. Arrival on a Final Dominant 188
  - 4.4.2. Arrival on a Terminal Dominant 192
  - 4.4.3. Premature Dominant Arrival 193
    - 4.4.3.1. PDA on a Final Dominant 194
    - 4.4.3.2. PDA on a Terminal Dominant 195
    - 4.4.3.3. Hyperdominant Prolongations 202
  - 4.4.4. Additional Issues 202
    - 4.4.4.1. Dominant Arrival of Limited Scope 202
    - 4.4.4.2. Reinterpreted Dominant Arrival 203
    - 4.4.4.3. Reopened Dominant Arrival 204
    - 4.4.4.4. Doppia PDA versus Doppia HC 205
    - 4.4.4.5. Burstein's Critique 207
- 4.5. Combinations of Deviations 208
- 4.6. Cadential Ambiguities 209
  - 4.6.1. Evaded versus Deceptive (Elided) 209
  - 4.6.2. Evaded versus Authentic (Elided) 211
  - 4.6.3. Evaded versus IAC (Elided) 213
  - 4.6.4. Evaded versus Covered PAC 214
  - 4.6.5. Evaded versus HC (Dominant Arrival) 217
  - 4.6.6. Abandoned versus Deceptive 217
  - 4.6.7. Multiple Ambiguities 218
    - 4.6.7.1. Mozart, Piano Sonata in A Minor, K. 310, i, mm. 1–10 218
    - 4.6.7.2. Haydn, String Quartet in D, Op. 71, no 3, iii, mm. 1–10 220

# 5. Cadential Expansion 223
- 5.1. Perfect Authentic Cadence 224

5.1.1. *Harmonic Content* 224

    5.1.1.1. *Stage 1—Initial Tonic* 224

    5.1.1.2. *Stage 2—Pre-dominant* 236

    5.1.1.3. *Stage 3—Dominant* 247

    5.1.1.4. *Diversity of Harmonic Content; Bass-Line Complexities* 250

    5.1.1.5. *Ambiguous Onset of an ECP* 257

5.1.2. *Melodic Content* 259

    5.1.2.1. *Basic Simple ($\hat{3}/\hat{2}/\hat{2}/\hat{1}$); with Cadential Six-Four ($\hat{3}/\hat{2}/\hat{3}\text{-}\hat{2}/\hat{1}$)* 260

    5.1.2.2. *Basic Soprano ($\hat{5}/\hat{4}/\hat{2}/\hat{1}$); with Cadential Six-Four ($\hat{5}/\hat{4}/\hat{3}\text{-}\hat{2}/\hat{1}$)* 260

    5.1.2.3. *Basic Alto ($\hat{3}/\hat{2}/\hat{7}/\hat{1}$); with Cadential Six-Four ($\hat{3}/\hat{2}/\hat{1}\text{-}\hat{7}/\hat{1}$)* 261

    5.1.2.4. *Basic Tenor ($\hat{8}/\hat{6}/\hat{5}/\hat{1}$); with Cadential Six-Four ($\hat{8}/\hat{6}/\hat{5}\text{-}\hat{4}/\hat{1}$)* 261

    5.1.2.5. *Varied Simple ($\hat{1}/\hat{2}/\hat{2}/\hat{1}$); with Cadential Six-Four ($\hat{1}/\hat{2}/\hat{3}\text{-}\hat{2}/\hat{1}$)* 261

    5.1.2.6. *Varied Soprano ($\hat{3}/\hat{4}/\hat{2}/\hat{1}$); with Cadential Six-Four ($\hat{3}/\hat{4}/\hat{3}\text{-}\hat{2}/\hat{1}$)* 263

    5.1.2.7. *Varied Alto ($\hat{1}/\hat{2}/\hat{7}/\hat{1}$); with Cadential Six-Four ($\hat{1}/\hat{2}/\hat{1}\text{-}\hat{7}/\hat{1}$)* 263

    5.1.2.8. *Varied Tenor ($\hat{5}/\hat{6}/\hat{5}/\hat{1}$); with Cadential Six-Four ($\hat{5}/\hat{6}/\hat{5}\text{-}\hat{5}\,(\hat{4})/\hat{1}$)* 263

    5.1.2.9. *Successive Combinations* 263

    5.1.2.10. *Simultaneous Combinations* 264

    5.1.2.11. *Additional Patterns* 265

5.2. Imperfect Authentic Cadence 267

5.3. Half Cadence 268

    5.3.1. *Minimum Length* 268

    5.3.2. *Harmonic Content* 271

        5.3.2.1. *Stage 1* 271

        5.3.2.2. *Stage 2* 272

        5.3.2.3. *Stage 3* 272

    5.3.3. *Melodic Content* 273

        5.3.3.1. *Simple HC* 273

        5.3.3.2. *Converging HC* 273

        5.3.3.3. *Expanding HC* 273

        5.3.3.4. *Converging/Expanding; Expanding/Converging* 273

5.4. Deviations 273

    5.4.1. *Minimum Size of Expansion* 274

    5.4.2. *One-More-Time and Related Repetitions* 274

    5.4.3. *Deceptive-Authentic Combinations (DCP-ACP); Melodic Content* 275

    5.4.4. *Abandoned ECP* 275

    5.4.5. *Dominant Arrival* 279

5.5. A Cadential Conundrum 280

5.6. Expanded Cadential Progressions in Beethoven's Symphonies 281

    5.6.1. *Symphony No. 1 in C, Op. 21, i, Subordinate-Theme Group* 281

    5.6.2. *Symphony No. 2 in D, Op. 36, iv, Coda* 282

    5.6.3. *Symphony No. 3 in E-flat ("Eroica"), Op. 55, i, Second Subordinate Theme* 284

    5.6.4. *Symphony No. 5 in C Minor, Op. 67, iv, Subordinate Theme, Coda Themes* 287

    5.6.5. *Symphony No. 6 in F ("Pastoral"), Op. 68, iv, Subordinate Theme* 292

    5.6.6. *Symphony No. 7 in A, Op. 92, i, Coda Theme* 294

    5.6.7. *Symphony No. 9 in D Minor ("Choral"), Op. 125, i, Main Theme* 294

    5.6.8. *Symphony No. 9 in D Minor ("Choral"), Op. 125, iv, Coda* 298

# PART II. CADENCE IN OTHER TONAL STYLES 303

## 6. Cadence in the High Baroque 305

6.1. Authentic Cadence 307

    6.1.1. *Perfect Authentic Cadence* 307

    6.1.2. *Harmonic Content* 307

    6.1.3. *Imperfect Authentic Cadence* 310

    6.1.4. *Cadential Deviations (Authentic Cadence)* 312

        6.1.4.1. *Deceptive Cadence* 313

        6.1.4.2. *Evaded Cadence* 317

        6.1.4.3. *Abandoned Cadence* 320

    6.1.5. *Cadential Extension and Expansion* 323

6.1.5.1. Consecutive PACs   323

6.1.5.2. Expansion via Slower Tempo; Hemiola; Change of Tempo Marking   325

6.1.5.3. Expanded Cadential Progression   326

6.1.5.4. Deceptive-Authentic Combinations (DCP-ACP); Pulcinella   329

6.2. Half Cadence   333

6.2.1. Harmonic, Tonal, and Formal Functions   333

6.2.2. Dominant Arrival   339

6.2.3. Precadential Dominant Expansion   340

6.3. Miscellaneous Issues   344

6.3.1. Cadential Content versus Cadential Function; Cadences of Limited Scope   344

6.3.2. Prolongational Closure   346

6.3.3. "Plagal" Cadence; Tonic Arrival   348

6.4. Cadence in Fugue: J. S. Bach's *Well-Tempered Clavier*   350

6.4.1. General Concepts and Terminology   351

6.4.2. Tonal Functions of Cadence in Fugue   352

6.4.3. Formal Functions of Cadence in Fugue   352

6.4.4. Subject-Ending Cadences   355

6.4.5. Expositions Concluding with an S-Ending Cadence   357

6.4.6. Final Cadence as S-Ending   361

6.4.7. Cadential Deviations and Cadential Blurring   364

6.4.8. Three Case Studies   367

6.4.8.1. Fugue in D, WTC 1   367

6.4.8.2. Fugue in E-flat, WTC 1   370

6.4.8.3. Fugue in G-sharp Minor, WTC 1   372

7. Cadence in the Galant Era   379

7.1. Morphology of the Galant Cadence   380

7.1.1. Gjerdingen's Galant Clausulae   380

7.1.2. Prinner Cadence   384

7.1.3. Miscellaneous Variants   391

7.1.4. Melodic "Overhang"   392

7.2. Cadential Deviations   396

7.2.1. Evaded Cadence   397

7.2.2. Deceptive Cadence   399

7.2.3. Abandoned Cadence   400

7.2.4. Dominant Arrival   402

7.3. Extension and Expansion Techniques   403

7.3.1. Consecutive Cadences and Codettas   404

7.3.2. Expanded Cadential Progression   405

7.3.3. Pulcinella   408

7.3.4. Dominant Expansions—Penultimate, Ultimate, Precadential   409

7.3.4.1. Expanded Penultimate Dominant   409

7.3.4.2. Internal HC (or Dominant Arrival)   409

7.3.4.3. Precadential Dominant Expansion   410

7.4. Galant Cadence in Relation to Formal Functions   412

7.4.1. Main Theme   412

7.4.2. Transition; Fusion Processes   415

7.4.2.1. Fusion of Main Theme and Transition   415

7.4.2.2. Fusion of Transition and Subordinate Theme   416

7.4.3. Subordinate Theme; Cadential Play   419

7.4.4. Development   423

7.4.5. Recapitulation   424

8. Cadence in the Romantic Era   431

8.1. Chromaticism and Dissonance   433

8.2. Root-Position Harmonies   435

8.3. Uniform Harmonic Rhythm and Density   437

8.4. Off-Tonic Openings; ECP Openings   438

8.5. Formal Circularity   441

8.6. Symmetrical Grouping Structures   443

8.7. Sequence versus Cadence   444

8.8. Prolongational Closure   447

8.9. Lack of Formal Closure   450

8.10. Cadential Deviations   453

8.10.1. Deceptive Cadence   453

8.10.1.1. "Mondnacht"   453

8.10.1.2. "Waldesgespräch"  455

8.10.2. Evaded Cadence  457

8.10.3. Dominant Arrival  458

8.11. Ultimate versus Penultimate Dominants; Dissipated Cadence  463

8.12. Prinner Cadence  470

8.13. Analytical Notes to Chopin's Preludes, Op. 28  472

    8.13.1. Prelude No. 1 in C  473

    8.13.2. Prelude No. 2 in A Minor  473

    8.13.3. Prelude No. 3 in G  475

    8.13.4. Prelude No. 4 in E Minor  475

    8.13.5. Prelude No. 5 in D  477

    8.13.6. Prelude No. 6 in B Minor  478

    8.13.7. Prelude No. 7 in A  478

    8.13.8. Prelude No. 8 in F-sharp Minor  480

    8.13.9. Prelude No. 9 in E  481

    8.13.10. Prelude No. 10 in C-sharp Minor  481

    8.13.11. Prelude No. 11 in B  482

    8.13.12. Prelude No. 12 in G-sharp Minor  484

    8.13.13. Prelude No. 13 in F-sharp  484

    8.13.14. Prelude No. 14 in E-flat Minor  485

    8.13.15. Prelude No. 15 in D-flat  486

    8.13.16. Prelude No. 16 in B-flat Minor  487

    8.13.17. Prelude No. 17 in A-flat  488

    8.13.18. Prelude No. 18 in F Minor  488

    8.13.19. Prelude No. 19 in E-flat  488

    8.13.20. Prelude No. 20 in C Minor  488

    8.13.21. Prelude No. 21 in B-flat  491

    8.13.22. Prelude No. 22 in G Minor  491

    8.13.23. Prelude No. 23 in F  493

    8.13.24. Prelude No. 24 in D Minor  493

9. Cadence in the Mid- to Late Nineteenth Century  495

9.1. Tonic Arrival  496

9.2. Pre-dominant Arrival; Subdominant Arrival  503

9.3. Plagal Cadence/Plagal Closure  511

    9.3.1. Theoretical Speculations  512

        9.3.1.1. Plagal Cadential Progression (PCP)  512

        9.3.1.2. Plagal Cadential Progressions: Moment-to-Moment Listening Contexts  514

        9.3.1.3. Plagal Cadence; Prolongational Closure; Plagal Closure  515

    9.3.2. Analyses of Plagal Closure  516

        9.3.2.1. Dependent Plagal Closure  516

        9.3.2.2. Independent Plagal Closure  523

    9.3.3. Plagal Closure versus Plagal Codetta  526

    9.3.4. Additional Characteristics of Plagal Closure  527

        9.3.4.1. $\hat{6}$–$\hat{5}$ Melodic Closure  527

        9.3.4.2. Phrygian Modality  528

        9.3.4.3. Home-Key Plagal Closure versus IV: HC  528

        9.3.4.4. Subdominant with Added Sixth; $\hat{1}$–$\hat{2}$–$\hat{3}$  528

        9.3.4.5. "Diminished" Plagal Closure  528

    9.3.5. Feigned Plagal Closure  529

9.4. Prolongational Closure  536

9.5. Detour Cadence  540

9.6. Iconic Cadence  544

9.7. Cadential Deviations  550

    9.7.1. A Deceptive Half Cadence?  550

    9.7.2. Evaded Cadence  551

9.8. Cadential Ambiguities  554

9.9. Four Case Studies  560

    9.9.1. Grieg, String Quartet in G Minor, Op. 27, Finale  560

    9.9.2. Dvorak, Symphony No. 7 in D Minor, Second Movement  564

    9.9.3. Liszt, Sonata in B Minor  570

    9.9.4. Wagner, Prelude to Tristan und Isolde  575

*Glossary of Terms*  583
*Bibliography*  593
*Index of Musical Compositions*  601
*General Index*  609

# Preface

How does music end? How do we know that a piece of music, or section thereof, is over? Most simply, we might assume that a work is complete when the music stops. But for most listeners, the mere cessation of activity is not the principal reason for believing that closure has been attained. Rather, they perceive that something in the music itself seems to signal its own end. The device that most readily expresses musical closure is *cadence*, a conventionalized configuration that brings specific melodic, harmonic, and formal processes to a degree of relative completion. Indeed, cadence is one of the most commonplace notions in all of music theory: musicians learn about cadence early in their training, and nonmusicians perceive cadences more readily than many other musical techniques. Yet for all its familiarity, cadence is an enormously complex concept, one that often conveys distinctly different connotations and embraces a multitude of musical phenomena. Cadence is thus entirely deserving of extensive theoretical treatment.

My own interest in the topic grew directly out of my investigations in the theory of musical form, more specifically, the ways in which formal processes play out in the instrumental works of Haydn, Mozart, and Beethoven. For it became clear early on in my research that my goal of constructing a comprehensive theory of formal functions, building on ideas of Arnold Schoenberg and his student Erwin Ratz, depended on formulating precise notions of cadence. The rather vague precepts that I had learned in my own musical education were entirely insufficient to the task, and I was forced to reconsider every element of cadence anew. And even though my treatise *Classical Form* (Oxford University Press, 1998) contains many refinements in the cadence concept, ones that are generally sufficient to undertake basic formal analyses, I realized that the need for even greater theoretical precision required more extensive examination. It also became evident that in the teaching of classical form, a sticking point for so many students involved the problem of cadential identification. Once they could determine cadences with clarity, the path toward a more comprehensive understanding of musical form opened up before them. Although the present study does not have the pedagogical slant found in my prior work on form, I am hopeful that teachers of tonal analysis will nonetheless find here useful material for explaining to students the wide variety of cadential situations that regularly occur in this repertory.

Following the completion of *Classical Form*, I continued to probe the many fascinating complexities that cadence offers the music theorist. I published the initial findings of that research in the 2004 article, "The Classical Cadence: Conceptions and Misconceptions." Though substantial in size, that study covered less than half of the topics that I had originally outlined for it. Indeed, it soon became obvious that a book-length project would be required to deal with the multitude of issues associated with cadence, even when restricting the notion to the works of the three major composers of what is frequently termed the Viennese high classical period.

This last consideration points to a particularly complicating factor in the study of cadence, namely the problem of musical style. For the way in which a given cadence is constructed—the details of its melodic, harmonic, and rhythmic content—and the precise manner in which it functions in shaping a composition are highly dependent on a given musical language, as operative in a particular historical, geographical, and cultural milieu. Moreover, I believe that a theory of cadence is most profitably accomplished by founding it upon a relatively restricted musical repertory, one in which cadence is a vitally important phenomenon. Thus focusing on cadence in the classical style seemed especially productive. As I noted in my 2004 article:

> In no other repertory does cadential articulation, and especially cadential play, assume such major significance for formal expression. Indeed, the highly teleological character of this music depends in no small measure on attempts to gain varying degrees of cadential closure at pivotal moments within a movement. If the concept of cadence can be successfully grounded for music of the classical style, then it might be possible to extend and refine the notion to earlier and later styles with greater confidence. (52)

Thus even for the present study, the "classical cadence" forms the core of the project, as detailed in the four chapters of Part I. The theoretical principles developed for this repertory then provide the conceptual framework for Part II, which attempts to "extend and refine" the theory to four additional style periods of tonal music—the high baroque, the galant, the early Romantic, and what I will call the mid- to late-nineteenth-century style. To be sure, the validity of such style periodization has often been challenged by musicologists, and in certain cases it is often far from certain to which style period a particular composer should be assigned, as in the cases of Domenico Scarlatti and Franz Liszt, to name two whose works play an important role in the present study. Indeed, music theorists have often shied away from examining distinctions among styles, especially those of tonal music, which are typically lumped together as a single "common-practice period." So despite the inherent difficulties associated with defining musical style, I nevertheless believe that differentiating among five styles for music composed within the more general system of tonal harmony, roughly 1690–1910, can serve to make more precise the manifold ways in which cadence and closure function within these two centuries of compositional practice.

As should be clear by now, I link cadence inextricably to musical form. Many of what I believe to be erroneous notions attached to the concept arise when cadence is formulated outside of a more comprehensive formal theory. Thus a general familiarity with my *Formenlehre* will aid considerably in understanding the contents of the present study. Since it is not feasible here to elaborate on many theoretical points of form and phrase structure, I regularly refer to pertinent passages from my treatise *Classical Form* (hereafter, *CF*) and my textbook *Analyzing Classical Form* (*ACF*). Since many readers may have access to only one of these publications, I will normally cite both the treatise and the textbook. I also include some explanatory material in the notes so as not to overburden the main text with definitions or elaborations of formal concepts.

My ideas on cadence are developed not only in the context of a theory of form, but are also associated with a particular stance on the theory of tonal harmony. Most importantly, I highlight a distinct *cadential* harmonic progression, one that differentiates itself from two other progression types—*prolongational* and *sequential*. Consequently, harmonic analysis plays a central role throughout this study, as will be evident by the extensive annotations in the musical examples. It will prove useful to the reader to consult the Guide to Analytical Annotations, which follows the Acknowledgments, for a detailed explanation of how the manifold elements of tonality, harmony, cadence, phrase structure, and larger-scale form are identified on the musical scores. As well, a comprehensive Glossary of Terms found at the back of the book provides definitions and abbreviations to the terminology employed throughout this study.

As mentioned earlier, this book is organized into two parts. Preceding Part I is a short chapter discussing the concept of *closure*, which I consider to be a more embracing phenomenon than the specific instance of cadential closure, the principal topic of this study. This chapter briefly considers some general notions of closure in our everyday lives, in the realm of perceptual psychology, and in the literary arts. I then turn to how some music theorists understand the role of closure for both musical composition and the listening experience.

The chapters of Part I are devoted to cadence in the classical style. Chapter 2 concerns itself with general concepts of the classical cadence. Here, I draw extensively from my 2004 article, along with a number of additional considerations, especially an introduction to a novel theory of bass melody and my response to James Hepokoski and Warren Darcy's critique of my distinction between cadential and postcadential formal functions. Chapter 3 details the morphology and function of the three basic cadence types—the perfect authentic cadence, the imperfect authentic cadence, and the half cadence. In addition to treating their harmonic content, I present a detailed theory of cadential melody, a topic often overlooked in the study of cadence. The chapter also considers how metrical and textural issues play a role in cadential analysis. I close the chapter by briefly discussing two other cadence types traditionally recognized by many theorists, the "contrapuntal cadence" and the "plagal cadence," and I explain why I deem such configurations noncadential in nature. Chapter 4 deals with cadential deviations, that is, specific techniques whereby a particular cadence fails to be realized as such. I explore three deviations associated with authentic cadences—the deceptive, evaded, and abandoned cadences—as well as the half cadential deviation of dominant arrival. Chapter 5 develops the topic of cadential expansion, building upon ideas presented in a number of my earlier studies on the expanded cadential progression (ECP). The chapter concludes with detailed analyses of selected ECPs in Beethoven's symphonic works.

Part II, the four "historical" chapters, extends my theory of classical cadence to earlier and later styles of tonal music. Chapter 6 on cadence in the high baroque (focusing on works by Corelli, Vivaldi, Handel, and J. S. Bach) highlights some specific morphological traits of baroque cadences that differ from later classical usage. I especially stress the formulaic nature of the baroque cadence and emphasize how the principle of "retaining the cadential formula" plays itself out in a number of formal contexts. As I did for the classical cadence, I consider how cadential deviations and expansions function in the baroque style. I conclude the chapter with a study of cadence in fugue, using Bach's *Well-Tempered Clavier* as the corpus of works for the investigation of this fascinating topic. Chapter 7 on cadence in the galant period (featuring works by Scarlatti and C. P. E. Bach) again considers some morphological features that are especially characteristic of this style, along with how cadences, and their associated deviations and expansions, function in the newly emerging formal types—sonata, rondo, and concerto—that continue to be employed in the classical style. Chapter 8, on cadence in the Romantic era (especially in works by Schubert, Schumann, and Chopin) examines a set of stylistic changes in compositional practice—emphasis on root-position harmonies, uniformity of harmonic rhythm, blurring of cadence and sequence, formal circularity, and symmetrical grouping structures—that result in new modes of thematic closure, including some novel uses of cadential deviations. The chapter concludes with a set of analytical notes to cadences in Chopin's Preludes, Op. 28. Finally, Chapter 9 surveys additional compositional techniques employed in the second half of the nineteenth century (particularly in pieces by Liszt, Wagner, Bruckner, and Brahms) that continue to modify the classical cadence in significant ways. Among the topics treated are alternative "arrivals" on tonic and pre-dominant (subdominant) harmonies, the problematic notion of plagal cadence (which I will term *plagal closure*), along with some special cadential techniques—the detour cadence and the iconic cadence. The chapter concludes with four case studies that consider longer passages containing a variety of cadential techniques typical of this style period.

Regarding the extensive use of musical examples in this book, it should be noted that, with the exception of a small number of vocal excerpts, all are set as a single system of two staves. For passages not written for a single keyboard, the examples are not necessarily "piano reductions," and so the music does not always lie conveniently for two hands. Rather, the examples are meant to provide as much harmonic and textural information as possible in order to illustrate the theoretical and analytical issues under consideration. Unfortunately, a companion website containing audio of the examples is not yet planned for this book. But seeing as many of the classical passages used in Part I are taken from examples found in *ACF*, the audio reproduction of those excerpts can be obtained on the textbook's website (www.music.mcgill.ca/acf/). Examples from the textbook, as well as the supplementary examples that only appear on the website, will be identified in the captions (e.g., "*ACF* Ex. 2.1," or "*ACF* Sup. 2.1").

Though this study dives deeply into a wide variety of issues of cadence in tonal styles, I still consider it to be largely introductory for many of the topics it raises. I fully expect, and indeed hope, that even more detailed investigations will refine (and perhaps even overthrow) some of the theoretical formulations and analytical conclusions presented here. I also understand that many, if not most, readers will simply dip here and there into the various topics that interest them. For this reason, I am hopeful that they will be aided by the glossary of terms, the indices, and the many cross-references to relevant earlier and later discussions of selected issues.

# Acknowledgments

Since 2012, when I formally began researching and writing this book, I have been aided by numerous friends, colleagues, and students. I begin by acknowledging the enormous help that I have received over many decades from Cynthia Leive, the former head librarian of the Marvin Duchow Music Library of McGill University. In so many ways, Cynthia has served as my professional guru, helping me over hurdles throughout my research career. Librarians often get short shrift in acknowledgments, but they are an invaluable resource for any scholar, especially in the humanities and fine arts. I am sure that I speak for my colleagues and students at McGill in recognizing Cynthia as a librarian of the first rank. Following her retirement, her successor Houman Behzahdi and his entire staff have continued to be enormously helpful and supportive of my research efforts.

Among my professional colleagues in music theory, I must mention the ongoing help and encouragement I have always received from my dear friend Janet Schmalfeldt, who carefully, and critically, read many chapters of this study and offered much sage advice, especially in the form of alternative analytical perspectives. I am also highly thankful to Julian Horton and Dean Sutcliffe, who read early drafts of Chapters 3, 6, 8, and 9 and who made suggestions that have significantly improved the present text.

A highly valuable resource for refining many of the theoretical issues addressed in this book were the interactive workshops that I was fortunate to hold in connection with the ideas developed for Chapters 6, 8, and 9. The series of workshops titled "Form Forum," initiated by Steven Vande Moortele and organized by him, Julie Pedneault-Deslauriers, and Nathan John Martin, permitted me to interact with students and colleagues at the University of Toronto and McGill University on the topics of cadence in Bach's Fugues and cadential practice in the second half of the nineteenth century. Additional discussions with Steven, Julie, and Nathan on all matters of form and cadence were a continuing source of encouragement during the research and writing of this book. I was also fortunate to have been invited to hold workshops on cadence at several other institutions in North America and Europe: for providing me the opportunity of presenting my ideas and receiving valuable input from themselves, their colleagues, and students, I thank Frank Heidelberger and Timothy Jackson

(University of North Texas), Paul Scheepers (for three days of workshops at the Royal Conservatory of The Hague, in association with the Dutch-Flemish Society for Music Theory), and especially Harald Krebs (University of Victoria), who worked with me through many analyses of nineteenth-century works. In my role as co-applicant of a research project "To Play the Cadence" (funded by the Katholieke Universiteit Leuven), I was fortunate to collaborate with Pieter Bergé on our mutual interest in the topic. In this connection, I gained much from a set of workshops organized by Pieter, along with Markus Neuwirth, that were held at the Academia Belgica in Rome. They assembled there a distinguished group of scholars, including Poundie Burstein, Vasili Byros, Felix Diergarten, Peter Hoyt, David Lodewyckx, Danuta Mirka, Martin Rohrmeier, Giorgio Sanguinetti, and David Sears, to address the question "What Is a Cadence?" The discussions associated with this gathering, along with the published collection of essays of the same title, resonate throughout the present book.

At many stages in the course of my research, I was offered assistance, inspiration, and even constructive pushback by many other professional colleagues, including William Benjamin, David Cohen, Richard Cohn, Erdem Çöloğlu, Karst de Jong, Ben Duane, Yoel Greenberg, Daniel Harrison, James Hepokoski, Graham Hunt, Clemens Kemme, Tomás Koljatic, John Koslovsky, Ralph Locke, Nicholas Marston, Scott Murphy, Dimitar Ninov, Mark Richards, William Rothstein, Mathew Santa, Ronald Squibbs, Peter Van Tour, and James Webster. In connection with my views on the "plagal cadence," I owe a special debt to Stephen Rodgers, who freely shared with me his own work on the songs of Fanny Hensel.

During my forty-four-year career in the Faculty of Music (later named The Schulich School of Music) at McGill University, I have been blessed with incredibly collegial colleagues in the music theory area. During the period of my work on this book, I had valuable discussions with Nicole Biamonte, Robert Hasegawa, Edward Klorman, Christoph Neidhöfer, René Rusch, Peter Schubert, and Jon Wild. I want especially to single out Jon, who spent many hours with me working through some particularly difficult issues of cadence and form. Among my friends in the music history and composition areas at the Schulich School, I am grateful for support and advice from Dorian Bandy, Brian Cherney, David Brackett, Julie Cumming, Steven Huebner, John Rea, and Lloyd Whitesell. I have also had the joy of working with many outstanding graduate students, including Ellen Bakulina, François de Médicis, Andrew Deruchie, Naomi Edemarian, Erin Helyard, Thomas Posen, Malcolm Sailor, and Andrew Schartmann, who engaged me constructively in many ideas reflected in this study. As well, I was aided by an excellent group of research assistants, who helped me uncover repertoires for analytical study and set the musical examples; in this connection I thank Evan Campbell, Mylène Gioffredo, Rachel Hottle, Hubert Léveillé Gauvin, Carlotta Marturano, Toru Momii, Corey Stevens, and William Van Geest.

I want to give special thanks to the former music editor of Oxford University Press, Suzanne Ryan, for her unwavering support of this project through the initial stages of submitting the proposal and the securing of a contract. Her successor, Norman Hirschy, along with his editorial staff (Sean Decker, Meredith Taylor) and production team (Koperundevi Pugazhenthi, Dorothy Bauhoff), have also been especially helpful in bringing this book to its final state.

Funding for this project has been generously supported by a Major Research Grant from the Social Sciences and Humanities Research Council of Canada, a Killam Research Fellowship from the Canada Council for the Arts, and research stipends from the James McGill Professor Program of McGill University.

Portions of this book have appeared earlier in article form. I want to thank the publishers for permission to incorporate material from the following publications:

"Analysis Symposium: The Andante of Mozart's Symphony No. 40 in G Minor." In *A Composition as a Problem 2: Proceedings of the Second International Estonian Music Theory Conference*, edited by Mart Humal, 155–62. Tallinn: Eesti Muusikaakadeemia, 2000.

"Beyond the Classical Cadence: Thematic Closure in Early Romantic Music." *Music Theory Spectrum* 40, no. 1 (2018): 1–26.

"Cadence in Fugue: Modes of Closure in J. S. Bach's *Well-tempered Clavier*." *Music Theory & Analysis* 7, no. 1 (April 2020): 190–249.

"Harmonic Variants of the Expanded Cadential Progression." In *A Composition as a Problem 2: Proceedings of the Second International Estonian Music Theory Conference*, edited by Mart Humal, 49–71. Tallinn: Eesti Muusikaakadeemia, 2000.

"Harmony and Cadence in Gjerdingen's 'Prinner.'" In *What Is a Cadence? Theoretical and Analytical Perspectives on Cadences in the Classical Repertoire*, edited by Markus Neuwirth and Pieter Bergé, 17–57. Leuven: Leuven University Press, 2015.

"Schoenberg's 'Second Melody', or, 'Meyer-ed' in the Bass." In *Communication in Eighteenth-Century Music*, edited by Danuta Mirka and Kofi Agawu, 160–88. Cambridge: Cambridge University Press, 2008.

"Structural Expansion in Beethoven's Symphonic Forms." In *Beethoven's Compositional Process*, edited by William Kinderman, 27–54. Lincoln: University of Nebraska Press, 1991.

"The Classical Cadence: Conceptions and Misconceptions." *Journal of the American Musicological Society* 57, no. 1 (Spring 2004): 51–117.

"The 'Continuous Exposition' and the Concept of Subordinate Theme." *Music Analysis* 35, no. 1 (2016): 4–43.

"The 'Expanded Cadential Progression': A Category for the Analysis of Classical Form." *Journal of Musicological Research* 7, no. 2–3 (1987): 215–57.

Finally, I have been sustained throughout by the love, patience, and understanding of my wife Marsha Heyman, and my children Adam and Rebecca. My sister Wendy was always available for support during challenging times, and in much gratitude, I dedicate this book to her.

W. E. C.
Montreal
August 2023

# Guide to the Analytical Annotations

This guide will help the reader understand the details of harmonic, cadential, and formal analyses represented in the musical examples. Though extensive, it does not cover every annotation found there; in such cases, the meaning of the label should be clear from the analytical comments in the text.

## Tonal and Harmonic Labels (below the score)

*Key*: A major key is indicated by a boldface, uppercase pitch name followed by a colon; a minor key, by a boldface, lowercase pitch name, e.g., **C:** for C major; **c:** for C minor.

*Harmony*: Each harmony built on a scale degree within a key is indicated by an uppercase roman numeral, irrespective of its "chord quality," e.g., major triad, minor triad, diminished triad, half-diminished seventh. Augmented sixth harmonies, *in any position*, are indicated by their "national" labels (It$^{+6}$, Gr$^{+6}$, or Fr$^{+6}$). Some harmonies include an added sixth ($^{a6}$) or added augmented sixth ($^{a+6}$) (see Ex. 9.3, m. 368, and Ex. 9.39, m. 10, respectively). A harmony that is sustained across a bar line is indicated by a straight line, e.g., I ——————— (see Ex. 2.4, mm. 1–2 and 4–5).

*Harmonic inversion*: Inversions are indicated by standard figured-bass symbols following the roman numeral, e.g., I$^6$, V$^4_3$. The cadential six-four is analyzed as a dominant harmony in root position, with the symbols for the six-four embellishments and their resolutions placed in parentheses, e.g., V($^{65}_{43}$). A change of position of the same harmony does not usually bring a repetition of the roman numeral, e.g., II$^6$–$^5_3$ (see Ex. 2.4, mm. 3–4).

*Harmonic functions*: Generalized harmonic functions—tonic (T), pre-dominant (PD), and dominant (D)—are annotated with a sans serif font: e.g., T–PD–D–T (see Ex. 5.37e).

*Modulation*: A pivot-chord modulation is indicated by a vertical brace connecting the harmonies of the prevailing key and the new key. The harmonic relation of the new key to the home key is indicated by a roman numeral placed in parentheses below the new key name (see Ex. 3.84, m. 7).

*Tonicization*: Secondary dominants are normally indicated by an arrow pointing to the tonicized harmony (usually forward, but sometimes backward), e.g., V⁷↪II or VI↩VII⁶₅ (see Ex. 2.4, mm. 2–3; Ex. 4.64, m. 295). If the secondary dominant is neither followed nor preceded by its expected tonicized degree, then that degree follows a slash, e.g., V⁷/II (see Ex. 2.6, mm. 48–49). Extended tonicizations are indicated by a horizontal brace enclosing the secondary harmonies, e.g., II⎵V; the tonicized scale degree is placed below the brace (see Ex. 4.2, mm. 44–45).

*Prolongational progressions*: Subordinate harmonies within a prolongation are sometimes placed in parentheses, especially when they do not significantly contribute to the basic harmonic rhythm of a passage, e.g., I⁶–(IV)–I⁶–(VII⁶)–I; II⁶–(VII⁷)↪–V (for a tonic prolongation with subordinate subdominant harmonies, see Ex. 2.20, m. 9–10; for a dominant prolongation with subordinate tonic harmonies, see Ex. 2.23, mm. 20–25; for a pre-dominant prolongation within a cadential progression, see Ex. 2.29a, m. 85). When it is useful to distinguish a prolongational progression from a different progression type (sequential or cadential), an under curved line connects the boundaries of the prolonged harmony (see Ex. 3.2).

*Cadential progressions*: The boundaries of a cadential progression are indicated by a horizontal square bracket placed below the roman numerals. *Exception*: to avoid clutter, an expanded cadential progression (ECP) omits the bracket; instead, the label "ECP" is placed directly after the first harmony of the progression, e.g., I⁶_ECP (see Ex. 2.16, m. 56).

*Sequential progressions*: Sequential progressions are indicated by the abbreviation "seq." following the initial harmony of the progression, e.g., I_seq. The subsequent harmonies of the progression are sometimes placed in parentheses, except for the final harmony of the sequence, which stands outside of the parentheses, e.g., I_seq.–(VII⁶–VI–V⁶)–IV⁶–V (see Ex. 2.6, mm. 48–49).

*Pedal point*: A pedal point is indicated by the abbreviation "ped." following the roman numeral of the prolonged harmony, e.g., I_ped. All subordinate harmonies within the pedal point are placed in parentheses; an inversion is not indicated for these harmonies because their bass notes are replaced by the pedal, e.g., I_ped.–(IV–V⁷)–I (see Ex. 2.1e).

*Contrapuntal functions*: Where helpful, some local neighboring, passing, and appoggiatura harmonies are labeled with "n," "p," or "app," respectively (see Ex. 2.1a and b; Ex. 4.8, m. 16).

*Nonfunctional sonorities*: Some nonfunctional sonorities lack a roman numeral; in its place, the sonority is labeled with its chord quality placed in parentheses, e.g., (°7) for "diminished-seventh chord" or (m⁷) for "minor-seventh chord." A nonfunctional diminished-seventh sonority often has a "common tone" ("ct") relationship with its subsequent harmony (see Ex. 5.15, m. 65).

*Omitted harmonic analysis*: The use of ellipses following a roman numeral (e.g., I...) indicates the omission of harmonic analysis either for the rest of the passage or until another roman numeral appears (see Ex. 2.6, m. 1)

*Square brackets*: Harmonies enclosed with square brackets can indicate a variety of harmonic situations: (1) an additional level of harmonic subordination within a prolongational or sequential progression (see Ex. 3.121, mm. 16–17; (2) an alternative harmonic interpretation (see Ex. 7.15b, m. 2); (3) a contextually implied harmony (see Ex. 2.18a, m. 66); (4) the diatonic source of a chromatically altered harmony, e.g., V⁷/II as a chromatically altered [VI] harmony (see Ex. 2.6, mm. 48–49).

*Scale degrees*: A scale degree in the bass voice is indicated by an arabic numeral enclosed in a circle, e.g., ①; a scale degree in any voice above the bass is indicated by an arabic numeral with a circumflex accent, e.g., $\hat{1}$. Scale degrees associated with a particular voice (e.g., alto) are indicated by an abbreviation of the voice preceding the degrees, e.g., A: $\hat{3}$–$\hat{7}$–$\hat{1}$ (see Ex. 3.38, mm. 11–13).

# Cadential Labels (below the score)

*Genuine cadences*: The label for a genuine cadence—perfect authentic, imperfect authentic (including the Prinner cadence), and half—is enclosed with a square box, e.g., PAC and placed below the final harmony of the cadential progression. If it is not feasible to distinguish between a perfect authentic cadence and an imperfect one, then the neutral label AC is used instead (see Ex. 4.85a, m. 9). Cadences of limited scope are enclosed with parentheses instead of a box, e.g., (PAC) (see Ex. 2.19, mm. 3 and 5).

*Deceptive cadence*: The label for a deceptive cadence appears below the final harmony of the deceptive cadential progression (see Ex. 2.19, m. 10); the label for a noncadential deceptive resolution (dec. res.) of the dominant is enclosed in parentheses and placed below the resolving harmony, e.g., VI (see Ex. 3.65, m. 14).

*Evaded cadence*: The cadential bracket is shown to be interrupted by a double slash (//), and the label for an evaded cadence ("ev. cad.") is placed below the "initiating harmony," e.g., I⁶, that stands in place of the expected final tonic (see Ex. 4.30, m. 60).

*Abandoned cadence; abandoned cadential progression*: The cadential bracket is left open-ended (except in the case of an ECP, which uses no bracket), and the label for an abandoned cadence appears below the harmony that stands in place of the expected final tonic (see Ex. 4.46, mm. 13–14). In the absence of an expected moment of cadence, the cadential bracket is left open-ended (except for an ECP) and the label for the abandoned cadential progression "abnd." is enclosed in parentheses and placed below the first harmony that departs from the ongoing cadential progression (see Ex. 4.47, m. 6).

*Dominant arrival*: The label for a dominant arrival is placed below the first appearance of the final dominant of the thematic unit (see Ex. 3.164a, m. 7). The same type of label is used for a pre-dominant (subdominant) arrival and a tonic arrival (see Ex. 9.1, m. 42 and m. 24, respectively).

*Prolongational closure; plagal closure*: Labels for noncadential thematic closure are placed below the tonic harmony that completes the prolongational progression (see Ex. 3.7, m. 4).

## Form-Functional Labels (placed above the score)

*Idea functions*: Labels for idea functions (e.g., basic idea, contrasting idea, codetta, model, sequence) are placed centered above the square bracket embracing the functional unit.

*Phrase functions*: Labels for simple phrase functions, e.g., presentation, cadential, compound basic idea, standing on the dominant, are set in lowercase and placed at the onset of the functional unit. Labels for compound phrase functions, e.g., compound antecedent, compound presentation, are set in bold typeface; the expression "compound" is not included in the label, being indicated as such by the bold typeface.

*Ternary or binary functions*: Labels for the three sections of a small ternary (or rounded binary) (A, B, A′) or the two parts of a small binary (1, 2) are set in bold typeface and enclosed with a box.

*Thematic functions*: Labels for thematic functions, e.g., main theme, transition, core, retransition, coda theme, are set with an initial uppercase letter and bold typeface.

*Section functions*: Labels for the section functions of a complete movement, e.g., exposition, development, slow introduction, coda, are set uppercase and in bold typeface.

*Fusion*: A case of form-functional fusion (usually for thematic functions) is indicated by a forward slash separating the functions, e.g., Main Theme/Transition (see Ex. 3.67, m. 1).

*Ongoing function*: Any form-functional label enclosed with square brackets, normally appearing at the start of an example, indicates that the function is already ongoing (see Ex. 2.23, m. 19).

*Intrinsic function*: In cases of a conflict between intrinsic and contextual formal functions, the intrinsic function is enclosed in vertical braces, e.g., {cad.} (see Ex. 2.17, mm. 1–2).

## Miscellaneous Annotations

*Descriptors*: Various cadential descriptors (e.g., elided, way station, premature, dissipated, iconic) are typically enclosed with parentheses and placed below the cadence or deviation label (see Ex. 2.25, m. 54). Various formal descriptors associated with a given function (e.g., repetition, extension) are typically enclosed in parentheses and placed beside the functional label (see Ex. 2.19, mm. 4–5).

*Galant schemata*: A galant schema is indicated by an uppercase label, e.g., PRINNER (see Ex. 3.67, mm. 3–4).

*Retrospective reinterpretation*: A retrospective reinterpretation ("becoming") of any tonal, harmonic, cadential, or form-functional situation is indicated by a double arrow (⇒) linking the two elements of the reinterpretation, e.g., cont.⇒cad., for a reinterpreted closing phrase (see Ex. 3.79, m. 5; PAC (⇒HC), for a reinterpreted half cadence (see Ex. 3.73, m. 36).

# 1

# Ideas of Closure

THE SINGLE-WORD TITLE OF THIS BOOK—*CADENCE*—will obviously be its central object of study. The subtitle delimits its scope by the well-known expression *tonal music*, designating European art music written largely in the eighteenth and nineteenth centuries. As well, the subtitle situates the idea of cadence within the domain of *closure*. Since cadence will preoccupy us throughout this book, it will be useful to consider briefly the more encompassing notion of closure. In this opening chapter, I present the idea in its simple, everyday senses, turning quickly to how psychologists of perception and cognition have understood the concept. I then discuss some ways in which closure has been treated by several scholars of the literary arts, especially poetry, and finally I look at how *musical* closure, broadly construed, has been conceptualized by some music theorists in the past forty years. Given the large scope of the topic, my remarks here are preliminary at best.[1] I largely focus on ideas that will resonate throughout the study of cadence in the rest of this book.

We are all familiar with some simple ideas of closure in our everyday life. We close the door of a car; we close our eyes to sleep; and we close a container by attaching its lid. In my own city of Montreal, where Canadian English is influenced by French, we speak of closing the lights of a room and closing the radio (American usage favors "to turn off" in both cases). Indeed, the idea of closure finds a place in a wide range of human experience: the Wikipedia article on the term references many specialized uses in the domains of psychology, computer science, mathematics, philosophy, sociology, business, atmospheric science, and poetry.[2]

---

1. For additional material on general concepts of musical closure and cadence, especially from recent music-psychological perspectives, see David R. W. Sears et al., "Expecting the End: Continuous Expectancy Ratings for Tonal Cadences"; David R. W. Sears et al., "Simulating Melodic and Harmonic Expectations for Tonal Cadences Using Probabilistic Models." The first appearance of a reference will contain the name of the author(s) and the complete title; all subsequent citations will use a shortened form of the reference. Full documentation can be found in the bibliography.

2. Wikipedia, s.v. "closure," last modified July 8, 2022, at 08:07 (UTC), https://en.wikipedia.org/wiki/Closure.

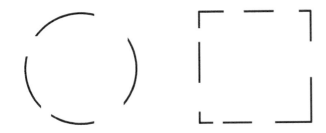

FIGURE 1.1. Law of closure.

Of particular interest in this study is how notions of closure play out in human psychology, because music creates a type of closure that we *experience*, not just understand intellectually. Early in the twentieth century, a group of Austrian and German psychologists, initiators of the movement called *Gestalt psychology*, studied mechanisms of human perception and cognition.[3] Among their general principles of *Prägnanz* (German, lit. "pithiness," but in psychological contexts, meaning "salience," "conciseness," and "orderliness"), they formulated the *law of closure*, which holds that given the appropriate cues, our perception of an object that is literally incomplete, say a circle or square (Figure 1.1), will actually appear to us as a complete whole, that is, closed. A number of other principles of *Prägnanz* (Figure 1.2), for instance the laws of (a) proximity, (b) similarity, and (c) continuity, indirectly pertain to closure in that they help to explain how we *group* (or conversely, *segment*) perceptual stimuli into more or less complete entities, thus implying that some kind of closure has taken place.

When considering the visual images of Figure 1.1 and Figure 1.2, the sense of closure appears to be largely *atemporal* in nature; that is, we almost immediately discern the completeness of the visual object in question. But many uses of closure arise within a temporal context, where we perceive that some *process in time*, usually involving an ordered set of elements, has reached its end, thus engendering a sense of completeness to the process. Indeed, the general idea of "ending" most often refers to a temporal context of some kind. We would not likely speak of our perceiving the closure associated with the circle and square in Figure 1.1 as something that has ended.[4] Rather, "the sense of an ending" (referencing the title of Frank Kermode's important study of closure in literary fiction)[5] normally pertains to a process that occurs in time, such that we can perceive that one or more elements in this temporal succession bring the process to an end.[6]

## 1.1. Closure in Literature

Moving beyond everyday ideas of closure, we encounter a temporally defined sense of ending arising in a number of art forms apart from music. Indeed, what may be the earliest—and most influential—statement on the construction of plot in the dramatic arts appears in Aristotle's *Poetics*:

> A whole is that which has a beginning, a middle, and an end. A beginning is that which does not itself follow anything by causal necessity, but after which something naturally is or comes to be. An end, on the contrary, is that which itself naturally follows some other thing, either by necessity, or as a rule, but has nothing following it. A middle is that which follows something as some other thing follows it. A well-constructed plot, therefore, must neither begin nor end at haphazard, but conform to these principles. (1.7)

This beginning-middle-end paradigm underlies most theories of narrativity in literary art forms. And within such accounts, theorists try to discern how concepts of ending and closure are applicable to the telling of a story.

> At the risk of much oversimplification, . . . one might distinguish five different senses of "closure" in recent criticism: (1) The concluding section of a literary work; (2) The process by which the reader of a work comes to see the end as satisfyingly final; (3) The degree to which an ending is satisfyingly final; (4) The degree to which the questions posed in the work are answered, tensions released, conflicts resolved; (5) The degree to which the work allows new critical readings.[7]

In addition to these meanings of narrative closure, most theorists readily agree that we must distinguish the literal end of a story—the final word that is read or uttered—from a broader sense of closure, one in which the perceiver senses that all of the strands of the narrative have been successfully disentangled.

> It is the impression that exactly the point where the work does end is just the right point. To have gone beyond that point would have been an error. It would have been to have gone too far. But to have stopped before that point would also be to

---

3. Ronald Thomas Kellogg, *Cognitive Psychology*, 59–62. Among its many meanings in German, *Gestalt* refers to a "shape" or "figure." Gestalt psychology is not to be confused with *Gestalt therapy*, a type of psychotherapeutic treatment.

4. As Eyal Segal notes, "The terms *closure* and *openness* were originally carried over from the visual field. So there is no point in talking about the 'end' of a visual shape, but there certainly is in talking about its closure—or the lack thereof—as demonstrated by numerous studies in perceptual psychology and art history" ("Closure in Detective Fiction," 154).

5. Frank Kermode, *The Sense of an Ending: Studies in the Theory of Fiction*. Though this work has been enormously influential on literary scholars (and others), its subject matter is not all that applicable to musical closure.

6. Whereas many temporal contexts consist of discrete elements, others occur through time in a fully continuous manner. Consider, say, a simple running race, where its end is marked by the first runner to cross the finish line. The temporal process from beginning to end does not normally comprise a series of discrete events, but transpires within a stretch of unbroken time. If the race is a relay, though, a number of specific moments in time will be articulated with each passing of the baton.

7. Don P. Fowler, "First Thoughts on Closure: Problems and Prospects," 78.

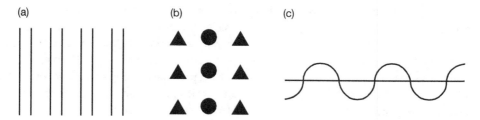

FIGURE 1.2. (a) Law of proximity; (b) law of similarity; (c) law of continuity (from Burkhard, "The Use of Complementary Visual Representations for the Transfer of Knowledge," 41, fig. 5).

have committed a mistake. It would be too abrupt. Closure is a matter of concluding rather than merely stopping or ceasing or coming to a halt or crashing.[8]

This last point—the distinction between "ending" and "stopping"—is referenced by most writers on closure, and indeed I will devote a section in the next chapter to the matter, one that often leads to problematic interpretations of cadence.

Perhaps the most influential study of closure in the literary arts is Barbara Herrnstein Smith's *Poetic Closure: A Study of How Poems End*. Speaking in a manner that is familiar to many music theorists, Smith characterizes poetic closure as occurring when:

> a sequence of events has a relatively high degree of structure, when, in other words, we can perceive these events as related to one another by some principle of organization or design that implies the existence of a definite termination point. Under these circumstances, the occurrence of the terminal event is a confirmation of expectations that have been established by the structure of the sequences, and is usually distinctly gratifying. The sense of stable conclusiveness, finality, or "clinch" which we experience at that point is what is referred to here as *closure* . . . a structure appears closed when it is experienced as integral: coherent, complete, and stable. (2–3)[9]

For Smith, closure is a manifestation of a poem's *structure*, of which she recognizes two basic types: *formal* and *thematic*. The formal structure concerns the "physical nature of words," such as "rhyme, alliteration, and syllabic meter." Thematic structure refers to the "symbolic or conventional nature of words" and includes "everything from reference to syntax to tone" (6). Both types of poetic structure address the question: "what keeps it going?" along with the corollary question: "what stops it from going?" The first question deals with modes of *continuation*, the second, with modes of *closure*. Most generally, Smith sees *repetition* (normally an immediate reiteration) as a primary means of continuation: "A systematic repetition is . . . a force for continuation that must be overcome if closure is to occur" (48). In the case of formal structures, what is typically repeated is the metrical organization, the rhyme scheme, and various syllabic utterances (e.g., alliterations). For thematic structure, repetitions include organizational schemes such as the paratactic or sequential patterning of ideas.[10]

In both types of structure, repetition creates expectations of further continuation and these, eventually, give rise to expectations for an ending of some kind, for closure:

> Closure . . . may be regarded as a modification of structure that makes *stasis*, or the absence of further continuation, the probable succeeding event . . . or, put another way, it creates in the reader the expectation of nothing. . . . That expectation of nothing, the sense of ultimate composure we apparently value in our experience of a work of art, is variously referred to as stability, resolution, or equilibrium. It is obviously a function or effect of closure. (34)

Closure, then, is intimately associated with the idea of tamping down any further expectations of continuation. But how does that denial of expectation come about? Smith's reference in this quote to a "modification of structure" provides the answer: the repetition pattern is broken by a modification of some kind, and particularly a change that brings a sense of "stability, resolution, or equilibrium." And in this connection, Smith speaks more specifically of *terminal modification* as a major technique for both formal and thematic closure.[11] In fact, it will be useful to identify here what I will call the *repetition/terminal-modification* paradigm, one that has broad application throughout the temporal arts. One example of this paradigm in poetry involves the use

---

8. Noël Carroll, "Narrative Closure," 2–3.

9. The language here is reminiscent of Leonard B. Meyer's *Emotion and Meaning in Music*. Indeed, Smith cites the importance for her of this music theorist's work in the preface to her study (p. x). I discuss Meyer's concepts of musical closure ahead in sec. 1.2.1.

10. Paratactic structures bring a set of statements that do not necessarily follow logically, but rather succeed each other like a list of items, as found frequently in nursery rhymes, lullabies, and folk songs. A sequential structure brings an ordering of the statements that follow a more logical, causal principle (Smith, chap. 3, secs. 2 and 3). At the end of her chapter on thematic structure, Smith also discusses more briefly what she terms "associative" and "dialectical" structures, those that arise from the sense of the poem reflecting an "interior monologue" or a stream of consciousness.

11. Smith, *Poetic Closure*, 53.

of a rhymed couplet as the terminal modification used to close Shakespeare's Sonnet No. 21:[12]

> (1) So is it not with me as with that Muse (a)
> Stirred by a painted beauty to his verse (b)
> Who heaven itself for ornament doth use (a)
> And every fair with his fair doth rehearse (b)
> (2) Making a couplement of proud compare (c)
> With sun and moon, with earth and sea's rich gems (d)
> With April's first-born flowers, and all things rare (c)
> That heaven's air in this huge rondure hems. (d)
> (3) O let me, true in love, but truly write (e)
> And then believe me: my love is as fair (f)
> As any mother's child, though not so bright (e)
> As those gold candles fixed in heaven's air (f)
> ("4") Let them say more that like of hearsay well (g)
> I will not praise that purpose not to sell. (g)

Among the formal repetitions in the first twelve lines of this poem, we can readily identify the consistent iambic pentameter, a pattern of four lines per stanza (each stanza indicated by an arabic numeral in parentheses), and an alternating scheme two rhymes per stanza (indicated by the letters in parentheses). The final two lines, however, produce a terminal modification in the form of a rhymed couplet, which breaks both the ongoing rhyme scheme and the stanzaic organization to achieve formal closure of the sonnet.

Smith points out that the rhymed couplet as terminal modification is particularly effective in cases of blank verse, where the sudden appearance of rhyming effectively signals the end of a poetic utterance that had no prior end rhymes. Shakespeare, for one, regularly uses the device in his dramas, especially to mark the exit of a character at the end of a scene:

> . . . The spirit that I have seen
> May be a dev'l, and the dev'l hath power
> T' assume a pleasing shape, yea, and perhaps,
> Out of my weakness and my melancholy,
> As he is very potent with such spirits,
> Abuses me to damn me. I'll have grounds
> More relative than this—The play's the *thing*
> Wherein I'll catch the conscience of the *King* [my italics].[13]

As Smith puts it, "Blank verse is most easily closed . . . when it ceases to be blank verse."

In addition to terminal modification, Smith discusses another type of formal closure, namely, the return at the end of the poem, or a major section, of its opening lines, sometimes lightly modified. "In certain poetic forms, such as the rondeau, closure may be secured through a structural principle analogous to that of the circle: and, in general, whenever a poetic form repeats at its conclusion a formal unit with which it began, closure will be thereby strengthened" (27). She cites in this connection a three-part poem by Thomas Wyatt (1503–42), "Lo, what it is to love!" In each part, the opening stanza is followed by four more stanzas, after which the opening stanza is restated in full to close the part. Here is the first stanza:[14]

> Lo, what it is to love!
> Lerne ye that list to prove
>   At me, I say,
>   No ways that may
> The grownd of grief remove.
>   My liff alweie
>   That doeth decaye:
> Lo, what it is to love.

In addition to restating this opening stanza after the four that follow, the stanza itself has a circular design: the same line opens and closes the stanza. Thus, the poem projects two levels of closure, both based on the principle of formal circularity.[15]

This brief presentation of selected ideas in Smith's rich and detailed study has focused on two techniques of formal structure: terminal modification and circularity. As we will see in our study of musical cadence, the first of these techniques strongly connects with an eighteenth-century aesthetic that prizes the attainment of formal goals. The second principle finds expression more in a nineteenth-century sensibility that emphasizes the importance of opening ideas, which are then brought back in a circular manner to end a musical utterance.

## 1.2. Closure in Music

Given that music is essentially perceived "in time," it is no surprise that issues of closure arise often enough in theoretical and aesthetic writings on this most temporal of art forms. Any theory of harmony, counterpoint, melody, rhythm, and form will by necessity have to deal with how these individual parameters achieve a satisfactory sense of ending. We possess, however, no large-scale study of closure in music of the kind offered by Smith's treatment of poetry. What follows, then, is a brief account of how selected music theorists have developed general notions of closure largely independent of a specific musical parameter.

### 1.2.1. Leonard Meyer

One theorist who consistently concerned himself with the topic in its foundational aspects is Leonard Meyer, whom Smith acknowledges as providing important stimulus for her own

---

12. Smith, *Poetic Closure*, 51–52; I have added the numbers and letters in parentheses.

13. *Hamlet*, 2.2.598–605; cited in Smith, 80.

14. Smith, *Poetic Closure*, 66–67.

15. Curiously, Smith does not point out this obvious bi-level structure.

project (see note 9 above). As early as his influential and enduring work, *Emotion and Meaning in Music*, Meyer addresses just what it means for musical closure to be experienced. Inspired by principles of Gestalt psychology, he notes that "the mind, governed by the law of *Prägnanz*, is continually striving for completeness, stability, and rest. But what represents completeness will vary from style to style and from piece to piece."[16] Thus, while Meyer appeals to fundamental principles of human cognition in our ability to grasp closure, he also affirms the role of cultural practices and conventions associated with the "style" of a group of works, along with processes arising within an individual composition. Like Smith, for whom closure involves a "structure" of some kind, Meyer notes that "[c]ompletion is possible only where there is shape and pattern" (129). He also appeals to the importance that immediate repetition plays in *inhibiting* completeness: "Repetition in itself does not make for completeness or closure." Furthermore, Meyer distinguishes between *reiteration*, an immediate repetition, and *recurrence*, a repetition that appears after some intervening, contrasting material, and observes that the latter concept exemplifies "the law of return."[17] "There can be a return to a pattern only after there has been something different which was understood as a departure from the pattern. Because there is departure and return, recurrence always involves a delay of expectation and subsequent fulfilment." Moreover, a "recurrence itself represents, not tension, but the relaxation phase of the total motion. It creates closure and a feeling of completeness" (151–52).[18] With these notions of recurrence or return, we again encounter the idea of formal circularity as a fundamental principle of closure, similar to what we found with Smith.

Perhaps owing to the influence of Gestalt psychology, Meyer's emphasis on "completeness," "pattern," and "shape" evokes a visual or spatial sense of closure. In fact, he seldom refers to "ending," an expression directed more to temporal processes than to spatial configurations. At a number of points in his discussion, though, he speaks in a manner that seems more attuned to an "in-time" experience of closure:

> Two types of incompleteness can be distinguished: (1) those which arise in the course of the pattern because something was left out or skipped over; and (2) those in which the figure, though complete so far as it goes, simply is not felt to have reached a satisfactory *conclusion*, is not *finished*. The first type of incompleteness may be said to be a product of a "structural gap," the second type, a product of a delay in the need and desire for "closure." (130, my italics)

Of the two forms of incompleteness proposed here, the first is rooted in the spatial image of a "gap," whereas the second—the reaching of a "conclusion"—is more grounded in a mode of temporality involving delay and subsequent ending.

In his later writings, Meyer continues to be concerned with general matters of musical closure. One passage from *Explaining Music* strongly reflects Smith's idea of terminal modification: "Particularly when they tend toward uniformity, so that no decisive points of structural stability are established, patterns [such as repeated linear sequences] develop a strong internal momentum. In such cases, a marked, unequivocal *break in process* is needed if closure is to be effective and convincing" (119, my italics). We see here a clear allusion to the repetition/terminal-modification paradigm, whereby repetitions promote openness and continuation, whereas a marked change in material is required to effect closure. Note as well that Meyer's appeal to "process," something that occurs through time, evokes a distinctly temporal conception of closure.

In his last book, *Style and Music*, Meyer discusses how musical closure is specifically linked to *syntactical* processes. "In order for syntax to exist . . . successive stimuli must be related to one another in such a way that specific criteria for mobility and closure are established."[19] Since we normally think of syntax (both in language and in music) as a *successive* arrangement of elements, this connection of closure and syntax operates in a context that is decidedly temporal. Meyer then inquires as to the conditions necessary for a given musical parameter to express syntactic relationships: "Such criteria [for syntax] can be established only if the elements of the parameter can be segmented into discrete, nonuniform relationships so that the similarities and differences between them are definable, constant, and proportional" (14). As he goes on to note, only certain parameters are capable of meeting these conditions, most principally, those of harmony, tonality, counterpoint, and meter. These *primary* parameters, as Meyer terms them, can give rise to syntax because their constituent elements are sufficiently *differentiated* as to permit our being able to perceive that in a pair of elements, one is unstable and mobile in relation to the other, which is stable and conclusive (e.g., dissonance vs. consonance, dominant vs. tonic, unaccented beat vs. accented one). On the contrary:

> A series of exactly equivalent elements (e.g., a succession of half steps or whole steps, of quarter-notes or, on a higher level, dotted rhythms), a series of entirely disparate stimuli (as occurs at times in random music), or a gradually graded continuum (e.g., a *crescendo* or *accelerando*) cannot establish criteria for closure. Each can stop at any point, at any time. But

---

16. Meyer, *Emotion and Meaning in Music*, 128.

17. Meyer attributes this "law" to the psychologist W. V. Bingham, who proposes that "other things being equal, it is better to return to any starting point whatsoever than not to return" ("Studies in Melody," 33).

18. In his subsequent writings, he emphasizes the same distinction, but uses the term "repetition" more restrictively to mean an immediate restatement (his earlier "reiteration"), as opposed to a "return," a restatement following other ideas (his earlier "recurrence"); see, e.g., Leonard B. Meyer, *Explaining Music: Essays and Explorations*, 49. In my own work, I follow Meyer's later terminology (repetition versus return); see *Classical Form: A Theory of Formal Functions for the Instrumental Music of Haydn, Mozart, and Beethoven* (henceforth, *CF*), 260, note. 12, and *Analyzing Classical Form: An Approach for the Classroom* (*ACF*), 83.

19. Leonard B. Meyer, *Style and Music: Theory, History and Ideology*, 14.

because no stability/instability relationship can establish preferential points of articulation, none can close. (14)

The absence of such functional differentiation renders the succession of elements just described as nonsyntactical. In particular, if the succession involves a sense of gradated accumulation or reduction, such as a tempo acceleration or deceleration, textural thickening or thinning, or a dynamic intensification or abatement, Meyer considers these parameters to be *secondary* and *statistical*, in that they "tend to be described in terms of amounts rather than in terms of classlike relationships" (15), as the syntactical parameters are normally expressed. Meyer is aware, however, that although the statistical parameters are incapable of creating syntax, they are nonetheless processive, in that once they are established, they tend to persist until the process simply stops or else is checked by one or more of the syntactical parameters. "Lacking syntax, . . . such processes cannot specify definite points of termination. . . . [t]hey may cease, but they cannot close" (15). Note that these descriptions evoke the repetition/terminal-modification paradigm, as well as the distinction between stopping and ending. Meyer's concerns, therefore, resonate closely with some fundamental conceptions of closure articulated widely in approaches advocated by scholars working outside of music.

## 1.2.2. Kofi Agawu

As we have seen, Meyer in his later work speaks of closure primarily in connection with syntax. Indeed, music theorists writing on matters of closure regularly recognize the importance of syntactical processes in producing what is frequently termed *tonal closure*, that is, the closing of a work's fundamental pitch-structural organization. And given the prominence of Schenkerian theory as a comprehensive model of such organization, theorists typically identify tonal closure as occurring at that point in a work where the *Ursatz* achieves its completion, though considerable ink has been spilled determining just where in a given piece such a moment actually occurs. In the past forty years or so, a handful of music theorists writing on generalized notions of musical closure have identified a wider range of meanings associated with the concept, especially involving modes of closure that transcend matters of tonal syntax. In an oft-cited article, Kofi Agawu proposes three general perspectives on how to view closure in music:[20]

> "1. *Closure is a function of formal principles and/or generic signs.*" Here, Agawu references Smith's work on poetic closure, and especially her notions of the background knowledge that a reader, say, of a Shakespearian sonnet, brings to a given poem in that genre. Like poetry, music in a particular style has "various types of signs—some conventional, others arbitrary—[that] are used to inform the listener of how or when a piece is going to end."

> "2. *Closure is not the same thing as an ending.*" As important as ending may be, our sense that a work is completed in a more comprehensive manner is dependent on a host of closural mechanisms, namely, "the sum total of all the tendencies to close that occur in the composition, whether or not these are actually fulfilled." In this respect, Agawu considers an ending to be representative of "local elements in the musical structure, whereas closure denotes a global mechanism."

> "3. *Closure is a function of both syntactic and semantic principles.*" We may largely know how syntactical processes work to create tonal closure, but Agawu appeals as well to a semantic component. He concedes, though, that music's semantics "is not so easy to decipher." Unlike poetry, whose constituent elements—words—express a set of literal and allusive meanings, music's semantic domain can only be marked by "certain rhetorical procedures." In order to account for a musical semantics, Agawu proposes a "series of dichotomies that carry roughly the same connotations as syntactic-semantics: structure-rhetoric, form-expression, and structure-utterance."

## 1.2.3. Robert Hatten

Robert Hatten also proposes a semantic component to musical closure residing in what he more specifically terms *dramatic closure*. Developing first a view of music's syntactic, tonal closure, Hatten notes that even in that domain, if some "unstable structures persist, or are heightened rather than transformed to stability, . . . then closure may nevertheless be achieved, but it must be understood as dramatic closure, strategically achieved, and appropriate to the semantic argument of the piece (whether serious or witty)."[21]

Among various strategies for dramatic closure, Hatten identifies a technique of "'summing up,' in which strategic instabilities are heightened in a terse or epigrammatic final statement" (197), as exemplified by the coda of the opening movement of Beethoven's first piano sonata. And in connection with the juxtaposition of highly diverse, conflicting material featured throughout that composer's String Quartet in B-flat, Op. 130, first movement, Hatten discusses a form of dramatic closure that he terms *integration*, defined as an "accommodation between (or among) conflicting materials or ideas, regardless of the means employed or the degree of tonal (or harmonic, or rhythmic) stability involved." He sees such integration as analogous to "resolution" in the domain of syntax, and notes that integration "may be possible even when resolution (of contradiction) is not." Moreover, in the coda of that movement, "Beethoven solves the problem of dramatic closure left unsatisfied by the syntactic formal closure at the end of the

---

20. V. Kofi Agawu, "Concepts of Closure and Chopin's Opus 28," 4–5.

21. Robert S. Hatten, "Aspects of Dramatic Closure in Beethoven: A Semiotic Perspective on Music Analysis via Strategies of Dramatic Conflict," 197.

recapitulation. He both *sums up* the problem situation and finds appropriate means of *resolution* or *integration* for the different kinds of conflicts involved" (205). Having established dramatic closure as conceptually distinct from syntactic closure, Hatten concludes his argument by emphasizing that a "high-level event for the dramatic argument of a movement may be represented by a surface structure in a syntactic hierarchy (such as Schenker's); the hierarchy of dramatic relevance or salience may not be congruent with the hierarchy of a purely syntactic analysis of a work" (208–9).

### 1.2.4. Patrick McCreless

Patrick McCreless, like Hatten and Agawu, also understands musical closure as embracing phenomena that are more than purely syntactical. A music theorist who has especially been inspired by ideas of literary closure, McCreless not only rehearses Smith's categories of formal and thematic closure in poetry but adds to the mix a concept of narrative closure proposed by Rolland Barthes, as well as Quintillian's ideas of rhetorical closure in the realm of oratory. McCreless's goal, then, is "to show more specifically how we can define syntactical, thematic, formal, and rhetorical closure in tonal music, in ways analogous to their use in the literary models."[22]

McCreless begins with Barthes's account of narrativity as presented in his extraordinarily detailed analysis of Balzac's short story *Sarrasine*.[23] Among the number of *codes* that Barthes identifies as operative in narrative genres, the *hermeneutic* code focuses on the description of an overarching plot, a structure that Barthes likens to a grammatically "well-made" sentence. The "subject" of this "hermeneutic sentence" sets out an enigma that launches the narrative. Following various delays, digressions, and interpolations, the sentence eventually yields a "predicate" that solves the enigma, thus bringing closure to the narrative. As McCreless notes, Barthes's hermeneutic sentence thus "provides for a syntax of narrative, one that metaphorically carries the notion of 'subject-predicate' to the broadest level of a narrative" (37). Moreover, McCreless sees here a powerful analogue to Schenker's *Ursatz*, which similarly finds at the highest level of musical organization, a structural model that replicates lower-level progressions of melody, counterpoint, and harmony.

Complementing syntactical closure are the two types—formal and thematic—offered by Smith's theory of poetic closure. Here, too, McCreless finds analogues in musical practice, with formal closure in music resulting from "the proportional balance of sections, thematic return, and the completion of formal prototypes" (50), for example, ternary, rondo, or sonata forms. Smith's thematic closure is less easy to analogize with music, but since it involves the "structure and progression of *ideas* in poetry," McCreless defines "thematic closure in tonal music as that type of closure which invokes the completion of themes or thematic processes, or thematic reminiscence and 'summing up'" (50).[24]

Finally, McCreless turns to concepts of rhetoric inspired by Quintillian's *Institutio Oratoria*. Among the main components of a rhetorically effective speech (Quintillian is specifically referring here to a legal oration in front of a judge), the final part, the *peroration*, is responsible for clinching the argument, for bringing a convincing conclusion. Of the main features of rhetorical closure, two in particular stand out for McCreless—those of convention and excess:

> In general, rhetorical closure involves both the importation of *conventions* that dramatize and call attention to closure, and the *exceeding* of already established internal norms in a work as a way of signaling closure. . . . [We] shall designate as rhetorical closure the importation of closural *conventions* or the use of harmonic, melodic, rhythmic, textural, orchestrational, articulative, or registral extremes as means of dramatizing the end of a piece. (51)

Among the corollary ideas that McCreless pursues in his essay are two general themes that we have already encountered in other writings on closure. First, he considers the extent to which his four types (syntactical, formal, thematic, and rhetorical) operate "in time" or "out of time." He notes, for example, that Smith would seem to favor a temporally ordered accounting of poetic elements; yet "we can still look back upon them once they are complete, and understand the formal and thematic structures that she uncovers as abstractions that we can perceive as a synoptic whole" (49–50). Compared to Smith, Barthes, a thorough-going structuralist, "is philosophically on the side of atemporality"; nevertheless, "his analysis . . . of the irreversible codes in *Sarrasine* . . . demonstrates (despite his own opposition) the power of classic narrative as it is experienced in real time" (50). In other words, the phenomenon of closure is amenable to description grounded in both spatial and temporal perspectives, a seeming dichotomy that nonetheless resides at the heart of the concept.

A second theme that McCreless broaches involves the distinction between processes that trace either linear or circular trajectories. "Narratives start at a point in time . . . where one or more enigmas are introduced, and progress to a point where those enigmas are solved" (55). Tonal music is likewise fundamentally linear, but it is also, "at least in a purely harmonic sense, circular" (55). With only a few exceptions, a tonal work starts with tonic of the home key and returns to that harmonic-tonal source at its end. The formal structures of many compositions also have pronounced elements of circularity. A narrative, on the contrary, rarely brings a "return" to the initial state of the story. For these reasons, then, there are limitations on the extent to which a theory of musical closure can find its analogues in models of narrative closure.

---

22. Patrick McCreless, "The Hermeneutic Sentence and Other Literary Models for Tonal Closure," 40.

23. Roland Barthes, *S/Z*.

24. Note that whereas Hatten saw "summing up" to be a technique of dramatic closure, McCreless assigns it to the realm of thematic closure.

## 1.2.5. Mark Anson-Cartwright

A more recent contribution to discussions of closure in music is offered by Mark Anson-Cartwright.[25] Like all of the theorists we have already examined, he strongly supports a multifarious view of closure, all the while acknowledging that closure in music is most often equated with tonal closure, especially in the Schenkerian sense of that expression. Similar to his predecessors, Anson-Cartwright identifies different senses of closure by defining three main types:

(1) that condition of rest or finality which a piece or movement attains at the moment of structural (tonal) resolution . . .

(2) that condition of imminent rest or finality which begins near the chronological conclusion of a piece or movement, and lasts until such rest is achieved . . .

(3) that condition of immanent rest or finality which a piece or movement possesses as a temporal whole, by virtue of all the tendencies to close projected within that whole. (3)

Note that all three definitions begin by characterizing closure "as a condition of rest and finality." By "rest," Anson-Cartwright seems to be alluding to a "cessation of activity," whereas "finality" clarifies that this cessation is associated with the temporal experience of ending (for we would unlikely speak of "finality" in a context of spatial closure, where a word such as "completeness" would be more apt). Moreover, the first type of closure involves listeners hearing a *moment* in time, whereas the two others engage our perception of closure over a *span* of time.[26] In the second definition, the time-span occurs near the end, whereas in the third, the span embraces the entire length of the musical work. In addition, Anson-Cartwright borrows a distinction drawn by Kermode between a span of closure that is "imminent" (in type 2) and one that is "immanent" (in type 3). The former refers to closure that is "about to happen," the latter, to closure that is "inherent in" or "intrinsic to" a span of time.[27]

Clarifying these definitions further, Anson-Cartwright sees the first type of closure as a moment in time where the "structure" of the composition finds resolution. In speaking of structure in this manner, he follows in a tradition, held by many adherents of Schenker, that distinguishes "structure," a specifically Schenkerian conception of tonal organization, from "design," a more traditional view of formal organization.[28] Thus his first definition of closure refers to the moment of time articulated by the final event of the *Ursatz*. In this respect, his view resembles McCreless's syntactical closure (as an analogue to Barthes's hermeneutic sentence). Inasmuch as Schenkerian theory stipulates that the *Ursatz* closes at *one* specific time point, considerable analytical work is often required to determine just which point in the piece satisfies this type of closure.[29]

Anson-Cartwright's second definition concerns a span of time leading up to the moment of structural (tonal) closure, as determined by type (1). Just where that span of time would begin is left rather open, but he notes that it would be "at least halfway (and usually more than two-thirds of the way) through the piece." As well, he speaks of a "listener's complicity in a set of stylistic conventions" that help to signal the onset of this time-span, such as a "strong turn to the subdominant [that] can project the condition of imminent rest" (3).[30]

Anson-Cartwright's third definition considers closure at the level of the entire work. Inspired by Agawu's idea that one view of closure includes the "sum total of all the tendencies to close that occur in the composition,"[31] Anson-Cartwright sees this type of closure as encompassing the time-span of the complete work, that is, "as a temporal whole." Indeed, from the perspective of this definition, "the listener is aware at all times—even in principle, before the piece begins—that the piece will end sooner or later." From this view, a fully synoptic one, closure seems as though it is operating in an atemporal manner, somewhat in the sense of spatial completeness, rather than in-time finality. Indeed, at the close of his article, Anson-Cartwright raises the question as to whether this type of closure necessarily arises from the specific order of events as actually presented to the listener: "can one conceive of closure—specifically in the sense of 'wholeness' or 'completeness'—without strict regard to the order or sequence of events?" Following in the spirit of his third type of closure, the answer would seem to be yes.

---

25. Mark Anson-Cartwright, "Concepts of Closure in Tonal Music: A Critical Study." Anson-Cartwright's article appeared after my own study, "The Classical Cadence: Conceptions and Misconceptions." He acknowledges being influenced by certain of my ideas on cadence and closure, yet also critiques aspects of my approach.

26. This distinction relates to a similar point that I propose in "Classical Cadence," 77–81, between cadential *arrival* as a moment of time and cadential *function* as a span of time; see ahead sec. 2.5 in Chapter 2.

27. Kermode, *Sense of an Ending*, 6.

28. The idea that a tonal composition's *structure* is revealed through a Schenkerian representation of its pitch organization seems to have originated with Hans Weisse, in his teaching of Schenkerian theory and analysis at Mannes College in the 1930s; see David Carson Berry, "Hans Weisse and the Dawn of American Schenkerism." Felix Salzer, another proponent of Schenkerian analysis, defines *design* as "the organization of the composition's motivic, thematic and rhythmic material through which the functions of form and structure are made clear. Design is instrumental in bringing about the formal subdivisions and repetitions and in shaping the prolongations into sections, themes and phrases. These subdivisions, specifically, may be accomplished through various techniques developed in past centuries, such as: thematic repetition, cadences (harmonic as well as contrapuntal), caesuras, change of tempo, rhythm or texture, etc." (*Structural Hearing: Tonal Coherence in Music*, 1: 224).

29. McCreless also discusses the problem of determining which moment, of several potential ones, counts as the real point of syntactical closure ("Hermeneutic Sentence," 56).

30. This example is somewhat confusing, however, because we normally associate a "strong turn to the subdominant" as occurring *after* a moment of syntactical closure—in a closing section or coda, for instance, rather than *before* the closure of the *Ursatz*. Perhaps he is referring to the conventional swerve to flat-side tonal regions (such as the subdominant) in early portions of a sonata-form recapitulation (e.g., in the main theme's return or in the subsequent transition).

31. Agawu, "Concepts of Closure," 4. This is Agawu's second type of closure discussed earlier.

Temporal linearity is not the only mechanism that can generate our sense of musical closure, even if it is the primary one. A spatial view seems often to be lurking in the shadows.

* * * * *

The preceding discussion of closure has, needless to say, been all too cursory. The writers I have discussed develop their ideas in greater detail and sophistication. My goal, however, has been to extract from their writings key concepts associated with closure that will gain pertinence as we consider the topic of cadence in music. These include: differentiating between ending and cessation of activity; outlining some general mechanisms of closure, such as the repetition/terminal-modification paradigm; distinguishing processes of linearity and circularity; and considering those experiences of closure that reside in-time or out-of-time (spatial closure).

Most of the writers we have looked at understand that closure is a multifaceted phenomenon. In that spirit, I argue throughout my study that whereas cadence is a powerful source of closure, it is not the exclusive source. Put conversely, I hold strongly to the view that closure can be perceived in contexts that are not cadential (as I define them). In the following chapter, especially, I highlight how a state of terminological inertia characterizes the disciplines of music theory and history, such that "cadence" has been used by many writers to embrace a host of compositional situations that I exclude as cadential; indeed, some of these contexts of cadence do not even project a process of closure. Some might see in this approach an impoverishment of the cadence concept; on the contrary, I would argue that by clearly delimiting the conditions for cadence, we enrich our understanding of how closure is effected in musical compositions, both cadentially and, just as important, noncadentially.

# Part I

# The Classical Cadence

The four chapters of Part I investigate cadential practice of the classical era, as exemplified by the instrumental works of Haydn, Mozart, and Beethoven. Following a chapter that develops some general concepts of the classical cadence, the second chapter defines the three genuine cadence types—perfect authentic cadence, imperfect authentic cadence, and half cadence—as regards their morphology (harmonic and melodic) and their function within broader formal contexts. The third chapter considers various deviations of these cadential types—deceptive cadence, evaded cadence, abandoned cadence, and dominant arrival. The final chapter demonstrates how cadences can become expanded in ways that contribute to a heightened rhetorical expression and the formal loosening of certain thematic units, especially subordinate themes.

# 2

# General Concepts of the Classical Cadence

THIS OPENING CHAPTER OF PART I EXAMINES GEneral concepts associated with the classical cadence, thus laying the groundwork for a further elaboration of cadence not only in the classical style, but also in earlier and later tonal styles, as presented in Part II of this book.[1] For the purposes of this chapter, I am assuming that the reader is familiar with the standard textbook definitions of cadences, especially the differences among the three fundamental cadence types: the *perfect authentic cadence* (PAC), ending on tonic harmony with the tonic scale degree in the upper voice; the *imperfect authentic cadence* (IAC), ending on tonic harmony, with the third scale degree on top; and the *half cadence* (HC), ending on dominant harmony, with no stipulation as to the scale degree of the soprano.

I begin this chapter with a brief sketch of some traditional notions of cadence—a full history of the concept far exceeds the confines of this study—and then move quickly to the fundamental ideas that underpin my own approach. I argue that cadence effects *formal closure* at a limited number of levels of musical structure, especially those associated with *thematic units* (main and subordinate themes, transitions, and developmental cores), but also to certain subthematic *phrases* (e.g., the antecedent and consequent phrases of the period theme type).[2] I propose that the underlying harmonic and bass-line support for a cadence is highly constrained to specific *cadential progressions*, ones in which the final dominant and tonic harmonies must reside in root position. I see *cadential function* embracing a time span from the beginning of the cadential progression to its end—the point of *cadential arrival*. I carefully distinguish such cadential function from *postcadential function*, which embraces the music that follows the

---

1. This chapter is based on my article "The Classical Cadence." I have updated a small number of references and have included some new topics (esp. in sec. 2.4 and 2.8).

2. The cadence closing the consequent also functions to end the complete period.

cadential arrival (and appears prior to a new thematic beginning). I further show how passages of *cadential content* do not always function as genuine cadences. I emphasize that cadential arrival represents a formal *end*, not a rhythmic or textural *stop*, and that the appropriate linguistic analogy for cadence is *syntactical closure*, not the external, written signs of *punctuation*. Finally, I distinguish between two types of cadential *strength—syntactical* and *rhetorical*—the former being the one aspect essential for the expression of formal functionality.

## 2.1. Traditional Notions of Cadence

Cadence (from Latin *caderer*, "to fall") has a long history as a theoretical term.³ It gained initial currency in late fifteenth-century Italian theory in reference to "closing gestures" (*clausulae*), that is, specific intervallic formations used to conclude passages in both monophonic and polyphonic textures.⁴ Throughout the sixteenth and seventeenth centuries, the term normally had attached to it a wide variety of qualifying expressions (such as *cadentia ordinaria, cadentia cantizans, cadentia simplex, cadentia perfecta, cadentia diatonica*) in order to distinguish closes based on the scale degree of the final pitch, the particular voice being closed, the style of counterpoint, the interval of melodic or contrapuntal progression, the modality, and many other compositional factors.⁵ As will be discussed in more detail in both Chapters 6 and 7 on cadential usage in the high-baroque and galant styles, theorists in the seventeenth and eighteenth centuries developed an extensive system of classifying cadential patterns, later termed *Kadenzlehre* (or *Klausellehre*),⁶ based on how clausulae formations are distributed among the various voices of a composition.

The eighteenth century also saw a profound impact of models of natural language on music theory in general, and thus the idea of cadence as a closing gesture strongly became associated with grammatical punctuation in language, especially in the writings of Mattheson, Riepel, Kirnberger, and Koch.⁷ With the origins of harmonic theory early in that century, cadential classifications became based primarily on harmony rather than on melodic or contrapuntal interval. Moreover, the sense of cadence enlarged considerably when Rameau took the fateful decision of recognizing the harmonic content of the *cadence parfait* (our authentic cadence) as the fundamental paradigm of harmonic progression in general.⁸ The concept of cadence was thus no longer confined to musical situations involving gestures of ending. From then on, any harmonic progression could be considered a cadence, whether or not it occurred at the end of a musical unit.

Well into the nineteenth century, a cadential progression was understood to involve just two harmonies. Toward the end of that century, however, Riemann extended the progression to embrace a complete functional succession, tonic–subdominant–dominant–tonic, and he deemed such a cadence the fundamental model of *tonality*, a broader conception of tonal relations than harmony alone.⁹ Twentieth-century theory, overwhelmingly concerned with musical hierarchies, saw the notion of cadence applied to multiple levels within a work, even invoking the idea of a large-scale cadence to account for the tonal progression of an entire piece.

The diverse elements associated with twentieth-century conceptions of cadence have been well analyzed by Ann Blombach.¹⁰ By reviewing definitions of cadence drawn from eighty-one pedagogical texts (whose median publication date is 1970), she identified how often various elements appear within those definitions.¹¹ Her results are summarized in Table 2.1, where the numbers represent percentages of occurrence of a given element.¹² It is no surprise that *end of phrase* and *conclusion* place high on the list. But it is telling that *harmony, chord progression* leads the group, thus revealing how powerful was

---

3. For a comprehensive account, see Hans Heinrich Eggebrecht, ed., *Handwörterbuch der musikalischen Terminologie*, s.v. "Kadenz," 1–23. For additional information on the history of the cadence concept, see Caleb Mutch, "Studies in the History of the Cadence"; Janet Schmalfeldt, "Cadential Processes: The Evaded Cadence and the 'One More Time' Technique"; Daniel Harrison, "Cadence." In addition to its more common meanings as "formal conclusion" and "basic harmonic progression," the term "cadence," in music, has also been used in reference to various types of melodic ornamentation in baroque vocal music and to regularly alternating rhythmic-metric accentuation in French Enlightenment theory. These senses of the term will not be treated in this study.

4. "Cadence" was originally used alongside *clausula* (fr. Lat., "to close"), but eventually replaced that earlier term. Harrison advocates for a renewed usage of cadence and clausulae as different, but highly related, ideas ("Cadence," 544–51); see Chapter 3, note 263.

5. The *Handwörterbuch* article cites over eighty cadential types (5–6).

6. Ludwig Holtmeier, "Kadenz/Klausel."

7. On the impact of language models for music theory, see Mark Evan Bonds, *Wordless Rhetoric: Musical Form and the Metaphor of the Oration*, chap. 2.

8. Jean-Philippe Rameau, *Treatise on Harmony*, 63–81.

9. See, e.g., Hugo Riemann, *Systematische Modulationslehre als Grundlage der Musikalischen Formenlehre*, 16, as discussed by Daniel Harrison, *Harmonic Function in Chromatic Music: A Renewed Dualist Theory and an Account of Its Precedents*, 278.

10. Ann K. Blombach, "Phrase and Cadence: A Study of Terminology and Definition."

11. Blombach, 231. She also proposes her own definition: "A *cadence* is any musical element or combination of musical elements, including silence, that indicates relative relaxation or relative conclusion in music. ('Conclusion' is intended in the sense of 'destination of ideas,' as opposed to merely stopping with no indication of finality or direction.)"

12. Blombach, 227. The first column contains percentages from textbooks published prior to 1970; the second column, textbooks published after 1970; the third column, percentages for all textbooks.

TABLE 2.1
*Elements of Cadence Definitions*

| Element | Percentage before 1970 | Percentage after 1970 | Percentage all |
|---|---|---|---|
| Harmony, chord progression | 77 | 63 | 70 |
| List of cadence (PAC, etc.) | 54 | 63 | 62 |
| End of phrase | 57 | 51 | 54 |
| Conclusion | 51 | 56 | 54 |
| Melody | 57 | 49 | 53 |
| Rest, pause | 43 | 49 | 46 |
| Rhythm | 46 | 37 | 41 |
| Language, punctuation | 29 | 49 | 39 |
| Formula | 40 | 22 | 30 |
| Relaxation | 31 | 27 | 29 |
| Formal indicator | 14 | 34 | 25 |
| "To fall" | 20 | 24 | 22 |
| Recognizes other styles | 23 | 15 | 18 |
| Other elements | 3 | 7 | 9 |
| Confirm tonality | 6 | 7 | 7 |
| Completion of formal unit | 9 | 2 | 5 |

Source: "Blombach, "Phrase and Cadence," 227, Table 1.

the conceptual enlargement effected by Rameau in the eighteenth century.[13] The inclusion of *language, punctuation* in more than a third of the definitions also attests to the influence that eighteenth-century models of natural language have continued to exert on our notions of cadence. Noteworthy is the prominent appearance of the element *rest, pause*. The idea that achieving formal closure entails a cessation of rhythmic activity is strongly entrenched in the cadence concept. The mention of *formula* in many of the definitions is also not surprising given that the content of cadences is normally conventional or repeatable from work to work. Finally, I must draw attention to the low rankings for *formal indicator* and *completion of formal unit*; as the rest of this chapter will make abundantly clear, these are precisely the elements that I find at the heart of the classical cadence.

## 2.2. Cadence as Formal Closure

Central to my concept of cadence is the fundamental idea that cadence effects *formal closure* at middle-ground levels in the structural hierarchy of a work. More simply put, a cadence must

---

13. Caution must obviously be exercised when trying to interpret data such as that shown in Table 2.1. It is most likely the case that, when taken together, either one of the two elements *end of phrase* and *conclusion* would occur in a very large percentage of the definitions, thus displacing *harmony, chord progression* from the leading position.

*end* something. Now this idea—the most pervasive and historically rooted of all cadence notions—might seem so trivial as not to require further elaboration. Yet many of the problems associated with conceptualizing and analyzing cadence result from not specifying (or even not being able to specify) exactly what formal unit a given cadence is actually ending. Since the implications of this premise are far-reaching, I want to address a number of major issues that ensue from it.

Cadence creates musical closure, but, as we amply observed in Chapter 1, not all closure in music is cadential. Indeed, the specific technique of cadence, while frequently associated with "tonal closure," by no means holds a central position within the studies on musical closure that we examined. Also discussed in the previous chapter was the fundamental idea that closure in general involves bringing to completion some process implicating one or more modes of musical organization at a variety of levels within the hierarchical organization of a work. Within this broad conceptual framework, I hold that cadence is only one device of musical closure and is operative at only a limited number of structural levels.

Determining which specific musical processes are ended by cadences can be somewhat complicated and will sometimes vary from case to case. At all times, however, a definite *harmonic* process is closed, since the harmonies associated with the cadence almost always bring to some degree of completion a broader harmonic trajectory established prior to the onset of the cadential harmonies per se.[14] Often we can identify a distinctly *melodic* process closed by cadences, such as when, in the case of a PAC, a melodic line descends to the tonic scale degree ($\hat{1}$). Some writers have also spoken of cadence achieving a sense of *rhythmical* or *metrical* close, though the actual mechanisms of such closure are often left unclear.[15] More importantly, however, the various types of closure associated with individual musical parameters are, in themselves, insufficient to create cadence unless a sense of *formal* closure is present as well.

---

14. For an exception to this rule, see Chapter 5, sec. 5.5.

15. Thus Meyer invokes rhythmic processes when noting that "a semicadence might be defined as one in which a mobile, goal-directed, harmonic process is temporarily stabilized by decisive rhythmic closure," but he does not specify any further just how such closure comes about (*Explaining Music*, 85). In Hugo Riemann's theory of meter, which posits a normative scheme of eight alternating weak and strong bars, metrical closure is achieved in measure "eight" of the scheme, the measure in which a cadence normally occurs; see, e.g., *System der musikalischen Rhythmik und Metrik*. Whether such metrical closure is responsible for cadence is not clear in Riemann's approach, however. That genuine cadences can occur on metrically weak measures (by any accounting of strong and weak) and even on weak beats within a measure prohibits us from establishing a determinate relation of cadence and meter. On this complicated relationship in Riemann's theories, see William E. Caplin, "Criteria for Analysis: Perspectives on Riemann's Mature Theory of Meter." I address the general topic of cadence and meter in Chapter 3, sec. 3.4.1.

When speaking of cadence achieving formal closure, I mean something like what Fred Lerdahl and Ray Jackendoff describe in connection with a "cadenced group," a unit of grouping structure that "at some level of reduction reduces to two elements, the second of which is a cadence. The first of these elements is the *structural beginning* of the group, and the cadence is the *structural ending*. . . . A cadence must be a cadence *of something*; a group that consisted only of the articulation of its ending would be unsatisfying."[16] The logic of formal closure thus requires that a cadence be grouped with at least one preceding event at the same level of structure and that the cadence would usually be the final event in the group.[17] If we cannot identify an initiating formal unit that precedes a potential cadence, then we cannot legitimately speak of a true cadence. Put somewhat differently, since the first idea of a group normally expresses the sense of formal initiation, this idea cannot itself be a cadence, for an essential condition of formal closure would no longer obtain: there would be no beginning for which such a cadence would be the ending.

---

16. Fred Lerdahl and Ray Jackendoff, *A Generative Theory of Tonal Music*, 168. It also seems reasonable to permit a cadenced group to contain an element standing between the functions of structural beginning and ending that would express the sense of structural middle, what I term a *medial* formal function (*CF*, 255, and *ACF*, 709). (The pervasively binary nature of Lerdahl and Jackendoff's system does not readily permit such tripartite formal structures, but see the upcoming statement by them in the text and referenced in note 24.)

17. This last point needs further refinement. On the one hand, it might be the case that the formal unit does not conclude with a structural end (i.e., that formal closure does not take place). In that case, the last event in the formal unit may not be a cadence. On the other hand, the cadential event might be followed by a postcadential event that still groups with the formal unit as whole.

18. Arnold Schoenberg, *Fundamentals of Musical Composition*; Erwin Ratz, *Einfuhrung in die musikalische Formenlehre: Über Formprinzipien in den Inventionen und Fugen J. S. Bachs und ihre Bedeutung für die Kompositionstechnik Beethovens*.

19. All genuine themes close cadentially; a "themelike" unit, though containing the same basic formal functions as a theme, sometimes closes in a noncadential manner or even remains open without any sense of formal closure. Most of *CF* and *ACF* is devoted to a detailed description of the structure and function of these various thematic units.

20. These theme types are treated in *CF*, part 2; *ACF*, part 1.

21. See Janet Schmalfeldt, "Phrase," and Schmalfeldt, "Coming to Terms: Speaking of Phrase, Cadence, and Form."

22. Blombach, "Phrase and Cadence," 226.

23. Roger Sessions, *The Musical Experience of Composer, Performer, Listener*, 12.

24. Fred Lerdahl and Ray Jackendoff, "Toward a Formal Theory of Tonal Music," 123.

25. Warren Darcy and James Hepokoski, "The Medial Caesura and Its Role in the Eighteenth-Century Sonata Exposition," 123. In their subsequent treatise, James Hepokoski and Warren Darcy, *Elements of Sonata Theory: Norms, Types, and Deformations in the Late-Eighteenth-Century Sonata*, material from their earlier article was revised (to some extent in response to my own work); as a result, references to that article in the present chapter may not entirely reflect their later formulations.

## 2.2.1. Formal Units Closed by Cadence; Cadence and Phrase

What, then, are the formal units closed by cadences? In my view, a cadence closes a *theme* and, in many cases, a component part of a theme. Unlike most traditional notions of theme, which primarily refer to relatively short melodic ideas, my notion derives from the usage of Arnold Schoenberg and his followers (especially Erwin Ratz) and refers to a complete formal unit, minimally eight measures in length, consisting of the clear articulation of a formal beginning, middle, and end (the latter being the cadence).[18] Such a formal unit can function in the broader context of a classical movement as a *main theme*, a *subordinate theme*, an *interior theme*, or a *coda theme*; the *transition* and *developmental core* are also constructed as themelike units, and these may also close with a cadence.[19] The basic theme types are the *sentence*, *period*, *small ternary*, and *small binary*; various *hybrids* of the sentence and period can also be identified, along with *compound* versions of the sentence and period.[20] All of these theme types achieve formal closure by means of cadence. Some of the component parts of these types have cadential ending as well. For example, the two parts of the period—the *antecedent* and *consequent*—each end with a cadence (the first one being weaker than the second). The A and A′ sections of the small ternary (also the first and second parts of the small binary) have cadential requirements as well. On the contrary, the sentence form has no cadential articulation prior to its closing cadence.

Traditionally, the formal unit considered to be closed by a cadence is the *phrase*.[21] Cadence and phrase are so intimately connected that the two terms are frequently defined in reference to each other, as in "a cadence is a melodic-harmonic formula ending a phrase," and "a phrase is a formal unit ending with a cadence."[22] Indeed many theorists posit cadential ending as a central component of their notion of phrase:

The phrase is a constant motion toward a goal—the cadence.[23]

A phrase can be roughly characterized as the lowest level of grouping which has a structural beginning, a middle, and a structural ending (a cadence).[24]

The concept of phrase is most productively understood, both historically and theoretically, as admitting only two choices for its end-point: a half cadence or an authentic cadence.[25]

This powerful connection of phrase and cadence, however, has led to a number of theoretical and analytical difficulties. On the one hand, some phrase endings are identified as cadences even though their concluding harmonic progression fails to satisfy the fundamental criteria for cadence (such as when the dominant is not in root position, an issue I will discuss shortly), or else because the last part of the phrase cannot be seen to represent a formal end for any one of a number of reasons. On the other hand, the concept of phrase is sometimes defined so broadly as to embrace not only relatively short groups (four to eight bars) but also large thematic regions consisting of multiple subgroups.²⁶ I would argue that many of the problems associated with cadence (and indeed with phrase) can be dispelled when the two concepts are entirely disengaged. *Cadence* can then be viewed as a manifestation of formal functionality, whereas *phrase* can be used as a functionally neutral term for grouping structure (embracing approximately four bars of music).²⁷

By separating cadence from phrase, it is possible to describe more clearly which phrases have cadential closure and which do not. As mentioned before, the antecedent and consequent phrases of the period theme type close with a cadence. So, too, does the second phrase, the *continuation*, of the sentence form.²⁸ But the initial four-measure phrase of the sentence, what I have termed a *presentation*, never closes with a cadence, even if its final harmonic progression (V–I) suggests one.²⁹ A presentation consists of a two-measure *basic idea* that is immediately repeated in measures three and four of the phrase. Inasmuch as the basic idea itself functions to begin the theme, its repetition should also be seen to express formal initiation; indeed, the repetition could even be said to intensify that sense of beginning.³⁰ As a result, the repeated basic idea should not be comprehended as concluding a formal process, and so we should not speak of a cadence closing the presentation phrase. To be sure, there are musical forces that effect closure of some kind for the phrase, or else we would not perceive it to be a unified group; but the nature of that closure—be it harmonic, melodic, rhythmic, textural—is not cadential.³¹

Since cadential formations normally occupy at least two measures of music and since a cadence must be preceded by an initiating event, which, in the classical style, itself is minimally two bars long, then the formal unit closed by a cadence is usually no shorter than four measures.³² We see, therefore, that cadential closure does not tend to operate at levels of musical organization lower than the four-measure phrase; instead, other modes of musical closure are used to bring motives and other short ideas to a conclusion. Thus most lower-level groups (i.e., at the levels of the two-measure "idea," the one-measure "fragment," and the individual "motives" that arise within a bar) have their boundaries defined through generalized gestalt perceptual mechanisms such as pitch and durational "proximity" or "change." Similarities and changes of texture, dynamics, articulation, timbre, register, and so on, are also responsible for our sense of what constitutes such lower-level groups. Cadence, on the contrary, would rarely be a factor in determining grouping structure below the level of the four-measure phrase.³³

### 2.2.2. Cadence and Higher-Level Formal Units

If cadence does not provide closure at the lower ends of a work's structural hierarchy, we might ask whether there are any constraints to cadences functioning at higher levels, namely, those above the level of the theme. The idea that large-scale formal units, including an entire movement, are closed by cadences finds repeated expression in music-theoretical literature of the twentieth century. Thus Schoenberg, on several occasions, takes the extreme position of seeing an entire piece as a large-scale cadence.³⁴ Edward T. Cone remarks that if "there is a sense in which a phrase can be heard as an upbeat to its own cadence, larger and larger sections can also be so apprehended. A completely unified composition could then constitute a single huge rhythmic impulse, completed at the final cadence."³⁵ Likewise, Lerdahl and Jackendoff extend their notion of cadenced group to the largest level of a piece.³⁶ Charles Rosen even considers that the last finale of every Mozart comic opera "serves as cadence to the entire opera."³⁷ At somewhat lower structural levels, we find Meyer referring to the entire slow introduction of Beethoven's "Les Adieux" sonata as a "high-level cadence."³⁸ William Rothstein speaks of a sonata exposition closing with a cadence, and localizes it specifically at the point where the "first

---

26. For example, William Rothstein identifies a single phrase lasting thirty-seven measures starting from the beginning of Chopin's Mazurka in G-sharp Minor, Op. 33, no. 1 (*Phrase Rhythm in Tonal Music*, 232).

27. Not all theorists link phrase and cadence so firmly as suggested in this discussion. Schmalfeldt ("Coming to Terms," 103) discusses how Peter Westergaard's notions of phrase do not require a cadential ending (*An Introduction to Tonal Theory*, 313–19). Schmalfeldt further observes that "even if we can agree that to describe a phrase calls for determining where it ends, there is simply no consensus within music-theoretical communities as to whether, by definition, a phrase within tonal music needs to end with one of the types of cadences I've described" (103).

28. The continuation *phrase* of the sentence fuses together two discrete formal *functions*—continuation and cadential. In many *looser* formal situations, such as in a subordinate theme or transition, these two functions can occupy their own unique phrases; in that case, the continuation phrase would not have cadential closure (*CF*, 40–41, and *ACF*, 35).

29. See ahead, the discussion of Ex. 2.5a; see also *CF*, 45, Ex. 3.13, and *ACF*, 59–60, Ex. 2.23.

30. Recall the discussion in Chapter 1 of Smith's and Meyer's notions of repetition as a force for continuation, not for closure.

31. An exception arises in the case of a basic idea that itself seems to close with a cadence, as considered later in connection with the idea of "limited cadential scope" (sec. 2.7 and the discussion of Ex. 2.19).

32. Rarely does a cadence close a three-measure unit; for such a case, see the opening of the slow movement of Beethoven's String Quartet in G, Op. 18, no. 2, analyzed in *CF*, Ex. 4.12.

33. See Lerdahl and Jackendoff, *Generative Theory*, 43–49, for their "grouping preference rules" for low-level groups. Similar to my view, they circumscribe cadence hierarchically by distinguishing cadenced groups from other, lower-level ones whose boundaries are closed noncadentially: "The smallest levels of cadenced groups correspond rather closely to the traditional notion of musical *phrase*" (168).

34. "In a general way every piece of music resembles a cadence, of which each phrase will be a more or less elaborate part" (Schoenberg, *Musical Composition*, 16). "To exaggerate a little . . . we can consider the chorale, as well as every larger composition, a more or less big and elaborate cadence" (Arnold Schoenberg, *Theory of Harmony*, 290–91). These references to cadence, along with others, are gathered together in the "Concordance of Terms" from Arnold Schoenberg, *The Musical Idea and the Logic, Technique, and Art of Its Presentation*, 358–59.

35. Edward T. Cone, *Musical Form and Musical Performance*, 26.

36. Lerdahl and Jackendoff, *Generative Theory*, 233.

37. Charles Rosen, *The Classical Style: Haydn, Mozart, Beethoven*, 305.

38. Meyer, *Explaining Music*, 266.

**18** General Concepts of the Classical Cadence

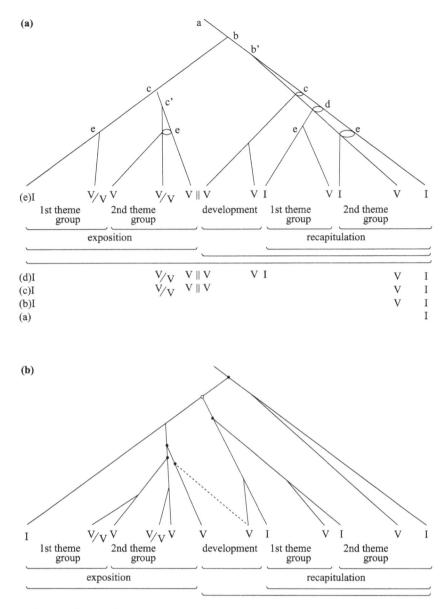

FIGURE 2.1. (a) Time-span reduction of sonata form; (b) prolongational reduction of sonata form (from Lerdahl and Jackendoff, *Generative Theory*, Ex. 9.29 and 9.35).

perfect cadence in the key of the second group" occurs.[39] James Hepokoski and Warren Darcy follow Rothstein in referring to the same cadential articulation as the "essential expositional closure" and the corresponding cadence in the recapitulation as the "essential sonata closure."[40]

It is difficult to evaluate and substantiate many of these claims. But given the pervasive reference to such high-level cadences in the theoretical literature, it is worth pursuing the matter in some detail. As far as an entire piece being a single cadence, the idea can quickly be dismissed as illogical, for such an overarching cadence could not be construed to end anything other than itself.

To say, however, that a given cadence appearing late (or even at the end) in a work represents cadential closure for the work as a whole is somewhat more viable, but still problematical. Take the case of a movement in sonata form, where a decisive cadence ends the subordinate-theme group in the recapitulation. What exactly would it mean to say that this cadence, per se, is responsible for creating closure for the entire movement, in the sense, say, of Hepokoski and Darcy's essential sonata closure?

Two hierarchical perspectives offer positions from which this question can be considered, corresponding essentially to Lerdahl and Jackendoff's distinction between "time-span reduction" and "prolongational reduction."[41] Their two representations of fundamental structures for sonata form are reproduced in Figure 2.1.

---

39. Rothstein, *Phrase Rhythm*, 116.

40. Hepokoski and Darcy, *Sonata Theory*, 18, 20.

41. *Generative Theory*, 118–23.

In both reductions, the local V–I cadence of the recapitulation's subordinate-theme group brings closure to the form. From the perspective of the time-span reduction (Figure 2.1a), the second highest level (labeled "b") would be, presumably, a cadenced group consisting of a structural beginning and a structural end.[42] The moment of structural beginning would be the initial I harmony, but this moment has attached to it a large time span embracing the entire exposition; thus the exposition would represent the subgroup expressing the structural beginning of the form (a notion that seems plausible enough). Likewise, the moment of structural end is articulated by the local V–I progression, but the entire subgroup representing this end comprises both the development and recapitulation.[43] What is not especially convincing, however, is the idea that the development and recapitulation together function as the cadence that closes the cadenced group (the movement as a whole). Even if we say that the development section expresses a structural middle and that the recapitulation represents the structural end (a somewhat more credible idea), it is not clear that we would want to say that the recapitulation, as a whole, is a single, large cadence, for its internal organization is considerably more complex than any kind of cadential formation ending a thematic unit.[44]

From the perspective of the prolongational reduction (Figure 2.1b), the ending of the complete movement only includes the actual V–I cadential formation closing the second-theme group. Everything that precedes that local cadence is connected as right-branching extensions to the initial tonic of the movement. As a cadenced group, the highest level in this representation would see the event that functions as the structural beginning embracing the entire exposition, the entire development, and most of the recapitulation; the event that functions as the structural ending would comprise the local cadence of the second-theme group. Although these two events reside on the same hierarchical level from a prolongational point of view, their actual durational dimensions are entirely disparate. Thus we could question whether we are really talking about a *formal* process at all.[45] To say that the movement as a whole is formally closed by this local cadence is thus problematic. It is perhaps more profitable to understand that, on the one hand, the principal *prolongations* of pitch organization (which are primarily harmonic for Lerdahl and Jackendoff) achieve closure at the same time as the second-theme group in the recapitulation is cadentially closed. On the other hand, the large-scale *formal* closure of the movement is achieved (according to the time-span reduction) by the development and recapitulation together in relation to the exposition (or in my alternative reading, by the recapitulation as ending in relation to the exposition as beginning and development as middle). And neither of these two higher-level closures—of formal time span and of harmonic prolongation—need be considered cadential, an ending function that is more appropriately understood to operate at middle-ground levels of formal organization.

Lerdahl and Jackendoff's prolongational reduction (Figure 2.1b) resembles in certain respects the hierarchy of a Schenkerian model of large-scale pitch structure. From a Schenkerian perspective, to say that an entire movement is closed by a cadence is tantamount to saying that the *Ursatz* itself closes with a cadence.[46] In this respect, Schenker's own writings on the matter are interesting, but somewhat inconclusive. At one time, he refers to the final $\hat{2}$–$\hat{1}$ (supported by V–I) component of the *Ursatz* as a "cadential formula," thus suggesting that the preceding $\hat{3}$ ($\hat{5}$ or $\hat{8}$) represents material of an initiating (as well as possibly medial) formal function.[47] The resulting hierarchical situation, then, could be analogous to Lerdahl and Jackendoff's prolongational reduction in that, as is often the case, the initial I of the *Ursatz* takes up a large percentage of the temporal duration of the movement, with the cadence of the *Ursatz* normally occurring in connection with a relatively foreground cadence closing some thematic unit. Thus my concerns raised before in considering such a closure to be formal and cadential in the context of a prolongational reduction would be applicable to an *Ursatz* closure as well. At other times, Schenker discusses at some length that the "forms of the fundamental structure [*Ursatz*] must not be confused with the cadences of the conventional theory of harmony" and points out that the similarity between a $\hat{3}$–$\hat{2}$–$\hat{1}$ (I–V–I) fundamental structure and a conventional cadence with this same melodic-harmonic

---

42. Lerdahl and Jackendoff do not speak explicitly of cadenced groups in connection with these reductions, so what follows is an interpretation that tries to follow the spirit of their ideas.

43. This interpretation assumes that the notions of structural beginning and ending are manifestations of actual time spans, not of time points; unfortunately, Lerdahl and Jackendoff are not entirely clear on this issue, though most of their discussion suggests that these structural events are groups, thus time spans. But at one point in their theory they refer to formal beginnings and cadences as "structural accents" (30–35), and since they explicitly associate "metrical accents" with time-points, it is possible that they mean "structural accents" to be durationless moments as well. I will return to this distinction between time span and time point when discussing cadential arrival versus cadential function, sec. 2.5.

44. There are also melodic-motivic considerations that make it difficult to hear the entire recapitulation as a cadence. Since the recapitulation begins with the same material that began the exposition (the structural beginning), it is not easy to hear this material as articulating the beginning of a cadential formation; at the level of the theme, it is rare in music of the classical style for the cadential unit to begin with the same melodic ideas that open the theme.

45. Indeed, when Lerdahl and Jackendoff acknowledge that Figure 2.1b "expresses the structural counterpoint between the major grouping divisions of the piece and the major patterns of tension and relaxation" (248), they strongly suggest that formal processes operate independently of prolongational ones, and that the former are represented more accurately by a time-span reduction than by a prolongational reduction.

46. The *Ursatz* as a whole cannot logically be conceived as a formal cadence, since it would not function to end anything.

47. Heinrich Schenker, *Free Composition*, 16. See also V. Kofi Agawu's characterization of the *Ursatz* as embodying the broad temporalities of beginning (e.g., $\hat{3}$/I–$\hat{2}$/V) and ending ($\hat{2}$/V–$\hat{1}$/I) (*Playing with Signs: A Semiotic Interpretation of Classic Music*, 53).

progression "is merely external"; he thus strongly suggests that *Ursatz* and cadence are conceptually distinct entities.[48]

Though I have tried to cast doubt on the validity of considering cadential closure to be operative at relatively high levels of formal organization, it is worth considering at least two reasons why the notion has become so ingrained in much contemporary theory. First, a cadence typically presumed to close an entire movement is often accorded a high degree of foreground rhetorical emphasis through such means as harmonic expansions, highly active surface rhythmic articulations (often culminating in the furiously shaking cadential trill), a loud dynamic, full textures, and the placement of the final cadential tonic on a hypermetrically strong position. All of these modes of emphasis render such cadential arrivals so prominent and forceful that they can give the impression that they must be concluding something more structurally significant than a thematic region alone.[49]

Second, since the hierarchies of both Schenker's model and the two reductive models of Lerdahl and Jackendoff are *uniform* and *continuous*, in that the same basic principles of harmony, voice leading, and reduction preference are applied at all structural levels, it is easy to assume that if formal closure at lower levels is primarily cadential, then formal closure at higher levels should be cadential as well.[50] But whereas models of pitch, grouping, and metrical hierarchies may effectively be conceived as uniform and continuous, it is not necessarily the case that models of *formal* hierarchies need to be understood in the same way; indeed, there are good reasons to believe that the forces defining formal functionality on lower levels of structure are essentially different from those that define it on higher levels. In other words, the modes of musical organization that permit the expression of a formal beginning, middle, and end at the level of the phrase may be unlike those expressing the same sense of functionality for the larger sections of a movement. If so, then the nature of formal closure need not be conceptualized as identical, namely, as cadential, for all levels.

That a hierarchy of formal closure may be fundamentally discontinuous is suggested by an analogy to literary closure. Consider the case of a generic murder mystery. A stereotypical element of discourse that functions to bring closure to the plot is the classic announcement by the detective: "the butler did it." This sentence, however, has its own formal (syntactical) organization, and the element that brings the sentence to a close is the appearance of a direct object ("it") required of the transitive verb ("did"); until that direct object is spoken, the sentence is technically open. It seems unlikely that the syntactical element of the direct object, which brings closure to the sentence, is also responsible for bringing closure to the entire course of the mystery plot; rather, it is the meaning of the sentence as a whole (one which admittedly needs to be closed) that effects the higher-level formal closure. Thus the mechanisms for closure at both local (sentence syntax) and global (plot syntax) levels remain distinctly different.[51] I would claim that a similar situation obtains for formal closure in classical music. At lower levels (but not the very lowest, as discussed earlier), the major means of closing some phrases and most themes is cadence. At higher levels, formal closure is achieved by other musical forces. Unfortunately, we have no simple, conventional term to label such closure. In that absence, theorists have all too quickly extended the term "cadence" to cover those situations. Such application of cadence is best understood in a *figurative* sense, not in its literal one.[52] I return to consider this issue further after I have clarified the distinction between cadential function and cadential arrival later in the chapter.

## 2.3. Cadence as Harmony; Harmony as Cadence

The important role that harmony plays in the articulation of cadence as a mechanism of formal closure is well-known to musicians and central to most conceptions of the classical cadence. Somewhat less familiar, but just as prominent, is the role that cadence has played in the theory of harmony. As mentioned earlier, the idea that harmony is conceived as a cadential phenomenon originates with Rameau. The traditional notion of cadence as ending formula provided Rameau with a musical construct whose patterns of dissonance resolution and fundamental-bass motion could form the basis of an explanatory model for why individual harmonic entities are motivated to progress from one to another. Rameau then extended the explanation of the "perfect cadence" (V–I) and the "irregular cadence" (I–V, IV–I; also

---

48. Schenker, *Free Composition*, 17. Note that Schenker speaks of the conventional theory of *harmony*, not the theory of *form*, thus revealing how powerfully cadence was conceived in his day as a harmonic construct.

49. Thus James Webster notes, in connection with the aria "Un'aura amorosa" from *Così fan tutte*: "Rhetorically, too, the final vocal cadence seems to round off not just the final section, but the entire aria" ("The Analysis of Mozart's Arias," 122). I raise again the notion of "rhetorically" strong cadences toward the end of this chapter (sec. 2.11).

50. On hierarchical continuity vs. discontinuity, see Leonard B. Meyer, *Music, the Arts, and Ideas: Patterns and Predictions in Twentieth-Century Culture*, 96–97, 257–59, 306–8, and Meyer, *Explaining Music*, 89–90. Akin to the models offered by Schenker and by Lerdahl and Jackendoff, Patrick McCreless, whose study on Barthes's "hermeneutic sentence" I discussed in Chapter 1, shows how Barthes takes a very low-level event—a single sentence of natural language—and elevates its internal structure (subject, predicate, etc.) to represent the very highest level of narrative form ("Hermeneutic Sentence," 35–36).

51. The analogy of music to crime fiction thus proposes a model of literary closure that, unlike the one of Barthes (as summarized by McCreless), features a discontinuous hierarchy.

52. Steven Huebner has observed similar extensions of local cadence to overall structure in the world of opera analysis: "such wide-spanning 'cadences' detected by [Sigmund] Levarie (and by analysts of opera from Mozart to Wagner) are unlike true cadences that involve adjacent chords. Nevertheless, like literary *figures* these cadences share at least one characteristic with the normative concept, here a succession of sonorities (however separated) reminiscent of real cadences" ("Structural Coherence," 148, my italics).

termed "imperfect cadence") to all harmonic progressions, irrespective of their position within a phrase. In these progressions he recognized various "imitations" of the cadence that arise through "evading" the cadence, which inverts one or both harmonies or adds a dissonance to the final harmony, or "breaking" the cadence, which allows the fundamental bass to ascend a step, thus creating a deceptive cadence (*cadence rompue*; lit. "broken cadence"). Some progressions do not fit well into Rameau's cadential model, especially various sequences, but as Joel Lester has observed, "it seems never to have occurred to him that harmonies could relate to one another in meaningful ways other than in terms of cadential progressions or their imitation."[53]

With some exceptions, the subsequent development of harmonic theory continued to be based upon a cadential model, such that harmonic progression and cadence became virtually synonymous.[54] Indeed the two major (and competing) systems of harmony developed in the course of the nineteenth century—Sechter's *Stufentheorie* and Riemann's *Funktionstheorie*—each were based, in manifestly different ways, on the cadence as a model for harmonic progression. Especially in Riemann's theories, the cadence not only provided the basis for harmonic relationships, but, more broadly, for *tonal* ones as well. The cadential progression—now expanded to include an initial tonic, a subdominant, a dominant, and a final tonic—was seen as the principal agent for establishing and confirming a tonal center, the sense of key (see note 9 above).

Though cadence served as the preeminent explanation for harmonic analysis, theorists recognized that some kinds of progression were not well covered by the model. In particular, most harmonic sequences, as well as some progressions involving "passing" harmonies, could not be regarded as fundamentally cadential.[55] Indeed, the increased recognition that passing harmonies were structurally subordinate to their surrounding harmonies led to Schenker's notion that an individual *Stufe* could be *prolonged* through various contrapuntal-harmonic techniques. Eventually the idea that harmonic progressions at one structural level principally acquire their meaning and raison d'être by serving to prolong various harmonies at higher levels of structure allowed this prolongational model of harmony to surpass the cadential model in a number of influential textbooks still consulted today.[56]

Despite the prominent use of the cadential model within the history of harmonic theory and its obvious explanatory utility, the linking of cadence and harmony has been detrimental in at least two ways to the concept of cadence in its primary sense of "formal conclusion." In the first place, the term *cadence* can be invoked in situations that entirely violate the hierarchical requirements for formal closure. Thus when we read, as we often do, that Beethoven's First Symphony in C opens with a cadence in F major, the term can logically refer to a harmonic situation exclusively, not a formal one.[57] Likewise, when Schoenberg speaks of an entire movement as an enlarged cadence, his idea has meaning only if taken in the sense of a large-scale harmonic-tonal progression. Even Schenker, who minimizes references to cadence in his writings, introduces the "auxiliary cadence" as a harmonic progression lacking an initiating root-position tonic. That his concept is only tangentially related to cadence as formal conclusion is clear when he cites examples of the auxiliary cadence serving "as the basis for the so-called second theme of a sonata movement" or "supporting even an entire piece."[58]

A second consequence of linking cadence so strongly to harmony is that many progressions that are considered cadential from an exclusively harmonic point of view are not actually associated with genuine formal cadences in the classical style. Thus when a progression such as I–II$^4_2$–V$^6_5$–I is described as "cadential" (as Meyer does when referring to the opening of the first prelude of Bach's *Well-Tempered Clavier*), the impression is given that this progression can be used at the basis of a formal cadence.[59] But even a casual examination of eighteenth-century instrumental repertories reveals that such progressions are rarely, if ever, used to close formal units at the hierarchical level of a theme.

### 2.3.1. Progression Types

If the wholesale equating of harmonic progression and cadence has led to the kinds of problems just mentioned, it is still possible to identify specific progressions as cadential in ways that are compatible with the concept of cadence as formal conclusion. In critiquing the traditional theory of harmony, Carl Dahlhaus points to a possible way out of the dilemma by taking formal context into account: "The widespread theory that in classical music all harmonic relationships can be seen as expansions or modifications of the cadence is thoroughly mistaken. It is necessary to distinguish between closing sections, whose harmony constitutes a cadence, and opening and middle sections."[60] Thus following Dahlhaus's cue, I propose that most harmonic progressions can be classified as one of three basic types: *prolongational*, *sequential*, and *cadential*.[61] Within themes, prolongational progressions are associated

---

53. Joel Lester, *Compositional Theory in the Eighteenth Century*, 119.

54. One eighteenth-century theorist who does not appeal to cadence in his theory of harmony is Heinrich Christoph Koch, who restricts the concept of cadence to "formal ending" (*Versuch einer Anleitung zur Composition*, 1: 240–44). Koch thus limits "cadential harmonies" to those in root-position exclusively; see Lester, *Compositional Theory*, 279.

55. Thus Riemann regarded sequences as essentially melodic in nature and not analyzable using functional harmonic labels.

56. Edward Aldwell, Carl Schachter, and Allen Cadwallader, *Harmony & Voice Leading*; Robert Gauldin, *Harmonic Practice in Tonal Music*; Westergaard, *Tonal Theory*.

57. *Grove Music Online*, s.v. "cadence," by William S. Rockstro et al., accessed July 23, 2022, https://doi-org.proxy3.library.mcgill.ca/10.1093/gmo/9781561592630.article.04523.

58. Schenker, *Free Composition*, 89.

59. Meyer, *Explaining Music*, 227.

60. *Grove Music Online*, s.v., "Harmony," 3.2 ("The Classical Era"), by Carl Dahlhaus, accessed July 23, 2022, https://doi-org.proxy3.library.mcgill.ca/10.1093/gmo/9781561592630.article.50818.

61. The following discussion summarizes a more extensive treatment of harmonic progressions in *CF*, chap. 2, and *ACF*, chap. 1. Many theories of

EXAMPLE 2.1. Prolongational progressions.

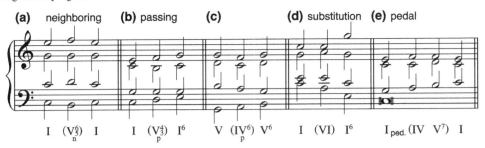

EXAMPLE 2.2. Sequential progressions.

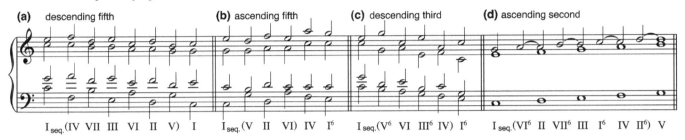

with most initiating contexts and some medial ones;[62] sequential progressions are normally tied to medial contexts; and cadential progressions form the basis of ending contexts.

### 2.3.1.1. Prolongational Progressions

From a more specifically harmonic perspective, a prolongational progression functions (within an implied tonality) to sustain in time an individual harmony, the *prolonged* harmony, by means of one or more *subordinate* harmonies (see Ex. 2.1); the latter (placed within parentheses) are deployed in the context of embellishing techniques such as (a) neighboring harmonies, (b and c) passing harmonies, (d) substitute harmonies, and (e) pedal point.[63] Most often the tonic harmony of some key is prolonged in this manner, but other scale degrees, especially the dominant, may also be prolonged. Though it is most often the case that the prolonged harmony literally frames the progression (as in Ex. 2.1), this situation is not a requirement for harmonic prolongation. It happens often enough that a prolongation may begin or end with the subordinate harmony.[64] Indeed, cases arise where it is not always clear whether a given harmony (say, a tonic) is functioning as the prolonged harmony or else as the subordinate harmony, within a prolongation of the dominant.[65]

### 2.3.1.2. Sequential Progressions

A sequential progression projects a consistent melodic-contrapuntal pattern for the purpose of temporarily destabilizing the syntax of harmonic functionality. In many cases, the sequence preserves an overall sense of tonality; at other times, the sequence may serve to move the music away from, or return it to, a particular tonal center. Sequential progressions are classifiable in terms of the interval generated by the roots of their component harmonies (e.g., descending fifth, ascending step). Example 2.2 shows some representative progressions, all of which reside in a single tonality. Such sequences are sufficiently familiar not to require further discussion at this point.[66]

### 2.3.1.3. Cadential Progressions

Whereas a prolongational progression emphasizes the identity of an individual harmony, thus implying a tonality in which that harmony receives its meaning (say, as tonic), the tonality itself is not made certain until its principal harmonic functions are

---

harmony separate off sequential progressions from other types. And some modern theories informally appeal to a prolongational model at some points and to a cadential model at other points. I am not aware, however, of a prior theory that so categorically distinguishes prolongational progressions from cadential ones or that systematically develops the consequences of this distinction as the basis for defining the relationship of harmony to form.

62. Prolongational progressions are also used in what I term *framing* formal contexts, namely, a *before-the-beginning* (such as a thematic introduction) or an *after-the-end* (such as a postcadential codetta); *CF*, 15–16, and *ACF*, 133–35.

63. As a preliminary caution to my readers, it is obvious that my speaking of harmonic "prolongation" is inspired by Schenkerian concepts, even though my application of the term departs in significant ways from Schenker's own usage.

64. See ahead, Chapter 3, Ex. 3.13, for a tonic prolongation that begins with a subordinate $V_2^4$ (upbeat to m. 1) to support a continuation phrase; in Ex. 3.99, we find a tonic prolongation ending with a subordinate $V_5^6$ (downbeat of m. 4).

65. See, e.g., the discussion in Chapter 4 of Ex. 4.57.

66. For a recent treatment of sequential harmonies, see Naomi Waltham-Smith, "Sequence."

EXAMPLE 2.3. Cadential progressions.

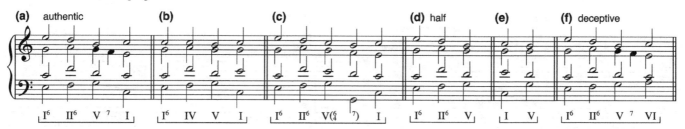

articulated in a sufficiently powerful manner. It is thus the role of a cadential progression to confirm a tonal center as such.[67] And it does so by introducing dominant harmony in its most stable form—*in root position*—thus strongly implying a resolution to a stable, *root-position* tonic. Example 2.3 illustrates some standard cadential progressions; the square brackets embracing the roman numerals indicate the boundaries of the progression.[68] In the case of an *authentic cadential* progression (a–c), the dominant (which frequently contains a dissonant seventh to aid in the implication of resolution) progresses to tonic; as such, the dominant functions as the *penultimate* harmony of the progression. This dominant is frequently embellished by a *cadential six-four* (c), whose resolution to a root-position triad or seventh I will term the *dominant proper*. With the *half cadential* progression (d–e), the dominant becomes the goal, the *ultimate* harmony, of the progression,[69] and thus the dominant must remain a stable, fully consonant triad; a subsequent resolution to tonic does not belong to the half cadential progression itself but occurs at the beginning of the next harmonic progression. (Less often, this resolution to tonic is omitted and a different harmony initiates the next progression.) A third general type of cadential progression sees the final tonic replaced by some other harmony, typically built over the sixth degree in the bass (as VI or VII$^6$/V) but sometimes over the third degree (as I$^6$). This *deceptive cadential* progression (f) is associated with various cadential deviations, as discussed more fully in Chapter 4.

A central tenet of my concept of cadence is the requirement that dominant harmony occur exclusively in root position prior to the moment of cadential arrival (or, in the case of a half cadence, just at the moment of arrival).[70] So essential is this harmonic condition that if a seeming penultimate dominant first appears inverted (say as V$^6_5$) or becomes inverted after initially being in root position, then either no sense of cadence will be projected or else a potentially cadential situation becomes *abandoned*.[71] In such cases, the ongoing cadential progression is converted into a prolongational one by virtue of the inverted dominant.

The dominant of a cadential progression is often introduced by one or two preceding harmonies—an initial tonic, usually placed in first inversion, and a pre-dominant harmony, usually built over the fourth scale degree in the bass.[72] That the progression typically includes a pre-dominant harmony is well known. The presence of an initial tonic is less often discussed by theorists, yet when mentioned, such a tonic is normally understood to be in root position (as in the textbook progression I–IV–V–I).[73] Much more frequently, however, the initial cadential tonic appears in first inversion and is often accorded emphasis as a sign that a cadential progression is indeed underway. A root-position tonic, on the contrary, is normally prolonged from the very beginning of a thematic unit and thus less often signals the start of something cadential. Indeed, following a prolonged root-position tonic, the appearance of I$^6$ to initiate the cadential progression later in a theme helps to lighten the harmonic texture, to provide greater dynamic momentum, and to motivate a return to the stability of the final cadential tonic (in root position). The cadential I$^6$, built over the third scale degree in the bass, combined with a pre-dominant, built over the fourth degree, provides a powerful melodic ascent in the bass toward the fifth degree, which supports the root-position dominant, the linchpin of the cadential progression. If the cadential progression includes all four harmonic functions—initial tonic, pre-dominant, dominant, and final tonic—then we can speak of a *complete* cadential

---

67. Though there is ample precedent for the idea that cadence is key confirming, it is surprising that only seven percent of the definitions of cadence surveyed by Blombach include that element; see Table 2.1.

68. Throughout this study I use such brackets to indicate cadential progressions, except in cases of *expanded cadential progressions*, those that last four measures or more (see ahead, Ex. 2.16 and 2.29c), where I use the abbreviation ECP at the start of the progression to avoid overly cluttering the analytical annotations.

69. The important distinction between a penultimate and ultimate dominant will frequently arise in our discussion of cadences throughout this study.

70. In a half cadence, the dominant triad may acquire a dissonant seventh or become inverted *following* the moment of cadential arrival without syntactically weakening the sense of cadence.

71. On abandoned cadence, see Chapter 4, sec. 4.3.

72. Pre-dominant harmonies (sometimes referred to as "dominant preparation" harmonies or even more generically as "subdominant" harmonies) include a wide variety of formations whose principal function is to progress to dominant. The main cadential pre-dominant in music of the classical style is II$^6$, though IV is often used as well. Other pre-dominants include a group of applied (or secondary) dominants to the dominant built over the raised fourth degree (typically VII$^7$/V), the various "nationalities" of augmented-sixth harmonies, and the Neapolitan in first inversion ($\flat$II$^6$).

73. As discussed in Chapter 8, sec. 8.2, this particular progression is more typical of nineteenth-century styles than of eighteenth-century ones.

EXAMPLE 2.4. Haydn, Symphony No. 87 in A, iii, mm. 1–8 (*ACF* 4.12).

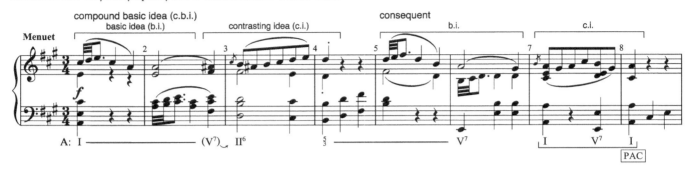

progression. Often, however, either the initial tonic or the predominant (or both) are excluded, thus giving rise to an *incomplete* progression.[74]

Inasmuch as one raison d'être of the cadential progression is to confirm a tonality, the *plagal progression* I–IV–I is entirely inadequate to the task.[75] The subdominant harmony does not contain the essential elements, especially the leading tone, to set up powerful expectations for a resolution to a stable tonic.[76] Instead, the progression is perfectly suited to a prolongational role, especially seeing as the common tone between the harmonies is the root of the tonic. If the plagal progression does not fulfill the requirements of a true cadential progression, then the concept of "plagal cadence," described in virtually every music theory textbook on rudiments and harmony, must be seen as a fiction, at least for the classical repertory (as well as for the other eighteenth-century styles—the high baroque and galant).[77] The situation that theorists normally identify as a plagal cadence is either a postcadential codetta (a topic to be discussed at greater length below, sec. 2.8) or a noncadential, prolongational articulation in the middle of a thematic unit, or, rarely, at its end.

### 2.3.2. Ambiguity of Progression Types

Though in theory we can distinguish harmonic progressions as prolongational, sequential, and cadential, in actual analytical practice, ambiguities in classification may well arise. Consider the simple progression I–V–I (ironically, the first one often taught to students of harmony). On the one hand, we could identify here an incomplete cadential progression, one whose initial tonic stands (less typically) in root position. On the other hand, the same progression can be considered prolongational, with the dominant—in root position, to be sure—functioning as a subordinate, neighboring harmony to the prolonged tonic. Typically, the formal context in which the progression appears clarifies the potential ambiguity: if it arises at the end of a thematic unit, and in conjunction with an appropriately closing melodic configuration, then the progression is likely to be heard as cadential, as seen in Example 2.4, measures 7–8.[78] On the contrary, if the progression appears at the beginning of such a unit, it is likely better understood as prolongational, Example 2.5a, measures 1–4.[79]

Note in this latter example that the progression supports a *basic idea* and its immediate repetition, thus creating a *presentation*, a formal phrase function that, in principle, is supported by a tonic prolongational progression. Alternatively, though, could we not say that the basic idea itself is supported by a prolongational I–V while the repeat of the basic idea is supported by the (very incomplete) cadential progression V–I? The problem with this interpretation hinges on the function of *repetition*. As discussed in Chapter 1, as well as earlier in this chapter (sec. 2.2.1), a repetition generates expectations for continuation that eventually promises closure of some kind, what I called generally, after Barbara Herrnstein Smith, the *repetition/terminal-modification*

---

74. The distinction between complete and incomplete progressions will be discussed more fully in the next chapter. For the time being, it is important to note that cadences supported by an incomplete cadential progression are not syntactically "weaker" or "less effective" than those containing a complete cadential progression.

75. Some other theorists seem to agree: "Plagal cadences . . . are only a means of stylistic expression and are structurally of no importance" (Arnold Schoenberg, *Structural Functions of Harmony*, 14); "Because motion between IV and I lacks the key-defining power of the V–I progression, plagal cadences have a much more limited function than authentic (V–I) cadences" (Aldwell, Schachter, and Cadwallader, *Harmony & Voice Leading*, 231).

76. For an important treatment of plagal harmonic progressions in relation to authentic progressions, see Deborah Stein, "The Expansion of the Subdominant in the Late Nineteenth Century." Stein's characterization of these progressions in light of their voice leading and tonal focus resonates well with the general views on plagal harmonies and cadence that I develop in this study; see Chapter 9, sec. 9.3.

77. We will encounter what appear to be genuine plagal cadences in nineteenth-century musical styles. As I will discuss in detail in the final chapter of this study, however, such situations are better regarded as instances of "plagal closure," not plagal cadence; see Chapter 9, sec. 9.3.

78. In the analytical annotations in this example, the term *compound basic idea* refers to an initiating phrase consisting of a basic idea and a contrasting idea that does not close with a cadence; see *CF*, 61, and *ACF*, 107–108. All of the form-functional labels, which appear throughout this study *above* the music, are defined in *CF* and *ACF*. Harmonic and cadential labels are placed below the music.

79. When useful, and especially when emphasizing the distinction between prolongational and cadential progressions (as in Ex. 2.5a), I use a curved line to embrace the harmonies of the prolongation. Normally, however, this annotation is unnecessary (and overly cluttering), because all cadential progressions will be bracketed (or indicated as an ECP).

EXAMPLE 2.5. Beethoven, Piano Sonata in C, Op. 2, no. 3, i, (a) mm. 1–4 (*ACF* 5.11); (b) mm. 11–13.

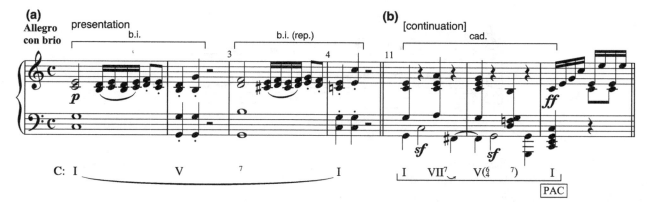

EXAMPLE 2.6. Mozart, Symphony No. 40 in G Minor, K. 550, i, mm. 44–51.

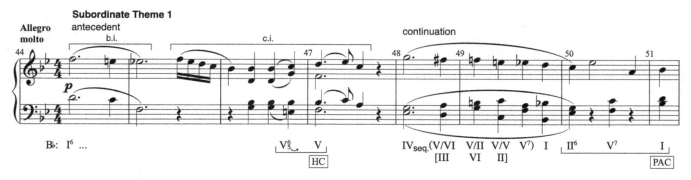

*paradigm*. Under these conditions, the repeated basic idea (mm. 3–4) does not engender formal closure; rather, the repeated idea itself implies an eventual terminal modification, which for the theme as a whole is represented by its cadence (Ex. 2.5b).[80]

A second type of harmonic ambiguity involves sequential progressions versus cadential ones. Let us take the progression VI–II–V–I. In one view, we can recognize a descending-fifths sequence. In principle (if not so much in practice), the same progression could be classified as cadential, here a complete progression, wherein VI functions as an initial tonic substitute and II serves as a pre-dominant. A standard context for the appearance of such a progression is in a formal continuation, such as at measures 48–49 of Example 2.6. Here, the progression is clearly sequential; in fact, the sequence even begins one step earlier with the chromatic V/VI replacing a diatonic III (as well, V/VII replaces VI, and V/V replaces II). Clearly, the arrival on tonic at the very end of measure 49 projects little in the way of anything cadential. Indeed, not until the sequence ends does a distinct cadential progression arise in measures 50–51, now with a conventional II⁶ as the pre-dominant. As a general rule, in fact, classical composers carefully distinguish between sequential and cadential progressions, and the reason should be clear by now. The essence of sequence is *repetition*, namely, of a given root interval (e.g., a descending fifth); in many situations, moreover, a sequential progression supports a complete musical idea, a *model*, that is repeated as a *sequence* (though not in Ex. 2.6, where we cannot really speak of the final quarter note in m. 48 as an "idea"). As discussed, such repetitions in themselves inhibit closure, though they also raise expectations for a subsequent ending, one that is likely to be fulfilled by a cadence. Returning to the harmonic ambiguity proposed for the progression VI–II–V–I, it turns out that in the classical style, this succession of harmonies is encountered so rarely as cadential that I cannot cite a single case of its use (though probably there exists one in this enormous repertory). In the following Romantic period, however, the strict separation of sequence and cadence begins to break down, and the ambiguity of this progression comes more to the fore (see Chapter 8, sec. 8.7).[81]

## 2.4. Bass-Line Melody and Cadence

Up to now, I have spoken of the harmonic content of the cadential progression in a manner that has emphasized the position or

---

80. I will return these issues later in sec. 2.8.5.

81. A second, more complex and quite rare, harmonic ambiguity arises between an ascending-stepwise sequence and a deceptive cadential progression; see ahead in Chapter 5, the discussion of the first movements of Mozart's G-Minor Symphony (Ex. 5.37d and f) and Beethoven's *Eroica* Symphony (Ex. 5.69 and 5.70a). We will also encounter the issue of sequential vs. cadential in the discussion of a deviation type I term *dominant arrival* (see Chapter 4, sec. 4.4.3.2).

EXAMPLE 2.7. Melodic analysis of "Twinkle, Twinkle."

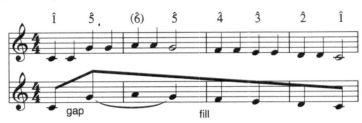

(inversion) of the component harmonies: initial tonic and predominant in first inversion; dominant and final tonic in root position. Another perspective in considering the relationship of harmony and cadence arises from a close analysis of the melodic nature of the bass voice in the classical style. In an earlier study, I proposed a theory of bass-line melody that builds upon the distinction between prolongational and cadential harmonies.[82] Let me now summarize the essential elements of that theory, for it will help clarify some basic tenets of my concept of cadence and prove useful in analyzing some complicated cadential situations arising in the various tonal styles to be considered in the present study.

I begin by reviewing a well-known distinction between *melodic* and *harmonic* relationships among pitches. A melodic relationship is established in reference to a *scalar* collection of pitches, and the basic unit of melodic motion is the individual step. If the melodic interval between two pitches exceeds a second, we sense that one or more notes of the scale have been skipped over. Indeed, the "gap" thus created may then be "filled in" by stepwise motion, as in the "Twinkle, Twinkle" melody of Example 2.7.[83] Indeed, the complete filling-in of the gap and the return to tonic creates melodic *closure* of the line. A harmonic relationship, on the contrary, is established in reference to a *triadic* collection. Thus the basic units of harmony are the intervals of the fifth and third (and their inversions). Unlike a melodic interval of these same sizes, however, a harmonic interval does not imply the presence of intervening notes: in other words, the interval between the root and fifth of a harmony does not create a gap implying a subsequent fill.

Harmonic relationships distinguish themselves from melodic ones in another important way, one less often considered by theorists. The pitches of a harmony are normally understood to reside in different *voices*; thus in the C-major harmony of Example 2.8a, the low C (the harmonic root) and the G (harmonic fifth) reside in the bass and alto voices, respectively; the E (third) lies in the tenor, and the doubled C appears in the soprano. Each of these notes has the potential of creating melodic

EXAMPLE 2.8. (a) C-major harmony; (b) harmonic progression in C major.

relationships with other notes in the same voice, as one harmony succeeds another, as shown in Example 2.8b. Thus the connections of pitches *within* one voice are normally melodic, while those *between* voices are harmonic. But there exists, at least in theory, one voice whose pitches are exclusively harmonic: this is Rameau's *basse fondamental*, which he conceptualizes as a single, distinct voice.[84] Yet what we have been considering thus far suggests that the pitches of the fundamental bass, as harmonic entities, should logically reside in different voices. In other words, as the fundamental bass progresses, its notes form a series of harmonic connections, and as such, each note in succession can be thought to leap from one voice to another. The fundamental bass, of course, is a theoretical construct. But there does exist a real sounding voice that normally includes elements of the fundamental bass: this is what Rameau calls the *basso continuo*, or, more simply, our regular "bass voice."[85]

What I am thus proposing is that the bass voice, as distinct from the upper voices, is, in principle, a two-voiced structure.[86] Following Schenker, we can say that the bass is anchored in the

---

82. William E. Caplin, "Schoenberg's 'Second Melody', or, 'Meyer-ed' in the Bass."

83. The notion of "gap-fill" melodic organization is advanced prominently in Meyer's "implication/realization" theory of melody (*Explaining Music*, 145–57).

---

84. Throughout his writings, Rameau notates the fundamental bass as a series of pitches residing in a single staff; see, for instance, Ex. 11.10 from *Treatise on Harmony*, 86.

85. The example from Rameau cited in the previous note clearly distinguishes the *basso continuo* from the fundamental bass as separate voices.

86. The idea of a single voice projecting multiple implied voices is akin to the notion of *compound melody*, as exemplified by the subject of the C-Minor Fugue in Bach's *Well-Tempered Clavier*, book 1 (see ahead, Ex. 6.90a in Chapter 6). Most instances of compound melody see the line regularly leaping back and forth from one implied voice to the next, as in this fugue subject. The kind of two-voiced structure I propose for the bass, however, sees a less frequent alternation between the implied voices compared to most compound melodies.

EXAMPLE 2.9. Prolongational and cadential streams under the rule of the octave.

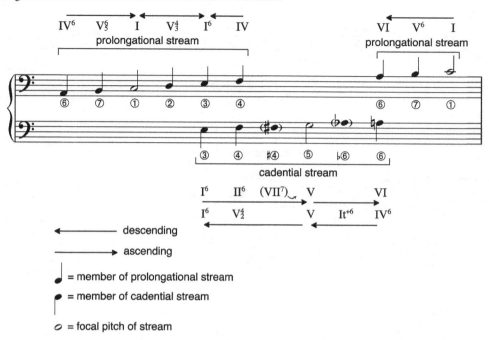

EXAMPLE 2.10. Basic model of bass-line melodic organization.

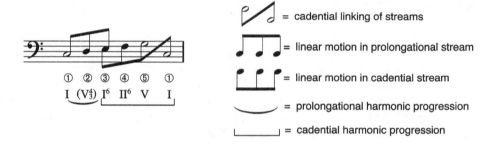

harmonic relationship of tonic and dominant. But as harmonic constituents, these two notes can be thought to reside in two different voices, and each note can become the focal point of melodic activity within its own voice. To avoid terminological confusion, I will now refer to these internal voices (within the single bass voice) as *streams*.[87]

Example 2.9, a modified *rule of the octave*, shows the pitches normally occurring within the two streams.[88] As well, I have indicated typical harmonic progressions associated with the ascending or descending melodic motions within each stream. In reference to these harmonies, I label the stream focused around the tonic as *prolongational*; that focused around the dominant, as *cadential*. Observe that the third, fourth, and sixth scale degrees belong to both streams: they can thus function as pivot notes linking the streams in an apparently melodic manner.

For a given thematic unit within a movement (in the classical style), such as a main theme or a subordinate theme, the bass line behaves roughly as follows. It begins with the tonic, the focal pitch of the prolongational stream (shown as a half note) and then explores various melodic motions within that stream. Eventually, it attains the third degree, which then pivots the line into the cadential stream for further ascent to the dominant, the melodic focal pitch of that stream (also, a half note). Bass-line *closure* is achieved when, in the context of a formal authentic cadence, the dominant leaps back to the tonic, thus forging a harmonic connection that links the two streams and purges the bass of all melodic tendencies that might generate further continuation. The simplest

---

87. Though there are some similarities, my use of "stream" does not refer to how that term is employed by Albert S. Bregman in his theory of "auditory stream segregation" (*Auditory Scene Analysis: The Perceptual Organization of Sound*).

88. Following the practice of Giorgio Sanguinetti, *The Art of Partimento: History, Theory, and Practice*, scale degrees in the bass voice will be indicated by circled arabic numerals (e.g., ④, ♭⑥) while scale degrees in the soprano voice (or some inner voice) will be designated by a circumflex accent over the numeral (e.g., $\hat{1}$, $\sharp\hat{4}$).

EXAMPLE 2.11. Modulating models.

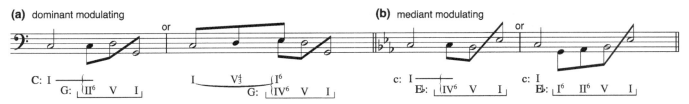

EXAMPLE 2.12. Period model.

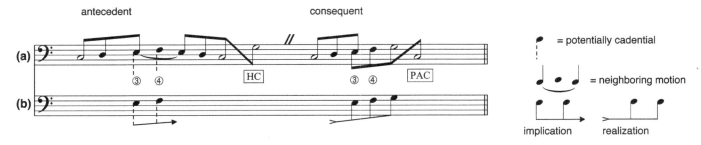

EXAMPLE 2.13. Two-gapped model.

manifestation of this process is shown in Example 2.10, which I offer as a *basic model* for classical bass-line melodies.[89] (Other tonal styles tend to feature different underlying bass motions: baroque and galant bass lines frequently include prominent stepwise descents, especially at the opening of thematic units,[90] while Romantic bass lines often take on a leaping, harmonic character, as a result of a predilection for root-position harmonies.[91])

Comparing this model to the "Twinkle, Twinkle" configuration of Example 2.7, we see that the melodic activity is entirely different:[92] the soprano line opens up an ascending gap that motivates a stepwise descending fill, which brings closure to the line; all of this melodic motion takes place within a *single* voice. By contrast, the linear ascent of the bass traverses *two* streams and closes with a harmonic leap, one that creates no sense of melodic gap for a subsequent fill. To be sure, the ascending motion in the bass is so linear that it does not necessarily give the impression of changing from one stream to the other. In actual musical realizations, however, the composer often articulates this shift by means of register, texture, grouping mechanisms, and so forth.

The basic model is subject to some important variants. Two arise with themes that *modulate* to the dominant or mediant regions, as shown in Example 2.11. Another variant, especially common in Mozart, underlies a *periodic* formal design (Ex. 2.12). Here, the bass of the antecedent phrase ascends to ③, which has the potential of shifting the melody into the cadential stream (as indicated by the descending dotted stem); a further rise to ④ reinforces that implication. But the melody returns to the initial tonic to complete a broad prolongation. The line then leaps directly to the dominant, thus bypassing cadential melodic activity, to create a half cadence. The consequent phrase reproduces the opening ascent; but this time, the potential for ③ and ④ to be cadential is fully realized, and the line continues up to the goal dominant, whose leap back to the tonic creates authentic cadential closure for the period. The notation in staff (b) shows the *implication/realization* (I/R) relationships of ③ and ④.[93] Another common variant, shown

---

89. This model of bass melody resembles some of the first-level middleground patterns of bass motion given by Schenker in Fig. 14.12 of *Free Composition*. Schenker's figure suggests that the melodic motion in the bass is an embellishment of a more structural bass arpeggiation (①–③–⑤). But the figure does not distinguish between the motion ①–③ (as prolongation) and ③–⑤ (as cadential).

90. On baroque descending bass lines as characteristic of the prelude style, see Joel Lester, *Bach's Works for Solo Violin: Style, Structure, Performance*, 31–33; on galant descending bass lines, see ahead in Chapter 7 the discussion of Ex. 7.18, 7.20, and 7.26.

91. See Chapter 8, sec. 8.2.

92. That the two patterns stand in a retrograde relation to each other seems incidental, though perhaps there is some further theoretical significance to this relationship that others may wish to explore.

93. A feature of Meyer's melodic theory is his general idea that melodic processes *imply* a set of continuations, some of which may become *realized* immediately, may be deferred to a later moment, or may remain unrealized. This "implication/realization" model has been a notable contribution to music theory applicable to other musical processes beyond the purely melodic.

EXAMPLE 2.14A. Mozart, Piano Trio in B-flat, K. 502, ii, mm. 1–8.

EXAMPLE 2.14B. Mozart, Piano Trio in B-flat, K. 502, ii, mm. 1–8, bass-line melody.

in Example 2.13, omits ②. With this *two-gapped* variant, it is often interesting to see whether the lack of the second degree is offset at some point by its appearing prominently later within the theme itself, or, more likely, after the theme has closed.

Let us now consider these abstract models in relation to actual music. In Example 2.14a, an eight-measure hybrid theme by Mozart,[94] the bass line of the four-measure antecedent phrase conforms entirely to the basic model. The following continuation begins at measure 5 with an unusual move from ⑤ down to ③, which I interpret as operating prolongationally, since nothing of the formal and harmonic context suggests cadence.[95] At measure 6, the bass returns to ① via the neighboring leading tone, and from here to the end of the continuation, we can recognize the dominant-modulating model (as in Ex. 2.11a). In Example 2.14b, staff 1 replicates the bass-line analysis; staff 2 shows a possible I/R relationship generated by the unusual bass descent of measure 5, whose continuation with F (②⇒⑤), at measure 7, is an essential element of the modulation.[96]

The period model is well illustrated by Example 2.15a. The antecedent begins with a double neighbor-note configuration in the bass that embellishes the initial tonic of the prolongational stream.[97] The leap to ③ at the end of measure 2 can be heard to initiate the cadential stream, and the ascent to ④ further supports that presumption. But when ④ returns to ③, which then pushes back down to ①, we recognize that all of this melodic activity takes place within the prolongational stream. The leap to the dominant at measure 4 supports the half cadence that closes the phrase. The opening of the consequent brings back the same basic pitches of the antecedent, but now with some upper-third embellishments (labeled motive "x"). The second embellishment in measure 6

---

94. On the structure of hybrid themes, see *CF*, chap. 5, and *ACF*, chap. 4.

95. Though ⑤ normally appears in the cadential stream, it may sometimes participate in prolongational activity when supporting a passing chord between the harmonies placed over ④ and ⑥ or when supporting a genuine tonic harmony in second inversion (as here).

96. Throughout this study, I use the symbol ⇒ to mean "becomes," in the sense of a *retrospective reinterpretation* of a harmonic or formal element, as promoted by Janet Schmalfeldt in many of her writings; see esp. *In the Process of Becoming: Analytic and Philosophical Perspectives on Form in Early Nineteenth-Century Music*.

97. The opening B♭, though not literally present in the score, is obviously implied as the bass support for the initial F in the soprano voice.

EXAMPLE 2.15A. Mozart, Piano Sonata in B-flat, K. 281, iii, mm. 1–8.

EXAMPLE 2.15B. Mozart, Piano Sonata in B-flat, K. 281, iii, mm. 1–8, bass-line melody.

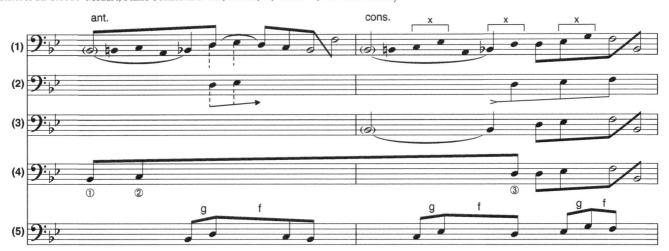

achieves ③, whose repetition and ascent to ④ fully realizes the cadential implications from the prior phrase. Example 2.15b, staff 2, shows this I/R relationship. As seen in staff 3, the consequent exhibits the ②-gapped variant of the basic model. But when we take the opening double-neighbor note configuration into account (opening of staff 1), we can discern (staff 4) a latent expression of the *complete* basic model.[98] Finally, staff 5 highlights a number of *gap-fill* (g-f) patterns that arise in the course of the theme.

---

98. Observe that if the double-neighbor configuration had been inverted, that is, B♭–A–C–B♭, then there would be no directed motion from ① to ② that would imply a continuation to ③. Perhaps this is why the opening double neighbor of so many classical bass lines is ①–②–⑦–① and not the inverse (①–⑦–②–①).

This introduction to my theory of classical bass-line melody helps us better understand some specific characteristics of the harmonic content of a cadential progression. The reason that the initial tonic is typically found in first inversion, that the predominant is most often built over ④ or ♯④, and that the cadential dominant must stand in root position, is owing as much to the nature of the melodic line of the bass voice as it is for the particular *positions* (or *inversions*) of those harmonies. This is not to say that the position is irrelevant. It is obviously not: the initial tonic gains a degree of mobility through its less stable position compared to the solid expression of root-position tonic appropriate to the beginning and end of the theme; and the cadential dominant also projects the stability of its harmonic function needed to help confirm the sense of key. But the melodic organization of the bass

EXAMPLE 2.16. Mozart, Piano Sonata in B-flat, K. 333, i, mm. 56–59.

also plays a decisive role, with its essential locking into place of ⑤, as the focal pitch of the cadential stream and as the scale degree that creates such strong closure by means of the direct harmonic connection to ① at the moment of authentic cadence. When dominant harmony is built over ⑦ or ②, on the contrary, the strong *melodic* connection to the subsequent ① or ③ reinforces the idea that the dominant is harmonically subordinate to the tonic, that it participates in a *prolongation* of the latter. If the dominant is supported by ⑤, however, the sense of harmonic subordination is reduced (though of course never obliterated—a dominant is always, in principle, subordinate to tonic to some extent), and the dominant gains a greater sense of independence from the tonic such that the former's connection to the latter is potentially cadential.[99]

As we attend carefully to the bass line, we can directly experience the interplay between prolongational and cadential streams. We can appreciate all the more that the bass motion ⑦–① or ②–① projects a powerful sense of harmonic prolongation, not harmonic cadence, and this awareness helps reinforce the fundamental axiom advocated in this study that the cadential progression—and thus genuine cadences themselves—must engage a root-position dominant, not an inverted one.

## 2.5. Cadential Arrival versus Cadential Function

Even in the sense of "formal conclusion," the term *cadence* is often used in two different ways. On the one hand, cadence signifies the actual moment of formal closure, that *time point* where the cadential dominant resolves to the final tonic (in the case of an authentic cadence). This is the place in the musical score where the analyst would place some symbol for cadence (e.g., a boxed PAC) and that the listener would say "here is where the cadence really happens." More precisely, we can term this moment in time the *cadential arrival* and define it as occurring where the final harmony of the cadential progression first appears. Often enough, the final note of the melody in the soprano voice also corresponds with the cadential arrival, but frequently the sense of melodic closure for the thematic unit occurs somewhat after the final cadential harmony appears, usually as a result of suspension resolutions or some further elaboration of the tones of the final harmony, what the eighteenth-century theorist H. C. Koch describes as an "overhang" (*Überhang*).[100]

But the phenomenon of cadence as closure consists of more than this moment of cadential arrival, for there must be some musical material immediately preceding that point whose formal purpose is to announce "a cadence is forthcoming." This *time span*, which also includes the arrival of the cadence itself, expresses *cadential function* because it sets up, and then usually fulfills, the requisite conditions for thematic closure through specific harmonic and melodic processes. Even if the implied cadential arrival fails to materialize—for example, via deception, evasion, or abandonment—we can still identify a passage of music whose formal function is cadential.[101] Sometimes the cadential function is relatively *compact*, roughly one to three bars in length; HCs, especially, are often very short (as seen earlier in Ex. 2.6, m. 47, and Ex. 2.15a, m. 4). At other times, the cadential function is more *expanded*, four or more bars, such as in subordinate-theme areas where the confirmation of the new key requires a more powerful rhetorical expression (Ex. 2.16).[102] But no matter what its length, the boundaries of the cadential function are essentially defined by the underlying cadential progression. To be sure, it is not so obvious in some situations just where that progression actually begins, and thus the onset of the cadential function may only

---

99. We know, of course, that a progression from a root-position dominant to a root-position tonic can also be prolongational in some formal contexts; see again Ex. 2.5a.

100. Heinrich Christoph Koch, *Introductory Essay on Composition: The Mechanical Rules of Melody*, Sections 3 and 4, 24. Koch understands the overhang as an appendix to the cadential melody, which he sees as effectively superfluous to the melodic closure. In such cases he regards as decisive the first pitch appearing in the soprano when the final harmony arrives. Koch's idea will be referenced again in subsequent chapters, but a more detailed discussion is postponed until Chapter 7, sec. 7.1.4, since the device is especially characteristic of galant repertories.

101. The cadential deviations of deception, evasion, and abandonment will be studied in detail in Chapter 4.

102. The opening of Chapter 5 deals in more detail with the distinction between compact and expanded cadences.

EXAMPLE 2.17. Haydn, Symphony No. 45 in F-sharp Minor ("Farewell"), v, mm. 1–10.

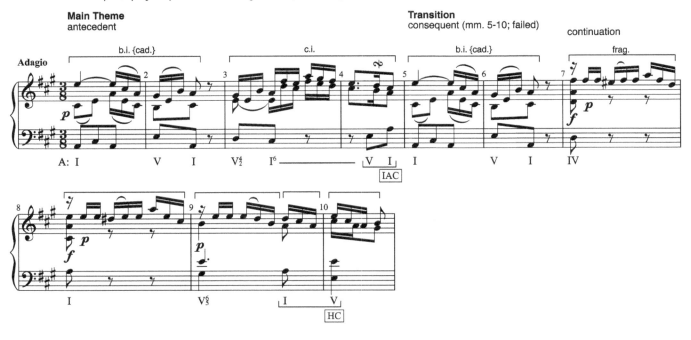

be understood retrospectively. Frequently enough, however, the composer decisively articulates the start of the progression by various means, such as a clear shift from a stable root-position tonic to its more mobile first inversion or a prominent change in the register of the bass voice.

The idea that cadence involves a time span leading up to and including the time point of arrival has been implicitly recognized by a number of theorists and historians. Thus Rosen identifies the final phrase of a subordinate theme (see again Ex. 2.16) as "four bars of cadence."[103] (The annotations in the example distinguish the cadential arrival, the PAC, as a point in time, whereas the cadential function, the entire phrase, is a span of time.) And Leonard Ratner recognizes a "grand cadence of first reprise" toward the end of an exposition in the first movement of Mozart's String Quintet in E-flat, K. 614.[104] Lerdahl and Jackendoff provide one of the more explicit formulations of the idea: after first defining a "cadential preparation" that consists of "events leading up to the cadence," they then speak of a "cadential nucleus" that includes both the cadential preparation and cadence proper.[105]

The more specific notion of "cadential function" also crops up now and then in the theoretical literature, though usually in ways that are rather vague and that differ considerably from the conception developed here. So, for example, Rosen discusses how:

> the exposition of a sonata is based on only one action, the establishment of one polarity . . . ; once it has arrived, everything remaining in the first half [i.e., the whole exposition] tends to have a purely cadential function. In a concerto, the withholding of this cadence is the simplest and most justifiable procedure, the occasion for virtuoso passagework from the soloist.[106]

Though it is not clear just how we are to understand "cadential function" in this context, the notion seems to apply to a fairly a large stretch of music, one that both precedes and follows a cadence. Following the lead of Rosen, Darcy and Hepokoski also recognize cadential function within the latter part of a sonata exposition: "The tonal function of S [the "secondary-theme zone"] is *cadential*: its purpose is to cadence decisively in the new key."[107] Again, it is uncertain what they mean by cadential function, except in the most general sense of "a cadence has to occur." To be sure, the secondary-theme area of a sonata exposition must close with a cadence, but their statement suggests that the entire zone has a cadential function, an idea clearly divergent from the concept of cadence that I have been presenting.

Even when not speaking explicitly of cadential "function," some writers characterize specific grouping structures as cadential, thus implying that they fulfill that formal function. Thus James Webster, in connection with Example 2.17, identifies measures 7–10 of this main theme as a "cadential phrase," though the

---

103. Rosen, *Classical Style*, 72.

104. Leonard G. Ratner, *Classic Music: Expression, Form, and Style*, 241.

105. Lerdahl and Jackendoff, *Generative Theory*, 191–94. Their cadential preparation includes any pre-dominant harmonies as well as the cadential six-four, whereas the cadence proper consists of the V–I progression exclusively. (That they conceptually separate the cadential six-four from the dominant is odd, since most theorists recognize this six-four harmony as expressing dominant function.) Lerdahl and Jackendoff do not specifically acknowledge the presence of an initial tonic as part of the cadential preparation, but their theory does not exclude that possibility.

106. Rosen, *Classical Style*, 269–70.

107. Darcy and Hepokoski, "Medial Caesura," 121.

actual half cadential progression begins only in the last eighth-note beat of measure 9.[108] Rothstein introduces the notion of "cadential theme," which he defines as a "new or striking melodic idea that appears shortly before, and that leads to, the closing cadence [of the second-theme group]."[109] And along similar lines, Darcy and Hepokoski refer to a "thematically profiled cadential module," typically used by Haydn at the end of an "expansion section" (a position corresponding to the close of what I would call the subordinate-theme area).[110] But by far the most influential references to "cadence phrase" or "cadence theme" arise repeatedly in the writings of Donald Francis Tovey, who employs these expressions in reference to passages that usually, but not always, *follow* a cadential arrival.[111] Such usage has been the source of great confusion for the concept of cadence, for it fundamentally mistakes cadential function with postcadential function, a crucial difference that I will address shortly below (sec. 2.8).

Having now distinguished between cadential function and arrival, I want to return briefly to the question of whether or not high-level formal closure should be conceptualized and experienced as specifically cadential. To support my contention that broad stretches of music, ones that embrace multiple thematic units, achieve closure in ways that are noncadential, let me propose the following analogical situation. As we have just discussed, the process for creating closure at the level of an individual theme takes place within the *time span* of the cadential *function*; what ultimately completes the process of thematic closure occurs at the *time point* of cadential *arrival*. I claim that a similar distinction obtains at higher levels of organization, say, of an entire exposition. To simplify the argument, let us take the case of a relatively short sonata exposition, one that contains a single subordinate theme. I would suggest that the process of creating expositional closure occurs within the time span of the entire subordinate theme, for even when that theme begins, we can hear ahead ("protend," as phenomenologists would say) to the eventual close of the exposition and already experience that the exposition is in the process of ending. And, to be sure, the ultimate realization of that expositional closure occurs at the time point of cadential arrival that decisively closes the subordinate theme. Although the time points for the fully realized closure of both subordinate theme and exposition occur at the same temporal location, the time spans of closing function are vastly different in size and internal organization. Hence it seems reasonable to differentiate these formal functions through our technical vocabulary. At the thematic level, the function can be termed *cadential* (with its conventional harmonic–melodic content); at the expositional level, we have no standard label. I would suggest, then, that the notion of *subordinate-theme function*, as a constituent formal function of an exposition, should incorporate the concept of closure just as *cadential function* incorporates closure for an individual theme.[112] It might seem at first far-fetched to ask us to hear such broad-range processes of formal closure at a multiplicity of levels, but such experiential demands have been part and parcel of Schenkerian approaches to harmonic-contrapuntal processes for many decades now, and to invoke the idea for formal functionality hardly seems a radical proposal.[113]

## 2.6. Cadential Function versus Cadential Content

In addition to its harmonic content, cadential function in classical compositions often projects melodic-motivic gestures that can generally be described as *conventional*, as opposed to the *characteristic* ideas typically used at the beginning of a thematic unit. In earlier style periods, the content of the cadence is so conventionalized that we can appropriately speak of a melodic formula, almost always of falling contour (hence the etymology of the term), that unequivocally signals cadential closure. The sense of formulaic gestures for thematic ending continued to be employed in the high classical period, but it became less and less the case, particularly with Beethoven, that the same cadential idea is used in multiple works.[114] Nonetheless, most cadential melodies

---

108. James Webster, *Haydn's Farewell Symphony and the Idea of Classical Style: Through-Composition and Cyclic Integration in His Instrumental Music*, 98. The analytical annotations in the example reflect my harmonic–formal interpretations, not Webster's. In my view, mm. 7–10 function as a *continuation* phrase (*CF*, 40–42, and *ACF*, 36–37) primarily because it initiates prominent phrase-structural fragmentation (i.e., a reduction in the size of the grouping structure from two measures to one measure). I see the cadential function occurring only at the very end of the phrase, as supported by the compact half cadential progression. The phrase that begins in m. 5 starts off as a *consequent*, but that function fails to be fully realized when it closes at m. 10 with an HC rather than with a PAC, as required by the definition of consequent function. Although the implied period form (ant. + cons.) fails to emerge, the syntactical logic of these two phrases is regained when we consider the level of *thematic* functionality, for in the broader context of an exposition, mm. 1–4 function as a main theme, while mm. 5–10 serve as the transition. From this perspective, the cadential logic also makes more sense, because the "stronger" IAC closes the main theme, while the "weaker" HC closes the transition. The situation is thus akin to cases of what some theorists have spoken of as a "reversed period" or an "anti-period"; see also note 129. For some different cadential and formal interpretations of this theme, see James S. MacKay, "A Case for Declassifying the IAC as a Cadence Type: Cadence and Thematic Design in Selected Early- to Middle-Period Haydn Sonatas," 8–12.

109. Rothstein, *Phrase Rhythm*, 118.

110. Darcy and Hepokoski, "Medial Caesura," 135.

111. Donald Francis Tovey, *A Companion to Beethoven's Pianoforte Sonatas*; references to "cadence theme," etc., are found throughout the analyses.

112. Likewise, the formal function of *recapitulation* would incorporate closure of the entire sonata form.

113. I elaborate further on the idea of multiple levels of functional closure in "What Are Formal Functions?," 24–28.

114. Thus I somewhat overstate the case in *CF* that a "conventional melody [of a cadence] . . . is interchangeable from piece to piece" (37). Although this notion may be appropriate for music of the early and mid-eighteenth century, the classical style already witnesses a wide diversity of melodic content. With Beethoven, cadential ideas become

of the classical style remain relatively conventional (if not formulaic) by projecting scalar or arpeggiated descending ideas that "shut down" melodic activity. On the contrary, the characteristic melodies of initiating gestures tend to feature an "opening up" of melodic space, with a diversity of intervallic content (i.e., combinations of leaps, steps, and directional changes). The process that achieves cadential conventionality has been emphasized by Schoenberg in his concept of motivic *liquidation*, which "consists in gradually eliminating characteristic features, until only uncharacteristic ones remain, which no longer demand a continuation. Often only residues remain, which have little in common with the basic motive [found at the beginning of a theme]."[115] Consider the melodic content of Example 2.16, which exemplifies well the kind of liquidation Schoenberg has in mind. The conventionalized scalar runs and arpeggiations culminating in the cadential trill leave little trace of the opening ideas of this thematic unit; indeed, we would hardly expect to find such material at the opening of a theme—where would the music go from there? That melodic-motivic conventionality inhibits formal continuation is also discussed by Jonathan Kramer, who convincingly summarizes the aesthetic rationale for composers' using conventionalized gestures in cadences: "The reason for simplification and convention rather than contextual references at the end [of a formal unit] is to avoid any implications toward the piece's future which would work against coming to a close."[116] These remarks resonate well with ideas we discussed in the preceding chapter, especially those that emphasize how closure can only exist in an environment that thwarts expectations for continuation. Note as well, that by distinguishing between characteristic and conventional ideas, we see a mechanism in place for the appearance of a terminal modification of the sort that Smith highlights for poetic closure; in the case of music, the conventionalized cadential content brings the necessary sense of modification in contrast to the individualizing content of initiating functionality.

Though we can speak of cadential function possessing a conventional cadential *content*, we must be careful not to assume that the presence of such content necessarily signals cadential *function*.[117] Indeed, confusing cadential content and function has led to problematic analyses of cadence, which, in turn, can lead to questionable interpretations of phrase structure and form. If the hierarchical conditions of cadence as formal ending are not met, then even passages whose material content is suggestive of formal cadence would not normally result in a cadential arrival (or the promise of one). Thus when Webster identifies "initial cadences" in measures 2 and 4 of Haydn's "Farewell" Symphony finale (see again Ex. 2.17), we must ask just what the first of these cadences is actually closing.[118]

In the appropriate formal context, of course, the musical content of measures 1–2 could very well serve to articulate a genuine cadence. And even in its position at the theme's opening, it projects a certain cadential quality independent of its actual location within the theme. As a formal unit, however, these measures are initiating in function (a basic idea), to which measures 3–4 could be seen as effecting cadential closure (by means of an IAC). To call the opening unit "a cadence" that is followed two measures later by another "cadence" misses the opportunity of making finer experiential distinctions. For the content of the two opening measures projects, paradoxically, what might be called "the material content of cadence" in the context of formal initiation, while the second two-measure unit actually functions as cadential closure for the four-measure phrase.

Another way of understanding the difference between cadential content and cadential function is to distinguish between two different manifestations of formal functionality, namely, the sense of *intrinsic function*, which is expressed by the musical material in isolation from the broader formal environment in which that content is placed, and its *contextual function*, which reflects the actual position within the form that the passage occupies.[119] In most formal situations, intrinsic and contextual functions are congruent (as in mm. 3–4 of Ex. 2.17), and the overall form-functional expression is unambiguous. In other cases, there arises a kind of *form-functional dissonance* (akin to Harald Krebs's idea of "metrical dissonance") between the intrinsic and contextual functionality of the passage, such as where a contextually opening idea brings intrinsically cadential content, as in measures 1–2 of the same example.[120]

When speaking of a formal unit that seems to open with a cadence, it is difficult not to think of the third movement of Mozart's "Jupiter" Symphony (Ex. 2.18). The beginning of the trio has frequently been cited as an example of a witty effect that arises from displacing a cadence from its normative formal position. Ratner's description is typical:

> The cadence is placed at the *beginning* of the period [mm. 60–61], not the end, as if it were a final cadence for the minuet. The half cadence in m. 4 of the trio [m. 63] loses much of its clarity and almost all of its emphasis because of the steady eighth-note motion in the melody. Throughout this trio, in fact, the cadence never seems to find its proper place; it is used for everything *but* a point of arrival, and this seems to be the point of the trio—to put the cadence out of countenance.[121]

---

more individualized, while in the nineteenth century, they can even be considered "characteristic" in their melodic-motivic content.

115. Schoenberg, *Musical Composition*, 58.

116. Jonathan D. Kramer, "Beginnings and Endings in Western Art Music," 4.

117. Further to this distinction between cadential content and form, see Naomi Waltham-Smith, "Haydn's Impropriety," 125–26.

118. *Haydn's Farewell Symphony*, 75.

119. Michel Vallières et al., "Perception of Intrinsic Formal Functionality: An Empirical Investigation of Mozart's Materials," 18; see also, William E. Caplin, "Teaching Classical Form: Strict Categories vs. Flexible Analyses," 132–35.

120. Harald Krebs, *Fantasy Pieces: Metrical Dissonance in the Music of Robert Schumann*, chap. 2. In the annotations of Ex. 2.17, and in similar cases throughout this study, I use vertical braces to enclose an *intrinsic* form-functional label, thus, {cad.}, as seen in mm. 1–2 and mm. 5–6.

121. Ratner, *Classic Music*, 39.

EXAMPLE 2.18. Mozart, Symphony No. 41 in C ("Jupiter"), K. 551, iii, (a) mm. 56–67; (b) mm. 76–87.

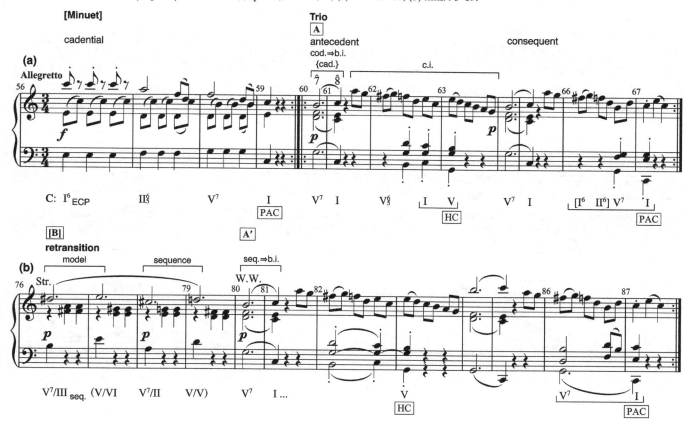

In light of the distinction that I am proposing between cadential content and cadential function, we need to inquire into the status of "the cadence" that Ratner identifies at the beginning of the trio. For although the content of this unit resembles a cadence, it is incapable of functioning as one for reasons already discussed—it cannot be construed to end a formal unit. Rather, this two-measure gesture is used throughout the trio as a *basic idea* to initiate both the antecedent and consequent phrases of the A and A' sections. That this basic idea contains cadential material is obvious enough: an authentic cadence must conclude with V–I, which often supports $\hat{7}$–$\hat{8}$ in the melody. But as I have discussed, the classical cadence more typically brings three to four harmonies; as a result, the absence of an initiating tonic ($I^6$) and pre-dominant ($II^6$) permits the simple $V^7$–I progression here to be interpreted as prolongational or even sequential (as will be discussed shortly).

Indeed, when it appears immediately after the cadential phrase that closes the minuet, the basic idea of the trio can very well give a first impression of ending the minuet not as a *cadence* (*pace* Ratner) but as a postcadential *codetta*, which follows directly upon the PAC in measure 59.[122] In other words, the content of measures 60–61 projects as much the idea of codetta as of cadence. The annotation cod.⇒b.i. captures the formal reinterpretation involved here; as well, I have indicated with the label {cad.} that this basic idea has an intrinsically cadential quality.

When the same gesture returns to initiate the A' section (Ex. 2.18b, m. 80), it makes a completely different effect. Following a long-held dominant of VI (mm. 68–75, not shown), a retransitional passage in measures 76–79 brings a descending-fifths sequence whose last link is the $V^7$–I progression of measures 80–81; that this final sequential link actually ends up functioning as a basic idea (seq.⇒b.i.) is signaled foremost by the change in instrumentation from the strings to the woodwinds. Seeing as classical composers are usually careful to distinguish sequential progressions from cadential ones, we should not jump to the conclusion that the final V–I motion of the sequence is necessarily cadential.

If Ratner's "cadence" actually turns out to be a basic idea disguised first as a codetta and then as a sequential link, what, then, is the status of the actual cadences needed to articulate musical form in this trio? Has Mozart really managed "to turn things topsy-turvy," as Ratner further describes it?[123] The fact is, both the antecedent and consequent phrases of the A and A' sections are completely in order. Nothing whatsoever is problematic with the HCs.[124] The PACs that close the periods are also normal, except in one fascinating respect. Given the bass quarter notes in measure 62 (Ex. 2.18a), we might believe

---

122. I develop in greater detail below (sec. 2.8) the distinction between cadential and postcadential functions.

123. Ratner, *Classic Music*, 39.

124. Later, in sec. 2.10, I consider Ratner's suggestion that continuity of musical motion weakens a cadential effect, as might be construed given the continuous eighth-note activity in mm. 62–63.

EXAMPLE 2.19. Mozart, Piano Sonata in C, K. 279, i, mm. 1–12.

## 2.7. Limited Cadential Scope

that the implied harmonic support for the melody of the authentic cadence in measures 66–67 is I⁶–II⁶–V⁷–I (as the square brackets around the tonic and pre-dominant indicate). But in the A′ section (Ex. 2.18b), Mozart shows us that the final cadence, measures 86–87, is really to be understood as supported exclusively by V⁷–I. He thus suggests, somewhat ironically in light of my previous discussion, that we might indeed regard the opening basic idea as having a fully legitimate cadential content after all.[125] The only cadential anomaly in this trio is the lack of closure for the B section, which normally would end with an HC. As already discussed, this cadential omission is motivated by the final sequential link becoming the basic idea of the A′ section. Ratner is right, of course, to stress the compositional play expressed in this trio, but the witty effects here arise from a rather more complicated set of references—both cadential and noncadential—than his comments might otherwise suggest. Indeed, the dissonance between intrinsic and contextual cadential functions is especially marked in this extraordinary passage.[126]

Distinguishing between cadential content and function is, in some cases, a matter of hierarchical perspective. For it is sometimes valid to speak of cadential content having an actual cadential function at one level of structure while also recognizing that this same content loses its function at a higher level. In these cases, it might be useful to invoke the notion of *limited cadential scope*. Consider the opening of Example 2.19. If we identify cadences at the downbeats of measures 3 and 5,[127] then we must ask exactly what formal unit is being closed by the cadence. Clearly, it is too early to speak of closing the main theme itself, for when we consider the broader context, we can identify a sentence-like structure for the theme as a whole, one whose promised cadential close is initially denied by the deceptive cadence at measure 10, but then realized by the PAC at measure 12. To the extent that we want to identify cadences at the downbeats of measures 3 and 5, it is best to see them functioning to provide closure to the basic idea itself, but having no further effect on the theme. For at the thematic level, a basic idea is exclusively an opening idea; it itself cannot produce a formal cadence.[128]

The notion of limited cadential scope also helps to clarify a problematic formal situation identified by Webster at the beginning of Example 2.20: "The slow introduction opens with what sounds

---

125. Note how Mozart subtly prepares the slurred dotted half-note G in m. 86 by changing the bass line of m. 82 (cf. Ex. 2.18a, m. 62).

126. For a study that raises issues similar to those discussed in this section, see John A. Rice, "The Bergamasca Schema in Late Haydn."

127. See, for example, Lerdahl and Jackendoff, *Generative Theory*, 62, and Hepokoski and Darcy, *Sonata Theory*, 80.

128. Here, and in other analyses of the similar situation to follow, I indicate a cadence of limited scope by placing the cadential label in parentheses, rather than in a box.

EXAMPLE 2.20. Haydn, Symphony No. 92 in G ("Oxford"), i, mm. 1–12.

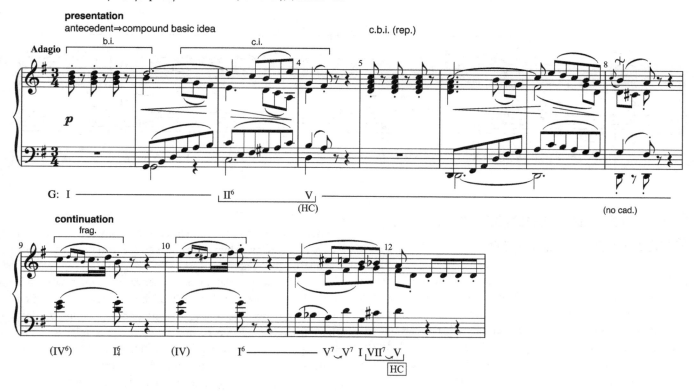

like the antecedent of a normal period.... But the following phrase cadences even more strongly on the dominant (m. 8)—is this then an anti-period?—; and worse yet, so does the third (m. 12)."[129] After highlighting the emphasis on dominant harmony throughout these bars, Webster proceeds to argue that in the context of the rest of the slow introduction and the beginning of the main theme of the exposition, this dominant is actually undermined and cannot be seen as structural after all. But leaving aside the broader role of dominant harmony in these measures, his analysis of cadences raises questions. Finding an HC at measure 4 seems, at first glance, reasonable enough: a clear half cadential harmonic progression leads to a sense of closure for a phrase that has all of the features of a four-measure antecedent, one that could begin a normal period, as Webster notes. But the idea of an HC at measure 8 is problematic due to the lack of harmonic progression into that bar.[130] Indeed, a single dominant is prolonged from measure 4 through measure 8. Moreover, it is not at all clear what makes this putative dominant cadence "stronger" than the first one (the embellished B in the first violin? the C♯ neighbor in the second violin?). Starting at measure 9, harmonic activity picks up again and the progression into measure 12 creates an unobjectionable HC.

If an HC at measure 8 should be ruled out, then what kind of formal situation obtains, and how does it relate to the HCs in measures 4 and 12? Given the lack of harmonic closure at measure 8, the idea of an (anti-)periodic structure for measures 1–8 can no longer be sustained. Yet the melodic-motivic content of the second phrase clearly repeats that of the first. Following this repetition, measures 9–12 bring fragmentation into one-measure units and a marked acceleration of the harmonic rhythm, the two major attributes of continuation function. In light of the two four-measure phrases that precede this continuation, the idea of a *compound sentence* (normatively sixteen measures in length) suggests itself, for this theme type often features a continuation that is compressed into four bars, thus resulting in a twelve-measure theme.[131] In this interpretation, then, the HC in measure 12 is the only one that truly effects thematic closure. As for the cadence in measure 4, the notion of limited scope can be of aid, for we can understand that this cadence may indeed close the first four-measure unit per se, but then have no further effect at the higher-level organization of the theme, where the individual units making up the eight-measure presentation should not, in principle, bring cadential articulations.[132]

---

129. Webster, *Haydn's Farewell Symphony*, 167. Webster defines an anti-period as "a period whose consequent cadences *off* the tonic and hence is more 'open' than the antecedent" (44). Other theorists and historians speak of this formal pattern as a "reversed" period. For a critique of this idea, see *CF*, 129, and *ACF*, 319–20.

130. The absence of a distinct progression of harmonies into a moment of a possible cadential arrival will again prove problematic for the identification of cadence in some passages that we will encounter ahead (Ex. 2.23, m. 25, and Ex. 2.26, m. 31).

---

131. *CF*, 69, and *ACF*, 180.

132. I thus analyze the opening four measures as an antecedent, which, *in retrospect*, functions in the manner of a *compound basic idea* (see note 78); a genuine compound basic idea then appears in mm. 5–8. In

EXAMPLE 2.21. Haydn, String Quartet in D Minor, Op. 42, iv, mm. 32–40.

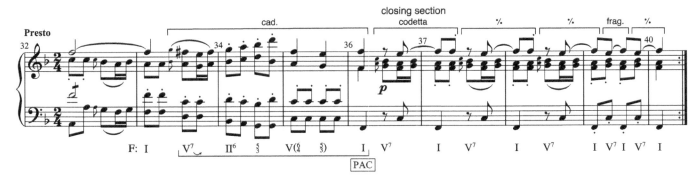

## 2.8. Cadential Function versus Postcadential Function

Perhaps the most pervasive confusion about the nature of cadence arises from the failure to distinguish conceptually between the time span of music that *precedes* the cadential arrival and the time span that *follows* that arrival. The former can rightfully be characterized as cadential in function since it provides the actual musical content for effecting formal closure. The latter should not be understood as cadential because the music following the moment of arrival can have no further impact upon the fact that formal closure has indeed been achieved. This music can instead be considered *postcadential* in function, as distinct from the genuine cadential function, which precedes (and includes) the cadential arrival. A truly cadential passage expresses the temporal sense of *end*; a postcadential passage expresses the distinctly different temporal sense of *after-the-end*.[133] Such material following the end is often motivated by the need either to dissipate the energy accumulated in the process of achieving the end or to sustain (or even to boost) such energy in order to reinforce the sense of arrival. Not all cadences require a postcadential passage (the HC internal to the period form rarely includes such material), but in many contexts, postcadential function is appropriate in order to avoid an overly abrupt cessation of musical activity at the moment of cadential arrival. In particular, the subordinate-theme group of a sonata exposition (and recapitulation) is normally followed by a postcadential unit, since the final PAC of the group usually is given such a strong articulation as to require further material to release the energy accrued by that arrival. Main themes of movements may also include a postcadential passage (as shown shortly in Ex. 2.22). The transition in the exposition (and recapitulation) and a core of a development section usually end with an HC, which is then followed by a subsequent postcadential extension, one that may be quite elaborate in scope.[134]

Postcadential material can be divided into two main categories on the basis of the final harmony of the cadence. Following an authentic cadence, the passage can be termed a *closing section*, which itself is made up of one or more *codettas*.[135] An individual codetta ranges in length from a single chord to a full four-measure phrase and prolongs the tonic harmony achieved at the end of the preceding authentic cadence. Following an HC, a comparable passage can be termed a *standing on the dominant*.[136] This unit prolongs dominant harmony and often consists of individual ideas that are comparable in nature to the codettas of a closing section.[137] The harmonic content of a postcadential passage usually consists of prolongational progressions, but frequently enough cadential progressions are used as well. Indeed, the individual codettas of a closing section often have cadential content, though their formal function is postcadential. And it is surely the appearance of such content that has reinforced the conceptual confusion between cadential and postcadential functions that so pervades our theoretical discourse.

### 2.8.1. Theoretical Background

One possible historical source for the confusion is that the German word *Schluß* has the general meaning of "close," as well as the more technical meaning of "cadence." Thus when speaking of the final phrase of a sonata exposition by Haydn (Ex. 2.21,

---

the classical style, a *compound presentation* (the initiating function of a compound sentence) is composed of two compound basic ideas. Haydn's theme is itself a kind of hybrid of this situation in that it uses an opening antecedent ("becoming" a compound basic idea) followed by a clear-cut compound basic idea.

133. The notion of after-the-end finds expression as well in temporal contexts that are nonmusical. If, for example, the formal closure of a mystery story occurs when the murderer is uncovered, as discussed earlier, the "after-the-end" of the plot concerns itself with the fate of the criminal and the other suspects of the crime, as well as the glorification of the detective. For additional cases of nonmusical, "after-the-end" temporalities, see ahead sec. 2.8.4.

134. On developmental cores, see *CF*, 141–47, and *ACF*, 429–40.

135. The term *closing section* is potentially misleading, since "closing" itself is suggestive of "cadential closure." I have resigned myself to the term, however, because such a passage within a sonata-form exposition (or recapitulation) has traditionally been called a "closing theme." I consider this terminological dilemma again in sec. 2.8.4.

136. The original German expression "*Stehen auf der Dominante*" is coined by Ratz, *Die musikalische Formenlehre*, 25.

137. For the sake of consistency, the postcadential passage following an HC could also be termed a closing section, with its individual units called codettas. But since such usage in connection with a prolongation of dominant harmony has no basis in traditional theory, I have elected

mm. 37–40), Tovey translates the widespread German term *Schlußgruppe* as "cadence-phrase," though he could have chosen the less specific term "closing phrase" as well.[138] But from the theoretical perspective developed here, the actual cadential function, which brings closure to the subordinate theme of the exposition, begins with the upbeat to measure 34 and ends with the cadential arrival on the downbeat of measure 36. The following phrase—Tovey's "cadence-phrase"—is a closing section consisting of codettas whose content may be cadential but whose function is entirely postcadential.

Tovey's tendency to label postcadential passages as various types of cadential units (phrases, groups, themes) exerted enormous influence on North American theory, especially in the writings of Charles Rosen. Thus when presenting a "textbook" definition of sonata form, Rosen states, "At the end of the second group, there is a closing theme . . . with a cadential function. The final cadence of the exposition, on the dominant, may be followed by an immediate repetition of the exposition."[139] Although it is difficult to know exactly what constitutes this "closing theme" (it may be the closing section proper, but it may also include the cadential component of the subordinate-theme group), the "final cadence" undoubtedly refers to the final *codetta*, since rarely does an exposition end with the actual PAC closing the subordinate-theme group. Rosen also speaks of a cadence and its "repetitions" (105). These repeated "cadences," however, are actually codettas within a closing section that follows the true cadence. (Thus, Tovey's "cadential-phrase" in mm. 37–40 of Example 2.21 contains codettas that might be taken as repetitions of the cadence.) Further confusion arises when Rosen refers to the entire closing section of a concerto ritornello as an "elaborate cadence" (74) and speaks of the coda to the finale of Beethoven's Eighth Symphony as "fifty bars of cadence in stretto style" (351). Many other writers invoke cadence in the same vein. Thus Cone, after correctly identifying the cadence closing a subordinate theme, labels the following material a "cadential phrase, confirming the key" of that theme.[140] Like Rosen, Webster refers to "final cadences" that are actually codettas and speaks of a true cadential arrival that is clinched "with four additional root-position V–I cadences";[141] again, these are better understood as codettas, not cadences. Similarly, Lerdahl and Jackendoff identify a cadence that is immediately followed by "additional cadences," though these are preferably seen as codettas that are structurally subordinate to the real cadence, as their tree graph reveals.[142] And Ratner uses the label "cadential phrase" to refer to a passage that actually functions as a standing on the dominant.[143]

In all of these cases, theoretical confusion arises because cadential function is not sufficiently distinguished from postcadential function, along with a further conflation of cadential content and cadential function. Especially in the case of codettas whose content is the same as, or very similar to, the actual cadence closing the theme, it is easy enough to assume that the cadence is merely being repeated (following Rosen and Webster), a point that I will develop later in this section. In such cases, it seems that theorists and historians rely on a kind of terminological inertia, such that if something looks like a cadence, then it might just as well be called a cadence, whether or not it actually functions as one. The theoretical problem, however, is that codettas of cadential content cannot usually be construed to "end" a prior initiating unit, and thus the basic hierarchical conditions of formal closure do not obtain. Beyond this logical consideration, the failure to differentiate cadential from postcadential can obscure our experience of musical temporality, namely our sense that such-and-such stretch of time creates ending, while a subsequent stretch affirms a coming-after-the-end. These are fundamentally different aesthetic sensibilities, and these differences deserve to be respected analytically whenever possible. To be sure, genuine cases of formal ambiguity sometimes arise, such that it can be difficult to specify exactly where the moment of cadential arrival separates the cadential function from the postcadential one, another topic to be considered later on.[144] But such cadential play is largely effective because, in principle, we are aware that there is a distinction to be made. We do a disservice to our listening experience by lumping together as "cadence" the variety of gestures that express both ending and after-the-ending.

To complicate the matter further, there are indeed cases where a closing section seems to contain real cadences, ones that function to conclude a distinct four-measure phrase. Here, however, the notion of limited cadential scope helps to clarify the situation. Consider Example 2.22, from the end of a main theme by Mozart. Built as a small ternary, the theme concludes formally with a PAC in measure 20. What follows is a closing section consisting of a repeated four-measure codetta. The codetta, however, is itself closed with a clear cadential progression. Within the limited scope of the codettas, these cadential figures have a genuine cadential function. From the perspective of the theme as a whole, however, they participate within a broader postcadential passage.

Despite the common confusion of cadential and postcadential functions, some scholars are clearly aware of the distinction. Blombach, for one, explicitly differentiates "the actual cadence" from "the repeated dominant-to-tonic pattern that frequently

---

to follow Ratz in using different expressions based on the underlying harmony, even though the formal situations are essentially the same. Unfortunately, we lack specific terminology associated with the individual units making up a standing on the dominant. No satisfactory term seems readily available, so I will speak generally of the "new idea(s)" at the basis of a standing on the dominant.

138. Donald Francis Tovey, *The Forms of Music*, 210. Tovey also regularly uses the expressions "cadence group" and "cadence theme."

139. Charles Rosen, *Sonata Forms*, 2. Other references to "final cadences" that are actually codettas appear on pp. 75 and 241–42.

140. Cone, *Musical Form*, 50.

141. Webster, *Haydn's Farewell Symphony*, 146, 78.

---

142. Lerdahl and Jackendoff, *Generative Theory*, 235.

143. Ratner, *Classic Music*, 42.

144. See the discussion of Ex. 2.24, ahead. I analyze a similar case in connection with the scherzo of Beethoven's Piano Sonata in E-flat, Op. 7, in *CF*, 221, Ex. 15.1, and *ACF*, 616, Ex. 18.3.

EXAMPLE 2.22. Mozart, Violin Sonata in E Minor, K. 304, i, mm. 18–28.

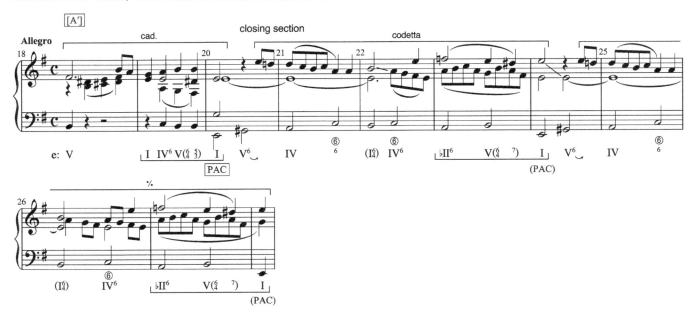

occurs at the ends of tonal compositions or major sections."[145] Likewise, Darcy and Hepokoski hold that the "closing zone (C)" of a sonata exposition embraces all of the material that follows their "essential expositional closure (EEC)," usually the first substantial authentic cadence in the new key, and they assign that zone a "postcadential" tonal function, whose "purpose is to solidify further the new key."[146]

## 2.8.2. Postcadential Function as "Confirmation"

Darcy and Hepokoski's description of postcadential function as a further solidification of a tonal region articulated by a cadence relates to another widely held view, namely, that the material following a cadential arrival—which, as we have seen, is termed "cadential" by other scholars—serves primarily to confirm, reinforce, or emphasize the cadence itself. Indeed, they are even more explicit on this point when they discuss how their closing zone (C) typically includes "a chain of cadential modules that confirm the PAC with varying degrees of strength."[147] A similar idea is expressed by Ratner. "The most powerful effect of arrival is created when the *cadential action* itself is *reinforced and extended*, forming an *area of*

arrival. This generally takes place toward the end of a large section of a movement." He then refers to the end of a duet in Mozart's *Don Giovanni*, in which the dramatic action "is underscored by a series of strong cadences in D minor, culminating in an extended play on the D minor chord,"[148] in other words, by what I would call a broad postcadential passage. Kofi Agawu, a student of Ratner, elaborates these ideas by distinguishing between "syntactic" and "rhetorical" components of closure. "The syntactic component is the melodic-harmonic event that closes the overall structure. . . . The rhetorical component . . . is the set of devices that emphasize the closure—notably, repetition in various dimensions and on various temporal levels."[149] Agawu's syntactic component is normally an actual cadence with its point of arrival. The rhetorical component occurs in a passage following this arrival, as exemplified by a codetta that appears after the end of the first-movement main theme of Mozart's String Quintet in C, K. 515. Agawu notes that the actual cadence closing this theme (mm. 56–57),

> while fulfilling a syntactical obligation, does not carry sufficient rhetorical weight to provide an effective balance for the period as a whole. The event necessitates a complementary confirmation, hence measures 57–60, which constitute a prolonged cadence. . . . It is not enough simply to supply a cadence in order to secure the tonal meaning of a period; it is also necessary to confirm it.[150]

---

145. Blombach, "Phrase and Cadence," 233.

146. Darcy and Hepokoski, "Medial Caesura," 121. With their treatise, *Sonata Theory*, Hepokoski and Darcy speak of something as "postcadential" in similar, but more restricted terms: "By definition, C is postcadential (post-EEC). . . ." But as they explain, "[i]n this context 'postcadential' means that it occurs after the first satisfactory PAC in the secondary key [i.e., their EEC]." Indeed, they acknowledge that the closing zone can include genuine cadences, some of which may even be more emphatic than earlier ones: "C-ideas often end with stronger cadences than had been articulated at the EEC" (181). I will shortly deal with their thoughts on these matters in a more extended discussion (see sec. 2.8.3).

147. Darcy and Hepokoski, "Medial Caesura," 121.

148. Ratner, *Classic Music*, 46.

149. Agawu, *Playing with Signs*, 67.

150. Agawu, *Playing with Signs*, 81–82. Agawu illustrates other cases of rhetorical endings with several examples in which the actual cadence (the syntactic component) is "repeated" multiple times (thus recalling Rosen and Webster); see Agawu's analyses of Mozart's Piano Sonata in C Minor, K. 457, ii, and Haydn's Piano Sonatas in C-sharp Minor, H. 36, i, and in D, H. 37, i, on pp. 69–71. These discussions give the impression that his

The idea that postcadential material confirms, emphasizes, or strengthens the cadential arrival or the tonal region associated with that arrival seems at first glance plausible enough; indeed, I specifically spoke of postcadential material as "reinforcing" the sense of arrival in the opening paragraph of this general section (2.8). But further reflection prompts a number of concerns, especially when speaking of postcadential function as *confirming* the sense of cadence. For instance, if a cadence is not followed by a closing section, does that mean that the cadence remains unconfirmed? Inasmuch as the word *confirm* "implies the making unquestionable of something in question by means of authoritative statement or indisputable fact,"[151] does the lack of a closing section undermine the existence of a cadence? Moreover, if, as argued earlier, a cadential progression is the principal means of confirming a tonality, then how could a subsequent postcadential passage (which is often made up exclusively of prolongational progressions) also be seen as confirmatory of a key? In response to these questions, I would hold that a real cadence need no further confirmation in order to have full legitimacy as an agent of formal closure (at the thematic level); as well, the need for a subsequent postcadential function entails other matters (dynamic, rhythmic, textural, grouping structure) that are not specifically cadential in nature.

Another concern involves the notion of cadential strength (a topic to be treated in greater detail in sec. 2.11). That a prominent postcadential area can reinforce and strengthen the sense of cadential arrival seems reasonable enough (especially when the constituent codettas seem to repeat the cadence). But another kind of cadential emphasis should be considered as well. Many cadences, especially those closing subordinate themes and codas, witness enormous expansions of the harmonies that *precede* the final tonic, thus delaying the cadential arrival and causing the listener to desire it all the more. Surely this expansion of cadential function also has an effect of making the cadence appear powerful. But the nature of this emphasis and strengthening of the actual cadential function is of a different kind than that created by a postcadential function. Just as it is important to differentiate cadential and postcadential as discrete formal functions, so too is it important to differentiate the aesthetic effects of emphasis that results from expansions associated with these differing functions.[152]

## 2.8.3. Hepokoski and Darcy's Critique

Though I have cited some statements by Hepokoski and Darcy indicating that they recognize a distinction between cadential and postcadential functions, their views in this respect are actually quite limited to a specific, large-scale situation involving their "essential expositional closure" (EEC)—the one PAC deemed necessary to close the fundamental formal processes of the exposition—and the following postcadential "closing zone" (C), which constitutes all of the remaining material of the exposition.[153] With respect to the more local situations involving what I term a closing section or a standing on the dominant, they actually back away from identifying these sections as postcadential, especially in the case of the latter (which they term a "dominant lock"). Thus when discussing the relationship of their "medial caesura" (MC) to the actual HC that closes the transition (TR), they seem intent on holding on to the idea that the "dominant lock" continues to be cadential in function, not postcadential:[154]

> [the dominant] of the half-cadence arrival is vigorously seized onto, frozen in place, kept alive by means of a specialized pedal-point effect that announces that TR is ending with a continued push toward the MC. The sense of an "HC-moment" is not released and left behind as a mere past event—as happens with most other kinds of HC phrase endings—but rather is held onto, brandished as an achievement, sustained as a continuing function with a specific role to play at this point in the form.[155]
>
> Thus our view differs from that of Caplin ... who ... regards this dominant-lock as "postcadential" in function. We find it preferable to think of this stretch of music not so much as existing "after" the half-cadence arrival (which in a literal sense, it does) as keeping that arrival alive, refusing to let it go, animatedly spreading its sense of being still active over several more measures. Put another way, the dominant-lock may be considered a special prolongational technique that extends and "holds in place" the HC-arrival effect for a specific rhetorical purpose.[156]

In a somewhat similar vein, they downplay the "postcadential" aspects of a closing section, at least one consisting of possible "cadence-like" gestures:

---

rhetorical component is congruent to my postcadential function. But in his analysis (pp. 67–68) of Mozart's String Quintet in C Minor, K. 406, i, he includes within the rhetorical component passages that both precede and follow a cadential arrival.

151. *Webster's Third International New Dictionary of the English Language Unabridged*, 476.

152. Karol Berger also notes that lengthening the duration of the harmonies preceding the cadence "will intensify the expectation of the arrival," yet he maintains that lengthening the final tonic through an "appendix" also yields cadential strengthening. In other words, he seems not to distinguish conceptually a cadential strengthening from a postcadential one ("The First-Movement Punctuation Form in Mozart's Piano Concertos," 244).

153. A comparable situation obtains in a sonata-form recapitulation, though they designate the articulative cadence as the "essential sonata closure" (ESC).

154. The "medial caesura" is a major element of Hepokoski and Darcy's theory of sonata form. This rhythmic-textural gap (which may sometimes be filled in) appears at the very end of the transition and prepares for the entrance of the "secondary-theme zone" (S). In the present study, I restrict the term to those cases where there exists a literal caesura created by a moment of silence, or else a fermata on the final sounding sonority of the transition.

155. Hepokoski and Darcy, *Sonata Theory*, 31.

156. Hepokoski and Darcy, *Sonata Theory*, 31, note 11.

EXAMPLE 2.23. Beethoven, String Quartet in C Minor, Op. 18, no. 4, i, mm. 19–27.

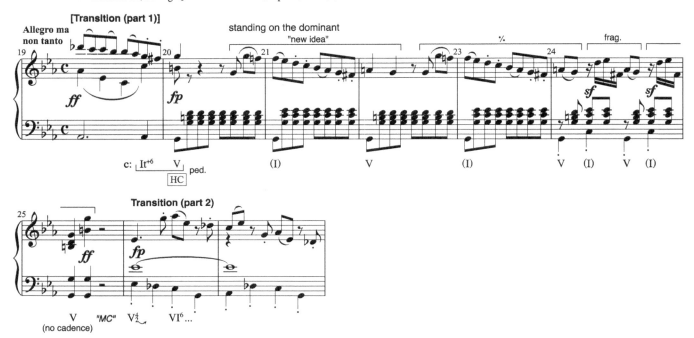

Another instance—similarly disallowed as "cadences" by Caplin . . .—would be the succession of emphatic V–I chords (often without preceding tonic and predominant chords) sometimes found at the end of expositions [see again Ex. 2.21, not specifically referenced by Hepokoski and Darcy but illustrating exactly their point]. We suspect that most listeners intuitively hear such chords as recrafted, emphatic reiterations of the final portion (the "cadence" element proper) of a more complete cadential progression heard just before them. To strip them of legitimate cadential status (in favor only of the "postcadential" role of "codettas") is counter-intuitive.[157]

In other words, Hepokoski and Darcy seem to maintain that cadential function embraces not only the music that precedes the point of cadential arrival but also any subsequent passage that prolongs the final harmony of that arrival, thus discounting a different, *postcadential* function for that latter passage.

Despite the vivid language that they use to describe how the cadential arrival is "frozen in place" and thus "kept alive" by the standing on the dominant (and, presumably, by a closing section), their idea is nonetheless problematic, as we can test out on a typical case (see Ex. 2.23).[158] Here, the first part of a *two-part transition* (which begins earlier at m. 13, not shown) leads to a powerful home-key HC at the downbeat of measure 20.[159] At that moment, the accompaniment changes and a postcadential standing on the dominant begins with distinctly new material within a prolongation of dominant harmony. The final liquidation of these postcadential ideas brings a textural break in the second half of measure 25, Hepokoski and Darcy's medial caesura (MC). The second part of the transition then begins in the following bar in the submediant region. To be sure, the accompanimental material supported by dominant harmony that begins on the downbeat of measure 20, whose initial time point marks the cadential arrival, also occupies a distinct time span, one that includes the point of arrival and lasts to the second half of beat 3 of that same bar. And this material indeed belongs to the cadential function (initiated by the pre-dominant, the augmented-sixth of m. 19). When, however, we hear the onset of a *new* event—the new idea of the standing on the dominant (upbeat to m. 21)—we understand, I believe, that another *formal process* is in the making, one that naturally follows upon the closure attained by the preceding cadential arrival, which itself had marked the end of the prior thematic process (the transition's first part). This formal process consists of a new two-measure idea, its repetition (mm. 23–24), subsequent fragmentation (m. 24), and ultimate liquidation (m. 25).[160] In other words, once cadential closure has been

---

157. Hepokoski and Darcy, *Sonata Theory*, 67, note 5.

158. This example is not specifically referenced in this connection in Hepokoski and Darcy's treatise, but is cited as a good example of a medial caesura in their earlier article on the topic: "At m. 25, the music reaches what at first sounds like an unambiguous i:HC . . . MC, complete with *fortissimo* double hammerstroke and GP [general pause]." They go on to explain that whereas this home-key medial caesura is initially "proposed," it is eventually "declined," such that the following music continues the "transitional zone," arriving finally at "a III:HC (first-level default) MC at m. 33" (Darcy and Hepokoski, "Medial Caesura," 141).

159. See *CF*, 135–38, and *ACF*, 339–42, for a discussion of the *two-part transition*, whose first part ends with a home-key HC, and whose second part typically begins off-tonic (often directly with submediant harmony, or as in Ex. 2.23, with a tonicization of that region).

160. Though the formal process just described reminds us of the sentence theme type, we cannot really speak of a genuine *thematic* process here, because of the lack of any harmonic progressions and subsequent

achieved (via the cadential arrival), we experience any subsequent material as something that no longer belongs to the cadential function per se, but rather projects either the beginning of an "after-the-end," postcadential function (the standing on the dominant) or the onset of a completely new thematic process (say, the second part of the transition).

Hepokoski and Darcy also strongly imply in the previous quotation that "stripping" the final V–I chords ending an exposition (such as Ex. 2.21) of "their legitimate cadential status" and thus characterizing such chords as postcadential reduces their import in some way. The question is, import in what sense? Most obviously, of course, every formal function in a musical composition has its appropriate role to the play in the work's temporal unfolding, and thus no single function is intrinsically more or less important than any other when it fulfills its intended role. But with respect to the formal closure of a thematic process per se, it is true that cadential function is more important than the following postcadential passage. It is the cadence, not the standing on the dominant, that brings thematic closure. Indeed, such postcadential passages are effectively optional to the form. A good number of sonata forms, especially in slow movements, dispense with a specific standing on the dominant at the end of the transition, and even a closing section at the end of the exposition is omitted now and then. Much less often, however, does the composer dispense with a cadence to close a transition (thus leaving it without a structural end),[161] and very rarely does the subordinate theme fail to bring authentic cadential closure.[162]

Why, then, are Hepokoski and Darcy so insistent that the "HC-arrival effect," and thus the cadential function itself, must be understood to retain its structural importance all the way through the standing on the dominant and right up to the medial caesura? I suspect it is because this latter moment of transition articulation is so crucial to their theory of sonata form, and so the MC must be accorded a formal status that is equally, if not more, significant than the earlier HC itself. Yet abolishing the difference between an "ending" and an "after the ending" seems more of a loss than retaining the distinction, despite the various complications that it can sometimes entail.

### 2.8.4. Two "Registers" of Closure

One such complication involves multiple ways of using the word "ending" (or any number of synonyms, such as "closing," "completing," "finalizing," or "terminating"). As Hepokoski points out in another context, my view of a sonata transition (to take the case that he is most interested in) identifies "two endings, albeit in two different registers of closure."[163] One ending is the HC that provides a conclusion to the formal processes of the transition; the other ending is the very final utterance that we hear associated with the transition as a whole, namely, the last event of the standing on the dominant, which immediately precedes the medial caesura. This latter event "literally" concludes the transition, in that what follows belongs to a subsequent thematic unit. In Example 2.23, the two "endings" can be identified, respectively, as the HC in measure 20 and the *fortissimo* dominant chord on the second quarter-note beat of measure 25.

In ordinary language, we use the words "ending," "closing," "concluding," and so on, to speak of both of these modes of closure, though experientially they are very different. Indeed such linguistic confusion is sown even by my speaking of the postcadential function of an authentic cadence as a "closing section." But if our language lacks a ready way of differentiating these two registers of closure, this should not prohibit us from appreciating the differences between them. I have already (in note 133) mentioned the dual nature of closure associated with a murder mystery. Let us consider some other nonmusical temporal experiences that exhibit similarly multiple types of "ending." Take the case of a running race. For any individual runner, the race "ends" when he or she crosses the finish line; this moment stops the clock that measures how fast it took the runner to complete the race (and thus to determine the winner). Yet, our experience of the race also includes the short period of time after the runner crosses the line and winds down with a brief walk or jog, and then leaves the track, thus "ending" the race as an entire event. Something similar occurs in everyday classroom teaching, to use another analogy that may relate to many readers of this study. A given class technically ends when the instructor finishes providing any further information to the students for that particular period (a moment sometimes prompted by a ringing bell to indicate the end of the session). But the experience of the class also includes the period of time when the students shuffle out of the class, some perhaps remaining behind to talk to the instructor about individual matters, and so on. Eventually the class as a complete experience "ends" when everyone has left the room, thus making way for another class to begin. In both cases, the running race and the classroom period, we can readily distinguish two different registers of closure: one that represents the essential, formal close of each event—crossing the finishing line, concluding the lecture—and a second, ancillary period of time that follows, whose "ending" (leaving the track; leaving the room) is also associated with the entire experience.

Understanding the differences between these two modes of closure is not difficult, but actually describing them in words is, since we do not have terms in our everyday language that readily differentiate these temporal experiences.[164] In the case of musical

---

cadential closure; see again my definition of theme in the earlier sec. 2.2.1 and note 19.

161. *CF*, 135, and *ACF*, 343; see also William E. Caplin and Nathan John Martin, "The 'Continuous Exposition' and the Concept of Subordinate Theme," 11–18.

162. For one exception, see the discussion of the finale of Beethoven's Fifth Symphony in Chapter 5 (Ex. 5.71).

163. James Hepokoski, "Sonata Theory, Secondary Themes and Continuous Exposition: Dialogues with Form-Functional Theory," 54.

164. In addition to English, I am not aware of any other European language that distinguishes these temporal realities with consistently different words; indeed, I already have discussed how the German *Schluß* so readily evokes precisely the problematic issue we are examining now.

EXAMPLE 2.24. Beethoven, Symphony No. 7 in A, Op. 92, iii, mm. 1–24 (R = 2N) (*ACF* 5.9).

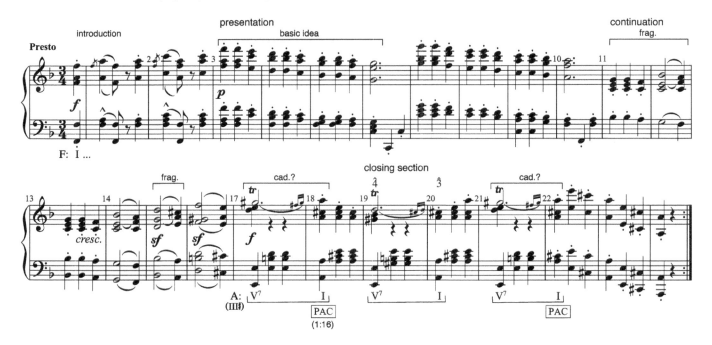

closure, we confront the same linguistic dilemma, thus resulting in multiples uses for "ending." One way of addressing this problem, however, is to confine the term *cadence* to only one of these modes, the one that provides formal closure, and to use other terms (such as *codetta*, *closing section*, *standing on the dominant*) to identify the other mode. In this way, at least, our more specifically musical terminology can project the various ways of "ending" that natural language fails to convey. And for this reason, among many others, my approach advocates limiting the identification of cadence. When we say that the last tonic event of an exposition (say, the last chord of Ex. 2.21) marks its "final cadence," we risk serious analytical confusion between the two registers of closure. If we restrict using cadence in the way proposed here, we can be more precise in our identification of how different kinds of endings, with diverse musical processes, can be projected and experienced.

## 2.8.5. Consecutive (Repeated) PACs

Another complication associated with cadential versus postcadential arises in a small number of cases in which a cadential unit (say, a 2-m. idea or a 4-m. phrase) ending with a PAC is immediately restated. Whereas such cadences typically bring the same musical content in the sense of a repetition, the content may sometimes vary from one cadential unit to the next. For this reason, I speak more generally of *consecutive* cadences, which embrace repeated cadences as well. (I am not referring here to consecutive codettas, a situation that has also been confused with consecutive cadences, as discussed earlier in sec. 2.8.1.) Moreover, I am concerned here with consecutive cadences of the same type (e.g., two or more PACs or HCs). A situation of consecutive cadences in which the first is syntactically "weaker" than

the second—say, an IAC followed immediately by a PAC—is not problematic, since we can readily ascribe full thematic closure to the latter.

One case of such consecutive cadences arises in the A section of a symphonic scherzo by Beethoven (Ex. 2.24). Following a brief thematic introduction (mm. 1–2), a basic idea of four notated measures is repeated as a response, thus creating the presentation phrase of a sentence (mm. 3–10).[165] A continuation (mm. 11–18) brings fragmentation into two-measure units (11–14) and then further fragmentation while the music modulates to A major, the III♯ region. A quick PAC at measure 18, consisting of the incomplete cadential progression V$^7$–I, confirms the new key.[166] In the following music, another V$^7$–I sees the melody conclude $\hat{4}$–$\hat{3}$, in the manner of an IAC (mm. 19–20), while the next two bars

---

165. The fast tempo and comparative paucity of musical material in each *notated* measure suggest that our sense of what comprises a *real* measure of music, for the purposes of identifying the theme type, is not reflected in the notation. In this case, I believe that we readily hear a real (R) measure embracing two notated (N) measures, thus R = 2N. Accordingly, the theme is not a sixteen-measure compound sentence but rather an eight-measure simple sentence, though one that is notated as sixteen measures. Another common situation, one that eighteenth-century theorists referred to as "compound meter," sees a real measure occupying only one-half of the notated measure (R = ½N). On compound meter, see Floyd K. Grave, "Metrical Displacement and the Compound Measure in Eighteenth-Century Theory and Practice." In order to avoid confusion, I will indicate all cases of R = 2N or R = ½N in the captions of the examples. Whereas determining the relationship between real and notated measures is important for a strictly *formal* analysis, it usually has little bearing on cadential analyses. More information on real versus notated measures is found in *CF*, 35, and *ACF*, 63–65; see also the discussion of cadence and meter in Chapter 3, sec. 3.4.1.

166. The indication "(1:16)" below the PAC sign refers to a metrical issue that will be discussed in the next Chapter 3, sec. 3.4.1.

replicate the PAC of measures 17–18. The very final two measures of the theme bring an obvious postcadential extension that continues to sound tonic of the new key.

The cadential situation just presented prompts a number of questions: which cadence—the PAC in measures 17–18 or the one in measures 21–22—represents true closure for the theme? (The potential, but weaker, IAC at m. 20 does not come into consideration here.) When we hear the first cadence, do we simply say that the theme is over and that everything else is postcadential? Or do we hear the second cadence as the more conclusive one (responding in some sense to the preceding IAC configuration)?[167]

In such an ambiguous situation, we can recognize three different perspectives from which to answer these questions. One perspective respects as much as possible the temporal ordering of events, so that we deem the first of the two cadential moments as creating closure and then interpret the second "cadence" as an after-the-end utterance, a codetta. After all, according to the fundamental logic of cadence, this second one cannot literally be construed to end a prior beginning (or middle), since what precedes—the first cadence—is itself the ending of an ongoing thematic process. Although we hear two musical ideas with the same content, we understand the first as cadential and the second as postcadential. Once closure has been achieved by the first cadence, there is nothing further in the way of a thematic process to conclude; the second "cadence" is functionally superfluous.

A second perspective on consecutive cadences gives greater structural weight to the second one as the *last* occurring moment of closure. Here, we perceive that a formal ending has been accomplished, but when we hear the same closing gesture sounding immediately again, it has the effect of "undoing" the first cadence and allowing us to hear the second cadence as the real, decisive moment of closure.[168] In other words, although we can perceive that closure seems at first to have been effected, we give up on this idea when we hear another attempt at closure. In this sense, it is almost as though the first cadence has been evaded, with the second cadence representing a "one-more-time" situation akin that advocated by Schmalfeldt.[169]

A third perspective does not ask us to decide which of these two cadences is the "real" one. It simply asserts that both cadences represent the very same musical event, one that closes the ongoing thematic process. In other words, "it's just a repeated cadence."[170] This view asks us to forgo the literal temporal ordering and to allow our experiential clock to be "wound back" for a second run-through. We understand that closure has occurred (the first time), but we allow ourselves to experience once again a sense of ending.

Each of these three perspectives has its own merits and inherent difficulties. And it is not clear that we can decisively invoke any one as the definitive way in which to handle all such ambiguous situations. Though my general approach to cadence tends to favor the first perspective, individual cases arise where the second one seems preferable. (The third perspective, in effect, is always available.) Moreover, the performer may help to sway our hearing by rhetorically emphasizing either the first or second cadential iteration.

With these general notions of consecutive cadences in mind, let us return to Beethoven's scherzo (Ex. 2.24). In this particular case, I prefer hearing the first PAC (m. 18) as ending the theme. I am motivated not only by my general predilection to perceive the first moment of closure as decisive, but also by another consideration that often plays a role as well, namely the symmetrical phrase grouping (or phrase rhythm) that is maintained when the cadence appears in the sixteenth bar of this sentential theme (though literally in m. 18, due to the 2-m. introduction). We thus recognize a continuation phrase of eight bars that matches the presentation phrase of the same length. In other words, listeners are primed by the conventions of tight-knit main themes to expect closure after sixteen bars, so that when it does occur there, they naturally assume it to be in just the "right place."[171]

Alternatively, let us consider a passage in a quartet by Haydn where we may want to give preference to the second of two PACs for a different set of reasons (Ex. 2.25). In the course of the first subordinate theme of the exposition, an internal dominant arrival occurs at measure 44 (not shown).[172] The example picks up with the extension of the dominant for another two bars. This dominant then resolves deceptively in measures 47–48 when ⑤ moves up chromatically (♯⑤–⑥) to support $V^6_4$/IV–IV$^6$. There follows a quick cadential progression that yields a PAC on the downbeat of measure 50. Immediately thereafter, another four-measure phrase (mm. 51–54) brings a varied repeat of the previous phrase. The chromatic $\hat{5}$–♯$\hat{5}$–$\hat{6}$ is then relocated to the upper voice, while the bass brings ③–④ (from the prior alto, mm. 47–48) to initiate an

---

167. A likely reason why this particular piece elicits ambiguity between cadential and postcadential functions is owing to its being a scherzo, a genre in which the accumulative energy and rhythmic momentum might be hindered by a sudden change to new material for a postcadential, closing section. As such, the theme is propelled through both PAC articulations up to the final event on the downbeat of m. 24.

168. Hepokoski and Darcy often speak of a cadence being "undone" in various contexts (*Sonata Theory*, 60, 123–24, 51). In a somewhat similar vein, Danuta Mirka speaks of "cancelling a caesura [i.e., cadence] effect" ("Punctuation and Sense in Late-Eighteenth-Century Music, 244).

169. Janet Schmalfeldt, "Cadential Processes." Cadential evasion and the one-more-time technique will be discussed in Chapter 4 on cadential deviations (see sec. 4.2.2.2).

170. I thank David Cohen for proposing this perspective to me. Elizabeth Hellmuth Margulis invokes a similar sentiment by Peter Kivy—"still, it repeats" (*The Fine Art of Repetition: Essays in the Philosophy of Music*). Margulis furthermore emphasizes the "double function" that lies at the heart of any repetition: "context reconfigures sound such that no repetition is truly redundant, but there are also senses in which we have to account for the fact that we do experience many reoccurrences as 'repetition'. . . . Repetitions are always repetitive in one sense, and divergent in another" (*On Repeat: How Music Plays the Mind*, 32).

171. On the concept of tight-knit formal organization, see *CF*, 84–86, and *ACF*, 203–5.

172. On an "internal half cadence (or dominant arrival)" within a subordinate theme, see *CF*, 115–17, and *ACF*, 376–80. As explained in Chapter 4, a dominant arrival is a type of half cadence deviation.

EXAMPLE 2.25. Haydn, String Quartet in F, Op. 50, no. 5, i, mm. 45–54.

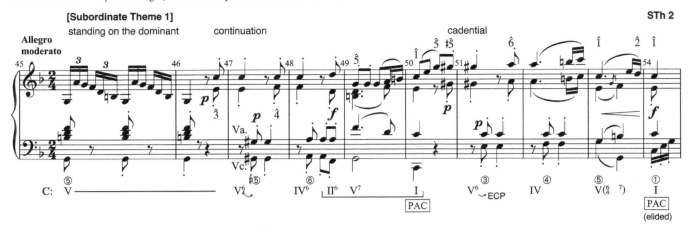

ECP, thus effecting a second PAC at measure 54. Subordinate theme 2 then elides with this second cadence.

We confront again the issue of consecutive PACs. This time, however, I prefer to accord greater status to the second cadence as the one that achieves thematic closure. Here, it is not a question of a symmetrical grouping structure within a tight-knit main theme, as in the prior example, but rather of a looser subordinate theme, one that brings a significant difference in the *rhetorical* weight of the two cadences. (I am anticipating a topic—syntactical vs. rhetorical strength—that I develop more fully at the end of this chapter.) A number of important details support this idea. First, the cadential melody of measures 49–50 sees a rising line from $\hat{5}$ to $\hat{1}$, a melodic configuration that, as discussed in the next chapter (sec. 3.1.2.4), is employed much less frequently in authentic cadences than any number of falling melodic contours. Moreover, the line continues to ascend, now as an arpeggio leading back up to $\hat{5}$, to initiate the next phrase. The arrival on $\hat{1}$ as a cadential goal is therefore rhetorically understated, even if it is syntactically sufficient to articulate a genuine PAC. As well, the expansion of the cadential harmonies in the second phrase generates a more powerful sense of closure than the compact cadence of the first phrase. Finally, the soprano voice in measures 51–54 brings a widely used configuration ($\hat{5}$–$\hat{6}$–$\hat{1}$–$\hat{2}$–$\hat{1}$), with its pronounced fall down to $\hat{1}$, as opposed to the rising melodic line of the first cadence. All of these details work together to create a more powerfully rhetorical expression for the second cadence, even if both have the same syntactical weight as genuine PACs. As a result, I hear the second phrase as an integral part of the subordinate theme, rather than as a postcadential extension.[173]

Consecutive cadences, such as those in the two examples just examined, arise infrequently in works of the classical style with its prizing an aesthetic of clear formal goals. In the earlier baroque and galant styles, however, such difficult cases appear more often, especially with Corelli (see Ex. 6.34–6.36) and Domenico Scarlatti (Ex. 7.52). As well, the early Romantic composers, Chopin in particular, will sometimes bring two cadences in a row, such that we hear the first cadence arriving "too early" in the theme (see Ex. 8.12, 8.29, and 8.44), a circumstance rarely encountered in eighteenth-century styles.

## 2.9. "End" versus "Stop"

Relatively high on Blombach's list of elements traditionally associated with cadence is "rest, pause" (see again Table 2.1). The idea that a cadence is normally associated with a cessation in musical activity has become highly entrenched in everyday notions of cadence, especially in pedagogical writings. Thus Joel Lester, in his textbook on harmony, considers a "break in rhythmic continuity" as a fundamental element of the concept, such that its absence converts a potential cadence into a "caesura," a different kind of phrase ending.[174] Harrison also invokes the idea of cadence as a mode of stopping: "How music starts and stops is one of the first things students of the art learn. Of the two, stopping—or pausing, articulating, and so forth—is the more conventional and therefore easier to name and to categorize. . . .Taken together, the stopping conventions are described as types of *cadence*. . . ."[175] Indeed, music students, in particular, often appeal to a criterion of rest or pause in their analyses of cadence. In my own teaching experience, I regularly encounter the following kinds of statements: "This must be a cadence because everything stops," or, conversely, "this cannot be a cadence because the music keeps on going." Most theorists and historians, however, understand, at least implicitly, that the stopping of motion is not essential to cadence: even a cursory examination of the tonal repertory reveals that although many cadences are followed by a break in activity, many others occur in contexts where rhythmical continuity is sustained beyond the moment of cadential arrival. In fact, some scholars are explicit on

---

173. Toward the beginning of Chapter 5 (see Ex. 5.4b), I consider a similar passage in the main theme group, comparing it to the subordinate theme just discussed.

174. Joel Lester, *Harmony in Tonal Music*, 1: 50, 53.

175. Harrison, "Cadence," 535–36.

this point. Blombach's broad definition of cadence, for example, appeals fundamentally to the notion of cadence as conclusion, noting that "'conclusion' is intended in the sense of 'destination of ideas,' as opposed to merely stopping with no indication of finality or direction."[176] Moreover, we saw in Chapter 1 that not only does one music theorist (Meyer) understand that closure is not essentially a matter of stopping, but the same idea also emerges in writings on closure outside of music.[177] In other words, formal "end" and rhythmic/textural "stop" may very well be associated in many cadential situations, but they are fundamentally different phenomena, both conceptually and experientially. Formal closure may take place in the context of rhythmic/textural continuity, and a decisive break in those parameters may occur at moments that are formally open.[178]

If some scholars do not consider a rhythmic stop to be a necessary condition for cadence, others still betray a lingering sense that they are significantly entwined. Ratner, for example, discusses how "*melodic action* [i.e., continuity through the cadential arrival] can reduce the effect of arrival even when the harmony clearly makes an authentic cadence."[179] In a similar vein, Douglass Green holds that "continuity often tends to obviate the conclusive quality of an otherwise strong cadence."[180] Berger notes that in the standard cadence, "there is at least one beat and at most three beats of general rest in both the melody and the accompaniment," and that an elimination of these rests (by means of elision, *inter alia*) results in cadential weakening.[181] The suggestion by these writers that formal closure is somehow diminished by the absence of a rhythmic break shows how persistent is the notion that ending and stopping are fundamentally linked.

The issue of end versus stop is also often implicated with that of cadential versus postcadential. If a cadence is followed by a closing section or a standing on the dominant, rarely do we see a complete break in rhythm and texture. Only after the postcadential section plays itself out does a genuine stop in the ongoing rhythmical activity take place, often to help set in relief the beginning of the next thematic unit. In such cases, the moments of cadential arrival and rhythmical stop are entirely nonconcurrent. Example 2.23, which we examined earlier, illustrates well the distinction between cadential (mm. 19–20) and postcadential (mm. 21–25) functions as well as their relationship to rhythmic continuity (the steady drum-bass accompaniment throughout m. 20) and rhythmic stopping (the pronounced caesura in m. 25). Indeed,

I have regularly observed students quickly slapping down a cadential label at the very final event of a standing on the dominant (such as m. 25 of Ex. 2.23) or a closing section (for instance, m. 40 of Ex. 2.21) because, as they report, of the obvious cessation of activity associated with these moments.

Example 2.26a, which shows the first-movement main theme of Haydn's "Military" Symphony, also illustrates how locating cadences on the basis of a criterion of rhythmic stopping can obscure the distinction between cadential and postcadential functions. At measure 31, a clear break in rhythm and texture occurs such that we might be led, as is Joel Lester in his introductory harmony text, to recognize there an HC, one that would mark the end of the theme's first part.[182] Such an identification, however, would be problematic due to the lack of harmonic progression from measure 30 into the downbeat of measure 31. As my analysis of shows, dominant harmony appears first at measure 29 and is prolonged for three bars. If an HC is to be identified anywhere, it is better seen to come on the downbeat of measure 29, with the following measures understood as postcadential in function. The issue of where to identify the HC in Haydn's theme is central to an assessment of its overall formal organization. For another motivating factor in preferring measure 31 is the tradition of identifying a cadence in the final bar of an eight-measure thematic unit.[183] And considering that the subsequent unit (mm. 32–39) also lasts eight measures, closing in its final bar with a PAC, we are readily inclined to identify a compound period form with a normative 8 + 8 grouping structure.

The formal and cadential organization of this theme is not, however, so neatly symmetrical. Indeed, attempting to analyze the form of the opening eight measures reveals a number of complexities: the initial two-measure basic idea (mm. 24–25) is followed immediately by fragmentation into one-measure units, in the sense of a continuation, and further fragmentation into half-bar units appears in measure 28. It would be possible, in fact, to reconstruct a more conventional eight-measure sentence (see Ex. 2.26b), such that measure 26 begins a repetition of the basic idea, which then leads into a regular continuation using the remaining material of the theme (though somewhat altered harmonically).[184] The compound antecedent of the actual theme (Ex. 2.26a) could thus be seen as a compressed sentence,

---

176. See again, note 11.

177. See in Chapter 1, sec. 1.2.1, the discussion of Meyer's "statistical" parameters, as well as the quotation by Carroll cited in note 8 in Chapter 1.

178. Both of these situations are discussed and illustrated in *CF*, 51, Ex. 4.7 and 4.3, and *ACF*, 88.

179. Ratner, *Classic Music*, 45. See also his remarks, cited earlier, on the HC of the "Jupiter" trio (Ex. 2.18a, m. 63).

180. Douglass M. Green, *Form in Tonal Music: An Introduction to Analysis*, 15.

181. Berger, "First-Movement Punctuation Form," 246–47.

---

182. Lester, *Harmony*, 1: 52. The motivation for Lester's analysis of a cadence at m. 31 clearly owes much to his definition of a true cadence, which, as discussed above, emphasizes the need for "a break in rhythmic continuity" at the end of a phrase (see note 174).

183. I, too, invoked this notion of "conventional thematic length," where in Beethoven's Seventh Symphony scherzo (Ex. 2.24), I favored finding the cadence in the sixteenth bar of the theme.

184. This reconstructed version also helps clarify what may seem to be an anomaly in my analysis of Haydn's theme (Ex. 2.26a). Although the "basic idea" and the first "fragment" each literally embrace three half-note beats, the initial gesture can be perceived as longer than the second from a formal perspective, because the basic idea contains two metrical downbeats, whereas the fragment contains just one. It is as though the initial basic idea lacks the upbeat figure that is given to the fragment.

EXAMPLE 2.26. (Haydn, Symphony No. 100 in G ("Military"), i, (a) mm 24–39; (b) reconstruction of mm. 24–31.

whose six-measure size is then extended postcadentially to fill out a more normative eight-measure length.[185] The compound consequent repeats the antecedent until measure 36, at which point the one-measure fragments are further extended until the cadential idea of measures 38–39 closes the theme.[186] Both units thus begin with a compression and close with an extension: however, in the former, the extension is postcadential, in the latter, it is precadential (as part of the continuation function). To be sure, it would be easy enough to understand the situation here as merely another example of Haydn's quirkiness, such asymmetries (even within broader symmetries) being standard fare of his compositional practice. But a further examination reveals that these various formal manipulations mark measure 28 for special attention, first by allowing it to occur "too early" in the antecedent of the main theme, and then by eliminating it in the consequent (in that m. 36 continues the one-measure fragmentation rather than bringing the new half-bar fragments). Being thus marked, measure 28 (both alone and in its relation to m. 36) becomes the source of powerful motivic and formal developments that occur throughout the movement.[187]

## 2.10. Cadence as Punctuation

Related to the association of cadence with rhythmic break is the notion that cadence represents a kind of musical "punctuation." As mentioned earlier, the eighteenth-century emphasis on linguistic analogies in describing and explaining strictly musical phenomena led theorists from that time to view various musical phrases or themes as ending with differing degrees of punctuation, usually called "resting points," just like the phrases and sentences of written language.[188] The persistence of this idea is revealed in Blombach's tabulations, with "language, punctuation," ranked only slightly lower than "rest, pause" (Table 2.1). Recent manifestations occur in Darcy and Hepokoski's characterization of structural caesuras

---

In the reconstructed version, the repeated basic idea includes the upbeat figure but also contains a second metrical downbeat.

185. For a discussion of similar nonconventional main themes in sonata expositions, see *CF*, 199, Ex. 13.1–13.3, and *ACF*, 289–91, Ex. 10.1–10.3.

186. For an alternative, more regularizing, form-functional interpretation of the compound consequent, see Jason Yust, *Organized Time: Rhythm, Tonality, and Form*, 136.

---

187. This is not the place for a detailed examination, but see mm. 79 and 86, as well as mm. 95 and 103.

188. Johann Phillip Kirnberger, *The Art of Strict Musical Composition*, 403–6; Koch, *Introductory Essay on Composition*, 1–3.

EXAMPLE 2.27. *Ruhepunkt des Geistes* (resting point of the spirit) (from Koch, Introductory Essay on Composition, Ex. 18, 97).

as "punctuation breaks,"[189] and even more pervasively in Berger's theory of "punctuation form."[190]

This recent emphasis on punctuation by many scholars of eighteenth-century music is surely inspired by a renewed interest in Koch's theories of melody and phrase structure,[191] and especially by his notion of *Ruhepunkt des Geistes* (resting point of the spirit).[192] This is Koch's expression for the sense of closure associated with phrases that are not concluded with an actual *Cadenz* (that is, a melodic figure supported by a harmonic progression from a root-position dominant to a root-position tonic).[193] Indeed, it is the idea of a "resting point," with its explicit sense of "stopping of musical motion" that seems to have especially influenced these modern theorists. Yet we must not forget the second part of the expression, "*des Geistes*."[194] For as Koch makes abundantly clear, this resting point of the spirit need not be associated with an explicit break in the rhythm or even necessarily a longer note value, as we see (Ex. 2.27a) in the case of the resting point that closes the "incise," a short formal unit, often comparable to a two-measure basic idea. Here, Koch explicitly notes that the resting point (indicated by the triangle) is "not revealed through anything external." He is further explicit on this point when discussing resting points that are decorated with an appoggiatura:

> In duple meters it often happens that the resting point is not marked by a rest. Indeed, that occurs every time the proper caesura note is delayed through an appoggiatura until the weak part of the measure and the following phrase is begun on the upbeat, as in [Ex. 2.27b, indicated by the square]. From this

it is apparent that in all these instances, which occur very frequently, there are no external signs which reveal the presence of a resting point; this must be determined by one's feeling.[195]

In other words, Koch's *Ruhepunkt des Geistes* is better understood as a "virtual resting point" or "conceptual resting point," whether or not literal "external" signs of resting are present in the music. To be sure, Koch explicitly speaks of "punctuation forms" later in his treatise, and in this manner gives rise to the analogy that has so captured modern scholars.

The idea of associating cadence with punctuation, however, is debatable on a number of grounds. In written language, punctuation is used as an aid to reading and as a kind of analysis of the grammatical structure of the individual sentence. As a guide to reading aloud (or in the imagination), punctuation can help render the syntax more obvious by interpreting the punctuation signs as indications for rests or pauses of various lengths. And in cases of grammatical ambiguity, punctuation marks can help indicate the intended syntax of the author. But punctuation is not a necessary requirement of written language, as witnessed by ancient texts, which contained no such signs. And, of course, punctuation per se does not exist in spoken language, though a sentence may be often uttered in a way that suggests a particular punctuation in written form.[196] In short, punctuation may be a visual sign of syntax but not a real source of syntax. A phrase or sentence in natural language achieves a degree of syntactical closure not by ending with any given punctuation mark, but by the meanings, inflections, and ordering of words.[197] Cadence, too, is an element of syntax, more specifically, an element that generates formal closure at specific levels of musical organization. Characterizing cadence as a type of musical punctuation is thus clearly problematic. Moreover, the relationship of cadence to punctuation has the potential of confusing

---

189. Darcy and Hepokoski, "Medial Caesura," 115.

190. Berger, "First-Movement Punctuation Form," 239–59.

191. For a comprehensive listing of "neo-Kochian" approaches to form and cadence, see L. Poundie Burstein, *Journeys through Galant Expositions*, 10–11, notes 11–13.

192. Koch, *Introductory Essay on Composition*, 1.

193. As mentioned in note 54, Koch's concept of "cadence" has major restrictions as to harmonic content, much like that presented in this study. Indeed, his notions are even more restrictive than mine, in that he does not recognize the standard "half cadence" as a cadential articulation ending a phrase or a theme. He uses the term *Halbcadenz* primarily in reference to the final HC of a movement that leads into a subsequent movement (*Introductory Essay on Composition*, 36, 49).

194. When first introducing *Ruhepunkt des Geistes*, Nancy Baker (the translator of Koch's text) uses the full expression "resting point of the spirit"; it is telling, however, that she then omits "of the spirit" in the rest of her translation, so that Koch's more complete *Ruhepunkt des Geistes* is rendered exclusively as "resting point." As a result, it is easy for the reader to believe that Koch is referring to a literal moment of "rest."

195. Koch, *Introductory Essay on Composition*, 31.

196. The absurd result of literally speaking punctuation marks is masterfully realized in a famous comedy sketch by Victor Borge, who invents actual sounds for the various marks and interpolates them into spoken texts; "Phonetic Punctuation," *Caught in the Act*, Columbia Records CL 646.

197. In this respect, it is interesting to observe that Koch, very early in his treatise, attempts to establish an analogy between musical phrase structure and linguistic syntax (not punctuation), whereby he associates an opening idea with a "subject" and a closing idea with a "predicate" (4–6). He eventually abandons the analogy, unfortunately, because he fears that his readers will not have "either grammatical knowledge or familiarity with that part of logic which explains the different types of phrases and their closures" (6, note 8).

EXAMPLE 2.28. Beethoven, Piano Sonata in E-flat, Op. 7, ii, mm. 1–8.

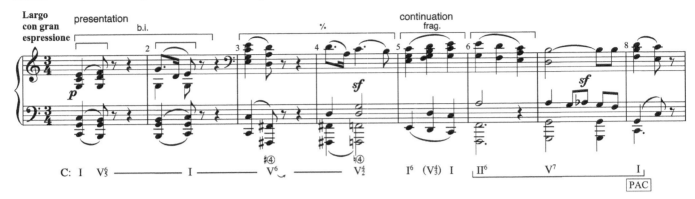

cause with effect: creating a musical pause does not in itself give rise to cadence, but a given cadence may manifest itself in such a way that it creates a punctuating effect. In other cases, a genuine cadence may result in no sense of punctuation, but that fact, in itself, does not diminish the syntactical function of the cadence.

To illustrate some consequences of the cadence-punctuation relationship, let us consider Example 2.28. In discussing a "rearrangement of the normal functions" of rhetorical discourse (opening, continuation, and completion), Ratner offers the following account:

> Each pause in mm. 1–3 . . . is a clear and emphatic articulation. Ordinarily, a half cadence would appear at m. 4 but the preceding pauses would reduce its punctuating effect. Hence, while m. 4 is actually a half cadence, the dissonance in the melody, the weak position of the bass, and the sustained tones in all voices disguise the effect of punctuation. Measure 4, presumably the end of phrase I, introduces the legato style of the latter half of the period, building to a broad authentic cadence in m. 8. The fragmentary beginning, three measures long, built from terse cadential gestures, is answered by a broadly scaled line—five measures long. Punctuation is *overstated* in the beginning and *understated* at the half cadence—a rearrangement of normal cadential functions.[198]

These remarks raise a number of questions. Does the punctuating effect of the pauses in measures 1–3 have form-functional consequences? Are the gestures in those measures truly cadential? Are the criteria for HC satisfied in measure 4? On this last question, the possibility for a real half cadential progression there is suggested by the pre-dominant V⁶/V, but the subsequent addition of a seventh and inversion of the harmony subverts a necessary condition for a true HC, namely, that a cadential dominant must appear exclusively in root position. But even if a root-position dominant triad had appeared on the second beat of measure 4, there would be contextual reasons for doubting a genuine HC at this point. Inasmuch as measures 1–2 contain the basic idea of the theme, measures 3–4 repeat that idea (though with an inverted contour at its beginning). The resulting phrase is a presentation, a formal function that creates an intensified sense of initiation. As discussed earlier, presentation phrases, in principle, do not engender cadential closure. Thus I would argue that for both harmonic and contextual reasons, measure 4 brings no cadential articulation. Moreover, it is questionable whether the opening three measures feature "cadential gestures," since their underlying harmonic support (especially given the inverted dominant) has no cadential implication. To be sure, the pauses create a punctuating effect, but the stopping of musical motion in these measures is not associated with formal ending: indeed, the sense of hesitancy projected by the pauses intensifies a feeling of opening, which, along with the repeated basic idea of the presentation, creates a strong sense for functional continuation and eventual closure (mm. 5–8).[199] We see here how a commitment to notions of musical punctuation as an essential component of cadence can lead to problematic conclusions about a presumed reordering of formal functions.[200]

## 2.11. Cadential Strength— Syntactical versus Rhetorical

Pervasive in the theoretical literature is the idea that cadences can project varying degrees of strength (or weight). We have

---

198. Ratner, *Classic Music*, 39.

199. The idea that rhythmic discontinuity is associated with formal initiation may seem counterintuitive, for we might, at first, assume such gestures of hesitancy to be more appropriately introductory in nature. Yet, the main themes of many classical movements feature frequent starts and stops, and it is often the role of the transition section (a middleground medial function) to get the movement truly under way (see *CF*, 197, and *ACF*, 300–301).

200. Though I am analyzing this theme as a standard sentence, it would not be incorrect to view the material in mm. 3 and 4 as projecting a "contrasting idea" due to the change in melodic contour (see *ACF*, 111–12). As a result, the theme would be considered one of the "hybrid" types (compound basic idea + continuation). Additionally, the irregular melodic organization of the bass line supporting this idea (especially the unusual motion from ♯④ to ♮④) engenders significant compositional implications for the rest of the movement, as I discuss in "Schoenberg's 'Second Melody,'" 173–77.

already encountered suggestions of this kind when Ratner, Green, and Berger see rhythmic continuity as an agent of cadential weakening,[201] or when Darcy and Hepokoski, Ratner, Agawu, and Berger understand a postcadential closing section as strengthening a prior cadential arrival.[202] We have also seen that cadences are sometimes considered more or less weighty if the harmonies preceding the final tonic are lengthened or contracted.[203] Other criteria invoked by theorists include the metrical placement of the final tonic (the infamous "masculine" vs. "feminine" cadence),[204] differing degrees of textural completeness,[205] rhythmic "noncongruence" (between melody and bass),[206] dynamic intensity,[207] and the presence or absence of a dissonant seventh in the penultimate dominant.[208] At times, what is described as cadential weakening is better understood as noncadential, such as when Berger sees a weakening occurring if the third of the final tonic is placed in the bass, though he acknowledges that "situations of this kind are invariably on the borderline between the cadence and the noncadence."[209]

How are we to evaluate the wide range of claims made for varying modes of cadential strength and weakness? To sort through this issue, it is helpful to distinguish between cadential *syntax* and *rhetoric* (along the lines suggested by Agawu, though somewhat differently formulated).[210] In its syntactical aspect, a given cadence represents a particular cadential *type* on the basis of its harmonic–melodic content exclusively. In its rhetorical aspect, that cadence has a unique compositional realization entailing the entire range of musical parameters, including rhythm, meter, texture, intensity, and instrumentation. Thus a particular HC may present itself as a metrically accented orchestral tutti within a *forte* dynamic, whereas another HC may take the form of a metrically weak, thinly textured event within a *piano* dynamic. From a syntactical point of view, both cadences are identical;[211] they are each a representative of the type "half cadence." From a rhetorical perspective, the two cadences have entirely different realizations and thus project opposing expressive effects.

When characterizing cadential strength and weakness, it is important that we distinguish between the syntactical and rhetorical aspects. For in the classical style, at least, differences in syntactical strength manifestly relate to the expression of formal functionality, whereas it is questionable whether rhetorical differences alone have such a form-defining potential.[212] Syntactically, there are only three, distinct degrees of cadential strength and weakness, and these are associated with the three fundamental cadence types of the classical style—HC, IAC, and PAC (ordered from weaker to stronger).[213] As agents of formal definition, any cadence representative of a given type is equally strong or weak in relation to any cadence of another type. Thus any particular manifestation of a PAC is syntactically stronger than any realization of an HC (within some given formal context, such as the antecedent and consequent phrases of the period form). Rhetorically, on the contrary, the multitudinous degrees of cadential strength are indefinite, even to the point of varying from one performance to another. Rhetorical differentiation of cadential strength does not seem to be directly implicated in the definition of classical formal functions (at least, according to the theory developed in my writings). Rhetorical strength may, of course, be congruent with syntactical strength. Typically enough, the HC closing the antecedent phrase of a period is rhetorically weaker than the authentic cadence closing the consequent. But noncongruence of syntax and rhetoric is regularly found as well. The PAC closing the main theme of a sonata exposition is often rhetorically weak compared to the HC closing the subsequent transition, yet, from a form-functional perspective, the former cadence is syntactically stronger than the latter. Similarly, a subordinate-theme group will typically consist of multiple themes, each ending with a PAC.[214] Syntactically, all of these cadences are of equal strength—they fully satisfy the requirements for thematic closure—yet they often have decidedly different rhetorical expressions.

In light of the distinctions just drawn, we can now see that many, if not most, of the criteria for cadential strength regularly cited in the theoretical literature relate more to the rhetorical aspect than to the syntactical one. For that reason, we should strive in analytical practice not to confuse those factors

---

201. See notes 179, 180, and 181.

202. See notes 147, 148, 149, and 152. Meyer, on the contrary, sees the immediate repetition of a half cadence (in the sense of an echo) as weakening the point of relative stability and arrival (*Explaining Music*, 257).

203. See note 152; see also Green, *Form*, 9; Lerdahl and Jackendoff, *Generative Theory*, 192.

204. Cone, *Musical Form*, 43–45; Green, *Form*, 9; Berger, "First-Movement Punctuation Form," 244.

205. Webster, *Haydn's Farewell Symphony*, 37.

206. Webster, *Haydn's Farewell Symphony*, 37. A criterion of rhythmic noncongruence is also cited by Green, *Form*, 9.

207. Webster, *Haydn's Farewell Symphony*, 147.

208. Green, *Form*, 8.

209. Berger, "First-Movement Punctuation Form," 246–47.

210. See note 149. Whereas Agawu relates the rhetorical components of cadence primarily to postcadential areas, I will focus on genuinely cadential functions.

211. McCreless asserts the same point: "... all perfect authentic cadences in music are syntactically the same" ("Hermeneutic Sentence," 57–58).

212. This is not to say that rhetorical matters play no role whatsoever in formal readings. Recall that my discussion of Ex. 2.25 engaged rhetorical differentiation when deciding to include the phrase closed by the second PAC (m. 54) as a constituent part of the subordinate theme rather than as a postcadential unit.

213. See *CF*, 53, and *ACF*, 80. The three basic cadences will be discussed in greater detail in the next chapter. As well, we will see that an IAC may sometimes emerge as syntactically weaker than an HC when a melodic perspective is emphasized (see the discussion of Ex. 3.74).

214. *CF*, 121, and *ACF*, 382.

responsible for one or the other aspect. If we identify varying degrees of cadential strength and weakness that are rhetorical in nature, then we should be careful not to allow these distinctions to distort our formal readings, which should be based essentially on syntactical strength. Beyond these considerations, we should take care not to assume that a musical event that is rendered rhetorically strong be taken as cadential primarily on that account.

To illustrate these points, let us consider a passage that arises in the opening movement of a Beethoven piano trio (Ex. 2.29a). At measure 86, the exposition's transition arrives, conventionally enough, at an HC in the new key of D major. There follows an extensive standing on the dominant. Example 2.29b starts with the final two measures of the prolonged dominant seventh, which resolves to a root-position tonic at measure 99. Immediately thereafter, the first of two subordinate themes begins with eighth-note pickups to measure 100. Considering the rhetorical strength accorded the harmonic resolution to tonic along with its location at the final moment of the transition, it might be tempting to recognize the presence of an authentic cadence. Indeed, such a view is offered by Darcy and Hepokoski, who want to identify there a "deformation" of a standard medial caesura:

> A clear approach is made to what we expect to be a normative triple hammer-blow V:HC MC [read: dominant-key half cadence, medial caesura] at mm. 97–98. At this juncture the violin and cello drop out for the remainder of the measure, while the right hand of the piano part traces out a melodic fill from $g^2$ down to $d^1$. More important, the usual caesura-fill energy-loss is absent here. On the contrary, the fill, continuing in aggressive triplet-sixteenth-notes, insists on retaining the full measure of gained energy and plunges precipitously to the new D-major tonic, now reinforced by the strings (m. 99), before S itself emerges, *piano*, at the upbeat to m. 100. The composer has wrenched a normal MC, V:HC (first-level default), into a strong V:PAC (third-level default) by brute force.[215]

As indicated by the set of images that they use in describing this passage—"aggressive triplet sixteenth-notes," "gained energy," "plunge," "wrenched," and "brute force"—Darcy and Hepokoski are clearly responding to the many rhetorical devices that effect a powerful resolution of dominant to tonic at measure 99. And they are surely correct in pointing out that the music expresses the sense of authentic cadence at this point. But we might further reflect on the possibility that this is more a case of cadential *content* than actual cadential *function*. For in order to hear a syntactical PAC at measure 99, the preceding dominant must be understood as the *penultimate* harmony of an authentic cadential progression. But earlier, at measure 87, the dominant unambiguously appears as the *ultimate* harmony of a half cadential progression, and throughout the subsequent standing on the dominant, there is no reason to believe that the formal context is anything but postcadential. So when the dominant resolves to tonic at measure 99, it would require a massive retrospective reinterpretation to hear the entire dominant prolongation as cadential in function inasmuch as we would have to understand that the ultimate dominant "becomes" a penultimate one.[216] To be sure, the resolution to this tonic is rhetorically powerful, but the "brute force" applied to this moment does not thereby cancel out the syntactical expression of an earlier HC and replace that with an authentic cadence. Undoubtedly something is unusual about the downbeat of measure 99. Normally, a standing on the dominant progresses to a tonic that initiates a new formal process. Here, instead, the first complete measure of the next unit, the subordinate theme, occurs at the upbeat to measure 100, as accurately noted by Darcy and Hepokoski. Consequently, the tonic of the downbeat of measure 99 groups backwards to the prior transition as its "final" event. Yet just because this tonic is the last member of the transition does not mean that it represents cadential closure; rather, for the reasons just discussed, this tonic is best understood as belonging to the postcadential function that has been in force since the half cadence at measure 87.[217]

---

215. Darcy and Hepokoski, "Medial Caesura," 129.

216. In a further discussion of this passage, Hepokoski and Darcy specifically endorse such a retrospective reinterpretation (*Sonata Theory*, 28, note 6). In responding to my criticism of their analysis, they note that my view "fails to consider the possibility that a dominant-lock might be abandoned en route—in other words, that it might be staged as 'changing its mind'—in order to proceed to a PAC. Such a procedure would 'unfreeze' the locked dominant . . . and treat it as more of a 'normal' $V_A$ [an 'active dominant,' i.e., one that is not tonicized and continues to imply its resolution to a tonic] that can proceed onward toward resolution." In a later chapter of the present study, I will consider the possibility of a penultimate dominant "becoming" an ultimate dominant through a process of cadential *dissipation* (see Chapter 8, sec. 8.11). Though I do not hear the reversed situation here, namely an ultimate dominant becoming penultimate, as suggested by Hepokoski and Darcy, I cannot rule it out as a theoretical possibility. Indeed, I will make a similar argument in connection with a passage by Dvorak (see in Chapter 9, Ex. 9.54b, mm. 88–91). For additional observations on the differences between Hepokoski and Darcy's analyses of this trio and my analysis (initially offered in Caplin, "The Classical Cadence," and largely reproduced here), see Joel Galand, review of *Elements of Sonata Theory: Norms, Types, and Deformations in the Late-Eighteenth-Century Sonata* by James Hepokoski and Warren Darcy, 390–92.

217. Though unusual, the resolution of a standing on the dominant (in root position) to tonic harmony prior to the onset of a subsequent formal function is by no means unprecedented: the same situation arises in the first movement of Mozart's Symphony No. 35 in D ("Haffner"), K. 385, i, mm. 48–58. A similar case can be found in Mozart's Symphony No. 39 in E-flat, K. 543, i, mm. 83–98, though here, the dominant undergoes inversion prior to the tonic resolution, so we cannot even speak of an authentic cadence in any case.

EXAMPLE 2.29. Beethoven, Piano Trio in G, Op. 1, no. 2, i, (a) mm. 85–89; (b) mm. 97–101; (c) mm. 136–40.

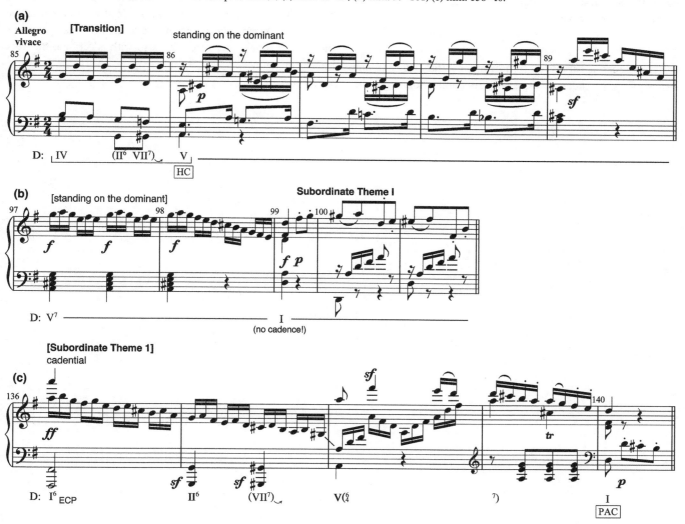

Inasmuch as the precipitous plunge of aggressive sixteenth-note triplets from mm. 98 to 99 suggests a cadence, but actually fails to create one, it is interesting to observe what happens the next time Beethoven brings back a similar plunge. Later in the first subordinate theme, a flowing sixteenth-note piano line gives way to a sixteenth-note triplet descent, which clearly references the earlier descent at measure 98, though now supported by a prominent I⁶ (mm. 132–35, not shown). Such a harmonic arrival conventionally signals the onset of the cadential function that we expect to end the subordinate theme. But, as typically occurs in such cases, the function fails to realize itself fully when the subsequent cadential six-four yields to V$^4_2$, forcing a resolution to another I⁶. At this point (Ex. 2.29c, m. 136), the piano repeats the precipitous plunge to initiate a second cadential function, one that fully satisfies all requirements for cadential closure four measures later. It is as though Beethoven, having projected rhetorically the "idea" of authentic cadence earlier at measure 99, now uses a similar (though even more intensified) gesture to actualize a syntactical PAC later at measure 140. Here, both rhetorical and syntactical forces align themselves at a moment of unquestionable cadential closure.

Finally, it should be noted that the PAC at measure 140 is not the final one of the exposition. Following that cadence, a second subordinate theme begins, which closes quickly with a rhetorically weak cadence at measure 147. The theme is immediately repeated and then considerably extended, leading eventually to another cadence (with expanded pre-dominant harmony) at measure 167. This final cadence of the exposition is rhetorically stronger than the preceding one at measure 147, yet it remains weaker than the one at measure 140 ending the first subordinate theme. Whereas all three PACs of the subordinate-theme group are rhetorically differentiated as to strength of expression, they are equally weighted syntactically: each provides the necessary and sufficient means of bringing their individual subordinate themes to a formal close.

\* \* \* \* \*

This concludes a survey of some fundamental issues in the theory of tonal cadence, especially in connection with the classical style. Throughout the rest of this study, we will touch base with most every one of the points dealt with here, usually via further exemplification by means of musical passages from the various tonal repertories, but also with additional theoretical clarifications.

# 3

# Basic Cadence Types: Morphology and Function

THE PREVIOUS CHAPTER LAID OUT THE FUNDAmental notions of the classical cadence that underlie the theoretical approach of this study. The chapter assumed that readers would already have a general knowledge of the three basic cadence types—PAC, IAC, and HC—that musicians learn early on in their music-theoretical education. The present chapter now examines these cadence types in detail, with an emphasis on their *morphology* (especially their harmonic and melodic content) and how they *function* within classical form. In addition, the chapter assesses the roles that meter and texture play in cadential morphology. Finally, I consider two other cadence types traditionally proposed by theorists—the "contrapuntal cadence" and the "plagal cadence"—and explain why I do not include them as legitimate types within my theory.[1]

The basic cadence types are identified as such because they alone have the capacity to create closure for a complete thematic unit, as confirmed by a remarkable consistency of usage in the instrumental works of Haydn, Mozart, and Beethoven. With very few exceptions (ones that seem more to prove the rule than to permit an expansion of the basic types themselves), no other cadential formations identified by theorists over the ages are used by the classical composers to mark the conclusion of a theme or themelike unit.[2] These other modes of closure are best understood as either deviations of the basic types (e.g., deceptive cadence,

---

1. The corpus of works used in researching this chapter (as well as the following two chapters of Part I) consists primarily of the large collection of classical passages found on the *ACF* website (www.music.mcgill.ca/acf/), which includes all of the examples in the printed text as well as supplementary ones (Sup.) found only on the website. To facilitate accessing the audio of the examples chosen for the present study, their captions identify the example number on the website; thus the first two examples of this chapter include the labels (*ACF* 2.22b) and (*ACF* Sup. 4.17), respectively. In addition, the corpus contains a wide range of other instrumental works by Haydn, Mozart, and Beethoven, ones regularly used in my teaching; examples from this group do not include an *ACF* label.

2. One formation, an ending on dominant harmony that I have termed *dominant arrival*, frequently enough closes transitions and developmental cores such that it plausibly could be considered a basic type due to its usage alone. But as will be developed fully in the following chapter, the

evaded cadence), which normally function to delay the arrival of the actual cadence, or as some kind of noncadential articulation, which only occurs *within* a theme to mark some moment of partial conclusion, not at the theme's actual end.³

To speak of *three* basic cadence types is by no means obvious, since the qualifiers "perfect" and "imperfect" suggest that there are actually only *two* fundamental categories—authentic and half. Moreover, a case can be made that the IAC is a variant that brings only provisional melodic closure on $\hat{3}$, which eventually leads to a more conclusive PAC.⁴ Nonetheless, I have retained the IAC as a separate category because it can be used, albeit infrequently, to end a theme and because absolute closure of all parameters need not be a requirement of a genuine cadence type, insofar as the HC is also incomplete, both melodically and harmonically.

## 3.1. Perfect Authentic Cadence

The perfect authentic cadence achieves the strongest degree of thematic closure of all possible cadential formations. Its moment of arrival brings to a close the essential harmonic processes of the theme by directly engaging the principal harmonic functions of the key in the form of a cadential progression. Melodically, the two fundamental voices of the cadence's contrapuntal construct achieve their full completion when the soprano reaches $\hat{1}$, normally by stepwise motion, and the bass regains ① via a direct leap from ⑤. Insofar as closure, most generally construed, obtains when the music projects no further expectations for something to continue,⁵ the PAC generally avoids promoting further development by introducing new motivic ideas or referencing earlier ones. As a result, the cadence tends to engage processes of motivic liquidation, as originally observed by Schoenberg.⁶

The following discussion on the morphology of the PAC is organized around the two principal parameters—harmony and melody—that go into making the material content of the complete cadential configuration. The most conventional parameter is *harmony*, the topic of the following section. In a subsequent section, I give detailed attention to the *melodic* component of the cadence. To facilitate reading throughout the entire unit on this cadence type, I will often refer to the PAC more simply as the "cadence" or the "classical cadence."

### 3.1.1. Morphology—Harmonic Content

Because of the severe limitations arising from the need to create complete harmonic and melodic closure, and thus to avoid arousing expectations for further continuation, the PAC tends to be a conventionalized construct, one that at times is highly formulaic in character. Indeed, my own approach to the syntax of cadence significantly limits the range of its component harmonies.⁷ Moreover, the formulaic nature of such harmonies allows cadence (of any type) to be defined as a *schema* along the lines initiated by Robert Gjerdingen and developed more fully by David Sears.⁸

#### *3.1.1.1. Stages of the Cadence Schema*

In connection with most schemata, Gjerdingen identifies a set of successively ordered entities, each consisting of specific pitches residing in the soprano and bass voices. He speaks of these entities as "events," but I will call them *stages*.⁹ The pitches of each stage are identified as scale degrees within the prevailing key, though Gjerdingen generally avoids associating these pitches with a broader harmonic context. Seeing as the melodic component of cadential stages is not nearly as formulaic as the harmonic one, it will prove practical to define *four stages* of the PAC in relation to the harmonies of the authentic cadential progression (as defined in the previous chapter, sec. 2.3.1.3 and Ex. 2.3a–c). Thus stage 1 embraces the musical content supported by the *initial tonic* of the progression; stage 2, by the *pre-dominant*; stage 3, by the root-position *dominant*; and stage 4, by the *final tonic*, also in root position.

In many situations, the first three stages may be divided into substages, indicated by letters. Working backwards from stage 4 (which is never subdivided), stage *3a* contains a cadential six-four, with *3b* bringing the dominant proper. The second stage can be divided into stage *2a*, whose pre-dominant harmony includes the subdominant scale degree ($\hat{4}$ or ④), or stage *2b*, which contains the leading tone of the dominant, that is, the chromatically raised fourth degree (#$\hat{4}$ or #④).¹⁰ Even stage 1 may be subdivided such that substage *1a* holds the tonic harmony proper, while *1b* brings

---

dominant arrival is better understood as a deviation of the HC than as a separate type unto itself.

3. The HC and IAC can also arise interior to a theme. Rarely does a PAC occur prior to the end of a theme; such cases include an "early" PAC in minuet form (see sec. 3.1.3.2, "A Section [Minuet Form]") and a PAC that becomes a "reinterpreted half cadence" (see sec. 3.3.5.1).

4. The exceptional case of an IAC seeming to close on $\hat{5}$ will be considered below (sec. 3.2.1.5).

5. See Chapter 1, the discussions of Smith and Meyer.

6. See Chapter 2, note 115.

7. For a richly formalized account of cadential harmonies, see Martin Rohrmeier and Markus Neuwirth, "Towards a Syntax of the Classical Cadence."

8. Robert O. Gjerdingen, *Galant Style*, chap. 11; David R. W. Sears, "The Perception of Cadential Closure"; David R. W. Sears, William E. Caplin, and Stephen McAdams, "Perceiving the Classical Cadence."

9. Gjerdingen limits the term *stage* to "the longer utterance into which the event is embedded" (*Galant Style*, 21–22). On the contrary, I will refer to cadential "stages" exclusively, thus saving the word "event" as an informal reference to a given musical idea in general, one that does not necessarily constitute a schematic stage (e.g., "Following *stage* 4 of the schema, the next *event* in the upper strings initiates a new thematic unit").

10. This ordering of the pre-dominant substages reflects conventional usage: in almost all cases, a pre-dominant containing the subdominant degree ($\hat{4}$, ④) precedes one containing the leading tone of the dominant (#$\hat{4}$, #④).

either a tonic substitute (e.g., VI) or a secondary dominant of the harmony in stage 2 (e.g., $V_5^6/IV$ or $VII_5^6/II$).

### 3.1.1.2. Stage 1—Initial Tonic

Let us now examine in more detail the harmonies of the classical cadence, starting with stage 1. The initial tonic is normally set in first inversion, $I^6$ over ③, thus allowing the bass to begin its stepwise melodic ascent through ④ to the cadential dominant ⑤ (as discussed in Chapter 2, sec. 2.4). Example 3.1 shows this highly conventionalized pattern, associated here with a simple melodic descent from $\hat{5}$ to $\hat{1}$ in the upper voice. Less often, stage 1 sees the initial tonic set in root position (Ex. 3.2). Here, this position is necessitated by the melody's ascent from $\hat{3}$ to $\hat{4}$ in measure 15, since parallel octaves would otherwise arise with the more conventional $I^6$. This example also shows that the harmony of stage 1, especially when it stands in root position, may well function as a *linking harmony*, that is, a harmony that represents both the end of one progression (here, a tonic prolongation) and the beginning of a different progression type (here, cadential).[11]

EXAMPLE 3.1. Haydn, Piano Trio in D, H. 16, iii, mm. 7–8 (*ACF*, Ex. 2.22b).

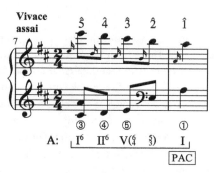

EXAMPLE 3.2. Beethoven, Piano Sonata in C, Op. 2, no. 3, iii, mm. 14–16 (R = 2N) (*ACF* Sup. 4.17).

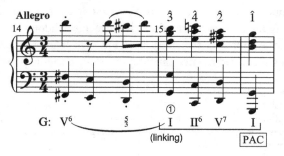

EXAMPLE 3.3. Mozart, Piano Concerto in A, K. 488, i, mm. 15–16 (*ACF* 6.6).

Now and then, the initial tonic is embellished through the use of the submediant harmony (VI), which either follows the initial tonic, as stage 1b (Ex. 3.3),[12] or fully substitutes for the tonic (see ahead, Ex. 3.16l, m. 7).[13]

The initial tonic of stage 1 can be chromatically embellished, as stage 1b, such that it functions as a secondary dominant that tonicizes either a subsequent subdominant or supertonic in stage 2. This secondary dominant is usually built over ③, either in the form of a dominant seventh ($V_5^6/IV$), a diminished triad ($VII^6/II$), or a diminished seventh ($VII^7/IV$), though now and then the harmony will appear over ① ($V^7/IV$) or even ♭⑦ ($V_2^4/IV$). Example 3.4 shows some cadences using these chromatic embellishments of stage 1. A somewhat rare case, though one commonly employed in the nineteenth century, sees $I^6$ substituted by the dominant of the submediant, which then resolves "deceptively" to the subdominant (i.e., $V^7/VI–IV$).[14]

On occasion, the initial tonic of the cadential progression is preceded by a dominant seventh that leads so strongly into the tonic that it seems to be an actual part of the cadential progression. Most typically that dominant stands in third inversion ($V_2^4$), thus demanding a resolution to $I^6$. Indeed, *expanded cadential progressions* (ECPs) often display a prominent "rocking" back and forth between the $V_2^4$ and $I^6$.[15] Example 3.5 shows a case where it seems reasonable to include this dominant as a genuine constituent of the cadential progression: following a two-measure basic idea (opening a consequent phrase), the concluding cadential idea clearly begins with the progression $V_2^4$–$I^6$.[16]

---

12. Gjerdingen speaks of the progression I–VI–IV–V–I as a "long cadence" (*Galant Style*, 169–70), though as we see in Ex. 3.3, it can actually be quite short. For a case of an embellishing VI that follows an initial $I^6$, see Mozart, Piano Sonata in F, K. 332, i, m. 10.

13. The annotation "1:8" below the PAC in Ex. 3.16l refers to a later discussion of cadence and meter.

14. On the nineteenth-century usage of this chromatic variant, see, in Chapter 8, the discussion of Ex. 8.4d, as well as the accompanying note 16. For a classical example, see Mozart, Piano Sonata in D, K. 576, i, m. 49.

15. See Chapter 5, sec. 5.1.1.1, "Rocking on the Tonic."

16. Ex. 3.23, ahead, is another such case where $V_2^4$ is appropriately grouped with the cadential progression. Whether or not to situate such a dominant seventh within the scheme of cadential stages is unclear and probably unnecessary for all practical purposes. Labeling it as a substage

---

11. For the use of a curved line to show harmonic prolongation, see again in Chapter 2, note 79. The harmonic linkage in Ex. 3.2 is made explicit by the intersection of the curved line and the cadential bracket. Finally, recall that an incomplete prolongational progression can sometimes begin with a subordinate harmony, as in this example ($V^6$–I). The annotation of the scale degrees in the upper voice of Ex. 3.1 and Ex. 3.2 (along with many subsequent ones) refers to a later discussion of the cadence's melodic content.

EXAMPLE 3.4. (a) Beethoven, Piano Sonata in D, Op. 28, ii, mm. 20–22 (*ACF* 7.10); (b) Mozart, Piano Sonata in D, K. 576, i, mm. 7–8; (c) Beethoven, Piano Sonata in B-flat, Op. 22, iv, mm. 14–16 (*ACF* 6.15).

EXAMPLE 3.5. Beethoven, String Quartet in G, Op. 18, no. 2, i, mm. 191–94 (*ACF* 3.24).

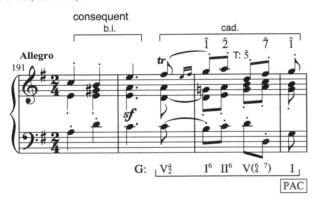

### 3.1.1.3. Stage 2—Pre-dominant

The second stage of the cadential schema comprises a wide variety of pre-dominant harmonies. In general, it is useful to distinguish between two main classes of pre-dominants: class one includes the fourth scale degree as a harmonic constituent, such as II⁶ and IV (most often with ④ in the bass voice); class two includes the raised-fourth degree as leading tone of the dominant, such as VII⁷/V (with #④ in the bass) and the various augmented sixths (with ♭⑥ in the bass). These two classes have a determinate temporal relation to each other, in that the first almost always appears before the second. So we can again invoke the notion of substages and associate class one with stage 2a and class two with stage 2b.[17] We can additionally divide the harmonies of stage 2 into those whose bass *ascends* to the dominant via the motion ④–(#④)–⑤ or those whose bass *descends* via ⑥–(♭⑥)–⑤. The former occurs more often than the latter, except in the minor mode, where the bass tends to emphasize the motion ♭⑥–⑤, often supporting an augmented sixth for stage 2b.[18]

The most frequently occurring harmony of stage 2 is the supertonic in first inversion. Though harmony texts traditionally identify the pre-dominant of a cadence as the subdominant, IV is used less often in the classical period than II⁶.[19] Many other pre-dominant harmonies can be formed by including various

---

of stage 1 is problematic because no letter precedes "a," and it does not seem sensible to consider the initial tonic proper as belonging to a substage 1b. A better option would see the dominant as a stage in its own right, namely stage "0," in the sense of it being a "before-the-beginning" stage. Again, this degree of theoretical precision rarely has any practical utility in cadential analyses.

17. A fascinating counterexample arises at the end of the slow movement of Beethoven's Piano Sonata in E-flat, Op. 7, where a stage-2b V⁶/V precedes a stage-2a II⁶; see Caplin, "Schoenberg's 'Second Melody,'" 176 and Ex. 6.16, mm. 88–89.

18. For authentic cadences, I have not found it necessary to provide a label for these two types of bass-line motion; however, the distinction will become more significant when differentiating half cadences as "converging" or "expanding" (see secs. 3.3.3.2 and 3.3.3.3).

19. IV gains greater frequency in the nineteenth century (see Chapter 8, sec. 8.2); indeed, this later usage probably accounts to some extent for why theorists of that time, especially Riemann (see Chapter 2, note 9), identify the subdominant as the principal constituent of the cadential progression (rather than II⁶).

EXAMPLE 3.6. (a) Pre-dominant diminished seventh; (b) Mozart, Piano Sonata in D, K. 576, ii, mm. 5–8 (ACF 7.15).

EXAMPLE 3.7. Beethoven, Piano Sonata in E Minor, Op. 90, ii, mm. 1–4.

dissonances or chromatic alterations; since these harmonies arise regularly enough in the literature and are generally unproblematic, it is not necessary to examine them further here. One particular pre-dominant is sufficiently unusual, however, to warrant special attention. On a small number of occasions, stage 2a includes a diminished-seventh harmony built over ④ (Ex. 3.6). Normally, this formation would be understood as VII$^4_3$, substituting for V$^4_2$, and would resolve to tonic (I$^6$). Here, however, the diminished seventh moves by ascending motion to VII$^7$/V (as stage 2b), thus no longer serving a dominant function. In this case, it is better to understand this diminished-seventh sonority as a *pre-dominant*, three of whose pitch constituents are shared with the II$^6$ harmony from the minor mode, and to identify it as a diminished-seventh pre-dominant substitute, notated °7-PD in the harmonic analysis.[20]

### 3.1.1.4. Stage 3—Dominant

The third stage of the cadence schema contains a root-position dominant. Most often, this harmony is accompanied by a seventh, though the inclusion of this dissonance is by no means a rule, since the dominant triad alone can fully satisfy the harmonic requirements of a cadence. Very frequently, the dominant is embellished with a cadential six-four, thus allowing us to identify two substages: the cadential six-four constituting stage 3a; the dominant proper, stage 3b. Like most theorists today, I recognize that the six-four intervals above the bass ⑤ function as suspensions (or appoggiaturas), such that the cadential six-four is understood to project *dominant* harmonic function, even if, as an isolated sonority, it is homologous with a second-inversion tonic.[21]

In tonic prolongational progressions, the diminished-seventh harmony VII$^7$ (and its inversions) can substitute for a dominant-seventh harmony when the root of the dominant, $\hat{5}$, is replaced by ♭$\hat{6}$ (e.g., I–VII$^7$–I, I–VII$^6_5$–I$^6$). Such a dominant-functioning diminished seventh, however, cannot be used to replace the root-position dominant in stage 3 of a cadential progression. For the resulting VII$^4_2$ (over ♭$\hat{6}$) would not only create a highly unstable sonority, but also eliminate ⑤ in the bass, an essential requirement of a cadential bass line.

As mentioned in the previous chapter (secs. 2.3.1.3 and 2.4), the dominant of stage 3 must initially appear, and then remain, in root position. With the exception of one situation to be discussed momentarily, an inversion at any point during the stage undermines the cadential status of the dominant and renders it prolongational. Consider Example 3.7, measures 3–4. Here, we might be tempted to recognize an IAC when a seeming root-position dominant (last eighth-note beat of m. 3) resolves

---

20. My label here thus differs from that in *CF*, 17, Ex. 2.7h, and *ACF*, 16, Ex. 1.13e, where I indicated this sonority as a passing chord without any functional meaning.

21. The latent tonic functionality of the cadential six-four is often exploited in situations of a marked expansion of this sonority; see sec. 5.1.1.3 and the discussion of Ex. 5.34.

EXAMPLE 3.8. Deceptive cadential progressions.

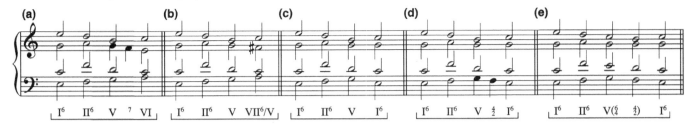

to a root-position tonic (downbeat of m. 4). But when we observe that the dominant has *initially* appeared in first inversion, thus participating in an ascending motion of the bass line, B–C♯–D♯–E (⑤–①), we understand that the root B of the dominant (end of m. 3) functions as an arpeggiated embellishment of the real bass, D♯ (second beat of m. 3) and that the motion into the final tonic at measure 4 completes a prolongational progression (IV⁶–V⁶₅–I), not a cadential one. The function of this opening phrase is thus better understood not as an antecedent, ending with an IAC, but rather as a *compound basic idea*, which, as is typical, ends noncadentially with what I term *prolongational closure*.²²

### 3.1.1.5. Stage 4—Final Tonic

The fourth stage of the cadence schema is supported by the final tonic, which appears as a consonant triad in root position. Indeed, to speak of a genuine authentic cadential progression, this requirement in the position and quality of the tonic must completely obtain. In some situations, however, the final tonic may be *replaced* by some other sonority, one that still fulfills a sense of tonic function. In such a case, we would identify a *deceptive cadential progression*. Among the various harmonies found in stage 4 of this progression type are, most typically, the submediant (VI), the secondary dominant VII⁶/V, and the tonic in first inversion (I⁶) (Ex. 3.8a–c). This progression is typically used to create a *deceptive cadence*, a deviation type to be discussed at length in the following chapter (sec. 4.1). Here, I am focusing on the harmonic progression itself.

The possibility of using I⁶ as a replacement harmony in a deceptive cadential progression may give rise to an exceptional situation involving stage 3. As seen in Example 3.8d, a passing ④ in the bass voice may be inserted between the dominant proper (⑤) and the I⁶ (③) of stage 4. We might then be tempted to speak of the resulting V⁴₂ harmony as an "inversion" of the dominant, thus undermining its cadential status. We can nevertheless retain the impression that the dominant has not lost its sense of being cadential, because we can easily hear the passing ④ as a local embellishment of a secure root-position dominant. Indeed, we could understand the passing seventh as "standing in" for the root of the harmony, thus not truly inverting the dominant. From another perspective, we could say that the segment of the melodic bass line that contains the motion ⑤–④–③ remains in the cadential stream (see again Ex. 2.9 from the previous chapter) and not that it shifts to the prolongational one. In some cases, the passing tone occurs already at the onset of stage 3b, following a cadential six-four in stage 3a (Ex. 3.8e), thus rendering the sense of "inversion" more marked, but not to the extent that it denies cadential status to the dominant proper.

### 3.1.1.6. Complete versus Incomplete Cadential Progressions

As briefly mentioned in the previous chapter, a cadential progression need not contain its complete set of harmonic functions. Stages 3 and 4 are absolutely required, but stage 1, in particular, is often omitted. Stage 2 is sometimes bypassed such that the initial tonic moves directly to the dominant. Now and then, the first two stages are eliminated and the cadence is articulated exclusively by a V–I progression. In all of these cases, we can speak of an *incomplete* cadential progression, as opposed to a *complete* progression containing all four stages.

The distinction between complete and incomplete cadential progressions might seem to provide grounds for differentiating some progressions as more or less strong or weak. But actual compositional practice does not support the idea that an incomplete progression is syntactically weaker than a complete one. Whether a composer chooses to employ one type or the other depends on circumstances unique to the given context at hand. To be sure, a complete progression offers more possibilities for cadential expansion, which could well endow the cadence with rhetorical emphasis. But from a purely syntactical perspective, even the most incomplete cadence can accomplish its task of providing full thematic closure.

### 3.1.1.7. Boundaries of the Cadential Progression

By definition, the time span of a given cadential formal function is congruent with its supporting cadential progression. So determining the boundaries of the progression is an important analytical task. The end is normally simple enough to locate, namely, where the final tonic appears. In some situations,

---

22. Both an antecedent and a compound basic idea consist of a simple two-measure basic idea followed by a two-measure contrasting idea. These phrase functions differ in their modes of closure, with the antecedent ending with a weak cadence (HC or IAC) and the compound basic idea ending noncadentially with prolongational closure, a concept that will be developed in more detail toward the end of this chapter (sec. 3.5.1).

EXAMPLE 3.9. Haydn, Piano Variations in F Minor, H.XVII:6, mm. 9–12 (*ACF* Sup. 5.6).

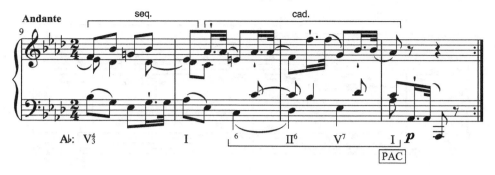

EXAMPLE 3.10. Mozart, Piano Sonata in B-flat, K. 570, iii, mm. 40–42.

however, identifying the beginning of the cadential progression can be more difficult. In most cases, the preceding progression (be it prolongational or sequential) ends with tonic harmony. (For the purposes of this discussion, I will refer to these as a *prolongational tonic* or a *sequential tonic*.) If the cadential progression also begins with tonic, the lack of harmonic change from one progression type to the next may obscure just where the second one begins.

Most often, these tonics are clearly distinguished one from the other. For example, if the prolongational or sequential tonic stands in root position then the shift to a first inversion tonic may be sufficient to articulate the onset of the cadential progression. As seen in Example 3.9, such a change in harmonic position can be even further associated with a new grouping structure—from a sequential idea in steady eighth notes in the melody to a cadential idea with dotted rhythms. The cadential harmony of stage 1 may even have its own additional characteristic, in this case, a chromatic alteration (E♮) that further differentiates the cadential tonic from the prior sequential one. If the prolongational or sequential tonic takes the same form as that of the cadential tonic, then some other features of the music may help clarify the boundaries of the progressions. Thus in Example 3.10, the final prolongational tonic (end of m. 40) and the initial cadential tonic (downbeat of m. 41) both stand in first inversion, but the two harmonies are articulated as quite different events based on the melodic-motivic content, the grouping structure, and the octave leap in the bass voice.

Complications arise, however, if a single tonic sonority can be seen as both sequential and cadential, or prolongational and cadential. Consider Example 3.11, where a *continuation phrase* begins with a descending-stepwise sequence concluding with I⁶ on the third beat of measure 3.[23] This moment also seems to bring the cadential idea, which begins with this same tonic. In this situation, we can recognize that the I⁶ is a *linking* harmony, namely, one that functions both as the final harmony of the sequence and the first harmony of the cadence.[24] Here, the sequential passage and the cadential idea clearly overlap. In some situations, however, the linking harmony seems to belong more to the cadential

---

23. Within a relatively tight-knit main theme of a classical movement, as are many of the themes discussed in this chapter, a *continuation phrase* combines together (*fuses*, to use my technical term for the situation) two distinct formal functions—continuation function proper and cadential function. The latter typically takes the form of a compact unit ending the theme, as generally defined in the previous chapter (sec. 2.5). Continuation function is characterized by four traits: fragmentation of the grouping structure, an acceleration in the rate of harmonic change, faster surface rhythmic activity, and sequential harmonies. (Not all of these attributes need be present in order to speak of continuation function.) What is potentially confusing is that I use the word "continuation" in two distinct ways: (1) as a complete *phrase* of music lasting four measures (more or less) and typically serving as the second, final phrase of a main theme, and (2) as a specific formal function (with the four characteristics just enumerated). To quote from my textbook: "The decision to label [this second phrase] a 'continuation phrase' is motivated by the fact that the continuation function is usually more salient throughout the entire phrase than is the cadential function, which does not normally appear until later in the phrase" (*ACF*, 35).

24. Unlike Ex. 3.2, which first introduced the idea of a linking harmony, I do not use in Ex. 3.11 a curved line that overlaps with the onset of the cadential progression, because the progression preceding the cadential one is sequential, not prolongational.

EXAMPLE 3.11. Haydn, Piano Sonata in G, H. 39, ii, mm. 3–5 (*ACF* Sup. 5.33).

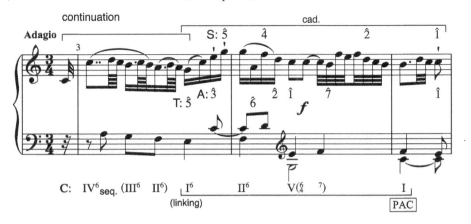

EXAMPLE 3.12. Mozart, Violin Sonata in B-flat, K. 454, iii, mm. 12–16 (*ACF* Sup. 6.2).

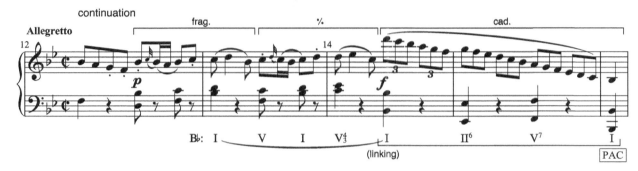

idea than to the preceding material. Thus in Example 3.12, the cadential idea begins evidently with the root-position tonic in the second half of measure 14. The prior continuational ideas (as expressed by the fragmentation and rapid harmonic changes) seem to end with the $V_3^4$ in the first half of that bar. In other words, little sense of functional elision arises here, as in the prior example. Nonetheless, we might still speak of the tonic as linking, since from a harmonic perspective exclusively, that tonic serves as the end of a prolongation supporting the continuation function, even while representing the start of the cadential progression (i.e., the prolongation does not conclude with $V_3^4$).

Finally, we can consider cases where an incomplete cadential progression begins with stages 2 or 3 (the latter being quite rare). As in the prior situations, the progression normally follows a prolongational or sequential tonic. But here, this harmony does not group with the cadential idea, which itself begins with a predominant or a dominant. Example 3.13 is a case in point. The ongoing continuational material, supported by a tonic prolongation, concludes on I at the second beat of measure 30, after which the cadential idea begins with II⁶. In this case, we would not speak of the tonic as a linking harmony, since it does not participate in the cadential progression proper, one that, by beginning with predominant, is incomplete. As these last examples show, the onset of the cadential progression depends on many factors—especially ones of grouping structure, bass-line contour, and formal function—that transcend considerations of harmony alone.

EXAMPLE 3.13. Beethoven, Piano Variations ("Diabelli"), Op. 120, mm. 29–32 (*ACF* Sup. 8.3).

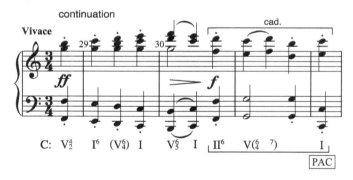

### 3.1.2. Morphology—Melodic Content

Given the conventionalized nature of the PAC's harmonic and bass-line content, we might suppose that the upper-voice melodic component would be equally conventional. And traditional accounts of cadential melody, especially those that only identify a dominant resolving to a tonic, would seem to support that view. For typically that melody is described as the stepwise motion from either $\hat{2}$ to $\hat{1}$ or $\hat{7}$ to $\hat{1}$. Indeed, the final melodic gesture of the vast majority of classical cadences conforms to this account, though a limited number of $\hat{5}$–$\hat{1}$ cadences occur as well. But this view, which focuses on stages 3 and 4 of the cadence, fails to consider the broader harmonic activity associated with stages 1 and

EXAMPLE 3.14. Basic simple pattern.

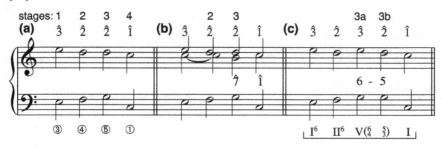

2. When we consider the complete cadential function, the melodic component becomes a more complicated affair; indeed, the large variety of melodic patterns that can be appropriately harmonized by a complete cadential progression casts doubt on the ability to find a limited number of conventional melodies to the cadence. Though we regularly speak of the cadence as formulaic, its melodic aspect actually presents considerable diversity, a fact that creates significant theoretical challenges. The following classification scheme is offered as an attempt to make sense of the multiplicity of melodic patterns presented by the classical cadence.[25]

### 3.1.2.1. Basic Patterns

In constructing this classification scheme, I assume that we can normally identify a single pitch associated with the top voice in each stage of the cadential progression, thus giving rise to a number of melodic *patterns*. We would then be able to recognize foreground embellishments of these more structural pitches, a technique widely used in most types of melodic analysis. Somewhat like what I propose for a bass-line melody (see Chapter 2, sec. 2.4), though differently conceived, I identify a set of *streams* that give shape to the basic melodic pitches. In so doing, I appeal to the fundamental idea that a cadential melody is largely a "falling" gesture, following the etymology of the word cadence. (The distinction between a pattern and a stream is subtle; I will clarify these terms after we have seen some specific examples of patterns and streams.)

With these general points in mind, let us consider a set of *basic* melodic patterns for the PAC. (I discuss these patterns at first in the abstract, turning then to specific manifestations in actual musical contexts.) The first such pattern consists of the simple descending motion 3̂–2̂–1̂ (Ex. 3.14a), which shows the pattern in counterpoint with the standard bass melody. Since this *basic simple pattern* contains only *three* different pitches, we have to specify how they relate to the *four* stages of the cadential progression. In this case, the harmonic context clearly associates 3̂ with stage 1 and 1̂ with stage 4; 2̂ is shared with stages 2 and 3. In order to clarify the relationship of melodic pitches to their cadential stages, I use a slash (/) to separate the stages, thus representing the basic simple pattern as 3̂/2̂/2̂/1̂.[26] When an alto voice is included (Ex. 3.14b), a harmonic dissonance in stage 2 is resolved downward in stage 3. The resolution brings the leading tone, which then resolves upward to the final tonic, a motion that will become important when considering some other basic patterns. If stage 3 is embellished with the cadential six-four (Ex. 3.14c), the intervallic "six to five" motion over the bass yields the scale-degree pattern 3̂/2̂/3̂-2̂/1̂. (Note that the substages are distinguished by the hyphen separating 3̂ and 2̂ within stage 3.)

Curiously, this basic simple pattern is not highly represented in the classical repertory. Rather, we more often find three other basic patterns in which each stage is accorded its unique scale degree. In these cases, it proves useful to distinguish three different streams of largely descending melodic action, which I relate to the three voices lying above the bass: soprano, alto, and tenor.[27]

---

25. The corpus of works examined for this study of cadential melody embraces roughly three hundred *main themes* found in chaps. 1–8 on the *ACF* website; see again, note 1. I restrict my corpus to tight-knit main themes because the looser organization of other thematic regions (e.g., transition, subordinate theme) often results in ECPs that can sometimes present more complicated melodies. The melodic organization of expanded cadences is examined in Chapter 5 (secs. 5.1.2, 5.2, and 5.3.3).

The scheme presented here is highly congruent with that devised for the HC by Nathan John Martin and Julie Pedneault-Deslauriers, who speak of *notional* soprano, alto, tenor, and bass patterns ("The Mozartean Half Cadence," 203–4); see ahead, sec. 3.3.3. Though their approach and mine were developed independently (theirs actually preceded the one presented here), it is not surprising that they have many features in common, ensuing as they do from the same basic conceptions of cadence and form. As for other approaches to cadential melody, Gjerdingen's cadential schemata include a variety of melodic patterns. Two of his melodic figures, the "Cudworth" and the "Prinner," will be introduced in the present chapter; others will be discussed in Chapter 7 on galant cadences (see sec. 7.1.1). For a cognitive study of Gjerdingen's cadential schemata, see Ben Duane, "Melodic Patterns and Tonal Cadences: Bayesian Learning of Cadential Categories from Contrapuntal Information." A recent study by Kyle Hutchinson and Mathew Poon proposes a different approach to cadential melody, one largely based on Schenkerian principles of upper-voice progressions ("Cadential Melodies: Form-Functional Taxonomy and the Role of the Upper Voice").

26. In the musical examples, it is not necessary to use a slash between the scale degrees, since their association with their respective stages, as defined by their harmonic context, is clear enough.

27. The identification of cadential melodic patterns based on their association with the standard four voices (soprano, alto, tenor, and bass) has a long history in the German *Klausellehre* (theory of clausulae) of the seventeenth and eighteenth centuries; see, e.g., Johann Gottfried Walther, *Praecepta der Musicalischen Composition* (1708); Andreas Werckmeister, *Harmonologia Musica* (1702). See also Markus Waldura, *Von Rameau*

EXAMPLE 3.15. Basic soprano pattern.

EXAMPLE 3.16. Basic soprano pattern with four-voice harmonization.

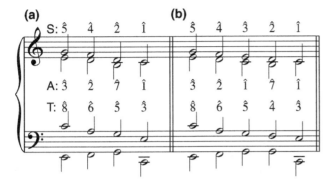

In the first pattern, which I call the *basic soprano pattern* (Ex. 3.15a), the fundamental melody begins on the dominant scale degree, thus yielding a descent to tonic $\hat{5}/\hat{4}/\hat{2}/\hat{1}$; if the cadential six-four is employed, then the gap between $\hat{4}$ and $\hat{2}$ is filled in by $\hat{3}$, thus creating a completely stepwise descent $\hat{5}/\hat{4}/\hat{3}$-$\hat{2}/\hat{1}$ (Ex. 3.15b). In that this pattern brings the final motion $\hat{2}$–$\hat{1}$, which we associated with the soprano voice of the basic simple pattern (Ex. 3.14), the melody of Example 3.15 can be seen as a notional *soprano stream*. If we then harmonize the basic soprano pattern in a four-voice realization that favors descending motion in the upper voices against the rising motion of the bass, as shown in Example 3.16, we witness the alto voice consisting of $\hat{3}/\hat{2}/\hat{7}/\hat{1}$ (with the six-four included, $\hat{3}/\hat{2}/\hat{1}$–$\hat{7}/\hat{1}$); the tenor voice, likewise, brings $\hat{8}/\hat{6}/\hat{5}/\hat{3}$ (with the six-four, $\hat{8}/\hat{6}/\hat{5}$-$\hat{4}/\hat{3}$).[28] I now propose that both the alto and tenor voices of this example can be conceived as a notional *alto stream* and *tenor stream*, respectively. When these streams are then placed in the upper voice, that is, when they function as the *literal* soprano voice of the cadential melody, we can identify a *basic alto pattern* (Ex. 3.17a and b) and a *basic tenor pattern* (Ex. 3.17c and d).[29] Note that the difference between a *pattern* and a *stream*

is somewhat complex. A stream is the more general concept, in that a given stream can appear in any literal voice, whereas a pattern (e.g., a "basic alto pattern") is identified on the basis of which stream (soprano, alto, or tenor) occurs predominately in the upper voice. We will also see cases where a cadential melody does not conform to one of the patterns, but rather is made up of a combination of different streams.

It could be objected at this point that the basic alto pattern of Example 3.17a and b is also perfectly suited to be described as a soprano melody. I do not disagree. Indeed, this pattern is highly representative of the upper voice in cadences of this repertory. Moreover, the basic alto could very well be seen as a variant of the basic simple pattern ($\hat{3}/\hat{2}/\hat{2}/\hat{1}$), whereby $\hat{2}$ of stage 3 is replaced by the leading tone (thus $\hat{3}/\hat{2}/\hat{7}/\hat{1}$). Indeed, a standard Schenkerian representation of that melodic motion (Ex. 3.18) would show the soprano melody moving into an inner alto voice, while conceptually retaining $\hat{2}$, supported by dominant harmony. In other words, this reduction suggests that the first two pitches of the stream ($\hat{3}$–$\hat{2}$), as well as its final pitch, project a normal soprano, while the leading tone alone would represent the alto. Such a view would further undermine the appropriateness of regarding the entire melody as an alto stream. Indeed, it might be questioned whether using the standard voice labels (soprano, alto, tenor) to identify the streams is even suitable. We need, however, to find some way of characterizing these cadential patterns, and although we could simply use neutral terms (such as the letter designations *x*, *y*, and *z*), it seems fitting nonetheless to invoke the concept of idealized (notional) voices. And as we saw in the harmonized basic simple pattern of Example 3.14b and the Schenkerian perspective of Example 3.18, the motion $\hat{7}$–$\hat{1}$ is already associated with an "inner" alto voice, while the motion $\hat{2}$–$\hat{1}$ seems especially characteristic of a soprano. In addition, the complete harmonization of the basic soprano pattern, shown in Example 3.16, sees the literal alto voice projecting exactly the same melodic configuration that I identify as an alto stream. For all of these reasons, I associate a basic, unembellished melodic line that ends $\hat{2}$–$\hat{1}$ with a soprano, and one that ends $\hat{7}$–$\hat{1}$ with an alto. In short, I continue to find it useful to label the basic melodic patterns in terms of these notional voices, understanding, of course, that any one of them in a real musical context will occur in the actual soprano voice.

Before considering some important variants to the patterns just laid out, it would be prudent to illustrate them with actual examples from the repertory. We will see that these passages often bring melodic embellishments (indicated by parenthetical scale degrees) on the very foreground of the musical surface; indeed, it is rare to find examples whose melodies conform strictly to the model. Despite such embellishments, it is usually possible to recognize the underlying pattern. As a general rule, I find the fundamental pitches of the melody to be associated with metrically

---

*und Riepel zu Koch: Zum Zusammenhang zwischen theoretischem Ansatz, Kadenzlehre und Periodenbegriff in der Musiktheorie des 18. Jahrhunderts*; Ludwig Holtmeier, "Kadenz/Klausel"; Gjerdingen, *Galant Style*, 139–41; Mutch, "History of the Cadence"; Vasili Byros, "Prelude on a Partimento: Invention in the Compositional Pedagogy of the German States in the Time of J. S. Bach." The labeling of the melodic streams that I present here do not correspond to those of the German tradition, because they are grounded in different theoretical principles; see also Chapter 7, sec. 7.1.

28. The pitches of this example lie an octave lower than in the previous ones in order to keep the four voices within their normal range.

29. When the tenor stream is placed in the upper voice, the final pitch $\hat{3}$ would create an IAC. In order to make a PAC, the stream either leaps from $\hat{5}$ directly to $\hat{1}$ (thus replicating the final motion of the bass) or else adds an embellishing $\hat{2}$ or $\hat{7}$ just prior to $\hat{1}$.

EXAMPLE 3.17. Basic alto and tenor patterns.

EXAMPLE 3.18. Schenkerian view of "alto stream."

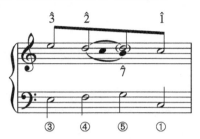

EXAMPLE 3.19. Haydn, Piano Trio in D, H. 7, iii, mm. 6–8 (*ACF* 2.32).

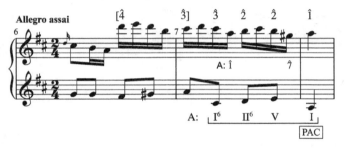

EXAMPLE 3.20. Beethoven, Piano Sonata in E, Op. 14, no. 1, ii, mm. 13–16 (*ACF* Sup. 3.8).

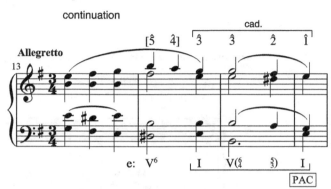

strong positions; as well, the attack-points of the pitches typically coordinate with those of the bass voice. In other cases, my choice of pitches as structural or ornamental is, admittedly, ad hoc and open to alternative interpretations. We will also observe that many examples bring incomplete cadential progressions, in which stage 1, but sometimes stage 2, is eliminated. In some cases of the former, we can still find the complete melodic pattern, since the melody of stage 1 may arise in connection with the event that immediately precedes the onset of the cadential progression proper. In the analytical annotations, scale degrees of a melodic stream that occur before the actual beginning of the cadential function are placed in square brackets.

**Basic Simple—$\hat{3}/\hat{2}/\hat{2}/\hat{1}$; $\hat{3}/\hat{2}/\hat{3}$-$\hat{2}/\hat{1}$ (with Cadential Six-Four).** Though the basic simple pattern would seem to represent the archetypical cadence melody, few cases appear in the classical literature of its use in an unornamented way. Rather, some degree of embellishment is usually present, though the underlying pattern nonetheless remains evident. The earlier discussed Example 3.3 shows a straightforward case, whereby the short upper-neighbor embellishments do not obscure the pattern. In Example 3.19, the pattern is emphasized by its rhythmic coordination with the bass. The descending third leaps at the end of each group of four sixteenths represent a quick "touching" on the alto stream in an inner voice.[30] Note, as well, that although the cadential function does not technically begin until the I$^6$ of measure 7, the sense of a more extended melodic descent already begins with the high D [$\hat{4}$] of the previous bar, thus alluding to the soprano stream ($\hat{5}$–$\hat{4}$–$\hat{3}$–$\hat{2}$–$\hat{1}$).

The basic simple pattern employing the cadential six-four ($\hat{3}/\hat{2}/\hat{3}$-$\hat{2}/\hat{1}$) seems to be rarely used.[31] Perhaps the redundant $\hat{3}$–$\hat{2}$ melodic motion accounts for its general unsuitability. One possible case (Ex. 3.20), which bypasses stage 2, yields the pattern $\hat{3}$// $\hat{3}$-$\hat{2}/\hat{1}$, thus eliminating a twofold $\hat{3}$–$\hat{2}$ motion.[32] Note that like the prior example, a more complete melodic descent, this time from $\hat{5}$, suggests the basic soprano pattern, even if the first two melodic components belong to the continuation function that precedes the cadence.

**Basic Soprano—$\hat{5}/\hat{4}/\hat{2}/\hat{1}$; $\hat{5}/\hat{4}/\hat{3}$-$\hat{2}/\hat{1}$ (with Cadential Six-Four).** Characteristic of this basic pattern is a problematic gap between $\hat{4}$ and $\hat{2}$.[33] As a result, it is hard to find examples that are completely unornamented. One case that is close to the model appears in Example 3.21, though here, the third scale degree, B, which could fill in the

---

30. Embellishments that touch on other streams are annotated with scale degrees in a smaller font size than those representing the fundamental pattern. Later, I consider more extensive cases, ones that seem to represent a genuine *combination* of two different streams (see sec. 3.1.2.3).

31. My corpus of classical themes does not contain a single case of this pattern involving a complete cadential progression.

32. The use of two slashes in a row (//) represents the absence of a stage, here, the elimination of stage 2.

33. A general principle of melodic writing shuns the use of a leap in the same direction as the ongoing melodic line; when such a leap occurs, it is generally preferable to fill the gap thus created with a reversal in the line's

EXAMPLE 3.21. Beethoven, String Quartet in G, Op. 18, no. 2, iv, mm. 26–28 (*ACF* 4.4).

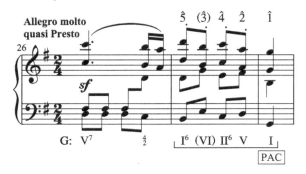

EXAMPLE 3.22. Beethoven, Piano Sonata in C Minor ("Pathétique"), Op. 13, ii, mm. 5–8 (*ACF* 4.7).

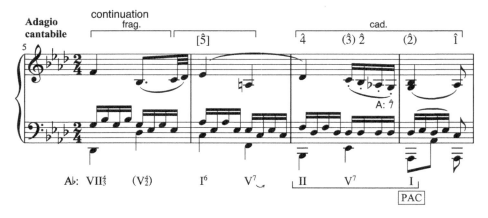

EXAMPLE 3.23. Beethoven, Piano Sonata in G, Op. 14, no. 2, ii, mm. 14–16 (*ACF* Sup. 8.14).

gap between C ($\hat{4}$) and A ($\hat{2}$), is at least anticipated by appearing in stage 1b, supported by VI. More often, the gap is directly filled in by an embellishing $\hat{3}$, as in Example 3.22. Here we also see stage 3 move into the alto stream to touch on $\hat{7}$ just prior to the moment of cadential arrival, which itself is embellished by the appoggiatura $\hat{2}$. This latter embellishment is often found at the start of stage 4, especially when stage 3 brings $\hat{7}$ as its literally sounding final degree.

The structural gap of $\hat{4}$ and $\hat{2}$ in the basic soprano pattern is most decisively filled by using a cadential six-four to support $\hat{3}$.

Example 3.1 illustrates the pattern without any ornamentations (save the octave grace notes). Example 3.23 brings another case of the pattern. Note that I include the V$^4_2$ at the end of measure 14 as part of the cadential progression due to the manifest grouping boundary immediately preceding this harmony.[34] In Example 3.24, the pattern begins with stage 2, thus bypassing an initial $\hat{5}$; as well, this example is notable for its four-part realization in which the alto and tenor streams of the fundamental model actually lie in their literal voices (cf. Ex. 3.16b). Example 3.25 shows another case of beginning the pattern with stage 2. We also see here a characteristic embellishment at the beginning of stage 3,

---

direction. We will shortly see how in the alto stream a reversal fills in the gap $\hat{2}$–$\hat{7}$ with $\hat{1}$; such a fill between $\hat{4}$ and $\hat{2}$ is not available to the soprano stream due to its required motion down to $\hat{1}$.

---

34. See the earlier discussion of this issue in sec. 3.1.1.2.

EXAMPLE 3.24. Mozart, Piano Sonata in A, K. 331, i, mm. 7–8 (*ACF* 3.17).

EXAMPLE 3.27. Beethoven, Piano Sonata in E, Op. 14, no. 1, ii, mm. 73–78 (*ACF* Sup. 3.14).

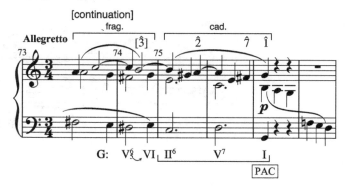

EXAMPLE 3.25. Beethoven, Violin Sonata in G, Op. 96, iii, mm. 6–8 (*ACF* Sup. 2.3).

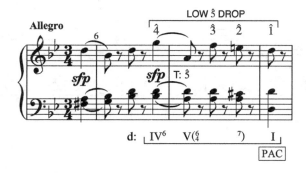

EXAMPLE 3.26. Haydn, Piano Sonata in D, H. 33, iii, mm. 5–8 (*ACF* Sup. 3.5).

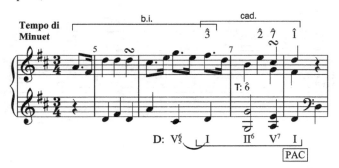

namely, the leap down to $\hat{5}$, which references the tenor stream. Though not so common in tight-knit main themes, this *low $\hat{5}$ drop* gesture emerges at the end of an ECP as a standard signal of closure in looser, subordinate themes (especially in the string quartet genre).[35]

**Basic Alto—$\hat{3}/\hat{2}/\hat{7}/\hat{1}$; $\hat{3}/\hat{2}/\hat{1}$-$\hat{7}/\hat{1}$ (with Cadential Six-Four).** Like the soprano pattern, the basic alto contains a melodic gap ($\hat{2}$–$\hat{7}$); but here it is immediately filled in by $\hat{7}$ resolving to $\hat{1}$ at stage 4, thus providing a particularly satisfying sense of melodic closure. Indeed, this feature may partly explain why the

pattern, along with its cadential six-four variant, is so highly represented in the repertory. Example 3.26 shows a relatively unornamented version, the main embellishment being the leap into the tenor stream ($\hat{6}$) at the start of stage 2 (downbeat of m. 7). This "drop" to $\hat{6}$ and the immediate return to the regular alto stream ($\hat{2}$) is reminiscent of the low $\hat{5}$ drop gesture of Example 3.25. Note that in Example 3.26, I identify the start of the cadential progression with stage 1 (upbeat to m. 7) due to the pervasive "upbeat" motives in the theme; however, this moment could also be heard as the final pitch of the basic idea, thus allowing the tonic of this upbeat to function as a linking harmony.[36]

When a given pattern of any kind begins with stage 2, as frequently happens, we sometimes find that the melodic pitch immediately preceding the cadential progression is taken from stage 1 of the pattern; see again Example 3.22. Another illustration of this technique, one that is especially typical of the basic alto, can be found in Example 3.27. The complete theme is a compound sentence; the example begins in the middle of the continuation phrase, which sees fragmentation into two-measure units (the final fragment being mm. 73–74), followed by the onset of the cadential function at measure 75. As a result, we can identify the alto stream beginning with stage 2 on the third beat of this bar. At the same time, we recognize that the final fragment ends with $\hat{3}$ (supported by VI), which represents stage 1 of the cadential melody, even if this harmony seems to belong more to the continuation function (as projected by the fragmentation) than to the cadential one.

As already discussed, it is not always certain just where a given cadential progression begins. Thus in Example 3.28, a plausible case could be made for seeing the cadential function proper beginning either at the end of measure 8 or at the beginning of measure 9. Such distinctions normally depend on different interpretations of the grouping structure. On the one

---

35. See Chapter 5, sec. 5.1.2.11, "Low $\hat{5}$ Drop." The label is inspired by Gjerdingen's terminological usage when identifying some conventional melodic patterns that he calls the "High $\hat{2}$ drop" and a variant "High $\hat{6}$ drop" (*Galant Style*, 74, 162, respectively).

36. That the tonic stands in root-position, resolving V$^6_5$, further supports interpreting I as prolongational, then linking with the cadential function. Alternatively, we need not be bound by the pervasive upbeat groups preceding the cadence and thus hear the cadential idea beginning with stage 2 on the downbeat of m. 7.

**68** Basic Cadence Types

EXAMPLE 3.28. Haydn, Symphony No. 101 in D, ii, mm. 7–10 (*ACF* 5.28).

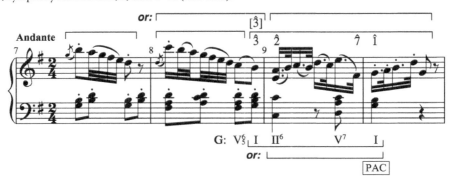

EXAMPLE 3.29. Haydn, Piano Trio in E, H. 28, i, mm. 1–4 (R = ½N) (*ACF* 3.11).

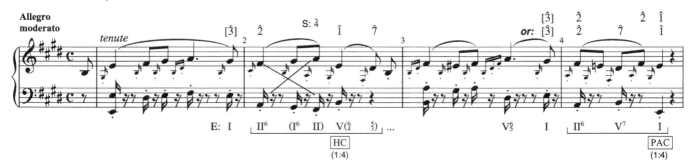

hand, we could understand measure 8 as a repetition of measure 7 and hear the descending scale ending on the third eighth note of measure 8, with the fourth eighth note representing the beginning of the next group. On the other hand, the manifest change in rhythm and texture on the downbeat of measure 9 suggests that here is the beginning of a new group, thus allowing us to hear the final eighth note of measure 8 as ending the prior group. No matter which interpretation we choose, we still find the complete alto pattern beginning on the upbeat to measure 9. This example also shows a type of embellishment often found in cadential melodies, namely, an upward thrusting elaboration within stage 2 (m. 9).

It often arises that we cannot determine which pitches in the cadential melody are fundamental to the melodic stream or which ones are ornamental. Take the case of Example 3.29, measures 3–4 (the opening two measures will be discussed later). Depending upon whether we hear as structural either the third or fourth eighth notes of measure 4, we can invoke the basic simple pattern $\hat{3}/\hat{2}/\hat{2}/\hat{1}$ or the alto $\hat{3}/\hat{2}/\hat{7}/\hat{1}$. Since I normally privilege the rhythmic coordination of harmony and melody, and thus would probably prefer the latter interpretation, the former is just as plausible. Indeed, I already have acknowledged how these two patterns are strongly related (see again the earlier discussion of Ex. 3.18).

The variant of the alto stream that brings the cadential six-four in stage 3 is the most highly represented pattern in the corpus. As with some of the issues we have already discussed, we often find the pattern beginning with stage 2, with the melodic content

EXAMPLE 3.30. Haydn, Piano Sonata in E-flat, H. 28, ii, mm. 5–8 (*ACF* Sup. 5.5).

of stage 1 represented at the end of the group that precedes the cadential function proper. Example 3.30 is a case in point. The cadence is probably best seen to begin with $\hat{2}$ on the downbeat of measure 7, since the preceding $\hat{3}$ seems more to group with the prior idea, as a resolution of the 4–3 suspension in the final beat of measure 6. Similar to Example 3.28, we find an upward-thrusting arpeggiation in stage 2.

**Basic Tenor—$\hat{8}/\hat{6}/\hat{5}/\hat{3}$; $\hat{8}/\hat{6}/\hat{5}$-$\hat{4}/\hat{3}$ (with Cadential Six-Four).** This pattern arises less often than others in the repertory, foremost because it naturally leads to $\hat{3}$, thus resulting in an *imperfect* authentic cadence (as will be discussed later in this chapter) and also because of the awkward gap ($\hat{8}$–$\hat{6}$) between stages 1 and 2. The pattern can be altered, however, by replacing $\hat{3}$ of stage 4 with $\hat{1}$, thus permitting closure with a PAC. Even then, the complete pattern seldom arises without some embellishment in stage 3 to bring a foreground stepwise

EXAMPLE 3.31. Varied patterns.

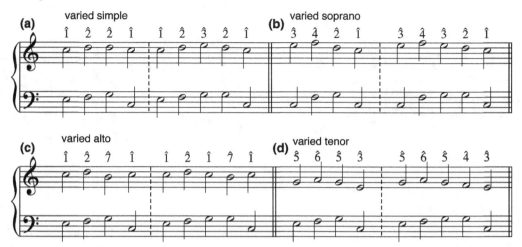

closure to the melody, as seen earlier in Example 3.10 and Example 3.4a.[37]

### 3.1.2.2. Varied Patterns

At this point, we have identified four *basic* patterns—simple, soprano, alto, and tenor. We can now introduce a significant variation, one that occurs regularly in the repertory of classical cadential melodies. With these *varied* patterns, the first pitch is placed one step lower than the second pitch. The first pitch thus steps *upward* to the second pitch, creating an ascending-descending contour. The resulting patterns are:

Varied simple—$\hat{1}/\hat{2}/\hat{2}/\hat{1}$; $\hat{1}/\hat{2}/\hat{3}$-$\hat{2}/\hat{1}$ (with cadential six-four), Example 3.31a;

Varied soprano—$\hat{3}/\hat{4}/\hat{2}/\hat{1}$; $\hat{3}/\hat{4}/\hat{3}$-$\hat{2}/\hat{1}$ (with cadential six-four), Example 3.31b;

Varied alto—$\hat{1}/\hat{2}/\hat{7}/\hat{1}$; $\hat{1}/\hat{2}/\hat{1}$-$\hat{7}/\hat{1}$ (with cadential six-four), Example 3.31c;

Varied tenor—$\hat{5}/\hat{6}/\hat{5}/\hat{3}$; $\hat{5}/\hat{6}/\hat{5}$-$\hat{4}/\hat{3}$ (with cadential six-four), Example 3.31d.

Note that the distinction between the soprano and alto streams is still grounded in the melodic motion of stages 3 and 4; that is $\hat{2}$-$\hat{1}$ (soprano) vs. $\hat{7}$-$\hat{1}$ (alto). Let us look at some specific examples of these varied patterns.

**Varied Simple—$\hat{1}/\hat{2}/\hat{2}/\hat{1}$; $\hat{1}/\hat{2}/\hat{3}$-$\hat{2}/\hat{1}$ (with Cadential Six-Four).** Example 3.32 illustrates the varied simple pattern, one that exhibits embellishments within stage 3. Note that because the cadential idea begins with the pre-dominant on the downbeat of measure 7, we cannot necessarily differentiate between the basic or varied patterns, because both are identical from stage 2

---

37. In Ex. 3.4a, the stage-3 embellishment, C♯, references the alto stream; the second embellishment, E, is placed in parentheses, since it resides in stage 4.

EXAMPLE 3.32. Mozart, String Quartet in B-flat, K. 589, iii, mm. 6–8 (*ACF* 4.6).

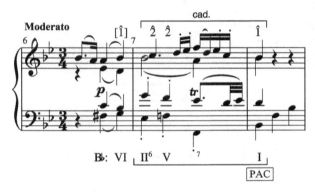

onwards. But when we look at the pitch immediately preceding the cadence (last beat of m. 6), we find a precadential [$\hat{1}$], thus suggesting that the *varied* pattern is at the basis of this cadential melody.

When stage 2 of the varied simple pattern is bypassed, as in Example 3.33, an incomplete I–V–I progression supports a straightforward $\hat{1}$-$\hat{2}$-$\hat{1}$ melody. The use of the cadential six-four in this pattern, as seen in Example 3.34, seems to be typical of Beethoven (at least as represented in the corpus).

**Varied Soprano—$\hat{3}/\hat{4}/\hat{2}/\hat{1}$; $\hat{3}/\hat{4}/\hat{3}$-$\hat{2}/\hat{1}$ (with Cadential Six-Four).** This pattern poses the problem of producing parallel octaves in stages 1 and 2 if the standard ③–④ motion of the classical bass line is used. As a result, this varied soprano normally employs either ① or ⑥ as the bass of stage 1; see Example 3.2 and Example 3.35, respectively. Recall that the basic soprano pattern ($\hat{5}/\hat{4}/\hat{2}/\hat{1}$) features a gap ($\hat{4}$-$\hat{2}$) between stages 2 and 3. The varied soprano ameliorates this situation by bringing $\hat{3}$ as an "anticipated" fill (in stage 1).

**Varied Alto—$\hat{1}/\hat{2}/\hat{7}/\hat{1}$; $\hat{1}/\hat{2}/\hat{1}$-$\hat{7}/\hat{1}$ (with cadential six-four).** The varied alto is well represented in the corpus. Example 3.5 (discussed earlier) shows how the pattern can be lightly embellished with the low $\hat{5}$ drop at the beginning of stage 3.

EXAMPLE 3.33. Beethoven, Piano Sonata in E-flat, Op. 31, no. 3, ii, mm. 7–8 (*ACF* 7.14).

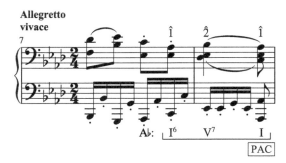

EXAMPLE 3.34. Beethoven, Andante in F ("Andante favori"), WoO 57, mm. 6–8 (*ACF* 4.15a).

EXAMPLE 3.35. Haydn, Piano Trio in A-flat, H. 14, ii, mm. 14–16 (*ACF* 8.1).

In Example 3.36, we see that another type of embellishment—a voice exchange between the outer voices on the first two beats of measure 9—permits the melody of stage 2 to touch on $\hat{4}$ (from the soprano stream). The cadential six-four version shown in Example 3.37 features a prominent upward arpeggiation of the pre-dominant.[38]

**Varied Tenor—$\hat{5}/\hat{6}/\hat{5}/\hat{3}$; $\hat{5}/\hat{6}/\hat{5}-\hat{4}/\hat{3}$ (with Cadential Six-Four).** Seeing as the varied tenor naturally yields an IAC, it is necessary

---

38. The cadential melody ends on $\hat{1}$, but a simultaneously occurring $\hat{5}$ is a "cover tone" that initiates the melody of the passage that follows. I return to this example in a later discussion of the *covered cadence* (sec. 3.4.2.3).

EXAMPLE 3.36. Haydn, String Quartet in G, Op. 54, no. 1, iii, mm. 8–10 (*ACF* 5.12a).

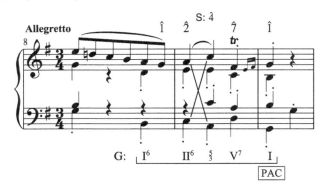

to substitute $\hat{1}$ for $\hat{3}$ in stage 4 in order to create a PAC. But unlike the basic pattern (see above, Ex. 3.4a and Ex. 3.10), I have not found any examples of this variant in the corpus. The first two stages ($\hat{5}$–$\hat{6}$), however, begin another, highly represented type of pattern, which will be discussed in the next section.

### 3.1.2.3. Combined Patterns

In the set of cadential melodies examined so far, each stage of the cadential progression has been represented by a melodic pitch drawn from a single stream (recalling, however, that for the *simple pattern*, both basic and varied, I do not recognize streams per se). Another set of patterns can be understood as *combining* two or more streams to produce the pitch content of the cadential melody. We have already seen the borrowing of pitches from other streams when we identified various embellishments, such as the low $\hat{5}$ drop and the voice-exchange. In those cases, the embellishing notes could be identified as members of a different stream. More genuine cases of combined patterns, however, take the *fundamental* pitches of the stages from two or more streams. With combined patterns, we can distinguish two general situations: (1) as the progression moves from stage to stage, the melody draws *successively* on different streams; or (2), we find a *simultaneous* expression of two or more streams providing the fundamental pitch content of the stages.

**Successively Combined Patterns.** In Example 3.38, the cadential melody begins with the alto stream ($\hat{3}$) for stage 1, leaps up to engage the tenor stream for stages 2 and 3a ($\hat{6}$–$\hat{5}$), and returns to the alto for stages 3b and 4 ($\hat{7}$–$\hat{1}$). With a similar contour, the cadence in Example 3.39 successively combines alto and soprano streams. Another successive combination of these two streams is favored by Mozart, who uses it in a number of works (see Ex. 3.40).[39]

Many successively combined patterns begin with the varied tenor stream, $\hat{5}$–$\hat{6}$, leaping then down to engage the soprano

---

39. Four other Mozart cadences feature practically the same melody, including the upward arpeggiation: Piano Sonata in C, K. 330, ii, m. 8; Rondo in D, K. 485, m. 16; Piano Sonata in C, K. 545, ii, m. 40; Piano Concerto in B-flat, K. 450, ii, m. 24.

EXAMPLE 3.37. Haydn, String Quartet in C ("Emperor"), Op. 76, no. 3, iv, mm. 9–13 (*ACF* Sup. 6.16).

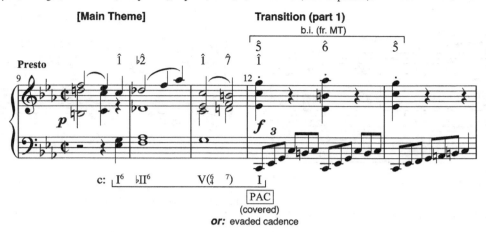

EXAMPLE 3.38. Beethoven, Piano Sonata in C, Op. 2, no. 3, i, mm. 10–13 (*ACF* 5.11).

EXAMPLE 3.39. Haydn, String Quartet in G, Op. 77, no. 1, ii, mm. 7–8 (*ACF* Sup. 3.10).

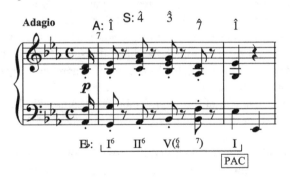

EXAMPLE 3.40. Mozart, Horn Quintet in E-flat, K. 407, ii, mm. 16–18.

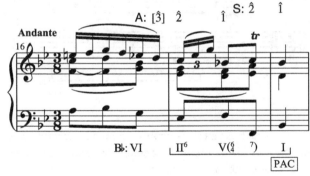

or alto (or both). The contrapuntal advantage of this melodic motion is owing to the parallel thirds created with the bass ③–④. In Example 3.41, the first two stages of the tenor stream yield to the final two stages of the soprano, thus producing the pattern $\hat{5}/\hat{6}/\hat{3}$-$\hat{2}/\hat{1}$ (T/T/S-S/S).[40] Another variant in Example 3.42 employs a combination of tenor and alto streams, $\hat{5}/\hat{6}/\hat{1}$-$\hat{7}/\hat{1}$ (T/T/A-A/A). Note that in the embellishments of stage 2, we find a downward

arpeggiation, akin to the upward arpeggiations we have already identified with this stage.

One of the most frequently found successive combinations (Ex. 3.43) begins with the tenor stream, but then engages both the alto and soprano stream successively to produce the pattern $\hat{5}/\hat{6}/\hat{1}$-$\hat{2}/\hat{1}$ (T/T/A-S/S), a considerably complicated combination

---

40. Ulrich Kaiser, in his study on Mozart's early compositions and the "Nannerl notebook," highlights a similar melodic component $\hat{8}$–$\hat{6}$–$\hat{3}$–$\hat{2}$–$\hat{1}$ as a *Kadenzmodell* (*Die Notenbücher der Mozarts als Grundlage der Analyse von W. A. Mozarts Kompositionen 1761–1767*). Curiously, this particular combination arises only once in my corpus; see Beethoven, Piano Sonata in F Minor, Op. 2, no. 1, ii, mm. 7–8 (*ACF*, Ex. 4.16a). The pattern seems to be used more in the galant style of the very young Mozart than with the more mature composer of the high classical style.

EXAMPLE 3.41. Beethoven, Symphony No. 2 in D, Op. 36, ii, mm. 5–8 (*ACF* 4.8).

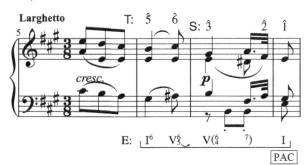

EXAMPLE 3.44. Haydn, Piano Trio in F, H. 6, ii, mm. 6–8 (*ACF* 4.11).

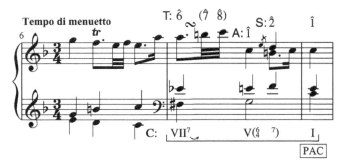

EXAMPLE 3.42. Mozart, Piano Sonata in C, K. 330, iii, mm. 14–16 (*ACF* 5.17).

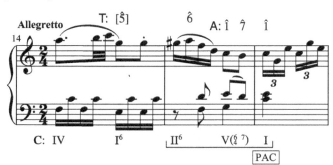

EXAMPLE 3.45. Haydn, Piano Trio in C Minor, H. 13, i, mm. 6–8 (*ACF* 4.14).

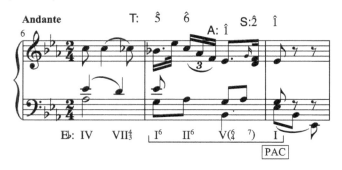

EXAMPLE 3.43. Mozart, Piano Trio in G, K. 564, ii, mm. 5–8 (*ACF* 8.11).

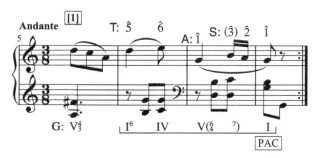

to be sure.[41] Yet this pattern is popular enough to warrant its own nickname, for which I propose the colloquial term *tenor combo*.

The tenor combo is noteworthy in a number of ways. For instance, the plunge from T: $\hat{6}$ down to A: $\hat{1}$ is a particularly expressive gesture, one that can even be more pronounced if $\hat{6}$ is embellished by a stepwise rise to $\hat{8}$, as we see in Example 3.44, such that the plunge is a complete octave. Alternatively, the gap between $\hat{6}$ and $\hat{1}$ can be filled with a downward arpeggiation of the pre-dominant (Ex. 3.45). The leaping approach to $\hat{1}$ also belies a dictate of strict counterpoint, namely, that the dissonant fourth of the cadential six-four should be prepared and then resolved by a stepwise descent (with the arrival of the dominant proper). The tenor combo, on the contrary, steps up from A: $\hat{1}$ to S: $\hat{2}$ rather than continuing the alto stream down to $\hat{7}$ (which would produce the combination already described in Ex. 3.42).[42] Indeed, the rise to $\hat{2}$ is almost always emphasized by an appoggiatura $\hat{3}$ (sometimes written out, as in Ex. 3.43). In this respect, Examples 3.44 and 3.45 are interesting for how the voice holding the stage-3a $\hat{1}$ splits into separate soprano and alto parts, the former with $\hat{2}$ (and its appoggiatura $\hat{3}$), the latter resolving more normally to $\hat{7}$. Example 3.46 not only shows this same voice splitting, but also presents a variant of the tenor combo that begins with the *basic* tenor stream ($\hat{8}$–$\hat{6}$), continuing on with the standard $\hat{1}$–$\hat{2}$–$\hat{1}$ for the rest of the combo.

**Simultaneously Combined Patterns.** In some cases, the degree of embellishment of a cadential melody is extensive enough as to suggest that multiple streams are being expressed simultaneously. Consider Example 3.47, where we find a clear case of the soprano and alto lines occurring over the same span of time. To be sure, the soprano line seems more salient due to its stronger metrical placement, but the alto stream is fully complete and seems more than just ornamental. In Example 3.48, we again find a combination of soprano and alto streams, but now the metrical

---

41. Note that at the top of this example (over m. 5), the boxed numeral "1" refers to this passage arising within an ongoing *first part* of a small binary theme type. Later, we will discuss the comparable passage ending the *second part* of the binary (Ex. 3.64), as indicated by the boxed "2" at m. 11.

42. Although I introduced Ex. 3.42 before speaking of the tenor combo, this example, along with Ex. 3.41, can rightfully be considered variants of that popular combination.

EXAMPLE 3.46. Mozart, Piano Sonata in F, K. 332, iii, mm. 29–32 (*ACF* 5.16).

EXAMPLE 3.47. Haydn, Piano Sonata in B-flat, H. 41, i, mm. 6–8 (*ACF* Sup. 2.1).

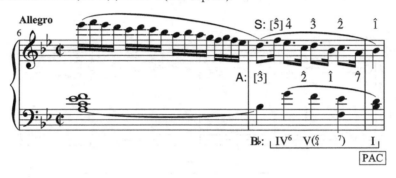

EXAMPLE 3.48. Beethoven, Piano Sonata in A-flat, Op. 26, iv, mm. 26–28 (*ACF* Sup. 8.7).

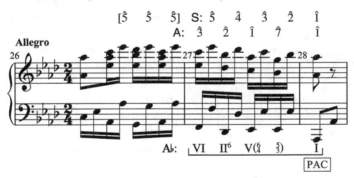

EXAMPLE 3.49. Haydn, String Quartet in F, Op. 77, no. 2, iii, mm. 6–8 (*ACF* 7.20).

EXAMPLE 3.50. Mozart, Piano Sonata in D, K. 284, iii, mm. 7–8 (*ACF* Sup. 4.9).

EXAMPLE 3.51. Mozart, *Eine kleine Nachtmusik*, K. 525, ii, mm. 6–8 (*ACF* 3.1).

EXAMPLE 3.52. Haydn, Piano Sonata in E-flat, H. 38, iii, mm. 6–8 (*ACF* Sup. 7.8).

placement gives greater emphasis to the latter. (The repeated 5̂s in m. 26 refer to a later discussion.)

Although we might expect that most simultaneous combinations would occur with the soprano and alto, the tenor stream can also come into play. In the earlier discussed Example 3.11, the melodic line is sufficiently complex that we can recognize the first two stages of the tenor stream lying below the soprano and alto. In other cases, the tenor may be placed above the other streams, as in Example 3.49, where an upper tenor is combined with an alto. Note that the tenor drops out at stage 4 so that the melody can close unambiguously on 1̂ (i.e., without an interfering 3̂, as called for by the normal tenor stream). Simultaneous soprano and tenor combinations are also well represented in the corpus, as seen in Example 3.50. Here, the tenor, lying mostly above the soprano, leaps into an inner voice at the very end of the configuration (see the line connecting the two 4̂s), again to allow 1̂ to appear without a covering 3̂.

The examples of simultaneous combinations discussed thus far involve just two streams. But all three can sometimes come into the picture. Example 3.51 is a complicated melody that primarily combines soprano and alto, with the tenor becoming prominent in stages 1 and 2. In Example 3.52, a highly leaping melody gives emphasis to the tenor stream in stages 1 through 3 (but then dropping out for the PAC), with the off-beat eighth notes referencing *successively* first the soprano and then the alto streams.[43] Such a combination of both simultaneous and successive streams can involve especially intricate situations, as in Example 3.53. Here, the melody begins with the tenor as primary for stages 1 and 2; halfway through stage 2 to the very end, the soprano and alto streams enter into a simultaneous combination. Similarly in Example 3.54, the first two stages feature a simultaneous combination of tenor and soprano, followed by a combination of soprano and alto.

Finally, a simultaneous combination of streams in a single voice can sometimes split into two actual voices representing the

---

43. The 5̂ on the second half of the first beat of m. 7 could also be thought of as expressing the first stage of the varied tenor stream.

same voice combinations. Thus in Example 3.55, stages 1 and 2 bring combinations of soprano and alto; at the start of stage 3, however, the texture thickens such that each prior stream now becomes its own literal voice.

### 3.1.2.4. Additional Patterns

The basic, varied, and combined patterns identified so far do not exhaust the possibilities of cadential melodies in the classical repertoire. A variety of miscellaneous configurations are found now and then. Two of these patterns, holdovers from the galant style, are discussed prominently in Gjerdingen's study—the "Cudworth" and "Prinner" schemata. The former, a PAC type, will be identified in this section; the latter, which produces an IAC, will be introduced later in this chapter (sec. 3.2.1.2) and then treated in greater detail in Chapter 7 (sec. 7.1.2).

**Ascending Melodic Pattern ($\hat{5}/\hat{6}/\hat{7}/\hat{8}$).** The harmonies of the authentic cadential progression permit the soprano voice to acquire a fully ascending profile, $\hat{5}/\hat{6}/\hat{7}/\hat{8}$ (Ex. 3.56a). Such melodic motion, of course, counters the normal descending contour reflected in the etymology of the word *cadence*. Moreover, the counterpoint between the standard bass line and this ascending melody brings consistent parallel motion for the first three stages, thus reducing the voice differentiation that is so characteristic of a cadence. In addition, the pattern can easily give rise to parallel fifths (as in Ex. 3.56b) or, if not handled carefully, a doubled leading tone. Perhaps for these reasons, the fully ascending cadential melody appears infrequently in the corpus examined for this chapter. One clear case (Ex. 3.57) features the complete pattern. Another possible candidate is shown in Example 3.58. Here, the cadential progression per se begins with stage 2, but the pitch content of stage 1 [$\hat{5}$] appears at the very end of the basic idea. Although metrical considerations favor an ascending melody, the leap-up to $\hat{2}$ within the pre-dominant of stage 2 and the use of the cadential six-four make it feasible to identify the basic alto (/$\hat{2}$/ $\hat{1}$-$\hat{7}$/$\hat{1}$) as well. Several instances of the ascending melodic pattern arise in connection with themes that modulate to the dominant region (such as Ex. 3.144a, to be discussed later in sec. 3.3.5.1).

EXAMPLE 3.53. Beethoven, String Quartet in C-sharp Minor, Op. 131, iv, mm. 21–24 (*ACF* 8.8).

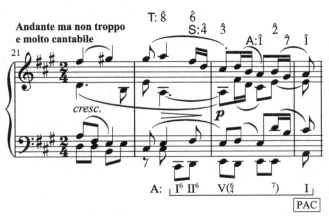

EXAMPLE 3.54. Haydn, Piano Trio in D, H. 7, iii, mm. 14–16 (*ACF* Sup. 8.6).

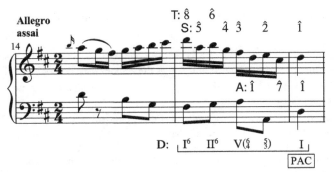

EXAMPLE 3.55. Beethoven, Violin Sonata in C Minor, Op. 30, no. 2, ii, mm. 6–8 (*ACF* Sup. 4.3).

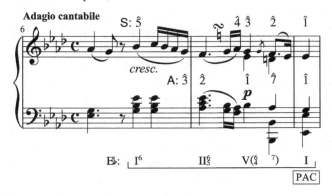

EXAMPLE 3.56. Ascending melody.

EXAMPLE 3.57. Beethoven, String Quartet in E-flat, Op. 74, iv, mm. 17–20 (*ACF* Sup. 8.2).

EXAMPLE 3.58. Haydn, String Quartet in D Minor, Op. 76, no. 2, ii, mm. 3–4 (R = ½N) (*ACF* Sup. 4.13).

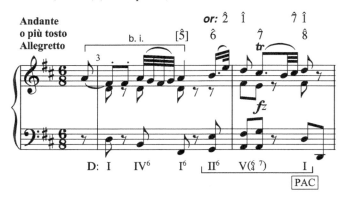

**Bass Melodic Pattern ($\hat{3}/\hat{4}/\hat{5}/\hat{1}$).** Now and then, the melodic component of the cadence appropriates the pitch content of a standard bass line ($\hat{3}/\hat{4}/\hat{5}/\hat{1}$). Example 3.59a shows one such case. In a main theme built as a small ternary, the A section features a texture in which all voices sound the same series of notes but in different octaves, a technique I call *doubled monophony*.[44] To close this section, measures 7–8 bring a conventional bass-line melody. Difficult to determine in these final bars, however, is whether the line sounded by the violin (notated in the right hand of the score) necessarily represents a soprano voice, or whether it merely doubles the bass voice, such that no independent soprano is even being expressed.

Considering the theme from its beginning may shed some light on this matter. The initial basic idea (mm. 1–2) is most likely a soprano, since a tonic arpeggiation is not typical of a bass line. But the following contrasting idea already brings the contour of a cadential bass, albeit in B major.[45] Unusually, this idea is then repeated, but the harmonic implications of the constituent scale degrees are no longer cadential. Finally, the cadence itself is clearly a further variant on the contrasting idea, though in order to reinforce the sense of closure, Mozart alters the melody to consistent quarter notes in measure 7.[46] What remains unclear, however, is whether or not the cadential idea continues to express itself as a genuine soprano voice. At this point, it is not really possible to know, for we could say that the doubled monophonic line changes from a soprano voice in the basic idea (mm. 1–2) to a bass voice in the cadential idea (mm. 7–8), with the middle measures 3–6 being uncertain as to voice function. When we examine the subsequent A′ section, we see that Mozart clarifies the situation by introducing a full melody and accompaniment texture (Ex. 3.59b). Here, the melodic line, which is identical to that of the A section, clearly functions voice, thus concluding in measures 19–20 with a cadential melody that imitates a cadential bass line ($\hat{3}/\hat{4}/\hat{5}/\hat{1}$). To avoid parallel octaves in stages 2–3, Mozart alters the actual bass to ⑥–⑤–①. (To be sure, the final progression brings parallel octaves, but this is an acceptable license at the very close of a thematic unit.)

In some cases, the fundamental pitches of the cadential melody begin by being associated with a typical bass line, but then receive embellishments that effect a final stepwise resolution to $\hat{1}$, a procedure prohibited for a genuine cadential bass, which must leap directly from ⑤ to ①. Thus in Example 3.60, the bass-like melody $\hat{8}/\sharp\hat{4}/\hat{5}/\hat{1}$ sees an insertion of the leading tone (from the alto stream) just before the final harmony, which itself adds $\hat{2}$ as an appoggiatura to $\hat{1}$, thus strongly implying upper-voice cadential motion.

**Cudworth.** Midway through the twentieth century, the music historian Charles Cudworth identified a cadential "cliché" arising prominently in galant instrumental music and termed it the "*cadence galante*."[47] More recently, Gjerdingen, who recognizes a wider variety of galant cadential schemata, has honored this historian by labeling this schema the "Cudworth."[48] Though ubiquitous in the galant era, the Cudworth continues to appear now and then in works of the classical composers.

Characteristic of the schema is the rapidly falling scale from $\hat{7}$ down to $\hat{3}$,[49] with a slower continuation to $\hat{1}$, as seen clearly in measures 9–10 of Example 3.61.[50] Note that this pattern normally occurs within stages 2–4 of the cadence. If stage 1 is present, as in this example, the note that immediately precedes the leading tone is either $\hat{8}$ (as here) or $\hat{5}$. Inasmuch as the leading tone serves as an appoggiatura to $\hat{6}$—indeed, this embellishment is often notated specifically as such—we can recognize that the opening of the Cudworth employs the first two pitches ($\hat{8}$–$\hat{6}$ or $\hat{5}$–$\hat{6}$) of the tenor stream. Moreover, the Cudworth as a whole is an embellished version of Kaiser's *Kadenzmodell* ($\hat{8}$–$\hat{6}$–$\hat{3}$–$\hat{2}$–$\hat{1}$), as cited in note 40. In the classical style, the Cudworth most often appears either embellished in various ways or embedded within a broader melodic gesture, as in Example 3.61. In Example 3.62, the Cudworth is preceded by various chromatic embellishments, and the appoggiatura gestures are led down further to $\hat{1}$ for the onset of stage 3.

**Deceptive-Authentic Combinations.** In some more complicated cadential situations, we find a deceptive cadential

---

44. This texture, along with other conventional ones of the classical style, is discussed again later in sec. 3.4.2.1.

45. With this reading, I am not suggesting an actual tonicization of (let alone modulation to) the key of B major, an unlikely tonal relation to the home key of E minor.

46. Here, Mozart would seem to be writing in the spirit of the repetition/terminal-modification paradigm (see Chapter 1, sec. 1.1) by ensuring that the cadential idea of a theme differentiates itself from prior material, at least to a minimal extent.

47. Charles L Cudworth, "Cadence Galante: The Story of a Cliché," 176–82.

48. Gjerdingen, *Galant Style*, 146–49.

49. In one variant, the first note brings the seventh scale degree lowered by a half step ($\flat\hat{7}$); in another, the pattern starts on $\hat{6}$ with an eighth-note triplet descent.

50. The first part of this example, which is supported by the initial tonic of an ECP will be discussed in Chapter 5, sec. 5.1.2.11, "Cudworth"; the term "rocking" will be clarified in sec. 5.1.1.1 ("Rocking on the Tonic"). A number of other examples of ECPs will be treated in the present chapter when appropriate to the topic under consideration.

3.1. PERFECT AUTHENTIC CADENCE 77

EXAMPLE 3.59. Mozart, Violin Sonata in E Minor, K. 304, i, (a) mm. 1–8; (b) mm. 17–20.

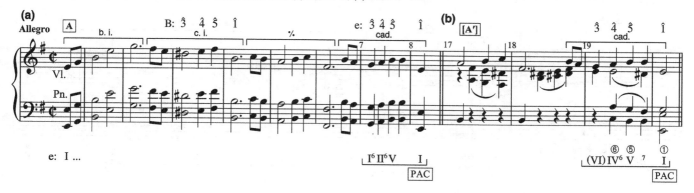

EXAMPLE 3.60. Haydn, String Quartet in F, Op. 74, no. 2, ii, mm. 6–8 (*ACF* Sup. 4.8).

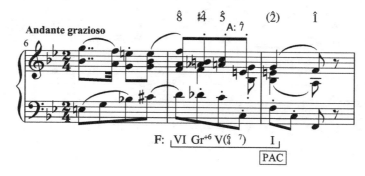

EXAMPLE 3.61. Haydn, Piano Sonata in B Minor, H. 32, ii, mm. 5–10 (*ACF* Sup. 5.24).

EXAMPLE 3.62. Mozart, Piano Sonata in B-flat, K. 333, ii, mm. 6–8 (*ACF* 3.10).

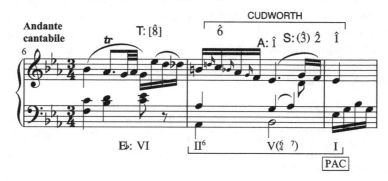

EXAMPLE 3.63. Haydn, Piano Sonata in F, H. 29, ii, mm. 3–6 (R = ½N) (*ACF* Sup. 5.18).

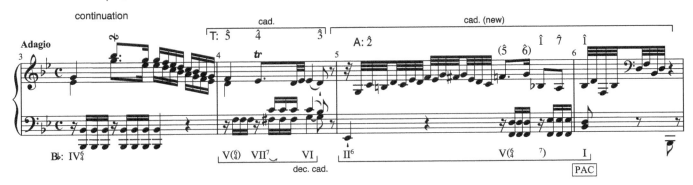

EXAMPLE 3.64. Mozart, Piano Trio in G, K. 564, ii, mm. 11–16 (*ACF* 8.11).

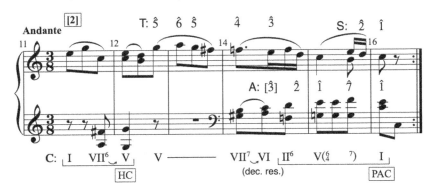

progression (DCP) and an immediately following authentic cadential progression (ACP) together supporting a single melodic pattern, which is distributed over the various stages of the two progressions. Example 3.63 is a case in point. The continuation phrase of the theme leads at m. 4 to an incomplete DCP, whose stages 3 and 4 support the tenor stream //$\hat{5}$–$\hat{4}$/3. There follows in measures 5–6 an ACP (also incomplete), whose stages 2–4 conclude the melodic descent with the alto stream /$\hat{2}$/$\hat{1}$–$\hat{7}$/$\hat{1}$. This second progression sees extensive melodic ornamentation within stage 2, and stages 3–4 bring, in diminution, what appears to be the complete successive combination $\hat{5}$–$\hat{6}$–$\hat{1}$–$\hat{7}$–$\hat{1}$. The first two degrees ($\hat{5}$ and $\hat{6}$), however, are not actually associated with their normal stages 1 and 2, but rather occur within stage 3a of the ACP.

Example 3.64 shows another case of this technique, though this time the deceptive progression is not actually cadential. Here, the second part of a small binary leads to an HC at measure 12, after which the dominant is further retained in measure 13, only to resolve deceptively in the next bar. A regular authentic cadence then closes the theme at measure 16.[51] Within this final four-measure phrase, the deceptive progression supports a complete varied tenor stream $\hat{5}$–$\hat{6}$–$\hat{5}$–$\hat{4}$–$\hat{3}$, while the following ACP supports a simultaneous combination of alto [$\hat{3}$]–$\hat{2}$–$\hat{1}$–$\hat{7}$–$\hat{1}$ and soprano $\hat{2}$–$\hat{1}$.[52] When we compare this cadence to the one that ends the first part of the binary, see again Example 3.43, we see that the final cadence of the theme is a remarkable variation (transposed up a fourth) on the earlier one, which brings a single cadential progression supporting a tenor combo.[53]

* * * * *

The theory of cadential melody outlined above is admittedly intricate and perhaps overly cumbersome. Indeed, a more efficient way of accounting for the diversity of PAC melodic patterns may yet be found. For the present, however, this attempt at classifying such patterns reveals at least that the phenomenon in question is indeed more complex than suggested by many theoretical accounts, which typically identify a simple $\hat{2}$–$\hat{1}$ or $\hat{7}$–$\hat{1}$ cadential melody. Above all, we learn that whereas we are accustomed to speaking of cadential melodies as "conventional" and "formulaic," the diversity of patterns employed by the classical composers calls into question such a simple description. In only a small number of cases, such as the successive combination of Example 3.40 (see also note 39), do we find the identical melodic configuration used in multiple themes. Much more often, the melody of a

---

51. Unlike the previous example, the deceptive resolution of the dominant in Ex. 3.64 (second eighth note of m. 14) does not create a deceptive cadence, primarily because the dominant is not a penultimate one; instead, it sustains the ultimate dominant of the HC.

52. The first pitch of the alto stream [$\hat{3}$] is placed in brackets because it precedes the onset of the ACP to which it is associated.

53. Additional DCP-ACP combinations will be considered in Chapter 4, sec. 4.1.2.5.

cadence—in all of its aspects (pitch, rhythm, texture)—is unique to the theme that it closes.

### 3.1.3. Function

The formal function of the various cadence types is extensively treated in my *Classical Form* and its textbook adaptation, *Analyzing Classical Form*. The purpose of this section (and the comparable ones for the IAC and HC below) is to summarize the standard functions of the PAC at various levels in the structural hierarchy of a movement. For more details, readers can consult these books (specific pages and examples are cited in the notes). In addition, I raise some new topics, ones not covered, or insufficiently considered, in these earlier works.

#### 3.1.3.1. Standard Functions of the PAC

As the syntactically strongest of the three cadential types, the PAC functions primarily to mark closure at the *thematic* levels of hierarchical structure.[54] By fully completing the ongoing harmonic and melodic processes of the theme, the appearance of this cadence effectively shuts down any expectations that something further should occur within the structural boundaries of the theme. Of course, a PAC may also generate expectations that a postcadential, closing section might occur or that a new thematic process might be initiated. Any one of these subsequent events, however, lies outside the formal boundaries of the theme proper.

As for the conventional theme types, the simple sentence and the compound sentence most often close with a PAC. The period form, with its two cadential articulations, typically uses the PAC only for the second cadence, never with its first (with one exception to be discussed later in sec. 3.3.5.1). The compound period seems always to close with a PAC.[55] The small ternary brings two PACs: one to end the A section, the other, the A′ section.[56] Of the two parts of the small binary, the first may close with a PAC (the HC is an alternative option), but the second must be a PAC.[57] In addition to concluding thematic structures, we sometimes encounter a PAC functioning with limited scope, especially in connection with a codetta of a closing section.[58]

Turning from individual themes in their own terms to the way in which a given theme itself functions within the larger structure of a movement, we can observe that in the full-movement forms of sonata, sonata without development, rondo, and concerto, a PAC primarily marks the closure of a main theme, a subordinate theme,[59] or a coda theme.[60] Now and then a PAC will arise within a development section as part of the pre-core or, more rarely, to end a core or core substitute (subordinate-themelike unit).[61] In rondo forms, the main theme appears always to close with a PAC (the HC or IAC seeming not to be an option). In concerto form, the opening and closing ritornellos end with a PAC in the home key; the subordinate-key ritornello usually closes with a PAC (naturally enough in the subordinate key), though sometimes this cadence will be bypassed in order to forge greater continuity into the development section.[62]

In the full-movement large ternary form, the PAC is used in its conventional manner to end the main theme and, occasionally, the interior theme; the latter, however, often fails to close with a PAC, ending instead with an HC or dominant arrival.[63] In the

---

54. In *CF*, 17, I spoke of two general categories of formal functions: *interthematic* functions (e.g., main theme, transition, subordinate theme), which comprise *intrathematic* functions (e.g., presentation, antecedent, continuation, cadential). I now prefer the simpler labels *thematic* functions and *phrase* functions, respectively (see *ACF*, 47). In the present study, see Chapter 2, sec. 2.2.1, for a more general discussion of the hierarchical levels associated with cadential closure.

55. I have yet to uncover a case of a compound period closing with the weaker IAC, but such a possibility exists theoretically.

56. Exceptionally, a small number of Haydn's small ternaries see the A section closing with an HC; see, e.g., Haydn, Symphony No. 100 ("Military"), ii, mm. 1–8 (with written-out repeat in mm. 9–16). The A′ section of this ternary is shown ahead in Chapter 8, Ex. 8.11.

Another kind of exception arises when, quite rarely, the A section fails to close cadentially; the ternary as a whole, however, receives cadential closure with a PAC at the end of the A′ section. One such case arises in Beethoven's Bagatelle in G, Op. 126, no. 1, m. 8 (and then m. 16 with the written-out repeat of the A section). When the A′ appears, the opening melody is now placed in the bass part, which is slightly modified to create a genuine PAC to close the entire theme at m. 35. This very late work by Beethoven, a harbinger of the "character piece" so typical of early Romantic practice, anticipates cadential manipulations that will be discussed in connection with movements by Schumann and Mendelssohn in Chapter 8, sec. 8.8, Ex. 8.15 and 8.16. Beethoven's Piano Sonata in C, Op. 2, no. 3, iv, m. 8, is another example of an A section that does not close cadentially. In this case, the complete small ternary also fails to end correctly when the A′ section "becomes" the transition; see the discussion of this unusual passage in *CF*, 131. Ex. 9.9, and *ACF*, 338–39, Ex. 11.18.

57. The IAC seems not to be employed in the various sections (or parts) of the small ternary (or small binary).

58. See Chapter 2, sec. 2.7 and Ex. 2.22.

59. With respect to a subordinate theme *group* containing multiple PACs, the theoretical utility of identifying only one of these as the "essential exposition closure" (EEC) or the "essential sonata closure" (ESC), as required by Hepokoski and Darcy (*Sonata Theory*, 18, 20), is a significant issue worthy of examination, but is one that more properly lies outside the scope of the present study. Suffice it to say that from the perspective of cadence developed here, a *syntactical* evaluation of cadential strength does not differentiate among any number of PACs—all are considered to have the same capacity for thematic closure. A *rhetorical* evaluation of cadential strength, however, does permit us to differentiate between PACs that are stronger or weaker based on a wide variety of parameters (dynamics, texture, metrical placement, etc.); see again, Chapter 2, sec. 2.11.

60. On coda theme, see *CF*, 179, 183, and *ACF*, 530.

61. On the use of a subordinate-themelike unit as a core substitute, see *CF*, 157, and *ACF*, 457.

62. See *CF*, chap. 17, and *ACF*, chap. 20.

63. On the closure of interior themes, see *CF*, 213–16, and *ACF*, 575–84. Interior themes, often lacking PAC closure, are also used in some rondo forms; see *CF*, 233, 238, and *ACF*, 653.

EXAMPLE 3.65. Haydn, String Quartet in A, Op. 20, no. 6, i, mm. 1–12.

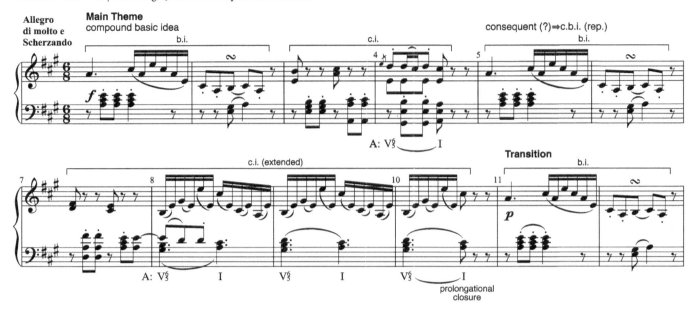

### 3.1.3.2. Exceptional Situations

Some exceptional situations arise in which an anticipated PAC fails to occur or in which a PAC appears in a place not normally expected. This section considers such departures from the norm in relation to some thematic functions in a number of full-movement forms. The standard cadential *deviations* of deceptive, evaded, and abandoned cadence, along with the dominant arrival, a deviation of the HC, will be treated in detail in the next chapter. What follows here deals with more unusual situations.

**Main Theme.** In the overwhelming majority of cases in the high classical style, the main theme of a sonata form (or sonata-related form) closes with some kind of cadence in the home key; indeed, we might even consider this to be a requirement of the form. As a result, any exception to the rule is noteworthy. In some cases, a putative main theme ends with a tonic prolongational progression, a noncadential situation that I term *prolongational closure*.[65] Consider, for instance, the main theme shown in Example 3.65. Following an opening compound basic idea in measures 1–4, the simple basic idea begins to be repeated at measure 5 in the manner of a consequent, but rather than closing this phrase with an expected PAC, Haydn stretches out for three bars (mm. 8–10) the $V^6_5$–I prolongational progression heard first at measure 4 closing the compound basic idea. A caesura in the second half of measure 10 prepares for another statement of the basic idea, which promises again to create a consequent phrase for the main theme. Instead, the passage (not shown) brings a new continuation that modulates to the subordinate key, as partially confirmed by an HC and standing on the dominant. Thus the structure beginning at measure 11 has all of the characteristics of a transition, as so labeled in the score. As a result, a syntactically adequate consequent of the main theme never emerges, and the theme ends instead at measure 10 with prolongational closure ($V^6_5$–I), though one strongly asserted through repetition.[66]

A somewhat more complicated situation arises when a distinct main theme, as a complete formal unit of some kind, cannot readily be identified. One such case occurs early in Mozart's "Facile" Sonata in C, i, a movement that is far from being "simple" from a formal perspective (Ex. 3.66).[67] The movement opens with a compound basic idea, followed by an extended continuation phrase (mm. 5–8) and an ECP leading to a home-key HC and standing on the dominant. The subordinate theme follows immediately (not shown).[68] Although we could perhaps consider the HC at measure 12 as ending the main theme, this would mean that the exposition lacks a transition, which rarely occurs.[69] But the formal loosening effected by the extended continuation and expanded cadential functions suggests that the music from measure 5 on projects a looser transition function. If so, main theme function would be reduced to the opening four bars. We

---

64. See *CF*, chap. 15, and *ACF*, chap. 18.

65. See below, sec. 3.5.1 for more examination of this idea.

66. I place the annotation "prolongational closure" at m. 10, even though it could be understood, retrospectively, at mm. 8 or 9. I favor the later bar because until we hear the caesura and the starting of something else (in m. 11), we do not necessarily think that the theme has ended: the prolongational progressions $V^6_5$–I in mm. 8 and 9 could easily have been followed by a cadential progression to make any type of cadence.

67. The annotations of "Prinner," as well as the designations of stages *a–d*, will be explained later in sec. 3.2.1.2.

68. For an analysis of the subordinate theme, see *ACF*, Ex. 12.1.

69. See *CF*, 211, and *ACF*, 592.

EXAMPLE 3.66. Mozart, Piano Sonata in C, K. 545, i, mm. 1–12.

would probably not want, however, to speak of this single phrase as a complete, discrete main theme, in that it consists exclusively of an initiating formal function (a compound basic idea).

We witness, therefore, a case of the main theme and transition functions *fusing* into a *single* thematic unit (mm. 1–12, annotated as "Main Theme/Transition") and understand that the former function fails to close cadentially.[70] As I discuss later in Chapter 7, such form-functional fusion is especially characteristic of the galant style, which more regularly omits cadential closure for a main theme than in the subsequent classical style.[71] The appearance of this technique in Mozart's sonata is probably owing to its strongly referencing the galant, where such fusion techniques abound, even though this is a "late" work by the composer.[72]

**Transition.** One of the more controversial aspects of my theory of classical form is its fundamental axiom that PAC closure is a central element of subordinate-theme functionality. Consequently, my theory denies, in principle, the possibility of a transition ending with a subordinate-key perfect authentic cadence (SK: PAC). The question then becomes: How do we handle cases where a *single* thematic unit not only brings about a modulation from the home key to the subordinate key but also confirms the latter key with a PAC? My solution is again to invoke the concept of form-functional fusion, in this case, a fusion of transition and subordinate-theme functions, thus holding on to the principal idea that a transition, per se, cannot end with an SK: PAC.[73] This position is countered by Hepokoski and Darcy's theory, which establishes this very cadential situation as a "third-level default" *medial caesura* (MC), thus explicitly allowing a transition to end with a PAC in the new key. The theoretical ramifications of this topic are too extensive to be treated here. Needless to say, though, high-classical compositional practice includes a small number of cases where a complete thematic unit—defined as a single group containing a full complement of initiating, medial, and ending functions—initially begins in the home key and ends with a PAC in the subordinate key. Seeing as we are so used to a *single* thematic unit having a *single* formal function, it is understandable that some

---

70. A fusion of main theme and transition occurs more commonly in a recapitulation than in an exposition; see *CF*, 165, and *ACF*, 502.

71. See Chapter 7, sec. 7.4.2.

72. Typical also of the galant style is the extensive use of the Prinner schema throughout the movement; see Gjerdingen, *Galant Style*, chap. 26. I return to this example in Chapter 7 in connection with Ex. 7.26, sec. 7.1.2.

73. As I discuss in *CF* (203), to speak of a transition ending with an SK: PAC "is to recognize authentic cadential closure as a legitimate deviation from the normal ending of a transition. But sanctioning this cadential possibility blurs a theoretical distinction fundamental to this study, namely, that the authentic cadential confirmation of a subordinate key is an essential criterion of the subordinate theme's function. It is thus theoretically more consistent to interpret such passages as cases of fusion than to risk confusing the fundamental characteristics of the interthematic [thematic] formal functions"; see also Caplin and Martin, "'Continuous Exposition,'" 23–28, 31–33.

theorists would want to label the kind of unit just described as a "transition," thus allowing this formal function to end with a PAC.[74] I would only counter that such a view oversimplifies the complexities offered by such a structure, and I would advocate recognizing in such cases a situation of form-functional fusion of transition and subordinate-theme functions.[75]

**Subordinate Theme.** As just discussed, the essential role in defining subordinate-theme function played by an SK: PAC means that any such theme identifiable in a sonata exposition or recapitulation must close with this cadence type. Some rondo forms feature what to all extent and purposes is a subordinate theme, but which fails to bring full confirmation of the subordinate key by means of a PAC.[76] Moreover, and very rarely, a subordinate theme of a sonata-form movement may lack its required PAC. In some cases, the theme may only end with an IAC.[77] In other cases, an authentic cadence of either type is entirely bypassed.[78] Both situations are clear departures from general classical principles.[79]

**A Section (Minuet Form).** In a modulating A section of the minuet form, one seemingly exceptional usage sees the appearance of a home-key PAC prior to the final cadence, a PAC in the subordinate key. In this situation, we can recognize that this *early PAC* marks the end of the main-theme function within the A section, while the subordinate-key PAC ends subordinate-theme function at the close of the section.[80]

**Development Section.** Unlike the exposition or recapitulation of the sonata form (and allied forms, such as the sonata-rondo and concerto), a development section has no predefined requirements for PAC closure. But the possibility of using that cadence arises in certain situations. For example, if the pre-core of the development is structured as a tight-knit, conventional theme (as occurs often with Mozart), that theme is likely to close with a PAC, either still in the subordinate key (from the exposition) or in one of the development keys (in a major-mode movement, VI, III, or II; in minor, IV or minor V).[81] We may also encounter a PAC at the end of a core substitute built like a subordinate theme, a technique favored by Haydn; such a unit will close with a PAC confirming one of the development keys.[82] This practice is somewhat of a holdover from the galant style, where development sections regularly end with a development-key PAC immediately prior to the onset of the recapitulation.[83]

## 3.2. Imperfect Authentic Cadence

The imperfect authentic cadence is defined as one whose harmonic processes are fully closed but whose melodic ones remain open by failing to conclude on the tonic scale degree in the soprano voice. Thus for the authentic cadence in general, the modifiers "perfect" and "imperfect" refer exclusively to the melodic dimension.[84] In all other respects, the IAC has the same morphology as the PAC. Form-functionally, the IAC can be considered a genuine cadence type because it is capable of effecting cadential closure (if not the strongest possible closure) to some complete thematic units. Such usage, however, is infrequent in the literature, being generally

---

74. Hepokoski and Darcy, *Sonata Theory*, 27–29; see also, Hepokoski, "Sonata Theory, Secondary Themes," 58–63. Given a fundamental assumption of their theory, namely that the absence of a medial caesura leads to the absence of a subordinate theme ("If there is no MC, there is no S"), it is understandable that Hepokoski and Darcy want to identify some SK: PACs as constituting a medial caesura. Nonetheless, from an experiential perspective not tied to their theoretical imperative, a concluding PAC MC creates an entirely different formal and aesthetic effect than a concluding HC MC. Whereas the latter sets up strong expectations for the start of a subordinate theme (one that would resolve the dominant of the MC), the former fully shuts down all ongoing formal processes, and although a subsequent thematic unit (their "real" S) may occur, the expectation for such a unit is not nearly as powerful as that following an HC MC. Moreover, whereas an HC ending a transition is usually followed by a postcadential standing on the dominant prior to the beginning of the subordinate theme, an SK: PAC MC rarely, if ever, has a postcadential closing section positioned before the onset of the next formal unit (their S). It is not clear, therefore, that these two cadential situations are sufficiently comparable to be embraced by the single category of "medial caesura."

75. For some specific examples, see *CF*, Ex. 13.8 and 13.9, and *ACF*, Ex. 12.16 and 12.17. See also Caplin and Martin, "'Continuous Exposition,'" Ex. 1, 8, 10, and 11. We argue this case with respect to Hepokoski and Darcy's idea of a "continuous exposition." Transition/subordinate-theme fusion is especially common in the galant style, as will be discussed in Chapter 7, sec. 7.4.2. It is therefore not surprising that L. Poundie Burstein readily identifies SK: PACs appearing midway through expositions by early Haydn and some other galant composers ("Mid-Section Cadences in Haydn's Sonata-Form Movements"; see also, L. Poundie Burstein, "Galant Expositions," 204–7. In line with Hepokoski and Darcy's theory, Burstein identifies the thematic unit closed by such cadences as a transition, thus explicitly allowing that thematic function to close with the third-level default MC. My form-functional approach, however, would recognize most all of these cadences as concluding a subordinate-theme function, sometimes in the form of a complete subordinate theme or sometimes as a case of transition/subordinate-theme fusion.

76. See *CF*, 233, 237, and *ACF*, 651.

77. See in Chapter 5, the discussion of Beethoven's "Hammerklavier" Sonata in Ex. 5.14, and esp. note 22.

78. See in Chapter 5, the discussion of Beethoven's Fifth Symphony finale, Ex. 5.71.

79. Hepokoski and Darcy also recognize a deformation in cases where an S-zone (in any sonata type, including rondo) fails to bring an EEC or ESC (*Sonata Theory*, 177).

80. On the early PAC, see *CF*, 221, and *ACF*, 614–15.

81. *CF*, 153, Ex. 10.13, and *ACF*, 444. Ex. 13.10. Though the expression "development key" is obviously applicable to actual development sections, we can also use the term more generally in the contexts of other formal units of a work, esp. those outside of the classical style.

82. *CF*, 157, Ex. 10.18, and *ACF*, 457, Ex. 13.16.

83. See Chapter 7, sec. 7.4.4.

84. This terminological usage is rooted largely in North American theoretical practice from at least the middle of the twentieth century. In British and French usage, a "perfect cadence" usually denotes any kind of authentic cadence, whereas an "imperfect cadence" refers to a half cadence. In some theoretical works, the label "imperfect" describes an authentic cadence whose last harmony is inverted (i.e., a final V–I$^6$ progression).

EXAMPLE 3.67. Beethoven, String Quartet in D, Op. 18, no. 3, i, mm. 37–39.

limited to the conclusion of a main theme in sonata form (see ahead, in sec. 3.2.2.3, "Ending a Complete Main Theme"). The IAC can also bring cadential closure to individual phrases within a theme, most often the antecedent of a period. In subordinate-theme contexts, the IAC is normally used to defer the required PAC, and thus functions, like deceptive and evaded cadences, to loosen the formal organization through extension and repetition.

### 3.2.1. Morphology

The material content of an IAC is largely the same as a PAC except that the soprano voice closes on the third scale degree.[85] In principle, the melody of an IAC could conclude on the fifth scale degree, but I have yet to find a clear-cut case in the classical literature. So for the purposes of the following discussion, I will consider the IAC to close only on $\hat{3}$. (At the end of this section, I discuss the complications arising in a small number of cases in which an authentic cadence seems to end with $\hat{5}$.)

Like the PAC, we can identify the same four stages comprising the harmonic content of the IAC. As well, the various harmonic options for each stage of the IAC are comparable to those of the PAC. Two differences, however, are notable. First, when the final melodic $\hat{3}$ is approached from $\hat{2}$ below, the dominant proper of stage 3 is frequently built as a triad, not as a seventh harmony.[86] This harmonic usage is perhaps owing to the composer wishing not to overemphasize $\hat{3}$ when the dissonant seventh resolves, as required, to that same scale degree in an inner voice. A second difference concerns the distinction between complete or incomplete cadential progressions. In the absence of reliable statistics, my general observations suggest that the IAC is more often incomplete compared to the PAC. Though no discernible syntactical difference obtains between complete or incomplete cadential progressions, in that both are fully capable of providing thematic closure, the former often projects a greater rhetorical strength.

Since the IAC tends not to be the final cadence of a theme, its projecting a weaker rhetorical effect is entirely fitting. The rest of this section will be devoted to the melodic content of the IAC, as this aspect primarily distinguishes it from the PAC.

#### 3.2.1.1. Basic Tenor Stream ($\hat{8}/\hat{6}/\hat{5}/\hat{3}$); Varied ($\hat{5}/\hat{6}/\hat{5}/\hat{3}$)

As noted in connection with the PAC, only one of its melodic patterns naturally effects closure on $\hat{3}$, namely, the *basic tenor*, $\hat{8}/\hat{6}/\hat{5}/\hat{3}$, or its varied form, $\hat{5}/\hat{6}/\hat{5}/\hat{3}$. When this pattern is used for a PAC, the melody of the final stage must be altered to obtain $\hat{1}$.[87] To create an IAC, the tenor stream can be used without alteration, and indeed, a good number of IACs in the literature employ this melodic pattern. Example 3.67 is a case in point. Though the melody is lightly embellished, the basic tenor emerges clearly in the upper voice. Note that the interval between $\hat{5}$ and $\hat{3}$ is filled in with a passing $\hat{4}$, in this case, as an appoggiatura at the start of stage 4. When a stage-3a cadential six-four is used (Ex. 3.68), then $\hat{4}$ will typically appear as the dissonant seventh in stage 3b.[88] One variant of the pattern sees the initial $\hat{8}$ of stage 1b replaced by $\flat\hat{7}$ (Ex. 3.69), due here to the use of V$^6_5$/IV as a chromatic substitute for I$^6$.

As mentioned before, the IAC often brings an incomplete cadential progression, such as that seen in Example 3.70, where stage 1 is omitted from the cadence. In this example, observe that stage 2 (upbeat to m. 81) supports $\hat{6}$, a component of the tenor pattern, which in this case passes over $\hat{5}$ to bring $\hat{4}$ within stage 3, resolving to $\hat{3}$ to complete the IAC. Note as well that stage 3 first brings $\hat{2}$ (downbeat of m. 81), which moves upward to obtain $\hat{4}$ of the tenor pattern. This $\hat{2}$ can be understood as the continuation of a (precadential) soprano line beginning at the upbeat of measure 79, which then leads to a complete stepwise descent (supported at first by the sequential progression), such that this $\hat{2}$ eventually descends to $\hat{1}$, now in an inner voice. We see, therefore, how the tenor stream ($\hat{6}$–$\hat{4}$–$\hat{3}$) has been placed over this soprano line in order to create an IAC rather than a PAC.

---

85. Up to now, the melodic dimension of the IAC has received little theoretical treatment, with the exception of Manfred Hermann Schmid's exhaustive catalogue of "falling third cadences" (*Terzkadenz*) ("Die 'Terzkadenz' als Zäsurformel im Werk Mozarts"). Most of his examples fit well my definition of an IAC, but many others are noncadential in my terms.

86. See ahead, Ex. 3.75–77, 3.81, and 3.88.

87. See Ex. 3.4a and 3.10.

88. The term "independent" placed below the cadence label in this example (and others to be encountered below), refers to a later discussion of the IAC's formal function (sec. 3.2.2.1).

EXAMPLE 3.68. Mozart, Violin Sonata in B-flat, K. 454, ii, mm. 3–6 (*ACF* 6.17).

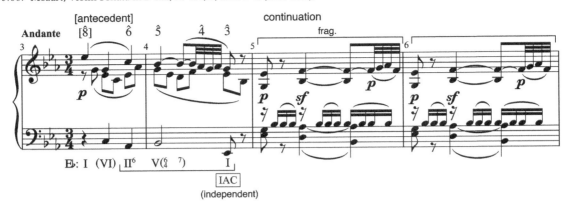

EXAMPLE 3.69. Haydn, Piano Sonata in D, H. 33, i, mm. 5–8 (*ACF* Sup. 5.21).

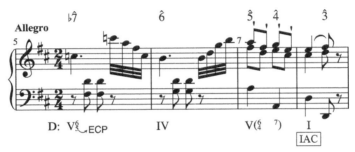

EXAMPLE 3.70. Mozart, Allegro and Andante in F Minor for Organ, K. 608, mm. 79–82 (*ACF* 4.18).

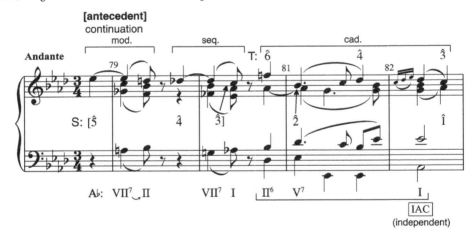

EXAMPLE 3.71. Mozart, Piano Sonata in C, K. 330, i, mm. 4–8 (*ACF* 2.14).

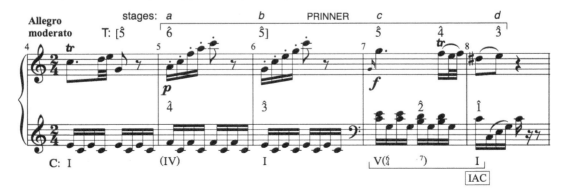

EXAMPLE 3.72. Mozart, Violin Sonata in E Minor, K. 304, i, mm. 29–40 (*ACF* 11.9).

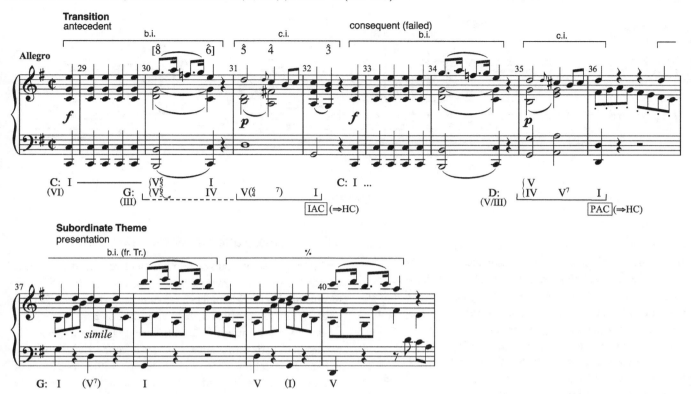

EXAMPLE 3.73. Prinner prototype.

The cadential progression of an IAC can be especially incomplete when both stages 1 and 2 are omitted, as seen in Example 3.71. As we have also discussed, moreover, the complete melodic stream—here, $\hat{5}/\hat{6}/\hat{5}$-$\hat{4}/\hat{3}$—can still be heard when taking the precadential material of measures 4–6 into account.[89] A similar, but more complicated, case arises in Example 3.72. At the start of the transition section of a sonata form, an initial two-measure basic idea in C major brings about a quick modulation to G major, confirmed by an IAC.[90] The cadential material itself occupies measures 31 and 32 (a contrasting idea following the basic idea) and consists of stages 3 and 4, which contains the second half of the tenor stream's melody, $\hat{5}$–$\hat{4}$–$\hat{3}$. Within the preceding basic idea, we can also find the first two elements of the stream, $\hat{8}$–$\hat{6}$, even supported by the harmonies of stages 1b ($V^6_5$/IV) and 2 (IV) of the G-major cadence. However, in the harmonic context of the basic idea, supported by a tonic prolongation in C major, we do not particularly hear these opening two stages as such; only in retrospect (as indicted by the dashed bracket) do we understand those harmonies completing the cadential progression in G. (The rest of this example will be discussed later in sec. 3.3.5.1.)

### 3.2.1.2. Prinner Cadence

One of the most important galant schemata identified by Gjerdingen is the "Prinner" (named after a rather obscure seventeenth-century theorist).[91] The schema (Ex. 3.73) brings a stepwise melodic descent from $\hat{6}$ to $\hat{3}$; the supporting bass line usually features a stepwise descent from ④ to ①, creating parallel thirds between the principal voices. The schema thus contains four stages (*a–d*), best defined as one stage for each note of the melodic pattern ($\hat{6}$–$\hat{3}$).[92] A clear example of the full schema is

---

89. The "Prinner" label, and the indication of stages *a–d* will be explained momentarily.

90. This cadence itself will then be reinterpreted as a kind of HC, as discussed ahead in sec. 3.3.5.1.

91. Gjerdingen, *Galant Style*, chap. 3.

92. In order to avoid confusion with the four stages of an authentic cadence, I use italicized letters for the stages of the Prinner schema. Unlike the cadence schema, in which the stages correspond to the harmonic content, the stages of the Prinner are best established in terms of its melodic component, which tends to be a stable element of the schema, as opposed to the supporting harmonies, which can vary extensively.

EXAMPLE 3.74. Haydn, Symphony No. 42 in D, ii, mm. 1–8.

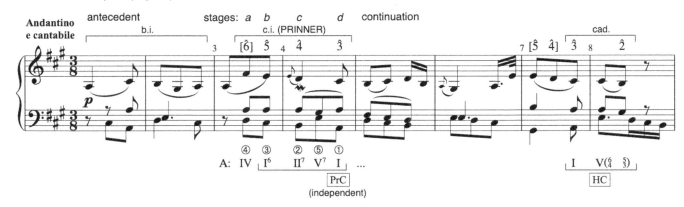

seen earlier in Example 3.66, measures 5–8. Here, the conclusion of the Prinner does not yield a cadence, because the schema's third stage *c* (m. 7) holds a noncadential VII$^6$.[93] If, however, as in Example 3.74 (m. 4), a bass ⑤, supporting a cadential dominant, is included in stage *c* (following ② and still supporting $\hat{4}$), then the conditions obtain for a genuine cadence. I term this mode of closure a *Prinner cadence* (PrC), a variant of the IAC.[94]

One might initially think that the melody $\hat{6}$-$\hat{5}$-$\hat{4}$-$\hat{3}$ of the PrC in Example 3.74 is a version of the tenor pattern $\hat{8}/\hat{6}/\hat{5}$-$\hat{4}/\hat{3}$; however, even if most of the same scale degrees are involved, their relation to the harmonies of the cadential progression differs. In the Prinner cadence, the initial $\hat{6}$ is supported on the second beat of measure 3 by a subdominant that *precedes* the onset of the cadential progression; $\hat{5}$ is found in the first cadential stage; $\hat{4}$ is included in both stages 2 and 3; and the final $\hat{3}$ supported by the stage-4 tonic. In other words, the first stage (*a*) of the Prinner schema (IV supporting $\hat{6}$) does not belong to the cadential progression proper, which, in the case of Example 3.74, only begins with the upbeat to measure 4. A similar situation is found in the earlier Example 3.71, except that here, the first two stages of the Prinner schema (mm. 5–6) are clearly seen as prolongational, with the very incomplete cadential progression arising in stages *c* and *d* (mm. 7–8). We thus clearly observe a Prinner melody, but the supporting bass line has been altered to yield a regular IAC, not a PrC variant. (For additional cases of the Prinner cadence, see ahead, Ex. 3.91, 3.92, and 3.145.)

### 3.2.1.3. Other Patterns; Melodic Diversion

An IAC may arise by means of the other standard cadential melodies, namely the simple, soprano, alto, and bass patterns. In such cases, the melodic line, which implies a resolution to $\hat{1}$ (to create a PAC) is *diverted* from its normal path in order to close on $\hat{3}$.[95]

**Basic Simple Pattern ($\hat{3}/\hat{2}/\hat{2}/\hat{3}$); Varied ($\hat{1}/\hat{2}/\hat{2}/\hat{3}$).** The simple pattern in its basic form seems to be rare in connection to the IAC, in that I have not uncovered a clear example within the corpus of works consulted for this study. Some cases, however, can perhaps be related to the varied version of the pattern ($\hat{1}/\hat{2}/\hat{2}/\hat{1}$), where the final pitch is diverted from $\hat{1}$ to $\hat{3}$, thus producing $\hat{1}/\hat{2}/\hat{2}/\hat{3}$. Stage 2 also seems normally to be omitted in these cases (thus $\hat{1}//\hat{2}/\hat{3}$), as seen in Example 3.75, measures 15–16. Note that in this period form, the IAC is matched by a closing PAC (m. 20) based on the same varied simple pattern ($\hat{1}//\hat{2}/\hat{1}$), though with light embellishments in measure 19 that touch on the tenor ($\hat{4}$) and alto ($\hat{7}$) streams.

**Basic Soprano ($\hat{5}/\hat{4}/\hat{2}/\hat{3}$); Varied ($\hat{3}/\hat{4}/\hat{2}/\hat{3}$).** A good number of IAC melodies employ the basic soprano pattern (Ex. 3.76, mm. 23–24). Though rather embellished in stages 1 and 2, the IAC in this example brings an identifiable soprano whose final pitch is diverted to $\hat{3}$. Again, a matching PAC four bars later (mm. 27–28) brings the same pattern, now in its normal form closing on $\hat{1}$.[96] Note that within the embellishments of this cadential melody we can also discern elements of the tenor stream (//$\hat{5}/(\hat{4})$-$\hat{3}$) that further supports the diversion up to $\hat{3}$. The same pattern also appears in Example 3.77, but here we might want to see the varied soprano

---

93. An additional Prinner is also found in the preceding mm. 3–4. Here, though, the bass line is significantly altered (①–⑦–①) to project the strong impression of a tonic prolongation, which supports the contrasting idea of the initiating compound basic idea.

94. The rest of this passage will be discussed later when considering the relative syntactical strength (or weight) of the cadential types; see sec. 3.3.4.1, "Periodic Forms." I discuss the Prinner cadence in more detail in Chapter 7, sec. 7.1.2; see also William E. Caplin, "Harmony and Cadence in Gjerdingen's 'Prinner.' " For a study that rejects the Prinner cadence as a genuinely cadential subtype of an IAC, see MacKay, "Declassifying the IAC," 14–15.

95. Markus Neuwirth thus distinguishes between two kinds of IAC: one that implies a melodic resolution to $\hat{3}$ and another that promises a resolution to $\hat{1}$ (thus proposing a PAC) but that is instead diverted up to $\hat{3}$ ("*Fuggir La Cadenza*, or, the Art of Avoiding Cadential Closure: Physiognomy and Functions of Deceptive Cadences in the Classical Repertoire," 129). In a very recent article specifically devoted to the IAC, Xieyi (Abby) Zhang further develops the significance of this distinction ("Apparently Imperfect: On the Analytical Issues of the IAC," 195). This important study treats many of the issues associated with the IAC that I develop in the present chapter, which was completed prior to the appearance of Zhang's article.

96. The words "way station" placed below the IAC in this example (and several others that follow) refer to the formal function of this cadence as discussed later in sec. 3.2.2.2.

EXAMPLE 3.75. Mozart, Piano Sonata in F, K. 332, i, mm. 13–20 (*ACF* 10.15).

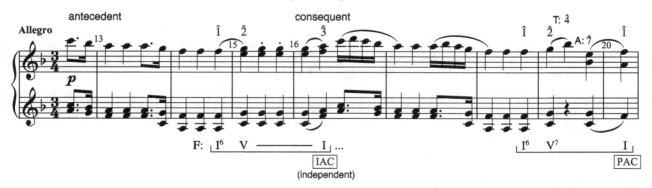

EXAMPLE 3.76. Mozart, Violin Sonata in E-flat, K. 481, ii, mm. 21–28 (*ACF* 19.12).

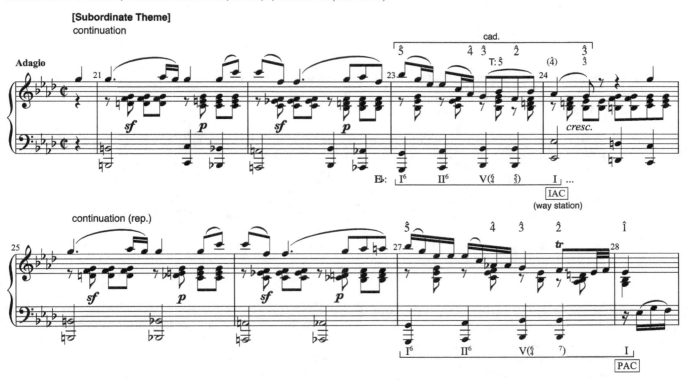

EXAMPLE 3.77. Beethoven, Piano Sonata in C Minor, Op. 111, ii, mm. 13–16 (*ACF* Sup. 8.15).

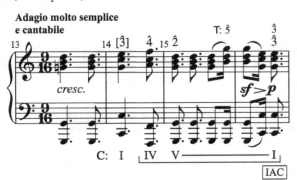

($\hat{3}/\hat{4}/\hat{2}/\hat{1}$) at play, since its initial pitch $\hat{3}$ appears in the tonic harmony (m. 14) that precedes the onset of the cadential progression proper. Again, we see the cadential melody touching on the tenor stream ($\hat{5}$) at the end of measure 15.

**Basic Alto ($\hat{3}/\hat{2}/\hat{7}/\hat{3}$); Varied ($\hat{1}/\hat{2}/\hat{7}/\hat{3}$).** The alto pattern is rarely used at the basis of an IAC melody because its penultimate pitch $\hat{7}$, the leading tone, demands resolution to $\hat{1}$, and so the melody is not easily diverted to $\hat{3}$. One such case might be seen to arise in Example 3.78.[97] Here, the extensive scalar motion

---

97. Each phrase in the example is labeled *continuation⇒cadential* (read "continuation becomes cadential"). Such a phrase initially projects continuation function (following some kind of initiating phrase), but when we understand retrospectively that the phrase as a whole is supported by an ECP, we reinterpret the phrase as also expressing cadential function in its entirety; see *CF*, 45–47, and *ACF*, 60–63.

EXAMPLE 3.78. Haydn, Piano Sonata in E, H. 31, i, mm. 5–8 (R = ½N) (*ACF* 6.18).

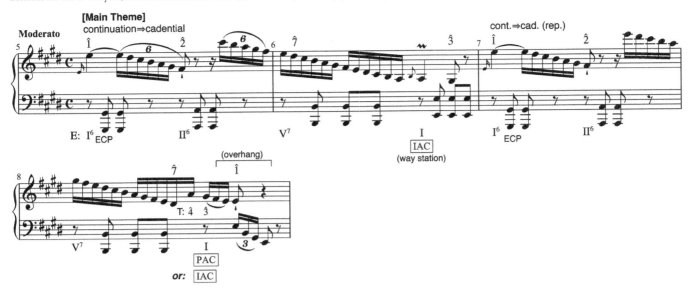

EXAMPLE 3.79. Beethoven, Piano Sonata in C Minor, Op. 10, no. 1, i, mm. 70–76 (R = 2N) (*ACF* 12.2).

surely obscures the underlying pattern. Focusing on the metrical emphasis accorded to beats 1 and 3 of measures 5 and 6, we can perhaps recognize the varied alto stream $\hat{1}/\hat{2}/\hat{7}/\hat{3}$. As a result of the scalar embellishments, the awkward gap between $\hat{7}$ and $\hat{3}$ is filled in with surface melodic activity. When the cadential idea is repeated to bring a closing PAC, the gap now appears on the very foreground (aided by a reference to the tenor stream) at the end of beat 2 in measure 8. The gap is then filled in immediately by additional melodic motion to achieve a concluding $\hat{1}$ for the PAC.[98]

**Bass Melodic Pattern.** The melody of an IAC may, on occasion, double the bass line, though in order to create a genuine IAC, the two voices must separate toward the end of the pattern. In Example 3.79, an expanded cadential progression begins at measure 70 with the melody in the following bar (third beat) replicating the bass stream. Toward its close (m. 74), however, the melodic $\hat{5}$ (stage 3a) is deflected toward $\hat{3}$ via a passing $\hat{4}$ in stage 3b, thus creating an IAC (and in so doing, invoking the tenor stream).

**Cudworth.** The Cudworth schema can also be diverted to close with an IAC, as shown in Example 3.80a, measures 2–4 (parts b and c will be discussed shortly).[99] Here the Cudworth literally begins at stage 2, having emerged from $\hat{8}$ in stage 1 and continuing on with $\hat{3}$–$\hat{2}$ in stage 3. The melodic line in measure 4 then ascends to $\hat{3}$ in stage 4 (via a passing ♯$\hat{2}$). Note the extensive melodic embellishment within the dominant proper (m. 3), whose upward motion is balanced by a another Cudworth descent.

### 3.2.1.4. Combined Patterns

As discussed in connection with the melodic content of the PAC, elements of two or more patterns can be combined successively. The most frequently used pattern of this type is the tenor combo $\hat{5}/\hat{6}/\hat{1}$–$\hat{2}/\hat{1}$.[100] Example 3.81 shows how this

---

98. The alternative of seeing this final cadence as an IAC will be raised in Chapter 7, sec. 7.1.4, when discussing H. C. Koch's concept of melodic *overhang*, an idea already mentioned in Chapter 2, sec. 2.5, and note 100.

99. Measures 6–10 will be discussed later, in sec. 3.3.5.1 on the "reinterpreted half cadence." The bass-line melody of the theme shown in Ex. 3.80a was also discussed in Chapter 2, Ex. 2.14.

100. For earlier examples of this pattern, see Ex. 3.43 and 3.44. To avoid cluttering the annotations, I will no longer routinely label the individual streams (e.g., T:, A:) of the combined patterns, except on occasion to highlight a particular point made in the text.

3.2. IMPERFECT AUTHENTIC CADENCE    89

EXAMPLE 3.80. Mozart, Piano Trio in B-flat, K. 502, ii, (a) mm. 1–10; (b) mm. 14–16; (c) mm. 18–20 (*ACF* 6.8).

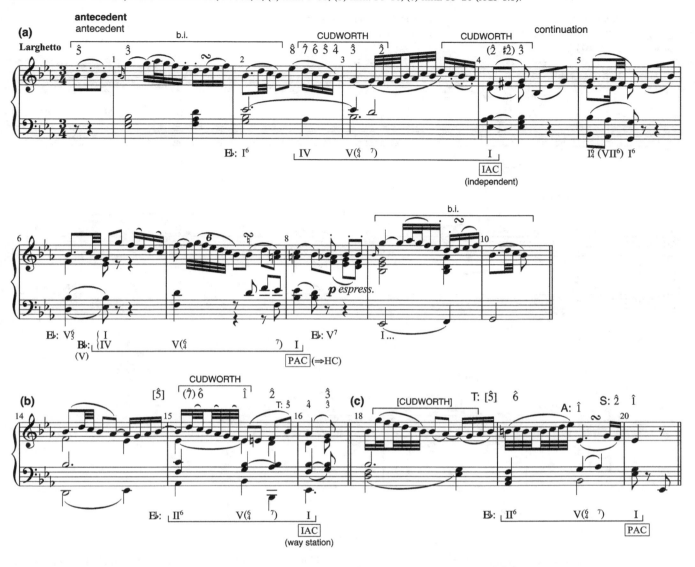

EXAMPLE 3.81. Beethoven, Piano Sonata in B-flat, Op. 22, iv, mm. 12–16 (*ACF* 6.15).

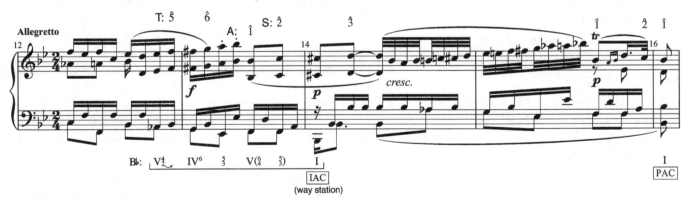

pattern can be diverted to close on $\hat{3}$, thus creating an IAC at measure 14. With the repetition of the cadential idea, the extensive embellishment created by the ascending chromatic line obliterates any clear melodic profile for the first two stages, but stages 3 and 4 of the pattern emerge at the end to create the matching PAC.

Another case of this diverted pattern arises in Example 3.80b. Here, the $\hat{6}$ of stage 2 (m. 15) is embellished by an appoggiatura

EXAMPLE 3.82. Beethoven, Violin Sonata in F ("Spring"), Op. 24, iv, mm. 25–38.

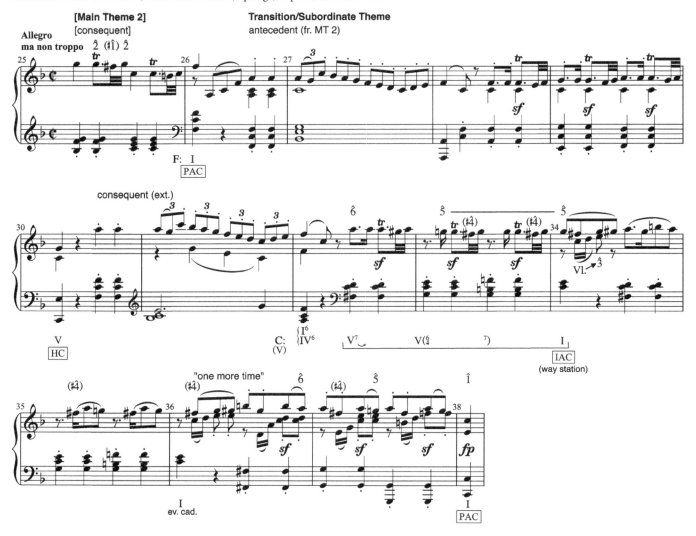

$\hat{7}$, which can also be seen to initiate a Cudworth-like descent that fills in the gap between $\hat{6}$ and $\hat{1}$ (thus referencing a similar Cudworth in the earlier-appearing IAC shown in Ex. 3.80a, mm. 2–3).[101] The matching PAC in Example 3.80c again brings the tenor combo to fully close the theme (m. 20).[102]

### 3.2.1.5. Ending on $\hat{5}$?

In that the IAC is fundamentally conceived as leaving its melodic processes open while its harmonic ones are fully closed, most definitions of this cadence type allow it to conclude melodically on the fifth scale degree ($\hat{5}$), albeit sometimes conceding that this ending is seldom encountered.[103] An examination of the classical literature reveals that few such cadences actually arise and that most of those seeming to end in this manner offer other ways of understanding how the dominant scale degree ends up in the highest sounding voice. After all, none of the melodic patterns that we have observed concludes on $\hat{5}$ or even provides an obvious way of diverting its melodic line up to that degree, other than by an awkward leaping motion. The one exception is the tenor stream ($\hat{8}/\hat{6}/\hat{5}$–($\hat{4}$)/$\hat{3}$), whose $\hat{5}$ at stage 3 could be retained into stage 4, thus yielding $\hat{8}/\hat{6}/\hat{5}/\hat{5}$.

Among the works analyzed for this study, only five cases arise where we might want to identify an IAC ($\hat{5}$) (i.e., an IAC ending on

---

101. Note again in Ex. 3.80b a reference to the conclusion of the tenor stream $\hat{5}$–$\hat{4}$–$\hat{3}$ as an embellishment of the diversion.

102. A final Cudworth reference in the broad melodic descent of m. 18 occurs prior to the onset of the actual cadential idea. All of the Cudworth configurations in this theme ultimately arise from filling in the melodic gap B♭4–G5 ($\hat{5}$–$\hat{3}$) opened up at the theme's very beginning, Ex. 3.80a.

103. See, e.g., Aldwell, Schachter, and Cadwallader, *Harmony & Voice Leading*, 118. My own definitions in some previous writings mention $\hat{5}$ as a "rare" option for melodic closure in an IAC (*CF*, 43, and "The Classical Cadence," 57, note 12). In *ACF*, 56, I no longer include $\hat{5}$ as an option. As early as the turn of the eighteenth century, a thorough-bass manual by Georg Muffat specifically characterizes the closing of a simple cadence (*cadentia simplex*) on the fifth degree as "bad" (*schlecht*) (*An Essay on Thoroughbass [Regulae Concentuum Partiturae, 1699]*, 108–109). I thank Edward Klorman for pointing me to this source.

EXAMPLE 3.83. Beethoven, Symphony No. 7 in A, Op. 92, ii, (a) mm. 1–10; (b) mm. 23–26.

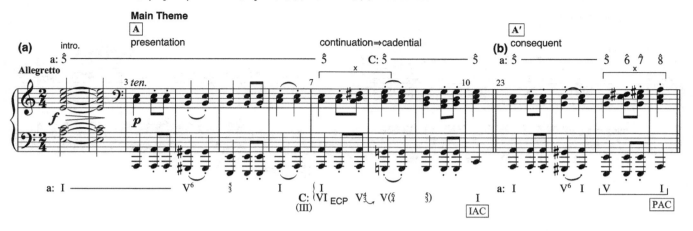

EXAMPLE 3.84. Haydn, String Quartet in D, Op. 50, no. 6, iii, mm. 1–8.

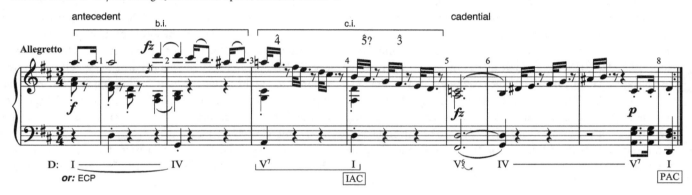

the fifth degree). The first case seems to be the most convincing, while the remaining ones pose some intriguing challenges for interpretation. Let us begin with Example 3.82, in which an IAC appears within a process of transition/subordinate-theme fusion. A second main theme, built as a tight-knit period, closes with an HK: PAC at measure 26. The theme then begins to be repeated. The opening antecedent (mm. 27–30) is identical to that of the second main theme proper. But the consequent is now altered to modulate quickly to the dominant region, initially confirmed by the IAC at measure 34. The melodic content engages the tenor stream (beginning with stage 2), and as just discussed, $\hat{5}$ of stage 3 is held through stage 4, thus bringing a rare IAC ($\hat{5}$). A repetition of the cadential idea in measures 35–36 tries for another cadence, though the absence of an actual melodic resolution on the downbeat of measure 36 prompts us to hear an evaded cadence instead of a genuine cadence. A "one-more-time" repetition of the same idea finally achieves PAC closure to fully confirm the subordinate key, thus bringing an end to the transition/subordinate-theme fusion, whose cadential extensions via the IAC and evaded cadence are typical of subordinate-theme structure.[104] (A sudden shift to C minor then begins a second subordinate theme, whose cadential complications will be treated later in Ex. 3.151.)

The use of $\hat{5}$ to close the IAC in measure 34 seems indisputable. We can likely understand the reason for this exceptional circumstance in the motivic emphasis that Beethoven accords to G ($\hat{5}$) by means of its embellishing lower neighbor, F♯ (♯$\hat{4}$). Indeed, the embellishment of this pitch persists up to the PAC in measure 38.[105] At the same time, it is interesting to observe that the violin enters the fray with a brief melodic snippet in measure 34 that ends on $\hat{3}$, the pitch that we would have expected to be the melodic goal of a normal IAC.

A second case of an IAC ($\hat{5}$) (Ex. 3.83a) is also explainable on motivic grounds. In this famous theme, built as a small ternary, Beethoven emphasizes $\hat{5}$ from the very beginning, first in A minor, then in C major (HK: III), when the continuation⇒cadential phrase (mm. 7–10) concludes with an IAC ($\hat{5}$). In fact, this scale degree is highlighted throughout the movement, and so the IAC ($\hat{5}$) is just one manifestation of this broader motivic process.[106] Another motivic detail might also play a role in this unusual IAC

---

104. Schmalfeldt's notion of the one-more-time technique, introduced in Chapter 2 (see note 169), is discussed in detail in Chapter 4, sec. 4.2.2.2.

105. The G–F♯–G gesture even appears earlier in the final cadence of main theme 2, m. 25, though in the home key with different scale degrees ($\hat{2}$–♯$\hat{1}$–$\hat{2}$).

106. Even the introductory chord in the winds, a literal I$^6_4$, finds $\hat{5}$ at the top and bottom of the sonority. I analyze this harmony as a root-position tonic, however, because the low E (in the second horn) is unlikely to be heard as a functional bass.

EXAMPLE 3.85. Beethoven, Piano Sonata in G, Op. 31, no. 1, ii, mm. 39–42 (*ACF* 17.16).

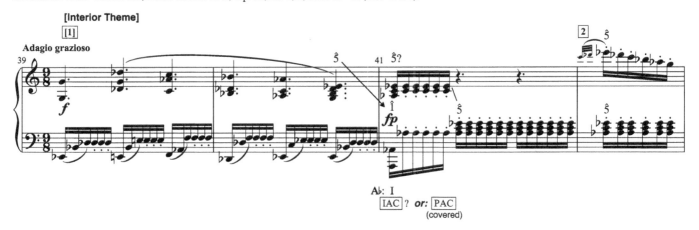

formation. As a way of connecting $\hat{5}$ in A minor to $\hat{5}$ in C major, Beethoven introduces a rising stepwise motive "x" (mm. 7–8); in the A′ section of the theme (Ex. 3.83b), he then brings back motive "x" in order to connect $\hat{5}$ with $\hat{8}$ of the concluding PAC. The earlier IAC ($\hat{5}$) thus helps forge this motivic connection, while also bringing a modicum of melodic activity to the A section.[107]

The remaining three cases of potentially $\hat{5}$-ending IACs are more difficult to understand. In Example 3.84, we encounter the opening section of a minuet, whose formal type seems to be a hybrid (antecedent + cadential). If we want to identify a cadence concluding the opening antecedent, we might see an IAC in measure 4 that ends with a melodic $\hat{5}$, which not only appears metrically strong within that bar but is also coordinated with the entrance of ① in the bass voice. Given the wholesale scalar line that descends throughout measures 3 and 4, however, it is not obvious that we should pick out $\hat{5}$ as the principal melodic goal of the phrase. Indeed, when we consider that the downbeat in the previous bar brings $\hat{4}$ supported by a dominant seventh, then we would hardly expect that scale degree to resolve by ascending to $\hat{5}$, in violation of basic voice-leading principles. Instead, we would be more inclined to hear $\hat{3}$ on the second beat of measure 4 as the true resolution of this dissonance, and thus recognize a standard IAC closing on $\hat{3}$.[108]

Another problematic case arises in Example 3.85. Here we find an IAC that seems to end on $\hat{5}$ in the course of an interior theme of the full-movement large ternary form. The cadence in question concludes (at m. 41) part 1 of the small binary residing at the basis of this interior theme. Note that throughout this part, the left-hand accompanimental figure consists of individual notes in sixteenth-note rhythm. At the cadence, the accompaniment continues in sixteenth notes, but now in the form of block chords.

The highest note of these chords is E♭, $\hat{5}$ of A-flat, the key in which the first parts ends and in which the second part begins. Since the first section of any interior theme would ordinarily conclude with either a PAC or HC, the use of an apparent IAC is highly exceptional.[109] Therefore we might wonder whether a better interpretation is to see the actual melodic line moving to A♭, in an inner part, to effect a normal PAC, while the notes C and E♭, lying above this melodic closure, represent accompanimental voices in the newly emerging chordal texture.[110]

A similar IAC ($\hat{5}$) closes the first part of a small binary form shown in Example 3.86, measures 10–12. The opening antecedent ends at measure 6 with an HC, whose melody has been "stuck" on $\hat{5}$ since the beginning of measure 5. As we will discuss later in this chapter, such melodic endings are, if not so common, entirely possible with an HC (see ahead, Ex. 3.110). Within the consequent, the cadential melody (mm. 10–13) begins with the tenor stream $\hat{8}$–$\hat{6}$–$\hat{5}$ for the first three stages, but then it too gets stuck on $\hat{5}$ throughout stage 3, never dropping to $\hat{3}$ as called for by the standard pattern.[111] To be sure, we could merely find this example to be a simple case of an IAC ($\hat{5}$), but when we take the broader formal situation into account, we recall that, just like the previous example, the first part of a small binary form almost always closes with either a PAC or an HC, not with an IAC. With this perspective in mind, we might then wonder whether the repeated E♭s in the upper part of measures 11–12 represent another pedal, one which has been placed above the genuine soprano voice. The latter voice is found in an inner part of the chords, thus referencing a varied soprano stream $\hat{3}/\hat{4}/\hat{2}/\hat{1}$ (as annotated in the score) for a more normative PAC. What seems to motivate

---

107. The B section of the theme (not shown) also exploits motive "x", so that its final use as a cadential gesture is especially satisfying.

108. Mirka, appealing to Koch's theories of phrase structure, speaks of an "overridden caesura" in connection with m. 4 (but also in connection with m. 6) ("Punctuation and Sense," 257–58). I revisit this example in Chapter 5 on cadential expansions (sec. 5.5), considering the appropriateness of even speaking of a formal cadence in m. 4 in light of a possible ECP supporting the entire first phrase.

109. A similar situation arises in Ex. 3.83, m. 10, seeing as the A section of a small ternary rarely closes with an IAC.

110. I will define this situation as a "covered cadence" in a later section of this chapter (sec. 3.4.2.3).

111. I am reading the pedal point ⑤ in mm. 9 and 10 as an embellishment of the true bass voice residing in the upper line of the left-hand part; otherwise, we could not speak of a genuine cadential progression throughout these measures.

EXAMPLE 3.86. Beethoven, Piano Sonata in A-flat, Op. 26, iv, mm. 3–12 (*ACF* Sup. 8.7).

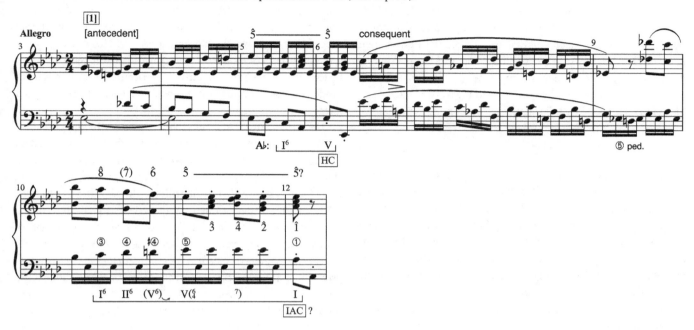

Beethoven to write this unusual cadence is his wish to maintain the same emphasis on $\hat{5}$ in the authentic cadence as he had given to the previous HC at measure 4.[112]

As we have seen, all of the five cases of IACs that seem to close on $\hat{5}$ are by no means straightforward: each brings something special with respect to motive, melody, or texture that challenges a simple interpretation of an IAC. Clearly the topic requires further research either to confirm our initial impression that an IAC ($\hat{5}$) is a highly exceptional situation, or to suggest that, while uncommon, this melodic close is nonetheless a standard form of the cadence. For the time being, we can note that the normative ending of an IAC melody is the third degree, issuing as the final pitch of the basic tenor or arising from a melodic diversion in one of the other melodic patterns applicable to an authentic cadence.[113]

### 3.2.2. Function

The IAC normally functions as a temporary goal of a thematic process in one of two ways: (1) as an *independent* cadence closing the antecedent phrase of a simple four-measure period (or periodic hybrid), akin to an HC; or (2) as a *way station* for an expected PAC toward the end of a theme, usually a subordinate theme, but sometimes a main theme. The two cases are similar in that for both, the IAC is followed by a more conclusive PAC. They differ in their formal effect, however, because in the first case, the approaching cadence does not imply a PAC—we do not expect that the strongest mode of closure will occur after only four bars of a simple theme. In the second case, on the contrary, we are waiting for a promised PAC, one that fails to materialize due to the appearance of the IAC. This cadence type may also arise in a variety of other formal contexts, such as the end of a compound antecedent, as the real end of a theme, and as a cadence of limited scope.

#### 3.2.2.1. Independent IAC

Most antecedent phrases of a periodic theme type (either simple or compound) conclude with an HC, thus bringing a form of weak ending that fails to fully close both the harmonic and melodic processes of the theme. A significant minority of such phrases may end with an IAC, whereby harmonic closure is complete but the melody remains active on $\hat{3}$. In that this cadence exists on its own and not as a substitute for an implied PAC, we can speak of the IAC as *independent*.[114] To be sure, any IAC tends to imply that a PAC will eventually occur; however, the sense of cadential independence here is associated with the IAC appearing at a moment in time that would not ordinarily

---

112. The second part of the binary also emphasizes an upper $\hat{5}$, but this time in a precadential position (see Ex. 3.48, m. 26), such that the melody ultimately steps down to $\hat{1}$ during the cadential idea proper in mm. 27–28.

113. For three nineteenth-century cases of IAC ($\hat{5}$), see ahead Ex. 8.34, m. 27, Ex. 8.43, m. 21, and Ex. 9.55c, m. 700.

114. In the course of this study, we will encounter two additional formal contexts in which I invoke the idea of cadential "independence." One involves the function of cadence in fugal composition, where I identify an *independent cadence* as one that stands apart from a fugal subject (see Chapter 6, sec. 6.4.3); the second involves cases of *independent plagal closure*, which arises in contexts that are relatively free from any prior cadential expression (see Chapter 9, sec. 9.3.2.2). To be sure, it is not ideal to use the same locution ("independent") for three different cadential-formal circumstances. I believe, however, that they are sufficiently distinct to avoid serious confusion; when in doubt, the reader is encouraged to consult the "Glossary of Terms" at the back of this book.

call for a PAC.¹¹⁵ As the opening phrase of a multi-phrase thematic unit, the listener has little cause to believe that a PAC will occur at the end of an antecedent. A clear case of an independent IAC ending such a phrase in a simple period is shown in Example 3.75, measure 16. The independent IAC in Example 3.68, measure 4, concludes the antecedent phrase of a hybrid theme, in that the phrase beginning with measure 5 is a continuation (as witnessed by the fragmentation in mm. 5–6).¹¹⁶

### 3.2.2.2. Way-Station IAC

A second conventional use of the IAC occurs toward the end of a thematic unit as the music strives to reach an expected PAC. At the PAC's anticipated point of arrival, an IAC appears instead. The theme then continues, eventually fulfilling the promise of a PAC. A number of examples already examined illustrate this technique well: Example 3.76, measure 24; Example 3.78, measure 6; and Example 3.81, measure 14. In such cases, the IAC represents a kind of *way station* in the course of the thematic process, providing strong harmonic closure, but leaving the melodic organization active on 3̂.¹¹⁷

What distinguishes an independent IAC from a way-station IAC is the cadence's relationship to the subsequent PAC that finally closes the theme. In the case of the former, the listener would not be expecting PAC closure at, say, measure 4 of a periodic theme, because according to the norms of classical thematic organization, this moment would be "too early" in the standard process of formal closure. In other words, the independent IAC is not *replacing* an expected PAC but stands on its own as an internal articulation, after which an eventual PAC will likely ensue. With a way-station IAC, on the contrary, the cadence appears in a context where we are expecting a PAC to occur; however, a weaker mode of closure occurs instead, one that puts off the PAC to a later moment in time.

The way-station IAC most typically arises in the course of a *subordinate theme* as a means, along with deceptive, evaded, and abandoned cadences (deviation types discussed in the next chapter) of deferring a PAC (see again, Ex. 3.76, m. 24, and Ex. 3.82, m. 34). In that a subordinate theme always ends with a PAC, strong expectations for this cadential goal are aroused in the listener as the cadential function begins to be engaged. And so, while the unexpected appearance of a way-station IAC provides a degree of closure, it is nonetheless experienced as provisional and requiring of further thematic work. Indeed, the music following the IAC typically "backs up" and runs through the previous phrase (or portion thereof) with the promise of fulfilling the expected PAC (Ex. 3.76).¹¹⁸ Sometimes, new material appears after a way-station IAC, but that material, too, will eventually lead to another try at a PAC (see ahead to the discussion of Ex. 3.87).

A way-station IAC is rarely, if ever, followed by the opening of the ongoing thematic unit. In other words, the music may back up to an earlier moment in the theme, but not normally as far back as its very beginning. If that were to happen, we might be led to re-evaluate the formal situation and think that the IAC was actually functioning as an independent cadence. For hearing the theme start over again could suggest that the prior unit was an antecedent of some kind, and that presumption would conflict with our original sense that the IAC is a way station.¹¹⁹

Though a way-station IAC eventually results in a PAC, that cadence may not be the very next cadential articulation to appear; indeed, it is quite common for the IAC to be followed by any number of deceptive, evaded, or even abandoned cadences prior to the arrival of the PAC. In such a combination of cadential deferrals, the IAC tends to be used relatively early, after which the various deviations follow, though now and then a deviation (especially a deceptive cadence) may precede the IAC.¹²⁰

The use of a way-station IAC relates to another expectation that arises in connection with subordinate themes in general, namely, that the theme will bring a variety of *loosening* devices whose effect is to extend the theme in time by pushing

---

115. For this reason, an IAC that functions to end a complete theme (see ahead sec. 3.2.2.3), where we would also expect a PAC, would not be suitably labeled an "independent" cadence.

116. For additional cases of independent IACs closing an antecedent phrase, see Ex. 3.80a, m. 4; Ex. 3.84, m. 4; Ex. 3.88, m. 33; and Ex. 3.157, m. 4. As well, the PrC in Ex. 3.74 is a variant of an independent IAC.

117. As Neuwirth has discussed ("*Fuggir la Cadenza*," 129–30), the effect is somewhat akin to a deceptive cadence, where the melody concludes on 1̂ but the harmony remains open (typically on VI). Indeed, he even proposes subsuming the IAC under the more general category of deceptive cadence for this very reason. Developing an understanding of this cadential deviation largely from a contrapuntal perspective, he finds a kind of equivalency in situations where either the soprano or the bass fails to reach its expected closing pitch, thus putting on the same plane the IAC (where the melody thus fails) and the deceptive cadence (where the bass thus fails). In that my own theory of formal functions normally sees harmony trumping melody as a structural component of a tonal composition, I find the effect of an IAC (with its full harmonic completion) to create a stronger sense of closure than the deceptive cadence (which leaves harmonic processes open), and so I regard them as quite separate cadential devices, the former actually constituting a unique cadence type. MacKay also identifies an IAC functioning like a deceptive or evaded cadence ("Declassifying the IAC," 16 and 23, note 49, in connection with his Ex. 9, m. 24). In many other passages, he goes further than Neuwirth by proposing that the IAC should not even be seen as a genuine cadence, but rather more as a form of noncadential closure, what he calls a "tonic arrival" (akin to what I define as *prolongational closure*; see sec. 3.5.1). Zhang also understands the IAC to function at times like a deceptive cadence ("Apparently Imperfect," 194–96), but aligned with the view advocated in the present chapter, he retains the IAC as a genuine cadence type.

118. The effect is similar to the "one-more-time" technique described by Schmalfeldt for evaded cadences ("Cadential Processes").

119. The same circumstances hold for any authentic cadential deviation that functions as a way station; seldom does the following material return to the beginning of the ongoing thematic unit. See in Chapter 4, secs. 4.1.2.1 and 4.2.2.2.

120. This general topic will be raised again in the following chapter, sec. 4.5.

EXAMPLE 3.87. Mozart, Piano Sonata in A, K. 331, i, mm. 13–18.

into the future the final PAC; in this way, the rhetorical effect of that PAC is rendered even more powerful when it finally arrives after such a long-fought struggle. The way-station IAC therefore engages two contradictory expectations: on the one hand, it *denies* one expectation by failing to bring a PAC; on the other hand, it *fulfills* a second expectation by contributing to structural loosening. Though seemingly paradoxical, the appearance of the same event can both frustrate and satisfy the listener's presumptions regarding the organization of a subordinate theme.

The earlier discussed Example 3.79 illustrates a clear way-station IAC. Following a repeated presentation phrase (not shown), a continuation⇒cadential phrase beginning at measure 70 quickly brings an ECP leading to the IAC at measure 76. In the context of a subordinate theme, this cadential progression appears rather abruptly and so, although we are expecting a closing PAC, we hardly think it likely to arrive this early in the theme. It is thus unsurprising that the authentic cadence ends up being imperfect. As will be discussed in Chapter 5 (Ex. 5.47), the continuation⇒cadential phrase is repeated, and then enormously expanded, thus deferring the PAC arrival all the way to measure 94.

When an IAC is used to end a presumed final phrase of a subordinate theme, which is then immediately repeated to achieve the required PAC, the two phrases can often be perceived to stand in an antecedent-consequent relation: the first phrase ending with a weak cadence is repeated to close with a stronger cadence. While such a general relationship evidently obtains, we should be careful in our analysis of the phrase functions not to assign automatically the labels "antecedent" and "consequent," thereby implying that a period theme type has emerged. In the first place, the two phrases themselves have a different role to play within the subordinate theme, most often as continuation or cadential functions. Were we to identify the first phrase as an antecedent, we would be suggesting that it fulfills an *initiating* formal function, not a medial or concluding one. In the second place, the phrases are likely not to contain a two-measure basic idea followed by a two-measure contrasting idea, the standard constituents of an antecedent and consequent. Instead, the material of the phrase may be made up of fragments typical of a continuation and receive harmonic support that is less stable than that of normal periodic phrases. Example 3.76, above, shows matching phrases at the end of a subordinate theme, the first ending with a way-station IAC, the second with the final PAC. Here, the temptation to label the first phrase an antecedent and the second phrase a consequent is strong, since the latter so obviously repeats the former with stronger closure. Yet in the course of the subordinate theme, these are repeated continuation phrases (fusing both continuation and cadential functions); and so, while they express a degree of antecedent-consequent functionality, their phrase functions within the theme as a whole are very different.

The way-station IAC is sometimes encountered toward the end of a *main theme*. In such cases, its appearance might be somewhat surprising because, unlike a subordinate theme, we are not expecting the formal loosening that this cadence can produce. Though not always possible, it is useful to seek out an explanation, usually an ad hoc one, for this usage. Thus in connection with Example 3.78, the opening of the theme brings a repeated compound basic idea (not shown), thus creating a compound presentation phrase of eight real measures (notated as four, given the compound meter). The subsequent continuation⇒cadential phrase, shown in measures 5 and 6 of the example, first achieves an IAC, followed then by a repetition for a PAC. As a result, the continuation and cadential functions occupy the same span of time as the initiating presentation, thus providing a degree of balance to the grouping structure of the theme.[121]

Another main theme, one quite famous in the analytical literature, features a way-station IAC toward the end of a small ternary (Ex. 3.87, m. 16). The A section (not shown) is built as a standard 8-measure period, antecedent plus consequent, using the same material shown in measures 13–16. Typically in such cases, the subsequent A′ section consists of only *one* phrase, a consequent ending with a PAC, in order to avoid undue redundancy in the musical material.[122] As a result, the listener is primed to expect a

---

121. To be sure, the continuation and cadential functions of a compound sentence do not have to match in length that of the presentation, as a number of examples discussed in *CF*, 69, and *ACF*, 180, attest.

122. See *CF*, 83, and *ACF*, 198.

final PAC at measure 16, and so the appearance of an IAC at this moment is clearly heard as a way station. But rather than "backing up" to repeat the same material (again, to prevent redundancy), Mozart adds a two-measure extension made up of new material (though motivically related to m. 15), which closes the theme with the expected PAC in measure 18. As we learn throughout the rest of the movement, a set of variations based on this theme, Mozart uses this extension not as a mere afterthought required to provide complete thematic closure, but rather as a major structural component of the theme, allowing it to generate elaborate textural connections from one variation to the next.[123]

### 3.2.2.3. Additional Functions of the IAC

Beyond the two principal uses of the IAC just discussed—as an independent cadence ending a simple antecedent or as a way station within a subordinate theme—this cadence type is found occasionally in a number of other formal situations, such as at the end of a compound antecedent, the A section of a small ternary, or a complete thematic unit (be it a main or subordinate theme). An IAC may also function as a cadence of limited scope (e.g., in a large-scale model, a compound presentation, or a closing section).

**Ending a Compound Antecedent.** Seeing that an independent IAC can readily be used to close the four-measure antecedent of a simple period, we might think that it could function similarly to end the eight-measure antecedent of a compound period. Surprisingly, I have found only a small number of examples in the corpus, one of which arises in the earlier discussed Example 3.70. Here, the IAC in measure 82 marks the end of a compound antecedent; the compound consequent (not shown) brings a final PAC to close the theme.[124]

A somewhat different situation occurs in Example 3.88, where the first of two subordinate themes in an orchestral ritornello is built as a compound period. The antecedent is an eight-measure sentence closing with an IAC at measure 33 (the example shows the continuation phrase leading to the cadence). Note that Mozart creates the IAC by *diverting* the cadential melody of a varied soprano pattern ($\hat{3}/\hat{4}/\hat{3}$-$\hat{2}/\hat{1}$) up to $\hat{3}$, via a passing $\sharp\hat{2}$. In other words, the melodic line is clearly heading toward a PAC to close the sentence, but is pushed open at the last second. The IAC thus seems at first like it is functioning as a way station, and so we would probably be expecting the continuation phrase alone to be repeated to create the PAC, such as what we saw earlier in Example 3.76. So it comes as a surprise when the entire eight-measure unit is repeated to create a compound consequent. The cadence is thus reinterpreted from being a way station to becoming independent.

**Ending the A Section of a Small Ternary (or the First Part of a Small Binary).** The opening unit of the small ternary (A section) and small binary (part 1) normally closes with a PAC, either in the home key or in a subordinate key.[125] This section seldom ends with an IAC. For one such case, see Example 3.89a, where the A section of the main theme takes the form of a simple period, whose consequent concludes in measure 8 with an IAC (following a weaker HC in m. 4). Normally in such cases, we would expect the final unit of the section to end with a PAC. In this respect, the end of the A′ section (Ex. 3.89b) is especially interesting, because it initially closes again, and surprisingly, with an IAC (not shown). But when Mozart repeats both the B and A′ sections together (the theme is actually a rounded binary version of a small ternary), the moment where the IAC would have occurred, measure 32, is converted into an elided deceptive cadence, thus prompting further continuational activity that eventually ends the theme, as initially expected, with a PAC.

The theme for variations in the Allegretto movement of Beethoven's Seventh Symphony (see again Ex. 3.83a, m. 10) features another case where an A section closes (at m. 10) with an IAC, though the cadence there is especially unusual owing to its melody ending on $\hat{5}$, as earlier discussed. Another unusual case appears in the first part of a small binary (Ex. 3.90a). The opening phrase ends at measure 4 with an HC in the home key to close an antecedent. The next phrase then seems to begin directly in the subordinate key of C major, thus continuing the same harmony from the prior phrase and ending with an IAC in that key.[126] The function of this second phrase, however, is uncertain. On the one hand, the unit clearly "answers" the first one: the C-major outburst matches the prior phrase as regards its rhythmic profile and cadential weights (a stronger IAC vs. the weaker HC). On the other hand, the second phrase also provides a significant contrast in terms of dynamics, articulation, harmonic rhythm, and melodic contour. Technically it is neither a consequent (it does not bring back the basic idea from the antecedent) nor a genuine continuation (there is no fragmentation, and the harmonic rhythm actually slows down). A somewhat more complex analysis (perhaps even a counterintuitive

---

123. In a number of the variations, the texture and style of the A section's consequent phrase is markedly different from the prior antecedent. In the A′ section, the phrase ending with the way-station IAC matches those same characteristics of the earlier antecedent, while the extension matches the consequent. Thus these individual variations contain within themselves "two variations," a unique take on the traditional "double variation" (or "alternating variation") technique, found typically in Haydn's variations practice. In "Schoenberg's 'Second Melody'" (178–80), I propose an additional reason for the appropriateness of the 2-m. extension, relating it to the odd structure of the bass-line melody (①–⑦–⑥–⑦–①) in the phrases of the A and A′ sections (see of the annotations of mm. 13–16), an anomaly that is normalized when the bass of the extension traverses the standard pattern ①–②–③–④–⑤–① (see again, Chapter 2, sec. 2.4).

124. See also Haydn, String Quartet in C, Op. 74, no. 1, i, m. 10; Mozart, Violin Sonata in E-flat, K. 481, i, m. 76; and Beethoven, String Quartet in D, Op. 18, no. 3, i, m. 9, for three other cases of a compound antecedent ending with an IAC.

125. Haydn now and then employs an HC to close the A section; Mozart and Beethoven rarely, if ever, do so; see *CF*, 268, note 5. The first part of a small binary by any of the classical composers may also close with an HC; see *CF*, 87–89, and *ACF*, 243–45.

126. Also unusual is that the normal subordinate key of F minor would be C *minor* (not major).

3.2. IMPERFECT AUTHENTIC CADENCE    97

EXAMPLE 3.88. Mozart, Piano Concerto in B-flat, K. 450, i, mm. 30–34.

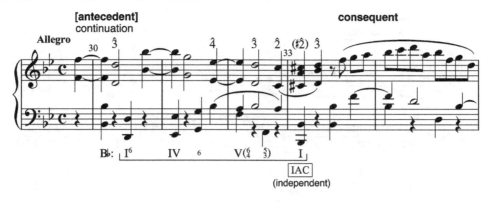

EXAMPLE 3.89. Mozart, Piano Concerto in D Minor, K. 466, ii, (a) mm. 1–8 (*ACF* 3.13); (b) mm. 31–36.

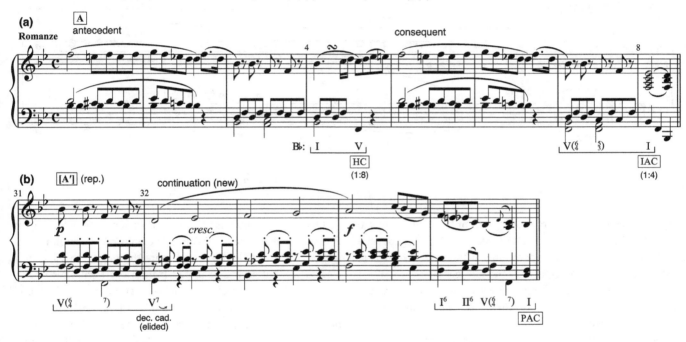

EXAMPLE 3.90. Beethoven, Piano Sonata in A-flat, Op. 110, ii, (a) mm. 1–8; (b) reconstruction 1 of mm 7–8; (c) reconstruction 2 of mm. 7–8.

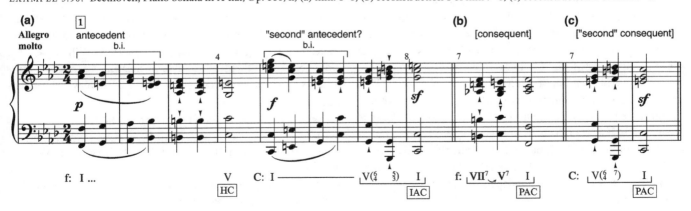

EXAMPLE 3.91. Mozart, Piano Sonata in E-flat, K. 282, i, mm. 1–4 (R = ½N).

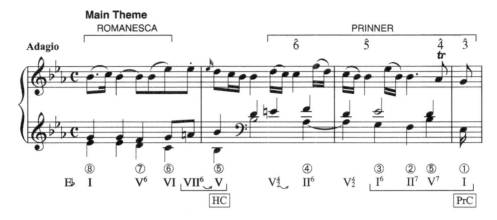

EXAMPLE 3.92. Mozart, Symphony No. 38 in D ("Prague"), K. 504, i, mm. 37–42.

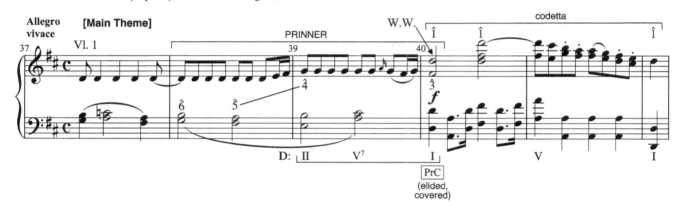

one) considers the second phrase in light of its intrinsic formal expression. By ending with a relatively weak IAC, it could be seen as a kind of "second" antecedent, one in the new key. Indeed, it would be easy to imagine what the two genuine consequent phrases would be like, by taking the basic idea of each antecedent and following it with the two-measure PACs shown in Example 3.90b and c, respectively.

**Ending a Complete Main Theme.** The great majority of main themes (of any formal type) end with a home-key PAC. If the home key is in the minor mode, the main theme, especially of sonata form, will often end with an HC. Infrequently does a main theme end with an IAC. As I discuss later in Chapter 7 on galant cadence (sec. 7.4.1), main themes in that style frequently conclude with that cadence type. So it is not surprising to find a number of examples of this practice in earlier works by Haydn and even the young Mozart (up to ca. 1780).

In that an IAC ending a main theme occurs where a PAC would be expected, we might wonder whether the former should be considered a way station. On first hearing, this is a plausible presumption, but when it turns out that the IAC is not a provisional substitute for a PAC, but rather its complete replacement, the idea of a way station must be cast aside. (That an IAC ending a complete theme is also not an independent cadence has already been mentioned in note 115 above.)

One type of IAC is directly associated with Gjerdingen's Prinner schema.[127] Since this PrC is employed widely in the galant period, it will be discussed more thoroughly in Chapter 7 (sec. 7.1.2), but several examples from Mozart will illustrate its use in closing a classical main theme. A good case can be found in Example 3.91, an early work by Mozart (the main theme is notated as four measures in compound meter).[128] Here a vestige of earlier eighteenth-century practice is witnessed by the Prinner cadence being paired with an initiating "Romanesca" schema;[129] as well, the overall descending bass line is especially characteristic of baroque and galant compositions, as mentioned in Chapter 2, note 90.

The rare use of a PrC in a high classical work can be seen in Example 3.92. The opening of the Prinner sounds in an inner voice, only shifting to the soprano at measure 39. When the melodic goal of the theme, $\hat{3}$, sounds in measure 40, another textural layer brings $\hat{1}$ to "cover" the $\hat{3}$. So, the effect may be heard as

---

127. See the earlier discussion of the Prinner, sec. 3.2.1.2.

128. For other examples of a main theme closing with a PrC, see Haydn, Piano Sonata in C Minor, H. 20, ii, m. 4 (R = ½N); Haydn, Piano Sonata in D, H. 24, i, m. 4 (R = ½N).

129. See Gjerdingen, *Galant Style*, 46–52. Typical of the schema is the opening harmonic progression I–V–VI.

EXAMPLE 3.93. Haydn, String Quartet in C ("Emperor"), Op. 76, no. 3, i, mm. 1–5 (R = ½N).

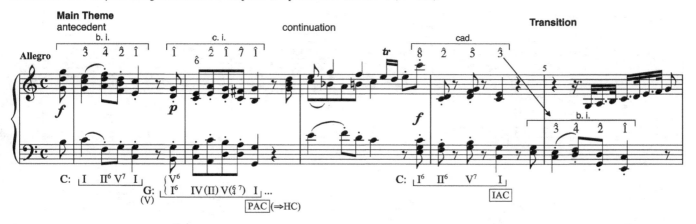

EXAMPLE 3.94. Beethoven, Piano Sonata in E, Op. 109, iii, mm. 13–16.

a kind of PAC, even though the genuine ending is a PrC.[130] The codetta that elides with the cadence then emphasizes $\hat{1}$ in such a manner as to reference the possibility that the cadence was a PAC after all, in conformance with classical norms.[131]

A case of a standard IAC ending a main theme can additionally be seen in Example 3.93. Note that this cadence type is particularly appropriate here since PAC content is found not only within the basic idea itself (notated as one measure in compound meter), but also in the contrasting idea, now in the dominant region of G major (creating what I term a "reinterpreted half cadence").[132] Moreover, when the transition picks up at measure 5, the return of the basic idea brings a pronounced $\hat{3}$–$\hat{4}$–$\hat{2}$–$\hat{1}$ motion, in C major, that "completes" the melodic descent checked by the IAC at the end of the main theme.[133]

In his later period, Beethoven ends a number of complete themes with an IAC in a manner that projects a distinctly expressive touch, as though the melodic openness seems less a structural matter and more a device that wistfully looks forward into the future. Such incomplete closure is especially found in themes for variations, as seen in the final movements of Opp. 109 and 111 (Ex. 3.94; and Ex. 3.77, above). In both cases, Beethoven retains the IAC through the variations themselves, even ending Op. 109 with an IAC in the return of the original version of the complete theme. (In Op. 111, he closes the work with a PAC at m. 176.)[134]

**Ending a Subordinate Theme.** As discussed earlier in sec. 3.1.3.2, "Subordinate Theme," a fundamental principle of classical form requires a subordinate theme to close with a PAC; the weaker IAC is rarely used. One case arises in Example 3.95. In the exposition, transition and subordinate-theme functions are fused into a single thematic unit, one that closes with an IAC in measure 54. In that this closure is not fully complete, as expected of any subordinate theme, we could well imagine that more of this theme must occur, in the sense of the IAC being a way station. What follows, however, is a manifestly new thematic process, a folksy tune of the type that Haydn often uses as either a second subordinate theme or a closing section. Here, the new tune first brings what seems to be an antecedent ending melodically with

---

130. The idea of a "covered" cadence will be explored later in sec. 3.4.2.3.

131. For another case of the closing section emphasizing $\hat{1}$ following a Prinner cadence (closing on $\hat{3}$), see ahead in Chapter 7, Ex. 7.21.

132. See ahead sec. 3.3.5.1.

133. For other examples of an IAC ending main themes, see Haydn, Piano Sonata in G, H. 39, iii, m. 7; Haydn, Symphony No. 92 in G, i, m. 32; Mozart, String Quartet in B-flat, K. 458, iv, m. 8.

---

134. For additional themes ending with an "expressive" IAC, see Beethoven, String Quartet in F Minor, Op. 95, ii, m. 33; Beethoven, Symphony No. 9 in D Minor, Op. 125, iii, m. 32.

EXAMPLE 3.95. Haydn, String Quartet in G Minor ("Horseman"), Op. 74, no. 3, i, mm. 53–63.

a suspension configuration that yields an independent IAC at measure 58. Upon repeating the phrase in the following bars, we expect a consequent to end with a PAC. Instead, Haydn closes the phrase with another IAC (m. 62).

At this point, we can now understand retrospectively that both IACs (mm. 58 and 62) only end their own four-measure phrases, not any larger formal unit, and thus the cadences emerge as ones of limited scope. As a result, a period structure fails to be realized (though the lack of a suspension helps to make measure 62 sound somewhat more decisive this second time around). The entire eight-measure structure, which must now be considered a closing section consisting of repeated four-measure codettas, is then sounded in full, again ending with an IAC (not shown). Only with further codettas does the melody finally attain the tonic scale degree. With its incessant repetitions, the IAC thus emerges as a motivic feature of the subordinate-theme area, which perhaps accounts for the major departure from sonata-form norms in this exposition. In the recapitulation, Haydn fulfills our expectations by allowing the transition/subordinate-theme fusion to achieve PAC closure (m. 168), though the subsequent folksy tune continues to remain open with its reiterated IACs.[135]

**Limited Cadential Scope.** An IAC sometimes appears in contexts in which its cadential scope is limited to a single phrase and as such loses its genuine cadential function with respect to the thematic organization as a whole.[136] One common context for an IAC of limited scope is in the codettas making up a closing section. We just observed an instance of this technique in Example 3.95, measures 58 and 62. Another more unusual case arises in Example 3.96. Here, the final four-measure phrase of a minuet (mm. 17–20), one that is identical to the opening four-measure antecedent (mm. 1–4, not shown), functions at this point in the form as a codetta ending with an IAC of limited scope. Real thematic closure for the minuet occurs with the PAC just before, at measure 16.

A compound presentation provides another context where an IAC of limited scope may occur. In this case, the presentation may be made up of two four-measure phrases, each ending with an IAC. As seen in Example 3.97, the opening phrase closes with an IAC in measure 4, thus suggesting an antecedent function. Its repetition proposes a consequent, but when the IAC returns again at measure 8, a period form fails to emerge, and we can hear the repeated four-measure phrases functioning together as a compound presentation, one that receives a continuation in the subsequent bars. The IACs in measures 4 and 8 thus have a limited cadential scope within their own antecedent phrases and do not function as genuine cadences within the context of the overall compound sentence, which concludes with an HC at measure 14 (not shown).

A related situation arises in the compound presentation of Example 3.98. Here, an initial compound basic idea (mm. 1–4) is repeated in the next phrase, one that might seem to end with an IAC. A closer look at the overall harmonic structure, however, reveals that the "cadential" dominant of measure 7 arises already at the upbeat to measure 5; this $V^7$ actually ensues from the prior $V^6_5$ ending the opening compound basic idea. In other words, we cannot speak

---

135. For another subordinate theme that ends with an IAC, see Beethoven, Piano Sonata in B-flat ("Hammerklavier"), Op. 106, i, discussed ahead in Chapter 5, Ex. 5.14a, m. 100. Here, a "second" subordinate theme follows, one that brings an eventual PAC at m. 116 (not shown). Inasmuch as this second subordinate theme begins with a "false closing section" (*CF*, 123, and *ACF*, 389), it affirms that the first theme had reached its genuine conclusion with the IAC.

136. See Chapter 2, sec. 2.7.

EXAMPLE 3.96. Haydn, String Quartet in A, Op. 20, no. 6, iii, mm. 15–20.

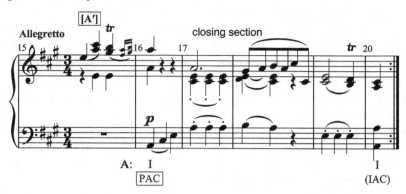

EXAMPLE 3.97. Haydn, Piano Sonata in C, H. 21, iii, 1–10 (*ACF* Sup. 6.22).

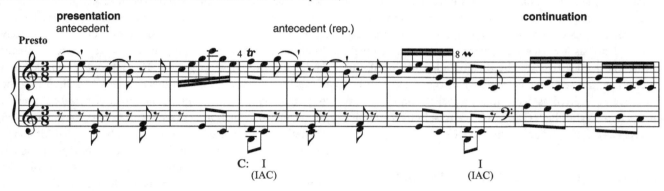

EXAMPLE 3.98. Mozart, String Quartet in A, K. 464, i, mm. 1–10 (*ACF* 6.16).

of a genuine cadential progression closing the second phrase, but rather understand the dominant underlying most of that phrase as prolonging the initial tonic of the compound presentation.[137]

## 3.3. Half Cadence

Throughout all tonal styles, and especially in the high classical period, the half cadence (also termed "semicadence") is a significant source of formal articulation. Indeed, this cadence is so fundamental that it is unimaginable how a comprehensive theory of musical form could be constructed without incorporating this mode of tonal closure. Yet the idea of an HC raises a major theoretical conundrum, such that conceptualizing this cadence type has regularly proven challenging for music theorists. The titles of two recent studies by Poundie Burstein betray these difficulties when he speaks of HCs and their related structures as "slippery events" and "analytic fictions."[138]

The central conundrum of the HC arises from the fact that its goal harmony, the dominant, is in principle an unstable entity, one that by nature demands resolution to a more stable tonic (or tonic substitute of some kind). Yet in the context of the HC, this

---

137. Other cases of questionable IACs in the context of a compound presentation arise in Mozart, Symphony No. 41 in C ("Jupiter"), K. 551, iii, mm. 4 and 8 (*ACF* Sup. 6.18), and Beethoven, Piano Concerto No. 1 in C, Op. 15, i, m. 8 (*ACF* Sup. 6.19).

138. L. Poundie Burstein, "The Half Cadence and Other Such Slippery Events"; Burstein, "The Half Cadence and Related Analytic Fictions."

dominant comes to project sufficient stability to mark an end—to be sure, a provisional one in most cases—of a thematic formal process. Further complicating the matter is the marked morphological similarities between authentic cadential progressions and half cadential ones. For the most part they are identical, except that in the former, the dominant is the second to last (penultimate) harmony of the progression, whereas in the latter, it is the final (ultimate) harmony. Indeed this strong relation between the two cadential progressions has led some theorists to regard the HC as a kind of "incomplete" authentic cadence. As Gjerdingen notes, "Perhaps the limit in [cadential] avoidance or evasion would simply be to stop a cadence short of its goal—to leave it 'half' finished. Half cadences would then be described as those that stop on the penultimate bass tone, ⑤. . . ."[139] But whereas this characterization makes sense from an exclusively *harmonic* perspective, it is highly problematic as regards *formal* closure, for it suggests that an HC appears in place of an authentic cadence as a device that avoids or evades a complete thematic ending, as suggested by the quotation just cited. But as Gjerdingen himself acknowledges, "half cadences seem not to have been perceived as deceptions or tricks," and thus most theorists understand the HC as a cadence type in its own right, not simply as a deformed authentic cadence.[140]

### 3.3.1. General Conditions for Half Cadence

What then accounts for the possibility of a dominant harmony being experienced as the ultimate harmony of a cadential progression so that the HC can emerge as its own category of thematic closure? This question is actually hard to answer with complete certainty, and a definitive account of just which musical forces are both necessary and sufficient to yield half cadential closure is not yet forthcoming. The organization of certain compositional parameters, however, evidently plays a role. For example, empirical evidence from eighteenth-century repertories suggests that the dominant itself must appear in its "most stable" configuration: in root position and as a consonant triad, without any added harmonic dissonances (a seventh or ninth).[141] Indeed, as already discussed on several occasions, the necessity for a cadential dominant to reside exclusively in root position is a central axiom of my approach to cadence.

This condition, though, is by no means accepted by many theorists. Burstein, for one, has recently challenged the requirement for a root-position dominant (along with the need for a triadic sonority), arguing that the close of the first phrase in Example 3.99 on $V^6_5$ is a perfectly adequate HC when recognizing a period form, antecedent + consequent.[142] In my view, on the contrary, the dominant articulation in measure 4 arises out of a *prolongational* progression and a bass line that traverses the prolongational stream. The voice-exchange in measures 3–4 especially supports a prolongational view of the harmony leading into measure 4. Moreover, the lack of any bass motion engaging ⑤ within the phrase discounts our speaking of a genuine cadence. I would thus analyze this opening unit as a compound basic idea, not an antecedent.

Since my position is axiomatic, and thus not provable in any logical manner, I cannot claim that Burstein's view is wrong in its own terms. I do believe, however, that significant theoretical advantages accrue from distinguishing categorically between prolongational and cadential progressions and that many disadvantages result from lumping a wide variety of dominant "endings" into a single category of HC. I return to a consideration of this issue toward the end of this chapter when discussing the long-standing idea of a "contrapuntal cadence," based on inverted dominants and (final) tonics (see sec. 3.5.1). As for the question of whether or not a dissonant seventh may be included within the root-position dominant of an HC, that issue is best postponed to Chapter 4 on cadential deviations, where I propose a distinction between the HC proper and various manifestations of *dominant arrival*.[143]

Though the harmonic requirements just laid out are a necessary condition for recognizing a HC (and distinguishing it, say, from a PAC), they are not sufficient ones: an AC also brings a cadential dominant in root position that can very well (even if not typically) consist of a consonant triad. We must therefore include another condition in the mix, namely one concerning the relation of harmony to *grouping structure*. For in order to hear a cadential dominant as *ultimate*, the musical event supported by this harmony must be experienced as the final event of a larger group; in other words, the HC must be associated with a grouping boundary in a manner that the subsequent event is heard to initiate a new group. To be sure, the various principles that determine grouping structure are manifold, involving matters such as similarity of melodic-motivic material, texture, rhythmic patterning, and so forth. And as Lerdahl and Jackendoff have shown, grouping structures are largely governed by "preference" rules, many of which, in a given analytical situation, need to be assessed on a case by case basis.[144] Since this study is obviously not the place to formulate and evaluate precise principles of grouping structure, I will assume that in most contexts, experienced listeners group musical events in largely the same ways, recognizing, of course,

---

139. Gjerdingen, *Galant Style*, 153. Other theorists have spoken in similar terms: "each schema of perfect authentic cadence can be turned into a half cadence by leaving out the final tonic" (Mirka, "Punctuation and Sense," 245–46); "This so-called *half* or *semi cadence* is in short, an authentic cadence that stops prematurely" (Harrison, "Cadence," 14).

140. Seeing as much of the following discussion will be comparing the HC to the authentic cadences (PAC and IAC), it will be useful to employ the more general initialism *AC* to indicate any type of authentic cadence.

141. In contrast, the penultimate dominant of an authentic cadential progression typically includes a dissonant seventh precisely to emphasize the harmony's need for tonic resolution.

---

142. Burstein, "Analytic Fictions," 101.

143. In nineteenth-century repertories, we will want to sanction a genuine HC ending with a dominant seventh; see Chapter 8, sec. 8.1.

144. Lerdahl and Jackendoff, *Generative Theory*, 43–55.

EXAMPLE 3.99. Haydn, String Quartet in G, Op. 17, no. 5, ii, mm. 1–8.

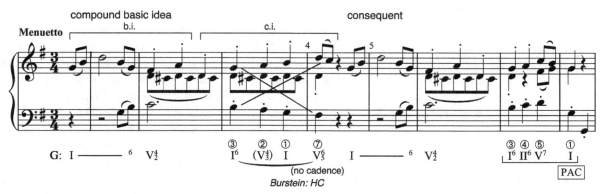

that many ambiguities may arise, thus affecting our identification of cadence. Indeed, many of the problematic cases that Burstein discusses in his studies—does such and such a phrase (or theme) close with an HC, an AC, or no cadence?—largely revert to conflicting interpretations of grouping structure.[145]

Like the harmonic criteria for an HC, the principle requiring it to be the final event of a group may be a necessary condition, but it is not a sufficient one. For in those situations that I and other theorists have identified as *evaded cadences*, the final harmony of the cadential unit is also a dominant, with the subsequent event (typically a tonic) marking the beginning of a new group. Although this grouping situation seems identical to that of an HC, the differences between the two cadential formations are experientially significant. In the case of an evaded cadence, the dominant is heard as the *last* event of the group, but it is not heard to *end* the group; rather, that harmony is experienced as the penultimate one of an authentic cadential progression, whose goal harmony has been omitted from the group. As a result, we experience a marked disruption to the formal processes of closure. With the HC, on the contrary, we are satisfied that the dominant itself is the goal harmony of the group, and while we expect an eventual resolution to tonic, that harmony will be understood to mark the beginning of the next group, not as something that was suddenly omitted from the cadential group. To be sure, cases arise where listeners may disagree about whether an HC or an evaded cadence has been created, thus revealing how difficult it is to formulate precise criteria for identifying these (and many other) cadential circumstances.[146]

In the context of relatively tight-knit themes, where highly symmetrical grouping structures tend to be based on exponentials of 2 (e.g., 2 + 2, 4 + 4, 8 + 8), cadential articulations tend to fall in measures 4 and 8 of the theme (or additionally with compound themes, in mm. 12 and 16). If, in such tight-knit situations, a cadential dominant arises in those bars (especially on their downbeats), we are disposed to interpret the harmony as ultimate (of an HC) rather than penultimate (of an AC). Some theorists speak of this as a "hypermetrical" situation, but the more general expression *phrase rhythm* might be more satisfactory, since the metrical weight (or accentuation) of the given bars is not so much the issue as is the overall regularity of grouping structures that arise.[147] Unlike the two prior sets of conditions (harmony and grouping structure), which are necessary in the case of the HC, the tendency for it to occur with symmetrical phrase rhythms is neither necessary nor sufficient: in looser formal contexts, an HC (or even an AC) may also appear with asymmetrical phrases.

### 3.3.2. Morphology—Harmonic Content

As just discussed, the notion of the HC as a kind of "incomplete" AC is highly problematic as regards the functional differences between these cadence types. But from a strictly morphological perspective, the idea makes a degree of sense. Thus whereas we recognize an AC as having four discrete stages, we can say that the HC consists of three stages, whose harmonic and melodic content strongly resemble stages 1 through 3 of an AC. We must understand, however, that although the stages of the two cadence types are comparable in their pitch content, stage 3, in particular, has very different temporal, and thus functional, expressions: with the HC, this stage represents the ultimate event, a stable goal, and the sense of cadential arrival. That same stage in the AC is the penultimate event, highly mobile in nature, and one that promises cadential arrival only with the subsequent stage 4. The following discussion, while revealing similarities of morphology between HCs and ACs, will largely focus on aspects that help differentiate the two types. For example, we can observe that in general the bass line of an HC, more often than an AC, approaches ⑤ (stage 3) from above, engaging ⑥ or ♭⑥ in stage 2, and sometimes even preceding

---

145. See the first two examples of Burstein's "Slippery Events" (Schubert, "Der Wegweiser," from *Die Winterreise*, mm. 6–11, and Mozart, Symphony No. 14 in A, K. 114, i, mm. 76–82), where the difference between identifying an HC or an AC essentially depends on which cadence represents the final event of the ongoing formal group. See also his Ex. 8a (Mozart, Piano Sonata in G, K. 283, ii, 1–4), where, given the continuity of rhythmic motion into the downbeat of m. 3, the distinction between a possible HC or no cadence again involves determining the grouping boundaries.

146. I explore such ambiguities in a later discussion of cadential deviations in Chapter 4, sec. 4.6.5.

147. See ahead, sec. 3.4.1.3.

these degrees by a stage-1 ♭$\hat{7}$ (supporting an initial tonic substitute V$^4_2$/IV).[148] This descending bass typically occurs in minor-mode contexts, not only in movements whose overall modality is minor, but also in situations of modal mixture in an otherwise major-mode movement. The prevalence of the descending bass in HCs means that a somewhat wider variety of harmonies tend to be used for stages 1 and 2 than are typically encountered for ACs, whose bass line normally ascends to the dominant degree.

### 3.3.2.1. Stage 1—Initial Tonic

Any of the harmonies used in stage 1 of an AC can be employed in that stage for the HC. Though the initial tonic may stand in first inversion, a *root-position* tonic for this stage arises more frequently for the HC than for the AC. In such cases, the tonic often moves directly to the dominant, thus bypassing the pre-dominant of stage 2. This *simple (I–V) half cadence*, as Martin and Pedneault-Deslauriers term it,[149] typically appears at the end of a four-measure antecedent phrase of a period. Looking back at Example 2.15a from the previous chapter, the arrival on I$^6$ at the upbeat to measure 3 might have signaled the onset of the cadential progression. Instead, the harmony returns to its root position on the last beat of that bar to complete a broader tonic prolongation. This root-position tonic then proceeds directly to V for the simple HC in measure 4. As seen in the consequent phrase, the arrival again on I$^6$ (upbeat to m. 7) now realizes its implication of being cadential by progressing to the pre-dominant and dominant harmonies of the concluding PAC.

In cases of the bass line descending to the dominant, the initial tonic will also tend to be in root position (over ⑧), with the bass then moving downward to ⑥ or ♭⑥ (holding a stage-2 pre-dominant) on its way to ⑤.[150] Seeing as the leading tone ⑦ does not support a harmony of either stages 1 or 2, it is typically omitted from the bass line or else supports a passing sonority of some kind (for a case of the latter, see ahead, Ex. 3.129, m. 3). The gap between ① and ⑥, however, can be filled in by ♭⑦ (holding V$^4_2$/IV, a tonic substitute), thus dividing stage 1 into two substages, I and V$^4_2$/IV (see ahead, Ex. 3.137).

### 3.3.2.2. Stage 2—Pre-dominant

The large set of pre-dominant harmonies in stage 2 of the AC are available for the HC as well. Even more often for the latter, this stage is subdivided into two substages: the first pre-dominant containing $\hat{4}$; the second, #$\hat{4}$, typically in the form of VII$^7$/V or V$^6_5$/V. These secondary dominants in stage 2b intensify the progression to the dominant by typically bringing its leading tone (#④) in the bass, thus helping to support our perception of V as a goal harmony. Within a four-measure antecedent phrase (as in Ex. 3.100), the use of two distinct harmonies facilitates extending the duration of the pre-dominant for the whole of measure 3, enabling the dominant to fall on the downbeat of measure 4. This pushing of the dominant all the way to the final bar of the phrase helps to project that this harmony is ultimate, in line with the symmetrical phrase rhythms typical of the period form. Note that in the consequent phrase, as so frequently happens, the stage-3 penultimate dominant is shifted back to the end of measure 7 in order for the final tonic to arrive on the downbeat of measure 8, again complying with the standard phrase rhythm of the theme type.[151] As a result, stage 2 of the authentic cadential progression eliminates VII$^7$/V over #④ found in stage 2b of the antecedent phrase.

The prevalence of descending bass lines in half cadential progressions promotes the use of pre-dominants built on ⑥ or ♭⑥ (or both). In minor-mode contexts, the progression IV$^6$–V gives rise to the traditionally termed *phrygian half cadence*, the characteristic half step in the bass being reminiscent of the first two steps of the phrygian scale (see Ex. 3.101).[152] Though widely described as an HC subtype, the phrygian HC is actually quite limited in the classical style. Found more regularly is a chromatically altered version of this phrygian progression, which yields an augmented-sixth sonority, most typically Italian (Ex. 3.102), but sometimes French.[153] Indeed the progression It$^{+6}$–V is especially characteristic of HCs used at the end of a contrasting middle of the small ternary (or binary) theme type, as well as the transition and developmental core of a sonata form. Just as a prominent arrival on I$^6$ often signals the onset of an authentic cadential progression, the appearance of an Italian sixth is tantamount to waiving a flag for an impending HC.

In major-mode contexts, the descending approach to ⑤ typically sees ♮⑥ supporting the secondary dominant VII$^6$/V (sometimes V$^4_3$/V); here, the leading tone of the dominant (#④) is often exposed in the soprano voice (Ex. 3.103).

### 3.3.2.3. Stage 3—Dominant

The harmonic content of this stage—a root-position dominant triad—has already been discussed, and little more needs to be

---

148. If stage 2 features ⑥ followed by ♭⑥, we can speak of substages 2a and 2b (just like the case of the ascending bass line that contains ④ and #④).

149. Martin and Pedneault-Deslauriers, "Mozartian Half Cadence," 192. Their three other HC categories will be discussed later, in sec. 3.3.3. A potential confusion of terminology must also be addressed at this point: the term *simple* in the context of HC subtypes is distinct from the same term when used for a cadential melodic pattern, e.g., the *simple* pattern ($\hat{3}/\hat{2}/\hat{2}/\hat{1}$). Additionally, the term is often applied to eight-measure theme types (e.g., a *simple* period) compared to *compound* themes of sixteen measures.

150. See ahead, Ex. 3.102, 3.103, and 3.136.

151. See *ACF*, 85.

152. See, e.g., *Grove Music Online*, s.v. "cadence," by William S. Rockstro et al., accessed July 23, 2022, https://doi-org.proxy3.library.mcgill.ca/10.1093/gmo/9781561592630.article.04523, ex. 5. The term is somewhat problematic, of course, in that the phrygian scale being referenced starts on the dominant degree of the prevailing key, not the tonic. For another case of a phrygian HC, see ahead Ex. 3.135.

153. The German augmented sixth creates parallel fifths when resolving to a dominant triad, so this "nationality" is used less frequently in HCs than in ACs, where it typically resolves at first to a cadential six-four, thus breaking up the problematic parallels.

EXAMPLE 3.100. Haydn, Piano Trio in C, H. 27, iii, mm. 1–8 (*ACF* 3.8).

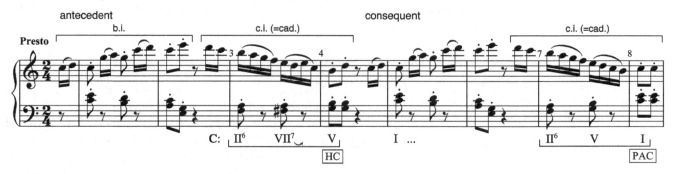

EXAMPLE 3.101. Beethoven, String Quartet in E-flat, Op. 74, iv, mm. 6–8.

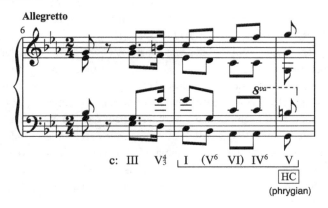

EXAMPLE 3.102. Beethoven, Piano Sonata in G, Op. 14, no. 2, i, mm. 106–107 (*ACF* 13.13).

EXAMPLE 3.103. Beethoven, Piano Sonata in B-flat, Op. 22, iii, mm. 3–5 (*ACF* Sup. 4.1).

EXAMPLE 3.104. Beethoven, Symphony No. 2 in D, Op. 36, ii, mm. 3–4 (*ACF* 4.8).

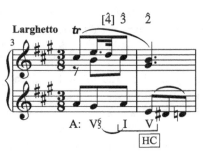

EXAMPLE 3.105. Mozart, Piano Sonata in F, K. 332, ii, m. 4 (R = ½N) (*ACF* 2.26).

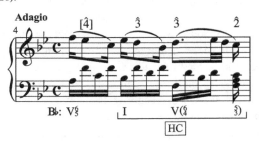

added here. The stage is sometimes divided into two substages (3a and 3b) through a six-four embellishment (see ahead, Ex. 3.105). Such usage occurs less frequently with the HC than with an AC for reasons that are not yet entirely clear. Inasmuch as a cadential six-four, especially when rhetorically emphasized, is often so strongly associated with authentic cadential closure, it is understandable that composers would shy away from this harmony in half cadential contexts, preferring instead to use an augmented-sixth or some secondary dominant of the dominant as the primary signal for this cadence type.

### 3.3.3. Morphology—Melodic Content

Just as for harmony, the melodic content of the HC can be analyzed with the model developed for the AC, except that stage 4 of the latter must be eliminated from the HC melodic patterns. In addition, the HC typology introduced by Martin and Pedneault-Deslauriers (see note 25) can help further refine our understanding of melodic processes in this cadence type. Using a methodology similar to mine, they identify melodic segments based on notional soprano, alto, tenor, and bass clausulae:

(1) a soprano clausula moving stepwise from $\hat{5}$ down to $\hat{2}$;

(2) an alto clausula understood to move $\hat{3}$–$\hat{2}$–$\hat{1}$–$\hat{7}$ but admitting the substitution of $\hat{1}$ for the initial $\hat{3}$, the antepenultimate $\hat{2}$, or both;

(3) a bass line moving $\hat{3}$–$\hat{4}$–$\hat{5}$ ($\hat{1}$ may be substituted for $\hat{3}$, and $\hat{4}$ may be intensified to $\sharp\hat{4}$);

(4) a tenor line moving $\hat{5}$–$\hat{6}$–$\hat{5}$ or $\hat{8}$–$\hat{6}$–$\hat{5}$.[154]

These patterns obviously correspond to the melodic streams that I used above in the analysis of authentic cadential melodies, though Martin and Pedneault-Deslauriers do not associate the individual pitches of their scheme explicitly in reference to the cadential stages.

Using these clausulae, Martin and Pedneault-Deslauriers further distinguish among various subtypes of the HC, based largely on harmonic and bass-line considerations.[155] One of their subtypes, the simple (I–V) HC has already been discussed (sec. 3.3.2.1). A second—the *converging half cadence*—employs an ascending bass line against a descending melodic line that projects either the soprano or alto clausulae.[156] A third—the *expanding half cadence*—features a descending bass, derived from the tenor stream, against an ascending melody consisting of the bass clausula: $\hat{3}$–$\hat{4}$–$\hat{5}$.[157] Finally, they introduce a subtype that they call the *doppia half cadence*, after an AC pattern common in the baroque era and termed the *cadenza doppia* (double cadence) by many theorists of the time.[158] Since this fourth subtype begins with a dominant-seventh sonority (though eventually ending with a dominant triad), their *doppia* HC does not conform to the definition of HC developed in this study, and so I will leave it aside for further discussion in Chapter 4 on cadential deviations (sec. 4.4.4.4).

---

154. Martin and Pedneault-Deslauriers, "Mozartian Half Cadence," 204.

155. Martin and Pedneault-Deslauriers actually speak of HC "types," but I will refer to them as *subtypes*, seeing as the HC itself is a genuine cadence type as defined in this study.

156. Martin and Pedneault-Deslauriers, "Mozartian Half Cadence," 186–89. They borrow the term from Gjerdingen's "Converging" schema (*Galant Style*, 159–62), a specific form of HC that always includes ④ and ♯④ in the ascending bass. Their converging HC has no such harmonic requisite.

157. Martin and Pedneault-Deslauriers, "Mozartian Half Cadence," 190–92. The term "expanding" in this context has a very different meaning from the similar term in the expression "expanded cadential progression," the topic of Chapter 5. Here, "expanding" refers to a contrapuntal contour; there, "expanded" refers to the temporal lengthening of the cadential progression.

158. Martin and Pedneault-Deslauriers, "Mozartian Half Cadence," 193–96. The authentic *cadenza doppia* is discussed in Chapter 6, sec. 6.1.2.

Let us now relate the first three of their principal HC subtypes more specifically to the various melodic patterns developed thus far in this study.

### 3.3.3.1. Simple (I–V) HC

The simple HC regularly appears within the corpus of works examined for this chapter. As already mentioned, the initial tonic normally stands in root position, and in the majority of cases, the melodic content is based on the *simple basic pattern* ($\hat{3}/\hat{2}/\hat{2}/\hat{1}$) of the AC.[159] Since this subtype only includes stages 1 and 3, the resulting pattern can be represented as $\hat{3}//\hat{2}$.[160] The initial tonic often functions as a linking harmony ending a prolongational progression, one that is typically achieved by the motion $V^6_5$–I, supporting $\hat{4}$–$\hat{3}$, as seen in Example 3.104. In some cases, stage 3 is embellished with a cadential six-four, thus yielding the pattern $\hat{3}//\hat{3}$-$\hat{2}$ (Ex. 3.105).

The *varied* version of the simple pattern ($\hat{1}/\hat{2}/\hat{2}/\hat{1}$) produces the half cadential ascending line $\hat{1}//\hat{2}$, shown in Example 3.106; note that the melodic ascent is reinforced by beginning on a precadential $\hat{7}$ (supported by $V^4_3$). A version using the cadential six-four ($\hat{1}//\hat{3}$-$\hat{2}$) appears in Example 3.107. Another variant sees the initial tonic supported by $I^6$ (Ex. 3.108).[161] In general, such ascending melodic motion ($\hat{1}$–$\hat{2}$) to the final cadential pitch occurs with HCs more frequently than with ACs. The effect is one whereby the HC's "question" (as a melodic ascent) is "answered" (as a descent) by a subsequent AC.

A surprisingly small number of simple HC melodies end on the leading tone approached above from the tonic; this $\hat{1}//\hat{7}$ pattern derives from deleting stages 2 and 4 of the varied alto stream ($\hat{1}/\hat{2}/\hat{7}/\hat{1}$). Example 3.109 is one such case.[162] Also rare are HCs built around the dominant degree in the upper voice; this $\hat{5}//\hat{5}$ pattern derives from the varied tenor stream ($\hat{5}/\hat{6}/\hat{5}/\hat{3}$), as illustrated in Example 3.110.[163]

### 3.3.3.2. Converging HC

The converging HC features a standard ascending bass line (③–④–⑤) that counterpoints a descending melody in the upper

---

159. As mentioned in note 149, "simple" is being used in two different ways here: as a distinct HC subtype and as a cadential melodic pattern.

160. The same melodic configuration can also be derived from the varied soprano pattern $\hat{3}/\hat{4}/\hat{2}/\hat{1}$, thus yielding $\hat{3}//\hat{2}$ for the simple half cadence. Recall that two slashes in a row indicate that stage 2 is omitted from the schema; stage 4 of the AC is, obviously, never included in melodic patterns of the HC.

161. The first inversion tonic is rarely used with the *basic* simple pattern $\hat{3}//\hat{2}$, most likely due to the weak effect of an octave doubling with the bass ③ in stage 1; see Mozart, Clarinet Quintet in A, K. 581, iv, m. 12 (*ACF* 7.17) for an exceptional case.

162. For a version using the cadential six-four, see Beethoven, Piano Sonata in C Minor, Op. 111, ii, mm. 3–4.

163. See also the earlier discussion of Ex. 3.86, mm. 5–6.

EXAMPLE 3.106. Beethoven, Piano Sonata in D, Op. 10, no. 3, i, mm. 25–26 (*ACF* 3.26).

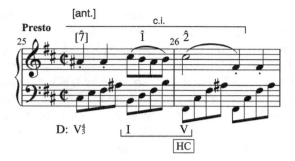

EXAMPLE 3.107. Mozart, Piano Concerto in B-flat, K. 450, ii, mm. 19–20 (*ACF* Sup. 8.4).

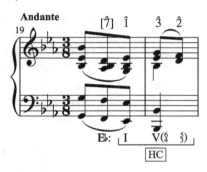

EXAMPLE 3.108. Mozart, Piano Sonata in D, K. 284, iii, mm. 130–31 (*ACF* Sup. 8.10).

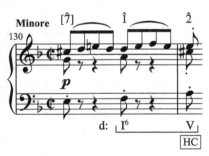

EXAMPLE 3.109. Mozart, Symphony No. 35 in D ("Haffner"), K. 385, iii, mm. 3–4 (*ACF* Sup. 4.18).

EXAMPLE 3.110. Beethoven, Violin Sonata in C Minor, Op. 30, no. 2, i, mm. 6–8 (*ACF* Sup. 6.4).

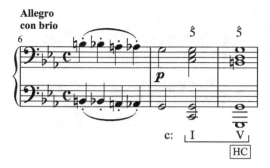

voice. This "coming together" (convergence) of the two lines accounts for Gjerdingen's choice of nomenclature and is cited as especially characteristic by Martin and Pedneault-Deslauriers.[164] Unlike the simple HC, the pre-dominant harmony of stage 2 is necessarily present in the converging HC, often in the form of two distinct substages (④–♯④). Indeed, many cases either omit stage 1 outright or find the melodic component of a possible stage 1 in the noncadential material that precedes the onset of the actual cadential progression. As mentioned earlier (in connection with Ex. 3.100), the durational emphasis often accorded stage 2, whereby pre-dominant harmony may occupy an entire bar of music, helps enable the goal dominant to appear on the downbeat of the subsequent bar, typically measures 4 or 8 of the theme. This emphasis also provides space for extensive melodic embellishment in the form of arpeggiations and scales. As a result, it can be difficult at times to decide just which scale degree should be chosen as the structural component of the stage. Due to its conventional bass line, the melodic content of the converging HC can engage all of the patterns associated with the authentic cadence. A variety of successive combinations of streams are also found, along with a handful of miscellaneous patterns. For reasons that are not yet clear, the use of simultaneous streams is not especially characteristic of HCs of any subtype.

**Basic Simple Pattern ($\hat{3}/\hat{2}/\hat{2}$); Varied ($\hat{1}/\hat{2}/\hat{2}$).** Like the authentic cadence, the basic simple pattern is used infrequently to form a converging HC. One of those few cases is seen in Example 3.111 ($\hat{3}/\hat{2}$-$\hat{2}/\hat{2}$), which shows how a subdivided stage 2 supports repeated $\hat{2}$s in the upper voice. In Example 3.112 (/♭$\hat{3}$/$\hat{2}$), the cadential progression begins with stage 2b, where we find ♯④ (VII⁷/V) supporting ♭$\hat{3}$ as a replacement for a diatonic $\hat{2}$. The varied version of the simple pattern ($\hat{1}/\hat{2}$-$\hat{2}$/$\hat{2}$) clearly appears in Example 3.113a, though the very high $\hat{1}$ is left stranded by the two-octave leap down to $\hat{2}$. Earlier in the theme, Haydn uses the same pattern with a cadential six-four ($\hat{1}/\hat{2}/\hat{3}$-$\hat{2}$) (Ex. 3.113b), but embellishes stage 2 with an ascending arpeggio ($\hat{2}$-$\hat{4}$-$\hat{6}$), a technique often seen in authentic cadences (see again Ex. 3.30).

**Basic Soprano ($\hat{5}/\hat{4}/\hat{2}$); Varied ($\hat{3}/\hat{4}/\hat{2}$).** Converging HCs employing the soprano stream are well represented in the corpus.

---

164. Martin and Pedneault-Deslauriers, "Mozartian Half Cadence," 186.

EXAMPLE 3.111.  Haydn, Symphony No. 93 in D, i, mm. 59–61 (*ACF* 12.16).

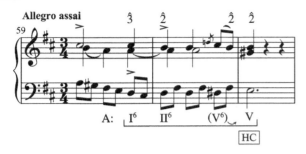

EXAMPLE 3.112.  Beethoven, Piano Concerto No. 2 in B-flat, Op. 19, iii, mm. 7–8 (*ACF* 6.5).

Almost always, the pattern begins with stage 2, though a pitch denoting stage 1 (usually $\hat{3}$ of the varied pattern) may appear at the end of the precadential passage. Thus in Example 3.114, the $\hat{3}$ over ① arriving on the second half of measure 7 belongs more to the prior tonic prolongation than to the cadential progression per se, where the bass-line leap down to ④ initiates stage 2. Note as well that the gap between $\hat{4}$ and $\hat{2}$ of the basic pattern is filled in with $\hat{3}$ by means of the six-four in stage 3a. Alternatively, this gap can be filled by using stage 2b, as seen in Example 3.115. Note that this example features the basic soprano as indicated by the precadential $\hat{5}$.

**Basic Alto ($\hat{3}/\hat{2}/\hat{7}$); Varied ($\hat{1}/\hat{2}/\hat{7}$).** The alto pattern accounts for the largest number of converging HCs in the corpus. Just why a converging cadence tends to end on an alto $\hat{7}$ more than a soprano $\hat{2}$ is unclear. Even if we include simple HCs ending on $\hat{2}$, the alto-stream converging cadence still accounts for almost double the number of examples, thus making this category the largest one among all HC types. Like the soprano pattern, the alto one almost always begins with stage 2, though the melodic content of stage 1 is often found in the preceding noncadential material (Ex. 3.116, middle of m. 11). Unambiguous cases including all three stages is rare; Example 3.117 shows one such instance. Sometimes the pitch content of stage 1 can be identified as arising out of a broader prolongation of the pre-dominant II, as seen in Example 3.118. Here, stage 1 (I⁶) can be found on the fourth eighth-note beat of measure 19. The question then becomes whether or not this moment is heard as the actual onset of the cadential progression. If so, then we can identify all three stages of the cadence. If not, we might regard the I⁶ as passing between II and II⁶, hearing the progression to begin instead with stage 2 on the downbeat of measure 19. In that case, the melodic pattern would begin with $\hat{4}$

from the soprano stream moving via a voice-exchange to the alto $\hat{2}$ when II⁶ appears. Thus whether or not a given HC of this sub-type contains stage 1 is usually a matter of interpreting the general grouping structure and the specific boundaries of the cadential progression, an issue we have encountered throughout this study.

The unembellished alto pattern contains a gap between $\hat{2}$ and $\hat{7}$, one that is almost always filled in by $\hat{1}$, either supported by the cadential six-four of stage 3a, $\hat{3}/\hat{2}/\hat{1}\text{-}\hat{7}$ (see the earlier discussed Ex. 3.29, m. 2), or by a pre-dominant built over #④ in stage 2b, $\hat{3}/\hat{2}\text{-}\hat{1}/\hat{7}$ (see again Ex. 3.117). Sometimes, both stages 2 and 3 are subdivided, yielding the pattern $\hat{3}/\hat{2}\text{-}\hat{1}/\hat{1}\text{-}\hat{7}$ of Example 3.116. Here, as is often the case, stage 1 is omitted from the cadential schema even if its melodic component ($\hat{3}$) appears immediately before the cadential melody proper.

Since most converging cadences begin with stage 2, it is worth considering in a little more detail the harmonic content out of which the pre-dominant emerges. In many cases, of course, it follows a prior tonic (typically I, but sometimes I⁶ or VI). At other times, stage 2 appears as the last link of a sequential progression, often a descending-step sequence, as seen in Example 3.116. Here, the downbeat of measure 11 holds IV⁶, which initiates the sequence. What breaks the sequential pattern is the ascending move of the bass to #④, which then marks stage 2b of the half cadential progression. The prior II⁶ thus functions as a linking harmony, ending the sequence and initiating the cadence.[165] A similar, but more extensive sequence occurs in Example 3.119. The uniformity of melodic-motivic material throughout the sequential passage means that the change in the second half of measure 25 from ④ to #④ is the decisive move that breaks the sequence and announces the half cadence; we thus perhaps experience less the sense of the II⁶ as a linking harmony compared to Example 3.116. (If we do hear the linking chord option, then the harmonic analysis would be that shown in the alternative annotations.) An ascending stepwise sequence can also be used to set up an initiating pre-dominant, as seen in Example 3.120. Here, I⁶ appears at the end of measure 17; however, in the context of the prevailing 5–6 ascending sequence, that harmony does not immediately register as initiating a cadential progression, but rather more as continuing the sequence. Only when the 5–6 pattern is broken by II⁶ on the downbeat of measure 18 (which replaces an expected IV) do we begin to think that the sequence might be over, an impression confirmed by the chromatic motion up to #④ in the second half of the bar.

Stage 2 of the converging HC is often the site of melodic embellishment, even quite considerable, especially when the pre-dominant lasts an entire bar of music. In the case of the alto pattern, we frequently encounter the initial pitch $\hat{2}$ moving upward to $\hat{4}$ (thus touching the soprano stream) before continuing on to $\hat{1}$ and $\hat{7}$. As seen in the earlier Example 3.29, the stepwise ascent in measure 2 from $\hat{2}$ to $\hat{4}$ may be accompanied by a

---

165. I indicate the II⁶ as linking by placing it within both the cadential bracket and the closing parenthesis of the sequential progression.

EXAMPLE 3.113. Haydn, String Quartet in F, Op. 74, no. 2, ii, (a) mm. 14–16 (*ACF* Sup. 7.3); (b) mm. 3–4.

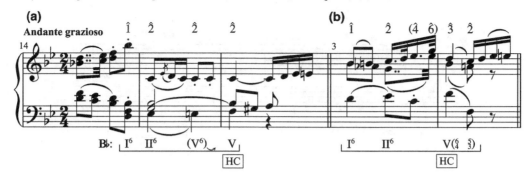

EXAMPLE 3.114. Beethoven, Violin Sonata in A, Op. 30, no. 1, iii, mm. 7–8 (*ACF* 8.3).

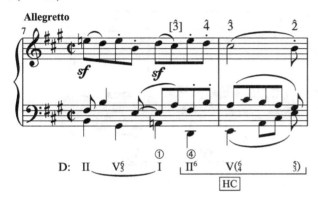

EXAMPLE 3.115. Beethoven, Piano Concerto No. 3 in C Minor, Op. 37, i, mm. 324–26 (*ACF* 14.13).

EXAMPLE 3.116. Haydn, Piano Trio in E-flat, H. 22, iii, mm. 11–12 (*ACF* 11.21).

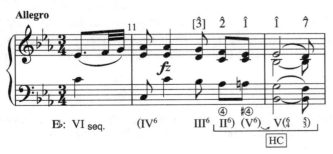

EXAMPLE 3.117. Beethoven, Cello Sonata in G, Op. 5, no. 2, ii, mm. 3–4 (*ACF* Sup. 3.3).

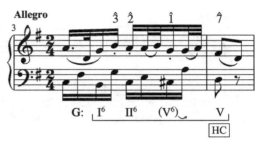

EXAMPLE 3.118. Haydn, Piano Sonata in E-flat, H. 49, i, mm. 19–20 (*ACF* 11.3).

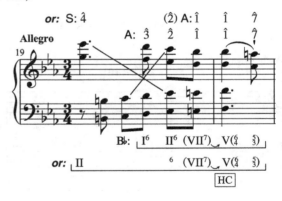

voice-exchange with the bass (④ to ②) thus supporting the predominant prolongation embedded within the broader cadential progression. The melody of Example 3.121 creates an initial gap from $\hat{2}$ up to $\hat{6}$ (of the tenor stream) followed by a quick descending scalar fill, reminiscent of the Cudworth authentic cadence. An even more rhythmically subtle embellishment can be seen in Example 3.122, where a scalar drive in stage 1 from $\hat{5}$ (of the soprano stream) down to $\hat{2}$ for the beginning of stage 2 leads to a return up to $\hat{4}$ and back down to $\hat{1}$ (at the start of stage 3a). The overall ascending/descending melodic contour is typical of a half cadential stage 2 (just as we discussed for the same stage in the authentic cadence). In addition, both of the scalar descents evoke the Cudworth formula. Finally, the complexity

EXAMPLE 3.119. Mozart, Piano Sonata in D, K. 576, i, mm. 24–26 (*ACF* 11.2).

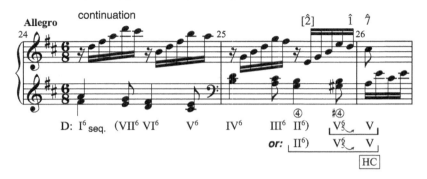

EXAMPLE 3.120. Beethoven, Piano Sonata in G, Op. 14, no. 2, i, mm. 15–19 (*ACF* 11.25).

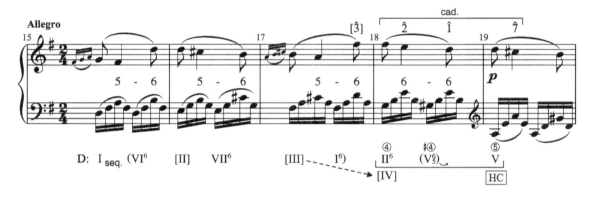

EXAMPLE 3.121. Mozart, Piano Sonata in B-flat, K. 333, ii, mm. 3–4 (*ACF* 3.10).

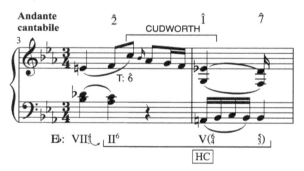

of this example can also be explained in terms of a *simultaneous* combination of soprano and alto streams.

**Basic Tenor (8̂/6̂/5̂); Varied (5̂/6̂/5̂).** Only a handful of converging HCs are based on the tenor pattern. Example 3.123 shows two cases where all three stages are used: in the first, stages 1 and 2 receive extensive scalar embellishments, which continue to develop the descending motive from measure 6 (a continuational fragment); in the second, the opening pitch of the pattern (8̂) lies an octave lower than usual, though the precadential tonic supports that pitch in the higher register.

**Combinations.** If the complete tenor is not commonly used for a converging HC, the tenor's opening two stages, especially of the varied pattern (5̂–6̂), are frequently employed in *successive*

combination with the soprano or alto, in the manner of a tenor combo. Thus in Example 3.124 the initial ♯5̂–6̂ motion for stages 1 and 2a derives from the tenor stream, while the leap down to 1̂–7̂ engages the alto. Similarly, the opening of the cadential progression in Example 3.125 draws on the tenor stream (5̂–6̂), which then combines with the soprano (4̂–3̂–2̂). The stepwise descent filling in 6̂ through 3̂ recalls the Cudworth schema. Observe as well that the notated appoggiaturas confirm that the structural melody of measure 7, beat 3, is 6̂–4̂; this motion to 4̂ following the high 6̂ of the tenor already references the soprano. Indeed, a number of HCs using this combination see a downward leap from 6̂ to 4̂ (and even sometimes further to 2̂) to help forge a tighter link between the tenor and soprano (or alto) streams.[166] Note that both the tenor 6̂ and the soprano 4̂ occupy the same cadential stage, thus forging a brief simultaneous combination. This use of both successive and simultaneous combinations is even more evident in Example 3.126a and b, where the opening two stages of each passage simultaneously combine a tenor and soprano and a tenor and alto, respectively, after which the "lower" stream emerges alone in stage 3 so that the cadence can conclude on 2̂ or 7̂. The relatively large number of HCs using a tenor combined with an alto or soprano stream is consistent with

---

166. See, for example, Mozart, Piano Sonata in D, K. 284, ii, 8, and, with considerably more embellishment, Mozart, Piano Sonata in D, K. 576, ii, 3–4.

EXAMPLE 3.122. Mozart, Piano Sonata in A Minor, K. 310, ii, mm. 2–4 (*ACF* Sup. 3.2).

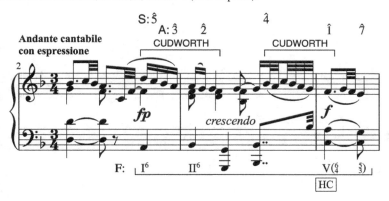

EXAMPLE 3.123. (a) Mozart, Piano Sonata in D, K. 311, iii, mm. 6–8 (*ACF* 2.16); (b) Beethoven, String Quartet in F, Op. 59, no. 1, iii, mm. 7–8 (*ACF* 6.20).

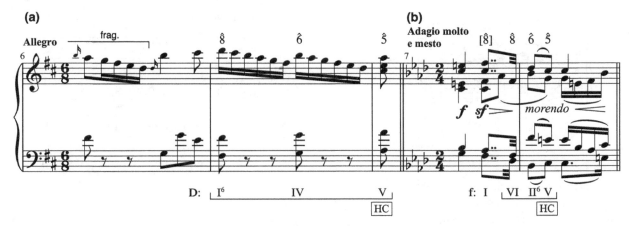

EXAMPLE 3.124. Beethoven, Violin Sonata in A Minor ("Kreutzer"), Op. 47, i, mm. 10–13 (*ACF* 16.4).

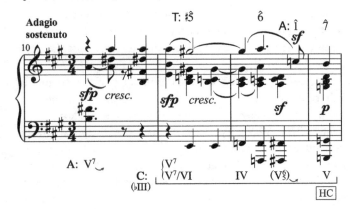

EXAMPLE 3.125. Mozart, Piano Sonata in C, K. 309, ii, mm. 7–8 (*ACF* Sup. 6.3).

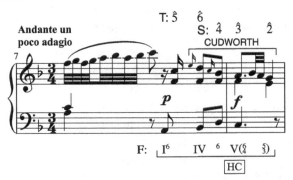

the many cases of ACs using similar combinations, especially the tenor combo.[167]

In addition to combinations involving the tenor stream, we find some that only engage the soprano and alto streams.

Thus the pattern $\hat{5}/\hat{4}$-$\hat{2}$/$\hat{1}$-$\hat{7}$ (Ex. 3.127) successively combines the soprano of stages 1 and 2a with the alto of stages 2b and 3, thus creating a completely stepwise descent (in the spirit of a Cudworth).

**Simple versus Converging.** Before leaving the converging HC, we can observe that in some cases, the cadence can be counted as simple or converging. Thus in Example 3.128, the ♯$\hat{4}$ on the last eighth note of measure 7 could be considered either an embellishment of a simple I–V HC (line 1 of the

---

167. It interesting to note, however, that an HC tenor combo $\hat{5}/\hat{6}$/$\hat{1}$-$\hat{2}$ (T/T/A-S) is not included in the corpus, perhaps reflecting the general preference for ending an HC on $\hat{7}$ rather than on $\hat{2}$.

EXAMPLE 3.126. (a) Mozart, Piano Sonata in D, K. 284, iii, mm. 3–4 (*ACF* 7.21); (b) Haydn, Piano Sonata in E-flat, H. 49, iii, mm. 15–16 (*ACF* 7.8).

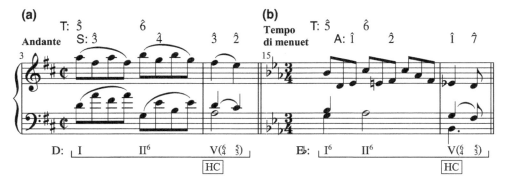

EXAMPLE 3.127. Haydn, Piano Sonata in E-flat, H. 38, iii, mm. 3–4 (*ACF* Sup. 7.8).

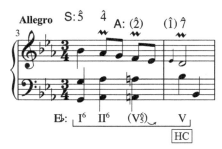

EXAMPLE 3.128. Haydn, Piano Sonata in F, H. 29, iii, mm. 7–8 (*ACF* Sup. 8.13).

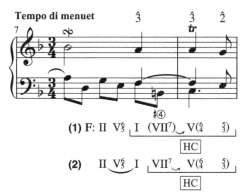

harmonic analysis) or as a genuine constituent of a converging HC, beginning solely with stage 2b (line 2). The issue here is more one of harmony than melody, namely, the attending to different levels of harmonic activity. Ultimately, classifying a given cadence is, in itself, not necessarily an interesting analytical act; rather, it is using the classifications to help understand the particularities of a given cadential formation that validates, one hopes, the construction and employment of the scheme in the first place.[168]

### 3.3.3.3. Expanding HC

The expanding HC is formed when the tenor stream ($\hat{8}$/$\hat{6}$/$\hat{5}$) is shifted into the actual bass (thus ⑧/⑥/⑤), while the bass stream is placed in an upper part ($\hat{3}$/$\hat{4}$/$\hat{5}$). At times, one of the other streams (soprano or alto) appears in the uppermost voice, with the bass stream occupying an interior position within the texture.

For the purposes of describing the melodic content that arises from this arrangement of the streams, it is useful to distinguish among situations where the dominant in the bass voice is approached: (1) by a whole step (⑧/⑥/⑤); (2) by a half step

(⑧/♭⑥/⑤); or (3) by two half steps (⑧/⑥–♭⑥/⑤), thus yielding a subdivided stage 2. Just like the converging HC, the expanding one more often than not omits stage 1 or else finds the content of that stage represented in the immediately preceding noncadential material. As well, the melodic content of stage 2 is often highly embellished, sometimes making it difficult to determine just which pitch is structural (i.e., represents the stage as a whole).

**Whole-Step Approach (⑥–⑤).** This form of the expanding half cadence occurs in major-mode contexts, with the predominant normally taking the form of a secondary dominant (VII⁶/V, V⁴₃/V). Typically, the bass stream appears in the very upper voice with the pattern $\hat{3}$–#$\hat{4}$/$\hat{5}$. As such, stage 2a is bypassed in favor of stage 2b (see again Ex. 3.103). In some cases, the gap in the bass line between ⑧ and ⑥ is filled in by ⑦, supporting a passing dominant (e.g., V⁶), as seen in Example 3.129. Depending upon where one wants to see the cadential idea beginning—either in the middle of measure 3 or on the downbeat of measure 4—we may or may not recognize the presence of stage 1. Note as well that the melodic line in stage 2b is quite embellished, yet the final sounding pitch of this stage is #$\hat{4}$, as called for by the pattern.

Now and then, the root of the secondary dominant in stage 2 is "cast out" (to speak with Rothstein, via Schenker's "*Auswerfen des Grundtons*") as ② below the structural bass ⑥ (Ex. 3.130,

---

168. In the case of Ex. 3.128, the analysis might actually have performance implications. The pianist could project a *simple* HC by emphasizing F in the left hand of beat 3, while underplaying the embellishing leap to B♭; alternatively, imparting an accent to that same B♭ could help convey the impression of a *converging* HC.

EXAMPLE 3.129. Beethoven, Piano Sonata in D, Op. 10, no. 3, iv, mm. 3–4 (*ACF* 5.8).

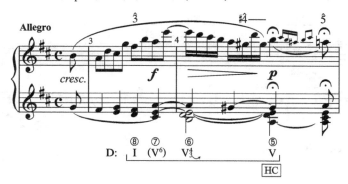

EXAMPLE 3.130. Haydn, Piano Sonata in C, H. 35, iii, mm. 11–14 (*ACF* Sup. 7.11).

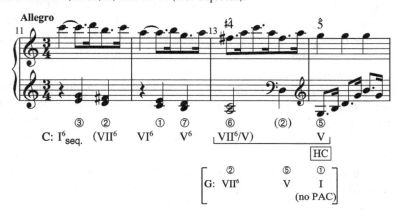

m. 13).¹⁶⁹ The reason for this embellishment here might be due to the way in which the onset of the cadential progression emerges, namely, as the final harmony of a broader descending-stepwise sequence. In order to help break out of the sequence and to suggest the change to a cadential progression, Haydn sounds ⑥ on the *downbeat* of measure 13 (in the prior bars, the bass appears only on the second and third beats) and then casts out the root ② for additional emphasis.¹⁷⁰

On occasion, the alto stream (1̂/-1̂-7̂) is placed in a separate voice above the bass stream, which then appears in an inner voice (Ex. 3.131). A comparable example featuring the complete soprano stream does not arise in the corpus, but a successive combination of alto and soprano (/-1̂/3̂-2̂) appears a number of times (see Ex. 3.132 for one such case).

EXAMPLE 3.131. Mozart, Piano Concerto in F, K. 459, i, mm. 74–75 (*ACF* 3.6).

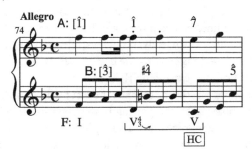

EXAMPLE 3.132. Haydn, String Quartet in C, Op. 50, no. 2, iii, mm. 3–4 (*ACF* 3.23).

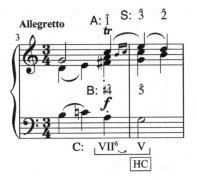

---

169. William Rothstein, "Transformations of Cadential Formulae in the Music of Corelli and His Successors," 255; Schenker, *Free Composition*, sec. 247. Rothstein remarks that "[Ernst] Oster translates Schenker's term here as 'addition of a root,' although in his oral teaching he used the more literal—and far more vivid—'casting out.' (He once compared the casting out of a root to a ship casting out its anchor.)" (Rothstein, 255, note 33).

170. We must be careful not to think that the motion D–G in the bass creates a PAC in G major (as annotated within the brackets), since the penultimate dominant appears first as an inversion (VII⁶) at the beginning of m. 13.

EXAMPLE 3.133. Haydn, Piano Sonata in G, H. 40, ii, mm. 12–14 (*ACF* 7.7).

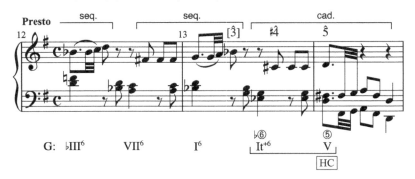

**Half-Step Approach** (♭$\hat{6}$–$\hat{5}$). The half-step approach to the cadential dominant, with its characteristic sixth degree from the minor mode (♭$\hat{6}$), takes place either in the broad context of an overall minor modality or, as a case of modal mixture within a more prevailing major modality. The pre-dominant of stage 2 normally takes the form of an augmented-sixth harmony of some kind (the Italian sixth being most preferred). Since that harmony contains ♯$\hat{4}$, the defining feature of stage 2b, we understand that stage 2a has been skipped over altogether; like so many other HCs, stage 1 is often bypassed as well.

As with the whole-step approach to the dominant, the half-step approach typically finds the bass stream shifted into the upper voice to yield the pattern $\hat{3}$/-♯$\hat{4}$/$\hat{5}$ (Ex. 3.133). Note that the pitch content of stage 1 ($\hat{3}$) appears on the second beat of measure 13, but since this pitch is the final one of a sequential fragment, it does not really belong to the cadential idea per se, and so the cadence more properly begins with the Italian sixth of stage 2b. As seen in Example 3.102 (discussed earlier), the initial pitch of stage 2b may sometimes be taken from a different stream, in this case $\hat{1}$ (from the alto), which leads through various embellishments to the final pitch ♯$\hat{4}$, thus creating the half-step ascending motion so characteristic of the expanding HC.

Another option sees the bass stream occupying an inner voice, with some other stream appearing in the upper-most voice (Ex. 3.134). Here, the soprano voice actually holds the soprano stream (/-4/3-2), while the bass steam resides in the alto (top strand of the left-hand part).

More complicated combinations may also be encountered. Thus in Example 3.135, the use of $\hat{1}$ for both stages 1 and 2 draws upon the alto stream, but rather than continuing with $\hat{7}$, the melody leaps down to double $\hat{5}$ from the bass stream, which appears in an inner voice. Note that this example does not use an augmented sixth; rather, stage 2 exclusively brings the diatonic IV⁶ (which itself ensues directly from the tonic substitute VI). We see here one of the few cases in the corpus of the so-called phrygian HC, a variant type more associated with the earlier baroque and galant styles than with the classical style.[171] Example 3.136 shows another complex melodic situation. The cadential idea begins with the basic alto stream ($\hat{3}$/-$\hat{1}$/$\hat{7}$) in the upper voice for stages 1 and 2, but then shifts to an inner voice for the final stage ($\hat{7}$). At the same time, ♯$\hat{4}$ from the bass stream's stage 2 shifts to the upper voice for $\hat{5}$. (It is not clear which pitch is meant to represent the inner voice of stage 1 in this dense symphonic texture.)[172] To be sure, the "melodic complications" of this and the previous example are due to how their leaping melodies relate to the models of cadential melody that I am proposing, ones based on predominantly descending scalar motion; the upper voices are obviously not "complicated" in themselves. At the same time, it must be observed that such leaping melodies occur in the great minority of cases encountered in the classical style, a fact that helps to validate the establishment of the models in the first place.

**Two-Half-Step Approach** (♮$\hat{6}$–♭$\hat{6}$–$\hat{5}$). Like the previous type, the appearance of ♭$\hat{6}$ associates this pattern with the minor mode and the use of an augmented-sixth harmony for stage 2b. The appearance of ♮$\hat{6}$ along with ♭$\hat{6}$ creates a heightened chromaticism that may be reflected as well in the upper voice (Ex. 3.137). Here, a fully chromaticized bass stream begins in the upper voice, until it is "covered" by the alto stream for stages 2b and 3 (/-$\hat{1}$/$\hat{1}$-$\hat{7}$). This example is also one of the few that subdivides all three stages of the half cadential progression. The types of melodic patterns seen for the other bass-line options apply as well to the two-half-step approach and thus do not need to be further illustrated here.

### 3.3.3.4. Miscellaneous Issues

Two miscellaneous issues—the *unison* half cadence and combinations of converging and expanding cadences—round out my discussion of the melodic content in HCs.

**Unison half cadence.** As we saw earlier in connection with Example 3.59a, measures 7–8, a PAC may be formed with only a single voice being expressed; by default, that voice would need to be a bass, otherwise, we would not be able differentiate

---

171. See the earlier discussion of Ex. 3.101 (sec. 3.3.2.2).

172. The unusual leap up to $\hat{5}$, rather than the more normal move from $\hat{1}$ to $\hat{7}$, is likely due to motivic grounds, namely as a means of continuing to emphasize $\hat{5}$ as the opening pitch of both the famous thematic introduction and the basic idea of the main theme.

EXAMPLE 3.134. Mozart, Piano Sonata in F, K. 332, iii, mm. 55–57 (*ACF* 1.4).

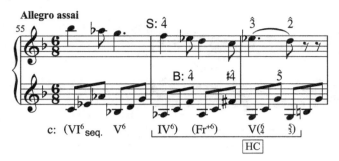

EXAMPLE 3.135. Beethoven, Piano Sonata in E, Op. 14, no. 1, ii, mm. 96–100 (*ACF* 18.16a).

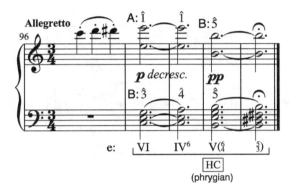

EXAMPLE 3.136. Beethoven, Symphony No. 5 in C Minor, Op. 67, i, mm. 18–21 (R = 2N) (*ACF* 2.27).

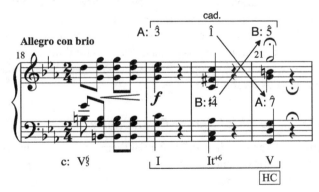

EXAMPLE 3.137. Mozart, Piano Sonata in D, K. 284, iii, mm. 122–23 (*ACF* Sup. 4.16).

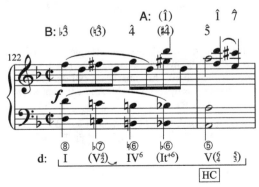

EXAMPLE 3.138. Mozart, Piano Sonata in D, K. 576, iii, mm. 22–23 (*ACF* 12.9).

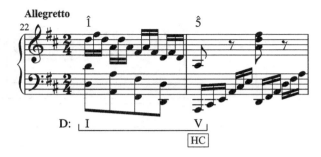

EXAMPLE 3.139. Mozart, Piano Sonata in G, K. 283, i, mm. 21–22 (*ACF* 11.11).

a prolongational situation from a cadential one. This *unison* (or doubled monophony) texture can arise with an HC as well.[173] Sometimes, the unison HC obviously references one of the standard types, such as the simple (I–V) HC (Ex. 3.138) or the bass line of the converging cadence (Ex. 3.139). At other times, no obvious cadential model is suggested by the melodic line, as in Example 3.140.

**Converging-Expanding (or Expanding-Converging) Combinations.** When presenting their HC subtypes, Martin and Pedneault-Deslauriers discuss a passage (their Ex. 19), shown here (with my annotations) in Example 3.141. It begins as a converging HC but transforms itself, via a voice-exchange process within stage 2, into an expanding HC. The opposite situation— the change from an expanding to converging cadence—also occurs and may actually be more common. Thus in Example 3.142, the descending bass line is suggestive of an expanding HC, but the further voice-exchange linking stages 2a and 2b yields an ascending bass approach to the dominant, and a converging cadence thus emerges in the end; the melody features a complete varied soprano ($\hat{3}/\hat{4}/\hat{3}$–$\hat{2}$).

An interesting play with descending and ascending approaches to the dominant can be seen in Example 3.143. Here, the Italian augmented-sixth harmony in the second half of measure 20 promises to produce an expanding HC for the downbeat of measure 21. But the dissonant seventh added to the dominant at that point disrupts the sense of cadence,

---

173. Martin and Pedneault-Deslauriers also speak of a *unisono* half cadence ("Mozartian Half Cadence," 195–96).

EXAMPLE 3.140. Mozart, Piano Sonata in C, K. 309, i, mm. 30–32.

EXAMPLE 3.141. Mozart, Piano Sonata in B-flat, K. 281, iii, mm. 55–59.

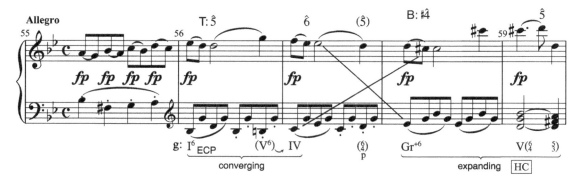

EXAMPLE 3.142. Mozart, Piano Concerto in F, K. 459, ii, mm. 3–4 (*ACF* 5.3a).

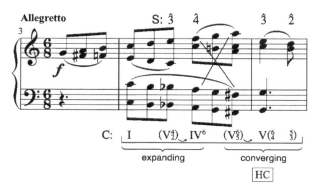

and this V$^7$ ends up functioning as a passing sonority within a pre-dominant prolongation, one that gives way to an ascending approach to the cadential dominant on the downbeat of measure 22. Even within this final pre-dominant in the second half of measure 21, the bass raises the possibility of maintaining the expanding HC when it moves from ♯④ back up to ♭⑥, only to revert to ♯④ to confirm the converging cadence. A nice touch occurs in the postcadential standing on the dominant, when the bass line again regains ♭⑥ to sound twice the expanding pattern.

### 3.3.4. Function

The HC is used to close a wide variety of phrase and thematic units, from a simple four-measure antecedent to a highly complex developmental core, one that can stretch to thirty or more measures. In this section, I first describe the units that can end with an HC in relation to various levels in the structural hierarchy of a movement and then propose some generalizations that account more broadly for this usage.

#### 3.3.4.1. Levels of Phrase Functionality

**Sentential Forms.** All of the sentential theme types—the simple eight-measure sentence (presentation + continuation), the sentential hybrids (compound basic idea + continuation, compound basic idea + consequent), and the compound sixteen-measure sentence—include only a single, final cadence of any type.[174] In the majority of cases, sentential forms end with a PAC, but a good number also close with an independent HC.[175] When so used,

---

174. The hybrid compound basic idea + consequent can, of course, also be considered a periodic hybrid, because of the prominent "return" of the basic idea at the start of the consequent phrase. From a cadential perspective, however, this hybrid resembles more the sentential forms by containing a single cadence.

175. As already discussed, the IAC is rarely used to end these formal types; see in sec. 3.2.2.3 "Ending a Complete Main Theme."

EXAMPLE 3.143. Mozart, Piano Sonata in G, K. 283, ii, mm. 20–23 (*ACF* 9.8).

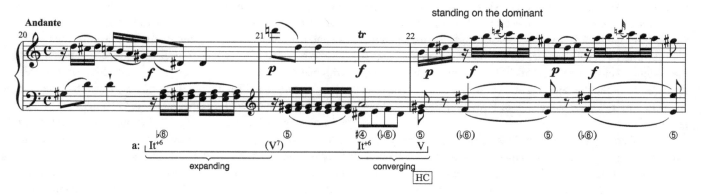

the HC tends to be a relatively brief segment appearing at the end of the continuation phrase (see again Ex. 3.119, upbeat to m. 26), though now and then, it may be sufficiently large to be considered a full two-measure "cadential idea" (Ex. 3.120, mm. 18–19). In the simple sentence or sentential hybrids, the HC normally occurs alone and is not followed by a standing on the dominant; the compound sentence, though, may well include such a postcadential unit.[176]

**Periodic Forms.** The independent HC is the principal device for ending the opening antecedent phrase of the simple period, with only a small number being closed by an IAC.[177] Within the antecedent, half cadential material is often a very brief segment at the end of a two-measure contrasting idea (see again, Ex. 3.106). Less often, the complete contrasting idea is supported by the half cadential progression (Ex. 3.100, mm. 3–4), in which case the contrasting idea effectively resembles the "cadential idea" of a sentence. (The contrasting idea of the consequent phrase of this example can similarly be labeled a cadential idea.)

The two periodic hybrids—antecedent + continuation; and antecedent + cadential—also normally bring an HC halfway through their durational span. Unlike the genuine period, however, this HC does not lead to a return of earlier sounding material but rather to new material constituting a continuation or cadential phrase.

The sixteen-measure compound period offers up to three places for half cadential closure. In almost all cases, the eight-measure compound antecedent ends with this cadence type (rarely is the IAC used for this purpose).[178] If the compound antecedent is built as the hybrid antecedent + continuation, the simple antecedent always ends with an HC as will the continuation most of the time. If the following compound consequent also begins with a simple antecedent, as usually occurs, we then encounter a theme containing three phrases in row that conclude with an HC. In such cases, the material content of the first and second cadence

is usually different, to avoid an obvious redundancy, while the third normally matches the first.[179]

All of the formal contexts mentioned thus far maintain the fundamental cadential syntax, which sees, within a given formal process, a weaker cadence followed eventually by a stronger one. Some exceptional cases, however, seem on the surface to violate this norm, though a closer consideration usually reveals that a convincing compositional logic can nonetheless be found. For example, we sometimes encounter the exceptional situation of a simple eight-measure hybrid whose opening antecedent phrase ends with an independent IAC, typically a "Prinner cadence" (PrC). There follows then a continuation phrase that closes with an HC (see again Ex. 3.74). This succession of cadence types raises the awkward circumstance of an AC preceding an HC. Normally the PrC (as a form of an IAC) in measure 4 should be syntactically stronger than the HC in measure 8, due to the priority we assign to harmonic processes. But in this particular case, the melodic structure of the theme may play a more important role. Note that the PrC brings the melody from $\hat{6}$ stepwise down to $\hat{3}$ as its provisional goal. The melody that ends the following continuation phrase regains $\hat{5}$ (downbeat of m. 7) but then descends stepwise past $\hat{3}$ and on to $\hat{2}$ for the HC, thus projecting forward to a $\hat{1}$ that will eventually be achieved by a final PAC.[180] In other words, some specific formal contexts make it seem as though an IAC is syntactically weaker than a subsequent HC, in seeming opposition to cadential norms.[181]

Another kind of syntactical disruption can occur in a context that some theorists and historians have termed a "reversed" (or "inverted") period.[182] Here, a consequent-like phrase ending with

---

176. See the main theme of Mozart's Symphony No. 40 in G Minor, K. 550, i, mm. 16–20 (*ACF*, 6.21).

177. See again the discussion of Ex. 3.68 and 3.75 (and note 116).

178. See, in sec. 3.2.2.3, "Ending a Compound Antecedent."

179. See Beethoven, Piano Sonata in A-flat, Op. 26, i, mm. 1–16 (*ACF*, Ex. 6.1), and Mozart, String Quartet in C ("Dissonance"), K. 465, iv, mm. 1–16 (*CF*, Ex. 5.13, and *ACF*, Ex. 6.7).

180. In connection with Ex. 4.74, the hybrid theme ending with the HC actually functions as the entire main theme of a larger sonata form; as a result, the promised home-key PAC is deferred until the recapitulation's closure of the subordinate theme (m. 147).

181. Zhang develops this point in greater detail ("Apparently Imperfect," 191, 194, and 197–201); see also Caplin, "Gjerdingen's 'Prinner,'" 38–42.

182. Webster speaks in this context of an "anti-period"; see in Chapter 2, note 129.

a PAC is directly followed by an antecedent-like phrase ending with an HC. As I have discussed elsewhere,[183] this reversal of periodic functions might seem to violate the norms of formal syntax, whereby an "ending" unit would appear to precede an "opening" one. But when we take a broader context into account, we find that the opening "consequent" is actually functioning as an initiating main theme, while the "antecedent" serves as a medial transition. As such, a more logical succession of formal functions is thereby regained.

**Small Ternary.** The three sections of the small ternary form have fairly rigid cadential requirements. The final A′ section always closes with a PAC in the home key. The opening A section also concludes with a PAC, but either of the home key or a subordinate key. Exceptionally, and only in a few works by Haydn, the A section may end with a home-key HC.[184]

The second section of the small ternary form—the contrasting middle (B section)—must close in such a way as to motivate the reappearance of the basic idea from the A section, thus marking the sense of recapitulation that is an essential aspect of the A′ section. This motivation for a return is largely brought about by harmonic means, namely, by the B section ending with dominant harmony, normally in the form of an HC. Adding a standing on the dominant further reinforces the need for tonic resolution to initiate the A′ section. In some cases, the B section consists entirely of a standing on the dominant.[185] In this case, the section "ends" with the dominant, but we cannot speak of a genuine HC given the absence of any harmonic progressions within the section.

At times, the B section modulates to a related tonal region, confirming that subordinate key with a PAC. In order for the music to return to the home key and to set up the A′ section, a *retransition* normally follows, itself ending with a home-key HC (and sometimes a further standing on the dominant). Indeed, retransitional passages of this sort are found in a number of formal contexts that require preparation for a return of opening material, such as at the end of a sonata exposition, a development section, or a rondo couplet.

**Small Binary.** The two parts of the small binary each end with a cadence of some kind. In all cases, the second part brings complete closure with an HK: PAC. And most often, the first part also closes with that cadence type, sometimes in a subordinate key. In a significant minority of cases, however, the first part ends with an HC, either in the home key or in some other key (not necessarily the standard subordinate key). When that cadence occurs, the first part of the form exhibits weaker cadential closure than the second part. Such a situation might raise the idea that the overall form is a period of some kind, especially if the second part begins with material that references the opening of the first part (as often happens with this formal type). But one important characteristic of the small binary counters the impression of a periodic design. In a normal period, the consequent first appears as a *repetition* of the antecedent, only then to close with a stronger cadence. In the small binary, however, the first part itself is almost always repeated prior to the onset of the second part; as a result, the latter part (the putative "consequent") sounds like a "different" unit after the first part, the "antecedent," has already been repeated, and so the effect of a periodic form does not truly emerge.[186]

The second part of a small binary may also include an HC if that part begins with a local B section, which, as already discussed, normally closes with that cadence type.[187] In this case, however, the HC will not engender a "return" of opening material from part one, for this would result in the overall form becoming a small ternary; rather, the contrasting middle will be followed by new material, usually of a continuational or cadential nature. Now and then, a consequent phrase with a "new" basic idea will bring the second part of a small binary to a close.

### 3.3.4.2. Levels of Thematic Functionality

**Main Theme.** Most units that function as a main theme for a movement close with a PAC in the home key. In certain formal types, such as the large ternary and the various rondo forms, the main theme invariably ends with a PAC. In sonata form (and its allied minuet and concerto forms), main themes may occasionally end with an HK: HC. Many of these cases arise in minor-mode contexts, suggesting a correlation between the relative instability of cadential closure and the more intense emotionality typically expressed by this mode.

When confronted with an eight-measure opening theme that ends with an HC, a listener could well believe that the ongoing thematic unit is functioning as a compound antecedent, one that will be answered by a consequent to close the main theme with a PAC. And if the unit following the HC begins with the main theme's basic idea, the expectation of a consequent is reinforced all the more. As noted as early as A. B. Marx, however, this presumed consequent may actually "dissolve" when the music modulates to a subordinate key and we recognize that a transition is already underway.[188] Thus in a series of retrospective reinterpretations, we

---

183. *CF*, 129, 274 (note 23), and *ACF*, 319.

184. Haydn, String Quartet in E-flat, Op. 76, no. 6, i, m. 8; Haydn, String Quartet in B-flat, Op. 55, no. 3, ii, m. 8; Haydn, Piano Trio in A, H. 18, iii, m. 8. I have not yet encountered a case by Mozart or Beethoven of an A section ending with an HC.

185. When the entire B section comprises a standing on the dominant, this unit should not be considered "postcadential," since it occurs immediately after a PAC (ending the A section), not an HC. It would be more proper, therefore, to speak of a *medial* standing on the dominant, in recognition of its broader formal function within the small ternary as a whole.

186. See *ACF*, 246.

187. On the use of a local contrasting middle at the start of a binary's second part, see *CF*, 89–91, and *ACF*, 239–40, 246–52.

188. Adolf Bernhard Marx, *Musical Form in the Age of Beethoven: Selected Writings on Theory and Method*, 107. Marx's notion of the "dissolved consequent" (*aufgelöste Nachsatz*) is one of his enduring theoretical legacies.

understand that the main theme actually did conclude with the HC and that the return of the basic idea (of the dissolved consequent) marks the start of the transition.

**Transition.** A transition is marked especially by its closing with an HC, normally of a newly achieved subordinate key, but sometimes of the home key. As discussed earlier (sec. 3.1.3.2), my theory of formal functions does not recognize the option of a transition closing with a PAC in the subordinate key; rather, I consider such apparent cases as engaging a *fusion* of transition and subordinate-theme functionalities. With Schubert, however, the use of a PAC in the subordinate key becomes a standard option for concluding a transition (while eliding with the beginning of the subordinate theme).[189]

**Subordinate Theme.** A fundamental function of a subordinate theme (in sonata and concerto forms) is to confirm fully the subordinate key with a PAC.[190] As a result, any weaker cadence that arises in the course of that theme must be deemed to have achieved only provisional closure. So if we encounter an HC in the course of a subordinate theme, we are certain that more material will follow, eventually forging the requisite PAC. For that reason, I speak in this context of an *internal* HC, since that cadence type cannot be used to end the theme proper. Most typically, an internal HC is followed either by new continuational material or immediately by cadential material promising authentic cadential closure. Less frequently, an internal HC leads to new material that projects an initiating function of some kind. In such a case, the sense of a *two-part subordinate theme* emerges, with the internal HC marking the end of the first part.

Once a subordinate theme is underway, we are always expecting a final PAC to close the theme. So any syntactically weaker cadential articulation (or any authentic cadential deviation) will seem to appear "in place of" a PAC. In that sense, we might wonder if an internal HC should be understood as a way station, akin to how an IAC functions within a subordinate theme. There are a number of reasons, however, for not including the internal HC as a way station. The most obvious difference between the two situations concerns their underlying harmony. Although half cadential progressions and authentic cadential ones are similar in many respects, we have noted some morphological differences between them. Thus characteristic of an HC is the prominent use of a stage 2b harmony (such as VII$^7$/V), the approach to ⑤ from above (via ⑥ or ♭⑥), or the appearance of a final dominant triad. Hearing such harmonic and bass-line features may account for our sensing in a given situation that an HC, not an IAC, is in the making, and so the internal HC does not seem like a "PAC replacement," an essential element of a way-station. Second, an internal HC frequently leads to a postcadential standing on the dominant, whereas a way-station IAC is never followed by a comparable closing section. Third, the material that comes after an internal HC (and standing on the dominant) is almost always new (to the subordinate theme), whereas a way station tends to repeat the ideas leading up to the IAC. For all of these reasons, we sense that a half cadential articulation within a subordinate theme lies "farther away" from the final PAC. And this perspective explains why an internal HC is almost always the first provisional goal of a subordinate theme, one that is rarely preceded by any type of authentic cadential articulation.[191]

**Pre-core of Development.** Among the many options for how a pre-core of a development section can be constructed, one of them involves a thematic unit whose organization resembles the transition of an exposition. Such a unit modulates, normally from the subordinate key at the beginning of the development to some other related region (typically IV, VI, or II) and closes with an HC in the new key.[192]

**Core of Development.** A core is defined as a broad thematic process consisting of a relatively large model (four to eight measures), one or more sequential repetitions, fragmentation of the grouping structure, cadential closure, and a postcadential unit appropriate to the cadence. In the vast majority of cases, the cadential goal of a core is an HC, followed then by a standing on the dominant.[193] If the core is the last thematic unit of the development, the HC will normally be in the home key so that the concluding dominant well prepares for the initiating tonic of the following recapitulation. In a small number of cases, this final cadence may occur within the development regions of VI or III, in which case the dominant can be heard as a "substitute" for the home-key dominant because both V/VI and V/III contain the leading tone of the home key.[194] If a retransition follows the core, that unit will, like all retransitions, end with an HC in the home key.

**Early in a Coda.** As explained in my books on classical form, I define the "start" of a coda as that place where the recapitulation ceases to correspond to the exposition.[195] In many cases, this moment is not associated with any initiating formal function, but rather occurs within an ongoing, continuational passage that ensues from the closing section of the recapitulation. This preliminary material often functions to set up a more obvious sense of the coda's "beginning" (as opposed to its non-functional "start"),

---

189. For important work on this topic, see Brian Black, "Schubert's 'Deflected-Cadence' Transitions and the Classical Style."

190. As mentioned in sec. 3.1.3.2, "Subordinate Theme," rondo forms are exceptional because a subordinate theme in that full-movement form may not necessarily end with a PAC.

191. As discussed in Chapter 7, subordinate-theme organization in a galant sonata form is less strict in the ordering of these cadential goals. Thus we will observe cases where a deceptive cadence, for example, is followed by an internal HC, or where a given subordinate theme contains two internal HCs; see sec. 7.4.3. Neither of these situations obtains in a classical subordinate theme.

192. On the pre-core of a development section, see *CF*, 147–55, and *ACF*, 440–46.

193. As discussed earlier in sec. 3.1.3.2, "Development Section," a PAC of some development key, most often VI, but also II or III, is sometimes used to end a core, especially in early Haydn. On the core of a development section, see *CF*, 142–47, and *ACF*, 429–40.

194. See *CF*, 141 (ex. 10.2), and *ACF*, 461.

195. *CF*, 181, and *ACF*, 526–27.

and the most direct way of doing so is by means of an HC. What follows this cadence may be the basic idea of the main theme, some other previously heard initiating passage, or even entirely new material.

### 3.3.4.3. Some Functional Generalizations

Having now summarized those specific phrases or thematic units that end with an HC, let us consider some generalizations pertaining to how this cadence functions. First, we have seen that in many contexts, the HC obviously represents a provisional goal of some broader formal process. In some cases, that goal closes the *first part* of some *two-part* structure. Such situations include the HC ending the first part of a periodic theme type, the first part of a small binary, and the first part of a two-part subordinate theme. Other cases see the cadence closing the *second part* of a *three-part* structure, such as the B section of the small ternary and the transition of a sonata exposition (the main theme and subordinate themes being parts one and three, respectively). An HC ending a main theme might seem exceptional, for we would be recognizing this cadence type as closing the *first* part of a three-part structure (the exposition as a whole). But in many such cases, as already discussed, the HC gives the initial impression of ending a compound antecedent (the first of a two-part structure at the phrase level), and only in retrospect, when the subsequent consequent is "dissolved," do we reinterpret that HC as effecting complete closure of the main theme (the first of a three-part structure at the thematic level).

Looking at even higher levels in the structural hierarchy, we can question whether or not a cadence per se is the operative mechanism of closure, as discussed at length in Chapter 2 (sec. 2.2.2). As argued there, I do not recognize a PAC (to take another case) as the primary means of ending a complete exposition or a complete recapitulation, let alone a complete sonata form. Likewise, I would normally not speak of the last occurring HC of the development as ending that complete section. Nonetheless, it is surely relevant that a PAC is the last major cadential articulation of both the exposition and recapitulation (i.e., the cadence ending their respective subordinate themes), while the HC is the last major cadential articulation of a development section (i.e., the cadence ending the core). As such, we strongly associate the development section, as the *second* part of a three-part structure (the entire sonata form), with an emphasis on half cadential closure.[196]

---

196. If the development consists of a pre-core made up of an *incomplete* thematic unit (thus concluding without any cadence) and followed by only a single core, then the HC ending the core will be the only cadence within the development and could thus be deemed as the primary mechanism for sectional closure. See, for example, Mozart's Piano Sonata in F, K. 280, iii, 78–106; the seeming PAC at m. 85 is a cadence of limited scope ending the first phrase of the pre-core, which, as a whole, remains incomplete when the core emerges at m. 90.

When considering the HC in its role as a formal end, the focus of our experiential attention is primarily *backwards*, in the sense that we hear the cadence as bringing a partial close to the form-defining processes (harmony, melody, grouping structure) that precede the cadence. But when recognizing the HC as a provisional end, our focus also shifts *forward* in anticipation of further processes that will fully complete the ongoing formal unit. This forward-hearing perspective also pertains to our expectations about the music (as regards both content and function) that we are likely to encounter following the HC. In this sense, the cadence seems to have not only an ending function, but also an *annunciating function*. And depending on our assessment of the ongoing formal context, we often have some idea of just what kind of musical material will be announced.

Three general situations typically obtain. First, and probably most often, the HC is followed directly by a *return* of the material that initiated the broader formal plan. The basic idea coming after an antecedent of a period is a prime example for two-part structures, and the same return, coming after the B section of a small ternary, for three-part structures. Also included here are a number of retransitional passages, especially the one at the end of a rondo couplet to announce the return of the refrain. The retransition that signals the return of the main theme's basic idea to begin a repeat of a sonata exposition is another case in point. Often, but not necessarily, the second part of a two-part transition opens with the basic idea of the preceding main theme.

Second, the half cadential articulation may be followed by *new* initiating material, that is, a beginning that does not obviously reference earlier ideas. The HC ending a transition is typical of this situation, since the subsequent basic idea that begins the subordinate theme normally brings melodic-motivic ideas not yet heard in the exposition. (Haydn's so-called monothematic expositions, of course, would fit into the first category discussed in the previous paragraph.) The internal HC closing the first part of a two-part subordinate theme also leads to a new initiating idea.

Third, the material following a provisional half cadence can sometimes bypass a new initiating passage and proceed directly to medial or closing functions. The majority of internal HCs in subordinate themes function in this manner, where following the cadence (including a standing on the dominant), the music brings a new continuational passage or even just a cadential one. The same situation applies to some lower-level hybrid themes, where an antecedent closing with an HC is followed by new continuation or cadential phrases. The second part of the small binary may also begin with continuational material.

The annunciating quality of the HC distinguishes itself from the attainment of complete closure by means of a PAC. For with the latter, our conjectures about what will ensue are considerably enlarged. To be sure, our knowledge of the broader formal structure at hand can give us some general clues as to what will follow a given PAC, but even then, the options are usually more varied than what we come to expect following an HC. To take just one example, in the course of a movement that we expect to be in sonata form (such as the opening movement of a string quartet or a symphony), the first home-key PAC will normally signal the end of a main theme. What occurs next can include a variety of options: we may hear a second main theme, which may or may not be based on the opening idea of the first theme,[197] or a transition, which may begin in any number of ways. More exceptionally, we might even perceive the immediate onset of a subordinate theme. In other words, we know that the movement will not end with this first PAC, but our specific expectations for what will continue are multifarious. The HC, on the contrary, generally elicits more specific expectations of what will follow, because the options are more restricted. By ending with dominant harmony, which, perforce, should resolve to tonic, an HC forges a stronger connection with what follows than does a PAC, whose final tonic may yield to any number of subsequent harmonic events. The HC thus promotes formal cohesion, while the PAC fosters formal separation. The balanced combination of the two cadence types helps contribute to the multitude of formal possibilities encountered in music of the high classical style.

### 3.3.5. Special Cases

Whereas I have presented the HC and AC as fully differentiated types, two additional cadential formations seem to combine both types in especially interesting ways, though in each case, the sense of HC emerges as the decisive mode of articulation. In the first situation, which I call a *reinterpreted half cadence*, a local PAC (or sometimes an IAC) in the dominant region of a prevailing key is readily heard to function like an HC when the music immediately returns to the original key. In the second situation, the *reopened half cadence*, the theme is clearly driving to a PAC but at the last second the cadence "reopens" to dominant harmony, thus creating a sense of HC instead.

I should note that technically speaking, the authentic cadence is the one that is reinterpreted or reopened. So the expressions "reinterpreted PAC" or "reopened PAC" might be more precise. However, since the upshot of the cadential conversion is an HC in both cases, I prefer to label the overall situation as a special case of that cadence type, in the sense that the cadential reinterpretation (or reopening) allows for the emergence of the HC. In other words, for the purposes of a broader form-functional analysis, it seems better to identify the cadential circumstances that result from the given technique, not those that precipitate its outcome.

#### 3.3.5.1. Reinterpreted HC

The reinterpreted HC arises when a thematic unit begins in a major-mode key (usually the home key, but possibly the subordinate key) and then, toward its end, quickly modulates to the dominant region of that key as confirmed by a PAC. The music then immediately returns to its starting key, which prompts the listener to reinterpret the PAC as a "kind of" HC because the tonic of the new key has the same pitch content as the dominant of the original key. Morphologically, the cadence in question is a PAC; functionally, however, it behaves like an HC.[198]

A reinterpreted HC typically occurs at the end of a compound antecedent of the compound period form, as seen in the earlier discussed Example 3.80a. The theme begins in the home key of E-flat major, which is confirmed in measure 4 by an IAC at the end of a simple antecedent. A continuation phrase begins in the same key but then effects a modulation to the dominant region, ending there with a completely standard PAC (m. 8), thus concluding a simple hybrid (antecedent + continuation). When the music modulates at once back to the home key, as signaled by the seventh added to the B♭ harmony in measure 8 (second half of beat two) and then starts up with the opening basic idea, we presume that a compound consequent is in the making, one that is realized first by the way-station IAC in measure 16 (Ex. 3.80b) and then by the decisive PAC at measure 20 (Ex. 3.80c). On the surface, it seems that a necessary cadential requirement for a periodic form is not forthcoming, since the cadences ending both the large-scale antecedent and consequent (mm. 8 and 20) are of the same type (PACs) and thus of the same syntactical weight. Yet the impression of an antecedent is nonetheless projected: upon hearing the immediate return to the home key, we can readily reinterpret the B♭ harmony of measure 8 from "having been" the tonic of the local subordinate key to "becoming" (⇒) the dominant of the original home key. As a result, this retrospective reinterpretation allows us to hear the effect of an HC, even if the morphology of that cadence conforms to that of a PAC. For some listeners, indeed, the tendency to retain the home key is so strong that they can perceive an HC without even being aware that, at a more local level, a PAC has been completely articulated.[199]

It is important to recognize that both the PAC in the new key and the *reinterpreted half cadence* (⇒HC) in the home key

---

197. See *CF*, 97, and *ACF*, 298–300.

198. The expression "tonicized half cadence" is occasionally encountered in connection with what I am calling a reinterpreted HC: "Sometimes... [an] antecedent phrase closes with an authentic cadence in the dominant area, which we can refer to as a *tonicized half cadence*. The authentic bass motion (V–I, often embellished with a V$^6_4$) and the cadential soprano $\hat{2}$–$\hat{1}$ or $\hat{7}$–$\hat{1}$ tonicize V to a greater extent than does a single applied chord; V is still heard in relation to the home tonic, as an intensified replacement of a semicadence, but it also may lead to a more extended dominant area should the composer desire" (Aldwell, Schachter, and Cadwallader, *Harmony & Voice Leading*, 252–53). This description well accords with my concept of the reinterpreted HC. Problematic with the term *tonicized half cadence*, however, is that it could equally well be applied to those frequent situations where the ultimate dominant of an HC is "tonicized" by any number of inverted secondary dominants (e.g., V$^6_5$/V, VII$^7$/V). Such cases prohibit us from initially hearing an authentic cadence in the "dominant area," an essential feature of the reinterpreted HC.

199. When teaching this example of a reinterpreted HC, a good number of my students immediately identify an HC at the end of the opening eight-measure phrase without even considering the option of an authentic cadence. When I then ask them to look up from the score, and I play the final two bars of the phrase *in isolation*, they readily report hearing a PAC, much to their surprise.

**122**  Basic Cadence Types

EXAMPLE 3.144. Mozart, Violin Sonata in B-flat, K. 454, iii, (a) mm. 6–10 (*ACF* Sup. 6.2); (b) mm. 7–8 as HC.

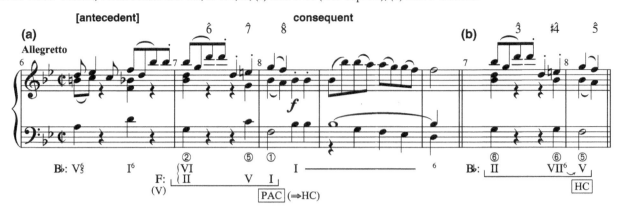

are entirely operative in our listening experience; they occupy, as David Lewin would say, different "phenomenological space-times."[200] Indeed, in the context of the compound antecedent itself, the final PAC in B-flat brings complete cadential closure, if not tonal closure, to that unit. In this particular case, moreover, the strong PAC in measure 8 matches the weaker IAC in measure 4. In the broader formal context, the PAC looks backward, so to speak, while the reinterpreted HC looks forward toward the conclusion of the complete compound period.

**Morphology.** The reinterpreted HC is constructed as a PAC (infrequently an IAC is used instead); that is, the final harmony is understood as a root-position tonic triad preceded by its own dominant, also in root position. Sometimes the cadential content is typical of the standard PAC, as seen in the previous example; more often than not, however, the reinterpreted HC brings some harmonic and melodic features that are less regularly associated with perfect-authentic closure. In particular, stage 2 frequently finds the pre-dominant II harmony standing in root position rather than in the more usual first-inversion form (see Ex. 3.144a). There, the modulation to the dominant region pivots in measure 7 with the VI harmony of the home key (B-flat) becoming II of the new key, which then moves directly to the cadential dominant.

This example also illustrates a melodic gesture often seen with the reinterpreted HC, namely, the ascending motion $\hat{6}$–$\hat{7}$–$\hat{8}$, a melodic profile less commonly used in regular PACs. When we consider both the bass line and the melody line together, we can observe that if the lower voice of the cadential dominant were changed from C to G, as shown in Example 3.144b, then the resulting configuration would correspond to that of an expanding HC, bringing, in the home key, the ascending line /$\hat{3}$–#$\hat{4}$/$\hat{5}$ against the bass /$\hat{6}$–$\hat{6}$/$\hat{5}$. But then, of course, we could not speak of a PAC in the dominant region (cf. Ex. 3.144a, m. 8). Given that the cadential content of this PAC so strongly resembles a regular HC, it is not surprising that some listeners might fail to register the sense of a reinterpreted cadence, and especially here, where the cadential dominant (stage 3 of the PAC) is of such a short duration. Nonetheless, we must recognize that the placing of this dominant in root position is not merely incidental, but presumably a deliberate move by the composer to provide a richer cadential experience at this moment in the form.

In light of the foregoing circumstances, where the root ($\hat{5}$) of the cadential dominant seems almost to have been "cast out" from the pre-dominant $\hat{2}$,[201] we must be careful not to confuse this genuine PAC with a similar situation we saw earlier in Example 3.130. As shown in the bracketed annotations, we again encounter a bass line $\hat{2}$–$\hat{5}$–$\hat{1}$ like that in Example 3.144a; in that earlier example, however, $\hat{2}$ already supports the dominant of the final harmony, and the cast-out root seems to be an embellishing tone, such that we continue to hear an originally inverted dominant (VII⁶/V). In this circumstance, then, we cannot identify a genuine authentic cadential progression in G, but must rather recognize a variant on the regular expanding HC (VII⁶/V–V) in C.

Though the reinterpreted HC normally has the morphology of a PAC, it may sometimes take the form of an IAC. The formation closing a large-scale antecedent in Example 3.145 features the galant-era "Prinner cadence," a subtype of the IAC introduced earlier in sec. 3.2.1.2 (and to be developed more prominently in Chapter 7, sec. 7.1.2). Following parallel motion with the soprano's descending scale from $\hat{6}$ to $\hat{3}$, the bass inserts $\hat{5}$ in order to create a root-position dominant for the authentic cadential progression in E major. In the broader formal context of a highly expanded periodic form, the initially heard PrC in the dominant key becomes a reinterpreted HC in the home key, following which (and after a brief standing on the dominant) the compound consequent begins at measure 21.

**Function.** As discussed several times already, the compound period theme type frequently employs the reinterpreted HC at the end of its compound antecedent.[202] And as already mentioned,

---

200. David Lewin, "Music Theory, Phenomenology, and Modes of Perception," 357, 369.

201. See note 169.

202. In *ACF*, compound periods employing a reinterpreted HC can be found in Ex. 6.8, 6.15, and 6.17, as well as in many "Supplementary" examples on the website (Sup. 5.14, 6.2, 6.10, 6.13, 6.15, and 6.20).

EXAMPLE 3.145. Beethoven, Piano Sonata in A, Op. 2, no. 2, i, mm. 15–22 (*ACF* 10.7).

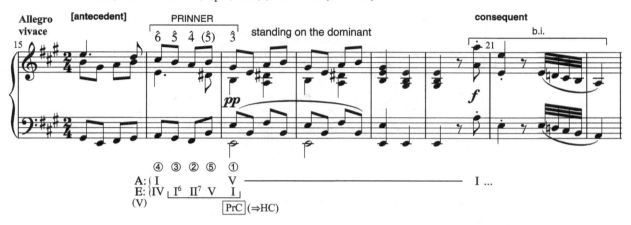

EXAMPLE 3.146. Mozart, Piano Sonata in A, K. 331, ii, mm. 1–7 (*ACF* 18.6).

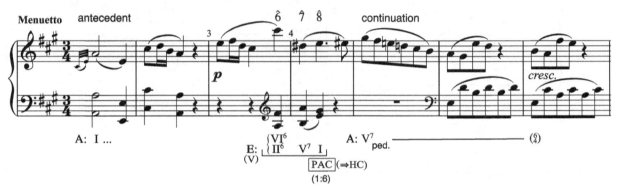

the device works especially well, since in the guise of a PAC, it provides stronger closure compared to a prior HC or IAC ending the simple antecedent (mm. 1–4 of the theme). As a type of HC, however, it still leaves the compound antecedent open-ended in relation to the subsequent consequent.

I have to date encountered only one *simple* period whose four-measure antecedent ends with a reinterpreted HC,[203] but a couple of simple hybrids from the corpus conclude their opening phrases with this cadential formation. As seen in Example 3.146, a reinterpreted HC closes a simple antecedent (m. 4), and the subsequent continuation phrase (which continues to prolong the home-key V$^7$ of the reinterpreted HC) appears in place of a possible consequent. Note that while the harmony of the PAC in E is routine (II$^6$–V$^7$–I), the melody features the less common $\hat{6}$–$\hat{7}$–$\hat{8}$ pattern, which is typical of so many reinterpreted HCs.[204]

Beyond the periodic formations just examined, the reinterpreted HC may also arise in other formal contexts that would close with a regular HC. Thus Example 3.147 shows this cadential device ending the B section of a rounded binary; note again the $\hat{6}$–$\hat{7}$–$\hat{8}$ melody, whose first pitch (like the previous example), lies an octave higher than the others. In Example 3.148, a reinterpreted HC closes the first part of a two-part transition. Although the melodic material leading into the local PAC is conventionally descending, the harmonic support features a root-position II (second half of m. 18), a regular element for this type of cadence. A reinterpreted HC can even arise in the course of a subordinate theme, as shown in Example 3.149, measure 36, where the music suddenly modulates to the dominant region of the subordinate key, only to return quickly back to the tonic of that key. Here, then, we reinterpret the local PAC in A as an internal HC in D, the subordinate key of the movement.

A particularly ingenious use of the reinterpreted HC occurs in the short, and strangely symmetrical, transition from the first movement of a violin sonata by Mozart (see the earlier Ex. 3.72). Following a closing section to the main theme in E minor (shown in Chapter 2, Ex. 2.22), the transition suddenly bursts out with a tonicization of the submediant region (C major); immediately, however, the music modulates to G (here, as the dominant

---

203. See Beethoven, Serenade for Violin, Viola, and Cello in D, Op. 8, iv, mm. 23–30 (discussed in *CF*, 57, in connection with Ex. 4.8). In *ACF*, I first illustrate the reinterpreted cadence appearing in Haydn's String Quartet in G, Op. 64, no. 4, i, 1–8 (Ex. 3.19) in a chapter on the simple period (see also *CF*, Ex. 4.15); I believe now that this theme is better understood as a compound period (notated as R = ½N).

204. See also Mozart, String Quartet in D Minor, K. 421, iv, mm. 97–104 (*ACF*, Ex. 17.18).

EXAMPLE 3.147. Beethoven, Piano Sonata in C Minor ("Pathétique"), Op. 13, iii, mm. 96–99 (*ACF* 19.2).

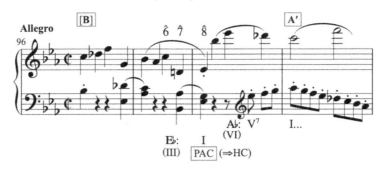

EXAMPLE 3.148. Beethoven, Violin Sonata in F ("Spring"), Op. 24, i, mm. 18–21 (*ACF* 11.26).

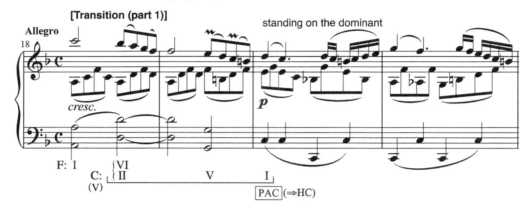

EXAMPLE 3.149. Beethoven, Piano Sonata in G, Op. 14, no. 2, i, mm. 33–37 (*ACF* 12.18).

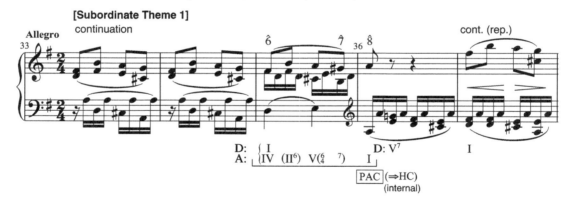

region of C), ending with an IAC in measure 32. When the music returns to the transition's basic idea (mm. 33–34), we understand that the first phrase (mm. 29–32) has closed with a reinterpreted HC ending a simple antecedent, followed by a presumed consequent. Yet this second phrase itself modulates to D major, ending with a local PAC in measure 36. When the music picks up with a basic idea in G (now understood as the subordinate key of the exposition), we recognize that this second cadence (mm. 35–36) is also a reinterpreted HC, and thus the consequent of the periodic formation fails. This use of two different reinterpreted HCs in a row is most unusual, but the logic makes sense from the perspective of the thematic purpose these cadences are intended to serve, namely, as modes of closure for a modulating transition, one whose (failed) periodic structure itself is highly nonconventional.[205]

### 3.3.5.2. Reopened HC

A second unusual type of HC, like the reinterpreted one just discussed, also combines aspects of both authentic and half

---

205. Note that the basic idea of the subordinate theme (mm. 37–38) is, most irregularly, derived from that of the transition. This motivic connection can result in a misunderstanding as to where the subordinate theme actually begins, for some listeners may want to hear the music at m. 37 as still part of the transition. That the subordinate theme begins at m. 37 is fully evident by the initiating presentation in mm. 37–40 (which is then repeated with a modal shift to minor, not shown), followed then by a cadential phrase (see ahead in Chapter 5, Ex. 5.60), which eventually leads to a PAC.

cadences. In this case, the music realizes (or promises to realize) an AC, usually a PAC, for the first phrase of a theme. But the final tonic of the cadence immediately leads to a root-position dominant to effect a simple HC instead. As a result, we sense that the original PAC has been "reopened" to create the HC. When the phrase is then repeated, the original PAC returns to effect full closure of the theme. This *reopened half cadence*, as I will term it, is relatively rare—I have to date uncovered only a handful of examples in the classical repertory. Most of them, however, are sufficiently interesting to warrant a detailed analysis here.[206]

A straightforward case occurs in the finale of Beethoven's Second Symphony (Ex. 3.150a). The main theme begins with a two-measure basic idea followed by a four-measure continuation. With the upbeat to measure 5, II$^6$ initiates a cadential progression that concludes with a PAC on the downbeat of measure 6. Of course, a PAC at this point in the theme seems quite premature. We would more likely expect a weaker cadence, normally an HC, but possibly an IAC. And in fact, the composer seems to agree: he forces the final tonic of the PAC to move to a root-position dominant triad, thus engendering a powerful sense of HC, one that is reinforced texturally by the subsequent caesura. When the following music repeats the opening material of the theme, we believe that the first phrase, an antecedent ending with an HC, is now being matched by a consequent, one that is completed by the PAC at measure 12, indeed, the very same PAC that had been "reopened" in measure 6. With the closure of this periodic main theme now fully secure, the transition can get underway with the upbeat to measure 13.

Let us return to the critical juncture at measure 6 of the theme. We see here that the morphological conditions for both a PAC and an HC are fully satisfied. And what permits these two cadences to appear back to back is the way in which the *final tonic* of the PAC "becomes" the *initial tonic* of a half cadential progression, which then moves immediately to a stage-3 dominant, thus bypassing stage 2 in the manner of a simple (I–V) HC. Functionally, however, it is illogical to speak of both cadences as fully operative for defining the phrase structure of the theme. For although we hear the formation of a perfectly legitimate PAC, that cadence is immediately overridden by the HC, which emerges as the functional cadence that closes the antecedent phrase. When the identical PAC returns to close the consequent, we appreciate all the more the game that the composer has played with this reopened HC.

Finding a rationale for the use of a reopened HC is not always easy, but normally worth the effort. In this example, we could readily observe that if the initial PAC had been fully realized, then a main theme closed at measure 6 would seem way too short for a symphonic finale. Beethoven, of course, could have avoided the problem by simply writing a regular HC. So we should try to find some additional reasons for his using a special technique. Indeed, the peculiar motivic content of the opening basic idea provides a clue. The abrupt stepwise ascent from $\hat{3}$ to $\hat{4}$, along with the immediate caesura and sudden downward plunge to the leading tone C♯, leaves the unstable $\hat{4}$ highly exposed and dangling in mid-air. The continuation phrase now repeats the $\hat{3}$–$\hat{4}$ ascent in the upper part of the melody, allowing it to reach a more stable $\hat{5}$, before heading down stepwise to the cadence. At the same time, another scalar ascent, from $\hat{1}$ to $\hat{4}$, appears in the metrically emphasized middle part of the continuation's melody. We therefore see a strong impetus for rising stepwise motion built into the first phrase of the theme, a gesture that is further propelled when the reopened HC moves from $\hat{1}$ to $\hat{2}$. This melodic ascent now motivates the return of the basic idea, which continues on from $\hat{3}$ to $\hat{4}$. As a result, the basic idea no longer appears "out of the blue," as it did at the very opening of the theme, but rather forges a powerful motivic connection with the end of the antecedent phrase. That Beethoven wants to throw special attention on the ascending stepwise ascent from $\hat{1}$ to $\hat{4}$ (motive "x") is further reinforced when that same motive reappears at the start of the first part of the transition (m. 13) as well as its second part (Ex. 3.150b). Returning to the main theme, we can further observe that the reopened HC, as is almost always the case, creates a metrical irregularity, in that the initial PAC occurs, as it normally would, on the downbeat (m. 6), but the HC then emphasizes the metrically weak, second quarter note of the bar. Beethoven thus creates a rhythmic rhyme with the two quarter notes ending the basic idea (see motive "y" connected by the dashed line). The combination of all these motivic, rhythmic, and metrical characteristics lends a high degree of jocularity to the theme, whose final punch line occurs right after the closing PAC in measure 12, where the move from $\hat{7}$ to $\hat{8}$ completes all of the ascending scalar gestures generated within the theme.

A somewhat more complicated reopened HC arises in Example 3.151. Within a subordinate-theme group in C major, a second subordinate theme begins with a modal shift to minor for its opening basic idea (mm. 39–40); the contrasting idea returns to major but also brings the cadential material for a projected IAC on the downbeat of measure 42. But like the Second Symphony example, the cadence is immediately reopened to create an HC on the second beat of the bar. The following consequent now tries to realize the potential for an IAC offered by the antecedent. Again, however, Beethoven does not allow that cadence to fully emerge, even though the melody stops on E ($\hat{3}$) at measure 46. For after reaching the cadential dominant in the middle of measure 45, the bass drops down (through V$^4_2$) to support I$^6$, thus creating a deceptive cadence instead of the implied IAC. A repetition of the contrasting idea then brings the closing PAC on the downbeat of measure 48. Note that if an actual IAC had been created at measure 46, it would have been a way station on the path to the subsequent PAC, one that is required to close a subordinate theme. The deceptive cadence, which occurs instead, nonetheless fulfills this way-station function (a topic to be addressed in the following chapter, sec. 4.1.2.2).

Here, like the previous example, an issue of motivic manipulation perhaps provides a reason for the use of the reopened HC to close the first phrase of this theme. Note that the basic idea

---

206. In addition to the passages discussed here, see Haydn, Symphony No. 61 in D, ii, m. 4.

126  Basic Cadence Types

EXAMPLE 3.150. Beethoven, Symphony No. 2 in D, Op. 36, iv, (a) mm. 1–14; (b) mm. 26–28.

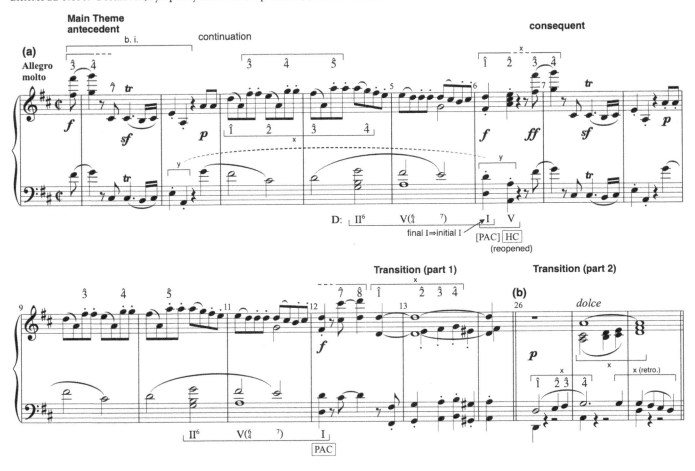

EXAMPLE 3.151. Beethoven, Violin Sonata in F ("Spring"), Op. 24, iv, mm. 39–48.

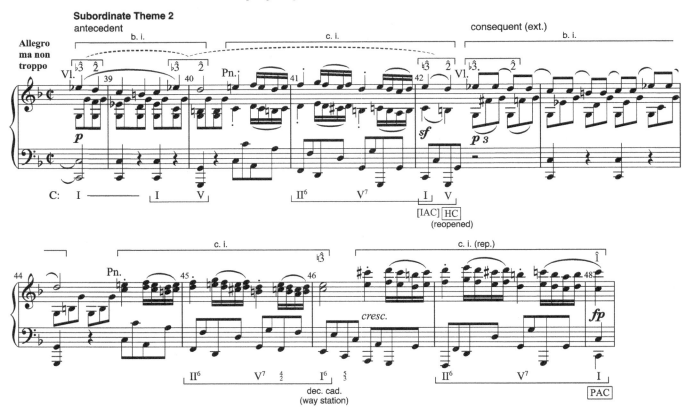

EXAMPLE 3.152. Mozart, String Quartet in B-flat ("Hunt"), K. 458, i, mm. 1–8.

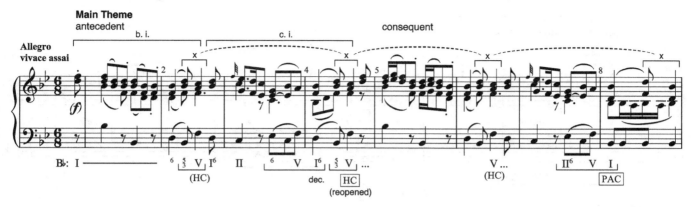

begins with the stepwise descent $\hat{3}$–$\hat{2}$, which is echoed at the very end of the idea. The reopened HC thus allows him to create another $\hat{3}$–$\hat{2}$ ending motion, one that is especially striking because we are expecting the melody to end on E, and we are thus surprised when it suddenly descends to D. Moreover, this motivic play emphasizes that the first descent is from ♭$\hat{3}$, while the second is from ♮$\hat{3}$, thus further reinforcing the modal mixture at the heart of this passage. At the same time, using the reopened HC allows Beethoven to avoid a rather awkward chromaticism that would result if an E♮ in the piano at measure 42, ending a potential IAC, were to move directly to E♭ in the violin, when the basic idea returns.

A more harmonic explanation for using a reopened HC may also be forthcoming. Note that the end of the basic idea itself brings the harmonic and melodic content of a simple (I–V) HC, though it is too early in the theme to speak of any genuine cadential closure. Still, the move toward a matching authentic cadence in the contrasting idea seems motivated by that earlier half cadential content. But then, perhaps wanting to save a genuine IAC for the purposes of a way station, Beethoven reopens that cadence to create the more typical HC of an antecedent phrase, one that will then be matched by the consequent, which closes at first with a way-station deceptive cadence and then with the expected PAC.

A similar harmonic motivation presents itself in the first-movement main theme of Mozart's Hunt Quartet (Ex. 3.152); for like the previous example, the basic idea itself contains elements of a simple HC, explaining perhaps why the following contrasting idea initiates a matching authentic cadential progression, one that promises to close with a PAC on the downbeat of measure 4. As already discussed with the previous examples, such a PAC would appear too early in the thematic process; so it is not surprising that Mozart denies that cadence. Indeed he does so in two different ways: first by inverting the final tonic (along the lines of a way-station deceptive cadence, such as we observed in the prior example) and then by leading that tonic directly to dominant, thus enacting a reopened HC. The subsequent consequent leads again toward a PAC, one that is fully achieved as a genuine cadence when the dominant resolves to tonic in root-position on the downbeat of bar 8.

Note that in the second half of measure 8, Mozart adds a little melodic "overhang" (D–B♭, motive "x") that both rhythmically and melodically rhymes with the earlier melodic configuration ending the reopened HC (m. 4).[207] We can further observe that the basic idea also closes with motive "x," supported by a simple half cadential progression. In fact, the musical content of bars 2 and 4 are practically identical. Yet I would suggest that a potential redundancy is far from obvious to the casual listener, because the harmonic context leading into each bar is entirely different. Bar 1 consists exclusively of a root-position tonic, whose move to I⁶ at measure 2 sounds like it is simply prolonging the same harmony. Measure 3, on the contrary, contains a pre-dominant and a dominant, such that the I⁶ on the downbeat of bar 4 does not function prolongationally, but rather as the disruption of a cadential progression. The logic of Mozart's compositional work is thus clear. Since the basic idea itself exhibits half cadential content, it makes sense to follow it with material that proposes an authentic cadence. But because he wants to create an antecedent phrase, he must deny the articulation of a PAC and close the unit half cadentially instead. Indeed, the technique of the reopened HC allows him to accomplish all of these tasks.

Another example featuring I⁶ in place of a root-position tonic, which appears just prior to the cadential reopening, arises in Mozart's String Quintet in C (Ex. 3.153a), a situation that Mirka describes as a "twisted caesura."[208] The main theme, stretching to 57 bars, is perhaps the longest in the entire classical repertory. In order to achieve such startling length and degree of complexity, Mozart employs a variety of devices that allow him to extend the theme in time, prominent of which is a reopened HC at bar 19. Up to this point, the theme has been forming itself into a sixteen-measure compound sentence, which promises to close with a PAC. In fact, the potential cadence is first preceded by a deceptive cadential progression to the submediant in measures 16–17, a technique that reinforces the idea that a PAC will shortly follow.

---

207. On "overhang," see note 98.

208. Mirka, "Punctuation and Sense," 235. The other "twisted" cadences that she presents in her article do not bring features of my reopened HC, and so our respective concepts are not actually congruent.

EXAMPLE 3.153. Mozart, String Quintet in C, K. 515, i, (a) mm. 16–21; (b) Mirka's reconstruction of mm. 16–18; (c) mm. 53–57.

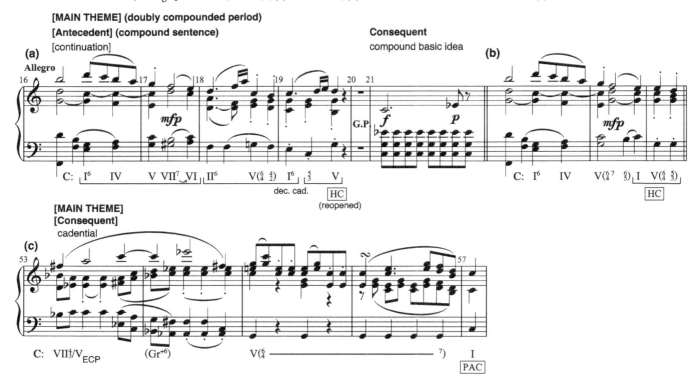

But rather than fully emerging as such, the PAC is undermined when the dominant moves to I⁶, just as we saw in the previous example. To be sure, Mozart could have written a standard HC, as Mirka reconstructs in Example 3.153b. But such a situation would hardly have created the sense of surprise that he achieves by suggesting that the theme will fully close at measure 19 (Ex. 3.153a), but then suddenly reopens onto an HC, thus paving the way to further thematic work.

As is typically the case, the rhythmic caesura immediately appearing after the reopened cadence helps to mark it as a genuine moment of closure. Here, though, Mozart extends the caesura into a complete general pause in bar 20, thus eliciting a degree of mystery as to how he is going to continue the theme. When it then backs up to its very beginning—with a most startling shift to minor (shown only in m. 21)—we eventually understand that the preceding compound sentence, ended by the reopened HC, ultimately functions as a large-scale antecedent to constitute the first part of a *doubly* compounded period, a theme type that does not normally exist in the classical repertory. In other words, when Mozart held out the option that the main theme would end with an authentic cadence at measure 19, we presumed that the theme would fully close at that point. The reopened HC is thus astonishing, especially when it yields a theme type that listeners of the time would never expect to encounter. Given the enormity of the main theme, it is not surprising that, unlike most other cases of the reopened HC, the original PAC configuration of measures 18 and 19 does not appear at the end of the giant consequent. Instead, Mozart writes a huge ECP as befits the massive enlargement enacted by the theme (see Ex. 3.153c, which shows the last part of the ECP).

Up to this point, I have examined the reopened HC in connection with the antecedent of a period theme type. Example 3.154 shows how this cadential anomaly can arise in a different, and rather unusual, formal context. Toward the end of a continuation phrase, an authentic cadential progression beginning at measure 6 is poised to create a PAC on the downbeat of measure 8. In a manner similar to the two previous examples by Mozart, however, the final tonic is initially inverted, such that a sense of deceptive cadence is created instead. When the tonic then regains its root position, it moves quickly to dominant to effect a reopened HC. Following this moment, the music does not back up to the beginning of the theme, in the sense of a compound consequent, but rather, returns to the start of the continuation, whose repeated attempt to gain a PAC is now successful at measure 12. Looking back, we see that the reopened HC functions not so much as an independent cadence to end an implied compound antecedent, but rather, most exceptionally, as a way-station cadence on the road toward the final PAC.

What motivates Haydn to write a reopened HC here, a situation that is not only rare in itself, but especially unusual in its functioning as a way station? Again, the answer may be found in the manner in which the opening of the theme is constructed. We find here a basic idea that opens up melodically, followed then by a contrasting idea that fully shuts the melody down, thereby bringing a PAC that seems premature after only four bars. The phrase is thus constructed like a consequent, one that is clearly

EXAMPLE 3.154. Haydn, String Quartet in A, Op. 55, no. 1, i, mm. 1–12.

missing its matching antecedent.[209] To be sure, the cadential progression supporting the PAC at measure 4 is quite incomplete, consisting only of a dominant to tonic motion.[210] As such, the listener is unlikely to believe that the main theme has actually concluded, and so the appearance of a subsequent continuation phrase is plausible enough. Yet if Haydn had closed that phrase with a standard HC on the downbeat of measure 8, then we would likely be confused by the logic of a PAC being followed by an HC. So instead measures 6–8 bring a longer, and more complete, authentic cadential progression (with an initial I⁶ and a pre-dominant II⁶), thus projecting the possibility of a rhetorically stronger PAC than the one opening the theme. But had Haydn realized this second cadence, he would have created a theme consisting of two PACs in a row, again, a formally problematic situation. He thus opts to reopen the cadence, so that an HC is created after all. Then, when the continuation begins to be repeated, we realize that the reopened HC was not meant to represent closure for the theme, but rather to function as a way station for the PAC that effects full closure at measure 12 (a cadence, moreover, that concludes with the same triplet gesture, labeled "x," as the upbeat to bar 4). The resulting twelve-measure theme is still nonconventional, but the succession of cadences makes more sense than if Haydn had written a PAC at measure 4, followed by a *regular* HC at measure 8, and followed again by a PAC at measure 12. The reopened HC, with its initial promise of an internal authentic cadence that is ultimately undermined, creates a more intricate and aesthetically satisfying cadential environment.

## 3.4. Additional Aspects of the Basic Cadence Types

Up to now, this chapter has largely considered the various harmonic and melodic processes that define the basic cadence types. Two additional parameters may also play a role—the metrical placement of the cadential arrival and the textural layout of the cadence. These aspects will now be examined in relation to all three cadence types.

### 3.4.1. Meter

The relationship of cadence to meter is a complicated matter. Many theorists since the eighteenth century associate cadential arrival (or some kind of phrase ending) with a strong metrical position.[211] At the same time, they recognize that exceptional

---

209. These circumstances give rise to a formal "dissonance," whereby the intrinsic function of the phrase is a consequent (that label, placed in braces), while its contextual function is obviously initiating, in the sense of a compound basic idea; see Chapter 2, sec. 2.6, and note 119.

210. Indeed, it might be questioned whether the entire opening phrase is better seen as supported by a prolongational progression. Normally, however, the harmonic distribution of such a prolongation over four bars would take the form of three main options: I–I–V–V, I–V–I–V, or I–V–V–I. The distribution here, I–V–V–I, is what one would find supporting an antecedent or consequent phrase ending with an authentic cadence (either an IAC or PAC); e.g., Haydn, Piano Sonata in F, H. 9, iii, mm. 1–4, 5–8 (*ACF*, Ex. 3.21).

211. "The most important cues used by eighteenth-century composers to indicate the metrical level of *Taktteile* [beats] are ending formulas represented by *Einschnitte* [incises], *Absätze* [phrases] and *Kadenz*. As repeatedly emphasized by authors of compositional handbooks

cases do arise, especially in some dance types, where a cadence may occur on a weak beat. Indeed, the notorious characterization of cadences as "masculine" or "feminine" is grounded in the possibility that some may occur on stronger or weaker metrical positions.[212] Of course, all such claims must be understood in relation to how a given theorist defines the concepts of "cadence" and of "strong metrical position," and since unanimity is far from assured in either of those domains, we must be cautious in evaluating the statements of any writer on the topic.

Nonetheless, a quick glance at the musical repertory suggests that most classical cadences occur on metrically strong positions as indicated by the notated meter; that is, cadences tend to fall on the first beat of any metrical type (duple, triple, or quadruple).[213] Metrical notation, however, can be difficult at times to interpret. For example, many theorists in the eighteenth century recognize the use of *compound meters*, which they define as the combination of two bars of a *simple* meter into a single bar of compound meter.[214] Thus one measure of 4/4 is often construed as a compound measure containing two simple bars of 2/4, and in this situation, a cadence can readily be placed on beat three (of 4/4) without violating the general principle that a cadence should fall on a strong beat, since this mid-bar location was deemed identical to the first beat of a simple meter. (A similar situation holds for 6/8 meter as a compounding of two 3/8 meters, thus allowing a cadential placement on the fourth eighth-note of a 6/8 bar.) In fact, theorists often suggest that the metrical placement of cadences can be a guide for determining whether a given metrical notation reflects simple or compound meter.

Such cases of compound meter give rise to the impression that a single *real measure* (R) of, say, 2/4 time, represents only one half of a *notated measure* (N) of 4/4, thus R = ½N. As a further complication, composers also employ a notation based on another relation of real to notated measures, especially in scherzo-like genres, In this second mode of notation, each real measure comprises two notated ones, thus R = 2N. Under these metrical conditions, a conventional theme consisting of eight real measures would be notated as sixteen. If the final cadence appears on the downbeat of the last notated bar (m. 16), it might seem to conform to the general rule relating cadence to meter, yet that cadence would still be perceived as occurring on a weak metrical position within the final "real" bar (mm. 15 and 16 together).

### 3.4.1.1. A Ratio Model of Metrical Strength

Clearly, then, we cannot rely on the notated measure as a complete guide to how a given cadence relates to our impression of just where it is placed within the metrical hierarchy of the passage in question. For this reason, it would be helpful to find a way of identifying the metrical strength of cadences independent of the notation as much as possible. One way would be to identify the *duration* of the final cadential event (that is, stage 4 of the PAC or stage 3 of the HC) in relation to the total duration of the formal unit that the cadence is closing. Take, for example, the typical case of the two cadences (an HC and a PAC) that end the two phrases of a simple period (or periodic hybrid, e.g., antecedent + continuation) consisting of eight real measures (Ex. 3.155). In the antecedent phrase, the onset of the final stage—the moment of cadential *arrival*—usually occurs on the downbeat of measure 4, and the duration of the stage occupies one-quarter of the entire duration of the antecedent. The resulting durational ratio of the final stage to the entire length of the phrase can be more simply denoted by the expression *1:4*.[215] Similarly, the final PAC occurring on the downbeat of measure 8 occupies one-quarter of the entire duration of the consequent, thus again the ratio is 1:4.[216] In these situations, each cadence occupies as strong a metrical position within the phrase as is possible given the constraints of the form.[217]

---

[e.g., Mathesson, Riepel, Kirnberger, and Koch], caesura notes of these formulas must fall on a strong *Taktteil* (downbeat)" (Danuta Mirka, "Metre, Phrase Structure and Manipulations of Musical Beginnings," 83). See also William Rothstein, "National Metrical Types in Music of the Eighteenth and Early Nineteenth Centuries," 112–13. For an important discussion of cadential-metrical relationships in Koch, see John Paul Ito, "Koch's Metrical Theory and Mozart's Music: A Corpus Study." Among nineteenth-century theorists, both Hauptmann and Riemann specify the connection; see Moritz Hauptmann, *The Nature of Harmony and Metre*, xlvi, 327–28; Caplin, "Criteria for Analysis," 432. More recent theory tends to be less assertive of a determinate relationship of cadence and meter, but see Berger, who in his summary of the "morphology of cadence," lists a metrical requirement as his first criterion ("First-Movement Punctuation Form," 244).

212. The gendering of cadences goes back at least as far as Koch, see ahead Chapter 7, sec. 7.1.4, and note 44.

213. This general observation is largely confirmed by Ito's corpus study of Mozart.

214. See again, Chapter 2, note 165.

215. The idea of speaking of metrical strength in terms of durational ratios is not common in traditional metrical theories, where degrees of metrical strength are normally described in relation to the various pulse-streams that make up the metrical hierarchy. But such pulse-streams are usually determined in relation to some notated durational value: we say, for example, that the first pulse (or beat) of the *quarter-note stream* in 2/4 is stronger than the second pulse, further observing that the first and third pulses of the *eighth-note* stream are stronger than pulses two and four. But to speak in this way ties us to the specific notation of the passage in question. In order to break free from this notational constraint, I will avoid speaking of pulse streams and refer instead, as mentioned in the main text, to the durational ratio of the time span of the cadential event (here, its final stage) to the total duration of the passage being closed by this event. In any given notational situation, we can convert this ratio into a description of the metrical position of the cadential arrival and observe where, in the pulse stream, this event lies.

216. Here, I am considering the duration of the unit that the cadence is closing to be the four bars of the consequent exclusively. From the perspective of the period as a whole, however, the durational ratio of the PAC would be 1:8.

217. The strongest metrical position would be for the two cadences to appear on the downbeats of mm. 3 and 7, respectively, with the final stage of each cadence continuing on for another bar (i.e., into mm. 4 and 8). In this situation, the durational ratio of each cadence would be 1:2. But this condition is difficult to obtain, since following a two-measure basic idea, little time would be available for a distinct cadential progression to arise.

EXAMPLE 3.155. Haydn, Symphony No. 100 in G ("Military"), iv, mm. 1–8 (ACF 3.9).

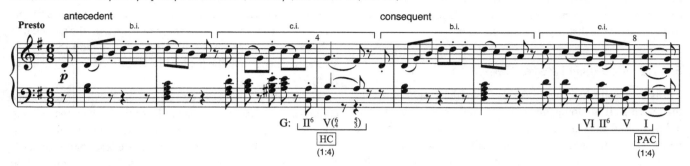

Consider now the case of a simple period notated in compound meter (R = ½N); see the earlier discussed Example 3.29. The two cadences appear on what may seem to be the metrically weak second half of measures 2 and 4, respectively. Yet these metrical positions are of the same strength, namely 1:4, as a simple period notated as R = N (Ex. 3.155). The same situation occurs in the context of R = 2N if the HC arises on the downbeat of measure 7 (and continues through m. 8) and the PAC, on measure 15. Both cadences would still be as metrically strong as those in the two previous examples, namely 1:4.[218]

Turning now to the simple sentence form (or the sentential hybrids),[219] the situation is somewhat different, since the one and only cadence of the standard eight-measure sentence normally appears on the downbeat of measure 8. In this case, the ratio of the final cadential event to the overall time span of the theme is 1:8, which is generally the strongest metrical placement for this theme type.[220] This ratio would be maintained if the sentence is notated R = ½N, such that the cadence appears in the second half of measure 4, or if the notation is R = 2N, with the cadence appearing in measure 15.[221]

Although it might seem that the one cadence of the sentence is metrically weaker (1:8) than either of the two cadences of the period (1:4), the metrical balance is regained when we evaluate the second cadence of the period in relation to the entire eight-measure span of the theme, in which case, the PAC acquires a 1:8 ratio, the same as that of the single cadence of the sentence. (In that we normally have no reason to compare metrically the cadence of a sentence with those of a period, the previous point is of more theoretical than practical concern.)

In the case of compound themes, that is, sentences or periods consisting of sixteen *real* measures—no matter how those measures are notated—the situation becomes more complicated. For the compound period, we would be considering just the two cadences ending the compound antecedent and consequent, which are normally found at the beginning of measures 8 and 16, thus creating a 1:8 ratio.[222] If the compound antecedent and consequent themselves contain internal cadences in (real) measures 4 and 12, then their metrical strength (maximally 1:4) would be measured in terms of the simple theme lying at the basis of their respective eight-measure compound phrases. In the case of the compound sentence, the single, final cadence most often appears in the final measure, thus creating a relatively weak 1:16 ratio.[223]

To summarize, we can establish a normatively *strongest* metrical position for cadences in the standard theme types as follows:

- simple period (or periodic hybrids): two cadences, each with a 1:4 ratio;
- simple sentence (or sentential hybrids): one cadence, with a 1:8 ratio;
- compound period: two cadences, each with a 1:8 ratio;
- compound sentence: one cadence, with a 1:16 ratio.

Each one of these theme types may be notated as R = N, R = ½N ("compound meter"), or R = 2N, and the standard ratios just defined will still be maintained. (I have not encountered any compound themes notated as R = 2N, which would give rise to a notated 32-m. theme.) If we find a higher ratio, say 1:8, for each cadence of a *simple* period, we can say that their metrical positions are relatively weaker than the norm for that theme type.

---

To be sure, Beethoven found a way to do something like this in the slow movement of his String Quartet in G, Op. 18, no. 2 (see CF, Ex. 4.12). In a compressed period lasting only six bars, a two-measure basic idea is followed by a quick HC, whose final stage arrives on the downbeat of m. 3 and then occupies only a single bar; the consequent then begins in m. 4. In this case, the ratio of the cadence is only 1:3. I have not encountered any situations where the cadential arrival obtains a 1:2 ratio in relation to the passage being closed by that cadence.

218. The corpus of themes used for this chapter does not contain an eight-measure period notated R = 2N, both of whose cadences are 1:4.

219. For the purpose of this discussion, sentential hybrids contain a single cadence closing the eight-measure theme, namely, the hybrids "compound basic idea + continuation" and "compound basic idea + consequent" (see CF, 63, and ACF, 110–11). (In other contexts, the latter hybrid might be considered "periodic" due to the return of the basic idea in mm. 5–6 of the theme.)

220. In the context of a normal sentence, the final cadence rarely arises earlier, such as in m. 7, which would yield a stronger 1:4 ratio.

221. For a case of R = ½N, see Mozart, Piano Sonata in F, K. 332, ii, 1–4 (ACF 2.26). For R = 2N, see above, Ex. 3.136; here, the concluding HC appears in m. 21, which, because of the five bars of thematic introduction, represents m. 15 of the theme proper.

222. See Beethoven, Piano Sonata in A-flat, Op. 26, i, 1–16 (ACF, 6.1).

223. See Beethoven, Piano Concerto in No. 3 in C Minor, Op. 37, i, 1–16 (ACF 6.2): single PAC in m. 16.

Likewise, if we encounter a lower ratio, then we can say that the cadence is given a stronger metrical weight than would normally be the case for the theme type in question.[224]

### 3.4.1.2. Metrically Weaker Cadences

Let us now examine cases where the cadential weight is weaker than normal. In so doing, however, we must be aware of one pitfall that could skew our interpretations. In some cases, the final harmony of the cadence may appear to fall on a weak metrical position, but a closer look reveals that the *implied* appearance of that harmony is on a stronger position. Consider the cadence shown in Example 3.156a, which ends a compound period. An ECP, which sets up a harmonic rhythm of one harmony per bar, promises to close with the final tonic on the downbeat of measure 16. The penultimate dominant, however, is syncopated over the bar line such that the tonic resolution is delayed until the second eighth-note beat within the bar. The final tonic thus seems to arrive on a weak metrical position (1:12 of a compound consequent). We can also recognize here that in standard classical practice, the composer would have normally moved the bass to E♭ on the downbeat of measure 16 and let the upper voices resolve as suspensions (see Ex. 3.156b), thus yielding a stronger, and more conventional, 1:8 ratio.[225] A similar situation of syncopating the penultimate cadential harmony occurs in Example 3.156c and d, though the latter is even more extreme in that the melody resolves to $\hat{1}$ before the bass reaches ①.[226] As a rule, I would advocate treating these cases as ones in which the sense of cadential arrival occurs on the downbeat of the bar, and is thus metrically strong, even though the final harmony literally arrives later (thus metrically weaker).

For an important counterexample to the situations just discussed, look again at Example 3.146, measure 4, where a reinterpreted HC falls on the weak, second beat of measure 4. Here, the harmonic situation does not imply that the final harmony of the progression (a PAC configuration in E major) would occur on the downbeat of measure 4, since this position is occupied by the stage-3 dominant, which itself is preceded by the predominant in measure 3. In this case, then, the cadence genuinely has the metrical ratio of 1:6, which is weaker than the standard 1:4 of a normative antecedent phrase.

**Simple Period (Eight Real Measures).** Given the fundamental notion that the cadence ending an antecedent must be syntactically weaker than the cadence ending the consequent, we might expect this stipulation to be reflected in the relative metrical strengths of the two cadences. And some cases do occur where the antecedent's cadence is metrically weaker than that of the consequent. In Example 3.89a, discussed earlier, the antecedent closes with an HC in the middle of measure 4, thus yielding a weak 1:8 ratio; the consequent, however, concludes on the downbeat of measure 8, thus conforming to the norm with a strong ratio of 1:4. A more extreme case can be found in Example 3.157a, where the antecedent ends with an IAC on the second half of beat 1 in measure 4, thus resulting in a 1:16 ratio that is considerably weaker than the final 1:4 PAC (Ex. 3.157b, downbeat of m. 8).[227]

The reverse situation can also arise, namely, where the cadence ending the antecedent is metrically stronger than that ending the consequent, thus conflicting with their syntactical weights. In Example 3.158a, the ratio for the antecedent's half cadence is 1:4 as normally expected, but the final PAC in the second half of measure 8 results in a weaker 1:8 ratio (Ex. 3.158b). The reason for these differing cadential weights is that in this particular period, Beethoven does not adjust the consequent phrase so that its penultimate dominant would appear earlier than the ultimate dominant of the antecedent. Consequently, the final tonic of the PAC does not arrive on the same metrical position as the final dominant of the prior HC, which is at odds with the standard construction of a period. In this case, the antecedent and consequent are fully conformant up to the dominant harmonies on the downbeat of measures 4 and 8; only when the second of these two dominants then resolves to tonic to create the PAC do the two phrases diverge, thus resulting in differing metrical weights for their two cadences.

When the notation is R = 2N, the metrical relationships of the cadences may be obscured, as seen in Example 3.159. Here, the final cadence of the consequent (Ex. 3.159b appears on the downbeat of measure 16, thus seemingly in a strong metrical position. But the actual ratios show that the antecedent's HC (1:4) (Ex. 3.159a, downbeat of m. 7) is stronger than the consequent's PAC (1:8) (Ex. 3.159b, m. 16).[228]

Finally, the two cadences of the simple period may exhibit the same metrical strength, yet both may appear relatively weak. In Example 3.160, which is clearly notated in R = 2N, both cadences of this periodic hybrid end on the downbeats of their respective notated measures (8 and 16) and thus project a 1:8 ratio. In terms of their real measures, however, both cadences occur in the *middle* of their final bar (4 and 8), which more obviously reveals their relative weakness as respects the norms of this theme type. Example 3.161 presents a similar situation: the cadences in the middle of measures 4 and 8 have a 1:8 ratio with respect to the phrases that they close. Here,

---

224. Though theoretically possible, occurrences of "stronger than normal" metrical positions for cadences within a theme are rarely encountered, for such cases give the impression that the cadence has arrived *prematurely* within the theme, that is, at an earlier point in time than would ordinarily be expected.

---

225. See also Ex. 3.75, where the independent IAC in m. 16 is implied to occur on the downbeat of the bar but is instead delayed until the second beat.

226. This technique of harmonic syncopation, particularly at cadences, is a well-known trait of Beethoven's late style.

227. The gesture of an abrupt, metrically weak cadence in m. 4 is a remnant of galant practice, as discussed in Chapter 7, sec. 7.1.3, in connection with Ex. 7.31a.

228. Like the previous example, the discrepant cadential weights are due to Beethoven's retaining the same relative positions of the two dominants in the phrases.

EXAMPLE 3.156. (a) Beethoven, Bagatelle in E-flat, Op. 126, no. 3, mm. 13–16 (*ACF* 6.19); (b) reconstruction of mm. 15–16; (c) Mozart, String Quartet in E-flat, K. 428, iv, mm. 5–8 (*ACF* 7.6); (d) Beethoven, String Quartet in B-flat, Op. 130, iv, mm. 21–24 (*ACF* Sup. 7.4).

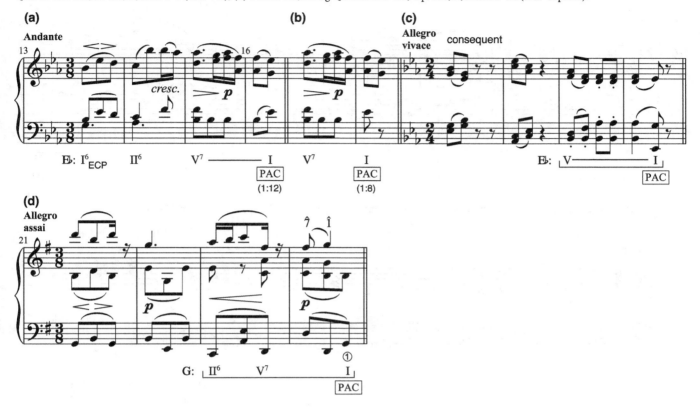

EXAMPLE 3.157. Mozart, Piano Sonata in B-flat, K. 281, i, (a) mm. 1–3; (b) mm. 7–8 (*ACF* 3.14).

EXAMPLE 3.158. Beethoven, Piano Sonata in E-flat, Op. 31, no. 3, ii, (a) 1–4 (*ACF* 7.14); (b) mm. 15–16.

EXAMPLE 3.159. Beethoven, Piano Sonata in E, Op. 14, no. 1, ii, (a) mm. 1–8 (R = 2N) (*ACF* Sup. 3.8); (b) mm. 13–16.

EXAMPLE 3.160. Beethoven, Piano Sonata in C, Op. 2, no. 3, iii, (a) mm. 1–8 (R = 2N) (*ACF* Sup. 4.17); (b) mm. 15–16.

though, we might wonder whether we are dealing with a compound period (thus R = ½N), not a simple period (R = N). I will return to this matter after we examine clearer cases of the compound period.

**Compound Period (Sixteen Real Measures).** For the purposes of this discussion, we will be considering the two cadences ending the compound antecedent and consequent, since, as noted earlier, the metrical placement of any interior cadences (ending a simple antecedent within each of these units) is already covered by the previous section on the simple period form. In the great majority of compound periods, the cadential ratios correspond to the normal situation, namely 1:8 in both units. Exceptionally, the cadence closing the compound antecedent is weaker than that of compound consequent, as seen in the following example, where the first cadence (Ex. 3.162a) has the weak 1:16 ratio, while the second (Ex. 3.162b) restores the normative 1:8 ratio.[229] The reverse situation arises in Example 3.163a, where the HC (1:4) ending the compound antecedent at measure 7 is stronger than the PAC (1:8) ending the consequent (Ex. 3.163b) at measure 16. In this case, however, the antecedent is structured as a simple sentence, whose HC (m. 7) appears one bar "too early" in the form; so although the cadence is metrically stronger than usual, it nonetheless creates an odd, disturbing effect due to its premature appearance.[230]

Finally, we sometimes come across situations in which both the compound antecedent and consequent are of equal metrical strength but metrically weaker than the norm. In Example 3.164a and b, both the antecedent and consequent units (each of which is built as a sentence) conclude on the second beats of measures 8 and 16, respectively. Though the resulting ratio, 1:12, is not standard due to the triple meter, it is obviously weaker than the 1:8 ratio normally seen for this theme type. Here, we may wonder whether Mozart's designation "Rondeau en Polonaise" may point to a stylized dance genre as the key to the weaker than usual metrical placement of the cadences.

**Sentence (Simple and Compound).** With only one cadence included in the sentence theme type, the consideration of a weaker

---

229. To be sure, the dominant harmony of the antecedent's reinterpreted HC is syncopated from the end of m. 7 into the downbeat of m. 8. But unlike the cases discussed in Ex. 3.156, the use of the cadential six-four throughout the second half of m. 7 prohibits us from expecting the final tonic to fall on the downbeat of m. 8; rather, we more strongly presume that the cadential six-four will resolve to the dominant proper before that tonic arrives, which is exactly what happens. As a result, the cadential arrival occurs in the second half of m. 8. Nonetheless, the appearance of the cadential six-four on a metrically weak position is unusual; in fact, we might suppose that this sonority is going to function as a passing chord

to another pre-dominant (say, II⁶) on the downbeat of m. 8. When the dominant proper appears instead, we can perceive a somewhat jarring effect from the syncopating dominant.

230. For this reason, I propose the alternative label "dominant arrival (premature)," as discussed in the following chapter, sec. 4.4.3.2.

3.4. ADDITIONAL ASPECTS OF THE BASIC CADENCE TYPES   135

EXAMPLE 3.161. Mozart, Clarinet Quintet in A, K. 581, iv, mm. 1–8 (*ACF* 7.17).

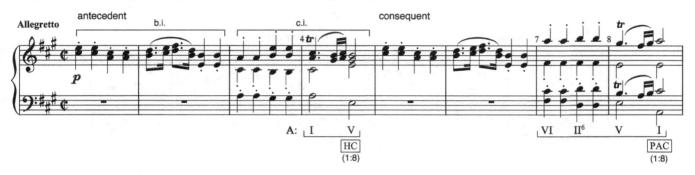

EXAMPLE 3.162. Mozart, Piano Sonata in D, K. 576, iii, (a) mm. 6–8 (*ACF* Sup. 6.15); (b) mm. 15–16.

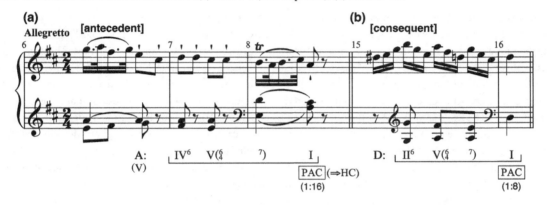

EXAMPLE 3.163. Beethoven, Violin Sonata in A, Op. 30, no. 1, ii, (a) mm. 1–10 (*ACF* Sup. 6.8); (b) mm. 14–16.

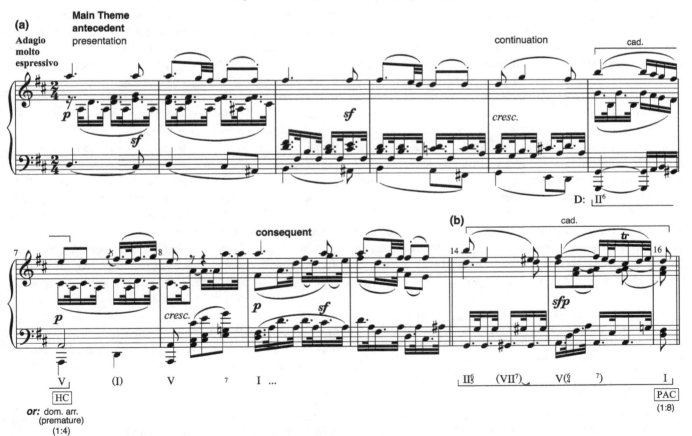

EXAMPLE 3.164. Mozart, Piano Sonata in D, K. 284, ii, (a) mm. 7–8 (*ACF* Sup. 6.1); (b) mm. 15–16.

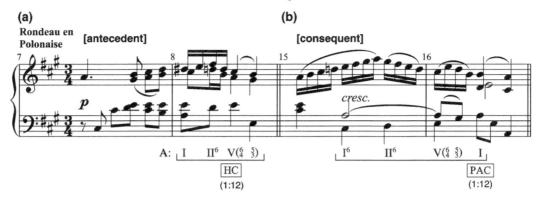

metrical placement is considerably easier to assess than in the case the two cadences of the period. Like the latter, the majority of simple sentences bring their final cadences in a normatively strong metrical position, that is, with a ratio of 1:8. A small group of cases finds the cadence in a weaker position, most often expressing a 1:16 ratio. As for the compound sixteen-measure sentence, I have not encountered any cases in which the final cadence is weaker than the norm (1:16).

A case of a simple sentence with metrically weak closure can be seen in Example 2.24 of the previous chapter. In an obvious notation of R = 2N, the final cadence (which is followed by its own repetitions as codettas) appears on the downbeat of measure 18, the second half of the real eighth measure of the form. The metrical ratio 1:16 is thus weaker than the 1:8 norm for this theme type. The same situation holds for Example 3.165 in the current chapter, where the IAC appears in the middle of measure 8 (1:16). It is interesting to observe, however, that Beethoven is obviously not entirely satisfied to allow this main theme to end with a cadence that is both syntactically and metrically weak; so he repeats the continuation phrase in a manner that effects a slight expansion of the cadential idea in order for it to appear on the downbeat of measure 13 as a PAC.[231]

Another metrically weak cadence of a sentence is somewhat more complex. In Example 3.166, a regular four-measure presentation is followed by a continuation that has been compressed into two bars. The final cadence, appearing in the second half of measure 6 (1:12 ratio) is weaker than the norm. But as both Mirka and Ito have discussed in connection with this example, it is as though Haydn had suddenly changed from a simple meter in the presentation to a compound meter in the continuation (R = ½N).[232] From that perspective, the placement of the cadence conforms more to the norms, in that within the continuation phrase itself, the cadence expresses a 1:4 ratio, as would be the case for the continuation of a standard eight-measure sentence.

**Simple versus Compound Themes.** The approach to cadence and meter taken here has tried to formulate their relationship as independently as possible from the musical notation, since composers use three different notational systems (R = N, R = ½N, and R = 2N) without indicating which one is operative in any given case. As a result, once we have determined the theme type in question, we can assess the metrical weight of its cadence(s) in terms of a durational ratio that can be calculated without having to ascertain the notational system. This leaves open the question, however, of whether or not we always know which theme type is actually operative. Whether a given theme is *simple* or *compound* is often a matter of interpretation, one that even depends at times on our intuitions about the notational system involved, that is, what exactly constitutes a "real" measure of music for a given theme. Let us return to Example 3.161. As originally discussed, we identified there a *simple* eight-measure period, thus assuming that R = N, and observed that both cadences occur on a weak metrical position (1:8). On the one hand, this situation is relatively rare in the literature, though still possible. On the other hand, the 1:8 ratio for both cadences is highly typical of the *compound* period. And when we look forward into the complete rounded-binary theme, of which this period constitutes the A section, we find that the HC ending the B section and the PAC ending the A′ section have the same metrical weight (1:8). Such consistency of cadential placement is highly suggestive of compound meter (R = ½N), which would support the idea that the A section is a compound theme, not a simple one. Yet if we undertake a harmonic-formal analysis of this period, the musical content does not seem sufficiently differentiated for us to identify with confidence a full basic idea in measure 1, a complete simple antecedent (or possibly compound basic idea) in measures 1–2, and a fully convincing continuation phrase for measures 3–4.[233] In fact, the problem boils down, as it often does, to just how much content there must be to speak of a "real" measure

---

231. It is not obvious just how one should determine the ratio of a cadence that results from a phrase deviation. Here, we should probably eliminate the first continuation phrase (mm. 5–8), seeing it replaced by mm. 9–13, with a one-bar expansion of the cadence. In that case, the ratio of the PAC in relation to the complete sentence would be 1:9, slightly weaker than what occurs in a regular, unexpanded sentence but stronger than the original IAC of m. 8.

232. Danuta Mirka, *Metric Manipulations in Haydn and Mozart: Chamber Music for Strings, 1787–1791*, 212–14; Ito, "Koch's Metrical Theory," 206–7.

233. Mozart's use of cut time rather than common time also inhibits our hearing a single notated measure as two real measures.

EXAMPLE 3.165. Beethoven, Piano Sonata in C, Op. 2, no. 3, i, mm. 1–13 (*ACF* 5.11).

EXAMPLE 3.166. Haydn, String Quartet in B-flat, Op. 50, no. 1, ii, mm. 1–6.

of music. In other words, an analysis of a compound theme for this example seems overly complex, compared to an analysis in relation to a simple period (basic idea, measures 1–2; contrasting idea, measures 3–4, etc.). In short, some themes are resistant to an unequivocal interpretation about their theme type (simple vs. compound), about the notational system being employed, and about the metrical weighting of their cadences. Indeed, all three aspects are sometimes so intricately entwined that in some cases it is not possible to use any one as a certain criterion for formal and metrical interpretation.[234]

---

234. For additional themes that bring similar problems to the interpretation of simple vs. compound theme type, see Mozart, Piano Sonata in D, K. 311, ii, 1–8 (*ACF*, Ex. 3.2); Haydn, String Quartet in G, Op. 64, no. 4, i, 1–8 (*ACF*, Ex. 3.19); Mozart, Piano Sonata in A Minor, K. 310, iii, 1–20 (*ACF*, Ex. 5.5); and Beethoven, Piano Sonata in G, Op. 14, no. 2, ii, 1–20 (*ACF*, Sup. 8.14).

**Reopened HC.** Before leaving the topic of metrically weak cadences, it is interesting to observe that all of the cases that we examined of the reopened HC result in the emerging HC falling on a weak beat of the bar. The reason, of course, is that the PAC, which reopens into an HC, is implied to occur on the downbeat of the bar. In other words, the surprising effect of the cadential reopening is dependent on our normal expectations that cadences, especially authentic ones, will occur on a strong metrical position. Indeed, in every one of the cases of reopened HC, the matching PAC that ends the subsequent phrase of the theme arrives on the downbeat of the final bar, thus producing a cadence that is metrically stronger than the prior reopened HC.

### 3.4.1.3. Hypermetrical Considerations

Up to now, our discussion of the metrical interpretation of cadence has been confined to the limits of a "real" measure, no matter what notational system is used. Metrical theory from the nineteenth century to the present, however, is often concerned with how individual measures themselves group into larger metrical units, what is normally called *hypermeter*.[235] In general, theorists divide themselves into two camps: those who, with respect to some predefined group of two or more measures, regard the *odd*-numbered bars as metrically strong, and those who consider the *even*-numbered bars to be strong.[236] As for the hypermetrical interpretation of cadences, the first camp usually sees them occurring on weak metrical positions (e.g., the even-numbered measures 4, 8, and 16), whereas the second camp accords hypermetrical strength to these same even-numbered bars.[237] Though these contradictory positions are well entrenched within both camps, one regularly arising hypermetrical situation perhaps lends support to the "odd-measure strong" interpretation. From that perspective, tight-knit conventional themes normally find cadences arising in even-numbered, "weak" measures. In some looser contexts, however, various processes of extension or expansion can result in a cadence arriving on an odd-numbered bar, sometimes even eliding with the onset of the next formal unit. Such cases can thus be seen to accord greater metrical strength to the moment of cadential closure than would normally be the case. Let us look again at Example 3.165. As earlier discussed, we find the IAC in measure 8 occurring on a weak metrical position *within* the bar; but measure 8 as a whole is already considered weak according to the "odd-measure strong" camp. Thus it is interesting to observe that when Beethoven repeats the continuation phrase, he expands the cadential progression such that it arrives not only on a notated downbeat but also in an odd-numbered measure; as a result, the cadential arrival achieves both metrical and hypermetrical strength. Along with the elision (m. 13 being simultaneously the final bar of the main theme and the first bar of the transition), the change to a *fortissimo* dynamic, and a new "brilliant" topic, the metrical status of the cadence adds another element that contributes to a powerful rhetorical articulation at this point in the form.[238]

### 3.4.1.4. Metrical Weighting—Syntactical or Rhetorical?

The appeal to a sense of rhetorical strength just invoked leads us now to a central question regarding the relationship of cadence to meter: Is metrical strength an essential criterion for assessing the *syntactical* strength of a given cadence, or is metrical strength better understood as an element contributing to a cadence's *rhetorical* strength?[239] On the one hand, that the overwhelming majority of cadences occur on metrically strong positions could lead to a presumption that if a cadence is placed on a metrically weak position, its status as a genuine cadence might be lessened or even undermined. On the other hand, we have observed that in the minority of cases where a cadence is metrically weaker than the norm, we have little reason to believe that formal closure is thereby thrown in doubt. Especially in those cases where a metrically strong HC of an antecedent phrase is followed by a metrically weaker PAC (see again Ex. 3.158, 3.159, and 3.163), we are still likely to perceive that a genuine period form has been created. In other words, neither the ontological status nor the syntactical strength of a cadence seems to come into question if it occupies a weak metrical position. Nonetheless, we evidently do perceive a certain sense of strength (or weakness) of a cadence in its association with its metrical position, namely, what I have been calling its *rhetorical* strength. Indeed, we can now add meter as a parameter, along with many others, that contributes to the rhetorical strength of a given cadence.[240] In short, we should not deny or undermine the status of a presumed cadence simply because it appears metrically weak.[241]

---

235. This term is normally accredited to Cone, though he speaks more of "hypermeasure" than hypermeter; *Musical Form*, 79. Many theorists use this term in connection with the two-measure groupings in the notational system that I identify as R = 2N. For the purposes of this discussion, I restrict the term to the metrical groupings of "real" measures, no matter how they are notated.

236. The theoretical literature on this matter is large: see, for example, Jonathan D. Kramer, *The Time of Music: New Meanings, New Temporalities, New Listening Strategies*, 84–86; William E. Caplin, "Theories of Musical Rhythm in the Eighteenth and Nineteenth Centuries," 688, notes 97 and 98; Rothstein, "National Metrical Types," 112–14. Today, we think of the first camp as especially associated with Schenker, the second, with Riemann. A third pattern is also sometimes invoked: within, say, a four-measure unit, measures one and four are considered metrically strong, with measures two and three being weak (see Cone, *Musical Form*, 26–31).

237. Indeed in Riemann's scheme, the final bar of an eight-measure theme (he calls all such formations a "period") is accorded the greatest hypermetrical strength; see Caplin, "Criteria for Analysis," 420.

238. Similar effects occur regularly in subordinate-theme construction, with various expansions of the grouping structure resulting in final PACs that arrive on hypermetrically strong measures (as defined by the "odd-number strong" camp). Of course, not all theorists concur with this account. Thus Yust proposes a different view of such elided cadences, which he finds as "*preventing* or *delaying* closure" (*Organized Time*, 148).

239. See again the distinction between syntactical and rhetorical strength in the previous chapter, sec. 2.11.

240. Paradoxically, Meyer considers meter, in its own right, to be a *syntactic* (*primary*) parameter, presumably because meter essentially engages the functionally differentiated categories of accent and unaccent; see the discussion of Meyer's notions of closure in Chapter 1, sec. 1.2.1. Though I generally agree with Meyer on this point, I would propose that meter *in its specific relation to cadence* is better seen as a secondary, statistical parameter, such that the degree of metrical weight associated with a given cadence affects its rhetorical strength, not its syntactical strength, as I have just argued in the text.

241. The idea that meter can be a criterion for the syntactical weighting of cadences is prominently advanced by Yust, especially for music in the late seventeenth and early eighteenth centuries; *Organized Time*, 146–47.

## 3.4.2. Texture

Texture is one of the most under-theorized concepts in music, and so providing a satisfactory textbook definition is far from easy. Generally speaking, texture involves the distribution of musical material across the pitch spectrum (from low to high) and especially, for tonal music, in reference to some notion of *voice* (often, but not necessarily, the standard S-A-T-B set of voices). Thus texture may refer to the number of voices employed in a given musical passage, the nature of the material associated with those voices, and various other relationships obtaining between them (excluding the intervallic and scale-degree relationships of their pitch content, which more properly belong to the domains of counterpoint and harmony, respectively). Texture also implicates the idea of *density* of material from thinnest to thickest. Though some common textural descriptors (such as monophony and homophony) apply to a wide range of musical styles, it would be more useful here to limit our discussion to the types of textures featured in music of the classical style, with an emphasis of course on the role that texture may play in the articulation of cadential closure.[242]

One characteristic of the classical style, especially in relation to the earlier baroque and later Romantic styles, is the high degree of textural variety that arises from idea to idea, phrase to phrase, theme to theme (works by Mozart are particularly subject to a regular flux of new textures). As a result, textural changes often support the segmentation of the musical material, and to that extent, texture is indirectly tied to issues of formal function, for which the identification of grouping structure can be decisive. Moreover, certain textural situations seem correlated with some general temporal functions, such as the tendency for monophonic passages to express the local sense of initiation,[243] and for polyphonic textures to be associated with medial functionalities.[244]

### 3.4.2.1. Textural Types

Among the more commonly described textures for music of the classical style, we regularly find the following types:

- *monophony*: The use of a single voice; multiple voices sounding the identical material but at different octaves result in what may be termed *doubled monophony*.

- *homophony*: The use of multiple voices (usually three or more) that exhibit a strong uniformity in musical material, especially, in durational values; the terms *chordal texture* or *block-like texture* are also frequently used to identify this textural type.

- *polyphony*: The use of multiple voices whose pitch contour and durational profiles are individualized and clearly differentiated. The non-simultaneous, often overlapping, use of similar melodic ideas results in *imitative* polyphony (such as canonic or fugal imitation).

- *melody and accompaniment*: A multi-voiced texture in which one voice (usually an upper one) carries salient melodic material supported by conventionalized accompanimental patterns in the other (lower) voices. Some conventionalized accompaniments include the *Alberti bass*, the *drum bass*, and the *murky bass*.[245]

### 3.4.2.2. Texture and Cadence

As regards the relation of texture to cadence, the topic has already been raised in the present chapter in connection with how a registral shift of the bass voice can help support the change from a prolongational stream to a cadential one (especially the leap from a prolongational ① down to a cadential ③). In the previous chapter (sec. 2.9), I examined the idea of a rhythmic caesura ("stop") and considered the role that the resulting textural gap may play—or not play—in characterizing points of cadential arrival. I also discussed there how texture contributes significantly to the *rhetorical* weight projected by a given cadence. Indeed, I generally follow Meyer in seeing texture as a secondary, or statistical, parameter, one that does not normally contribute in a direct manner to the syntactical organization of tonal music.[246] Even in these kinds of associations between texture and cadence, the former component is by no means a necessary condition for the latter. If, for a given passage, we can identify the essential harmonic and melodic elements of cadential content and can validate an appropriate context of formal ending, we should be able to speak confidently of genuine cadential closure irrespective of the passage's texture. Whether a cadence features a massive orchestral tutti or a lone pitch (as in Ex. 3.167, downbeat of m. 29), the syntactical requirements of cadence are entirely fulfilled if the requisite morphological and functional conditions are present or clearly implied (in the case, say, of harmonically incomplete textures).[247]

---

242. For a considerably more sophisticated treatment of texture than what I present in this section, see Jonathan De Souza, "Texture." See also a number of empirical studies by Ben Duane, e.g., "Auditory Streaming Cues in Eighteenth- and Early Nineteenth-Century String Quartets: A Corpus-Based Study"; "Thematic and Non-Thematic Textures in Schubert's Three-Key Expositions."

243. Janet M. Levy, "Texture as a Sign in Classic and Early Romantic Music," 498–518.

244. Polyphony is frequently featured in the contrasting middle (B section) of the small ternary theme type and in development sections of sonata form, both of these units being medial functions. See Ratz, *Die musikalische Formenlehre*, 25; Olga Ellen Bakulina, "The Loosening

---

Role of Polyphony: Texture and Formal Functions in Mozart's 'Haydn' Quartets."

245. See *ACF*, 315, for examples of these accompanimental patterns.

246. Meyer, *Style and Music*, 14–15; see also Leonard B. Meyer, "A Universe of Universals," 8–10.

247. In connection with these matters, Hepokoski and Darcy introduce the notion of "attenuated cadence," one that involves a sudden reduction in dynamics and textural density (*Sonata Theory*, 170). Seeing as they generally regard an attenuated cadence as providing genuine formal

EXAMPLE 3.167. Haydn, Piano Variations in F Minor, H.XVII:6, mm. 28–29.

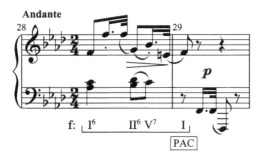

Situations arise, however, where a textural issue may impede our assessment of a cadence's morphology, thus presenting potential ambiguities in cadential identification. These problems can include cases where an incomplete texture obscures our recognition of the bass voice, as well as cases that permit multiple options for which pitch projects the soprano voice.

Textural gaps, especially when they concern the bass, can create ambiguities that call into question whether or not a particular musical configuration acquires genuine cadential status. Consider how the second subordinate theme of Beethoven's *Waldstein* sonata reaches its end (Ex. 3.168). As the culmination of an enormous ECP, which begins at least as early as measure 59 (not shown),[248] measure 66 brings a stage-3a cadential six-four supported by ⑤. In the course of prolonging dominant harmony, the left hand arpeggiates upward in a manner that metrically weakens the bass pitch B; indeed, ⑤ disappears entirely with the left-hand trill in measures 72–73. When the final tonic appears at measure 74, it seems on the surface as though it is achieved by means of the prolongational (and thus noncadential) progression V$^6_5$–I. If this is our understanding, then we must say that the impending cadence has been *abandoned*.[249] Alternatively, we could understand that Beethoven has manipulated not the position of the dominant but rather the texture of that harmony, literally omitting the bass voice in measures 72–73, but still implying its presence in our aural imagination. Seeing as what follows is obviously the closing section, the interpretation of abandoned cadence makes little sense here, and so we understand that an incomplete texture results in the temporary suppression of the bass, not its complete disappearance.[250]

In some cases, texture leads to ambiguities about which pitch represents the actual upper voice at the moment of cadential arrival. In string quartet writing, especially, the first and second violins sometimes intertwine their lines in ways that obscure which structural voice (soprano or alto) is being taken by which instrument. In Example 3.169a, an opening main theme, set in a straightforward homophonic texture, closes with an unambiguous PAC on the downbeat of measure 8. The theme is then repeated, with the original melody now sounding in the second violin (cf. mm. 1–2 and 9–10). Toward the end of the repetition (Ex. 3.169b), the first violin becomes ever more florid and even references the melodic content of measures 5–6 (see the pitches with the elongated stems in mm. 14–15). Indeed, it seems obvious that violin 1 is now fully projecting the soprano voice, that is, until the second beat of measure 15, when it suddenly leaps below the second violin, to bring a $\hat{4}$–$\hat{3}$ resolution within the final harmonic progression V$^7$–I. (The first violin is thus replicating a similar gesture from m. 13 to m. 14.) At the same time, the second violin in measures 15–16 (shown in the upper voice of the left hand) effects a $\hat{7}$–$\hat{8}$ resolution, lying above violin 1.[251] The question then becomes: Which cadence type is operative here—an IAC conveyed by the first violin, or a PAC, by the second violin? From a purely formal perspective, the PAC interpretation seems to make more sense, in that we are hearing a repeat of the main theme that has already closed with that cadence, and we would not be expecting the repeated theme to end with a weaker IAC.[252] From the point of view of string quartet texture, where we normally associate the first violin with the soprano voice, it remains a viable listening option to hear an IAC, especially because we are clearly focusing on the first violin as the leading voice up to the final downward leap. In short, the textural complexities of this passage produce cadential ambiguities that are not fully resolvable.[253]

### 3.4.2.3. Covered Cadence

A special case of the textural problem identified in the previous paragraph arises when, in the context of an elided authentic

---

closure, their identification of texture relates primarily to the rhetorical aspect of cadential strength. They normally hold, however, that an attenuated PAC is not a viable candidate for their EEC or ESC, and so in this respect, their concept enters into the realm of the syntactical. Since my own theory of formal functions does not subscribe to the idea of a single EEC or ESC, those cadences that Hepokoski and Darcy deem to be attenuated are still perfectly acceptable cadences for me from a syntactic point of view, even if they are rhetorically weak.

248. The first two stages of this ECP are discussed in Chapter 5, Ex. 5.39.

249. As will be discussed in the next chapter (sec. 4.3.1), one means of abandoning a cadence is to invert the cadential dominant prior to its resolution to tonic.

250. I thank Pieter Bergé for drawing my attention to this example as particularly illustrative of the issue at hand.

251. In fact, the second violin in m. 15 is referencing the opening motive ($\hat{8}$–$\hat{7}$–$\hat{8}$) of the theme in m. 1.

252. When a sonata-form main theme that closes with a PAC is repeated, even in a highly varied form (e.g., the first movement of Beethoven's String Quartet in A, Op. 30, no. 1), the repetition ends again with a PAC. I have not yet encountered a case where the repeated theme closes obviously with an IAC. More likely, the repeated theme might conclude with an HC, such that we would interpret the repetition as functioning as a transition (see the discussion of the "reversed" or "inverted" period in in sec. 3.3.4.1, "Periodic Forms," and note 182).

253. See ahead Ex. 3.171a, where textural matters also complicate the analysis of thematic closure.

3.4. ADDITIONAL ASPECTS OF THE BASIC CADENCE TYPES  141

EXAMPLE 3.168. Beethoven, Piano Sonata in C ("Waldstein"), Op. 53, i, mm. 65–75.

EXAMPLE 3.169. Haydn, String Quartet in B-flat, Op. 76, no. 4, ii, (a) mm. 1–10; (b) mm. 13–16.

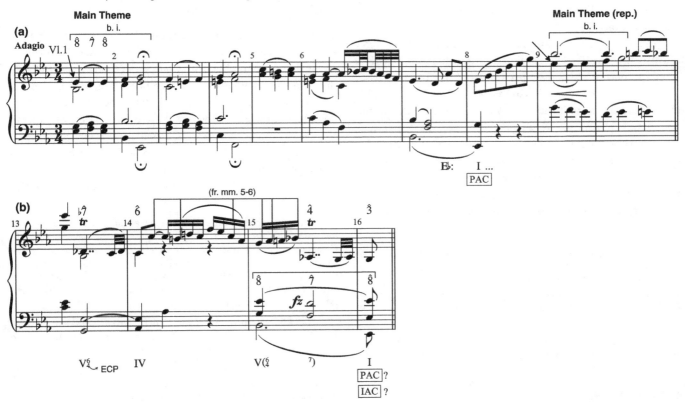

cadence, the initial pitch of the subsequent thematic unit begins on scale degree $\hat{3}$ or $\hat{5}$, which lies *above* the final of the pitch of the cadence (usually $\hat{1}$). Such a situation can give the impression that the authentic cadence is imperfect because the "highest" pitch at the moment of cadential arrival is not the tonic. If we sort out the texture, however, and understand that this higher pitch does not belong to the cadential configuration per se, we realize that the authentic cadence is better understood as perfect. Steven Vande Moortele has proposed the term *covered cadence* to identify this situation, since, in a nod to Schenker's notion of a "covering tone," the initiating pitch of the next unit covers the goal pitch of the cadence.[254]

A clear covered cadence has already been seen in Example 3.37, where the main theme is obviously heading toward a PAC on the downbeat of measure 12, with the leading tone as the penultimate melodic pitch. The onset of the transition, however, elides with this cadence, by bringing back the opening basic idea ($\hat{5}$–$\hat{6}$–$\hat{5}$) of the main theme. As a result, the initial pitch of the basic idea "covers" the final pitch of the cadence, $\hat{1}$, which is buried in the triple stop of the first violin. To claim that the cadence is an IAC is to assert that $\hat{5}$ is the melodic goal of the main theme, which seems patently false given the conventional varied alto pattern ($\hat{1}/\flat\hat{2}/\hat{1}$–$\hat{7}/\hat{1}$) of the cadential melody. Alternatively, we could argue that the cadence has been *evaded*, such that the musical event on the downbeat of measure 12 does not group with the preceding cadential material but rather exclusively belongs to the opening of the transition. Such an interpretation is also problematic, for it would leave the main theme unclosed, since no other cadential candidate is forthcoming (the subsequent home-key HC at measure 18, not shown, clearly functions to end the first part of a two-part transition).[255]

Example 3.85 also raises the possibility of recognizing a covered cadence (measure 41). Once again, two alternative interpretations come into play: the first, the rare case of an IAC ($\hat{5}$) (as discussed in sec. 3.2.1.5); the second, a covered PAC, with $\hat{1}$ concealed in the chordal accompaniment. Somewhat unusual for the normal understanding of a covered cadence is that $\hat{5}$ on the downbeat of measure 41 does not represent the opening pitch of the next thematic unit, but rather the upper note in a new accompanimental drum-bass texture. (To be sure, the next thematic unit, part 2 of the ongoing interior theme, does begin on $\hat{5}$ in m. 42, but it is functionally not the same $\hat{5}$ as the one in the previous bar.)

Another kind of covered cadence can be seen in Example 3.92, measure 40. Here, the cadential situation is inverted, in that the goal pitch of the PrC (a type of IAC) is $\hat{3}$, while the covering pitch is $\hat{1}$, introduced by the newly entering woodwinds. Though we normally expect a main theme to conclude with a PAC, we must be careful not to let this assumption color our view of what really seems to be happening in the melody, which, as discussed earlier, is clearly heading to close on $\hat{3}$. The elided formal unit is a simple codetta, operative not in a cadential context, but rather in a postcadential one.[256]

## 3.5. Other Cadence Types

In addition to the three cadence types treated thus far (PAC, IAC, HC), theorists have regularly proposed two other types, ones that are not deemed genuine in my theory of cadence, but which deserve mention here, since they will prove important for the treatment of thematic closure not only in the classical style, but in other tonal styles as well. The first type has been identified by a variety of terms, *contrapuntal cadence* being the one most typically found nowadays. The second type is the *plagal cadence*, cited in virtually every textbook of musical rudiments, harmony, and form. This section evaluates the status of these two cadential options and concludes that neither finds a comfortable home in the notions of *cadential* closure developed in this study.

### 3.5.1. "Contrapuntal Cadence"; Prolongational Closure

Over many centuries, most music theorists have included in their concept of cadence instances where either the final dominant or the final tonic (or both) are inverted; some, though, speak of only the dominant changing its position.[257] In addition, various leading-tone harmonies (typically VII$^7$ or VII$^6_5$) may be substituted for the dominant of stage 3.[258] Theorists have used a variety of terms to characterize these cadences, such as *imperfect*, *medial*, *inverted*, and *contrapuntal*, the latter seeming to be the preferred choice in recent years. In describing the function of such cadences, most theorists note that they are relatively weak, less conclusive, and

---

254. Steven Vande Moortele, *The Romantic Overture and Musical Form from Rossini to Wagner*, 53, note 23. He also alludes to the covered cadence in his earlier study, *Two-Dimensional Sonata Form: Form and Cycle in Single-Movement Instrumental Works by Liszt, Strauss, Schoenberg, and Zemlinsky*, 58, note 13. See also Zhang, "Apparently Imperfect," 196–97 and 205–11.

255. Textural issues often arise when considering cadential deviations, especially when deciding among genuine, deceptive, and evaded cadences, where grouping structure, a factor that often involves texture, is a central criterion. The topic of texture and cadence will thus arise again in the following chapter.

256. Other examples of the covered cadence will arise now and then in the rest of this study; see especially Chapter 4, sec. 4.6.4, Ex. 4.81a. In Chapter 6, we will even see that a covered cadence can appear as the final cadence of the movement (see Ex. 6.15a); in this case, the covering tone, as part of the final sonority, neither groups forward, to represent the start of a new thematic process, nor groups backward with the cadence, but rather seems to exist on its own.

257. Aldwell, Schachter, and Cadwallader, *Harmony & Voice Leading*, 156; Steven G. Laitz, *The Complete Musician: An Integrated Approach to Theory, Analysis and Listening*, 108.

258. Stefan M. Kostka, Dorothy Payne, and Byron Almén specifically speak of a "leading-tone IAC" in such cases (*Tonal Harmony: With an Introduction to Twentieth-Century Music*, 147).

generally confined to ending phrases that are internal to broader thematic processes.²⁵⁹ To be sure, whereas some writers confine contrapuntal cadences to such interior positions, they still leave open the possibility, albeit remote, that a cadence ending a complete theme may include an inverted dominant.²⁶⁰

Needless to say, the idea of a contrapuntal cadence runs counter to the fundamental concept of the classical cadence presented in this study. As discussed on a number of occasions in Chapter 2, the distinction that I propose between prolongational and cadential harmonic progressions prohibits me from speaking of inverted dominants as participating in any phenomenon that I deem cadential.²⁶¹ The issue involves not only the sense of requisite stability associated with a root-position dominant and tonic, but as well, the melodic organization of the bass line, which I have conceptualized as divided into two streams (using again the distinction between prolongational and cadential).²⁶² Unlike most other theorists, who see a continuous spectrum of varying degrees of cadential articulation from the weakest contrapuntal cadence at one extreme to the strongest PAC at the other, my view of what is, or is not, cadential is categorical and absolute.²⁶³ In the history of cadence theory, my position is admittedly an extreme one. Yet I am convinced that it not only avoids many problems in cadential identification, but also promotes considerable analytical insights into the nature of musical *form*. Indeed, most of the writers that I have cited present the contrapuntal cadence in the context of a *harmony* textbook embracing multiple tonal styles (usually ranging at least two centuries), without considering how their ideas would become fully integrated into a comprehensive theory of form and phrase structure for some relatively specific musical style.

In short, I am claiming that the contrapuntal cadence does not have the capacity to create closure for a complete thematic process, unlike the three cadence types PAC, IAC, and HC, each of which is suitable for ending a thematic unit. Empirical evidence, moreover, largely confirms this statement, for in the classical style, a thematic unit (one consisting of distinct initial, medial, and concluding formal functions) is rarely closed with such a contrapuntal cadence.²⁶⁴

At the heart of the dilemma posed by the contrapuntal cadence is my rejection of the idea that all formal closure should be conceptualized and experienced as *cadential*. Put more positively, I entirely accept the proposition that certain forms of *noncadential* closure have the capacity to project the sense that a formal unit has achieved a degree of completion. With this view in place, it then remains to characterize the nature of this noncadential closure for the musical events that other writers identify as contrapuntal cadences. And here we can return to the fundamental distinction between harmonic environments that are prolongational as opposed to those that are cadential. For the contrapuntal cadence clearly inhabits the world of harmonic prolongation. The kinds of progressions identified with the contrapuntal cadence are prolongational ones: they *propose* a potential tonality, but they do not *confirm* it, and for this reason, they occur internal to the harmonic, melodic, and tonal processes that constitute a complete thematic utterance. At the same time, these contrapuntal cadences do close something, for example, a single musical idea or certain phrases consisting of multiple ideas. It is extremely important to understand that I am not denying that a certain degree of closure is associated with what others have called the contrapuntal cadence. In order to distinguish this type of closure from that which is truly cadential, however, I propose using a different term, namely, *prolongational closure* (as already introduced in connection with Ex. 3.65, m. 10) to cover such situations.²⁶⁵ In other words, such passages of music do project a degree of self-containment, of having a clear grouping boundary, or put otherwise, of being closed to some extent. And what seems to be the characteristic harmonic feature of this closure is the prolongational progression lying at the basis of the passage.

Some writers who otherwise advocate for contrapuntal cadences betray their own understanding that there is something not quite cadential about them. Thus in connection with Example 3.170, Ellis B. Kohs speaks of a weak IAC on the downbeat of measure 33. He then notes that "[w]ith so many weakening factors [continuous motion, phrase elision, and inverted dominant], the very presence of a cadence in measure 33 may be questioned."²⁶⁶ That Beethoven does not write a genuine cadence

---

259. Jane Piper Clendinning and Elizabeth West Marvin, *The Musician's Guide to Theory and Analysis*, 215; Kostka, Payne, and Almén, *Tonal Harmony*, 147. Green bucks the trend by speaking of such cadences as "conclusive" (*Form*, 9–10).

260. Thus Aldwell, Schachter, and Cadwallader note that "[s]uch cadences are virtually never used at the end of a piece" (*Harmony & Voice Leading*, 152). L. Poundie Burstein and Joseph Nathan Straus warn the student that at a PAC or HC, "it is normal for V to be in root position" (*Concise Introduction to Tonal Harmony*, 125).

261. I am referring here to genuine cadences only, not to the cadential deviations that may include inverted harmonies in stages 3 and 4.

262. See the discussion in Chapter 2, sec. 2.4.

263. Harrison also proposes a broad conception of harmonic and formal closure that distinguishes categorically between a musical configuration that is termed *cadence* from one that is not a cadence, namely, *clausulae* of various types, these effectively being the kinds of configuration that other theorists term *contrapuntal cadences* ("Cadence," 550, Fig. 19.13). But Harrison's choice of terminology betrays a degree of discomfort with denying these structures cadential status, for the term that he uses to identify them—*clausulae*—is historically a synonym for cadence, as he himself acknowledges (548).

---

264. Some of these exceptional cases have already been discussed above in sec. 3.1.3.2; some additional ones (Ex. 3.172 and 3.173) will be investigated shortly.

265. Mark Richards develops a similar idea, which he terms "closural function" ("Closure in Classical Themes: The Role of Melody and Texture in Cadences, Closural Function, and the Separated Cadence," 31–35). MacKay describes a number of cases in which he denies the cadential status of a putative IAC, arguing instead for a situation that is essentially comparable to my notion of prolongational closure ("Declassifying the IAC").

266. Kohs, *Musical Form: Studies in Analysis and Synthesis*, 31.

EXAMPLE 3.170. Beethoven, Piano Sonata in C, Op. 2, no. 3, i, mm. 31–33.

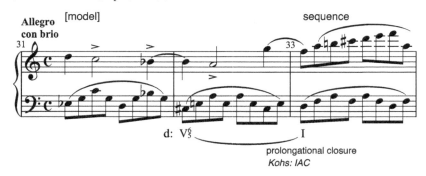

at this point makes perfect compositional sense, because what is being "ended" by this prolongational closure is a model for immediate sequential repetition (in mm. 33–39, not shown), not anything fully thematic.

Similarly, consider Laitz's analysis and commentary on the opening vocal phrase of Schubert's song "Die Krähe" (Ex. 3.171a), which he sees concluding with a contrapuntal cadence at measure 9, supported by the progression VII⁶–I.[267] Laitz notes, however, that "[i]t is also possible to view the four-measure excerpt as merely a tonic expansion and therefore not a phrase, since there is no strong root-position harmonic motion from T[onic] through D[ominant]." By speaking of a "tonic expansion," he alludes to the harmonic situation that I have been calling a tonic prolongation, and to the extent that we recognize a degree of ending when the progression is completed, we can speak of prolongational closure for the phrase as a whole.

Unfortunately, Laitz's harmonic analysis of this passage is problematic, since the left hand of the piano is doubling the melody and therefore does not represent an actual bass voice. As a result, we cannot say for sure just how this four-measure phrase ends harmonically. We are left uncertain as to whether the passage exhibits prolongational closure or an actual cadence (assuming a bass line that would bring a root-position dominant). It is interesting to note, however, what happens in the immediately preceding piano introduction (Ex. 3.171b), which brings a similar melodic line supported by a genuine bass, one that creates a PAC on the downbeat of measure 5. What occurs in the introduction, of course, does not prove that the closure in measure 9 is to be understood as cadential; indeed, finding weak closure there (to yield a compound basic idea) probably makes sense in light of the following consequent phrase, which modulates to the relative major and ends with a PAC. Here then is another case where textural matters complicate an analysis of closure.

The morphology of prolongational closure is easy to describe, in that it consists harmonically of a prolongational progression ending most typically with tonic in root position (less often in first inversion) and a melodic conclusion on $\hat{1}$, $\hat{3}$, or $\hat{5}$.[268] Functionally, prolongational closure can end any number of lower-level units: a simple basic idea; an initiating four-measure phrase, such as a presentation (Ex. 3.166, m. 4) or a compound basic idea; a model for sequential repetition (Ex. 3.170), and, especially in looser formal contexts, a continuation phrase that is followed by an exclusively cadential phrase (Ex. 3.66, mm. 5–8).[269] Where prolongational closure is rarely used, at least in the classical style, is at the end of a thematic unit, which, as has been elaborated at length, is one of the principal reasons why I do not regard this mode of closure to be genuinely cadential.

Needless to say, some highly exceptional situations arise in which a thematic unit ends prolongationally. The main theme in Example 3.65 has already been discussed (sec. 3.1.3.2). Two additional cases from the string quartet literature are also worthy of examination. The first, shown in Example 3.172a, sees the A′ section of a minuet form closing with its requisite, and fully unproblematic, PAC at measure 33.[270] There follows a coda, whose coda theme begins with polyphonic imitations. The theme heads toward a PAC at measure 47 (not shown) but fails to close due to a deceptive cadence at that point. A second try for the cadence occurs in the following bars (Ex. 3.172b), which is again unrealized via the deceptive cadence at measure 51. Here, the violins approach the cadential goal with a broad stepwise descent from B down to D (mm. 49–51, motive "x"). A third attempt sees the violins playing the same descending line, now up an octave (mm. 53–55). At measure 55, however, Beethoven does not even allow a cadential situation to arise when the cello firmly holds on to ⑤, not letting it ascend to ⑥ for another deceptive cadence. Over this dominant pedal, the viola now has a chance to sound the descending line (mm. 55–57), which is finally picked up by the cello at measure 57 and repeated down an octave (mm. 59–61). When the cello completes motive "x," the tonic thereby achieved

---

267. Laitz, *Complete Musician*, 254–55 (Ex. 17.7).

268. It is not easy to find a tonic prolongation that concludes on an unstable second inversion tonic, but for an example of a brief prolongation that begins with a tonic six-four, see Ex. 3.80a, m. 5.

269. To avoid cluttering the analytical annotations, I do not normally indicate phrase-level prolongational closures, saving the use of that term for the end of a thematic unit, in which the prolongational closure replaces an expected authentic cadence.

270. The A′ section itself is unusual in that it opens with a subdominant version of the A section. Eventually the music modulates to the home key, confirmed by the cadence at m. 33. The addition of a lengthy coda, to be discussed immediately, thus helps to compensate for the tonal instabilities of the A′ section.

3.5. OTHER CADENCE TYPES 145

EXAMPLE 3.171. Schubert, "Die Krähe," *Die Winterreise*, (a) mm. 6–9; (b) mm. 3–5.

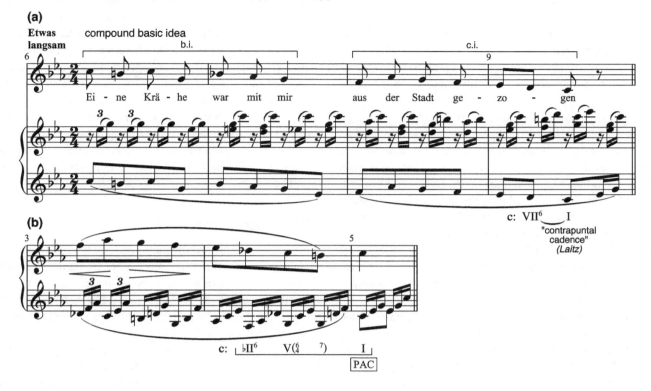

EXAMPLE 3.172. Beethoven, String Quartet in D, Op. 18, no. 3, iii, (a) mm. 31–37; (b) mm. 48–62.

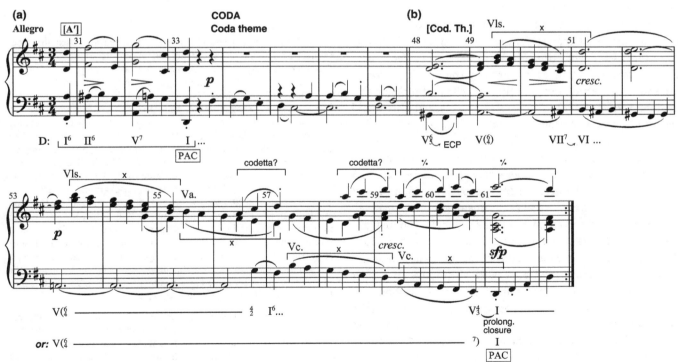

is sustained into the downbeat of the following bar. Given the decisive *melodic* closure attained throughout the previous measures, we have the impression that the coda theme finally reaches its conclusion at measure 61. A closer examination reveals, however, that dominant harmony becomes inverted at the end of measure 60, thus prohibiting us from recognizing a genuine PAC and understanding that the coda theme ends instead with prolongational closure.

This exceptional situation can be explained, of course, by Beethoven's insistence on letting all four parts perform the descending scalar line. Thus motivic and textural concerns override the normal demands of a true cadential articulation. To be sure, we have heard the cadential dominant literally sounding in root position for a total of ten bars during this entire cadential process (mm. 43–46, not shown, mm. 49–50, and mm. 53–56), so we can perhaps retain this pitch in our imagination, even when we hear that the cello in measures 57–61 is performing an "upper voice" melody, not a true bass line. If so, then we could speak of a cadence to end the coda theme after all, despite the lack of a literally sounding bass voice.

Before leaving this example, it is interesting to observe that this analysis finds no postcadential passage literally concluding the coda. Yet it is not difficult to hear the music from the upbeat to measure 57 through to measure 61, especially in the upper voice, as sounding like a series of codettas. Problematic in this interpretation, of course, is the lack of any clear cadence upon which such a closing section would follow. Beethoven seems to want to have it both ways: saving the final thematic closure for measure 61—be it prolongational or cadential—but also referencing the gestures of codettas in the music that precedes this ending.

A second, similar case for how motive and voice articulation can complicate thematic closure arises in Example 3.173a. Here, the A section of a trio begins with a series of three leaping gestures that arpeggiate tonic harmony (motive "a"). Toward the end of the section (Ex. 3.173b), the cello part picks up this opening idea to effect a closing $V^6_5$–I progression. This would seem to be a case of prolongational closure, not cadence, because the potentially cadential dominant on the downbeat of measure 78 becomes inverted. (Alternatively, this moment could be considered a case of *abandoned cadence*; see sec. 4.3.) It is obvious that the license here is dependent upon Mozart continuing to let the cello realize the opening motivic material. At the same time, and compared to the original ascending gesture (Ex. 3.173a), the cello motive is actually cut slightly short, thus failing to complete the melody of the full compound basic idea, which concludes with a stepwise fill (motive "b"). So it is no surprise when, at the beginning of the A′ section (Ex. 3.173c), the cello finally gets the opportunity of performing the opening material in full. It is as though the cello had entered "too early" toward the end of the A section (Ex. 3.173b) and finally, at the opening of A′, gets the chance to repair the damage caused by bringing in a prolongational close in place of a genuine cadence. Following this opening, the A′ section ends quite regularly with a standard PAC (not shown).

Up to this point, I have been framing the issue of prolongational closure as a noncadential mode of ending within the formal syntax of the classical style. The topic will also arise prominently when we look at nineteenth-century practice in Chapters 8 and 9. There we will discover that composers gradually come to accept prolongational closure as a means of ending not only internal phrases, but also complete thematic units and even larger-scale sections of a movement. If, for the classical style, we had simply accepted prolongational closure as a genuine cadence—a contrapuntal one—we might have failed to appreciate the significantly different ways in which this mode of noncadential closure operates over a wider stylistic purview.

### 3.5.2. "Plagal Cadence"

In all of music-theoretical discourse, perhaps the most egregious disconnect between theory and practice arises with the idea of the "plagal cadence." Given how widespread the term appears in the music-theoretical literature,[271] it is astounding that for all practical purposes there is no such thing as a plagal cadence in music of the eighteenth century and the first decade or so of the nineteenth.[272] For that reason, I postpone a more complete discussion of this problematic issue until the final chapter of this study, where I deal with manifestations of the plagal cadence in the rest of nineteenth century.

A major source for this discrepancy between theory and practice is surely the confusion between cadential and postcadential functionalities (see Chapter 2, sec. 2.8). For when we observe in

---

271. Indeed, I am not aware of any standard harmony text that does *not* define a specific plagal cadence. For recent iterations, see Aldwell, Schachter, and Cadwallader, *Harmony & Voice Leading*, 231–32; Laitz, *Complete Musician*, 239; Clendinning and Marvin, *Musician's Guide*, 301; Burstein and Straus, *Tonal Harmony*, 169; Robert Gauldin, *Harmonic Practice*, 135–36; Kostka, Payne, and Almén, *Tonal Harmony*, 148–49. Lester even recognizes a "half plagal cadence" (with a phrase-ending motion of I–IV) (*Harmony*, 52–53); Green also echoes this idea when speaking of "half cadences ending with IV" (*Form*, 14). On the historical origins of the term *plagal cadence*, see Caleb Mutch, "Blainville's New Mode, or, How the Plagal Cadence Came to Be 'Plagal.'" For more on the "plagal half cadence" and its theoretical background, see Harrison, *Harmonic Function*, 29, note 16. As an example of a plagal HC, Harrison cites the minuet of Mozart's Symphony No. 39 in E-flat, K. 543, m. 4. In my view, this excerpt does not bring opening antecedent and consequent phrases as proposed by Harrison. Rather, I hear a compound basic idea (supported by I–IV) followed by its repetition (V–I), thus forming a compound presentation; a continuation eventually modulates to the subordinate key, as confirmed by a closing PAC (m. 16). This PAC is thus the only cadence in this compound sentence.

272. Indeed, this fact has already been recognized by Rosen: "Cadences had still been formed in the seventeenth century with either dominant or subdominant triads, but as the significant advantages of emphasizing the built-in imbalance of the system (the strength of the sharp over the flat direction) began to be realized, the subdominant or plagal cadence was dropped. The dominant cadence became the only one, and was reinforced by the increased importance of the dominant seventh chord" (*Classical Style*, 26).

EXAMPLE 3.173. Mozart, String Quartet in C ("Dissonance"), K. 465, iii, trio, (a) mm. 64–67; (b) mm. 76–79; (c) mm. 89–93.

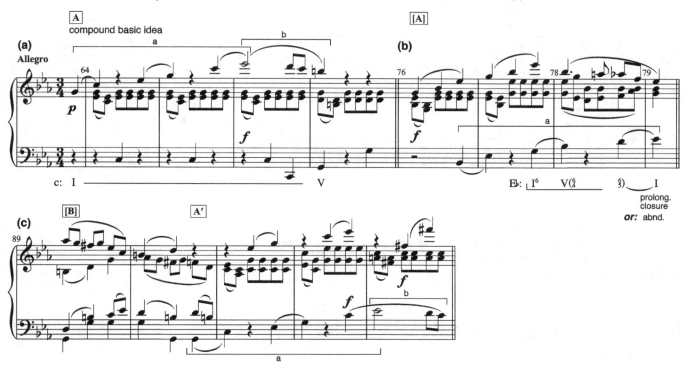

musical writings just which formal situations involve the plagal cadence, they almost always are *codettas* supported by the plagal progression I–IV–I, or some variant thereof, what many texts also call the "Amen" cadence.[273] When we exclude all postcadential passages, the number of plagal cadences that actually seem to involve thematic closure drops significantly.

As also mentioned in the previous chapter (sec. 2.3.1.3), the plagal progression at the basis of the cadence is essentially *prolongational*, as witnessed by the tonic scale degree held in common between the subdominant and tonic. Thus if we are tempted to associate that progression with a sense of genuine formal close (and even these cases are few and far-between in the classical literature), we should speak more properly of this ending as a type of prolongational closure, one that employs the subdominant as subordinate to the tonic, compared to most other tonic prolongations, which see the dominant assuming the subordinate role.[274]

Though I have claimed that the plagal cadence is virtually unknown in the classical style, one passage, arising in the first movement of Beethoven's "Ghost" Trio (Ex. 3.174) may seem like a genuine case. Quite unusually, the subordinate theme in the exposition takes the form of a tight-knit sentence of nine bars, ending with the PAC at measure 51. At the same moment, the theme begins to be repeated, now with a different instrumentation. According to the plan of the theme's first iteration, measure 59 should bring the closing PAC. Given how tight-knit the formal situation has been up now, it is not surprising that a structural expansion ensues as the music gets stuck on the penultimate dominant, now with an added minor-ninth embellishment (♭6̂). Measures 60 and 61 repeat the idea supported by this dominant and even extend it by a bar (m. 62). When this harmony, which we have been taking as cadentially penultimate, finally resolves to tonic at measure 63, a dissonant seventh is added to the harmony, thus converting it into a secondary dominant of the subdominant. In other words, the V$^7$/IV "replaces" the expected cadential tonic in the manner of a *deceptive cadence*, as will be discussed in the next chapter. What follows, however, is not a repetition of earlier material that would bring a final PAC, but rather a plagal progression V$^7$/IV–IV–I, whose tonic at measure 67 is the final harmony of the exposition.[275] To speak of a plagal cadence here is tempting, but perhaps not quite accurate. For with the appearance of the replacement harmony V$^7$/IV, it seems as though the music were jumping the gun by entering already into a postcadential area. Indeed, the harmonic context here strongly references a galant schema identified by Gjerdingen as a "Quiescenza," a device regularly used in postcadential

---

273. To be sure, most writers acknowledge that plagal "cadences" occur effectively in postcadential situations, that is, following an authentic cadence (the "Amen" situation is routinely cited in this respect). These writers then continue to speak of plagal cadences instead, more accurately, of plagal codettas.

274. In Chapter 9, I term the device *plagal closure*, as a subset of prolongational closure; for simplicity's sake, I continue to use the locution "plagal cadence" in the remainder of the present chapter.

275. In m. 66, the use of an "added sixth" (2̂) above the root of IV, as part of a melodic 1̂–2̂–3̂ motion becomes a standard feature of plagal progressions in the nineteenth century (see Chapter 9, sec. 9.3.4.4).

EXAMPLE 3.174. Beethoven, Piano Trio in D ("Ghost"), Op. 70, no. 1, i, mm. 50–68.

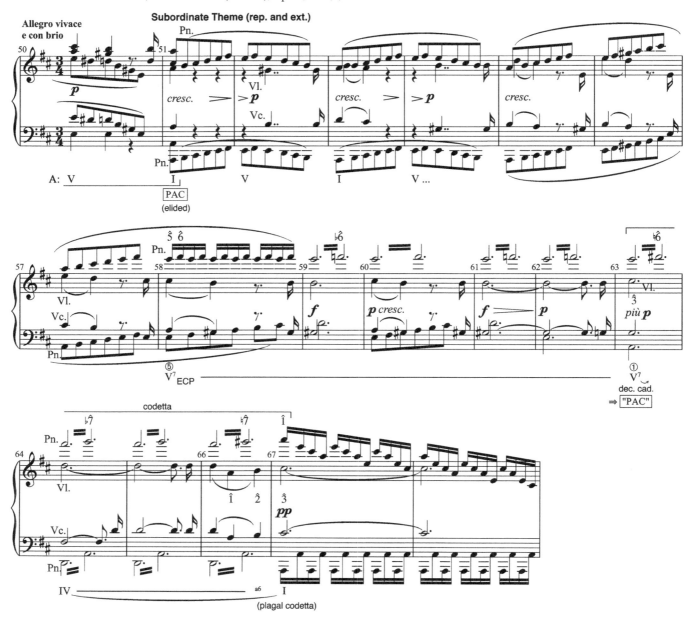

formal positions.[276] Here, however, a cadential close has not yet occurred, upon which postcadential material would logically follow. In fact, the absence of cadence prompts us to reinterpret the deceptive cadence at measure 63 as "a kind of" PAC (thus dec. cad.⇒"PAC"), even if the morphological conditions for such a cadence are not fully fulfilled. Thus when the subdominant of measures 64–66 finally resolves to tonic at measure 67, I would propose that the formal context is postcadential and

the harmonic context, prolongational, as would be appropriate for a closing section, not a cadence. As such, employing the expression plagal "codetta" (embracing m. 63ff.) makes more sense than speaking of a real plagal "cadence" at measure 67.[277]

Before leaving this example, let me mention a couple of other details that further complicate an already complex cadential situation. First, the emphasis on subdominant harmony that occurs at the end of this repeated subordinate theme is especially appropriate

---

276. Gjerdingen, *Galant Style*, chap. 13. Gjerdingen identifies the melodic component of the schema as $\hat{1}$–♭$\hat{7}$–$\hat{6}$–♮$\hat{7}$–$\hat{1}$, supported by the harmonic progression I–V$^7$/IV–IV–V$^7$–I set over a tonic pedal. (Gjerdingen, quite intentionally, does not use roman numeral analyses in his treatise, but the harmonic content of his examples illustrating the Quiescenza can readily be analyzed in this manner.)

277. I return to this line of argumentation in connection with some deceptive cadences by J. S. Bach (Chapter 6, Ex. 6.19–6.22) and Schumann (Chapter 8, Ex. 8.19). In Chapter 9, sec. 9.3.5, and in connection with Ex. 9.35, I situate the "Ghost" trio passage within a broader conceptual framework that opens up the possibility of alternative analytical interpretations (see also Chapter 9, note 93).

given that the harmonization of the original theme consisted of tonic and dominant exclusively. So we are primed, perhaps, to understand the subdominant in measures 64–66 as a pre-dominant cadential harmony, even though its function more properly emerges as postcadential. Second, an additional detail further problematizes the idea of a genuine plagal cadence here. As early as measure 58, the highest part (in the piano) initiates a written-out trill that ends up tracing an ascending chromatic line from $\hat{5}$ up to $\hat{1}$ at measure 67.[278] As a result, the final plagal progression contains the leading tone, an essentially "dominant" element of the denied PAC.

---

278. This line contains the melodic components of a standard Quiescenza, $\hat{1}-\flat\hat{7}-\hat{6}-\natural\hat{7}-\hat{1}$ (see note 276) but presents them in an order that is fully ascending ($\hat{5}-\flat\hat{6}-\natural\hat{6}-\flat\hat{7}-\natural\hat{7}-\hat{1}$) and thus more goal directed than the Quiescenza, which is more curvilinear in contour.

# 4

# Cadential Deviations

CADENTIAL FUNCTION ENGAGES TWO general conditions: first, specific harmonic progressions and melodic patterns generate expectations for a cadential arrival; second, the actual occurrence of that proposed arrival achieves the goal of genuine formal closure. Both conditions are often present, thus allowing us to recognize a PAC, IAC, or HC. Regularly, however, expectations for a cadential arrival may be aroused but fail to be realized. Classical composers employ a variety of devices to deny the attainment of a promised cadence. These *cadential deviations*, as I call them, were inherited from compositional practice in the earlier baroque and galant styles, as discussed in later chapters of this study, and some techniques even extend back to Renaissance practice, as first described by Zarlino.[1]

In connection with an authentic cadence, I recognize three basic types of deviation: the *deceptive cadence*, the *evaded cadence*, and the *abandoned cadence*. As for the half cadence, I speak of a *dominant arrival* as the principal deviation type (of which a number of subtypes can be identified).[2] Although distinguishing theoretically among the various deviation types is generally straightforward, applying them

---

1. "To make intermediate divisions in the harmony and text, when the words have not reached a final conclusion of their thought, we may write those cadences which terminate on the third, fifth, sixth, or similar consonances. Such ending does not result in a perfect cadence; rather this is now called 'evading the cadence' (*fuggir la cadenza*)"; Gioseffo Zarlino, *The Art of Counterpoint: Part Three of Le Istitutioni Harmoniche, 1558*, 151. Almost all theories of form and harmony recognize the idea of cadential deviation. It would require a study of its own to sort through the wide variety of concepts and terminology introduced by theorists to account for this phenomenon. Among recent contributions, the writings of Schmalfeldt are especially to be singled out, since they are rooted in the same basic conceptions of cadence developed in the present study; see "Cadential Processes," and "Coming to Terms." Other recent contributions of note include: Danuta Mirka, "Absent Cadences"; Mirka, "Punctuation and Sense"; Neuwirth, "*Fuggir la Cadenza*"; and Carl Schachter, "*Che Inganno! The Analysis of Deceptive Cadences*." Studies of cadential deviation in other tonal styles are cited in the relevant chapters of Part II.

2. In Chapter 9, sec. 9.7.1, I raise the possibility of recognizing a *deceptive half cadence*. I have not yet encountered such a situation in the classical style.

analytically can at times be difficult. As well, many situations present uncertainties about whether a genuine cadence has been realized or whether a deviation has occurred instead. The final section of this chapter considers a range of cadential ambiguities involving deviations that may arise in the classical repertory.

It is important to emphasize that, whereas any cadential deviation represents a departure from the norms of cadential closure, the idea of deviation itself is not meant in any negative sense. On the contrary, cadential deviations have positive roles to play, and it hardly needs saying that many cases of cadential deviation are of special aesthetic interest and beauty. Classical composers clearly relish the idea of proposing, but then withholding, the attainment of closure, only then to eventually realize the cadence, thus satisfying the powerfully aroused expectations for harmonic, melodic, and formal completion. As Agawu notes, "The phenomenon of closure is as dependent on specific closes that occur in the piece as it is on closes that do not occur. The effect of a promised cadence is in some ways comparable to that of an actual cadence."[3]

To be sure, modern *disability theory* encourages music theorists to be sensitive to their use of technical vocabulary. Thus the word "deviation," along with a host of related expressions in the general category of the non-normative, may well irritate some readers.[4] Yet it is not clear how the kind of theory and analysis practiced in this study—and in many similar ones—can dispense with terms used both to establish theoretical norms and to identify departures from such norms. Even if the binary "normative/non-normative" inherently evokes a "positive/negative" correlation, the pejorative associations with terms such as "deviation" and the like can perhaps be overcome in the course of detailing technical aspects of harmonic and formal syntax in an emotionally neutral and nonjudgmental manner. The irony, of course, is that in the hands of accomplished composers, the expression and manipulation of the non-normative is most often of aesthetic value, whereas the dogged pursuit of standardized procedures can easily lead to boredom and dissatisfaction.

The idea of cadential deviation typically raises the issue of *surprise*, since we normally would assume that the failure to realize a highly expected musical event—the moment of cadential arrival—might readily elicit that emotional response. Among the various modes of surprise discussed by David Huron, his notion of "schematic surprise" seems especially apt in relation to cadential deviations. Such a surprise occurs when "the music is constructed so that it violates some existing schema that listeners have brought to the listening experience."[5] Since the previous chapter has shown that a cadence can be regarded as a strongly established schema, any cadential deviation would be a likely source for schematic surprise. Indeed, Huron cites the deceptive cadence as the "quintessential example of a schematic violation" (271) in Western art music. I have no doubt that some listeners experience a surprise when first encountering deceptive cadences in tonal compositions. I imagine, though, that a growing familiarity with the technique quickly leads to a lessening of that reaction. And given the pervasive use of deceptive cadences in the music of Wagner, to take an extreme case, those rare moments where the composer actually realizes a genuine PAC might instead elicit a pronounced surprise in many listeners.

Surprise may be a byproduct (albeit a minimal one) of cadential deviations, but most occur not because the composer wishes to confound the listener, but rather for other compositional goals associated with the specific formal context in which such deviations occur. As we will see, they normally arise in situations where a *loosening* of the phrase structure is intended and where the *deferral* of cadential closure is especially desired.[6] An implicit knowledge of formal context, in fact, plays a large role in whether or not a given deviation is perceived as surprising. For example, the appearance of a deceptive or evaded cadence in the course of a subordinate theme should rarely arouse astonishment, since such deviations are part and parcel of this unit's typical goal of loosening the form by postponing cadential closure as long as possible. In contrast, the use of a deceptive cadence in measure four of an opening main theme could be truly surprising, because in this formal context, the deviation seldom occurs.[7] In short, deviations may now and then elicit a sense of surprise, but most often they do not.[8]

## 4.1. Deceptive Cadence

Theorists regularly speak of a *deceptive cadence* when the final root-position tonic of the authentic cadential progression, stage 4, is replaced by some other harmony.[9] I term the resulting succession of harmonies a *deceptive cadential progression* (DCP). Most often, the *replacement harmony* is a root-position submediant (VI) built over ⑥ (see Ex. 4.1a; the other DCPs in this example will be discussed shortly).[10]

---

3. Agawu, "Concepts of Closure," 7.

4. The foremost proponent of disability theory, Joseph N. Straus, discusses at length how dependent music theory has been on concepts that evoke some sense of disability; his critique of the *Formenlehre* tradition in this regard is carefully argued in "Normalizing the Abnormal: Disability in Music and Music Theory."

5. David Brian Huron, *Sweet Anticipation: Music and the Psychology of Expectation*, 269.

6. Speaking of looser organization, I should note that cadential deviations often work in conjunction with various types of cadential *expansions*, the principal topic of the following chapter. As a result, many of the examples in the present chapter feature expanded cadential progressions (ECPs), and many in the next chapter engage cadential deviations.

7. See ahead sec. 4.1.2.4, in connection with Ex. 4.20 and 4.21.

8. John Y. Lawrence proposes some other ways of framing some of the issues just raised by considering the sense of *prediction* that a listener brings to various aspects of formal closure ("Toward a Predictive Theory of Theme Types," 11–12).

9. The theoretical literature on deceptive cadences is extensive in textbooks on harmony and form; most treatments, however, are cursory, largely confining their observations to the harmonic component of the device. For an excellent introduction to the history of the concept, see Neuwirth, "*Fuggir la Cadenza*."

10. All of the progressions in Ex. 4.1 begin with stage 2, built over ④; of course, any DCP may employ various other harmonic options, including those of stage 1.

EXAMPLE 4.1. Deceptive cadential progressions.

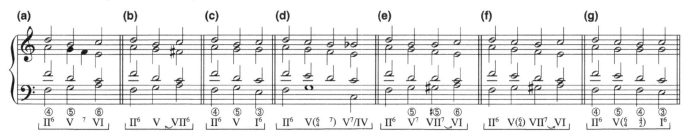

EXAMPLE 4.2. Mozart, Piano Sonata in C Minor, K. 457, i, mm. 44–59 (*ACF* 12.5).

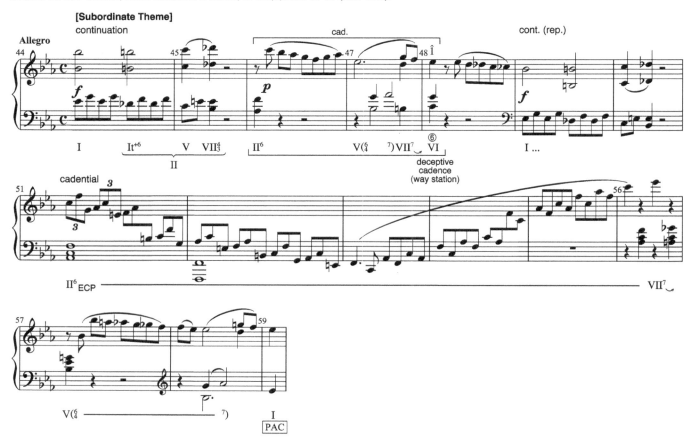

Every deceptive cadence requires a DCP. Additionally, this deviation type must end melodically on $\hat{1}$ (or less often, $\hat{3}$) in order to provide a degree of melodic completion in the absence of harmonic closure. Two other factors are also essential for producing this deviation type, namely, our perception that the musical event associated with the replacement harmony (1) *groups backward* with the prevailing cadential function and (2) marks its *final* event. In other words, a deceptive cadence engages not only harmonic and melodic processes, but grouping ones as well. Thus identifying a replacement harmony following a cadential dominant is a necessary condition, but not a sufficient one, for recognizing a deceptive cadence. If we perceive that the tonic replacement only *groups forward* with the subsequent formal unit, then we might identify another type of deviation—an evaded cadence—or even possibly an HC, in which case the dominant would function as the *ultimate* harmony of the cadential progression. There remains to note one further grouping possibility—the replacement harmony may not only group backward with the prevailing cadential progression, but also may simultaneously group forward to mark the start of a new formal group. In this case, we would speak of an *elided* deceptive cadence.

The technique of deceptive cadence is well illustrated in Example 4.2. In the context of a subordinate theme, a continuation phrase beginning at measure 44 promises to close with a PAC at measure 48. Though the melody ends as expected on $\hat{1}$, a final root-position tonic is replaced by the submediant (VI), thus yielding a DCP. As well, the event on the downbeat of measure 48 clearly groups backward as the final event of the cadential idea. Since the formal context is appropriate for cadential closure, we can speak of a genuine

EXAMPLE 4.3. Mozart, Violin Sonata in B-flat, K. 454, i, mm. 149–53 (*ACF* 15.2a).

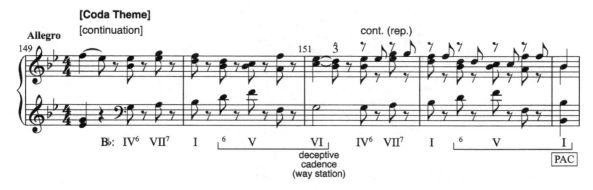

EXAMPLE 4.4. Haydn, String Quartet in C Minor, Op. 17, no. 4, i, mm. 39–41.

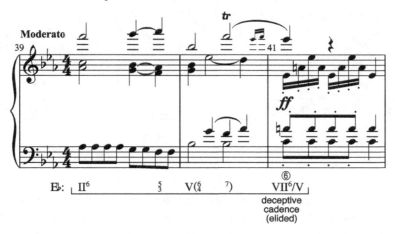

deceptive cadence arising at this moment.[11] Following the deviation, the continuation phrase begins to repeat, but the cadential *idea* is replaced by a large cadential *phrase* supported by an ECP, which eventually realizes a PAC at measure 59.

### 4.1.1. Morphology

The morphology of the deceptive cadence derives largely from that of the authentic cadence (either PAC or IAC). As just discussed, the deviation is supported harmonically by a DCP, which is identical to an authentic cadential progression (ACP) save for stage 4, whose harmony must *replace* a final root-position tonic triad. Most often the replacement harmony is VI, though now and then we find the less stable VII⁶/V also set over ⑥ (Ex. 4.1b). We sometimes encounter a deceptive cadence whose final tonic appears in first inversion (Ex. 4.1c). Rarely, the stage-4 tonic may remain in root position but fails as a cadential tonic by including a minor seventh, thus functioning as a secondary dominant seventh of IV (Ex. 4.1d).

Though the harmony of a deceptive cadence must be altered from that of an ACP, its melodic content usually brings the same patterns presented in the previous chapter for authentic cadences.

A deceptive cadence replacing an implied PAC ends on $\hat{1}$, whereas a deceptive cadence replacing an IAC ends on $\hat{3}$.[12] Since the essential difference between authentic and deceptive cadences resides in the harmonic content of stage 4, the remaining discussion can focus on details of harmony, especially in connection with the bass line.[13]

The bass of a complete DCP generally takes one of two forms: (1) the voice continues its stepwise ascent, thus ③–④–⑤–⑥; or (2) the line returns back to its start, ③–④–⑤–③. In both cases, a passing tone may be inserted between the pitches of stages 3 and 4: thus ⑤–♯⑤–⑥ (see Ex. 4.1e and f) or ⑤–④–③ (Ex. 4.1g). In the first bass pattern (③–④–⑤–⑥), the final harmony is almost always the submediant triad (VI), a tonic substitute that functions well as a replacement for stage 4 (see Ex. 4.3, m. 151): not only does VI contain two of the three pitches of tonic harmony, but it also can support the melodic goal of $\hat{1}$ or $\hat{3}$. Another effective harmony built on ⑥ is VII⁶/V (see Ex. 4.4); an even more dissonant

---

11. The label "way station" for this deceptive cadence relates to its function of cadential deferral, one that is akin to the way-station IAC discussed in the previous chapter (see sec. 3.2.2.2).

12. If a deceptive cadence concludes on I⁶, it is possible for the melody to close on $\hat{5}$, usually as a result of an upward leap from $\hat{7}$ or $\hat{2}$. This situation is rare in classical instrumental music, but occurs now and then in the vocal literature; see the discussion by Schmalfeldt of passages from Mozart's *Die Zauberflöte*, Act 1, nos. 1, 3, and 4 ("Cadential Processes," 25–30).

13. For additional discussion of the melodic component of a deceptive cadence when followed directly by a PAC, see Chapter 3, sec. 3.1.2.4, "Deceptive-Authentic Combinations," and Ex. 3.63 and 3.64. In the present chapter, see ahead sec. 4.1.2.5.

EXAMPLE 4.5. Haydn, Piano Sonata in C, H. 48, i, mm. 128–29.

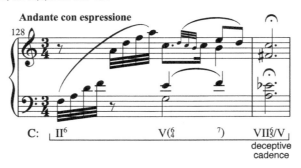

EXAMPLE 4.6. Haydn, String Quartet in B-flat, Op. 50, no. 1, i, mm. 7–12 (ACF 5.35).

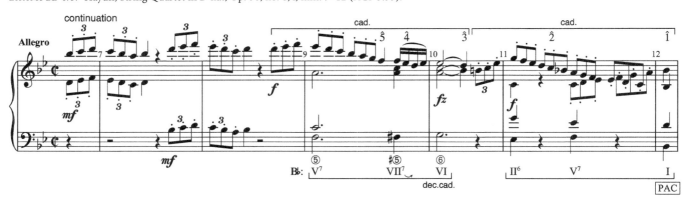

variant uses the fully diminished VII$^6_5$/V (Ex. 4.5).[14] Seeing as these diminished harmonies are considerably less stable than the consonant VI, the harmonic closure effected by these deceptive cadences is especially weak.[15]

If the passing tone ♯⑤ connects the primary bass pitches of stages 3 and 4, then it normally supports a secondary dominant of the submediant (V$^6_5$/VI or VII$^7$/VI). The passing harmony may follow the cadential dominant proper (Ex. 4.1e and Ex. 4.6, m. 9), or may occur directly after the six-four embellishment of the dominant, thus substituting for the dominant proper (Ex. 4.1f, and, in Chapter 3, Ex. 3.63, m. 4).

In some cases, the metrical context may suggest that the chromatic harmony functions as an appoggiatura within stage 4 (Ex. 4.7, m. 16, and in Chapter 2, Ex. 2.19, m. 10). In minor-mode contexts, the flat-submediant (♭VI) normally marks the goal of the DCP (Ex. 4.8, m. 45). In such cases, the passing tone ♯⑤ is obviously not available, since this pitch is enharmonically equivalent to ♭⑥, which supports the final harmony of the progression.[16]

It is interesting to observe that when these passing harmonies are used in stage 3, we already have the impression that a potential deceptive cadence may arise. In other words, our experiential sense of "surprise" occurs earlier then in a regular deceptive cadence, where the harmonic deviation only involves stage 4.

The second bass pattern ③–④–⑤–③ (Ex. 4.1c) occurs less often than the first. In this case a tonic in first inversion (I⁶) replaces the expected root-position harmony (Ex. 4.9, m. 8). When the bass brings a passing tone between ⑤ and ③, ④ supports V$^4_2$, which demands resolution to I⁶ (Ex. 4.1g and Ex. 4.10a, m. 82).[17] We encounter here an exception to the rule that a cadential dominant must never be inverted. Inasmuch as ④ functions as a passing tone, it continues to *represent* the root of the harmony (⑤), and thus does not generate a genuine harmonic inversion.[18]

Now and then an unusual harmony appears in stage 4 of the DCP. In Example 4.11, the downbeat of measure 20 brings a deceptive cadence whose final harmony is built over ♭⑦, a pitch

---

14. VII⁶/V does not include ♭$\hat{3}$, so it cannot be used for a deceptive cadence that replaces an IAC. VII$^6_5$/V contains ♭$\hat{3}$, but I am unaware of any case that employs this harmony to create a deceptive cadence.

15. See also Haydn, Piano Sonata in C, H. 21, ii, m. 20, discussed by Neuwirth, "*Fuggir la Cadenza*," 138.

16. In principle, stage 3 could repeat ⑤ as a support for a V$^6_5$/♭VI, but I have not encountered such a case in the classical repertory. A variant on this idea arises in Haydn's String Quartet in E-flat, Op. 50, no. 3, i, m. 81, where immediately following the dominant proper, V⁷/♭VI appears

as the final harmony of the cadential progression, a most unusual "tonic replacement" but one supported by ③, a conventional final bass note (as will be discussed momentarily). Rosen refers to this cadence as "abortive" (*Sonata Forms*, 158).

17. See also in Chapter 3, Ex. 3.151, m. 46.

18. See ACF, 19. The same harmonic situation can arise with an evaded cadence, as discussed earlier in Chapter 3, sec. 3.1.1.5, Ex. 3.8d, and ahead in the present chapter, sec. 4.2.1.1, Ex. 4.31, mm. 68–69; see also ACF, 373. I discuss a variant of this pattern in connection with the abandoned cadence (sec. 4.3.2.1).

EXAMPLE 4.7. Mozart, Rondo in A Minor, K. 511, mm. 9–21.

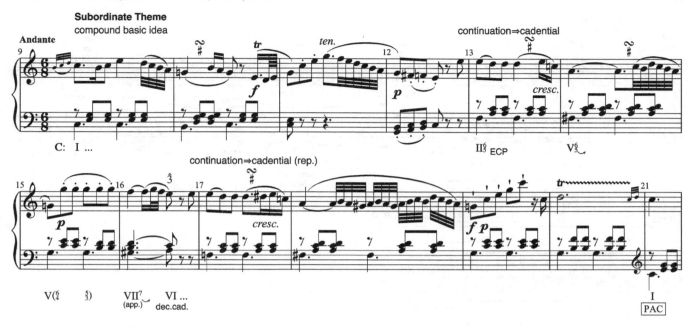

EXAMPLE 4.8. Beethoven, Piano Sonata in F, Op. 10, no. 2, i, mm. 38–55 (*ACF* 12.22).

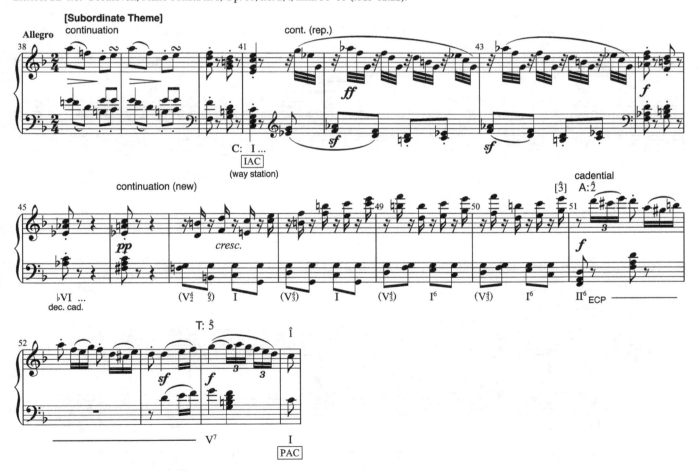

**156** Cadential Deviations

EXAMPLE 4.9. Beethoven, String Quartet in C Minor, Op. 18, no. 4, i, mm. 5–13 (*ACF* Sup. 5.12).

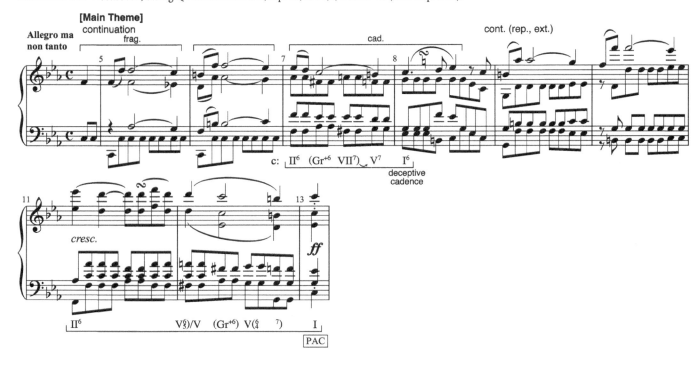

EXAMPLE 4.10. Mozart, Violin Sonata in F, K. 547, ii, (a) mm. 79–87 (*ACF* 13.20); (b) reconstruction of mm. 81–82.

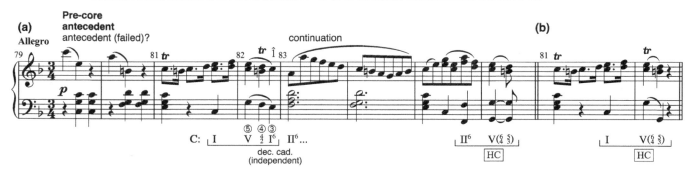

EXAMPLE 4.11. Beethoven, Piano Sonata in E-flat, Op. 7, ii, mm. 17–20 (*ACF* 7.11).

EXAMPLE 4.12. Mozart, String Quartet in D Minor, K. 421, iii, mm. 20–23.

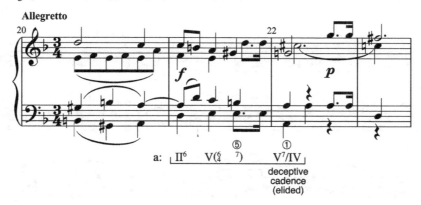

that substitutes for ⑥, as verified immediately when VII♯$^4_2$/II "reverts" to V$^7$/II, the harmony for which the initial diminished seventh is substituting.[19] This secondary dominant, of course, is a chromatic alteration of a regular VI harmony of the standard deceptive cadence. That Beethoven employs this unusual harmonic variant may be owing to its sinister quality, projected as well by the tritone leap in the melody from $\hat{5}$ to ♯$\hat{1}$. We should also note that the prior ascending sequence in measures 17–18 ends with VI, which would render redundant the use of this harmony for the following deceptive cadence.

Another nonstandard replacement harmony occurs when the bass of stage 4 moves to ①, just like a regular ACP, but a dissonant minor seventh is added to the tonic, thus converting it into a secondary dominant of IV (Ex. 4.1d and Ex. 4.12, m. 22).[20] A deceptive cadence using this rare replacement harmony has already been encountered in Chapter 3 (see again Ex. 3.174, m. 63). There, it is especially unusual that the deceptive cadence emerges as the very last cadential event in the movement, such that the deceptive cadence appears, highly in retrospect, to function as a kind of PAC.[21]

### 4.1.2. Function

In principle, a deceptive cadence can be used at any point in a piece to replace an implied authentic cadence, either perfect or imperfect. But insofar as such usage results in a cadential deferral and a concomitant phrase-structural extension, the deceptive cadence normally occurs in contexts that promote formal loosening, such as in a subordinate theme, a small-ternary recapitulation, and a coda theme. By contrast, contexts that lead conventionally to HCs, such as the end of a ternary B section, a transition, or a developmental core, rarely give rise to cadential deception. This deviation is also frequently encountered in the A' section of the minuet form (Ex. 4.13, m. 34).[22] Although main themes are relatively tight-knit in their organization, deceptive cadences nonetheless occur in those themes often enough.

In most cases, a deceptive cadence functions as a *way station* on the path toward eventual authentic cadential closure (almost always a PAC).[23] In some cases, the deviation seems as though it were to function as a way station, but that status is denied if a subsequent PAC fails to arrive or if the music leads instead to an HC. Now and then, a deceptive cadence does not behave as a way station because it occurs in a context in which PAC closure is not expected. In such cases, the deviation functions instead as an *independent* deceptive cadence, like that of an IAC or HC ending the antecedent of a period.[24]

Many contexts arise where a DCP does not produce a genuine deceptive cadence. Like a regular cadence, a deceptive one must conform to the general principles that hold for all situations of cadential closure, especially the need for the deceptive cadence actually to be *ending* a formal process (provisionally, of course). To speak of a deceptive *cadence*, as opposed to a deceptive *resolution* (of the dominant), we must be able to identify a point in time that can potentially create a genuine cadence if the requisite morphology were actually at hand. In other words, we can distinguish deceptive *content* from deceptive *function*, just like any regular cadence.

---

19. I speak of here of a diminished seventh reverting to (not "resolving to") the dominant seventh for which it substitutes, since both sonorities express the same basic harmony.

20. Neuwirth ("*Fuggir la Cadenza*," 147) points out that in the eighteenth century, Johann Georg Sulzer ("assisted by Kirnberger") speaks of this situation as a *vermiedene Kadenz* (avoided cadence); Johann Georg Sulzer, "Cadenz," 186.

21. I discuss other cases of this type in the baroque and Romantic style periods; see Chapter 6, sec. 6.1.4.1 (Ex. 6.19, m. 32; Ex. 6.20, m. 37; Ex. 6.21, m. 22; and Ex. 6.22, m. 143), and Chapter 8, sec. 8.10.1.1 (Ex. 8.19, m. 59).

22. See *CF*, 227, and *ACF*, 625.

23. The notion of a way-station cadence was introduced in the previous chapter in connection with the function of an IAC, see sec. 3.2.2.2. Neuwirth also discusses how both the IAC and the deceptive cadence function as way stations, though he does not use this specific term ("*Fuggir la Cadenza*," 129). Largely for that reason, he wants to expand the category of deceptive cadence to embrace what he calls the "deceptive imperfect authentic cadence" (which for me, would be a way-station IAC). See again my reservations with this proposal in Chapter 3, note 117.

24. On the notion of an independent IAC and HC, see Chapter 3, sec. 3.2.2.1 and 3.3.4.1.

EXAMPLE 4.13. Haydn, String Quartet in G, Op. 54, no. 1, iii, mm. 25–44 (*ACF* 5.12a and 18.1b).

### 4.1.2.1. Way-Station Deceptive Cadence, Replacing a PAC

A cadence or cadential deviation functions as a way station when expectations are aroused for the appearance of a PAC, but instead, a syntactically weaker articulation ends up occurring at the moment of expected arrival, thus deferring the PAC to some later moment in time. In the previous chapter (sec. 3.2.2.2), I discussed how the IAC can function as a way station precisely in this manner. The vast majority of deceptive cadences in the classical style also function as way stations. They can even serve to replace an IAC (when the melody closes on $\hat{3}$). As such, the technique will then lead to further thematic work that eventually effectuates full cadential closure via a PAC, though additional deferments (in the form of evaded, abandoned, or other deceptive cadences) may occur prior to the arrival of the final cadence.

Most typically, the music that follows a way-station deceptive cadence repeats the material (usually of continuation or cadential function) that initially preceded the deviation. Less often, the deceptive cadence is succeeded by new material that leads in due course to a PAC. As explained in connection with the IAC, a way-station deviation (of any type) seldom brings about a return of opening ideas of the ongoing thematic unit.[25]

**Repeated Material.** The idea of repeating material that initially led to a way-station deceptive cadence makes obvious compositional sense. For when that material sounds again, we expect more than ever the arrival of the earlier promised PAC. In other words, the procedure likens to the "one-more-time technique" introduced by Schmalfeldt; indeed, many theorists employ this expression in connection with deceptive cadences.[26]

Examples 4.2 and 4.3, discussed earlier, illustrate well a way-station deceptive cadence that is followed by a repeat of continuation material, leading eventually to a PAC. Another case of a repeated continuation phrase, this time in a main theme, is found in Example 4.9.[27] At times, a continuation⇒cadential phrase leads to the deceptive cadence, which is then repeated for the PAC (Ex. 4.14). Even less frequently, a periodic formal context may bring a consequent phrase closing with a way-station deceptive cadence (Ex. 4.15, mm. 245). Here, the repeated material only consists of the immediately preceding cadential idea, not the complete consequent phrase. Following a second deviation at measure 247, the cadential idea is even used a third time to bring the final PAC. (A closing section continues to use the same material.)

When a deceptive cadence functions as a way station, and when the material following the deviation repeats that which proceeds it, the effect can resemble an antecedent phrase (with weak cadential closure) followed by a consequent (with stronger closure).[28]

---

cadential deviation ("Cadential Processes"). Since her introduction of this highly popular locution, however, many theorists apply it in other contexts, including deceptive cadences and even IACs. Following the lead of my esteemed colleague and friend, I restrict using "one more time" to cases of evaded cadence and speak more generally of "repeated material" in connection with the deceptive cadence (as well as the way-station IAC).

27. Since "way-station" deceptive cadences are so ubiquitous, I will no longer include the label in the analytical annotations unless particularly useful for the discussion at hand.

28. Thus Aldwell, Schachter, and Cadwallader note in this connection, "the deceptive cadence provides the impetus for a varied repetition of the whole four-bar phrase in a kind of antecedent-consequent grouping" (*Harmony & Voice Leading*, 200). In a similar vein, Neuwirth discusses how such a situation is "analogous to the type of Schenkerian interruption structure found in a parallel period, in which the V chord ending the first phrase is disconnected from what immediately ensues in the second phrase and resolves only when the final tonic enters" ("*Fuggir la Cadenza*," 131).

---

25. See Chapter 3, sec. 3.2.2.2.

26. Schmalfeldt defines the one-more-time technique exclusively for evaded cadences and is adamant that the term only be used with that

EXAMPLE 4.14. Mozart, Clarinet Trio in E-flat, K. 498, i, mm. 7–16 (*ACF* 6.10).

EXAMPLE 4.15. Haydn, Piano Trio in C, H. 27, iii, mm. 242–50 (*ACF* 15.7a).

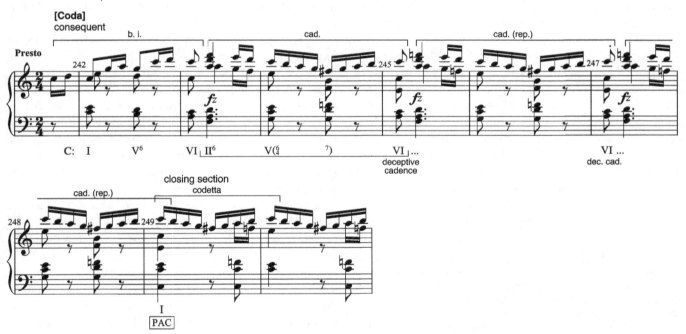

To speak of the repeated material of a way-station deceptive cadence as producing a periodic design, however, is problematic in a number of ways.[29] First, the internal organization of the paired phrases does not normally contain a recognizable basic idea followed by a contrasting idea; rather, each phrase usually has marked qualities of continuation or cadential function.

Thus in Example 4.9, it would be unconvincing to extract this passage from its formal context and expect that listeners would hear this music as a periodic main theme. The same could be said for measures 9–16 of Example 4.14. Indeed, neither of the opening phrases in these two examples sounds like an antecedent. Second, the deceptive cadence is understood to represent a replacement of an implied PAC; as such, the listener is not expecting that the cadence ending the first phrase will be "independent" in the manner in which an HC (or even an IAC) may function midway through a standard periodic theme. Finally,

---

29. For the analogous situation with respect to a way-station IAC, see Chapter 3, sec. 3.2.2.2.

when the deceptive cadence replaces a PAC, the melodic dimension does not normally resemble that of a period. Seeing as the upper voice in the first of the paired phrases descends fully to $\hat{1}$, thus projecting strong melodic closure, the phrase hardly sounds like an antecedent. In short, it is not productive, and possibly quite misleading for the formal interpretation, to consider a way-station deceptive cadence as a kind of independent cadence within a periodic design.[30]

**New Material**. In some cases, a way-station deceptive cadence is followed by *new* material.[31] In Example 4.13 the A′ section of this minuet form brings back the identical period from the A section, except that the implied PAC of the consequent is replaced by the deceptive cadence at measure 34. The material that follows is not a repeat of the consequent, but rather a new continuation, one, to be sure, that obviously references motivic ideas from prior phrases as well as projecting a rhyming effect in its final two bars (cf. mm. 33–34 and 43–44).[32]

New material also follows the deceptive cadence in Example 4.8, measure 45. Here, a continuation phrase first closes with a way-station IAC at measure 41, after which an elaborated repeat of the continuation, with modal shift, leads to the deceptive cadence at measure 45. Having once repeated the continuation, Beethoven would likely not want to sound the same phrase again. So he writes a new "oomp-chink" figure in the context of a different continuation and then lets an ECP finally effect PAC closure for this subordinate theme.

At times, a deceptive cadence may elide with the start of a new passage that temporarily deflects the trajectory of thematic closure into more distant harmonic realms. Schachter highlights one such case, shown in Example 4.16a, in which the music following the deceptive cadence functions as an interpolated episode.[33] In the course of a subordinate theme (within the concerto's opening ritornello), a deceptive cadence at measure 49 suddenly shifts the music to the ♭VI region (E-flat), supporting a new presentation phrase in that key. The following continuation⇒cadential phrase then brings the music back on track for the promised PAC closure in the home key. Although I see the ♭VI harmony of measure 53 as initiating the ECP, it would not be unreasonable to regard the progression as beginning back at measure 49. But given the sudden change to the flat-side tonal region and a completely new melodic gesture (the rising arpeggios and sudden downward leap into a trill), I believe that measure 49 projects an interpolated "new beginning" (a presentation phrase) and not the sense of impending cadential closure.

### 4.1.2.2. Way-Station Deceptive Cadence, Replacing an IAC

The way-station deceptive cadences we have examined so far bring melodic resolution to $\hat{1}$ and thus replace an anticipated PAC. Sometimes, however, the deceptive cadence concludes on $\hat{3}$, thereby substituting for an IAC. In such situations, the implied cadence, if it had actually been realized, would be considered a way station on the path toward a PAC. Like the previous cases, the material following the deceptive cadence may be a repetition or may be new. In the earlier discussed Example 4.3, the continuation phrase of a coda theme leads to a deceptive cadence with $\hat{3}$ at measure 151.[34] The final segment of the continuation is repeated, but this time it brings a PAC to close the theme. A similar situation arises in Example 4.7, except that now the repeated material (mm. 13–16 and 17–21) constitutes a continuation⇒cadential phrase supported by an ECP.

With Example 4.6, the idea of the deceptive cadence ($\hat{3}$) at measure 10 as motivating a repetition of prior material is less certain: to be sure, the descending triplets of measure 11 refer to the ideas leading up to the deceptive cadence; however, they bring completely different scale degrees, ones that, when reduced to their basic melodic motion, complete a descending melodic line, from $\hat{5}$ (m. 9) to $\hat{1}$ (m. 12), which embraces both the DCP and APC. As a result, the two segments, measures 9–10 and 11–12, present a more integrated whole than a more normal repetition would project.

A clear-cut case of new material arising after a deceptive cadence ($\hat{3}$) is seen earlier in Chapter 3, Ex. 3.63. Following the deceptive cadence (m. 4), the ACP (mm. 5–6), and the material content that it supports, is entirely different from the ideas preceding the deceptive cadence. Note that the DCP in measure 4 is very incomplete, consisting exclusively of stages 3 and 4; the ACP (mm. 5–6) is rendered more complete by including the pre-dominant harmony of stage 2, which thus necessitates the appearance of different material.

The situation of a way-station deceptive cadence replacing an implied IAC raises again the issue of whether or not to consider the relationship of the paired phrases as one of antecedent to consequent. After all, the first phrase not only leaves the harmonic

---

30. Indeed, Schachter later changes his position on the formal implications of the deceptive cadence: "The restlessness built into submediant harmony directs the VI chord toward some kind of short-range goal at or near the beginning of the music that follows. This differentiates a passage like the one in [Ex. 4.14] from the typical parallel period, where the two segments are more sharply articulated, where the closing dominant of the first one is resolved only by the closing tonic of the second, and where there is no deep connection from the end of one segment to the beginning of the next" ("*Che Inganno!*" 284).

31. When I speak of new material, I more precisely mean music that does not restate the immediately prior melodic-harmonic content. Most often this material is truly new, in that we have not yet heard it at any earlier moment in the movement; however, it is also possible that this material references previously sounding ideas, just not those that precede the deceptive cadence.

32. I also discuss this passage in *ACF*, 610.

33. Schachter, "*Che Inganno!*" 289. Ex. 4.16b is discussed later in sec. 4.1.2.3.

34. From now on in the text, I indicate a deceptive cadence that replaces an implied IAC as a *deceptive cadence* ($\hat{3}$) in order to distinguish it from those that imply PAC closure. In the musical examples, $\hat{3}$ is indicated above the final soprano pitch, but (to avoid redundancy) not in the deviation label that appears below the replacement harmony.

EXAMPLE 4.16. Mozart, Piano Concerto in G, K. 453, i, (a) mm. 47–57; (b) mm. 317–28.

processes open-ended (e.g., VI instead of I) but denies closure for the melody as well (3̂ instead of 1̂). Nonetheless, a periodic interpretation still seems unsatisfying in most cases, for the material content of the first phrase strongly projects either continuation or cadential function, nothing that sounds convincingly initiatory. Moreover, the broader formal context also plays a role: in Example 4.7, for instance, interpreting measures 13–16 as an "antecedent" begs the question of why this phrase is positioned immediately after another initiating unit (the compound basic idea in mm. 9–12).[35] As a general rule, then, it is best to see a way-station cadence as a functional substitute for a goal, not as a potentially independent cadence ending a genuine antecedent, one matched with a following consequent, as closed by a PAC.[36] To

---

[35]. For similar cases, see also Ex. 4.3, 4.6, and, in the prior chapter, Ex. 3.63.

[36]. In the later sec. 4.1.2.4, I discuss cases where a deceptive cadence followed by a PAC more plausibly engenders an antecedent–consequent relationship.

EXAMPLE 4.17. Haydn, Symphony No. 89 in F, ii, mm. 44–47 (*ACF* 17.2).

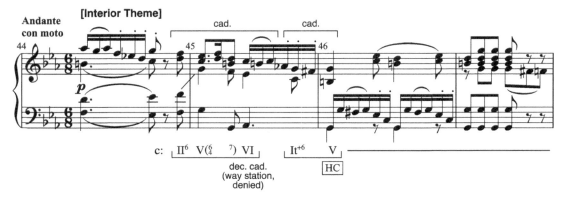

EXAMPLE 4.18. Haydn, Symphony No. 8 in G ("Le soir"), i, mm. 141–52.

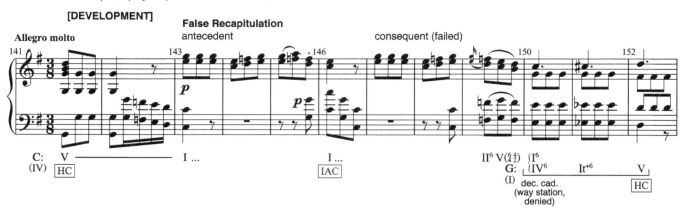

be sure, a highly generalized expression of periodic organization is undoubtedly associated with the two phrases in question, but their actual formal function should be determined primarily on the basis of their material content and phrase-structural context.

### 4.1.2.3. Way-Station Deceptive Cadence, Denied

Any deceptive cadence appearing at a point in time where we rightly expect a PAC to occur would seem to express a way-station function. That function is denied, however, when a matching PAC either fails to materialize or else arrives considerably later than expected, usually after a deflection of the thematic process owing to a substantial excursion that introduces new material. In retrospect, we can often understand why a way-station function is denied because of the broader formal context in which the cadential deception occurs. In Example 4.17, a cadential idea promises to close the interior theme of a large ternary form with a PAC in the middle of measure 45. When the final tonic is replaced by the submediant, a way-station deceptive cadence is proposed but is then quickly denied when VI is transformed into a predominant augmented sixth, whose resolution to V brings about an HC. The interior theme thus remains only partially closed, rather than ending fully with a PAC. This compositional situation, however, should not be considered a weakness, since in the context of a large ternary, an interior theme typically concludes with dominant harmony in order to prepare for the return of the main theme on the tonic.[37]

When a putative way-station deceptive cadence fails to acquire its matching PAC, the former may provide the opportunity of modulating to a different key. Neuwirth discusses several cases of this phenomenon, including the passage shown in Example 4.18.[38] Late in the course of the development section, an HC in C major at measure 141 sets up a false recapitulation at measure 143 when main theme material returns in the subdominant region of the home key (G major). A four-measure antecedent closing with an IAC at measure 146 is followed by a consequent, whose anticipated PAC is denied by the deceptive cadence on I⁶ at measure 150. Ordinarily, we would assume this to be a way-station deviation that would pair with a subsequent PAC in the same key. Instead of allowing that cadence to occur, however, Haydn immediately uses the I⁶ as a pivot chord IV⁶ to effect a modulation back to the home key of G, as signaled by the HC at measure 152, which represents the structural end of the development. Like the previous example, the local formal context proposes a way-station function for the deceptive cadence of measure 150, but

---

37. See also *ACF*, Ex. 17.4, for another Haydn large ternary, whose interior theme closes in a similar manner.

38. Neuwirth, "*Fuggir la Cadenza*," 145–47. Ex. 4.18 reproduces his Ex. 20 (with my analytical annotations).

EXAMPLE 4.19. Haydn, Piano Trio in E, H. 28, i, mm. 21–32 (R = ½N).

this function is superseded by the broader formal goal that the return of main theme material serves, namely to express a false recapitulation. Indeed, the true recapitulation (not shown) brings the identical passage back into the home key, this time closing with a PAC, as expected.

In the prior two examples, the deceptive cadences lead to an HC instead of the implied PAC, each for its own appropriate compositional rationale. In Example 4.19, we encounter a way-station denial within a subordinate theme that eventually produces a PAC, but only after a relatively long digression, such that this authentic cadence seems no longer to match the earlier deception. To begin the theme,

Haydn employs his famous *monothematic* technique by bringing back main-theme material in the subordinate key. In fact, the entire periodic structure of the main theme (shown in Chapter 3, Ex. 3.29) returns in B major (HK: V), save for a final deceptive cadence at measure 24 in lieu of the expected PAC.[39] Ordinarily, this deceptive cadence would be a regular way station, but that function is denied

---

39. Actually, given the context of a subordinate theme, we would not be expecting the entire main theme to return. Here is a good case where the listener might be truly surprised if a PAC had emerged instead of the deceptive cadence (or some other deviation).

when the music is deflected by a new continuation in the relatively remote region of G major (♭VI). Indeed, we witness here an exemplary case of a subordinate theme heading off "somewhere else," as Erwin Ratz so aptly puts it.[40] Eventually the music attains an IAC at measure 29, which gives rise to a completely different continuation. An ECP begins with pre-dominant harmony toward the end of measure 30 and finally leads to full closure of the subordinate theme in the middle of measure 32. By the time we hear this PAC, we are unlikely to forge a strong connection between it and the earlier deceptive cadence at measure 24, especially considering the intervening IAC at measure 29. As such, the interpretation of a "way station denied" seems sustained, despite the eventual appearance of the closing PAC.

An even more complex set of implications arises in Example 4.16b. As discussed by Schachter, the final subordinate theme in the solo recapitulation promises to close with a PAC at measure 319.[41] A completely unexpected deceptive cadence appears instead, one that brings back material from the interpolated episode of the opening ritornello, which we examined earlier in Example 4.16a, measure 49ff. The deceptive cadence at measure 319 (Ex. 4.16b) is especially unexpected, because a marked cadential trill in the solo part almost always results in PAC completion. Seeing as the solo piano drops out following the deceptive cadence, we can well imagine that the music has moved from the solo recapitulation into the closing orchestral ritornello. And this interpretation is further sustained when the music arrives at the cadential six-four (m. 327) that announces the pianist's cadenza, which in Mozart's concerto practice almost always occurs *within* the closing ritornello. (Other composers of the period, including Haydn, tend to place the cadenza at the very end of the recapitulation, just prior to the closing ritornello.)

As is normally the case, the cadential six-four links up, as noted, with the penultimate dominant of the PAC closing the cadenza. According to Schachter, the deceptive cadence back at measure 319 "prevents any feeling of completeness at this critical point [in the form].... Only after the cadenza does the resolution of dominant to tonic redeem the broken promise at the end of the solo recapitulation" (291). By speaking of a "broken promise," Schachter tacitly acknowledges the deceptive cadence's potential to function as a way station, which is effectively denied when no further PAC brings a sense of "completeness" to the recapitulation proper. But when he also explains that the promise is in fact "redeemed," he seems to be saying, using my language, that the initially denied way station recovers that function after all, namely, by means of the PAC ending the cadenza. Indeed, Mozart actually makes it relatively easy to connect the cadenza's PAC with the supposedly denied way station of measure 319. For if we compare Example 4.16b to Example 4.16a, we see that the music following both deceptive cadences is largely the same. In other words, the manner in which the earlier way-station deceptive cadence of measure 49 links up with the PAC of measure 57 is almost identical to the way in which the cadential deception at measure 319 is fulfilled by the PAC of measure 328, the only significant difference being the insertion of the cadenza in the latter case. Though Schachter maintains that the solo recapitulation remains incomplete, it seems to me that by using virtually the same music here as with the deceptive cadence of the opening ritornello, Mozart in effect *fuses* the end of the solo recapitulation and the opening section of the closing ritornello into a single formal unit, one that finds its proper PAC closure at measure 328.[42]

What makes Example 4.16b so fascinating is the way in which we can recognize three levels of formal implication: first, the deceptive cadence of the recapitulation (m. 319) promises to be a way station; second, the sudden silencing of the solo piano as the music moves into a new formal region, the closing ritornello, suggests a denial of way-station function; and third, the recovery of that function by means of the PAC closing the cadenza (m. 328), which both effects a form-functional fusion and restores a semblance formal completeness to the recapitulation.[43]

### 4.1.2.4. Independent Deceptive Cadence

Now and then, a deceptive cadence arises in formal contexts that do not generate expectations for PAC closure. Such cases usually involve a deceptive cadence occurring at the end of an opening phrase, since such a phrase would not ordinarily conclude with a PAC. After all, few themes in the classical style consist of only a single phrase. If the phrase following the deceptive cadence repeats the material of that prior phrase and then ends with a PAC, a periodic formation emerges, as seen in Example 4.20. At the start of a subordinate theme (m. 57), a two-measure basic idea is followed by a contrasting idea, which leads at measure 60 to a deceptive cadence ($\hat{3}$) (i.e., one that replaces an implied IAC). In all respects other than its closing with a deviation, the phrase functions as an antecedent, with the following phrase providing a matching consequent.[44] Here, the deceptive cadence does not function as a way station, because we would not be expecting a PAC after only four bars of a new theme; moreover, if Haydn had actually written

---

40. Ratz, *Die musikalische Formenlehre*, 31.

41. Schachter, "*Che Inganno!*" 291.

42. Though not invoking my own technical sense of form-functional fusion, Schachter nonetheless speaks of an "extraordinary fusion through harmony of solo recapitulation, cadenza, and closing ritornello" when pointing to Beethoven's similar procedure in his Violin Concerto (mm. 473–97) ("*Che Inganno!*" 291).

43. In connection with the same Mozart concerto, Schachter discusses a third deceptive cadence to the ♭VI region using the same material as Ex. 4.16a and b. Indeed, he regards all three ♭VI deceptive cadences as "a recurrent feature in the design [of this movement]—almost a kind of motive" ("*Che Inganno!*" 289). This third case, however, does not involve a genuine deceptive cadence, but rather a deceptive *codetta* (at m. 184), which follows upon a clear PAC (m. 178) ending the subordinate-key ritornello. I discuss the use of such deceptive codettas shortly in sec. 4.1.2.5.

44. Though I analyze this second phrase as ending with a PAC (mm. 63–64), we should note that the harmonic implications of the bass line, played by the second violins, as in the first phrase, conflicts with that of the melody: the bass of m. 63 suggests two cadential harmonies, a pre-dominant over ④ followed by a dominant over ⑤. The melody beginning on B♭, however, expresses dominant harmony for the entire bar.

EXAMPLE 4.20. Haydn, Symphony No. 67 in F, i, mm. 55–64.

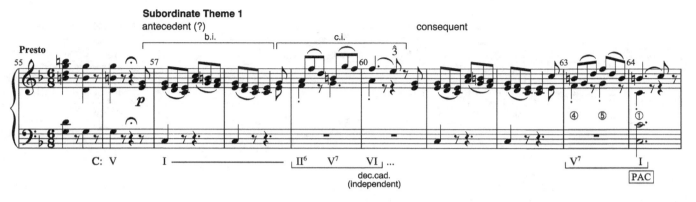

EXAMPLE 4.21. Haydn, Piano Sonata in C, H. 21, ii, mm. 1–6.

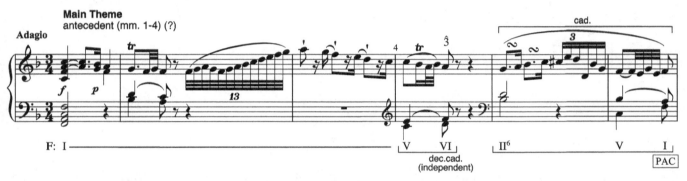

an IAC, that cadence would have been heard as *independent* (as explained in Chapter 3, sec. 3.2.2.1). Consequently, the deceptive cadence replacing the IAC also acquires an *independent* status. We thus recognize here a most unusual periodic formation.[45]

Example 4.21, measure 4, shows another case of an independent deceptive cadence (3̂) replacing an IAC at the end of what seems like an antecedent phrase. But rather than being followed by previous material, the deceptive cadence leads immediately to a cadential idea, thus producing a compressed hybrid theme.[46]

One final case of an opening phrase that ends with a deceptive cadence (3̂) is especially interesting; see Example 4.22. This theme stands as the *third* main theme of an overall rondo form.[47] The first phrase ends with a deceptive cadence (3̂) in measure 26. Though the phrase is contextually initiatory, its intrinsic content is manifestly continuational. So if the phrase had ended with an IAC, we might have wanted to consider that cadence to be a way station, and thus to accord the same function to the deceptive cadence that replaces this IAC. In its actual formal context as a period-like main theme, the deceptive cadence at measure 26 could also be seen as independent. That Mozart begins this main theme with continuational expression is entirely understandable in that the two previous main themes each began with an initiating unit. So to avoid overburdening the main-theme group with opening tonic prolongations, he eliminates a functional beginning to the third theme, starting it directly with continuation function.[48] In the end, the function of the deceptive cadence—independent or way station—remains ambiguous, as my analytical annotations suggest.

Unlike the three previous examples, the deceptive cadence that ends the opening phrase of Example 4.23a, measures 1–4, has 1̂ as

---

45. In the recapitulation (mm. 214–21), Haydn normalizes the theme in a number of ways. First, he replaces the independent deceptive cadence with a regular IAC. Second, he eliminates the harmonic conflict of the penultimate bar (m. 220) by having it express dominant harmony exclusively in root position. And third, he gives the bass line entirely over to the cellos and contrabasses (rather than having it played by the second violins, as in the exposition). But just when the theme proposes to close with a PAC at m. 221, Haydn most unexpectedly allows the melody to push back up to 3̂, thus ending the theme with another IAC. And so for that reason, a normal period form fails to emerge. The theme then begins to be repeated just as in the exposition, and Haydn closes the antecedent again with an IAC (m. 225). The subsequent consequent is then highly extended, eventually achieving a PAC at m. 238. Thus prior to the extension, the composer has written three IACs in a row, a most unusual (and difficult to justify) cadential situation.

46. In the recapitulation (see *ACF*, Ex. 14.14), Haydn fuses main theme and transition functions by writing a way-station deceptive cadence in place of the PAC ending the main theme of the exposition. As a result, we encounter two deceptive cadences in a row, each having a different function—the first being independent, the second, a way station.

47. A main-theme group consisting of three themes is unusual in this repertory.

48. This situation is akin to what often happens in a subordinate-theme group, where the second or third subordinate theme dispenses with a functional initiation; see *CF*, 111–15, and *ACF*, 390–95.

EXAMPLE 4.22. Mozart, Piano Sonata in F, K. 332, iii, mm. 21–32.

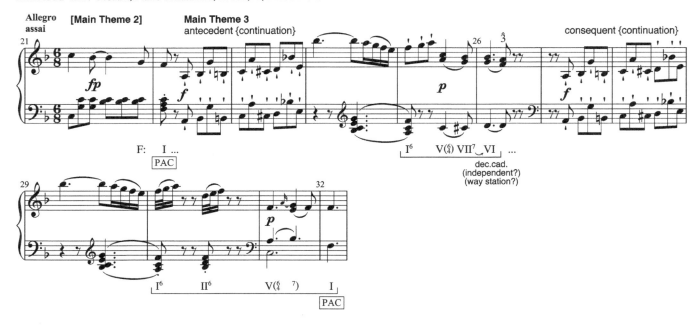

EXAMPLE 4.23. Haydn, String Quartet in C, Op. 64, no. 1, i, (a) mm. 1–8; (b) reconstruction of mm. 3–4.

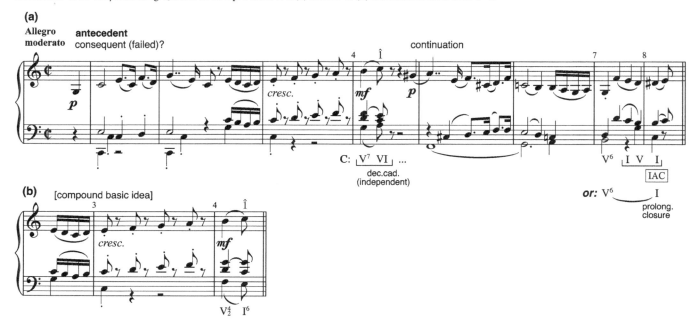

its melodic goal and therefore replaces an implied PAC. It is thus unclear how to label the formal function of this opening phrase, for the idea of its being some kind of antecedent is perhaps belied by its melody closing as it does on 1̂. We might instead recognize a kind of *failed consequent*. Yet the ascending melodic gestures found in this phrase make it appropriate as an initiating unit, not an ending one, as the idea of a consequent might suggest. Indeed, the phrase could easily have been transformed into an opening compound basic idea, if, in place of the V–VI ending, Haydn had written, say, V$_2^4$–I$^6$ (see Ex. 4.23b), thus creating an overall tonic prolongation. Despite the formal ambiguities that the deceptive cadence in measure 4 creates, we can still understand that it does not function as a way station, but rather as an independent deviation matched by the subsequent IAC in measure 8.[49]

---

49. This entire eight-measure unit itself functions as a compound antecedent concluding with the IAC. The theme is then completed by a following compound consequent (not shown) ending with a PAC. One additional note: in order to identify a cadence in m. 8, I am finding an implied root-position tonic on the third beat of m. 7. Otherwise, if we hear the first three beats of that bar as V$^6$, the inversion of the penultimate dominant would fail to qualify as truly cadential, and we would have to recognize the continuation ending with prolongational closure instead of a real cadence. The resulting form for the theme as a whole would thus be some kind of compound hybrid, a form rarely encountered in this literature.

EXAMPLE 4.24. Mozart, Piano Trio in G, K. 496, ii, mm. 8–12 (*ACF* 5.22).

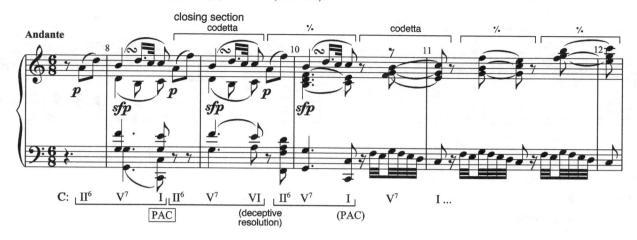

Looking back to Example 4.10a, we encounter a deceptive cadence ending the opening phrase of a developmental pre-core. And like the previous example, this deceptive cadence replaces an implied PAC given its melodic closure on $\hat{1}$. For this reason, it is again unclear how to label this obviously initiating four-measure unit. One interesting possibility is to observe that the phrase could easily have closed with an HC, as shown in Example 4.10b. In that case, the phrase would have been a simple antecedent.[50] But rather than allowing an HC to emerge by ending the melody on $\hat{2}$, Mozart pushes the melodic line down to $\hat{1}$, even adding a cadential trill to make the deceptive cadence all the more emphatic. Thus an interpretation of "failed antecedent" might reasonably be applied to this passage. Note that by allowing the phrase to end with a replacement tonic (I⁶) rather than a dominant, Mozart achieves a smoother harmonic connection to the pre-dominant II⁶ opening the continuation phrase at measure 83. The deceptive cadence thus ends up functioning as independent within a periodic hybrid, with no implications of its being a way station of any kind.[51]

### 4.1.2.5. Noncadential Uses of a Deceptive Cadential Progression

As is the case with some authentic cadential progressions (ACP), the use of a deceptive cadential progression (DCP) does not necessarily result in a genuine deceptive cadence, because a more general condition for closure may be lacking. One common case sees the DCP supporting a codetta within a closing section (Ex. 4.24). The main theme of the movement ends with a PAC in the second half of measure 8. A repeat of the cadential idea then finds the dominant resolving deceptively to VI, after which a repeat of this codetta resolves to I (m. 10). Additional half-bar codettas in measures 11–12 complete the closing section.

We see in this example a DCP pairing directly with an ACP, just like what frequently happens in cases of a genuine deceptive cadence followed by a PAC.[52] But here, both the DCP and ACP are rendered noncadential, because each supports a codetta, not a cadence. Frequently, however, we find DCP-ACP combinations in which the former is noncadential while the latter brings genuine cadential closure. In such cases, the DCP usually concludes with $\hat{3}$, thus allowing the ACP to bring the melody down to $\hat{1}$. In some cases, the DCP-ACP pair together can effect a single melodic descent from $\hat{4}$ to $\hat{1}$. In Example 4.25, the DCP beginning in measure 20 sees IV⁶–V supporting $\hat{4}$, VI supporting $\hat{3}$, and the ACP supporting the final $\hat{2}$–$\hat{1}$ descent (via $\hat{7}$ for stage 3). Note that for any number of contextual reasons (melodic, rhythmic, metric, textural), we have little sense, if any, that the DCP in measures 20–21 achieves a genuine deceptive cadence: the appearance of VI supporting $\hat{3}$ on the second quarter of measure 21 does not represent a formal end of any kind. Whenever a DCP is rendered noncadential, as in this case, we can rightfully speak of a "deceptive resolution" (of the dominant) but not of a "deceptive cadence," as we find so frequently identified in the theoretical literature.

Another, more complex, combination appears in Example 4.26. This subordinate theme, the first of two in the exposition, is largely supported by an ECP beginning with I⁶. But the dominant in measures 50–51 resolves deceptively (via a passing VII⁷/VI) in the following bar, after which a compact ACP brings the closing cadence (m. 53). A melodic analysis of the passage reveals that the entire ECP features the basic tenor pattern $\hat{8}/\hat{6}/\hat{4}/\hat{3}$, which elides with a varied soprano $\hat{3}/\hat{4}/\hat{2}/\hat{1}$ in the compact ACP of measures

---

50. One might argue that an HC at m. 82 would be redundant given the HC at m. 86 that closes the compound antecedent (the theme as a whole being a compound period ending with a PAC in m. 94, not shown). The classical repertory, however, regularly features compound periods whose compound antecedents begin with a simple antecedent, thus bringing two HCs in a row.

51. Similar cadential complications arise in two other works by Mozart: Piano Sonata in E-flat, K. 282, ii, mm. 15–16; Piano Concerto in G, K. 453, i, 113–14.

52. Also see the earlier discussion in Chapter 3, sec. 3.1.2.4, "Deceptive-Authentic Combinations," and Ex. 3.63.

EXAMPLE 4.25. Haydn, Piano Sonata in G, H. 40, ii, mm. 19–22 (*ACF* 7.7).

EXAMPLE 4.26. Beethoven, Piano Sonata in E-flat, Op. 31, no. 3, i, mm. 46–54 (*ACF* 12.12).

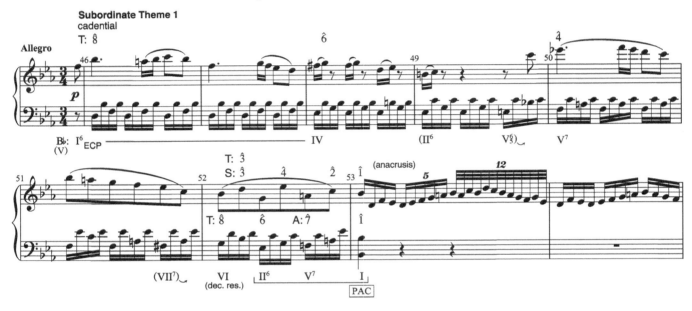

EXAMPLE 4.27. Bass-line reductions of DCP-ACP pairs.

52–53, thus bringing a full octave melodic descent for the entire theme. (As well, the soprano melody of the ACP combines simultaneously with a successive tenor and alto 8̂/6̂/7̂/1̂.)

When considering DCP-ACP pairings of the type shown in the last number of examples, some theorists, especially those of a Schenkerian bent, might want to hierarchize the harmonies of the two progressions in some way. As Schachter notes, "Many deceptive cadences are followed by a repetition of some of the music that precedes the V–VI. Usually . . . the first segment and its repetition will join together and form a single larger harmonic entity."[53] Thus in Examples 4.25 and 4.26, we might hear the dominant of the DCP being prolonged through to the dominant of the ACP, thus rendering as harmonically subordinate stage 4 of the DCP and stages 1 and 2 of the ACP, as represented in the bass-line reduction of Example 4.27a.[54] In this reading, one overall ACP embraces the DCP-ACP pair. Such a harmonic interpretation is, of course, perfectly valid in many cases. But if the lower-level DCP is ignored—reduced out of the picture, so to speak—and the cadential situation is described exclusively as a single ACP with an expanded dominant, there arises the potential to neglect the important cadential

---

53. Schachter, "*Che Inganno!*" 284.

54. Depending on the details of the context, two other viable interpretations might find the initial tonic of stage 1 (Ex. 4.27b) or the pre-dominant of stage 2 (Ex. 4.27c) as the higher-level prolonged harmony.

EXAMPLE 4.28. Mozart, Piano Sonata in B-flat, K. 333, ii, mm. 5–6 (*ACF* 3.10).

play engendered by the complete DCP-ACP combination, a situation that often contributes to processes of formal loosening. Indeed, both of these examples arise in contexts that tend to employ loosening devices: the A′ section of a small ternary and a subordinate theme, respectively.[55]

### 4.1.2.6. Deceptive Resolution of a Noncadential Dominant

As discussed in the previous section, a deceptive resolution of a cadential dominant (normally to the submediant) may occur without creating a genuine deceptive cadence. It is also possible for a *noncadential* dominant to resolve deceptively (whereby obviously no deceptive cadence would result). Among the numerous contexts in which a noncadential V–VI progression can arise, the following general situations are often encountered:

- following a prolonged dominant in the part 2 of a small binary (Ex. 3.64, m. 14);
- as the last link of a harmonic sequence (Ex. 4.11, end of m. 18);
- at the end of an initiating unit, such as a basic idea (Ex. 4.28, m. 6).

In none of these, or similar, noncadential situations would it be appropriate to identify a deceptive cadence.

### 4.1.2.7. Elided Deceptive Cadence

Just as the final tonic of an authentic cadence may both end an ongoing thematic process and simultaneously begin a new one, thereby creating a structural elision, the replacement harmony of the deceptive cadence can also function to link two formal units. A number of the deceptive cadences discussed thus far are elided. Example 4.16 a and b shows two such cases. The resolutions to ♭VI at measure 49

and at measure 319 clearly articulate a temporary cadential goal, thus satisfying the necessary and sufficient conditions of a deceptive cadence. At the same time, we readily hear these bars projecting the beginning a two-measure idea, which marks a new thematic process. The manifest overlapping of the grouping structure results in elided deceptive cadences. Additional cases appear in Example 4.4, measure 41; Example 4.12, measure 22; and Example 4.19, measure 24. In that the elided deceptive cadence groups forward as the first element of a new phrase or idea, it can sometimes be confused with an evaded cadence, which, as will now be discussed, features this specific grouping situation. Later in the chapter I return to this matter by considering some ambiguous cases of these two cadential deviations.

## 4.2. Evaded Cadence

An expected authentic cadence is *evaded* when stage 4 of the cadential schema fails to materialize and in its place appears an event, supported by any number of *initiating harmonies*,[56] that groups *forward* as the start of a new phrase or idea.[57] The lack of a final cadential event results in an abrupt cutting off, or interruption, of the ongoing cadential process, thus strongly motivating another try for cadential closure. Frequently, this attempt has the effect of winding back the clock, so to speak, by repeating the same material that had originally led up to the evaded cadence, an effect that Schmalfeldt terms the *one-more-time* (OMT) technique.[58] Less often, the evaded cadence is followed by new material. In either case, the promised PAC is eventually achieved to conclude the ongoing thematic process.

Example 4.29 illustrates a clear-cut case of an evaded cadence with one-more-time technique. An ongoing continuation phrase

---

55. I return to this topic in Chapter 5, when considering cadential expansion in greater detail (sec. 5.4.3). The importance of DCP-ACP combinations is also raised in Chapter 6 on cadence in the high baroque (see Chapter 6, sec. 6.1.5.4).

56. In discussing the evaded cadence, it will prove useful to have a general term that identifies the *first harmony* of the progression (of any type) that supports the phrase (or idea) following the evasion. I introduce the term *initiating harmony* with some trepidation, since it could easily be confused with the expression *initial tonic*, which refers to stage 1 of a cadential progression. Moreover, if an evaded cadence is followed by a new cadential progression, as occurs often enough, then the *initiating harmony* may also be an *initial tonic*. Finally, the term *initiating harmony* need not be restricted to evaded cadences. It may be applied to the first harmony of any discrete harmonic progression or to the first harmony of any given grouping structure, be it an idea, a phrase, or a complete theme.

57. Unlike the term *deceptive cadence*, which is usually defined in similar ways in most theory texts, the term *evaded cadence* sees little consensus in the scope of its application. For a good introduction to the background literature on this deviation type, see Schmalfeldt, "Cadential Processes," note 12.

58. Schmalfeldt," Cadential Processes." We have already discussed in connection with both the way-station deceptive cadence and IAC a similar form of backing up and repeating prior material for another run at the cadence. As mentioned in note 26, I follow Schmalfeldt in not speaking of the one-more-time technique in these cases, though I acknowledge that the general situation is comparable to what happens with the evaded cadence.

EXAMPLE 4.29. Haydn, Piano Sonata in C, H. 35, i, mm. 56–62 (*ACF* 12.7).

is poised to close with a PAC on the downbeat of measure 60. But in place of the expected stage 4, which would consist of a root-position tonic and a melodic $\hat{1}$, measure 60 brings $I^6$ as an initiating harmony, which supports a leap up to $\hat{5}$ and a broad scalar descent that is virtually identical to the music of measure 58. What follows continues the same cadential formula, this time realizing the appropriate stage 4 of the PAC at measure 62. The music in measure 60 thus groups forward as the first bar of this one-more-time technique that follows the evaded cadence.

Note that the analytical annotation that brackets the harmonies supporting the evasion ends with a double-slash sign (//) to suggest graphically a "cutting off," or "interruption," of the ongoing cadential progression.[59] As for the label "evaded cadence," its ideal placement is perhaps somewhat equivocal because this deviation type does not result in any kind of cadential *arrival*. As a result, it would make some sense to place it at the same point as the harmonic interruption, that is, at the end of stage 3. But I have chosen rather to locate it at the moment where the final tonic is expected, that is, where the initiating harmony appears. In this way, the label's position is identical to where the "deceptive cadence" label would be found if that deviation had been used instead.

Unlike the deceptive cadence, we seldom speak of an evaded cadence replacing an expected IAC. In order for that situation to arise, the ongoing melodic process would have to clearly imply a cadential ending on the third degree. For all practical purposes, that would require the final melodic pitch of stage 3 to conclude on $\hat{4}$, which is the only scale degree that demands resolution to $\hat{3}$. Any other candidate for the penultimate melodic pitch ($\hat{7}$, $\hat{2}$, and even $\hat{5}$) would normally imply a resolution to $\hat{1}$. Since an IAC ending, in principle, represents incomplete closure, there is no particular aesthetic reason for that cadence type to be evaded, and indeed such a variant of the regular evaded cadence rarely arises in the classical repertory. One such case does occur in Example 4.30, beginning with an ECP at measure 64. If we look at the melodic highpoints in the opening four-measure phrase, we see the pitches of the tenor stream ($\flat\hat{7}/\hat{6}/\hat{5}$-$\hat{4}/\hat{3}$) clearly implying a close on $\hat{3}$.[60] Instead, the final stage of the cadence is bypassed, and the melody reverts to $\hat{5}$ at measure 68. Inasmuch as the melodic goal is projected to be $\hat{3}$, we can probably speak in this case of an evaded cadence standing in for an IAC.

### 4.2.1. Morphology

Up until stage 4 is omitted, the morphology of an evaded cadence is identical to that of any other PAC. The only topic that needs further discussion in this section is to consider the harmonic and melodic content of the music that stands in place of stage 4, that is, the music that groups forward with the next phrase or idea.

#### 4.2.1.1. Harmonic Content

The most commonly employed initiating harmony of an evaded cadence is $I^6$. This harmony works well because, as a tonic, it often provides appropriate support for the beginning of the material following the cadential evasion, yet its being inverted helps to deny our hearing a cadential arrival. The $I^6$ at measure 60 of Example 4.29 and at measure 68 of Example 4.30 is typical of this deviation.

At times, the use of a passing ④, supporting $V^4_2$ in stage 3b, already signals a possible evasion, as seen in Example 4.31. Here, the $I^6$ at measure 69 must necessarily arise due to the preceding $V^4_2$.

---

59. I borrow the double slash from the practice of many Schenkerian analysts, who use it to indicate an "interruption" of the *Urlinie* (or *Urlinie*-like processes); needless to say, my use of this symbol differs from that of Schenker and his followers.

60. Stage 1 of the pattern, which normally contains $\hat{8}$, is replaced by the passing seventh ($\flat\hat{7}$) due to the harmonic support of $V^6_5/IV$ in place of a diatonic $I^6$.

EXAMPLE 4.30. Mozart, Piano Concerto in E-flat, K. 482, i, mm. 64–72 (*ACF* 20.1).

EXAMPLE 4.31. Beethoven, Symphony No. 1 in C, Op. 21, i, mm. 65–70.

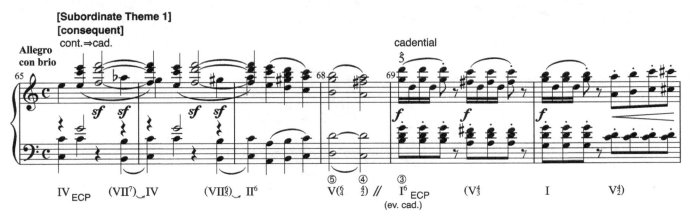

Note that the harmonies here, V($^6_4$ $^4_2$)–I$^6$, resemble a situation that arises now and then with a deceptive cadence (as discussed in connection with Ex. 4.10a, m. 82). The difference between the two situations depends entirely on the grouping structure that obtains with the event that replaces stage 4 of the cadential process. If that event groups backward with the ongoing the cadential function, then a deceptive cadence ensues. If that event groups forward, then an evaded cadence results instead. In Example 4.10a, the I$^6$ on the third beat of measure 82 obviously groups with the prior cadential dominant and thus can clearly be heard as stage 4 of a deceptive cadence. On the contrary, Example 4.31 brings at measure 69 a sudden change in texture, along with a melodic leap up to $\hat{5}$, both of which strongly prevent us from hearing the I$^6$ at measure 69 as the goal of the prevailing cadential process. As a result, we perceive an evaded cadence, not a deceptive one.

Though I$^6$ appears frequently with an evaded cadence, the expected final tonic may be replaced by various other harmonies, some of which are illustrated in the following examples:

Example 4.32: the V$^6_5$ at measure 10 appears in place of the expected stage-4 tonic and initiates a one-more-time technique by "backing up" to the music of measure 7ff.

Example 4.33a: IV$^6$ serves as the initiating harmony of a one-more-time technique associated with the evaded cadence at measure 4. Somewhat unusual, though, is that this harmony can also been seen to function as a passing sonority between the cadential V$^7$ and the V$^6_5$ on the second beat of measure 4. Indeed, a more literal one-more-time technique would have brought V$^6_5$ on the downbeat of that bar in reference to the content of measure 2. (The complicated formal situation that arises from this evaded cadence will be discussed later in sec. 4.2.2.1.)

EXAMPLE 4.32. Mozart, Piano Sonata in F, K. 280, i, mm. 6–11 (*ACF* 5.1a).

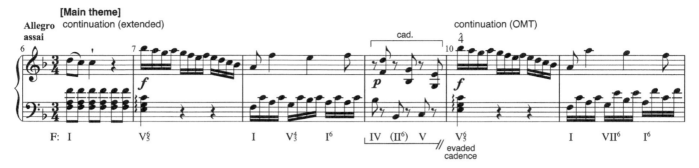

EXAMPLE 4.33. Mozart, Piano Sonata in C, K. 279, ii, (a) mm. 1–6 (*ACF* 5.37); (b) reconstruction of mm. 3–4.

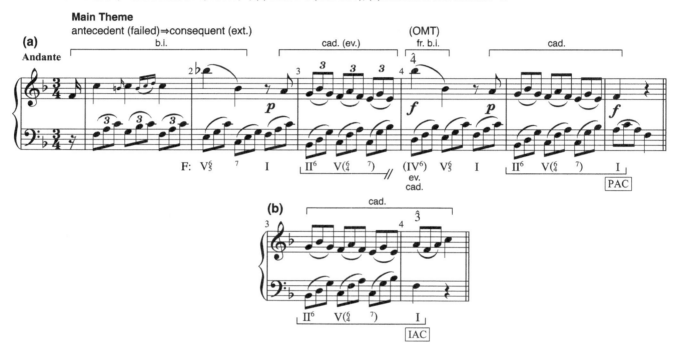

EXAMPLE 4.34. Haydn, Symphony No. 104 in D ("London"), iv, mm. 261–67 (*ACF* 15.6).

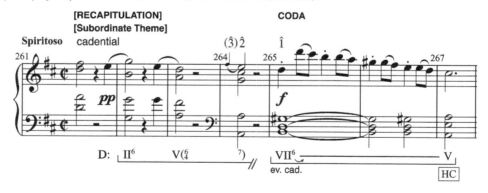

Example 4.34: the VII⁶/V at measure 265 is an initiating harmony of an evaded cadence. Note that the harmonic and melodic content of measure 264 into the downbeat of measure 265 could also render a deceptive cadence (cf. Ex. 4.4, which also uses VII⁶/V in place of the implied stage-4 tonic). But the grouping structure in Example 4.34 speaks against the interpretation of deceptive cadence. The textural caesura in the second half of measure 264, along with the sudden change to

EXAMPLE 4.35. Beethoven, Violin Sonata in A Minor, Op. 23, i, mm. 237–52 (*ACF* 15.15).

EXAMPLE 4.36. Beethoven, Piano Sonata in A, Op. 2, no. 2, i, mm. 83–92 (*ACF* 12.8).

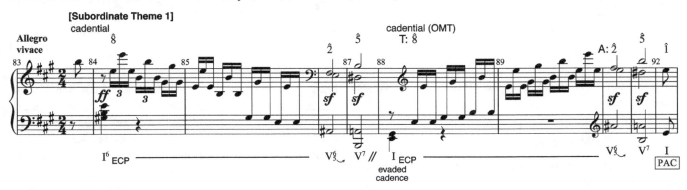

*forte* in measure 265, suggests that the VII⁶/V groups forward to the subsequent HC at measure 267, thus yielding a prior evaded cadence.[61]

Example 4.35: the cadential pre-dominant II⁶₅ reappears as the initiating harmony for a couple of one-more-time repetitions, after which new material at measure 244 (based on main-theme motives) brings a final PAC at measure 250.

Example 4.36: now and then, the initiating harmony of an evaded cadence is a root-position tonic, precisely the harmony that is expected to appear in stage 4 of the cadential progression. This seemingly paradoxical situation can only arise when we clearly perceive the event supported by this tonic to group forward with the subsequent phrase. Just such a case arises at measure 88, where I occurs following the cadential dominant. Yet the sudden change of texture, the lack of a melodic event on the downbeat of measure 88 (cf. m. 92), and the clear impression that the content

of that bar refers back to the I⁶ of measure 84 all contribute to us hearing measure 88 as grouping forward and thus producing an evaded cadence, despite the presence of a root-position tonic. Putting it most concisely, measure 88 holds an *initiating* tonic, not a *final* one.

Example 4.37: Toward the close of a written-out cadenza at the end of a development section, an ECP in measures 56–58 promises PAC closure in B minor at measure 59. In place of a final tonic, we encounter V⁷/IV, which, along with the diversion of the cadential trill upward to 3̂, effects an evaded cadence. The evasion then initiates a retransition that leads the music back to the home key for the onset of the recapitulation (m. 61). Supporting the interpretation of evaded cadence is our recognizing that a cadential trill is used almost always in connection with a PAC, so that Haydn's diverting the melody interrupts a melodic process as well as a harmonic one. In addition, measure 59 brings a new model-sequence technique, along with a sudden change to a drum-bass accompaniment. All of these factors suggest that the downbeat of that bar

---

61. This example is a seldomly encountered case of an evaded cadence that leads to an HC instead of a PAC.

EXAMPLE 4.37. Haydn, Piano Sonata in D, H. 37, i, mm. 56–61.

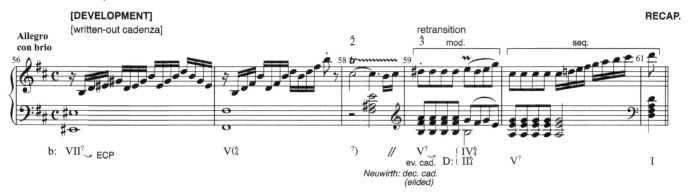

EXAMPLE 4.38. Mozart, Piano Sonata in C, K. 309, iii, mm. 13–19 (*ACF* 5.13).

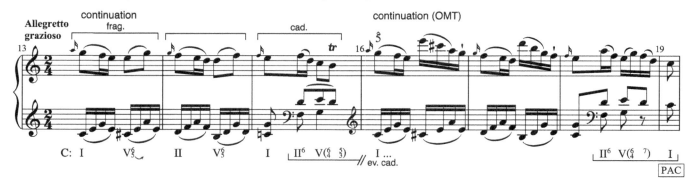

represents the start of a new group rather than the formal goal of the cadenza.[62]

### 4.2.1.2. Melodic Content

In order to speak of a genuine evaded cadence, we must normally perceive a harmonic interruption following the cadential dominant. Usually the melodic goal projected by the ongoing cadential process is similarly interrupted, typically by an upward motion so as to deny a melodic resolution to $\hat{1}$. When the initiating harmony is $I^6$, the melody often leaps up to $\hat{5}$ to begin the next phrase, as seen already in Examples 4.29–4.31. A melodic leap to $\hat{5}$ is especially effective when the initiating harmony is a root-position tonic, because the resulting melodic disruption compensates for the lack of a literal harmonic interruption, as witnessed at measure 16 of Example 4.38. If the initiating harmony is not a tonic, other scale degrees can result from the leaping motion (Ex. 4.32, m. 10, $V^6_5$, with a leap to $\hat{4}$; Ex. 4.33, m. 4, $IV^6$, with a leap to $\hat{4}$).

Frequently enough, the melodic line of an evaded cadence resolves to its expected goal of $\hat{1}$. When this occurs, the initiating harmony will not be a root-position tonic, since the combination of I supporting $\hat{1}$ would almost always create a PAC rather than a cadential evasion. Example 4.34 is a case in point: measure 265 brings $\hat{1}$ as expected from the preceding melodic line. The cadential evasion is thereby effected primarily by harmonic means (the use of $VII^6/V$ as an initiating harmony), along with the secondary parameters of texture and dynamics, as discussed earlier. Another such case (Ex. 4.39) sees a sudden turn to minor with the initiating $I^6$ at measure 26 supporting the melodic resolution to $\hat{1}$. Again, the sense of evasion is projected largely by the harmonic inversion, though the surprising modal shift, the marked change in texture, and the *forzato* articulations also help dramatize the cadential deviation.[63]

On occasion, the material following stage 3 has the same harmonic-melodic content that would be expected to effect a PAC, namely a resolution to both a root-position tonic and $\hat{1}$. In such cases, the composer must create a marked sense of interruption in the non-pitch parameters (e.g., rhythm, texture, dynamics) in a convincing enough manner so that the event supported by I is not perceived as a final cadential tonic; otherwise, we would hear a regular PAC at this point. We have already discussed such a case in Example 4.36, measure 88, and have observed those factors that create the sense of cadential evasion.

---

62. I return to this example in sec. 4.2.2.1 on the function of evaded cadences. Toward the end of the chapter (sec. 4.6.1), I consider Neuwirth's alternative analysis of an elided deceptive cadence at m. 59.

63. The following measures of this example will be discussed later (sec. 4.3.3) in connection with the abandoned cadence. I return again to this example toward the end of the chapter (sec. 4.6.1) when discussing the option of hearing an elided deceptive cadence at m. 26 in lieu of an evaded one.

EXAMPLE 4.39. Haydn, String Quartet in B Minor, Op. 64, no. 2, i, mm. 24–34 (*ACF* 12.6).

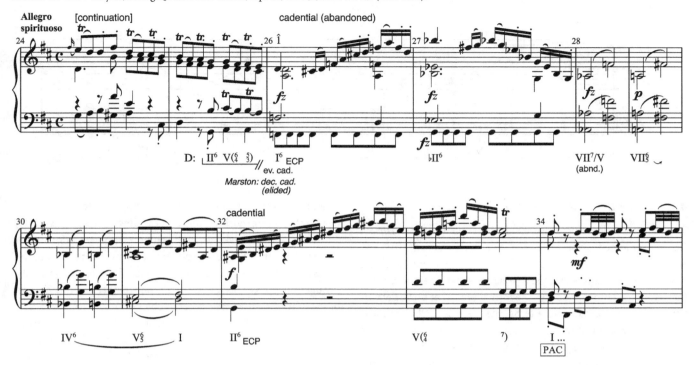

### 4.2.2. Function

Like the deceptive cadence, the evaded cadence can be used in any formal context where the music is likely to close with a PAC, such as at the end of a main theme, a subordinate theme, and a coda theme. A transition or retransition, which normally closes with an HC, rarely, if ever, brings this deviation. A developmental core (or core-like substitute) also normally ends with an HC, but now and then promises instead to close with a PAC to confirm a development key; in that case, an evaded cadence may be used to precede that PAC or may represent a failed attempt at such closure, as we already observed in Example 4.37.

Due to the evaded cadence's inherently dramatic effect, caused by an abrupt interruption of the cadential process just prior to its realization, this deviation is especially associated with subordinate themes and coda themes, where the confirmation of the subordinate key (in the exposition) or the home key (in the recapitulation or coda) tends to be dramatized. Unlike the deceptive cadence, which appears occasionally in main themes, the evaded cadence is less likely to occur in relatively tight-knit formal contexts (but see Ex. 4.32, 4.33, and 4.38, for such a usage).

#### 4.2.2.1. Way Station

Almost all evaded cadences operate in a manner that is akin to the way-station function of many deceptive cadences and some IACs. The metaphor of a way station is, however, not quite apt for the evaded cadence, since reaching a way station normally implies an arrival of some sort, albeit a provisional one. Yet it is entirely in the nature of the evaded cadence to thwart the attainment of a goal by significantly interrupting the ongoing cadential processes; indeed, we cannot really speak of a cadential arrival in the case of this deviation type. For all intents and purposes, nonetheless, the formal function of an evaded cadence is essentially the same as a way station. And like any way station, the evaded cadence is almost always followed eventually by the PAC that is implied by the overall formal context within which the deviation occurs. Now and then that PAC fails to appear, as already seen in Examples 4.34 and 4.37. Such cases are like those of a way station that has been *denied* (see above sec. 4.1.2.3). As for an evaded cadence that does not function like a way station, I have yet to encounter an unequivocal case, though Example 4.33a comes close. Following an opening two-measure basic idea, a contrasting idea at measure 3 heads directly for cadential closure on the downbeat of measure 4 to produce an antecedent phrase. Given this formal context, we presume that the cadence would be an independent IAC (such as that reconstructed in Ex. 4.33b), since a PAC occurring after only four bars of a main theme is a less likely scenario. Following the cadential evasion, the music "backs up" to the content of measure 2, and the repetition of the contrasting idea brings a PAC at measure 6 (not the earlier expected IAC). As a result, an antecedent function fails to emerge, and we understand in retrospect that the entire phrase, extended by the one-more-time technique, ends up functioning as a consequent, albeit one that is missing its matching antecedent, although such a function had initially been implied. In addition, we now see that the evaded cadence eventually functions like a way station, even if that was not our initial impression of the situation.

EXAMPLE 4.40. Mozart, Piano Concerto in G, K. 453, iii, mm. 324–30.

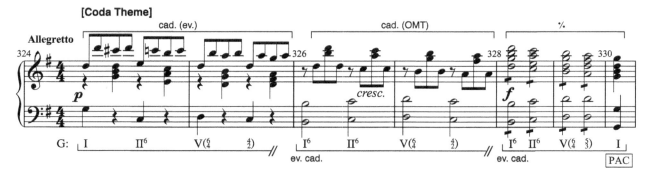

### 4.2.2.2. One-More-Time Technique

The inherently dramatic character of the evaded cadence is even further reinforced when the attempt to achieve the cadential goal, which initially fails, is immediately tried "one more time." As discussed earlier, this technique repeats the same, or similar, music that led to the evaded cadence. The formal units that normally participate in the one-more-time technique are essentially like those discussed earlier in connection with "repeated material" following a deceptive cadence (e.g., a continuation phrase, a cadential idea or phrase) and thus require no further explication or specific illustration. And like the deceptive cadence and the way-station IAC, it is rare for an evaded cadence to return to the very beginning of the ongoing thematic unit.[64] When that situation does arise, the beginning, to which the music has backed up, normally has intrinsic continuational characteristics (i.e., that it is not an inherently *initiating* unit, such as a presentation or compound basic idea).[65]

Unlike the other way-station types (the IAC and the deceptive cadence), where only a single instance of the way station is normally used,[66] the one-more-time technique is itself often repeated, thus enhancing the dramatic effect: "try it once . . . try it twice . . . third time's the charm." Example 4.40, discussed by Schmalfeldt, illustrates this situation well.[67] Toward the end of a coda theme, a cadential idea beginning at measure 324 is evaded two bars later, and a one-more-time approach is likewise evaded at measure 328; a second repetition finally achieves the PAC at measure 330.

Example 4.41 shows a particularly intricate series of possibly three evaded cadences in a row. Within the course of a subordinate theme, a continuation leads to a dominant arrival at measure 27, which is prolonged until the middle of measure 28.[68] A short cadential idea then appears in the following bar. To be sure, this idea reaches a root-position tonic on the downbeat of measure 30, and the melody resolves to $\hat{1}$; so the necessary conditions for a PAC are present. Yet the displacement of the melodic arrival to the second sixteenth note, as well as the sustained rhythmic continuity throughout this bar, casts some doubt on whether genuine closure for the subordinate theme has been achieved. When we then hear a repeat of the same dominant prolongation and cadential idea from the prior phrase, we are encouraged to understand that the potential cadence at measure 30 was evaded. What is not in doubt is the clear cadential evasion at measure 34 when the melody, which promises to close on $\hat{1}$, leaps up to $\hat{5}$. This evasion is then followed by new material, another evaded cadence at measure 36 (with one-more-time technique), and a decisive PAC two bars later. If we accept hearing an evaded cadence at measure 30, we find a series of three evasions as well as the one-more-time repetition of two different phrases. Though this view favors an evaded cadence, the idea of a genuine PAC occurring at measure 30 should not be discounted entirely. Yet an examination of subordinate-theme structures in the classical repertory reveals that composers normally postpone cadential closure as long as possible and avoid bringing a PAC that is internal to the broader thematic processes.

A similar problem in cadential interpretation arises in Example 4.42, where our hearing a potential one-more-time technique again helps tip the balance in favor of an evaded cadence over that of a PAC. Within a subordinate-theme group, an opening compound presentation (not shown) is followed by a continuation featuring fragmentation (mm. 31–33), model-sequence technique (m. 34), an internal dominant arrival (m. 35), and a new cadential idea (mm. 36–37), which promises to close with a PAC on the downbeat of measure 38. This moment indeed brings the necessary conditions for a PAC—a root-position tonic and a melodic $\hat{1}$. The rhythmic displacement of the latter and the sudden change to *piano* nonetheless help to signal an evaded cadence. But what seems to really clinch the sense of evasion is the one-more-time technique that we hear when the downbeat of measure 38 backs up the music to the upbeat of measure 33 for a

---

64. See Chapter 3, sec. 3.2.2.2. For an exception to this rule, see ahead Ex. 4.82a, discussed in sec. 4.6.5.

65. For more on this point, see in Chapter 5, the discussion of Ex. 5.71a, and note 117.

66. For an exception, see Ex. 4.15, where we find two deceptive cadences prior to the PAC; see also Beethoven, Piano Sonata in A-flat, Op. 26, iv, mm. 42–48.

67. Schmalfeldt, "Cadential Processes," 5–6.

68. The dominant at m. 27 does not effect an HC, because the preceding harmony in m. 26 is VII[6]. This variant of the dominant arises from an ongoing Prinner pattern (IV–I[6]–VII[6]–I), one that begins two bars before

the I[6] in the opening bar of the example; indeed the harmony promised for m. 27 is a root-position tonic. As a result, the V at m. 27 is better understood to mark a dominant arrival (even a slightly premature one) rather than an actual cadence. The concept of dominant arrival will be developed later in this chapter (sec. 4.4).

EXAMPLE 4.41. Mozart, Piano Sonata in B-flat, K. 281, i, mm. 24–40.

repeat of the immediately prior material. The unambiguous PAC at measure 43 then brings full closure to this loose subordinate theme.[69]

### 4.2.2.3. New Material

Though evaded cadences are most typically followed by the one-more-time technique, this cadential deviation now and then leads to new material.[70] We have already seen such cases in Example 4.30, measure 68; Example 4.31, measure 69; Example 4.37, measure 59; and Example 4.41, measure 34.

When the melodic line of an evaded cadence actually achieves $\hat{1}$, this pitch will likely initiate new material rather than a one-more-time repetition (see Ex. 4.34, m. 265; Ex. 4.39, m. 26; and ahead, Ex. 4.76, m. 178). The reason probably lies in the fact that the initial scale degree of melodic material leading to most PACs begins higher than $\hat{1}$ so that the line can then descend to that goal. Put another way, if the melody of an evaded cadence reaches $\hat{1}$, it is not likely to create a one-more-time situation, because the prior material more typically began on some higher scale degree. Some exceptions to this rule occur when the goal $\hat{1}$ of the evaded cadence is supported by tonic in root position (Ex. 4.36, m. 88; Ex. 4.41, m. 30; and Ex. 4.42, m. 38). In these circumstances, the one-more-time technique is essential for allowing us to hear an evaded cadence rather than a PAC.

---

69. Note that the last two examples come from early Mozart. I suspect, but cannot yet verify, that his more mature compositional practice tends to avoid such cadential ambiguities in favor of a clearer deferral of cadential closure.

70. See again note 31 for a clarification of what I mean by "new" material.

EXAMPLE 4.42. Mozart, Piano Sonata in G, K. 283, i, mm. 31–44.

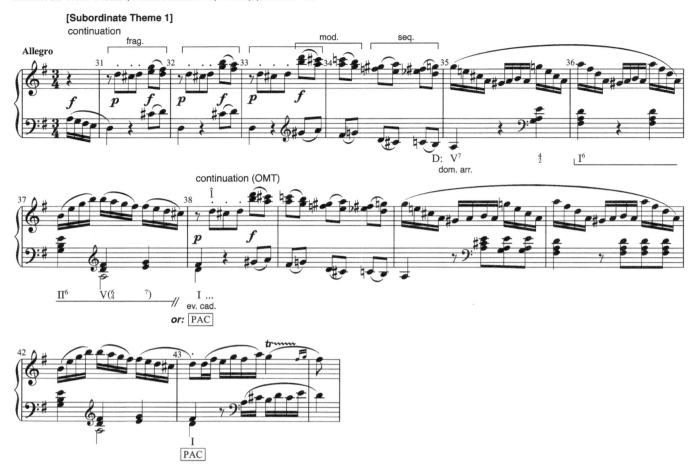

## 4.3. Abandoned Cadence

Of the three cadential deviations of an authentic cadence—deceptive, evaded, and abandoned—the latter occurs less frequently and generally presents a more complicated set of harmonic-formal circumstances. If the deceptive and evaded cadences implicate stage 4 of the schema, either by replacing the normal harmony of that stage (deceptive) or by eliminating that stage entirely (evaded), the abandoned cadence arises from a problem with stage 3, the dominant. Three general situations can produce a cadential abandonment: (1) the sounding root-position dominant is undermined by shifting to its first-inversion ($V^6$ or $V^6_5$), thus converting a cadential dominant into a noncadential one; (2) the expected dominant appears immediately in inversion, thus never even attaining cadential status; or (3) the predominant of stage 2 leads to no cadential dominant.

Cadential abandonment is further complicated because we often cannot identify an actual point in time that represents the moment of "abandoned cadence" proper (akin to that place in the score where we position the labels for deceptive and evaded cadences). Rather, the ongoing cadential process, as defined foremost by its underlying harmonic progression, is abandoned without there being a definitive location where a cadence would be expected to appear. In such cases we must understand the cadential *progression* alone as being abandoned in the absence of an implied moment of formal closure.

Since the rest of this discussion will largely concern the morphological conditions giving rise to the abandoned cadence, let me first offer some brief comments on the function of this deviation. Like the deceptive and evaded cadences, cadential abandonment (either of a determinate cadential arrival or of just the cadential progression) normally arises in the context of an expected authentic cadence. Depending on the melodic content, this implied cadence may be a PAC or an IAC. Now and then, the abandonment is followed by a repeat of prior material in the sense of the one-more-time technique. More often than not, however, the abandoned cadence is continued by new material, which eventually becomes cadential, either to realize a PAC or to be subjected to another deviation technique. An abandoned cadence occurs most often in loosely organized subordinate themes or coda themes; main-theme usage is less common. A cadence of limited scope can also be abandoned, though that situation seldom arises.[71] Finally, because of the underlying harmonic prolongation that results in all cases of abandoned cadence,

---

71. See Mozart, Clarinet Quintet in A, K. 581, i, mm. 71–74 (*ACF* 12.11a).

EXAMPLE 4.43. Haydn, String Quartet in E-flat, Op. 33, no. 2, i, mm. 21–28 (R = ½N) (ACF 12.21).

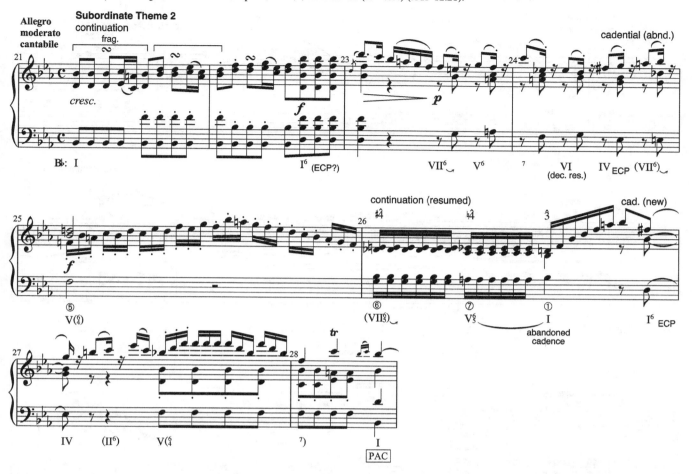

this mechanism of formal ending must be considered a type of *prolongational closure*.[72]

An abandoned cadence arising within a subordinate-theme group is well illustrated in Example 4.43. Following a first subordinate theme, a second one begins at measure 21 directly with a sense of continuation due largely to the half-bar fragments.[73] The shift to a prominent $I^6$ at the upbeat to measure 23 suggests the possibility of a cadential progression, but the following prolongational activity, along with the harmonic acceleration, sustains the expression of continuation function. After the deceptive resolution of the dominant that straddles measures 23–24, a clearer cadential progression begins with pre-dominant harmonies (IV and $VII^7/V$), leading at measure 25 to an expanded cadential six-four, which signals the onset of stage 3. But rather than resolving to the dominant proper, the harmony is undermined when the bass ascends ⑤–⑥–⑦ to yield $V^6_5$, which then resolves as a *prolongational* dominant to I in the middle of measure 26, thus producing an abandoned cadence.[74] Note that the melodic content $\sharp\hat{4}$–$\natural\hat{4}$–$\hat{3}$ suggests that had a genuine cadence been realized, it would have been an IAC. What then follows must be reckoned as a new cadential process leading to a PAC in measure 28, though the rhythmic configuration of the melody in the first half of measure 27 alludes (in a slightly one-more-time manner) to the prior continuation of measures 23–24.

### 4.3.1. Cadential Dominant Undermined by Inversion

A fundamental axiom of cadential practice for the classical style (and a principle that I retain for all tonal styles) holds that the dominant harmony constituting stage 3 of the cadential schema must appear initially in root position and retain that position throughout the stage. In cases of genuine authentic cadences and the deviations of deceptive and evaded cadences, this condition is strictly maintained. With one type of abandoned cadence,

---

72. See Chapter 3, sec. 3.5.1. In the analytical annotations, the use of both labels "abandoned cadence" and "prolongational closure" for the same moment of cadential deviation would be cumbersome; so I will only indicate the former, as a more specific case of the latter.

73. For the idea that a second subordinate theme may "begin" with continuation function, see *CF*, 111–13, and *ACF*, 391.

74. In beats 2 and 3 of m. 26, the viola sounds the pitch F lying a third and a fourth below the bass line ⑦–①. In such cases, we ordinarily do not take the viola to represent the bass voice, which continues to be expressed by the cello. Since there is no easy way of showing this pitch in a two-staff reduction, I have eliminated this F from the score.

EXAMPLE 4.44. Beethoven, Violin Sonata in E-flat, Op. 12, no. 3, i, mm. 1–13 (*ACF* 5.6).

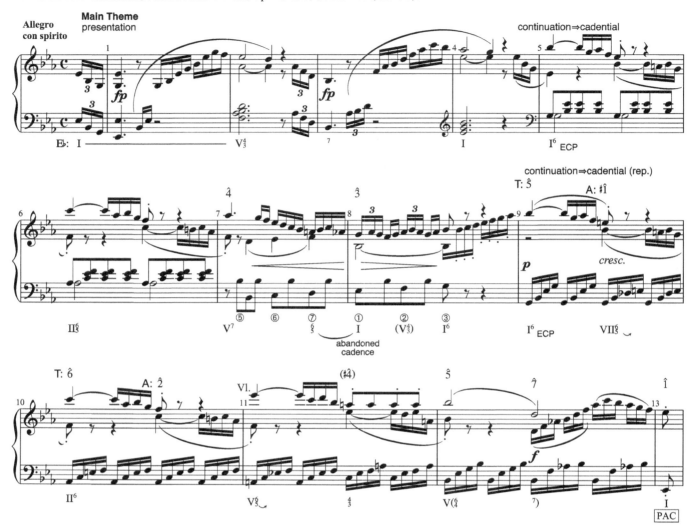

however, the dominant loses its cadential status by means of inversion to $V^6$ (or $V^6_5$), thus converting the cadential dominant into a prolongational harmony, which normally resolves to I. A cadential dominant could, in principle, be undermined by changing to its second inversion ($V^4_3$), but I have not yet found such a case in the classical style.[75] If the dominant moves to its third inversion ($V^4_2$), then the situation becomes, in effect, what I have already described as a variation of the *deceptive cadential* progression (which may be used for both deceptive and evaded cadences; see Examples 4.10a and 4.31, respectively). Here, then, is a seeming exception to the rule that a dominant can be undermined by inversion for the purpose of cadential abandonment. But as discussed before, the motion from ⑤ to ④ within the dominant motivates us to hear ④ more as a passing tone to ③ (supporting $I^6$) than as a genuine positional change that subverts the cadential status of the dominant. For all practical purposes, then, the condition of undermining the cadential dominant applies to a shift from root position to first inversion exclusively.

We have already seen an abandoned cadence produced by inverting the dominant to $V^6_5$ in Example 4.43, measure 26. Another case, this time in a main theme, arises in Example 4.44. Here, an opening presentation phrase (mm. 1–4) is followed by a presumed continuation⇒cadential phrase, as supported by an ECP. A dominant seventh, representing stage 3, arrives on the downbeat of measure 7, but the bass line then begins to ascend, passing through a $V^6_5$ on the way up to I, which arrives as expected on the downbeat of measure 8. (The bass then continues up to ③ to support $I^6$ at the very end of the phrase.) The bass line in measure 7 thus undermines the cadential status of the dominant, such that the resolution to tonic is prolongational, not cadential. As a result, the downbeat of measure 8 projects an abandoned cadence, since we had been expecting some kind of cadential closure at this moment.

---

75. Cadential abandonment in association with a descent of the bass line down to ②, supporting $V^4_3$ (or $VII^6$) becomes common in the second half of the nineteenth century; see Chapter 9, sec. 9.4, and Ex. 9.36, m. 8; Ex. 9.37, mm. 422 and 426; Ex. 9.54a, m. 31. Abandonment via the progression V–IV also occurs in nineteenth-century cases of plagal closure; see sec. 9.3 and Ex. 9.19a, m. 28; Ex. 9.20a, m. 32; and Ex. 9.21a, m. 35.

EXAMPLE 4.45. Beethoven, String Quartet in E-flat, Op. 127, i, mm. 1–32.

Following the abandonment, the continuation⇒cadential phrase is repeated and subjected to an extension by one bar (m. 11), with a PAC occurring on the downbeat of measure 13. Like Example 4.43, the abandoned cadence at measure 8 finds a melodic $\hat{4}$ resolving to $\hat{3}$, thus implying that an IAC would have been created if the cadence had not been abandoned. Since we normally expect an eight-measure main theme to end with a PAC, the abandoned cadence thus functions as a way station.

Unlike the previous example, the way station here motivates a repetition of the prior phrase, akin to the one-more-time technique.[76]

A similar, but more complicated case, appears in Example 4.45, another main theme by Beethoven. Following a short slow

---

76. The rest of the annotated melodic scale degrees in this example will be discussed in the following chapter, sec. 5.1.2.10.

introduction, which itself ends with a cadential abandonment (to be discussed shortly in sec. 4.3.2.1), an eight-measure hybrid (compound basic idea + consequent) is prepared to close with an authentic cadence at measure 14. Note that the melodic scale degrees of each phrase point to the Prinner schema ($\hat{6}$-$\hat{5}$-$\hat{4}$-$\hat{3}$), but one that remains incomplete when the melody pushes back up to $\hat{5}$ at the end of the first phrase. When it begins to be repeated, in the manner of a consequent, a compact cadential progression, beginning with $I^6$ in measure 12, reaches V on the downbeat of the next bar. Like the previous two examples, the bass then pushes upward to produce a final prolongational progression, $V^6_5$–I, to yield an abandoned cadence on the downbeat of measure 14.[77] As a result, the consequent fails to be fully realized, although the Prinner schema is rendered complete with a final $\hat{3}$, thus implying that the cadence would have been a PrC, a version of the IAC.

What follows is a repetition of the entire theme, which this time abandons an implied PAC (m. 22) when the melody pushes down to $\hat{1}$. Given the melodic differentiation created by these two statements of the theme—the first ending on $\hat{3}$, the second, on $\hat{1}$—a compound periodic organization is strongly suggested, even if the compound "antecedent" (mm. 7–14) and "consequent" (mm. 15–22) do not end with genuine cadences, but rather, most exceptionally, with abandoned ones. And seeing as this compound period would represent the main theme of the movement, it would seem that Beethoven has violated a central norm of classical form, namely, that a main theme should close with a home-key cadence. This formal oddity appears to be confirmed by the following material: the continuous drum-bass accompaniment and *forte* dynamic at measure 22 both propose that a transition is underway. But the composer then surprises us and allows this new thematic unit to close with a genuine PAC at measure 32, still in the home key, thus forcing us to reinterpret the transition as a second main theme. Even if he failed to end a first main theme cadentially, at least he concludes a second one (and thus the main-theme group as a whole) with a proper cadence.[78]

## 4.3.2. Cadential Dominant Replaced by Inverted Dominant

A second type of abandoned cadence occurs when what we anticipate to be a cadential dominant is immediately *replaced* by an inverted form that functions noncadentially. In other words, rather than the dominant becoming undermined by inversion, this type of cadential abandonment takes place at the very moment we are expecting the stage-3 dominant to appear. The majority of abandonments of this type feature the third inversion $V^4_2$, which can easily appear when the bass ④ of the preceding pre-dominant is held in place, rather than rising to ⑤, which would then have engaged a cadential dominant. Alternatively, the expected dominant may be replaced directly by $V^6_3$. (A second inversion $V^4_3$ is also a viable option, but extremely rare in the classical repertory. I discuss one such case toward the end of Chapter 5, Ex. 5.75a, m. 27, where $VII^6_5$ stands in place of $V^4_3$.)

### 4.3.2.1. Replaced by $V^4_2$

Example 4.46 well illustrates a cadential abandonment via $V^4_2$. This continuation phrase of an eight-measure sentence initiates a possible cadential progression with the $I^6$ at the upbeat to measure 6. When the pre-dominant on the downbeat of that bar is followed directly by a dominant in third inversion, with the bass holding steady on ④, the progression is abandoned. The required resolution to $I^6$ at measure 7 begins a second cadential progression, which brings true closure to the theme on the downbeat of the next bar. Note that it is not immediately obvious just where the first cadential progression would have achieved its moment of arrival. If the second beat of measure 6 had alternatively contained a root-position dominant, then we probably would have expected a PAC on the downbeat of measure 7. Yet that arrival would likely have felt premature, given the normal length of a tight-knit sentence. In this situation, which is very common for this deviation type, it seems preferable to regard the cadential *progression* as having been abandoned without specifying an abandoned *cadence* per se (as we do for the deceptive or evaded cadence).[79]

At this point, I must clarify why I do not consider the $V^4_2$ in Example 4.46 to represent a cadential dominant in root position with a passing ④ in the bass, as I have done for deceptive and evaded cadences that also feature this harmony (see again Ex. 4.10a, m. 82, and Ex. 4.31, m. 68). In these latter cases, a root-position dominant with cadential status has already been locked into place; that is, the bass line has achieved the focal pitch ⑤ of the cadential stream.[80] The subsequent $V^4_2$ thus arises not as a genuine inversion of the dominant but rather from a melodic passing motion in the bass (④), all taking place within the *cadential*

---

77. In the analytical annotations, I indicate the abandonment of a compact cadential progression by means of an open-ended cadential bracket, which is cut off where the progression becomes prolongational (see Ex. 4.45, mm. 12–13). If the abandoned progression is followed by a discernible moment of formal arrival, I use the label "abandoned cadence" to identify that cadential deviation (m. 14). In cases of an abandoned ECP (for which there is no cadential bracket), I use the label "(abnd.)" placed below the harmony that *departs* from the cadential progression, as seen with the $V^4_2$ at m. 7 (to be considered shortly ahead). If the abandoned ECP leads to a moment of formal arrival, I avoid redundancy by eliminating that abbreviation in favor of the label "abandoned cadence," placed at that arrival moment (see again Ex. 4.43, m. 26, and Ex. 4.44, m. 8).

78. We might even be tempted here, following ideas developed by Steven Vande Moortele (see Chapter 8, note 56), to take a more global perspective on this main theme group and see the first theme and its repetition as a magnified *presentation*, whose constituent units remain structurally open due to the lack of cadences. The second main theme could then be seen as a corresponding *continuation* to close this highly expanded sentential form.

79. In the absence of a specific moment of formal arrival, I supplement the open-ended cadential bracket with the abbreviation "(abnd.)" (see again note 77).

80. See again my discussion of bass-line motions revolving around the focal pitch ① for the *prolongational stream* and ⑤ for the *cadential stream* (Chapter 2, sec. 2.4, and Ex. 2.9).

EXAMPLE 4.46. Beethoven, Piano Trio in B-flat, Op. 11, ii, mm. 4–8 (ACF. 2.34).

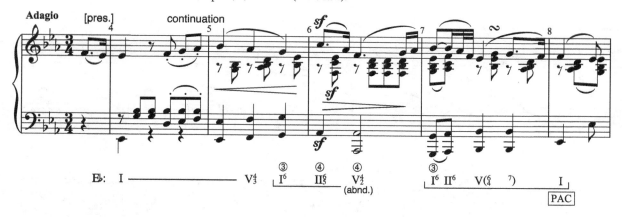

EXAMPLE 4.47. (a) Motion within the cadential stream; (b) shift from cadential stream to prolongational stream.

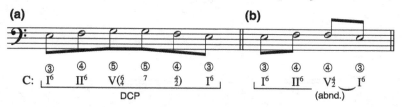

stream (Ex. 4.47a) as part of a deceptive cadential progression. The case of an abandoned progression (Ex. 4.46, m. 6, and Ex. 4.47b), by contrast, is different. The motion from ③ (I⁶) to ④ (II⁶) is initially construed as cadential, but then the bass fails to achieve ⑤, remaining fixed instead on ④. When the harmony progresses to the dominant, as V$^4_2$, the return, perforce, to I⁶ represents a shift to the *prolongational* stream and thereby abandons the cadential progression. To be sure, the differing interpretations that I give to the V$^4_2$—as cadential, when emerging from a root-position V, or as prolongational, when following upon II⁶ (or IV)—is a subtle one. I believe, however, that it helps account for the different impressions accorded to a deceptive cadential progression and an abandoned one.

Another case of this type occurs at the beginning of Example 4.45. In a very brief slow introduction, the shift from I to I⁶ at measure 5 suggests the possibility of a cadential progression in the making. And the move to IV in the next bar helps support that presumption. But then, at the beginning of the *Allegro*, the subdominant in measure 7 is followed by II⁶ and V$^4_2$, the latter replacing the expected root-position dominant and thus abandoning the ECP. Alternatively, because the V$^4_2$ is so fleeting as hardly to be heard as the primary mechanism of the abandonment, we might claim that the ECP is abandoned instead by the I⁶ at measure 8 (thus exemplifying a third type of abandonment to be discussed shortly ahead in sec. 4.3.3). This second possibility shows that analyzing different types of abandoned cadence is hardly a sure endeavor.[81]

---

81. For another case of an abandoned cadential progression via V$^4_2$, see ahead Ex. 4.79, m. 38.

### 4.3.2.2. Replaced by V$^6_5$

Example 4.48 shows how an expected cadential dominant can be replaced by its first inversion form. The second theme of a subordinate-theme group begins in measure 65 (eliding with the end of the first subordinate theme) and results in a relatively tight-knit, though nonconventional, structure, one that closes at measure 71 with a PAC. Given that this subordinate theme is rather compressed compared to the norms of this thematic function, the theme's immediate repetition, with the melody now shifted to the cello, is hardly surprising. When the repeated theme approaches its projected end (m. 77, cf., mm. 70–71) the cello melody is altered in such a way that it moves stepwise down to ⑦ to support V$^6_5$ on the downbeat of measure 77, thus abandoning the cadence at this point. The inverted dominant then becomes highly expanded and eventually resolves to the dominant seventh of IV (m. 81), a tonic substitute that functions as the initial stage of an ECP, one that closes the theme with a PAC at measure 90 (not shown).

### 4.3.3. Cadential Dominant Replaced by Nondominant Harmony

A third way of abandoning a presumed cadential progression sees the expected cadential dominant replaced by a nondominant harmony of some kind. Sometimes, a tonic (typically I⁶) stands in place of the dominant; at other times, a different harmony may come into consideration.

In Example 4.49a, a subordinate theme opens with a presentation phrase in measures 9–10 (R = ½N). At measure 11, the bass moves up to ③ to support an expanded I⁶, which suggests that a

**184** Cadential Deviations

EXAMPLE 4.48. Beethoven, Cello Sonata in A, Op. 69, i, mm. 65–83.

continuation⇒cadential phrase is in the making, an impression further reinforced by the ascent to ④ holding the pre-dominant IV. But when that harmony moves back to I⁶ to initiate a new, compact cadential progression (m. 12), we understand that the ECP has been abandoned, with its expected dominant replaced by the initial tonic of the second cadential progression. As it turns out, Mozart evades the promised PAC on the third beat of measure 12, already signaling that evasion by the passing $V_2^4$ in stage 3b (fourth eighth note of m. 12).[82] He then runs through

---

82. Alternatively, we might want to hear a deceptive cadence on the third quarter-note beat of m. 12, seeing as the melody reaches its goal on 1̂ at that point. Yet the sudden change to *forte*, along with the manifest one-more-time technique, suggests more the option of an evaded cadence.

EXAMPLE 4.49. Mozart, Piano Sonata in G, K. 283, ii, (a) mm. 9–14 (R = ½N) (*ACF* 9.4); (b) reconstruction of mm. 13–14.

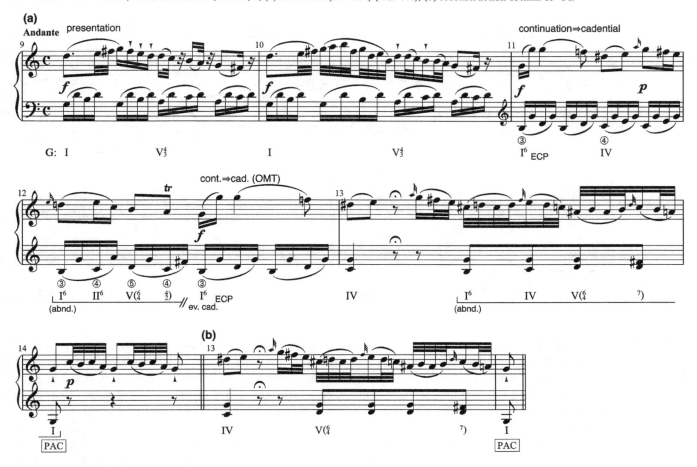

the cadential processes again as a one-more-time technique. The fermata in measure 13, beyond its more obvious expressive intent, has an interesting structural function, for it permits the listener to ponder the possibility that the ongoing ECP might be realized with the subsequent appearance of a cadential dominant (as reconstructed in Ex. 4.49b) or that the progression will be abandoned, as it was the first time. We quickly learn that the composer opts for the latter.[83]

In the earlier discussed Example 4.39, the dramatic shift to minor at the evaded cadence (m. 26) proposes the start of an ECP when I⁶ moves directly to ♭II⁶. What follows in measure 28 is definitely not a cadential dominant. The doubled monophonic texture indeed makes it difficult to say exactly what the harmonies are (and the notation obscures the situation all the more); the reading of consecutive diminished-seventh harmonies (VII⁷/V–VII⁶₅/IV) is one possible interpretation. What makes the passage cohere, of course, is the chromatically ascending bass line, which ultimately becomes diatonic to bring the standard prolongational progression IV⁶–V⁶₅–I. A fully realized ECP (mm. 32–34) then concludes this very loose subordinate theme.[84]

### 4.3.4. Prolongational versus Cadential; Harmonic Expansion

As just presented, cadential abandonment occurs in three main ways: (1) undermining the cadential dominant via inversion, (2) immediately inverting an expected cadential dominant, and (3) fully replacing that dominant with a harmony of a different function. When the deviation involves option 1, it is evident that the ongoing progression is truly cadential, because the root-position dominant has been locked into place prior to the inversion. In the case of option 2, and even more so for option 3, we

---

83. The melody in m. 13 of Ex. 4.49b does not assimilate perfectly to a harmonization by an expanded dominant, esp. in the sixth eighth note of that bar. Had Mozart taken this harmonic option, he presumably would have fashioned a more suitable melodic line.

84. It is perhaps debatable whether this final cadential progression is long enough to be considered an ECP, which, as discussed in the next chapter, is minimally four bars. Here, however, some additional factors come into play. First, the movement could perhaps be understood as notated in compound meter (i.e., R = ½N), seeing as the exposition consists of only 40 measures, thus considerably shorter than a typical first-movement sonata form notated as R = N. Second, the abandoned ECP in mm. 26–27 "protends" (as phenomenologists would say) a full four measures of cadential content, with each stage accorded a full bar. In this sense, we could understand the second ECP picking up with stage 2 and completing the abandoned ECP, to hear a combined ECP of four virtual measures.

EXAMPLE 4.50. Mozart, Piano Sonata in B-flat, K. 333, ii, (a) mm. 14–21 (*ACF* Sup. 5.3); (b) reconstruction of mm. 19–21.

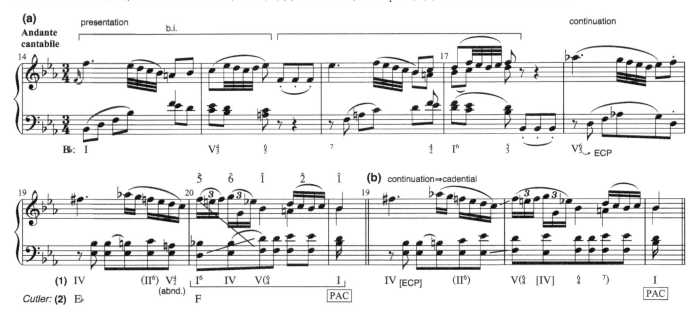

### 4.3.5. Cadential Abandonment and Harmonic Reduction

Some recent work on harmonic analysis from a Schenkerian perspective has identified passages in which what appears to be a $I^6$ on the very surface of the music is explained alternatively as an "inversion" (or more accurately, a "re-inversion") of a cadential six-four. Timothy Cutler, building on ideas of Rothstein (who himself was inspired by some comments in Schenker's writings), has identified a variety of voice-exchange situations in which he proposes that a foreground $I^6$ does not have tonic function, but rather stands for a dominant-functioning six-four residing at a higher level of harmonic motion.[85] Without speaking in these terms, Cutler offers a number of examples that involve abandoned cadential progressions, but in which his own analyses propose ECPs instead. One case is shown in Example 4.50a. This subordinate theme begins with a presentation phrase in measures 14–17 that features a statement-response repetition (I–V–V–I) of a two-measure basic idea. When the continuation phrase begins with $V^6_5/IV$, a chromatic substitute for $I^6$, and then carries on with IV in the next bar (m. 19), we strongly suspect that an ECP is in the making (along the lines discussed in the previous example), especially when the pre-dominant shifts to $II^6$, a harmony that is less likely than IV to function prolongationally as a neighbor to the prior $I^6$. Suddenly, on the very last eighth note of the bar, the $II^6$ yields to $V^4_2$, which abandons the ECP (in the same manner as discussed for Ex. 4.46). The resolution to $I^6$ on the downbeat of measure 20 initiates a compact cadential progression that realizes the expected PAC.

are not always certain that the progression in question is cadential. This is especially true when the pre-dominant is IV, since that harmony frequently functions prolongationally as a neighbor to I. Thus in Example 4.49a, the subdominant in the second half of measure 11 comes from $I^6$ and returns to that same harmony on the downbeat of the next bar. In that sense, the progression could be regarded as tonic prolongational. If we hear the passage in that way, then we cannot speak of an abandoned cadential progression.

What then, might prompt us to hear such a cadential abandonment? First, of course, is the direct shift from a prolonged root-position tonic to its first inversion, a typical marker of an impending cadential progression. Second, we are encouraged to hear the harmonies as cadential by the broader formal context, namely, the onset of a continuation phrase following a presentation. Moreover, we perceive that the harmonic rhythm does not accelerate in the manner of a standard continuation; instead, the pacing of the harmonies remains the same as that of the prior phrase. All of these factors contribute to the progression sounding cadential, only then to be abandoned. The important role that harmonic *expansion* can play in our perception of cadential function becomes evident when we observe that many cadential abandonments occur in the context of an ongoing ECP (e.g., Ex. 4.39, 4.43, 4.44, and 4.45). Since I deal with the topic of cadential expansion in the next chapter, I return to the issue of abandoned cadences there (sec. 5.4.4) and consider more cases in which the effect of abandonment relates to an initial expansion of stages 1 and 2 of the cadential progression.

According to Cutler, the voice-exchange involving the pitches F and D (shown by the lines in m. 19) permits us to hear that bar as a single harmonic entity—a dominant functioning

---

85. Timothy Cutler, "On Voice Exchanges"; Rothstein, "Transformations of Cadential Formulae." See the earlier discussion (Chapter 3, sec. 3.3.3.3, esp. note 169) of Schenker's "casting out of the root" and Rothstein's development of this idea. Since Rothstein deals largely with baroque music in his study, I return to a discussion of his ideas more fully in Chapter 6, sec. 6.1.2.

cadential six-four beginning with its "inverted" form, the I$^6$.[86] (The intervening IV is relegated to a subordinate status as a passing chord within this prolongation of the cadential six-four.) Cutler's own harmonic analysis, shown in line 2 below the score (and using root letters rather than roman numerals), assigns a single dominant function to measure 19, thus continuing the ECP initiated in the prior two bars. In its own terms, with its emphasis on the prolongational consequences of a voice exchange, nothing is objectionable with Cutler's analysis.[87]

His approach, however, raises the question of why Mozart does not just write a literal six-four on the downbeat of measure 19 to produce a single ECP in support of a continuation⇒cadential phrase, as reconstructed in Example 4.50b. One problem with this version is quickly evident in the hidden octaves arising in the outer voices on the downbeat of measure 20. Indeed, Cutler himself discusses (though not specifically in the case of this example) that the "inverted six-four" helps to eliminate this particular contrapuntal weakness. A second problem concerns the status of the V$^4_2$ at the end of measure 19 in Example 4.50a: How is that harmony to be understood within a prolongation of IV, as indicated by Cutler's root analysis (line 2)? Additionally, there is the matter of the harmonic rhythm of the theme as a whole. For Cutler's analysis proposes a pacing of harmonic change that is highly uniform: one harmony per bar (with the exception of a single dominant in mm. 2–3), a consistent rhythm that is uncharacteristic of most classical themes. Thus in this example, Mozart abandons the ECP and effects an acceleration in the harmonic rhythm by changing the harmonies on each eighth note (starting with the II$^6$ in m. 19). Given the slow tempo, we can easily hear each of these beats as containing individual harmonic entities in their own right. A final consideration involves the melodic component of the cadential material in measures 20–21. Note that by abandoning the initial ECP, Mozart is able to use one of his favorite cadential melodies, the "tenor combo" $\hat{5}/\hat{6}/\hat{1}$-$\hat{2}/\hat{1}$, set against its conventional bass line ③–④–⑤–①.[88] In short, Cutler's analysis, while convincing in its own terms, ignores lower-level harmonic, melodic, rhythmic, and cadential features that are essential to the full effect of this theme.[89]

## 4.4. Dominant Arrival

Conventional theories of cadence have not proposed any cadential deviations associated with the half cadence. An investigation of the classical repertory, however, reveals many instances where a formal section, which would normally end with an HC, concludes instead in a manner that conflicts with the requirements of this cadence type. In my writings on form and cadence, I have termed such situations a *dominant arrival*.[90]

In order to clarify the conditions that give rise to this deviation, it will be useful to establish a terminological distinction regarding the dominant as an ending harmony. Throughout this study, I have been referring to the last stage of a cadential progression as its *final* harmony. In the case of a half cadential progression, the final harmony, occurring in stage 3, is a dominant triad in root position. As we will see, some dominant arrivals modify this harmony by adding a destabilizing, dissonant seventh. But many other cases of dominant arrival involve a dominant that arises out of other harmonic progressions, but that nonetheless ends up representing the last harmony of a thematic unit. I label this noncadential harmony a *terminal* dominant.[91] In short, two general conditions can engender a dominant arrival: (1) a potential half cadential progression is undermined when its *final* dominant (in root position) is rendered unstable by the addition of a dissonant seventh; and (2) the last harmonic event of the thematic process is a *terminal* dominant, one that arises from a prolongational or sequential progression. Within the purview of this basic distinction lies a wide variety of manifestations, such that the expression "dominant arrival" ends up covering a multiplicity of compositional devices.[92]

In most cases, a terminal dominant appears to be an ending harmony because (among other possibilities) it may mark the beginning of a standing on the dominant, feature liquidation and textural reduction, or be especially elongated relative to its preceding harmonies. Indeed, many dominant arrivals, especially those involving a terminal dominant, occur with a fermata, which not only supports our hearing that harmony as an ending, but also helps to arouse expectations for the resumption of the prevailing tempo in the context of a new formal beginning.

---

86. Cutler, "On Voice Exchanges," 205, Ex. 14.

87. Indeed, he effectively buttresses his argument by appealing to a chain of motivic connections involving a set of these voice-exchange patterns (205–6).

88. See Chapter 3, sec. 3.1.2.3.

89. A similar issue obtains with Ex. 4.46. One might consider the I$^6$ on the third beat of m. 5 to be prolonged by the neighboring II$^6_5$ and V$^4_2$ harmonies until the downbeat of m. 7, thus recognizing a single ECP, whose initial bass line ③ would be embellished by ④ in m. 6. Like what happens in Ex. 4.50a, this reading is perhaps too reductive, such that it would identify a marked slowing of the harmonic rhythm in the second half of the theme (mm. 5–8). My analysis of an abandoned cadential progression thus focuses on a more nuanced hearing of the harmonies, one that is readily perceivable at the slow tempo of this passage.

90. In Chapter 9, sec. 9.7.1, Ex. 9.45, I entertain the idea of another type of HC deviation, namely, a "deceptive HC" (for a late nineteenth-century theme by Tchaikovsky). I have not yet encountered a case of this particular deviation in the classical style.

91. The distinction between a *final* and *terminal* dominant must not be confused with another pair of terms that can characterize this cadential harmony, namely, that between an *ultimate* dominant (ending a half cadential progression) and a *penultimate* one (ending an authentic cadential progression). To be sure, a final dominant is coequal with an ultimate dominant, but a terminal dominant is noncadential and differs essentially from any dominant associated with stage 3 of a half (or even authentic) cadential progression.

92. Indeed, Burstein finds that my usage of dominant arrival is too broad and proposes instead to retain the term half cadence for such situations, but qualifying them as, for example, a "half cadence on a V$^7$" or a "half cadence on a V$^6$" ("Slippery Events," 213, note 26). I return to Burstein's concept of half cadence later in sec. 4.4.4.5.

EXAMPLE 4.51. (a) Mozart, Violin Sonata in C, K. 296, ii, mm. 1–5; (b) Haydn, String Quartet in G, Op. 54, no. 1, iv, mm. 1–4; (c) Beethoven, String Quartet in B-flat, Op. 130, iv, mm. 10–14.

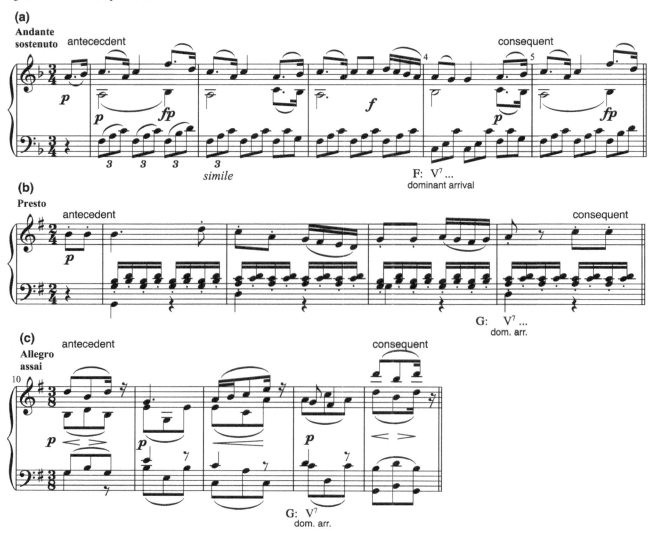

One broad category of dominant arrivals involves cases where the dominant—be it cadential and final or noncadential and terminal—seems to arrive earlier than what we otherwise hear as the "end" of the prevailing phrase-structural process. I term this situation a *premature dominant arrival* (see sec. 4.4.3).

### 4.4.1. Arrival on a Final Dominant

Compositional practice in the classical style reveals that the final harmony of a half cadential progression is overwhelming a dominant triad in root position. In a relatively small number of situations, which would otherwise be considered half cadential, a dissonant seventh is added to the final harmony of the progression. I propose that such cases be understood as a cadential deviation, a dominant arrival.[93] A selection of antecedent phrases ending with this type of dominant arrival is shown in Example 4.51. In each case, the conditions for a genuine half cadence are operative, except for the dissonant sonority of the final dominant. Given how infrequent this usage is, we are encouraged to seek reasons for why the seventh is employed. Sometimes a recomposition may reveal a problem with using a dominant triad in measure 4. But in these examples, changing the final harmony to a triad does not present any apparent difficulties.[94] For Example 4.51c, we might consider the late date of composition (1825–26) already to reflect nineteenth-century practice,[95] but this reason would not apply to any works by Haydn and Mozart. One textural feature, however, is associated with all three cases, including a number of others not

---

93. In later repertories, the use of $V^7$ becomes sufficiently normative such that I follow Schmalfeldt in sanctioning this "nineteenth-century half cadence" as a genuine cadence type (*Process of Becoming*, 202); see Chapter 8, sec. 8.1.

94. For Ex. 4.51b, in fact, later in the movement (m. 77) Haydn writes a minor-mode version of the theme that brings a dominant triad, thus creating a genuine HC.

95. The same point can perhaps be made for a similar case in Beethoven's Bagatelle in A Minor, Op. 119, no. 9, m. 4, written in 1820–22, as cited by Burstein, "Slippery Events," 215, Ex. 12d.

EXAMPLE 4.52. Beethoven, Cello Sonata in A, Op. 69, iii, mm. 19–31.

shown here: namely, each brings an uninterrupted, relatively rapid, accompanimental pattern that is sustained through all of measures 4 and 5 and even continued up to the final PAC (not shown). As a result, the grouping boundary between the antecedent and consequent phrases is somewhat obscured by this aspect of the texture. Indeed, a continuous accompaniment through the initial cadence of a periodic structure seldom arises in the classical literature.[96] With this aspect in mind, we could say that the dissonant seventh, which destabilizes the final dominant in measure 4, also contributes to blurring the boundary between the phrases. Indeed, we might even consider the opening four-measure phrase in Example 4.51b to be supported by a tonic prolongation, thus recognizing a hybrid theme (compound basic idea + consequent).

An interesting counterexample to the textural circumstance just discussed presents itself with the theme shown in Example 4.52. Here, the dominant seventh in measure 22 (the fourth bar of the theme) occurs with an abrupt stop in the accompanimental pattern, thus delimiting the boundary of the contrasting idea in a most decisive manner; but so too does measure 20, which articulates the end of the basic idea in the same way. From the beginning of the consequent on, however, this drum bass accompaniment is entirely continuous until the PAC at measure 26. When the theme is then repeated (so that the piano can sound the melody), the accompaniment, now an Alberti bass, is continuous throughout; moreover, the cello sustains a tonic pedal right through what was originally a dominant arrival (cf. m. 30 to m. 22). Both the textural continuity and the tonic pedal obscure the fourth bar of the repeated theme as an arrival moment thus significantly blurring the grouping boundaries. As the movement progresses, every return of the basic and contrasting ideas is clothed in a continuous accompaniment of some kind. Only the very first statements in measures 19–22 project a marked caesura, and in a manner that provides a striking textural gap that is always filled in by later appearances of the ideas.[97]

Dominant arrivals that feature a final, root-position seventh are frequently associated with a descending half step in the bass, ♭⑥–⑤. The fourth scale degree, located in some upper voice of the pre-dominant (typically IV⁶ or II$^4_3$), can then be held over as a common tone to provide the dissonant seventh in the final dominant. Consider Example 4.53, which arises toward the end of a development section. A PAC at measure 82 confirms the submediant region as a development key (a common procedure in early Haydn). Following a brief closing section, a retransition at measure 85, which quickly modulates back to the home key of C major, ends with a dominant arrival in the next bar, followed by a standing on the dominant.[98] Note that the modulation is achieved by a chromatically descending bass line ⑥–♭⑥–⑤ and that the

---

96. A quick look at the periods found in chapter 3 of *ACF* (including the supplementary examples on the website) will confirm this observation.

97. If the caesuras quickly disappear from the main theme, they nevertheless return in the first subordinate theme to mark the end of the repeated compound basic ideas (mm. 49 and 53, not shown), as well as the deceptive cadential phrase that follows at m. 57. In other words, Beethoven is not really finished with the caesura "motive" when he abandons it in the main theme and all subsequent appearances of main-theme material.

98. The standing on the dominant could be seen to begin already in m. 86, but since that bar is still sounding rhythmic motives from the closing section, I have indicated the standing on the dominant to begin with the textural change in the middle of m. 87.

EXAMPLE 4.53. Haydn, Piano Trio in C, H. 21, i, mm. 81–88 (*ACF* 13.23).

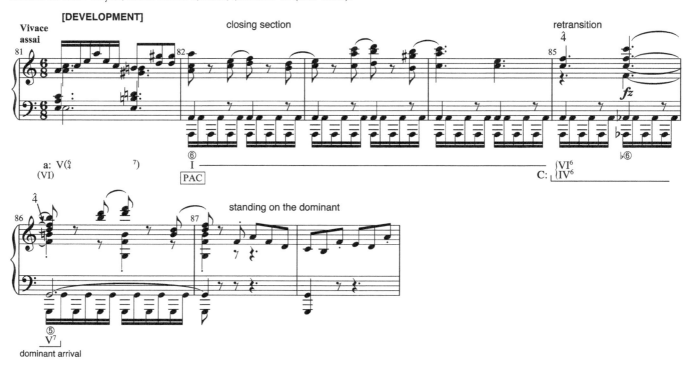

EXAMPLE 4.54. Beethoven, Piano Sonata in C Minor, Op. 10, no. 1, ii, mm. 17–23 (*ACF* 11.27).

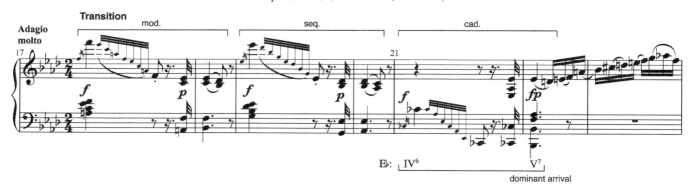

note F, as $\hat{4}$, is retained as a common tone (in an inner voice) to create the dominant seventh. A similar approach to a dominant arrival occurs in Example 4.54, which shows a complete, and very short, expositional transition. The section begins directly with a two-measure model that is repeated sequentially. When the idea starts up again in measure 21, now led by the left hand, we might wonder whether another sequence will sound. Instead, Beethoven alters the harmony to yield a half cadential progression ending with a final dominant seventh. Here, the sequence is not maintained, but we will see later examples where a premature dominant arrival emerges directly out of sequential repetitions.

Sometimes the seventh of a dominant arrival, rather than being somewhat buried in an inner voice (as in the last two examples), is made more prominent by appearing in the melody, as seen in Example 4.55. Toward the end of a development section, and within an elaboration of C-sharp minor (HK: VI), the music temporarily tonicizes A major (C-sharp: VI), which then becomes a pre-dominant German sixth (m. 133) to effect a dominant arrival in C-sharp at measure 137. Not only is the bass of the dominant approached from above by a half step (A–G♯), but the melody itself, starting in measure 131, descends by half-step motion A–G♯–F𝄪–F♯ (see the scale degree analysis in the score). Indeed, we might see the melodic arrival on the dissonant seventh F♯ emerge from a broader motivic process, whereby the A–G♯–F♯–E idea (bracketed in mm. 128 and 130) undergoes substantial rhythmic augmentation beginning in measure 131, finding its "motivic goal" with the resolving E ($\hat{3}$) on the downbeat of measure 138.

If the motivic interpretation just offered is a viable one, then it raises an issue that relates back to the fundamental conundrum of the half cadence, namely, how it is that an essentially unstable harmony, the dominant, can acquire the condition of being a *formal* goal, when, in principle, that harmony should resolve to tonic as a *harmonic* goal. As discussed in the previous chapter

EXAMPLE 4.55. Haydn, String Quartet in E, Op. 17, no. 1, iv, mm. 127–38.

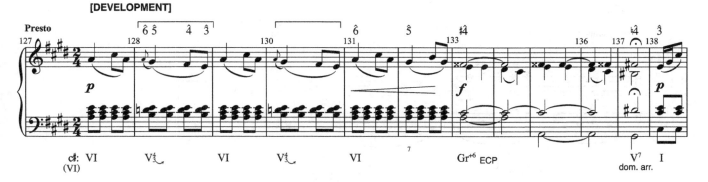

(sec. 3.3.1), the major way the dominant gains sufficient solidity to project an ending is for it to appear in its most stable form, as a consonant triad in root position. The half cadence paradox is obviously exacerbated by adding a dissonant seventh, especially if placed in the most salient voice, the soprano—just the situation that we confront in Example 4.55, m. 137. The problem facing the composer (and performer) becomes one of convincing the listener that the V⁷ functions as a formal arrival, even when powerful forces of pitch organization lead us to hear that dominant as pointing toward a different point of arrival, namely, the resolving tonic in the following bar.

Although the parameters of harmony, melody, and dissonance counteract our hearing the dominant seventh at measure 137 as a formal goal, other parameters may come to its aid. And here we find an explanation for why the harmony in that bar is given a *fermata*, a device that not only accords durational emphasis to the event, but actually pulls it out of the ongoing stream of pulses that underly the meter and tempo of the passage. If the fermata were not employed, we might not hear measure 137 as a goal at all and perceive instead an authentic cadence on the downbeat of the next bar.⁹⁹ The fermata thus functions as an external intervention to enforce our hearing the dominant arrival as a genuine end. As we will see, many of these deviations either employ an actual fermata or the duration of their final event is notated sufficiently long in order to give the effect of a fermata.

In Example 4.56a, from a sonata-form coda, we find a passage that features descending parallel six-three chords leading to a dominant arrival (m. 195), whose dissonant seventh appears in the upper voice, also elongated by a fermata. Once again, the bass of the dominant is approached by a chromatic descent ⑥–♭⑥–⑤, while the seventh (♯4̂) in the upper voice arises when

the preceding ♯4̂ bypasses its normal resolution to 5̂, which would have created a regular HC.

To understand Haydn's writing a dominant arrival instead of a cadence, it is instructive to compare this passage to an earlier version (see Ex. 4.56b, mm. 22–24), which occurs at the end of the exposition's transition (in the subordinate key of B-flat). The continuation phrase of the transition reaches its goal with a regular HC at measure 20; there follows a standing on the dominant, which I hear as supported entirely by the F in the bass of measure 20 to the dominant seventh of measure 24.¹⁰⁰ Here, the final V⁷ does not function as a dominant arrival, because an earlier HC has already formally closed the transition; instead, the melodic 4̂ of measure 24 appears as a "passing seventh" of the type that is frequently found following the dominant triad of an HC. In the recapitulation, Haydn eliminates this passage for various reasons, and so it is not surprising that he brings it back toward the start of the coda (Ex. 4.56a). This time the music is not part of a standing on the dominant, but rather occurs as the conclusion of a new continuational phrase emerging from the closing section of the recapitulation.¹⁰¹ Haydn's use of a dominant seventh, rather than a triad (to make an HC), is obviously explained by his wanting to match what happened earlier at the literal end of the exposition's transition (Ex. 4.56b, m. 24, with fermata). In the coda, in fact, Haydn plays a fun trick with this dissonant seventh A♭ (4̂) and its expected resolution to G (3̂). In the transition of the exposition (in the subordinate key), the seventh, E♭, receives its resolution to D at the start of the subordinate theme, though an octave lower than expected. And in typical Haydnesque fashion, the opening idea of the subordinate theme references that of the main theme, as shown in the recapitulation's version in Ex. 4.56c, measures 137–38. Indeed, the basic idea here is preceded by a prominent dominant seventh, whose A♭ resolves to G (now, in the same register). By the time we get to the coda (Ex. 4.56a) and Haydn brings back the material from the *close* of the transition, we highly anticipate the music of measure 196 to bring back some variant of the main theme's basic idea (thus directly resolving the seventh),

---

99. A metrical problem would actually arise with the situation just described, for given the clear hypermeter projected in the passage (under the "odd-bar-strong" interpretation), the direct move (with no fermata) to tonic at m. 138 would be metrically weak and thus seem to appear one bar too early. To create a more effective PAC, the dominant should last two full bars. For this reason, the performer might consider holding the fermata even longer to counteract the potential effect of an authentic cadence.

100. In other words, the left hand of this postcadential passage sounds as an inner voice.

101. See my discussion of this passage in *ACF*, Ex. 15.13.

EXAMPLE 4.56. Haydn, Piano Sonata in E-flat, H. 49, i, (a) mm. 192–96 (*ACF* 15.13); (b) mm. 19–26 (*ACF* 11.3); (c) mm. 131–33.

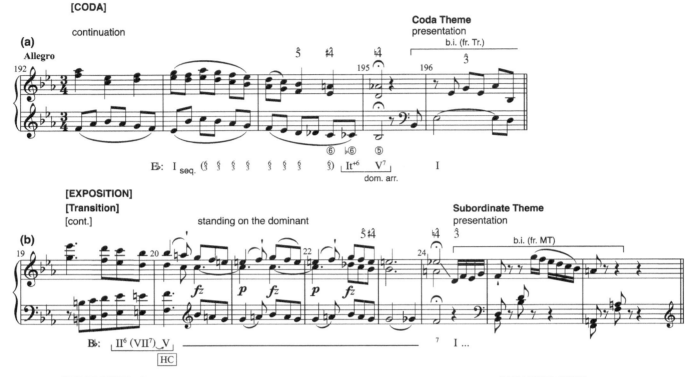

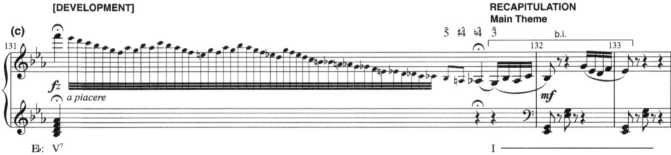

especially since a coda typically references main-theme material.[102] Instead, he surprises us by using motives found at the *beginning* of the transition, thus foiling our expectations for a final return of the main theme. In fact, and most exceptionally, main-theme ideas never once appear in the coda.[103] In short, the use of a dominant arrival early in that section is part of a broader motivic narrative that spans the entire piece.

### 4.4.2. Arrival on a Terminal Dominant

As defined earlier, a dominant arrival using a terminal dominant does not ensue from a half cadential progression, yet nonetheless serves as the last harmonic event of the thematic unit. A terminal dominant typically ends a contrasting middle, a transition, a developmental core, an interior theme, or a retransition.[104] The great majority of these cases are phrase-structurally "premature," an idea to be discussed shortly. One case that is not premature is shown in Example 4.57. At first

---

102. See *CF*, 186, and *ACF*, 538.

103. To be sure, the dissonant A♭ receives a proper resolution with the G of m. 196, but this note is not a salient pitch in its own right, but rather part of an accompanimental figuration to the main motive of the transition, now transferred to the bass voice.

104. It is possible for a terminal dominant to close an *initiating* phrase of a theme, but genuine cases are rare in the classical literature. The phrase in question has to be a compound basic idea, for an antecedent must end with an HC, or as seen above in Ex. 4.51 and 4.52, an antecedent-like unit ending with a final dominant. (A presentation, with its repeated basic idea, brings no formal ending.) Most compound basic ideas end with tonic harmony. A small number see dominant arise in bar three of the phrase and continue on to the fourth bar, a situation that is not comparable to a cadential ending of any kind; very few actually close with a noncadential dominant. One case, from the previous chapter (Ex. 3.99), has already been discussed. As seen in the analysis, I simply label this ending dominant as noncadential, contrary to Burstein's "HC on V$^6_5$" ("Analytic Fictions," 101, Ex. 5c). Could this better be called a terminal dominant arrival? Seeing as the movement is only four bars long at this point, it is perhaps overly fussy to regard this moment as some kind of cadential deviation; rather, the dominant seems to arise more simply from an incomplete tonic prolongational progression, one that is completed with the resolution to tonic in m. 5.

EXAMPLE 4.57. Beethoven, Piano Sonata in G Minor, Op. 49, no. 1, ii, mm. 7–13 (ACF 7.12).

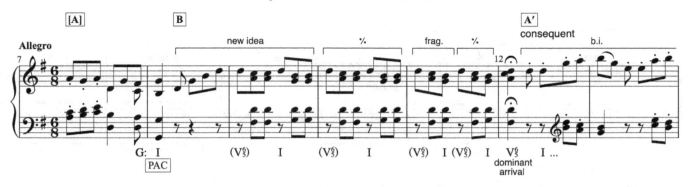

EXAMPLE 4.58. Haydn, String Quartet in G Minor, Op. 20, no. 3, iv, mm. 54–59.

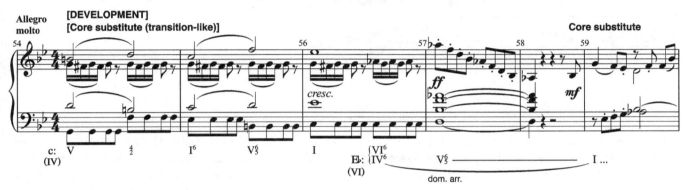

glance, this seemingly simple contrasting middle (B section of a small ternary) might seem to be built exclusively as a standing on the dominant, in which case we could not speak of any "arrival" on the $V^6_5$ at measure 12, due to the lack of any harmonic progression into this moment. A closer look, however, suggests that the actual harmony being prolonged throughout the passage is a root-position tonic, because the $V^6_5$ on the downbeat of each bar, though metrically emphasized, still sounds subordinate to its resolving tonic. As a result, the terminal dominant in measure 12 is part of this ongoing prolongation, and we can understand that its accompanying fermata is almost required to give the effect of an ending. We should note, of course, that it would have been very simple and entirely normal for Beethoven to have concluded the section with a regular HC, namely, by writing a root-position dominant triad on the downbeat of measure 12. That he does not do so attests to the perceptual differences between these types of ending and his clearly preferring one type over the other in this particular case.

Example 4.58 offers another case of a terminal dominant arrival, one that arises within a more elaborate harmonic-tonal context than the previous example. In the course of a development section, a transition-like core substitute,[105] one largely focused around C minor (HK: IV) and its local tonic (mm. 54–56), suddenly swerves in the middle measure 56 to E-flat (HK: VI), closing abruptly in the next bar with a terminal dominant arrival

on $V^6_5$ of that new region. Note that this harmony cannot be understood as cadential, but rather as part of a prolongational progression $IV^6$–$V^6_5$–I, which is completed with the tonic of measure 59. Though the terminal dominant is not given a fermata, as is so often the case with such arrivals, the harmony is elongated (compared to the previous ones) and followed by a prominent caesura in measure 58. This rhythmic rupture reinforces the sense of this harmony as an ending, an impression quickly confirmed when a new core substitute begins at measure 59.

### 4.4.3. Premature Dominant Arrival

In many dominant arrivals, especially those using a terminal dominant, the moment of arrival does not coordinate with what we hear to be the "end" of various melodic or grouping processes within the ongoing thematic unit. In these cases, the music gives the impression of getting stuck on the dominant "too early." In such situations, we can speak of a *premature dominant arrival* (PDA).[106] To be sure, it is not easy to define just what constitutes a dominant arrival as preceding its more natural ending point, since so many factors come into play; moreover, some cases are ambiguous as to whether a given dominant arrival is premature or is effectively congruent with other forces of closure (such as melody, grouping, and texture). It is to be hoped that the following examples will illuminate

---

105. See *CF*, 155–57, and *ACF*, 452–57.

106. I hesitate to introduce another initialism into the discussion, yet it will prove useful to avoid overly encumbering the prose.

EXAMPLE 4.59. Mozart, Piano Sonata in F, K. 332, i, mm. 31–40 (*ACF* 11.23).

the kinds of musical features that can elicit the sense of a PDA. For the purposes of this discussion, I will group the examples according to whether their ending dominant is final or terminal.

### 4.4.3.1. PDA on a Final Dominant

If the final dominant of a half cadential progression is a consonant triad, then the morphological conditions for an HC are clearly present. And when that V occurs, it normally marks the end of a thematic process in such a manner as to project a genuine cadence. Now and then, however, the final dominant triad seems to arise earlier within the prevailing thematic processes, so that it may seem appropriate to invoke the idea of a PDA. Consider Ex. 3.163a from the previous chapter. In the context of a sixteen-measure compound period, the compound antecedent appears to close with an HC at measure 7, whose dominant is prolonged into the following bar (via a neighboring I). The compound consequent then concludes with a matching PAC at measure 16 (Ex. 3.163b). To be sure, we can simply identify measure 7 as an HC and leave it at that. Such a labeling, however, would not reflect our impression, as discussed in Chapter 3, that this moment of closure seems premature, such that Beethoven needs to prolong the harmony by an extra bar in order to restore the standard eight-measure length of the antecedent. Qualifying this moment as a PDA seems like an appropriate option. Just why the composer does not create a standard HC at measure 8 is not at all clear; indeed, I cannot find anything in the rest of the movement that might justify or explain the oddity of this cadential situation.

At times, the moment of half cadential closure can acquire a certain premature quality because of its placement within a broader process of phrase-structural fragmentation. In Example 4.59, an ongoing expositional transition brings a half cadential progression $Gr^{+6}$–V in measures 35–37. The HC thus created then elides with a four-measure standing on the dominant. (The subordinate theme follows directly thereafter.) If we consider the overall grouping structure of the transition—compound presentation (2 × 4, not shown)[107] + continuation (3 × 2) + standing on the dominant (4 × 1)—we see that this cadence arises within an extensive fragmentation technique, namely at the border between the two-measure groups of the continuation and the one-measure groups of the standing on the dominant. In most cases of the latter, the grouping structure broadens out following the cadence so that this postcadential area can bring its own fragmentation process. Here, however, the effect is of a cadence that seems to arise *prior* to the end of the grouping processes, and so the idea of this formal articulation as a PDA definitely presents itself for consideration.

In the two previous examples, a degree of ambiguity of cadential category—HC versus PDA—clearly comes into play. Certainly unambiguous is the dominant articulation in Example 4.60. Within a polyphonic passage ending the transition of the exposition, a half cadential progression I–$VII^6$/V–V in measure 33 confirms the modulation to the subordinate key of E major (HK: V). But do we want to recognize a genuine HC in the middle of this bar? The ongoing polyphony hardly makes this moment sound like the end of anything. That point seems more to be reached on the downbeat of measure 36, after which a standing on the dominant made up of new material prepares for the entrance of the subordinate theme at measure 40. It is thus preferable in this case to speak of a PDA in measure 33, even though the final dominant is a consonant triad and thus could, if properly placed within the transition, be heard as marking a true HC.

---

107. Read "2 × 4" as "a twofold statement of a 4-m. group."

EXAMPLE 4.60. Mozart, String Quartet in A, K. 464, iv, mm. 29–41 (*ACF* 11.16).

In the cases of PDA that we have been considering thus far, the final dominant takes the form of a consonant triad, so that the potential for a genuine HC must be taken into account. In Example 4.61, a final dominant appears at measure 35 already as a dissonant seventh, so the question becomes, is it a regular dominant arrival or a premature one? Here, what seems to be the beginning of the transition starts with a four-measure compound basic idea (mm. 22–25), which is then repeated twice (mm. 26–29, 30–33). At first, we may believe that the underlying harmonic progression supporting the original compound basic idea and its first repetition is prolongational, because this time span (mm. 22–29) begins and ends with tonic harmony. A more detailed look, however, one that also takes into consideration the second repetition (mm. 30–33), reveals a more pervasive ascending-step, *sequential* progression at the harmonic basis of the passage.[108] The last link of this harmonic sequence begins with the IV⁶ of measure 34. Were the sequence to continue, it would lead to III⁶ in the next bar, an unlikely harmonic goal for the overall progression. So instead, Mozart breaks the sequence and has the IV⁶ pivot to become a cadential pre-dominant, resolving to V⁷ at measure 35. Several repetitions of this progression ensue, after which the dominant seventh (m. 40) sounds alone up to the fermata at measure 43. Clearly, a final cadential dominant emerges as the goal harmony of this entire thematic process. But within the grouping structure, this dominant first arises in the middle of a fragmentation process and continues to be prolonged while the motives are eventually liquidated. In other words, the dominant arrival occurs not at the end, but rather in the middle of the broader thematic processes at play and can thus rightly be heard as a PDA.[109]

### 4.4.3.2. PDA on a Terminal Dominant

The preceding example showed a PDA based on a half cadential progression, whose initial pre-dominant (IV⁶) functions as a linking harmony with the preceding sequential progression. In other cases, the dominant itself can represent the last element of the sequence. As such, the harmony has no cadential status and the PDA thus engages a terminal dominant (see Ex. 4.62). Within the course of a lengthy transition, a continuation phrase

---

108. Complicating the harmonic analysis is Mozart's very odd use of a six-four sonority both to begin each primary harmony supporting the model and its repetitions (downbeats of mm. 22, 26, 30, and 34). The norms of voice leading, however, suggest that we choose the first-inversion form of the primary harmonies of the sequence, appearing on the final eighth note of the bar, as the essential representatives, thus yielding an alternation of six-three sonorities descending by a step and ascending by a third, the overall result being an ascending stepwise sequence. A further complication arises with the second repetition at m. 30. Here, the next harmony of the sequence should be III⁶₄. But Mozart lowers the fifth of that harmony by a half step (C♮ instead of C♯), the effect of which is to make the harmony sound like VII⁶/IV, which then resolves (deceptively) to II⁶ (m. 31).

109. When, immediately following the fermata in m. 43, the dominant resolves to tonic of the home key in the next bar, we may think that the second part of a two-part transition were getting underway. But Mozart eventually brings a home-key PAC (m. 59, not shown) to close a most unconventional ternary theme, one that replaces its A′ section with new material. As a result, we have to reinterpret the presumed opening of the transition (m. 22) as the start of a contrasting middle. A final oddity concerns the A section, which seems not to have a genuine cadential close: the final V–I progression (mm. 20–21) actually supports a codetta in the absence of any obvious prior PAC. A most unusual main theme, indeed.

EXAMPLE 4.61. Mozart, String Quartet in D, K. 499, iv, mm. 20–45.

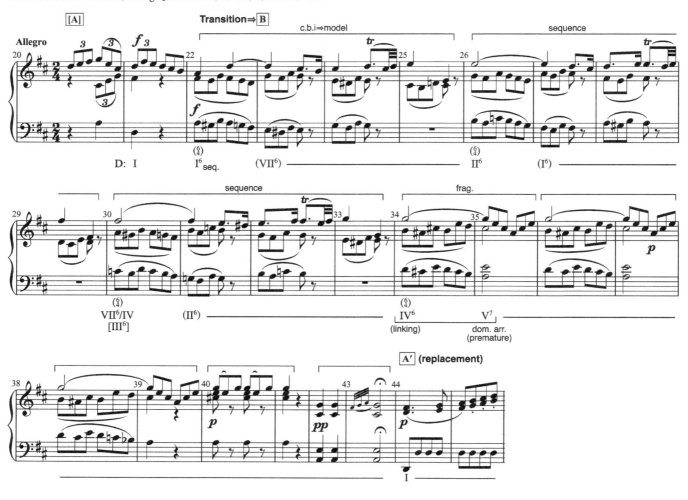

EXAMPLE 4.62. Beethoven, Symphony No. 4 in B-flat, Op. 60, i, mm. 85–99 (*ACF* 11.14).

## 4.4. DOMINANT ARRIVAL

EXAMPLE 4.63. Beethoven, String Quartet in F, Op. 18, no. 1, i, mm. 272–303 (*ACF* 15.1).

at measure 89 begins with model-sequence technique. As the harmonic analysis shows, the underlying root motion consists of a descending-fifth sequential progression. The sequence ends on a root-position dominant at measure 92, which is prolonged through the rest of the transition. Although the last harmonic move, VII$^4_3$/V–V, resembles stages 2 and 3 of a half cadential progression, the broader context for these harmonies is clearly sequential, not cadential, and so the dominant emerges as terminal. The ongoing melodic activity, however, does not conclude with the dominant arrival at measure 92, but rather continues on to measure 95, after which new ideas initiate a standing on the dominant. The terminal dominant thus arises prematurely within the prevailing melodic, rhythmic, and textural processes, which only find their end three bars later.

Sometimes a terminal dominant appears so prematurely that it conveys little sense of being an arrival, until we eventually realize that the music has been stuck on this dominant for quite some time. In Example 4.63, a sonata-form coda "starts" at measure 274 with a

EXAMPLE 4.64. Haydn, String Quartet in C, Op. 20, no. 2, iii, mm. 69–80 (*ACF* 18.13).

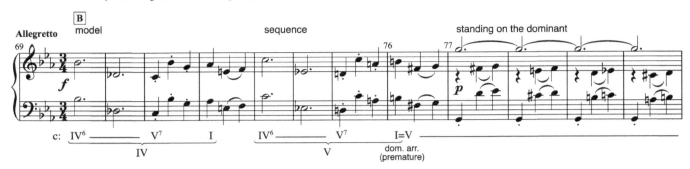

passage of doubled monophony:[110] an ascending scale, whose final note is sustained by a fermata, is then sequenced down a third (mm. 278–81). The passage seems highly introductory,[111] and we feel that the coda more rightly "begins," as a coda theme proper, with the new four-measure phrase at measure 282, which re-engages rhythmic momentum and brings back a salient main-theme motive. This new phrase, which is supported harmonically by $V^7/V$, is itself sequenced down a fifth at measure 286.[112] The formal situation thus reminds us of a developmental core, though the music does not stray from the home key, as befits a coda. This idea of a core is further reinforced when the music fragments into two-measure units (mm. 290–91, 292–93). Note, however, that the harmony does not change in the course of this fragmentation, but has effectively been "stuck" on the home-key dominant seventh from the prior four-measure sequence. When the dominant finally resolves deceptively at measure 294, a new continuational passage eventually leads to an ECP, which closes the coda theme with a PAC at measure 302. In retrospect, we understand that the extended dominant from measures 286–93 represents a situation that is analogous to an *internal* HC and standing on the dominant, which we find frequently within a subordinate theme, but which can occur in a coda theme as well. If we try to identify a moment of HC, however, we realize that one does not exist and that the extended dominant first "arrives," quite prematurely, at measure 286, as the last link of a sequence.[113]

As just discussed in the present example, the moment of dominant arrival can often be hidden from the listener. The composer can even more overtly mislead us by bringing a rhetorical "moment of arrival" that in fact continues to sound the same harmony from the end of a prior sequence. In Example 4.64, the second half of a trio begins with a four-measure model that is immediately sequenced up a step. At measure 77, the sudden change of dynamics (from *forte* to *piano*) and texture (from doubled monophony to what best might be called "accompaniment 'without' melody") suggest a standing on the dominant to conclude this truncated trio.[114] The powerful forces that articulate a grouping change at measure 77 can give the impression that a dominant arrival occurs at this point. But a closer look reveals that this dominant already appears in the prior bar as the last harmony of the sequence (m. 76).[115]

Until now, the examples of PDA that we have been considering find the terminal dominant in root position, which may deceive the listener into confusing this moment with a genuine HC. Often, however, such arrivals bring *inverted* dominants, usually $V^6_5$, which should not give any impression of a half cadential articulation.[116] Similar to what we have already seen, a PDA can arise immediately following a sequential progression or as the last link of such a progression.[117] Other harmonic contexts may also be involved. Sometimes the terminal dominant results from a prolongational progression (Ex. 4.65). Following the close of the exposition in B-flat (HK: V) with a series of codettas based on main-theme material, measure 51 starts off in the manner of another codetta. But as signaled by the modal shift to B-flat minor, the music quickly leads off toward F minor (HK: II), with the prominent appearance of $V^6_5$ (downbeats of mm. 52–53), approached prolongationally from a neighboring $IV^6_4$. A third statement of this idea takes the bass down a third, so that the last harmony of the passage (m. 54) is $V^7$, coming from $IV^6$. The caesura in this bar, extended by the fermata, seems to project this dominant as a point of structural arrival, and what follows brings a transition-like core substitute in

---

110. I define a coda as "starting" where the music of the recapitulation no longer corresponds with the exposition. This moment often occurs prior to a more intrinsic sense of "beginning" the coda; see *CF*, 181, and *ACF*, 526–27.

111. Indeed it resembles a *transitional introduction* that is sometimes found at the start of a developmental pre-core (*CF*, 147, and *ACF*, 459).

112. The descending-fifths sequential *progression* actually begins earlier with $V^7/II$ at m. 278.

113. Indeed, the internal dominant arrival is so premature that I myself was deceived when discussing this passage in *ACF*, 521–23 (Ex. 15.1); there, I incorrectly identified the premature dominant as arriving first at m. 290, failing to note that the harmony had already arrived four bars earlier at the start of the sequence.

---

114. On a truncated trio, see *CF*, 229, and *ACF*, 629–30.

115. And I was fooled yet again when in *CF*, 229, Ex. 15.13, and in *ACF*, 629–30, Ex. 18.13, I mistakenly identified a PDA at m. 77, rather than at the prior bar.

116. A first inversion dominant is probably preferred because it arouses a stronger sense of resolution to a root-position tonic (to begin the next formal unit) than the other inversions, though, as we will see, $V^4_3$ can also come into play.

117. See, respectively, *ACF*, Ex. 17.19, m. 144, PDA on $V^6_5$, and *ACF*, Ex. 18.20, m. 30, PDA on $V^4_3$.

EXAMPLE 4.65. Mozart, Clarinet Trio in E-flat, K. 498, i, mm. 49–56.

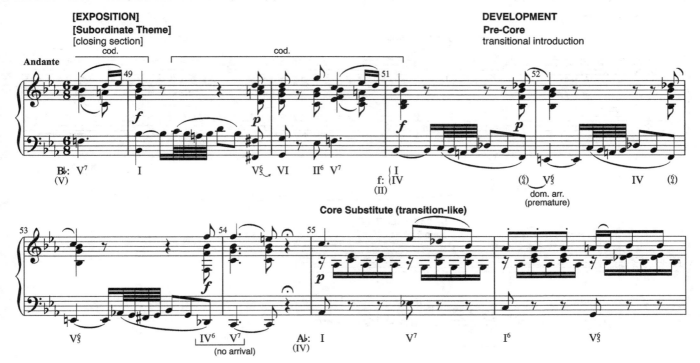

A-flat (HK: IV).[118] Given the stability of the root-position dominant seventh in measure 54, accompanied by a *forte* dynamic and a fermata, it is not surprising that some listeners would hear a final dominant arrival (arising out of the half cadential progression IV$^6$–V$^7$). Indeed, Burstein regards this passage as ending with a "half cadence on V$^7$."[119] But to be more precise about what is happening, we must take into account the inverted dominant sevenths in the preceding bars and recognize that a terminal dominant has prematurely arrived at measure 52 via an incomplete prolongational progression, whose final tonic is only implied (i.e., IV$^6_4$–V$^6_5$ [–I]). The inverted dominant is itself prolonged through measure 54 even when the harmony changes to root position.[120]

One particular type of PDA, used frequently by Mozart, occurs when a developmental core concludes by confirming the submediant region with an HC or dominant arrival, and a simple chromatic lowering of the submediant's leading tone effects a short retransition to the home-key dominant, usually in second inversion (Ex. 4.66).[121] The core closes in measure 123 with an HC confirming the development key of D minor (HK: VI). The leading tone of the dominant (C♯) is naturalized in measure 127 to render a diatonic III of the home key, F major. A stepwise descent in the bass at measure 129 brings V$^4_3$, which is then inverted to a root-position dominant seventh (m. 131) to prepare the way for the recapitulation at measure 133. In that the terminal dominant appears prior to the retransition's "end," which seems to be signaled by the V$^7$ in measures 131–32, we can speak of a PDA on an inverted dominant.[122] (The annotation of a "hyperdominant" prolongation connecting measures 123 and 129 will be discussed in the next section.)

A more complicated chromatic scenario arises when a diminished-seventh sonority is transformed enharmonically to produce a PDA (Ex. 4.67). The second, and final, core of the development section features a stepwise-ascending model-sequence passage (the first part of which is not shown). The final link (mm. 121–22) reaches the dominant of C minor (HK: VI), first in the form of a triad (embellished by six-four suspensions), and then as a diminished-seventh substitute, VII$^4_3$. When the low B♮ in the middle of measure 123 slides chromatically down to B♭ in measure 125, a V$^7$ in the home-key (E-flat major) marks the last harmonic event of the development. Although it is tempting to identify this dominant as the onset of a PDA, we can see that the first appearance of this harmonic function reaches back to the diminished-seventh sonority, E-flat: VII$^6_5$ (m. 122), a harmony that arises through an enharmonic reinterpretation to effect the modulation back to the home key. Thus the diminished seventh emerges (quite retrospectively) as the PDA of the development, and the entire passage from measure 122 forward functions as a

---

118. With this interpretation, we can go back and see a pre-core (mm. 51–54) built as a transitional introduction; *CF*, 147, and *ACF*, 459–60.

119. Burstein, "Analytic Fictions," 102, Ex. 5f.

120. Burstein analyzes a prolonged *pre-dominant* (F: IV) through mm. 51–53, finding the dominant to arrive only at m. 54 ("Analytic Fictions," 102, Ex. 5f). He thus regards the V$^6_5$ harmonies in mm. 52–53 as structurally subordinate, in contrast to the reading that I propose.

121. David Beach, "A Recurring Pattern in Mozart's Music."

---

122. A number of variants to this basic pattern can also be found, such as the use of V$^6_5$ to replace the V$^7$ (see *ACF*, Ex. 13.21. m. 60), the omission of the III harmony (*ACF*, Ex. 13.12, mm. 86–87), or the chromatic alteration of the V$^4_3$ into VII$^6_5$ (*ACF*, Ex. 13.20, m. 110).

EXAMPLE 4.66. Mozart, Piano Sonata in F, K. 332, i, mm. 121–34.

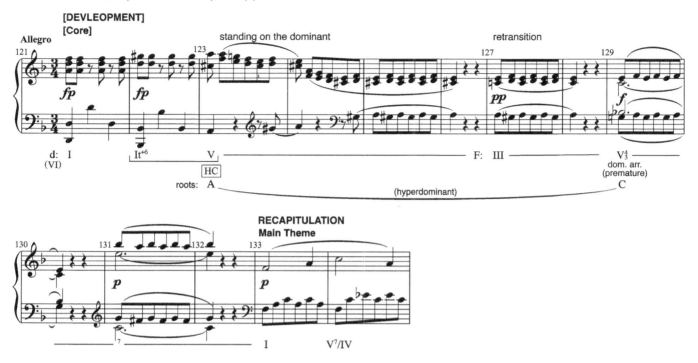

EXAMPLE 4.67. Haydn, Piano Sonata in E-flat, H. 49, i, mm. 119–27.

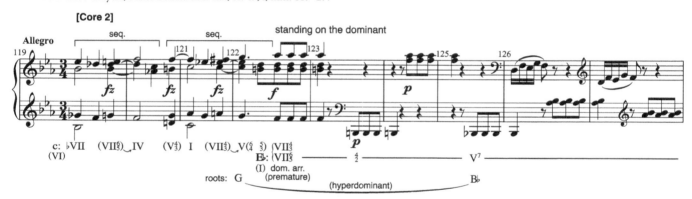

standing on the dominant (whose final, cadenza-like flourish can be seen back in Ex. 4.56c).

A similar, but even more complex, set of enharmonic transformations is found in Example 4.68, which appears toward the end of a development section of a sonata-rondo form. A core, beginning in B-flat major earlier at measure 35 (not shown), features a descending-third model-sequence pattern, whose final link on E♭ (beginning of the excerpt) gets stuck in measures 41–43. In the actual context of the core, this passage functions to prolong E♭ as a local tonic supporting a continuation that follows the sequential activity. At measure 44, a diminished-seventh harmony, G–B♭–D♭–F♭ (notated with E♮) emerges that could be understood to have E♭ as its implied root (that is, F♭ replacing the root E♭). With this interpretation, the diminished seventh functions as a dominant of A-flat (IV of E-flat), further suggesting, in retrospect, that the prolonged E♭ harmony of measures 41–43 could also be understood as projecting the same dominant, in the sense of a PDA followed by a standing on the dominant. Problematic with this reading, however, is that A♭ is the ♭V region of the home key (D major), a scale degree not normally available for tonicization. So it is not surprising—and Beethoven gives away the game with his notation of E♮ in the bass of measure 44—that the diminished seventh is better reinterpreted as the dominant of F (HK: ♭III), the region in which the main theme's antecedent returns at measure 46 as a false recapitulation.[123] In this reading, the real PDA of the

---

123. Since the diminished-seventh sonority no longer sounds acoustically in m. 45, with only a diminished triad in "root" position literally occurring there, it would not be unreasonable to analyze the harmony as F: $V^6_5$, with an implied C that resolves the D♭. Nonetheless, the D♭ is made quite salient by being doubled in the right hand of m. 44, so it is just as possible to hear that note continuing on to the next bar. Indeed, if

EXAMPLE 4.68. Beethoven, Piano Sonata in D, Op. 10, no. 3, iv, mm. 39–57.

core arises at measure 44 as a reinterpreted diminished seventh, A♭ (♭V): VII$^4_2$ ⇒ F (♭III): VII$^7$.

The false recapitulation that now follows does not get very far, for its opening antecedent phrase is not completed, but rather is prematurely cut off by another diminished-seventh sonority on the last beat of measure 48.[124] As a result, we could say that this harmony also pivots when F: VII$^7$ becomes d: VII$^6_5$.[125] And

---

we think that D♭ is still active in our imagination in m. 45, then we could see it resolving upward (as C♯) to D♯ in m. 46 (see the dashed curved line). An intriguing melodic relationship would thus be initiated, as discussed ahead in note 125.

---

124. It is not entirely clear if B♭5 arising on the second beat of that bar is heard as part of the harmony of the fourth beat, though the low B♭s at the upbeat to m. 50 could also be heard as belonging to this harmony. So my analysis suggests that the final sonority of m. 48 is a diminished seventh, not a diminished triad, which in any case would not change the basic harmonic analysis.

125. Note that the melodic configuration D to C♯ in m. 48 is critical in effecting the enharmonic reinterpretation. The special emphasis given to

when V⁷ of D minor (the home-key minor) is then prolonged throughout measures 50–55, we can recognize that the false recapitulation (becoming a retransition) concludes at the end of measure 48 with a PDA and standing on the dominant, a harmony that, like the previous one at measure 44, arises out of an enharmonic reinterpretation.[126] Indeed all three dominants in this entire excerpt—E♭ (V/A-flat), C (V/F), and A (V/d)—enharmonically share the same diminished-seventh sonority; a fourth dominant (not found here) would include F♯ (V/B). As such, Beethoven engages key relationships that divide the octave into minor thirds, a procedure that anticipates Schubert's pervasive use of such tonal and harmonic symmetries.

### 4.4.3.3. Hyperdominant Prolongations

That one diminished-seventh sonority can function as the dominant of four different tonal regions suggests that we might posit the notion of a single *hyperdominant* harmonic function. Such a hyperdominant does not have a single root (like a normal dominant), but rather references four different roots, pitches that relate to each other by the intervals of a minor third, an augmented second, or a tritone. Thus in Example 4.67, the G dominant at measure 122 and the B♭ dominant at the upbeat to measure 126 are components of the same hyperdominant (G, B♭, D♭, E); indeed, their shared diminished seventh at the upbeat to measure 123 literally connects the two dominants. As such, we could speak of a hyperdominant *prolongation*, as indicated by the slur. A similar situation occurs in Example 4.66, except that here we do not encounter a shared diminished seventh; rather, the two regular dominants are linked at measure 127 by the diatonic III, which thus functions as a passing chord within the hyperdominant prolongation.

With Example 4.68, the harmonies are more intricate, for here we can recognize two hyperdominant prolongations: one connecting the E♭ harmony in measures 41–43 with the implied "C" harmony of measures 44–45; the second, connecting the "C" at the end of measure 48 with A at measure 50. Indeed, both of these prolongations engage the same hyperdominant (E♭, G♭, A, C). The intervening tonic of F major in measures 46–48 connects these two prolongations as a passing harmony. Complicating this reading is the fact that the E♭ harmony initially sounds as a tonic, and only in retrospect can be understood as the dominant of A-flat.

How, then, does an interpretation of hyperdominant prolongation affect our experience of PDAs in these examples? Continuing to look at Example 4.68, and in light of the idea that the "tonic" E♭ in measures 41–43 might be thought of as a dominant (of A-flat), then we could presumably find the onset of a dominant arrival in measure 41, though again, only greatly in retrospect. As for Example 4.67, a hyperdominant interpretation would shift the PDA from the diminished seventh in the upbeat to measure 123 back to the beginning of measure 122, a relatively minor correction. Recognizing a hyperdominant prolongation in Example 4.66, however, results in a significantly different interpretation of how the goal dominant is projected, for if the hyperdominant starts with the A harmony of measure 123, then we could say that the HC there becomes the final harmonic goal of the development section, and the category of premature dominant arrival would no longer apply; moreover, we would then recognize an extensive "standing on the hyperdominant" from measure 123 to the literal end of the development at measure 132.

At this point I should make it clear that I am not suggesting that the original analyses of PDAs, as annotated in the three examples, should be overthrown. Rather, these hyperdominant considerations can perhaps enrich our understanding of the chromaticism in these passages, revealing an underlying logic to the successions of their harmonies and key relations.[127]

### 4.4.4. Additional Issues

Whereas most manifestations of dominant arrival are covered by the concepts laid out thus far, other cases call for additional elaboration. Some complications that arise with regular HCs, such as those of limited scope, the reinterpreted HC, and the reopened HC, also find expression as dominant arrivals. A particular configuration that Martin and Pedneault-Deslauriers term a *"doppia HC"* can engage this deviation type as well. Finally, I end this section by considering Burstein's trenchant critique of my dominant arrival concept, along with his redefinition of half cadence to permit its including a dissonant seventh and inverted dominant.

### 4.4.4.1. Dominant Arrival of Limited Scope

Like the deviations of the authentic cadence, a dominant arrival may appear in a formal context in which the extent of its closure has a limited scope; that is, the dominant arrival does not participate in ending the broader thematic process at hand (see Ex. 4.69). Within a contrasting middle of a small ternary, an opening four-measure phrase (mm. 9–12) in the subordinate key of G-flat modulates to A-flat minor. A half cadential progression, whose final dominant contains a dissonant seventh, thus produces a dominant arrival at measure 12. A second phrase begins as though it were to be a sequence of the first, but then quickly changes course by modulating back to the home key, as confirmed by a genuine HC at measure 16, one that we understand to conclude the B section as a whole when the basic idea of the theme returns in the next bar. Here, our expectations of how a contrasting middle normally ends, namely by a *home-key*

---

the appoggiatura D via the fermata draws even more attention to how D eventually resolves; indeed, this melodic configuration reverses the proposed D♭⇒C♯ to D♯ of mm. 44–46 that I discussed in note 123. The dashed curved lines connect the pitches of this configuration.

126. The doubled monophony texture of this standing on the dominant references the earlier passage starting in m. 41, which I also proposed as a possible standing on the dominant (of A-flat).

127. I raise the topic of hyperdominant prolongation again in Chapter 9, in connection with an analysis of the Prelude to *Tristan und Isolde*, Ex. 9.56d.

EXAMPLE 4.69. Haydn, Piano Trio in E-flat Minor, H. 31, i, mm. 9–17.

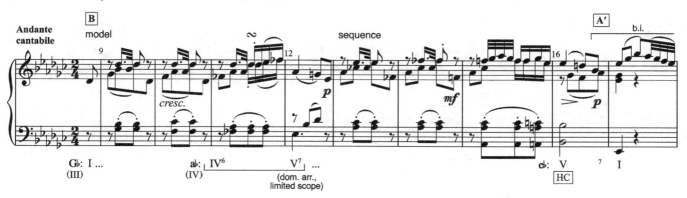

EXAMPLE 4.70. Beethoven, Cello Sonata in A, Op. 69, iii, mm. 1–9.

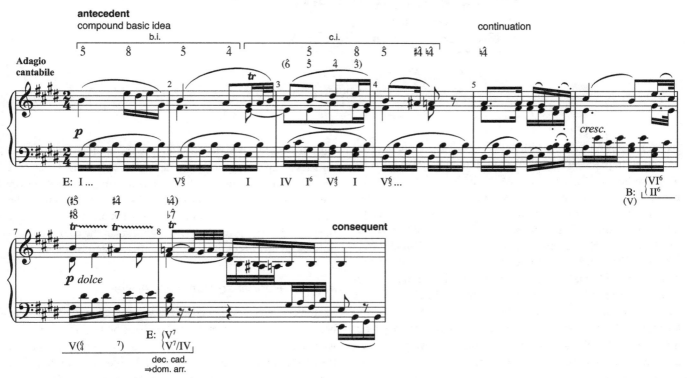

HC (or dominant arrival), lead us to understand that the earlier dominant arrival in measure 12 cannot represent closure for the B section as a whole, even while concluding its opening phrase. The dominant arrival thus has a limited structural scope. To be sure, Haydn could have written a genuine HC at measure 12, and we would still understand it to be of limited scope. Yet by writing a dominant arrival instead, he downplays even more the sense of structural closure for this opening phrase.[128]

### 4.4.4.2. Reinterpreted Dominant Arrival

Now and then a dominant arrival appears in the context of what seems to be an ongoing authentic cadential progression (Ex. 4.70). The slow introduction to the finale of this cello sonata begins with a simple eight-measure hybrid theme (c.b.i. + cont.).[129] At the end of measure 6, the music begins to modulate to the subordinate key (B major) as proposed by the ACP. The cadential

---

128. It is instructive to compare the two dissonant sevenths in mm. 12 and 16. In the former, the seventh appears in conjunction with the resolving appoggiatura (at the beginning of beat 2), and thus seems to be a true member of the harmony ending the model, thus resulting in a dominant arrival. In the latter, the dissonant seventh arising at the very end of m. 16 does not belong to the B section, but rather to the upbeat of the A′ section; thus a genuine HC closes there with a consonant dominant triad.

129. Alternatively, this theme could be considered a sentence, given that the basic idea's underlying harmonic structure (I–V$_5^6$) and melodic structure ($\hat{5}$–$\hat{8}$–$\hat{5}$–$\hat{4}$) is reproduced in mm. 3–4, thus permitting the interpretation of a presentation phrase. The accelerated harmonic rhythm in m. 3, however, supports hearing a contrasting idea. In fact, all four stages of a Prinner riposte are clearly evident in that bar (with the melodic component moving from the soprano, $\hat{6}$–$\hat{5}$, into the alto, $\hat{4}$–$\hat{3}$); on the contrary, this schema finds no expression in the preceding basic idea.

EXAMPLE 4.71. Mozart, Fantasia in C Minor, K. 475, (a) mm. 26–29; (b) reconstruction of m. 27.

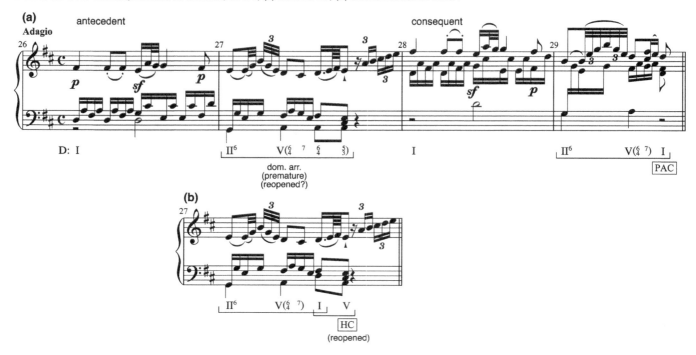

six-four resolving to the dominant seventh proper prepares for an impending SK: PAC on the downbeat of measure 8; however, when we hear the leading tone (A♯) of the local B major resolve not up to 1̂ but rather down to ♭7̂ (A♮), we hear an exceptional type of deceptive cadence (akin to that shown in Ex. 4.12), whereby a final tonic of the ACP is replaced by V⁷/IV. If Beethoven had resolved the penultimate dominant to a final tonic (a B-major triad with 1̂ in the soprano) and then continued by immediately returning to the home key to start a presumed repetition of this theme, we would have said that the resulting PAC had become reinterpreted as an HK: HC, one that would then be seen to end a compound antecedent, whose matching consequent begins in measure 9.[130] In this light, we can be justified in saying that what actually occurs is a deceptive cadence "becoming" a reinterpreted dominant arrival.

Note that this deviation brings, in the home key, the melodic motion 5̂–♯4̂–♮4̂, a pattern that we have frequently seen in connection with regular dominant arrivals (see Ex. 4.55 and 4.56a). The difference here, however, is that these degrees must now be first interpreted as 8̂–7̂–♭7̂, as supported by the DCP in the subordinate key. Nonetheless, the appearance of this pattern is clearly motivated by an earlier motivic emphasis on the motion from 5̂ to 4̂, seen at the end of the basic idea in measure 2 as well as in measure 4, where the chromatic passing tone ♯4̂ is introduced. Though 4̂ in measure 2 resolves directly to 3̂, the addition of the trill and subsequent sixteenth-note upward motion suggest that 3̂ initiates an upbeat to the next idea; the basic idea might then best be seen to end on 4̂ (despite Beethoven's slurring), just as it does in measure 4. This emphasis on 4̂ continues in measure 5, only to be further reinforced by the dominant arrival in measure 8, whereby the fundamental motive 5̂–(♯4̂)–4̂ reappears in the course of a sophisticated process of tonal and cadential reinterpretation.

### 4.4.4.3. Reopened Dominant Arrival

Examples of actual reopened half cadences are already few and far between, but one such case could perhaps be seen in connection with a PDA (Ex. 4.71a). Here, a seemingly tight-knit period (notated in compound meter, R = ½N) appears in the course of a keyboard fantasia. A close look at the end of the antecedent phrase shows that the final dominant of an expected HC arises at beat 2 of measure 27, one beat earlier than anticipated. The dominant is then held through the third beat to what appears gesturally to be an HC on the second part of that beat. Since the arrival on the final dominant occurs prior to the end of the ongoing melodic process, we should more rightly consider this form of closure to be a PDA. But we must note that a genuine HC could have been created if Mozart had brought a tonic harmony in root position at the beginning of beat 3, rather than prolonging the dominant by means of the six-four at that same location. If we rewrite the passage in this way, shown in Example 4.71b, we recognize a reopened HC as defined and illustrated in Chapter 3 (sec. 3.3.5.2). We would then see that the cadential progression in measure 27 is authentic, not half cadential, and the PAC thus created at the start of beat three is reopened to become an HC. Indeed, Mozart

---

130. The consequent fails, however, when the music modulates from E major, the opening key of the slow introduction, to A major, the key of the finale. This harmonic-formal move is surprising, since listeners are likely expecting the E-major music to be the sonata's actual slow movement, which Beethoven ultimately forgoes.

EXAMPLE 4.72. (a) *Doppia* HC (from Martin and Pedneault-Deslauriers, "Mozartian HC," 194, Ex. 9a; (b) *cadenza doppia* (from ibid., Ex. 9b); (c) *doppia* HC variant (from ibid., 201, Ex. 15).

EXAMPLE 4.73. Mozart, Piano Sonata in E-flat, K. 282, i, mm. 6–8 (R = ½N) (from ibid., Ex. 9d).

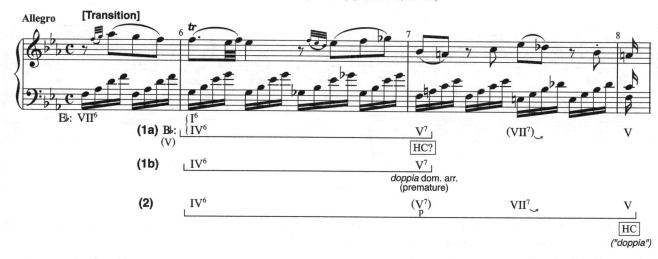

then completes the period (Ex. 4.71a, mm. 28–29) by bringing a consequent, whose final PAC realizes the same cadence that would have been reopened in the antecedent, had he written the reconstructed version. By actually writing a six-four position for the tonic, thus prolonging the final dominant, the composer creates a PDA while also alluding to the idea of the reopened HC. The cadential oddities thus presented make the theme an appropriate one for a fantasia, a genre that abounds in nonconventional formal structures.[131]

### 4.4.4.4. Doppia PDA versus Doppia HC

In their typology of half cadences for Mozart's piano sonatas, Martin and Pedneault-Deslauriers identify a relatively rare type that they term the "*doppia* HC," one that shares certain features with an authentic cadential configuration that baroque theorists called a *cadenza doppia* (lit., "double cadence").[132] Example 4.72a presents the basic harmony and voice leading of this HC type, and Example 4.72b shows its relation to the *cadenza doppia*. (Ex. 4.72c is discussed in the next paragraph.) Example 4.73 illustrates the technique in an actual passage. As they note, the *doppia* HC (Ex. 4.72a) raises the question:

> where does the final dominant of the half cadence occur? Is it (1) the first dominant chord, in which case the goal dominant bears a dissonant seventh; or is it (2) the second dominant, in which case the dissonant seventh ($f^2$ in the example) discharges to the third scale degree ($e♭^2$) contained in the second sonority. (193–94)

As a general rule, they prefer the second option (see Ex. 4.73, analysis in line 2), thus hearing $V^7$ on the downbeat of measure 7 as a passing harmony that prolongs two pre-dominants ($IV^6$ and $VII^7/V$).[133] They further note that the first option (line 1a) would violate the principle that the final dominant of an HC must contain a consonant triad (193, note 17). In addition to the two options they discuss, a third one (line 1b), which they do not mention, could see the dominant seventh (first harmony in Ex. 4.72a and the downbeat of m. 7 in Ex. 4.73) as a *doppia* PDA and thus not a genuine HC. The following progression, $VII^7/V$–V, would then be understood as prolonging the dominant.

Later in their article, Martin and Pedneault-Deslauriers observe that if, in place of the pre-dominant $VII^7/V$, a six-four position of the tonic were to appear (Ex. 4.72c), the situation

---

131. William E. Caplin, "Fantastical Forms: Formal Functionality in Improvisational Genres of the Classical Era."

132. Martin and Pedneault-Deslauriers, "The Mozartean Half Cadence," 193–95. The baroque *cadenza doppia* will be treated in detail in Chapter 6, sec. 6.1.2.

---

133. See the voice-leading sketch in their Ex. 9d, p. 195.

EXAMPLE 4.74. Haydn, Symphony No. 104 in D ("London"), ii, (a) mm. 1–6; (b) reconstruction of mm. 3–4; (c) mm. 122–27.

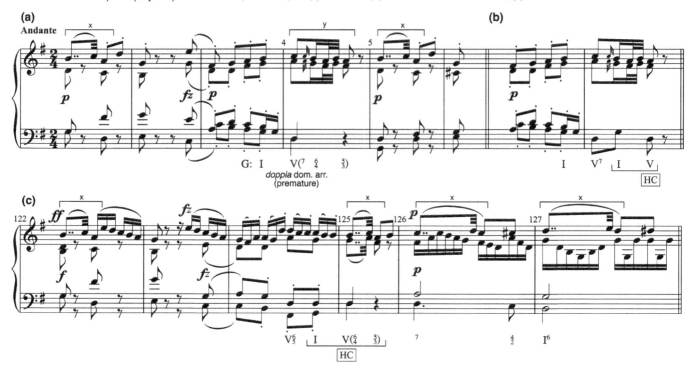

would resemble even more the *cadenza doppia* proper (Ex. 4.72b). And while acknowledging that this variant of the *doppia* HC does not arise in Mozart's piano sonatas (the corpus of their study), they observe that "it does do so elsewhere in the classical repertory" (201).[134] Indeed, Example 4.74a (which they do not discuss) is a case in point. In the context of a tight-knit main theme, an opening phrase ends with dominant harmony in measure 4 to create what seems to be an antecedent. The dominant entering on the downbeat of that bar, however, contains a dissonant seventh (C), which resolves to a sixth (B) on the second eighth note of the first beat. The passage then ends with a consonant triad on the second beat, followed by a caesura. The harmonic content of measure 4 is effectively the same as that shown in Example 4.72c. Given the dominant seventh's placement on the downbeat of measure 4, where most HCs would appear, the sense of a *premature* arrival is not so evident. Yet if we reconstruct a more normative HC (Ex. 4.74b), we observe that the dominant arrival in Example 4.74a precedes in time this potential HC.

Example 4.74b stays close to the model given by Martin and Pedneault-Deslauriers (Ex. 4.72c), but in fact, Haydn provides two of his own "reconstructions," as Schmalfeldt explains:

> Has a phrase ended at m. 4 [Ex. 4.74a]? This seems undeniable. Does it really matter whether we call this phrase ending a case of "HC on V⁷" . . . ? Some may think not; but the affective difference between a phrase ending on V⁷

and one that ends on the root-position dominant triad has apparent relevance for Haydn. Within two later returns of the antecedent, . . . the composer replaces his "HC on V⁷" with the much more common triad on the dominant—no seventh.[135]

Example 4.74c shows the second of these two returns in measures 122–25. (The first return, mm. 98–101, has the same melody and harmonic support.) Here, Haydn brings an HC in which the cadential six-four appears in the first half of measure 125, resolving then to the dominant proper in the second half of the bar. Schmalfeldt continues, "The unalloyed dominant triad returns as the antecedent's HC at m. 125, this time within a tutti texture and a fortissimo dynamic. Its greater stability as a phrase ending contributes to the exultant character of that final reprise" (309).

In addition to the differing rhetorical qualities projected by the two endings (the PDA in Example 4.74a, m. 4, and the genuine HC, Example 4.74c, m. 125), some clever motivic manipulations are operative as well. Note that the melody of the HC in Example 4.74c (motive "x") is identical to opening motive of the basic idea. If Haydn had written that same HC at measure 4 (Ex. 4.74a), the return of the basic idea at measure 5 might have been redundant. So the use of the *doppia* PDA (motive "y") brings sufficient contrast (even if the general contour is similar) to avoid a repetition from measure 4 to measure 5. In the case of the later return (Ex. 4.74c), what follows the HC at measure 125 is no longer a simple repeat of the basic idea (starting on B), but rather a stepwise-ascending version, starting on C, still supported by dominant

---

134. They specifically cite the main theme of Pamina's aria "Ach, ich fühl's" from Mozart's *The Magic Flute*.

135. Schmalfeldt, "Phrase," 215, Ex. 12b.

EXAMPLE 4.75. Haydn, String Quartet in D, Op. 71, no. 2, ii, mm. 13–17.

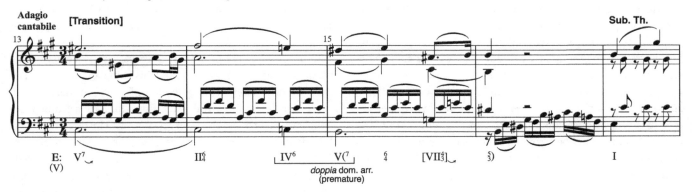

harmony. As such, motivic redundancy is avoided and a regular HC can be used to end the antecedent phrase.[136]

If the sense of *premature* dominant arrival is minimal (but still palpable) in the Haydn example just discussed, it is more salient in Example 4.75, a passage that arises at the end of an expositional transition. In the process of modulating to the subordinate key, a final dominant appears in the form of a dissonant seventh on the downbeat of measure 15 and becomes prolonged in the manner of Martin and Pedneault-Deslauriers's *doppia* HC. Here, the impression of the dominant arrival being premature is projected by the continuity of texture, rhythm, and melodic motion that continues beyond the V$^7$ at measure 15, finding the sense of an "end" only on the downbeat of the next bar.

### 4.4.4.5. Burstein's Critique

In his two studies on the half cadence, Burstein has argued that some modern definitions of this cadence type for eighteenth-century compositional practice are overly restrictive. In particular, he objects to any requirement that the final dominant of the half cadential progression be a consonant triad in root position: "it has been argued that by definition the appearance of an inverted V or V$^7$ at the onset of a phrase ending *automatically* rules out the possibility of a half cadence, regardless of whatever melodic, rhythmic, and formal features might otherwise support such a reading."[137] He thus advocates that an HC definition should include the options of the final dominant being dissonant and inverted. Burstein recognizes, of course, that my own concept of dominant arrival covers many of these cases, but he finds my usage overly extensive, especially when it describes "a host of other situations in which no phrase ending is implied."[138] He recommends instead that "terms such as 'half cadence on a V$^7$' or 'half cadence on a V$^6$' are far more descriptive, allow for greater subtlety of distinctions, and avoid the looseness of the term 'dominant arrival.'"[139] Burstein thus recognizes both a dominant triad and a dominant seventh in any position as an acceptable harmony to end a half cadential progression. As a result, he does not speak of any deviation techniques for an HC, since those cases that I would deem to be dominant arrivals would be contained under his broader concept of a genuine HC.

Burstein supports his position by three main arguments: (1) a harmonically restrictive view of the HC flies in the face of eighteenth-century theoretical formulations (e.g., Marpurg, Kirnberger, Koch), which are considerably more flexible in this regard; (2) the half cadence is already intrinsically unstable due to its ending on a dominant (instead of a more stable tonic) and so additional forces of instability could well include "the lack of caesura, volatile texture, an acceleration, or the presence of an inverted V or V$^7$";[140] and (3) the classical repertory provides ample cases whereby a phrase ending is articulated by a dominant seventh or inverted dominant.[141]

As for the first point, it is hardly an imperative for modern-day music theory to adopt a strong historicist stance. My entire project on musical form in general, and on cadence in particular,

---

136. The motivic ascent from B to C (mm. 125–26) is taken much further in the ensuing music; indeed, the way in which motivic work is carried out beyond m. 126 (not shown) is extraordinary, especially in relation to the similar continuation in mm. 102–124. Note, in particular, the play of the enharmonic E♭/D♯ in mm. 105 and 128, which alludes back to the *minore* interior theme of the overall large ternary form of the movement.

137. Burstein, "Slippery Events," 97.

138. Burstein, "Slippery Events," 213, note 26. It is not entirely clear just what Burstein means when he says that I apply my dominant arrival label to situations that do not involve a phrase ending. In "Analytic Fictions" (104, note 35), he speaks in similar ways, and then cites my discussion of dominant arrival in *Classical Form* (75). In reference to the B section of a small ternary form, I mention there that "even though the section contains a definite harmonic progression that concludes with dominant harmony, we sometimes may be reluctant to speak of a genuine cadence at that point, because the dominant takes the form of a seventh or *because the onset of the dominant seems not to mark the actual end of the melodic, rhythmic, and phrase-structural processes*" (italics added). In other words, Burstein seems to be alluding to my notion of *premature* dominant arrival (though he never references this term in either of his articles). To be sure, the location of a PDA will, by definition, never be made at the point of literal phrase ending; still, the overall circumstances involving this concept pertain to mechanisms of formal closure, though ones that deviate from the HC.

139. Burstein, "Slippery Events," 213, note 26.

140. Burstein, "Analytic Fictions," 97.

141. Burstein, "Analytic Fictions," 98–105.

is grounded in the belief that an examination of a given musical repertory need not be constrained by, or beholden to, theoretical conceptions promulgated by theorists who are contemporaneous with that repertory, as interesting and suggestive as such views may be.[142] And the same can be said for many other approaches regularly used today—Schenkerian theory, Schoenberg's developing variations, Forte's set-theory, and Lewin's transformational approach, to name but a few. Even Gjerdingen's theory of galant schemata is far from being historicist, in that almost all of his melodic-contrapuntal patterns were not explicitly recognized as such by eighteenth-century theorists, but are newly identified and defined by himself.

Concerning the second point, Burstein lumps together a variety of destabilizing forces without distinguishing between their syntactical and rhetorical effects. As to whether or not a given HC exhibits a "lack of caesura, volatile texture, [or] an acceleration," such features engage textural and rhythmic issues that are rhetorical in nature and not directly associated with cadential syntax. Questions of harmonic dissonance and inversion, however, are syntactical matters essential to the definition of the classical cadence. As has already been discussed, adding a dissonant seventh to a cadential dominant risks obscuring whether that harmony is perceived as ultimate (thus creating an HC) or penultimate (thus proposing a PAC), since the powerful need to resolve the dissonance tends to favor the latter interpretation. And for that reason (among others), my definition of half cadence sees the presence of a final dominant seventh as a cadential deviation. With respect to an inverted dominant, that matter goes straight to the heart of what constitutes a specifically cadential progression as opposed to a prolongational one, an issue I have raised repeatedly in the course of this study.

The third point, that half cadences on a $V^7$ or a $V^6$ occur with sufficient frequency to suggest that they should be subsumed within a wider definition of that cadence type, is problematic in a number of ways. For it is difficult to know just how often such situations actually occur in the repertory, and the methods we currently have for making such a determination are complex and fraught with pitfalls. As of now, we do not possess a fully reliable database of the classical repertory that would permit an enumeration of dissonant or inverted half cadences. Burstein himself cites "literally *hundreds* of examples from 1750 to 1825—by dozens of composers and from a wide variety of genres—that include a strong phrase ending on an inverted V or $V^7$ [my italics]."[143] Yet it is surely plausible to say that a comparable survey of HCs ending on a consonant triad would yield *thousands* of examples, in that almost every classical movement contains at least a couple of these cadence types. If the ratio of HC on a $V^7$ or a $V^6$ to HC on a $V^5_3$ were even as high as 1:10, that could well be comparable to the ratio of authentic cadential deviations (deceptive, evaded, abandoned) to authentic cadences proper. In terms of frequency of appearance, therefore, it seems to be an entirely reasonable proposition to consider Burstein's HCs on a $V^7$ or a $V^6$ as *deviations* (dominant arrivals) of a genuine half cadence with a final root-position dominant triad.

To be sure, my use of dominant arrival covers a multiplicity of situations, and in this sense, Burstein's complaint that the term is insufficiently precise has some merit. But to consider cases of what I call a dominant arrival as additional forms of a genuine HC has its own share of problems. Especially when inverted positions of the dominant come into consideration, the very nature of what it means to be cadential is, in my view, seriously compromised. Finally, if the authentic cadence can be subjected to various deviations, it hardly seems problematic to find a deviation form for the half cadence as well, even if that deviation type is complex in its various manifestations.[144]

## 4.5. Combinations of Deviations

Up to this point, I have been dealing primarily with individual cadential deviations. Let us now briefly consider how a given thematic unit, especially one that is loosely organized, may feature two or more deviations prior to the attainment of the final PAC. (For this discussion, it would be useful as well to include the internal HC and the way-station IAC, since they often work together with the genuine deviations toward the goal of PAC deferral.) We have already seen a number of cases where deviations and weak cadences participate together in loosening the formal organization of a theme. Thus Example 4.19 shows how a potential tight-knit period becomes loosened through a deceptive cadence at measure 24 and a subsequent IAC at measure 29, with the theme eventually concluding with a PAC at measure 32. In Example 4.39, an evaded cadence at measure 26 is followed by an abandoned ECP (m. 28). And in Example 4.41, an internal dominant arrival (m. 27) leads to a series of evaded cadences before a PAC finally brings full thematic closure (m. 38).

In principle, the organization of weak cadences and deviations is entirely flexible, but we can discern in the repertoire some preferred orderings. Thus an internal HC (or dominant arrival) usually precedes the other cadential articulations, probably to respect the syntactical order of a dominant articulation followed by a tonic one, inasmuch as the way-station IAC and the deceptive, evaded, and abandoned cadences stand in place of a final PAC. An evaded cadence (or cadences, as often occurs) will usually be the final deviation in the theme. The effect of a grouping rupture is more highly charged, and thus more appropriately placed toward the end of a theme, than the IAC and deceptive cadence,

---

142. See *CF*, 5.

143. Burstein, "Slippery Events," 213, note 25. This list is found in "Analytic Fictions," 100–1, Table 2.

144. Taking Burstein's critique into account, I have indeed given careful thought to the idea of introducing different terms to cover the admittedly wide application of dominant arrival that I detail above. Unfortunately, no such set of labels has yet come to mind, though my distinction between a "final" and "terminal" dominant arrival is one step toward refining the concept.

which bring a semblance of harmonic goal. As for the abandoned cadence (or abandoned progression), I have not yet observed any particular preference for where in a theme this deviation may occur, except that it will not normally precede an internal HC.

Needless to say, it is possible to find exceptions to any of these general rules of thumb; see ahead in Chapter 5, Ex. 5.36a, for a slow introduction whose first theme brings an evaded cadence (m. 8) followed by a deceptive cadence (m. 12). And in that same chapter, Ex. 5.72a finds an evaded cadence (m. 100) followed by an IAC (m. 107). The entire topic of deviation combinations, indeed, is worthy of more empirical examination, a project that exceeds the scope of the present study. I return to the issue in Chapter 7 on galant music, where we see cases that run quite counter to the generalizations just proposed for the manipulation of cadential deviations in the classical style.

## 4.6. Cadential Ambiguities

It is one thing to develop criteria for defining cadential deviations; it is another to apply those criteria in actual musical situations. Of course most cases are straightforward, thus permitting an easy identification of a given deviation. We nonetheless encounter difficult cases where more than one cadential label—be it a deviation or a regular cadence—seems to be a reasonable option for analysis. We have already seen, for instance, situations where it is uncertain whether we are dealing with an HC or a dominant arrival (see Ex. 4.59, m. 37, and Ex. 3.163a, m. 7). In such circumstances we must try to identify just which musical forces come to bear on our perception of the cadential anomaly at hand. For example, our understanding of the grouping structure (which itself is determined by a host of compositional processes) will usually play a critical role in resolving cadential ambiguities. Details of texture, rhythmic activity, repetition schemes (such as the one-more-time technique), dynamics, along with various types of harmonic progressions and melodic patterns, all participate in helping us sort out varying cadential possibilities. It is also important to take into account the formal context in which the problematic cadence or deviation arises, for our expectations of closure will often influence our perception (and thus our analysis) of a potential ambiguity. Finally, cadential ambiguities can sometimes be "resolved" by a particular performance. Matters of phrasing, articulation, dynamic shading, and rhythmic nuance—variables that are under some degree of control by performers—can often play into a listeners' experience of grouping structure, perhaps the most important criterion for differentiating among various cadential options.

The following discussion, consisting of individual case studies, is organized according to a variety of analytical oppositions among deviation types themselves (such as deceptive cadence vs. abandoned cadence) or oppositions between a deviation and a genuine cadence (evaded cadence vs. HC). I conclude with a couple of examples where multiple cadential categories come into play.

### 4.6.1. Evaded versus Deceptive (Elided)

A frequently encountered cadential ambiguity involves a possible evaded cadence or an elided deceptive cadence.[145] An exemplary case of the problem arises in a passage that I have already examined when discussing the melodic content of the evaded cadence (see again Ex. 4.39). I argued that the downbeat of measure 26 is marked by a surprising modal shift to minor, a sudden *forzato* articulation, and a striking change of texture, all of which combine to make this moment appear highly initiating, thus evading the promised cadence. As Nicholas Marston has pointed out, however, this is not the only way to hear the passage. "Why may we not understand bar 26 as the consequence of a functional elision . . . , making it simultaneously the (deceptive) goal of the preceding cadential progression and the beginning of the ensuing, abandoned one"?[146] When Marston hears measure 26 as a goal, as a moment in time that groups backward with the ongoing cadential material, he is hearing a deceptive cadence, not an evaded one. But what specific musical forces prompt such an interpretation? Here, the obvious one is the powerful *melodic* resolution to $\hat{1}$, which marks the end of a long stepwise descent in the violins. Listeners who focus their attention to the upper voice and hear the *forzato* sign as a confirmation of the melodic goal, will thus rightly experience a sense of deceptive cadence, one that is elided with the next phrase. On the contrary, those who hear a marked disruption in the cadential process, despite the melodic resolution to $\hat{1}$, will experience an evaded cadence instead. Can we claim that only one hearing is to be preferred? I doubt it, for by acknowledging the individual parameters (melody, dynamics, texture) that lead to these different hearings, we can hardly say that one interpretation must necessarily exclude the other: both are grounded in fully perceivable features that are intrinsic to the music.

Another case (Ex. 4.37), discussed earlier as an evaded cadence, also may be perceived as an elided deceptive cadence. Indeed, Neuwirth hears it just that way: "Although the expected cadence is interrupted in m. 59, there is also a sense of elision conveyed at this point, as the harmony replacing the tonic is a closely related substitute for the tonic of B minor and thus articulates both an endpoint and the initial event of the subsequent phrase."[147] His justification for hearing a deceptive cadence seems largely grounded in the harmonic circumstance that the $V^7/IV$, as a chromatic variant of the expected root-position tonic, is so strongly linked syntactically to the preceding cadential

---

145. For an excellent discussion of this general issue, see Schmalfeldt, "Cadential Processes," 18–21.

146. Nicholas Marston, "Review of *Classical Form: A Theory of Formal Functions for the Instrumental Music of Haydn, Mozart, and Beethoven* by William E. Caplin," 146. In my discussion of this passage in *CF*, Ex. 8.6 (reproduced in *ACF*, Ex. 12.6), I speak only of an evaded cadence and did not even develop a specific concept of "elided deceptive cadence." I thank Marston for drawing my attention to this important source of cadential ambiguity.

147. Neuwirth, "*Fuggir la Cadenza*," 148.

EXAMPLE 4.76. Mozart, Piano Sonata in D, K. 576, iii, mm. 175–84 (*ACF* 19.16).

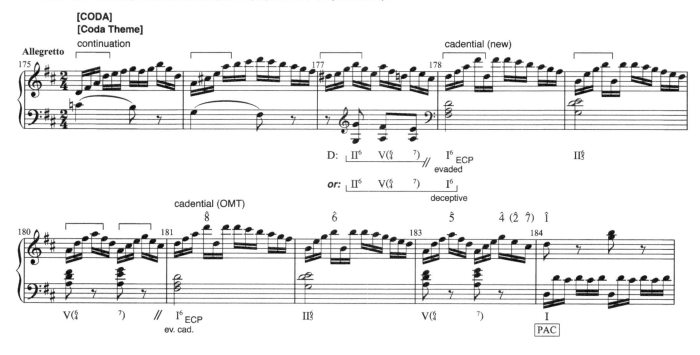

dominant that this replacement harmony is readily heard as a formal goal (i.e., that it groups backward with the ongoing cadential progression).[148] Yet Neuwirth also betrays a sense that the deviation here may also be understood as evaded, when he characterizes the cadence as being "interrupted." Moreover, when explaining that the idea of a replacement V⁷/IV is referenced by Sulzer's notion of a *vermiedene Kadenz* (avoided cadence, see again note 20), he observes further that what Sulzer seems to have in mind is something like an evaded cadence (in my sense), more than a deceptive one.[149]

Example 4.76 presents another interesting case of an ambiguous deviation involving an evaded cadence or an elided deceptive one. Within the coda of a sonata-rondo form, the final refrain brings a compact cadential progression in measure 177 that implies authentic cadential closure on the downbeat of the following bar, just as it had done twice before in the movement.[150] Though the melody resolves to 1̂, the expected root-position tonic is inverted to I⁶, which initiates an ECP, whose final harmony is projected to occur on the downbeat of m 181. Again an inverted tonic creates a deviation and the same passage is repeated "one more time." The refrain finally closes with a PAC at measure 184. What, then, is the status of the two moments of cadential deviation, measures 178 and 181? Both cases could rightfully engage the categories of elided deceptive cadence or evaded cadence, with legitimate arguments found for both options. On the one hand, the complete melodic closure on 1̂ permits us easily to hear the downbeats of measures 178 and 181 as grouping backward with the ongoing cadential progressions, and the use of I⁶ as a *replacement harmony* supports the possibility of hearing elided deceptive cadences. On the other hand, the melodic 1̂ also represents the first pitch of an ascending arpeggiated motive that sounds on the downbeats of measures 175–77 and that continues within the ECPs (see brackets). In all of these cases, the upward-thrusting energy of this motive seems to undermine the potential of its initial note functioning as a melodic goal. For this reason, it is not difficult to hear the I⁶ as an *initiating harmony* and the melodic 1̂ that it supports as exclusively defining the start of a new group, thus legitimizing an interpretation of evaded cadence.[151]

Moreover, another factor comes into play. As Schmalfeldt emphasizes in her study of cadential processes, the use of a one-more-time repetition is so strongly connected with evaded cadences that its presence can often be helpful in supporting an

---

148. On the use of V⁷/IV as a replacement harmony (albeit a rare one) of a deceptive cadential progression, see the discussion of Ex. 4.1d and Ex. 4.12, m. 22.

149. "[I]n the manner of an evaded cadence, the applied dominant [V⁷/IV] groups forward with the following unit.... Anticipating Schmalfeldt's (and Caplin's) grouping-based distinction between deceptive and evaded cadences, Sulzer does not consider this progression to belong to the category of 'cadence' at all. Unlike the deceptive cadence, the chord replacing the tonic in a *vermiedene Kadenz* is a forward-looking dissonant harmony that propels the music onward instead of articulating a point of rest" (Neuwirth, "*Fuggir la Cadenza*," 147).

150. See m. 16 (end of refrain 1) and m. 80 (end of refrain 2); Mozart modifies the sonata-rondo by deleting refrain 3 at the start of the recapitulation; the coda begins with a "fourth refrain" (as defined by sonata-rondo form), whose final portion is shown in Ex. 4.76.

151. A number of other passages with ambiguous deviations also feature a prominent ascending gesture initiated by a potential goal 1̂, thus promoting an interpretation of evaded cadence over that of elided deceptive cadence; see Haydn, Symphony No. 104 in D, i, m. 80 (discussed by Schmalfeldt, "Cadential Processes," 17); Mozart, String Quartet in D, K. 575, ii, m. 16; Beethoven, Piano Sonata in G, Op. 14, no. 2, i, m. 45.

EXAMPLE 4.77. Haydn, String Quartet in D, Op. 50, no. 6, i, mm. 35–40.

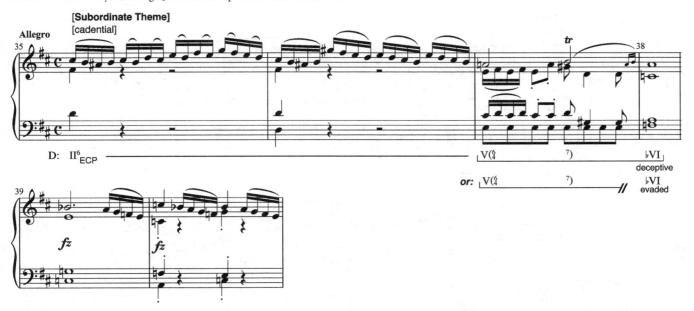

analysis of that deviation type, especially in ambiguous cases.[152] Thus our hearing a "one more time" at measure 181 is especially compelling. Even if we were inclined to regard measure 178 as a deceptive cadence, we might reverse our interpretation at measure 181 in favor of an evaded cadence when perceiving the onset of a one-more-time technique.[153]

In the three cases of ambiguous deviations just discussed, I tended to come down more on the side of the evaded cadence than the deceptive one. In Example 4.77, I prefer the latter option, while still recognizing the possibility of hearing the former. Toward the end of a subordinate theme, an ECP, with an emphasized pre-dominant II⁶, heads toward PAC closure on the downbeat of measure 38. The resolution of the cadential dominant to the replacement harmony ♭VI, while not common, is entirely possible for creating a deceptive cadence.[154] What is so striking about the appearance of that harmony, of course, is the sudden change in texture, a force for discontinuity that could well lead to an interpretation of evaded cadence. One detail, though, is perhaps worthy of greater reflection: the single whole-note chord perhaps magnifies the sense of the ♭VI harmony as a real goal, especially since rhythmic activity does not resume until the next bar (and even then, it takes three quarter-note beats to get significantly underway). In short, my preference would be to find a deceptive cadence here, even while I recognize—and fully validate—the option of evaded cadence.

One final example of deceptive versus evaded cadences is particularly interesting as regards texture and melodic activity. Like the previous case, Example 4.78 arises in the course of a subordinate theme. The passage starts with a continuation⇒cadential phrase that implies a PAC on the downbeat of measure 38. When, in the previous bar, the bass supporting the cadential six-four drops down a step to create V$^4_2$, we know that something is going awry, and the resolution to I⁶ as a replacement harmony, one that supports the melodic resolution in the violin to 1̂, fully expresses a deceptive cadence. Yet if we focus our attention to the newly appearing piano's right-hand melody, with its prominent upward leap to the high F (downbeat of m. 38), the sense of a one-more-time technique is highly palpable. For that repetition can easily prompt us to experience an evaded cadence, especially since the suddenly appearing piano melody may distract from hearing the melodic resolution in the violin. In this passage, like the others we have discussed, the nature of the ambiguity can be identified by the conflicting musical forces at play, even if we cannot necessarily come to a definitive decision that resolves our cadential analyses one way or the other.

### 4.6.2. Evaded versus Authentic (Elided)

An ambiguity between an evaded cadence and a genuine authentic one can only arise when the harmony following the cadential dominant appears as a tonic in root position (otherwise we could not even speak of a genuine cadence). In those cases, a significant grouping discontinuity must be manifest for us *not* to hear a PAC (or IAC). In order to establish firm criteria for the evaded cadence, and to distinguish it from an authentic cadence, I already have treated in detail a number of potentially ambiguous cases (see the earlier discussions of Ex. 4.36, 4.41, and 4.42).[155]

---

152. Schmalfeldt, "Cadential Processes," 20–21.

153. The melodic analyses of scale degrees in mm. 181–84 refers to a discussion of this example in Chapter 5 (sec. 5.1.2.4).

154. We have already considered some prominent cases from Mozart's Piano Concerto in G, K. 453, see again Ex. 4.16a and b.

155. See also Haydn, Symphony No. 104, i, m. 32 in comparison to m. 80 (as discussed by Schmalfeldt, "Cadential Processes," 17–18).

EXAMPLE 4.78. Mozart, Violin Sonata in B-flat, K. 454, ii, mm. 34–44 (*ACF* 12.20).

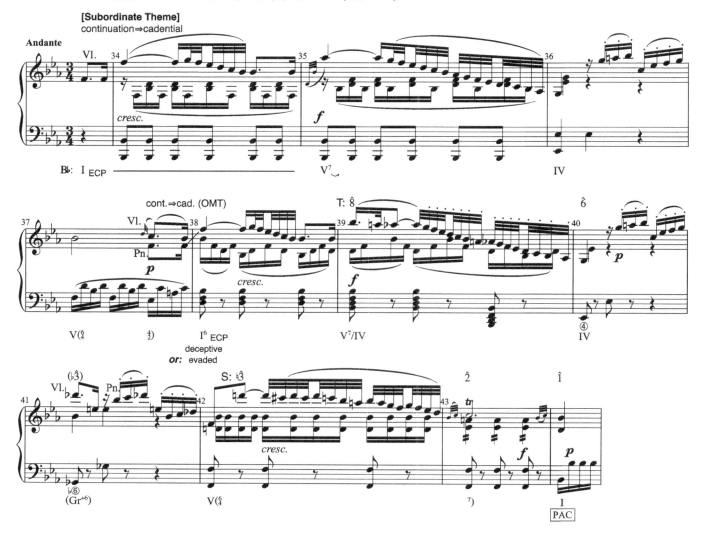

One additional example can be dealt with here, since it involves some interesting matters of texture not yet considered. Toward the end of a subordinate theme (see Ex. 4.79), three locations can potentially be identified as a PAC inasmuch as a cadential dominant resolves to a final tonic in root position: measure 35, measure 40, and measure 45. Each case, however, disrupts our hearing a texturally completely cadence. At measure 35, the melodic goal proposed by the trill in the previous bar is replaced by an eighth-note rest; at measure 40, the melody reaches its moment of resolution, but an anticipated bass on the downbeat is missing; and at measure 45, although both the melody and bass occur at the very start of the bar, the latter lies two octaves higher than where we would expect it to appear (given the contour of the bass within the penultimate dominant). Of these three potential PACs, the first is most likely to be interpreted as an evaded cadence, since the failure to realize the goal of a cadential trill is a well-established means of supporting an evaded cadence (see Ex. 4.38, m. 16, and Ex. 4.41, m. 34). The second case (m. 40) is more problematic, since a handful of examples contain a perfectly legitimate PAC whose bass is delayed for various textural reasons.[156] But what helps support the idea of an evaded cadence here is the one-more-time technique, whereby the music backs up to the melodic material of measure 35. Once we recognize the repetition, we understand that the left-hand part lacks the expected bass C on the downbeat of the bar precisely in order to project an exchange of the parts—what was in the right hand of measure 35 is now in the left hand at measure 40. As for the third cadence at measure 45, if we agree that the two prior ones are best analyzed as evaded cadences, then we are fully prepared to find an acceptable PAC for the theme, especially since an obvious closing section ensues. We could moreover consider that the textural gap between where the bass actually appears (on a middle C) and its implied appearance (two octaves lower) is systematically filled in by the elaborate stepwise descending patterns in the left hand of the closing section.[157]

---

156. See in Chapter 3, Ex. 3.76, m. 28; Ex. 3.78, mm. 6 and 8; Ex. 3.167, m. 29. Ahead in Chapter 5, we find in Ex. 5.41, m. 178, a textural situation very similar to that of Ex. 4.79, m. 40, in the present chapter.

157. Note that the middle C bass of m. 45 realizes the earlier implication at m. 40 that a bass note could have occurred at this same pitch-level.

EXAMPLE 4.79. Mozart, Piano Sonata in A Minor, K. 310, i, mm. 31–47.

Though I have presented an analysis of two evaded cadences and a final PAC for this *single* subordinate theme, it is not out of the question to recognize three PACs here: one at measure 35 to close a first subordinate theme; the next at measure 40 ending a second subordinate theme; and the third at measure 45 to conclude an extended repetition of this second theme. Finally, we should consider the overall symphonic character of this movement, perhaps the only one of Mozart's opening piano sonata movements that we might imagine orchestrating.[158] If this were a work with multiple instruments, it is likely that the composer would have normalized some of the textural oddities so as not to have presented the same degree of cadential ambiguity that arises from the constraints afforded by a single instrument.

---

158. As Alfred Brendel puts it, "The first movement of . . . K310 is to me a piece for symphony orchestra" (*Music Sounded Out: Essays, Lectures, Interviews, Afterthoughts*, 3).

### 4.6.3. Evaded versus IAC (Elided)

For reasons discussed earlier, the cadential evasion of an implied IAC is uncommon. Even so, we now and then find a case where it is not entirely clear whether that cadence type has been realized or evaded. In Example 4.80, an extended continuation phrase of the main theme proposes to close with a PAC on the downbeat of measure 18. But the melody line, which resides in the piano part, is diverted up to $\hat{3}$ to realize an IAC instead (see the line connecting the F at the end of m. 17 to the G at beginning of m. 18). At the same time, the violin re-enters above the piano to initiate (along with the piano lying below), a varied repeat of the continuation passage from measure 15 on. As a result, we can speak of the IAC being elided with this repeated material, which eventually reaches a PAC at measure 21. An alternative interpretation presents itself as well. Rather than hearing the piano note G ($\hat{3}$) on the downbeat of measure 18 as a melodic goal, we could

EXAMPLE 4.80. Mozart, Violin Sonata in B-flat, K. 454, ii, mm. 14–21 (*ACF* 6.17).

understand it as exclusively initiating, which in association with the newly entering B♭ (5̂) in the violin, effects an evaded cadence supported by a one-more-time technique. One detail, the diversion of the cadential trill up to 3̂, perhaps tilts toward hearing a cadential evasion, as discussed earlier with Example 4.37, measure 59. Otherwise, nothing else in the musical notation supports one or the other of the conflicting interpretations—IAC versus evaded cadence. It thus remains largely a matter of how the performers phrase this boundary moment (or how listeners themselves interpret the phrasing in their imagination). In other words, it is again a question of the grouping structure. If we hear measure 18 as belonging to the ongoing cadential process, we would hear an IAC; if we hear that bar as marking an initiation only, then an evaded cadence would emerge. Both are plausible options.

### 4.6.4. Evaded versus Covered PAC

One feature of Example 4.80 is worthy of further note. When at measure 17 the violin leaps away from the leading tone and up to the B♭ (5̂) on the downbeat of measure 18, a *covered* cadence might be said to emerge.[159] The idea that a cadential ambiguity could involve an implied PAC and a covered cadence was raised in the previous chapter in connection with Ex. 3.37. I discussed there that the marked change of texture and dynamics at measure 12 of this main theme could give the impression that the promised PAC becomes evaded, inasmuch as that bar seems not to group with the ongoing cadential process. And though I quickly dismissed this interpretation for reasons of formal context—to

hear an evaded cadence would leave the main theme completely unclosed—the sense of evaded cadence is pronounced nonetheless. We should not, then, entirely repress that impression, even if the effect of a covered cadence emerges as the preferred interpretation from a broader formal perspective.

A related, but more complex, case arises at the end of another main theme (Ex. 4.81a). The many problems of closure in this theme are best approached by working backward from measure 13, at which point the transition begins by bringing back the material and texture from the opening of the main theme. The preceding measures 11 and 12 bring a cadential progression promising an authentic cadence. But the note B, which has been stubbornly emphasized in the upper part from the beginning of the theme (see the scale-degree annotations), resists resolving to 1̂ for an obvious PAC (as reconstructed in Ex. 4.81b). Instead, B is retained as the opening note of the transition, thus functioning as a covering tone over an implied E, which literally appears (in its implied register) only in the second half of measure 13. This cadential analysis would understand an elided, covered PAC closing the theme (see option 1). Alternatively, we could recognize an evaded cadence (option 2), as marked by the complete change in texture and rhythmic patterning, thus inhibiting our wanting to group measure 13 backward with the cadential progression. We thus encounter an ambiguity between a possible covered cadence and an evaded one. Like the covered cadence identified in Example 3.37, this second interpretation (for Ex. 4.81a) is problematic because the main theme would be left without any cadential closure.

Before considering any further how this cadential ambiguity might be resolved, let us move backward in the theme and observe what happens in measures 9–10, whose cadential progression

---

159. See Chapter 3, sec. 3.4.2.3. Alternatively, we might find that this covering tone projects even more the sense of an evaded cadence.

EXAMPLE 4.81A. Beethoven, Piano Sonata in E, Op. 14, no. 1, i, mm. 1–13 (*ACF* 10.14).

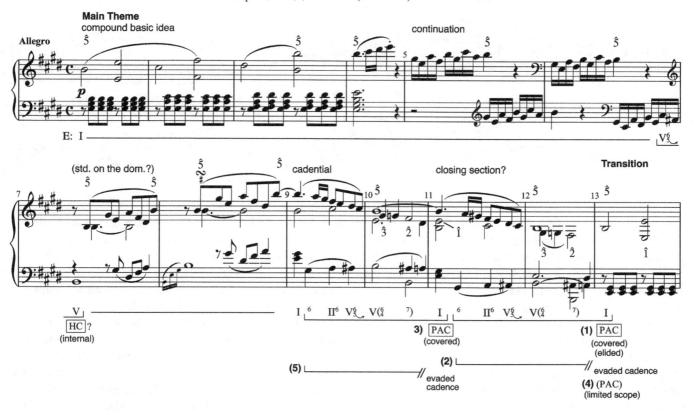

EXAMPLE 4.81B. Beethoven, Piano Sonata in E, Op. 14, no. 1, i, reconstruction of mm. 11–13.

proffers a PAC on the downbeat of measure 11. This passage uses the same material of measures 11–13, only this first time an octave higher. Here, the upper note B in measure 10 is retained into the downbeat of measure 11 (now literally held as a tied note), though at least the conventional melody $\hat{3}$–$\hat{2}$ in the alto voice completes its descent to $\hat{1}$. If we take this alto line as the structural one, we could recognize a PAC, one that is covered by the high B (option 3). Unlike the following unit (mm. 11–13), however, the strong continuity of texture and rhythm from measure 10 to measure 11 evinces little, if any, sense of evaded cadence.

But now we confront the tricky situation of a cadential passage that is immediately repeated, a matter that was discussed earlier in Chapter 2 (sec. 2.8.5). There I proposed three alternatives for considering which of the cadences might be considered the truly structural one. (The third alternative considers both cases to be equally effective of closure, so that possibility will not come into further play here.) In line with the first alternative, we would regard measures 9–11 as creating a covered PAC (option 3) to end the main theme. We would then have to hear measures 11–13 as a postcadential codetta, one that is either a "covered cadence" of limited scope (option 4) or incomplete, due to the "evaded cadence" (option 2). Following the second alternative of repeated cadences, we would hear the first cadence (m. 11) as initially structural, but then undermined as such by the second cadence (m. 13), which we would hear as either a covered PAC (option 1) or else an evaded cadence (option 2), which, to be sure, would leave the theme structurally incomplete. This second interpretation of repeated cadences could also consider the possibility that

EXAMPLE 4.81C. Beethoven, Piano Sonata in E, Op. 14, no. 1, i, string quartet version (transposed to E major), mm. 8–14.

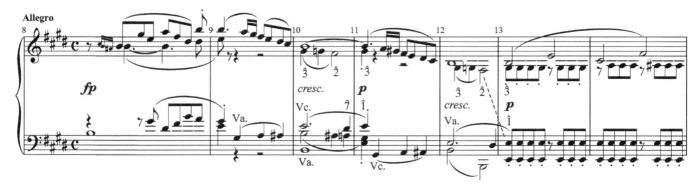

the first cadence is evaded (option 5), though little in the way of genuine musical forces contribute to project that impression.

Although it is probably best at this point to avoid a definitive decision regarding the complicated ambiguities of this main theme, it is worth noting that Beethoven himself provides some additional evidence in connection with the string quartet version that he made of this same sonata.[160] Example 4.81c shows the measures in question, and we can observe some important details that may shed light on some of the problems we have been considering.[161] First, the initial cadence (mm. 9–11) reduces the texture (compared to the piano version): in measure 9, the second violin and cello rest on beats 2–4, and the viola is given the bass line of the cadential progression, with the cello in measure 10 lying above, thus taking on the role of an inner voice. With the fuller texture of measure 10, the second violin, which brings the conventional $\hat{3}$–$\hat{2}$ descending approach to the cadence, gets diverted up to $\hat{3}$, thus failing to reach $\hat{1}$ for a PAC, though the cello, with its resolving $\hat{7}$–$\hat{1}$ motion, achieves the implied melodic close (below, of course, the covering B in the first violin). These features together result in a sense of closure for the first cadence that is less secure than the one in the piano version. Indeed, when the second cadence (mm. 11–13) begins, the cello now sounds the bass voice on the downbeat of measure 13, which imparts a more solid, decisive feel to this cadence.[162] Additionally, the drum bass accompaniment begins directly on the downbeat, as opposed to the second eighth note in the sonata version.[163] These features of the quartet perhaps mitigate the strong sense of *evaded* cadence that was found in the concluding bar of the piano sonata. And so in general, this version would seem to support well the second alternative of interpreting consecutive cadences, mentioned before, where a more affirmative closure occurs with the second PAC (m. 13).

Finally, one more detail of the quartet theme is worth mentioning, namely, Beethoven's use of dynamics. Outside of the opening *piano*, the sonata is devoid of any such indications; the quartet, on the contrary, contains a number of markings. Of particular note are the crescendos within stage 3 of the cadential progressions (mm. 10 and 12), and especially their leading to a sudden shift back to *piano* at the downbeat of the subsequent bars (stage 4). These crescendos are particularly suitable to string instruments and are not especially effective in a passage that features relatively long-held notes on the piano.[164] As for their cadential implications, they undoubtedly support the idea of evaded cadences in both cases, for they create a rupture in the dynamic curve that helps separate measures 11 and 13 from their ongoing cadential processes. In other words, our suspicion that measure 13 of the sonata is an evaded cadence (or evaded codetta) is underscored by the dynamics of the quartet version, despite the forces of continuity that we otherwise observed.

As mentioned before, I hesitate to find a single interpretation of the cadential ambiguities exhibited here. Ironically, this otherwise simple sonata begins with a theme whose modes of closure are especially intractable. And although the quartet version complicates matters all the more, it nonetheless further highlights the rich set of musical factors that contribute to the multifarious hearings offered by this intriguing passage.[165]

---

160. Documentary evidence, including a letter that Beethoven wrote to Breitkopf und Härtel, leaves no doubt that he is the composer of this arrangement. Whether the quartet version may have been written *before* the sonata, as some have speculated, has been well disproven by Michael Broyles, "Beethoven's Sonata Op. 14 No. 1—Originally for Strings?"

161. Beethoven transposed the quartet version up a step into F major, presumably to accommodate better the range of the instruments (and especially so that the lowest note on the viola and cello would be available to play a low ⑤). My example transposes the music back into E major for easier comparison with the piano version, and so some of the notes lie outside of the range of the instruments.

162. But even here the quartet differs from the piano: the A♯–A♮ move in the second half of m. 12 is missing in the quartet, due to the inability of the upper strings to fit this part into their ranges, or, perhaps, because a certain muddiness might ensue were the cello to play the A♯–A♮–G♯ line with a double stop.

163. And unlike the sonata, Beethoven also starts the main theme of the quartet (not shown) with a complete chord in the lower strings on the downbeat of the first bar.

164. It is also the case that the pianist might already know to make a slight crescendo in mm. 10 and 12, something that would have to be more literally indicated for four instrumentalists.

165. In addition to the cadential difficulties just discussed, the phrase-structural organization of the theme is hardly clear-cut: the initiating four-measure phrase is rather nonconventional even if I tend to find there a compound basic idea. Consider as well whether or not an HC is

EXAMPLE 4.82. Mozart, Piano Sonata in F, K. 280, iii, (a) mm. 45–51; (b) reconstruction of mm. 47–50; (c) mm. 59–62.

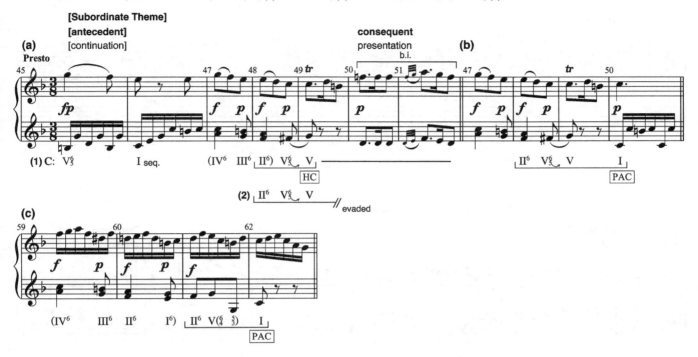

### 4.6.5. Evaded versus HC (Dominant Arrival)

The morphological conditions for an evaded cadence can sometimes resemble those of a half cadence. The difference between these two cases resides in how we interpret the status of the cadential dominant, as either penultimate (for an evaded cadence) or ultimate (for an HC).

Example 4.82a shows a case in point. In the course of a subordinate theme, a descending stepwise sequence in measures 47–48 leads (via a linking II⁶) to a cadential progression of some kind. The use of V$^6_5$/V in stage 2b suggests our hearing the dominant as ultimate, thus proposing an HC (line 1 of the analysis). Yet the melody of measure 49 can also be heard to drive forward toward an eventual goal of 1̂, as illustrated by the recomposition in Example 4.82b, which shows the theme ending with a PAC in measure 50. With that understanding of the cadential context, what occurs in the original would result in an evaded cadence (Ex. 4.82a, line 2 of the analysis). Very unusual for this deviation type, however, is that the subsequent one-more-time technique does not "back up" to some continuation or cadential material, but rather to the very opening of the theme (m. 38ff., not shown, but see the opening basic idea in mm. 50–51).[166] For this reason alone, we might be suspicious of an evaded cadence interpretation. Additionally, however, the concluding cadence at measure 62 (Ex. 4.82c) sees a significant alteration in the cadential progression (compared to the ambiguous cadence at m. 49): the descending sequence (mm. 59–60) pushes all the way down to I⁶; the pre-dominant consists exclusively of II⁶ (thus no V$^6_5$/V); and the bass voice continues with steady eighth notes all the way until the PAC, measure 62.[167] In that the content of an evaded cadence is often replicated in the final cadence (though by no means always), the differences between the two cadential progressions strongly suggest that the first is an HC, the second, an authentic cadence. Finally, an HC interpretation at measure 49 yields a compound periodic formal plan for the subordinate theme as a whole, which, although rather tight-knit, makes more sense than seeing a single thematic impulse becoming evaded (at m. 49) and then being entirely repeated. If I tend toward an HC interpretation here, I by no means want to imply that the evaded cadence option is nonsensical; rather, I believe that Mozart presents us with a genuine case of cadential ambiguity.

### 4.6.6. Abandoned versus Deceptive

When presenting the criteria for abandoned cadences, I noted that the cadential dominant in root position can lose its cadential status when undergoing inversion into a six-three (or six-five) position. In such cases, we often find a passing harmony built on ⑥, which stands between ⑤ and ⑦ (see Ex. 4.43, m. 26; Ex. 4.44, m. 7; and Ex. 4.45, m. 13). A potential ambiguity of cadence type can arise if the harmony over ⑥ could be heard as a replacement harmony of a deceptive cadence, especially when marking the provisional end of a phrase structural process. To illustrate

---

projected on the downbeat of m. 7, especially with the small chromatic change to A♯ in the left-hand part at the very end of m. 6, which suggests a pre-dominant V$^6_5$/V. If so, we could perhaps recognize an internal HC and standing on the dominant in mm. 5–6, a most unusual situation for a main theme.

166. See above, sec. 4.2.2.2 and notes 64 and 65.

167. The continuation phrase is then immediately repeated to create a second PAC at m. 66 (not shown).

EXAMPLE 4.83. Haydn, Piano Sonata in C, H. 21, ii, mm. 18–22.

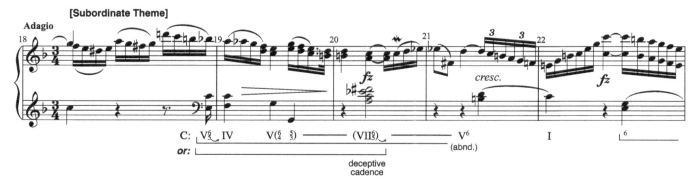

EXAMPLE 4.84A. Mozart, Piano Sonata in A Minor, K. 310, i, mm. 4–9 (*ACF* 5.40).

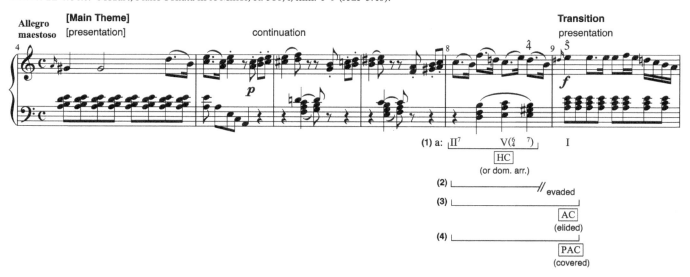

this scenario, Neuwirth points to Example 4.83 and notes that following the cadential dominant in measure 19,

> there is no tonic harmony provided at this point, but rather a fully diminished sonority (VII$^6_5$/V) based on A—a dissonant harmony that propels the music further instead of allowing a resting place. The diminished chord is prolonged into the next bar [m. 21], where it resolves into a V$^6$ chord; this in turn leads to a root-position tonic preparing a second attempt to achieve a complete cadence.[168]

Neuwirth thus describes well the conditions of an abandoned cadence (though without using that term). Yet given the slow tempo, it is not unreasonable for a listener first to hear the sense of deceptive cadence on the second beat of measure 20, especially given the sarabande style of the movement, which finds many points of closure on the second beat of the bar (as witnessed already in the main theme, Ex. 4.21 above). As the music progresses and the VII$^6_5$/V over ⑥ moves on to V$^6$, the listener may reassess the situation and recognize an abandoned cadence in place of the initially assumed deceptive one.

### 4.6.7. Multiple Ambiguities

#### 4.6.7.1. Mozart, Piano Sonata in A Minor, K. 310, i, mm. 1–10

An especially complex set of circumstances may give rise to three or more cadential interpretations. Burstein has drawn attention to two of these exceptional cases, the first of which is shown in Example 4.84a, "one of the warhorses of music analysis classes."[169] Burstein offers three possibilities for how this sonata-form main theme closes: with an HC in measure 8, an evaded cadence at the end of the same bar, and an elided authentic cadence on the downbeat of measure 9. Let us consider each of these options in turn, noting that by not specifying which type of authentic cadence comes into play at measure 9 (IAC or PAC), Burstein leaves the door open for a fourth option, namely, a *covered* authentic cadence.

---

168. Neuwirth, "*Fuggir la Cadenza*," 138, in reference to his Ex. 12. The second attempt is evaded at the end of m. 23, only to find its closing PAC at m. 26. Note, by the way, that when Neuwirth speaks of the diminished-seventh harmony in mm. 20–21 being "based on A," he is referring to the harmony being set over the bass note A, and not its being a dominant substitute with an implied root of A.

169. Burstein, "Slippery Events," 221–22, Ex. 21.

EXAMPLE 4.84B. From Burstein, "Slippery Events," Ex. 21c.

Burstein supports a reading of HC in measure 8 (annotated in option 1) by appealing to an important convention of sonata form, characterized most recently by Hepokoski and Darcy as a "grand antecedent," but first described as an *aufgelöste Nachsatz* ("dissolved consequent") by A. B. Marx in the nineteenth century.[170] As discussed already in the previous chapter (sec. 3.3.4.2), this technique sees a main theme closing with an HC, thus suggesting an antecedent function for the theme as a whole. When the theme begins again in the manner of a matching consequent, that function eventually "dissolves" when a modulation to the subordinate key reveals this failed consequent to be the real start of the exposition's transition. The main theme thus consists of an antecedent alone. Hearing an HC in measure 8 of Example 4.84a, however, is rather precarious due to the dissonant seventh ($\hat{4}$) lying prominently at the top of the texture. Burstein acknowledges this harmonic detail, but justifies it as a case of his "HC with $V^7$." As mentioned earlier (sec. 4.4.1), however, I would understand this situation to be a dominant arrival. Here, the deviation functions within the context of a main theme to end an antecedent unit. Problematic, though, is the lack of a true consequent that would close the theme with a PAC. As a result, the dominant arrival would represent the final cadential articulation of the main theme, a circumstance that is extremely rare.[171]

Burstein also mentions the possibility of the theme ending with an evaded cadence (what he calls a "disrupted ending") and notes that choosing this interpretation over that of an HC "depends on one's own tolerance for half-cadential abruptness."[172] Since I have a difficult time hearing an ultimate dominant in measure 8, but rather perceive a penultimate one (embellished with the conventional $^{6-7}_{4-3}$ pattern), I find the idea of an evaded authentic cadence considerably more palatable than an HC. Again, this reading leaves the main theme without any cadential closure.[173]

The third option discussed by Burstein sees the theme ending with an elided authentic cadence on the downbeat of measure 9. In support of this reading, he notes "the stylistically idiomatic loop structure that would result [i.e., the elision of the main theme and transition], the presence of $V^7$ in m. 8, the acceleration from m. 8 into m. 9, and the more normative hypermetric layout in which m. 9 would stand at the end of a four-measure hypermeasure" (see his voice-leading and hypermetrical interpretation shown in Ex. 4.84b).[174] Countering this reading, he alludes to the problematic parallel fifths in the left hand and outer voices if we were to group measure 9 with measure 8. What Burstein does not explicitly mention is which type of authentic cadence would arise—an IAC or a PAC.[175] If we consider the melody on its own, we might find here an IAC ending on $\hat{5}$, recalling, however, that this situation is highly exceptional and normally explained in some other manner (see Chapter 3, sec. 3.2.1.5). Indeed, as discussed in the previous chapter, one way of accounting for such an IAC ($\hat{5}$) is to recognize instead a *covered* cadence (sec. 3.4.2.3), whereby we understand $\hat{5}$ to function exclusively as the beginning note of a new unit, not as the cadential close of the ongoing theme, which usually ends on $\hat{1}$ for a PAC. Though he does not refer to this fourth option, Burstein would seem to support it because his voice-leading sketch shows the melodic line of the theme concluding on A, not E, as indicated by the end of the slur. And even if the pitch A is not literally present in the musical texture, it is implied by the preceding cadential melody. The idea of a covered PAC is especially compelling in this particular movement due its highly orchestral character.[176] It is easy to imagine that following a tutti presentation phrase (mm. 1–5), the woodwinds alone would sound the plaintive circle-of-fifths sequence, beginning with the

---

170. Burstein, 221; Hepokoski and Darcy, *Sonata Theory*, 77–80; Marx, *Musical Form*, 107. See *CF*, 129, and *ACF*, 310–11, for my own analytical application of this idea.

171. The only other case I have found appears in the first movement of Beethoven's "Appassionata" sonata, Op. 57, whose main theme ends with a terminal dominant arrival on $V^6$ (m. 16). That case, however, does not raise any of the other cadential ambiguities that we see in the present theme by Mozart.

172. Burstein, "Slippery Events," 221. His "disrupted ending" is a broad category that embraces what I call evaded cadence among other cadential situations.

173. Even the case of the "Appassionata" sonata, mentioned in note 171, seems more closed by a dominant arrival than would any main theme ending exclusively with an evaded cadence. An additional problem with the evaded cadence interpretation of Ex. 4.84 involves the music to which the cadential evasion backs up, namely to the *beginning* of the theme. As discussed earlier in sec. 4.2.2.2, a one-more-time repetition rarely returns to the opening of the ongoing thematic unit.

174. Burstein, "Slippery Events," 221, Ex. 21c.

175. For this reason, I annotate option 3 with the cadence symbol "AC," which does not indicate the degree of melodic closure of the cadence.

176. See again, note 158.

EXAMPLE 4.85. Haydn, String Quartet in D, Op. 71, no. 2, iii, mm. 1–10.

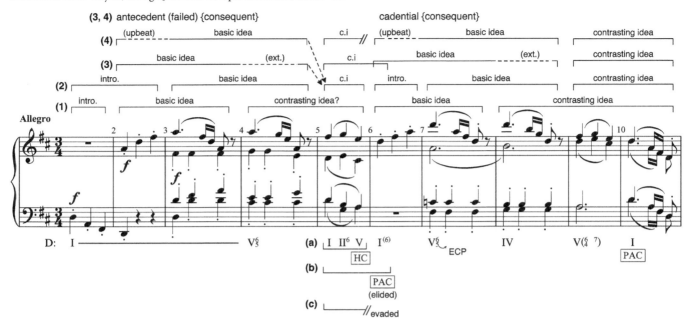

upbeat to measure 6, and continue with the cadence in measures 8 and 9, at which point the full orchestra would bring a *forte* return of the opening $\hat{5}$, to "cover" the cadential $\hat{1}$, presumably buried in the winds. With this view, the seeming parallel fifths are due to limitations of the piano texture, which, in order to effect the return of the tutti, must sound again the drum-bass pattern from the opening of the movement.

Though I prefer this fourth interpretation of a covered PAC, I fully endorse Burstein's insistence that we keep all of these possibilities in mind, especially since each option may be suggested by an actual performance.[177] Indeed, as I have continually stressed throughout this section on cadential ambiguities, the goal is not to come up with a definitive decision, but rather to expose, and then to weigh against each other, those factors that point toward various alternatives.

### 4.6.7.2. Haydn, String Quartet in D, Op. 71, no 3, iii, mm. 1–10

The second case of multiple ambiguities discussed by Burstein is shown in Example 4.85, the A section of a minuet form. As regards the first cadential articulation, he points out three possible interpretations: an HC at the end of measure 5 (option a);

an elided PAC on the downbeat of measure 6 (option b); and a "disrupted ending" (i.e., evaded cadence) at the same location (option c).[178] In my view, additional ambiguities of grouping structure, cadence, and formal functionality are also offered by this theme.

Seeing as the cello's descending arpeggio in quarter notes (m. 1) neither appears again in the entire minuet nor belongs to any unit we would think to be a basic idea, we can confidently consider it to be an introduction that lies outside of the thematic boundaries (see line 1 of the analyses placed above the score). (To be sure, a descending arpeggio is clearly motivic, as seen in mm. 3–4, 7–8, and 10, yet each time it reappears with a dotted rhythmic profile, not with the steady quarter notes of m. 1.) With this option, we would likely hear a two-measure basic idea in measures 2–3, such that measure 4 would presumably begin a contrasting idea. Alternatively (see line 2), we might imagine measure 2 as part of a larger thematic introduction, due to the content of that bar being related to measure 1 through contour inversion. If so, then the basic idea would embrace measures 3 and 4, a feasible proposition since a basic idea may consist of a repeated one-measure motive.[179] As well, the sense of the theme "beginning" at measure 3 is supported by the newly entering drum-bass accompanimental pattern.

These two grouping options (lines 1 and 2) assume that each bar in the opening four-measure unit has an independent role to play within the phrase. But a somewhat more complicated picture also emerges. On the one hand, we might hear measure 4 not as the start of a contrasting idea (line 1), but rather as an *extension* of the basic idea via a repetition on its second half, as represented in line 3. On the other hand, we could hear measure 2 not as part of

---

177. In this connection, Burstein refers to eight different performances that can be heard in audio clips found on the *Music Theory Spectrum* website associated with "Slippery Events." Especially admirable in Burstein's study is his consideration of performances that seem to "realize" the cadential possibilities that he discusses. Limitations of space prohibit my own examination of these issues using multiple performances, but the examples of ambiguities discussed in this section (including other cases dealt with earlier on) may provide useful material for future research along these lines.

178. Burstein, "Slippery Events," 220–21.

179. See *CF*, 37, and *ACF*, 39, 88–89.

a thematic introduction, but rather as an "extended upbeat" to the basic idea beginning at measure 3, as shown in line 4.[180]

The next issue to consider is the unit following the basic idea. In none of the views just offered do we find the idea being repeated to make a presentation phrase. So we are likely to be looking for a two-measure contrasting idea. As shown in line 1, I already raised the possibility of that idea appearing immediately after the basic idea; further supporting that view is the cadential progression in measure 5, which could yield an HC at the very end of the bar, as proposed by Burstein (see line "a" in the harmonic analysis).

The three options shown in lines 2–4 find the basic idea lasting through measure 4, so in these cases, the contrasting idea would begin at measure 5. If, like the previous option in line 1, we hear the harmonies in that bar as half cadential (line a), then the contrasting idea would last only one bar (line 2), thus yielding an opening antecedent phrase of only three bars. A one-bar contrasting idea ending with an HC could also follow the basic ideas in lines 3 and 4 (see the dashed arrows).

Another possibility would find the contrasting idea concluding on the downbeat of measure 6, as shown in line 3. This option would normalize the idea as a two-measure unit, as well as result in our hearing an authentic cadential progression ending with a PAC (line b). This interpretation would also be possible following the basic ideas of lines 2 and 4. (I forgo the dashed lines in these cases to avoid unduly cluttering the annotations.)

Finally, we could experience the contrasting idea as being only one bar long as the result of an evaded cadence, shown both in lines 4 and c. (Again, this option is also available for lines 2 and 3.) The grounds for hearing a cadential evasion lie with the abrupt cessation of the accompanimental pattern at the end of measure 5, as well as the change in articulation from *legato* to *staccato*. In sum, the opening phrase, following the introduction of measure 1, can be construed as lasting three bars (line 2), four bars (lines 1 and 4), or five bars (line 3). Moreover, the phrase could close with an HC, a PAC, or an evaded cadence (lines a, b, and c, respectively). As mentioned, various other combinations of basic and contrasting ideas are also available. With respect to the form-functional interpretation of the entire first phrase, I will consider some options after having examined the following phrase.

Turning now to this second phrase, the situation is (thankfully) less complex. In the first place, it unambiguously closes with a PAC in measure 10. Moreover, the cadential progression is now expanded to support measures 7–10. As for measure 6, the tonic harmony there might be considered to be in root position, assuming a PAC in that bar, or it might imply being a $I^6$, assuming an evaded cadence. (In the case of a preceding HC in measure 5, both I or $I^6$ can reasonably initiate the second phrase.) The internal grouping structure of phrase 2 is still complex, but it models the options already discussed for phrase 1. Thus the various versions of the basic idea are seen in lines 1 through 4. In the case of line 1, there would be no thematic introduction, and in the case of line 2, that introduction would be only one bar long (m. 6). The contrasting idea would then last two bars in most of the interpretations, except for line 1, where it would be extended to three bars by the PAC in measure 10.

At this point we are ready to consider which form-functional descriptors are best assigned to the two phrases of the theme. An interpretation of "antecedent" would be apt for any of the cases that recognize an HC at measure 5. But for those that find either a PAC or an evaded cadence in measure 6, the label "consequent" (either realized or failed, due to the evasion) would appropriately identify the phrase's *intrinsic* functionality, even if this interpretation belies the *contextual* function of the phrase, which is obviously one of formal initiation.[181] As for the second phrase, its containing a single ECP suggests a label of "cadential." At the same time, its constituent ideas so closely match those of the opening phrase, it seems legitimate as well to identify basic and contrasting ideas. And for that reason, speaking of measures 6–10 as a "consequent" is viable, even if somewhat odd due to the ECP supporting the complete phrase.

Up to now, I have adopted a neutral stance as regards the many differing interpretations of grouping, cadence, and formal function identifiable in this theme, since they all have a degree of validity. I am, however, skeptical of some of the readings and more persuaded by others. As proposed in the analysis of line 1, for example, I find it difficult to hear measures 4 and 5 grouping together as a contrasting idea: first, such an idea rarely begins with material from the latter half of the basic idea; second, measures 4–5 seem hardly to belong to each other as a unified melodic gesture; and third, the HC occurring on the weakest beat of the bar seems highly abrupt.

As for line 2, I do not readily hear an HC at the end of measure 5 because (excluding the introduction) we rarely find a cadence in the third bar of a theme.[182] More convincing is the possibility of an HC for lines 1, 3, and 4, since at least there, the cadence would be occurring in the fourth bar of the phrase. Yet the appearance of the HC on the metrically weak third beat is somewhat questionable. To be sure, Burstein argues that "as has been acknowledged since the eighteenth century, occasionally phrases can plausibly be interpreted as terminating on the final beat of a measure," and he cites an example discussed by H. C. Koch that would appear to feature an HC on the third beat of a minuet.[183] Moreover, my discussion of cadence and meter in the

---

180. Ryan C. McClelland, "Extended Upbeats in the Classical Minuet: Interactions with Hypermeter and Phrase Structure," 43–45, Ex. 18. McClelland's discussion of this movement largely deals with hypermetrical issues, but his analysis also touches on some of the issues of form and cadence raised in connection with my Ex. 4.85.

181. We sometimes find such intrinsically "ending" phrases opening a minuet form, as discussed in *CF*, 222–23, Ex. 15.2, and *ACF*, 617–18, Ex. 18.4. In such circumstances, however, the following phrase (or phrases) modulate to the subordinate key, ending the opening section with an SK: PAC that matches the "early HK: PAC" (as I call it). With Haydn's theme of Ex. 4.85, however, the second phrase remains in the home key.

182. For an exception, see again in Chapter 2, note 32.

183. Burstein, "Slippery Events," 220–21; Koch, *Introductory Essay on Composition*, 125, Ex. 286. In the absence of a bass line for this example (identified as a "Menuet" by C. G. Scheinpflug), it is difficult to

previous chapter concluded that an identification of cadence is not dependent on any particular metrical placement. In my own research, however, I have not yet uncovered a classical minuet in which an opening antecedent ends with an HC ($II^6$–V) on beat three of the phrase's final bar, though such a case may eventually be found.[184] I find it very difficult, in fact, to hear this interpretation in Haydn's minuet. With a relatively slow performance, I can "force" myself to perceive an HC, but at moderate and relatively fast tempi, I hear the progression I–$II^6$–V (m. 5) as projecting an impending authentic cadence, with the dominant functioning as a penultimate harmony. I fully recognize, of course, that other musicians may be convinced by an HC interpretation here.[185] As regards a PAC for measure 6 (the option shown in line 3, but also available for lines 2 and 4), the issue is one of formal convention. It is rare in the classical style to find a period-like structure whose phrases are closed by cadences of the same syntactical weight.

My preferred hearing of the grouping structure of this theme is reflected in either lines 3 or 4. I have already discussed the problems I experience with line 1. For line 2, the completely different contour and instrumentation of measures 1 and 2 militate against my finding a two-measure introductory gesture. Rather, I lean toward hearing a three-measure basic idea containing a motivic extension (line 3) or an extended upbeat (line 4). Of the three cadential options offered for measures 5–6 of this example, my preference goes to the evaded cadence shown in line 4 (but available for all of the other grouping options). Yet I must also acknowledge a weakness with this choice. To speak of an evaded cadence following measure 5 is to recognize an *independent*, as opposed to a way-station, deviation. As discussed earlier in connection with Example 4.33, the use of an evaded cadence ending the first phrase of a periodic formation is rare.

To conclude this discussion of Haydn's minuet theme, I cannot find any fully satisfactory solutions to the many complications it presents. In fact, this is perhaps one of the most unusual themes in the classical repertory. Were I to be pinned down for a single phrase-structural and cadential analysis, I would tend toward the options shown in line 4 and line c as being the most coherent, though the idea of an evaded cadence at measure 6 is surely odd. That the theme offers so many possibilities for grouping, cadential, and form-functional interpretations attests to the composer's remarkable abilities. For despite all of its ambiguities, the theme nonetheless sounds compositionally effective, containing as it does so many witty touches and fanciful gestures, an aspect of Haydn's musical aesthetic that has been admired by scholars, performers, and audiences for more than two centuries.

---

ascertain whether the third beat actually contains an HC or some type of prolongational closure.

184. For a minuet whose opening phrase cadences with a reinterpreted HC on the *second* beat, see Mozart, Piano Sonata in A, K. 331, ii, m. 4, in the previous chapter (Ex. 3.146); another example by Mozart (Piano Sonata in D, K. 284, ii, m. 8; see Ex. 3.164) contains a compound antecedent closing on beat two of a triple meter.

185. Thus McClelland explicitly annotates an HC at this point in the piece ("Extended Upbeats," 46, Ex. 18).

# 5
# Cadential Expansion

A STYLISTIC HALLMARK OF MUSIC IN THE high classical era is the practice of considerably lengthening cadential passages, compared to the relatively brief configurations favored in earlier tonal works.[1] As I highlight in the following two chapters, baroque and galant styles favor formulaic, *compact cadences*, even in contexts of significant formal loosening. By contrast, composers in the final quarter of the eighteenth century found the means of controlling the pace of harmonic activity such that a powerful sense of closure could be achieved by enlarging the cadential progression within a thematic unit. This chapter considers in detail such *expanded cadences*, focusing on the morphology of the three cadence types (PAC, IAC, and HC) as well as their various deviations (deception, evasion, abandonment, and dominant arrivals). (It will not be necessary to include a specific section on the function of such expansions since they can be used wherever it is appropriate to loosen the cadential function.) Along the way, I will revisit a number of issues raised in prior chapters, but now more specifically related to cadential expansion.[2] The chapter concludes with a detailed examination of selected passages of cadential expansion in Beethoven's symphonic oeuvre.

Insofar as I define the boundaries of cadential function as coinciding with the temporal extent of its supporting harmonies,

---

[1]. Many of the theoretical principles and individual analyses presented in this chapter derive from four of my earlier publications: "The 'Expanded Cadential Progression': A Category for the Analysis of Classical Form"; "Harmonic Variants of the Expanded Cadential Progression"; "Analysis Symposium: The Andante of Mozart's Symphony No. 40 in G Minor"; and "Structural Expansion in Beethoven's Symphonic Forms." The ca. 150 works examined for this chapter include pieces discussed in these publications, as well as many found on the *ACF* website (see again Chapter 3, note 1).

[2]. Examples of cadential expansion have already been discussed and illustrated on earlier occasions. For Chapters 2 and 3, see Ex. 2.16, 2.18, 2.25, 3.69, 3.78, 3.79, 3.84, 3.141, 3.153, 3.156, 3.168, 3.172, and 3.174. Chapter 4 includes many cases, because the techniques of cadential deviation and expansion typically work hand in hand to effect formal loosening (see Ex. 4.2, 4.7, 4.8, 4.14, 4.16, 4.26, 4.31, 4.36, 4.37, 4.39, 4.43, 4.44, 4.49a, 4.50a, 4.63, 4.76, 4.78, 4.79, and 4.56). To avoid duplicating musical examples, I will often discuss ones shown in these chapters.

EXAMPLE 5.1. Haydn, Piano Sonata in E-flat, H. 25, i, mm. 4–8 (R = ½N) (*ACF* 10.12).

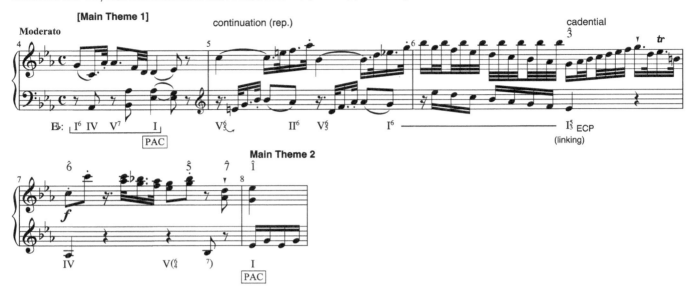

we must first consider how much lengthening they must undergo in order to speak of their forming an *expanded cadential progression* (ECP).³ As a rule of thumb, I identify an ECP when the authentic cadential progression is expanded to support a least a full phrase of music. Since most phrases within a classical theme consist minimally of four real measures, I tend not to recognize as ECPs authentic progressions that are any shorter in length.⁴ To be sure, circumstances arise where we may question whether or not the progression is sufficiently long to be considered a genuine ECP, though admittedly such a determination is often of little analytical import. Still, it would be useful to examine some of these ambiguous cases if for no other reason than to help sharpen our classification of cadential function and grouping structure. Cases of an ECP that yield a half cadence may involve a shorter progression, inasmuch as that cadence type contains only three harmonic stages (rather than the four stages of the authentic cadence). A discussion of HC expansion is postponed to a later section (5.3.1) of the chapter.

## 5.1. Perfect Authentic Cadence

The morphology of an expanded perfect authentic cadence is essentially the same as that described in Chapter 3, except that the lengthening of the harmonic progression permits room for a greater diversity of harmonic and melodic content. As regards harmony, composers can take advantage of an ECP in order to bring a wider variety than is normally found in a compact progression. Indeed, the specific choice of harmonies and their disposition within one or more ECPs of a formal unit often prompt considerable analytical interest, as will be apparent in many cases discussed throughout the chapter. With respect to melody, the various patterns outlined in Chapter 3 (e.g., "simple basic," "varied soprano," "successive combinations") are often identifiable in ECPs. Extensive surface embellishments (scales, arpeggios) arising in the drive to the cadential goal, however, can sometimes obscure the presence of an underlying melodic pattern or even render it impossible to be identified.

### 5.1.1. Harmonic Content
#### 5.1.1.1. Stage 1—Initial Tonic

As with compact cadential progressions, stage 1 of an ECP frequently consists exclusively of tonic harmony in first inversion (I⁶). This usage is so common as not to require further illustration here.

**Root-Position Tonic.** The initial tonic of an ECP infrequently appears in root position, most likely because an expansion of that tonic would more likely be associated with initiating or medial formal functions than with cadential ones. Example 5.1 illustrates a root-position tonic that functions as a linking harmony to connect the continuation and cadential functions. A first main theme closes with a compact cadence in measure 4. The continuation phrase begins to be repeated in measure 5 but is extended through the first half of measure 6. The root position tonic supporting the second half of that bar can then be understood as belonging both to the prior continuation and to the onset of the ECP. Haydn could easily have added ③ in the bass on the last

---

3. For my first theoretical articulation and analytical application of this idea, as well as references to its antecedents in earlier writings, see Caplin, "'Expanded Cadential Progression,'" 246. More recently, Gjerdingen has coined the term "Grand Cadence" for what is essentially an ECP (*Galant Style*, 152).

4. I should note in this connection that I normally accord only a single measure for the final stage of the progression (stage 4, for authentic cadential progressions; stage 3, for half cadential ones). I do so because any further expansion of the final harmony is normally heard as *postcadential*, and thus not belonging to the ECP proper.

EXAMPLE 5.2. Haydn, String Quartet in F, Op. 77, no. 2, iii, mm. 16–22 (ACF 7.20).

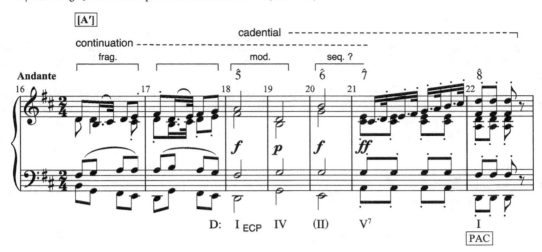

eighth note of bar 6, thus beginning the progression with I⁶, but since he does not, we can hear the expanded I as the first harmony of the cadence. Since this movement is notated in compound meter (R = ½N), we see here a short ECP lasting only four (real) measures.[5] With such a minimally sized ECP, the harmonies of each stage are normally distributed one per bar, as seen in this example.[6]

In Example 5.2, the A′ section of a rounded binary movement also uses a root-position tonic to initiate an ECP. Up to this point, the rhythmic texture of the movement's main theme has its accompanimental voices predominantly strolling along in eighth notes, as seen in the opening bars of the excerpt. Following a four-measure presentation (not shown), these bars (mm. 16–17) function as the beginning of a continuation phrase, as projected by the fragmentation into one-measure units. Most surprising, then, is the abrupt halt in motion at measure 18, brought about by a *forte* half-note, root-position tonic, which throws the formal functionality into doubt. The following half-note subdominant, with a *piano* dynamic, further clouds the picture. When measure 20 returns to *forte* with yet another half-note triad, now built over II, we might believe that an ascending-stepwise sequence were in the making, thus furthering the continuation function. Indeed, the following bar brings the sequential V (corresponding to IV of m. 19), yet with the now *fortissimo* dynamic and the resumption of the eighth-note accompanimental texture, the resolution of this dominant to tonic clearly effects a PAC on the downbeat of measure 22. We can now look back at the tonic of measure 18 and reinterpret it as the start of an ECP, one that contains root-position triads exclusively.[7]

**Harmonic Variants.** As for the harmonic variants that may constitute stage 1b, we occasionally encounter the tonic substitute VI (see ahead, Ex. 5.14a, m. 79, and Ex. 5.28, m. 98), though rarely as the initial harmony of an ECP.[8] A more common embellishment sees I⁶ converted into a secondary dominant of IV. Usually this harmony is built over ③ as V⁶ or V⁶₅ of the subdominant (refer back to Ex. 3.69, m. 5), but this dominant can be manifested by a variety of harmonies, such as V⁷/IV (over ①), V⁴₂/IV (♭⑦), VII⁷/IV (③) (see earlier, Ex. 4.63, m. 298), and VII⁴₃/IV (⑤).[9] In addition, the supertonic (usually II⁶) of stage 2a may be tonicized in stage 1b by its own secondary dominant, such as VII⁶₅/II (③) or VII⁴₃/II (⑤). Both of these latter harmonies appear in a large-scale ECP in the subordinate-theme group of Mozart's Symphony No. 39, first movement (Ex. 5.3). In the first subordinate theme (not shown), a couple of compact cadences omit an initial tonic over ③. The presentation phrase of the second subordinate theme then emphasizes this bass degree, supporting I⁶, after which a brief continuation leads to an ECP at measure 125 that begins with VII⁶₅/II over ③. The cadence is then evaded at measure 130, and a one-more-time repetition is projected by the melody. When we attend to the bass voice, however, we see that rather than backing up to ③, Mozart holds on to ⑤, supporting a different inversion of the previous secondary dominant of stage

---

5. To save space, the full length of the stage-4 harmony will not always be shown in the examples.

6. The analysis of the principal melodic scale degrees of this ECP (as well as many others that follow) refers to a later discussion of melodic content (sec. 5.1.2).

7. Another textural anomaly of this first-movement main theme is worthy of mention (the entire theme is reproduced in Ex. 7.20 on the ACF

website). Both the A and B sections of the ternary are given to the first violin and cello alone; only with the beginning of the A′ section do the second violin and viola join in, producing a marvelous effect of the full quartet sounding a lush harmonization of the melody. The root-position chordal texture of the ECP (mm. 18–21), which suddenly slows down the ongoing motion, underlines even more the full four-voice sonority of the complete quartet.

8. One case of an initial VI arises in Haydn's Symphony No. 98 in B-flat, iv, mm. 98–102. A most unusual use of ♭VI⁵ is discussed ahead in Ex. 5.44, m. 58; see also CF, Ex. 8.11, and ACF, Ex. 12.11a).

9. For V⁷/IV, see Beethoven String Quartet in F, Op. 18, no. 1, i, m. 26; for V⁴₂/IV, see Haydn, Piano Sonata in D, H. 37, iii, m. 17 (ACF, 7.2); for VII⁴₃/IV, see Haydn, Symphony No. 98 in B-flat, iv, m. 112.

EXAMPLE 5.3. Mozart, Symphony No. 39 in E-flat, K. 543, i, mm. 124–35.

EXAMPLE 5.4. Haydn, String Quartet in F, Op. 50, no. 5, i, (a) mm. 12–20; (b) mm. 1–8.

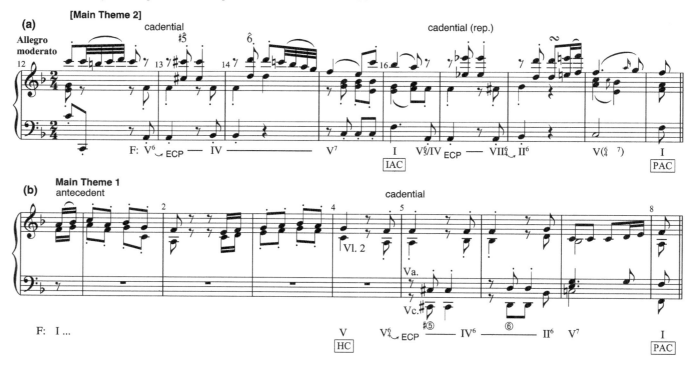

1b, namely, VII$^4_3$/II (m. 130). In the next bar, the bass drops down to ④ for the II$^6$ of stage 2a, but Mozart again varies the harmony by inverting the pre-dominant of stage 2b as VII$^6_5$/V, thus engaging ⑥. The ensuing dominant finally resolves to tonic to create the PAC at measure 135. Here, then, is one of several cases that we will examine in this chapter where the composer, in the context of a one-more-time (or similar) repetition, does not bring a conventional twofold occurrence of a standard cadential bass line, but rather uses harmonic variants to fashion a *single* line, one that may be somewhat unidiomatic in its melodic shape.

If the fifth of an initial tonic is raised by a half step (♯5̂), thus promising resolution to 6̂, the resulting augmented triad functions as a secondary dominant of IV. We find an instance of this harmonic variant (V$^+$/IV–IV) in Example 5.4a, measures 13–14, which shows the final two phrases of the second main theme (a variation of the first main theme, to be discussed shortly). When the cadential phrase concludes with a way-station IAC in measure

EXAMPLE 5.5. Beethoven, Piano Sonata in E, Op. 14, no. 1, i, mm. 38–46.

10. The opening of the first cadential phrase of the second main theme (Ex. 5.4a, mm. 13–14) returns, with some variation, in the second phrase of the first subordinate theme (Ex. 2.25, mm. 51–54). Note, as well, that in Ex. 5.4b, I identify mm. 5–8 as a phrase supported by an ECP in the home key of F major, beginning with the unusual initial tonic (V$_4^6$/IV). In Ex. 2.25 (mm. 47–48), on the contrary, I consider the same progression (now in the subordinate key of C major), as effecting the sense of a deceptive resolution of the dominant (V–V$^6_5$/IV–IV$^6$). The difference in the harmonic analysis is due to the instrumentation. In the latter case, the viola's and cello's G♯ (♯5) in m. 47 ensues from a sounding G♯ (⑤), mm. 45–46, thus rendering the deceptive resolution. In the former case (Ex. 5.4b), the C♯ (♯5) comes in "out of the blue" with the first entrance of the cello and viola (second staff of the score), and thus does not connect directly with the bass of the half cadence in m. 4 (second violin). In contrast, it would not be unreasonable to consider the second phrase of the subordinate theme (Ex. 2.25, mm. 51–54) to be supported by an ECP, just as we heard earlier in the main theme (Ex. 5.4b, mm. 5–8).

16, a repetition brings two other stage-1 secondary dominants (V$^6_5$/IV and VII$^6_4$/II) to reinforce the move to stage 2.

The use of an augmented sonority to begin the ECP is already found in the first main theme (Ex. 5.4b). There, the opening compound basic idea, sounded by the violins alone, exploits the hunting topic of horn fifths. In keeping with this topic, the opening of the second phrase (upbeat to m. 5), retains the interval of a sixth between the two violins (cf., m. 2). As a result, when the two lower instruments finally appear at measure 5, they complete the initial tonic harmony while chromatically altering the bass (♯5) to create a most unusual six-four position of the secondary dominant. The consequences of this harmonic choice are then further played out in the first subordinate theme, as previously discussed in Chapter 2 (in connection with Ex. 2.25).[10]

**Rocking on the Tonic.** When stage 1 of an ECP is represented by a single harmony, this initial tonic (or tonic variant) is rarely more expansive than the remaining stages of the progression. One such case, though, has already been illustrated in the previous chapter (Ex. 4.36), where the first stage of each ECP lasts twice as long as the other stages. Frequently, a significant expansion of the tonic is produced by its prolongation via subordinate, neighboring harmonies. Most often we find a dominant seventh in third inversion (V$^4_2$) serving to expand I$^6$, often with the impression of a "rocking back and forth" of these two harmonies. Indeed, it is useful to speak colloquially in these circumstances of a *rocking on the tonic* in the spirit of a "standing" on the dominant.[11] Occasionally a neighboring subdominant is used to prolong the tonic.

In most cases of a rocking on the tonic, the neighboring V$^4_2$ is metrically stressed in relation to the resolving I$^6$, either as the strong beat within the bar, Example 5.5 (mm. 39–40 and 43–44), or in what we take to be a hypermetrically accented bar (Ex. 5.6), normally the "odd-numbered measures" within a clear grouping structure. Now and then, V$^4_2$ is metrically weak (Ex. 5.7); note in this case that measure 17, the final bar of stage 1, retains I$^6$ throughout (thus deleting an expected V$^4_2$ on beat 3) so that the pre-dominant in the following bar can be approached by a tonic, rather than, non-syntactically, by a dominant.

11. I concede that "rocking on the tonic" is perhaps overly colloquial, but given how pervasive this technique is—practically every case of an ECP in Beethoven's symphonies (to be discussed at the end of this chapter) features this device in some way or another—it is necessary to have a concrete label at hand.

228  Cadential Expansion

EXAMPLE 5.6. Beethoven, String Quartet in F, Op. 59, no. 1, i, mm. 73–77.

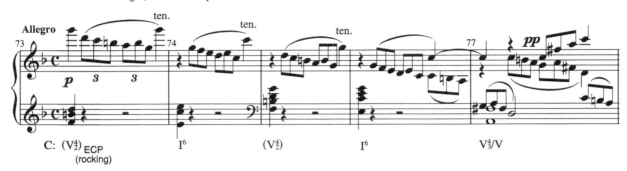

EXAMPLE 5.7. Haydn, Symphony No. 101 in D, iii, mm. 14–20 (*ACF* 18.2).

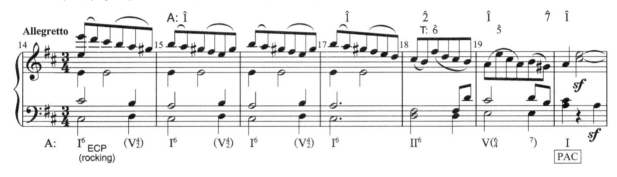

EXAMPLE 5.8. Haydn, String Quartet in F, Op. 77, no. 2, i, mm. 48–54.

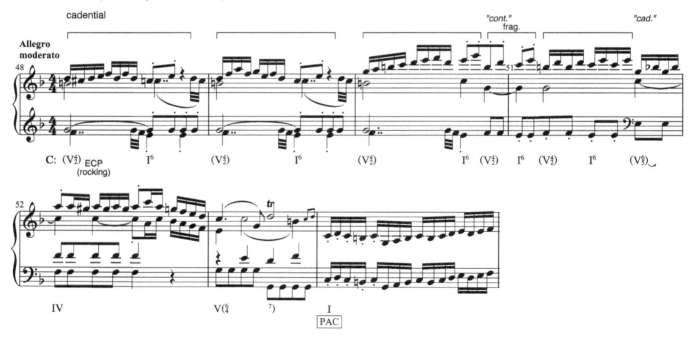

At times, the rocking on the tonic can be sufficiently extensive as to incorporate a process of phrase-structural fragmentation into this first stage of the cadential progression (Ex. 5.8, upbeat to m. 51). Note that this fragmentation (along with the harmonic acceleration) conveys a sense of "continuation" function embedded within the overall cadential function. As such, when the bass at the end of measure 51 leaps down an octave to support a stage-1b shift to $V^6_5$/IV, this important textural marker can project the idea that a more exclusively "cadential" expression is being renewed following the brief "continuational" passage.

A rocking on the tonic most often engages a neighboring $V^4_2$, since this harmony demands resolution to $I^6$. Sometimes,

EXAMPLE 5.9. Beethoven, Piano Sonata in E-flat, Op. 31, no. 3, ii, mm. 43–50 (*ACF* 12.14).

EXAMPLE 5.10. Mozart, Symphony No. 36 in C, K. 425, i, mm. 67–71 (*ACF* 12.10).

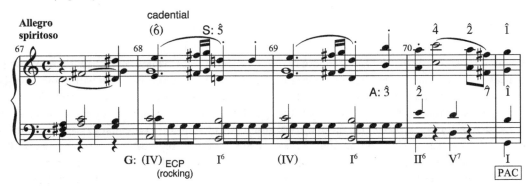

however, variant subordinate harmonies are employed, such as the diminished-seventh substitute, VII$^4_3$ (Ex. 5.9). Note again how the extensive rocking engenders fragmentation within stage 1 (mm. 47–48), with additional fragmentation in stages 2 and 3 (m. 49). In fact, we could even speak of this ECP as being organized like a simple eight-measure sentence, as annotated with the italicized phrase functions embedded within a broader cadential function of the subordinate theme as a whole.

Now and then the initial tonic will be embellished by a rocking subdominant harmony (see Ex. 5.10); not surprisingly, Mozart then chooses an alternative pre-dominant II$^6$ for stage 2. In Example 5.11, a Neapolitan, along with a dominant VII$^4_3$, is found rocking with I$^6$ in this continuation⇒cadential phrase.[12]

In the cases of rocking on the tonic so far observed, we have little hesitation in viewing the V$^4_2$ (or its substitute VII$^4_3$) as a genuine harmony of the ECP's stage 1, because the multiple occurrences of a back-and-forth bass motion yield an unambiguously expanded stage. But how are we to regard cases of a single subordinate dominant moving to I$^6$, such as that seen in Example 5.12, measures 45–46? In the context of a small binary theme, a contrasting middle concludes with an HC in measure 44. The following phrase begins with one bar of VII$^4_3$ followed by a bar of I$^6$ (m. 46). The cadential progression continues with stages 2 and 3 in measure 47, and the PAC closes the theme in the next bar. Considering the final phrase as whole, it is easy to hear one-bar

---

12. That the second quarter-note beat of m. 63 should be understood as a diminished seventh VII$^4_3$ with an implied E♮ and not as some kind of augmented-sixth harmony with E♭, is confirmed by the sixteenth-note melodic embellishment, which includes an explicit E♮ in the second beat of the following measure. To speak of a VII$^4_3$ (as opposed to a more literal VII$^4_2$), I am taking G to represent the bass in the first two quarter-note beats (just as I am not reading a change to I$^6_4$ on the last quarter note of m. 63).

EXAMPLE 5.11. Mozart, Rondo in F, K. 494, mm. 63–67 (*ACF* Sup. 6.6).

EXAMPLE 5.12. Mozart, Piano Sonata in C, K. 545, ii, mm. 44–48 (*ACF* Sup. 8.1).

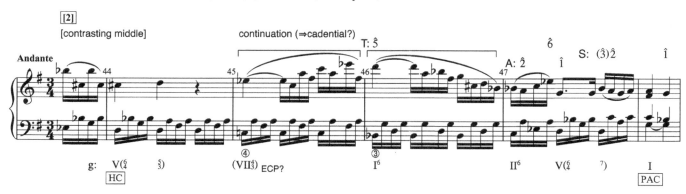

fragments in measures 45 and 46, followed by an increasing harmonic rhythm in measure 47. So continuation function is clearly expressed within these four bars. But should we also conclude that this phrase is supported entirely by an ECP, such that the label continuation⇒cadential is more accurate? On the one hand, we cannot speak here of a standard rocking on the tonic, since the ④–③ bass motion occurs but once. On the other hand, the strong harmonic connection between the VII$^4_3$ and the I$^6$ renders it plausible to hear measures 45–46 as an expanded initial tonic of an ECP. To be sure, this situation probably does not demand an unequivocal decision as to where, exactly, to analyze the onset of the cadential progression (this is more of a concern to students seeking the "correct" answer), so I am content to raise the issue here, but to leave it unresolved for the time being.[13]

To conclude this discussion on the morphology of a rocking on the tonic, I present in detail three cases that are particularly noteworthy for the harmonic variants contained within their cadential progressions.[14]

---

13. For other cases that raise the same problems, see *ACF*, Ex. 4.17, mm. 5–8; *ACF*, Ex. 5.33, mm. 5–8; *ACF*, Ex. 13.2, mm. 55–59; and *ACF* Website, Supplementary Ex. 8.9, mm. 13–16. *ACF*, Ex. 8.6, mm. 5–8, presents a similar case, though here, we might be more tempted than otherwise to hear an ECP, since the analogous fourth and sixth phrases of the theme (mm. 13–16 and mm. 21–24) contain unambiguous ECPs.

14. Throughout this chapter, we will observe additional examples of the rocking technique.

*1. Haydn, Symphony No. 45 in F-sharp Minor ("Farewell"), i.* The first case features two ECPs within the three-key exposition of Haydn's "Farewell" Symphony, first movement (Ex. 5.13).[15] Following the presentation and continuation phrases of the transition (not shown), a cadential passage in A major (the first of two subordinate keys) begins at measure 29 with I$^6$. There ensues a rocking back and forth with a dominant that seems to be in root position. This harmony is most unconventional here, since within a cadential progression, a root-position dominant is, with few exceptions, exclusively confined to stage 3.

What motivates this unusual position of the neighboring dominant is Haydn's transferring of the soprano's eighth-note motive ("x") of measure 29 into the bass of the following bar. To be sure, we might want to choose the upper note D as representing the true bass of measure 30, in accordance with the voice-leading conventions of a rocking on the tonic. The lower E would then be regarded as a "casting out of the root" (as Schenker would say). Ultimately, this ECP is abandoned when the presumed cadential II$^6$ of measure 34 becomes a sequential harmony, moving up to III$^6$ in measure 35 and eventually reaching V$^6$ (not shown).

Haydn's use of a root-position V in this rocking on the tonic foreshadows an even more peculiar ECP in the subordinate theme that follows (Ex. 5.13b). After modulating from A minor

---

15. For a detailed phrase-structural analysis of the transition and subordinate theme of this exposition, see Caplin and Martin, "'Continuous Exposition,'" 11–18.

EXAMPLE 5.13. Haydn, Symphony No. 45 in F-sharp Minor ("Farewell"), i, (a) mm. 29–35; (b) mm. 54–65.

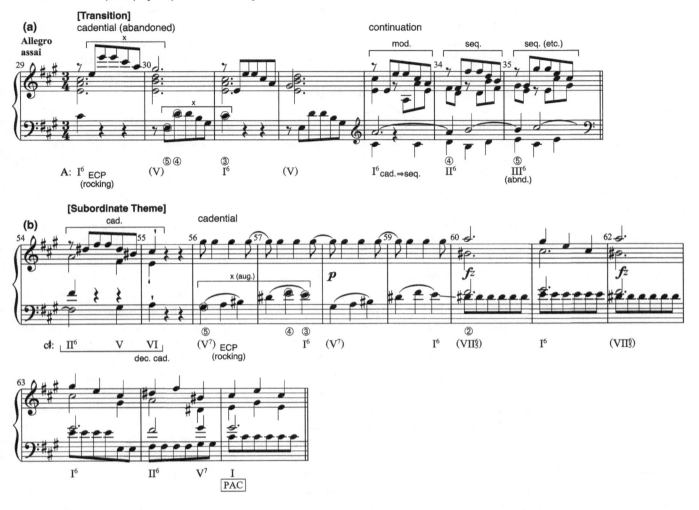

to C-sharp minor, the theme is abruptly closed by the way-station deceptive cadence in measures 54–55. But rather than repeating the prior continuation (in the sense of a one-more-time technique), Haydn launches into a most "creepy" ECP. It begins with a quarter-note motive in the bass part, which rises from ⑤ up to ④ by means of an arpeggiated diminished seventh, resolving to ③ in support of the prolonged cadential I⁶ (last beat of m. 57). Note that this motive represents an augmented version of motive "x" in Example 5.13a, measure 30 (cf. the circled notes). As a result of this motivic play, the neighboring dominant within the subordinate-theme's rocking on the tonic stands again in root position (Ex. 5.13b, mm. 56–59).

Following this passage, the rocking continues in measures 60–63 with a substitute diminished seventh (VII⁶₅ over ②) as the subordinate dominant of the I⁶ prolongation. This, of course, is the same diminished-seventh harmony found within the ascending arpeggiation of the creepy motive ("x" aug.). It is not clear why Haydn chooses this less conventional position of the diminished seventh, which would normally be VII⁴₃ over ④, as a substitute for V⁴₂. Perhaps he prefers to let the quarter-note motive continue on with a linear descent from F♯ and E (end of m. 59) to D♯, rather than returning to F♯ (for a more conventional VII⁴₃). There may also be a hypermetrical reason for this odd harmonic usage, since Haydn continues to let D♯ in the bass appear on the accented measures 60 and 62 (taking an "odd-measure-strong" view of the prevailing phrase rhythm), just as this note had similarly appeared on the downbeats of measures 57 and 59.[16] Together with the root-position dominant, this unusual inversion of the diminished seventh renders the ECPs in this movement entirely unconventional, just as so many other features of this symphony as a whole are especially strange.[17] Indeed, other than these two occurrences within the "Farewell," I have not encountered any other examples in the classical repertoire of V⁷ (in root position) participating in a rocking on the tonic.

2. *Beethoven, Piano Sonata in B-flat ("Hammerklavier"), Op. 106, i.* A massive ECP arising in the first subordinate theme

---

16. Measures 60 and 62 are "odd" measures (5 and 7) when starting to count the phrase rhythm from m. 56 at the beginning of the new cadential phrase.

17. For a detailed account of the complete work, see Webster, *Haydn's Farewell Symphony*.

in the opening movement of Beethoven's "Hammerklavier" (Ex. 5.14a) also involves the use of a neighboring dominant set over ② within a rocking on the tonic. Unlike Haydn's ECP (Ex. 5.13b, mm. 60–63), which uses the diminished seventh VII$^6_5$ over ②, the rocking passage in the "Hammerklavier" (mm. 75–78) is produced by a regular dominant seventh in second inversion, V$^4_3$ (②), rather than the conventional V$^4_2$ (④). In order to understand Beethoven's usage here, we need to examine the entire subordinate theme, which witnesses major extensions and expansions of its constituent sentential functions. The presentation (mm. 47–54, not shown) contains a repeated basic idea, which itself is expanded to four bars. The resulting eight-measure presentation is then completely repeated (mm. 55–62), yielding an initiating area of sixteen bars and setting the stage for even more elaborate structural expansions. The continuation that follows (shown at the start of Ex. 5.14a) immediately effects an acceleration of the harmonic rhythm, fragmentation into two four-measure phrases (mm. 63–66, 67–70), and further fragmentation into one-measure units, which feature a stepwise-descending sequence (mm. 70–74). In addition to these continuational traits, the makings of another thematic structure are found embedded within this larger-scale continuation, namely, a periodic formation: a four-measure antecedent (ending with a reinterpreted HC in m. 66) and a subsequent consequent, which is extended to eight bars via the one-measure model and descending sequence in measures 70–74. Yet this consequent fails because a matching authentic cadence does not materialize. This lack of cadential closure is necessary, of course, for the broader continuation of the subordinate theme to project its medial function. This process of embedding one theme type (the failed period) within a single expansive function of a higher-level structure (the continuation of the subordinate theme as a whole) is then replicated in a more complex thematic embedding within the large-scale cadential function of this theme, namely, a two-level sentential process in measures 75–100.

The opening of the ECP (upbeat to m. 75) features a rocking on the tonic whose neighboring dominant is V$^4_3$ over ②. A two-measure basic idea (mm. 75–76) is repeated to form a local four-measure presentation, one that is followed by a two-measure continuation, which brings a modicum of harmonic acceleration in comparison to that of the presentation. These harmonies also continue the ECP (starting from m. 75), which ends with a dominant in the middle of measure 80. It is not immediately clear, though, how to interpret the cadential function of this harmony. On the one hand, it could represent an ultimate dominant, thus yielding an HC (and thereby ending a kind of antecedent unit, mm. 75–80); indeed, the cadential progression here contains both a pre-dominant VII$^7$/V and a consonant dominant triad, both conventional markers of an ultimate dominant for an HC. On the other hand, and my preferred interpretation, the dominant could be heard as penultimate, thus creating an evaded cadence when followed by the V$^4_3$ in measure 81.

When the six-measure cadential phrase is repeated, a larger-scale twelve-measure presentation-like unit emerges (mm. 75–86).[18] Following the end of this higher-level presentation, a new continuation at measure 87 arises out of the sequential repetitions of measures 85–86. To sum up so far, we can recognize four levels of form-functional organization operating here (see the formal labels at m. 75):[19] (1) a local sentential structure, the presentation and compressed continuation of measures 75–80; (2) the function of these six measures as "cadential" in relation to the prior antecedent plus failed consequent of measures 63–74 (which themselves project a continuation function of the overall subordinate theme); (3) the formation of a middle-ground sentential structure—presentation, measures 75–86, continuation, measures 87–90, and (as yet to be discussed) cadential, measures 91–100; and (4) the function of this structure (mm. 75–100) as the complete cadential area for the entire subordinate theme.

Before continuing further, let us pause to examine the specific harmonies that Beethoven selects for the cadential progressions appearing thus far in the subordinate theme, since these choices will have major ramifications for what follows. Looking first at the reinterpreted HC in measures 65–66, we see that the cadential progression occurs in the dominant region (D major) of the subordinate key. As such, none of the standard cadential bass-line scale degrees in G major is touched upon, such as B (③), C (④), or C♯ (♯④), save for D (⑤), which, of course, we first hear as ① in D major, only then to be reinterpreted as ⑤ in G major. Moving on to the start of the broader cadential function at measure 75ff., I have already observed that the rocking on the tonic engages a second-inversion dominant seventh built over ②. As such, the bass avoids the more conventional C (④) (supporting a V$^4_2$), a fact whose significance will become clearer as the music progresses. The initial I$^6$ is furthered prolonged in measure 79 by the tonic substitute VI on the second half of the bar, and the cadential progression continues with a pre-dominant VII$^7$/V built on C♯, the raised fourth degree. By employing this particular pre-dominant, Beethoven once again shuns ④ in the bass. He thus cleverly signals that the cadential progression is somewhat incomplete, and we very well may expect the future appearance of a more conventional II$^6$ or IV as a cadential pre-dominant.[20]

As already mentioned, the composer repeats the opening six-measure unit of the broad cadential function (starting at m. 75, repeated at m. 81), thus creating a middle-ground presentation (mm. 75–86) and a new continuation with the sequencing in measures 87–90. By the downbeat of this last bar, the bass line has arrived back at B (③), and what could have been a simple I$^6$ is now converted, in line with the sequencing, into a VII$^7$/IV, whose move to the subdominant in the second half of measure 90 finally

---

18. If we believe that an HC has been satisfactorily articulated in the middle of m. 80, this cadence, as well as the subsequent one at m. 86, must then be understood to have a limited structural scope.

19. In order to help sort out these multifarious formal interpretations, I have used varying sizes and styles of annotation, which depart somewhat from my standard practice.

20. As discussed, the use of VII$^7$/V also supports the interpretation of an HC at mm. 80 and 86.

5.1. PERFECT AUTHENTIC CADENCE 233

EXAMPLE 5.14A. Beethoven, Piano Sonata in B-flat ("Hammerklavier"), Op. 106, i, mm. 63–101.

EXAMPLE 5.14A. Continued

EXAMPLE 5.14B. Beethoven, Piano Sonata in B-flat ("Hammerklavier"), Op. 106, i, bass-line reduction of mm. 74–100.

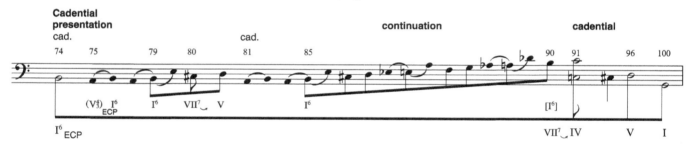

brings C♯ (④), just the note that Beethoven had so systematically avoided in the preceding bars. As if to celebrate this arrival, the music breaks forth (in m. 91) with a rhythmic motive that recalls the bombastic opening gesture of the movement.[21] Moreover, this fortissimo outburst allows the left hand to regain the original register of the ECP in measures 79–80. The pre-dominant is then further prolonged by a return in measure 94 of VII⁷/V, an allusion to the role that this chromatic harmony played in the small-scale cadential progressions of measures 75–89. Four measures of dominant harmony then lead to the authentic cadence in measure 100, which closes this huge subordinate theme.[22]

In retrospect, we can now understand, with the aid of the bass-line reduction in Example 5.14b, that the passage from the end of measure 74 to measure 90, which contains the local evaded (or half) cadential progression, its repetition, and continuation, features an enormous prolongation of a I⁶ harmony. This I⁶ functions as the initial component of a more expansive ECP, one that continues with the subdominant (m. 91) and stretches to the end of the theme at measure 100. By first withholding the regular predominant built on ④, and then letting it finally appear majestically in measures 90–91, Beethoven finds an effective way of assimilating the lower-level cadential phrases to the higher-level one and, at the same time, creating a climactic moment of enormous effect. We can further marvel at the extraordinary way in which the composer has manipulated the ECPs in order to create

---

21. The label "cadential," which I place at m. 91 to reflect the manifest change in musical material of this bar, more properly belongs in the middle of m. 90, as the beginning of the final ECP.

22. The final cadence of the theme is, most unconventionally, an IAC, though one that is conclusive (i.e., not a way station), because an entirely different thematic region—a second subordinate theme—elides with this cadence. Alternatively, we could propose the possibility of a covered cadence, with 3̂ covering a presumed 1̂. Problematic, however, is that the final melodic gesture of the cadential dominant 5̂–4̂ leads naturally to

3̂ for the IAC. Here, then, is a clear exception to the rule that a classical sonata-form subordinate theme must close with a PAC. To make up for this omission, the second subordinate theme closes with that cadence type in m. 118 (not shown), so the subordinate *key* is at last confirmed by this syntactically strongest cadence.

EXAMPLE 5.15. Beethoven, Violin Concerto in D, Op. 61, i, (a) mm. 64–77; (b) mm. 10–13; (c) mm. 1–3.

a cadential area that balances the larger-scale presentation and continuation functions of this immense subordinate theme.

*3. Beethoven, Violin Concerto in D, Op. 61, i.* My final case of an unusual rocking on the tonic presents a fascinating, and quite rare, variant on the traditional harmonies of an expanded stage 1 (Ex. 5.15a). Within the subordinate theme of the opening ritornello, and following upon a formal continuation, the passage beginning in measure 65 is poised to express cadential function, and indeed, the alternating bass line, ③ and ④, suggests a rocking on the tonic. Here, however, the tonic is replaced by a diminished-seventh sonority with ③ in the bass, which effects a common-tone ("ct") connection to the following dominant in third inversion. As is always the case with such embellishments, the tone in common (A) is the root of the resolving harmony.

Thus we easily hear the diminished seventh as a neighboring harmony to V$^4_2$, a situation that reverses the normal hierarchical relationship in such a rocking, where the dominant is subordinate to the tonic. In this particular case, it is possible to find grounds for Beethoven's unusual harmonic choice, for the diminished-seventh harmony allows him to bring back the four-note repeated D♯ motive from the continuation phrase of the main theme (Ex. 5.15b, m. 10), which itself is a variant on the quarter-note D♯s in the famous timpani motive from the opening bar of the movement (Ex. 5.15c).[23]

---

23. On the broader significance of D♯ within the movement, see Joseph Dubiel, "Hearing, Remembering, Cold Storage, Purism, Evidence, and Attitude Adjustment."

EXAMPLE 5.16. Haydn, Piano Sonata in E-flat, H. 52, i, mm. 23–27.

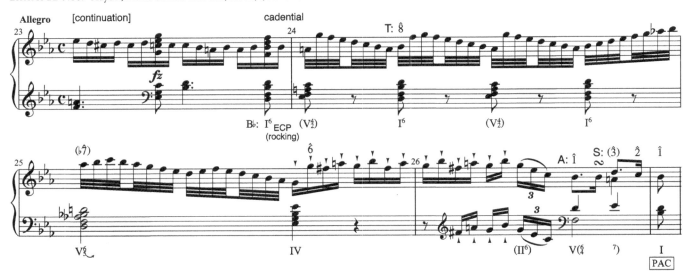

Though I have identified measure 65 as the onset of an ECP, we may not be so sure that cadential function is necessarily being expressed, since the unusual progression (°7)–V$_2^4$ may not immediately invoke the impression of being cadential. So in order to express more fully the sense that an ECP is underway, Beethoven dwells on the diminished seventh for two bars (mm. 69–70) and effects a powerful crescendo into the pre-dominant II$^6$. As a consequence, we now must reinterpret the diminished-seventh as a dominant functioning VII$_5^6$/II, a chromatic variant for stage 1b of a cadential progression. Ultimately, this ECP is abandoned when ④, supporting II$^6$, fails to reach ⑤, and the resulting V$_2^4$ resolves to I$^6$, to support the climactic D of measure 73, a pitch that "naturalizes" the prior D♯s.[24] The ECP that follows then brings full closure to the subordinate theme at measure 77.[25]

**Stage 1b.** In that a rocking on the tonic brings two distinctly different harmonies (V$_2^4$ and I$^6$), we might be tempted to recognize the presence of two substages, one for the dominant, a second for the tonic. Such usage does not seem quite appropriate, however, because we would then be identifying a regular alternation between the stages of the cadential schema, a situation we do not normally observe in the substages of the pre-dominant and dominant. Moreover, how would we label the stages? 1a for the V$_2^4$ and 1b for the I$^6$? Instead, it seems more consistent to include these harmonies together as stage 1a and to recognize stage 1b as an enhancement, or intensification, of the harmonic content, such as what occurs in stages 2b (e.g., VII$^7$/V following II$^6$) and 3b (V$^7$ following the cadential six-four). Thus after I$^6$ (with or without rocking), stage 1b normally holds either a tonic substitute VI or, more typically, a secondary dominant of the pre-dominant, such as V$_5^6$/IV or VII$_5^6$/II (Ex. 5.16). Following a rocking in measure 24, whose harmonies are lightly punctuated by eighth-note chords, the change in stage 1b to V$_5^6$/IV, as a full two-beat chord in the first half of measure 25, forcefully propels the cadential progression onward to stage 2.[26]

### 5.1.1.2. Stage 2—Pre-dominant

Even in relatively compact cadential progressions, stage 2 offers many different harmonic options from which the composer can choose. When this stage is expanded, it is even easier to employ a variety of pre-dominant harmonies. As discussed in Chapter 3, the host of pre-dominants is divided into two main classes—(1) those that contain the unaltered fourth degree, such as II$^6$, IV, and ♭II$^6$; and (2) those that contain the raised-fourth degree (the leading tone of the dominant), such as VII$^7$/V and the three "nationalities" of augmented-sixth harmonies. Indeed, this division underlies the distinction between stage 2a (using ♮4̂) and stage 2b (using ♯4̂). The temporal ordering of these two classes of harmonies is almost always respected, such that those containing the raised fourth follow those with the unaltered degree.[27] The following discussion will focus first on the harmonies of class 1, though many of the examples also contain a class-2 harmony (in stage 2b); the latter is specifically treated later.

**Pre-dominants Containing the Fourth Scale Degree–Stage 2a.** In compact authentic cadences, stage 2 is most typically occupied by II$^6$, with IV or IV$^6$ being secondary options. In ECPs, II$^6$ is found often enough, but it is not so preponderant, with IV

---

24. On this type of cadential abandonment, see in Chapter 4, sec. 4.3.2.1.

25. Another instance of this unusual harmonization in a rocking on the tonic is found in connection with the second movement of Beethoven's Seventh Symphony, as discussed in (Caplin, "Harmonic Variants," 54–55).

26. See also Ex. 4.78, mm. 35 and 39.

27. For an exceptional case of stage 2b appearing before 2a, see ahead, Ex. 5.28, m. 99. For a particularly intriguing case, one that engages some long-term motivic play in the bass line, see Beethoven, Piano Sonata in E-flat, Op. 7, ii, mm. 88–89, as analyzed in Caplin, "Schoenberg's 'Second Melody,'" 173–77.

EXAMPLE 5.17. Mozart, String Quartet in C, K. 465, iv, mm. 11–16 (*ACF* 6.7).

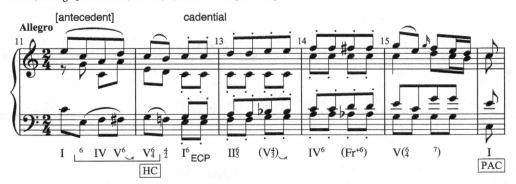

EXAMPLE 5.18. Haydn, Piano Sonata in A, H. 26, i, mm. 17–27 (R = ½N).

gaining considerably greater usage. (Just why the subdominant is favored in ECPs is not yet clear.) Like compact cadences, an ECP can find II⁶ directly following IV (less often in reverse) to make a broader pre-dominant prolongation. Diatonic variants of an expanded II⁶, such as II⁶₅ or simply II (in root position) are occasionally used in stage 2 of an ECP, but I have not yet encountered cases of II⁴₃ or II⁴₂ (the latter being fairly unimaginable given its required resolution to V⁶, which finds no place in a cadential progression).[28] A passing prolongation linking II⁶₅ and IV⁶ (via V⁴₃/IV) also arises now and then, as seen in Example 5.17, measures 13–14.

In simple, four-measure ECPs, stage 2 often occupies a single bar. But this stage can also undergo extensive expansion (Ex. 5.18). Within a subordinate theme, a continuation closes with a compact cadential progression leading to a deceptive cadence (3̂)

---

28. A case of stage 2 beginning with II⁶ will be discussed below in connection with Beethoven, Piano Sonata in E-flat, Op. 31, no. 3, i (see ahead Ex. 5.34b, mm. 1–3). The use of a root-position II can be seen above in Ex. 5.2, m. 20.

EXAMPLE 5.19. Haydn, Symphony No. 67 in F, ii, mm. 28–43.

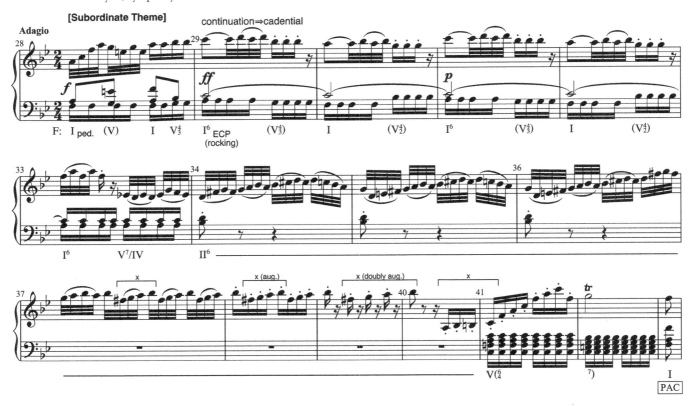

on VI (m. 18). The cadential idea is immediately repeated and ends again deceptively (m. 19). A third attempt at a cadence now brings a substantial ECP, whose pre-dominant, first represented in stage 2a by II⁶, is significantly expanded (mm. 19–21). A shorter, half-bar stage 2b (m. 22) then brings VII⁷/V, followed by stage 3, whose cadential trill reaches its melodic goal on $\hat{1}$ (m. 23). Once again, however, a deceptive cadence, now with a new replacement harmony, VII⁶/V, denies cadential closure. Further noncadential material reminiscent of the earlier continuation (not shown) leads to a dominant-seventh sonority, whose fermata teases us by continuing to withhold a cadential progression. When the music starts up again, it brings another ECP, this one also emphasizing stage 2, but now exclusively using subdominant harmony (mm. 25–26). Stage 3 appears and finally brings a genuine PAC to close the theme.

One additional detail is worth noting in connection with this example. We have observed that Haydn emphasizes stage 2 harmonies in both of the ECPs of this subordinate theme. It is especially interesting to see, then, how he subtly anticipates this harmonic expansion by slightly elongating the pre-dominant within the compact cadential formula of measures 17–19. A surface reading of measure 17 would find a change of harmony on each eighth note (I⁶–IV– I⁶–IV–V⁷; see line 1 of the harmonic analysis). The metrical and motivic context, however, renders the I⁶ on the second half of beat three as a neighbor to IV, and so a more nuanced analysis would see this pre-dominant prolonged for one and one-half beats (line 2). Perhaps Haydn is already signaling in this first cadential progression that the pre-dominant will be the most prominent harmony within the two ECPs that follow.

A highly expanded stage 2 can be seen in another subordinate theme by this composer (Ex. 5.19). At the end of a four-measure initiating unit grounded solidly in the prolongation of a root-position tonic (not shown), the bass in measure 28 moves up to I⁶ to initiate a continuation phrase that brings harmonic acceleration in the form of alternating tonic and dominants, much like a rocking on the tonic, though one that also embellishes tonic in root position via V⁴₃.²⁹ As a result, we could hear measures 29–33 as projecting an expanded stage 1a of an ECP, which moves to stage 1b with V⁶₅/IV in the second half of measure 33. The ECP then continues with a stage-2 predominant (II⁶), a harmony that is expanded to almost absurd lengths. Indeed, when the bass drops out after the downbeat of measure 36 and the violins continue with a single four-note ascending motive "x" (see brackets in m. 37ff.), whose durational values are systematically halved (from thirty-seconds, to sixteenths, to eighths), it is as though the

---

29. Note that despite the presence of tonic in root position, the expansion here seems to privilege I⁶ as the prolonged the harmony, seeing as it both begins and ends the rocking and also acquires hypermetrical emphasis by its placement on the downbeats of mm. 29, 31, and 33. We will later encounter a very similar rocking passage in the first movement of Beethoven's First Symphony (see ahead Ex. 5.67a, mm. 69–73).

EXAMPLE 5.20. Mozart, Piano Concerto in A, K. 488, ii, mm. 7–12 (*ACF* Sup. 5.2).

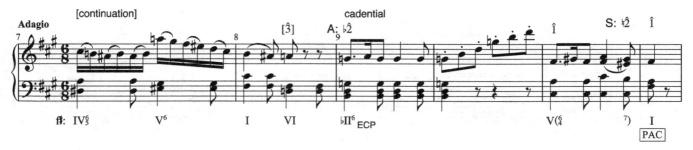

EXAMPLE 5.21. Haydn, Piano Trio in C, H. 21, i, mm. 77–82 (*ACF* 13.23).

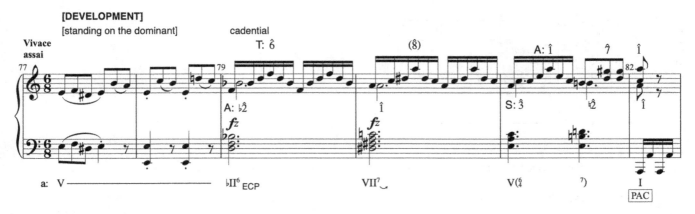

ECP has completely run out of steam before even reaching the dominant. Things pick up again with the sudden drop in register (upbeat to m. 41), and a new sixteenth-note version of motive "x" finally leads into stage 3 and the completion of the ECP.[30]

The striking sonority of a Neapolitan sixth (♭II⁶) lends itself well to cadential expansion.[31] In Example 5.20, an ongoing continuation in measures 7–8 is followed by a four-measure ECP beginning directly with ♭II⁶ (m. 9). The startling effect of this harmony is especially forceful in Example 5.21. Toward the end of the development section, a dominant arrival in measure 73 (not shown) brings a standing on the dominant that suddenly, at measure 79, lurches back (syntactically speaking) to a pre-dominant Neapolitan for an ECP that confirms A minor as a development key via the PAC at measure 82.

A particularly clever use of an expanded ♭II⁶ takes advantage of the possibility that the Neapolitan region of a minor-mode key can readily be tonicized (Ex. 5.22). Within a subordinate theme in the key of B minor (the minor dominant of the home key, E minor), a sequentially organized continuation leads in the second half of measure 48 to a diminished seventh of the Neapolitan (VII$_2^4$), which reverts to a root-position dominant (V⁷/♭II) at measure 49.[32] The emphasis on this dominant creates the sense of a premature, internal dominant arrival, as if the key of the subordinate theme were actually C major. The bass then steps down in the second half of measure 50 to support V$_2^4$ in that same key. The next bar initiates a prolongation of B-minor's ♭II⁶ that is reminiscent of a rocking on the tonic (in C major), though of course, the rocking is really on the Neapolitan (in B minor). The ECP, which this prolongation initiates, continues on at measure 55 with an enharmonic reinterpretation of V$_2^4$/♭II to become a pre-dominant German augmented-sixth for stage 2b. The dominant follows in measure 56 and is expanded for an additional nine bars in a powerful drive to the PAC at measure 66 (not shown). Note how Beethoven's dynamic indications support the effect here. The *subito piano* at measure 51, further softened by the *pianissimo* two bars later, evokes an other-worldly setting wherein C major feigns being the tonic of the theme, only to have the *crescendo* in measures 55–56 pull the music out of its dream-like state into the more menacing B minor, the true tonic of the subordinate key. In this striking passage, Beethoven would seem to be relying on his

---

30. This passage is an obvious example of Haydn's famed wit. Indeed, the movement is full of such comic passages, starting off with the immediate appearance of music that sounds more like a closing section than a structural beginning. Haydn brings this music back at the very end, but only after the movement seems to have finished itself off with an entirely different closing section. The development also features a bizarre passage (mm. 56–67), one that brings another wholesale reduction in texture to violins alone, obviously inspired by the ECP in the exposition just examined.

31. See earlier, Chapter 4, Ex. 4.39, m. 27, for a case of an abandoned ECP following ♭II⁶ of stage 2.

32. On the idea of a diminished seventh "reverting" to the dominant, for which it substitutes, see in Chapter 4, note 19.

EXAMPLE 5.22. Beethoven, Piano Sonata in E, Op. 109, ii, mm. 48–58.

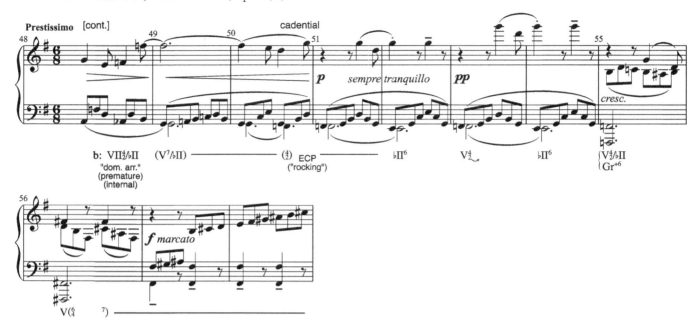

EXAMPLE 5.23. Beethoven, Piano Sonata in D, Op. 10, no. 3, ii, (a) mm. 1–9 (*ACF* Sup. 5.4); (b) reconstruction of m. 6.

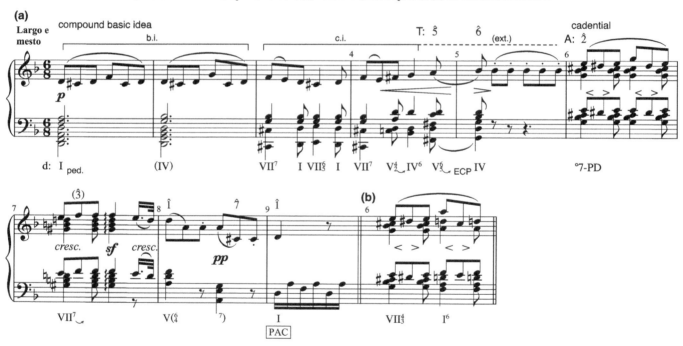

listeners' implicit knowledge of the conventional rocking on the tonic, a device that he transfers to a different tonal region, while still conforming to the standard syntax of an ECP.[33]

---

33. In principle, it is possible to tonicize the "natural" II⁶ in the major mode with a similar rocking effect, yet this formation is rare, perhaps because the bass of V⁴₂/II (or VII⁴₃/II) is ③, which would normally be saved to support the cadential dominant. For one case, see ahead, Ex. 5.36a, m. 9.

A relatively rare pre-dominant consists of the diminished-seventh sonority built over ④, which functions as a pre-dominant substitute (°7-PD). Example 5.23a illustrates this situation well, in addition to revealing a complicated relationship between the grouping structure of the phrases and the boundaries of the cadential progression. This main theme seems clearly divided into two phrases (mm. 1–5 and 6–9), the second of which begins with a diminished-seventh notated as VII⁴₃. As such, the phrase could have continued as shown in Example 5.23b, whereby the

EXAMPLE 5.24. Mozart, Piano Concerto in C Minor, K. 491, iii, mm. 10–16 (*ACF* Sup. 8.8).

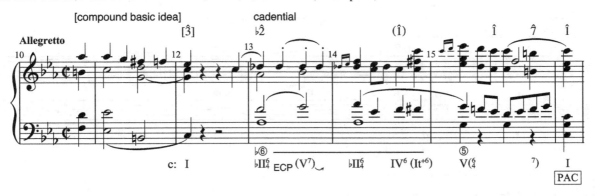

VII$^4_3$ resolves to I$^6$. Instead, the diminished seventh (as stage 2a) moves up a half step to create a second diminished-seventh sonority, which functions as a secondary VII$^7$/V (stage 2b);[34] the ECP continues with the dominant in measure 8 to effect the PAC in the following bar.

The question now arises as to where this ECP actually begins. Looking back to the first phrase, we find a two-measure basic idea followed by a contrasting idea, leading to IV$^6$ in middle of bar 4. The resulting four-measure compound basic idea then seems to be extended by an additional bar, when IV is prolonged into the downbeat of measure 5. With respect to its material content, this fifth measure seems most naturally to belong with its ongoing group (as an extension). Yet when we consider the harmonic progression, we recognize an initial tonic V$^6_5$/IV moving to a predominant IV, thus beginning an ECP that continues with the diminished-seventh pre-dominant in measure 6. In other words, the ECP straddles two phrases, such that we can recognize here a noncongruence of progression boundary and grouping structure, which yields a complex thematic organization for the opening of this highly expressive movement.[35]

Every so often we encounter a particularly unusual harmony within stage 2 of an ECP. One case by Mozart and two by Haydn are worthy of consideration. The first arises in Example 5.24 in the context of the second part of a small binary. The final phrase is supported by a four-measure ECP that most unusually begins directly on ♭II$^6_4$ (m. 13), built over ♭$\hat{6}$, a bass pitch that normally would support VI or IV$^6$. This strange Neapolitan six-four is even prolonged by its own passing dominant seventh, after which it eventually yields to a more conventional IV$^6$ on the second half of measure 14. A stage 2b augmented-sixth then quickly leads to the cadential dominant in measure 15. In all, Mozart brings three different pre-dominants over the same bass ♭$\hat{6}$.

A second case of a strange pre-dominant in an ECP is shown in Example 5.25, which arises in the second of two subordinate themes (taken here from the recapitulation). A continuation, featuring model-sequence technique in the context of a rhythmical hemiola, leads on the last beat of measure 177 to V$^7$/II, which itself resolves deceptively on the downbeat of the next bar to ♭VII, a relatively remote region of the home key E-flat major. There then follows one of Haydn's characteristic mid-phrase pauses, after which the music continues to reiterate, in alternating hands, the same replacement harmony of the deceptive resolution. The immediate sense here is one of formal *interpolation*, a passage that stands apart from the logical flow of the formal functions, due largely to the sudden shift to a *piano* dynamic, the focus on a single rhythmic and melodic motive, and the marked stasis of a remote harmonic region, all of which project the sense of "being somewhere else." In measure 183, Haydn pulls the music out of the interpolation and resumes its regular path, whereby a German sixth on beat 3 signals the start of a cadential idea, supported by a light expansion of the dominant. A final PAC brings thematic closure at measure 186.

A closer examination of the interpolation, however, reveals an alternative harmonic interpretation. In the more local context of a deceptive resolution, the harmony of measure 178 could be understood as the submediant of the supertonic (VI/II), thus a *substitute* for the supertonic and one that expresses (somewhat remotely, to be sure) pre-dominant function in the home key. As such, we might want to locate the onset of the cadential progression (now a full ECP) as far back as measure 178. To be sure, this interpretation is far from obvious, and so I would not advocate simply discarding the interpolation effect. It is nonetheless useful to recognize the ingenious way in which Haydn establishes a broader logic to the ongoing harmonic and formal processes of this theme. (Note by the way, how cleverly Haydn returns from the world of ♭VII by way of C in the bass [m. 183, beat 2], which supports II$^6_4$, thus connecting back to the implied resolution to II at m. 178.)

A third case of a surprising harmony for stage 2 of an ECP is seen in Example 5.26. In this minuet A' section, a presumed

---

34. A case could be made that all of m. 7 should be understood as V$^6_5$/V, with the emphasized diminished seventh as subsumed within this dominant. But the overall context better suggests reading VII$^7$/V for the whole bar, emerging as this harmony does out of a prior diminished-seventh sonority in m. 6.

35. I place the label "cadential" at the beginning of m. 6 to help clarify the boundaries of the second phrase, even though by definition the label should be situated at the upbeat of m. 5. For an additional case of a diminished-seventh pre-dominant, see ahead, Ex. 5.44, m. 59, as discussed in *CF*, 119, Ex. 8.11a, and *ACF*, 398, Ex. 12.11a.

EXAMPLE 5.25. Haydn, Piano Sonata in E-flat, H. 49, i, mm. 176–86 (*ACF* 14.20).

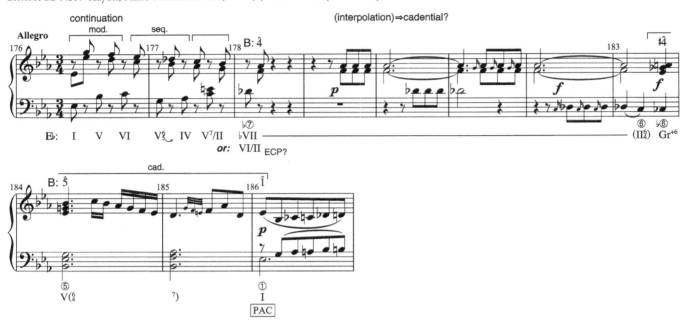

EXAMPLE 5.26. Haydn, String Quartet in B Minor, Op. 64, no. 2, iii, mm. 30–42 (*ACF* 18.15b).

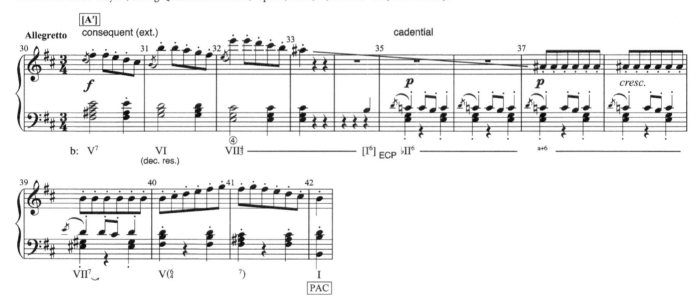

consequent phrase (in relation to a consequent in the A section) closes with a dominant seventh resolving deceptively to VI (mm. 30–31). (Though we might recognize a deceptive cadence here, the ongoing melodic line pushes through this moment to suggest that we speak more of a deceptive resolution than a cadence per se.) The harmony that follows in measures 32–33 should probably be understood as VII$^4_3$, whose resolution to tonic is interrupted by the mid-phrase pause that immediately ensues. When the music starts up again at measure 35, the pickup B suggests a resolving I$^6$ (albeit without a bass support). The quick move to an expanded Neapolitan-sixth in measure 35 suggests that we see the start of an ECP with that pick-up I$^6$. At measure 37, the first violin returns, an octave lower and with the same note, A♯, that had been broken off by that part at measure 33 (see the connecting line). Within the context of a ♭II harmony still sounding by the other three instruments, and in light of the ascending resolution of the A♯ to B at measure 39, we must recognize a dissonant "added-sixth" element to the harmony. Added sixth sonorities are actually quite rare in the eighteenth century (Rameau's theories notwithstanding), and when they occur, they more normally arise in the context of a subdominant harmony. Here, however, Haydn not only includes a dissonant sixth to the Neapolitan, but also chromatically raises that pitch to become an added *augmented* sixth ($^{a+6}$), thus creating an even

EXAMPLE 5.27. Mozart, String Quartet in B-flat ('Hunt'), K. 458, i, (a) mm. 71–77; (b) mm. 53–54.

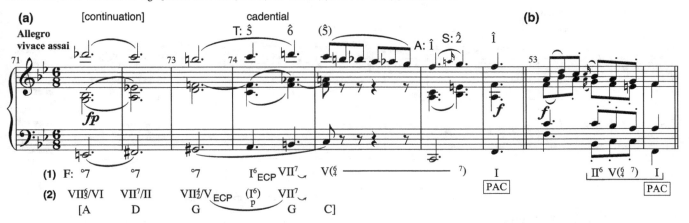

stronger dissonant effect.[36] When the bass rises to ♮④ at measure 39, the ongoing ECP moves into stage 2b with VII⁷/V, followed by the remaining two stages to effect a PAC at measure 42.

**Pre-dominants Containing the Raised-Fourth Scale Degree—Stage 2b.** An ECP frequently uses harmonies from the second class of pre-dominants, namely, those that contain the raised-fourth scale degree. These include various secondary dominants of the dominant along with the augmented-sixth harmonies. These pre-dominants belong to stage 2b of the cadential progression because they typically follow a pre-dominant of stage 2a (or directly after a stage-1 harmony if stage 2a is bypassed).

The most frequently used pre-dominants in stage 2b are V⁶₍₅₎/V and VII⁷/V; these harmonies appear often enough not to require exemplification here. Both are built over ♯④ and normally occur after a pre-dominant built over ♮④. Now and then, a stage 2b pre-dominant is placed over ⑥, such as V⁴₃/V or VII⁶/V.[37] The various augmented-sixth harmonies are usually built over ♭⑥. They sometimes follow IV⁶ over ♮⑥ in stage 2a; see above, Example 5.17, measure 14. An augmented sixth placed over ♭⑥ may also emerge directly from a stage 2a pre-dominant built over ④, as shown in Chapter 4, Ex. 4.78, measures 40–41. The exceptional situation of an augmented sixth ensuing from a stage 2a II⁶₄ over ⑥ has already been observed in Example 5.25, measure 183.

**ECP Bypasses Stage 2a.** On occasion, stage 2b of an ECP appears immediately following stage 1, thus passing over stage 2a. In such cases, it is often worthwhile to seek a rationale for this occurrence. One such passage arises in Example 5.27a. At the start of an ECP closing the final subordinate theme of the exposition, the I⁶ of measure 74 moves quickly to VII⁷/V and on to the cadential dominant in the following bar, thus skipping over a pre-dominant built over ④ (line 1 of the harmonic analysis). If we consider this excerpt in a broader formal context, we can note that within the subordinate-theme group, Mozart has brought four previous cadential progressions (albeit compact) that employ the standard pre-dominant II⁶ without any stage 2b built on ♯④ (see Ex. 5.27b for the first instance of this compact progression). So it is not surprising that for the final cadence of the subordinate-theme group, Mozart omits II⁶ in favor of VII⁷/V (m. 74, beat 2).[38] Another motivation for his using this chromatic pre-dominant may be seen in light of the highly chromatic context established at the end of the continuation function, which brings the three acoustically unique diminished-seventh harmonies in a row (Ex. 5.27a, mm. 71–73). Thus by using VII⁷/V as the exclusive pre-dominant of the ECP, the composer sustains an emphasis on a diminished-seventh sonority from the end of the continuation through to the cadential dominant.[39]

A similar chromatic context also perhaps motivates the bypassing of stage 2a in an ECP from the first-movement coda of Beethoven's first string quartet, discussed in Chapter 4, Ex. 4.63. Following an internal standing on the dominant (mm. 286–93),

---

36. This added augmented sixth A♯, of course, is the leading tone of B minor, so including this pitch within the Neapolitan represents a functional mixture of pre-dominant and dominant in a single harmony. In Chapter 3, Ex. 3.174, m. 66, we have already seen how Beethoven sneaks in the leading tone just prior to the tonic resolution of a plagal progression. In Chapter 9 on music in the second half of the nineteenth century, we will encounter a number of other cases that mix subdominant and dominant functional elements: see Ex. 9.10, 9.26, 9.30c, and 9.56a (the Tristan chord itself); see also in Chapter 9, note 84, for references to some important secondary literature on this topic.

37. For a case of V⁴₃/V, see Ex. 5.6, m. 77; for VII⁶/V, see Ex. 5.3, m. 132.

---

38. The closing section that follows Ex. 5.27a (not shown) contains codettas that bring back II⁶ as the pre-dominant for two cadences of limited scope (mm. 80 and 84).

39. If we want to find a harmonic interpretation of the diminished-seventh chords in mm. 71–73 (see line 2), we could understand each sonority as substituting for a dominant seventh, whose roots project a descending-fifths sequence (the implied roots are bracketed below the roman numerals). This analysis shows that VII⁴₃/V (m. 73) is prolonged by a passing I⁶, which leads to VII⁷/V in the second half of m. 74. If this is our hearing, then we could find the ECP beginning earlier at m. 73 directly with a stage 2b VII⁴₃/V, thus bypassing both stages 1 and 2a. Problematic in this harmonic interpretation of these consecutive diminished sevenths is the overall voice leading, which, except for the upper voice, largely consists of ascending motion, untypical of a descending sequence.

EXAMPLE 5.28. Beethoven, String Quartet in F, Op. 18, no. 1, i, mm. 76–101.

a new continuation (m. 294) highlights a number of diminished-seventh sonorities, the last two of which (mm. 298–299) comprise stages 1b (VII$^7$/IV) and 2b (VII$^7$/V) of the concluding ECP.

Another case of bypassing stage 2a of an ECP occurs in the subordinate-theme group of the same Beethoven quartet (Ex. 5.28). To conclude the second of three themes within this group, an ECP at measure 78 begins with II$^6$, which launches a flurry of sixteenth-note activity that extends this harmony for four full bars.[40] Stages 3 and 4 then yield a PAC at measure 84. At this

---

40. We might consider the VII$^6_5$/II in mm. 76–77 as stage 1b of the ECP, but the melodic-motivic context suggests that these bars are heard more as a third statement of the basic idea within an extended presentation than as anything cadential at this point in the theme.

EXAMPLE 5.29. Haydn, Symphony No. 97 in C, i, (a) mm. 236–50 (*ACF* 15.5); (b) mm. 96–103.

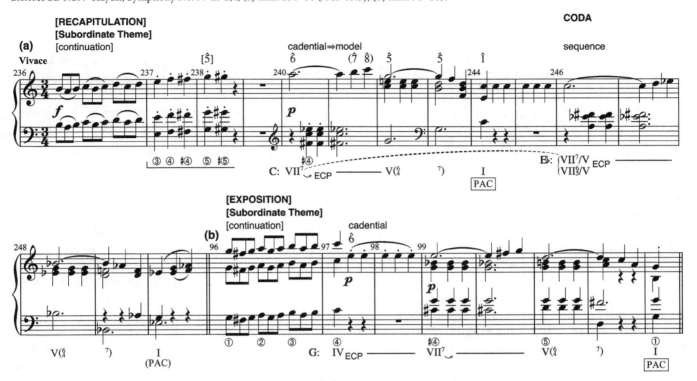

point, a third subordinate theme begins directly with continuation function but suddenly breaks off with a Haydnesque mid-phrase pause in measure 87. When the music starts up again at measure 89, a new ECP, beginning with a root-position tonic for stage 1, bypasses stage 2a to bring V⁶₅/V for stage 2b; the PAC is then quickly attained at measure 92. The reason that Beethoven bypasses stage 2a for this ECP is likely found in his emphatic marking of the II⁶ (mm. 78–81) in the prior ECP. We might even say that Beethoven "used up" this harmony in the first ECP and thus needed to supply a different pre-dominant (m. 90) for the second cadence. (I return to this example later to discuss the rest of the third subordinate theme and to summarize the wide variety of cadential harmonies employed throughout the subordinate-theme group.)

In the three previous examples, I proposed that a rationale for skipping over stage 2a of an ECP can be found in the music that precedes it. Some other cases suggest that an explanation for this bypassing may involve the music that follows the cadential progression.[41] Consider Example 5.29a, which shows the end of a symphonic recapitulation and the beginning of a coda. The continuation of the final subordinate theme in the recapitulation suddenly stops short in measure 238 with a mid-phrase pause (this time actually by Haydn). On the downbeat of measure 240, an ECP to close the theme not only bypasses stage 2a, but stage 1 as well, thus beginning directly with a stage-2b pre-dominant, VII⁷/V. In trying to understand what may have motivated this harmonic choice, we could look at the chromatic line that ends the continuation (mm. 237–38) and recognize that the doubled monophonic passage concludes by replicating the bass line of a deceptive cadential progression (though stopping just short of the goal ⑥). With this in mind, we could say that Haydn returns to the first chromatic pitch of that bass, F♯ (m. 237), to begin the ECP with VII⁷/V, thus realizing the potential for that chromatic line to be cadential (as opposed to merely continuational). But a stronger rationale can be found in what happens after the PAC. For at measure 246, Haydn suddenly sequences the ECP down a sixth, into the relatively remote region of E-flat (HK: ♭III) to start the coda.[42] And what makes this sequence sound so smooth is that Haydn can use the enharmonically equivalent diminished-seventh sonority, shown in the analysis at measure 246, as the pre-dominant of the sequenced ECP (see the dashed line connecting the diminished sevenths). In short, Haydn's skipping over stage 2a may well be explained by how he wants to continue the music following the recapitulation's PAC at measure 244.

At this point, we might wonder how the analogous passage in the exposition played itself out (see Ex. 5.29b), especially since the same explanation for skipping stage 2a, namely, the swerve to E-flat, would presumably not be available within the expositional space. The first thing to observe is that the continuation now concludes on ④ (m. 97), rather than moving up chromatically to ♯⑤, as had taken place in the recapitulation (Ex. 5.29a,

---

41. I have already examined such a situation in connection with Beethoven's "Hammerklavier" sonata (Ex. 5.14a, mm. 79–80 and 85–86).

42. See *CF*, 181, and *ACF*, 529, for more details on the formal situation arising at this point in the movement.

EXAMPLE 5.30. Mozart, Piano Sonata in C, K. 545, i, mm. 20–23 (*ACF* 12.1).

m. 238). And instead of introducing a mid-phrase pause, Haydn has the first violins alone repeat the pitch E, $\hat{6}$ of the subordinate key (Ex. 5.29b, mm. 97–98). Since we can still hear the bass pitch C in our imagination throughout these bars, we can understand that the harmony projected there is IV (or II⁶). What then follows at measure 99 is VII⁷/V to introduce the full-textured passage that corresponds to the ECP of the recapitulation. In other words, the exposition's ECP does not skip over stage 2a, since the IV of measures 97–98 represents that substage as the real start of the exposition's final ECP. One additional detail in connection with Example 5.29b is noteworthy here. Following a standard closing section in measures 103–107 (not shown), the development begins directly in E-flat major, the very same tonal region that Haydn so cleverly reintroduces at the start of the coda (m. 246) via the sequence of the recapitulation's ECP.

In some cases, a rationale for bypassing stage 2a of an ECP is difficult to find. Consider, for example, a passage from a Beethoven piano sonata discussed in the previous chapter (Ex. 4.36). In both of the ECPs, the initial tonic (first I⁶, then I) moves directly to V⁶₅/V for stage 2b. I can find nothing in the preceding or following music that suggests a reason for Beethoven omitting a pre-dominant built on ④. I suppose he just liked the more chromatic, edgy sound of the V⁶₅/V suddenly stopping the rhythmic motion at that point. To be sure, the cadence closing the final subordinate theme (not shown) brings a regular II⁶, thus naturalizing the V⁶₅/V of the prior ECP and concluding the exposition in a completely diatonic manner.

**ECP Begins with Stage 2.** Just like many compact cadential progressions, an ECP may be *incomplete*, that is, it may omit stage 1, stage 2, or both. Of these three possibilities, the latter two are relatively rare; however, stage 1 is frequently left out of the progression. We have already considered one case, Example 5.29a, where both ECPs bypass not only stage 2a, but stage 1 as well.

In the large majority of cases where an incomplete ECP begins with stage 2, a strong grouping boundary separates the onset of the ECP from prior material. Often, the boundary is articulated by a sudden contrast in melodic-motivic ideas, as well as a marked change in dynamics, texture, and rhythmic patterning. A number of examples discussed earlier illustrate this situation: Example 5.28, measures 78; Example 5.21, measure 79; and in Chapter 4, Example 4.8, measure 51. Sometimes the material content is less contrasting, but the grouping boundary is clearly evident, such as when an incomplete ECP follows upon a phrase ending with an HC or some other prominent caesura.[43]

Additional factors may also be associated with, or help provide a rationale for, an ECP skipping stage 1. For example, the material preceding the ECP may give special emphasis to tonic harmony, especially in first inversion, such that it might seem redundant to use that harmony at the start of the ECP (see again Ex. 4.8). Following two way-station cadences (an IAC in m. 41 and a deceptive cadence in m. 45), a new continuation features rapidly alternating chords that prolong tonic via neighboring dominants, the last two bars of which (mm. 49–50) emphasize I⁶. It would make little sense for Beethoven to continue tonic harmony within the ECP, so he initiates the cadential phrase with a pre-dominant II⁶ at measure 51.

When a continuation phrase preceding an ECP is organized by model-sequence technique ending on tonic, the ECP tends to begin with a pre-dominant (Ex. 5.30). The end of the continuation in this subordinate theme completes a full circle-of-fifths sequence, one that begins on I⁶ (not shown) and concludes on I in the middle of measure 21. The ECP that follows opens directly with II⁶. Moreover, since the theme begins with a presentation phrase (not shown) that gives special emphasis to a prolonged I⁶, this harmony is especially inappropriate for further emphasis in the ECP.

Cadential units that strongly emphasize the Neapolitan often begin immediately with this harmony so as to magnify the dramatic effect that it often makes. The ECPs in Example 5.20, measure 9, and Example 5.21, measure 79, illustrate well this situation. As described earlier, the ECP in Example 5.22 begins at measure 50 with a rocking on the Neapolitan. Here, though, the material content of the passage is somewhat less contrasting with what comes before than is typically the case when a cadential unit begins with stage 2. Beside the Neapolitan, the expansion of other unusual pre-dominants normally occurs with those harmonies initiating the ECP; see again, Example 5.24, measure 13, and Example 5.25, measure 178.

In some cases, it is not clear whether the ECP starts with stage 1 or stage 2. The problem usually involves the tonic: Is it better

---

43. In Ex. 5.24, the ECP follows a literal caesura in m. 12; see also Mozart, Symphony No. 35 in D ("Haffner"), K. 385, iii, mm. 4–5 (*ACF* Supp. 4.18), for a caesura appearing after an HC.

EXAMPLE 5.31. Beethoven, Piano Sonata in G, Op. 14, no. 2, i, mm. 37–42.

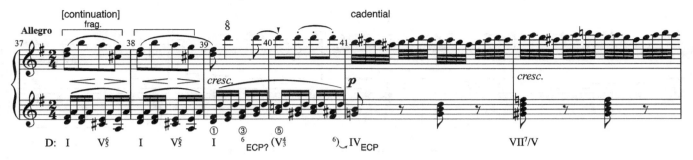

heard as continuational or cadential? Consider Example 5.31, which begins in the middle of a subordinate-theme continuation. Fragmentation into one-measure units in measures 37–38 leads at measure 39 to a melodic stasis (on $\hat{8}$) and an ascending bass line, which passes from ③ to ⑤ in supporting $I^6$ and $V^4_3/IV$, respectively. Thus tonic function alone is expanded in measures 39–40 in comparison to the more rapid harmonic changes in the preceding two bars. For this reason, it is plausible to regard the expansion of this $I^6$ (middle of m. 39) as the onset of an ECP. Yet when the resolution to the subdominant occurs in measure 41, it brings a marked change in texture, dynamics, and melodic material. So it would also be viable to hear this pre-dominant as opening the cadential progression. In this particular case, I tend to hear the powerful grouping boundary at measure 41 as projecting a clear change from continuation to cadential function, since the texture of measures 39–40 is largely the same as the preceding music. Nonetheless, hearing the expansion of a cadential tonic in these bars remains a legitimate analytical interpretation.[44]

### 5.1.1.3. Stage 3—Dominant

Compared to the first two stages of an ECP, the harmonic content of stage 3 is highly constrained. Absolutely required is a dominant that first appears in root position and remains as such until the tonic of stage 4 arrives. Most of the time, stage 3 is divided into two substages, stage 3a containing a cadential six-four, stage 3b, the dominant proper (usually $V^7$). In my corpus of movements containing ECPs, a cadential six-four occurs in approximately three-quarters of the cases (in the remaining quarter, stage 3 consists perforce of the dominant proper alone). This latter circumstance normally arises when the duration of stage 3 is comparable in size, or even compressed, in relation to the prior stages.[45] When the ECP includes a cadential six-four, approximately two-thirds witness stage 3a having the same duration as stage 3b.[46] In the remaining third, 3a is longer than 3b, being equally divided into cases where the ratio is 2:1 or 3:1. A handful of cases feature a more extensive ratio, ranging from 5:1 (Mozart, Piano Concerto in C, K 467, i, mm. 188–93) to 15:1 (see Ex. 5.14a, mm. 96–99). I have uncovered only two cases where the dominant proper is longer than the cadential six-four.[47]

These informal statistics suggest a couple of interpretations. First, that the use of both substages is considerably more prevalent than using the dominant proper alone makes sense seeing as the presence of two distinct sonorities better enables the kind of passage-work that normally accompanies cadential expansion. Second, that the duration of the cadential six-four is either equal to, or greater than, the dominant proper is likely explainable when recognizing that the former has the same pitch content as a tonic triad, whose inherent harmonic stability (irrespective of its unstable six-four position) facilitates extensive melodic embellishments (esp. arpeggiations and scalar runs) compared to the destabilizing dissonance of $V^7$, the dominant proper.

**Embellishing Harmonies in Stage 3.** In a small number of ECPs, one of the two harmonies of stage 3 (the cadential six-four or the dominant proper) may be embellished with neighboring harmonies. Two such cases are worthy of discussion.[48] In Example 5.32, the cadential six-four in measures 150–51 is suddenly interrupted on the downbeat of measure 152 by what seems to be a backward shift to a stage-2b $VII^7/V$. The following bar brings more local embellishments of this harmony, after which the cadential six-four resumes on the downbeat of measure 154, resolving quickly to the dominant proper in the second half of that bar.[49] From a "first-time" listening perspective, the effect here is

---

44. A similar ambiguity as to where to locate the beginning of the ECP can be found in Ex. 5.28, mm. 76–77, as discussed already in note 40.

45. See Ex. 5.2, m. 21; Ex. 5.9, m. 49; Ex. 5.10, m. 70; and Ex. 5.28, m. 100.

46. See Ex. 5.1, m. 7; Ex. 5.17, m. 15; Ex. 5.23a, m. 8; Ex. 5.25, mm. 184–85; and Ex. 5.26, mm. 40–41.

47. See Ex. 5.22, mm. 56; the cadential six-four lasts a half bar, after which the dominant proper continues for another 9½ measures (the example shows only 2½ bars), a considerably unusual relationship of stage 3b to 3a. See also Haydn, String Quartet in E, Op. 54, no. 3, ii, mm. 29–32.

48. An additional case arises in Mozart, Violin Concerto in A, K. 219, i, m. 31 (ACF 20.4), where a neighboring I briefly appears within a prolongation of the dominant proper.

49. One might notice the very brief appearance of the cadential six-four on the third eighth-note beat of m. 153. I hear this potential harmonic resumption as subsumed within the broader neighboring embellishment of the cadential six-four between mm. 151 and 154. But a legitimate, alternative reading would find stage 3a resuming on the downbeat of m. 153. I will return to this interpretation when looking later at the melodic component of this ECP.

EXAMPLE 5.32. Mozart, Piano Sonata in D, K. 576, i, mm. 147–55 (*ACF* 14.10).

EXAMPLE 5.33. Haydn, Symphony No. 104 in D ("London"), iv, mm. 304–309 (*ACF* 15.6).

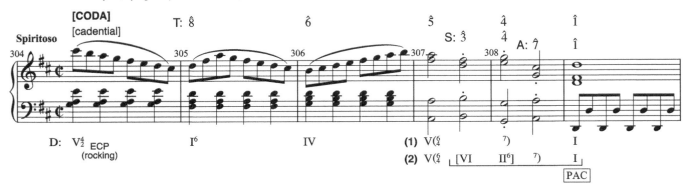

somewhat like that of turning the clock back to an earlier moment in time, namely to a stage 2b harmony that could have preceded the onset of stage 3 at measure 150; in fact prior to that stage, Mozart had only used a stage-2a pre-dominant, so the "late" appearance of a stage-2b harmony is at least not redundant. From a more synoptic viewpoint (i.e., a prior knowledge of the whole passage), we can understand the VII⁷/V more simply as a neighboring harmony to the cadential six-four.

Example 5.33 illustrates a second case of neighboring harmonies occurring within stage 3a. Following a prominent rocking on I⁶ in measures 301–305 (the last two bars of which are shown), a pre-dominant IV in measure 306 leads to a cadential six-four supporting $\hat{5}$ in the upper voice, which descends eventually to $\hat{1}$ via the leaping motion $\hat{5}$–$\hat{3}$ and $\hat{4}$–$\hat{7}$. Most simply, this cadential melody could be harmonized with the cadential six-four in the whole of measure 307, followed by V⁷ in measure 308, as seen in line 1 of the harmonic analysis. Instead, Haydn supports the melodic descent by adding two neighboring harmonies, VI and II⁶, between the cadential six-four and the dominant proper (see line 2). As a result,

he thus embeds a compact cadential progression within the broader ECP.[50]

**ECP Proceeds from Stage 1 to Stage 3, Bypassing Stage 2.** Very rarely, an ECP skips over stage 2 by moving directly from stage 1 to stage 3. It is not difficult to understand why this situation would seldom occur. The majority of ECPs include a cadential six-four, which has the local sonority of an inverted tonic. Thus bypassing stage 2 has the potential of overemphasizing tonic harmony in the progression. In fact, I have so far uncovered only a single example in the classical repertory of an authentic ECP that moves from stage 1 directly to stage 3 (see Ex. 5.34a).

The excerpt begins in the middle of the second subordinate theme with a continuation featuring model-sequence technique and a hemiola rhythmic pattern. After the sequence concludes on I at the last quarter-note beat of measure 70, Beethoven reiterates

---

50. Haydn thus produces the sense of "retaining the cadential formula," a technique that I will discuss in the next two chapters as typical of both the high-baroque and galant styles; see Chapter 6, sec. 6.1.1 and 6.1.5.3; see also Chapter 7, sec. 7.3.4.3.

EXAMPLE 5.34. Beethoven, Piano Sonata in E-flat, Op. 31, no. 3, i, (a) mm. 69–82; (b) mm. 1–10 (*ACF* 10.10); (c) mm. 33–34.

a couple of more times the final progression V$^6_5$–I, while still maintaining the melodic-motivic material of the continuation phrase. All of this changes at measure 72, when the left hand drops out and the right hand fully liquidates the continuation ideas by bringing a sixteenth-note flurry of arpeggiations of tonic harmony. Seeing as the bass note B♭ remains in our imagination to support the music of measures 72–74, we can comfortably analyze these bars as expressing a root-position tonic. Things become more complicated in the ensuing measures, however, where Beethoven lightly applies the brakes, so to speak, and introduces arpeggiated eighth notes. Observe that in measure 75, the lowest note of the new arpeggiations is now F (⑤), which gets shifted down two octaves in measure 76. In the following bar, the melody briefly breaks out of the arpeggios to bring a stepwise descent to

2̂, which is sustained by a cadential trill for the next four bars. The appearance of 2̂ forces a change in harmony away from tonic. The left hand responds by continuing the eighth-note arpeggiation motive of the previous bars, but now projecting a dominant harmony, with F continuing to be the lowest note of the arpeggiated gestures. The dominant finally resolves to tonic at measure 82 for the PAC that ends the theme.

Looking back, it is clear that cadential function has taken over from the continuation at measure 72. And supporting this function is an ECP initiated by a root-position tonic and concluding with V$^7$ resolving to I at the moment of cadential arrival. Most exceptionally, then, the ECP begins with a stage 1 tonic (atypically, in root position), bypasses a pre-dominant, and moves directly to stages 3 and 4. Still, the passage raises a number of questions. Just what constitutes the harmonic content of stage 3? Is it the dominant seventh alone at measures 78–81, or has a cadential six-four entered into the picture somewhere? Why does stage 1 employ a root-position tonic, rather than a standard I$^6$? And finally, why has Beethoven chosen to eliminate any pre-dominant function from the ECP? As for the harmonies of stage 3, it would seem that Beethoven has subtly shifted the tonic from root position to second inversion somewhere along the way. Exactly where, though, is somewhat hard to say, especially when listening without the aid of a score. Two possibilities are suggested in my annotations: measure 75, as articulated by the change in melodic material, or measure 76, in which the low F definitively displaces the prior bass B♭ from measure 72.

To understand why Beethoven begins the ECP with a root-position tonic and then passes over a stage 2 pre-dominant, we need to examine earlier passages of the exposition, starting with the very first bar (Ex. 5.34b). For here we encounter one of the most unusual main themes in all of Beethoven's oeuvre, namely one that is supported exclusively by an ECP and that furthermore omits stage 1 to open with the pre-dominant II$^6_5$. Three bars later, the progression moves on to stage 2b with VII$^7$/V (mm. 4–5) and a cadential six-four (sustained by a fermata in m. 6), finally closing with V$^7$–I for the PAC at measure 8. In short, we encounter a main theme that begins directly with a cadential function, thus bypassing initiating and medial phrases. I know of no other classical main theme constructed in this manner; indeed, the technique looks forward to the Romantic era, especially in works by Schumann.[51] Immediately following the PAC, Beethoven writes an extended anacrusis leading upward to a repeat of the entire theme in measures 10–17 (not shown). The first part of a two-part transition then gets underway, leading eventually to the second part (see Ex. 5.34c), which restates the main theme's opening idea, now shifted into the minor. Thus three times within the main theme and transition we hear thematic units beginning with an emphatic cadential pre-dominant.

Moving further into the exposition, let us turn to the first subordinate theme, as already discussed in Example 4.26 in the previous chapter. There, we focused on the combination of an expanded DCP supporting most of the theme and a compact ACP producing its closure. Now, we must attend to the opening harmony of the DCP, and observe that Beethoven begins the theme with a cadential I$^6$. In a manner resembling the main theme, he supports most of the first subordinate theme with an ECP (albeit one that becomes deceptive, as earlier discussed). Furthermore, the close at measure 53 is followed by an anacrusis figure that recalls the same situation in the main theme, except that now, this upbeat extends four bars (not shown) before bringing back a complete restatement of the subordinate theme—again, just like what happens with the main theme.

At this point it should be easy to suggest some answers to our original questions as to why the cadential function of the second subordinate theme (Ex. 5.34a) begins with a root-position I and then bypasses a pre-dominant. The more conventional I$^6$ for a stage 1 ECP has previously been emphasized ("used up," perhaps) by two statements of the first subordinate theme. As well, the main theme gives considerable weight to stage 2 of its ECP by beginning directly with pre-dominant harmonies. So to end his second subordinate theme, Beethoven choses a novel, and highly exceptional, option, one that does not utilize either of the previous ECP's opening harmonies (I$^6$ and II$^6_5$).

### 5.1.1.4. Diversity of Harmonic Content; Bass-Line Complexities

In his *Einführung in die musikalische Formenlehre*, Erwin Ratz now and then appeals to what he calls the "law of artistic economy": "if one of two possibilities is employed at a given place, then one endeavors to employ the other possibility at an analogous place."[52] This compositional rule of thumb sometimes plays itself out in cases of multiple ECPs, where it seems as though the composer were attempting to achieve maximal diversity of harmonic content within the cadential function of a thematic unit or, as in the previous example, across a wider formal scope. Indeed, Example 5.34 just discussed well illustrates the idea, for Beethoven brings a completely different set of specific harmonies for stages 1 and 2 in the three ECPs closing the main theme and the two subordinate themes. (As is always the case, we find little variation in stage 3, which is so highly constrained harmonically.) To be sure, the details are subtle: an emphatic II$^6_5$ and VII$^7$/V in the main theme (Ex. 5.34b, mm. 1–5) compared to a full bar of IV followed by a fleeting a II$^6$ and V$^6_5$/V in the first subordinate theme (Ex. 4.26, mm. 48–49). But it seems clear that the composer carefully chooses the harmonies of the three ECPs to attain the greatest possible variety.

Another instance of this technique arises in the earlier discussed Example 5.28. There, I proposed that because the second subordinate theme's ECP so strongly emphasizes II$^6$ (mm. 78–81), the third subordinate theme bypasses stage 2a to bring a stage-2b V$^6_5$/V (mm. 90–91). Following the PAC, the third subordinate theme immediately begins to be repeated. This time, stages 1 and 2 of the ECP (mm. 97–100) bring six different harmonies, none of which had sounded in either of the two previous ECPs: in stage 1 (m. 97), a minor tonic in root-position, prolonged by a substitute ♭VI; in stage 2 (mm. 99–100), three different pre-dominants—VII$^7$/V, IV$^7$, and II. And for good measure, Beethoven slips in VI$^6_4$ (m. 100) as a passing chord within the prolongation of stage 2, this harmony perhaps substituting for I$^6$, which, ironically, is not included in any of the prior ECPs. Indeed, those cadential units brought distinctly different harmonies for stage 1, as detailed before.[53] Beethoven thus manages to bring an entirely varied

---

51. See in Chapter 8, sec. 8.4.

52. Ratz, *Die musikalische Formenlehre*, 28 (my translation).

53. As mentioned in note 40, we may want to include mm. 76–77 as representing stage 1 of the second subordinate theme's ECP, in which case this VII$^6_5$/II contrasts with the harmonic content of this stage in the two ECPs of the third subordinate theme (m. 89 and mm. 97–98).

EXAMPLE 5.35. Mozart, Symphony No. 39 in E-flat, K. 543, i, mm. 62–71 (*ACF* 10.8).

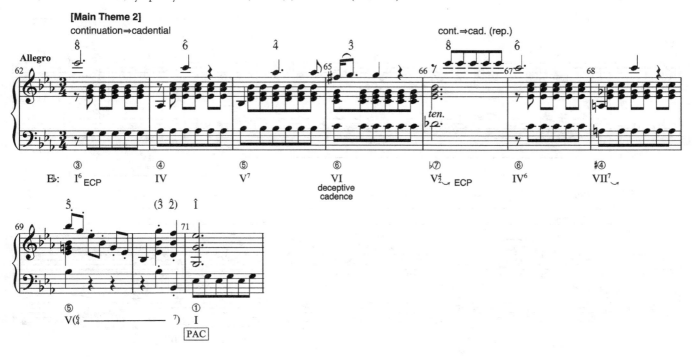

harmonic content (and thus prevents any redundancy) in all three of the ECPs of this expansive subordinate-theme group.

Sometimes, the diversity of harmonic content in multiple ECPs results in varied bass-line melodies as well. Thus in the example just discussed, the first two cadential progressions feature standard bass lines that ascend to ⑤, the third one (mm. 97–100), by contrast, brings a most unconventional descending bass: ⑧–♭⑥–♯④–♮④–③–②.

Two other interesting bass lines arise in a symphonic exposition by Mozart. The first case concludes a second main theme (Ex. 5.35), which features a deceptive-authentic combination of two ECPs.[54] The DCP (mm. 62–65) brings a standard bass line, ③–④–⑤–⑥; when the passage is repeated, Mozart does not write the same bass line, as would normally be the case. Rather, he continues the bass ascent up to ♭⑦ (m. 66), thus chromatically inflecting the initial tonic as V$^4_2$/IV, which moves as expected to IV$^6$ over ⑥ for the pre-dominant. He then further embellishes stage 2 via VII$^7$/V over ♯④ in measure 68, which arrives to ⑤ for the final V–I motion that completes the ACP. We see, therefore, that rather than bringing a two-part bass line, as is the norm with such DCP-APC combinations, Mozart fashions a single, unique line that snakes around the dominant: ③–④–⑤–⑥–♭⑦–⑥–♯④–⑤, thus creating a more integrative cadential function than would ordinarily be the case.[55]

Something similar then occurs later in the second subordinate theme (see again Ex. 5.3). Here we find two successive ECPs, the first being evaded, the second fully complete. As discussed, the standard procedure in such circumstances is to repeat the same bass line in order to achieve the final tonic. Here, however, Mozart begins the usual ascent ③–④–♯④–⑤, but at the moment of evasion (m. 130) surprisingly retains ⑤ (VII$^4_3$/IV) for the one-more-time repeat of stage ①, rather than reverting to ③. Then the bass, most unusually, steps down to ④ in order to support a stage-2a pre-dominant, only to leap up to ⑥ for the VII$^6_5$/V of stage 2b. The return back down to ⑤ initiates the final two stages of the ECP. Again, the diversity of harmonic content in these two progressions yields a single bass line that pulls together the two cadential units despite the disrupting evaded cadence.

A bass-line pattern that has marked similarities to those just considered (Ex. 5.3 and 5.35) arises in the slow introduction to Mozart's "Prague" Symphony (Ex. 5.36a). Here, though, we see that the composer's particular choice of harmonies not only affects the bass voice, but also engenders a particularly complex interaction of continuation and cadential functions. The movement begins with *coup-d'archet* flourishes by the strings. The absence of any clear basic ideas or contrasting ones prohibits us from speaking of a standard opening phrase (e.g., presentation, antecedent), but the sustained root-position tonic for these three bars projects a general sense of formal initiation. There follows a continuation (mm. 4–6) featuring a descending-thirds sequence

---

54. Such deceptive-authentic combinations (DCP-ACP) were introduced and discussed in Chapter 4, sec. 4.1.2.5. I return to the topic toward the end of the present chapter when considering the melodic content of ECP deviations (sec. 5.4.3).

55. DCP-ACP combinations are widely used in the baroque era (see Chapter 6, sec. 6.1.5.4, Ex. 6.47–6.49) as well as in the galant period (see Chapter 7, sec. 7.2.2, Ex. 7.44 and 7.46b). As a general rule, the bass lines of the cadential progressions conventionally ascend to ⑤.

EXAMPLE 5.36A. Mozart, Symphony No. 38 in D ("Prague"), K. 504, i, mm. 1–16.

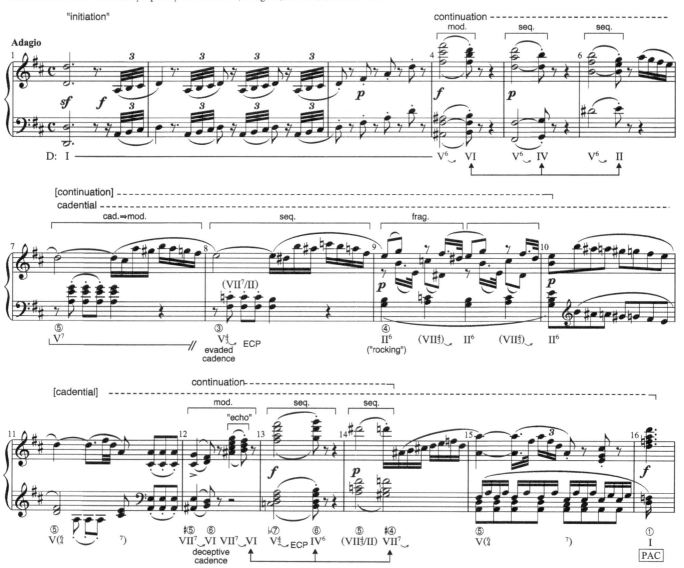

(see the arrows), each link of which is tonicized by its own dominant. The appearance of V⁷ in measure 7 holds out the possibility of a simple authentic cadence to conclude a thematic unit on the downbeat of measure 8. Mozart evades the cadence, however, with a surprising V₃⁴/II in measure 8,[56] which supports an ascending sequential repetition of the cadential idea of measure 7. Note that the sequence is not exact, for the bass voice does not follow the melody by rising up a step (for a V⁷/II) but rather descends to ③ to support the four-three position of the secondary dominant. This harmony, besides being sequential (looking backward), can also be understood (looking forward) as a chromatic substitute for a cadential tonic in stage 1b. The use of this particular position is especially noteworthy, because the bass line ⑤//③ now conforms to the conventional situation of an evaded cadence, whereby a root-position dominant (⑤) moves to a first-inversion tonic (③), which then marks the beginning of a one-more-time repetition. Indeed, V₃⁴/II signals the beginning of an ECP, which continues with II⁶ in measures 9–10 and the cadential dominant in the following bar.[57] Usually, the onset of an ECP is associated with a marked change in musical material, thus creating a phrase that is distinct from the preceding one (be it continuational or cadential). Here, however, Mozart obscures such a grouping boundary by employing harmonic material that permits a fusion of both continuation and cadential functions at least to the downbeat of measure 10.

---

56. The harmony on the downbeat of this bar is initially presented as a diminished-seventh sonority, but the motion of the inner voice C to B (in the left hand) reveals that the former is an embellishing tone, thus yielding an overall dominant-seventh formation for the measure as a whole.

57. Due to the neighboring VII₃⁴/II (substituting for V₂⁴/II), we might want to speak of a "rocking" on the supertonic in m. 9, a situation that is rarely encountered; see again note 33.

EXAMPLE 5.36B. Mozart, Symphony No. 38 in D ("Prague"), K. 504, i, bass-line reductions of mm. 8–16.

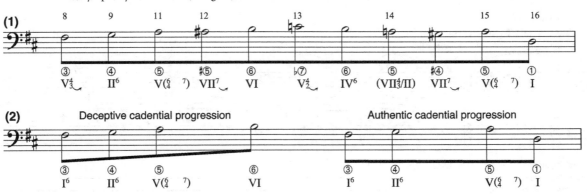

Once again, though, the ongoing thematic process fails to fully close, when the bass of measure 11 ascends chromatically to create a deceptive cadence in measure 12. Following an "echo" repeat in the woodwinds of the deceptive gesture, the harmonies in measures 13 and 14 (combined with those of m. 12) again play out the descending-thirds sequence of measures 4–6, though with important harmonic variants: thus, VII⁷/VI–VI (mm. 11–12), V$^4_2$/IV–IV⁶ (m. 13), and VII$^4_3$/II–VII⁷/V (m. 14), the latter harmony (VII⁷/V) being a chromatic substitute for II. Since the bass line does not follow the sequential plan, we can understand the harmonies in measures 13–14 as also projecting a cadential quality: stage 1, V$^4_2$/IV over ♭⑦; stage 2a, IV⁶ (⑥); stage 2b, VII⁷/V (#④); stage 3, V($^6_4$ ⁷) (⑤); and stage 4, I (①), the modal shift at the cadence signaling an elision with the next formal section of the introduction. Notice that in this scheme, the VII$^4_3$/II (first half of m. 14) functions as a passing harmony between the two pre-dominants of stages 2a and 2b.[58]

Let us consider more closely the bass line that Mozart forges with his two ECPs (see Ex. 5.36b) and especially with his choice of specific harmonies in this final phrase of the theme (mm. 13–16). First, we see that in this phrase he twice prohibits the bass from moving to G (④), the standard support for a cadential pre-dominant: first, in measure 13, by inverting the subdominant, as required by the preceding V$^4_2$/IV, and second, in measure 14, by employing VII⁷/V as a chromatic substitute for an implied II⁶. And like similar situations we have discussed before, we can easily understand his avoidance of ④, seeing as this scale degree is given such marked emphasis in measures 9–10. As such, the G is used up, so to speak, and thus no longer available to support a cadential pre-dominant. Second, and like the previous Symphony No. 39 examples, the resulting bass line creates a single melodic curve (line 1) rather than the more usual situation of repeated bass lines for the two ECPs—the first, deceptive, the second, authentic (line 2).

Finally, Mozart's choice of harmonies in this passage (along with other details of motive and grouping structure) has a profound effect on the form-functional expression in this slow introduction (see again Ex. 5.36a). We have already noted that as early as measures 7 and 8, a brief cadential moment is retrospectively reinterpreted as sequential, thus sustaining the continuation function during what are otherwise the cadential harmonies of these bars. All of the harmonies throughout measures 7–16 can thus be heard to support a cadential function. At the same time, the interpenetration of continuation and cadential functionalities re-emerges in measures 12–14 with the appearance of another sequential passage, one that references the earlier sequences in measures 4–6. Indeed, the fusions of continuation and cadential functions encountered in this slow introduction are considerably more extensive and complex than what we typically find in a simple continuation or continuation⇒cadential phrases of a sentential thematic design.

The cases of harmonic diversity that we have been considering up to now involve the normal circumstance of distinct harmonies that succeed one another in time. One extraordinary case of harmonic diversity in an ECP involves the expression of multiple harmonic functions that occur *simultaneously*, a situation that poses fascinating challenges to our standard modes of perception and cognition. The ECP in question (Ex. 5.37a) arises in the first movement of Mozart's Symphony No. 40 in G Minor. The subordinate-theme group of the exposition begins with an eight-measure hybrid theme, antecedent + continuation (shown earlier in Ex. 2.6). That theme is closed by a compact PAC in measures 50–51 (reproduced in Ex. 5.37b). Given the tight-knit construction of this first subordinate theme, we certainly expect to encounter more thematic activity that will achieve the obligatory loosening in compliance with the norms of sonata form. So it is no surprise that the theme starts up again and then undergoes a significant expansion of its cadential function. Example 5.37a begins at measure 56 with the continuation phrase of the theme. Formal loosening is then achieved by the lengthy ECP in measures 58–66. Note that this progression begins with the same bass note E♭ (④) that opens the compact cadence of the initial subordinate theme (Ex. 5.37b, m. 50). In that earlier cadence, E♭ holds a conventional pre-dominant II⁶ of the subordinate key B-flat major.

---

58. One further detail of harmony is worth mentioning. The diminished-seventh VII$^4_3$/II at the start of m. 14 alludes to the similar sonority on the downbeat of m. 8, though this time, the diminished-seventh alone represents the secondary dominant, without reverting into a form of V⁷/II (see note 56). The resulting succession of two diminished sevenths in m. 14 thus contributes to the rhetorical intensification of the ongoing ECP.

EXAMPLE 5.37(A-C). Mozart, Symphony No. 40 in G Minor, K. 550, i, (a) mm. 56–66; (b) 50–51; (c) reconstruction of mm. 58–59.

In the expanded version of the theme, measure 58 suddenly shifts the music into the remote key of A-flat major (SK: ♭VII). This tonal shift is prepared by the descending-fifths sequence in measures 56–57, such that the E♭⁷ harmony of measure 58 represents the final link in this sequential chain.[59] In the new tonal context of A-flat major, the bass, which is held as a pedal for five bars, now supports a dominant seventh that sounds through measure 62 (see line 2 of the harmonic analysis). The following bar sees the bass ascending to E♮, which contains a diminished-seventh sonority, one that not only continues to prolong the dominant of A-flat (as a substitute VII$^4_2$), but pivots to become a pre-dominant VII⁷/V of the true subordinate key, B-flat (line 3). The dominant of that key then appears as a cadential six-four in measure 64, and the theme closes with a PAC two bars later.

Looking back at measures 58–62 more closely, we can discern three levels of harmonic activity, each projecting a different harmonic function. At an intermediate level (line 2), the *dominant* of A-flat is prolonged by virtue of the bass pedal-point E♭. At a more local level, however, the passage seems more to express *tonic* harmony of the same key (line 1). Indeed, if we temporarily ignore the pedal, the melody suggests that an appropriate harmonization for each bar might have seen V$^4_2$ alternating with I⁶ (Ex. 5.37c),

entirely in the manner of a rocking on the tonic. Yet by placing an E♭ pedal below this prolonged I⁶, Mozart is able to assimilate the remote tonicization of A-flat within a cadential progression of B-flat, since the E♭⁷ could also be heard as an unconventional stage-2a *pre-dominant* IV⁷ (a major-minor-seventh sonority) in B-flat (line 3). The move to the stage-2b VII⁷/V (m. 63) continues to prolong pre-dominant function. This highest level of harmonic activity, of course, accounts for our hearing an ECP in the subordinate key stretching to the PAC at measure 66. As a result of this complicated manipulation of harmonic functions, Mozart creates the illusion that the ECP begins with a conventional rocking pattern (in the key of A-flat, of course), even though the progression as a whole is actually initiated by a pre-dominant (in the correct key), analogous to that of the compact cadential formula back at measure 50 (Ex. 5.37b). Providing the glue that holds these two interpretations together is the bass pedal, which creates an initial sense of dominant prolongation (in A-flat) that is retrospectively reinterpreted as a pre-dominant prolongation (in B-flat).

In light of the harmonic complexities exhibited by the ECP in this subordinate theme of the exposition, we might look at what happens in the recapitulation and consider whether Mozart will simply replay the same harmonic game of multiple harmonic reinterpretations by transposing the passage down a third (from B-flat of the exposition into G minor of the recapitulation). Not surprisingly, he does not, but what he does write is even more complicated (see Ex. 5.37d). First, let us look at the bass voice, starting at measure 241. Here, Mozart brings ③, in G minor, as a pedal point for five bars. This ③ is the perfect note to support an initial tonic (I⁶) of an ECP. Moreover, we again hear at the very

---

59. Note one small change to the end of the continuation phrase in the repeat of the subordinate theme. The final B♭ harmony of m. 57 takes the form of a dominant seventh, rather than remaining a triad, as found earlier at m. 49 of the original subordinate theme (Ex. 2.6). As a result, we feel that in the expanded version, the sequential pattern continues through to the E♭⁷ of m. 58. In the first version (Ex. 2.6), the B♭ triad (end of m. 49) could rightly be considered the close of the sequence so that the following II⁶ at m. 50 is heard as exclusively cadential.

EXAMPLE 5.37D. Mozart, Symphony No. 40 in G Minor, K. 550, i, mm. 239–54.

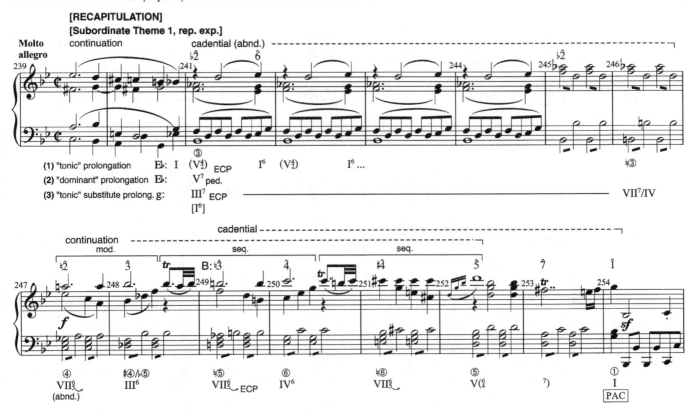

foreground of the music a rocking on the tonic, which further supports the idea of an ECP occurring at this moment in the theme. It is all illusory, however, since the harmony built over ③ is not I⁶, but rather a dominant-seventh, which shifts the music to the flat side, E-flat major, HK: ♭VI (line 2 of the analysis), the key in which the rocking on the tonic occurs (line 1). So the question now becomes: Is there a way of understanding this passage as cadential in the home key of G minor? Recall that in the exposition (Ex. 5.37a, m. 58) the bass ④ supports a dominant-seventh (of A-flat), which ultimately functions as a cadential pre-dominant IV⁷ in B-flat (the subordinate key). In the recapitulation (Ex. 5.37d), however, the harmony built over ③ (m. 241) cannot be seen as any kind of pre-dominant in G minor (the home key).

What then might corroborate the idea of an ECP beginning at measure 241? One option worth considering is to hear the B♭⁷ harmony in G minor as III⁷ (a major-minor-seventh sonority), which can then further be seen as a substitute for I⁶ (the notes B♭ and D being common tones with that harmony). The four systems shown in Example 5.37e provide a context for understanding this ECP beginning with an initial tonic substitute. System 1 shows the basic diatonic cadential progression as a framework for the more elaborate progressions in the other lines. System 2 adds major-minor sevenths (the star-shaped symbols) and secondary dominants (VII⁷) as representatives of the prolonged harmonic functions of stages 1 and 2 (T and PD). This system also includes a cadential six-four, as found in the actual ECPs that Mozart writes in the exposition and recapitulation. These harmonies of system 2 thus constitute the elements that Mozart chooses for his two ECPs, with the exception of the opening I⁶, which cannot be employed if the two ECPs are to support the same basic music (though set in different keys).

System 3 shows the actual harmonies in the ECP of the recapitulation (Ex. 5.37d). The progression begins with the major-minor seventh (B♭⁷). To be sure, some readers may be skeptical as to whether this harmony is an actual tonic substitute. Nevertheless, if Mozart wants to write an analogous passage to that of the exposition (m. 58ff.), then this particular sonority over ③ is the only option available (I will explain this choice of bass note shortly): this is the only sonority that can also function as a dominant seventh in the flat-side region of E-flat, which is needed to enact the *faux* rocking on the tonic. At measure 246, the bass moves up to B♮ (♮③) to support VII⁷/IV, a stage-1b chromatic variant of an initial cadential tonic. The following two harmonies (bracketed in mm. 247–48 and to be discussed shortly) no longer project a cadential progression, so we understand that the ECP has been abandoned at measure 247. The ECP resumes at measure 249 with the same stage-1b harmony (though positioned differently) that was the final harmony of the abandoned ECP; the dashed curve line shows this harmonic connection. The rest of the ECP follows as a matter of course. System 4 presents the harmonies of the ECP that Mozart uses in the exposition (Ex. 5.37a). These correspond to the final harmonies of the recapitulation's ECP (save for the initial IV⁷, which would have no necessary function to fulfill within the latter ECP).

EXAMPLE 5.37E. Mozart, Symphony No. 40 in G Minor, K. 550, i, harmonic derivations of the ECPs.

EXAMPLE 5.37F. Cadential vs. sequential.

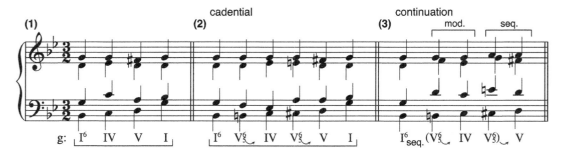

At this point, we have largely accounted for the harmonies making up the two subordinate-theme ECPs in this symphonic movement. Some additional complexities of harmony and formal function, however, remain to be discussed. But before tackling these issues, we have to step back and consider an interesting ambiguity in my classification of harmonic progressions. The first pattern of Example 5.37f shows a simple cadential progression in G minor. The second and third patterns add secondary dominants to the IV and V harmonies. These more elaborate versions, however, are now subject to two interpretations. Pattern 2 analyzes the progression as cadential, but pattern 3 proposes that the same harmonic succession can be heard as sequential, especially when the upper voices are rearranged to project a clear model-sequence repetition.[60] Inasmuch as patterns 2 and 3 reflect different progression types, they also support different formal functions: the first, cadential, the second, continuational. Throughout the classical repertory, the potential ambiguity of these two progressions rarely materializes, but in two cases that I have uncovered so far, the double nature of these progressions becomes a resource for significant compositional play.

One case appears in the recapitulation of Mozart's symphony under consideration in Example 5.37d.[61] Picking up where we left off in our earlier discussion, the stage-1b VII$^7$/IV at measure 246 does not resolve as expected (to a pre-dominant IV) but rather slides up by a half step to another secondary dominant, VII$^6_5$/III♭, which resolves to III$^6$ at measure 248. Since this tonicization of minor III has no place within a G-minor cadence, we recognize that the ongoing ECP has been abandoned. Indeed, measures 247–48 constitute a model for two sequential repetitions (mm. 249–50 and 251–52), and all of these harmonies support the resumption of *continuation* function. Note that the harmonies in measures 249–52 conform to pattern 3 of Example 5.37f, except that the secondary dominants take the form of diminished-seventh substitutes (in six-five position) and the subdominant at measure 250 is placed in first inversion. Given the VII$^6_5$/V in measure 251, we might also expect the dominant in the following bar to be found in first inversion as well; instead, that harmony appears in root position with six-four embellishments. With this change to a root-position dominant, Mozart clarifies that we can hear the ongoing progression not only as sequential but also as cadential, conforming to pattern 2 in Example 5.37f. As a result, a renewed *cadential* function brings decisive closure for the theme in measure 254. Note, as mentioned earlier, that the return of the cadential function at measure 249 links up with the abandoned ECP via the same diminished-seventh sonority—VII$^7$/IV, measure 246, and VII$^6_5$/IV, measure 249.

To summarize, Mozart takes the complex cadential function from the exposition's subordinate theme and extends it more significantly in the recapitulation. He is able to effect this extension by starting the ECP one step lower in the bass (on ③) rather than on ④, as in the exposition. In this way, he has more room to expand the cadential progression in the later section compared to the earlier one. And he does so by ramping up the harmonic tension by means of an ascending chromatic bassline from ③ up to ♮⑥, thus ending one step higher than the ECP bass of the exposition. The resulting progression supports an elaborate interaction of sequential and cadential harmonies, thus forging a remarkable fusion of continuation and cadential functions (comparable in complexity to the slow introduction of his "Prague" Symphony that we saw in Ex. 5.36). Moreover, the intricacies uncovered in this analysis make heavy demands on the listener's cognitive ability to negotiate the various reinterpretations of harmony and formal function that occur both successively and simultaneously. Finally, the ECPs of the exposition and recapitulation taken together present an astounding degree of harmonic diversity (see again, Ex. 5.37e), far surpassing the number of cadential harmonies typically found in this formal unit of a symphonic sonata form.

### 5.1.1.5. Ambiguous Onset of an ECP

To conclude our discussion of the harmonic content of the ECP, I want to return to a topic broached at the start of this chapter, namely, the minimum length sufficient to identify cases of cadential expansion. I proposed that authentic and deceptive ECPs need to last at least four measures (including a single bar for the final harmony of the progression) and that half cadential and evaded ECPs are minimally three bars in length. More precisely, an ECP should embrace the metrical downbeats of four or three bars, depending on its type. Such a stipulation, of course, is rather arbitrary, a mere rule of thumb that probably carries little analytical significance. Since it is normally clear where an ECP ends, the question reverts to where the expansion is thought to begin, and this more general problem can involve not only minimum-sized ECPs but longer ones as well. The matter seems to hinge largely on the status of stage 1, most notably, whether a given tonic harmony is thought to be included in the ECP, or whether it more appropriately belongs to a preceding continuation (or possibly initiating) function. Issues of bass line contour and grouping structure also have a role to play in determining where to locate the onset of an ECP.

Consider, for instance, Example 5.38a. This main theme, built as a compound period, begins with a presentation phrase that is followed by a continuation at measure 5 and concludes with an HC at measure 8, thus giving rise to a compound antecedent. (A compound consequent follows, Example 5.38b, whose presentation is not shown.) Returning to the antecedent, we see that the root-position tonic on the downbeat of measure 5 clearly functions to complete the tonic prolongation (I–V$^6_5$–I) supporting the presentation. The shift to first inversion in the second half of the bar leads to a root-position subdominant that also becomes inverted. The resulting IV$^6$, which is rather oddly syncopated across of the bar line of measure 7 (and is even emphasized by the *fp* accent), eventually resolves to V$^6_5$, which moves to I in order to complete a broader tonic prolongation (from the beginning of the continuation). A compact HC concludes the compound antecedent. In the matching consequent (Ex. 5.38b), measure 14 sees a full measure of II$^6$ leading to another complete bar of dominant in measure 15, which effects a PAC on the downbeat of the theme's final bar. A look at the bass line of each continuation phrase suggests that I$^6$ of both measures 5 and 13 can be heard to initiate a cadential progression, leading to a stage-2 predominant in the following bar (mm. 6 and 14). In the antecedent, this incipient cadential progression is abandoned when the IV$^6$ (which

---

60. Pattern 3 omits a final cadential tonic, as seen in patterns 1 and 2, because the harmony implied to follow the dominant is V$^6_5$/VI, which would continue the ascending sequence.

61. The second case will be discussed later in connection with Beethoven's *Eroica* Symphony; see Ex. 5.69 and 5.70.

EXAMPLE 5.38. Beethoven, Piano Sonata in C Minor, Op. 10, no. 1, ii, (a) mm. 1–8, (b) mm. 13–16 (*ACF* 5.14).

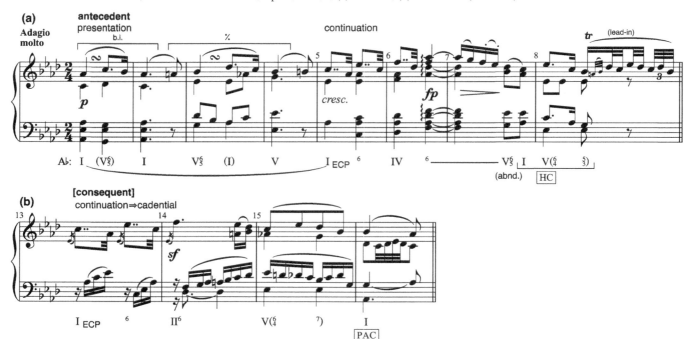

could still be heard as cadential) moves to V$^6_5$. In the consequent, on the contrary, the cadential progression is fully realized by the PAC. In short, we have a process of cadential abandonment and subsequent fulfillment.[62]

The one remaining question is whether we can identify an ECP in either one, or both, constituent units of the compound period. On the one hand, the downward leap of the bass to I$^6$ over ③ in the second half of measures 5 and 13 strongly signals cadential initiation.[63] If so, then the resulting authentic cadential progression in the consequent can be said to last only three bars, inasmuch as the I$^6$ is an upbeat to the first of three metrical downbeats. In that case, the minimum length for an ECP would not be forthcoming (and the same would hold for the abandoned progression in the antecedent). On the other hand, the consistent rhythm of one harmony per bar in the consequent's continuation phrase (and the first two bars of the antecedent's continuation) might prompt us to recognize the onset of a genuine ECP on the downbeats of measures 5 and 13. That in all other respects the first half of these two bars clearly *groups* with the material that follows also argues for hearing a cadential expansion as supporting the full extent of both phrases (though the first progression becomes abandoned, as already discussed). Is it analytically necessary to make a final determination on where the cadential progressions are heard to begin? Clearly not; but the attempt at doing so is a productive heuristic in foregrounding many details of melodic, harmonic, rhythmic, and motivic organization of the theme.[64]

If we hear the ECPs in Example 5.38 beginning with the root-position tonic in measures 5 and 13 (as annotated in the score), then we de facto recognize that tonic to function as a linking harmony, since it simultaneously represents both the end of one progression type (prolongational) and the beginning of another (cadential). In some cases, as in this example, it can be uncertain whether or not a given tonic has such a dual role, thus rendering ambiguous just where we want to locate the onset of the cadential progression. Another, more complicated, case arises in the enormous ECP closing the subordinate-theme group of Beethoven's "Waldstein" sonata, first movement (Ex. 5.39). In a second subordinate theme beginning at measure 49, an extended presentation, consisting of a threefold statement of a two-measure basic idea, leads at measure 55 to a continuation with an extensive process of fragmentation: 2 × 1 (mm. 55–56); 2 × ½ (m. 57); and 4 × ¼ (m. 58). This process culminates in a thorough-going liquidation (mm. 59–60) and a harmonic intensification by means of V$^6_5$/IV. The resolution to the subdominant at measure 61 brings stage 2a of the ECP, whose stage 2b V$^6_5$/V (m. 63) leads to a massively

---

62. The topic of abandoned ECPs will also be taken up toward the end of the present chapter (sec. 5.4.4); as well, we will see that Ex. 5.62, discussed there, brings many features in common with Ex. 5.38 being considered now.

63. See Chapter 3, sec. 3.1.1.7, and the discussion of Ex. 3.9 and 3.10.

64. One detail not entirely relevant to this discussion, but of analytical interest nonetheless, is the unusual disposition of melodic highpoints in the two phrases. In the antecedent, the melody achieves a higher pitch (the emphasized A♭$_5$ in m. 6) than in the consequent (F$_5$ in m.14). Normally the reverse situation is the case. But as this exposition continues, the transition that immediately follows (see in Chapter 4, Ex. 4.54) dramatically opens up the melodic space to F$_6$, while the subordinate theme, not shown, markedly exploits the highest register of Beethoven's piano.

EXAMPLE 5.39. Beethoven, Piano Sonata in C, Op. 53 ("Waldstein"), i, mm. 49–63.

expanded dominant at measure 66 (not shown).[65] The IV harmony of measure 61 is obviously part of the ECP. Moreover, this moment effects a new grouping unit as characterized by the change in accompaniment to a drum-bass variant. But what is the status of the preceding V$^6_5$/IV (mm. 59–60)? That we might want to include it as part of the cadential progression seems likely, especially given the sudden octave drop of the bass to G♯, a standard textural signal of cadential onset. But this secondary dominant emerges from a clear I$^6$ in the previous bar, which features an intense rocking on the tonic. Should that harmony also be included as part of the cadential progression? Even more puzzling is trying to determine just where the root-position tonic, which supports the presentation, actually moves to its first inversion. For a change in position evidently takes place somewhere along the way. Indeed we can see I$^6$ becoming more metrically prominent

as the passage progresses, though the root E is ever-present in the bass through measure 57. In short, a moment of clear bass-line shift from E to G♯ cannot be discerned, which further complicates determining just where the onset of the ECP might be located. Again, it is probably not even necessary to make this decision, but considering the issue nonetheless encourages to give a close look at how Beethoven subtly blurs the boundaries of the theme's continuation and cadential functions.

### 5.1.2. Melodic Content

Let us now turn from the harmonies of cadential expansions to their melodic content. Given that an ECP opens up a greater span of time than a compact cadential progression, considerably more melodic activity may occur with the former compared to the latter. As a result, it might seem that the classification of an ECP's melodic content would pose special problems. And to be sure, when the melodic line is highly embellished, it is often difficult,

---

65. The expansion of this dominant has already been discussed in Chapter 3, Ex. 3.168.

EXAMPLE 5.40. Mozart, Violin Concerto in A, K. 219, i, mm. 28–33 (*ACF* 20.4).

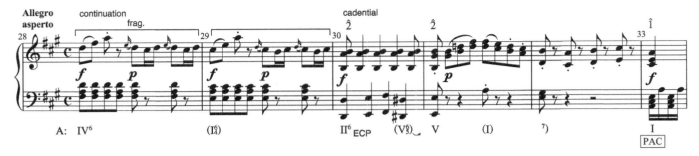

EXAMPLE 5.41. Mozart, Piano Concerto in E-flat, K. 482, i, mm. 174–78 (*ACF* 20.8).

if not fully impractical, to designate a single pitch as representing the melodic component of a given stage, especially in stage 3, where the cadential six-four can often support highly virtuosic displays of melodic outpouring. Nonetheless, the classification scheme proposed in Chapter 3 is still useful in many cases for understanding the melodic scaffolding behind the foreground embellishments. The following discussion is organized in a similar manner to that presented in the earlier chapter.

### 5.1.2.1. Basic Simple ($\hat{3}/\hat{2}/\hat{2}/\hat{1}$); with Cadential Six-Four ($\hat{3}/\hat{2}/\hat{3}\text{-}\hat{2}/\hat{1}$)

The basic simple pattern is rarely used for an ECP, probably because it does not provide as much differentiated pitch content as the other, more extended, basic patterns (soprano, alto, tenor and bass). One case of the simple pattern (/$\hat{2}/\hat{2}/\hat{1}$), though actually incomplete due to its bypassing stage 1, can be seen in Example 5.40, measures 30–33. Following the one-bar fragments in measures 28–29, which can readily be heard as continuational (subsequent to a compound presentation, not shown), the cadential pre-dominant in measure 30 supports $\hat{2}$, which reiterates this scale degree as the principal content of stages 2 and 3, resolving naturally to $\hat{1}$ at measure 33.

As discussed in Chapter 3, cases of the simple pattern using the cadential six-four ($\hat{3}/\hat{2}/\hat{3}\text{-}\hat{2}/\hat{1}$) occur infrequently, due most likely to the repetition of the $\hat{3}\text{-}\hat{2}$ motion. This redundancy can be overcome, however, if the pattern skips over $\hat{3}$ of stage 1 and begins instead with stage 2. Looking back to Example 5.34b, we see that the ECP opens with a pre-dominant supporting $\hat{2}$, which moves chromatically up to $\hat{3}$ for the cadential six-four (m. 6) and a quick $\hat{2}\text{-}\hat{1}$ resolution in measures 7–8. The overall /$\hat{2}/\hat{3}\text{-}\hat{2}/\hat{1}$ configuration thus avoids a repetitive $\hat{3}\text{-}\hat{2}$ motion of the complete simple pattern.

### 5.1.2.2. Basic Soprano ($\hat{5}/\hat{4}/\hat{2}/\hat{1}$); with Cadential Six-Four ($\hat{5}/\hat{4}/\hat{3}\text{-}\hat{2}/\hat{1}$)

The basic soprano pattern arises now and then in ECPs. In the earlier discussed Example 5.10, the initial $\hat{5}$ in measures 68–69 is embellished by $\hat{6}$ in the rocking on the tonic (via IV). A move to $\hat{4}$ within stage 2 yields a leap down to $\hat{2}$ for stage 3, thus bypassing $\hat{3}$ of a cadential six-four.[66]

The use of a cadential six-four to supplement stage 3 can be seen in Example 5.41, measures 175–78. Though the passage exhibits extensive arpeggiations, which could inhibit our recognizing a structural melody, the pattern formed by the

---

66. We might also recognize a *simultaneous combination* with the alto stream ($\hat{3}/\hat{2}/\hat{7}/\hat{1}$), as annotated in the score.

EXAMPLE 5.42. Haydn, Symphony No. 87 in A, iii, mm. 39–44 (*ACF* 18.12).

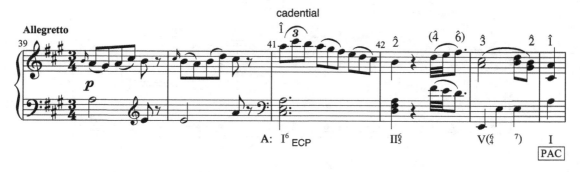

### 5.1.2.3. Basic Alto (3̂/2̂/7̂/1̂); with Cadential Six-Four (3̂/2̂/1̂-7̂/1̂)

The earlier discussed Example 5.24 illustrates the basic alto pattern with a cadential six-four. Though the cadence bypasses stage 1, the pitch content of that stage (3̂) appears precadentially at the end of the preceding compound basic idea. In the previous Example 5.23a, we considered the question of where to locate the onset of the cadential progression. If we take it to begin with the new phrase at measure 6, thus bypassing stage 1, then we can find the complete basic alto pattern /2̂-(3̂)/1̂-7̂/1̂. If, on the contrary, we want to see the progression starting with a stage-1 V$^6_5$/IV at the end of measure 4, then the opening of the varied tenor 5̂-6̂ comes into play (as a successive combination).

### 5.1.2.4. Basic Tenor (8̂/6̂/5̂/1̂); with Cadential Six-Four (8̂/6̂/5̂-4̂/1̂)

Among compact cadential progressions, the tenor pattern is found infrequently. With ECPs, however, the pattern appears more regularly.[67] As mentioned in Chapter 3 (sec. 3.1.2.1), the structural gap between stage 3 (5̂) and stage 4 (1̂) is most often filled in by various embellishments (esp. arpeggiations and scales). Exemplary in this respect is an ECP shown in Chapter 4, Example 4.76. In the complete ECP starting at measure 181, the structural tones in the melody stand out at the peaks of the arpeggios and scales, with those same tones receiving metrical emphasis an octave lower (save for the final 4̂). In stage 3 (m. 183), the upper notes correspond to the model (5̂-4̂), but the gap between 4̂ and 1̂ is partially filled in by the descending arpeggio on the last eighth note of the bar, such that the final tonic is locally approached from both 2̂ and 7̂.

In the present chapter, we have already looked at two ECPs featuring the basic tenor pattern. An especially clear case is shown in Example 5.9, where the rocking on the tonic (mm. 43–48) prolongs 8̂ via an upper neighbor 2̂. The progression concludes quickly (mm. 49) with 6̂ of stage 2, followed by 5̂ and leading directly to 1̂. A second case arises in Example 5.33, where scalar patterns are the primary mode of embellishment. Again, a rocking on the tonic supports 8̂ in the melody (m. 305). Stage 2 brings a drop to 6̂, and the structural 5̂-4̂ appears in the highest voice of measures 307–309. The particular way in which Beethoven harmonizes the descent from 5̂ to 1̂ has already been discussed, but from a melodic perspective, we can see that the compact cadential progression analyzed in line 2 supports a soprano-alto combination 3̂/4̂/7̂/1̂.

### 5.1.2.5. Varied Simple (1̂/2̂/2̂/1̂); with Cadential Six-Four (1̂/2̂/3̂-2̂/1̂)

As discussed in Chapter 3 (see Ex. 3.31), all of the basic melodic patterns regularly appear in a *varied* form, whereby the first pitch, stage 1, is lower than that of the basic patterns, so as to rise by a step to the regular pitch of stage 2. The rest of the melody then continues with the same notes of the basic pattern. Thus, whereas the basic simple pattern begins on 3̂, the varied one begins a third lower, on 1̂, and then steps up to 2̂, which eventually arrives back on 1̂. The varied soprano and alto also begin a third lower (3̂ and 1̂, respectively), but the tenor pattern begins a fourth lower (5̂ in place of 8̂).

The varied simple pattern arises in a handful of cases within the ECP corpus. In Example 5.42, the melody of the ECP begins on 1̂ (m. 41), which is followed by a broad descending scale that reaches 2̂ for the pre-dominant in the next bar. The melody continues with 3̂, supported by the cadential six-four, and concludes with the stepwise motion 2̂ to 1̂. Note that stage 2 brings an ascending arpeggio 2̂-(4̂-6̂), a standard technique that I already have highlighted in Chapter 3.[68] Though each bar of this ECP exhibits a fair degree of embellishment, the metrical downbeats clearly articulate the varied simple pattern.[69]

---

67. I am not entirely sure what accounts for this different usage. Perhaps the reason lies in the wider pitch space that the melodic line in this stream traverses, a full octave from 8̂ to 1̂. The ECP gives sufficient scope for this broad melodic descent to take place (usually with many attendant embellishments).

68. Sec. 3.1.2.1 and the discussion of Ex. 3.30.

69. It would be possible to take 3̂ in m. 41 as the structural pitch (of a basic simple pattern) if we focus our hearing on the very top note of the scale.

EXAMPLE 5.43. Haydn, String Quartet in G, Op. 64, no. 4, ii, mm. 5–8 (*ACF* 4.9).

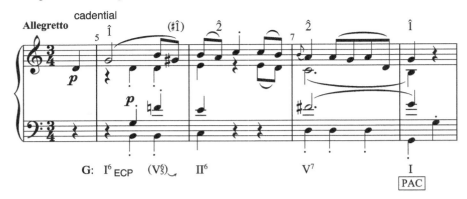

EXAMPLE 5.44. Mozart, Clarinet Quintet in A, K. 581, i, mm. 57–65 (*ACF* 12.11a).

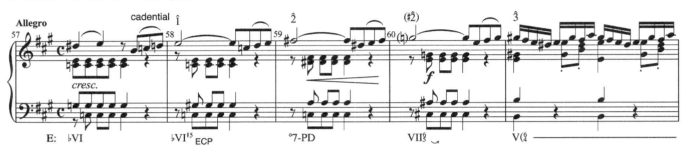

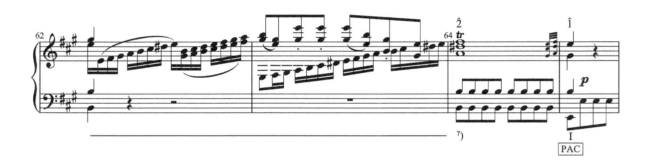

The example just examined is fully diatonic. For reasons that are unclear to me, however, a number of the ECPs in the corpus that employ the varied simple pattern feature an ascending chromatic motion in their melodic lines. Consider Example 5.43. A chromatic rise in stage 1 is clearly evident in measure 5. Such directed motion from G to G♯ encourages us to hear A ($\hat{2}$) in the following bar as the structural pitch of stage 2. When the dominant proper arrives in measure 7, the $\hat{2}$ is retained until its resolution to $\hat{1}$, which thus concludes the varied simple pattern.

A second case of a chromatic ascent within this pattern can be seen in Example 5.44. Following a descending-fifths sequence that arrives in measure 57 on ♭VI, an ECP begins in the following bar with $\hat{1}$ in the melody. Stage 2 follows in the next bar with a stepwise ascent to $\hat{2}$, and a further stage 2b brings ♯$\hat{2}$ (notated as ♭$\hat{3}$). Stage 3 arrives with $\hat{3}$ and a bursting forth of running sixteenths in the clarinet. It is as though the half notes in measures 58–60 are hemming in the eighth-note anacruses leading into those bars, such that the triumphant appearance of the cadential six-four breaks the logjam and sets the clarinet free.[70] The final stages (3b and 4) bring the cadential trill on $\hat{2}$ (m. 64) and the cadential close on $\hat{1}$. Reviewing the melodic scaffolding here, we find a clear example of a varied simple pattern (with cadential six-four), one that moves chromatically stepwise up from $\hat{1}$ to $\hat{3}$ and diatonically back down again to $\hat{1}$.

---

70. Robert S. Hatten specifically identifies such an "arrival six-four" as a significantly marked event within his theory of musical meaning (*Musical Meaning in Beethoven: Markedness, Correlation, and Interpretation*, 15, 288).

### 5.1.2.6. Varied Soprano ($\hat{3}/\hat{4}/\hat{2}/\hat{1}$); with Cadential Six-Four ($\hat{3}/\hat{4}/\hat{3}$-$\hat{2}/\hat{1}$)

An ECP that projects the varied soprano pattern can be seen in the earlier discussed Example 5.28. Following the mid-phrase pause in measures 95–96, a new cadential unit consisting entirely of block-chord texture brings a sudden shift to the minor mode. A varied succession of harmonies ultimately results in the major-mode, final PAC of the exposition. The upper voice of these block chords highlights the modal shifts, bringing ♭$\hat{3}$ for the two initial-tonic harmonies (I and VI). That same degree remains as a common tone to the first of two pre-dominants in measure 99 (VII$^7$/V and IV$^7$), but then, with a passing VI$^6_4$ harmony moving to II in measure 100, a corresponding ♭$\hat{3}$–$\hat{4}$ motion achieves the second structural pitch of the varied alto pattern ($\hat{4}$), which quickly leads to a final $\hat{2}$–$\hat{1}$ melodic close.

### 5.1.2.7. Varied Alto ($\hat{1}/\hat{2}/\hat{7}/\hat{1}$); with Cadential Six-Four ($\hat{1}/\hat{2}/\hat{1}$-$\hat{7}/\hat{1}$)

A number of examples already introduced illustrate the varied alto pattern. In Example 5.5, an ECP beginning in the second half of measure 38 leads to an IAC on $\hat{3}$, approached by a tenor $\hat{4}$. When the phrase is repeated, the melody touches again $\hat{4}$ (m. 45), but pulls away at the last second with a leap down to $\hat{7}$ in order to effect a matching PAC (and to avoid any implications of another IAC). The resulting melody, now with $\hat{2}$ for stage 2, thus fits the varied alto pattern.[71]

A considerably more complicated cadential melody in Example 5.7 also expresses the varied alto pattern (with cadential six-four). Starting with measure 15, a structural $\hat{1}$ is prolonged by the rocking on the tonic (which actually begins a bar earlier). The motion to $\hat{2}$ is effected by the scalar descent leading to the first beat of measure 18; another descending scale brings $\hat{1}$ on downbeat of measure 19, and the pattern can be completed with $\hat{7}$ appearing at the very end of that bar and resolving to $\hat{1}$ for the PAC. To be sure, some other melodic streams are touched upon in the course of the embellishing figurations (esp. the tenor stream with $\hat{6}$–$\hat{5}$ in mm. 18–19), but the overriding varied alto emerges with sufficient clarity.[72]

### 5.1.2.8. Varied Tenor ($\hat{5}/\hat{6}/\hat{5}/\hat{1}$); with Cadential Six-Four ($\hat{5}/\hat{6}/\hat{5}$-$\hat{5}$ ($\hat{4}$)/$\hat{1}$)

Like the case of the basic tenor pattern, the varied version finds frequent use among ECPs. As seen earlier in Chapter 4, Ex. 4.63, an ECP beginning at measure 298 features a melodic profile that assimilates easily to the model. In the present chapter, we encounter the same pattern in Example 5.29a, measure 240, this time beginning first with stage 2 (as already discussed). At the end of the stage, we see a characteristic embellishment, whereby $\hat{6}$ rises up to $\hat{8}$ before falling down to $\hat{5}$.[73]

### 5.1.2.9. Successive Combinations

The extra room for melodic activity afforded by an ECP leads to a wide variety of successive combinations.

**Tenor Combo ($\hat{5}/\hat{6}/\hat{1}$-$\hat{2}/\hat{1}$).** Just as with compact cadences, we can observe ECPs whose structural melodic pitches are drawn successively from two or more streams. The most common pattern involves the melodic profile $\hat{5}/\hat{6}/\hat{1}$-$\hat{2}/\hat{1}$, which in terms of successive streams can be interpreted as T/T/A-S/S. As discussed in Chapter 3, we can use the colloquial term *tenor combo* to reference this pattern. Many slight variants of this combination are found, some of which are seen in the following examples from earlier in the chapter.

Turning back to Example 5.12, we can observe that the cadential progression brings $\hat{5}$ from the tenor stream for stage 1 (m. 46). The upward arpeggio within stage 2 allows for two different interpretations of the structural pitches: (1) we could hear the $\hat{5}$ of stage 1 connecting to the E♭ ($\hat{6}$), thus yielding a literal tenor combo (T/T/A-S/S); or (2) we could hear the principal pitch of stage 2 as $\hat{2}$, from the alto stream, thus creating a variant combination T/A/A-S/S. Note that irrespective of these two possibilities, the structural $\hat{2}$ (S) of stage 3b is embellished by the upper neighbor $\hat{3}$, which further supports an interpretation of a closing soprano line. Indeed, we find this embellishment, ($\hat{3}$)-$\hat{2}$, in the majority of cases where the tenor combo (or its variants) underlies the ECP.

Example 5.16 shows a variant of the tenor combo in which $\hat{5}$ from the varied tenor pattern is replaced by $\hat{8}$ from the basic tenor (m. 24). The gap that opens up with the next structural pitch, $\hat{6}$, is filled in by the passing ♭$\hat{7}$ (of stage 1b), which is well projected in the upper voice in the first half of measure 25. Note also how stage 2 brings the highly conventionalized descending arpeggio leading to the alto stream's $\hat{1}$ in the middle of measure 26. The $\hat{2}$ of stage 3b also receives the almost obligatory appoggiatura ($\hat{3}$), which confirms our hearing the soprano stream.

Example 5.27 shows another variant of the tenor combo. The first two stages witness the typical $\hat{5}$–$\hat{6}$ motion. But instead of moving down to $\hat{1}$ at the start of stage 3a, the melody initially retains the tenor's $\hat{5}$; a scalar descent then achieves the alto $\hat{1}$ that is so characteristic of the pattern.

**Tenor-Soprano ($\hat{8}/\hat{6}/\hat{3}$-$\hat{2}/\hat{1}$).** A related pattern to the tenor combo sees the whole of stage 3 occupied by pitches from the soprano stream (thus T/T/S-S/S). A passage examined in Chapter 4, Example 4.78, measures 38–44, illustrates well this successive combination even in the presence of extensive embellishments. On the downbeat of measure 40, note that the stage-2 $\hat{6}$, the low G in the right hand, is chromatically shifted to the bass voice (♭$\hat{6}$) to support a German sixth in the next bar. This harmony allows

---

71. The melody of the first phrase (mm. 39–42) will be discussed later in sec. 5.2.

72. Another case of the varied alto can be seen in Ex. 5.11, which needs no further commentary.

73. See Chapter 3, sec. 3.1.2.3 and the discussion of Ex. 3.44.

the melody to leap up and capture ♭$\hat{3}$ (first in the violin, then in the piano), which beautifully anticipates the following ♭$\hat{3}$ of the soprano stream in measure 42.

Another tenor-soprano combination can be observed in Example 5.18. Following the fermata in measure 24, the continuation of the descending scale in the next bar means that the literal opening pitch of the ECP is $\hat{8}$ (over ③), which moves stepwise down to $\hat{6}$ for stage 2. Further scalar embellishments within stage 2 (note the characteristic rising and falling contour in m. 26) allows $\hat{3}$ (with metric emphasis) to emerge as the structural pitch of stage 3a, followed by the standard $\hat{2}$–$\hat{1}$ resolution.[74]

**Alto-Tenor-Alto ($\hat{3}/\hat{6}/\hat{5}$–$\hat{7}/\hat{1}$).** Another pattern, more distantly related to the tenor combo, sees stage 1 articulated by the alto's $\hat{3}$. Stages 2 and 3a bring $\hat{6}$–$\hat{5}$ from the tenor stream, and the pattern is completed by a $\hat{7}$–$\hat{1}$ resolution back to the alto. Example 5.28, measures 89–92, clearly shows this successive combination. The probable reason why the melody begins with an alto $\hat{3}$, rather than $\hat{5}$ or $\hat{8}$ of the tenor stream, is due to the opening tonic being in root position, the required resolution of the previous V$^6_5$, which appears in measure 87 just prior to the pause. The bass ⑦–⑧ makes its most effective counterpoint with $\hat{4}$ resolving to $\hat{3}$, to start the ECP's melody. A similar situation obtains in Example 5.1, where an opening root-position tonic supports an alto $\hat{3}$ for the initial stage of the ECP.

**Alto-Soprano ($\hat{3}/\hat{2}/\hat{1}$–$\hat{2}/\hat{1}$).** A variety of successive combinations exclude the tenor altogether. Example 5.20 illustrates a pattern that only uses alto and soprano streams. The ECP begins at measure 9 with stage 2, whose Neapolitan sixth supports the alto ♭$\hat{2}$. (The $\hat{3}$, associated with an alto of stage 1, appears precadentially in the second half of m. 8.) The final $\hat{1}$–$\hat{2}$–$\hat{1}$ formula continues with the alto stream ($\hat{1}$), then shifting to the soprano for the last two pitches of the pattern ($\hat{2}$–$\hat{1}$). Note that the potential redundancy of the motion $\hat{2}$–$\hat{1}$–$\hat{2}$–$\hat{1}$ is mitigated by the chromatic lowering, thus ♭$\hat{2}$–$\hat{1}$–♯$\hat{2}$–$\hat{1}$.

A more complex version of this same combination arises in Example 5.32. In measures 148–49, stages 1 and 2 support the alto stream's $\hat{3}$ and $\hat{2}$.[75] The following two bars bring the cadential six-four, supporting an embellishing line for which a structural pitch $\hat{5}$ is barely perceivable. As discussed earlier on, we can then observe at measure 152 a neighboring harmony (VII$^7$/V) that suddenly intrudes into the proceedings. This harmony supports a dramatic ♭$\hat{3}$ as the climax of the preceding upward sweep. What happens next is even more complicating: the downward leaping configuration in measure 152 lands on a long-held $\hat{1}$ at the start of measure 153. If, on the one hand, we hear the left-hand of that bar as continuing to prolong the diminished-seventh sonority, then the melodic $\hat{1}$ of that bar would not be deemed structural—it would be melodically parenthetical, just like its supporting diminished-seventh harmony—and the overall pattern would then continue with the soprano's ♭$\hat{3}$ of measure 154, which clearly connects to the ♭$\hat{3}$ left hanging in the air at the start of measure 152. Stages 3b ($\hat{2}$) and 4 ($\hat{1}$) then complete this soprano stream. On the other hand, and as discussed already in note 49, we could hear stage 3a already arriving on the downbeat of measure 153, signaling a continuation of the alto stream from $\hat{2}$ (m. 149) to $\hat{1}$ (m. 153) for the resumed cadential six-four. In either case, the melodic profile successively combines alto and soprano streams.

**Tenor-Alto ($\hat{8}/\hat{2}/\hat{5}/\hat{1}$).** Example 4.36 from the previous chapter illustrates well an alternating combination of tenor ($\hat{8}$, $\hat{5}$) and alto ($\hat{2}$, $\hat{1}$) streams. (The evaded cadence omits the final $\hat{1}$, which eventually appears in the one-more-time repetition.) The same combination occurs as well in Example 4.8, measure 51, though this time beginning directly with $\hat{2}$ of stage 2. (A precadential $\hat{3}$ on the last pitch of m. 50 immediately precedes the onset of the ECP.)

**Additional Combinations.** At this point, I have illustrated a number of the possible successive combinations that can arise in connection with an ECP. Three additional combinations can be observed in passages found on the *Analyzing Classical Form* website:

**Alto-Tenor-Soprano (/$\hat{2}$–$\hat{6}/\hat{5}$–$\hat{2}/\hat{1}$):** *ACF* Ex.14.2, Mozart, Piano Sonata in C, K. 545, i, measures 67–71; begins with stage 2.

**Tenor-Soprano-Alto ($\hat{5}/\hat{6}/\hat{3}$–$\hat{7}/\hat{1}$):** *ACF* Ex. 2.24, Haydn, String Quartet in D Minor, Op. 42, i, measures 5–8.

**Tenor-Alto ($\hat{5}/\hat{6}/\hat{1}$–($\hat{2}$) $\hat{7}/\hat{1}$):** *ACF* Ex. 5.7, Beethoven, Piano Sonata in B-flat, Op. 22, ii, measures 6–9.

### 5.1.2.10. Simultaneous Combinations

Some ECP melodies are sufficiently complex as to suggest that two (or more) melodic streams are occurring simultaneously. I already have raised that possibility when discussing Example 5.10. I initially identified a soprano stream ($\hat{5}/\hat{4}/\hat{2}/\hat{1}$) for this melody, but then acknowledged (in note 66) that the alto stream ($\hat{3}/\hat{2}/\hat{7}/\hat{1}$) can be found in all stages as well, as shown in the annotations on the score. A particularly clear case where we can say that the melody is truly *compound* appears in Example 5.45. Here, a complete varied tenor ($\hat{5}/-\hat{6}/\hat{5}$–$\hat{4}/\hat{1}$) resides above a complete varied alto ($\hat{1}/\hat{2}/\hat{1}$–$\hat{7}/\hat{1}$).

Somewhat more intricate is the melody of a passage discussed in Chapter 4 (see Ex. 4.44). The high notes of the violin in measures 9–10 project a tenor stream $\hat{5}$–$\hat{6}$, while the lower notes (the first being chromatically raised) are members of the varied alto pattern, ♯$\hat{1}$–$\hat{2}$. After reaching up to a high E♭ in measure 11, the violin moves down to ♯$\hat{4}$ and $\hat{5}$. These latter two pitches clearly

---

74. My classification of this melody depends on regarding $\hat{3}$ as the structural pitch for stage 3a. If, instead, we were to take the sixteenth note following the two thirty-second notes on beat three as the structural pitch, then this stage would begin with an alto-stream $\hat{1}$, and the overall pattern would be a regular tenor combo featuring a T/T/A-S/S succession of streams.

75. I am taking the first and last $\hat{3}$ of the sweeping up and down scales in m. 148 as the structural pitch of stage 1. Likewise, I regard the first and last chord-tone ($\hat{2}$) of m. 149 as structural. Alternatively, we could hear the "highest pitch" in each measure ($\hat{8}$ and $\hat{6}$) as the principal tones, in which case the pattern would begin with the tenor stream.

continue the tenor line, thus $\hat{5}/\hat{6}\text{-}(\sharp\hat{4})/\hat{5}\text{-}/$. The alto is picked up again with the final $\hat{7}\text{-}\hat{1}$ resolution, thus $\sharp\hat{1}/\hat{2}/\text{-}\hat{7}/\hat{1}$.

Returning to an earlier example from the current chapter (Ex. 5.21), we can recognize in the ECP, which begins at measure 79 directly with stage 2, a *simultaneous* combination of two *successively* combined patterns. One pattern, in the violin part (the downward-stemmed notes in the right hand of the score), brings an alto-soprano combination ($/\flat\hat{2}\text{-}(\hat{1})/\hat{3}\text{-}\sharp\hat{2}/\hat{1}$); a second pattern in the right hand of the piano (upward-stemmed notes) brings a tenor-alto combination ($/\hat{6}\text{-}(\hat{8})/\hat{1}\text{-}\hat{7}/\hat{1}$).

### 5.1.2.11. Additional Patterns

**Ascending Melodic Pattern ($\hat{5}/\hat{6}/\hat{7}/\hat{8}$).** Despite what is often taught in elementary harmony classes, a melodic line that ascends to its goal tonic occurs infrequently in the classical repertory. In the context of an ECP, a straightforward case arises at the end of the main theme group shown in Example 5.46, where the process of attaining the high F ($\hat{8}$) represents the melodic, dynamic, and textural climax of the section. A similar, but more complex case, is seen in the earlier discussed Example 5.2. Like the previous example, this passage also produces the climactic moment of the main theme, though the sudden shift to *piano* in measure 19 slightly delays the ongoing progressive dynamic. In both cases, we sense the composer giving special emphasis to the ascending line in a manner that highlights all the more this nonconventional melody.

**Bass Melodic Pattern ($\hat{3}/\hat{4}\text{-}\sharp\hat{4}/\hat{5}/\hat{1}$).** As discussed in Chapter 3, some cadential melodies appropriate their pitches from those normally given to the bass voice. In some cases, we have the sense that the texture has simply been conflated to express a bass voice in all sounding parts (a doubled monophony texture). At other times, the actual bass voice engages other pitches (e.g., $\flat\hat{7},\hat{6}$, or $\flat\hat{6}$) while the melody continues to project the standard bass stream. In both situations, we may also find that the melody eventually drops to $\hat{2}$ or $\hat{7}$ just prior to the cadential arrival on $\hat{1}$.

In Chapter 3 (refer back to Ex. 3.79), we saw the case of an ECP (mm. 70–76), whose texture is such that the "melody" (right-hand part) effectively doubles the bass, at least through stage 3a, at which point the melody descends from $\hat{4}$ to $\hat{3}$ (in the manner of a tenor line) to create an IAC. After this way-station cadence, a repetition of the ECP (shown in Ex. 5.47 of the current chapter) begins at measure 78. A marked expansion of the cadential six-four (starting at m. 82) then features a variety of double-neighboring harmonies, first by VI and $V^6_5/V$, and then, with the change of texture at measure 87, by the more chromatic $VII^6_5/V$ and $VII^7/V$. Measure 87 also sees the melody break away from the bass in order to leap up to $\hat{8}$ and then to $\hat{3}$ (m. 90). The melodic line eventually draws on the alto stream, $\hat{7}\text{-}\hat{1}$, for the PAC arrival at measure 94.

Earlier in Example 5.25 we encountered an ECP that, starting with stage 2 (m. 178), brings an *ascending* bass-line melody that complements a *descending* melody in the real bass voice (left-hand part).

A particularly interesting relationship plays out in Example 5.37d between an ascending bass-line melody in the upper part and the actual bass, also ascending. Given the harmonic complexities at the start of the ECP in measure 241, neither $\flat\hat{2}$ nor $\hat{6}$, the two pitches competing for prominence in stage 1, is a normal constituent of that stage. Beginning at measure 245, $\flat\hat{2}$ wins out, and the melody then proceeds to rise in parallel sixths with the bass (sometimes notated as diminished sevenths). As a result, the melody of the upper voice lags two bars behind the lower voice such that the melody does not engage the bass stream until measure 249, the start of the second ECP, when the bass has already achieved ⑤. As that voice continues on to ♮⑥ in measure 251, the melody finally reaches $\sharp\hat{4}$, with both voices then converging on $\hat{5}/⑤$ for the powerful arrival of the cadential six-four at measure 252.

EXAMPLE 5.45. Mozart, Piano Sonata in C, K. 330, iii, mm. 73–76.

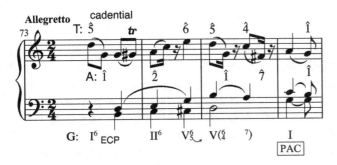

EXAMPLE 5.46. Beethoven, String Quartet in F, Op. 18, no. 1, i, mm. 26–29.

EXAMPLE 5.47. Beethoven, Piano Sonata in C Minor, Op. 10, no. 1, i, mm. 76–94 (R = 2N) (*ACF* 12.2).

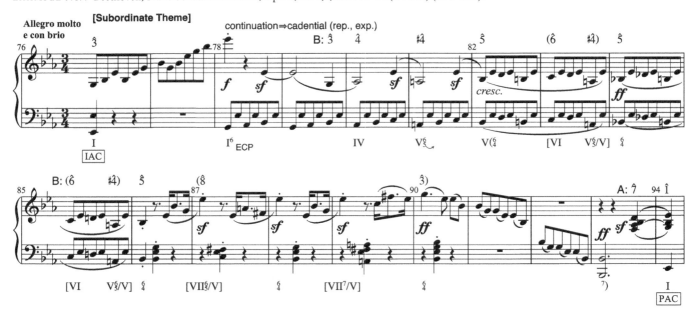

EXAMPLE 5.48. Haydn, Symphony No. 93 in D, i, mm. 71–74 (*ACF* 12.16).

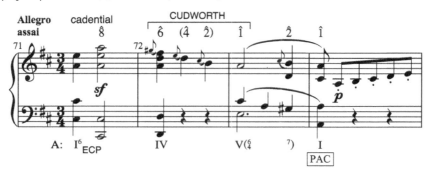

**Cudworth.** The Cudworth cadence, being characterized foremost as a quickly falling descent from $\hat{7}$ or $\hat{6}$ within stage 2, is, as Gjerdingen notes, "not easily enlarged."[76] Therefore it is no surprise that we do not find many examples of this schema associated with ECPs. If, however, the expansion of the cadential progression is confined largely to stage 1, the remainder of the progression may be relatively compact, such that a Cudworth could enter within stage 2. Turning back to Chapter 3, Example 3.61, we can observe just this situation: a rocking on the tonic in measures 5–7 yields to a flurry of running sixteenths within a long-held I$^6$ (m. 8). A Cudworth then occurs with stage 2 (IV) in the following bar.

Returning to the present chapter, we see in Example 5.48 how a Cudworth can be suggested even if stage 2 is expanded to last a full bar (m. 72). With appoggiaturas filling in a conventional downward arpeggiation in stage 2, we can readily hear a somewhat slower version of the schema.

**Low $\hat{5}$ Drop.** In a finely detailed article, Floyd Grave observes a particular melodic convention arising in connection with Gjerdingen's "Grand Cadence" schema (effectively, my ECP).[77] A characteristic element of this convention, shown in Example 5.49, is a highly embellished cadential melody featuring an "upward surge, highpeak, daring leap, and sparkling trill."[78] Particularly characteristic is the sudden drop down to $\hat{5}$, which then leaps back up to $\hat{2}$ for the cadential trill, and final resolution to $\hat{1}$. Grave is reluctant to give a new schematic label to this convention, but as discussed in Chapter 3, I call it a "low $\hat{5}$ drop."[79] More precisely, stages 1 and 2 of the ECP bring an embellished melodic line in a relative high tessitura; the precipitous drop down to a low $\hat{5}$ occurs with the onset of the cadential six-four in stage 3a, while the return back up to $\hat{2}$ and the cadential trill articulates stage 3b, the dominant proper.

---

76. Gjerdingen, *Galant Style*, 152.

77. Floyd K. Grave, "Freakish Variations on a 'Grand Cadence' Prototype in Haydn's String Quartets"; Gjerdingen, *Galant Style*, 152–53. I briefly describe the "Grand Cadence" schema in Chapter 7, sec. 7.1.1.

78. Grave, "Freakish Variations," 121.

79. Sec. 3.1.2.1, "Basic Soprano," and note 35.

EXAMPLE 5.49. Mozart, Violin Concerto in B-flat, K. 207, i, mm. 45–48.

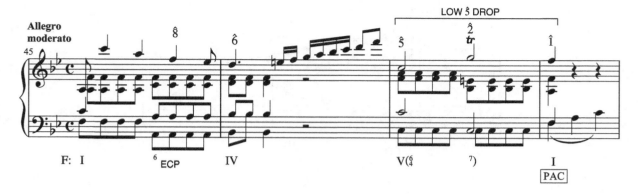

Grave spends most of his discussion detailing many significant issues of motive and texture associated especially with the elaborating melody that precedes the drop to $\hat{5}$. He mostly discusses cases drawn from Haydn's string quartets, which makes sense, because this configuration seems especially characteristic of the quartet genre.[80] But perhaps more importantly, this cadential melody seems exclusively associated with the closure of a subordinate theme. Indeed, I have not yet encountered a low $\hat{5}$ drop closing a main theme or any other formal unit requiring a PAC. The pattern further helps in generating excitement for the cadential arrival, since the effect of the pattern is to accelerate the rhythm in the course of stages 1 and 2 (and possibly including precadential, continuation material), while the sudden drop to the low $\hat{5}$ seems prematurely to slam on the melodic brakes (even though the accompaniment continues to be active); the leap back up to $\hat{2}$ and the cadential trill then resume the action by giving the greatest rhythmic activity to the melodic line, just prior to the resolution to $\hat{1}$. Among the examples already discussed in this chapter, we can look back to Example 5.28 and see a low $\hat{5}$ drop in measures 82–84 of Beethoven's first string quartet.

## 5.2. Imperfect Authentic Cadence

Let us now examine the morphological characteristics of the expanded IAC and compare them to those of the PAC. These differences are principally melodic, since the harmonic support for both cadence types is effectively identical. Unfortunately, the very small number of ECPs leading to an IAC that I have uncovered (ca. 15) limits making any kind of significant generalizations. Nevertheless, the melodic patterns typically associated with a compact IAC, as discussed in Chapter 3, can still be considered in relation to ECPs ending with that cadence type.

But first let us recall three important points raised in that earlier chapter. First, we observed that compact IACs often feature an incomplete cadential progression, as is rhetorically appropriate for a weaker cadence providing partial closure. Given that an ECP provides sufficient duration for a complete cadential progression, we would not necessarily expect ECPs leading to an IAC to be incomplete. Second, we discussed that the tenor pattern (basic or varied, with or without cadential six-four) is, along with the Prinner cadence, the only one that leads naturally to $\hat{3}$ in its final stage.[81] Given the tenor pattern's popularity in compact IACs, we might expect to see something similar with ECPs, but among the limited cases in the corpus, the pattern is not especially used over others. Third, an IAC is often produced by means of a melodic *diversion*, namely, where a penultimate $\hat{2}$ (in stage 3) promises to resolve to $\hat{1}$ but is redirected upward instead to close on $\hat{3}$. With these points in mind, let us consider some melodic patterns used in ECPs that result in an IAC.

A straightforward basic tenor ($\hat{8}/\hat{6}/\hat{5}/\hat{3}$) appears in Example 5.50; though somewhat elaborated with arpeggiations and stepwise motions, the pattern projects itself clearly as the highest notes of each stage. As discussed in Chapter 3, a chromatic variant for stage 1 finds $\flat\hat{7}$ substituting for $\hat{8}$ (Ex. 3.69). As well, the dominant proper of this example supports $\hat{4}$, which fills in the gap between $\hat{5}$ and $\hat{3}$. Although the tenor pattern here achieves its melodic goal directly through a descent from $\hat{4}$ to $\hat{3}$, the modest leaps of a third in stage 3 see the final E pitch (m. 7) held over the bar-line and resolved as an upward-rising suspension. As a result, the very foreground yields the sense of a melodic diversion. The soprano pattern, in particular, is prone to this technique, such that $\hat{2}$ in stage 3 is diverted upward to $\hat{3}$ rather than falling as normally expected (Ex. 5.51). Note that the final harmony I contains a doubled third (E♭). As discussed in Chapter 3 (sec. 3.2.1), this situation tends to be avoided by using a dominant *triad* in stage 3. In this example, the dissonant seventh ($\hat{4}$) is added to the dominant (on the last quarter-note

---

80. Graves duly notes, though, that the device can widely be used in "music that accommodates solo display, a broad category that ranges from sonata to opera" ("Freakish Variations," 121), including the concerto, as seen in Ex. 5.49.

81. None of the ECPs in the corpus create a Prinner cadence (see Chapter 3, sec. 3.2.1.2), so matters pertaining to this schema will not come into question in the current chapter.

EXAMPLE 5.50. Haydn, Symphony No. 95 in C Minor, iii, mm. 5–8 (*ACF* 4.10).

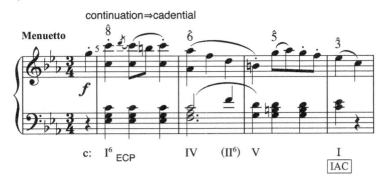

EXAMPLE 5.51. Beethoven, Piano Sonata in E-flat, Op. 7, iii, mm. 58–62 (*ACF* 18.11).

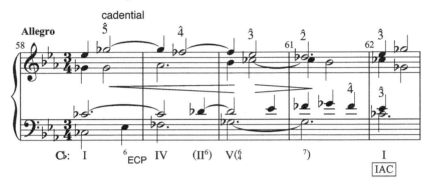

beat of measure 61, in the left hand's tenor voice), such that its required resolution down to $\hat{3}$, along with the melodic diversion up to that pitch in the soprano voice, yields a doubled third.[82]

Successive combinations can also lead to an IAC. One case, seen earlier in Example 5.5, measures 39–42, brings a pattern that can be reduced to the following set of scale degrees: $\hat{1}/\hat{2}/\hat{4}/\hat{3}$. This configuration, which is popular as an initiating cantus-firmus for polyphonic elaboration (e.g., the finale of Mozart's "Jupiter" Symphony), is here pressed into service as a cadential melody, one that exhibits a successive combination of alto ($\hat{1}$–$\hat{2}$) and tenor ($\hat{4}$–$\hat{3}$) streams.[83]

Another combination (Ex. 5.52, from a slow introduction) begins in the middle of measure 5 with a tenor line $\hat{8}$–$\hat{6}$, which then moves down (via stepwise motion) to capture a soprano $\hat{2}$ for stage 3 (m. 6). The final note D ($\hat{3}$) is then technically achieved by means of an upward diversion. On the very foreground, however,

the leap up from C ($\hat{2}$) to F ($\hat{5}$) in the second half of measure 6 is filled in by the surface $\hat{4}$–$\hat{3}$ descent, thus suggesting an overlying "tenor voice" that has been regained in order to provide a direct connection to the melodic goal $\hat{3}$.

A bass melody can also be used to generate an IAC, as seen earlier in Chapter 3, Example 3.79. There, the doubled soprano and bass voices (mm. 71–74) diverge in measure 75 so that the melody can move from $\hat{4}$ to $\hat{3}$ while the bass brings its required ⑤–① cadential leap (mm. 75–76). (Ex. 5.47, discussed earlier, repeats this phrase, but expands it considerably.)

## 5.3. Half Cadence

Within the classical repertory, the approach to the final dominant of a half cadential progression occasionally brings a modest degree of harmonic expansion. Indeed, the large expansions seen with authentic cadential progressions arise less frequently with half cadential ones. Thus within the small corpus of half cadential ECPs (ca. 30), the seven-measure expansion witnessed in Example 5.53 is especially large.

### 5.3.1. Minimum Length

If the size of any ECP has no maximum limit, determining a minimum length for an expanded half cadential progression is somewhat problematic. As discussed at the opening of this chapter,

---

82. The lack of a fifth in the final tonic, due to the doubled thirds, is immediately rectified by the doubling of G♭ ($\hat{5}$) in the second beat of m. 62.

83. The standard pitch of stage 3 in the tenor pattern is $\hat{5}$, which may bring $\hat{4}$ for the dominant proper when following a cadential six-four. In this example, $\hat{4}$ appears directly with the dominant proper in the second half of m. 41 even though the cadential six-four is not used in the progression. In m. 45 of the second ECP, the melody touches again on $\hat{4}$, but since this degree does not lead naturally to $\hat{1}$, it is preferable to take $\hat{7}$ as the principal pitch of the dominant proper.

EXAMPLE 5.52. Mozart, Violin Sonata in B-flat, K. 454, i, mm. 5–7 (R = ½N) (ACF 16.1).

EXAMPLE 5.53. Mozart, Piano Sonata in F, K. 332, i, mm. 167–73 (ACF 14.17).

EXAMPLE 5.54. Beethoven, Piano Sonata in G Minor, Op. 49, no. 1, i, mm. 7–15 (ACF 11.1).

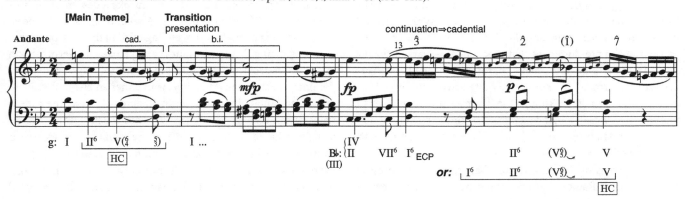

I normally consider an authentic ECP to last at least four bars, sufficient in scope to support a full phrase of music. This minimum makes sense, since it allows all four stages to occupy a full bar, a situation that regularly obtains (see again Ex. 5.48, 5.49, and 5.50). This criterion, however, is not entirely adequate for a half cadential ECP, which contains only three harmonic stages. If each harmony were accorded a single bar, then such a three-measure unit may prove somewhat short to support what we normally take to be a complete phrase. Yet, it seems reasonable that if each harmony of the progression lasts one measure, then, like the case of an authentic ECP, we should probably accept three bars as a practical minimum for a half cadential expansion.

For reasons that remain unclear, the small corpus of half cadential ECPs includes only a few instances where each of the three harmonic stages takes up a complete bar; Example 5.54, measures 13–15, is one such case. If we consider that the progression embraces the I⁶ in the whole of measure 13, then we can recognize the three-bar minimum ECP as previously defined. Alternatively, we could hear the cadential idea only beginning with the fourth quarter-note upbeat to measure 14 (thus regarding most of m. 13 as precadential). In that case, it would be preferable to analyze a compact HC. In either event, when we compare the length of the cadence closing the main theme (mm. 7–8) with that closing the transition (mm. 13–15 or 14–15, depending on one's analysis), we see that the latter is more expansive, which accords with the norms of tight-knit versus loose organization for a sonata-form exposition, even a miniature one.

We often find that a three-measure half cadential ECP sees the first two bars filled with pre-dominant harmony, with the final dominant in the third bar (Ex. 5.55). In this nonconventional

EXAMPLE 5.55. Haydn, String Quartet in G Minor ("Horseman"), Op. 74, no. 3, iv, mm. 1–8 (*ACF* 10.1).

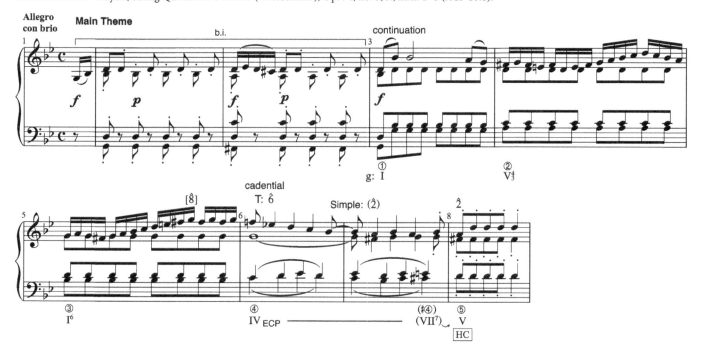

main theme, an opening two-measure basic idea (made up of repeated one-bar segments) is followed by a continuation (m. 3) that brings a flurry of sixteenth notes, with the bass rising from ① to ③ at the rate of one harmony per bar. With measure 6, the texture changes again, and the rise to ④ now supports an expansion of the pre-dominant that precipitates a marked slowing down in the rate of fundamental harmonic change (to be sure, the very foreground harmonies are quite active, yet all within a prolongation of stage 2). Though the I⁶ at measure 5 could constitute the first stage of a half cadential ECP, this bar clearly groups backward and thus represents the end of the continuation, not the beginning of the ECP.[84]

Not all cases of a three-measure half cadential progression express an ECP. Rather, the sense of a genuine harmonic expansion sometimes depends on various contextual circumstances, including issues of grouping structure, the general pace of harmonic activity, and other ad hoc concerns. For example, an apparent half cadential ECP is sometimes better understood as the last part of a broader continuation, because the cadential progression itself does not slow down the ongoing rate of harmonic change. Thus in the previous chapter, in Example 4.59, a sonata-form transition opens with a compound basic idea in the home key (not shown); a repetition of this unit modulates to the subordinate key of C, with modal mixture. The example begins with the continuation phrase, whose initial two-measure fragment is supported by I⁶. Though this harmony is potentially cadential, a

repetition of the fragment in measures 33–34 sees the bass descend by a third, to support VI⁶, a harmony that has no particular cadential implications; instead, it seems like a descending-thirds sequence (I⁶–VI⁶) is in the making. A second repetition in measures 35–36 brings another descending third in the bass, but rather than supporting IV⁶, to continue the sequence, the German sixth in these bars projects a cadential pre-dominant, which resolves to dominant to close the transition (with either an HC or dominant arrival, an ambiguity discussed in Chapter 4). Here, the cadential function lasts three bars (35–37) with the first two measures bringing what might be thought of as the minimally necessary expansion of the half cadential pre-dominant. But in the context of the ongoing continuation, with its rate of harmonic change at one harmony per every two bars, we have little sense of the cadential harmonies being expanded.

In this respect, it is revealing to compare what happens here in the exposition to the analogous passage in the recapitulation (see again Ex. 5.53 in the current chapter). Here, the continuation begins in measure 167 with a modally mixed IV⁶, a pre-dominant that is potentially cadential, especially since that harmony occurs in the analogous place where the exposition brought a I⁶ harmony (Ex. 4.59, mm. 31–32), whose cadential potentiality remained unrealized. In the recapitulation (Ex. 5.53), the following harmony in measures 169–70 is a passing six-four, which continues to prolong pre-dominant function by leading to VII⁷/V in the following two bars, resolving then to the dominant in measure 173. Unlike the exposition, which organized the continuation phrase sequentially, with little sense of cadential expansion, the analogous phrase in the recapitulation emphasizes more readily an expansion of the cadential pre-dominant to effect a half cadential ECP lasting seven bars. As a result, we can hear a retrospective

---

84. My recognizing a half cadential ECP represents a change of interpretation from my analysis of this theme in *CF*, Ex. 13.1, and *ACF*, Ex. 10.1, where I bracketed the cadential harmonies, thus proposing a compact HC for mm. 6–8.

EXAMPLE 5.56. Haydn, Piano Trio in D, H. 24, i, mm. 23–26.

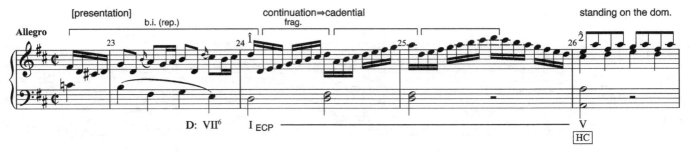

reinterpretation of continuation⇒cadential for the phrase as a whole.

### 5.3.2. Harmonic Content

The harmonic content of a half cadential progression is largely the same as an authentic one, except that the former lacks a stage-4 tonic and the stage-3 dominant is a consonant triad. Otherwise, stages 1 and 2 offer the same harmonic options for both types of cadential progression, though the presence of a stage-2b VII⁷/V is especially common in HCs.

#### 5.3.2.1. Stage 1

The standard use of I⁶ to initiate a cadential progression continues to be found with half cadential ECPs (see Ex. 5.54, m. 13), though less often than with authentic ECPs. Chromatic alterations of the initial tonic into a secondary dominant of IV or II are also encountered. One case, not shown, uses ♭III as a substitute for I⁶ in a minor-mode context.⁸⁵ These tonic-substitute harmonies may take up the entire stretch of stage 1, or they may appear in stage 1b, following a regular I⁶ (or I) in stage 1a (see Ex. 3.141, fourth beat of m. 56).

One of the standard subtypes of HC that I discussed in Chapter 3 is the simple (I–V) HC, as Martin and Pedneault-Deslauriers term it, which sees a root-position tonic in stage 1, followed immediately by the dominant of stage 3, thus bypassing stage 2.⁸⁶ In compact HCs, the simple HC tends to be especially short,⁸⁷ so it is hardly surprising that this subtype is not often encountered with ECPs. A couple of cases arise in the corpus, one of which is shown in Example 5.56 of the current chapter. Toward the close of the first part of a two-part transition, a repeat of the opening basic idea (upbeat to m. 23) leads at measure 24 to an expansion of root-position tonic. Though we are probably expecting an HC eventually to appear (since the music is still projecting a formal transition), it is not at all certain that this tonic is cadential; indeed, the fragmentation and surface-rhythm activity point to a continuation function. Still, the harmonic expansion in measures 24–25 is striking, and when a root-position V triad arrives at measure 26, followed by a standing on the dominant (of which only the first bar is shown), we can understand that the expanded tonic initiates a simple HC, one that is modestly expanded.⁸⁸

Now and then, stage 1 of a half cadential ECP witnesses a rocking on the tonic—an alternation of I⁶ and V⁴₂ (or IV). A clear case appears in Example 5.57. Within a transition, a compound basic idea (not shown) modulates to the subordinate key of F (HK: V); the final bar of this phrase at the beginning of Example 5.57 completes the tonic prolongation that brings the music into the new key. There follows a rocking on the tonic (mm. 15–16), which effects what is formally best described as a continuation⇒cadential phrase, ending at measure 18 with an HC (and subsequent standing on the dominant, not shown). The continuational aspects include the fragmentation into one-measure units and an increased pace of the harmonic rhythm.

A second case of such rocking, Example 5.58a, initiates a more expansive cadential progression. Following a compound presentation (whose final bar opens the example), this famous main theme continues with a rocking on the tonic that brings fragmentation into two-measure units (in comparison to the repeated four-measure compound basic ideas). The rocking is then followed by a progression in measures 14–15 that is somewhat difficult to analyze. The second harmony (m. 15) is a clear pre-dominant augmented sixth. The harmony in measure 14, however, presents two analytical options: (1) in reference to the stacked thirds, E-G-B♭-D, the lowest pitch is seen as the "root" of a VI⁷ harmony, an unusual tonic substitute that continues to prolong the tonic of the prior rocking; (2) the soprano D of the first harmony (measure 14) is heard as initiating a 7–6 appoggiatura, such that the resolution to C♯ in the following bar is taken as a harmonic constituent, thus yielding a pre-dominant VII⁶₅/V, and where the bass of that harmony is lowered by a half step when the suspension resolves, thus forming the augmented sixth.⁸⁹

---

85. See Beethoven, Piano Sonata in E-flat, Op. 7, iii, 104–105.

86. Martin and Pedneault-Deslauriers, "Mozartean Half Cadence," 192.

87. See in Chapter 3, Ex. 3.104–107.

88. See also, Beethoven, Symphony No. 4 in B-flat, i, mm. 365–69.

89. As shown in Ex. 5.58b, the harmonies in mm. 14–15 feature the "Tristan progression" with parsimonious voice leading, what David Lewin terms the "DOUTH2 relation" ("Cohn Functions," 207). See ahead

EXAMPLE 5.57. Mozart, Piano Sonata in B-flat, K. 333, i, mm. 14–18.

EXAMPLE 5.58. Mozart, Symphony No. 40 in G Minor, K. 550, i, (a) mm. 9–16 (*ACF* 6.21); (b) mm. 14–15 ("Tristan progression").

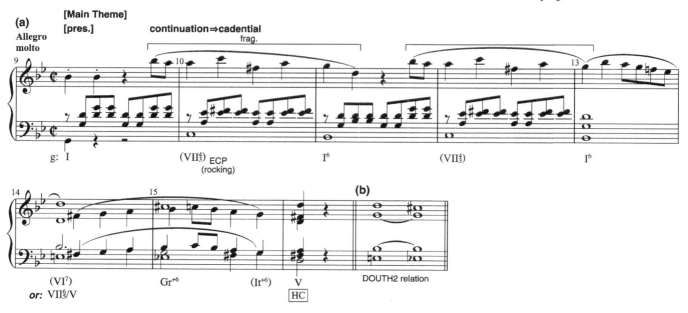

One question raised by this example is whether the cadential function is best understood to arise first with the 3-bar half cadential ECP marked by the change in texture at measure 14, in which case the rocking passage would be heard as exclusively continuational, or whether we should recognize the I⁶, prolonged in measures 10–13, as participating in both continuation and cadential processes. This question—just where does the cadential function first appear?—arises frequently when dealing with ECPs, and we cannot always find a definitive answer. For Mozart's passage, I lean toward the second option (as shown in the annotations), probably because of the rocking gesture, which is so suggestive of cadential function, but I validate the alternative view as well.

Chapter 9, Ex. 9.56a and d, mm. 2–3, for how this progression is used in Wagner's *Tristan*. Robert Gauldin finds the DOUTH2 progression at the end of the first-movement development of Mozart's G-Minor Symphony (mm. 150–52) but does not mention its appearance in the main theme, as seen in Ex. 5.58 ("The DOUTH2 Relation as a Dramatic Signifier in Wagner's Music Dramas," 181).

### 5.3.2.2. Stage 2

The wide variety of harmonies available for stage 2 are well exploited by half cadential ECPs; in fact, the use of pre-dominants containing ♯4 (e.g., VII⁷/V, Gr⁺⁶, see Ex. 5.57 and 5.58a) is especially prominent in half cadential ECPs, just as with compact HCs. Moreover, a good number of ECPs skip over stage 1 and start directly with a stage 2 pre-dominant. In such cases, we are still likely to find an initial tonic as the end of a continuation immediately preceding the ECP. And in some situations, the question may be posed as to whether this harmony stands distinct from the ECP (as we saw in Ex. 5.55, m. 5) or is preferably included in the progression (as discussed in Ex. 5.58a).

### 5.3.2.3. Stage 3

The final stage of a half cadential ECP yields an ultimate dominant triad in root position. An inversion of this dominant may arise as a result of abandoning the progression or may occur in connection within the deviation of a dominant arrival (both

EXAMPLE 5.59. Haydn, Piano Trio in D, H. 24, i, mm. 34–39.

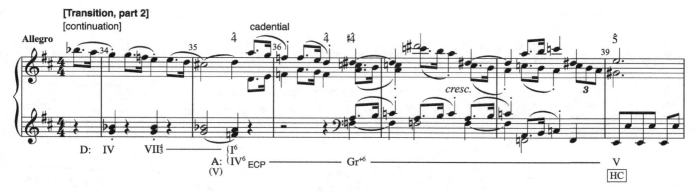

topics to be treated below). Normally stage 3 consists of a single harmony (V); presumably a cadential six-four may precede the dominant proper, though I did not encounter that option in the corpus.

### 5.3.3. Melodic Content

As presented in Chapter 3 (sec. 3.3.3), compact HCs can be assigned to one of the three subtypes formulated by Martin and Pedneault-Deslauriers—simple, converging, and expanding. The melodic patterns associated with these subtypes are also available for half cadential ECPs, though given the small size of the corpus, many of the possible melodic patterns associated with these types are not represented.

#### 5.3.3.1. Simple HC

The one case of a simple HC discussed so far, Example 5.56, presents the varied simple pattern ($\hat{1}//\hat{2}$).[90]

#### 5.3.3.2. Converging HC

The cases of converging half cadential ECPs in the corpus exhibit none of the simple, soprano, or tenor patterns (basic or varied). Only those based on the alto pattern arise among this small collection of ECPs. Example 5.54 shows the basic alto $\hat{3}/\hat{2}-(\hat{1})/\hat{7}$.

A small number of successive combinations arise in the corpus, including some that bring a tenor pattern combined with a simple pattern, as seen in Example 5.55. The line begins in measure 6 with a pre-dominant supporting $\hat{6}$ from the tenor stream (note as well the precadential appearance of the stage-1 tenor $\hat{8}$ as the melodic goal of the continuation phrase). In the course of stage 2, the melody descends stepwise to $\hat{2}$ (from the simple stream) and continues to sustain that degree into stage 3.

---

90. As mentioned in Chapter 3, note 149, I am using the term *simple* in two different ways: as a subtype of half cadence and as a particular melodic pattern.

#### 5.3.3.3. Expanding HC

The expanding HC frequently sees the final pitches of the melodic line ascend from $\hat{4}$ (through $\sharp\hat{4}$) to $\hat{5}$, thus expressing a cadential bass line in the upper voice. Example 5.59 illustrates this situation well. Within the second part of a two-part transition (the ending of part one was discussed in Ex. 5.56), the ongoing continuation shifts the music into the home-key minor (mm. 34–35), which pivots into the subordinate key (also minor at first). The resulting IV⁶ at beat three of measure 35 supports $\hat{4}$, which rises chromatically in the next bar to $\sharp\hat{4}$ (within a Gr⁺⁶); that pitch is then held until its resolution to $\hat{5}$ for the HC at measure 39. In retrospect, we can hear the half cadential ECP beginning at the upbeat to measure 36.

#### 5.3.3.4. Converging/Expanding; Expanding/Converging

As discussed in Chapter 3 (see Ex. 3.141), an initial converging pattern may shift to become an expanding one. In this example, the resulting melodic line begins with a tenor stream $\hat{5}$–$\hat{6}$, but then continues with a bass $\sharp\hat{4}$–$\hat{5}$.

The opposite situation, where an anticipated expanding HC turns into a converging one can be seen in Example 5.53. Here, an opening soprano $\hat{4}$–$\hat{3}$ (mm. 167–72) suddenly leaps up to the bass-line $\hat{5}$ for the stage-3 dominant (m. 173).

## 5.4. Deviations

Like compact cadential progressions, ECPs may be subjected to the deviation techniques of cadential deception, evasion, and abandonment. An ECP can lead as well to a dominant arrival as a deviation of the HC. Indeed, the previous chapter on deviations included a number of ECPs, some of which will be reviewed again in this section. Since the processes of harmonic progression and grouping structure that drive deviations in ECPs are essentially the same as for those in compact progressions, it is not necessary here to define or illustrate these mechanisms yet again. Instead, the discussion will focus on aspects of deviation most germane to cadential expansion. A word of caution: the number

EXAMPLE 5.60. Mozart, Violin Sonata in E Minor, K. 304, i, mm. 45–59.

### 5.4.1. Minimum Size of Expansion

In that a complete deceptive ECP includes the same four stages as an authentic one, the minimum size of expansion for the former, like the latter, can be defined as four bars in length. A clear case of these minimum-sized ECPs is shown in Chapter 4, Example 4.14, measures 9–12. With evaded cadences, the situation resembles the half cadential ECP, since both of these types bring only three stages, for different reasons, of course. A half cadential progression naturally contains three stages; the evaded cadential progression lacks a promised stage 4. The minimum size for an evaded ECP can thus be set at three full bars, as seen in Chapter 4, Example 4.76, measures 178–80.

### 5.4.2. One-More-Time and Related Repetitions

Both the deceptive and evaded deviations can motivate a repetition that attempts (and usually attains) complete closure in the sense of "one more time." Seeing as Schmalfeldt defines the one-more-time technique exclusively in reference to the evaded cadence, it is not surprising to find that ECP versions of this deviation frequently engage this technique, and most typically with the repeated phrase corresponding in material content and overall length to the original phrase. In principle, of course, the repeated phrase will last one bar longer than the original, deviational one, since the evaded cadential progression omits a final tonic, which is supplied by the authentic ECP that follows. Two such passages have already been discussed in Chapter 4 (see Ex. 4.36, mm. 84–87, 88–92, and Ex. 4.76, mm. 178–80, 181–84).

Now and then, the one-more-time effect brings an expansion, thus even further delaying the promised PAC; see Example 4.78, where the ECP starting at measure 38 finds stages 2 and 3 (mm. 40–43) lasting twice as long as those same stages in the preceding ECP (mm. 36–37). An especially impressive pair of ECPs arises in Example 5.60 of the present chapter. Within a subordinate theme, a six-measure ECP supporting a continuation⇒cadential phrase is evaded at measure 51, which then sees a one-more-time repetition that considerably expands stage 2 (mm. 53–56).[91]

---

91. A reason for this particular expansion of pre-dominant harmony built over C in the bass (④) may be found in a series of bass-line motivic connections involving the main theme and the start of the transition. As seen in Chapter 3, Ex. 3.59b, m. 19, the harmonized version of the main theme's cadence introduces a bass C (⑥) for the pre-dominant IV⁶. In this

Rarely is an evaded ECP not followed by the one-more-time technique. Example 4.30 in the previous chapter brings one such case. An ECP begins in measure 64 with V$^6_5$/IV. The progression continues with the subdominant, a cadential six-four, and a dominant proper in the following three bars. The cadence is evaded when measure 68 brings I$^6$ in place of a final tonic, thus initiating a completely new two-measure idea, one that itself promises to close cadentially. This idea, too, is evaded, and a one-more-time repetition achieves a PAC at measure 72. Note that the new idea that follows the first ECP concludes with its own, highly compact, cadential progression at measure 69. This shutting down of any further cadential expansion prior to the PAC is perhaps owing to the passage's function as the final subordinate theme of an opening ritornello, where according to the conventions of concerto form, loosening procedures—especially ECPs—are typically held in check.[92]

Schmalfeldt advocates that the one-more-time technique is most appropriately identified in relation to evaded cadences exclusively. But as discussed in the preceding chapter (sec. 4.1.2.1 and note 26), both the way-station IAC and the deceptive cadence can yield a repetition of preceding material that is obviously analogous to that technique. A clear case can be seen in Example 4.14. In the context of a main theme, built as a compound sentence, a continuation⇒cadential phrase (m. 9) leads to a deceptive cadence at measure 12; a matching phrase then brings a PAC at measure 16. Curiously, however, a number of the deceptive ECPs in the corpus continue with cadential progressions that are more compact than the original ECP. In Chapter 4, Example 4.26, a subordinate theme opens with an ECP that resolves deceptively in measure 52, without, however, creating a sense of genuine deceptive cadence; the resolution is then followed immediately by a compact PAC.

### 5.4.3. Deceptive-Authentic Combinations (DCP-ACP); Melodic Content

The two previously discussed examples fall into the general category of deceptive-authentic combinations, as presented earlier in Chapters 3 and 4.[93] In the case of Example 4.14, the melodic content of the deceptive ECP is effectively replicated in the repeating authentic ECP. In more complicated cases, such as Example 4.26, the melodic line may be more difficult to discern. In this example, taking the pitches that are relatively high and metrically strong yields a succession of scale degrees, T: $\hat{8}$–$\hat{6}$–$\hat{4}$–$\hat{3}$, S: $\hat{3}$–$\hat{4}$–$\hat{2}$–$\hat{1}$, that embraces both harmonic progressions.

Something similar, though somewhat inverted as regards the relation of the upper voice to the bass, occurs in the expanded DCP-ACP combination seen earlier in this chapter's Example 5.35, whose cadential bass line we examined in detail (see toward the end of sec. 5.1.1.4). The deceptive ECP in measures 62–65 supports a conventional tenor stream that only reaches $\hat{3}$ to effect a genuine deceptive cadence. With the repeat of the melody (somewhat altered) in measures 66–71, the authentic ECP sees the melodic line reach down to $\hat{1}$. Thus in its melodic component, the DCP-ACP combination brings two distinct, descending lines, each associated with one of the harmonic progressions (deceptive and authentic). Unlike this two-part melody in the upper voice, however, the two progressions sound more cohesive due the bass melody, which as discussed earlier, creates a single melodic trajectory without any internal repetitions.

### 5.4.4. Abandoned ECP

The nature of cadential abandonment was treated in detail in the previous chapter. I emphasized there that the effect of this deviation requires us to perceive that a cadential progression is clearly in the making. I further pointed out that the use of cadential expansion is a particularly effective way of indicating that such a progression is actually underway. When, following a continuational passage, we hear a manifest slowing down of the harmonic rhythm associated, say, with a shift to I$^6$, we likely assume that the music has entered into cadential territory. If something goes awry with stage 3 of the proposed progression, then we understand that the ongoing ECP has been abandoned. Indeed, the majority of the examples of abandoned cadential progressions discussed in Chapter 4 involve expansion in some way or another (see Ex. 4.39, 4.43, 4.44, 4.45 [mm. 5–7], 4.49, and 4.50).

As we have seen in the present chapter, one of the premier modes of signaling the onset of an ECP is the emphasis given to an expanded initial tonic through its rocking back and forth with a subordinate dominant (usually V$^4_2$) or, less often, a subdominant. It is therefore no surprise that cadential abandonments are often preceded by a rocking on the tonic. We have already discussed two such situations, the first arising in Example 5.13a. Following a continuation (not shown), measure 29 brings a prolongation of I$^6$ via a subordinate dominant (unusually in root position, as discussed earlier). This rocking on the tonic signals cadential expansion, and when the proposed ECP moves to II$^6$ in measure 34, our sense of an ongoing ECP is all the more substantiated. When the bass moves up to ⑤ in the following bar, however, the potential for a stage 3 dominant is presented, but immediately

---

way, the upper voice, sounding a bass melody, can distinguish itself from the actual bass voice. In the closing section to this main theme, shown in Chapter 2, Ex. 2.22, we can observe that the bass C (⑥) occurs twice within each codetta (mm. 21–22 and 25–26). At the beginning of the transition, seen in Ex. 3.72, mm. 29–30, the C not only appears in the bass, but that pitch represents as well the root of a C-major harmony, one that is emphasized by opening both phrases that make up this unusual transition (see the details in the discussion of this example in Chapter 3). Finally, the bass C, now in the subordinate key of G major, is given the greatest emphasis in the second ECP of the first subordinate theme (Ex. 5.60, mm. 53–56 in the current chapter). We thus see an increasing importance accorded this "marked" pitch throughout the exposition of the sonata, especially in connection with the cadential content of the main and subordinate themes. (The transition, on the contrary, brings the C harmony in an initiating position.)

92. See *CF*, 244, and *ACF*, 681.

93. See Chapter 3, sec. 3.1.2.4, "Deceptive-Authentic Combinations," and Chapter 4, sec. 4.1.2.5.

EXAMPLE 5.61. Mozart, Piano Sonata in B-flat, K. 570, i, mm. 41–57 (*ACF* Sup. 6.21).

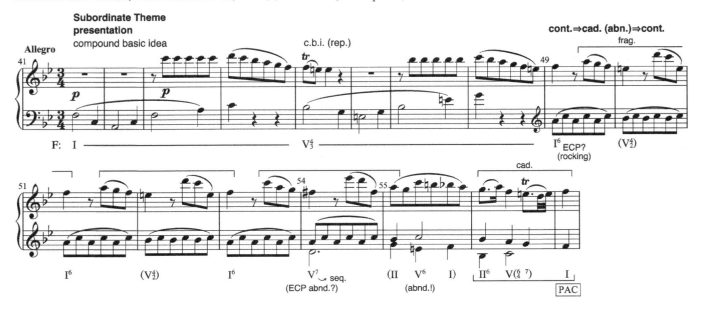

denied, when ⑤ supports III⁶, confirming the possibility that the move from I⁶ to II⁶ is not cadential, but rather sequential, hence yielding a new continuation. As a result, the ECP proposed by the rocking on the tonic is effectively abandoned.

A second case of a rocking on the tonic that leads to cadential abandonment has been treated in Example 5.15a. Following the unusual nature of the rocking (as earlier discussed), the predominant II⁶ in measure 71 moves to a dominant in the following bar. The bass ④ is retained, however, to support V$_2^4$, which forces a resolution to I⁶ at measure 73 that initiates a second, complete ECP, the first having been abandoned by failing to secure a root-position dominant.

In the two examples just discussed, the rocking on the tonic easily projects cadential function because the harmonic expansion follows upon material that was clearly continuational, and so the listener is already primed to expect cadential material. In some cases, however, the rocking is not so obviously associated with a pending cadence. In Example 5.61, for instance, a subordinate theme begins with a compound presentation consisting of two four-measure compound basic ideas, the first of which is supported exclusively by tonic, the second, by dominant. Measure 49 then brings a standard rocking between I⁶ and V$_2^4$. But rather than projecting harmonic expansion, the music accelerates the harmonies and is even accompanied by fragmentation into two-measure units. In other words, the passage expresses a continuation function as much, if not more, than a cadential one. In fact, the continuation is further enhanced when the harmony shifts at measure 54 to V⁷/II, which initiates a short descending-fifth sequential progression. Upon returning to I at the end of measure 55, a compact PAC brings closure to the theme. Mozart's careful placement of the sequential dominant in first inversion (V⁶, second beat of m. 55) guarantees that the potentially ongoing cadential progression is understood to have been abandoned.[94] All of these harmonic manipulations suggest that the formal function of the passage starting at measure 49 could be analyzed as continuation⇒cadential (abandoned)⇒continuation, an unusual, but ultimately logical, formal interpretation.

Cadential abandonment is sometimes associated with a situation that arises with some periodic structures, as discussed in Chapter 2 in connection with a bass-line pattern I call the *period model*; see Example 2.12 for the model in the abstract and Example 2.15a for its use in an actual period. In this latter passage, an opening antecedent arrives on I⁶ (upbeat to m. 3), which, together with the move to IV, implies the start of a cadential progression. The bass line, however, then continues in manner that is prolongational, eventually leading to a compact HC at measure 4. The matching consequent achieves the same I⁶ (upbeat to m. 7), but this time a genuine cadential progression emerges to close the period with a PAC. In this case, the cadential function beginning with the move from I⁶ to IV in measures 2–3 is barely incipient, such that speaking of a genuine abandonment is perhaps overly stretching the matter. But with an analogous case involving an ECP, this deviation type can come more prominently into play. In Example 5.62 of the present chapter, an opening compound basic idea, built largely over a tonic pedal (mm. 1–4), is followed by a phrase that begins with I⁶ moving to IV (m. 6), which is prolonged by a shift to IV⁶ on the downbeat of measure 7. The harmonic situation thus strongly implies the formation of an ECP. But when the bass moves further up to ⑦, to yield a V$_5^6$, which resolves prolongationally to I, we understand that the ECP has

---

94. The abandonment may already have been heard with the V⁷/II in m. 54, but this harmony could also be a cadential stage 1b tonic substitute on the way to a pre-dominant II in the following bar. Thus the abandonment is only fully confirmed by the subsequent V⁶.

EXAMPLE 5.62. Beethoven, Bagatelle in E-flat, Op. 126, no. 3, (a) mm. 1–8; (b) mm. 13–16 (*ACF* 6.19).

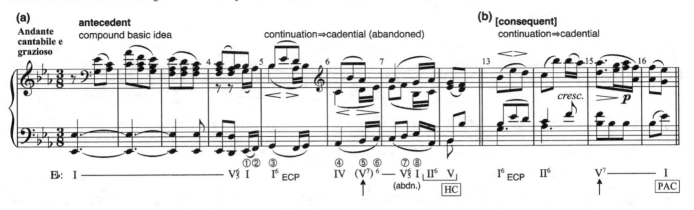

EXAMPLE 5.63. Mozart, Violin Sonata in E-flat, K. 380, i, mm. 22–27 (*ACF* 12.17).

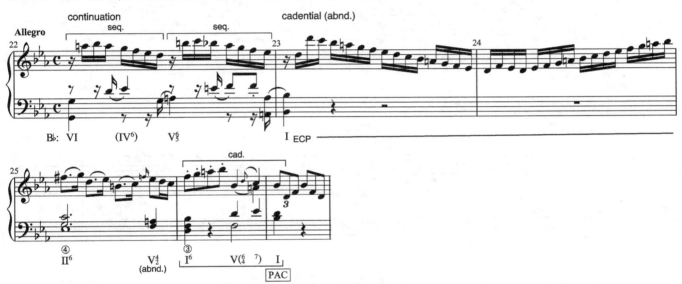

been abandoned. The phrase then quickly concludes with a compact HC to form a potential compound antecedent, an interpretation that is further supported when the compound basic idea returns at measure 9 (not shown). The same ECP is then proposed at measure 13 (Ex. 5.62b) and this time is completed to form a matching compound consequent. Note that the vertical structure of the cadential $V^7$ in measure 15 is almost identical to the passing $V^7$ in measure 6 (see arrows), thus forging a clear connection between the abandoned ECP and the fully realized one.[95]

Most of the abandoned ECPs just discussed are followed by a new continuation, which eventually brings PAC closure. In some cases, however, the cadential abandonment leads directly to new cadential material, which may also be expanded (see again Ex. 5.15a). As well, an abandoned ECP that is associated with a clear moment of arrival may be immediately repeated in a manner that is analogous to the one-more-time technique;

such is the case with Example 4.44, measures 5–8 and 9–13, from the previous chapter. Sometimes, the abandoned ECP leads immediately to a compact PAC (Ex. 5.63, in the present chapter). Following a continuation featuring an ascending-stepwise sequence (the last bar of which opens the excerpt), a flurry of sixteenth notes accompanied by an expansion of tonic harmony in measures 23–24 suggests the start of an ECP. And with the move to the pre-dominant $II^6$ at measure 25, that impression is further supported. The ECP is abandoned, however, when the $V^4_2$ on the last beat of that bar pushes the bass down to ③, holding $I^6$, and a second, compact cadential progression brings a PAC to close the subordinate theme.[96]

With one exception, all of the abandoned ECPs discussed in this section see the initial tonic (often expressed through a

---

95. The formal and cadential organization of this example is very similar to the theme discussed earlier in Ex. 5.38.

---

96. More accurately, the passage closes a case of transition/subordinate-theme fusion, as discussed in *ACF*, Ex. 12.17. The use of a root-position tonic to initiate the ECP in m. 23 is explainable in light of an earlier, expanded noncadential $I^6$ (mm. 19–20, not shown), which leads to the model-sequence technique.

EXAMPLE 5.64. Mozart, Piano Quartet in E-flat, K. 493, i, mm. 28–59.

rocking motion) move to the pre-dominant prior to the abandonment, thus allowing stage 2 of the progression to help solidify the sense of an ongoing ECP all the more. (Ex. 5.61 is an exception, but there, as discussed, the rocking already seems more continuational than cadential.) In one particularly interesting case (Ex. 5.64), the initial tonic of an ECP, signaled clearly by its rocking, is abandoned prior to the appearance of a pre-dominant.

When the cadential progression is eventually resumed, beginning precisely with the expected pre-dominant from the prior ECP, a complex interaction of formal elements results from the initial abandonment, as I will now detail.

The subordinate theme opens with a presentation phrase. After the dominant that ends the repeat of the basic idea resolves deceptively to VI (m. 32), the following continuation⇒cadential

EXAMPLE 5.65. Haydn, Piano Trio in E Minor, H. 12, iii, mm. 15–22 (*ACF* Sup. 7.2).

phrase begins on I⁶. The cadence is not realized, however, because the dominant resolves once again to VI, this time creating a genuine deceptive cadence at measure 35. Another I⁶ follows immediately, now embellished by a neighboring V$^4_2$, and the conventional rocking on the tonic signals that a more expansive cadential progression is in the making.

At this point we could easily "hear ahead" and project a normal conclusion to the cadential phrase via a PAC. Mozart deceives us, though, when the ECP loses its way through the changing function of the diminished-seventh sonority in measure 40, and the progression arrives on a pre-dominant augmented-sixth of G minor (SK: VI) in measure 41. (This tonicization of the submediant region has been well prepared, of course, by the two preceding deceptive resolutions, each yielding a G-minor triad.) The German sixth thus abandons the prior ECP in B-flat and at the same time initiates a modest ECP in G minor, which like the first one (mm. 32–35), resolves deceptively on the downbeat of measure 44. As a result, we can identify a cadential formal function for these measures (see the "cadential" label and the dashed line beginning at m. 41). We should not speak of a genuine deceptive cadence, however, due to the sudden return in measures 42–43 of the opening basic idea, now in G minor. Indeed, we might suspect that a new presentation were in the making, except that the extended repeat of the idea (mm. 44–46) is sequenced down a third. Consequently, a potential presentation becomes a continuation due to the sequential support of its constituent ideas. This continuation, now highly extended (mm. 46–54), brings the music back to the home key while fragmenting and liquidating the melodic material over an expanded dominant in first inversion (mm. 47–51). This harmony then "casts out" its root at measure 52 in order to re-enact, for a final time, a deceptive resolution to VI at measure 54. Mozart then begins a fourth, and final, ECP directly with II⁶ and at last completes the theme at measure 59 with a PAC. It is not surprising that this ECP omits an initial tonic: this harmonic function had already been expanded in the abandoned progression of measures 36–40 and thus could be eliminated here for the sake of artistic economy (to speak with Ratz; see note 52). But more interesting is the possibility that we could hear the II⁶ harmony of measure 54 linking back the earlier I⁶ at measure 38, just after which the ongoing ECP goes "off the rails." In other words, the material from measures 39–54 can be seen as a digression that has been interpolated between the I⁶ of measure 38 and the II⁶ of measure 54.

Two different views of the overall organization of this subordinate theme now emerge. At first glance, it would seem to divide itself into two more or less independent sections, each of which is sentential in structure. But this is perhaps too mechanical an interpretation because the first section (mm. 28–41) receives no genuine cadential closure, and the second section (mm. 42–59) does not project a strong enough sense of tonic opening. A second, subtler view recognizes that one structurally complete theme (from m. 28 to the end of m. 38 and from the second half of m. 54 to m. 59) has embedded within itself another, incomplete theme (from m. 39 to the first half of m. 54). Mozart has thus discovered an ingenious way of significantly loosening the phrase structure of this subordinate theme through the use of an abandoned ECP that is ultimately resumed and completed at the end of the theme.

### 5.4.5. Dominant Arrival

Though rare, an ECP may lead to a dominant arrival in place of an expected HC. We saw one such case in Chapter 4, Example 4.55, where a pre-dominant augmented sixth is expanded to four bars (mm. 133–36) before resolving to a final dominant seventh in measure 137. A more elaborate ECP, taken from the contrasting middle of a small ternary, can be seen in Example 5.65 of the present chapter. A rocking on the tonic (mm. 15–18) uses the subdominant as a subordinate harmony to prolong I⁶. A modal shift to the tonic minor in measure 19 then leads to a pre-dominant V⁷/V in the following bar, after which the resolution to V⁷ produces the dominant arrival. To be sure, the rocking on the tonic may alternatively be seen as continuational, rather than cadential, since these harmonies follow upon a passage (not shown) of relatively slow harmonic rhythm at the start of the B section, and thus the rocking may be heard to present a modest harmonic acceleration. Nonetheless, the shift to minor I⁶ breaks out of the rocking and can clearly be heard as cadential, in which case the ECP would still meet the minimum size of three bars (mm. 19–21).

EXAMPLE 5.66. Haydn, Symphony No. 97 in C, iv, mm. 1–8.

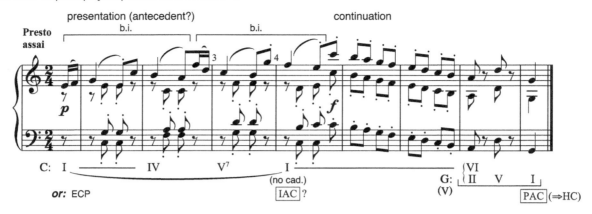

## 5.5. A Cadential Conundrum

In a small number of cases in the classical style, we encounter an *opening* four-measure phrase that seems to be supported exclusively by an ECP leading to an authentic cadence (either an IAC or a PAC). Since the fundamental logic of cadential closure holds that a cadence is a functional end "of something" (i.e., some material that precedes the cadence), the circumstances just described would have to recognize cadential content in the absence of genuine cadential function. Yet in these circumstances, it seems difficult to give up the idea that the fourth bar is concluding a distinct unit of form, the four-measure phrase. In such a situation, we could have recourse to an often played "escape card," by claiming that an imaginary passage of music begins the thematic process, such that the actually sounding first phrase represents a conclusion. But other resolutions of this conundrum are also sometimes available.

One such instance has already been presented in Chapter 3. Example 3.84 shows an opening four-measure phrase supported by the progression I–IV–V⁷–I, which in principle could be identified as an ECP. Yet this theme does not sound as though it were beginning with an "end"; rather, we can hear a two-measure basic idea followed by a contrasting idea, closing with an IAC (whose melodic complications were discussed in the earlier chapter).[97] What also contributes to making this phrase sound like an initiating unit, not a concluding one, is the opening progression from a root-position tonic to a root-position subdominant, harmonies that do not immediately signal themselves as cadential. It is perfectly normal for I–IV to sound prolongational (perhaps followed by I⁶ to clinch the prolongation). Only in retrospect, when the subsequent V⁷–I in measures 3–4 concludes the phrase, might we reconsider the entire progression as cadential. But then, when we hear the following phrase beginning with V⁶₅/IV–IV, harmonies that are more obviously cadential, we are more likely to understand the onset of an ECP for the second phrase exclusively.

Something similar occurs in Example 5.66. Again, an opening phrase begins with I–IV–V⁷–I. Here, however, an initial two-measure basic idea is obviously repeated in measures 3–4, such that the effect of a sentential presentation vies for prominence with the idea of an underlying ECP. As well, the ascending melodic leaps in the basic ideas inhibit an expression of cadential function for the phrase as whole. Indeed, the following continuation sees a descending scale filling in most of the melodic gaps opened up in the presentation. In short, it makes more sense to hear the harmonies of the first phrase as entirely tonic prolongational rather than cadential.[98]

Where our conundrum comes into full force is in that most exceptional opening written by Beethoven in the first movement of his Piano Sonata in E-flat, Op. 31, no. 1 (shown earlier in Ex. 5.34b). Here, the underlying progression, beginning with a stage-2 pre-dominant (II⁶₅) is entirely cadential, with no sense of an initial tonic prolongation. With this audacious gesture, Beethoven anticipates formal moves encountered more often in the Romantic era, especially with Schubert (see ahead Ex. 8.8 and 8.9) and Schumann (Ex. 8.7). When considering such opening units, it perhaps makes the most sense to distinguish between their intrinsic cadential expression—as an "ending"—and their contextual location—as a "beginning"—and thus validate the inherent conflict presented by these two modes of formal functionality.[99] As just mentioned, we will encounter in later chapters

---

97. Considering the extensive Scotch snaps beginning in m. 2 and continuing through m. 4, my analysis of the boundary between the basic idea and contrasting idea requires some justification. Here, I am appealing to the melodic turn figure in m. 2, C–B–A♯–B (supported by IV), as creating the effect of a momentary hesitation within the basic idea, prior to the downward scalar plunge that starts with the contrasting idea on the following downbeat. (Alternatively, the contrasting idea could be seen to start with the snaps on the second beat of m. 2.)

98. Zhang raises similar issues in connection with the opening four-measure phrase of Mozart's Piano Sonata in B-flat, K. 333, i ("Apparently Imperfect," 193 and Ex. 4b). Though he recognizes the possibility of hearing an IAC at m. 4, he prefers hearing here a noncadential mode of phrase closure (akin to my concept of prolongational closure).

99. As introduced already in Chapter 2 (see note 120 in connection with Ex. 2.17), I annotate a formal unit's *intrinsic* functionality with the

some nineteenth-century works where the cadential conundrum raised here becomes something of a stylistic norm, one that distinguishes itself prominently from classical cadential practice.

## 5.6. Expanded Cadential Progressions in Beethoven's Symphonies

By virtue of their large performing forces and capacity for intense rhetorical expression, orchestral music, especially the genre of symphony, inspires some of the most expansive and complex ECPs in the classical repertory.[100] Indeed, we have already seen some impressive cases in a selection from Mozart's symphonic oeuvre (Ex. 5.3, 5.35, 5.36, and 5.37). I close this chapter, and Part I of the book, with a sample of ECPs culled from Beethoven's nine symphonies. The examples I have chosen do not constitute the complete set of ECPs in these symphonic works, but rather those that either further illustrate some of the techniques already discussed above or that bring more novel means of cadential expansion and harmonic variation.

### 5.6.1. Symphony No. 1 in C, Op. 21, i, Subordinate-Theme Group

The opening movement of the First Symphony features three subordinate themes, the first and third of which close with ECPs. The first subordinate theme (Ex. 5.67a) is built as a compound period, whose sentential consequent, beginning at measure 61, brings a continuation⇒cadential phrase (mm. 65–69) that is evaded on the downbeat of measure 69. As so indicated, the ECP bypasses stage 1 and begins with a stage 2 subdominant (mm. 65–66), which continues with $II^6$ in measure 67. Stage 3 arrives in the next bar, and the cadential evasion is signaled by the $V^4_2$ that immediately follows the cadential six-four. Note, however, that an opening stage 1 finds expression in two ways. First, the preceding presentation concludes its underlying tonic prolongation in measure 64 with a secondary dominant of IV, a potential stage 1b harmony. As such, we could perhaps, in retrospect, come to hear it as the onset of the ECP, even though the evident 4 + 4 grouping structure does not align with such an interpretation. Second, we can observe that within the prolonged pre-dominant (mm. 65–67), Beethoven uses two enharmonically equivalent forms of the same diminished-seventh harmony, the first of which continues to tonicize IV, the second, $II^6$. These neighboring harmonies built over ③ thus allude to stage 1 of an ECP; in fact, they could be seen as creating a kind of "rocking" on the pre-dominant.

Following the evaded cadence at measure 69, another sentential structure begins. A new basic idea and its repetition arise within a tonic prolongation. The second phrase brings continuation⇒cadential function as supported by an obvious ECP (mm. 73–76), one that leads to an elided deceptive cadence on the downbeat of measure 76. There follows a highly compact cadential idea to close the entire subordinate theme.[101] Though the final ECP of this theme may seem to begin at measure 73, it is not unreasonable to locate its real onset back at measure 69, especially since the supporting harmonies prolong $I^6$ in a manner that projects a kind of rocking on the tonic (very much like a similar rocking passage seen earlier in Ex. 5.19, mm. 29–33). Indeed, this view seems to make the most sense, since the ongoing compound period has not yet achieved any closure due to the evasion at measure 69 (Ex. 5.67a), and so the formal environment does not suggest that a genuinely new initiation is getting underway. Rather, it is preferable to see the evaded cadence leading to a resumption of cadential function. In short, even though we can recognize the semblance of a sentence beginning at measure 69, the broader context allows us to understand that a new cadential unit (albeit one that is rendered deceptive) is sufficiently expanded as to permit it to acquire a sentence-like formation.[102]

A second subordinate theme follows, one that begins with continuation function.[103] Though the cadential expression in this theme is complex, none of its constituent cadential progressions is expanded. Indeed Beethoven's decision to use only compact progressions in this theme makes sense so as to permit a third subordinate theme to bring another ECP without the fear of formal redundancy (Ex. 5.67b). This final subordinate theme, like the second one, begins directly with continuation function.[104] Four bars later, an ECP, signaled by the $I^6$ at measure 92, slows down the harmonic rhythm to one change in each measure (from a prior two harmonies per bar in mm. 90–91). Within stage 1 of

---

function label placed in vertical braces; thus in Ex. 5.34b, the main theme's single phrase function is labeled {cadential}. No conventional formal term is available to indicate the phrase's *contextual* function as initiating. In contrast, the Romantic themes of Ex. 8.7–8.9 are structured in such a way as to yield an initiating "antecedent" as a contextual function that can be identified as such in the annotations.

100. Concertos also often bring massive ECPs, but normally with the substantial expansions applying largely to stage 3, in a show of virtuosic, cadenza-like passage-work and without the kinds of harmonic complications in stages 1 and 2 seen in other instrumental genres.

101. It is possible to hear another evaded cadence at the downbeat of m. 76, but the forces of continuity, especially melodically but rhythmically as well, strongly mark that moment as the formal goal of the ongoing ECP, thus projecting a cadential deception, more than an evasion.

102. See again Ex. 5.9 and Ex. 5.14, mm. 75–80, for other cases of ECPs that embed a sentential organization within the broader cadential function.

103. For an analysis of this second subordinate theme, see Caplin, "What Are Formal Functions?" 31, and Caplin, "Structural Expansion," 35–36.

104. In "What Are Formal Functions?," Fig. 1.4 and Ex. 1.1, as well as in "Structural Expansion," 36, I identify this third theme as beginning with a compressed presentation. I prefer now to see the sense of a continuation (with one-measure fragments) being expressed at the very opening of the theme.

EXAMPLE 5.67A. Beethoven, Symphony No. 1 in C, Op. 21, i, mm. 61–77.

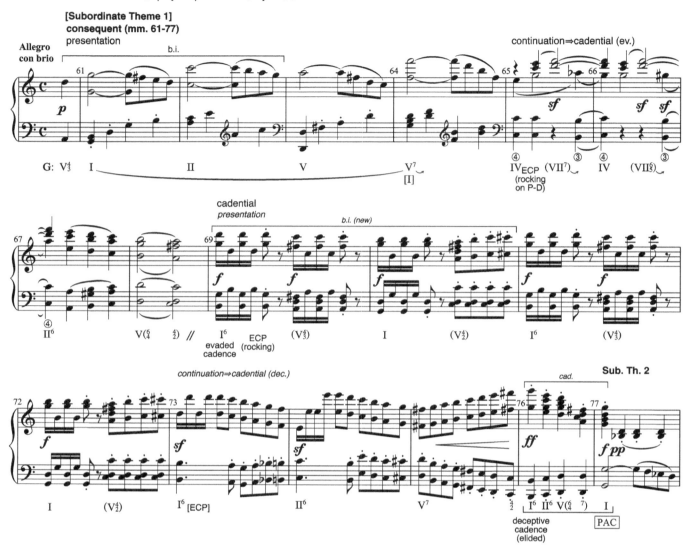

this ECP, we find four distinct harmonic sonorities: an initial I⁶, a passing VII⁴₃/VI (m. 93), and two manifestations of a secondary dominant of the subsequent pre-dominant (namely, V⁶/II and VII⁴₃/II, mm. 94–95), the latter two being understood as chromatic substitutes for VI, itself a tonic substitute. In other words, rather than prolonging the initial tonic with simple passing dominants, as in the opening of the large ECP in the first subordinate theme (Ex. 5.67a, mm. 69–72), Beethoven achieves in the third theme a chromatically enriched prolongation of stage 1, which continues with the pre-dominant (m. 96) and its conventional chromatic embellishment (VII⁷/V, m. 97). He then alludes to the compact cadences that end both the first and second subordinate themes by bringing a double-neighboring configuration that suggest VI and II⁶ harmonies within the expanded dominant of stage 3 (see the dashed cadential bracket).[105] Looking back over the entire subordinate-theme group, we see a considerable harmonic diversity within their three different ECPs (Ex. 5.67a, mm. 65–68 and 69–76; Ex. 5.67b, mm. 92–100).

### 5.6.2. Symphony No. 2 in D, Op. 36, iv, Coda

As we saw in connection with Mozart's Piano Quartet (Example 5.64), a pronounced *harmonic* expansion is not always a sign of *cadential* expansion. In that example, the expanded dominant in measures 47–53 forms part of a highly extended continuation. A somewhat similar kind of expansion arises in the first coda theme of the finale of Beethoven's Second Symphony (Ex. 5.68a). In the formal context of a broad continuation, stepwise descending scalar motion in the bass (mm. 350–58) consists of a four-note motive ("x"), which is repeated sequentially, as supported by a descending-fifths progression (see arrows under each principal harmony of the sequence). As well, this bass motion is complemented by inversions of motive "x" (shown in the lower

---

105. See again Ex. 5.33, mm. 307–308 for a similar embedding of a compact cadential progression within stage 3 of an ECP.

EXAMPLE 5.67B. Beethoven, Symphony No. 1 in C, Op. 21, i, mm. 88–100.

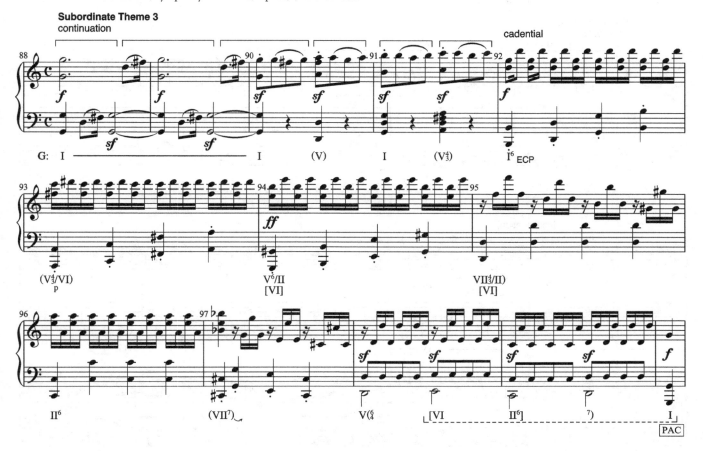

voice of the right-hand part of the example).[106] At measure 356, Beethoven discontinues the harmonic sequence and now repeats the motive with the same notes through to measure 366, thus effecting an enormous prolongation of subdominant harmony. Although the pattern of notes remain static during this ten-bar expansion, the motive's rhythm is systematically augmented, starting at measure 358, with a further stage of augmentation at measure 362. Finally, the motive becomes fully liquidated in measures 366–71. This enormous expansion of subdominant harmony might well suggest that the music has entered into cadential territory. This view is problematic, however, because that harmony arose initially at measure 356 as the final link of a sequential progression starting at the opening of the excerpt (m. 350). As discussed on many occasions in this study, the classical composers carefully distinguish a sequential harmony from a cadential one. Moreover, if we look to the rhetorical dimension, the expanded subdominant takes place within a *recessive dynamic* beginning at measure 358 and continuing through measure 371.[107] The effect is of a gradual winding down, a lulling to sleep. At the same time, this subdominant is charged with expectations that something will restore the music to the frenetic pace appropriate to the finale's coda. Indeed, the sudden *fortissimo* at measure 372 is a wakeup call that wrenches the music out of its temporary stupor and propels it toward cadential closure. This new *cadential* harmony is a chromatically charged stage-2b German augmented-sixth, inverted to stand over ♯④ (spelled "incorrectly" as ♭⑤) at measure 372. Two bars later, this ECP quickly leads to the dominant of stage 3 and the PAC at measure 382. In retrospect, of course, we could look back to the expanded subdominant and find there a stage-2a cadential harmony. Yet I doubt that we would want to consider the ECP to have started all the way back at measure 356, where this harmony first appears and is then prolonged, the context there being so manifestly continuational. At best, we might locate the ECP's onset at measure 366, yet even here the cadential status of this harmony is by no means evident. From both form-functional and rhetorical perspectives, the sudden appearance of the German sixth seems to be the real signal that the music has entered its cadential phase.

Beyond the intrinsic analytical interest of this passage, it further gains importance in relation to a similar passage arising in

---

106. Motive "x" is prominent throughout the finale, arising already in the main theme and then more obviously at the beginning of both parts of the two-part transition; see Chapter 3, Ex. 3.150.

107. My reference to a "recessive" dynamic follows the use of this term by Wallace Berry (*Structural Functions in Music*, 7), who speaks of a "recessive" intensity as a deintensification of many parameters, especially ones that Meyer would call "statistical" (see Chapter 1, sec. 1.2.1), including not only loudness but also rhythmic activity, texture, and contour. Berry terms the opposite process "progressive."

EXAMPLE 5.68A. Beethoven, Symphony No. 2 in D, Op. 36, iv, mm. 350–82.

the slow movement of the symphony, namely, in the exposition's subordinate theme (Ex. 5.68b). In the course of a continuation, a brief descending-third model-sequence technique in measures 66–68 (see arrows), engaging the same motive "x," leads to a significant expansion of subdominant harmony (mm. 68–73). The harmonic sequence continues down a third to II in measure 74, after which the bass (if not the harmony) falls another third to support $V^6_5$ (which resolves to tonic at m. 76). This $V^6_5$ connects back to the same harmony at measure 66, thus framing the harmonic sequence (VI-IV-II). A compact cadential idea in the following two bars completes the theme with a PAC. With this description, it should be clear that the expanded subdominant is embedded within a broader sequential process, such that even if we may have wondered whether that harmony were serving a cadential function, due to its marked expansion, that possibility is shut down when the dominant is inverted at measure 75.

Turning back to Example 5.68a, we can see some striking resemblances between the slow movement and the finale, including the use of a highly expanded subdominant within the broader context of a sequential progression. Despite its expansion, the subdominant in the finale seems, to my ears at least, to sustain the continuation, which is only broken by the German sixth, whose cadential function is fully realized. As discussed, of course, we could still be influenced by the expansion of the subdominant per se in suggesting cadential function, in which case an ECP would be completed by the remaining harmonies starting at measure 372. In this sense, Beethoven realizes in the finale an implication—that the expanded subdominant becomes cadential—that is otherwise denied in the slow movement.[108]

### 5.6.3. Symphony No. 3 in E-flat ("Eroica"), Op. 55, i, Second Subordinate Theme

As befitting its reputation for significant structural expansion, the opening movement of the Eroica contains a number of prominent

---

108. A precedent for Beethoven's motivic, harmonic, and formal manipulations in his Second Symphony finale can perhaps be found in an earlier examined symphonic movement by Haydn (see again Ex. 5.19), in which the composer highly expands a pre-dominant II⁶ (mm. 34–40) within a broadly recessive dynamic and the augmentation (doubly so in Haydn's case) of a four-note ascending motive. Unlike Haydn's expanded pre-dominant, which is manifestly cadential in expression, Beethoven's expansion is ambiguous as to its formal function.

EXAMPLE 5.68B. Beethoven, Symphony No. 2 in D, Op. 36, ii, mm. 65–78.

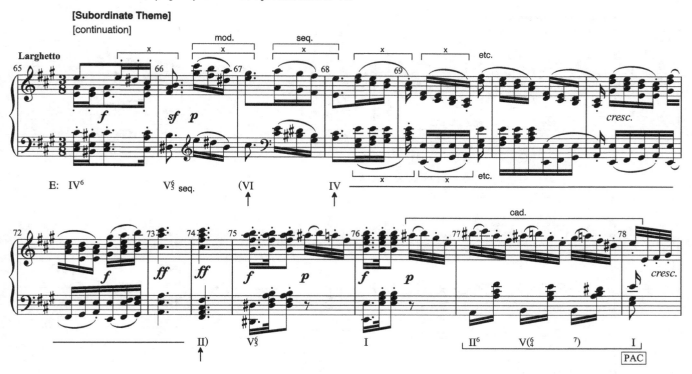

EXAMPLE 5.69. (a) Deceptive cadential progression; (b) deceptive cadential, chromaticized; (c) ascending-step sequential.

ECPs.[109] Those closing the first subordinate theme as well as the first coda theme are straightforward and easy to identify.[110] The second subordinate theme, part 2, presents a more interesting case, one that exploits an ambiguity in the classification of harmonic progressions similar to the one we examined in Example 5.37f. Example 5.69a shows a simple deceptive cadential progression; Example 5.69b, a chromaticized variant. Note that this variant is harmonically identical to the ascending-stepwise sequential progression of Example 5.69c, the basic difference between them being the realization of a clear model-sequence technique in the latter by means of a repetition pattern in the upper voices.

Looking now at the close of the second subordinate theme (Ex. 5.70a), a new presentation of part 2 (not shown) is followed by a continuation featuring an ascending-stepwise sequence in measures 119–21. Having achieved a sequential ascent from IV to I, supporting parallel tenths in the upper voice ($\hat{6}$–$\hat{3}$), the music continues with additional chromatic activity in measure 122. The following bar sees a textural change to quarter-note block chords while tonicizing VI. Beethoven then transposes the second and third chords down a third to fashion a second model in measure 124. He uses this model to initiate again an ascending-stepwise sequential pattern, one consisting of the same contrapuntal scaffolding as the first sequence (cf. the scale-degree analysis in the upper and lower voices of mm. 124–26 with mm. 119–20). Note, moreover, that this second sequence closely relates to the schematic model shown in Example 5.69c.[111]

This second sequence only gets as far as tonicizing VI (m. 126), after which, in the following bar, the music reverts to the

---

109. For a detailed harmonic and phrase-structural analysis of the complete subordinate theme group, see Caplin, "Structural Expansion," 36–44.

110. Subordinate theme 1 in the exposition, mm. 75–83; coda theme 1, mm. 625–31.

111. One difference between the actual sequence and the schematic pattern is that the model in the former tonicizes II[6] rather than IV.

EXAMPLE 5.70A. Beethoven, Symphony No. 3 in E-flat ("Eroica"), Op. 55, i, mm. 117–44.

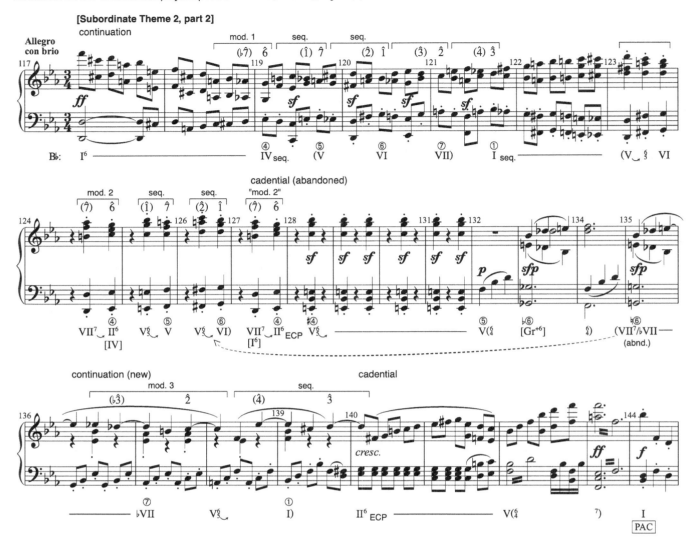

model of measure 124. As a result, it seems as if the sequence is about to occur all over again, a repetition that clearly risks becoming redundant. So to avoid that problem and to push the thematic process along, he *expands* the opening harmony of the second link, V$^6_5$/V, to four bars (mm. 128–31), thus leading the listener to suppose that the theme has finally entered into its cadential function. Indeed, we can then retrospectively hear the "sequential" VII$^7$/II of measure 127 reinterpreted as a stage-1b initial tonic substitute, continuing the cadential progression on to II$^6$. Following the expanded V$^6_5$/V, the arrival on the cadential six-four (m. 132), embellished by a neighboring German-sixth (♭$\hat{6}$), seems to confirm our suspicion that a PAC is close at hand.

But now Beethoven effects a startling turn of events: when the bass rises to ♮$\hat{6}$ at measure 135 to support VII$^7$/♭VII, the ongoing ECP is abandoned, and a new, third model is introduced, which allows the music to reconnect—both harmonically and contrapuntally—with the sequence that was interrupted back at measure 126 with the tonicization of VI (see the backward-directed dashed arrow).[112] The pattern is then completed by one further link that rises to I (m. 139). After all of this sequential activity and the frustration of not having fulfilled the obvious cadential implications of measures 127–34, Beethoven writes a second ECP (mm. 140–44) that finally closes the subordinate theme. This progression is entirely diatonic and not suggestive of sequence in the least. In sum, the composer has taken full advantage of the dual harmonic meanings offered by the schematic patterns of Example 5.69b and c, by switching from a sequential usage to a cadential one, only to abandon the latter by reverting to the sequence once again. This ingenious exploitation of harmonic ambiguity yields a massive structural enlargement, thus contributing to

---

112. The secondary dominant of ♭VII (mm. 135–36) initially takes the guise of a diminished-seventh sonority (VII$^7$), which connects well to the VII$^7$/VI of m. 126. But when the E♮ (really an F♭) in the upper voice of m. 135 moves down to E♭ in m. 136, we understand that the "substitute" VII$^7$ has reverted to V$^6_5$, the more fundamental form of the secondary dominant, and the one that is used in the sequence of model 2.

EXAMPLE 5.70B. Beethoven, Symphony No. 3 in E-flat ("Eroica"), Op. 55, i, continuity sketch of mm. 128–44 (from Beethoven, "*Eroica*" *Sketchbook*, p. 26, staves 6–7, 15).

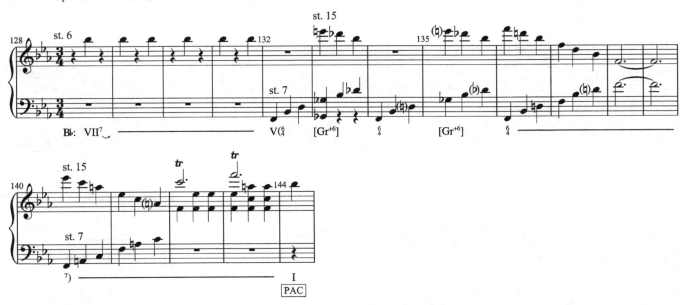

broader formal goals that this symphonic movement successfully achieves.

Finally, a note concerning one of Beethoven's continuity sketches for this passage (Ex. 5.70b):[113] the most "advanced" sketch (i.e., the one closest to the final version) shows the syncopated chords associated with measures 128–31, which initiate the ECP (staff 6 in the sketchbook). The cadential six-four and its embellishments by the German augmented sixth (mm. 132–35) is evident as well in the sketch (staves 7 and 15). From this point up to the final cadence at measure 144, the sketch suggests that Beethoven was planning to continue the six-four, unembellished, for an additional four bars, matched by the dominant proper for the same length. That the stretch of time in the sketch is identical to that found in the final version, reveals that Beethoven was sure of the phrase rhythm involved in closing the theme. Sometime between this sketch and the final version, however, he conceived of abandoning the ECP and reconnecting the music to the previous sequence, as discussed above. To be sure, nothing is wrong with the option shown in the sketch; many of Beethoven's ECPs are filled with such conventionalized arpeggiated figures as shown there. At the same time, it cannot be denied that his final version exploits harmonic progression, formal functionality, and retrospective reinterpretation in a considerably more sophisticated manner than in the sketch.

### 5.6.4. Symphony No. 5 in C Minor, Op. 67, iv, Subordinate Theme, Coda Themes

The finale of Beethoven's Fifth Symphony presents an extraordinary diversity of cadential harmonies within a formal context that contravenes some fundamental precepts of sonata form. I focus primarily on the recapitulation's subordinate theme as well as the coda. First, though, I must point out a striking irregularity in the exposition that proves consequential for what happens later in the movement. Unlike practically all cases within the classical repertory, the subordinate theme of this sonata-form exposition does not close with a PAC.[114] Indeed, a "first-time" listener might hear this lack of closure as a sign that the finale will be constructed as a sonata-rondo, a form that permits its subordinate themes to conclude noncadentially;[115] however, the wholesale repetition of the exposition eventually dispels that presumption.

The subordinate theme (Ex. 5.71a) begins with a compound presentation (not shown). There follows a brief sequential continuation in measures 53–55. An ECP starts up at measure 56 when the sequence to the subdominant gets stuck on $V^7/IV$, which is further intensified by the chromatically raised fifth (D♯) in the following bar. The resolution to IV brings a further expansion, yielding to $II^6$ and V in measures 62–63. Were the theme to cadence at measure 64, it would acquire the overall form of a compound sentence.

The promised PAC, however, is evaded (m. 64), and with this evasion comes a new two-measure basic idea, whose repetition produces a simple presentation (mm. 64–67). A continuation begins at measure 68 and a compact cadential idea proposes

---

113. The sketch appears in the "Eroica" sketchbook (Landsberg 6) on p. 26, and the version shown here combines staves 6 and 7 with staff 15, following note 4 of Lewis Lockwood and Alan Gosman's transcription (Ludwig van Beethoven, *Beethoven's "Eroica" Sketchbook: A Critical Edition*). (The harmonic analysis is mine.) I thank Barry Cooper for drawing my attention to this sketch and its relevance for the argument I am pursuing in this analysis. I also thank Thomas Posen for helping to clarify additional aspects of the sketch.

114. Hepokoski and Darcy also highlight this "failed exposition" as a sonata-form deformation (*Sonata Theory*, 178).

115. *CF*, 237, and *ACF*, 651.

EXAMPLE 5.71A. Beethoven, Symphony No. 5 in C Minor, Op. 67, iv, mm. 53–82.

PAC closure at measure 72 to form a slightly extended, simple sentence. The question now arises: Is this a new subordinate theme, and if so, what happened to the cadence promised for the preceding compound sentence left hanging by the way-station evaded cadence at measure 64? As a rule, a way-station evasion (or deception) is not followed by a strongly expressed sense of formal initiation (nor does an evasion back up to the start of the theme with its initiating material).[116] To do so would give the impression that a new formal unit were in the making, thus leaving

the prior unit without any cadential closure. So in such a circumstance, we normally find that the seeming "initiating unit" contains intrinsic qualities of a formal continuation, thereby leaving open the possibility that the ongoing thematic process (that is, the music prior to the evasion) will continue on and eventually attain full closure. Given the degree of harmonic instability projected by the new basic idea at measure 64—the opening I⁶ and concluding V⁶, connected by chromatic, diminished-seventh harmonies—we indeed could hear the new idea and its repetition projecting a palpable sense of continuation function. We would therefore not necessarily believe that a new subordinate theme

---

116. See in Chapter 4, sec. 4.2.2.2 and 4.1.2.1.

were in the making (thus rendering the first subordinate theme completely open-ended). And we would then understand that the simple sentence beginning at measure 64 is actually embedded within a new continuation of the original compound sentence.[117]

Confident that full closure will eventually be achieved for the compound sentence, we hear a second evasion at measure 72; indeed, the ensuing one-more-time repetition further holds out the promise of a future PAC to close the subordinate theme. So it is quite a shock, therefore, when at measure 77, the music suddenly departs from its expected course and brings an F-minor six-four harmony, which suddenly brings back the home key for a repeat of the exposition. The subordinate theme is thus left without any cadential closure whatsoever, in direct violation of sonata norms.

To understand the origin of the unusual six-four in measure 77, we can look back to the analogous moment in measure 69 and observe that the melodic G♯, supported by VII$^6_5$/II, is enharmonically altered to A♭ in measure 77 to accommodate the IV$^6_4$ (see the circled notes in mm. 69 and 77). This detail is significant for what happens in the recapitulation, where the subordinate theme returns largely intact, though now transposed to the home key of C major (Ex. 5.71b).[118] If the theme were to continue exactly as in the exposition, the melodic C♯ of measure 278 (see circled notes) would have been changed to D♭ in measure 286 and be harmonized by a B♭-minor six-four. Instead, Beethoven continues to use the C♯ for measure 286 and supports it, as in the earlier measure 278, with VII$^6_5$/II. This harmony now functions as a chromatic variant for the initial stage of a new ECP. But when stage 2 arrives in measure 289, the expected resolution to II$^6$ does not occur. Rather, we encounter a B♭-minor six-four built over ④ (though now enriched with a suspended 9th), a version of the harmony that had been avoided three bars earlier. Since the music must remain in the home key, the six-four ends up functioning as a most unusual, but comprehensible, pre-dominant substitute within the ECP of C major.[119] The resolution of the suspension in measure 290 also brings a number of chromatic alterations in this and the following bar (D♭ to D♮, B♭ to B♮), which do not overly disrupt the sense of pre-dominant prolongation.[120] The progression then continues on to stage 2b with VII$^7$/V at measure 292 and the arrival on the dominant (with six-four embellishment) two bars later, thus suggesting imminent closure for the subordinate theme.

Beginning with the upbeat to measure 295, the music ceases to correspond with that of the exposition and thus must be heard as initiating the coda, even though the recapitulation, like the exposition, has not brought a final PAC for its subordinate theme.[121] Indeed, the ongoing ECP continues into the coda by prolonging stage 3a, the cadential six-four, for eight bars, during which we hear what sounds like a new four-measure presentation (mm. 295–98), which itself is immediately repeated. To speak of a presentation means that the cadential six-four achieved at measure 294 must be reinterpreted as a prolongational, tonic six-four. As a result, and in light of what transpires, the ongoing ECP must be abandoned, though in a most unconventional way.

A subsequent continuation (mm. 303–305) sees the harmonies move off from the dominant pedal and become more active. At measure 306, the bass has regained ③ to support a diminished-seventh harmony. Earlier, at both measures 278 and 286, the same sonority functioned as a secondary dominant of II; here, it is reinterpreted enharmonically to tonicize IV (along with an intervening V$^6_5$/IV in m. 307) in order to initiate a new stage-1 variant of another ECP. The subdominant at measure 308 then receives significant expansion, after which the music seems desperately trying to close by means of the percussive V and I chords beginning at measure 312. The effort fails, however, as the dominant of measure 317 wins out in the end. As a result, this first coda theme ends noncadentially (like the previous subordinate theme of the recapitulation).

The subsequent "call to arms," given first by the bassoons and then by the horns, initiates a second coda theme, which takes place over a dominant pedal. Once more, the cadential six-four must ultimately be seen as a tonic, to provide the required harmonic support for the presentation beginning at this point (m. 318). And again, the ongoing ECP of coda theme 1 would seem to be abandoned, somewhat like what happened at measure 294. As the new tune is further developed by the winds at measure 322, we find the familiar rocking on the tonic via a neighboring V$^4_2$, the conventional sign for the beginning of yet another ECP. This one is also abandoned when, at the end of measure 332, the pre-dominant VII$^6_5$/V (⑥) moves to V$^6$ (⑦) and I (⑧). The rather feeble compact progression that follows can hardly do the trick, so when the cadence is evaded, a one-more-time technique repeats the entire sentential structure.[122]

---

117. See again the similar situation in the First Symphony's subordinate theme 1 (Ex. 5.67a, mm. 69–77), where a new cadential unit comprises a sentential structure.

118. To save space, this example omits the whole first part of the theme and begins with the first evaded cadence at m. 273; as well, a large-scale repetition (mm. 319–35, 336–49) is placed within double-bar repeat signs rather than being written out, as in the original score.

119. Though remote, a B♭ harmony can be understood as a submediant substitute for a D-minor pre-dominant in C major (i.e., VI/II). We will see a similar pre-dominant substitute in the finale of the Ninth Symphony (Ex. 5.76d, m. 883).

120. To be sure, the leading tone B♮ in m. 291 does not normally belong in a pre-dominant, but the resulting diminished triad is a simplified version of a °7-PD, a harmony we have seen on other occasions (e.g., Ex. 5.23, m. 6).

---

121. I present my rationale for locating the start of any sonata-form coda at that point where the music of the recapitulation stops corresponding to the exposition in *CF*, 181, and *ACF*, 526–27.

122. Here we find a true exception to the rule that a one-more-time repetition does not back up to the beginning of the thematic process. We can still note, however, that the tonic six-four supporting the presentation (mm. 318–21) hardly represents a stable sense of initiating function.

At measure 350, the cadential progression is about to be abandoned, as before, but now something new happens. Whereas the bass line of all the previous ECPs approached the dominant from below, starting with ③, the new ECP begins with a stage 1 that tonicizes IV at measure 350 with $V^4_2$/IV over ♭⑦. The bass then descends to ♭⑥ (holding IV⁶, borrowed from the minor mode), which in turn moves down a half step to the cadential dominant.

Although this cadence too is evaded (m. 353), the excitement generated by the tempo acceleration (*sempre piu Allegro*) as the progression is repeated suggests that maybe this new approach to the dominant might succeed where the other attempts had failed. Indeed, after a second evasion in measure 357, the momentum for cadence becomes overwhelming, and the dominant finally achieves a root-position tonic at the *Presto* of measure 362. Here,

EXAMPLE 5.71B. Beethoven, Symphony No. 5 in C Minor, Op. 67, iv, mm. 273–365.

EXAMPLE 5.71B. Continued

then, is the first authentic cadence since the beginning of the subordinate theme over one hundred bars earlier.

As far as I am aware, this symphony brings the most expansive series of cadential progressions within the classical repertory. One mechanism that Beethoven exploits to create such expansions is the conversion of a cadential six-four into a prolongational tonic six-four, such that the new presentations in measures 295 and 318, which mark the onsets of the two coda themes can also be heard, more broadly, to assimilate themselves (because of the sustained dominant pedal) to the ongoing cadential functions (mm. 286–302 and mm. 306–62).[123] As well, he is able to build cadential areas of such enormous scope by drawing upon a wide range of harmonic variants to the cadential progression itself. Moreover, the choice of harmonic variants is far from arbitrary, but rather is related to particular compositional goals and modes of expression. He thus uses specific diminished-sevenths and unusual six-four sonorities to help forge connections among events separated in time. And when at the end he introduces the descending bass motion ♭⑦–♭⑥–⑤, along with harmonies borrowed from the minor mode, he replays one final time the large-sale progression from C minor to C major that represents the fundamental modal drama of the entire symphony.[124]

### 5.6.5. Symphony No. 6 in F ("Pastoral"), Op. 68, iv, Subordinate Theme

Whereas many cases of notable ECPs involve a significant degree of chromaticism, the subordinate theme in the first movement of Beethoven's "Pastoral" Symphony is especially interesting due to a kind of extreme simplification in the constituent harmonies of its cadential area (Ex. 5.72a). The opening twenty measures of the theme (not shown) consist of a series of four-measure "snippets" that are presented in the manner of a musical round; the supporting harmonies are entirely prolongational of root-position tonic. From a functional point of view, these measures project a general sense of formal initiation, since we cannot quite speak of distinct basic or contrasting ideas. A continuation emerges at measure 87 (shown at the start of Ex. 5.72a), in which the surface rhythm accelerates via the accompanimental sixteenth notes and the bass line becomes more active and directional.[125] In measures 87–92, the bass rises ⑦–①–②, thus implying that it may well reach ③ at measure 93, which brings a complete change in material.[126] Indeed, if Beethoven had continued the bass up to ③, that pitch would have supported a I⁶, which would conventionally have projected the start of an ECP. Instead, the tonic remains in root position until its move to the subdominant at measure 96, after which IV returns to I (m. 98) in a manner that seems prolongational. I would propose, however, that we can identify the onset of an ECP at measure 93, with the first I and IV constituting stages 1 and 2 of the progression.

With stage 3a, measure 98, we encounter a particularly interesting situation: recognizing that a cadential six-four not only can be understood as a dominant harmony with double suspensions, but also can be considered a tonic in second inversion, Beethoven "re-inverts" the cadential six-four by placing it in root position and then follows it with a normal stage-3b dominant proper in the following bar.[127] The upshot of these harmonic manipulations is an ECP built exclusively out of root-position harmonies. Indeed, a simple reconstruction bringing a standard cadential bass line could easily have been set against the melody (Ex. 5.72b).

With this understanding of the cadential harmonies at play in this passage, let us look more carefully at the actual cadential articulations effected by the progression (refer back to Ex. 5.72a). At measure 99 a penultimate dominant resolves to a root-position tonic on the downbeat of measure 100; as well, the first oboe, which has been playing the upper line since measure 97, concludes its melody on E (3̂) at the same downbeat. The conditions are thus ripe for an IAC. Yet at this moment, the upper strings, led by the first violins, bring back the very opening of the cadential unit (fr. m. 93), beginning on G (5̂). Given the sudden change to a *fortissimo* dynamics and a tutti strings instrumentation, along with a turning back to the start of the cadential function, a sense of evaded cadence and one-more-time technique is strongly projected.[128] When this second attempt for a cadence reaches measure 107, the oboe's completion of its melody on 3̂ is no longer obliterated by a *fortissimo* entrance of the strings; as a result, we can clearly hear an IAC on the downbeat of measure 107. At this point, the music brings a varied repeat of the second phrase of the melody for another try at full cadential closure, but again, the line is diverted up to 3̂ for a second IAC at measure 111. In the last phrase of the theme (mm. 112–15), and for the first time in the cadential area, Beethoven finally allows the harmonies to break free from their obsessive placement in root position. In measure 112, the subdominant shifts to its first inversion, and the same thing happens to the tonic of the following bar. In fact, this touching upon I⁶ in the second half measure 113 creates the brief impression of a compact cadential progression embedded within the ECP. Beethoven's motivation here is likely due to his wanting to create a greater sense of harmonic momentum in the final drive to the PAC, aided in that effort by an acceleration of the note values from eighth notes to triplets.

---

123. Such a global perspective, of course, ends up denying the sense of abandoned cadence that I proposed as a means of permitting the coda themes to project their own initiations. In other words, the cadential abandonment operates a lower structural level than the cadential expansions just identified for mm. 286–302 and mm. 306–62. (Moreover, I have not found an entirely satisfactory way of annotating these broader expansions on the musical score.)

124. As we will see below, Beethoven re-enacts a similar change in bass-line direction along with a modal shift in the finale of the Ninth Symphony, sec. 5.6.8.

125. The three snippets of the initiating passage (labeled "x," "y," and "z") remain sounding throughout the continuation.

126. Supporting that implication even more is how snippet "z" leaps up from ② to ④ (middle of m. 92), thus encircling a potential ③ for the downbeat of the next bar.

---

127. On the idea of re-inverting a cadential six-four (promoted by Rothstein and Cutler), see Chapter 4, sec. 4.3.4 and note 85.

128. Alternatively, we could consider the entrance of the violins on 5̂ at m. 100 to create a "covered" IAC; see Chapter 3, sec. 3.4.2.3.

EXAMPLE 5.72. Beethoven, Symphony No. 6 in F ("Pastoral"), Op. 68, i, (a) mm. 87–115; (b) reconstruction of mm. 93–100.

Looking over the cadential area as a whole, we see four attempts to close the subordinate theme: the first is evaded, the second two are IACs, and the fourth one reaches its PAC goal. And until the final bars, every harmony stands solidly in root position. It is not difficult to understand Beethoven's harmonic usage in a work that Frank Kirby situates within a tradition of *sinfonia caracteristica*.[129] One of the conventional devices for projecting a pastoral affect in eighteenth-century music involves an emphasis on root-position harmonies, especially as a drone. As Kirby and many others have noted, Beethoven employs root-position harmonies in prominent ways throughout the entire symphony. That he also extends this technique to the cadential progression of the subordinate theme follows directly from the aesthetic values he wishes to convey in this especially "characteristic" piece.[130]

---

129. F. E. Kirby, "Beethoven's Pastoral Symphony as a 'Sinfonia Caracteristica.'"

---

130. In the trio section of the scherzo (third movement), mm. 103–106, Beethoven again employs root-position harmonies (①–⑤–⑤–①) for the cadential progression, where he could have used a more conventional bass line (③–④–⑤–①).

### 5.6.6. Symphony No. 7 in A, Op. 92, i, Coda Theme

The coda theme from the first movement of the Seventh Symphony brings what may be the longest rocking on the tonic (22 measures) as well as the longest *individual* ECP (31 mm.) in the classical repertory. Before looking at the coda, however, let me offer a couple of points about the ECP ending the subordinate theme in the recapitulation (see Ex. 5.73a).[131] First, the ECP begins (m. 370) with tonic in root position, not with the more anticipated I⁶; we will see a consequence of this harmonic choice shortly. Second, since this is a subordinate theme, we are expecting the ECP to yield a PAC; but elided with the authentic cadence (m. 376) comes a return of main-theme material for the closing section, which starts on $\hat{5}$ (indeed, this scale degree is highly emphasized throughout the symphony).[132] As a result, we might wonder if this is an IAC. As discussed in Chapter 3, I have proposed that this cadence type almost always ends on the third degree and generally found various ways to account for those that seem to end on $\hat{5}$. Here, I believe, we encounter an excellent example of a covered PAC (covered by $\hat{5}$). Otherwise, we must then recognize the unusual situation of a sonata-form subordinate theme closing with an IAC, such as we saw in connection with the "Hammerklavier" sonata in Example 5.14. For the symphony, on the contrary, I prefer the covered cadence interpretation, though the IAC option is also plausible.

Following the end of the recapitulation, a coda theme begins directly with a sequential continuation, one that sees the bass descend stepwise to a I⁶₄ over ⑤ (Ex. 5.73b, m. 399). (Given the sequential nature of the progression leading into this six-four, we are unlikely to think of it as an embellished cadential dominant.) When the bass then descends one step further to ④ (m. 401), V⁴₂ initiates a rocking on the tonic, I⁶ (m. 402), which continues on for 22 measures (Ex. 5.73b shows only the first ten bars). During this rocking, the rhythmic activity within the two-measure unit embracing the V⁴₂ and the I⁶ gradually accelerates. Starting at measures 409–10 (not shown), and continuing on for an additional twelve bars, the texture becomes progressively thicker and the sound intensity increases. At the climax of the rocking (see Ex. 5.73c, m. 423), an orchestral tutti *fortissimo* brings I⁶ alone for two bars, after which the ECP continues with the pre-dominant IV (m. 425) and a cadential six-four (m. 427). In light of the powerful emphasis on I⁶ in the coda, we now appreciate why Beethoven chose to begin the ECPs of the subordinate theme with a root-position tonic.

The ongoing coda ECP eventually sees the bass push down to ♯④ to support V⁶/V (Ex. 5.73d, m. 432), ♮④, for V⁴₂, and it eventually reaches ③ at measure 436 to initiate a series of relatively compact deceptive progressions. It is difficult to say whether at measure 432 we are dealing here with a case of cadential deception, evasion, or abandonment, though the latter option seems most appropriate in the given context.[133] The subsequent deviations at measures 438 and 440 are clearly deceptive. Finally, the third compact progression in measures 440–42 yields a closing cadence at measure 442. Unlike the earlier PAC ending the subordinate theme, here we can speak more confidently of a covered cadence, given the clear resolution of the first violins to $\hat{1}$, covered by $\hat{5}$ in the woodwinds. Though the details of harmony and cadence in the coda's ECP are interesting in their own right, the aesthetic effect of this massive expansion clearly resides in the juggernaut *crescendo* that it projects, an orchestral gesture that fully rivals, and perhaps even pre-dates, Rossini's famous exploitation of this device.[134]

### 5.6.7. Symphony No. 9 in D Minor ("Choral"), Op. 125, i, Main Theme

Hearing the extraordinary opening ("the journey out of the sphere of the inaudible into that of the audible") as a thematic introduction,[135] I understand the main theme (Ex. 5.74a) to begin at measure 17 with an extended three-measure basic idea matched by a three-measure contrasting idea to create a compound basic idea. At the start of the continuation (m. 23), the final two bars of the contrasting idea are sequenced up a fourth such that the melody reaches its high point on $\hat{6}$. The IV harmony of measure 24 is then quickly replaced by a substitute, root-position Neapolitan that is syncopated and sustained, during which time the melody steps down to the leading tone ($\hat{7}$) on the downbeat of measure 27. At this moment, the Neapolitan resolves, most unusually, to VII⁶₅ over ②. A root-position Neapolitan occurs rarely in the classical style, but when it does, it almost always resolves with the bass leaping down a diminished third (♭②–⑦) to support V⁶, which then resolves to I in order to complete a tonic prolongation.[136] So when the bass moves from ♭② up to ♮②, it seems well advised to consider the implications of a *rising* bass line for what transpires in the rest of the theme.

---

131. Within the recapitulation, this passage starts with a one-more-time repeat of the cadential phrase, which follows upon an evasion of the same phrase in mm. 364–69, not shown.

132. See, e.g., the discussion of the slow movement's main theme in Chapter 3, Ex. 3.83.

133. Normally, an abandoned cadential progression does not see the cadential six-four locked into place, but given the absence of a dominant proper, we can perhaps find here an exception to the rule. For that matter, the two abandoned cadences identified in the finale of the Fifth Symphony (mm. 294 and 318) are similarly exceptional.

134. The Seventh Symphony was composed in 1811–12, just around the time that Rossini's first mature overtures began to appear. Philip Gossett sees the overture to Rossini's *L'inganno felice* (1812) as "the first overture to have a proper crescendo," though he notes that the crescendos in Rossini's overtures around this time are relatively modest in scope ("The Overtures of Rossini," 17).

135. William Kinderman, *Beethoven*, 267.

136. See, for instance, Beethoven, Piano Sonata in D Minor ("Tempest"), Op. 31, no. 2, iii, mm. 10–12.

5.6. EXPANDED CADENTIAL PROGRESSIONS IN BEETHOVEN'S SYMPHONIES

EXAMPLE 5.73. Beethoven, Symphony No. 7 in A, Op. 92, i, (a) mm. 370–76; (b) mm. 399–408; (c) mm. 423–27; (d) mm. 432–42.

EXAMPLE 5.74. Beethoven, Symphony No. 9 in D Minor ("Choral"), Op. 125, i, (a) mm. 17–35; (b) reconstruction of mm. 27–32.

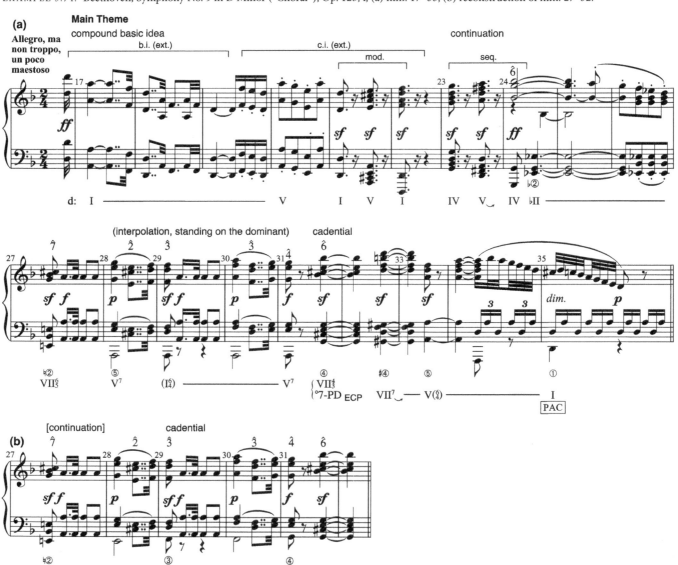

The only precedent I know for this odd resolution of ♭II, which permits the bass to ascend to ②, occurs at the end of the *minore* theme of Haydn's great set of keyboard variations in F Minor (Ex. 5.75a). Here, an ECP begins with a chromatic V⁷/IV (upbeat to m. 25) resolving to IV. The progression then continues quickly with an accented and syncopated ♭II, which is sustained (not literally, but in our imagination) to support a high melodic D♭ (6̂) and its arpeggiated descent to 7̂ (middle of m. 27). At that point, the Neapolitan resolves to VII⁶₅, thus abandoning the ECP due to the diminished-seventh substituting for an *inverted* dominant seventh, V⁴₃. This entire configuration is remarkably similar to Beethoven's gesture in measures 24–27 (Ex. 5.74a),[137] though there the melody descends stepwise from the high 6̂. In Haydn's theme, the bass then steps up to ③ for a cadential I⁶, after which a concluding PAC shortly follows.[138]

Beethoven's continuation, on the contrary, is more complex. Returning to Example 5.74a, we see that the VII⁶₅ of measure 27 is followed by a four-measure standing on the dominant, after which the bass ⑤ steps down to ④ at measure 31 to initiate a standard cadential bass line ④–♯④–⑤–①. Before considering the

---

137. I have no knowledge of whether or not Beethoven was familiar with this theme (though presumably he was), nor am I suggesting that he deliberately modeled it on that of his predecessor.

138. Haydn's use here of a rising stepwise bass, from ♭② to ⑤, is perhaps owing to a somewhat premature bass-line gap that he opens up from ① to ③ at the very beginning of the theme (see Ex. 5.75b), well before a cadential I⁶ would ordinarily be expressed. Following this gap, the harmonies continue to be cadential in nature, leading eventually to a premature dominant arrival (m. 5). So at the end of the theme (Ex. 5.75a), Haydn ingeniously fills in this third gap with the root-position Neapolitan (♭②) and its strange resolution to VII⁶₅ (♮②).

EXAMPLE 5.75. Haydn, Piano Variations in F Minor, H. XVII:6, (a) mm. 24–29; (b) mm. 1–6.

unusual formal placement of the standing on the dominant in the middle of this theme, let us observe some harmonic details of the ECP in measures 31–35. First, ④ supports a diminished-seventh sonority that has two harmonic functions. In light of where the harmony comes from, we can hear it as VII$^4_3$, still participating in the standing on the dominant. Looking forward, however, it now becomes a pre-dominant diminished seventh (see the earlier discussion of Ex. 5.23, m. 6), resolving to a stage-2b VII$^7$/V over ♯④. Following the arrival of the cadential six-four in the middle of measure 33, the texture and dynamics collapse down to I at measure 35, entirely bypassing the dominant proper. Although this peculiar harmonic situation is not without precedent, it is unusual enough to prompt our seeking an explanation for this harmonic anomaly.[139] First, the unusual standing on the dominant in the middle of the theme has perhaps "used up" that harmony, and thus to mitigate redundancy, Beethoven bypasses the dominant proper in the ECP. A second, and more compelling, reason may be found in the textural and dynamic collapse that occurs from the cadential six-four to the tonic in root position. For within that gesture, Beethoven already brings in the open-fifths (D–A, upper part of the left hand) from the thematic introduction, the same sonority that resumes immediately following the PAC at measure 35. To achieve that effect, he needs to banish the pitches C♯ and E from the accompanimental voices, thus eliminating the dominant proper.

Let us now turn to the dominant prolongation of measures 27–31. Rarely do we find a standing on the dominant occurring within the formal continuation of a simple theme, for the resulting harmonic stasis in antithetical to the nature of a continuation.[140] And so this passage might better be understood as an interpolation, one that interrupts the logical succession from the continuation to the cadential function. One additional consideration, however, needs still to be taken into account. As we saw in the Haydn theme (Ex. 5.75a, which I am taking as a template for understanding Beethoven's theme), the VII$^6_5$ over ② (m. 27) moves to I$^6$ over ③ before reaching the pre-dominant ④. Beethoven, in contrast, brings a root-position prolongation of V standing between ② (m. 27) and ④ (m. 31), such that the cadential progression starts first with the stage 2 pre-dominant. In other words, the theme has skipped over an initial tonic built over ③.

One element of the standing on the dominant, however, prompts further speculation, namely, the six-four harmony in measures 29–30. On the one hand, this sonority participates as a neighboring embellishment within the dominant prolongation. On the other hand, if we see the harmony as having a *tonic* function in its own right, then we could regard it as a stand-in for stage 1 of the ECP. In this interpretation, we would understand the low A in measures 28–31 not as the genuine bass voice, but rather as an embellishment lying *below* the "real bass," which, as reconstructed Example 5.74b, moves stepwise ascending, ②–③–④.

---

139. A similar omission of the dominant proper arises in the finale of Beethoven's Eighth Symphony, mm. 321–22 and 350–51. There, it is much more difficult to account for this exceptional circumstance.

140. One earlier case arises in Mozart's Piano Sonata in C Minor, K. 457, i, mm. 9–13.

EXAMPLE 5.76A. Beethoven, Symphony No. 9 in D Minor ("Choral"), Op. 125, iv, mm. 809–15.

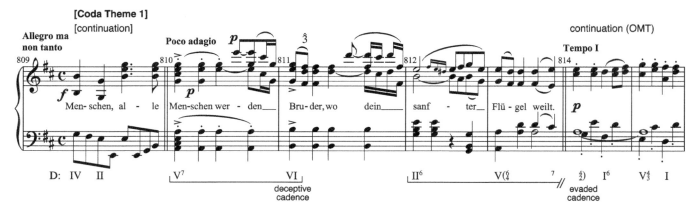

An additional factor, a more technical one, may also explain what is happening here. If the normal procedure (i.e., the way Haydn does it) would see the VII$^6_5$ moving to I$^6$, the bass line (②–③, ③–④) would create parallel octaves ($\hat{2}$–$\hat{3}$, $\hat{3}$–$\hat{4}$) with the melodic ideas that Beethoven uses in measures 28–31. In short, Beethoven finds a clever way of accommodating his melodic material within a harmonic and bass-line syntax that is unusual, but ultimately understandable. I concede, of course, that this is a highly speculative reading, but it is one worth considering, not for the purposes of downplaying the unusual harmonic-formal use of the standing on the dominant and the seeming passing over of the initial I$^6$, but rather just the opposite, to highlight how exceptional, yet convincing, are Beethoven's compositional decisions in this most unusual and complicated main theme.

## 5.6.8. Symphony No. 9 in D Minor ("Choral"), Op. 125, iv, Coda

The finale of Beethoven's Ninth Symphony has generated a substantial literature devoted to its *formal* organization.[141] This is not the place to rehash these many opposing perspectives, but in my view (shared, of course, by many), the *genre* most operative in this movement is that of theme and variations.[142] To be sure, the movement presents formal situations, such as interpolated recitatives and fugal passages, that transcend the simple case of a theme followed by a series of variations employing the same basic phrase-structural organization. Yet earlier variations by the classical composers (and especially Beethoven's "Eroica" Variations, Op. 25, and the finale of the "Eroica" symphony) provide precedents for almost all of the formal techniques used in the Ninth Symphony's finale. What is also clear is that its final two sections constitute a *coda*,[143] which features harmonic, tonal, and phrase-structural plans that are largely congruent with how an instrumental coda of any classical movement would be formally arranged.[144] And given the loose organization typically associated with coda themes, it is not surprising that ECPs play an important role.[145]

The coda (section 10) begins with a brief instrumental introduction (mm. 763–66, not shown). The first coda theme brings a broad presentation (mm. 767–82, "*Freude, Tochter aus Elysium*") and a highly extended continuation (mm. 783–801, "*Deine, Zauber...*") that leads to an internal HC and standing on the dominant (mm. 801–805). There follows a new continuation built on a descending-thirds sequence (mm. 806–11, "*Alle Menschen...*"), while the shift in tempo to *Poco adagio* brings a quick deceptive cadence ($\hat{3}$); see Example 5.76a, measures 810–811, followed by an evaded cadence at measure 814.

An enormous one-more-time repetition (not shown) brings back the first continuation (less extended this time), the internal HC and standing on the dominant, and the new continuation. The final link of the descending-thirds sequence, II (see Ex. 5.76b, mm. 830–31), undergoes a modal shift when its third is raised by a half step, thus facilitating a modulation to B major (HK: VI). An ECP, with a prominent expansion of stages 2 and 3, confirms this new key with a PAC (m. 841).[146] Another modal shift returns the

---

141. Two of the more important analyses are James Webster, "The Form of the Finale of Beethoven's Ninth Symphony," and Ernest H. Sanders, "The Sonata-Form Finale of Beethoven's Ninth Symphony."

142. My rationale for this viewpoint involves far too many considerations to be presented here; fortunately, my phrase-structural observations on the coda are not dependent upon any particular overarching formal or generic interpretation of the movement as a whole.

---

143. I am adopting Webster's very helpful eleven-section outline of the overall form: the coda embraces section 10, *Allegro ma non tanto*, mm. 763–850, and section 11, *Prestissimo*, mm. 851–940 ("Form of the Finale," 30, Table 1, and 32–33, Table 2).

144. On the structure of coda themes, which in their looser organization are essentially like subordinate themes, see *CF*, 183–86, and *ACF*, 529–37.

145. From its first appearance, the final phrase of the "Joy" theme has the potential to be realized as an ECP (as is the final phrase of the "Prometheus" theme in the Eroica finale). Perhaps to avoid too great a redundancy, as the harmonic framework of the theme is repeated in the variations, Beethoven does not provide such an ECP harmonization for this final phrase until the seventh variation (mm. 367–74).

146. The PAC in B major is atypical, since codas rarely modulate out of the home key. This cadential articulation, though, serves a number of motivic purposes, largely related to the "B(♭)–A" motive that is exploited

EXAMPLE 5.76B. Beethoven, Symphony No. 9 in D Minor ("Choral"), Op. 125, iv, mm. 830–42.

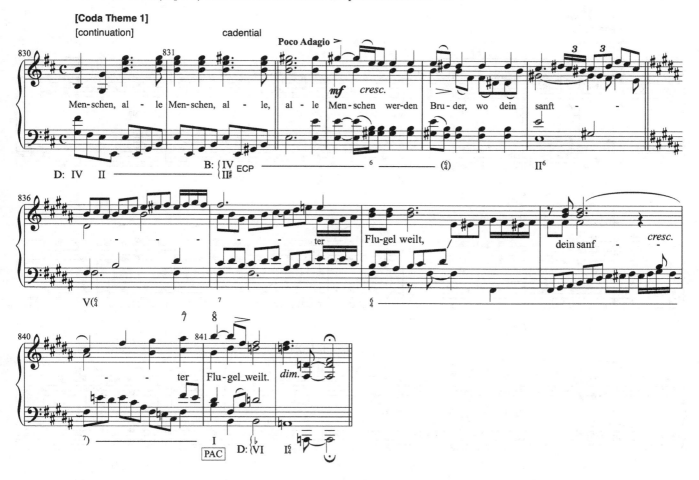

music to the home key of D major for the next section of the coda. Note that the ECP in this example begins with stage 2 (m. 831), thus bypassing an initial tonic. This maneuver is appropriate considering the extensive tonic emphasis accorded to the first continuation ("*Deine Zauber*").

Other than the modulation to the VI region, everything we have seen thus far is part and parcel of techniques used to build a coda theme. With section 11 of the movement, a second coda theme is prepared by an extended thematic introduction (not shown), which oscillates between the pitches A and B, a principal motive throughout the movement. The theme then begins with a four-measure antecedent phrase (Ex. 5.76c, mm. 851–54) ending with a quick HC; the phrase is then repeated by the chorus (mm. 855–58, "*Seid umschlungen ...*"). Taking the two antecedents together, and thereby demoting the two HCs to ones of limited scope, we could recognize a compound presentation initiating

this second coda theme.[147] Following the second HC, the antecedent is extended by a varied repeat of its contrasting idea (mm. 859–60), after which a new passage clearly projects an extended rocking on the tonic (mm. 861–69), thus signaling the onset of an ECP.[148] Though the formal context at this point would most accurately be labeled continuation⇒cadential, following as it does upon a presentation,[149] the sense of harmonic and motivic stasis puts much more weight on the cadential component than the continuational one (which I indicate by the parentheses around

---

throughout the movement at many pitch, harmonic, and tonal levels. As well, this cadence sees the solo soprano breaking through the high $A_5$ ceiling, which has largely capped all of the vocal writing, in order to reach $B_5$, the highest vocal pitch used in the movement (that pitch having only appeared twice before as an embellishment of the high A in mm. 309–10).

147. Such a compound presentation, made up of two antecedent phrases, arises rarely in the classical style (for one such case, see Ex. 3.97), but becomes more prominent in nineteenth-century works. It is even possible for the component units of the presentation to bring differentiated cadences (e.g., an HC followed by an IAC, both of limited scope), thus yielding a structure that Steven Vande Moortele calls a "large-scale sentence with periodic presentation" ("In Search of Romantic Form," 412–17).

148. I am including m. 869 as part of the ECP's stage 1, even though the bass steps down from ③ to ①. This move avoids potential parallel octaves with the upper voice were the measure to be harmonized by $V_2^4$–$I^6$. An alternative reading finds the ECP being abandoned only then to be followed by a relatively compact cadential progression in mm. 870–71. Given the fast tempo and uniform texture of the passage, I find this interpretation to be overly fussy and thus prefer the analysis annotated in the score.

149. See *CF*, 45–47, and *ACF*, 60–63.

EXAMPLE 5.76C. Beethoven, Symphony No. 9 in D Minor ("Choral"), Op. 125, iv, mm. 851–76.

"continuation"). And this cadential emphasis makes sense given the extensive continuational units in the previous coda theme. The rocking then leads at measure 870 to a quick pre-dominant II⁶, a dominant, and a subsequent evaded cadence. The one-more-time technique repeats the last portion of the ECP and achieves PAC closure at measure 876.

A third coda theme (Ex. 5.76d) now brings back the motives from the beginning of the second theme, but rather than being fashioned into a clear initiating unit, a two-bar model (mm. 877–78) is immediately sequenced up a step to tonicize II, thus launching this new theme directly with continuation function. What follows at measure 880, with the words "*diesen Kuss der ganzen Welt*," brings a clear case of harmonic expansion: a V⁷/II continues to tonicize the supertonic, after which a deceptive resolution (VI/II) brings a C-major triad (m. 883). This harmony then leads at measure 885 to what we probably would think to be an F-major triad, ♭III, even though the harmonic fifth is not literally sounding (though we could certainly retain the pitch C in our memory from the prior harmony). This F dyad then allows us to reinterpret the prior C major as a secondary dominant (V/♭III). Immediately thereafter, in the second half of measure 885, the pitch D is added into the mix, yielding a tonic harmony (borrowed from the minor mode), whose possible cadential meaning is further suggested by the dominant in the next bar. This short authentic cadential progression (I–V) is then evaded, thus bringing a one-more-time repetition of the entire "*diesen Kuss*" passage.[150]

Before preceding any further, let us step back and consider the constituent harmonies of this passage in greater detail. Along the lines of the analysis I have just presented, the first three harmonies (V⁷/II, ♭VI/II⇒V/♭III, and ♭III) would most readily be associated with a formal *continuation*, due to their relative instability in relation to the home key of D major, and thus these harmonies could serve to extend the short continuation from the beginning of the theme. Two other aspects could point us in a different direction, however: (1) the harmonic expansion—especially seeing as the harmonic rhythm of a continuation normally brings acceleration, not such a marked deceleration; and (2) the simple melodic descent from $\hat{5}$ to $\hat{2}$, promising to end on $\hat{1}$. Both of these aspects suggest that we consider the harmonies to be *cadential*, even though they are by no means obviously so (save for the I♭ and V already identified). In particular, we can observe that the

---

150. That the I–V progression is not signaling an HC is clear by the text "*der ganzen Welt*," which concludes on *Welt*, not *ganzen*.

EXAMPLE 5.76D. Beethoven, Symphony No. 9 in D Minor ("Choral"), Op. 125, iv, mm. 877–903.

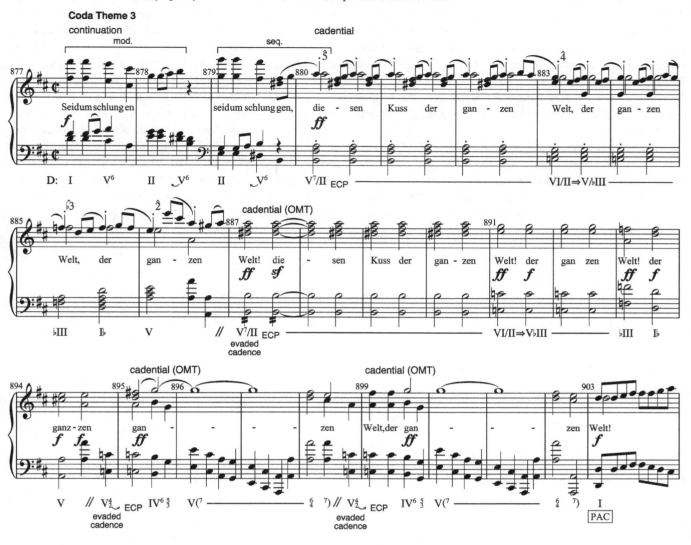

EXAMPLE 5.76E. Beethoven, Symphony No. 9 in D Minor ("Choral"), Op. 125, iv, schematic version of "Diesen Küss" passage.

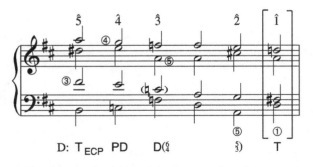

harmonic progression (see the schematic layout in Ex. 5.76e, which includes the implied resolution to tonic) not only supports a cadential soprano pattern $\hat{5}/\hat{4}/\hat{3}$-$\hat{2}$-[$\hat{1}$], but also contains among its harmonic members all of the pitches of a standard bass line, ③-④-⑤-[①], located, of course, in upper voices (until the final ⑤-①, which belongs to the bass). In this light, we can consider the functions of these harmonies as follows: the B seventh ($V^7/$ II), a chromatic alteration of VI, an initial-tonic substitute; the C triad (♭VI/II), a pre-dominant substitute;[151] the F dyad and D triads, cadential six-four substitutes (i.e., "re-inversions" of a "tonic" six-four); the A triad, the dominant proper. From this perspective, Beethoven has written the most original, and, I venture to say, entirely unique ECP in the tonal literature. We must, of course, seek some kind of explanation for his harmonic choices here, and the obvious place to look is at the text. For by setting *Welt!* (world) to the C triad (m. 883) and F dyad (m. 885), he clearly gives this most significant word—the Ode to Joy being addressed to the entire world ("*Millionen*," "*alle Menschen*")—a striking "color" in the midst of what up to this point has been a predominantly D *major* diatonicism for most of the coda. With the evaded cadence he even sets *Welt* to the bright B-seventh harmony (m. 887). A second consideration is the matter of the shift to the minor mode, which accounts for the C triad, the F dyad,

---

151. We saw a similar pre-dominant substitute in an ECP from the finale of the Fifth Symphony (Ex. 5.71b, m. 289).

and the D triad. Given an overall trajectory from D minor in the first two movements to D major in the finale, this late reference to the minor mode recreates at the very end of the work a similar move from minor to major. Recall that we saw this same process occurring in Beethoven's only other minor-mode symphony, the Fifth, in the discussion of the ECPs of that work's finale (see again Ex. 5.71b, m. 350ff.). His reworking of this idea in the Ninth, now in the context of an extremely unusual ECP, makes full compositional sense.

The one-more-time repetition of the "*diesen Kuss*" passage creates another evaded cadence (Ex. 5.76d, m. 894), this time followed by a new ECP, beginning with a stage-1 chromatic substitute, $V_2^4/IV$, resolving to $IV^6$ for stage 2. Note that neither of these two harmonies were used in any of the ECPs of the coda, thus showing the composer's continued sensitivity to Ratz's principle of "aesthetic economy."[152] The ECP quickly moves to the dominant proper (m. 896), at first bypassing a cadential six-four, though that harmony appears immediately before yet another evaded cadence (the third one in a row) at the upbeat to measure 899. The one-more-time technique uses the new ECP yet again, which is finally allowed to achieve PAC closure for the third coda theme at measure 903. What follows (not shown) is a fourth coda theme, this one ending with a compact cadence (mm. 918–19) employing the simplest cadential progression I–IV–$V^7$–I within the slow-moving *Maestoso* passage.[153] Looking back over the coda as a whole, we must marvel at the way in which Beethoven caps his symphonic oeuvre with a most astonishing set of cadential expansions, ones rivaled in scope only by the coda to the finale of the Fifth Symphony.

---

152. It so happens, as well, that the very first ECP in the finale (the one closing variation no. 7, mm. 367–74) begins with the same tonicization of the subdominant ($V_2^4/IV$–$IV^6$), thus bringing the harmonic usage of the ECPs full circle at the very end of the movement.

153. This slower *Maestoso*, ending with a home-key PAC, clearly references the two prior *Poco adagio* passages, the first of which (Ex. 5.76a) brings deceptive and evaded cadences and the second (Ex. 5.76b), which concludes with a PAC in the submediant region, thus completing a process of increasing cadential strength among the three passages of slower tempo.

# Part II

# Cadence in Other Tonal Styles

The four chapters of Part II broaden the historical scope of this study by investigating cadential practice in four other style periods of tonal music—the high baroque (e.g., Corelli, Vivaldi, Handel, J. S. Bach), the galant (D. Scarlatti, C. P. E. Bach), the early Romantic (Schubert, Schumann, Chopin, Mendelssohn), and, in the absence of a traditional expression, what might be termed the mid- to late-nineteenth-century style (Liszt, Wagner, Brahms, Bruckner). Each chapter continues to consider the morphology and function of the basic cadence types, along with how cadential deviations and expansions are deployed. The chapters especially consider how cadential usage in these style periods distinguishes itself from that of the classical style, due to the employment of differing compositional techniques in the service of differing aesthetic goals.

# Cadence in the High Baroque

THE CLASSICAL CADENCE, OF COURSE, DID NOT arise in the style period we call "classical" (ca. 1780–1810). Most of its constituent elements and associated techniques were firmly in place by the beginning of the eighteenth century. A good deal of seventeenth-century music also features structures whose morphology and function fall within the category of classical cadences developed in Part I of this study. Indeed, a historical account of the origins of the classical cadence begins many centuries earlier and thus lies considerably beyond the scope of this book. A brief survey, however, will prove useful for a more extensive discussion of cadence in the high-baroque era (ca. 1680–1740).[1]

Early in the history of Western polyphony, medieval theorists recognized that the primary mechanism for obtaining pitch closure entailed the two-voice progression from an imperfect consonance (typically a sixth, sometimes a third) to a perfect octave or unison (Ex. 6.1). At the time, the lowest voice was termed a *tenor*, usually bearing melodic material derived from plainchant. The upper voice was identified by a variety of names (*duplum*, *triplum*, *cantus*, *superius*), but for our purpose I will simply call it a soprano. This *soprano-tenor construct* continued to be defined by theorists well into the Renaissance as the primary means of creating a "perfect cadence."

EXAMPLE 6.1. Two-voice soprano-tenor construct.

---

1. Subsequent references to "baroque" will denote more specifically what many historians speak of as the *high-baroque* period, beginning typically with the works of Corelli and extending through to the mature compositions of Bach and Handel.

EXAMPLE 6.2. Three-voice cadences (from Randel, "Emerging Triadic Tonality," Ex. 1b–e).

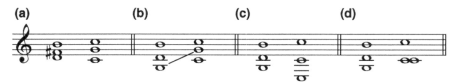

When vocal compositions started to employ more than two voices, the lowest voice continued to be a tenor well into the first half of the fifteenth century, and thus the cadential motion of a sixth expanding to an octave engaged the outer voices of the texture. Around the middle of the fifteenth century, a voice started to be used that normally sounded below the tenor. Originally this voice was identified as a *contratenor*, but eventually the term *bass* came into prominent usage. As Don Randel has ingeniously explained, the prevalent rules of consonance and dissonance, along with those of basic voice leading (esp. prohibited parallel motions), highly constrained the pitch content of this third voice as it engaged the soprano-tenor construct in the perfect cadence.[2] Randel demonstrates that the four cadential options shown in Example 6.2 "are the only possibilities which comply with . . . fifteenth-century rules." Option *a* shows the third voice, an alto, lying between the soprano and tenor, thus creating what later historians would call a "double leading tone" cadence. In option *b*, the third voice appears at first below the tenor, but then leaps an octave above it, so that the moment of cadential arrival finds the tenor continuing to occupy the lowest position in the texture. Option *c* illustrates what happens when the third voice, now a full-fledged bass, is placed a fifth below the tenor and then leaps down a fifth to conclude the cadence. Option *d* is similar, except that the bass leaps up a fourth to double the tenor. The resulting structure of these third and fourth options resembles, of course, the V–I cadence of the tonal era.

Throughout the Renaissance, moments of significant formal closure, especially those cadences found at the end of a major section or of a complete work, usually featured the leaping bass of options *c* and *d*, while the soprano-tenor construct was found in the upper voices, though not necessarily in the literal soprano and tenor. Indeed, a *notional* soprano-tenor structure could also involve the bass, thus yielding a cadence in which the final harmony is approached stepwise in that voice. Such cadences were typically used in interior formal positions and were a precursor to the tonal technique of *prolongational closure* (involving an inverted dominant).[3]

Inasmuch as the *content* of the soprano-tenor construct was not necessarily confined to those specific voices, but could migrate to other voices as well, theorists began to label such content, typically referred to as *clausulae*, in terms of the original voices of the cadence formula. Seventeenth-century German theorists, especially, developed an extensive *Kadenzlehre* (or *Klausellehre*), in which cadences were identified largely on the basis of which clausula appeared in the lowest voice.[4] Thus they recognized "tenor cadences" (*clausula tenorizans*) if the final motion in the bass descends stepwise, or a "soprano cadence" (*clausula cantizans*) if the bass ascends by a step. If the lowest voice descends a fifth (or ascends a fourth), the cadence was considered "perfect," the cadential type most worthy of bringing the strongest sense of closure for a work. Gradually from the sixteenth century through to the earlier part of the seventeenth century, the soprano-tenor construct for modal polyphony gave way to a completely bass-oriented conception of tonal pitch organization, codified by thoroughbass theorists.

Turning now to the central topic of this chapter, cadence in the high-baroque period, I first explore issues associated with the authentic cadence (perfect and imperfect), including its morphology and function, deviation processes (deceptive, evaded, and abandoned), and various modes of cadential extension and expansion. I then consider the half cadence and its deviation (the dominant arrival), along with a variety of other issues associated with cadence and closure: content versus function; postcadential situations, including the "plagal cadence"; and noncadential, prolongational closure. I conclude with a section devoted to a genre especially characteristic of the baroque era—fugue—exploring how cadence operates to effect closure at various levels of formal organization in the fugues of J. S. Bach's *Well-Tempered Clavier* (*WTC*).[5]

---

2. Don M. Randel, "Emerging Triadic Tonality in the Fifteenth Century," 78–79.

3. We can see, therefore, that the idea of a *tonal* cadence involving stepwise motion in the bass voice—a position that I have rejected in this study, as argued vigorously in Part I—reveals a continuity of music-theoretical thought with a long heritage.

4. For more background information, see in Chapter 3, note 27; also see ahead in Chapter 7, sec. 7.1.1.

5. The observations and generalizations offered in this chapter are based on an analysis of representative instrumental works by four major composers of the era: the corpus includes Corelli's Trio Sonatas Op. 1 and 2, Violin Sonatas, Op. 5, and Concerto Grossi, Op. 6; Vivaldi's Violin Concerti, Op. 8; Handel's Concerto Grossi, Op. 6, *Music for the Royal Fireworks*, and *Water Music*; and J. S. Bach's *Well-Tempered Clavier*, *Art of the Fugue*, and *Brandenburg Concertos*. Other individual pieces by these composers (including some vocal compositions) and a handful of works by other composers were examined as well. Needless to say, a broader survey, taking into account more genres and composers, may well modify, or even undermine, some of the conclusions presented here.

# 6.1. Authentic Cadence

## 6.1.1. Perfect Authentic Cadence

Phrase and thematic closure in works of the high baroque is principally achieved by means of the perfect authentic cadence; the imperfect authentic cadence occurs only sporadically. The half cadence appears as well, but not as frequently as in the classical style. The PAC is used, of course, to confirm the home key of the movement, but this cadence type also tends to confirm every other key to which the movement modulates. The home key is almost always re-established at the end of the movement with one or more PACs. Some internal slow movements within an instrumental cycle may literally conclude with an HC, one that normally appears after a PAC has brought full confirmation of the home key; such an HC provides a strong harmonic connection when resolving to tonic at the start of the subsequent fast movement.[6] With the earlier composers of this style period, such as Corelli, PACs saturate the musical texture, and it is possible to find multiple HK: PACs at various points in the movement. Later, such as with Bach and Handel, the tonal organization becomes more regularized, with a fairly systematic move from the home key to a subordinate key and then to one or more development keys, each one of which receives a PAC confirmation. Typically, a single home-key PAC is saved for the very end of the movement.[7]

Even more so than in the classical style, the baroque PAC is a highly conventionalized, relatively compact, harmonic-melodic *formula*. Many of the same basic melodic patterns (predominantly scalar and descending) are found in the upper voices, and the bass line is largely restricted to some standard patterns, including the "classical bass line" ③–④–⑤–①. Rarely can we hear a PAC in isolation and identify it as belonging to a particular work, as we occasionally can with Haydn and Mozart, and fairly often with Beethoven. Even in passages that are formally loose and where a sense of prominent cadential expansion is manifest, the very final gesture will bring a compact PAC of some sort. As we will see throughout this chapter, *retaining the cadential formula* is a guiding principle of baroque compositional practice.

## 6.1.2. Harmonic Content

Despite the variety of harmonic possibilities that the "classical" authentic cadence can employ, it remains useful to identify the prototypical form of that cadence as the progression $I^6$–$II^6$–$V(^6_4{}^7)$–$I$ and to see other options as variants on this basic scheme. Whether the harmonic content of the baroque PAC can be said to exhibit the same degree of conventionality is still an open question, for

EXAMPLE 6.3. Vivaldi, Violin Concerto in E, Op. 8, no. 1 ("Spring"), i, mm. 9–10.

it is not clear that a single progression can be identified as so stylistically defining. To be sure, the final two stages of the cadential progression require the penultimate dominant and final tonic to stand in root position. The cadential six-four, however, is used much less frequently in stage 3 than in the classical period; instead, a simple 4–3 suspension often suffices to embellish the dominant. As for stages 1 and 2, they are not so strongly characterized by a typical harmonic usage. In the baroque, the initial tonic of stage 1, when present, often stands in root position, and the pre-dominant of stage 2 does not so regularly bear $II^6$. In the same stage we sometimes find $IV^7$, whose dissonant seventh resolves when the harmony moves to the dominant.[8] In cadences of the Bach chorales, with their regular melodic descent from $\hat{2}$ to $\hat{1}$, the pre-dominant supporting the second scale degree is usually $II^6_5$ (followed then by V). Neither the dissonant $IV^7$ nor $II^6_5$ is typical of the classical cadence, which tends to favor the consonant $II^6$ or IV triads.

Whereas the simple I–V–I progression appears infrequently as a cadential option later in the eighteenth century, it is regularly employed in cadences of the baroque era. Indeed, this cadence formation was normally the first to be discussed by partimento theorists of the period, who termed it the *cadenza simplice* (simple cadence).[9] Thus the first movement of Vivaldi's "Spring," from *The Four Seasons*, sees every authentic cadence taking this form (Ex. 6.3 shows the first such case), and in the second movement of "Summer," we even find an expanded cadential progression (ECP) using I–V–I (Ex. 6.4).

Another type of embellishment of the cadential dominant became sufficiently widespread as to acquire a distinct name by the partimento theorists—the *cadenza doppia* (double cadence); see Example 6.5a.[10] In this formation, stage 3 consists of four distinct metrical articulations, each containing a specific sonority

---

6. The movements of most multi-movement works in this era normally reside in the same key, so that the dominant of an interior slow movement ending with an HC and the initial tonic of the subsequent movement are most often in the same tonality, and thus strongly connected syntactically.

7. Writing in the 1770s, but reflecting the principles of his teacher, J. S. Bach, Johann Phillip Kirnberger describes quite accurately this tonal-cadential practice (*The Art of Strict Musical Composition*, 112).

8. See ahead by Corelli, Ex. 6.14, m. 49; Ex. 6.15b, m. 58; and by Bach, Ex. 6.19b, m. 21; Ex. 6.53, m. 36.

9. Sanguinetti, *Art of Partimento*, 105–106; Gjerdingen, *Galant Style*, 466.

10. Sanguinetti, *Art of Partimento*, 105–107. I have added my own melodic, harmonic, and cadential annotations to Sanguinetti's examples. Gjerdingen also includes the *cadenza doppia* among his cadential schemata (*Galant Style*, 169, 466). I will thus identify the *cadenza doppia* in my annotations as a schema (i.e., with an upper-case label). For a detailed study of this baroque cadence type, see Johannes Menke, "Die Familie der Cadenza Doppia."

EXAMPLE 6.4. Vivaldi, Violin Concerto in G Minor, Op. 8, no. 2 ("Summer"), i, mm 48–52.

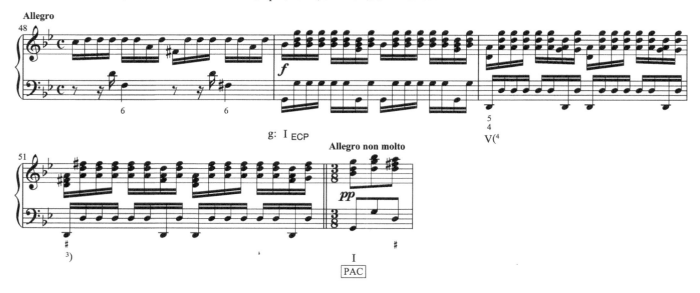

EXAMPLE 6.5. *Cadenza doppia* (from Sanguinetti, *Art of Partimento*, Ex. 9.2d and 9.3b).

as indicated by the figured bass $^5_4 \, ^6_4 \, ^5_4 \, ^5_3$. The first chord may also be a seventh chord ($^7_3$), as in Example 6.5b. Just why this configuration is called a "double" cadence is perhaps not immediately obvious. Presumably, the idea is that two V–I progressions are involved: in the first, stage 3 begins with a dominant appearing on beat 1 and resolving to a metrically weak tonic in second inversion ($I^6_4$); in the second, another dominant takes up beats 3 and 4, resolving to a stage-4 root-position tonic on the downbeat of the following bar. Associated with the *cadenza doppia* is the final two stages of the melodic alto pattern //$\hat{7}$–($\hat{1}$–$\hat{7}$)/$\hat{1}$. This configuration may occur in the highest voice (Ex. 6.5a) but also appears frequently in an inner voice (Ex. 6.5b) with the true soprano voice projecting its conventional scalar descent $\hat{5}$/$\hat{4}$/$\hat{3}$–$\hat{2}$/$\hat{1}$. As we will see in the course of this chapter, the sense of a *cadenza doppia* is often primarily signaled by the alto pattern (in any upper voice), while the cadential harmonies may vary from the strict succession of Example 6.5. One prominent variant sees the cadential six-four "re-inverted" into a root-position tonic (see ahead, Ex. 6.7b). In this case, the sense of a "double"

cadence (V–I, V–I supporting $\hat{7}$–$\hat{1}$, $\hat{7}$–$\hat{1}$) is even more strongly expressed.

To be sure, the "classical" progression $I^6$–$II^6$–V–I appears regularly enough in baroque practice, and even ECPs featuring this progression appear now and then. Indeed, William Rothstein, in a brilliant study of Corelli's cadences, finds the classical cadential progression as the reference for understanding most cadential formations in that composer's oeuvre.[11] He presents four models of how a single cadential bass line (the classical ③–④–⑤–①) interacts with a stepwise descending melody from $\hat{5}$ to $\hat{1}$ (Ex. 6.6). He then demonstrates that various transformations of these models can create more complex patterns using techniques such as "inversion, substitution, and elision of the bass."[12] Rothstein's account of Corelli's cadences is compelling; he convincingly shows that many of the composer's cadential formations can be

---

11. Rothstein, "Transformations of Cadential Formulae."

12. Rothstein, "Transformations of Cadential Formulae," 254.

EXAMPLE 6.6. Rothstein's four models (from "Transformations of Cadential Formulae," Ex 1)..

EXAMPLE 6.7. (a) Rothstein's Ex. 4 (from "Transformations of Cadential Formulae"); (b) after Rothstein, Ex. 5b.

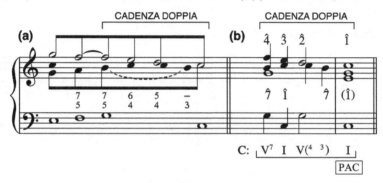

EXAMPLE 6.8. Corelli, Trio Sonata in E Minor, Op. 1, no. 2, iii, mm. 24–29.

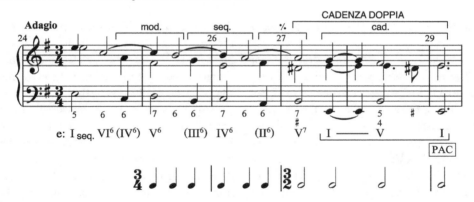

reduced to one of his four models. But for our purposes, revealing commonalities of structure in a wide variety of individual cases can potentially obscure some local details of harmony that are stylistically telling and that help differentiate baroque cadences from later classical ones.

For now, let us consider just one situation, which Rothstein calls (after Schenker) the "casting out" of the tonic degree in the bass from a more structural tonic six-four (what I referred to in earlier chapters as "re-inverting" the cadential six-four).[13] Example 6.7a shows Rothstein's three-voice elaboration of his model 4 (Ex. 6.6d), a pattern that clearly references the *cadenza doppia*.[14] Example 6.7b then shows how the six-four sonority can itself be re-inverted into a root-position tonic in order to support the melodic resolution of $\hat{4}$ to $\hat{3}$. He further cites a specific case from a Corelli Trio Sonata (Ex. 6.8) to illustrate this transformation. In relation to his model 4, the cadential progression would presumably begin with II⁶ in the last beat of measure 26 because an initial tonic is not present in the example. According to Rothstein, the cadence "shows the six-four chord of model 4 [Ex. 6.6d] transformed into a consonance in the simplest possible way, by casting out the root" to make an apparent tonic in root position on the third beat of measure 27 in Example 6.8. He notes as well that "the consonant chord on

---

13. Rothstein, "Transformations of Cadential Formulae," 255. See the discussions of "casting out of the root" in Chapter 3, sec. 3.3.3.3, Ex. 3.130, and note 169, and "re-inverting" a cadential six-four in Chapter 4, sec. 4.3.5 and Ex. 4.50.

14. Except for the figured bass and the dashed slur in Ex. 6.7a, the analytical annotations to Rothstein's examples are my own.

EXAMPLE 6.9. Corelli, Trio Sonata in B Minor, Op. 1, no. 6, i, mm. 10–11.

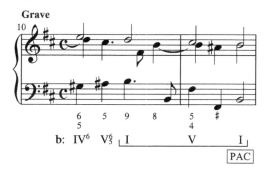

EXAMPLE 6.10. Corelli, Trio Sonata in A Minor, Op. 4, no. 5, iii, mm. 33–39.

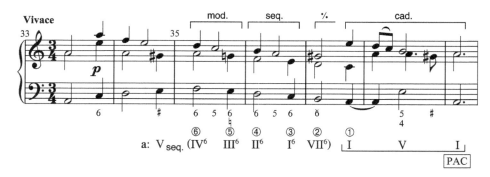

E [I] and the hemiola rhythm both help to reinforce the upper voice's descent."[15]

Nothing is objectionable in what Rothstein proposes, for recognizing an "apparent tonic" is clearly valid within a process of harmonic reduction to a more basic voice-leading model. But we should perhaps not dismiss too quickly the idea that the root-position tonic might be construed nonetheless as the first harmony of a compact cadential progression. After all, the simple I–V–I cadence, if not common in Corelli, appears now and then in his works (see Ex. 6.9) Here, the cadential configuration does not readily assimilate to any of Rothstein's models. In connection with Example 6.8, moreover, it is not clear that we would even want to speak of a cadential formal function arising with the pre-dominant II⁶ at the end of measure 26 and continuing with the dominant seventh on the downbeat of the next bar. For these harmonies arise out of a broader stepwise-descending sequence begun back at measure 24. In other words, in order to keep the cadential process separate from the sequential one—a goal that we have attributed to the classical style and one that manifests itself in the baroque as well—Corelli may have introduced the root-position tonic in measure 27 in order to break the sequence and to permit the simple cadence to emerge as its own formal function. Note as well, that whereas we can recognize the *cadenza doppia* as a *melodic* schema, its boundaries may not always be congruent with the specific *harmonies* of the actual cadence. In fact, we will observe this parametric overlapping in many cases of the *cadenza doppia* discussed in the course of this chapter.[16] Thus the simple cadence (*cadenza simplice*), characterized primarily by harmony (I–V–I), can be used together with the *cadenza doppia*, characterized primarily by melody, even though these patterns were considered distinct cadence types by partimento theorists.

A similar simple cadence by Corelli can be seen at the end of Example 6.10. Here, the music could easily have moved from the final VII⁶ of the sequence to I⁶, which could then initiate a cadential progression, presumably continuing on with some pre-dominant. Instead Corelli completes the descending bass line from ⑥ (m. 35) down to ①, thus initiating the cadential progression with a root-position tonic. I will return in connection with some later topics to Rothstein's models, but for now, I want to emphasize one main point: whereas the local details of harmony of a baroque cadence can frequently be reduced to a single (often expanded) cadential progression, it is sometimes useful to recognize at the very foreground a compact, formulaic progression articulating the final cadence of a thematic unit.

### 6.1.3. Imperfect Authentic Cadence

Like the classical style, most authentic cadences in the baroque period are perfect, with the final harmony supporting scale degree 1̂ in the upper voice. But the imperfect authentic cadence arises now and then in a variety of form-functional contexts. At times, the IAC may appear in isolation as the ending of a

---

15. Rothstein, "Transformations of Cadential Formulae," 263–64, Ex. 13.

16. The use of hemiola in this example will be treated later in sec. 6.1.5.2.

EXAMPLE 6.11. Bach, Prelude No. 9 in E, *WTC* 1, mm. 11–13.

EXAMPLE 6.12. Bach, Prelude No. 5 in D, *WTC* 2, mm. 48–56 (R = ½N).

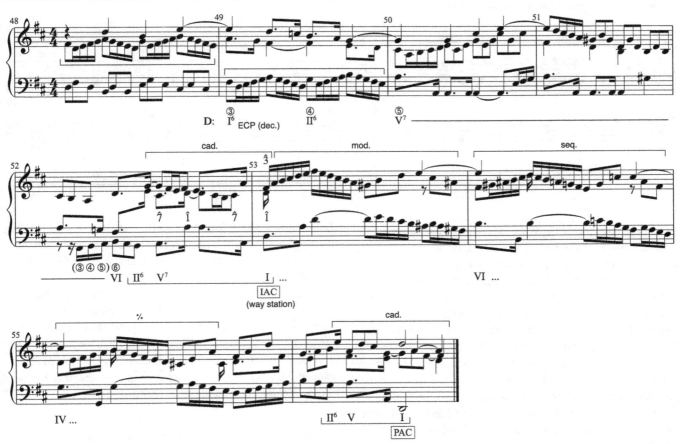

substantial thematic unit (Ex. 6.11). At other times, it is paired as a way station with a subsequent PAC, as in Example 6.12. At measure 53, an IAC leaves the upper voice of the cadence open on $\hat{3}$, thus motivating a new phrase whose initial descending-third sequence leads to a PAC in the final bar of the prelude. The impression that the IAC is less structurally conclusive than the PAC is clearly manifest here, a cadential differentiation that points directly to standard classical practice later in the century. (I return to this example in a discussion of the deceptive ECP leading to the IAC.)

On occasion, an IAC is found as the last cadence of a movement. Example 6.13 shows a case in point, one that is quite striking in that a home-key PAC appears nowhere in the piece, contrary to Bach's general practice.[17] A number of complete movements by Corelli also end with IACs. Example 6.14 is a particularly interesting case, especially in light of our discussion of the *cadenza doppia* and its embellishments. Typical of Corelli, the final cadence (mm. 46–47) is repeated (mm. 48–50), most likely to allow each of the two solo violins to sound the cadential melody.[18] (Violin 1 is notated with upward stems, Violin 2 with downward ones.) The first IAC has a "classical" bass line, whose initial I⁶ is

---

17. An earlier HK: IAC occurs at m. 13, and additional PACs confirm the related keys of F-sharp (V), m. 18, and C-sharp minor (II), m. 26.

18. The topic of consecutive (or repeated) cadences will be raised later in sec. 6.1.5.1.

EXAMPLE 6.13. Bach, Fugue No. 23 in B, *WTC* 1, mm. 33–34.

EXAMPLE 6.14. Corelli, Concerto Grosso in D, Op. 6, no. 1, i, mm. 43–50.

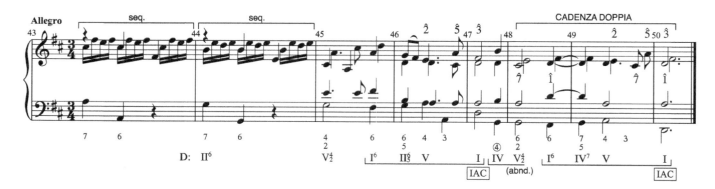

embellished by a preceding $V_2^4$ (m. 45). The second cadence seems similar, but actually is slightly expanded, in that it begins with the pre-dominant IV on the upbeat to measure 48. What follows in the final three bars is clearly an embellished version of the *cadenza doppia*, the melodic line in the first violin (sounding the alto voice) making this especially clear. As well, we find the hemiola effect so typical of a baroque cadence ending a triple-meter movement. Note, however, that instead of bringing ⑤ in the bass to support the entire *doppia* configuration, as the basic model would call for, Corelli initially *abandons* a potential cadential progression, beginning with the subdominant, by straddling ④ in the bass over measure 48, at which point the dominant seventh is again placed in third inversion (as on the downbeat of m. 45). The expected resolution to I⁶ then initiates the final compact cadential idea. We see, therefore, that the *cadenza doppia*, as befitting its name, actually contains two cadential progressions—the first abandoned, the second, realized. Moreover, the particular form of the melody, $\hat{2}$–$\hat{5}$–$\hat{3}$, allows the *cadenza doppia* to seem as though it were a repeat of the first cadence, even though the former cannot be construed as that schema.

In both of the cadences in Example 6.14, the melody leaps up from $\hat{2}$ to $\hat{5}$ and then back down to $\hat{3}$ (many of Corelli's IACs bring this melodic gesture). Given that the melody could easily have progressed from $\hat{2}$ to $\hat{1}$, it is as though the composer were hinting at a PAC but decided at the last moment to bring $\hat{3}$ instead. The IAC thus appears as a kind of replacement for an expected PAC, with the sense that the actual melody leaps over a more structural melody, which descends to $\hat{1}$. The same cannot be said for the IAC that ends Bach's fugue in Example 6.13, where the melodic line is not heading toward closure on $\hat{1}$. The effect in the Corelli is more of a harmonic "sweetening" by the third degree up on top, than a cadence that is formally open.

A similar, even stronger, effect arises with the apparent IACs of Example 6.15.[19] In Example 6.15a, $\hat{3}$ is placed above the expected $\hat{1}$ in a manner that is more textural than structural, the ongoing *cadenza doppia* finding its final pitch as $\hat{1}$, with $\hat{3}$ as a covering tone.[20] In Example 6.15b, the IAC is even preceded by an explicit PAC that brings $\hat{1}$ as expected, and so the final $\hat{3}$ makes the sweetening effect all the more prominent.[21]

### 6.1.4. Cadential Deviations (Authentic Cadence)

The three principal cadential deviations of an authentic cadence that we saw in connection with the classical style—deceptive,

---

19. The fifth movement of this sonata ends with a similar IAC; see also Corelli, Concerto Grosso in D, Op. 6, no. 4, of which two movements (i and iv) end with IACs.

20. On the covered cadence, see Chapter 3, sec. 3.4.2.3. Unlike most covered cadences, however, the covering tone here does not initiate a new thematic unit.

21. The voice leading of this cadence is not entirely clear, such that the $\hat{3}$ could be seen either as covering the genuine soprano ($\hat{1}$) in the sense of Ex. 6.15, or as a diversion of the soprano line up to $\hat{3}$. See also Corelli, Concerto Grosso in B-flat, Op. 6, no. 11, i.

EXAMPLE 6.15. Corelli, Violin Sonata in F, Op. 5, no. 4, (a) ii, mm. 59–61; (b) iii, mm. 57–61.

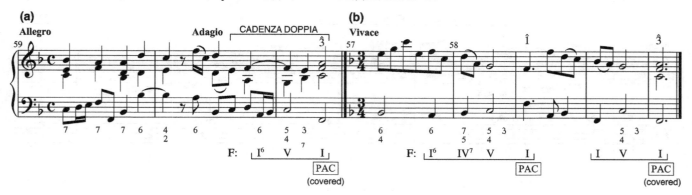

evaded, and abandoned—can be observed in the baroque as well, although the latter two deviations appear much less frequently than the former. The dominant arrival, a fourth classical deviation technique, will be discussed later with the half cadence (sec. 6.2.2). As well, some special types of cadential deception and abandonment, especially associated with J. S. Bach's fugues, will be treated in the final unit of this chapter (sec. 6.4.7).

### 6.1.4.1. Deceptive Cadence

As defined in Chapter 4, a potential authentic cadence can fail to be realized if the final root-position tonic (stage 4) is replaced by a different harmony (most often VI, but sometimes VII⁶/V or I⁶).[22] If the event that follows the cadential dominant is perceived as a formal goal, that is, if the replacement harmony groups backward with the ongoing cadential progression, then the necessary conditions for a *deceptive cadence* are satisfied. This deviation type rarely stands on its own, but most always functions as a way station, one that motivates another attempt at genuine cadential closure. In most deceptive cadences, the melodic line closes properly on $\hat{1}$, and so the deviation can be said to stand in place of an unrealized PAC. Occasionally, though, the melody of a deceptive cadence concludes on $\hat{3}$, in which case the effect is one of deviating from an implied IAC.

Deceptive cadences as so defined appear regularly in the baroque repertory, as seen in Example 6.16. Here, the cadential progression, which begins with II⁶ on the second half of beat 1 in measure 68, concludes with VI on the downbeat of the next bar, supporting the melodic resolution $\hat{2}$–$\hat{1}$. The deceptive cadence thus created motivates further continuational passagework, and a PAC finally arrives on the downbeat of measure 73, after which a brief closing section follows.[23] Lurking behind both cadences is the *cadenza doppia*, as proposed by the bracketed harmonies in line 2 of the harmonic analysis and the repeated $\hat{7}$–$\hat{1}$ melodic formula in the alto voice. In each case, though, the actual cadential progression does not start until after the *doppia* formula has already begun. As well, each of these progressions is preceded by a noncadential VI.[24] Were Handel to have employed an actual *cadenza doppia* harmonization beginning with a dominant seventh (supporting $\hat{4}$), a marked sense of harmonic expansion, and a concomitant slowing down of the harmonic rhythm, would have been expressed. Instead, he maintains the prevailing rapid rhythm of harmonic change and bass-line motion through the course of the hemiola, thus creating cadential progressions that are relatively compact in scope, as is so typical of cadences in the baroque era.

The case of a deceptive cadence produced by the cadential dominant yielding to I⁶ appears in another Handel Concerto (Ex. 6.17, middle of m. 85). As often occurs in these situations, the resolution of V to I⁶ sees a passing seventh (④) in the bass voice. A genuine PAC arises at the end of the subsequent phrase (in the last bar of the movement). Note that both the deceptive and authentic cadences in this passage are immediately preceded by a "deceptive resolution" of V to I⁶ (mm. 84 and 90, see the dashed brackets) thus anticipating the real cadence to come. The first may be considered to close a deceptive ECP, but the second case does not seem particularly cadential in implication. (The expansion of the Neapolitan sixth, mm. 82–84, will be discussed later in sec. 6.1.5.3.)

A similar deceptive cadence occurs toward the end of a Bach prelude (Ex. 6.18). A cadential progression begins to sound in measure 39, and the melodic goal arrives prominently on $\hat{1}$ at the downbeat of the following bar. Like the previous example, a passing tone in the bass disrupts the cadential dominant, this time, however, leading to the chromatic V⁶₅/IV substituting for I⁶. The cadential deception motivates additional motivic development and another try for a PAC, one that again becomes deceptive

---

22. Other options for replacement harmonies built over ⑥ include IV⁶ (see Handel's Concerto Grosso in G, Op. 6, no. 1, ii, three bars before the end). We can also find a replacement VII⁷/V built over #④ in Bach's Sonata in G Minor for Solo Violin, i, m. 13. I thank Edward Klorman for alerting me to this last example.

23. Note that the melody of the final codetta ends on $\hat{3}$, thus projecting the "sweetening" effect discussed for the IACs in the two previous examples.

24. That the first two beats of these potential *cadenza doppia* formulas are actually noncadential is clear by the use of an intervening III harmony between V and VI in m. 67 and especially the inverted dominant V⁶₅ in m. 71.

314  Cadence in the High Baroque

EXAMPLE 6.16. Handel, Concerto Grosso in E Minor, Op. 6, no. 3, iv, mm. 66–75.

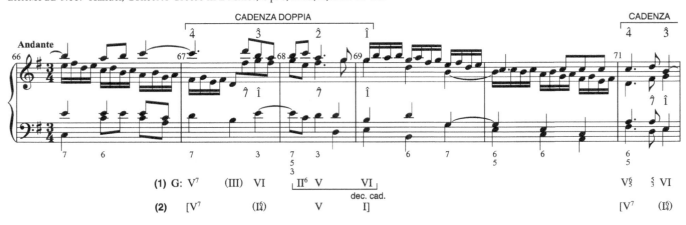

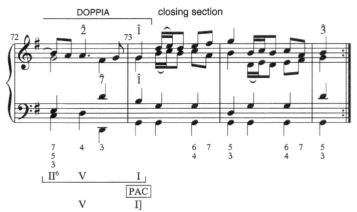

EXAMPLE 6.17. Handel, Concerto Grosso in G Minor, Op. 6, no. 6, iv, mm. 81–91.

EXAMPLE 6.18. Bach, Prelude No. 14 in F-sharp Minor, *WTC* 2, mm. 38–43.

on the downbeat of measure 42, now with the diatonic I⁶.²⁵ The final two bars see a genuine PAC decisively closing the movement.

Bach's use of a secondary dominant of the subdominant to create the first deceptive cadence in this example (m. 40) relates to a special kind of deceptive cadence found especially in the preludes of the first book of the *Well-Tempered Clavier*.²⁶ As noted by Mark Anson-Cartwright in a detailed investigation of this technique, Bach employs a V⁷/IV (in root position) for what seems to be the final, yet deceptive, cadence of a work.²⁷ We find this deviation technique already at the end of Prelude No. 1 in C (Ex. 6.19a). A highly expanded cadential dominant, which appears earlier at measure 24 (see the skeletal harmonic progression in Ex. 6.19b), resolves at measure 32 not to a final tonic triad, but rather to its chromatic alteration, V⁷/IV, to mark a deceptive cadence. A tonic pedal then remains in the bass for the rest of the prelude, within which a progression typically used in a postcadential closing section, one that Gjerdingen terms a *Quiescenza*,²⁸ finally brings tonic harmony as the last event of the piece. As a result, the prelude does not end with an actual authentic cadence. Yet our sense that the final bars are postcadential suggests that the V⁷/IV represents the real moment of structural closure. It is as though a consonant tonic triad, which should have appeared on the downbeat of measure 32, has been skipped over, elided, as Anson-Cartwright emphasizes.²⁹ One further anomaly must be highlighted: the expanded cadential dominant supports 4̂ in the upper voice, which eventually resolves to 3̂ at the deceptive cadence. Implied, of course, is an IAC, which, though possible (as discussed for Ex. 6.13, 6.14, and 6.15), is hardly the expected cadence type to close a complete movement. Eventually, the melody arrives on 1̂, with the tonic harmony of measure 35, not in a context that is genuinely cadential, but rather in a postcadential setting.³⁰ Taking a more in-time listening perspective, the cadence at measure 32 is initially heard as a manifest deceptive cadence. When we reach the end of what sounds like a closing section, however, we understand retrospectively that this *"final" deceptive cadence* becomes a kind of IAC, one that marks the structural close of the prelude, and so the abbreviation *dec. cad.⇒"IAC"* seems appropriate for labeling this complex cadential situation.

Before leaving this example, we might consider some additional complications, this time involving the cadential dominant (see again, Ex. 6.19b).³¹ As analyzed here, the dominant is the penultimate harmony of an ECP initiated by a stage-1 V⁷/IV and

---

25. To be sure, the ongoing triplet motion with scalar ascent rhetorically weakens this deceptive cadence's effect as a genuine formal goal. Note, moreover, that this deceptive cadence is anticipated by a noncadential, deceptive resolution in the middle of m. 41, similar to what we saw in the preceding concerto by Handel.

26. One case also appears in book 2 at the end of the prelude in D minor.

27. Mark Anson-Cartwright, "Elision and the Embellished Final Cadence in J.S. Bach's Preludes." Anson-Cartwright proposes six cadential models for what he calls "embellished final cadences," two of which (models Ia and IIa) involve the type of deceptive cadence under consideration now. The other models pertain to related techniques involving VI and IV⁶ as replacement harmonies. As for Bach's usage, Anson-Cartwright discusses cases from the *WTC* 1 as well as from a variety of chorale preludes; see his table 1. This technique seems to be a specialty of Bach; no cases arose in the works of the three other composers examined for this chapter.

28. Gjerdingen, *Galant Style*, chap. 13. For the harmonic content of this schema, see above, Chapter 3, note 276.

29. See the discussion of his Ex. 3, which details the harmonic situation at the end of the prelude; "Embellished Final Cadence," 270.

30. The notion of a final IAC bringing a further melodic descent to 1̂ within a postcadential context will be raised again in Chapter 7, in connection with Ex. 7.21.

31. The cadential label *PrC* at m. 19 refers to a *Prinner cadence*, a particular type of IAC. The topic was raised in Chapter 3 (see sec. 3.2.1.2) and will be elaborated on more fully in the next chapter (see sec. 7.1.2). The PrC of m. 19 is a home-key version of the same PrC (in the subordinate key) found earlier in the prelude (as discussed ahead in Ex. 7.25, m. 11).

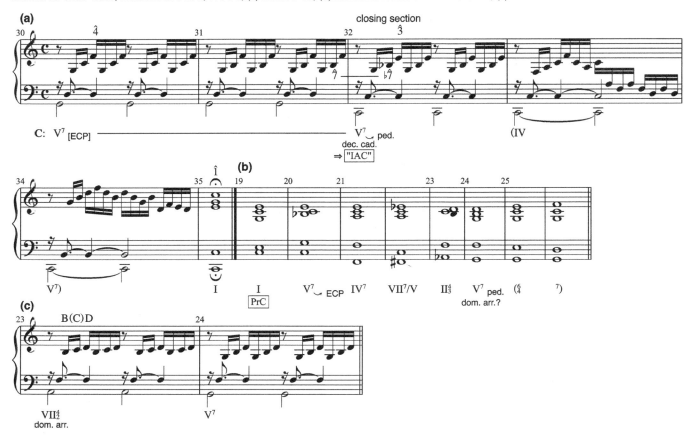

EXAMPLE 6.19. Bach, Prelude No. 1 in C, *WTC* 1, (a) mm. 30–35; (b) harmonic reduction of mm. 19–26; (c) mm. 23–24.

followed by three different pre-dominants in measures 21–23. It is not out of the question, however, that the dominant seventh in measure 24 could be heard as an ultimate dominant (of a half cadential ECP), thus yielding a dominant arrival, and not a genuine HC, due to the dissonant seventh. If this is our hearing, then the lengthy expansion of this harmony (mm. 25–31) would be understood as a postcadential standing on the dominant. When, however, this "ultimate dominant" yields to V⁷/IV at measure 32 (Ex. 6.19a), we should not be speaking of any cadential articulation at this point, because no *penultimate* dominant is available to create the cadence. In this reading, the prelude would not end with any authentic cadence whatsoever, a situation that might be difficult to accept given our expectations of baroque compositional practice.

Finally, let us consider one further harmonic complication. Thus far I have identified the harmony in measure 23 as a pre-dominant II⁴₃. This analysis understands the B♮ as a non-chord tone (shown by the black notehead), a position strongly advocated by Donald Francis Tovey.[32] But an alternative reading is also available, namely, hearing the B♮ as a genuine chord-tone, with the C as passing between the B and D (Ex. 6.19c). The harmony would then be a dominant substitute VII⁴₂. This interpretation undermines our recognizing the V⁷ in measure 24 as

penultimate, due to the inversion of the dominant-functioning VII⁴₂, and thereby encourages us to hear a premature dominant arrival at measure 23. Of course this view then leads to the same problem of denying any cadential status for measure 30, as discussed before. Given the complexities of this seemingly simple piece, we might wonder whether it is the improvisatory nature of the prelude genre itself that allows Bach the freedom to play with the conventions of harmony and cadence that he otherwise regularly follows in genres with more conventional formal processes.[33]

Another prelude with a "final" deceptive cadence implies a pending PAC (Ex. 6.20). The melodic content of the cadential idea beginning in measure 36 clearly points to a resolution to $\hat{1}$, which, when it occurs on the downbeat of the following bar, is supported by V⁷/IV for the cadential deception.[34] (I return to this example later to discuss the music that precedes the final cadence.)

Prelude No. 9 in E (Ex. 6.21) shows, exceptionally, that a "final" deceptive cadence may bring the more typical progression V–VI (middle of m. 22) instead of V⁷/IV, as in the previous examples of this technique. Observe as well, that at the end of the passage, the progression IV–I might lead us to recognize a concluding "plagal

---

32. Johann Sebastian Bach, "Forty-Eight Preludes and Fugues," 1: 23.

33. I thank Dean Sutcliffe for raising this issue of genre and form in a private communication.

34. See also Prelude No. 21 in B-flat, m. 18, and Prelude No. 24 in B Minor, m. 46.

EXAMPLE 6.20. Bach, Prelude No. 8 in E-flat Minor, *WTC* 1, mm. 28–40.

cadence"; however, the context in which these harmonies arise seems entirely postcadential, as the sustained $\hat{1}$ in the upper voice from measure 22 to the end makes clear. We should thus speak of a "plagal codetta," not of a genuine plagal cadence.[35]

Something similar, but even more complicated, occurs at the end of Bach's Toccata in D Minor (Ex. 6.22). On the downbeat of measure 143, the penultimate dominant of a cadential progression (beginning with $I^6$ and passing over stage 2) initiates what we are sure to hear as a 4–3 suspension in the alto voice, one that would continue an incipient *cadenza doppia*. Rather than resolving the suspension to the leading tone, as expected, the resolution to C♮ (♭$\hat{7}$) entirely undermines the dominant quality of the harmony.[36] Yet the move to VI that follows gives the impression of being a kind of deceptive cadence nonetheless, especially as the melody resolves to $\hat{1}$, which is held until the end of the piece. To be sure, the lack of a genuine leading tone in the penultimate dominant calls into question our finding a normal deceptive cadence or reinterpreted "PAC." Nonetheless, Bach's procedure clearly references the cadential situations that we have been surveying in the last number of examples. Following this potential deceptive cadence, the plagal motion IV–I seems like a postcadential embellishment, one that restores the final tonic that was replaced by the deceptive resolution of the (minor) dominant (as well as bringing a subdominant that was passed over in the previous cadential progression). Like the prior Example 6.21, a case could be made for hearing a "plagal cadence" to conclude the toccata, though the context here suggests more an interpretation of plagal codetta.[37]

### 6.1.4.2. Evaded Cadence

A cadence is evaded when the dominant is locked into place, but the harmony to which it progresses fails to represent stage 4 of the cadence; more precisely, the event associated with that harmony does not *group* with the prevailing cadential processes. Instead, an *initiating harmony*, typically $I^6$ (but even sometimes a root-position tonic), functions exclusively to begin another formal unit, one that often repeats the prior continuation or cadential material "one more time." Evaded cadences, so defined, occur with less frequency in the high-baroque style than later in the eighteenth century. Perhaps one reason why baroque composers do not regularly exploit the evaded cadence lies in the motoric rhythmic patterns that characterize so much of this music: the

---

35. Anson-Cartwright shows this situation in his model Ib ("Embellished Final Cadence," 279, Ex. 7).

36. See Anson-Cartwright's model IIb ("Embellished Final Cadence," 279). A related cadential deviation involving an anticipated leading-tone, which I term a *lowered leading-tone abandonment*, is discussed later in this chapter (sec. 6.4.7).

37. A classical example of a "final" deceptive cadence (dec. cad.⇒"PAC"), as illustrated in the last number of examples by Bach, was already raised at the end of Chapter 3, Ex. 3.174, in connection with Beethoven's "Ghost" Trio. In Chapter 8, I will discuss a Romantic case of this general technique, one that uses $V^6_5/IV$ (as a $I^6$ substitute) to replace the final tonic at the close of Schumann's song "Mondnacht" (see Ex. 8.19).

EXAMPLE 6.21. Bach, Prelude No. 9 in E, *WTC* 1, mm. 22–24.

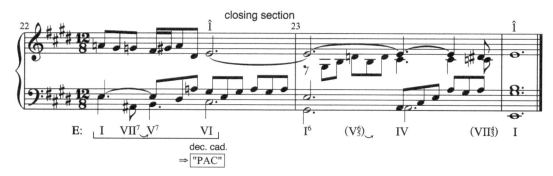

EXAMPLE 6.22. Bach Toccata in D Minor, BWV 565, mm. 141–44.

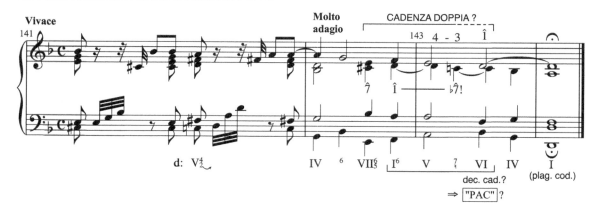

grouping disruption that typically accompanies this cadential deviation might overly inhibit the ongoing rhythmical flow.

Cases of evaded cadence nonetheless appear now and then, even as early as Corelli (Ex. 6.23). Here, the implied cadential resolution to I (and $\hat{1}$) are denied at measure 8 by the first violin's leap from the leading tone up to $\hat{6}$, accompanied by VI$^6_5$, an initiating harmony that does not group at all with the preceding cadential idea, despite the bass moving as expected to ①.[38] A particularly dramatic evaded cadence arises in Example 6.24, since no event at all arrives on the downbeat of measure 27, where a PAC is implied to appear.[39] Note, as well, that the varied repeat of the *cadenza doppia* material hints at the one-more-time technique, a very early example of this procedure.[40]

Some unusual evaded cadences arise now and then, showing that the deviation was not yet fully conventionalized in its usage,

as it eventually becomes in the galant period (to be discussed in the next chapter). Thus in Example 6.25, a *cadenza doppia* occurs in measures 29–30. The cadence begins to be repeated, now with an "echo" effect created by the sudden change to *piano*. But this time the cadence is suddenly evaded with the return to *forte*, and we have the impression that the downbeat of measure 32 exclusively marks the beginning of the next formal unit. We see here a reversal of the usual course of events (i.e., from a "classical" perspective), whereby an already sounding PAC begins to be repeated, only then to be evaded.

An especially odd evaded cadence arises in another highly dramatic passage, this time by Handel (see Ex. 6.26). The hemiola *cadenza doppia* in measures 17–18 promises to cadence at measure 19. But the resolution to the final tonic appears first in the guise of an upbeat anticipation, promising all the more the tonic proper on the subsequent downbeat. The sudden change to *forte* for the anticipation, along with the unexpected move to a secondary dominant at measure 19, evades the cadence in a most unusual manner. Rather than the anticipation grouping back with the cadential idea, it now functions as an anacrusis to the unexpected

---

38. See also Corelli, Concerto Grosso in B-flat, Op. 6, no. 5, iv, mm. 5–6. A similar harmonic-melodic situation, but with a different grouping structure, results in what I term an *inverted deceptive cadence*, a deviation technique especially associated with Bach's fugal practice; see sec. 6.4.7 and the discussion of Ex. 6.91b, m. 13.

39. The absence of any event immediately following an evasion is a technique that re-emerges in the nineteenth century; see in Chapter 8, the discussion of Ex. 8.14c, mm. 61–62, and Ex. 8.23d, mm. 111–12, and in Chapter 9, Ex. 9.46, mm. 20–21.

40. Schmalfeldt, who first introduced the "one-more-time" idea, does not mention Corelli in her historical survey of the technique ("Cadential Processes"). Another evaded cadence using this device is found ahead

in Ex. 6.39. See also Corelli, Concerto Grosso in D, Op. 6, no. 4, i, m. 21; Vivaldi, Violin Concerto in D, Op. 8, no. 11, i, m. 22; Handel, Concerto Grosso in C Minor, Op. 6, no. 8, i, m. 18; and Handel, Concerto Grosso in F, Op. 6, no. 9, ii, m. 108.

6.1. AUTHENTIC CADENCE 319

EXAMPLE 6.23. Corelli, Concerto Grosso in D, Op. 6, no. 4, ii, mm. 7–8.

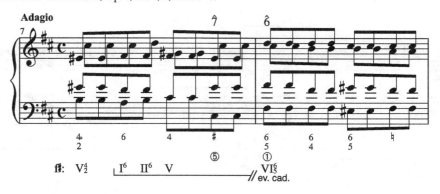

EXAMPLE 6.24. Corelli, Concerto Grosso in D, Op. 6, no. 1, iv, mm. 24–29.

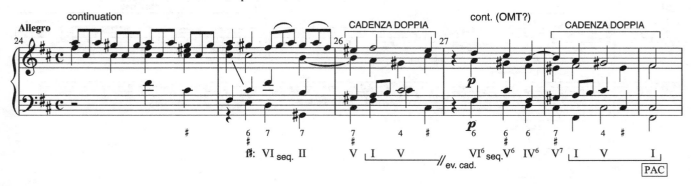

EXAMPLE 6.25. Corelli, Concerto Grosso in B-flat, Op. 6, no. 5, i, mm. 29–32.

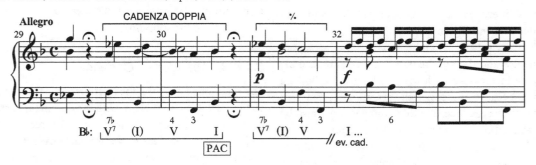

EXAMPLE 6.26. Handel, Concerto Grosso in G Minor, Op. 6, no. 6, i, mm. 16–21.

EXAMPLE 6.27. Bach, Prelude No. 15 in G, *WTC* 2, mm. 12–16.

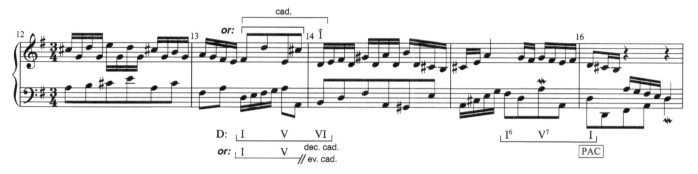

EXAMPLE 6.28. Bach, Prelude No. 24 in B Minor, *WTC* 2, (a) mm. 58–60; (b) mm. 1–2.

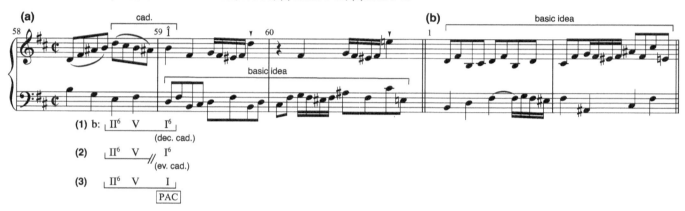

$V^7/\flat VII$. The effect of evaded cadence is clear, but the manner in which it is produced is entirely unique.

As in all tonal style periods, ambiguous cases of cadential deviation occur now and then in the baroque. In Example 6.27, the cadential idea in measure 13 leads to VI on the following downbeat, which, because of the melodic arrival on $\hat{1}$, may well be heard as a deceptive cadence. But this moment could also be understood as evaded if we hear measure 14 grouping forward with the following music, which drives to the genuine cadence at measure 16. In such a case of cadential ambiguity, performers may help resolve the matter by articulating one or the other deviation, or they may simply decide to leave the matter unsettled. An even more complicated ambiguity arises in Example 6.28a. The cadential idea in measure 58 leads to I⁶ supporting $\hat{1}$ on the downbeat of measure 59. For similar reasons to the previous example, this moment could be heard as either a deceptive or evaded cadence. But a third alternative presents itself as well. Seeing as the melodic material in the bass voice in measures 59–60 brings the basic idea of the prelude (introduced in the right hand at the opening of the piece, Ex. 6.28b), we might be inclined to accept the downbeat of measure 59 as a genuine PAC, whose bass, by taking on a "melodic" role, implies ① even if not actually bringing that note until the second beat of the bar. The situation is thus analogous to a covered cadence, whereby the upper voice implies a cadential $\hat{1}$, which instead is replaced by some other scale degree representing the beginning of a new formal unit.[41]

Here, however, the new melodic idea appears in the bass voice rather than in the soprano.

### 6.1.4.3. Abandoned Cadence

The abandoned cadence, the least dramatic form of cadential deviation, involves a "problem" with the dominant harmony of stage 3. In Chapter 4 (sec. 4.3) we observed three conditions under which an abandonment may arise: (1) a cadential, root-position dominant appears as expected, but then becomes inverted to its six-five position, thus losing its cadential status; (2) an expected cadential dominant is immediately replaced by an inverted form (sometimes $V^6_5$, but more typically $V^4_2$); and (3) a cadential progression, normally engaging stages 1 and 2, fails to achieve any dominant whatsoever.[42] We also noted that if these harmonic conditions point to a specific moment of pending cadential arrival, we can speak of an *abandoned cadence* associated with that point in time. Such an abandonment, which even in the classical

---

41. See Chapter 3, sec. 3.4.2.3.

42. I have not found any straightforward instances of this third option in the corpus for this chapter, though I have proposed one potential case ahead in Ex. 6.34. There the move from I⁶–II⁶ (end of m. 16) suggests itself as cadential but is then abandoned when the expected dominant is replaced by a root-position tonic (see line 1 of the harmonic analysis). As discussed later, I find this analysis less persuasive than the alternative of recognizing a single cadential progression, as annotated in line 2.

EXAMPLE 6.29. Corelli, Concerto Grosso in B-flat, Op. 6, no. 11, iv, (a) mm. 9–16; (b) reconstruction of mm. 13–16.

style appears infrequently, does not arise in the baroque works examined for this chapter.

If we rarely speak of abandoned cadences per se, we can nonetheless recognize many cases where an ongoing cadential progression is effectively disrupted in the ways just described. In other words, we can readily observe *abandoned cadential progressions* in the baroque style (just as in later tonal styles). Most often, such an abandoned progression is immediately followed by another cadential progression, one that is fully realized as a formal cadence.

Example 6.29a, the second half of a binary-form sarabande by Corelli, illustrates the first type of cadential abandonment. Though the bass line beginning at measure 9 looks like it might be cadential in nature, the actual harmonies form an ascending-stepwise sequence (based on a 5–6 contrapuntal pattern).[43] The beginning of measure 13 sees a return to ③, now supporting what could very well be the start of a cadential progression. The move to ④ brings the pre-dominant, with ⑤ appearing on the downbeat of measure 14. At this point, the dominant could have been locked into place to effect the PAC (as reconstructed in Ex. 6.29b). Instead, the bass keeps rising all the way to ⑧, thus inverting the dominant along the way and abandoning the cadential progression. A quick leap down to ④ in the second eighth of measure 15 initiates another cadential progression, this one yielding a true cadence. Note that the potential dominant at measure 14 might seem to arrive too early within the phrase, thus providing motivation for the abandonment; however, Example 6.29b shows how an ECP could have supported a *cadenza doppia* with hemiola. Such a cadence, though, would have resulted in a marked deceleration of the harmonies at measure 14, an effect that Corelli avoids by the continuous rhythmic motion prompted by the abandoned cadential progression.[44]

A particularly striking cadential abandonment of this type occurs toward the end of a Bach fugue (Ex. 6.30). The excerpt begins midway through a passage of stretto with the bass arriving on ♮③ at the downbeat of measure 78. Though this moment may not seem like the start of anything obviously cadential, if we follow the course of the bass from this point on, we see the formation of a large-scale, highly embellished ECP. The progression briefly pauses on ④ with the fermata at measure 80. At this point, $V_2^4$ seems like it might be abandoning the progression, but when the bass ascends to ♯④ to support $VII^7/V$, we understand that the prior $V_2^4$ is not functioning as a dominant, but rather as a passing, pre-dominant harmony (akin to a °7-PD over ④). The cadential progression finally reaches ⑤ at measure 81 for a genuine cadential dominant. In the second half of the following bar, however, that harmony fails to resolve cadentially as the bass continues its upward trajectory, reaching a noncadential tonic on the downbeat of measure 83. As a result, the cadential progression is now truly abandoned, thus realizing the potential for abandonment back at measure 80. Following this expansionary process, Bach tacks on a compact cadence to close the passage in the middle of the same bar.

A second way of abandoning a proposed cadential progression sees an expected cadential dominant immediately replaced

---

43. This potential ambiguity between cadential and sequential progressions associated with the bass pattern ③–④–⑤ was treated in the previous chapter; see Ex. 5.37f and 5.69.

44. For a similar case, see Bach, English Suite No. 3 in G Minor, i, mm. 27–33. See also the earlier discussion of Ex. 6.16, where the use of deceptive resolutions of the dominant (mm. 67 and 71), which precede the actual cadence, promote greater rhythmic activity compared to the realization of an implied *cadenza doppia*.

EXAMPLE 6.30. Bach, Fugue No. 20 in A Minor, *WTC* 1, mm. 78–83.

EXAMPLE 6.31. Vivaldi, Violin Concerto in C ("Il Piacere"), Op. 8, no. 6, iii, mm. 21–25.

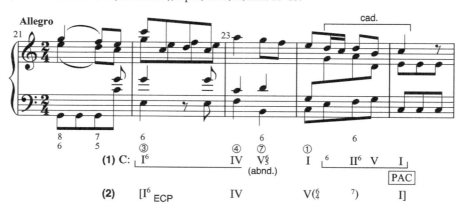

by an inverted form of this harmony (Ex. 6.31). In this passage by Vivaldi, the cadential progression reaches stage 2, with the bass ④ in measure 23. Instead of moving up to ⑤ to support a cadential dominant, the bass leaps down to the leading tone for a noncadential V$^6_5$, whose resolution to tonic then leads to a compact, formulaic cadence to close the phrase. To be sure, we could recognize a latent ECP supporting the entire four-measure unit, as shown in the second line of the analysis; however, such a harmonization would inhibit the use of both a rhythmically active bass line and a compact cadential formula—two features, found in the actual passage, that are important stylistic markers of baroque compositional practice.

Example 6.32, by Corelli, shows another way in which an expected cadential dominant may be replaced by its inverted form. Following an IAC in measure 12, a new cadential progression begins with I$^6$ on the upbeat to measure 13, leading to the pre-dominant II$^6$ in that bar. The progression is abandoned, however, when ④ is checked in its ascending motion and holds firm in measure 14 to support V$^4_2$. The required resolution to I$^6$ signals a second cadential progression, one that realizes the PAC at measure 16.[45]

A similar situation, closely related to the previous example, sees the bass line actually reaching ⑤ to hold a root-position dominant. Rather than resolving cadentially, the harmony moves to I$^6$ (over ③) via V$^4_2$ (Ex. 6.33, m. 36). Here we cannot speak literally of an abandoned cadential progression, since the dominant in root position has been achieved. The progression is therefore more properly labeled as deceptive, even if an actual deceptive cadence does not emerge (the I$^6$ on beat two of m. 36 hardly represents a provisional goal of the ongoing thematic process).[46] Stepping back from the very foreground, we recognize again the *cadenza doppia* configuration, such that I$^6$ and IV$^7$ of measure 36 could be seen as embellishments of a prolonged dominant within a broader ECP

---

45. See also, Corelli, Violin Sonata in B-flat, Op. 5, no. 2, i, mm. 20–21; and Bach, Prelude No. 17 in A-flat, *WTC* 2, mm. 14–17.

46. See, in Chapter 4, the discussion of Ex. 4.47, which distinguishes deceptive cadential progressions from abandoned ones.

EXAMPLE 6.32. Corelli, Concerto Grosso in B-flat, Op. 6, no. 11, v, mm. 11–16.

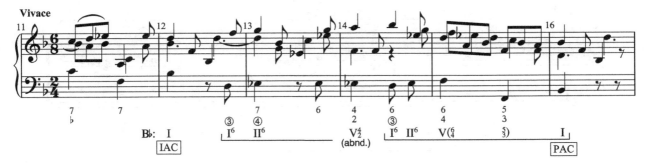

EXAMPLE 6.33. Corelli, Concerto Grosso in B-flat, Op. 6, no. 11, ii, mm. 35–38.

(see line 2 of the analysis). The purpose of these harmonies, once again, is to provide a compact cadential progression on the surface of the musical texture.[47] When Corelli repeats the cadential unit (as he is accustomed to do), he writes a more standard *cadenza doppia*, since the resulting slowing down of the harmonic rhythm and bass motion is now appropriate for the final cadence of the movement.[48]

### 6.1.5. Cadential Extension and Expansion

In prior chapters on the classical cadence, we discussed how a significant way of creating a rhetorically powerful sense of closure can involve the delay, or postponement, of an implied cadential arrival. We identified two general techniques to help achieve that effect—cadential *extension*, normally via deviations techniques (Chapter 4), and cadential *expansion* (Chapter 5). Extension procedures involve *adding on* cadential units that are not necessarily required in order to create closure. Expansion procedures involve temporally *lengthening* the component parts of an individual cadential process. Both techniques result in putting off into the future the goal of formal ending, thus arousing even stronger expectations that it must eventually arrive. And when the promised closure is fulfilled, it feels all the more satisfying and effective.

The baroque period employs a variety of devices that help achieve a sense of strong cadential finality. We have already observed some cases when discussing cadential deviations in the previous section. With most of these procedures, the initial failure to realize an implied cadence is overcome with another attempt that actually succeeds. Normally, such deviations involve formal extension, since additional cadential units are employed in order to realize a successful ending after a prior failure to close.

### 6.1.5.1. Consecutive PACs

Another kind of extension, one infrequently found in the classical style but regularly in the baroque, especially with Corelli, sees the use of two immediately consecutive authentic cadences of the same type, usually PACs.[49] We have already encountered three such cases by this composer, as just seen in Example 6.33, as well as earlier in Examples 6.14 and 6.15b (the former involving consecutive IACs).

Sometimes the material content of the first cadential idea is largely repeated in the second cadence. Example 6.34 presents a particularly simple repetition, with the only difference being the explicitly notated change to *piano*, which creates an echo effect. We observe again that, on the very surface of the musical texture, two cadential progressions literally support the cadential idea (a Cudworth pattern). Given the slow tempo, it is feasible to hear stages 1 and 2 being abandoned by the return to root-position tonic (shown in line 1), which then

---

47. See also, Handel, Concerto Grosso in A, Op. 6, no. 11, ii, mm. 48–50.

48. As an aside, note the melodic configuration in the second violin (with downward stems) in m. 36, one that anticipates the *tenor combo* of the classical style (see Chapter 3, sec. 3.1.2.3).

49. The issue of consecutive (or repeated) cadences is first raised in Chapter 2 (sec. 2.8.5).

EXAMPLE 6.34. Corelli, Trio Sonata in G Minor, Op. 2, no. 6, i, mm. 16–18.

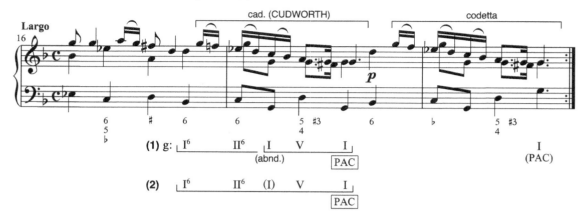

EXAMPLE 6.35. Corelli, Trio Sonata in A, Op. 1, no. 3, i, mm. 13–17.

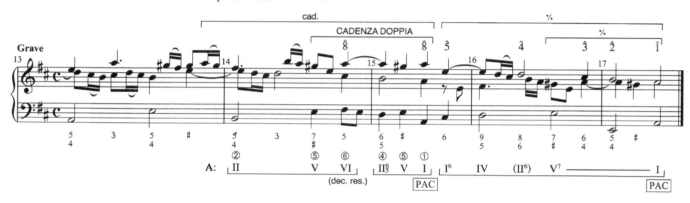

produces a simple I–V–I cadence. But we could also hear the root-position tonic as a passing chord between IV and V (see line 2). In this example, the reduction to a single cadential progression probably makes more sense than the analysis of two progressions in line 1, especially given the unity of the melodic line and the prevailing harmonic rhythm of one harmony per quarter-note beat.

At other times, the content of the consecutive cadences differs, as already observed with Example 6.33. Another such case appears in the trio sonata shown in Example 6.35. Here, the cadential repeat seems motivated by the desire to give each violin a chance to present one, and then the other, of the two upper voices in this *cadenza doppia* (mm. 14–15 and mm. 16–17). Note, however, that the bass voice is not simply repeated. Instead, it reflects a change in the harmonization of the cadences. Whereas the first one consists of two progressions—one, deceptive (②–⑤–⑥); the other, authentic (④–⑤–①)—the repeated cadence (mm. 16–17) contains just a single progression, one that represents a reduction of the harmonies (in the manner of Rothstein's analyses). As a result, both the harmonic rhythm and the bass voice become slower, thereby putting on the brakes, so to speak, an appropriate effect for the final utterance of the movement.[50]

When confronting consecutive PACs, the question is often raised, which is the *real* cadence, the one that produces the sense of complete formal closure? As discussed in Chapter 2 (sec. 2.8.5), a general principle holds that the first PAC should normally be accorded structural priority; after all, this is the one we initially hear, and as long as it is a fully legitimate cadence, then it should be capable of achieving full closure on its own. The repeated cadence would then be deemed to function postcadentially, a kind of non-essential supplement. Such seems to be the case with Example 6.34, where the shift to a softer dynamic gives rise to the echo effect, thus suggesting that the first cadence is the genuine one and that the second is a codetta closing with a cadence of limited scope. Sometimes, however, a cadential repetition can give the impression, for various reasons, that the second cadence is stronger, that it is the one more effective in asserting closure. Thus in Example 6.35, the second cadence, lying an octave lower than the first, projects a decisive melodic *descent* from $\hat{5}$ to $\hat{1}$, whereas the first PAC's melody circles around the high A ($\hat{8}$). The second cadence thus seems to be more essential in some respects than the first one. (Ex. 6.33 projects a similar registral shift accompanied by a rhythmic deceleration.)

Another case where the second of two consecutive cadences appears more structurally significant arises in Example 6.36, a solo violin sonata, again by Corelli. Like the previous example, the second PAC engenders a slowing of the rhythmic motion,

---

50. We saw a similar kind of harmonic reduction (along with a concomitant slowing of rhythmic activity) in Ex. 6.33; cf. mm. 35–36 and mm. 37–38.

EXAMPLE 6.36. Corelli, Violin Sonata in B-flat, Op. 5, no. 2, iii, mm. 63–68.

due to how the upper voice changes from triplets to mostly eighth notes (with a dotted quarter thrown in at the end for good measure). And as discussed, this reduced activity is appropriate for the final gesture of the movement. An additional consideration, however, may account even more for our hearing the second PAC in Example 6.36 as decisive, namely, the complete change in its melodic content and overall texture. Whereas the first cadence continues with the same general material as the passage that precedes it (mm. 63–64), the second cadence brings something new. As discussed in the opening chapter of this study, the effect of closure is often well projected when a closing element—a "terminal modification," as Smith calls it—contrasts with its preceding material, rather than seeming like a mere continuation.[51] Of course, a terminal modification has to involve more than mere contrast, it must possess an *intrinsically* ending quality for it to be perceived as conclusive. In the case of the two cadences of Example 6.36, both contain the necessary elements for formal closure, but the second cadence adds material contrast into the mix, thus providing additional grounds for regarding that cadence as the primary one reponsible for formal closure.

We see, therefore, that the experiential circumstances of the last two examples are more complex than when the first of two consecutive cadences is taken as structural (as proposed for Ex. 6.34). For after we hear the first cadence effecting a sense of closure, we nonetheless must reinterpret its status in light of the second cadence, which feels even more conclusive. For this reason, a latent ambiguity of form-functional expression is normally attached to the use of consecutive cadences. And although we find a baroque composer such as Corelli being fond of the technique, it is understandable that this cadential usage appears less often in works of the classical style, where the clarity of cadential goals is of particular aesthetic significance.

### 6.1.5.2. *Expansion via Slower Tempo; Hemiola; Change of Tempo Marking*

In the two previous examples of consecutive cadences, the second cadential idea exhibits a marked slowing down of the harmonic and surface rhythms. Two other techniques of generalized rhythmic deceleration—(1) hemiola and (2) a sudden change to a slower tempo—can impart a sense of *expanding* the cadence, thereby delaying the cadential goal to some extent. The use of hemiola at the cadence, a hallmark of baroque style,[52] has already been observed in a number of earlier examples. Example 6.8, measures 27–29, is a particularly clear case, where all of the voices of the texture participate in the hemiola, thus producing the impression of a slower tempo: the quarter-note beats in measures 24–26 create a pulse stream that becomes one-half as fast during the hemiola of measures 27–29.[53] Other cases are less clear in their effect, because the ongoing motion (usually in quarter notes) is maintained by one or more voices, thus countering the sense that the primary pulse stream is actually changing tempo. Thus in Example 6.16, measures 71–73, the lower voice for the most part marches along in quarter notes, while the upper voice articulates the hemiola. In the case of Example 6.29b, we identified a hemiola associated with the *cadenza doppia* figure that emerges via harmonic reduction, but the actual passage (Ex. 6.29a) features a regularity of eighth and quarter notes that projects little sense of a slower tempo on the musical surface.

A more drastic effect of cadential expansion occurs when the composer specifically notates a tempo change from a prevailing fast tempo to a markedly slower one, most often an *Adagio*. This technique, which is rare in the classical style, is common in the baroque, with Handel being a frequent practitioner of the device, though we find some cases in Corelli as well. In Example 6.37, the change to *Adagio* emerges directly out the preceding *Allegro* tempo. In a passage from Handel (Ex. 6.38), the *Adagio* at measure 112 is set up by the immediately preceding fermata. So it might seem as though the cadence only begins with the change of tempo at measure 112. Looking back, however, we can see the start of an ECP, which itself elides with a deceptive cadence, supporting cadential function as early as the initial tonic of measure 107. The progression continues until the fermata, at which point a melodic *cadenza doppia* pattern begins in the alto voice and continues into the change of tempo. With Example 6.39, the *Adagio* coincides with an HC tacked on to

---

51. Smith, *Poetic Closure*, 53.

52. For more on the rhythmic-metric effect of baroque hemiolas, see Channan Willner, "Metrical Displacement and Metrically Dissonant Hemiolas."

53. See also Ex. 6.14, mm. 48–50.

EXAMPLE 6.37. Corelli, Violin Sonata in B-flat, Op. 5, no. 2, ii, mm. 60–61.

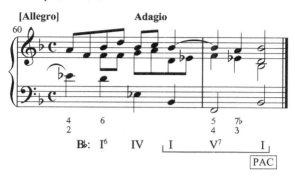

EXAMPLE 6.38. Handel, Concerto Grosso in F, Op. 6, no. 2, iv, mm. 105–13.

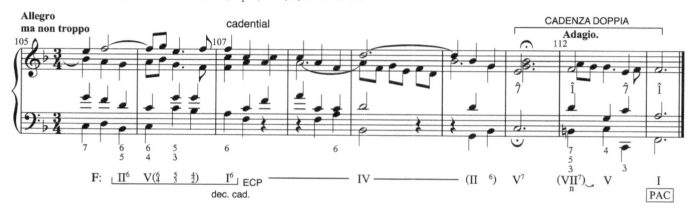

EXAMPLE 6.39. Handel, Concerto Grosso in B-flat, Op. 6, no. 7, iv, mm. 55–60.

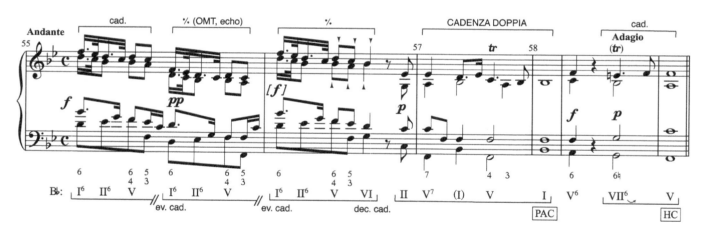

end the movement. We also see in this example a series of cadential techniques that extend and expand cadential action, beginning with two evaded cadences in measure 55 and a deceptive cadence in the following bar. A *cadenza doppia* in measures 57–58 then effects a slowing down in the tempo due to the marked change in note values, and the half cadential idea represents a final stage of deceleration with the actual shift to *Adagio*.

### 6.1.5.3. Expanded Cadential Progression

Compared to classical practice, expanded cadential progressions arise infrequently in the baroque repertory and rarely with the major expansions of individual harmonic functions often seen, for example, toward the end of a classical subordinate theme. Most typically, the progression is restricted in scope, normally allowing each harmony to occupy only a single bar of music. Several reasons perhaps account for the limited usage of the technique by baroque composers. First, an ECP typically brings a marked deceleration of harmonic rhythm and bassline motion, features that run counter to the baroque tendency toward uniformity of rhythmic activity in these parameters. Second, an ECP, which stretches out the length of the component cadential stages, makes it difficult for baroque composers to realize what appears to be a central aesthetic goal, namely,

EXAMPLE 6.40. Vivaldi, Violin Concerto in G Minor ("Summer"), Op. 8, no. 2, iii, mm. 66–70.

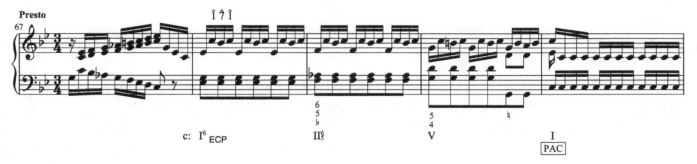

EXAMPLE 6.41. Vivaldi, Violin Concerto in E-flat ("La Tempesta di Mare"), Op. 8, no. 5, iii, mm. 156–64.

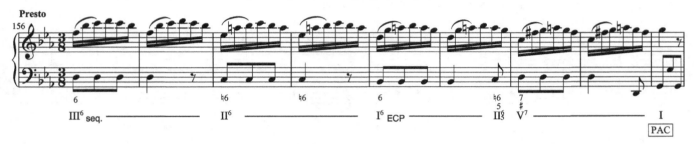

EXAMPLE 6.42. Bach, "Goldberg" Variations, mm. 11–16.

to project thematic closure by conventionalized, and relatively compact, cadential formulas.

In order to preserve rhythmic momentum in the face of a markedly slower harmonic pacing, the melodic content of an ECP often features a good deal of "passage work," which is especially suited to show off the virtuosic abilities of a concerto soloist. It is not surprising, therefore, that we find the baroque composers using ECPs in concertos more than in other genres.[54] Observe Example 6.40, where a flurry of ascending and descending scales is followed by an ECP, in the which a compound melody's upper strand alternates between $\hat{1}$ and $\hat{7}$, while a lower strand doubles the bass; little in the way of a specifically cadential melody arises from the rush of sixteenth notes. Another concerto excerpt from Vivaldi (Ex. 6.41) sees the melodic component supported by the ECP emerging out of the prior sequential material, such that a standard cadence formula is not particularly projected. Besides concertos, an ECP is likely to be used in a theme for variations (normally featuring ground-bass technique), as seen in Example 6.42. The relatively slow harmonic rhythm of the cadential phrase is especially appropriate so that the variations can bring a wide array of figurational passage work within the harmonic skeleton.

The inclination for baroque composers to "retain the cadential formula," one that is relatively compact, can be hard to realize in the case of a standard ECP. We see this tendency playing itself out, however, in a number of cases where an ECP is in the making, yet the composer still finds a way to close the thematic unit with a compact cadential idea at the very end. Thus in Example 6.43, the second half of the penultimate bar (m. 83) suddenly sees the melody slow down to eighth notes, while what we expect to be a half-measure of exclusively dominant harmony finds a root-position tonic wedged into the second half of beat three (see arrow). Of course, this tonic is easily understood to embellish the overall dominant, but the presence of that harmony is nonetheless necessary in order to project a compact *cadenza doppia* in the second half of the bar. Something similar occurs in Example 6.12, examined earlier. When the melodic idea sounding in the inner voice of measure 48 gets shifted to the bass at measure 49, the resulting harmonies give rise to an ECP that emphasizes dominant harmony in measures 50–51. Shortly into the next bar, the dominant resolves deceptively to VI on the second beat, such

---

54. And we can recall that the massive ECPs of the classical style are also typically associated with, or expressive of, the concerto.

EXAMPLE 6.43. Vivaldi, Violin Concerto in C, Op. 8, no. 12, i, mm. 81–84.

EXAMPLE 6.44. Corelli, Violin Sonata in E Minor, Op. 5, no. 8, i, mm. 9–17.

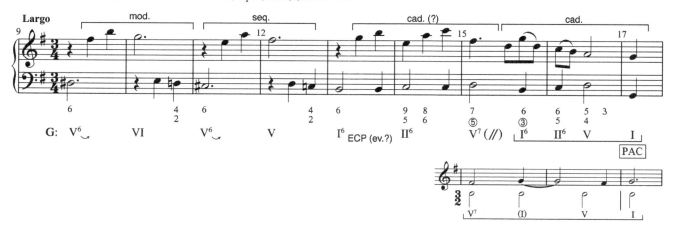

that a new, relatively compact progression effects an IAC.[55] This compact cadential idea thus fully liquidates all of the preceding motivic material (running sixteenths and triplet arpeggiations), such that the cadence appears as entirely formulaic in character. Indeed, the middle voice even brings a hint of the *cadenza doppia*.

With Example 6.12, the ECP begun at measure 49 becomes deceptive. In other cases, the progression is abandoned, as we discussed in connection with Example 6.30. Sometimes, it is difficult to pin down just which deviation technique is responsible for the ECP not being realized. What we find in Example 6.44 is typical of this problem, yet clearly related to other cases we have discussed already. Following sequential work in measures 9–12, an ECP begins in the following measure, with a steady rhythm of one harmony per bar. After the dominant arrives at measure 15, the bass leaps back down to ③ to initiate another, more compact, cadential progression, which closes the thematic unit in the subordinate key of G major. We cannot quite say that the ECP has been abandoned, because a root-position dominant has been achieved; nor does it seem like the following I⁶ is the goal of a deceptive cadential progression. Instead, what is expressed is a kind of evaded cadential progression (though not an evaded cadence per se). No matter what the cause, we see that an ongoing ECP fails to complete itself, thus yielding to a compact cadential formula on the very surface of the piece.[56] Again, as in so many cases already observed, we find at a slightly reduced level, a hemiola *cadenza doppia* supported by two bars of dominant (see the cue staff below mm. 15–17). Such a reduction reveals a single, complete ECP in the spirit, if not in the details, of Rothstein's models.

As a general rule, a baroque ECP tends to give equal emphasis to each harmony of the progression. Now and then, one of the harmonic functions is more expanded in relation to the others. In a manner that looks forward to classical practice, the ECP in Example 6.45 gives greater durational value to the dominant harmony (mm. 93–96), thus significantly delaying the cadential goal. A case of pre-dominant lengthening can be seen in Example 6.17, where the ♭II⁶ (mm. 82–84) is prominently expanded. The ECP is eventually given up, in the manner discussed earlier, so that a compact cadential formula (which itself becomes deceptive) can be tacked on to the end of the phrase.[57] Another passage by Handel (Ex. 6.46, mm. 90–95) shows almost the same situation, this time with a highly expanded initial tonic. Again, the ECP is not fully realized on the surface, so that a compact *cadenza doppia* can emerge at the end. Note, however, that the boundaries of the

---

55. Note how the highly compressed sixteenth-note bass line ③-④-⑤-⑥ in m. 52 beautifully echoes the genuine bass of the ECP (mm. 49–52).

56. See also Corelli, Concerto Grosso in D, Op. 6, no. 7, v, mm. 5–8.

57. See also Handel, Concerto Grosso in F, Op. 6, no. 2, ii, mm. 28–31.

EXAMPLE 6.45. Bach, Brandenburg Concerto No. 3 in G, i, mm. 91–97.

EXAMPLE 6.46. Handel, Concerto Grosso in A Minor, Op. 6, no. 4, iv, mm. 87–99.

schema embrace the end of the ECP and a very compact cadential progression.

### 6.1.5.4. Deceptive-Authentic Combinations (DCP-ACP); Pulcinella

In a number of cases examined so far, we have seen the inception of a cadential progression (sometimes expanded) whose dominant resolves deceptively, only then to be repeated with a fully realized authentic cadence. This combination of a deceptive cadential progression (DCP), with the bass line ③–④–⑤–⑥, followed by an authentic cadential progression (ACP), ③–④–⑤–①, appears in many guises throughout the baroque repertory.[58] One simple case is shown in Example 6.47. Here, we see a regular deceptive cadence (3̂) followed by a matching PAC. Sometimes, the DCP is stated twice before the subsequent ACP appears (Ex. 6.48). The upper voice of this

---

58. The technique of a DCP pairing with an ACP has already been discussed in Chapter 3, sec. 3.1.2.4, "Deceptive-Authentic Combinations," and Chapter 4, sec. 4.1.2.5.

EXAMPLE 6.47. Corelli, Violin Sonata in E, Op. 5, no. 11, ii, mm. 12–16.

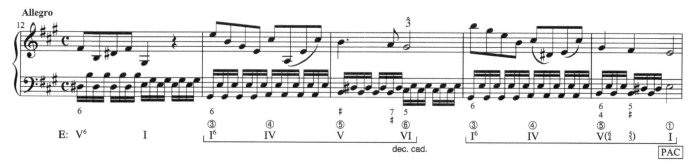

EXAMPLE 6.48. Corelli, Violin Sonata in E Minor, Op. 5, no. 8, ii, mm. 14–17.

passage displays an important detail: a pedal on $\hat{5}$, which is dissonant with the IV and VI harmonies. As a result of this static soprano, neither of the DCPs can create an actual cadence, which does not occur until $\hat{5}$ finds its descending resolution to $\hat{1}$ in measure 17. Note moreover, that the active inner voice in the DCP moves by stepwise ascent ($\hat{5}$–$\hat{6}$–$\hat{7}$–$\hat{8}$), thus creating parallel thirds with the bass (③–④–⑤–⑥), a feature we will observe in other related cases.

Example 6.49 illustrates a variant of this idea, whereby the first pair of melodic pitches $\hat{5}$–$\hat{6}$ lies above the second pair $\hat{7}$–$\hat{8}$, which is shifted down an octave. The third statement of the idea finally becomes realized as an ACP, though Corelli characteristically supports $\hat{3}$ with a root-position I, thus creating a highly compact *cadenza doppia* at the end.[59] One other detail to note: like the previous Example 6.48, an internal pedal appears in conjunction with the second DCP (second half of m. 11). This time the sustained pitch is $\hat{8}$ in the first violins (while the second violins play the $\hat{5}$–$\hat{6}$, $\hat{7}$–$\hat{8}$ pairs), thus creating a dissonance with the V at the very end of measure 11.

Some other harmonic variants on the DCP bass line are strongly related to the cases already examined. A number of these involve a schema that Gjerdingen terms the "Pulcinella," whereby $\hat{1}$ (sometimes along with $\hat{5}$ or $\hat{3}$) is sustained in an upper or middle voice while the bass brings the standard ③–④–⑤–⑥ of a DCP.[60]

In such cases, ⑤ tends to support a tonic six-four so that a DCP is not actually expressed (Ex. 6.50, mm. 25–27).[61] Rather, the sense is more of an overall tonic prolongation (with the final VI in its normal role of tonic substitute). For this reason, I do not place a cadential bracket beneath the harmonies of the Pulcinella progression, but rather use a slur to indicate its prolongational nature. Another case, this one by Corelli (Ex. 6.51) is slightly more complicated, for the figured bass indicates that in the second half of measures 55 and 57, ⑤ supports a dominant harmony. With the sustained $\hat{1}$ in the upper voice, however, this dominant seems more like a passing sonority rather than one that anchors a clear cadential progression. One additional detail is interesting. The beginning of the *cadenza doppia* melody (m. 59), played by the first violin (upward stems), is harmonized with II⁶. As a result, the $\hat{7}$ on the downbeat of the bar is a non-chord tone, although in most other cases of this schema, the pitch is a full-fledged member of a dominant harmony occurring at this point.[62] We can thus observe here an amalgam of cadential possibilities, such

---

59. See also Corelli, Concerto Grosso in C Minor, Op. 6, no. 3, i, mm. 17–20; Corelli, Trio Sonata in F-sharp Minor, Op. 2, no. 9, i, mm. 18–20.

60. "The Pulcinella cadence ignores the strictures of conventional counterpoint and instead revels in the free interplay between the moving bass and the static upper parts" (Gjerdingen, *Galant Style*, 154–55).

61. The two-part texture of the Pulcinella in Ex. 6.50 does not yield a complete tonic six-four, though it is the harmony clearly implied. The examples of the Pulcinella discussed by Gjerdingen (Ex. 11.27 and 11.28) have a fuller texture and explicitly bring that harmony.

62. This configuration (but not the work by Corelli) is cited by Menke ("Cadenza Doppia," Ex. 5f) as one of a host of variations of the

EXAMPLE 6.49. Corelli, Concerto Grosso in D, Op. 6, no. 7, iii, mm. 10–13.

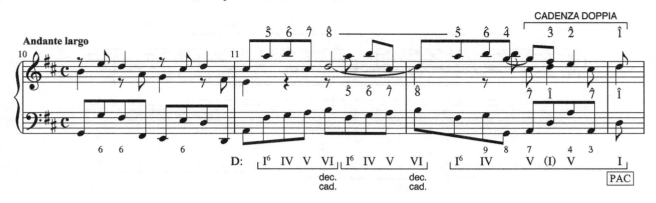

EXAMPLE 6.50. Handel, Concerto Grosso in F, Op. 6, no. 9, ii, mm. 24–28.

EXAMPLE 6.51. Corelli, Concerto Grosso in G Minor ("Christmas"), Op. 6, no. 8, v, mm. 54–60.

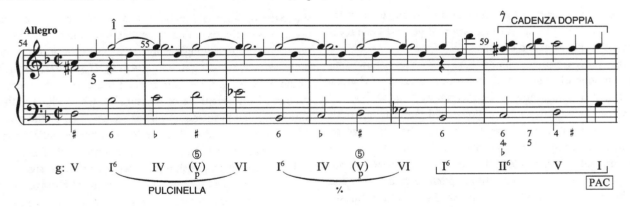

that the melodic component of this cadence expresses the *cadenza doppia*, a formula that largely dies out with the high baroque, while the bass line and resulting harmonization presents a "classical" configuration that endures throughout the entire eighteenth century and beyond.

A further harmonic variant of the Pulcinella schema sees ⑥ supporting what appears on the surface to be a pre-dominant harmony of some kind: II$^4_3$ in Example 6.52, measure 10 (the figured bass $^4_3$ indicates the fuller harmonic texture), and IV$^6_5$ in Example

6.53, measure 35. Although we see an emphasis on pre-dominant associated with the motion from ④ to ⑥, there remains the sense of a broader tonic prolongational progression, as projected by the upper-voice pedal on $\hat{1}$ and $\hat{5}$ (in Ex. 6.52) and on $\hat{1}$ and $\hat{3}$ (in Ex. 6.53).

Seeing as the Pulcinella schema is effectively tonic prolongational, it might be questioned whether we are dealing with a cadential situation at all. Three factors, however, need to be taken into consideration: (1) the resemblance of these Pulcinella examples to other DCP-ACP combinations that are more obviously cadential; (2) the formal positioning of the Pulcinella directly before the actual cadence; and (3) the bass line's traversal

---

*cadenza doppia* that results from "diminutions" of the standard bass progression ⑤–①.

EXAMPLE 6.52. Corelli, Violin Sonata in E, Op. 5, no. 11, iv, mm. 9–12.

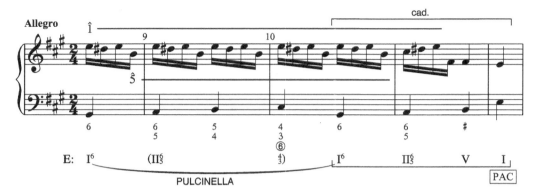

EXAMPLE 6.53. Bach, Brandenburg Concerto No. 3 in G, iii, mm. 35–36.

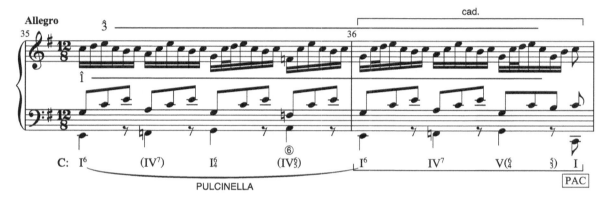

of the cadential stream. All of these considerations warrant including these examples in our discussion of general techniques for cadential extension and expansion.[63]

Finally, an excerpt by Handel (Ex. 6.54) shows how difficult it can be to distinguish fully between a genuine DCP and a Pulcinella. At the beginning of the excerpt, we find the ③–④–⑤–⑥ bass line common to both situations. And the sustained tonic pedal in an inner voice (upper part of the left hand) also suggests the Pulcinella schema. However, the actual harmony over ⑤ is dominant, which supports $\hat{7}$ in the upper voice; indeed, the soprano pattern brings the conventional pitch pairing of $\hat{5}$–$\hat{6}$ and $\hat{7}$–$\hat{8}$ (the latter, an octave lower, as in Ex. 6.49). Both features—harmony and melodic patterning—argue for the DCP interpretation, which is reflected in my enclosing the harmonies within a cadential bracket and my indicating the resultant two deceptive cadences. Particularly complicated is the progression beginning on the fourth beat of measure 43. The motion of the bass up to ⑤ on the downbeat of measure 44 yields a six-four sonority that could have two interpretations. First, it could represent a tonic as part of a Pulcinella prolongational schema. At this point, however, the internal tonic pedal has been given up, and the melody from the end of measure 43 now brings a scalar descent ($\hat{5}$ to $\hat{1}$)

suggestive of cadential function. Thus a second, more likely, interpretation sees the six-four as cadential, resolving to the dominant proper on the fourth eighth note of measure 44; in this slightly more reductive reading, the intervening VI and VII$^6_4$ harmonies would be passing.[64] In either case, a third deceptive cadence on I$^6$ emerges on beat three of measure 44, which elides with another cadential progression, this one abandoned by the inverted dominant at the end of that bar. Yet another cadential progression leads to a fourth deceptive cadence on VI (middle of m. 45). A final cadential progression (somewhat more expansive than all of the previous ones) brings PAC closure to the passage. We find throughout this excerpt a full array of techniques that keeps the bass melody in constant motion, largely focused on the cadential stream, but now and then breaking out into the prolongational stream with ⑦–⑧. As well, Handel realizes four deceptive cadences (in mm. 42–45) before achieving the final PAC. The wide variety of techniques used here to create cadential deferral looks forward to classical practice, but the texture, with its constantly moving bass melody and rapid harmonic changes, grounds this passage fully in the baroque style.

---

63. Recall from note 60 that Gjerdingen also speaks of a "Pulcinella cadence."

64. There is an unusual discrepancy with the notes of the third eighth-note beat of m. 44, in that the literally sounding pitches constitute an unusual VII$^6_4$ sonority, whereas the figured bass symbol $^6_5$ suggests the more conventional pre-dominant II$^6_5$.

EXAMPLE 6.54. Handel, Concerto Grosso in B Minor, Op. 6, no. 12, ii, mm. 42–46.

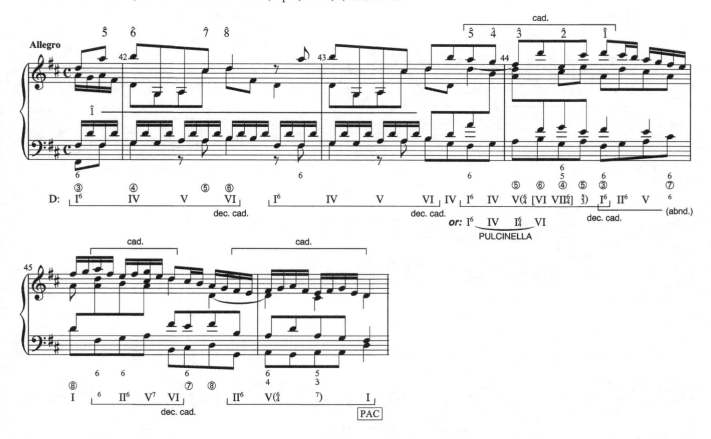

## 6.2. Half Cadence

### 6.2.1. Harmonic, Tonal, and Formal Functions

The half cadence, whose harmonic goal is an *ultimate* dominant triad in root position, is employed in the baroque repertory to mark a degree of incomplete formal closure and to partially confirm a tonal region as a genuine key. This cadence type, however, is used considerably less often in the early decades of the eighteenth century than in later tonal styles, largely because the formal contexts that conventionally lead to an HC are not characteristic of baroque phrase structure. For example, tight-knit periodic structures, which include an antecedent ending with an HC matched by a consequent (or continuation) with a PAC, appear infrequently in this repertory.[65] As well, the half cadential articulations associated with a transition or a development section are rarely encountered, seeing as sonata form, along with its allied minuet, rondo, and concerto forms, is not yet fully developed during this period. Analogous situations do arise now and then. For instance, we sometimes find a transition-like unit that partially confirms a subordinate key (Ex. 6.55). In the course of modulating away from the home key, B-flat, a sequential passage leads to a prominent arrival on the dominant of the new key, F major (HK: V), thus projecting a formation that clearly resembles the end of a transition in the classical sense, along with new material that sounds much like the beginning of a subordinate theme.[66]

Relatively late in a baroque movement, we sometimes find an HC that both marks the return to the home key and sets up a reappearance of opening material, much the way the end of a sonata-form development prepares the way for a recapitulation of the main theme. Example 6.56 illustrates well this technique, which occurs a number of times in the Preludes from the second book

---

65. For an example of the simple eight-measure period, see Vivaldi, Concerto for Violin in F ("Autumn"), Op. 8, no. 3, iii, mm. 69–76; for the compound, sixteen-measure period, see Corelli, Violin Sonata in D Minor ("Follia"), Op. 5, no. 12, i, mm. 1–16, and Bach, Partita for Keyboard in C Minor, v ("Rondeaux"), mm. 1–16. For periodic hybrids, see Corelli, Concerto Grosso in D, Op. 6, no. 7, v, mm. 1–8 (antecedent + cadential); Handel, Concerto Grosso in C Minor, Op. 6, no. 8, iv, mm. 1–4 (antecedent + continuation, R = ½N).

66. Whether the articulation on the downbeat of m. 12 is an HC or a dominant arrival is not entirely clear. Problematic is the way in which the dominant emerges as the last link in a circle-of-fifths sequence, and so a fully distinct half cadential progression is not forthcoming. As discussed in Chapter 4 (sec. 4.4.3.2), such a *terminal* dominant arising from a sequence typically brings a *premature* dominant arrival. Here, in the Bach partita, m. 12 still sounds very much like a genuine formal goal, especially with the medial caesura effect in the melody, so an HC designation is a viable interpretation. As for the incipient subordinate theme, it is difficult to say whether it opens with a standing on the dominant or a presentation, whose tonic prolongation is supported by a dominant pedal (on this distinction see *CF*, 19, 113–14, and *ACF*, 269, 393).

EXAMPLE 6.55. Bach, Partita No. 1 in B-flat, ii, mm. 10–15.

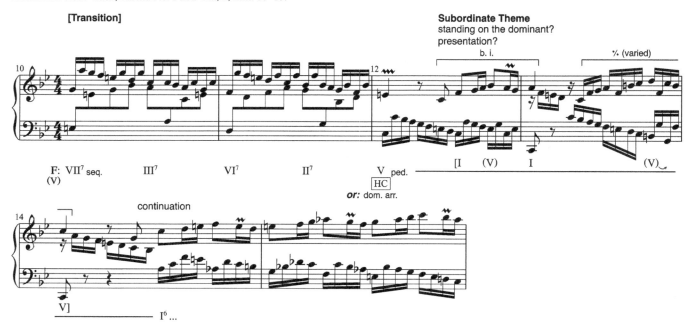

EXAMPLE 6.56. Bach, Prelude No. 5 in D, WTC 2, mm. 39–43 (R = ½N).

of Bach's *WTC*.[67] The HC in the middle of measure 40 liquidates the texture so as to facilitate a return of the opening basic idea in the following two bars.

The HC in baroque repertories is typically found in main-theme structures that exhibit the *Fortspinnungstypus*, as defined by Wilhelm Fischer.[68] In these cases, an initiating *Vordersatz* (antecedent) ends with an HC, after which a continuational *Fortspinnung* (spinning-out), with marked sequential organization, eventually leads to a closing *Epilog* (epilogue). The form thus resembles a loosely organized hybrid, with strong sentential qualities.[69] In Example 6.57, an opening ritornello begins with a four-measure *Vordersatz*, which ends with an HC.[70] There follows

---

67. Book 2 of the *WTC*, compiled in 1742, exhibits many formal procedures that reflect aspects of the galant style; see ahead, note 137. For other examples of the technique described for Ex. 6.56, see Prelude No. 7 in E-flat, m. 56ff., and Prelude No. 14 in F-sharp Minor, m. 29. Prelude No. 12 in F Minor, m. 56, which is especially galant in style, will be discussed shortly (Ex. 6.65).

68. Wilhelm Fischer, "Zur Entwicklungsgeschichte des Wiener klassischen Stils."

69. Though Fischer sometimes identifies an *Epilog* in connection with actual cadential closure, more often he refers to this third constituent of the *Fortspinnungstypus* in connection with a postcadential closing section made up of codettas, while the formal cadence actually appears as the last element of the *Fortspinnung*. On the relation of the *Fortspinnungstypus* to the classical sentence theme type, see William E. Caplin, "Funktionale Komponenten im achttaktigen Satz," 255–57.

70. More precisely, we might want to speak of a dominant arrival here, since the figured bass includes a seventh within this dominant harmony. Besides the continuo, the other instrumental parts give no evidence of the

EXAMPLE 6.57. Vivaldi, Violin Concerto in D Minor, Op. 8, no. 7, iii, mm. 1–7.

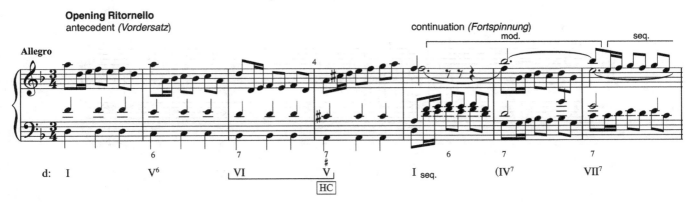

EXAMPLE 6.58. Corelli, Violin Sonata in E Minor, Op. 5, no. 8, iii, mm. 5–8.

EXAMPLE 6.59. Bach, Prelude No. 24 in B Minor, *WTC 1*, mm. 14–17.

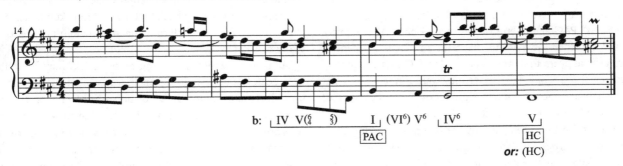

a *Fortspinnung*, featuring model-sequence technique and an expansion of dominant harmony, which eventually achieves PAC closure in measure 17.[71] A related structure sees a four-measure antecedent-like phrase ending with an HC; when the phrase is immediately repeated, a compound presentation emerges, upon which follows the *Fortspinnung*. In such cases, the two HCs have limited cadential scope.[72]

Half cadences are often used to close the first half of a *baroque binary* form, as found typically at the basis of a dance suite movement (allemande, courante, etc.) or of a prelude. For reasons that are not immediately clear, minor-mode movements seem particularly amenable to such closure (Ex. 6.58). Note that the HC in measures 7–8 is of the phrygian type, whereby the bass descends stepwise from ⑧ through ⑦ to reach ⑥ for the start of the cadence. This version of the HC commonly appears in this location within a baroque binary form.

Sometimes, the first half of the binary ends with a home-key PAC, after which an HC follows almost as an afterthought (Ex. 6.59). In such cases, it is not always evident just which cadence should be considered structural—the syntactically stronger PAC or, as here, the rhetorically stronger HC (stronger, due to the slower rhythmic pacing and bass trill). Seeing as the section has

---

dissonant seventh until the last beat of the bar, so an interpretation of HC remains a viable option.

71. I discuss the latter part of this ritornello and the particulars of the dominant expansion ahead in connection with Ex. 6.70.

72. See Vivaldi, Violin Concerto in F ("Autumn"), Op. 8, no. 3, i, mm. 1–11; Vivaldi, Violin Concerto in G Minor, Op. 8, no. 8, i, mm. 1–12.

EXAMPLE 6.60. Handel, Concerto Grosso in G Minor, Op. 6, no. 6, i, mm. 51–58.

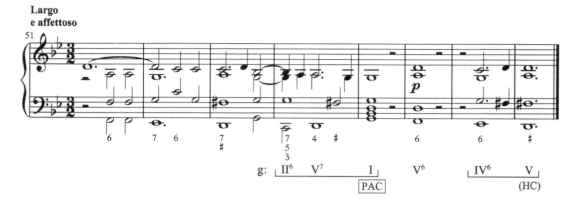

EXAMPLE 6.61. Handel, Concerto Grosso in B-flat, Op. 6, no. 7, iii, mm. 37–43, and iv, m. 1.

not modulated, it perhaps makes most sense to regard the first part as remaining "open" with the HC, which will then be matched by a "closed" PAC at the end of the second part. Alternatively, we could consider the PAC to mark the principal moment of closure as it appears first, and thus see the HC as a cadence of limited structural scope. Finally, we may want to recognize what happens here as a more elaborate, slowed down, manifestation of a *reopened HC* (see Chapter 3, sec. 3.3.5.2).

Even an entire movement, usually one that resides in the minor mode, may literally end with an HC. Again, the phrygian progression is the favored half cadential formation (Ex. 6.60). And similar to the case of an HC ending the first part of a binary, the final half cadential idea of a complete movement almost always follows a genuine PAC.[73] In this case, though, the syntactically stronger PAC is obviously meant to represent the movement's true structural close, with the HC gesture as a kind of postcadential transition to set up the subsequent (fast) movement. Indeed, the performer often takes the opportunity here of improvising on this standard cadence configuration, thus further suggesting that the cadence resides outside the scope of the movement's structural boundaries. One characteristic variant on this type sees the subsequent movement beginning in a different key from that of the slow movement. In most such cases, like that in Example 6.61, the slow movement itself resides in the relative minor of the overall tonality of the instrumental cycle, with the subsequent fast movement bringing back that major-mode key. In relation to what follows, then, the half cadential dominant functions as V/VI of the new key.[74]

As in the classical style, the baroque HC may be followed by a postcadential standing on the dominant, which prolongs that ultimate harmony. It is not necessary to illustrate various baroque standings on the dominant, since they do not differ substantially from what we have already observed in the later classical period. But one somewhat "primitive" type occurs now and then with Corelli (but not with the other composers surveyed for this chapter) and is especially associated with the style of the gigue (Ex. 6.62). Here, the end of the gigue's first section brings a home-key PAC on the downbeat of measure 13. In the manner described earlier, the music quickly leads to a phrygian HC in the following bar. The dominant of the cadence idea is then prolonged in a postcadential manner by a simple

---

73. Handel's Concerto Grosso in G, Op. 6, no. 1, iii, is exceptional in that the half cadential idea comes after a deceptive cadence.

74. The "bifocal" nature of this cadence—looking back to one key, looking forward to another—was first described by Jan LaRue, "Bifocal Tonality: An Explanation for Ambiguous Baroque Cadences." This cadential situation is not to be confused with Robert S. Winter's "bifocal close," a home-key HC that closes a nonmodulating transition in a classical sonata exposition ("The Bifocal Close and the Evolution of the Viennese Classical Style"). Winter acknowledges that his use of the term "bifocal" stems from La Rue's study.

EXAMPLE 6.62. Corelli, Trio Sonata in G Minor, Op. 2, no. 6, iii, mm. 12–15.

EXAMPLE 6.63. Corelli, Concerto Grosso in G Minor ("Christmas"), Op. 6, no. 8, vi, mm. 15–20.

alternation of block-chord tonic and dominant harmonies, all in root position.[75]

In the classical period, an HC and standing on the dominant can sometimes appear *internal* to the formal unfolding of a subordinate theme. In such cases, the prolonged dominant is usually followed by new material that expresses continuation and cadential functions.[76] In the baroque period, we do not usually speak of subordinate themes, though the concept has some legitimacy in certain formal contexts.[77] Nonetheless, we can sometimes encounter a similar half cadential articulation, but normally toward the close of a movement, where we would be expecting the kinds of loosening techniques associated with subordinate-theme organization. In Example 6.63, measure 16 brings a home-key HC, followed by a standing on the dominant (a rather eerie one at that) for the solo instruments. At measure 19, the tutti resumes and leads quickly to PAC closure on the downbeat of measure 20. Example 6.64 shows a situation where following the internal HC, a new continuation is bypassed. At measure 98, the music arrives at an HC in the home key, after which a standing on the dominant sounds through measure 106. A general pause then brings an ECP to close the ongoing thematic unit and the movement as a whole.[78]

With the classical composers, an internal HC and standing on the dominant can sometimes participate in a broader formal process of transition/subordinate-theme fusion.[79] Such cases often arise in what Hepokoski and Darcy call a "continuous exposition" of sonata form.[80] But they also occur in other formal types as well, such as the minuet and rondo.[81] As we will see in the following chapter, fusion processes are employed on a regular basis in the galant style; however, we sometimes find comparable situations in the high baroque. The very forward-looking Prelude No. 12 in F Minor, from Bach's *WTC* 2 (Ex. 6.65), takes the form of a baroque binary, whose first part can be construed easily enough as a continuous exposition. An opening antecedent phrase leads to an HC at measure 4 and a standing on the dominant.[82] The return of the opening basic idea at measure 9 suggests the start of a possible consequent phrase for the main theme, but the music then modulates to the relative major, partially confirming that subordinate key with

---

75. See also Corelli, Trio Sonata in F-sharp Minor, Op. 2, no. 9, iii, mm. 14–15; Corelli, Violin Sonata in G Minor, Op. 5, no. 5, iii, mm. 8–9.

76. On the notion of an internal HC, see Chapter 3, sec. 3.3.4.2; see also *CF*, 115–117, and *ACF*, 376–81.

77. See again the discussion of Ex. 6.55.

78. Observe that m. 109 brings the hemiola of a *cadenza doppia* notated as a single measure of 3/2 meter (but without a time signature change).

79. *CF*, 201–203; *ACF*, 403–408.

80. Hepokoski and Darcy, *Sonata Theory*, chap. 4. Though I disagree with Hepokoski and Darcy's concept of the continuous exposition as a fundamentally distinct mode of formal organization (distinct, that is, from a "two-part exposition"), as well as their understanding of how a continuous exposition is internally organized, I have no problem with the general idea, one that focuses on the textural continuities found within such an exposition; see Caplin and Martin, "'Continuous Exposition.'"

81. On form-functional fusion in minuet forms, see Caplin and Martin, "'Continous Exposition,'" 26–30.

82. Such a standing on the dominant following an opening antecedent would be unusual for a galant or classical exposition of any form.

EXAMPLE 6.64. Corelli, Concerto Grosso in C Minor, Op. 6, no. 3, ii, mm. 96–110.

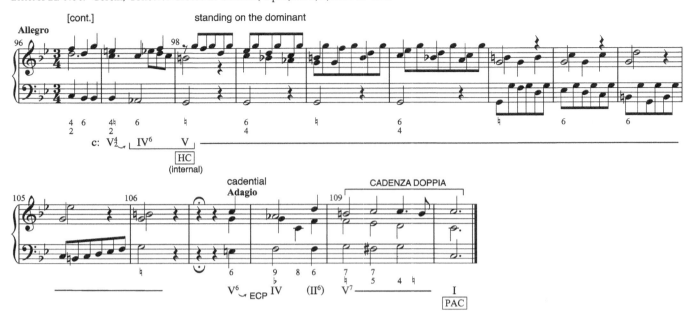

EXAMPLE 6.65. Bach, Prelude No. 12 in F Minor, *WTC* 2, mm. 1–28.

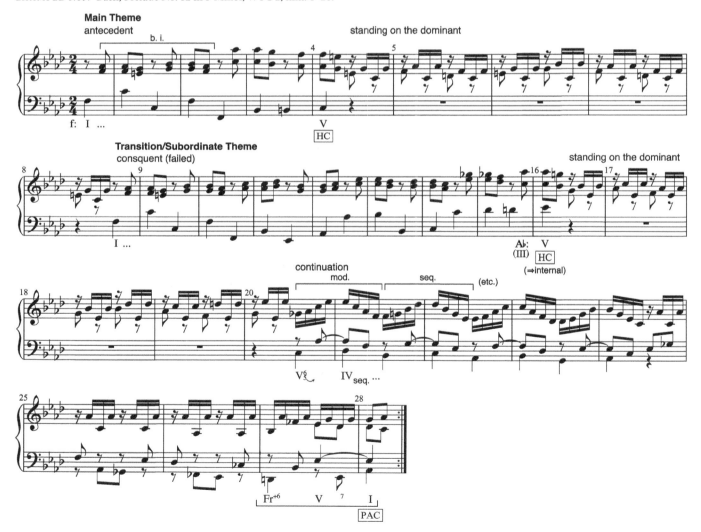

EXAMPLE 6.66. Vivaldi, Violin Concerto in G Minor ("Summer"), Op. 8, no. 2, i, mm. 8–12.

EXAMPLE 6.67. Handel, Concerto Grosso in G Minor, Op. 6, no. 1, i, mm. 30–34.

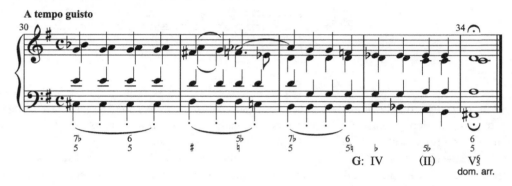

another HC at measure 16. We are reminded of the formal situation where a (failed) consequent "becomes" the beginning of the transition (Marx's *Periode mit ausgelöstem Nachsatz*).[83] A standing on the dominant now follows (mm. 17–20), which matches the melodic-motivic content of the previous one (mm. 5–8). If this were to be a standard sonata-like exposition, we would expect an initiating phrase in the new key to mark the entrance of the subordinate theme; instead, the music that follows the standing on the dominant (m. 20ff.) initiates sequential activity. The sense of a "new" continuation, followed eventually by an SK: PAC at measure 28, suggests that the prior HC (m. 16), which appeared to occur at the end of the transition, can be reinterpreted retrospectively as being "internal" to a subordinate theme. In this way, transition function fuses with subordinate-theme function within this continuous exposition.

### 6.2.2. Dominant Arrival

The principal HC deviation is the dominant arrival. As discussed in Chapter 4, this deviation typically arises through one of two circumstances: (1) a half cadential progression brings a *final* dominant that is rendered unstable by containing a dissonant seventh, or (2) a dominant that appears as a kind of "ending" is not associated with a specific cadential progression; in such cases, I identify the dominant as *terminal* (as opposed to the *final* dominant of a half cadential progression). If the final or terminal dominant of a thematic unit appears prior to when the unit seems to formally conclude, then we identify a *premature dominant arrival*, one that often gives the impression of the music being stuck on that harmony as the rest of the unit plays itself out.

Though by no means common in the baroque era, cases of dominant arrival do arise now and then. Example 6.66 shows a half cadential progression whose final dominant includes a dissonant seventh, thus converting a potential HC into a dominant arrival. With Example 6.67, which shows the final bars of a concerto grosso first movement, we cannot even identify a specific cadential progression associated with the terminal dominant at measure 34. So a dominant arrival is projected in place of a possible HC. This movement is highly exceptional because, unlike most others of its type, the dominant articulation at the end does not follow upon a prior PAC that represents true closure; the movement thus concludes with no cadential expression.

Looking back to Example 6.55, we raised the possibility of considering the dominant in measure 12 to arise from a sequential progression; as such, we would have to consider that dominant to be terminal (not final), thus rendering a dominant arrival in lieu of a genuine HC. (As discussed, though, this latter option is still available if we recognize the dominant as ensuing from a half cadential progression II$^7$–V.)

---

83. Marx, *Musical Form*, 107. See the discussion of this technique in Chapter 3, sec. 3.3.4.2.

EXAMPLE 6.68. Bach, Fugue No. 9 in E, *WTC* 2, (a) mm. 5–10; (b) reconstruction of mm. 7–9.

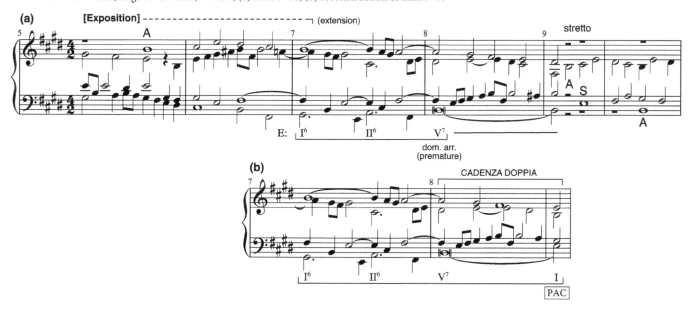

A good case of a *premature* dominant arrival arises in connection with a fugal exposition by Bach (Ex. 6.68a). The passage literally concludes on the downbeat of measure 9, with various melodic arrivals in the upper voices.[84] The bass, however, has already achieved its goal one bar earlier, and the dominant harmony arising at that point is sustained through measure 8 and into the concluding moment at measure 9. The sense of premature arrival can thus be understood, though, as is often the case in these situations, only retrospectively. It is interesting to note that the $V^7$ at measure 8 first appears as the possible penultimate dominant of a *cadenza doppia*, which could have been realized as shown in Example 6.68b.[85] But this cadential formation would have resulted in an HK: PAC arising shortly after the end of the exposition, a procedure that Bach rarely employs.[86]

### 6.2.3. Precadential Dominant Expansion

Throughout this chapter, I have been stressing the tendency for baroque composers to retain a compact cadential formula for effecting phrase and thematic closure. To be sure, we have seen some instances of genuine cadential expansion, but this technique occurs much less frequently than in the classical style. Rather, cadential extension, involving repeated cadential gestures and deviations, is more widely used to effect a general broadening out, or loosening, of the cadential context,

especially toward the end of a theme or movement. The goal, as already discussed, is to push into the future the actual moment of cadential arrival.

If composers of this period tended to eschew expansion of the cadence per se, they nevertheless developed another procedure, one rarely encountered in the later classical style, to help accomplish the goal of cadential deferral. The technique involves elongating a noncadential dominant just prior to the onset of an authentic cadential progression, a process I term *precadential dominant expansion*.[87] Several clear instances are found in Vivaldi. In Example 6.69, the concerto's opening ritornello heads toward formal closure with a large-scale ascending stepwise sequence that arrives back to tonic at measure 16. The bass then rises up another step to bring $V^4_3$, which is sustained in measures 17–19. After this dominant resolves to I at measure 20, the bass quickly marches up for a compact cadential formula to end the ritornello with a PAC. The three measures (17–19) where the music gets "stuck" on dominant harmony clearly precede the onset of the actual cadence. Nothing about the dominant in these bars suggests that it belongs to any cadential progression, yet that harmony helps provide a sense of expansion that raises strong expectations for cadential closure finally to appear. Similarly in Example 6.70, the dominant that appears at measure 11 of this opening ritornello emerges directly out of an ongoing circle-of-fifths sequence and thus has little in the way of cadential character. Yet it becomes expanded for five bars before finally giving way to a highly compact cadential idea in measures 16–17.

At this point, we might wonder whether we are dealing in both this and the preceding example with cases of premature dominant

---

84. The annotations "S" (subject), "A" (answer), and "stretto" refer to techniques of fugal composition presented in the final section of this chapter (sec. 6.4) "Cadence in Fugue."

85. As discussed in Chapter 4, sec. 4.4.4.4, Martin and Pedneault-Deslauriers would identify the situation in Ex. 6.68a, mm. 8–9, as a case of their "*doppia* half cadence" ("Mozartean Half Cadence," 193–95).

86. I discuss the contentious issue of whether or not a fugal exposition normally ends with a cadence in sec. 6.4.3 and 6.4.5.

87. I thank Naomi Edemarian for bringing this technique to my attention. In the musical examples, I shorten the term for this technique to "precadential expansion" to avoid overcrowding the annotations, since the expansion of dominant harmony is made clear by the roman numeral preceding the term.

EXAMPLE 6.69. Vivaldi, Violin Concerto in E, Op. 3, no. 12, iii, mm. 13–22.

EXAMPLE 6.70. Vivaldi, Violin Concerto in D Minor, Op. 8, no. 7, iii, mm. 9–17.

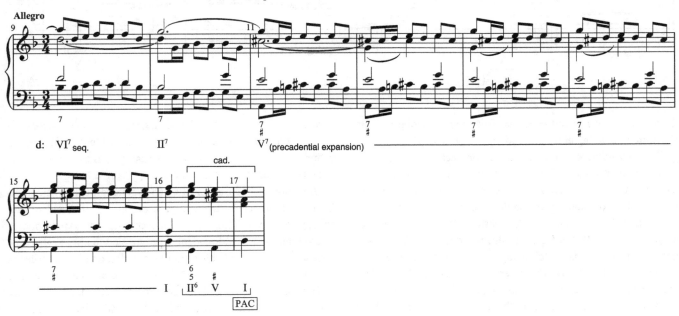

arrivals. To be sure, the morphological conditions are fully in place for such an interpretation. Problematic, however, is their general formal context, for both passages occur toward the end of a concerto ritornello, a unit of form that requires closure with a PAC. If we have little expectation for an HC here, we similarly do not expect to encounter a premature dominant arrival as a deviation of that cadence type.

A more elaborate case of such precadential dominant expansion arises in a Bach prelude (see again Ex. 6.20), whose "final" deceptive cadence (m. 37) we have already examined. Let us now look at how that cadence is set up. Earlier at measure 29, another deceptive cadence (using IV⁶ over ⑥ in the bass) leads to an ECP beginning with V⁶/IV (m. 30), which moves on to several pre-dominants in the next bar (IV and ♭II). Rather than bringing a cadential dominant, however, the progression is abandoned by the noncadential VII⁶₅ at measure 32. This diminished seventh is then prolonged by way of various changes of positions in measures 33–35, ending up on VII⁷, whose resolution to I, in the following bar (m. 36) initiates the compact "final" deceptive cadence at measure 37. Like the previous cases, the expanded

EXAMPLE 6.71. Bach, Brandenburg Concerto No. 1 in F, iii, (a) mm. 10–15; (b) reconstruction of mm. 11–15.

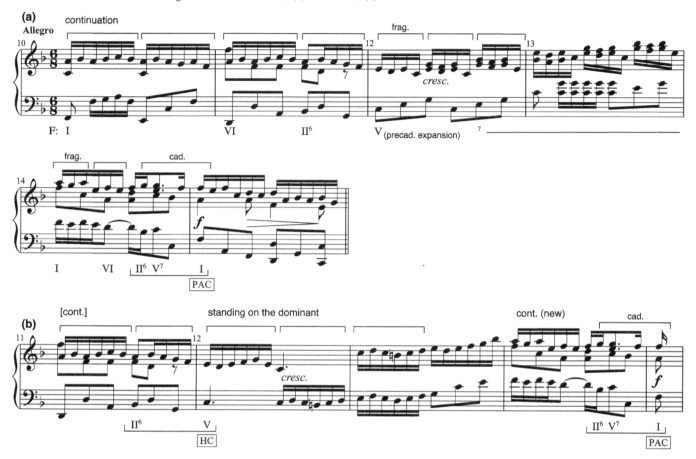

dominant is not in itself cadential, but arouses strong expectations for an ensuing authentic cadence nonetheless.[88]

The precadential dominant expansion seen in the last three examples is strongly related to two other kinds of dominant elongations already discussed in this chapter. One case is the "internal" HC and standing on the dominant that we examined in connection with Example 6.63, measures 16–19, and Example 6.64, measures 98–106. Here, an ultimate dominant harmony is given marked emphasis, following which a new cadential idea (often compact) appears. The difference between an internal HC with standing on the dominant and a precadential dominant expansion is, in principle, clear: in the former, the expanded dominant emerges as a prolongation of an ultimate harmony of a half cadential progression; the prolonged dominant is then heard as postcadential. In the latter, however, the expanded dominant appears as noncadential, and it occurs, moreover, in a formal context that does not raise expectations for half cadential closure, but rather for a concluding PAC as, for example, in a concerto ritornello (see again the discussion of Ex. 6.69 and 6.70).

A second related case involves an expanded penultimate dominant of an authentic cadential progression, one that ends up resolving deceptively, being evaded, or becoming abandoned; another, often compact, authentic cadential progression follows to effect the cadence. We observed this kind of expanded dominant earlier in Example 6.12, measures 50–52 (with deception), and in Example 6.30, measures 81–82 (with abandonment).[89] Again, the difference between such deceptive or abandoned cadential dominants and a precadential dominant expansion involves the cadential status of the dominant itself: in the case of the former, the dominant is penultimate, whereas in the latter, the dominant is not cadential at all.

Though these distinctions are relatively clear in theory, in practice it is not always so straightforward to determine which option is being employed, even if the overall effect is largely the same. It is nonetheless worthwhile examining some of these problematic cases in order to reveal some hidden complexities of compositional technique. Example 6.71a, the final portion of an opening

---

88. The baroque technique of precadential expansion continued to be used in the galant era (see Chapter 7, sec. 7.3.4.3). The technique largely died out in the classical style, but a subordinate theme by Mozart, which we earlier examined in reference to its abandoned cadential progression (see Ex. 5.64), features a highly expanded, *noncadential* dominant (mm. 47–53) that immediately precedes the final ECP of the theme. Another prominent case of a precadential dominant expansion arises in Beethoven's Piano Sonata in A, Op. 2, no. 2, i, mm. 74–83 (ACF, 12.8), where a noncadential VII$^6_5$ is expanded for ten measures immediately prior to a cadential progression (one that is also expanded, but only for four bars; see Ex. 4.36).

89. I have not yet discussed the case of an evaded ECP, but this possibility will be raised shortly in connection with Ex. 6.72.

EXAMPLE 6.72. Corelli, Violin Sonata in G Minor, Op. 5, no. 5, ii, mm. 88–104.

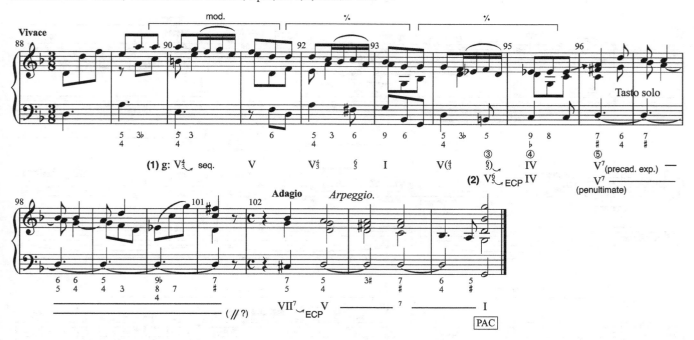

ritornello, presents an interesting ambiguity as to whether the expanded dominant in measures 12–13 is cadential or noncadential. On the one hand, we could see a possible half cadential progression (II⁶–V) leading into the downbeat of measure 12. A rewritten version (see Ex. 6.71b), shows how a pause in the bass could help make palpable the HC effect. On the other hand, what Bach actually writes (Ex. 6.71a, mm. 12–13) is a hemiola that produces fragmentation of the grouping structure within the dominant expansion. This process, combined with the overall melodic ascent, intensifies the ongoing continuation function, such that the dominant expansion may well be interpreted as precadential. The resolution to tonic on the downbeat of measure 14 brings further fragmentation, with the ritornello finally achieving a PAC via a compact cadential progression. Although the alternative possibility of hearing an internal HC and standing on the dominant has some validity, I prefer to recognize a precadential dominant expansion in measures 12–13, especially in light of the formal context, namely the closing part of a concerto ritornello, whose goal is a PAC, not an HC.

Another ambiguous case arises in Example 6.72. Focusing exclusively on the harmonic progression leading into the expanded dominant of measure 96ff., we can observe, as analyzed in line 2, an ECP beginning on V⁶₅/IV at the upbeat to measure 95, moving to IV, and arriving on V⁷, which is highly expanded in measures 96–101. As so analyzed, we would regard that dominant as cadentially penultimate. The ECP would then seem to be evaded at measure 102, when a second one begins with the *Adagio* tempo change and the pre-dominant VII⁷/V in measure 102. This interpretation is problematic, however, when we examine the broader formal context within which this passage arises. For with the upbeat to measure 90, Corelli establishes a two-measure model that is repeated sequentially two more times. As a result (see line 1 of the harmonic analysis), we are inclined to hear the V⁶₅/IV–IV progression (mm. 95–96) as a sequential link (analogous to the V⁶₅–I of mm. 92–93), not necessarily as something cadential. Further disrupting a cadential expression is the awkward leap of a tritone in the melody, E♭–A, into the V⁷ harmony (see arrow). From this perspective, the dominant expansion that follows could well be considered *precadential*, with the actual cadential progression only arising with the *Adagio* (m. 102).

Finally, a number of ambiguities are presented by Bach's Prelude in F Minor from the first book of the *WTC* (Ex. 6.73a). The middle of measure 16 brings a deceptive cadence, when V⁷ from the start of the bar resolves to VI. At that moment, the melody brings back the opening idea of the prelude (Ex. 6.73b). On the downbeat of measure 17, a pedal bass ⑤ appears, which is sustained all the way to the first beat of measure 21. At that point, the melody ($\hat{7}$–$\hat{1}$–$\hat{7}$) suggests the *cadenza doppia* pattern to bring about a PAC at measure 22. What, then, is the status of the long-held dominant (mm. 17–21)? To speak of a *cadenza doppia* here would be to suggest that the dominant on the first beat of measure 21 is penultimate. But if so, where exactly does this penultimate dominant first appear, and how is it set up cadentially? We might be tempted to find ♭⑥ on the second half of measure 16 as supporting a pre-dominant of some kind; however, that interpretation is problematic. In the first place, the VI on the third beat of that bar is clearly functioning as a tonic substitute (of the deceptive cadence), not as a pre-dominant. Moreover, the fourth quarter note, with the leading tone as part of the structural melody, actually projects a dominant harmonic function VII⁴₂.[90] In other

---

[90]. Dominant is also suggested as the harmonic support at the comparable moment at the opening of the movement (Ex. 6.73b, m. 1, beat 2).

EXAMPLE 6.73. Bach, Prelude No. 12 in F Minor, *WTC* 1, (a) mm. 15–22; (b) mm. 1–2.

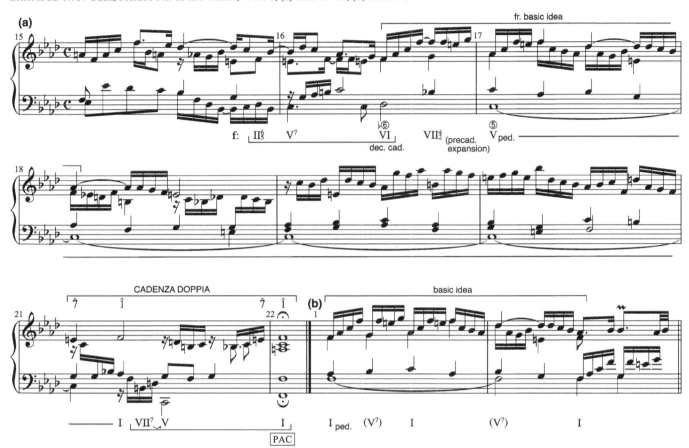

words, the expanded dominant first appears "inverted" on the last beat of measure 16 and is then prolonged (in root-position) from measure 17 on. For these reasons, it is difficult to hear the dominant as a penultimate (or even ultimate) harmony of a specifically cadential progression. As such, we might be rather inclined to perceive the long-held dominant as precadential, along the lines that I have been developing in this section. But then, what are we to make of the *cadenza doppia* of measure 21? As we have seen a number of times already, such a cadential pattern may reside in the near middleground, even when we recognize a compact cadential progression on the very foreground. If so, then we must understand the precadential dominant as resolving to tonic on the second beat of measure 21; immediately thereafter, a short pre-dominant (VII$^7$/V) initiates the actual cadential progression that ends the prelude.

As the last number of examples have shown, baroque composers employ a variety of techniques for delaying the moment of cadential arrival while preserving the compact cadential formula, which so strongly signifies closure in this style. Expanding the dominant prior to the onset of this formula is especially favored, though as we have seen, that dominant can come to have at least three different interpretations: as an ultimate dominant that represents an internal HC; as an expanded, penultimate dominant of an authentic cadential progression, which is eventually surrendered in some manner; or as a noncadential dominant that precedes the actual cadence. And by no means is it always clear just which function this dominant is serving, as the ambiguous cases just discussed make clear.

## 6.3. Miscellaneous Issues

### 6.3.1. Cadential Content versus Cadential Function; Cadences of Limited Scope

At times, baroque compositions seem almost saturated with cadential content. Corelli's music, in particular, brings cadential progressions on a regular basis. But not all of these progressions bring moments that effect genuine closure or, if they do, that closure may be limited in formal scope.[91] A formal context especially conducive to this situation arises when a *subject*, one that is restated in various voices, ends with a cadential figure, as seen in Example 6.74, from the opening of a fugal movement by Corelli. The subject (S), sounding in the upper voice, concludes with a *cadenza doppia* melody ($\hat{7}$-$\hat{1}$-$\hat{7}$-$\hat{1}$) in the second half of measure 2. Corelli supports this melody with a cadential progression concluding on the downbeat of measure 3. A short linking idea

---

91. On cadences of limited scope, see Chapter 2, sec. 2.7.

EXAMPLE 6.74. Corelli, Violin Sonata in C, Op. 5, no. 3, ii, mm. 1–9.

EXAMPLE 6.75. Bach, Prelude No. 14 in F-sharp Minor, *WTC* 1, mm. 21–24.

then leads to an *answer* (A) in the alto voice, which closes with another cadential idea in measure 5, now in the subordinate key of G.[92] The two PACs ending the subject and answer, coming as they do right at the beginning of the movement, seem not to have any broader formal effect; rather, they are limited in scope to the subject and answer themselves.[93] (I deal with the rest of this example shortly.)

Another context for the appearance of a limited-scope cadence is in a postcadential closing section (Ex. 6.75). The prelude as a whole achieves its structural close with the PAC at measure 22. What follows is a closing section signaled foremost by the lack of any motion in the upper voice, which clearly prolongs 1̂ until the very end, where a PAC of limited scope concludes the section.

In the classical style, the *core* of a development is characterized by the establishment of a large-scale model that is sequenced once or twice, after which fragmentation leads to an HC and a standing on the dominant.[94] In the baroque period, we rarely encounter such a classical core, but we often find analogous formal contexts that feature prominent model-sequence technique. These sequential repetitions usually appear early in the second part of a binary form or, in the case of freer forms, following an SK: PAC. Especially with Corelli, such models for sequence often include substantial cadential content (Ex. 6.76). Following a PAC (m. 16) in the subordinate key of A major (III of the home key, F-sharp minor), we find PAC gestures leading to the downbeats of measures 18 (C-sharp minor), 20 (E major), and 22 (B minor). The first two of these "cadences" do not end any broader formal unit as such, so we can recognize cases of cadential content in the absence of genuine cadential function.[95] We might say the same

---

92. I have slightly altered Corelli's original notation in mm. 4–5 in order to show that the answer resides fully in the alto voice.

93. The idea that cadential content associated with a subject or answer is normally of limited scope will be developed more extensively in the discussion of *subject-ending cadences* later in this chapter (sec. 6.4.4).

94. See *CF*, chap. 10, and *ACF*, chap. 13.

95. See also Corelli, Concerto Grosso in G Minor ("Christmas"), Op. 6, no. 8, ii, mm. 29–32.

EXAMPLE 6.76. Corelli, Violin Sonata in A, Op. 5, no. 6, iv, mm. 14–23.

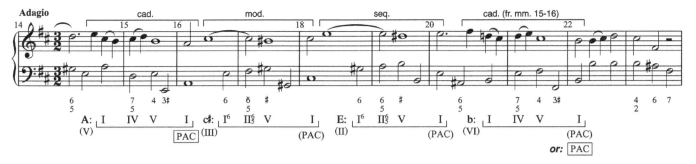

EXAMPLE 6.77. Bach, Prelude No. 6 in D Minor, *WTC* 1, mm. 5–10.

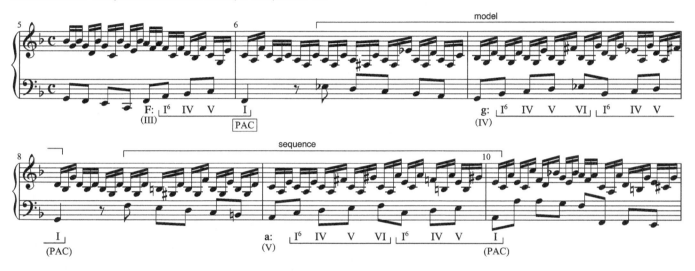

for the third cadence in B minor at measure 22; alternatively, it is perhaps better to understand that cadence as functional, that is, as embracing the structural scope of measures 16–20, especially since that cadence brings back the same melodic and harmonic idea used to confirm the subordinate key at measure 16.

A somewhat more elaborate case is found in a Bach prelude (Ex. 6.77). Measure 6 brings a PAC in the subordinate key, after which a model is established in measures 6–8, which ends with a PAC in G minor (HK: IV). The model is then sequenced up a step, ending with another PAC on the downbeat of measure 10 in A minor (HK: V). More sequential activity follows. Not only does the model end with an authentic cadential progression, but it includes a preceding deceptive cadential one as well (in short, a DCP-ACP combination; see sec. 6.1.5.4). In other words, much of the unit is cadential in content. We would not want to speak of genuine cadences, however, since the overall formal process is sequential. Instead, we would recognize cadences of limited scope concluding the model and its sequence.

Sometimes we find cadential bass lines and their associated cadential harmonies in formal contexts that are not seemingly appropriate moments for closure. Turning back to an excerpt that we have already examined (Ex. 6.74), we see that the subject itself contains a melodic figure (see bracket) that mimics a cadential bass line. Following a retransitional episode in measure 6, which takes the music back to the home key, the subject appears at measure 7 in the bass, and its cadential implications suggest the possibility of a cadence on the downbeat of measure 8. We know, though, that this moment is not an appropriate one for formal closure since it arises in the middle of the subject itself; moreover, the upper-voice melody (with the continuous sixteenth-note motion and $\hat{6}$-$\hat{7}$-$\hat{8}$ ascent) hinders the expression of melodic closure. Note that the bass subject is broken off with the F on the second beat of measure 8. The bass is then given another melodic profile to bring a more proper close to the subject, whose melody (see circled notes) is transferred to the soprano.

### 6.3.2. Prolongational Closure

The idea that a formal unit can express a modest degree of ending in the absence of a genuine cadence has been raised earlier in connection with the concept of *prolongational closure* (or, as many theorists label it, "contrapuntal cadence").[96] In such a case, we normally recognize that a phrase has been closed by a prolongational progression, whose penultimate dominant is inverted. Such processes of prolongational closure are rarely, if

---

96. See Chapter 3, sec. 3.5.1.

EXAMPLE 6.78. Bach, Fugue No. 6 in D Minor, *WTC* 2, mm. 12–14.

EXAMPLE 6.79. Handel, Concerto Grosso in D, Op. 6, no. 5, iii, mm. 125–30.

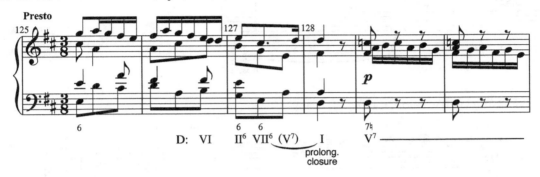

ever, found ending a complete theme in the classical style. The same can be said for the baroque period. The corpus of works analyzed in connection with this chapter (see note 5) reveal scant instances of thematic units closed prolongationally. One case of a formal division articulated by a prolongational progression arises in Example 6.78. Midway through this fugue, and just prior to a set of subject entries in stretto, an episodic passage, which would normally end with a genuine cadence of some kind, closes instead with a prolongational progression on the downbeat of measure 14. That Bach employs this mode of closure may be explained by the highly unusual circumstance that this fugue does not reside in any other tonal region outside of D minor, the home key. As he had already provided a PAC in that key to close the prior episode on the downbeat of measure 10 (see ahead, Ex. 6.99a), he may have wanted to avoid overburdening the fugue with too many D-minor cadences (of course, a final PAC occurs in the last bar of the fugue; see ahead Ex. 6.99c).

One anomalous moment of noncadential closure arises in a Handel Concerto Grosso (Ex. 6.79). At measure 128, an ongoing unit of continuous eighth notes comes to what seems to be a standard PAC, reinforced rhetorically by the caesura that follows. But a closer look at the harmonies reveals that the penultimate dominant initially appears as VII⁶ on the second beat of measure 127. Even though a root-position dominant immediately follows, the harmonic progression is technically prolongational, not cadential. We could of course just consider this to be an exception that proves the rule, and we might wonder whether Handel's listeners would have doubted the cadential effect here. Yet in all of the many prior places in the same movement where the composer brings the music to a comparable "stop" (mm. 40, 48, 68, 72, 84, and 88), he

consistently employs a normal cadential progression, whose dominant is first sounded in root position (on the second beat of the penultimate bar). Moreover, nothing could have prevented him from placing ⑤ on the second beat of measure 127. That it could not have been a mistake in notation is clear from Handel's specifically adding "6" to the figured bass at this point. It seems evident, then, that this is a deliberate choice on the composer's part to make this moment of formal articulation syntactically weaker than it might ordinarily have been. And we might find the reason for his decision in the fact that the only home-key PAC to appear in the entire movement is saved for its very final bar (sixteen measures later). Thus to keep the music open at measure 128, he effects prolongational closure rather than a real cadence.

In my survey of baroque compositions, I have found only a handful of instances where a complete movement ends with prolongational closure. Three of these arise in Corelli's Op. 1 Trio Sonatas, his earliest published work. In one case, Example 6.80, he lets a home-key PAC close the overall structure at measure 32, but he then writes a descending-stepwise (7–6) sequential passage that concludes with a prolongational progression VII⁶–I. I cannot provide any explanation for why Corelli did not write a genuine PAC in the final bars, except for his wanting to maintain the stepwise descending motion in the bass to the bitter end.[97] Another case is particularly strange (Ex. 6.81). A PAC (m. 27) in the subordinate key of F major arises four bars before the end of the movement, one that has featured a consistent alternation

---

97. See Corelli, Trio Sonata in D, Op. 1, no. 12, ii, for a very similar case of a movement closing with a large-scale descending stepwise sequence, whose last link brings the prolongational closure.

EXAMPLE 6.80. Corelli, Trio Sonata in F, Op. 1, no. 1, ii, mm. 30–36.

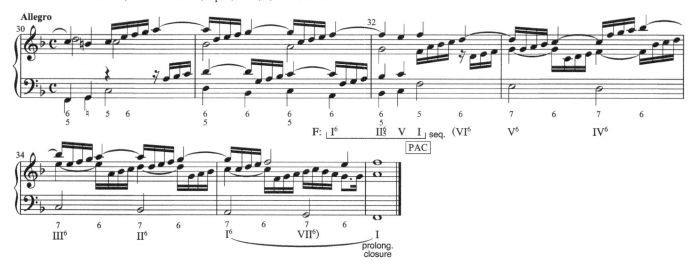

EXAMPLE 6.81. Corelli, Trio Sonata in B-flat, Op. 1, no. 5, iii, mm. 25–30.

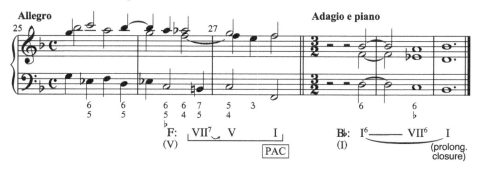

of *Allegro* passages with brief homophonic ones in *Adagio*.[98] The final *Allegro* brings a series of suspensions ending with the aforementioned SK: PAC at measure 27; the final *Adagio* consists of a single prolongational progression in the home key, I⁶–VII⁶–I, to mark the end of the movement. Nothing so odd is found in any other of Corelli's works examined for this chapter.

Prolongational closure for an entire movement is found in a pair of invertible fugues from Bach's *Art of Fugue*. If one fugue is an inversion of another, then it is not normally possible for both fugues to conclude with the same PAC because the descending leap of a fifth in the bass voice required to create the authentic cadence cannot survive the process of inversion, for example, A–D (V–I), would invert to D–A (I–V). In Contrapunctus 12 (Ex. 6.82), which does not contain a single genuine cadence, both the *rectus* and *inversus* fugues end prolongationally, though at different places (m. 54 for the rectus, m. 56 for the inversus). In Contrapunctus 13 (Ex. 6.83), the two versions also end in different bars: the inversus brings a genuine PAC on the downbeat of measure 70; the rectus closes prolongationally at measure 71. But the situation for the rectus is more complicated (if that is even possible in these already complex works). The literally notated bass voice seems to support the prolongational progression V⁶–I (with the B♮ and A sounding as embellishing tones). But just as the bass reaches C♯, the alto pushes down below the bass to sound A (see the circled note), the root of the dominant. When played on a keyboard, which most historians now believe was Bach's intended instrument for the *Art of Fugue*, it is easy to hear the penultimate dominant standing in root-position, thus creating the effect of an authentic cadence.

### 6.3.3. "Plagal" Cadence; Tonic Arrival

Problems associated with the so-called plagal cadence have been discussed in earlier chapters (in Chapter 2, sec. 2.3.1.3, and in Chapter 3, sec. 3.5.2), where I claimed that this cadence type is not operative in the classical style. The same assertion holds for the baroque period (and the following galant style as well). The survey of compositions for this chapter uncovered no clear-cut plagal cadence. I did find several cases that suggest the possibility of a plagal cadence occurring at the very end of a movement, two of which were presented earlier (Ex. 6.21 and 6.22). There I discussed that the final IV–I motion seemed entirely

---

98. Given the key signature, we might suppose that F major is the home key; however, this is a conventional case of the composer using a "Dorian" key signature for a home key of B-flat.

EXAMPLE 6.82. Bach, Contrapunctus No. 12, *The Art of Fugue*, mm. 53–56.

EXAMPLE 6.83. Bach, Contrapunctus No. 13, *The Art of Fugue*, mm. 69–71.

postcadential in function, even though the preceding "final" cadence is deceptive.[99]

Contrapunctus 3 from Bach's *The Art of Fugue* may also be a case of plagal cadence that marks final closure of a work (Ex. 6.84). Toward the close of the piece, and without any prior home-key authentic cadence, the music at measure 66 begins to focus around the subdominant region. In the middle of measure 68, the bass gets stuck on ①, which holds firm until the embellishments at the end of measure 71. If we feel that the reactivated bass line at this moment is structural, then the very local harmonic progression to the tonic is plagal, IV⁶–I. The progression back at measure 68 that established ① is plagal as well. Either one of these progressions might be considered cadential, though each is problematic in its own way. The possible cadence at measure 68 hardly seems like an ending moment, seeing as none of the other voices above the bass achieves any sense of closure. Rather, the situation might remind us of a *premature* dominant arrival, where what turns out to be an ending harmony for a passage arises earlier than where the passage seems really to end. In this case, the ending harmony is not dominant, but rather tonic, and so we might invoke the idea of a *tonic arrival*. In fact, we will observe such arrivals when considering some similar cases in the nineteenth century.[100] As for a possible cadence in the final bar, what undermines that interpretation is the sense that the bass motion

---

99. See also Bach, *The Art of Fugue*, Contrapunctus 2.

100. See Chapter 9, sec. 9.1.

EXAMPLE 6.84. Bach, Contrapunctus No. 3, *The Art of Fugue*, mm. 66–72.

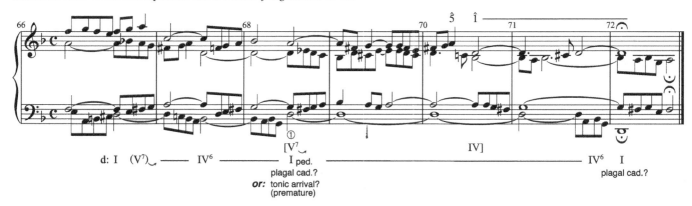

EXAMPLE 6.85. Vivaldi, Violin Concerto in D, Op. 8, no. 11, iii, (a) mm. 205–14; (b) Amsterdam print (1725), mm. 211–16.

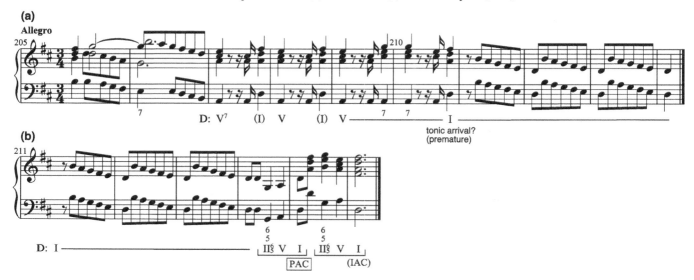

appears merely ornamental (for the purpose of maintaining eighth-note activity through all of the voices). More importantly, the soprano already finds its closure (in a most unidiomatic way, via the motion $\hat{5}$–$\hat{1}$) in the middle of measure 70. Nonetheless, it must be conceded that other than these potential plagal cadences, each one of which is problematic, no other candidate for authentic cadential closure materializes, so it is not unreasonable to regard the work as "ending" with some kind of plagal expression, cadential or otherwise.

The idea that Bach's fugue closes with a tonic arrival (comparable to a dominant arrival) is a concept that finds little empirical support in the baroque literature. A most interesting case, however, arises at the end of Vivaldi's Violin Concerto in D, Op. 6, no. 11, finale. In the 1995 edition published by Eleanor Selfridge-Field (Ex. 6.85a), the final measures of the movement end the same way as the opening ritornello, with a series of alternating V–I chords and descending scales, with no authentic cadence in sight. We perhaps encounter here another premature tonic arrival, beginning on the last quarter note of measure 210 and continuing, through the scalar descents, to the final bar. According to the editor, this ending "represents Vivaldi's original manuscript version, insofar as it can be determined."[101] But the major printed edition (Amsterdam, 1725), which many current performances follow, includes a different ending (Ex. 6.85b). Here, we see that two authentic cadential progressions are tacked on to the end of the scales. If not Vivaldi himself, some performers or editors must have felt that the "original" ending, with the premature tonic arrival, was unsatisfactory and needed a stylistically appropriate close.[102]

## 6.4. Cadence in Fugue: J. S. Bach's *Well-Tempered Clavier*

Like so many of the topics raised in this book, the way in which cadence appears and functions in the genre of the fugue is worthy of its

---

101. Antonio Vivaldi, "'The Four Seasons' and Other Violin Concertos in Full Score: Op. 8, Complete," 207. Further to this concerto, Selfridge-Field notes that, "in the case of No. 11, manuscript sources suggest ... that Vivaldi never settled on a final version of the work" (223).

102. Selfridge-Field provides another variant that features a full-textured PAC to close the movement ("Four Seasons," 218).

own large-scale study, especially since the general topic of analyzing form in fugue has lagged woefully behind other genres, with only sporadic contributions scattered among the standard theory journals.[103] This discussion, therefore, will only scratch the surface of this fascinating aspect of tonal closure, laying out what I see as the main issues that need to be explored. I limit the scope of my inquiry to the fugues in the two books of Bach's *Well-Tempered Clavier* (*WTC*), the core fugal repertory for most musicians, and so the observations made here may well require modification if an investigation with a broader repertorial scope is eventually attempted.[104]

Within traditional fugal theory, cadence is relegated to a minor role, with only cursory attention given to modes of closure within a fugue. To be sure, we find some general comments on how cadences can confirm various tonal regions and how they may be used in connection with fugal techniques such as subject, answer, episode, and stretto. But for the most part, theorists of fugue are principally concerned with the potential for cadence to inhibit rhythmic continuity and melodic flow:

> The very best is when the fugal phrase is so arranged that one rather avoids true cadences, and knows how to set its limits so that no actual cadence would result: inasmuch as the resting places are not at all appropriate in fugues and counterpoints; but are such strangers that they seldom occur earlier nor can appear in their own form until the whole chase has run its course.[105]

> The purpose [of avoided cadences] is to keep the music moving for a long time; [they are] of the greatest necessity in a fugue for the uninterrupted continuation of a harmonic fabric.[106]

> The maintenance of continuity is an important element in any fugal composition. Frequent cadences are to be avoided; indeed, it may almost be laid down as a rule that perfect cadences should only occur at the close of the entire composition, or at the end of the most important modulations; and in the latter case they generally serve as the basis from which a new attack of the subject springs.[107]

> The perfect cadence, however, should only be used when it is clearly motivated by the melodic sense of the parts; . . . only the logic and good sense of the composer will serve as guides. . . .

However, in the exposition, perfect cadences must be avoided. There all the entries should form an uninterrupted chain, and the least break in the melodic continuity and writing of the parts must be avoided.[108]

Thus many considerations of cadences in fugue are directed to how they can be used in a way that minimizes the cessation of musical motion. This attitude, however, betrays a fundamental misconception about cadence, namely that a cadential arrival, in principle, creates a "stop" of some kind. As discussed in Chapter 2 (sec. 2.9), however, cadence primarily functions to create formal closure. The degree to which a given cadence effects an actual interruption in motion depends on its particular rhythmic profile and texture. As this one issue of cadential theory shows, any study of cadence in fugue gains its validity and significance from the general concept of cadence employed by its author.[109]

### 6.4.1. General Concepts and Terminology

To begin, let me quickly dispatch one of those persistent conundrums of music theory: Is fugue a form, a genre, a set of compositional procedures, or all three? That fugue is the latter two cannot be denied. The numerous works entitled "Fugue" certainly establish it as a distinct genre. Moreover, specific compositional techniques are so regularly associated with fugue that we can readily identify fugal procedures no matter the genre in which they appear. (Thus, we often identify fugal writing in sonata-form developments.) As for fugue as a form—the crux of the controversy—the answer is also clear-cut: if we mean by fugue anything comparable to, say, sonata, rondo, or concerto form, then no one has yet demonstrated that a distinct fugal form contains a conventional set of formal functions that could constitute a specific formal type. To be sure, some fugues are manifestly bipartite in design, others tripartite, and indeed, cadence can help define the parts making up these forms. But many fugues are through-composed, and the ways in which cadence is deployed in those works resist any generalizations that would yield a definition of fugal form.

Given the widespread variance in traditional fugal terminology, let me define some concepts relating to fugue that I use throughout this discussion. A fugue begins with an opening section, an *exposition*, in which the fugal *subject*, the principal melodic idea of the work, is sounded successively in all voices of the fugue. An *answer* version of the subject, which emphasizes dominant-oriented scale degrees, harmonies, or tonal regions,

---

103. See, e.g., John S. Reef, "Subjects and Phrase Boundaries in Two Keyboard Fugues by J. S. Bach"; Nicholas Stoia, "Triple Counterpoint and Six-Four Chords in Bach's Sinfonia in F Minor."

104. An earlier version of the following material appears in William E. Caplin, "Cadence in Fugue: Modes of Closure in J. S. Bach's *Well-Tempered Clavier*." Some errors in the musical examples of that article have been corrected for the present study.

105. Johann Mattheson, *Johann Mattheson's Der Vollkommene Capellmeister: A Revised Translation with Critical Commentary*, 695.

106. Friedrich Wilhelm Marpurg, *Abhandlung von der Fuge*, 112 (translated and cited by Peter Schubert and Christoph Neidhöfer, *Baroque Counterpoint*, 219).

107. James Higgs, *Fugue*, 79.

108. André Gédalge, *Treatise on the Fugue (1901)*, 253.

109. One major difficulty with interpreting the variety of ways in which theorists speak of cadential articulations in fugue is the lack of uniformity in their understanding of the phenomenon. Thus, when Percy Goetschius flatly declares that "the Exposition ends, as a rule, with a perfect cadence," it is important to understand that for this type of cadence he is including any progression from dominant to tonic, no matter what the position of the harmonies (*Applied Counterpoint*, 228).

alternates in the exposition with the original subject version.[110] An exposition often employs a *countersubject*, literally a "counterpoint to the subject," consisting of melodic-motivic material that contrasts with the subject but also rhythmically complements it. Like many prior theorists, I define the end of the exposition as that moment when the final voice concludes its subject or answer version.[111] Following the exposition's end, the rest of the fugue brings a succession of *passages*, of which we can identify three different types: (1) a single *subject entry*, the reappearance of the complete subject (or answer) in one voice, perhaps accompanied by a countersubject; (2) an *episode*, typically featuring model-sequence technique and containing contrasting material or individual motives drawn from the subject; and (3) a *stretto*, which constitutes overlapping subject entries in two or more voices.[112] At a higher level of formal organization, we can speak of a *section* as a group of passages; thus, according to this definition, the exposition is a section. Another type of section that may occur later in the fugue is a *counter-exposition* consisting of alternating subject and answer versions in the manner of an exposition. Finally, we can identify the highest-level organization of a fugue as consisting of two or more *parts*.[113]

### 6.4.2. Tonal Functions of Cadence in Fugue

As in all tonal forms and genres, cadences in fugues are used to confirm the establishment of a key: always, of course, the home key, but also other tonal regions that may be explored in the work. Confirmation of the home key normally takes place toward the end of the fugue, though now and then a home-key cadence may occur earlier.[114]

---

110. When the distinction is helpful, I will differentiate subject from answer; otherwise, I will use subject as a general term embracing both versions.

111. Some theorists see the exposition as including an episodic extension closed by a cadence; see note 123 below for one such case.

112. All of Bach's fugues in the *WTC* bring one or more subject entries following the exposition. Moreover, a group of fugues emphasizes episodic passages that alternate with such entries. Another group gives prominence to passages of stretto. This distinction between *episode fugues* and *stretto fugues*, as they can be termed, may well have been recognized by Bach himself in light of how he presents the first two fugues in book 1 of the *WTC*. The C-Major fugue consists largely of stretto passages with only two isolated subject entries and not a single episode; the C-Minor fugue brings exclusively a series of episodes that regularly alternate with subject entries, with no stretto technique at all. Between these extremes, the remaining fugues of the *WTC* present a wide array of options, sometimes residing clearly in one camp or another, but oftentimes including both episodes and strettos, thus lying somewhere in the middle of the spectrum.

113. The distinction between section and part is relatively arbitrary and not of great theoretical import. I normally refer to a fugue's overall formal plan as made up of parts, because it seems more idiomatic to speak, say, of a "two-part" (or "bipartite") fugue rather than a "two-section" one.

114. *WTC* 1:3, 1:5, 1:16, 1:20, 2:6, 2:18.

As for the tonal regions confirmed by cadences, one interesting anomaly is worthy of mention. In most instrumental genres in the eighteenth century, the first tonal region to be explored (after the home key) and confirmed cadentially is the subordinate key, either the dominant region (for a major-mode home key) or the relative major (for a minor-mode one). The minor dominant is also a subordinate-key option in minor-mode movements, much more so in the baroque than in later galant and classical styles. In Bach's *WTC* fugues, exceptionally, the subordinate key is by no means the first region to which the music modulates. Indeed, a handful of fugues do not confirm the subordinate key at all,[115] and several fugues only bring a subordinate-key cadence later, after one or more other keys (typically minor-mode regions such as VI or III) have already been confirmed.[116] All of these cases but one (*WTC* 2:16, in G minor) are major-mode fugues, and perhaps one reason the subordinate key is not so emphasized is that the dominant region may well receive a degree of expression in the course of the exposition via the alternation of subject and answer versions.

### 6.4.3. Formal Functions of Cadence in Fugue

How does Bach use cadences to help articulate form in connection with the variety of compositional techniques we find in a fugue? Obviously, the fugue as a whole will conclude with a *final cadence* in the home key, almost always a PAC.[117] In a small number of cases, this may be the only PAC in the entire fugue.[118] All cadences appearing earlier, which I will term *interior cadences*, may vary in a number of ways: by cadence type, by tonal region, or by the use of a deviation technique. In slightly less than half of the fugues, a cadence appears around the midpoint of the work. In some cases, this *midway cadence* is a decisive marker, helping to divide the piece into two distinct parts. At other times, the midway cadence does not seem to have any particular formal role, yet that Bach so often introduces such a cadence halfway through suggests that he may have attached some special significance to this moment that is otherwise not so evident.[119]

---

115. *WTC* 1:1, 1:11, 2:16, 2:17.

116. *WTC* 1:15, 1:17, 2:9.

117. Only two of the forty-eight fugues (1:23 and 2:15) end with an IAC.

118. *WTC* 1:9, 1:10, 2:13, 2:15, 2:19, 2:20. Moreover, only two fugues (1:12 and 1:21) contain no other cadences than a single PAC (at the end, of course).

119. The idea of a midway cadence has not gone unnoticed in the secondary literature on fugue and the *WTC*. Thomas Benjamin notes, "Many shorter fugues have one clear internal cadence, placed roughly midway through the fugue, dividing it into two balanced sections" (*The Craft of Tonal Counterpoint*, 211). In connection with the F-Minor fugue, book 2, David Ledbetter identifies a "section-ending cadence at the halfway point (b. 40), the only one in the piece other than at the end" (*Bach's Well-Tempered Clavier: The 48 Preludes and Fugues*, 290). Joseph Kerman speaks of a "central cadence," one that "rhymes" with the final cadence and divides the piece into two main parts (*The Art of Fugue: Bach Fugues for Keyboard, 1715–1750*, 121). Such a central cadence, though, does not necessarily appear at, or even near, the midway point, as his analysis of

EXAMPLE 6.86. Bach, Fugue No. 2 in C Minor, *WTC* 2, mm. 12–16.

With most baroque forms (such as the binary, minuet, or ritornello forms), the use of specific cadences to close distinct formal functions is highly conventionalized and thus somewhat predictable. But since a fugal work does not necessarily engage any particular formal type, we initially confront a given fugue without any preconceptions as to the appearance or function of cadences, except, of course, for a final one at the close of the piece. Most fugues, however, do contain one or more interior cadences, and we must then try to ascertain just what formal function they are serving. At times, a particular interior cadence functions to end a section, or even a higher-level part. Furthermore, a cadence may seem to end just a single passage, such as an especially complex episode or stretto. The number of sections or parts thus defined by cadential closure can sometimes suggest an overall binary or ternary form, but often no conventional plan emerges from the succession of formal units articulated by cadences.

In the course of a fugue, we sometimes sense that a given cadence participates in the broader formal expression more by what comes after the cadence than by what precedes it, especially when followed by a new passage that has a strongly initiating quality.[120] Thus in the C-Minor fugue, book 2 (Ex. 6.86), a cadence confirming the minor-dominant key appears at measure 14, exactly midway through the fugue. Immediately thereafter, the texture is suddenly reduced with the introduction of two completely new transformations of the subject (first by augmentation, then by inversion) and the use of stretto. Indeed, the midway cadence here clearly divides the fugue into two distinct parts. A second case of a cadence that seems to gain prominence as a structural marker as much by what follows as by what comes before arises midway through the F-sharp-Minor fugue, book 2 (Ex. 6.87). In this triple fugue, the cadence in measure 37 helps to signal the start of the third subject, which enters in the alto with the sixteenth notes in the middle of the previous bar, and then continues with entries in the soprano (middle of m. 37) and bass (middle of m. 38). As such, the music following this midway cadence, and continuing on to the end of the fugue, creates a new rhythmic expression of ever-flowing sixteenth notes, which markedly contrasts the prevailing eighth-note motion in the first half of the fugue.[121] With an HC, in particular, we often feel that the cadence is more forward-looking than conclusive, as if "announcing" that a new section is to begin.[122] Toward the end of the G-Minor fugue, book 1 (Ex. 6.88), a prominent HC at measure 28 alerts us to a stretto passage that initiates the final section of the piece.

Up to now I have focused on the role of cadence in closing off a formal unit and, as well, in calling forth the onset of a new one. One unit, however, is rarely closed cadentially, namely, the exposition that begins the fugue.[123] If that section is defined as

---

the B-flat-major fugue, book 2, makes clear: "But most sly and artful of all is the phrase leading to the very strong cadence in the middle of this fugue—actually, not halfway through, more like a third" (119).

120. "Typically in fugues—though not always, of course—a strong structural cadence . . . *prepares* a subject entry" (Kerman, *Fugue*, 89). "Sometimes a subject that begins on the tonic can be *introduced* by a perfect cadence that ends an episode" (Gédalge, *Fugue*, 250). "Usually we find cadences *preparing* new thematic statements and/or new contrapuntal devices, such as stretto" (Schubert and Neidhöfer, *Baroque Counterpoint*, 222). (Italics added in all three quotations.)

121. With these entries of the new subject, a sense of a subject alternating with an answer is not projected; rather, the entries are organized sequentially by descending fifths (beginning on G♯, C♯, and F♯, respectively), as befits their medial position in the overall form.

122. Recall the discussion of the annunciatory function of HCs in the classical style, see Chapter 3, sec. 3.3.4.3.

123. In note 109 we encountered one theorist, Goetschius, who claims that expositions in principle end with a cadence. The reason his view so flatly contradicts my own is largely attributable to two factors: he has both a different concept of cadence and a different notion of what constitutes "ending an exposition" from mine. When we examine the cases that Goetschius provides of his "rule" (and helpfully, he comments on eleven expositions from the *WTC*), it emerges that some of his examples, such as

EXAMPLE 6.87. Bach, Fugue No. 14 in F-sharp Minor, *WTC* 2, mm. 34–38.

EXAMPLE 6.88. Bach, Fugue No. 16 in G Minor, *WTC* 1, mm. 26–30.

being concluded when the final voice has finished stating the subject (or answer), then we can well understand why this moment is not suitable for cadential closure: the subject is, in principle, an initiating idea, and repeated initiations—like the presentation phrase of a classical sentence—inhibit closure, rather than promote it.[124] For this reason, the end of the exposition is typically followed by an episode or (less often so early in the fugue) by a stretto. This passage introduces sufficiently contrasting content so as to motivate a potential cadence—an *independent cadence*, as I will call it—that stands apart from the subject itself.[125] Although an independent cadence, by definition, does not close a complete subject, individual motives from the subject may appear in the context of an independent cadential idea. On occasion, the literal end of the exposition may be *extended* by contrasting material that is not sufficiently developed to be considered an episode, and then be concluded by a cadence. A case in point, which we have already seen in Example 6.68a, finds the end of the exposition on the downbeat of measure 7 with the final pitch of the soprano completing the last entry of the subject (the answer version). There follows a brief extension and closure with a premature dominant arrival on the downbeat of the next bar.

---

the A-Minor fugue, book 1, involve an exposition whose final subject (or answer) concludes with prolongational closure (a I⁶ harmony at m. 14), not a genuine cadence, as I understand it. In other cases, he sees the exposition as closing with an episodic extension *after* the final subject sounds, which runs counter to my definition (as well as that of most other theorists) of where an exposition ends.

124. Indeed, the presentation phrase of a classical sentence likely developed out of the fugally inspired practice of opening a baroque instrumental form with a tonic version of its initiating idea or phrase, followed immediately by a dominant version.

125. By speaking of an "independent cadence" in fugue, I am using the word "independent" in a different sense than an "independent IAC" or "independent deceptive cadence": these latter are cadences that do not appear in a context implying PAC closure (see in Chapter 3, sec. 3.2.2.1, and in Chapter 4, sec. 4.1.2.4). See also ahead Chapter 9, where I introduce a third sense of "independent" associated with my notions of plagal closure (sec. 9.3.2.2 and note 66). For further on these distinctions, consult the glossary of terms at the end of the book.

EXAMPLE 6.89. Bach, Fugue No. 1 in C, *WTC* 1, mm. 1–2.

With only four exceptions, which I will discuss later, the exposition of a fugue in the *WTC* concludes with the last statement of the subject (or answer) in a harmonic context that is noncadential. To say that this section does not end cadentially does not mean, however, that it projects no sense of closure whatsoever. At times we can perceive that a goal has been achieved, thus allowing something new to begin. But instead of a genuine cadence, the moment is marked by prolongational closure, as seen ahead in Example 6.90b. Here, the exposition ends on the first beat of measure 9, with the conclusion of the subject in the bass voice. The harmonic progression thus created, $V^4_2$–$I^6$, is prolongational, not cadential.

### 6.4.4. Subject-Ending Cadences

Seeing as expositions rarely close with a cadence, the idea that the subject has an intrinsically initiating function is further reinforced. Yet the melody of many subjects includes a final gesture that may well be harmonized with a cadential progression, especially when the melody ends with descending stepwise motion to $\hat{3}$ or to $\hat{1}$.[126] The subjects of the first two fugues in the *WTC* (Ex. 6.89 and 6.90a) are both amenable to cadential closure, and in the case of the latter, Bach shows us twice just how it can be done.

The first time (Ex. 6.90c) occurs in measures 15–17, where the alto presents the answer, a modulating version of the subject, that deflects the music into G minor, as confirmed for the first time in the fugue by a PAC. Shortly thereafter (Ex. 6.90d), the subject version appears in the upper voice of measure 20 and leads to a home-key IAC on the downbeat of measure 22. Such moments, which realize the cadential implications of the subject, can now be termed *subject-ending* (or *S-ending*) cadences.[127] Within the confines of a subject entry, such a cadence functions as one of limited scope, because we sense that the cadence is closing the subject itself, not necessarily some larger unit of form. Indeed, in both cases from the C-Minor fugue (Ex. 6.90c, m. 17, and Ex. 6.90d, m. 22), it is not clear just what broader formal functions these cadences serve, for in the context of the fugue as a whole, neither cadence ends either of the fugue's two main parts, as defined more by the distribution of melodic-motivic material than by cadence per se. As we see in Figure 6.1, the second part introduces a succession of subject entries and episodes that largely corresponds with what happens in the first part, except that at the start of part 2, the counter-exposition omits an initial subject entry.[128] Within this *rotational* binary plan,[129] the two subject-ending cadences do not close either part. In fact, part 1 receives only prolongational closure ($VII^6$–$I^6$) at measure 15 (Ex. 6.90c). Our two S-ending cadences thus seem to exist primarily to show how the potential for closing a subject cadentially can indeed be realized, and in two different ways—first as a PAC in the subordinate key, and then as an IAC in the home key. Actualizing compositional implications intrinsic to the subject is a principal aesthetic goal of fugal technique, one that Bach achieves in many different ways. Here he does so by means of two S-ending

---

126. Most theorists on fugue recognize that the subject brings melodic closure on these stable scale degrees. Goetschius even speaks of the subject ending with a "distinctly *cadential* effect" (*Applied Counterpoint*, 212). Recall, however, that his concept of cadence embraces any dominant-to-tonic harmonic progression, meaning that the close of almost any subject could be a cadence (see again notes 109 and 123).

127. Some writers on fugue recognize the general notion of an S-ending cadence, though they do not develop the idea to the extent that I do in this study. Thus Marpurg, in his general guidelines for the broader form of a fugue, notes that one can make a "cadence immediately after the completion of the first group of themes [the exposition], in the case where the melody of the subject is inclined that way" (*Fuge*, 121); translated and cited by Schubert and Neidhöfer (*Baroque Counterpoint*, 351). But because Marpurg's concept of cadence, like that of many of his contemporaries, embraces inverted positions of the dominant-to-tonic progression, his identification of an exposition ending with a "cadence" is vastly broader than my notion of an S-ending cadence. Gédalge discusses how "the perfect cadence is sometimes used to begin an episode after the end of the entry of the subject" (*Fugue*, 252). Although he does not specifically define the harmonic content of his "perfect cadence," all of his examples of this cadence type feature the progression V–I, with both harmonies in root position, and so the case he identifies conforms to my idea of an S-ending cadence. Schubert and Neidhöfer distinguish between "formal" and "subordinate" cadences, the latter defined as occurring "within complete themes or sequences, that is, within some ongoing process" (*Baroque Counterpoint*, 217). In this context, they even speak of individual ideas of the subject as having a "cadential potential" (221). But since they are actually referring to individual motives from the subject—not necessarily the end of the complete subject—their idea of a subordinate cadence is considerably broader in scope than my S-ending cadence.

128. The second part does not start with an unaccompanied subject as at the opening, because once a fugue is under way, Bach never (in the *WTC*) so drastically reduces the texture to a single voice.

129. For the concept of formal rotation, see Hepokoski and Darcy, *Sonata Theory*, esp. appendix 2. As regards the formal organization of this fugue, Schubert and Neidhöfer compare a variety of formal analyses, most of which propose alternative readings to the binary view given in Figure 6.1 (*Baroque Counterpoint*, 363–64).

FIGURE 6.1. Chart of rotations, Bach, Fugue No. 2 in C Minor, *WTC* 1.

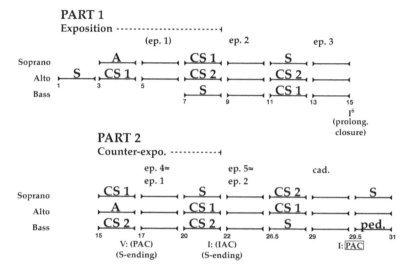

cadences, ones that have only limited cadential scope in relation to the overall form of the fugue.[130]

Not all S-ending cadences, however, are cadentially limited to the subject alone. Some, such as the midway cadence of the B-Major fugue, book 1, seem to close broader sections of the work. As shown in Example 6.91a, the subject closes with the melodic descent $\hat{4}$–$\hat{3}$–$\hat{2}$–$\hat{1}$, the penultimate note even bringing with it a tell-tale "cadential" trill. These features strongly imply that an S-ending cadence will occur at some point in the fugue. Following the close of the exposition, a very brief episode (see Ex. 6.91b) leads to a subject entry in the tenor toward the end of measure 11, which, with the appropriate bass-line support, promises to close cadentially as an S-ending IAC in the middle of measure 13.

The cadence is denied, however, when the leading tone in the alto fails to move to $\hat{1}$ and functions instead as a suspension resolving downward to $\hat{6}$. The resulting VI$^6$ replaces the final tonic, thus creating a type of deceptive cadence.[131] The music then pushes forward (Ex. 6.91c), modulating to the dominant region as confirmed by the S-ending midway cadence at measure 18—one that not only closes the first half of the fugue, but also helps to announce the start of a new section, which features an inversion of the subject. This section, too, receives cadential closure with an S-ending cadence in the supertonic region at measure 26 (Ex. 6.91d).

Before leaving this fugue, it is interesting to observe a number of details in the S-ending cadences. Note that in Example 6.91c (mm. 17–18), Bach alters the end of the subject (in the alto) by adding an embellishment (as bracketed) that, instead of leading as expected to $\hat{1}$, concludes on $\hat{3}$, in order to fill out the tonic harmony of the cadence. And in Example 6.91d (mm. 25–26), the subject in the tenor also ends with a new embellishment leading to $\hat{3}$ (bracketed); this time, however, not because of any change to the implied final note of the subject, but because the subject's pitches largely project the key of E major rather than C-sharp minor, the key confirmed by the cadence.[132] Thus, in both cases the alterations to the subject, along with its being somewhat hidden in an inner voice, perhaps allow us to hear the semblance of an *independent* cadence, the type we would normally expect as form-defining, especially for a midway cadence.[133]

Even if a subject is amenable to cadential closure, an S-ending cadence will not necessarily arise. The very first fugue in C major (see again Ex. 6.89) is one such case, for at no point does Bach write a cadential end for the subject. In fact, quite a number of fugues whose subjects are potentially suitable for such closure are simply not realized, most coming from book 2.[134] Of course, some subjects are simply not able to be closed cadentially, either because they do not finish on $\hat{1}$ or $\hat{3}$, or because they feature an ongoing rhythmic element that renders their end points somewhat obscure (see Ex. 6.92a and b).

---

130. Another factor plays into the disposition of cadences in this fugue, namely, the use of triple invertible counterpoint among the subject and its two countersubjects. Seeing as Bach uses all three ideas for every subject entry (save the first two), Bach has to place CS2 in the bass voice in order to realize an S-ending cadence, since that idea ends with the leap of a fifth and thus has the potential for a cadential articulation. Yet even if we can explain the S-ending cadences in mm. 17 and 22 as constraints of the invertible counterpoint, it still befits us to consider possible tonal and formal grounds for the choice of these particular locations within the fugue. I thank Julian Horton for prompting me to consider the connection here between invertible counterpoint and cadence.

131. I will define and discuss the resulting *inverted* deceptive cadence later in sec. 6.4.7.

132. The chromatic alteration of B♯ in the subject (tenor, m. 24, beat 4) is the one touch that betrays the key that will be confirmed by the S-ending cadence at m. 26.

133. Would it be overly speculative to suggest that a reason this fugue is one of only two in the *WTC* whose final cadence is an IAC (as mentioned in note 117) is that this highlighting of $\hat{3}$ at the very end of the fugue references the prior alterations of the two subjects just discussed to conclude on the same scale degree?

134. Indeed, the second book brings considerably fewer S-ending cadences than book 1. I posit a reason for this difference in note 137 below.

EXAMPLE 6.90. Bach, Fugue No. 2 in C Minor, *WTC* 1, (a) mm. 1–5; (b) mm. 7–9; (c) mm. 13–17; (d) mm. 20–22.

### 6.4.5. Expositions Concluding with an S-Ending Cadence

Having introduced the idea of the subject-ending cadence, I can return to an earlier topic left unfinished, namely, those four exceptional fugues whose expositions seem to conclude cadentially. One case appears in Example 6.93, the four-voice D-Major fugue, book 1. Here, the subject and answer versions enter consistently upward, from the bass to the soprano. The subject closes with a descending melodic line ($\hat{6}$–$\hat{5}$–$\hat{4}$–$\hat{3}$) that is entirely suitable for IAC closure. Of course, the first entry in the bass suggests nothing cadential because of the implied inversions of the final harmonies ($V^4_2$–$I^6$); however, each successive entry is supported by a cadential

EXAMPLE 6.91. Bach, Fugue No. 23 in B, *WTC* 1, (a) mm. 1–3; (b) mm. 11–13; (c) mm. 15–18; (d) mm. 24–26.

bass line to yield S-ending IACs in measures 3, 5, and 6. Though it might seem that the exposition thus "ends" with a cadence, the S-ending IAC at measure 6 is clearly limited in scope to the answer itself and does not close the entire exposition, because the two previous entries (in the tenor and alto, respectively) also conclude with the same S-ending cadences. Thus, what seems to be an exception to the rule is illusory, and we can say that the exposition as a whole remains formally open-ended.

A second exceptional case appears in the three-voice F-sharp-Major fugue, book 1 (Ex. 6.94). Again, the subject is entirely amenable to cadential closure. Only one detail is potentially confusing—determining the final pitch of the subject. Is it $\hat{3}$, which, following a leap from $\hat{5}$, appears on the downbeat of measure 3? Or $\hat{1}$, which follows $\hat{3}$ via another leap and elides with the onset of the answer? The overall harmonic context, not only at the beginning but throughout the fugue, suggests that the leap from $\hat{5}$ to $\hat{3}$, supported by a dominant-to-tonic progression, represents the principal melodic closure, with the subsequent $\hat{1}$ functioning as a kind of overhang, as Koch would say.[135] Unlike in the previous fugue, the subject enters in the order of voices from top to bottom. As a result, the subject appears each time in

---

135. On Koch's overhang, see earlier in Chapter 2, note 100, and ahead in Chapter 7, sec. 7.1.4.

EXAMPLE 6.92. (a) Bach, Fugue No. 9 in E, *WTC* 1, mm. 1–3; (b) Bach, Fugue No. 15 in G, *WTC* 2, mm. 1–6.

EXAMPLE 6.93. Bach, Fugue No. 5 in D, *WTC* 1, mm. 1–6.

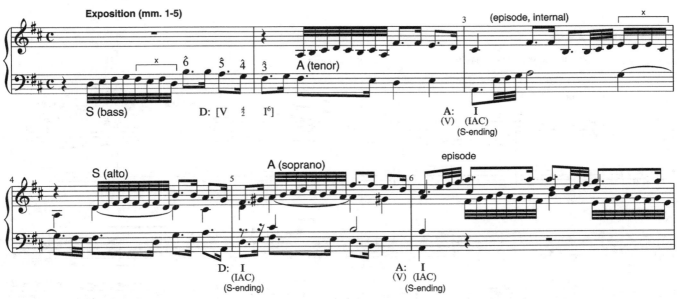

the lowest sounding voice. And for that reason, the possibility of a cadence would always be frustrated, because the final harmony would bring a melodic 3̂, thus concluding with I⁶. So for the first two entries, the moment of subject closure at measures 3 and 5 is prolongational, not cadential. When the bass voice finally enters at measure 5, we continue to expect that the subject will again fail to close with a cadence. This time, however, Bach tricks the listener and bypasses 3̂, thus allowing 1̂ to mark the end of the subject. As a result, the bass leaps from ⑤ to ①, creating an IAC at measure 7. The exposition thus closes, most exceptionally, with an S-ending cadence, one that extends in its structural scope to the beginning of the fugue.

Like the previous example, a third case of ending an exposition with a cadence finds the bass voice changing the subject's final pitch from ③ to ①. As seen in the four-voice fugue in A-flat from book 2 (Ex. 6.95a), the subject, appearing first in the alto, closes with 5̂ leaping down to 3̂ (downbeat of m. 3). When the soprano sounds the answer, it too closes on the third degree (downbeat of m. 5), as does the subject in the tenor (not shown). So when the bass finally has its turn with the answer, we expect that it will follow suit and end on ③, as in the previous entries. Instead (see Ex. 6.95b), Bach leaps the melody down from ⑤ to ①, thus permitting the harmonic context to realize an IAC at the downbeat of measure 10.

Unlike the previous Example 6.94, where a rationale for the same kind of bass-line change could be found in an ambiguity as to which pitch (3̂ or 1̂) represents the actual end of the subject, the exposition of the A-flat fugue does not seem to offer any hints for why Bach changes the bass's final pitch to effect a cadence. A possible explanation may be found, however, in what happens in the bass voice following this cadence. As shown in the annotations, the bass picks up a motive ("x") originally appearing at the close of the soprano's answer (first two beats of m. 5), and over the course of four bars systematically exploits

EXAMPLE 6.94. Bach, Fugue No. 13 in F-sharp, *WTC* 1, mm. 1–7.

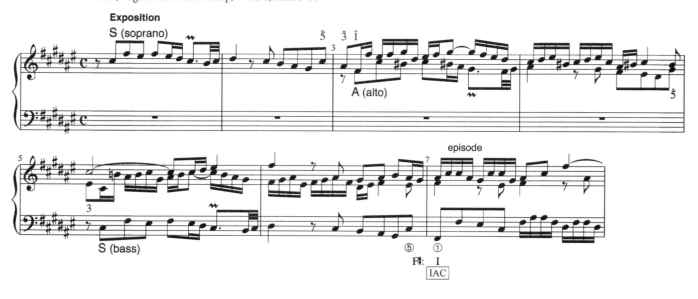

EXAMPLE 6.95. Bach, Fugue No. 17 in A-flat, *WTC* 2, (a) mm. 1–5; (b) mm. 9–13.

that motive by transposing it up one step at a time to traverse a complete octave, starting from E♭3 and ending on E♭4. Moreover, once the bass attains the higher E♭, it leaps down an octave to begin a subject entry on that same pitch. Thus in order to accomplish this extravagant motivic display, it is necessary for the bass to begin on the lower E♭, which is provided by Bach having altered the end of the ongoing answer and thus creating at the same time an IAC to end the exposition.

The final exceptional case of an exposition closing with a cadence occurs in the G-sharp-Minor fugue, book 1. I postpone my discussion of this exposition until I consider the work as whole at the end of the chapter (sec. 6.4.8.3).

EXAMPLE 6.96. Bach, Fugue No. 16 in G Minor, *WTC* 1, mm. 31–34.

EXAMPLE 6.97. Bach, Fugue No. 14 in F-sharp Minor, *WTC* 1, mm. 36–40.

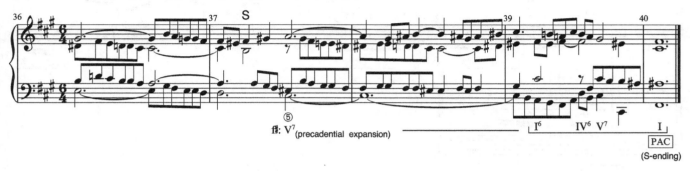

## 6.4.6. Final Cadence as S-Ending

From the discussion up to now, it should be evident that from a rhetorical perspective, S-ending cadences are inherently weaker as markers of formal closure than are independent cadences, which contain conventionalized material standing apart from the subject. And indeed, a survey of Bach's practice in the *WTC* reveals that in the majority of cases, the cadences most responsible for articulating the main structural components of the fugue are independent. Consider the final cadence, which we would assume to be the strongest one of all. Of the forty-eight fugues, only four conclude with an S-ending cadence, thus supporting the view that independent cadences are better suited than S-ending ones to mark a fugue's important boundaries. And this proposition makes sense because, as already mentioned, the subject is in principle an initiating idea, even if it may sometimes conclude with a degree of cadential expression. Thus the strongest kind of closure sees the fugue ending with a cadence that stands apart from, and thus contrasts with, the subject.[136] And this is precisely the situation that Bach exploits most of the time.[137]

Though they are exceptional, it would be instructive to examine the four S-ending final cadences of the *WTC* in order to understand why they are nonetheless effective in the contexts in which they arise. Consider the close of the G-Minor fugue, book 1 (Ex. 6.96). The lead-up to the end sees a subject entry in the alto in the third beat of measure 31, accompanied by various melodic motives featuring the durational pattern of two sixteenth notes followed by an eighth note. This material has been used throughout the fugue, its source being the final motives of the subject. At measure 33, where the last subject entry appears in the tenor, the accompaniment suddenly changes: all of the sixteenth notes are eliminated, and voices are added to effect a fuller chordal texture. This powerful textural contrast, whose rhythmic uniformity helps to blur our hearing of the subject, distinguishes this measure from all that have come before and thus prepares the way for the S-ending cadence that concludes the fugue. Two factors contribute to make this cadence sound "independent," even if it really is not: first, the markedly different texture of measure 33, and second, the downplaying of the subject in an inner voice, so as not to interfere with the more structural, outer-voice cadential framework.[138]

The final subject entry of the F-sharp-Minor fugue, book 1 (Ex. 6.97), lies in the soprano voice in measures 37–40, so that unlike

---

136. This principle thus conforms to the more general idea of closure as involving a "terminal modification," proposed by the literary critic Barbara Herrnstein Smith; see Chapter 1, sec. 1.1.

137. As mentioned in note 134, the fact that book 2 of the *WTC* (ca. 1744) contains many fewer S-ending cadences than book 1 (ca. 1722) perhaps reflects a tendency on Bach's part to highlight the structural function of independent cadences. In this respect, he may have been influenced by an emerging galant aesthetic that, in comparison to baroque practice, favors a greater transparency of formal goals; for more

on Bach's awareness of galant practices, see Robert L. Marshall, "Bach the Progressive: Observations on His Later Works."

138. To be sure, the returning sixteenth notes in the final bar belong to the end of the subject, thus permitting us to realize that this fugue is closing with a genuine S-ending cadence after all.

EXAMPLE 6.98. Bach, Fugue No. 17 in A-flat, *WTC* 2, mm. 44–50.

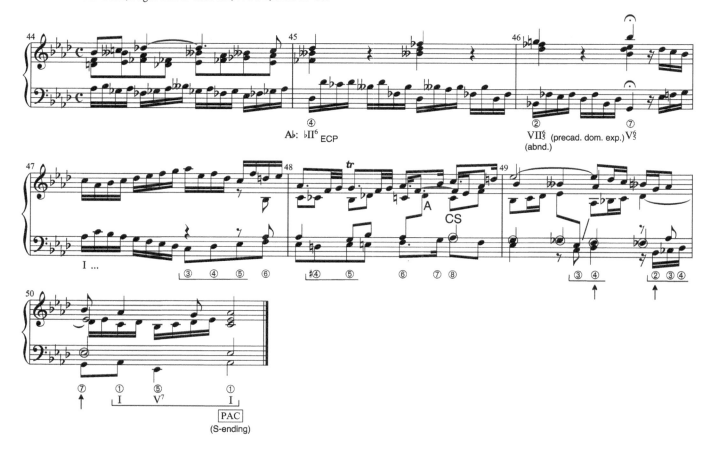

the previous example, we readily hear that the final cadence is S-ending. But given the slow tempo usually adopted for this piece and a subject that lasts four full bars, it is not so difficult to sense that this S-ending cadence has a somewhat more extensive structural reach than is ordinarily the case. Moreover, Bach provides one important cue that makes the final cadence seem more marked than it might otherwise be: in the middle of measure 37, right after the start of the subject, he employs a ⑤ pedal in the bass and then supports much of the subject with dominant harmony, which holds until the resolution to I⁶ on the second quarter note beat of measure 39. The cadence then appears shortly thereafter. We therefore see Bach using a *precadential dominant expansion* (see sec. 6.2.3) as a means of helping to signal the cadence as structurally significant.

The four-voice A-flat-Major fugue, book 2, combines techniques that we have seen in the previous two fugues to help make the final S-ending cadence an especially powerful one. The earlier discussed Example 6.95a shows the opening subject and answer entries along with the descending chromatic quarter notes that constitute the countersubject. Turning to the close of the work, Example 6.98, we can observe that the final cadence sees the answer at measure 48 buried in an inner voice, the tenor, as in the G-Minor fugue of Example 6.96; moreover, Bach obscures our hearing the answer all the more by adding a fifth voice to the texture, namely, the chromatic countersubject, shown by the circled notes. Given the textural complexities of these final two bars, our listening attention is probably drawn more to the outer-voice motions, which are fully conventional in their cadential expression, than to the inner-voice answer. As in the F-sharp-Minor fugue of Example 6.97, Bach signals the final cadence of the A-flat-major fugue considerably earlier than the appearance of the final answer entry, for back at measure 45 he writes a pre-dominant ♭II⁶, in a significantly reduced, homophonic texture, that is expanded for an entire bar, thus suggesting that an ECP is in the making. The progression is abandoned, however, when the bass twice leaps down a third to create inverted dominant-functioning harmonies in measure 46 (VII⁶₅ and V⁶₅), thus projecting a precadential dominant expansion, emphasized by the fermata in the middle of that bar.[139] The resolution to tonic on the downbeat of measure 47 leads to three attempts to realize a complete authentic cadential bass line, which, however, consistently fail to create final closure: (1) by allowing the bass to move up deceptively to ⑥ (at the end of m. 47); (2) by having the bass stride all the way up to ⑧ in measure 48; and (3) by leaping the bass from ④ down to ② (m. 49, see arrows) and then again from ④ down to

---

139. Here, unusually, the two techniques of an abandoned ECP and a precadential dominant expansion are combined together in a single passage.

EXAMPLE 6.99. Bach, Fugue No. 6 in D Minor, *WTC* 2, (a) mm. 1–10; (b) mm. 14–17; (c) mm. 25–27.

⑦ (end of m. 49 to m. 50) in a manner that imitates in diminution the same leaping bass in measures 45–46. After all of these failed attempts to create a standard ③–④–⑤–① cadential bass line, Bach concludes the fugue with a simple cadence, employing a ①–⑤–① bass that gives up even trying to engage ③ and ④. That we have entered into a broad cadential zone starting at measure 45 and continuing to the very end is clear, and the long-fought-for final cadence—S-ending that it may be—creates a powerful moment of arrival and closure.

The fourth case of an S-ending final cadence closes the D-Minor fugue in book 2. In order to understand the rationale for this cadence, we need to consider earlier passages, starting with the first entry of the subject in the exposition (Ex. 6.99a). Following the flurry of sixteenth-note triplets, a partially chromaticized, scalar eighth-note descent from $\hat{8}$ down to $\hat{2}$ concludes with a leap up to $\hat{5}$ and then down again to $\hat{3}$. At this point the answer enters, thus marking that the subject technically ends on this third degree. But like the situation we saw earlier in the F-sharp-Major fugue (Ex. 6.94), the melody leaps further down to $\hat{1}$. This detail is important, because the tonic scale degree has been implied to be the real ending of the subject, as a realization of a complete octave descent from $\hat{8}$ to $\hat{1}$. Here, however, $\hat{1}$ seems to come after the

EXAMPLE 6.100. Bach, Fugue No. 3 in C-sharp, *WTC* 1, mm. 52–55.

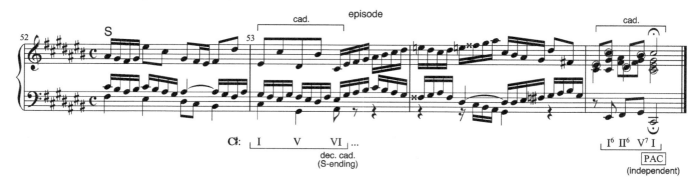

conclusion of the subject on $\hat{3}$. With the answer in the soprano, this implication of tonic closure is realized when the melody into measure 5 now leaps from $\hat{5}$ directly to $\hat{1}$ (in A minor), thus bypassing $\hat{3}$, as in the subject version. The final entry of the exposition, in measures 6–8 of the bass voice, also features a final leap of a fifth. Indeed this ⑤–① motion might have created an S-ending PAC to close the exposition. Yet in line with his normal practice of not letting that section end cadentially, Bach abandons the cadence in a particular manner, which will be discussed shortly. Even with this emphasis on a final tonic, one melodic implication is still left unrealized, namely, that $\hat{1}$ would be approached stepwise directly from $\hat{2}$ in a way that fully completes a scalar descent.

As the fugue progresses, the opportunity for the subject to conclude with stepwise motion arises with the subject and answer stretto in measures 14–16 (Ex. 6.99b). In this case, a complete scalar descent from $\hat{8}$ to $\hat{1}$ is realized, but not so as to see $\hat{1}$ functioning to end the subject: by the time the tonic pitches arrive in measure 16 (D, in the alto, downbeat of the bar; A in the soprano, one and a half beats later), the harmonies have already begun a sequential progression rendering these moments formally open, and the scalar descent continues in both voices. Only at the very end of the piece, now securely in D minor (Ex. 6.99c), does Bach finally bring a subject entry—well exposed in the soprano—that fully realizes the complete scalar descent from $\hat{8}$ to $\hat{1}$ without the interfering leap from $\hat{5}$. The use of an S-ending cadence here is thus fully justified and makes a highly conclusive effect.

### 6.4.7. Cadential Deviations and Cadential Blurring

Up to this point I have largely been discussing the genuine cadence types of PAC, IAC, and HC. Let us now consider some cadential deviations to see how they function in the context of Bach's fugal practice.[140] Of the three standard types—deceptive, evaded, and abandoned—only the first and third techniques appear in the *WTC*. The lack of any evaded cadences is perhaps explainable by the disruption to the grouping structure that this deviation produces, an effect that would run counter to the normal aesthetics of rhythmic continuity so prized in the genre of fugue.[141] Cadential abandonment occurs only now and then, whereas the deceptive cadence is the deviation type most used in the corpus. A typical case of the latter can be seen toward the close of the C-sharp-Major fugue, book 1 (Ex. 6.100), which uses an S-ending deceptive cadence in the middle of measure 53. The cadential deception is immediately followed by episodic material with pervading sixteenth-note motion that leads to a final, independent PAC of contrasting texture. This cadence also includes the leaping motive that ends the subject, shown by the circled notes, which nicely references the previous deceptive cadence.[142] Abandoned cadential progressions also can be found in the fugal repertory, one case of which has been discussed in connection with Example 6.98, measure 46.

In the *WTC* fugues, Bach sometimes uses two forms of cadential deviation that are related to the standard types of deceptive and abandoned but do not fit so comfortably into these established categories. Both forms involve the leading tone, or an expected leading tone, within the cadential dominant, and both find a bass line that remains conventionally cadential with a final ⑤–① leap. In the first case, the leading tone is suspended over the harmonic resolution from dominant to tonic; but rather than resolving upward to complete the latter, the suspension resolves downward to create, in effect, a VI$^6$ harmony in place of the final tonic. We have

---

140. If the general cadence concept of most prior theorists of fugue is problematic, as discussed earlier, their treatment of cadential deviations is at times remarkably comprehensive. J. J. Fux, especially, discusses a number of techniques that yield what he calls a "deceptive cadence" (Alfred Mann, *The Study of Fugue*, 91–92). Using modern terminology, these include changing the expected bass (⑤–①) to yield a different harmonic progression (e.g., ⑤–⑥, V-VI; ③–③, V-I$^6$; or ⑤–④, V-IV); retaining the expected bass ⑤–① but changing an upper voice ($\hat{5}$–$\hat{6}$, V-VI$^6$); and lowering the expected leading tone ($\hat{7}$) by a half step ($\flat\hat{7}$). Marpurg also discusses the same types as Fux, but adds to the mix the omission of the final pitch of the expected cadence, which results in what I would consider a cadential evasion (*Fuge*, 112–13). See also Schubert and Neidhöfer, *Baroque Counterpoint*, 219–20.

141. Recall, of course, that the evaded cadence in general is used less frequently in the baroque than in later eighteenth-century styles; see above, sec. 6.1.4.2.

142. See also *The Art of Fugue*, Contrapunctus 2, m. 83, for a similar deceptive cadence, one that becomes "final" (as discussed in sec. 6.1.4.1).

EXAMPLE 6.101. Bach, Fugue No. 8 in D-sharp Minor, *WTC* 1, mm. 15–18.

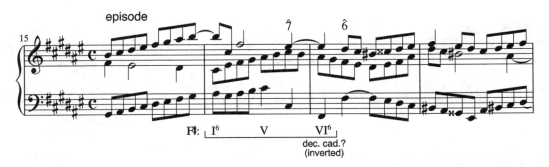

already seen a case of this deviation in Example 6.91b, measure 13, where, in connection with a potential S-ending IAC in the middle of the bar, the leading tone A♯ in the alto voice fails to resolve to 1̂, remaining instead as a suspension that descends to 6̂ (with an ornamental decoration) on the fourth beat. Technically speaking, this is a deceptive cadence, because the final tonic of an authentic cadential progression is replaced by VI. But the material content here is different from that of the normal deviation, which typically sees the leading tone rising to 1̂ while the bass moves up stepwise to support a root-position VI. In this less common form, the bass resolves correctly, ⑤–①, but the leading tone descends, and so the term *inverted deceptive cadence* might be an appropriate one here.[143] Because the "problem" resides in the upper voice, rather than the bass, this type of deviation is akin to the "final" deceptive cadence where V⁷/IV replaces the tonic, in which case the leading tone, rather than being a suspension, directly resolves downward to ♭7̂ (see again, Ex. 6.19a, mm. 31–32, in the alto voice).

In Example 6.91b, the sense of denying a cadence is fairly strong because its coming at the end of the subject raises our expectations for cadential closure. But sometimes, as we see in Example 6.101, a similar formation arises in a context that seems less closing in function. Here a new episode begins on the downbeat of measure 15, using material that has no direct relationship to the subject. Measure 16 contains a cadential progression whose bass line is completed on the downbeat of the following bar. But the cadence is denied when the leading tone in the soprano fails to resolve correctly, functioning instead as a downward-resolving suspension. Since no particular expectation of a cadence arises at this point, a new episode having just begun, analyzing a genuine inverted deceptive cadence is perhaps questionable, though we likely perceive a trace of this deviation nonetheless.[144]

A different kind of deviation occurs when the ongoing context leads us to expect the appearance of a cadential dominant with its leading tone. Instead, the seventh scale degree is immediately lowered by a half step, thus canceling the effect of a genuine cadential dominant.[145] Inasmuch as the expected dominant fails to appear, this deviation falls into the category of the abandoned cadence. Yet the effect of a possible cadence is somewhat different here than in most such cases, since, as in the inverted deceptive cadence, the bass line retains its conventional pattern, ⑤–①. One case of this deviation, which I now term a *lowered leading-tone abandonment*, arises at the end of the exposition of the D-Minor fugue, book 2 (see again Ex. 6.99a, mm. 7–8).[146] As discussed earlier, the exposition is poised to conclude with an S-ending cadence when the subject makes a final leap from ⑤ to ① on the downbeat of measure 8. In line with his normal practice of ending an exposition noncadentially, however, Bach abandons the potential cadence by failing to include a leading tone in the cadential dominant over ⑤; instead, he lowers the expected C♯ to C♮, thus converting the harmony into a nondominant, minor-seventh sonority. Seeing as this chromatic alteration denies expectations for a final D-minor tonic, Bach alters the harmony over ① into an applied dominant seventh, which briefly tonicizes the subdominant.[147] Within this context,

---

143. Jean-Phillipe Rameau identifies a similar deceptive cadence (*cadence rompuë*) when first introducing that idea early in book 2 of *Treatise on Harmony*, 61–63. Rameau's cadence, however, sees the upper voice resolving to 1̂ rather than descending to 6̂, which is Bach's practice. One of Fux's examples of a deceptive cadence likens to Rameau's (Mann, *Fugue*, 92, Ex. 56). See again Ex. 6.23 by Corelli for a morphology similar to the inverted deceptive cadence, except that this case creates an evaded cadence rather than a deceptive one.

144. A similar situation arises in *WTC* 1:4, m. 59.

145. Neuwirth traces this particular form of cadential deviation back to Gottfried Walther and Angelo Berardi, the latter speaking of *motivo di cadenza* for the technique (Neuwirth, "*Fuggir La Cadenza*, 122; Johann Gottfried Walther, *Musicalisches Lexicon*, 125; Angelo Berardi, *Documenti Armonici*, 152). Berardi's example arises within a broader descending-fifth sequential pattern, so its cadential implications are somewhat obscured; yet we will see momentarily that Bach also employs this deviation within a sequential context (see ahead Ex. 6.102a, mm. 20–21). A number of specifically fugal theorists also identify the chromatic lowering of an expected leading tone as a technique of cadential deviation: Fux (in Mann, *Fugue*, 91, Ex. 54), Marpurg (*Fuge*, 113 and Table 31, Fig. 12x), Gédalge (*Fugue*, 251), and Ebenezer Prout (*Fugue*, 74).

146. Both Fux and Prout specifically identify this deviation using the Italian expression *inganno* ("deception"), but Marpurg references the same term for any kind of cadential deviation. Berardi's *motivo di cadenza* ("motive for cadence") is not helpful, since it conveys no particular sense of deviation. To be sure, the term I have adopted—lowered leading-tone abandonment—is rather cumbersome but at least is accurately descriptive.

147. The tonicized IV barely appears in m. 8 as a six-four sonority on the second half of beat 1, before the harmonic context changes again in order to tonicize C major (HK: ♭VII).

EXAMPLE 6.102. Bach, Fugue No. 17 in A-flat, *WTC* 2, (a) mm. 18–22; (b) mm. 25–27.

the minor seventh over ⑤ thus functions as a pre-dominant II⁷. Though the bass line may be heard to project a cadential moment associated with the home key of D minor, Bach redirects the harmonic focus to the subdominant side of the tonal spectrum, thus ensuring that the exposition closes without any cadential expression. Shortly thereafter, however, an episode initiated by the abandoned cadence in measure 8 succeeds in confirming the home key with a genuine, and independent, PAC on the downbeat of measure 10.

The A-flat-Major fugue, book 2, whose beginning and ending I discussed earlier (Ex. 6.95 and 6.98), is saturated with this deviation type (see Ex. 6.102a and b). Starting at the end of measure 18, the alto sounds a subject entry, whose final pitches lead to a potential cadence in measure 20 when the progression I–II⁶₅ points toward a cadential dominant to appear on the second half of beat 2. If the soprano voice had introduced a G♮ at this point, resolving to A♭, the harmonic progression would have yielded an S-ending cadence. As actually composed, however, the cadence is abandoned when G♭ appears in the soprano, thus deflecting the tonal context one step to the flat side (D-flat). Note that unlike most abandoned cadences, the bass line continues to project its conventional pattern of ④–⑤–①. A sequence of this same pattern then appears in the first half of the following bar. Immediately thereafter (second half of m. 21) we hear in the alto the standard melodic configuration for a *cadenza doppia* except that ⑦, on the last eighth-note beat of the bar, is once again flattened. A final case (Ex. 6.102b) then occurs toward the end of measure 25,[148] after which the section concludes in the middle of measure 27 with an independent cadence in C minor (HK: III). Looking over these four cases of lowered leading-tone abandonment, it is important to distinguish those that seem to have a genuine potential to *function* cadentially from those that merely include cadential *content* in noncadential formal contexts. The first and fourth cases (Ex. 6.102a, m. 20, and Ex. 6.102b, mm. 25–26) appear at the close of subject entries, thus failing to fulfill a potential S-ending cadence. The other two cases (Ex. 6.102a, m. 21 and mm. 21–22) occur within an episode; they represent sequential repetitions of

---

148. This last case is further muddied when what we expect to be a V⁷/IV (downbeat of m. 26) sees the third of that harmony lowered by a half step (to A♭), thus denying its true dominant function, which instead becomes a pre-dominant II⁷ of E-flat. To avoid an overly complicated analysis on the score, I have not annotated this additional tonicization, instead showing the altered dominant as V⁷.

the initial abandonment and thereby cannot be seen to mark the end of any broader formal unit. The difference between cadential function and cadential content is manifest in many of Bach's fugues. Indeed, the third case study to be examined below (the G-sharp-Minor fugue, book 1) plays extensively with this distinction in ways that promote some interesting processes of retrospective reinterpretation.

The various cadential deviations just discussed involve cases where an implied cadence fails to be fully realized. Very often, and especially in fugal genres, a closing configuration meets the harmonic, melodic, and formal requirements for genuine cadence, yet elements of the texture *blur* an unambiguous expression of cadential closure. Most typically, the blurring arises from various embellishments, especially suspensions and their resolutions, within the cadence's individual voices, which may result in incomplete harmonies at the moment of arrival. The practice of maintaining ongoing rhythmic activity in one or more voices can produce a modest degree of blurring as well. A cadence can also be blurred when, shortly prior to the moment of cadential arrival, one or more voices initiate a subject entry, thus creating a formal overlap.[149]

Cadential blurring affects the rhetorical expression of cadence, not its syntactical function, since we still recognize that closure has been obtained, even if it is to some extent blurred. If the blurring in a given case does not in itself allow us to deny its status as a genuine cadence (otherwise the situation would be one of cadential deviation), the practice of blurring tends to correlate with the cadence's formal significance: those that mark major divisions tend to have little or no blurring effects, while those that arise within a section, and especially in the context of S-ending cadences, may well become blurred. Finally, the technique is not associated with genuine cadences exclusively, for often a cadential deviation may also feature such elements (e.g., the 7–6 suspension in an inverted deceptive cadence, Ex. 6.91b, m. 13). This usage makes sense, of course, since the composer specifically wishes in such cases to avoid a genuine cadence, and techniques of blurring in themselves help rhetorically to inhibit that sense of closure. (To save space, I will not introduce any new examples of cadential blurring here but rather will discuss such situations as they arise in the G-sharp-Minor fugue, book 1, as part of a case study at the end of the chapter.)

### 6.4.8. Three Case Studies

This discussion of cadential deviations and blurring concludes the presentation of theoretical issues pertaining to the use of cadence in the fugues of the *WTC*. Because the examples up to now have been excerpted from a variety of pieces, I devote the rest of this discussion to three case studies in order to show how the ideas presented above can help illuminate cadential processes in a complete fugue.

#### 6.4.8.1. *Fugue in D, WTC 1*

I start with the D-major fugue, book 1, whose exposition we studied earlier (see again Ex. 6.93). This fugue, in the style of a French overture, is largely homophonic in texture, and so its cadential articulations emerge with clarity. We have already seen the extensive use of S-ending cadences in the exposition. Two other details, however, are worthy of note. First, two of the three S-ending IACs confirm the subordinate key of A major (mm. 3 and 6). Therefore, not surprisingly, this key receives no further cadential confirmation in the course of the fugue. Second, the right hand of measure 3 brings an innocent sixteenth-note melodic configuration, labeled motive "x," that ends a brief internal episode. The motive is derived from the final four thirty-second notes of the subject's head motive (as identified in m. 1), though in that context it hardly stands out as an individual idea. We will see shortly how Bach develops this motive extensively, in its sixteenth-note version, in some later episodes of the fugue. Turning now to Example 6.103a, the music that follows the exposition, we encounter at measure 9 another S-ending cadence, an IAC in B minor (HK: VI). That this cadence has a larger scope than those in the exposition can be explained by its being heard to embrace both an episode (in m. 6) and a pair of subject entries, the first of which lies in the bass (in m. 7) and cannot therefore create a cadence on the downbeat of measure 8.

Looking ahead, the cadence at measure 9 signals a clear sectional division, since what follows is a markedly new episode, one that exploits motive "x," which I highlighted from the exposition. Measure 10 continues the episode by sequentially repeating measure 9, and the beginning of measure 11 seems like it, too, might be another sequence. But when the bass proceeds with the dotted rhythm on beat 2, it suggests the possibility of a full subject entry. The rest of the subject, however, does not appear—not surprising perhaps, because throughout the fugue every subject entry begins on the second quarter-note beat of the bar, not on the downbeat. So instead of concluding the subject, the bass voice in the second half of measure 11 takes on the conventional bass line of a cadence, thus supporting a genuine subject entry in the soprano and concluding (downbeat of m. 12) with an S-ending IAC in G major (HK: IV). Unlike the previous cadence, this one is not a sectional marker since the texture remains unbroken; moreover, a subject entry in the alto follows immediately, one whose cadential possibility is denied by the deceptive cadence on the downbeat of measure 13. Note that for the first time thus far in the fugue, a subject entry does not occur as the highest sounding

---

149. These various modes of cadential blurring are frequently identified in the secondary literature on the *WTC* as well as more generally by theorists of fugue. Most often these techniques are associated with the goal of furthering rhythmic and textural continuity, an aesthetic ideal of fugue that is repeatedly invoked. Thus Kerman speaks of "undercutting" a cadence (*Fugue*, 23) and Benjamin, of "obscuring" it (*Tonal Counterpoint*, 211). Fux specifically discusses how a subject entry that overlaps a cadential arrival can help "maintain the continuous flow" that should prevail in a fugue (Mann, *Study of Fugue*, 94). Schubert and Neidhöfer note that the use of suspensions at a cadence can "continue the forward momentum, but do not necessarily weaken the sense of arrival. Indeed, sometimes they can be thought of as heightening it" (*Baroque Counterpoint*, 219).

EXAMPLE 6.103A. Bach, Fugue No. 5 in D, *WTC* 1, mm. 6–17.

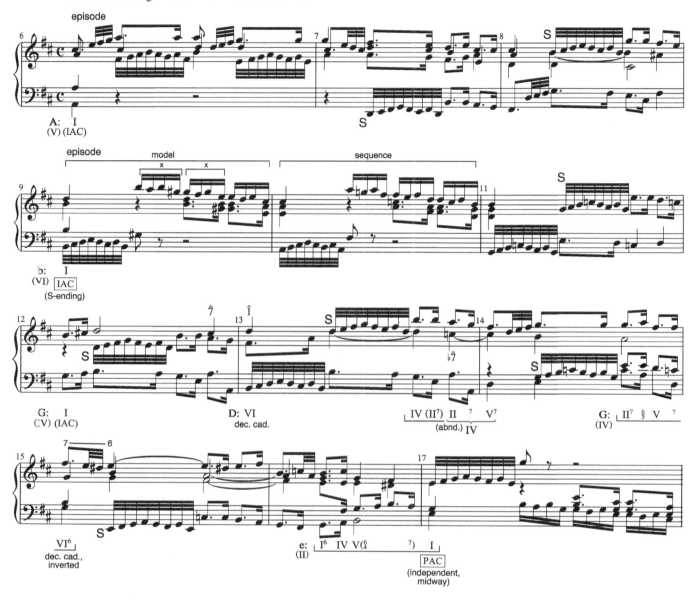

part, hence allowing the soprano lying above to be directed toward melodic closure on $\hat{1}$. The implied S-ending PAC is unrealized, as just mentioned, owing to the harmonic deception at the opening of measure 13.

The deceptive cadence now leads to those two exceptional deviation types discussed earlier. First, another home-key S-ending cadence is promised for the first beat of measure 14, but the dominant fails to materialize when the expected leading tone, on the last beat of measure 13, is lowered (to C♮), and the resulting tonicization of IV abandons the cadential progression. Subsequently, an S-ending PAC, still in the subdominant region, is projected to appear on the downbeat of measure 15. This one is also denied, due to the 7–6 suspension and the resulting inverted deceptive cadence. In light of these three failed cadences (deceptive, abandoned, and inverted deceptive), it is no surprise that Bach finally gives up on the subject as a source of cadential closure and employs instead an independent midway PAC in E minor (HK: II) to end part 1 of the fugue at measure 17. In fact, Bach has not only exhausted the potential for S-ending cadences but has no more interest in sounding the complete subject. The rest of the fugue thus remains entirely episodic.

Proceeding to Example 6.103b, we first encounter another episode based on motive "x." This episode, more extensive than the previous one, is initially closed in the home key by an independent IAC at measure 21. Note that the imperfect melodic closure here arises as a diversion from an expected PAC when the leading tone shoots up stepwise to reach $\hat{3}$ rather than concluding more normally on $\hat{1}$. Moreover, the cadential progression emerges from a descending-fifths sequential pattern (see the root motion

EXAMPLE 6.103B. Bach, Fugue No. 5 in D, *WTC* 1, mm. 17–27.

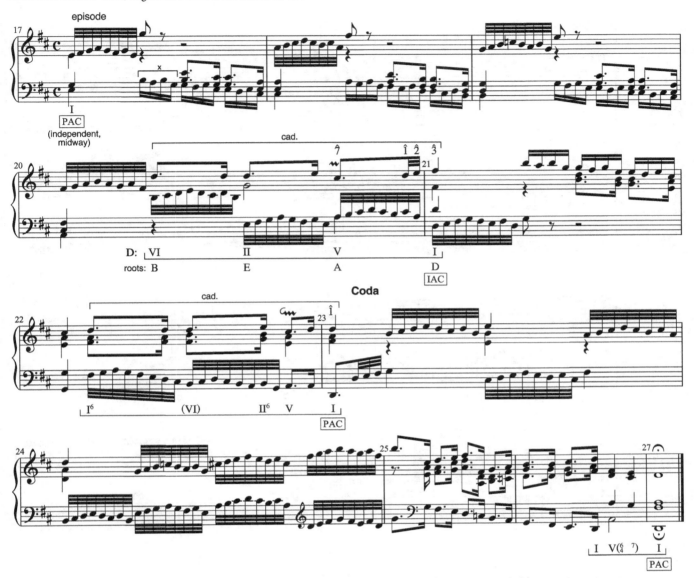

shown beneath the roman numerals), thus undermining to a degree the expression of cadential function.[150] Supported by these blurring details, the episode continues on, and the cadential melodic idea in measure 22, the same one from measure 20, resolves as expected to 1̂, thereby yielding an independent PAC at measure 23. Note that the harmonic support, beginning with I⁶ and including the pre-dominant II⁶, is more conventionally cadential than the previous one, which could also be heard as sequential.

From a purely tonal perspective, measure 23 could have functioned as the end of the fugue. But Bach has more to say, and thus in a coda, he finally dispenses with the motive "x" material of the prior episodes and focuses instead on the subject's head motive. This idea bounces back and forth between the outer voices so as to create a pervasive running sixteenth-note effect, one that climaxes in measure 24 with sixteenth notes together in the outer voices. Measure 25 sees a sudden liquidation of the fast notes and a new focus on the dotted rhythms of the subject (the feature that most clearly defines the French overture style). The fugue finishes by liquidating these dotted rhythms, leaving a completely conventional PAC for final closure, a cadence that clearly matches in content the midway PAC back at measure 17.

Looking at the broader cadential picture, we see the fugue starting with an exaggerated emphasis on S-ending cadences in the exposition and moving then to further employment of that device up to measure 12, after which all subsequent S-ending implications fail to be realized. The independent midway cadence at measure 17 brings the strongest cadential articulation thus far in the piece. Bach then abandons the complete subject

---

150. As discussed on other occasions in this study, eighteenth-century composers were normally careful to distinguish between sequential and cadential material; see Chapter 2, sec. 2.3.2. The clear-cut separation of these two harmonic and formal categories begins to break down in the early Romantic style (see Chapter 8, sec. 8.7).

EXAMPLE 6.104A. Bach, Fugue No. 7 in E-flat, *WTC* 1, mm. 1–17.

(and its potential for S-ending cadences) and develops instead a large episode based on motive "x" and the subject's head motive. This second part of the fugue quickly brings the music back to the home key, which Bach initially confirms with an independent, yet also problematic, IAC at measure 21. Two subsequent PACs, each of which is also independent of the subject, conclude the fugue. With respect to fugal technique and cadential content, the two parts of this fugue could hardly be more different. Yet the piece seems highly unified nonetheless, owing no doubt to the consistent development of ideas derived from a relatively short subject and an even shorter contrasting motive ("x").

### 6.4.8.2. Fugue in E-flat, WTC 1

The E-flat-major fugue, book 1 (Ex. 6.104a), features a subject that modulates to the dominant region, as projected by its

EXAMPLE 6.104B. Bach, Fugue No. 7 in E-flat, *WTC* 1, mm. 25–37.

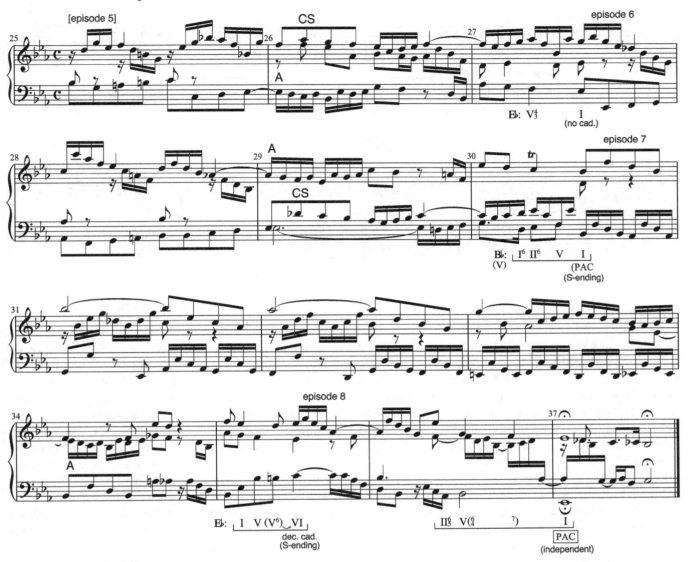

closing scalar descent from $\hat{4}$ to $\hat{1}$ (with a cadential trill on $\hat{2}$). The answer is tonal, being adjusted to remain in the home key, and ends with the same cadential melody. Both versions are thus crying out to receive an S-ending cadence at some point in the fugue. Yet within the exposition, Bach makes certain that such a cadence cannot emerge by having the voices enter from the top voice down (soprano, alto, bass) such that a cadential bass line cannot be set below either version of the subject. As a result, the exposition ends with prolongational closure on the third beat of measure 7. An episode starting in the middle of that bar leads to an answer entry in the soprano at the upbeat to measure 11.[151] For this passage, Bach could potentially have created an S-ending cadence; instead, he places in the bass the countersubject (from m. 3), a melodic idea that has no resemblance to a cadential bass

line. Ending on the third scale degree, the bass creates again a case of prolongational closure (middle of m. 12). Another episode then moves the music off to C minor (HK: VI) and finishes off with conventionalized passagework closed by an independent PAC in measure 17.

This midway cadence closes off the first part of the fugue. The second part, like the C-Minor fugue, book 1 (Figure 6.1), employs a modified rotation of material from part 1. We first hear a counter-exposition in C minor, one that omits the initial subject. The following episodic material (not shown) quickly brings the music back home to E-flat, which (as seen in Ex. 6.104b) is announced by an answer entry in the bass at measure 26. Unlike the soprano entry that it matches within the rotational scheme (namely, the one at m. 11, Ex. 6.104a), this answer, by being placed in the bass voice, has no potential to produce an S-ending cadence (in the middle of m. 27). At measure 29 the subject enters in the soprano, thus finally allowing a cadential bass line to realize a long-awaited S-ending cadence. Because the subject is modulating, this PAC

---

151. The episode at m. 7 is actually the second one in the fugue, since a short internal episode appeared in mm. 4–5.

EXAMPLE 6.105A. Bach, Fugue No. 18 in G-sharp Minor, *WTC* 1, mm. 1–9.

confirms for the first time the subordinate key of B-flat major, albeit late in the game. Though the cadence is syntactically strong, it seems to function as one of limited scope, thus not rivaling the structural significance of the midway cadence in C minor back at measure 17. Like the two S-ending cadences that we saw earlier in the C-Minor fugue (Ex. 6.90c, m. 17, and Ex. 6.90d, m. 22) the cadence in our E-flat fugue (Ex. 6.104b, m. 30) seems designed more to achieve the goal of realizing this type of cadence than to articulate any broader formal design.

If Bach has finally written an S-ending cadence, he has done so only in the subordinate key, and we may wonder whether a comparable cadence will confirm the home key. In fact, that possibility arises when the non-modulating answer appears for the last time at measure 34, now in an inner voice, thus enabling the bass to effect cadential closure. Yet even here, Bach fails to deliver a true S-ending cadence, providing instead a deceptive one, which defers until measure 37 the fugue's closing PAC, one that is entirely independent and thus structurally stronger than any S-ending cadence would have been.

### 6.4.8.3. Fugue in G-sharp Minor, WTC 1

My final case study, the G-sharp-Minor fugue, book 1 (Ex. 6.105a), is notable not only for its modulating subject, but for having one that closes with a melodic pattern $\hat{3}$–$\hat{4}$–$\hat{5}$–$\hat{1}$ (motive "x") that obviously has the potential of functioning as a cadential bass line (③–④–⑤–①), the only clear-cut case of such a configuration in the whole of the *WTC*.[152] In addition, this is the fourth exceptional case of an exposition ending with a cadence (the three others having already been discussed in sec. 6.4.5).

Given the subject's distinctive melodic close, an S-ending cadence can only arise when the subject appears in the lowest sounding voice. So if Bach wants to ensure that the exposition of this fugue, like almost all others, does not end with a cadence, he must not let the final entry appear in the bass. Looking at how he handles this opening, he seems to be aware of the issue, since he places the first entry moderately low in the keyboard's range. The remaining subject entries of the exposition could then occur above the lowest sounding voice, thus precluding a cadence. Because the first entry sounds alone, the close of the subject projects, by default, an S-ending cadence, one that is obviously limited in scope to the subject itself. With the second entry, a tonal answer that remains in the home key, the first sounding voice, as usual, continues to reside below, such that no cadence can occur. The same situation obtains when the third entry brings back the subject version at measure 5. It, too, cannot close with an S-ending cadence.

Now, to understand the wonderful game that Bach seems to be playing here, we need to put ourselves in the position of listeners who know that this is a four-voice fugue but have neither heard the piece before, nor are observing the score during the performance. Under these circumstances, they might have

---

152. Two other subjects in the collection conclude with the cadential bass motion ⑤–①. The subject of the A-Minor fugue, book 1, generates its cadential implications in the context of a ④–③–②–⑤–① construct, which is conventionally associated with Gjerdingen's Prinner schema (*Galant Style*, chap. 4). When functioning cadentially, this formation yields an IAC, as realized twice in this fugue (mm. 35 and 46); for more on this *Prinner cadence*, see in Chapter 3, sec. 3.2.1.2, and ahead in Chapter 7, sec. 7.1.2. In the E-flat-major fugue, book 2, the subject, which toward its end projects a $\hat{3}$–$\hat{5}$–$\hat{1}$ line, seems more like an upper voice than that of a bass; moreover, it is not entirely clear just where the subject actually ends (on the downbeat of m. 6 or m. 7?); indeed, the subject is never realized with a clear S-ending cadence at any point in the fugue.

EXAMPLE 6.105B–C. (b) Bach, Fugue No. 9 in E, *WTC* 2, mm. 1–7; (c) Bach Fugue No. 18 in G-sharp Minor, *WTC* 1, reconstruction of mm. 1–9.

the impression that the subject appears first in the bass, followed by the tenor and alto. They might then expect the soprano to complete the exposition, thus making certain that it does not end with a cadence. But when the fourth entry arrives in measure 7, Bach reveals the trick he has been setting up all along: he closes the exposition with the answer version placed *below* all of the other voices, that is, in the *real* bass. As a result, the conditions are ripe for a subject-ending PAC, one that could be heard, most exceptionally, to end the exposition as a whole.[153] Moreover, this cadence confirms the home key, since the answer, unlike the subject, is non-modulating.[154]

Let me note two additional points in connection with this exposition. First, one might object that the tessitura of Example 6.105a is too high for Bach to be playing the game I have proposed, and that listeners would automatically assume that the exposition begins with the tenor voice. Yet if we consider the opening of the E-major fugue, book 1 (Ex. 6.105b), we see an exposition that starts with the bass and brings its subject entries systematically upward. Comparing this section to the G-sharp-Minor fugue, we see that Example 6.105a is pitched only a couple of tones higher than Example 6.105b. In other words, that the former might be heard to start with the bass voice is not out of the question. Second, if the G-sharp-Minor fugue had actually begun with the bass (as represented in Ex. 6.105c), then the final voice, the soprano, would have started on a high D♯. With that possibility in mind, and looking ahead to Example 6.105e, it is fascinating to observe how Bach realizes this pitch level the very next time the soprano sounds the subject (at m. 24).

Having concluded the exposition with an S-ending cadence (Ex. 6.105d, m. 9), Bach immediately undermines the sense of closure by reinterpreting the cadential idea to "become" (⇒) a short model for sequential repetition, twice up a third (mm. 9–11). These sequences create a brief episode before the answer enters again in measure 11, this time in the tenor. Since the bass drops out after completing its threefold sequence of the cadential idea, the tenor now represents the lowest voice (as it did at the opening of the fugue) and therefore realizes another S-ending cadence on the downbeat of measure 13.[155] This cadence is rhetorically *blurred* by the 4–3 suspension in the alto, which does

---

153. Note that the texture of this cadence is entirely homophonic, since the inner voices follow the rhythmic eighth-note-eighth-rest pattern of the countersubject in the soprano. As a result, this S-ending cadence may actually seem like an independent one, whose texture and rhythm stand apart from the more pervasive polyphony in the rest of the exposition.

154. That the first cadence (aside from the one of m. 3) confirms the home key may seem natural from the perspective of later compositional styles. As discussed earlier, however, such a practice is relative rare in the fugues of the *WTC* and in the baroque style generally (with the exception of a concerto form, whose opening ritornello normally closes with an HK: PAC).

155. Note that the passage in mm. 11–13 resides in a high tessitura for all three upper voices. This would have been the placement of these voices if the initial subject entry of the exposition had been set in the bass voice, as discussed earlier (see again Ex. 6.105c). This fact, in addition to the tessitura of the soprano at m. 24, further supports the idea that a first-time listener may have been surprised when the true bass voice effects a cadence at the end of the exposition.

EXAMPLE 6.105D. Bach Fugue No. 18 in G-sharp Minor, *WTC* 1, mm. 8–17.

not resolve until the second beat of the bar and over which the soprano quickly steps down from its melodic close. Once again, Bach subverts the effect of cadence by sequencing it twice, this time downward. Following the sequence, a subject entry appears at measure 15, now back in the bass voice, and an S-ending cadence arises at measure 17, blurred again by a 4–3 suspension but now in the soprano, whose decorated resolution features a prominent upward skip that recalls the leaping motive "y" from the subject (see the first half of mm. 12 and 16).

In the entire section shown in Example 6.105d, the cadential bass line ending the subject, motive "x," obsessively appears in the lowest sounding voice. From this point forward (Ex. 6.105e), Bach permits this motive to migrate to the upper voices, thus denying its potential for cadencing. We first hear a subject entry in the tenor at measure 17 while the bass continues to sound below. At measure 19 the alto is permitted a subject entry (in the answer version) for the first time since the start of the piece, after which motive "x" completely drops out for the ensuing episode (mm. 21–23). This relatively extended episode closes with the first independent cadence of the piece in the middle of measure 24. In a forty-one-bar fugue, this cadence may qualify as a midway one (though occurring somewhat later than the exact midway mark).

Unlike many midway cadences, which help divide a fugue into two major parts, this potentially formal marker in measure 24 is blurred in a number of ways. First, the soprano, having remained out of sight since measure 19, enters with the subject at measure 24 (in the high part of the tessitura, as mentioned earlier in connection with Ex. 6.105c, m. 7), thus overlapping the formal boundary defined by the cadence. Second, the cadence promises to confirm the supertonic key of A-sharp minor, a region rarely tonicized, much less modulated to, in a minor-mode work, since the second degree normally supports a diminished triad. Owing to the intervallic demands of the subject, however, Bach must raise the third of the implied minor-mode tonic to C×, and though we might be tempted to hear a Picardy effect, we could also perceive a deceptive cadence if we take this harmony as a secondary dominant of the local subdominant, to which it quickly heads for another couple of beats.[156] In other words, whereas the bass line and harmonic content articulate an acceptable cadence on the third beat of measure 24, several factors help to obscure this midway cadence as a decisive formal boundary.

Indeed, the material that follows (Ex. 6.105f) does not suggest the start of a new section, but rather continues to develop ideas and motives in largely the same textural and rhythmic context as that which preceded the cadence. At measure 26 the bass again enters with the answer, realizing at measure 28 an S-ending cadence in B major (HK: III, rather late for confirming a standard subordinate key). The cadence is blurred, however, by double suspensions and the downward stepwise motion of the bass. As in earlier cases (at mm. 9 and 13), the cadence at measure 28 is followed by model-sequence technique, but this time the cadential idea is not reinterpreted to become the model. Instead, a new model appears whose bass uses a varied cadence-like pattern, ③–②–⑤–① (motive "z"), one that differs from that used in the subject

---

156. This type of deceptive cadence—involving the use of $V^7/IV$ to replace the final tonic—was discussed earlier in this chapter (sec. 6.1.4.1).

EXAMPLE 6.105E. Bach Fugue No. 18 in G-sharp Minor, *WTC* 1, mm. 17–25.

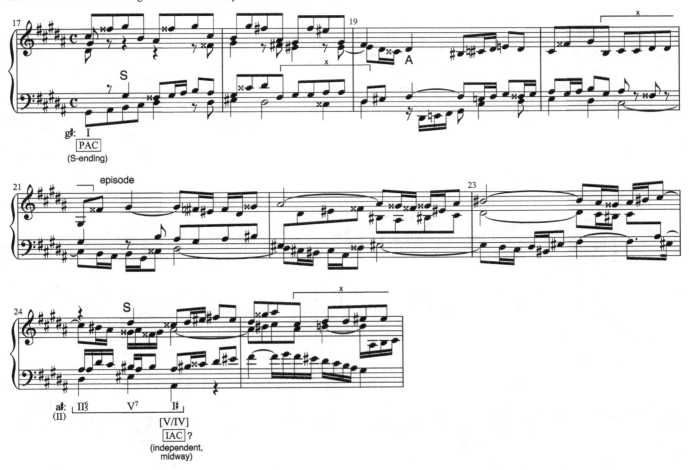

(③–④–⑤–①, motive "x").[157] Although this variant provides some relief from the potential overuse of motive "x," Bach nonetheless returns to that motive in the second half of measure 30, thus creating a cadence (downbeat of m. 31) that is blurred by a 4–3 suspension in the alto.

This second cadence in the subordinate key is especially interesting. In respect of its content, it sounds like the many S-ending cadences we have heard throughout the fugue, since it brings with it motives associated with both the end of the subject (motive "x" in the bass) and the end of the countersubject (in the soprano). In fact, however, the complete subject has not been sounded, so the designation "S-ending" is definitionally incorrect; instead, this cadence is more accurately identified as independent, one that closes off the preceding three-bar episode and that differentiates itself from the actual S-ending cadence back at measure 28. As the music continues, though, the cadential idea of measure 30 then functions as the model for a sequential repetition in measure 31, thus giving rise to the kind of retrospective reinterpretation so characteristic of this fugue.

A subject entry in the tenor at measure 32 is supported by free counterpoint in the bass, so an S-ending cadence is avoided on the downbeat of measure 34. Then, in the middle of that bar, Bach drops out the bass so that the tenor can continue with yet another statement of motive "x" in the lowest sounding voice. Here, in measures 34–35, we are surprised to hear another potential cadence in B major (an IAC, with a 4–3 suspension in the soprano), for it would be especially odd to encounter a *third* cadence in the same key. But when we recognize that the bass line supporting this cadence actually lies in the tenor voice, we can understand that this tenor (as well as the material it supports in the upper voices) sequentially repeats the final idea of the immediately preceding subject, and as such, identifying a genuine cadence at measure 35 must be rejected. When two more sequential repetitions occur in measures 35–36, motive "x" first returns to the true bass voice (m. 35) but then again moves back into the tenor (m. 36). Moreover, Bach accords even greater attention to motive "x" in these measures, first doubling it at the third in the alto and then, in the following bar, at the sixth in the tenor and soprano. Given the pervasive model-sequence technique exhibited from the noncadential end of the subject entry in measure 34 through to measure 37, Bach may allude to a redundant third cadence in B major at measure 35, but in fact, he cleverly makes sure not to realize one.

---

157. As discussed in note 152, this new bass pattern is typically associated more with a Prinner cadence than with a standard authentic cadence.

EXAMPLE 6.105F. Bach Fugue No. 18 in G-sharp Minor, *WTC* 1, mm. 25–37.

As the fugue approaches its end (Ex. 6.105g), a final subject entry in the soprano in measure 37 is completed on the downbeat of measure 39 without any cadential effect, given its placement on top of the texture. But as a kind of last gasp of the subject's end, with its characteristic cadential bass line (motive "x"), Bach immediately imitates that idea in its "proper" voice, the bass, in the second half of measure 39. Tonally, this cadential figure is pointing to C-sharp minor, the subdominant region of the home key. And the appearance in measure 39 of that key's leading tone (B♯) in the soprano moving up to tonic (C♯) even raises the possibility that a *cadenza doppia* might emerge, as reconstructed in Example 6.105h. Instead, Bach performs a lowered leading-tone abandonment, thus yielding a B♮ in the soprano on the last beat of measure 39 (Ex. 6.105g), which keeps the music oriented around the home key.[158] As a result, the C♯ harmony on the downbeat of measure 40 functions not as a tonic, but rather, and most appropriately here, as the pre-dominant for the *independent* cadence that ends the fugue, a *cadenza doppia* configuration that realizes the abandoned one just preceding it.

Before further considering this final cadence, let us observe several other aspects of the emphasis Bach accords to the subdominant immediately preceding that cadence. First, it is general baroque practice to give significant expression to this region toward the end of a work, perhaps as a kind of counterbalance to the emphasis that the dominant often receives earlier on, and more specifically in fugues, through the alternation of subject and answer versions in the exposition. Second, it is understandable that in this particular fugue, Bach would begin the final subject version in C-sharp minor (soprano voice, mm. 37–38), because its modulating structure would naturally lead it to close in the home key of G-sharp minor.

---

158. Note that the return to G-sharp minor is anticipated by a chromatic alteration to motive "x" in the bass of m. 39, whereby the use of ♯④ brings an F𝄪, the leading tone of the home key. The leap down from ③, another variant to the motive, especially highlights this chromatic change.

EXAMPLE 6.105G-H. Bach Fugue No. 18 in G-sharp Minor, *WTC* 1, (g) mm. 37–41; (h) reconstruction of mm. 39–40.

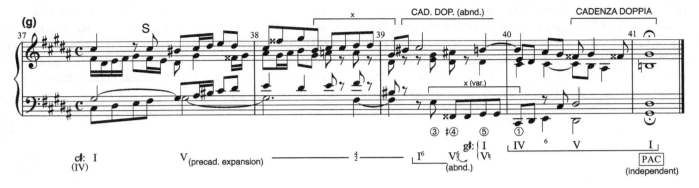

Yet he shuns that modulation by continuing to set the final pitches of the subject (motive "x" in m. 38) within the realm of C-sharp minor (as expressed by the A♮ and B♯). Finally, most of the subject is set against a G♯ pedal in the bass voice that stretches to the fourth beat of measure 38. Though we might be tempted to recognize a tonic pedal in the home key, the context makes clear that this is a *dominant* pedal in the prevailing region of C-sharp minor. Indeed, dominant harmony continues to be expressed when the bass moves down to F♯ on the fourth quarter note of measure 38. The resulting V$^4_2$ is syncopated into the next bar, where it resolves to I$^6$, setting in motion the cadential progression that becomes abandoned.[159] This prolonged dominant thus produces a precadential expansion that highlights all the more the continuing expression of C-sharp minor right up to the last cadence in the home key.

Turning now to that final PAC, we can observe that Bach employs a cadential progression that stretches over two bars (mm. 40–41); the expansion here may seem modest enough, but the progression is twice as long as any seen earlier in the fugue. Moreover, he entirely shuns referencing the cadential bass line, motive "x," which was so prominent with all of the S-ending cadences and in so many of the sequential passages, in favor of a bass that is (esp. in its rhythmic profile) entirely conventional in content and that does not allude to the subject at all. To modern sensibilities (conditioned perhaps by nineteenth-century attitudes of formal circularity),[160] the idea of allowing the cadential idea from the subject to close the fugue itself might seem like an obvious compositional choice; yet it is one that Bach does not make, holding closer to an eighteenth-century aesthetic that understands closure to be most strongly created when using material that is not associated with initiating ideas.

To conclude this analysis, let us review how Bach uses cadences in the G-sharp-Minor fugue as a whole. As with almost any fugue, a good deal depends upon the nature of the subject itself. Here, that it closes with a cadential bass line determines much of what happens cadentially throughout the work. At the start (Ex. 6.105a), we saw the clever game Bach plays of pretending to avoid an S-ending cadence to close the exposition (in line with his standard practice of keeping this section open-ended), only then to place the final entry in the real bass voice so that motive "x," the cadential bass line, could realize an implied S-ending cadence (m. 9). We then observed (Ex. 6.105d) how he immediately undermines that cadence by taking the cadential idea as a model for sequential repetition. This mode of retrospective reinterpretation (cad.⇒mod.) occurs several times throughout the fugue, each instance finding motive "x" appropriately placed in the bass voice. As the piece progresses, a number of S-ending cadences in the home key arise, again, when motive "x" occurs in the bass (mm. 13 and 17). Given this rather unusual emphasis on the home key, it is high time to explore other tonal regions. The first is the rarely tonicized supertonic (A-sharp minor), which receives an independent cadence around the midway point of the fugue (Ex. 6.105e, m. 24), though the many blurring devices used there almost totally obscure this cadential articulation. Next, Bach turns to the more conventional subordinate key, B major (III), providing an S-ending cadence at measure 28 (Ex. 6.105f), followed then by an independent cadence (m. 31),

---

159. Here we may find another reason for Bach's choosing to use ♯④ in this final appearance of motive "x" in the bass: he may have not wanted to sound again the diatonic F♯, which just before had been emphasized in the same voice via the syncopation.

160. See Chapter 8, sec. 8.5.

which, as we saw, imitates the material content of an S-ending cadence. A potentially third, fully redundant cadence in B major at measure 36 fails to function cadentially owing to its being placed in the heart of a broad model-sequence technique (mm. 33–37). At this late point in the fugue (Ex. 6.105g), Bach then turns, conventionally, to the subdominant region, providing a precadential dominant expansion within that key and the makings of an independent *cadenza doppia* using a chromatic variant of motive "x" in the bass (m. 39). At the last second, however, a lowered leading-tone abandonment leads quickly to a realization of the *cadenza doppia* pattern in the home key with an independent final cadence that has no relation to the subject whatsoever, thus capping a virtuosic display of cadential options within this remarkable fugue.

# 7

# Cadence in the Galant Era

THE GENERAL STYLE PERIOD OFTEN REFERRED TO as *galant*,[1] flanked by the high baroque of the first third of the eighteenth century and the high classical in the last third, has traditionally been a dead zone for music theory.[2] Whereas music historians have devoted much energy to this period, often concerning themselves with establishing the origins of the Viennese classical style, theorists have rarely dealt with galant music, with excerpts from the two major composers of the era—Domenico Scarlatti and C. P. E. Bach—appearing infrequently in music-theoretical texts.[3] This situation, however, has changed markedly in the past number of decades with the emergence of three significant initiatives: a revival of the *partimento* pedagogical tradition that flourished in eighteenth-century Italy;[4] new avenues of phrase structure and form based on the galant theorist Heinrich Christoph Koch;[5] and a novel *schema theory* of stock patterns especially associated with galant compositions.[6]

---

1. In addition to *galant*, the terms *rococo*, *pre-classical*, and *mid-century* are regularly used to label this style period.

2. Research for this chapter is based to a large extent on analyses of selected keyboard sonatas by Domenico Scarlatti and C. P. E. Bach, with a scattering of pieces by lesser-known composers of the period. That I am including Scarlatti's works within the domain of the galant is perhaps problematic in that many, perhaps the majority, of his sonatas were composed before 1740. Few historians, however, place his works comfortably in the baroque period, and at least for matters of harmony, cadence, and phrase structure, Scarlatti's keyboard sonatas align more with galant practice than with the earlier style. For more on the problematic chronology of these works, see W. Dean Sutcliffe, *The Keyboard Sonatas of Domenico Scarlatti and Eighteenth-Century Musical Style*, 43–45.

3. A recent study by Ben Duinker and Hubert Léveillé Gauvin confirms these observations on the relative paucity of music-theoretical scholarship and pedagogy surrounding galant composers ("Changing Content in Flagship Music Theory Journals, 1979–2014").

4. Sanguinetti, *Art of Partimento*; Peter van Tour, *Counterpoint and Partimento: Methods of Teaching Composition in Late Eighteenth-Century Naples*.

5. Burstein, *Galant Expositions*; Kaiser, *Die Notenbücher der Mozarts*; Wolfgang Budday, *Grundlagen musikalischer Formen der Wiener Klassik*.

6. Gjerdingen, *Galant Style*; Vasili Byros, "'*Hauptruhepuncte des Geistes*': Punctuation Schemas and the Late-Eighteenth-Century Sonata."

Both schema and partimento theories focus on formulaic, melodic-contrapuntal relationships obtaining between the outer voices of the musical texture, and thus these approaches accord well with the theoretical perspectives developed in this study of tonal cadence, including my formulation of the classical cadence as a distinct schema, my emphasis on bass-line activity, and my references to specific schemata such as the Prinner, Cudworth, Quiescenza, and Pulcinella. Schema theory and Koch's views on phrase structure, in particular, will continue to prove useful in the present chapter on the galant cadence.

Cadential practice in the galant is not substantially different from that of the preceding baroque period, though some changes are clearly manifest and certain tendencies arise that look forward to the classical procedures discussed in Part I of this study. As well, the galant sees the appearance of new forms of cadential content that are especially associated with that style. Techniques of cadential extension and expansion become more prominent compared to earlier baroque practice, yet the ideal of "retaining the cadential formula," so important for baroque composers, continues to influence the galant style. This period also sees the origins of new formal types—sonata, rondo, and concerto—that play a central role in the classical style. As a result, we are in a better position to observe how cadence relates to formal functions, compared to the baroque era, where such functionality is more nascent.

## 7.1. Morphology of the Galant Cadence

Cadences in the galant era continue to use melodic-harmonic patterns inherited from baroque practice. But now the "classical" bass line ③-④-⑤-① comes more to the fore, and the simple I–V–I cadence is used less frequently. Moreover, the *cadenza doppia*—a hallmark of baroque usage—begins to drop out of favor by the middle of the eighteenth century. The galant repertoire also sees some new cadential patterns, ones that typify that period in relation to earlier baroque and later classical styles.

### 7.1.1. Gjerdingen's Galant Clausulae

A good starting point for a discussion of the galant cadence is found in the eleventh chapter of Gjerdingen's treatise devoted to *clausulae*, formulas of "closing." Building on the *Klausellehre* of seventeenth- and early eighteenth-century theorists of counterpoint, especially Johann Gottfried Walther,[7] Gjerdingen presents a version of Walther's *clausula formalis perfectissima* (Ex. 7.1) showing the stepwise motions of four "melodic clausulae" that Gjerdingen identifies by the voice in which the motion appears.[8] The soprano and tenor voices duplicate the early Renaissance soprano-tenor construct of moving from an imperfect to a perfect consonance (as discussed at the opening of Chapter 6). The bass brings the leap of a descending fifth (or ascending fourth), and the alto fills in the texture with stepwise motion from 5̂ to

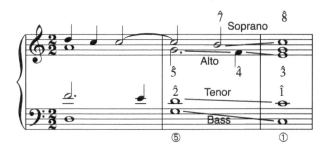

EXAMPLE 7.1. Walther's *clausula formalis perfectissima* (G11.2).

3̂. Following a *Klausellehre* approach, Gjerdingen notes that each of these melodic motions can be placed in the real bass voice to create a wide variety of clausulae. When the bass clausula of a descending-fifth leap actually appears in the bass voice, there arises a *clausula perfectissima* (the most perfect or, as Gjerdingen prefers, the most "complete" close).[9] This pattern, of course, relates strongly to the model of the classical cadence as I have defined it in this study. When any of the other melodic clausulae are placed in the actual bass, then Gjerdingen (after Walther) identifies the resulting formulas by their model voice motion as *clausulae cantizans* (closes characteristic of a soprano), *clausulae tenorizans* (characteristic of a tenor), or *clausulae altizans* (of an alto). These less complete forms of closing—which in my theory would not be considered genuinely cadential, but rather prolongational in nature—are nonetheless subsumed by Gjerdingen under the general concept of *cadence*, though he tends to shun using this term, since he associates it more with nineteenth-century, harmonically oriented modes of thinking.[10]

As already mentioned, the *clausulae perfectissimae* include genuine cadences (as so defined in this study). Within this category, Gjerdingen identifies the pattern supported by the bass line ③-④-⑤-① (Ex. 7.2) as the "standard clausula in galant music" (141), which, following the practice of the partimento theorists, he further classifies as a *cadenza simplice* (simple cadence)

---

7. Walther, *Praecepta Der Musicalischen Composition*. See Chapter 3, note 27, for additional items associated with the *Klausellehre* tradition.

8. *Galant Style*, 139–40. A number of the examples used in this chapter are drawn from Gjerdingen's treatise; in such cases, the original example number is identified in the caption (e.g., G11.2). For some of his examples, I have added harmonic and cadential analyses and have sometimes modified the labels of the schemata, eliminating ones that might obscure the central point being made. For upper-voice scale degrees, I have replaced his use of a blackened circled number by a circumflex accent over an arabic numeral to conform with the annotation style of the present study.

9. Gjerdingen sometimes identifies this cadence with the schema label "Complete" (*Galant Style*, 139); see ahead Ex. 7.6, mm. 67–70, and Ex. 7.13, m. 24.

10. "Since the mid-nineteenth century, each ostensibly fixed type of cadence has been taught as a 'chord progression' with a descriptive title intended to 'grasp its essence' (e.g., 'perfect,' 'imperfect,' 'deceptive,' 'plagal,' 'Phrygian' and so forth). The delicate interactions of galant basses and melodies, however, were not fixed and go well beyond simple ascriptions of an essence" (Gjerdingen, *Galant Style*, 142).

7.1. MORPHOLOGY OF THE GALANT CADENCE  381

EXAMPLE 7.2. Standard galant clausula (G11.3).

EXAMPLE 7.3. (a) Cimarosa, Keyboard Sonata C30, Allegretto, mm. 1–2 (G11.4); (b) Gaviniès, Violin Sonata in B-flat, Op. 3, no. 5, ii, mm. 29–32 (G11.6); (c) Schobert, Keyboard Sonata, Op. 6, no. 1, i, mm. 7–8 (G11.7); (d) Boccherini, String Quintet, Op. 11, no. 1, ii, mm. 23–24 (G11.10); (e) J. C. Bach, .Keyboard Sonata, Op. 12, no. 6, ii, mm. 6–7 (G11.11).

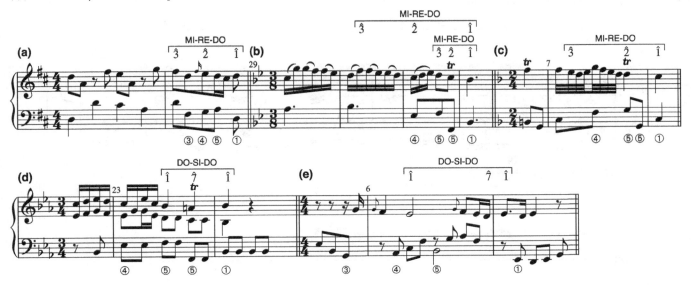

EXAMPLE 7.4. (a) Tartini, Violin Sonata, Op. 6, no. 4, i, mm. 17–18 (G11.13); (b) Cimarosa, Keyboard Sonata C37, Andantino, mm. 11–12 (G11.15).

or *cadenza composta* (compound cadence), depending upon whether the bass note ⑤ appears once or twice, the latter case bringing the cadential six-four.[11] Among the melodic patterns that can be associated with the standard galant clausula (Ex. 7.3), Gjerdingen cites the ubiquitous $\hat{3}$–$\hat{2}$–$\hat{1}$, which he calls the "Mi-Re-Do" schema (142–44), as well as $\hat{1}$–$\hat{7}$–$\hat{1}$, "Do-Si-Do" (146).

He also draws attention to a melodic formula first identified by the mid-twentieth-century musicologist Charles Cudworth (who specifically called this the "galant cadence"), one that features a rapidly descending scalar motion from $\hat{8}$ (or $\hat{1}$, as Gjerdingen analyzes it) to $\hat{1}$ an octave lower, with the leading tone typically appearing directly with the onset of ④ in the bass. In his honor, Gjerdingen labels this the "Cudworth" cadence (147–49), two cases of which are shown in Example 7.4.[12] He further identifies a "Grand Cadence" (152–53) that brings the melodic motion $\hat{8}$–$\hat{6}$–$\hat{5}$–$\hat{2}$–$\hat{1}$ over ③–④–⑤–⑤–①, respectively. Three of the four examples

---

11. As discussed early in Chapter 6 (in connection with Ex. 6.3 and 6.4 as well as note 9), the *cadenza simplice* of the baroque partimento theorists is most often supported by the "simple" bass motion ①–⑤–①. Gjerdingen's use of the ③–④–⑤–① pattern for this cadence aligns more with galant practice.

12. Gjerdingen notes that $\hat{7}$ is sometimes lowered by a half-step, as seen in the second excerpt of this example. For the use of the Cudworth cadence in the classical style, see Chapter 3, sec. 3.1.2.4, "Cudworth."

EXAMPLE 7.5. Clementi, Keyboard Sonata, Op. 4, no. 5, ii, mm. 109–115 (G11.23).

EXAMPLE 7.6. Barbella, Six Solos, No. 4, iii, mm. 63–70 (G11.27).

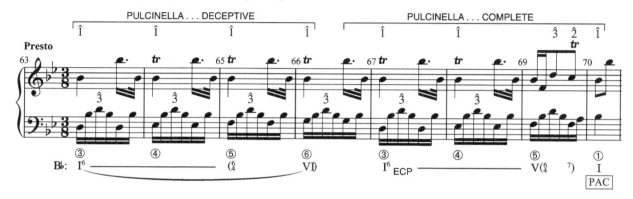

EXAMPLE 7.7. Cimarosa, Keyboard Sonata C78, Allegro brioso, mm. 26–29 (G20.2).

that he gives of this complete pattern occur in connection with an ECP,[13] and one of them (Ex. 7.5, m. 5) features what I call the "low $\hat{5}$ drop" configuration that frequently closes subordinate themes (esp. in string quartets), as discussed earlier in Chapter 5, sec. 5.1.2.11, "Low $\hat{5}$ Drop."

The Pulcinella schema (Ex. 7.6), which emphasizes a sustained $\hat{1}$, is another cadential variant for Gjerdingen, who notes that the schema is often paired with a "deceptive" version (154–55).[14] Like the Grand Cadence, the Pulcinella tends to be used in ECPs.

---

13. His Ex. 11.23, 11.24, and 25.5; Ex. 25.2 is one bar too short to be considered an ECP. One additional passage by Haydn, analyzed in his Ex. 27.7, mm. 35–36, shows the start of a grand cadence that remains incomplete; indeed, it is not even clear that this passage is functioning cadentially.

14. See the discussion in Chapter 6, sec. 6.1.5.4. As mentioned there, the Pulcinella is not actually a cadential schema, but rather a prolongational one.

EXAMPLE 7.8. "Long Cadence," after Nicola Sala (G11.50).

When the pre-dominant II⁶ of a cadence is especially expanded, Gjerdingen terms the resulting schema an "Indugio," which he discusses in chapter 20 of his treatise. Though the Indugio may bring an authentic cadence, most of his examples lead to an HC (Ex. 7.7) and often feature a final ♯④–⑤ motion in the bass, a separate schema that he calls the "Converging" (160–62). Gjerdingen further identifies a "Long Cadence" (cadenza lunga), as termed by the partimento theorist Nicola Sala. This schema brings a descending third motion ①–⑥–④ prior to the final ⑤–① close (Ex. 7.8).

All of the clausulae schemata mentioned up to now contain a bass that ends ⑤–①, ⑤–⑥, or just ⑤, and, except for the Pulcinella (see again note 14), can be considered, assuming an appropriate

EXAMPLE 7.9. Mozart, Piano Sonata in C, K. 545, i, mm. 3–4 (G11.29).

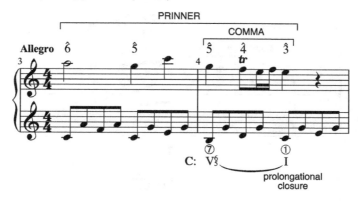

EXAMPLE 7.10. Castrucci, Violin Sonata in F, Op. 2, no. 4, i, mm. 4–7 (G11.33).

EXAMPLE 7.11. Jommelli, *Demofoonte*, Act. 2, scene 10, mm. 31–33 (G11.34).

formal context, genuine cadences (or cadential deviations) as defined in this study. When Gjerdingen considers the three other clausulae categories—the *clausulae cantizans* (⑦–①), *clausulae tenorizans* (②–①), and *clausulae altizans* (⑤–④–③)—the idea that these types are truly cadential is thrown into doubt, because in each case, the dominant is inverted and the bass melody traverses the prolongational stream, not the cadential one.[15] Sometimes, one of these clausulae may actually conclude a complete phrase and thus express *prolongational closure*.[16] His first example of the "Comma" (Ex. 7.9, m. 4), a type of *clausula cantizans* (⑦–①), serves to end the opening phrase of this well-known movement, but not in a manner that is cadential, due to the inverted dominant.[17] Consider as well the first two Commas in Example 7.10. Following an opening "Romanesca," a ubiquitous initiating schema of the galant style, the two commas clearly project continuation function, bringing fragmentation into half-measure units, only followed then by prolongational closure, using the "Long Comma" (a version of the Comma that includes ⑥ along with ⑦ and ①).[18] Another *clausula cantizans*, the "Jommelli" (159), shown in Example 7.11, seems in

---

15. The ⑤–④–③ pattern of the *clausulae altizans* could, in principle, represent a deceptive cadence (see in Chapter 4, sec. 4.1.1); however, we will shortly see that Gjerdingen's main type (the "Passo Indietro") is prolongational, not cadential.

16. See Chapter 3, sec. 3.5.1.

17. Gjerdingen, *Galant Style*, 156. I have added m. 3 to Gjerdingen's example to provide a broader formal context. I have also included the harmonic analysis to m. 4, as well as the "Prinner" label, a schema that will receive more extensive treatment shortly. For the complete phrase, see in Chapter 3, Ex. 3.66, mm. 1–4.

18. Gjerdingen, *Galant Style*, 158. Gjerdingen's scale-degree numerals associated with the Long Comma (mm. 6–7) can be confusing until one

EXAMPLE 7.12. Galuppi, *Concerto a quattro* in B-flat, i, mm. 24–25 (G11.43).

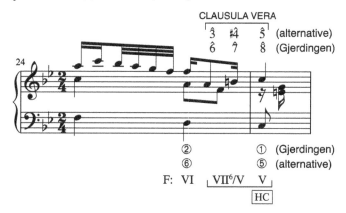

EXAMPLE 7.13. Quantz, Trio Sonata in G Minor, iii, mm. 23–25 (G11.46).

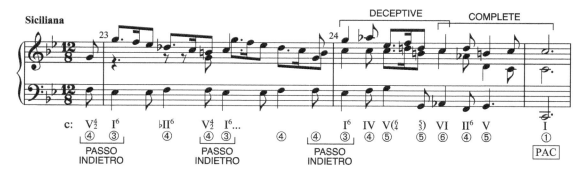

context to be medial in function, followed as it is by a Cudworth, a genuine cadential schema.

When Gjerdingen turns to the *clausula tenorizans* (②–①), the main type that he discusses is the "Clausula Vera" (164–66).[19] This schema can sometimes effect prolongational closure. Often enough, though, the bass does not move from ② to ①, but rather from ⑥ to ⑤ (supporting ♯$\hat{4}$–$\hat{5}$), thus creating an HC, as shown in Example 7.12.[20] The principal schema associated with the *clausula altizans* (④–③), the "Passo Indietro" ("step to the rear"), sees ④ stepping "backward" to ③, normally harmonized by V$^4_2$–I$^6$ (Ex. 7.13).[21] In the passage shown here, the I$^6$ indeed functions cadentially, but not as an ending gesture, rather as the initial tonic of the progression (even being prolonged by ♭II and V$^4_2$, in the sense of a rocking on the tonic).

In short, the three clausulae that see the soprano, alto, or tenor melodies placed in the actual bass voice do not represent true authentic cadences as defined and illustrated throughout the present study. In a small number of cases, they may effect a local HC or provide prolongational closure to a phrase, but most often they participate as a component of a medial function (normally a continuation), being followed then by a real cadence of some type.

### 7.1.2. Prinner Cadence

Among the many schemata defined by Gjerdingen, the melodic-contrapuntal pattern that he terms the "Prinner" is perhaps his most important theoretical discovery.[22] Once our attention has been drawn to this schema, we readily encounter it in a multitude of compositional contexts throughout the eighteenth century.[23] In the course of his treatise, Gjerdingen details many ways in which the Prinner can be employed, with a special emphasis on how it relates to other schemata. Curiously, he does not specifically deal

---

realizes that the passage modulates from C to F, a fact that he does not indicate in his example. Thus in my own annotations, I have added this change of key, along with a harmonic analysis of the complete passage.

19. Explaining the name of this schema, Gjerdingen notes that "[t]he term *clausula vera* [true cadence] appears frequently in nineteenth- and early twentieth-century manuals for students of counterpoint, but infrequently in historical [i.e., eighteenth-century] sources" (*Galant Style*, 490, note 21).

20. Gjerdingen analyzes the scale degrees in this example in C major, but it is clear from the context that the passage actually resides fully in F major, as my alternative annotations show.

21. Gjerdingen, *Galant Style*, 167. Gjerdingen seems to define the Passo Indietro in terms of bass motion and harmonic setting; he does not specifically identify (or annotate) a prototypical melody for this schema.

22. Gjerdingen, *Galant Style*, chap. 3. The discussion in this section is largely based on Caplin, "Gjerdingen's 'Prinner.'"

23. See Chapter 3, sec. 3.2.1.2, for an introduction to the Prinner's use in the classical style. We also find it occasionally in nineteenth-century repertories (see Chapter 8, sec. 8.12).

EXAMPLE 7.14. Prinner prototype.

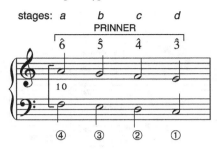

with one of its central functions, especially in the galant period, namely, as a variant of the IAC. Before focusing on the Prinner's cadential role, however, we must examine some of its special melodic and contrapuntal properties, as well as its possible harmonic and form-functional realizations, thus going beyond Gjerdingen's normal concerns.

The prototypical Prinner, shown schematically in Example 7.14, consists of a two-voice framework. Each voice contains a descending scalar tetrachord: the soprano voice moves stepwise from $\hat{6}$ to $\hat{3}$; the bass, from ④ to ①. The resulting counterpoint yields descending parallel motion by thirds (or tenths). In addition to labeling the individual scale degrees, it is useful to specify four *stages* of the Prinner schema (*a–d*), corresponding to each pair of pitches in the two voices. So as not to confuse the four stages of the Prinner with those of an authentic cadence, I use italicized letters for the stages of the former. The relationship of the stages is as follows: stage *a* is precadential; stage *b* corresponds to stage 1 of a cadence, while stage *c* comprises stages 2 and 3; stage *d* then corresponds to stage 4.

With respect to harmony, most of Gjerdingen's schemata are associated with one type of progression—be it prolongational (e.g., "Do-Re-Mi," "Fenaroli"), sequential (e.g., "Monte," "Fonte"), or cadential (e.g., "Complete," "Cudworth," "Indugio"). What is remarkable about the Prinner, and what explains its compositional flexibility, is that unlike any other schema, it can be harmonized to yield any one of the three progression types. Some cases of a *prolongational* Prinner can be seen in Example 7.15; note that the second passage sees an inserted bass ⑦ between ② and ① of the prototype. Such bass insertions are especially used for a *sequential* Prinner, two cases of which are shown in Example 7.16.[24] Finally, a *cadential* Prinner can emerge (Ex. 7.17) when ⑤, supporting a root-position dominant, is inserted after ②, which brings a predominant (usually II$^7$). In connection with this added ⑤, it is useful to distinguish cases where this bass creates a *metrical extension* of stage *c* (Ex. 7.17a) from those in which ⑤ appears as a *submetrical insertion* within that stage (Ex. 7.17b).

In an appropriate formal context (i.e., one where we can expect cadential closure to occur), such a cadential progression gives rise to a special form of the IAC, one that I term the *Prinner cadence* (PrC).[25] This cadence type is well illustrated in Example 7.18, a passage made famous by Stravinsky's adaptation in his *Pulcinella* ballet. The analysis of a PrC is shown in line 1. (The analysis in line 2 sees the Prinner as prolongational, as will be discussed later.)

As for the Prinner's generalized form-functional expression, Gjerdingen repeatedly refers to it as a "riposte," a conventional rejoinder to some immediately prior statement. He thus implies that the schema occupies a generalized "second" position, one that follows directly upon a formal "first," an *initiating* function of some kind.[26] If this second position is the final one of the phrase, then the Prinner can express a sense of functional *ending*, either as a genuine cadence (Ex. 7.18, line 1) or as a prolongational closure (Ex. 7.15b). If the schema itself is followed in the phrase by another event, the Prinner then assumes a *medial* function, and the subsequent event usually brings a cadence, such as the HCs ending Examples 7.15a and 7.16a, or the PAC of Example 7.16b. The prototypical Prinner (Ex. 7.14) does not normally occupy an *initiating* formal position in a theme, largely because the scale degrees of stage *a* ($\hat{6}$ and ④) cannot project tonic, the harmonic function most suitable for a formal opening. In some situations, however, a *modulating* version of the Prinner (Ex. 7.19) can be used to begin a new unit (such as the transition of a sonata exposition, where this variant is frequently employed), because the pitches of stage *a* can express an initiating tonic before being reinterpreted as a new set of scale degrees in the key to which the schema modulates—the dominant region.[27]

The remainder of this section focuses on the Prinner as a cadential function; prolongational and sequential Prinners will be mentioned where appropriate in order to contrast their usage with the cadential Prinner.[28] The specific PrC defined above tends to be used within the main themes of a movement, either

---

24. The inserted bass notes and the added harmonies they support are often necessary to avoid parallel fifths, which would arise if the prototypical Prinner alone were harmonized sequentially (e.g., IV-III-II-I); for more discussion on this point, see Caplin, "Gjerdingen's 'Prinner,'" 27–30. In Ex. 7.16b, the sequential harmonies supporting the model-sequence technique only involve stages *a* and *b* of the Prinner; the second two stages are prolongational. Note that in this example, as well as some others below, I use the Prinner label without a bracket to avoid cluttering the annotations.

25. I am unaware of any prior proposals for a specifically Prinner cadence. Gjerdingen gives examples of such a case, but does not explicitly link the Prinner to a cadence or clausula per se. Schmid's category of "falling-third cadences" embraces examples that I would identify as PrCs; however, many others are either cadences of a different type or are noncadential ("Die 'Terzkadenz'").

26. In many of Gjerdingen's examples, the "Romanesca," ①–⑤–⑥–③ supporting $\hat{1}$–$\hat{5}$–$\hat{1}$–$\hat{1}$ (and other melodic variants), typically appears as an initiating schema before the Prinner (see Ex. 7.15a and 7.18, and ahead, Ex. 7.20 and 7.23). In such cases, the Romanesca projects a tonic *prolongation*, as is appropriate to its opening function. These elements of the schema are also the ones presented in appendix A of *Galant Style* (454). When Gjerdingen first defines the Romanesca (29), however, he details a more extended version that includes two additional bass notes ④–① as well as a different melodic line: $\hat{3}$–$\hat{2}$–$\hat{1}$–$\hat{7}$–$\hat{6}$–$\hat{5}$ (as in Pachelbel's canon), thus giving rise to a descending-thirds *sequence*. For this reason, the Romanescas found in the four examples just mentioned are indicated as incomplete (by a dashed line that overlaps with the onset of the subsequent Prinner).

27. See ahead, Ex. 7.25. For more on the modulating Prinner, see Gjerdingen, *Galant Style*, 52–53.

28. Prolongational and sequential Prinners are treated in greater detail in Caplin, "Gjerdingen's 'Prinner,'" 22–27 and 27–30, respectively.

**386** Cadence in the Galant Era

EXAMPLE 7.15. (a) Galuppi, *La diavolessa*, mm. 1–4 (G23.1); (b) Graun, Trio Sonata, mm. 1–2 (G9.5).

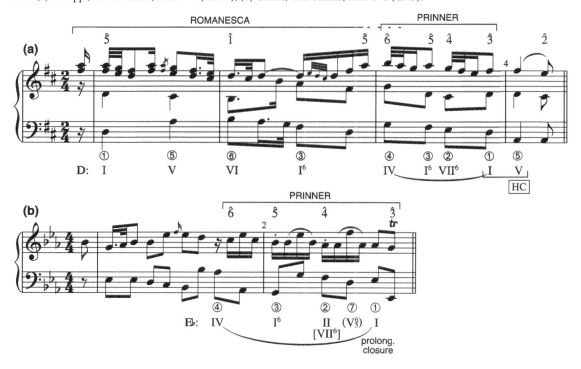

EXAMPLE 7.16. (a) Gaviniès, Violin Sonata in A, Op. 3, no. 1, i, mm. 10–19; (b) Ferrari, Violin Sonata in A, Op. 1, no. 3, i, mm. 13–18.

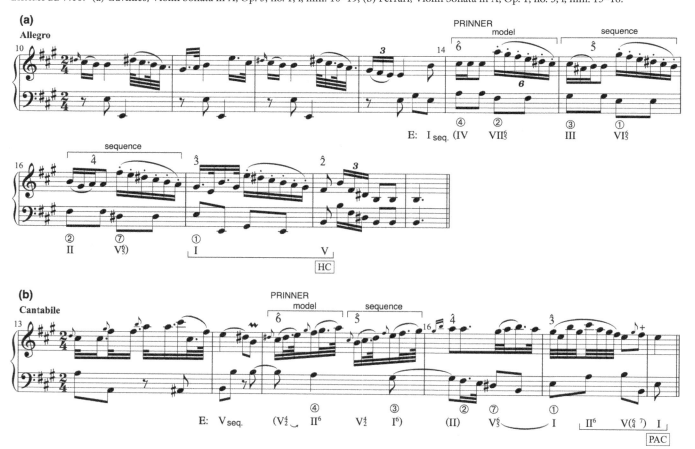

EXAMPLE 7.17. (a) Cadential Prinner, metrical extension; (b) submetrical insertion.

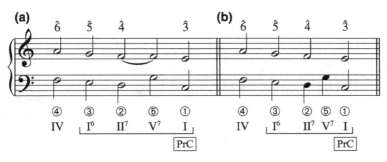

EXAMPLE 7.18. Gallo, Trio Sonata in G, i, mm. 1–2 (G3.9).

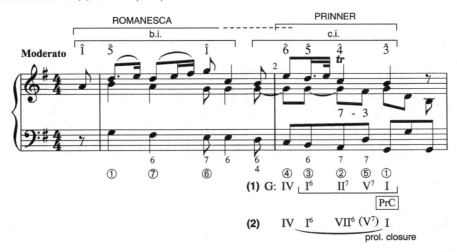

EXAMPLE 7.19. Modulating Prinner.

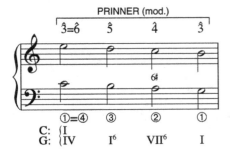

as the final event of the complete theme or as an internal articulation (ending an antecedent phrase) within a periodic structure. A Prinner cadence cannot end a subordinate theme of sonata form (or any allied form, such as minuet, rondo, or concerto), since such a function requires closure by means of a PAC; moreover, the Prinner cadence is rarely, if ever, used as a way station within subordinate themes, though other forms of the IAC may function in that way.

A typical case of a PrC with a metrically extended ⑤ has already been seen in Example 7.18. The opening basic idea, built as a Romanesca, is followed by a contrasting idea, a Prinner riposte, which creates a palpable sense of closure aided by the cadential trill on $\hat{4}$. A similar cadence arises in Example 7.20,

though here the situation is somewhat more complex. Following the Romanesca, the contrasting idea, beginning with the upbeat to measure 2, sees $I^6$ leading to IV on the downbeat of the bar. This harmonic move suggests that a standard cadential progression were in the making, and we might expect a cadential root-position dominant to follow. Instead, IV initiates the Prinner, which forces the bass downward, thus abandoning the cadential progression, though leading immediately to a second one that creates the PrC. While we clearly hear IV as signaling the start of the Prinner proper, this harmony also seems to function as a neighbor that embellishes the $I^6$ introduced on beat four of the first bar. I return to this example shortly and discuss how in some other cases, the initial cadential progression, which here is abandoned, can actually be realized.

Example 7.21 shows the schema at the basis of two continuation phrases. Following a presentation (mm. 1–3), the Prinner of the first continuation is highly prolongational due to the use of ① in stages *a* and *b* (replacing ④ and ③) in m. 4 and the inversion of the dominants ($V^{4-6}_{3-5}$) in the first half of measure 5. The resulting lack of cadential closure then motivates a repetition of the continuation at measure 6. Here, the bass line now conforms more to the Prinner prototype, with a submetrical insertion of ⑤ leading to a genuine PrC. Note by the way, that this cadence type, by definition, leaves the melody open on $\hat{3}$. It is therefore interesting to observe how following the PrC, Galuppi adds a brief

EXAMPLE 7.20. Marcello, Keyboard Sonata in F, Op. 1, no. 1, i, mm. 1–2 (G3.4).

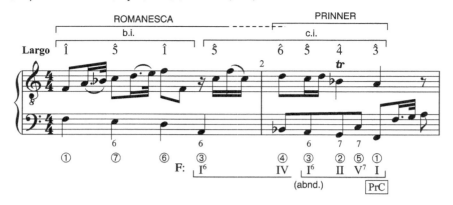

EXAMPLE 7.21. Galuppi, Keyboard Sonata in B-flat, I. 40, i, mm. 1–8.

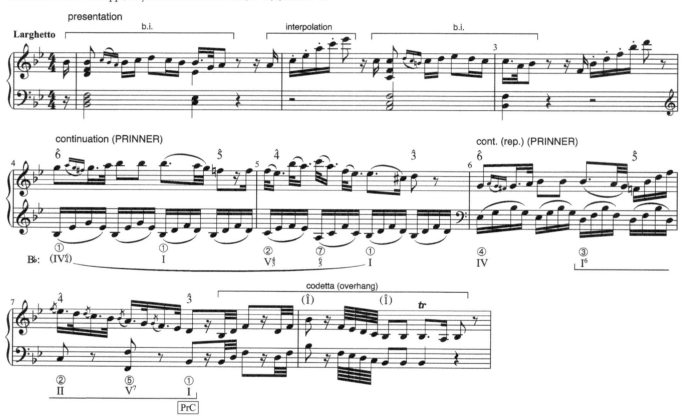

codetta that compensates for this incomplete melodic closure by emphasizing $\hat{1}$.[29]

An important caveat must be raised at this point. In order to speak of a genuine cadential Prinner, the bass ② must first support a pre-dominant harmony (II or II$^7$). If, on the contrary, ② already brings dominant harmony in the form of V$^4_3$ or VII$^6$ (Ex. 7.22a), then the added ⑤ will no longer be heard as cadential because the dominant initially appears inverted. In such cases, the following root-position V gives the impression of being an embellishment of the inverted dominant (a "casting out" of the root), thus rendering the progression prolongational. Example 7.22b provides a concrete illustration. Here, the appearance of VII$^6$ at the beginning of stage c (second half of m. 31) results in a prolongational Prinner, and so a genuine HC immediately follows to conclude the phrase.

With this consideration in mind, it must be recognized that in a passage with a two-voice texture, such as Example 7.20, we may not always know just what the implied harmony of stage c really is, especially in the absence of a figured bass that might give some clues as to a more complete harmonic texture. But even when the

---

29. As will be discussed shortly (sec. 7.1.4), this codetta can also be understood as an extended "overhang." For another case of a codetta that emphasizes $\hat{1}$ following a PrC, see Ex. 3.92.

EXAMPLE 7.22. (a) Prolongational Prinner with added ⑤; (b) Johann Stamitz, Flute Concerto in D, i, mm. 29–32.

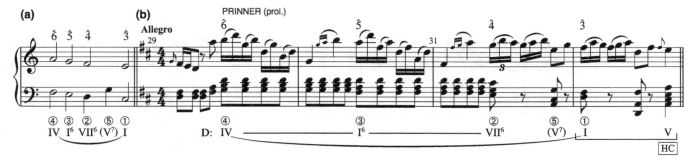

EXAMPLE 7.23. Castrucci, Violin Sonata in F, Op. 2, no. 4, i, mm. 1–2 (G3.5).

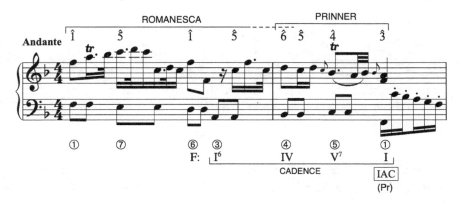

figured bass is present, as with this example, the situation may remain ambiguous. Typically, we find the figures "7–7" associated with the ②–⑤ bass. When realized (as with the second violin of Ex. 7.18), an inner, third voice lies a dissonant seventh above the bass ②, resolving stepwise down to creating a consonant third, as the bass leaps to ⑤.[30] In such cases, it would be possible to understand the seventh (over ②) in one of two ways: either as an "essential" dissonance (to speak with Kirnberger) within a pre-dominant harmony (II[7]), which resolves to a dominant seventh (over ⑤), see line 1 of Example 7.18; or as a "non-essential" dissonance, a suspension, within a single dominant harmony embracing both ② and ⑤, see line 2. The former case can be construed as cadential, but the latter cannot, since the dominant would initially appear inverted. It is more likely, however, that our hearing would gravitate toward the first interpretation, namely, that of a cadential Prinner, since, as Kirnberger observes, the progression of the roots by an ascending fourth is usually indicative of a resolving essential seventh, not a suspension.[31] Nonetheless, a certain harmonic ambiguity remains, which can contribute to some uncertainty about the cadential status of the Prinner configuration.

The PrC as defined and exemplified above is not the only cadential articulation associated with the melody of this schema.

Look again at Example 7.20 and recall how the move from I[6] to IV has the potential of becoming a standard cadential progression (by continuing on to V). There, this progression ends up being abandoned, leading instead to a second progression that effects a PrC. The possibility of realizing this opening cadential progression, however, is shown in Example 7.23. Here, the use of a standard cadential bass line to support the Prinner melody yields an unequivocal IAC.[32] In order to distinguish this cadence from the Prinner cadence proper, I use the label *IAC (Pr)*, which stands for *imperfect authentic cadence (Prinner type)*.[33]

The essential difference between the two cadence types associated with the Prinner involves the motion of the bass: in a PrC, ⑤ is immediately preceded by ②, which itself is either approached from ③ above, or occasionally, as a variant, from ① below. In an IAC (Pr), on the contrary, ⑤ ensues directly from ④. I consider this distinction to be both conceptually and perceptually significant. The IAC (Pr) is a standard variant of the genuine IAC; its bass line is fully differentiated from its melodic line. The PrC, on the contrary, always brings with it vestiges of a schema prototype that has strong sequential and prolongational implications, since its bass line derives from a situation of parallel motion and is thus not as differentiated from the melody as a standard cadential bass. The

---

30. I have slightly altered the notation of the inner voice in Ex. 7.18, m. 2, in order to show more clearly the 7–3 intervallic succession.

31. "It can be taken as a general rule that every essential seventh is followed by a bass progression by ascending fourth or descending fifth" (Kirnberger, *Strict Musical Composition*, 82).

32. The Prinner melody itself is assimilated to the varied tenor stream, 5̂/6̂ (5̂)/4̂/3̂.

33. Note that I have included Gjerdingen's label of "Cadence" that he adds to the bass line of Ex. 7.23, thus explicitly recognizing that such a bass differs markedly from the Prinner bass of Ex. 7.18 and 7.20.

EXAMPLE 7.24. Corelli, Concerto Grosso in F, Op. 6, no. 9, iii, mm. 7–11.

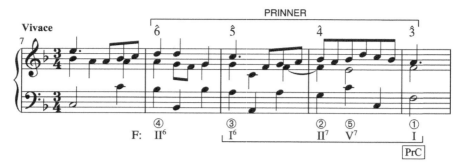

EXAMPLE 7.25. J. S. Bach, Prelude No. 1 in C, *WTC I*, mm. 4–11.

PrC brings, of course, a cadential dominant exclusively in root position; if it did not, we could not speak of a cadence. Yet this ⑤ still conveys the sense of embellishing a more prototypical ②. This impression is especially strong when the added ⑤ takes the form of a submetrical insertion. In other words, the PrC seems to occupy a middle position between the purely prolongational Prinner, which can, in certain formal contexts, bring about prolongational closure (as in Ex. 7.15b), and the IAC (Pr) (Ex. 7.23), which effects an entirely cadential process of ending.

The Prinner cadence did not originate in the galant style, although there, the cadence type appears most commonly. Already with Corelli we find a number of cases, one of which is shown in Example 7.24. Occasional PrCs arise in works by J. S. Bach as well; indeed, the famous first prelude of the *WTC* 1 contains two prominent instances, one articulating the subordinate key of G major (Ex. 7.25), the other, confirming the return of the home key (mm. 13–19, not shown).[34]

The PrC declines markedly in the high classical style (ca. 1780 onward), even while the prolongational and sequential Prinners continue to be used extensively. A comparison of remarkably similar passages, one from a piano sonata by Peroti (1756, Ex. 7.26), the other by Mozart (1788; see in Chapter 3, Ex. 3.66), who perhaps knew the earlier work, is highly telling in this respect.[35] Whereas the galant sonata employs three PrCs (mm. 3–4, 5–6, 7–10), the classical piece brings none, Mozart's Prinners (mm. 3–4, 5–8) being entirely prolongational. The PrC does, however, occur now and then in the classical repertoire,[36] even finding expression in the early Romantic period, as discussed later in Chapter 8, sec. 8.12.[37]

---

34. Note that with respect to the prototypical Prinner, the soprano and bass voices of Ex. 7.25 are not fully aligned, for the bass descent is delayed by one bar in mm. 6 and 8. Observe, as well, how the multi-voiced texture makes it clear that the harmony supported by ②, m. 9, clearly projects the pre-dominant II⁷ and not an inverted dominant (e.g., VII⁶). (Recall the earlier discussion of this issue in connection with Ex. 7.18.)

35. Gjerdingen, *Galant Style*, 359–68; see also Kaiser, *Die Notenbücher der Mozarts*, 183.

36. See Ex. 3.74, 3.91, 3.92, and 3.145.

37. For a more extended discussion of the Prinner cadence, including additional examples of the IAC (Pr), see Caplin, "Gjerdingen's 'Prinner,'" 46–52. This essay also assesses the PrC's cadential strength in relation to other cadence types, along with its propensity for being undermined in various ways.

EXAMPLE 7.26. Peroti, Keyboard Sonata in B-flat, iii, mm. 1–10.

EXAMPLE 7.27. C. P. E. Bach, Keyboard Sonata in F, Wq. 48, no. 1, i, mm. 26–31.

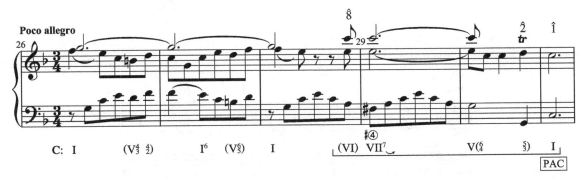

### 7.1.3. Miscellaneous Variants

The galant style employs a number of characteristic morphological variants of the tonal cadence. One type—found especially in the works of C. P. E. Bach—features a major-mode context in which a cadential pre-dominant built over #4̂ supports a half-diminished-seventh sonority (VII⁷/V).[38] (In the classical style, the seventh harmony over #4̂ normally takes the form of a fully diminished sonority, even in the major mode.) Example 7.27 shows a typical use of this harmony by Bach, one that is especially highlighted by the melody leaping up to 8̂ (upbeat to m. 29) and left dangling there while the melodic close 2̂–1̂ occurs an octave below. In Example 7.28, Bach emphasizes his characteristic sonority with a *forte* accent (mm. 48–49), though in this case, the cadential dominant that follows at measure 50 is quickly abandoned when the bass leaps down to ⑦; the required resolution to I is followed immediately by a compact cadential progression, which realizes the expected PAC.[39] Although Bach especially favors this pre-dominant, we find it used by Scarlatti as well (Ex. 7.29, m. 26), this time associated with an HC closing a transition.

A second variant, found typically with Scarlatti, involves a melodic quirk in connection with an HC (Ex. 7.30).[40] When the dominant arrives on the downbeat of measure 12, the penultimate 1̂, supported by tonic, moves *upward* to 2̂, with a delayed resolution. More typically in such a simple HC, 1̂ would descend to 7̂. We also find Scarlatti using the technique in connection a phrygian HC (see ahead Ex. 7.78c). At measure 52 (first bar of the example), the resolution from 1̂ to 2̂ is delayed as an ascending suspension. He can also allude to this configuration in the context of a standing on the dominant that follows an HC (or dominant arrival), as seen in Example 7.51a, measure 25. Just why Scarlatti

---

38. From now on in this chapter, I will reference C. P. E. Bach with his family name only. Any mention of the other members of the Bach family will include the initials of their given names (except where redundant).

39. Alternatively, the emphatic VII⁷/V following upon IV could give the impression of a *converging* half cadential progression, thus yielding an HC on the downbeat of m. 50. This reading would thus not recognize a subsequent cadential abandonment.

40. I thank Janet Schmalfeldt for alerting me to this HC variant.

EXAMPLE 7.28. C. P. E. Bach, Keyboard Sonata in C Minor, Wq. 48, no. 4, ii, mm. 46–52.

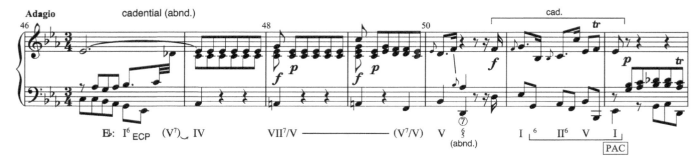

EXAMPLE 7.29. Scarlatti, Keyboard Sonata in C, K. 309, mm. 23–28.

EXAMPLE 7.30. Scarlatti, Keyboard Sonata in C, K. 587, mm. 9–12.

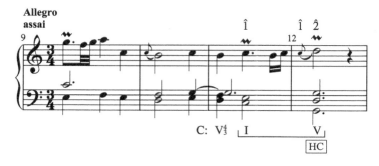

favors these particular sonorities, which have a certain "hollow" sound to them, is by no means clear.[41] In the absence of any obvious compositional explanations, the device seems simply to be part of the composer's harmonic palette.

A third cadential variant, identified by Yoel Greenberg, is especially typical of the galant style. As seen in Example 7.31a, a six-measure main theme concludes with an extremely compact PAC, whose closure on such a weak metrical position is decidedly *abrupt*. "This kind of cadence was a very common way to end opening ideas in mid-century works, especially for the keyboard, and still featured in some early Haydn sonatas.... Probably owing to the metrical weakness of the tonic, this cadence was only sufficient to end small-scale units—almost exclusively opening ideas."[42]

(We will encounter additional cases of this variant and return again to this example, including a discussion of system b, toward the end of the chapter, when considering main theme structures in the galant style.)[43]

## 7.1.4. Melodic "Overhang"

In his monumental treatise on composition, H. C. Koch describes how the final note of a (four-measure) phrase or a (two-measure) "incise" may be decorated "by means of striking afterward [*Nachschlag*] other tones contained in the triad at its basis [Ex. 7.32, m. 4, etc.].... In this case the caesura acquires an overhang [*Überhang*], or a feminine ending, which in addition can be mixed with passing notes and appoggiaturas in various

---

41. The final harmony of Ex. 7.30 is especially hollow with its absence of a third in a full chordal texture.

42. Yoel Greenberg, "Tinkering with Form: On W. F. Bach's Revisions to Two Keyboard Sonatas," 210.

43. For an (early) classical example of this gesture, see Chapter 3, sec. 3.4.1.2, in connection with Ex. 3.157, m. 4.

7.1. MORPHOLOGY OF THE GALANT CADENCE 393

EXAMPLE 7.31. W. F. Bach, Sonata in F, Fk. 6, (a) mm. 1–6 (early version); (b) mm. 1–4 (R = ½N) (later version).

EXAMPLE 7.32. Koch, *Introductory Essay on Composition*, Ex. 69a–d.

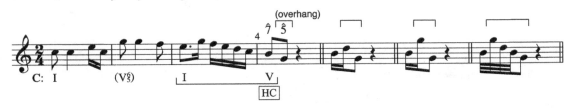

EXAMPLE 7.33. Koch, *Introductory Essay on Composition*, Ex. 71a–c and 72a–b.

ways [Ex. 7.33]."[44] As Koch continues to develop his idea of the overhang, it becomes clear that for the purpose of determining the degree of melodic closure associated with a given phrase, the notes of the overhang are discounted. In Example 7.32, in other words, the note B ($\hat{7}$), measure 4, is taken as the structural pitch defining the close of the phrase. And this determination holds for the additional overhangs in this example, as well as those in Example 7.33.

Despite the lack of a bass line, it is evident that in these examples, Koch is describing a phrase ending with an HC. And in this connection, the question of which note represents the "end" of the melody has no analytical impact as regards a determination of the cadence type: we would recognize an HC no matter which note of the ultimate dominant is taken as the structural close of the phrase. In the case of an implied authentic cadence, however, our differentiating between a PAC and an IAC depends entirely on our assessment of which note represents melodic closure. And in this connection, two of Koch's passages (Ex. 7.34, staves a and b), reveal again that the initial pitch of the overhang configuration is definitive. In staff a, Koch recognizes a "closing phrase," one that "can close the whole after other preceding sections" (7); here, the obvious cadential situation (assuming an appropriate cadential bass line) is that of a PAC. Staff b, however, shows how this closing phrase can be converted into an "internal phrase"

---

44. Koch, *Introductory Essay on Composition*, 23–24. All of the analytical annotations in Ex. 7.32–7.34 are mine; they are based on an interpretation of the implied bass-line and harmonic context.

EXAMPLE 7.34. Koch, *Introductory Essay on Composition*, Ex. 10 and 14.

EXAMPLE 7.35. C. P. E. Bach, Keyboard Sonata in B Minor, Wq. 49, no. 6, ii, mm. 1–6.

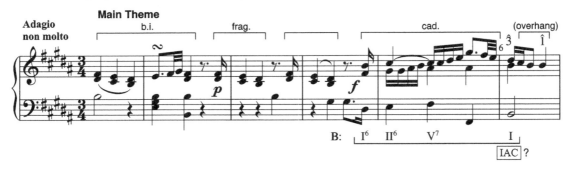

EXAMPLE 7.36. Galuppi, Keyboard Sonata in D, I. 39, ii, mm. 1–5.

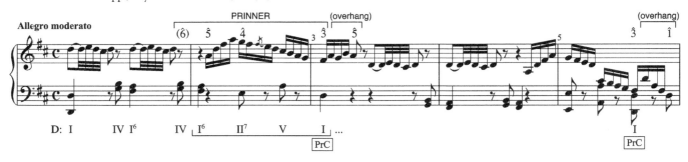

by changing its "ending formula" (7). Seeing as the phrase now exhibits a melodic overhang, the structural pitch must be taken as $\hat{3}$, even if $\hat{1}$ is achieved at the end of the overhang. Such a cadence (again, assuming a cadential bass line) would be an IAC.[45]

To explore this topic further, let us consider some actual passages from the galant literature. In Example 7.35, a main theme closes in measure 6 with an authentic cadence: Is it a PAC or an IAC? Following Koch's prescripts, it would be the latter due to the overhang. Frequently in the galant repertory, such overhangs involve paired phrases, as seen in Example 7.36. Here, an opening phrase closes with a PrC (m. 3), after which an overhang rises from $\hat{3}$ to $\hat{5}$;[46] a matching phrase then brings the same cadence (m. 5), this time with a descending overhang from $\hat{3}$ to $\hat{1}$. Sometimes the overhang can be extended to such a degree that it might be considered a kind of codetta, as seen in the earlier discussed Example 7.21 by Galuppi. A PrC ending on $\hat{3}$ at measure 7 receives what we now can understand as a substantial, postcadential overhang, which achieves $\hat{1}$ as the ultimate melodic, if not formal, goal.

If we accept Koch's description of melodic overhangs, we must acknowledge that Examples 7.21, 7.35, and 7.36 close with an IAC ending on $\hat{3}$, with the overhang being purely ornamental. In

---

45. Koch does not recognize an IAC as such, since his cadence concept is largely confined to our modern PAC. His restrictive notions about cadence (both authentic and half) have been outlined in Chapter 2; see notes 54 and 193.

46. The harmonies supporting the Prinner are clear enough; the melody is somewhat less discernible, especially the opening $\hat{6}$ (B), which is found only in the piano's left-hand part.

EXAMPLE 7.37. C. P. E. Bach, Keyboard Sonata in E, Wq. 62, no. 5, i, mm. 1–5 (R = ½N).

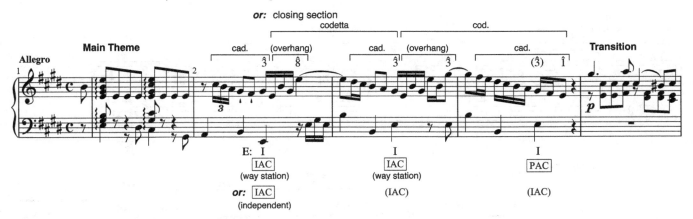

some cases of an overhang from 3̂ to 1̂, however, we may have the distinct impression that the melodic goal is more structurally decisive, and we might question whether the cadence should better be described as a PAC rather than an IAC. Consider Example 7.37 by Bach, notated in compound meter (i.e., R = ½N). An opening phrase (of four *real* measures) closes with a clear IAC in measure 2, followed by an ascending overhang to 8̂, which upon a cadential repetition is extended even further up to a high 3̂. An additional repetition sees a powerfully descending scale from that 3̂ all the way down to 1̂. Like the previous two cadences, the arrival of the bass ① is coordinated with the lower 3̂, yet the melodic goal of the descent, 1̂, seems to override the sense of an IAC, thus projecting the final cadence as a PAC. This analysis suggests that we hear the first two IACs (mm. 2 and 3) as way stations to a final PAC; moreover, this perspective would also deny the final 3̂–1̂ melodic descent (m. 4) its status as a genuine overhang. Alternatively, we could accept a more Kochian viewpoint and understand all of the material following the first 3̂ (m. 2) as a closing section consisting of overhangs *cum* codettas, along the lines of Galuppi's sonata in Example 7.21.

Another consideration can be brought to bear on the question of which cadence type is expressed when confronting an overhang. As we know, the final cadence of a classical subordinate theme must be a PAC. This principle holds as well for the galant repertory. If the composers of this period considered the cases of overhang discussed in the prior examples to be PACs, then we might expect them to use such configurations to close subordinate themes. Yet such seems not to be the case, at least for the works surveyed for this chapter. So it is probably best to regard such overhangs as arising from an IAC, albeit one that is potentially ambiguous.

A nice play on the ambiguities just discussed arises in Example 7.38. The first part of a baroque binary form (Ex. 7.38a) begins with an antecedent phrase that closes in measure 4 with an IAC and a downward overhang.[47] The contrasting idea begins to be repeated for a second IAC at measure 6. This time, in what seems more like a continuation than an extension of the antecedent, the melodic line pushes upward in a way that overrides the potential cadence, eventually leading to an HC at measure 8, which emerges as the genuine close of the theme.

Toward the end of the movement (Ex. 7.38b), Bach writes an expanded dominant (mm. 57–64), whose ambiguous formal status will be discussed later in this chapter.[48] This dominant then directly leads into the main theme's contrasting idea (mm. 64–65, cf., Ex. 7.38a, mm. 3–4).[49] When this idea begins to be repeated in measures 66–67, the piece could have concluded with an IAC and overhang, as reconstructed in Example 7.38c. But this cadence type is inappropriate for the final cadence of the movement, so Bach writes an additional cadential progression that allows the "overhang" 2̂–1̂ to be supported harmonically in such a way as to create a clear PAC, and to accord a way-station function to the prior IAC.

In the high classical style, where cadential identification is so important for formal articulation, melodic overhangs are less often encountered—they would seem to be "used up" as a mannerism of an older style—and as a result, the kinds of cadential ambiguities we have been dealing with occur less frequently. One such case, though, arises in a main theme discussed earlier in Chapter 3; see Example 3.78 (R = ½N), a piano sonata by Haydn from the mid-1770s, when galant characteristics are still discernible. Following a compound presentation (not shown), a continuation⇒cadential phrase leads to an IAC in the middle of measure 6. In principle, this cadence could mark the end of the main theme. But when we hear the phrase being repeated, we can easily believe that this cadence is a way station en route to a PAC. Indeed, the close of the melody on 1̂ (m. 8, second half of beat 3) would seem to fulfill that expectation. But one detail is telling. The actual arrival on tonic harmony occurs directly on

---

47. The unusual formal layout of this binary will be discussed later in note 74.

---

48. See below, sec. 7.3.4.3.

49. The idea in mm. 64–65 cannot effect a real cadence (nor a real overhang) because its dominant is not "penultimate," as will be explained later in the chapter.

EXAMPLE 7.38. C. P. E. Bach, Keyboard Sonata in A Minor, Wq. 49, no. 1, ii, (a) mm. 1–8; (b) mm. 50–69; (c) reconstruction of mm. 66–67.

the third beat (as shown in the analysis). Since this harmony initially supports $\hat{3}$, the following melodic embellishments could be understood as an overhang, achieving (and then sustaining) $\hat{1}$. If so, and following Koch's directives, we would have to understand the cadence as a second IAC, and therefore see a case of consecutive cadences. Of the two options, I prefer a PAC interpretation as conforming more to the conventions of main-theme organization in the classical style, though I am prepared to validate the ambiguities that Haydn builds into this particular theme.

## 7.2. Cadential Deviations

The principal types of cadential deviation witnessed in the classical style are already fully evident in works of the galant period. The deceptive cadence, which appeared widely enough in the baroque, continues to be used by mid-century composers. And even some genuine abandoned cadences can be identified in the repertory. The evaded cadence—employed sporadically in the baroque—now comes fully to the fore, especially in the works of Scarlatti.

EXAMPLE 7.39. Scarlatti, Keyboard Sonata in B-flat, K. 545, mm. 22–49.

## 7.2.1. Evaded Cadence

As discussed by Schmalfeldt in her groundbreaking study of the evaded cadence, this cadential deviation, especially in association with the "one-more-time" technique, is a hallmark of Scarlatti's keyboard works.[50] In Example 7.39, the entire subordinate-theme group of the exposition is marked by extensive cadential evasions, beginning first with a brief cadential progression in measure 22, which is evaded by the $I^6$ *initiating harmony* on the downbeat of the following bar.[51] There follows a new continuation, whose promised cadence at measure 28 is also evaded by $I^6$; the one-more-time technique is evident here when the music backs up to measure 23 and runs through the same passage, finally bringing a

---

50. Schmalfeldt, "Cadential Processes," 2; see also her detailed analysis of Scarlatti's Sonata in D, K. 492, on pp. 7–10.

51. Unusually, the subordinate key is the submediant (G) of the home key (B-flat), a situation almost unheard of in the classical style, save for the first movements of Beethoven's String Quintet in C, Op. 29, and his "Hammerklavier" sonata; see in Chapter 5, Ex. 5.14.

EXAMPLE 7.40. Scarlatti, Keyboard Sonata in C, K. 309, mm. 41–51.

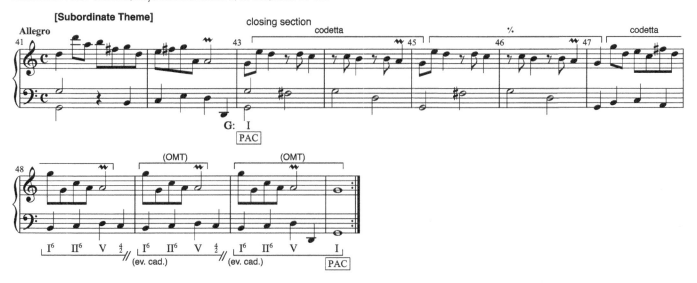

PAC at measure 34. A second subordinate theme, beginning with a series of half cadential gestures, closes with a PAC at measure 38. The unit is then repeated in full except that the final cadence is evaded at measure 42, thus producing an enormous extension. A passage of new material brings another evasion at measure 45, prompting a one-more-time technique with the reference back to measure 42. Measure 48 effects a final evaded cadence. Note that this time, the bass moves down from ④ to ③, which supports I⁶ for an immediate repeat of the progression and a final PAC at measure 49. As a result of this small change, the bass is not interrupted rhythmically, as it was on the downbeats of measures 42 and 45, but rather pushes on in steady quarter-note motion all the way to the final bar of the exposition.[52]

As we see in this sonata, the powerful rhythmic drive associated with the various cadential evasions and final attainment of the PAC literally brings an end to the exposition, since no further closing material follows this cadence.[53] In many of Scarlatti's expositions, however, the final subordinate theme leads to a distinct closing section. Even here, he often brings the one-more-time technique, something we rarely find with composers of the classical period. Example 7.40 is a case in point. The subordinate theme concludes with a PAC at measure 43. A closing section then begins consisting at first of a two-measure codetta, which is repeated in measures 45–46. At measure 47 another codetta promises to close with a PAC (of limited scope), but the cadence is evaded twice, with one-more-time technique, before attaining the final event of the closing section (and the exposition).[54]

Example 7.41 provides a final illustration of Scarlatti's propensity to use evaded cadences right up to the very last moment of the exposition (and, usually, of the matching recapitulation). Here, the end of the transition brings a medial caesura at measure 21. The following subordinate theme, which begins directly on VI with continuation function, leads quickly to a promised cadence for the downbeat of measure 26.[55] Whereas the dominant resolves deceptively to VI, the effect is more of an evaded cadence than a deceptive one, since the melody breaks off and leaps up an octave to repeat the continuation one more time. Another evaded cadence at measure 30 yields one-measure fragments made up of new material along with evaded cadences at measures 31 and 32.[56] Yet after all of these evasions, Scarlatti is still not ready to write a cadence. So an abandoned cadential progression (IV–V⁶) leads to a new idea at measure 33, and one more evasion finally achieves the long-promised PAC at the last bar of the exposition. Note that the use of deceptive resolutions and abandoned cadential progressions helps relieve what might have been an overburdening of standard evaded cadences beginning on I⁶.[57]

---

52. Inasmuch as the melody leading into m. 48 resolves 7̂–1̂ without any interruption, unlike the two prior evaded cadences, our hearing an elided deceptive cadence cannot be ruled out as an alternative option.

53. We might be tempted to consider the passage starting at m. 34 as a closing section consisting at first of a five-measure codetta that begins to be repeated. But a couple of factors militate against this idea. First, the emphasis on dominant harmony (via the half cadential gestures) at the beginning of this "codetta" is unusual for a passage that is supposed to be emphasizing the attained tonic of the cadence. Second, an individual codetta is rarely more than four bars long in this style, and the "closing section" that would result, lasting until m. 49, seems overly long.

54. Schmalfeldt's analysis of Scarlatti's Sonata in D, K. 492, also shows a case of one-more-time technique embedded within the closing section of the exposition ("Cadential Processes," 9–10).

55. As Schmalfeldt has pointed out to me in a personal communication, this unusual opening of a subordinate theme on VI foreshadows the extensive set of cadential evasions that occur with that same harmony (mm. 26, 30, 31, and 32).

56. These two evaded cadences might alternatively be heard as deceptive, if one focuses on the inner voice, whose 7̂–1̂ resolutions help to make the downbeats of mm. 31 and 32 sound like cadential goals.

57. Evaded cadences are such a key part of Scarlatti's compositional style that it comes as somewhat of a shock when an exposition fails to bring this deviation type, as in, for example, the Sonatas in F, K. 366, E Minor, K. 394, and E, K. 403.

EXAMPLE 7.41. Scarlatti, Keyboard Sonata in C, K. 308, mm. 20–35.

Cadential evasion is not always associated with the one-more-time technique. C. P. E. Bach, in particular, tends not to use this device (Ex. 7.42). A promised cadence on the downbeat of measure 26 is evaded when the melody leaps back up for another attempt. Though the descending melodic contour in measure 26 resembles that of the previous bar, the details of the melody are essentially different; moreover, the cadential progression supporting this descent is even abandoned. So rather than creating a one-more-time repetition, Bach seems to have in mind a broader, multi-level melodic process, as indicated by the stepwise descending "high points" in measures 24–28 (see the elongated stems connected by a beam).

Example 7.43 shows another evaded cadence (m. 19) that eschews the one-more-time technique. As a result, Bach does not need to restore the steady eighth-note motion that precedes the evasion. He can thus allow the downbeat of measure 19 to significantly disrupt the rhythmic-textural flow, an effect that is further enhanced by the quarter-note rest on the third beat of that bar.

### 7.2.2. Deceptive Cadence

The deceptive cadence continues to be used in the galant period much in the same way as in the earlier baroque and later classical styles.[58] Notable is the occasional galant use of the deceptive cadence in a series of deviations, such as what often occurs with evaded cadences. In Example 7.44, for instance, Bach writes two deceptive cadences in row (mm. 30 and 32) before finally achieving the PAC at measure 34.

Scarlatti even outdoes Bach with the passages shown in Example 7.45, where the deceptive cadence at measure 64 is followed in the next bar by a return to the material of measure 59ff., thus alluding to the one-more-time technique.[59] A second deceptive cadence at measure 69 leads this time to new material, which emphasizes both $V^7$ (metrically) and VI (durationally). For a third time within the theme, the phrase ends with a deceptive cadence, measure 72, whose following phrase repeats the new material of measure 69ff., finally resulting in the promised PAC at measure 75.

That a string of deceptive cadences can play a similar role as that of evaded ones is particularly clear in Example 7.46a. Here, Scarlatti closes the exposition with a series of evasions (of limited scope, since the music is actually part of an ongoing closing section). In the analogous place in the recapitulation (Ex. 7.46b), he replaces the evaded cadences with deceptive ones. The general function of both

---

58. J. S. Bach's penchant for using $V^7/IV$ as the final harmony of the cadential progression (especially in the first book of the *WTC*), however, seems rarely to be adopted by later eighteenth-century composers.

59. Recall that I restrict using the term "one more time" to situation of evaded cadences; see Chapter 4, sec. 4.1.2.1, and note 26. Observe as well that the repetition of previous material does not occur until m. 65, which follows the deceptive cadence in m. 64, a situation that is unlike a real one-more-time technique, which normally takes place at the very moment of cadential evasion.

EXAMPLE 7.42. C. P. E. Bach, Keyboard Sonata in B-flat, Wq. 48, no. 2, i, mm. 24–28.

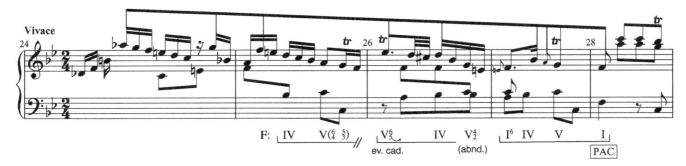

EXAMPLE 7.43. C. P. E. Bach, Keyboard Sonata in F Minor, Wq. 62, no. 6, ii, mm. 16–21.

EXAMPLE 7.44. C. P. E. Bach, Keyboard Sonata in F, Wq 62, no. 8, i, mm. 27–34.

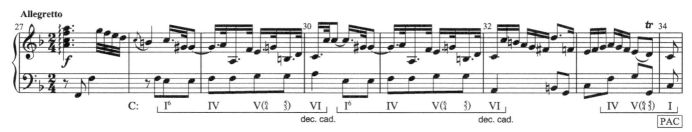

deviation types is the same—to postpone the arrival of the PAC.[60] But the effect is quite different between the exposition and recapitulation. In the former, the evaded cadences disrupt the melody, rhythm, and texture on the downbeats of measures 33–35. In the latter, the deceptive cadences promote greater continuity of these parameters. The change in deviation type is perhaps motivated by Scarlatti's playing with register: in the exposition, the implied melodic goal is always $C_5$, so the one-more-time technique keeps the melody leaping up to $B\flat_5$. In the recapitulation, the melodic goal is shifted down an octave from $F_5$ (m. 64) to $F_4$ (m. 65) and finally to $F_3$ (m. 66). The deceptive cadences allow for a more direct articulation of these goal tones than would be the case with evaded cadences.[61]

### 7.2.3. Abandoned Cadence

As discussed in the previous chapter, my survey of baroque compositions did not turn up any cases of a genuine abandoned cadence—that is, a specific point of anticipated formal arrival that fails to materialize due to the abandonment of the cadential progression. Such situations, which are even infrequent in the classical style, seldom appear in the galant as well. One such case may arise toward the end of the subordinate theme in Example 7.47. Following a deceptive cadence (3̂) in measure 26, the next bar initiates a cadential progression IV–V. Rather than letting the harmony resolve directly to I, Bach allows the bass line to fill in the melodic space between ④ and ⑧ with an ascending scale (accompanied by parallel 10ths in the upper voice). As a result, the dominant is inverted prior to the appearance of I in the middle of measure 28. A variation on these two bars then occurs immediately in measures 29–30. A final cadential progression (mm. 31–32) yields a PAC to close the theme. We could thus speak of abandoned cadences in the middle of measures 28 and 30 because these moments represent a degree of harmonic and melodic closure.[62]

---

60. Indeed, Schmalfeldt considers the cadences in Ex. 7.46b, mm. 64 and 65, as "evaded," though she notes that each replaces "the tonic with a deceptive VI chord" (Janet Schmalfeldt, "Domenico Scarlatti, Escape Artist: Sightings of His 'Mixed Style' Towards the End of the Eighteenth Century," 279).

61. I compare additional expositions and recapitulations by Scarlatti in the final unit of this chapter (sec. 7.4.5).

62. Alternatively, we might hear a deceptive cadence on the downbeats of mm. 28 and 30, with the rising gesture in the melody as a kind of upward

7.2. CADENTIAL DEVIATIONS   401

EXAMPLE 7.45. Scarlatti, Keyboard Sonata in E Minor, K. 402, mm. 55–75.

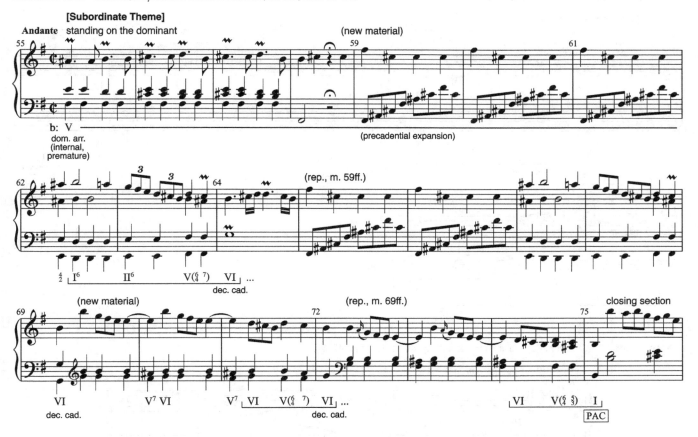

EXAMPLE 7.46. Scarlatti, Keyboard Sonata in F Minor, K. 481, (a) mm. 31–36; (b) mm. 61–66.

overhang. I find this interpretation less satisfactory, since the outer-voice parallel tenths seem to have as their goal the tonic harmony in the middle of mm. 28 and 30, not the VI on the downbeats of these bars; moreover, the prior deceptive cadence in m. 26 occurs in the middle of that bar, so our expectation of a "matching" PAC is likely to be focused on the middle of m. 28.

EXAMPLE 7.47. C. P. E. Bach, Keyboard Sonata in C, Wq. 62, no. 10, i, mm. 25–32.

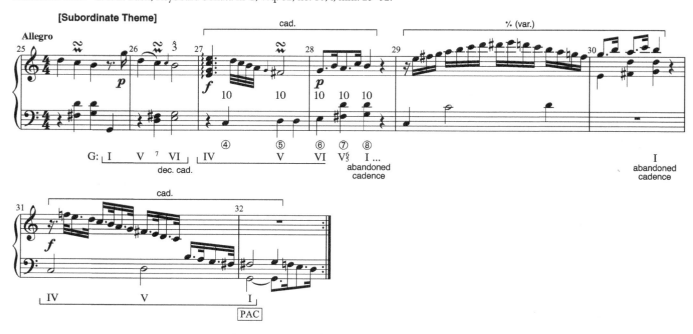

EXAMPLE 7.48. C. P. E. Bach, Keyboard Sonata in E, Wq. 48, no. 3, i, mm. 47–52.

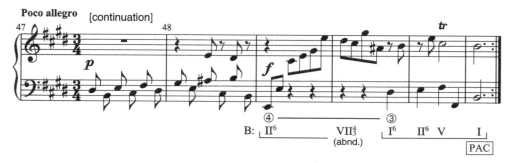

If actual abandoned cadences are rare in the galant period, the appearance of abandoned cadential progressions occurs now and then, especially in Bach's sonatas. Thus in Example 7.48, a continuation in measures 47–48 leads to a modestly expanded pre-dominant II⁶, thus proposing a possible cadential progression, one that is abandoned when the bass ④ is retained (not literally, but in our imagination) to support VII⁴₃, leading back to I⁶. A compact cadential progression immediately follows to bring the final PAC of the exposition.

A more complicated abandonment occurs in Example 7.49. At measure 11, an ECP begins with I⁶ moving to two bars of pre-dominant (IV and VII⁷/V). The arrival at measure 14 on the cadential six-four seems to clinch the deal, but this dominant strangely reverts to IV on the second beat of the bar. The single note D that follows in the right hand on beat three is harmonically ambiguous. It could seem at first to prolong the subdominant, with an implied bass of ④; however, the subsequent move to VII⁷/VI on the last beat of the bar would create a most unusual bass motion from ④ to #⑤ (see line 1 of the analysis). Perhaps a better interpretation is to understand the D as prolonging the cadential six-four, such that the implied bass is

actually ⑤, which then is chromatically altered on the next beat (see line 2). The IV would then be relegated to a subordinate status as a neighbor within the prolongation of the cadential six-four. When the rising bass continues to ⑥, eventually reaching ⑦ to support V⁶, we understand that the ongoing cadential progression has been abandoned. The return to root-position tonic on the second beat of measure 16 leads to another cadential progression, which gets as far as the resolution of the cadential six-four to five-three. Again, however, the bass returns to ④, thus creating a most unusual deceptive cadence (m. 17), though one that is motivically connected to the ⑤–④ bass motion in measure 14. A new cadential progression begins on the next bar with the pre-dominant VII⁷/V (the subdominant having been "used up"), which moves to dominant and a final tonic resolution at measure 19. The oddities of harmony in this passage are part and parcel of Bach's overall quirky style of composition.

### 7.2.4. Dominant Arrival

Dominant arrivals, an HC deviation, appear more often in the galant style than in the earlier baroque, but still infrequently

EXAMPLE 7.49. C. P. E. Bach, Keyboard Sonata in B Minor, Wq. 49, no. 6, i, mm. 11–19.

EXAMPLE 7.50. Scarlatti, Keyboard Sonata in D Minor, K. 141, mm. 31–39.

compared to later practices. Especially in Scarlatti, we find cases of prominent arrivals on a dominant seventh—not the more standard dominant triad—which is then extended in the manner of a standing on the dominant, typically to end a transition or as an internal articulation within a subordinate theme. In Example 7.50, a pre-dominant IV at measure 32 leads to a dominant seventh, which is prolonged, via a neighboring $IV^6$. Note how the trills in each measure of the standing on the dominant push upward, such that the final figure leads to the high A (m. 37), an arrival moment supported by a dominant triad (and a falling arpeggiation) to conclude this nonmodulating transition. Whereas measure 37 seems like the goal of the passage as a whole, the harmony has been stuck on a dominant seventh as early as measure 33, so a premature dominant arrival is thereby projected. A similar situation obtains in Example 7.51a, where a dominant seventh at measure 21 appears as a premature dominant arrival.[63] Here, though, the dissonant seventh only lasts a single bar, after which the subsequent dominants consist of open fifths (thus, with the octave doubled, suggesting a more complete consonant triad), and so the premature quality is rather minimal. Note also that the $V^7$ at measure 21 suggests itself as a penultimate dominant of a *cadenza doppia*. A rewritten version (Ex. 7.51b) realizes this possibility (though a PAC is not expected to end a transition).[64]

## 7.3. Extension and Expansion Techniques

As mentioned on a number of occasions in this study, the various deviation techniques just discussed normally give rise to cadential *extensions*, inasmuch as the failure to realize an expected cadence usually prompts one or more attempts that eventually succeed. And as discussed in connection with the baroque style, even simple cases of cadential repetition, without

---

63. See again Ex. 7.45, m. 55, for the comparable dominant arrival later in the recapitulation.

64. The procedure here is reminiscent of a similar situation by J. S. Bach that we observed in the previous chapter; see Ex. 6.68, m. 8. See also Scarlatti, Sonata in C, K. 421, m. 26, and Sonata in F Minor, K. 481, m. 18, for premature dominant arrivals that hint at the *cadenza doppia*.

EXAMPLE 7.51. Scarlatti, Keyboard Sonata in E Minor, K. 402, (a) mm. 19–25; (b) reconstruction of mm. 21–22.

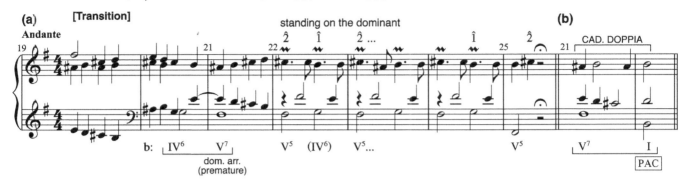

EXAMPLE 7.52. Scarlatti, Keyboard Sonata in D Minor, K. 141, mm. 79–85.

any particular deviations, can push the goal of thematic closure further into the future. The sense of deferring the cadential arrival can also be accomplished by cadential *expansion*, whereby the individual harmonies of the cadential progression are lengthened (in comparison to a relatively compact, normative version). These techniques of extension and expansion can be used together to create the formal loosening that is especially associated with certain thematic units of larger-scale forms, most prominently, the subordinate-theme area of a sonata-like exposition or recapitulation. Compared to the baroque period, the galant composers employ these procedures to a much greater extent, and thus they continue on a path that leads to the enormous cadential loosening exploited by composers of the high classical style.

### 7.3.1. Consecutive Cadences and Codettas

In a manner reminiscent of Corelli, Scarlatti sometimes directly repeats a cadential idea, perhaps down an octave, as seen in Example 7.52, from the end of the exposition. The question of just which of these two cadences is the "real" one continues to be somewhat unresolved, just as we discussed in connection with the similar situation in Corelli.[65] Though as a general rule, we would normally accord structural significance to the first PAC (m. 83), the wholesale *melodic descent*, from $A_5$ to $A_3$, drives the music to a decisive goal at the second PAC.[66] A similar case occurs at the end of Example 7.53 (mm. 28–32). Like the prior example, the downward octave shift encourages us to hear the second cadence as the true melodic goal; at the same time, the first PAC (m. 30) matches the way-station IAC of measure 24 by residing in the same register, and this cadential completion may well be taken, alternatively, as structurally definitive.

One other detail in this example is worthy of note. In the approach to the IAC at measure 24, Scarlatti accelerates the harmonies by evading a first progression at the beginning of measure 23 and immediately repeating the progression (one more time) in an even more compact manner. The same cadential situation occurs in measures 28–30 and is immediately repeated in measures 30–32, as previously discussed. Note that I speak here of evading the *progression*, not of an evaded cadence per se, because the pulling away from the dominant (on the third eighth-note beat of m. 23) is not associated with a moment in time that would seem to represent a point of formal arrival. Moreover, I do not identify a cadential abandonment, because nothing really goes wrong with the dominant; it simply is not allowed to make its expected resolution to tonic; instead, the evaded dominant suddenly "backs up" to another $I^6$ for a second try. In short, the cadential situation here is quite complex, even if Scarlatti makes it sound so natural and convincing.

---

65. See again, Chapter 6, sec. 6.1.5.1. The general topic of cadential repetition is also discussed in Chapter 2, sec. 2.8.5.

66. Cf. Ex. 6.35 by Corelli. In the Scarlatti example, one can even imagine a performer wanting to convey at m. 83 the effect of an evaded cadence, Scarlatti's favorite cadential deviation, by slightly breaking the rhythmic flow just before the downbeat of that bar.

EXAMPLE 7.53. Scarlatti, Keyboard Sonata in F, K. 525, mm. 16–32.

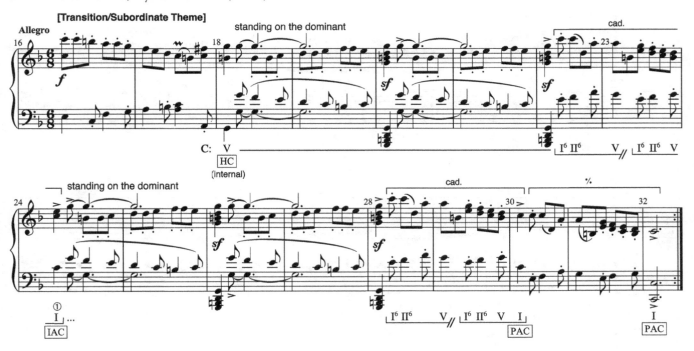

Formal extensions via repetition can also arise within a closing section whose codettas prominently feature repeated cadential gestures (Ex. 7.54). Here, an ongoing subordinate theme reaches closure on the downbeat of measure 13 by means of a deceptive-authentic combination. The latter part of the subordinate theme is then repeated, bringing the same cadence at measure 16. There follows a closing section consisting of codettas made up almost exclusively of cadential progressions. Looking first at the bass line of measures 16–17, we see the typical scale degrees of a deceptive cadential progression (③–④–⑤–⑥), repeated once. The actual harmonization, however, is not that of a DCP (cf., m. 12); rather, in measure 16, we first hear an initial tonic leading to a slightly expanded pre-dominant (II$^6_5$ $^4_3$). When the bass returns to ③, again supporting I$^6$, that ongoing cadential progression is abandoned. The subsequent progression then features a considerably more expanded II$^6_5$, still supported by a DCP bass line as well as the onset (④) of the final PAC. In short, the two iterations of the DCP bass line only engage stages 1 and 2 of the progression, a considerably more enriched cadential expression than that found closing the subordinate theme back at measures 12–13 (and repeated in mm. 16–15).

Although we can say that the cadence at measure 13 technically represents the formal close of the subordinate theme, such that everything that follows is in some sense postcadential, the relentless repetitions of cadential content suggest that a different aesthetic is at play, namely, a continual striving to rearticulate the attainment of thematic closure, which finds its final utterance only at the very end of the exposition. Such an aesthetic is not common in the classical era, where the final goal of a theme is typically followed by postcadential material that differs significantly from

the structural cadence.[67] Of course what Scarlatti writes here also reminds us of his using ever shorter evaded cadences toward the final goal of an exposition or recapitulation, either with a closing section (Ex. 7.40 and 7.46a) or without (Ex. 7.39 and 7.41).

### 7.3.2. Expanded Cadential Progression

I discussed in the previous chapter that expanded cadential progressions are fairly limited in the baroque repertory. The reasons for this restricted usage are grounded in a variety of compositional features typical of that style, such as a uniform and relatively rapid rate of harmonic rhythm and the retention of the "cadence formula." In the galant era, the trend toward simpler homophonic textures and a less active bass line, one that supports a slower change of harmonies, offers more opportunities for expanding the cadential progression. Example 7.55 is a clear-cut case, one that strongly resembles classical practice. Following an ongoing continuation ending with a model and its sequence, a new phrase (mm. 41–44), with its own motivic and textural profile, is supported by a single cadential progression, each harmony of which lasts a full bar. Example 7.56 by Scarlatti is similarly straightforward, though ECPs are not commonly found in his works.

Though most ECPs lead to a PAC, the technique is sometimes associated with a half cadential articulation (Ex. 7.57). Within a

---

67. Something similar to what we see here with Scarlatti happens now and then in the classical scherzo genre, whereby a series of repeated cadences can obscure just which moment is best taken as closing; see the discussion in Chapter 2, sec. 2.8.5, and Ex. 2.24.

EXAMPLE 7.54. Scarlatti, Keyboard Sonata in G Minor, K. 450, mm. 12–21.

EXAMPLE 7.55. C. P. E. Bach, Keyboard Sonata in E, Wq. 62, no. 5, iii, mm. 37–45.

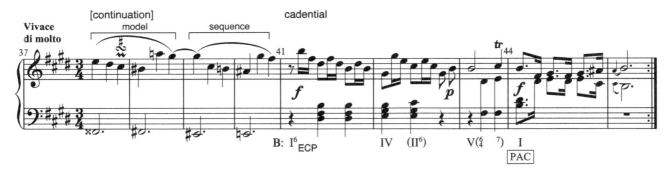

transition/subordinate-theme fusion, measure 15 begins a cadential progression that is quickly abandoned when IV moves to V$^4_2$. A second progression starts up with the I$^6$ of measure 16. This one is rendered deceptive when the bass at measure 18 moves from ⑤ to ⑥, supporting a replacement VII$^6$/V. Since beat 2 of measure 18 does not seem like a cadential goal, I analyze here a deceptive resolution, not a deceptive cadence proper. Finally, a half cadential ECP passes over stage 1 (having sounded already twice before) and expands the pre-dominant harmony for three bars, leading to an internal HC at measure 22. Though the three progressions represent different cadential situations—abandoned, deceptive, and half cadential—they are woven together as a more coherent whole by virtue of the bass melody, which traces a stepwise curve from ③ up to ⑥ and a return back to #④ before achieving the final ⑤ of the HC.

In the classical style, ECPs are typically used as the final technique for loosening a thematic unit (most often a subordinate theme), with various other deviations (deceptive, evaded, abandoned) preceding the cadential expansion, whose final dominant often marks the high point of rhythmic energy. In the galant style,

EXAMPLE 7.56. Scarlatti, Keyboard Sonata in E Minor, K. 402, mm. 32–37.

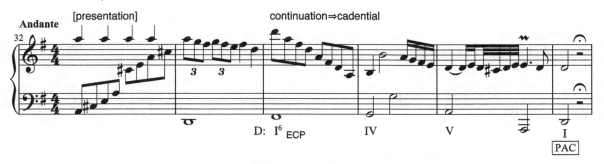

EXAMPLE 7.57. C. P. E. Bach, Keyboard Sonata in C, Wq. 62, no. 7, iii, mm. 15–22.

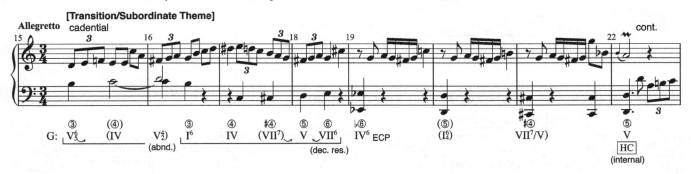

EXAMPLE 7.58. C. P. E. Bach, Keyboard Sonata in E, Wq. 62, no. 5, ii, mm. 14–22.

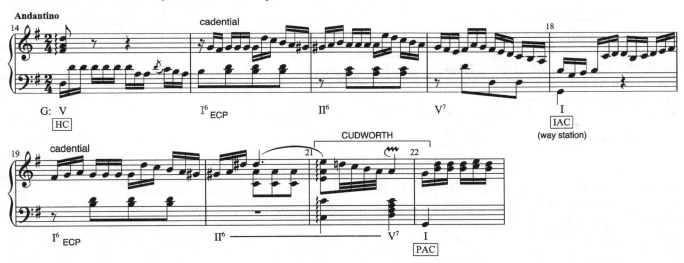

we frequently encounter situations where an ECP gets underway, but fails, for a variety of reasons, to achieve the final PAC.[68] In some cases, the expanded progression yields a way-station IAC, as seen at measure 18 of Example 7.58. At that point, the music continues on and the ECP begins to be repeated. But now we can observe an important aspect of style: in the repeated version, the pre-dominant is extended for an extra beat (downbeat of m. 21), with the dominant being equally shortened. As a result, the final cadential gesture in measures 21–22 has a more formulaic quality—a Cudworth variant—compared to the prior ECP. We thus see here a residual baroque tendency to retain the compact cadence. Something along these lines occurs in the earlier discussed Example 7.28. There, the ECP beginning in measure 46 never even achieves partial closure, but rather is abandoned by the inversion of the dominant at measure 50, after which a compact cadential idea closes the theme. An even more elaborate case arises in Example 7.59. Following a long standing on

---

68. To be sure, many ECPs in the classical style initially are unsuccessful in producing the anticipated PAC for a variety of reasons. Unlike what happens in the galant examples to be discussed presently, however, the initial (but failed) ECP is normally repeated using the same, or minimally varied, material content.

EXAMPLE 7.59. C. P. E. Bach, Keyboard Sonata in C, Wq. 48, no. 5, ii, mm. 29–46.

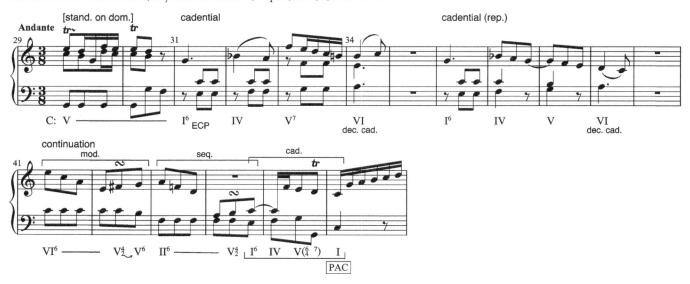

EXAMPLE 7.60. Nardini, Violin Sonata in D, Op. 5, no. 4, iii, mm. 32–47 (G11.28).

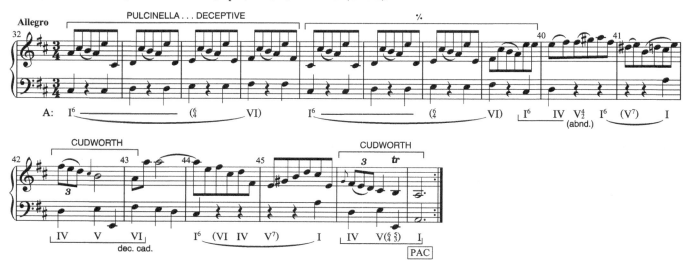

the dominant, an ECP starting in measure 31 leads to a deceptive cadence at measure 34. There ensues a general pause (a quirk of Bach's style that may well have influenced Haydn's mid-phrase caesuras), after which the deceptive cadence, along with the pause, is repeated. When the music gets going again, it now brings a model-sequence technique that projects continuational characteristics, as if the music were backing up to some earlier moment in the form. Finally, the theme is closed off by a compact PAC.

### 7.3.3. Pulcinella

As discussed in the previous chapter, one cadence-like schema, identified as the *Pulcinella* by Gjerdingen, is related to the deceptive cadential progression, though it actually features a tonic prolongation built over bass notes from the cadential stream (③–④–⑤–⑥).[69]

---
69. See Chapter 6, sec. 6.1.5.4.

Gjerdingen's first example of the schema (Ex. 7.6, above; the harmonic analysis is mine) shows a typical usage, whereby the progression leads initially to VI at measure 66 and is then repeated to yield a PAC on I. Note that Gjerdingen identifies a Deceptive schema in measures 65–66, yet a genuine deceptive cadence is not actually forthcoming, since the harmony of measure 65 is better understood as a *tonic* six-four, not a dominant. That situation is rectified when the progression is repeated, and measure 69 sees the six-four resolving to five-three to create a real PAC.

In Gjerdingen's second illustration of the schema (Ex. 7.60; my harmonic analysis), neither of the two Pulcinellas creates a cadence, despite his indicating the Deceptive schema. When the music continues with $I^6$ at the upbeat to measure 40, and a third progression seems to be in the making, its potential for cadence is quickly abandoned by $V^4_2$. After arriving on a root-position tonic at the end of measure 41, a compact Cudworth cadence promises closure in measure 43. A deceptive cadence appears instead, and a varied repeat brings the expected PAC, again as a Cudworth.[70] The seeming "cadential" expansion effected by the Pulcinella actually is actually prolongational, despite utilizing the cadential bass stream. And true to galant fashion, the final cadence is a compact formula.

### 7.3.4. Dominant Expansions—Penultimate, Ultimate, Precadential

In the previous chapter, I discussed three techniques that baroque composers employ to expand dominant harmony preceding a compact PAC. One technique sees an expansion of the penultimate dominant of an ECP; however, the progression fails to be fully realized due to a cadential deception, evasion, or abandonment (see Ex. 6.12, mm. 50–52, and Ex. 6.30, mm. 81–82). A second technique involves the ultimate dominant of an HC, followed by a standing on the dominant, which proves to be "internal" to the formal processes of the thematic unit when the music eventually reaches PAC closure (Ex. 6.63–6.65). A third technique features the expansion of a noncadential dominant that is positioned shortly before the final cadence of the theme; I speak in this case of a precadential dominant expansion (see Ex. 6.20, 6.69, and 6.70). I also discussed how ambiguous cases can arise in which it is not entirely clear which of these techniques is being employed (see Ex. 6.71–6.73). These three means of expanding dominant harmony continue to be used in the galant style, although some additional complications may sometimes ensue.

#### 7.3.4.1. Expanded Penultimate Dominant

The works investigated for this chapter did not yield many expanded penultimate dominants in which the failure to bring PAC closure (due to a deviation of some kind) is rectified instead by a subsequent compact cadence. Two examples, though, illustrate the general idea, though to be sure, the dominant itself is not markedly expanded within the ECP.[71] In a subordinate theme by Bach (see ahead Ex. 7.74), an ECP beginning with VII$^7$/V at measure 43, and followed by an equally expanded dominant in measures 45–46, is evaded on the downbeat of measure 47, as signaled by the abrupt change in dynamics (to *forte*) and rhythm (to dotted eighths). (Later, in sec. 7.4.3, I will consider the possibility of seeing this ECP close with an IAC.) What then takes place is a compact deceptive cadence, which presumably functions as a way station. After a new continuation (mm. 49–52) and a brief precadential dominant expansion (upbeat to m. 53), the same deceptive cadence appears again, with its way-station function finally confirmed by the compact PAC that follows immediately.

A second example of an ECP giving way to a compact cadence can be seen in a subordinate theme by Scarlatti (see ahead Ex. 7.77b). At measure 117, an ECP (with a mildly expanded V) concludes directly with a deceptive cadence, after which a compact cadence brings full closure to the theme. What happens here occurs infrequently in the classical style; instead, such a deceptive ECP would more likely be followed by an equally expansive cadential progression (or even more so), not by a compact PAC.[72]

#### 7.3.4.2. Internal HC (or Dominant Arrival)

An internal HC, with its standing on the dominant, is regularly encountered in the galant repertory.[73] Two options typically follow the elongated dominant: (1) a *new* continuation (i.e., one not using previous material); or (2) a cadential unit, often relatively compact. A case of the first option is seen earlier in Example 7.38b, where an internal HC at measure 51 is followed by a standing on the dominant. The harmony sounds longer than what appears on the score due to the sudden change of tempo in measure 52. The following bar brings a new continuation made up of a one-measure model for extensive sequential repetition.[74] (The subsequent dominant expansion in mm. 57–64 will be dealt with shortly.)

At times, a continuation is bypassed and the standing on the dominant leads directly to a cadential idea, as seen in Example 7.53. In the course of a transition/subordinate-theme fusion, an internal HC arrives at measure 18; the subsequent standing on the dominant expands that harmony, which is followed by a way-station IAC on the downbeat of measure 24. The lack of full closure thus motivates a return to the standing on the dominant after which a PAC appears at measure 30, which, as discussed earlier, is immediately repeated an octave lower. An interesting detail of style can be observed in this example, since later classical composers do not, as far as I am aware, back up the music to repeat a standing on the dominant. But for Scarlatti, at least, this repetition is a possible option.

---

70. The harmonic content of mm. 40–41 and mm. 44–45 is somewhat problematic given the single voice texture. To my ears, both passages feature a prolongation from I$^6$ to I; more specifically, the melody of m. 40 suggests an abandonment of the cadential progression, while m. 41 brings a passing dominant, like the clearer expression of that harmony in the matching m. 45.

71. I am asking the reader to look ahead to the following two examples because they are better positioned later in the chapter, where each will be discussed more fully.

72. For a classical abandoned ECP that is immediately followed by a compact cadence, see Ex. 5.61, mm. 49–57; for a comparable case employing a deceptive ECP, see Ex. 4.26.

73. On the internal HC, see in Chapter 3, sec. 3.3.4.2, "Subordinate Theme."

74. The nonconventional form of this movement most resembles a baroque binary. At this point, the music is clearly in the second part of the form. (Unusually, a presumed repeat of the first part, beginning at m. 21 [not shown], ends up *fusing* with the second part.) The HC at m. 51 could be seen to mark the end of a retransition back to the home key, but its status as "internal" can nonetheless be sustained, seeing as what follows does not represent a re-initiation of any kind, but rather a continuation of the ongoing part 2.

EXAMPLE 7.61. C. P. E. Bach, Keyboard Sonata in B-flat, Wq. 62, no. 1, iii, mm. 24–40.

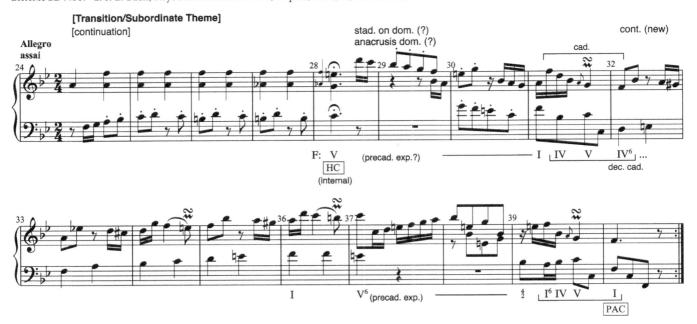

### 7.3.4.3. Precadential Dominant Expansion

A third technique of expanding dominant harmony in connection with cadential closure involves a noncadential dominant appearing immediately prior, or in close proximity, to a compact cadential idea. I introduced this form of harmonic expansion in the previous chapter (sec. 6.2.3) since the technique is particularly associated with the baroque. Some interesting examples can also be found in the galant style, whereas the procedure largely vanishes in the classical period.[75] A clear-cut galant case can be seen in Example 7.61, measures 37–39. Following a deceptive cadence at measure 32, a continuation phrase with rapidly changing harmonies eventually settles on a dominant in first inversion (m. 37), which is sustained until the downbeat of measure 39, where a compact PAC closes the theme. What then is the function of the expanded dominant? Evidently, it cannot be seen as anything cadential due to its inversion, and its formal position accords it a precadential status. Because the harmony is relatively expanded, it thus participates in a set of loosening devices, including the prior deceptive cadence and the extended continuation, all of which defer cadential arrival. We can also add into the mix the internal HC of measure 28, which seems at first glance to be followed by a standing on the dominant in measures 29–30. Something is peculiar about this elongated dominant, however, for it occurs *after* the fermata associated with the internal HC. As a rule, such a fermata occurs either at the very end of a standing on the dominant or is directly associated with the HC proper, as here at measure 28. So the idea of this expanded dominant as postcadential is brought into question. In fact, the harmony seems to be functioning as an *anacrusis dominant* (a before-the-beginning function) to the compact deceptive cadence into which that dominant leads.[76] And since this harmony appears immediately before the cadential idea, including it within the general category of precadential dominant expansion is worth considering.

Something similar arises in a sonata by Scarlatti (see again Ex. 7.45). At the start of this excerpt, an internal premature dominant arrival at measure 55 brings a standing on the dominant, whose final articulation is marked by a caesura with fermata. Normally what follows would be seen as the beginning of a new formal process (though still within the scope of the subordinate theme). Like what we saw in Example 7.61, the continuance of dominant supporting new material in Example 7.45, measures 59–61, no longer seems postcadential. Instead, we can speak of a precadential dominant expansion leading to the deceptive cadence in measure 64. Scarlatti then backs the music up to this dominant expansion (though this time compressing it by one bar).

Another, somewhat more complicated precadential dominant expansion can be seen toward the end of Example 7.62. A continuation phrase (late in the subordinate theme group) begins at measure 26 and eventually drives toward the dominant at measure 29 with an ever-accelerating harmonic rhythm. Once the dominant is reached, it is sustained for two beats, which, following a passage of rapid harmonic change, presents a distinct sense of expansion. Immediately thereafter, a compact Cudworth ends the subordinate theme (and the exposition). Note that the harmonic progression leading to V at measure 29 is half cadential, but the sense of a genuine HC at this late stage seems unlikely. The continued rhythmic drive through this moment and the upward thrusting melody also counters a sense of closure. As a result, this lightly elongated dominant seems not to be part of the theme's

---

75. For two such examples, see in Chapter 6, note 88.

76. I thank James Hepokoski for suggesting this term to me.

EXAMPLE 7.62. C. P. E. Bach, Keyboard Sonata in C Minor, Wq. 48, no. 4, i, mm. 11–30 (R = ½N).

cadential process, thus allowing us to speak of a precadential expansion of the harmony.

If we were inclined, however, to recognize an HC at measure 29, then this would be the *fourth* such cadence within the theme, the three others occurring in measures 17, 19, and 25. All of these more obvious cases function as internal HCs; indeed, this threefold use exploits the technique more extensively than what we normally find in either the galant or classical styles. (I am unaware of any classical work that brings more than a single internal HC within a subordinate theme.) Thus when confronting the possibility of yet another HC at measure 29, we are likely to dismiss the idea, preferring instead to hear a precadential dominant emphasis.

As just discussed in this example, a degree of ambiguity can arise as to whether a given dominant expansion is associated with an HC or whether it is genuinely precadential.

A similar uncertainty can surround a dominant arrival versus a precadential dominant expansion. Returning to Example 7.38b, we can recall identifying an internal HC and standing on the dominant in measures 51–52. We also observed that what follows is a new continuation, one that in this case features a modal shift and a descending-thirds sequence. The final link in the sequential chain sees $V^7/V$ (a chromatic alteration of II) moving to the dominant at measure 57. We could potentially recognize another internal HC, but in the sequential context here, the idea of a *terminal* dominant arrival perhaps makes more sense (as annotated in option 1 of the harmonic analysis below the score). If so, then the passage that follows would be a standing on the dominant (option 1 above the score). But seeing as this highly expanded dominant leads directly into two compact cadential progressions (whose own ambiguities were discussed earlier in sec. 7.1.4), an alternative interpretation would recognize a precadential dominant expansion in measures 57–64. Morphologically, a terminal dominant arrival (with standing on the dominant) and a precadential expansion can be indistinguishable: in both cases, the dominant arises in a noncadential manner. But the formal context can sometimes sway us toward one interpretation over the other. Here, at such a late moment in the form, we hardly expect a dominant arrival, especially having just heard an HC just prior to the new continuation (mm. 51–52). So when we find the dominant prolongation in measures 57–64 leading directly to the final cadences of the movement, the idea of a precadential expansion, as a means of further extending the ongoing continuation, is a reasonable analysis (option 2).

We see from the examples discussed in this section that all three techniques of dominant expansion can be used in connection with a loosely organized thematic region (typically a subordinate theme, or some analogous structure). In both the baroque and galant styles, the principle of "retaining the cadential formula" means that most often these techniques immediately precede a relatively compact cadence. By the time of the high classical style, the commitment to such a formulaic cadence is relinquished, especially in connection with subordinate-theme closure, and the use of a precadential dominant emphasis effectively disappears. The techniques of penultimate dominant expansion (within an authentic ECP) and the standing on the dominant (following an internal HC) still continue to be important sources of formal loosening in that later style.

## 7.4. Galant Cadence in Relation to Formal Functions

Though the formal types regularly employed by the classical composers find incipient expression as early as the high baroque, these forms, along with their constituent formal functions, emerge with a fair degree of clarity in the galant style. This period sees the rise of the sonata, rondo, and concerto forms that continue to be employed throughout all later tonal styles. And the roles that cadence plays in articulating formal functionality in the mid-eighteenth century are often quite similar to those found later. Nonetheless, some aspects of cadential usage are especially characteristic of the galant, as I describe in this final part of this chapter.

### 7.4.1. Main Theme

Classical main themes are normally structured as units of eight or sixteen measures. The simple sentence, period, and hybrid types, along with the compound period and sentence, the small ternary, and small binary make up a large majority of main themes in this repertory. In the earlier galant period, such themes are less often so conventional in organization. In particular, they frequently last four or six bars, and their constituent formal functions may not project the organization typical of a sentence, period, or hybrid. Indeed, it is not surprising that Koch's theory of phrase structure, which is largely modeled on galant compositional practice, sees the four-measure unit as the "basic phrase" (allowing, of course, for various extensions and expansions). He does not define as a standard case any of the eight-measure theme types more characteristic of the classical style.[77]

As regards cadential usage, classical main themes almost always close in the home key with a cadence of some kind, most often a PAC, occasionally an HC (especially for minor-mode works), and rarely, an IAC.[78] In the galant, all three cadential options are available, but the IAC is especially typical, often with an overhang that brings the melody from $\hat{3}$ down to $\hat{1}$. (The potential ambiguity of this usage has already been discussed in sec. 7.1.4.) Unlike in the classical style, we find many cases of galant main themes ending with no cadence whatsoever, concluding instead in a manner I have termed *prolongational closure*.

To begin, let us consider the main theme shown in Example 7.63. Here, the theme concludes after six bars, in that what follows initiates the transition with its characteristic tonicization of VI as a means of modulating to the subordinate key. The main theme begins with a two-measure basic idea, whose melody in the second bar, $\hat{4}$–$\hat{3}$, already projects the kind of melodic close that is associated with an IAC. There follows a contrasting idea that promises to realize this cadence type, with the melodic descent $\hat{5}$–$\hat{4}$ proposing $\hat{3}$ for the cadence. And indeed, this melodic resolution does occur, except that the bass line is somewhat delayed, such that we could hear dominant harmony syncopated across the bar line. Moreover, the bass in measure 4 is identical

---

[77]. Koch never quite describes all of the elements of the sentence form; the closest he gets are some cases of his "compound phrase"; see *Introductory Essay on Composition*, 57, Ex. 187 and 188. Later in his treatise (172), he eventually delineates the period theme type (without giving it any special nomenclature), but sees the form associated with rondo themes only. Many of his examples feature some of the hybrid types, but he does not identify them as such.

[78]. Main themes ending without any cadential closure are rare in the classical style; see Chapter 3, sec. 3.1.3.2, and Ex. 3.65.

EXAMPLE 7.63. C. P. E. Bach, Keyboard Sonata in F, Wq. 48, no. 1, i, mm. 1–9.

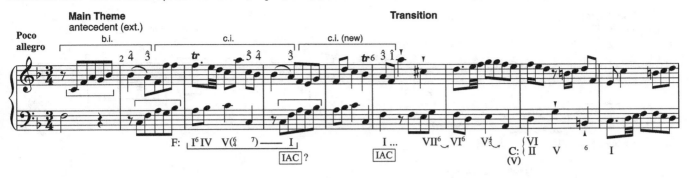

EXAMPLE 7.64. C. P. E. Bach, Keyboard Sonata in F, Wq. 48, no. 1, iii, mm. 1–8.

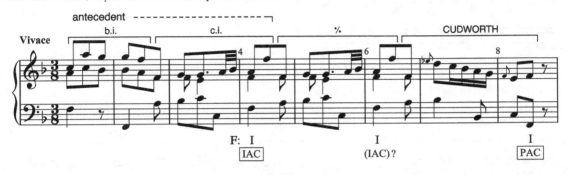

to that of measure 2 (which itself is an imitation of the opening melody of the basic idea), so an IAC is definitely blurred. Finally, a somewhat different contrasting idea brings an unequivocal IAC on the downbeat of measure 6 (with an overhang leap to $\hat{1}$). The nonconventional set of idea functions (b.i. + c.i. + new c.i.), which suggests that a four-measure antecedent phrase has been extended by an additional two bars, along with the emphasis on IAC content and function, typifies the galant nature of this theme, one that is markedly different in structure from that ordinarily found in the classical style.

The main theme from the third movement of this same sonata (Ex. 7.64) seems on the surface to resemble a classical theme, with its eight-measure length and its concluding PAC. But the internal organization is quite different: following an opening basic idea, a contrasting idea leads to an IAC, closing what we might take to be an antecedent phrase.[79] But rather than being followed by a subsequent consequent (for a period) or a continuation (for a hybrid), the contrasting idea is literally repeated, bringing again its IAC, only then to yield to a Cudworth-like idea that effects the more decisive PAC (a fine case of an "abrupt" cadence of the type identified by Greenberg).[80] The structure is entirely nonconventional and filled with cadential content. Like other cases of consecutive cadences discussed in this study, the question is raised as to which one is truly functional; the first two, or at least the second, might also be seen to have a limited scope. Indeed, such ambiguity of cadential content and function is characteristic of galant main themes.

The high degree of cadential material found in the previous two examples can be witnessed again in Example 7.65. Here, the opening four-measure phrase is supported by an ECP that ends melodically on $\hat{1}$, thus suggesting a PAC.[81] There follows a varied repeat of the cadential idea, thus again projecting a PAC.[82] At this point, the bass drops out and the melodic ideas seem to form a series of one-measure codettas concluding on the downbeat of measure 8. The left hand alone then returns as a lead-in to the beginning of the transition at measure 10. The theme, as projected by the melodic line alone, thus seems to fill a standard eight-measure length, but the internal organization is nonconventional and replete with cadential content.

As opposed to the main themes just examined, we regularly encounter galant themes that conclude with no cadence (Ex. 7.66). All of the harmonic progressions throughout the eight-measure extent of this theme are prolongational. Even if the closing melodic line is suggestive of an IAC, a genuine

---

79. Note that the melodic overhang leaps upward, a possibility also described by Koch, thus creating a melodic "reopening" that interferes with the sense of closure projected by the cadence (*Introductory Essay on Composition*, 25, Ex. 73 and 74).

80. See above, sec. 7.1.3.

81. It is not obvious that the opening is cadential from the start, since the first two stages of the presumed ECP are both in root-position. But if we consider the cadential harmonies to include only V and I, then it is not clear what to consider the opening progression from I to II—a sequence? a prolongation? This second option raises the possibility of hearing the entire phrase as tonic prolongational, though this view is belied by the clear cadential melody, employing the basic alto stream.

82. Here, stage 2 now occurs more conventionally over ④.

EXAMPLE 7.65. C. P. E. Bach, Keyboard Sonata in C, Wq. 48, no. 5, iii, mm. 1–12.

EXAMPLE 7.66. C. P. E. Bach, Keyboard Sonata in B-flat, Wq. 62, no. 1, iii, mm. 1–10.

EXAMPLE 7.67. C. P. E. Bach, Keyboard Sonata in C, Wq. 62, no. 7, iii, mm. 1–6.

cadence does not emerge (though the weak metrical placement of the closure in measure 8 is reminiscent of Greenberg's abrupt cadence).[83] The closing idea of Example 7.67 also hints at an IAC, but closer examination reveals that the final dominant initially appears inverted, thus canceling out a real cadence and prompting us to recognize prolongational closure for this six-measure theme.

Sometimes a theme will end noncadentially, yet still project a semblance of cadential content prior to the actual end. Example 7.68 opens with an antecedent phrase ending with an IAC in measure 4. The contrasting idea is then repeated to bring another IAC. The theme continues in measure 6 with fragmentation supported by a firm root-position tonic. The shift in measure 7 to $I^6$ followed by $II^6$ proposes another cadence, but the progression is abandoned and the closing harmonies of the theme end up being tonic prolongational ($V^6_5$–I). Though a cadential progression fails to materialize, the melody of the final idea projects a conventional tenor stream ($\hat{8}/\hat{6}/\hat{5}$–$\hat{4}/\hat{3}$), one that implies IAC closure. We see that even if the theme abounds in cadential expression, it ultimately closes prolongationally, thus upsetting the standard syntax of form and harmony in a manner that is utterly nonclassical.

---

83. Note that in a reversal of classical norms the most unstable harmonies of the theme ($V^4_2$–$I^6$) appear at its beginning.

EXAMPLE 7.68. C. P. E. Bach, Keyboard Sonata in C, Wq. 48, no. 5, i, mm. 1–8.

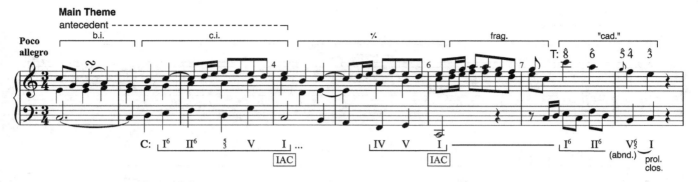

The difference between the kinds of galant main themes just discussed and the more conventional theme types of the classical style is especially highlighted in a later revision that W. F. Bach makes to his Sonata in F, discussed earlier in Example 7.31. As Greenberg shows, the original version (system a), written ca. 1735–40, was later revised a couple of decades later (system b).[84] In so doing, Bach discards the earlier abrupt PAC of measure 6: "By the 1760s it was falling out of fashion, which is probably why Friedemann replaced it with a more familiar half cadence in the revised version." In addition, Bach alters the overall structure of the theme: "The original opening consisted of an imitative six-measure statement, yet in the revised version, he adds the equivalent of two measures of 'continuing function.' As a result, the rather quirky original is transformed into a typical exemplar of a Classical sentence." The two versions thus well encapsulate important differences between galant and classical phrase structure.

## 7.4.2. Transition; Fusion Processes

The galant period sees the emergence and widespread use of a distinct transition. This formal function either remains in the home key or modulates to a new, subordinate key, closing in either case with an HC or dominant arrival.[85] At times, both a nonmodulating transition and a modulating one can occur successively, thus creating an overall two-part transition. The closing HC is often dramatized by a standing on the dominant and an eventual caesura effect (Hepokoski and Darcy's "medial caesura") prior to the onset of the subordinate theme.[86] The history of how transition function arises out of baroque practice (where it is encountered infrequently) is a significant topic worthy of its own study.[87]

### 7.4.2.1. Fusion of Main Theme and Transition

In the classical style, the three principal expositional functions of main theme, transition, and subordinate theme normally occupy their own unique grouping units as demarcated by cadences appropriate to their function. In the galant, however, the boundaries of these functions are often obscured in ways that create form-functional *fusion*, a process that merges two (or even three) successive functions into a single thematic unit. One such fusion combines the main theme of the exposition with the transition, a technique rarely occurring in the classical style.[88] In these cases, the main theme lacks cadential closure (or sometimes any sense of closure whatsoever), and the transition bypasses a formal beginning. Frequently, main-theme function is expressed exclusively by an initiating unit (a presentation or compound basic idea), whereas the subsequent continuation seems more to belong to the transition, which ends with an HC (and standing on the dominant). Example 7.69 illustrates this technique well. The one-measure opening basic idea (R = ½N), with its attention-grabbing flourishes, is repeated to make a presentation phrase. A one-measure extension of the flourishes leads to a new idea (m. 4) with accelerated harmonic and surface rhythms, supported by a continuous accompanimental pattern, a standard Alberti-bass variant, all regular features of a continuation phrase. In measure 6, VI$^6$ pivots to become II$^6$ of the subordinate key, and the passage ends with an HC on the downbeat of measure 9. This entire continuation phrase thus projects transition function, one that fuses with the main theme, which only consists of the initiating presentation.[89]

---

84. Greenberg, "Tinkering with Form," 210–11.

85. For a dominant arrival ending a transition, see Ex. 7.51.

86. Hepokoski and Darcy, *Sonata Theory*, chap. 3.

87. See Chapter 6, Ex. 6.55, mm. 10–12, for the end of a passage that suggests transition function.

88. In sonata forms of that period, main theme/transition fusion normally occurs in the recapitulation (see *CF*, 165, and *ACF*, 502–504), not in the exposition. One famous exception arises in the opening movement of Mozart's Piano Sonata in C, K. 545, as already shown in Chapter 3, Ex. 3.66.

89. An alternative interpretation, one that I find less convincing, could see mm. 1–3 as a kind of extended thematic introduction, with the main theme proper beginning at m. 4, a presentation whose continuation at m. 6 would still represent fusion with the transition function. Problematic in this interpretation is that the "basic idea" of the main theme would begin with the less stable V$^6_5$ and immediately bring a continuous accompaniment, the latter a standard feature of continuation (and indeed, transition) function.

EXAMPLE 7.69. Galuppi, Keyboard Sonata in E, I. 41, i, mm. 1–9 (R = ½N).

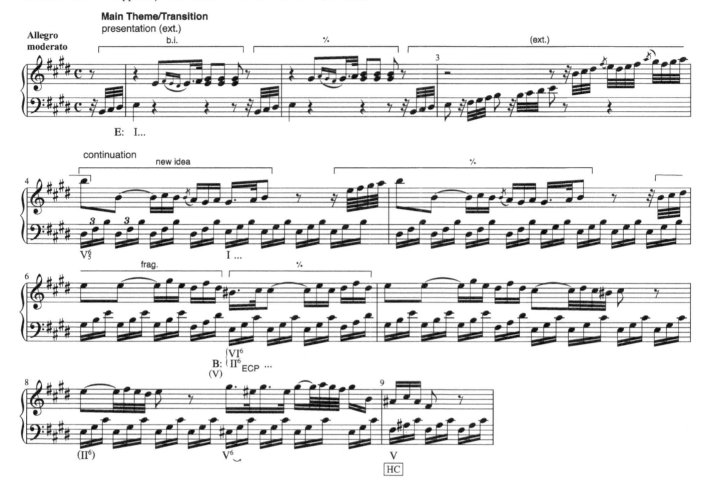

The opening of a toccata by J. C. Bach shows a main theme fusing with a non-modulating transition (Ex. 7.70). An opening presentation phrase in measures 1–2 (R = ½N) is followed by a continuation in which the bass descends chromatically down to ⑤, leading to a home-key HC at measure 8 and a subsequent standing on the dominant. We may not be certain at first that the continuation (mm. 3–5) necessarily belongs to the transition (as opposed to the main theme), but the standing on the dominant seems to suggest that function, in that main themes ending with an HC rarely feature such a postcadential passage. But our sense of a main theme/transition fusion becomes even more apparent when the next passage (m. 9) initiates the subordinate theme directly in the relative major.

An additional feature in the last two examples helps support the case for thematic fusion. Following the presentation phrase (the "main theme" component), the continuation does not immediately result in fragmentation. Instead, the grouping structure continues to project two-measure units (in real measures). As a result, the new material in these bars can represent a "basic idea" for the transition component, even if, from a more global perspective, we perceive this idea as continuational within a broader main theme/transition fusion.

### 7.4.2.2. Fusion of Transition and Subordinate Theme

The fusion of transition and subordinate-theme functions has engendered considerable theoretical debate in the context of the classical style, especially in connection with Hepokoski and Darcy's notion of "continuous exposition."[90] Such fusion, which is fairly infrequent in the classical style, occurs regularly in the galant. In such cases, two techniques of fusion typically apply: (1) an HC and standing on the dominant that at first marks the end of the transition is retrospectively reinterpreted as an internal HC of a subordinate theme; (2) the transition lacks any cadential close and attaches itself directly to the subordinate theme, which itself is missing a functional beginning.[91]

The first technique is illustrated in Example 7.71. The transition begins at measure 13 in the home key and quickly modulates to the dominant region, confirming the subordinate key with an HC (m. 21) and standing on the dominant, which lasts through

---

90. Hepokoski and Darcy, *Sonata Theory*, chap. 4, and Hepokoski, "Sonata Theory, Secondary Themes."

91. Caplin and Martin, "'Continuous Exposition,'" 11, fig. 1, final two categories.

EXAMPLE 7.70. J. C. Bach, Toccata in B-flat Minor, mm. 1–9 (R = ½N).

measure 26.[92] The next passage introduces a one-measure model that is twice sequenced down a third, concluding with the dominant of measure 30. The I⁶ in the following bar introduces an ECP that achieves PAC closure at measure 34 to fully confirm the subordinate key. The material from measure 27ff. clearly expresses subordinate-theme function, but inasmuch as it immediately brings continuation and cadential units, the theme expresses no formal initiation. Instead, we have the impression that the HC (along with its standing on the dominant) first functions as the end of the transition, but is then retrospectively reinterpreted as an internal HC, followed, as is conventionally the case, by new continuation and cadential functions. The HC of measure 21 thus does double duty in this transition/subordinate-theme fusion.[93]

---

92. We might wonder whether an HC in the new key already arises on the downbeat of m. 16. The melodic line in that bar, however, seems rather to have as its goal a $\hat{4}$–$\hat{3}$ configuration, supported by I of the new key. This moment, itself, might be understood as an IAC, but what then follows is a half cadential ECP, leading to the HC at m. 21. The ECP of mm. 17–21 thus seems to match that of mm. 14–16. This redundancy of cadential expansion, along with the confusion of cadence in m. 16, may be grounds for recognizing a degree of compositional weakness in this passage.

93. See also Ex. 7.53 for an instance of this technique in a sonata by Scarlatti.

A second way of fusing a transition and subordinate theme arises when the former lacks cadential closure (an HC or dominant arrival), and the latter dispenses with any sense of beginning (e.g., a basic idea supported by tonic of the new key). Example 7.72 illustrates this technique. Following a main theme, which itself eschews a cadence in favor of prolongational closure (mm. 7–8), the transition begins with an ascending arpeggiation at measure 9. The music then quickly modulates to the dominant region in the next bar and heads toward an IAC at measure 12, thus signaling that the music is already expressing subordinate-theme function. The middle of this same bar initiates another cadential progression, which might be seen to effect a PAC on the downbeat of measure 14. The lack of a bass note and the obvious return to another cadential progression, analogous to that of measure 12, suggests, however, that the cadence at measure 14 is better seen as evaded with a one-more-time technique. This second progression itself is abandoned as the bass marches up from ③ to ⑧, leading then to a mid-phrase fermata in measure 17, which brings the music to an unusual halt. The resumption of rhythmic activity in the following bar promises a PAC at measure 20, but the cadence is now obviously evaded, and a second one-more-time repetition finally achieves the PAC. From early in this thematic unit, one that begins in the home key but then quickly moves to the subordinate key, we recognize that all of the cadential play involves

EXAMPLE 7.71. Rutini, Keyboard Sonata in F, Op. 8, no. 1, i, mm. 13–34.

techniques associated with authentic cadential closure, which, in principle, clarifies that this music is expressing subordinate-theme function. At the same time, there is neither an obvious ending of the transition nor an opening of the subordinate theme, and so we can confidently speak of a fusion of the two functions into a single thematic unit.

In some highly compressed expositions, we occasionally find that all three thematic functions—main theme, transition, and subordinate theme—are fused into one unit. Example 7.73, from an oft-played sonata by Scarlatti, illustrates well this technique, one that clearly derives from earlier baroque practice, where these functions are often only incipiently expressed. The main theme begins in C major with a two-measure basic idea, whose repetition produces a presentation phrase. A continuation (mm. 5–8)

features parallel thirds with one-measure fragments, which together regroup into a two-measure unit, one that itself undergoes a varied repetition in measures 7–8. A second, related, continuation (mm. 9–12) immediately modulates to the subordinate key of G major.[94] A quick IAC at measure 14 then brings a degree of closure to the ongoing formal process. What follows is yet

---

94. The complicated relation of these two continuations is as follows: the original one (mm. 5–8) is a two-voiced construct in descending parallel thirds between the soprano and alto; a sustained G lies above these voices as a kind of extra soprano. The repeated version (mm. 9–12) sees a third voice, a bass, added to the parallel descent, with the very top voice sustaining a high D. To make this second continuation, the alto voice remains the same: C descending to G; the soprano of the first continuation, E to B, is shifted to the bass of the second continuation. The

EXAMPLE 7.72. C. P. E. Bach, Keyboard Sonata in E, Wq. 48, no. 3, iii, mm. 7–23.

another, and new, continuation (mm. 14–18), effecting another IAC, which motivates a repetition in measures 18–21. This time, the cadence is evaded at measure 22, and two more evasions eventually result in PAC closure at measure 26, a typical procedure of Scarlatti that we have already examined (cf., Ex. 7.39–7.41).

Taking a synoptic view of the complete exposition, we see that main-theme function is expressed exclusively in measures 1–8, a sentence that has no concluding cadence. The second continuation, which modulates to the new key, is associated, at first, with transition function, which, as well, receives no cadential closure. Instead, the IAC at measure 14 already tells us that the preceding music is part and parcel of subordinate-theme function, which continues to be expressed through the IACs and evaded cadences that follow. The lack of closure for the main theme and transition, combined with the omission of any beginning for the subordinate theme, allows all three functions to fuse together into a single thematic unit—the exposition.

### 7.4.3. Subordinate Theme; Cadential Play

To the extent that a movement confirms a subordinate key with a PAC, it exhibits some degree of subordinate-theme function. Such tonal confirmation in the baroque era is rarely associated with a distinct subordinate theme, that is, one containing a full complement of initiating, medial, and concluding phrase functions. With the galant style, such a theme appears more regularly as the baroque binary form becomes expanded into sonata form. Such expansion came about as galant composers developed specific compositional techniques for loosening the phrase structure of thematic units associated with the confirmation of a subordinate key. Foremost were those techniques that facilitated the deferral of complete cadential closure, such as cadential deviations, extensions, and expansions, all of which help to postpone the arrival of a PAC, the required cadential type for full closure of subordinate-theme function. Though I have already discussed these deferral devices individually, it would be useful here to see how they can work together to create broad spans of cadential play.

Turning back to Example 7.62, whose precadential dominant emphasis just prior to the final cadence has already been examined, we find Bach employing many ways of delaying the final cadence of the subordinate theme, which begins at measure 12.[95] Following a four-measure initiating phrase, which in this notated compound meter (R = ½N) can be identified as a repeated presentation, a continuation leads to an "abrupt" internal HC in the middle of measure 17, followed by a caesura.[96] But rather than

---

soprano of the second continuation then picks up from the final G of the alto in the first continuation (see the line connecting these pitches) and descends from there. Although I am analyzing the first continuation still in the home key of C, it is possible, as proposed by Schmalfeldt, to hear this music already in G, namely as a modulating Prinner, a device frequently used in a transition to effect a move to a subordinate key ("Domenico Scarlatti, Escape Artist," 273, Ex. 6). Note, though, that Scarlatti uses an F♮ embellishment at m. 7, and then introduces F♯ only at m. 9, thus perhaps justifying our hearing the first continuation in the home key.

---

95. The transition ends noncadentially, with prolongational closure, V$^6_5$–I.

96. This rhythmic break would not be a "medial caesura" in Hepokoski and Darcy's sense, because the subordinate theme has already begun with a clear initiating function (mm. 12–15), and nothing that follows the caesura in m. 17 can be construed as an alternative beginning of the theme.

EXAMPLE 7.73. Scarlatti, Keyboard Sonata in C, K. 159, mm. 1–26.

bringing a new continuation, as is usual after this cadence, the music backs up to repeat the prior continuation, embellished this time by the sixteenth-note alternating voices. Such an allusion to the one-more-time technique might be found with a way-station IAC or deceptive cadence, but is quite rare for an internal HC. The second such cadence at measure 19, however, is indeed followed by a "new" continuation. This one leads first to a deceptive cadence at measure 21, also followed by a caesura. The continuation is then restated an octave lower and with a *piano* dynamic, arriving again at a deceptive cadence (middle of m. 23). This time, the music does not pause as it had in the three previous cadential articulations (the HCs of mm. 17 and 19 and the deceptive cadence of m. 21). Rather, it continues on with an ECP, one that most surprisingly concludes yet again with an internal HC and prominent caesura (m. 25). And for a third time, there follows the new continuation first heard at measure 20, but now more obviously referencing that bar with the same high register and *forte* dynamic. With measure 27, Bach finally begins to generate a degree of rhythmic drive with the shift to sixteenth-note triplets in the right-hand part, though the momentum thus generated is twice interrupted by quarter-note caesuras (at the end of m. 27 and the second beat of m. 28. The motion is recovered in the middle of the bar and continues all the way to the final compact PAC at measure 30, preceded, as we already have discussed, by the precadential dominant expansion in measure 29.

Though this example brings many of the maneuvers that classical composers draw on to defer cadential arrival, their use here is very different from later practice. Typically a classical subordinate theme contains at most a single internal HC, followed by a new continuation. The music then heads toward an authentic cadence through various way stations (IAC, deceptive, evaded) that thwart a definitive arrival, and the theme finally concludes with one or more ECPs. Bach, by contrast, brings two internal HCs in a row, only the second one being followed by a new continuation. He then moves on to two way-station deceptive cadences, the first of which brings back the same "new" continuation. Most unusually, this leads to a *third* internal HC, again succeeded by the new continuation, also for a third time.

EXAMPLE 7.74. C. P. E. Bach, Keyboard Sonata in B Minor, Wq. 65, no. 13, i, mm. 19–56.

The one case of genuine cadential expansion (mm. 24–25) occurs relatively late in the theme but leads, most unusually, to a half cadence, not an authentic one. Finally, another harmonic expansion (m. 29) arises toward the very end, but emerges as precadential, so that a highly compact Cudworth PAC is all that is left to conclude the theme.

Another excerpt by Bach (Ex. 7.74) shows some of the same tendencies. Following a transition that ends at measure 20 with an HC of the new key (D major), the subordinate theme begins by prolonging root-position tonic. A presentation in measures 21–25 (with m. 21 as a kind of extended anacrusis) yields to a continuation, as projected by fragmentation, while still maintaining the tonic prolongation. Indeed, the insistence on ① throughout measures 21–28 seems rather excessive, and so we are relieved when ⑦ of measure 29 moves to #① in the next bar to animate

the harmonies via a descending-fifths sequence, which eventually leads to an internal HC at measure 35. Following a brief standing on the dominant, a "new" continuation (mm. 39–42), with chromatically imitative ascending lines, moves on to a cadential unit in measures 43–46. As discussed earlier (sec. 7.3.4.1), we can hear an evasion of the ECP on the downbeat of measure 47, followed immediately by a compact, way-station deceptive cadence in the next bar. To be sure, it is possible to hear an IAC at measure 47. But what then are we to make of the subsequent deceptive cadential idea? What unit of form would that deviation be ending? Indeed, the resulting lack of formal clarity here perhaps tilts us toward our original interpretation of an evaded cadence at measure 47, such that a deceptive cadence alone is heard as providing a semblance of authentic cadential closure to the ongoing subordinate theme.

EXAMPLE 7.75. Scarlatti, Keyboard Sonata in C Minor, K. 115, mm. 21–33.

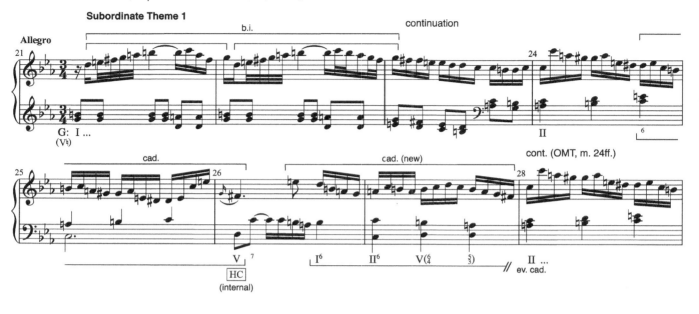

The deceptive cadence then leads to another "new" continuation, one that ends with a modest precadential dominant expansion (mm. 52–53). The dotted-rhythm passage returns and produces the same deceptive cadential gesture that we heard earlier at measure 47. Note that this time, however, the prolongational progression V$^6_5$–I in measures 53–54 does not raise the option of either an evaded cadence or an IAC, such as what confronted us at the analogous place in measures 46–47. Finally, the deceptive cadence at measure 55 motivates a highly compact authentic cadence to close the subordinate theme at measure 56.

In both of the preceding examples by Bach, there is a kind of bumbling quality to the succession of cadential devices, with no clear plan in the way they are ordered. Such eccentricities, of course, can be attributed to the composer's own personal style, but they do betray a sense that the galant era had not yet found the clarity of cadential loosening achieved later in the century. Coming closer to that aesthetic is Scarlatti, who, as we have seen in some of the earlier examples, finds ways of creating an inexorable drive to the final cadence.[97]

Whereas Scarlatti's use of cadential devices is often confined to the evaded cadence, some cases in his oeuvre include several different techniques (Ex. 7.75). The subordinate theme begins in G major with a two-measure basic idea (consisting of two one-measure motives). The following bars are continuational, with stepwise descending parallel thirds leading to II at measure 24. This harmony is then prolonged by a passing sonority on the way to a cadential pre-dominant II$^6$, which is sustained in the following bar before proceeding on to a dominant at measure 26. Inasmuch as the goal of the melodic line is F♯ on the downbeat of that bar, we can readily hear an internal HC, despite the dissonant seventh in the left-hand part (which, because it appears after the consonant dominant arrives, still permits us to speak of a legitimate HC). Bypassing a "new" continuation, Scarlatti then writes a compact cadential idea, which he evades at the downbeat of measure 28. A one-more-time repetition makes another run at the internal HC (m. 30), and this time the subsequent cadential idea realizes a PAC at measure 32.[98] Note that like the first

---

[97]. This characterization of galant cadential techniques vis-à-vis classical procedures is essentially descriptive and not meant pejoratively—galant music has its own aesthetic charms, as projected by its particular cadential practice.

[98]. In that the soprano voice does not literally sound the expected 1̂ on the downbeat of m. 32, we could possibly recognize another cadential evasion. But because what follows is so obviously a new thematic unit, it is probably better to hear a genuine cadence at this point and to understand that the implied soprano is omitted because of the new material that characterizes the right-hand part of the second subordinate theme. The resulting cadence can thus be seen as a "covered" PAC.

EXAMPLE 7.76. (a) C. P. E. Bach, Keyboard Sonata in F, Wq. 48, no. 1, i, mm. 53–57; (b) C. P. E. Bach, Keyboard Sonata in C, Wq. 62, no. 10, i, mm. 51–55.

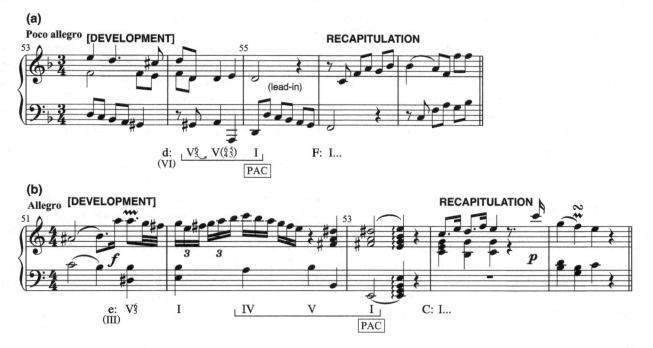

subordinate theme by Bach examined in this section (Ex. 7.62), Scarlatti employs more than one internal HC in his theme, a redundancy that later classical composers always avoid.

## 7.4.4. Development

Essential to the evolution of sonata form is the consolidation of a central section that stands between the opening exposition and the closing recapitulation. This *development* section, as it came to be termed, normally focuses its harmonic-tonal action on minor-mode regions of the home key: for a major-mode movement, these "development" regions (or keys, if they receive cadential confirmation) include VI, III, and II (in order of preference); for a minor-mode movement, they include minIV and minV. The melodic-motivic material of the development is usually based on ideas presented in the exposition, though some new material may be used on occasion. Phrase-structurally, development sections feature extensive use of model-sequence technique.[99]

Inasmuch as the development, in broad terms, functions as a kind of large-scale contrasting middle (in analogy to the B section of a small ternary), one of its central tasks is to prepare for the return in the home key of the main theme (or at least its opening basic idea) to signal the onset of the recapitulation. In the classical style, this return is most often marked by a prominent emphasis on the home-key dominant, as the most effective way to project an imminent return to tonic for the recapitulation's beginning. As such, the final phase of the development is normally closed by an HC (or dominant arrival) and standing on the dominant, which often includes motivic anticipations of the main theme's basic idea. In the galant period, many development sections end in this manner (though the standing on the dominant is often kept in check), so it is not necessary to illustrate this technique any further.

The influence of baroque tonal organization, however, with its emphasis on authentic cadential articulations of every key explored within a movement, can still be felt, especially in the works of C. P. E. Bach. As such, we frequently find the composer closing the development sections of major-mode movements with a decisive PAC in a development key, typically the submediant (Ex. 7.76a, m. 55) and, somewhat less often, on the mediant (Ex. 7.76b, m. 53). A short lead-in often keeps the rhythmic momentum alive through the boundary (Ex. 7.76a); however, a decisive caesura may also appear at the very end of the development (Ex. 7.76b).[100] Note that in these cases, the final harmony of the development is minor, while the opening harmony of the recapitulation is major. This modal change seems important, because in the case of minor-mode movements, galant developments most often end on the home-key dominant, a major triad. Ending the development with a PAC in one of the standard development keys

---

99. See *CF*, 139–41, and *ACF*, 420–23.

100. "Bach seems to have thought of the development as a section defined not by its emphasis on the dominant preparing the tonal return but by its formal closing cadence in a key that is closely or somewhat more distantly related to the tonic. For Bach, once the development section has reached that cadence, nothing further is usually required, and the recapitulation is free to begin" (Wayne C. Petty, "Koch, Schenker, and the Development Section of Sonata Forms by C. P. E. Bach," 152).

(minIV or minV) would not engender any modal change into the beginning of the recapitulation.[101]

One proto-sonata design, especially popular in the galant period, finds the development section moving imperceptibly into what is effectively the recapitulation of the subordinate-theme area from the exposition, thus bypassing a return of the main theme. This "binary sonata" form, as it is sometimes called,[102] will thus avoid a cadential articulation to mark the end of the development, since the return of the main theme is no longer necessary. Scarlatti's sonatas are largely written in this form, so we tend not to find in his music the kinds of cadential articulations just discussed in connection with Bach.

## 7.4.5. Recapitulation

In that the recapitulation is basically modeled on the exposition, this final section of a sonata (and its allied forms) often contains the same cadential plan of the earlier section (though all in the home key). In the classical style, two changes in cadential articulation may nevertheless occur: (1) the main theme may lose its final cadence, since home-key cadential confirmation will eventually be produced in the subordinate theme; and (2) the rhetorically strongest cadence of the exposition's subordinate theme (one usually associated with an ECP), will sometimes be rendered even stronger in the recapitulation, so that the final home-key confirmation can surpass that of the earlier subordinate key.[103] These cadential alterations may also occur in the galant repertory, and thus require no further discussion.

With Scarlatti, especially, the subordinate-theme group of the exposition so closely matches the recapitulation that it can be easy to overlook some particularly interesting changes that may arise in the latter section, especially as regards the *clarification* of cadential goals. We have already discussed one such case in connection with Example 7.46 (sec. 7.2.2). Two additional examples are sufficiently interesting to warrant a detailed examination.

Let us begin with the Sonata in A, K. 26 (Ex. 7.77a). Following a premature dominant arrival in the subordinate key of E minor, which marks the end of the transition (m. 30, not shown), a standing on the dominant plays itself out at measure 36.[104] The liquidation of material in that bar helps us to hear the following passage as the onset of the subordinate theme, which still stands on the dominant.[105] Note that $\hat{1}$ of the subordinate key appears buried within the left-hand chordal texture (see arrow) to create the kind of guitar-strumming effect that is so typical of Scarlatti's style. The long-held dominant finally resolves to tonic at measure 43, which immediately brings an authentic cadential progression. Seeing as the melody achieves $\hat{1}$ on the downbeat of the next bar, we might recognize a PAC to close the theme, though this moment seems highly premature. So it is not surprising that Scarlatti keeps up the rhythmical momentum by introducing a series of authentic cadential progressions in measures 44–48, though the melodic closure alternates between $\hat{1}$ and $\hat{3}$.

As we already have discussed in connection with consecutive PACs in Scarlatti (sec. 7.3.1, Ex. 7.52 and 7.54), it is not always clear which articulation represents the genuine cadence. In the present example, we could choose measure 44 or 48 (m. 46, being in the middle of the repetitions, hardly comes into question). And like the cases discussed before, we are probably tempted to choose the final cadential gesture as the decisive moment of closure, especially since measure 48 is also associated with a marked change of material.[106] Indeed, that bar brings a new subordinate theme, one that begins with continuation function as expressed by the one-measure units and the quasi-sequential progression of the harmonies.[107] This second subordinate theme is closed off with a PAC in measure 56 using the similar material as the PACs of the first subordinate theme. The second theme is then repeated, and again the PAC at measure 64 uses melodic content resembling the series of cadences in the first subordinate theme (mm. 44–48). This time, though, the PAC at measure 64 seems less premature than the earlier cadence at measure 44, because the later one also corresponds more directly to the unambiguous PAC at measure 56, which ends the first statement of the second subordinate theme. Still, a degree of cadential uncertainty remains, because the "final" arrival at measure 68 can also lay claim to being the decisive moment of thematic ending.[108]

If the overabundance of authentic cadential content in this exposition obscures moments of thematic closure, what happens in the recapitulation is remarkable for the way in which Scarlatti avoids such ambiguities (Ex. 7.77b). To begin

---

101. Thus Bach's Sonata in B Minor, Wq. 49, no. 6, iii, is exceptional in that the development ends with a PAC in F-sharp minor, after which a linking phrase leads to the B-minor harmony opening the recapitulation.

102. Hepokoski and Darcy term this a "type 2" sonata form (*Sonata Theory*, chap. 17).

103. See *CF*, 163, 167, and *ACF*, 478–79.

104. That the subordinate key of this major-mode sonata is the minor dominant is most unusual.

105. On the possibility of a subordinate theme beginning with a standing on the dominant, see *CF*, 113–14, and *ACF*, 393–95.

106. Schmalfeldt, in a private communication, advocates for hearing m. 44 closing the subordinate theme. Presumably the two subsequent articulations (mm. 46 and 48) would be heard as postcadential. Problematic with this reading is finding a closing section standing between two subordinate themes. I know of no such case in the classical style and have not yet encountered one in the galant.

107. I say quasi-sequential, because although the bass and soprano lines appear to be transposed down a step, the inner voice sustains a tonic pedal, thus permitting us also to hear a broader root-position tonic prolongation leading from m. 48 to m. 54. The prominence of continuation function (combined with the tonic prolongation) compensates for the utter lack of that function (and harmony) in the first subordinate theme.

108. If, on the contrary, we opt for m. 64 as the real cadence of the subordinate-theme group (also Schmalfeldt's position), then the exposition would end with a closing section made up of repeated cadential ideas.

EXAMPLE 7.77A. Scarlatti, Keyboard Sonata in A, K. 26, mm. 33–68.

with, he largely rewrites the first subordinate theme to create a more pronounced sense of initiating function. A new basic idea sounds three times in measures 104–109, thus producing an extended presentation, though one still supported by a dominant pedal (cf. Ex. 7.77a, m. 37ff.).[109] A continuation begins at measure 110 with model-sequence technique, whose overall descending contour is similar to that found at the start of the second subordinate theme in the exposition (cf. m. 48ff.). Rather than leading, as earlier, to a series of compressed cadential ideas (cf. mm. 43–48) whose closure is ambiguous, the recapitulation's theme (Ex. 7.77b) begins its process of ending with a deceptive ECP in measures 117–20, followed by a single

---

109. On this type of initiating unit, which sees a local tonic prolongation loosened by being set over a dominant pedal, see the discussion of Beethoven's Piano Sonata in F Minor, Op. 2, no. 1, i, in *CF*, 19, and *ACF*, 268–70. For the difference between beginning a theme with a regular standing on the dominant (as in Ex. 7.77a) and the weak type of tonic prolongation seen in Ex. 7.77b, see *ACF*, 395, and William

E. Caplin, "The *Tempest* Exposition: A Springboard for Form-Functional Considerations, 97–103.

EXAMPLE 7.77B. Scarlatti, Keyboard Sonata in A, K. 26, mm. 104–48.

PAC at measure 121. At this point, the second subordinate theme appears, whose construction is largely the same as that in the exposition (cf. Ex. 7.77a, m. 48ff.). When the theme is repeated (m. 130ff.), it too leads to a deceptive ECP (mm. 138–41), whose resolution to VI initiates a series of compressed cadential ideas, akin to those closing the exposition (cf. mm. 63–68). Again, what happens in the recapitulation clarifies the conditions for closure, for now a second, compact deceptive cadence is then followed by an abandoned progression leading to a PAC at measure 144 to end the theme. The melodic spinning out continues after this point, but rather than bringing additional cadential progressions (as at the end of the exposition), a clearly articulated closing section arises by virtue of the tonic pedal, which is sustained until the final bar of the recapitulation. We see, therefore, that whereas the structural goals of the exposition were blurred by a repetition of compact cadential figures, the recapitulation (in a manner that looks forward to the classical style) mixes together a variety of deviations, some expanded, to create a single, unambiguous PAC for each of the two subordinate themes.

EXAMPLE 7.78A–B. Scarlatti, Keyboard Sonata in G, K. 169, (a) mm. 11–32 (R = ½N); (b) m. 1.

Scarlatti's Sonata in G, K. 169, brings another case of the recapitulation clarifying cadential goals in relation to ambiguities presented in the exposition (Ex. 7.78a). Compared to the previous example, we encounter here an even greater abundance of authentic cadential content—*eleven* cadential progressions within the confines of the subordinate-theme group. Moreover, the situation is further complicated in six of those cases when the final bass ① is displaced by an eighth-note rest (see downbeats of mm. 16,

18, 24, 26, 28, and 30) in order to draw attention to an ascending scalar motive ("x"), appearing first in the left hand at the start of the subordinate theme (upbeat to m. 12) and then used copiously throughout the rest of the exposition. The lack of a bass tone at the moment of apparent cadential arrival opens up the possibility of perceiving an evaded cadence at each of these junctures. Such a hearing, however, makes it difficult to come up with a coherent interpretation of the formal organization of the subordinate-theme area, and for that reason I am going to offer an analysis that understands the upper voice's arrival on 1̂ as permitting us to hear PAC content at each of these six moments. Of course the formal status of these PACs must be carefully considered since it is not possible for all of them to function as moments of genuine thematic closure; rather, I will consider many to be cadences of limited scope.

Further complicating the formal analysis is the question of which notation system is operative in this movement. Seeing as the main theme comprises repeated units that last only one measure each (Ex. 7.78b), and given the overall length of the exposition at thirty-two bars, it is not unreasonable to understand here a case of compound meter (R = ½N).[110] We can thus hear the subordinate-theme area beginning at measure 12 with a presentation phrase, as annotated in the score. A brief continuation sees an acceleration of the surface rhythm, leading to an evaded cadence. A repeat of the continuation produces a PAC on the downbeat of measure 16 to end this subordinate theme. As mentioned before, the cadential arrival delays ① due to the immediate appearance of motive "x" in the left-hand. This motive is then set against a new basic idea, followed by a contrasting idea, one that is melodically related to the basic idea but now supported by a cadential bass line.[111] Seeing as the resulting one-measure unit begins on a high 1̂ and then shuts down on the same scale degree an octave lower (downbeat of m. 18), it would not be unreasonable to consider this idea as a codetta, closed by a cadence of limited scope. And when the codetta is then repeated, we could hear them together as constituting a closing section to the subordinate theme.

What follows at measure 20 sees fragmentation into half-bar units, thus proposing a continuation, signaled as well by the more energetic surface rhythm. This interpretation now allows us retrospectively to regard the closing section, with its constituent codettas, as a compound presentation made out of two consequent-like phrases, each of which ends with a PAC of limited scope. As such, a second subordinate theme emerges, one that achieves closure via the PAC at measure 22. Immediately eliding with this cadence, the continuation phrase is repeated, bringing another PAC at measure 24. What appears next might give the impression of being yet another closing section that becomes reinterpreted as the opening of a new subordinate theme. But whereas measures 24–27 may project a retrospective compound presentation, what follows in measures 28–29 does not quite seem like a continuation; in fact, these bars sound like a variation of the prior codettas, thus extending the closing section through to the end of the exposition. One complicating feature, though, is the deceptive cadence that arises immediately prior to the final cadential idea; this deviation alludes more to a subordinate theme than to a closing section.

Though I have tried to give a reasonable formal reading of the subordinate-theme group, the plethora of authentic cadential articulations unquestionably clouds the picture, and other formal options are available.[112] Of course, this entire discussion is leading to what happens in the recapitulation (Ex. 7.78c), where Scarlatti finds ways of presenting a much clearer formal plan. Following a phrygian HC that concludes the development, the recapitulation starts with the presentation (mm. 53–54) of a subordinate theme. A continuation at measure 55 leads to a manifest evaded cadence, which is repeated in the following bar.[113] New continuational material arrives at an internal HC at measure 59. Such a cadence is normally followed by a new continuation (or cadential) passage; however, Scarlatti writes a new presentation (mm. 59–61) drawn from the final codetta of the exposition (cf. Ex. 7.78a, mm. 28–29). As a result, we can speak of a *two-part* subordinate theme, whose second part has a clear initiating function.[114] The continuation of this second part leads quickly to another set of authentic cadential deviations, this time, two deceptive cadences (mm. 62 and 63),[115] whereupon a third try for a PAC is successful in the

---

110. Further supporting this view are the many cadential articulations, mostly in the recapitulation, that occur in the middle of the compound measure (C = 2 × 2/4); see ahead, Ex. 7.78c, mm. 62–64 and 67–69.

111. This basic idea is also related both rhythmically and melodically to the opening of the main theme's basic idea, Ex. 7.78b.

112. For example, Schmalfeldt (in a personal communication) proposes that m. 16 is not a functional PAC, and thus sees the first subordinate theme ending at m. 20. She then finds a second subordinate theme beginning with a large-scale presentation (mm. 20–23), upon which follows a continuation beginning at m. 24 and a concluding PAC at m. 28. Her formal reading thus largely depends on an alternative interpretation of which cadences are genuinely functional. That we are drawn to different views confirms the ambiguities of cadential articulations in this exposition. Not surprisingly, we concur in our analysis of the recapitulation, which, compared to the exposition, features a more coherent deployment of the cadences.

113. This second cadential deviation could alternatively be heard as deceptive, since the melodic goal of the cadential idea, G, appears in its expected register (unlike the prior evaded cadence, whose melodic goal is disrupted by a leap up to D, downbeat of m. 56). I lean toward the evaded cadence option for m. 57, however, to respect the parallelism otherwise projected here. A performer wishing to project the evasion would likely find a way to minimize articulating the G as a cadential goal.

114. *CF*, 117, and *ACF*, 380.

115. Though the material content leading to the two deceptive cadences (mm. 62–63) is identical to that of the evaded cadences in mm. 56–57,

EXAMPLE 7.78C. Scarlatti, Keyboard Sonata in G, K. 169, mm. 52–69 (R = ½N).

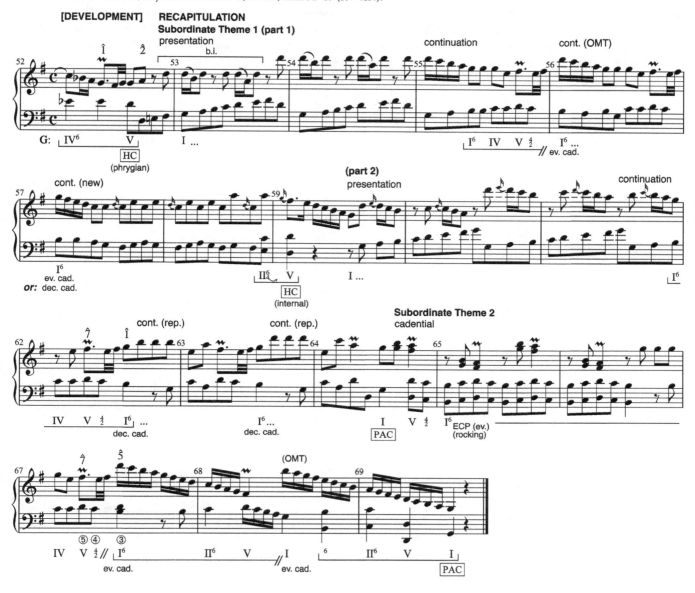

middle of measure 64, thus bringing this two-part subordinate theme to a close.

Immediately following this cadence, Scarlatti introduces new material not heard in the exposition. The underlying harmonic support prolongs I⁶, thus suggesting an ECP in the making (using a variant of the classical rocking on the tonic), which is confirmed at measure 67 with the move to stages 2 and 3 of the progression. The bass, however, pushes down ④–③ as the leading tone leaps up to 5̂, thus evading the ECP. A second, more compact cadential progression is also evaded in the middle of

measure 68, and a one-more-time repetition of the descending sixteenth-note scales effects a final PAC, which closes this second subordinate theme.

Unlike the exposition, which contained eleven PAC articulations, thus rendering a complex, uncertain formal plan, the recapitulation brings three unambiguous cadences—one internal HC (m. 59), and two PACs (mm. 64 and 69)—each of which achieves a high degree of formal clarity. All of the other cadential gestures are deviations that drive the music forward toward these formal goals. Though Scarlatti's deployment of cadential passages surely looks forward to the classical style, a number of elements are not entirely typical of that later practice. For instance, an internal HC is not usually *preceded* by evaded cadences (as in mm. 56–57), since those deviations are way

---

the melodic resolution 7̂–1̂ in middle of these bars clearly represents the melodic goal (unlike the leap up to 5̂ that occurs at m. 56).

stations that point to authentic, not half cadential, closure. As well, a classical ECP tends not to follow directly upon a goal PAC (as in mm. 64–65); instead, a standard classical technique would see an evaded cadence in the middle of measure 64 motivating the ECP. Finally, a classical ECP is normally the last harmonic event of a subordinate theme, with the final tonic of the progression bringing the long-anticipated PAC. Scarlatti, however, concludes the formal process with two relatively compact cadential progressions, thus firmly adhering to the standard practice of the baroque and galant styles.

# Cadence in the Romantic Era

BEGINNING WITH THIS CHAPTER, AND CONtinuing into the following one, we will examine cadential practices in tonal music written after the high classical style. The present chapter deals with music that is today generally termed *Romantic*, embracing composers working largely in the second quarter of the century, such as Schubert, Schumann, Chopin, and Mendelssohn.[1] The following chapter considers compositions from the mid- to late nineteenth century by a wider range of composers.[2] Before turning to the specific compositional techniques that typify cadential usage in these style periods, we must acknowledge a central fact—nineteenth-century composers continue to employ the classical cadence extensively throughout their compositions. Many phrases and most thematic units close cadentially in the manner described

---

1. Although Liszt is often included in this style period, I discuss him in the following chapter, since his works are cadentially more adventurous than many of his contemporaries in the second quarter of the century. The absence in both chapters of examples by French composers (esp. Berlioz) reflects what seems to be the general case: the classical cadence is retained more firmly in France throughout the nineteenth century than by composers of the German school and their "nationalist" compatriots (e.g., Dvorak, Grieg). To be sure, further examination of French compositions may well turn up cases of nonclassical cadential usage that differs from that discussed here.

The selection of nineteenth-century works examined for both chapters was not conducted as systematically as for the earlier ones. In the first instance, I consulted pieces that I was already familiar with analytically (esp. ones that I taught in my classes) and from there, I branched out to additional works in a variety of genres by the major composers of the period. At a rather late stage in my research, I realized that I had not given sufficient attention to the works of Mendelssohn, so additional investigations will be necessary to treat more fully cadential usage by this significant composer.

2. There seems not to be a well-recognized style label (akin to baroque, galant, classical, and Romantic) for music in the second half of the nineteenth century. We encounter "post-Romantic" now and then, but mostly in connection with music toward the very end of the century or even in the early decades of the twentieth. Perhaps this lack of an obvious term, along with my referencing a number of Romantic works in Chapter 9, suggests that the stylistic differences within nineteenth-century practice are not as strongly delineated as they are within the prior century, where we can readily distinguish between baroque, galant, and classical styles.

in Part I of this study. Indeed, classical cadences are so widespread in this music that it is unnecessary to highlight up front any specific cases; a quick glance through the repertoire (or even just the examples chosen for discussion in both chapters) will reveal easily enough the ubiquity of this mode of thematic closure. Yet despite the powerful influence that the classical cadence continued to exert, composers in the nineteenth century explored some new compositional procedures that modify, or distort, in interesting ways the classical means of creating closure. This and the following chapter will discuss in detail those novel techniques.[3]

A number of general factors contribute to the decline of cadential closure throughout the nineteenth century. Most obviously, the bonds of functional tonality begin to loosen under the impact of ever-increasing degrees of chromaticism and the employment of nonfunctional harmonies, especially the symmetrical, third-related progressions that lend themselves well to modeling by "neo-Riemannian" approaches.[4] As a result, the tonic-dominant polarity, which is central to the harmonic dimension of the classical cadence, begins to lose force in the course of the century. Additionally, the subdominant emerges as an alternative, or complementary, pole to the tonic, as reflected in the greater use of plagal progressions and the concomitant appearance of dualist harmonic theories. Eventually the "emancipation of the dissonance" and the wholesale relinquishing of the tonal system, which occurred in the early decades of the twentieth century, led to the elimination of the classical cadence as a device for formal closure.

Purely harmonic considerations alone, however, do not fully account for the change in cadential practices witnessed during the nineteenth century. Another factor plays a significant role as well, namely, some important changes in the nature of the bass voice. As we have seen, the classical bass line consists of two melodic streams—prolongational and cadential—that at the moment of authentic cadence are directly connected by means of the harmonic interval of the fifth.[5] This unification of melodic (upper-voice) and harmonic (bass-voice) closure accounts for my requirement that the cadential dominant appear exclusively in root position. (The stability associated with this position is another contributing factor.) Starting with the Romantic style, we can recognize two somewhat dichotomous tendencies in the organization of the bass voice. On the one hand, we find a greater use of harmonies standing in root position. The melodic character of the bass is thus reduced such that often this voice literally reproduces the fundamental bass of the harmonic progressions. This plethora of root-position harmonies can sometimes obscure the distinction between those that function to create a genuine cadence from those that are noncadential. On the other hand, the bass voice begins to acquire a distinctly *motivic* quality, thus resembling the motion of upper voices. In such cases, motivic reasons can often account for the final tonic of a thematic unit being approached by stepwise motion in the bass, giving rise to inverted dominants that create prolongational closure, not cadential closure strictly speaking.

In addition to these matters affecting the harmony and bass line, another issue of general aesthetic orientation had a profound impact on the use of the classical cadence. Under the sway of the "aesthetics of originality,"[6] nineteenth-century composers tended to shun the conventional, the formulaic, striving instead to make each moment of the composition a unique, individualized utterance. Insofar as the cadence is a highly conventionalized gesture, the kind of pervasive cadential usage witnessed in the classical style is less sustainable in nineteenth-century works, with their need for ever original content. Indeed, concerns with aesthetic originality tended to focus musical listening on the *opening* ideas of thematic units, on their characteristic, individualistic properties. Much more than for earlier styles, nineteenth-century compositions were prized for the quality of their "tunes." As a result, the highly teleological aesthetic of the classical style, as manifest in the constant striving toward cadential goals, loses ground in later styles. With a shift in preference toward the beginning of formal units, it sometimes occurs that a listener perceives that one such unit has ended not so much because a particular musical device, such as a cadence, has articulated decisive closure, but rather because something *new* has begun. In short, the need to articulate thematic closure in its own right gradually diminishes in the course of the century.

Just as we can speak with confidence of a classical cadence, we should ask if it is possible to identify a specifically defined "nineteenth-century cadence," one that has a set of morphological and functional features that distinguish it decisively from the classical cadence. Thus far the answer seems to be no. We can, of course, observe some modifications in the harmonic and melodic component of cadences in this century. For example, Schmalfeldt has coined the term *nineteenth-century half cadence* (19cHC), for situations in which the ultimate dominant of a half cadential progression includes the dissonant seventh (counter to classical practice, which requires the dominant to be a consonant triad);[7] however, this relatively minor modification of harmony and dissonance does not involve any further changes to what would otherwise be a regular, classical HC, and in any case, the idea has no application to authentic cadences. My investigation of the nineteenth-century repertory has failed to yield a consistent

---

3. For the most part, the compositional techniques discussed in these two chapters involve relatively local cadential-formal contexts, ones largely confined to a single thematic unit. In other words, I have not extended my investigation into the role of cadence in effecting larger-scale tonal and formal dimensions in nineteenth-century works. Significant research in this area, however, has recently been undertaken by Julian Horton, "Formal Type and Formal Function in the Postclassical Piano Concerto"; Horton, "Criteria for a Theory of Nineteenth-Century Sonata Form"; Peter H. Smith, "Cadential Content and Cadential Function in the First-Movement Expositions of Schumann's Violin Sonatas"; and Vande Moortele, *Romantic Overture*.

4. David Kopp, *Chromatic Transformations in Nineteenth-Century Music*, 21; Richard Cohn, *Audacious Euphony: Chromaticism and the Consonant Triad's Second Nature*.

5. See in Chapter 2, sec. 2.4.

6. Carl Dahlhaus, *Nineteenth-Century Music*, 27, 40.

7. Schmalfeldt, *Process of Becoming*, 202–3.

harmonic-melodic-rhythmic configuration that could warrant a label anything comparable to that of the "classical cadence."

If empirical studies have yet to yield a clearly identifiable nineteenth-century cadence, how then are we best able to describe thematic closure for this music? The working methodology I pursue here is one of *comparison*, namely, using the classical cadence as a measuring stick for observing to what extent moments of potential thematic closure in nineteenth-century works do, or do not, conform to classical norms. When those instances of closure largely replicate the classical model—recalling again that this is predominantly the case—we can simply analyze those situations as genuinely cadential. When they do not comply with those norms, we are prompted to describe as carefully as possible just how such modifications occur and attempt to explain their source and effect. This methodology, which emphasizes in the first instance why a given moment of closure is *not* classical, can give the impression that something is compositionally defective or abnormal, and the entire discussion can seem to be framed in largely negative terms.[8]

Unfortunately, this problem seems endemic to approaches that attempt to establish norms and then identify violations of them. Of course, if it can be shown that the norms are no longer really applicable (for example, using principles of tonal harmony to analyze twelve-tone music, to take an extreme case, though one that has occasionally been pursued), then such an approach is less compelling and potentially useless. As I have already stated, however, the classical cadence continues to be found widely in nineteenth-century music, especially at key moments of formal articulation, so employing this model as a measuring tool to gauge conformance seems entirely reasonable. More importantly, it is not a question of using the classical norms in order to show what is *wrong* with nineteenth-century music, but rather to highlight what is *different* about it. Given that so many theories of tonal music propose a "common practice period" that embraces multiple historical styles (baroque, classical, Romantic), many musicians fail to attend to significant differences in harmonic, cadential, and formal practices among these styles. Thus even if a norm-deformation model tends toward generating negative statements, such a model at least helps to clarify differences in compositional technique, leading ultimately to an enriched hearing experience of the music.

The rest of this chapter, focusing on music in the second quarter of the century, will be organized around a series of topics involving harmonic, rhythmic, and formal techniques that have the potential of affecting cadential usage in the Romantic period. A similar set of topics will be brought forth in the following chapter on music in the mid- to late nineteenth century. As just discussed, the goal will be to see how the technique in question represents a change in practice from what is typically found in the classical style, with the ordering of topics generally progressing from lesser to greater degrees of cadential alteration. Along the way, we will observe some important modifications in cadential morphology and in the formal functions of various modes of thematic closure, cadential or otherwise. I conclude the chapter with a series of "analytical notes" devoted to cadence and closure in Chopin's Preludes, Op. 28, a work of enduring popularity and critical attention that occupies a central position in any study of Romantic music.

## 8.1. Chromaticism and Dissonance

As is obvious to any casual listener, music in the Romantic era witnesses a marked increase in chromaticism and dissonance compared to the prior century. We might even think that this change would significantly influence, perhaps even distort, cadential expression. In fact, this seems not to be the case. Most often, chromatic alterations can be understood in relation to a basic diatonic harmony, and the harmonic function defined by that harmony is normally retained in the chromatic version. Thus, even if a given cadential harmony is extensively chromaticized, its syntactical function within the cadential progression remains comprehensible.

In addition to chromaticism arising from alterations of diatonic harmonies, a second general source of chromaticism derives from dividing the octave into equal-sized intervals: three major thirds or four minor thirds.[9] Due to their origins in a symmetrically divided octave, as opposed to the asymmetrical divisions of the diatonic system, these harmonies do not normally yield a clear functional interpretation—as tonic, pre-dominant, or dominant—in relation to a single tonal center. Instead, the smooth voice leading often connecting such harmonies allows their progressions to be modeled by neo-Riemannian operations rather than by traditional harmonic-tonal theory. At levels of harmonic motion within a phrase, this type of chromaticism normally involves *sequential* progressions. In some cases, minor-third related harmonies, especially as major-minor-seventh sonorities, can give the impression of prolonging a single harmonic function, as in the case of a *hyperdominant*, which I defined and analyzed in Chapter 4.[10] Otherwise, symmetrically derived harmonies are rarely used within cadential progressions, since the latter depend upon a functional succession of harmonies in order to confirm a tonal center and to create harmonic closure.[11]

---

8. Thus what follows may incur the kind of critique that Suzannah Clark levels at Hepokoski and Darcy's theories, when she notes that "given that their treatise focuses on musical instances where composers break the norm, there is hardly a positive adjective in the book" (*Analyzing Schubert*, 206, note 5. For an insightful discussion of the problems in approaching nineteenth-century form from a "positive" or "negative" perspective, see Vande Moortele, "Romantic Form," 408–11.

9. A tritone division can be assimilated within minor-third divisions; a "whole-tone" scale, into major-third divisions; and a chromatic scale, into any other interval divisions.

10. See sec. 4.4.3.3 for how this idea relates to the general domain of HCs and dominant arrivals. I raise the idea of hyperdominant again in Chapter 9, in connection with an analysis of the *Tristan* prelude, Ex. 9.56d.

11. At broader levels of a composition, the various key areas of a movement may be related by symmetrical divisions. These tonal relations, though,

EXAMPLE 8.1. (a) Donizetti, "Una furtiva lagrima," *L'elisir d'amore*, mm. 23–25; (b) Bellini, "Corre a valle," *I puritani*, mm. 11–12.

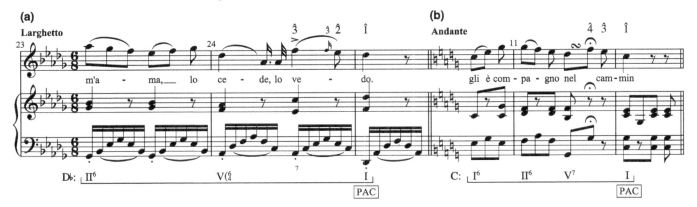

EXAMPLE 8.2. (a) Schumann, "Am Kamin," *Kinderszenen*, Op. 15, no. 8, mm. 31–33; (b) Schumann, "Volksliedchen," *Album for the Young*, Op. 68, no. 14, mm. 7–8; (c) mm. 23–24.

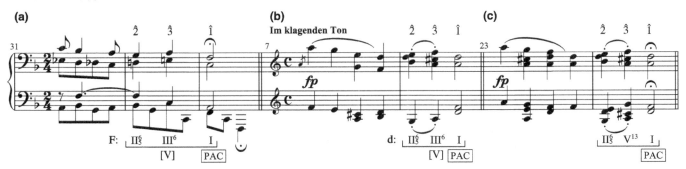

As for the greater dissonances generally employed in nineteenth-century styles, such usage does not usually disrupt the functional expression of cadential harmonies. Nonetheless, several relatively minor manifestations of greater dissonance treatment are especially characteristic of the Romantic era. With some composers and genres, we encounter particular melodic or harmonic embellishments that otherwise appear infrequently in eighteenth-century cadences. In Italian opera, especially, we can observe a predilection for including the third scale degree within the dominant proper, thus creating an added dissonance between the non-chord tone $\hat{3}$ and the dissonant seventh ($\hat{4}$). More specifically, special durational emphasis is often given to $\hat{3}$ prior to its resolution to $\hat{2}$ (Ex. 8.1a). When the cadential six-four resolves to the dominant proper in the second half of measure 24, the melody leaps up to $\hat{3}$, which acquires both durational and dynamic accentuation, and for good measure, an additional grace note $\hat{3}$ is added in the resolution to $\hat{2}$. A different technique sees $\hat{3}$ becoming an incomplete passing tone between $\hat{4}$ and $\hat{1}$, thus bypassing $\hat{2}$ (Ex. 8.1b). Here, $\hat{4}$ at the end of measure 11 is emphasized, but its resolution to $\hat{3}$ takes place still within dominant harmony, before skipping over $\hat{2}$ to reach $\hat{1}$ on the downbeat of the next bar.

Several passages from Schumann show how similar techniques emphasizing $\hat{3}$ were extended to instrumental music. Example 8.2a sees III$^6$ used as a dominant substitute, thus supporting $\hat{3}$ in the melody.[12] In Example 8.2b, the first PAC of this little folk song uses the same harmony, but now as a plaintive (*klagend*) augmented triad, while the song's final cadence (Ex. 8.2c) brings a more pungent V$^{13}$ sonority. In all three cases, $\hat{2}$ appears in the pre-dominant, with $\hat{3}$ occupying all of the dominant proper, thus skipping over $\hat{2}$ on the way to $\hat{1}$.

Another dissonance modification involves the ultimate harmony of a half cadential progression. Throughout the eighteenth century, composers scrupulously use a consonant dominant triad at the moment of cadential arrival in order to project a sense of stability for a harmonic function that is intrinsically unstable (in that it always wants to resolve to tonic). Exceptionally, a dissonant seventh ($\hat{4}$) can be added to the dominant, especially one closing a broader thematic unit, such as a transition or developmental core. In such a case, the deviation of *dominant arrival* comes into play.[13] In the Romantic period, this restriction begins to be eased. With Chopin and Schumann especially, the effect of an HC continues to be projected even when the final harmony is represented by a dominant seventh. For this reason, Schmalfeldt has specifically identified a 19cHC at points where a classical HC would be expected (such as at the end of an

---

normally take place at levels of structure that exceed those involving thematic closure.

12. Although I use the roman numeral III$^6$, the actual harmonic function expressed here is dominant, one in which $\hat{3}$ replaces $\hat{2}$. For a late nineteenth-century case of this same usage, see in Chapter 9, Ex. 9.54a, m. 4.

13. See Chapter 4, sec. 4.4.

EXAMPLE 8.3. Chopin, Waltz in A Minor, Op. 34, no. 2, mm. 17–36.

EXAMPLE 8.4. Nineteenth-century cadential progressions.

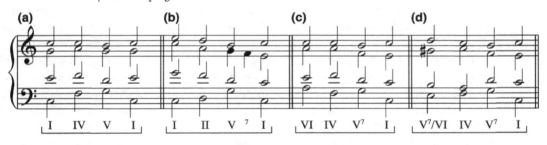

antecedent phrase).[14] She thus validates this harmonic usage as conventional, rather than being a deviation.

Since Schmalfeldt identifies many such cadences, it is not necessary to dwell on the technique here. The excerpt shown in Example 8.3 will suffice for the moment to illustrate the practice. The overall form of this theme is a compound period, whose opening compound antecedent is structured as a simple sentence (pres. + cont.⇒cad.) and whose bass line features a classical stepwise ascent from ① to ⑤. Two small harmonic details are worthy of note, namely, the use of VI$^6_4$ (m. 20) together with V$^6_5$/IV (m. 21) as substitutes for the more conventional I$^6$. Whereas the latter substitute is found now and then in classical practice, the former is most unconventional in that style. As the pre-dominant IV$^6$ in measure 23 moves to the dominant in the following bar, D ($\hat{4}$) in an inner voice is held over, thus creating a clear dissonant seventh within the dominant of this 19cHC. Seeing as Chopin regularly employs the dissonant seventh in this kind of formal context, not to recognize here a genuine cadence seems overly restrictive. (I return to this example to discuss its consequent phrase after introducing some other characteristics of the Romantic style.)

## 8.2. Root-Position Harmonies

One striking feature of Romantic harmony has largely gone unremarked by theorists: harmonies frequently succeed each other in root position. In fact, such a succession is regularly found in this style, whereas long strings of root-position harmonies arise less frequently in eighteenth-century works.[15] This emphasis on root-position harmonies affects the specific ones that tend to be used cadentially. Example 8.4 illustrates some commonly employed cadential progressions found in Romantic works (various

---

14. Considerably more work is needed to flesh out aspects of the 19cHC, investigating, in particular, which composers tend favor the technique and the extent of its employment.

15. When such progressions do occur in earlier styles, they are typically part of an extensive sequence, e.g., a descending-fifth pattern, as seen in Chapter 2, Ex. 2.6, mm. 48–49.

EXAMPLE 8.5. Chopin, Nocturne in G Minor, Op. 37, no. 1, (a) mm. 41–44; (b) mm. 1–8.

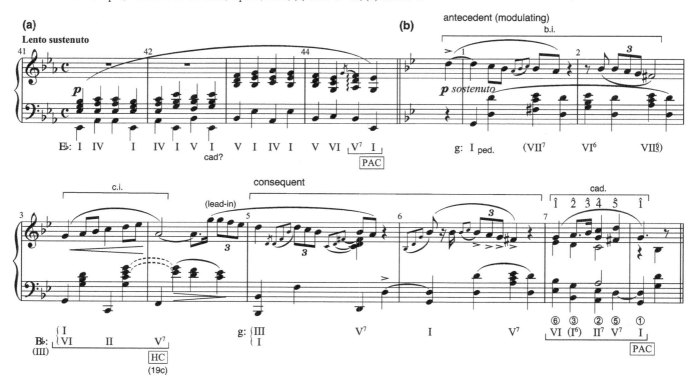

dissonances or chromatic alterations can be included, of course). Note that the pre-dominant of stage 2 tends to favor either the subdominant or the supertonic in root position (a) and (b), rather than the more typical II⁶ of the classical style. The initial tonic of Romantic cadences often stands in root position, and VI may fully substitute for that tonic (c). Another initial tonic substitute sees the third degree in the bass (which would normally support I⁶) holding a III harmony, or chromatically, a dominant of the submediant (V⁷/VI), which resolves deceptively to the subdominant (d). The resulting bass line resembles a classical one, but the chromaticism betrays a Romantic touch.[16]

An emphasis on root-position harmonies can sometimes yield ambiguities of progression type. For example, in cases of a descending-fifth sequential progression leading to I, the final harmonies (say, II–V–I) could also be associated with the last three stages of an authentic cadential progression. Likewise, a simple I–V–I progression might be construed as either prolongational or cadential. Example 8.5a shows an extreme case of root-position harmonies in a passage that obviously references the genre of chorale.[17] The final beat of measure 44 seems to be

a clear enough PAC, which itself is preceded by a deceptive resolution of the dominant.[18] And we also cannot entirely rule out the expression of the same cadence at the end of measure 42. In both places, however, the progression is quite incomplete and, especially in the case of the opening two-measure unit, we might want to regard the final two beats of measure 42 as continuing the tonic prolongations of the prior measure and a half. Indeed, an excessive use of root-position harmonies helps blur the fundamental distinctions among prolongational, sequential, and cadential progressions that are so essential to classical harmony in its relation to form.

Although this kind of chorale texture is not unique in Chopin's oeuvre, it still remains somewhat exceptional.[19] Yet the root-position emphasis found here is also present at the very opening of the Nocturne (Ex. 8.5b), which features a more standard melody-and-accompaniment texture. We might initially be tempted to identify various harmonic inversions within the first two measures: VII⁷, VI⁶, and VII⁶₅; however, the functional bass seems to sound in a lower tessitura of the piano. If so, we can hear the opening two bars as projecting a tonic pedal and then observe

---

16. Alternatively, V⁷/VI may be understood as III♯. For an insightful discussion of the latter usage, see Nathan John Martin, "Schumann's Fragment," 93–99. Martin shows how this harmony can function as both a *tonic* substitute (I⁶) and a *dominant* substitute (V/VI); on this point, he also cites L. Poundie Burstein, "A New View of 'Tristan': Tonal Unity in the Prelude and Conclusion to Act I," 20–24.

17. This passage, of course, is not in the chorale style of J. S. Bach, which rarely employs a series of root-position harmonies. It would be interesting to examine the historical sources for Chopin's reference here; is there a Polish, or a more general, chorale tradition that emphasizes root-position harmonies?

18. Note three differences associated with the penultimate dominant: the addition of a dissonant seventh (all of the prior chords being consonant triads), the "rolling" of the chord, and its embellishment by 3̂. All of these details provide a sense of terminal modification that helps project a cadential quality to this final progression (see Chapter 1, sec. 1.1; and Smith, *Poetic Closure*, 53).

19. For other cases, see Nocturne in G Minor, Op. 15, no. 3, m. 89ff. (marked "religioso"), and Prelude No. 20 in C Minor, Op. 28, to be discussed in a later section on Chopin's preludes (Ex. 8.45).

that every harmony in the theme stands in root position, with the exception of I⁶ in measure 7.[20]

Though I am using this example to illustrate the Romantic tendency to exploit root-position harmonies, it is worth pausing briefly to examine some details that reveal other nonclassical traits. In the first place, the form of the theme seems to be a standard period—an opening antecedent with weak cadential closure, followed by a consequent bringing a stronger cadence. Counter to classical norms,[21] however, the antecedent phrase modulates to the relative major, ending there with a 19cHC.[22] (Note, by the way, that the local E♭ sonority, VI⁶, on the downbeat of the second bar not only adds a major-mode coloration to the otherwise pathos-laden minor quality of the basic idea, but also subtly alludes to the upcoming modulation to B-flat major.) The consequent begins with tonic of the new key, but quickly modulates back to G minor. To solidify this return, Chopin brings a more marked sense of harmonic progression in measures 5–6 (four distinct harmonies compared to a single prolonged harmony in mm. 1–2) and makes sure that the downbeat of measure 6 holds a strong root-position tonic, rather than the more luminous VI⁶ of the antecedent (cf. m. 2). The final cadential idea is especially interesting, since its upper-voice melodic content ($\hat{1}$–$\hat{2}$–$\hat{3}$–$\hat{4}$–$\hat{5}$–$\hat{1}$) brings the elements of a classical bass line (the scalar rise from ① to ⑤ and subsequent leap back down to ①), a melody that regularly supports an entire thematic unit. To avoid parallel octaves (except at its end, a license found frequently enough in most tonal styles), Chopin introduces a nonclassical cadential bass line (⑥–③–②–⑤–①), featuring a root-position VI as the initial tonic of the progression. After a subsequent I⁶—an embellishing chord and the sole genuinely inverted harmony in the theme—the bass pushes downward to support a root-position half-diminished II⁷, a predominant rarely used in a classical cadential progression.[23] Thus the theme exemplifies many ways in which what might seem to be a fairly ordinary period departs considerably from the norms of the classical style, while bringing a series of typically Romantic elements of harmony and form.

## 8.3. Uniform Harmonic Rhythm and Density

In a manner that harkens back to baroque practice, the Romantic style often features a relatively uniform rhythm of harmonic change, especially compared to the classical style. In many cases, this harmonic-rhythmic uniformity arises from the use of various dance genres (mazurka, waltz) or from character pieces that tend to feature a single emotional affect, thus emulating, again, a baroque aesthetic.[24] This rate of harmonic change can often be quite fast, thus yielding a textural density, especially at the very opening of a thematic unit. (In the classical style, on the contrary, the harmonic rhythm tends initially to be relatively slow and then increases in the course of the theme.) To avoid overburdening the harmonic texture with rapidly changing prolongational progressions, Romantic composers will vary the progression type by introducing both sequential and cadential progressions in initiating formal positions. Moreover, the possibility of embedding one progression type within another emerges as an option for creating harmonic diversity within a foreground of uniform harmonic rhythm.

The opening of Example 8.6 illustrates the kind of consistency and density of harmonic activity found in a Romantic character piece. Measure 1 already brings a cadential progression in C minor, which upon repetition in the following bar proves to be a mere accompaniment to a rather fragmented melodic gesture. Taken together, and in the context of the entire theme, these opening two measures represent a basic idea. The accompanimental pattern in measure 3 is then varied to become a cadential progression in E-flat (HK: III), and the melodic fragment is sequenced a third higher, thus allowing us to reinterpret the basic idea as a model for sequential repetition. We thus see that Schumann embeds cadential progressions within a broader ascending-third sequence.[25] The use of these progression types for the very opening of a theme—here, a kind of "presentation" phrase—is especially characteristic of the Romantic style.[26] At the beginning of the continuation, measure 5, the progression resolves deceptively, thus shifting the tonal focus back to C minor. Observe that up to this

---

20. Since I consider the subordinate harmonies in mm. 1–2 to occur in the context of a tonic pedal, they should not be identified as being in any particular "inversion," since their bass is replaced by the pedal. I have retained the figured-bass labels for inversion, nonetheless, in order to acknowledge the alternative, first mentioned in the text, of hearing more literal changes of harmony within these bars. It should be further noted that the "VII⁷" on the third quarter-note beat of m. 1 may seem as though it stands in root position, but this harmony is really a functional substitute for an inverted dominant seventh (V⁶₅).

21. See *CF*, 55, and *ACF*, 90.

22. This interpretation of a 19cHC assumes that the seventh literally entering on the second beat of the measure genuinely belongs to the dominant harmony, which appears as an incomplete sonority on the downbeat. The seventh E♭ (along with the ninth G) continuing on from the previous II (see the dashed ties) suggests this harmonic reading. If, on the contrary, we hear the seventh as passing, the implied dominant triad on the downbeat would project a classical HC.

23. The cadential progression of mm. 7–8 could also be seen as a descending-fifth *sequential* progression, a potentially ambiguous situation that I mentioned earlier and will treat more extensively later in sec. 8.7.

24. A significant difference between the baroque *Affektenlehre* and the early Romantic portrayal of "character," however, lies in the conventionalized nature of the former compared to the more individualistic sense of personal expression in the latter.

25. Schmalfeldt identifies the ascending-third sequence as the initial component of a more complete pattern, I–III–V–I, which she associates especially with Chopin, calling it his "signature progression" (*Process of Becoming*, chap. 8). In Ex. 8.6, we see Schumann also using the sequence. The pattern is rare in the classical style, especially within an opening unit.

26. I enclose the term "presentation" in quotation marks, because the sequential repetition of the initiating idea does not result in an obvious *tonic prolongation*, an essential element of a classical presentation. For important discussions of the use and modification of sentential themes in the nineteenth century, see Matthew BaileyShea, "The Wagnerian Satz: The Rhetoric of the Sentence in Wagner's Post-Lohengrin Operas," and Steven Vande Moortele, "Sentences, Sentence Chains, and Sentence Replication: Intra- and Interthematic Functions in Liszt's Weimar Symphonic Poems," 124–30.

EXAMPLE 8.6. Schumann, *Davidsbündlertänze*, Op. 6, no. 8, mm. 1–7.

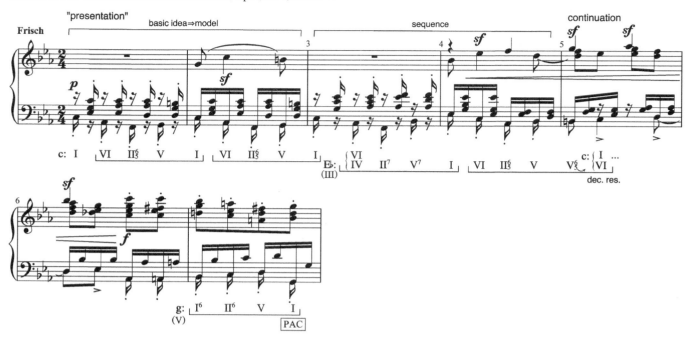

point, most of the harmonies of measures 1–4 stand in root position. With the deceptive resolution at the beginning of measure 5, the bass line now acquires an ascending-stepwise profile, which lasts most of the way through the modulation to the minor dominant and the confirmation of the new key by a genuine cadence. The cadential arrival, however, appears on the metrically weakest position within the final bar of the theme, not the typical location for what otherwise is a classical cadence. This placement permits the harmonic rhythm to remain entirely uniform throughout the theme (which functions as the A section of a small ternary).[27] Returning to the opening, it should go without saying that the embedded cadential progressions project cadential *content*, not any sense of cadential *function*, since no larger formal unit is ended by these cadence-like ideas.[28]

Let us now return to Example 8.3 and consider the compound consequent phrase (beginning at m. 25) in light of the uniform harmonic rhythms typical of a Romantic theme. Measure 29 sees the start of an ECP, analogous to the one in the second half of the compound antecedent (mm. 21–24), but now with a new one-measure melodic motive in the right-hand part, which is repeated in the following bars. The insistent upper pedal on the high A inhibits melodic closure, and so the ECP is abandoned when, at measure 33, the bass leaps down to the leading tone to support a noncadential $V^6_5$. Following the resolution to I, a simple $V^7$–I progression creates the final PAC. Note that it would have been perfectly possible for the ECP that began at measure 29 to have continued all the way to the end of the theme by progressing to a root-position dominant at measure 33 (see the bracketed roman numeral) and sustaining that harmony until the tonic at measure 36. Such an option would have been entirely conceivable within the classical style. Chopin, however, avoids the harmonic deceleration that would thus arise, probably for several reasons. First, he has established throughout most of the theme a fairly uniform rhythm of each measure bringing either a new harmony, or a change of bass, or both. By abandoning the cadential progression, he is able to maintain this consistent harmonic rhythm to the end of the theme. Second, by bringing the progression $V^6_5$–I in measures 33–34, he can provide the same harmonic support to those bars as for the similar material in measures 29–30. As a result, measure 33 sounds like the beginning of a sequential repetition, which is effectively relinquished with the need to create thematic closure, now by means of a compact, and highly incomplete, cadential progression. (That the cadence emerges out of what is initially heard as something sequential is a Romantic characteristic to which I will return in sec. 8.7.)

## 8.4. Off-Tonic Openings; ECP Openings

Only a handful of classical main themes begin with a harmony other than tonic in root position.[29] Many Romantic themes,

---

27. In the rest of the movement, Schumann shifts the cadential arrival back to the metrically stronger third eighth note (m. 21), and the last codetta even sees the final tonic appearing at the very downbeat of m. 26.

28. See also Ex. 8.45, Chopin's C-Minor Prelude, mm. 1–2, to be discussed in the "analytical notes" (sec. 8.13.20) at the end of this chapter.

29. Two striking cases appear in Beethoven's Op. 31 piano sonatas. In the "Tempest" sonata, Op. 31, no. 2, the main theme famously begins with $V^6$ as an extended *Largo* anacrusis. In the E-flat sonata, Op. 31, no. 3, the main theme begins with an expanded cadential predominant, $II^6_5$ (see

EXAMPLE 8.7. Schumann, *Davidsbündlertänze*, Op. 6, no. 5, mm. 1–8.

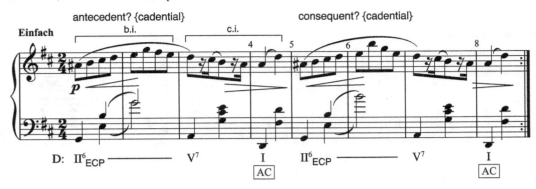

however, open "off-tonic."[30] Such an opening can sometimes give the effect of the theme beginning *in medias res*, especially if the supporting harmonic progression is cadential. Indeed, the use of an opening ECP, though relatively rare in the classical period,[31] is found more regularly in the nineteenth century, particularly with Schumann.[32] Another *Davidsbündler* dance (Ex. 8.7) begins with pre-dominant harmony of an ECP supporting the opening phrase. The melody of the cadence created at the end of that phrase (m. 4) is somewhat odd due to the ascending leap from $\hat{5}$ to $\hat{1}$. It is not clear if we are dealing with an IAC or a PAC, an ambiguity that arises now and then in the Romantic repertoire.[33] When the phrase is repeated, a period form seems to be in the making, except that the cadence at measure 8 is identical to the prior one; only the higher melodic rise to B in measure 6 gives the impression that the second phrase is a kind of "answer" to the first, in the sense of a periodic formation. The incipient antecedent-consequent relationship just identified involves the *contextual* functionality of these two phrases; however, their *intrinsic* functions are cadential, as indicated by the braces surrounding that label.[34]

That Schumann ends the first phrase of this period-like theme with tonic harmony, as opposed to a dominant for an HC, is explainable by the harmonic connection he needs to forge into the beginning of the second phrase, namely a syntactically appropriate progression from tonic (m. 4) to pre-dominant (m. 5);

moving from a cadential dominant to an initiating pre-dominant would rupture the harmonic syntax. Here, by the way, we find an example of the "cadential conundrum" raised in Chapter 5 (sec. 5.5), namely, whether we can even speak of a formal cadence concluding the opening four-measure phrase. For we would have to ask, what unit of form is this cadence actually ending? As discussed, I tend toward affirming a sense of cadence in such a situation, even while recognizing the logical difficulty attendant to such an interpretation.

In Example 8.8, a small binary theme begins by tonicizing the supertonic degree. As the music continues, we realize that the opening $\text{VII}^7/\text{II}$ initiates an ECP, similar to how the previous example begins. Unlike the Schumann, however, Schubert builds a more standard eight-measure period, in that he ends the first phrase with a clear IAC at measure 4 and repeats the phrase to conclude with a PAC at measure 8. Whereas the contextual functions of the two phrases can be understood as antecedent and consequent, respectively, each phrase has an intrinsic cadential function. Notice how in both phrases the opening tune shifts to an inner voice, as two new upper voices (in parallel thirds) enter to create the melody of the cadences.

The second part of the binary begins with a contrasting middle (mm. 9–12) featuring model-sequence technique. The descending-fifths sequence leads to $\text{I}^6$ at measure 13, a harmony well suited to begin a classical ECP to close the binary form. Indeed, Schubert initiates a cadential progressions at this bar, but then continues it with $\text{VII}^7/\text{V}$, the harmony that begins the two ECPs in part 1. As a result, the progression is displaced by one bar compared to the opening of the theme. In order to bring the final tonic in its normal position on the downbeat of measure 16, the preceding dominant does not a get a full bar of its own, but rather is squeezed back onto the final beat of measure 15. Observe how Schubert accentuates this third beat to help draw attention to this "early appearing" dominant. Looking at the melodic line, we see that measures 13–14 seem to bring a second sequence of the model that begins the second part. This reading is problematic, however, because the harmonic content is altered to create the ECP. At the same time, the contour and pitch content of these two bars, especially measure 14, remind us of the opening basic idea, thus imparting a sense of "return" within the overall form, akin

---

Chapter 5, Ex. 5.34b). The first sonata of the set, in G major, begins as usual with a root-position tonic but in a most exaggerated and comical manner.

30. Many of the pieces discussed by Martin concern thematic units that begin off-tonic ("Schumann's Fragment").

31. Beethoven's Op. 31, no. 3, i, just mentioned in note 29, is an obvious precursor of this technique.

32. Schumann's propensity to initiate thematic units with cadential content is also discussed by Peter Smith in connection with the composer's Violin Sonata in D Minor, Op. 121 ("Cadential Content," 36–37).

33. In such cases, I will drop the melodic qualifier (perfect or imperfect) and speak here (and in the next chapter) more simply of an "authentic cadence" (annotated "AC" in the musical example).

34. On the distinction between intrinsic and contextual formal functionality, see Chapter 2, sec. 2.6.

440  Cadence in the Romantic Era

EXAMPLE 8.8. Schubert, Ländler, Op. 171, no. 3, D. 790, mm. 1–16.

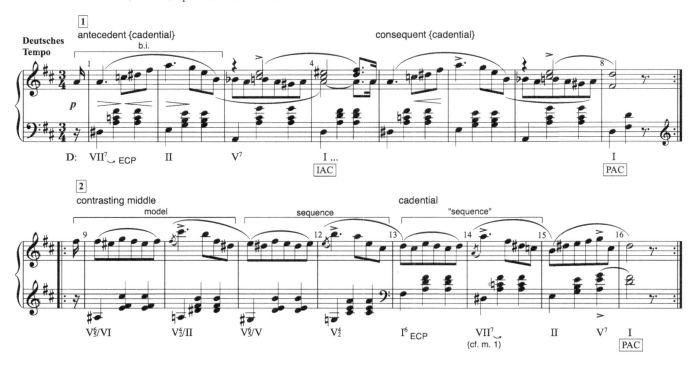

EXAMPLE 8.9. Schubert, String Quartet No. 8 in E-flat, D. 812, iii, mm. 1–16.

to a small ternary. Finally, unlike the phrases of part 1, whose intrinsic and contextual functions conflict, the concluding phrase of part 2 (mm. 13–16) now takes on a uniquely cadential function appropriate to its content and formal placement.

Another passage by Schubert (Ex. 8.9), which constitutes the A section of a minuet, also begins with an ECP, though not off-tonic. Unlike the two previous examples, the conclusion of the progressions (m. 7) does not seem to mark the end of the ongoing formal unit, which instead sees the melody pushing on to 1̂ at the downbeat of measure 8. After all, the theme up to the end of the ECP consists exclusively of a two-bar basic idea that is repeated twice;[35] no contrasting or continuational material appears that could function to create a sense of formal closure at measure 7. When the melody suddenly changes into steady eighth notes, we can identify a contrasting idea to effect a closing PAC for the first thematic unit of the A section. To speak of a cadence at this point, however, we must also recognize another, highly compact, cadential progression starting on the second beat of measure 7, one whose bass line is now taken over by the viola, as the cello drops out after the downbeat of that bar. As a result of the reduced texture, this music also gives the impression of being an embellishment, of sorts, of the rhetorically stronger tonic harmony that marks the end of the ECP at measure 7. In other words, the contrasting material of measures 7–8 gives a mixed message: on the one hand, it functions as structurally significant for creating formal closure; on the other hand, it has the character of an afterthought, in an almost postcadential sense.

As for the formal function of this initial eight-measure unit, it would seem on the surface to be a compound antecedent, one matched a compound consequent beginning at measure 9. The opening unit closes, however, with a PAC, thus projecting an intrinsically consequent function.[36] At the same time, though, the underlying ECP followed by a compact cadence suggests that this contextual antecedent is also intrinsically cadential in function. These complexities thus yield a unit with three different phrase-functional descriptors. (For the remainder of this analysis, I will speak of this unit more simply as an antecedent, thus privileging its contextual function.)

The second thematic unit of the A section (mm. 9–16) begins with the same material as the antecedent, and thus proposes to be a (compound) consequent. But the cadential situation is more complex than expected, because the ECP is changed from being an authentic cadential progression to a half cadential one, thus ending with a dominant on the downbeat of measure 15 (preceded by a conventional V$^6_5$/V). As in the antecedent, this "closing" moment seems formally premature; moreover, an HC is not the expected type of closure for a minuet's A section. As a result, Schubert follows the threefold statements of the basic idea with a contrasting idea, whose harmony could be heard either to extend the dominant (of E-flat) or, as I prefer to hear it, to effect a modulation to the subordinate key of B-flat, closing there with a PAC, the conventional cadence for ending an A section. (Note that this time, the cello participates in this compact, and highly incomplete, cadential progression.) In both units, therefore, the opening ECP seems to be more prominent rhetorically than the compact progressions that actually effect closure. Finally, the complications of cadential expression and formal functionality that emerge in this seemingly innocent minuet are surprising, yet also telling of a significant shift in style from the classical to the early Romantic.

## 8.5. Formal Circularity

In the classical style, themes normally begin with a relatively "characteristic" idea, which, in accord with the powerfully teleological aesthetic of the style, leads to the goal of cadential closure. Part of the broader mechanism for motivating that closure resides in breaking down, and eventually eliminating, this opening material—Schoenberg's "liquidation"—such that all that remains by the end of the theme is a relatively "conventional" cadential idea. In contrast, a newly arising Romantic orientation begins to favor a more circular mode of formal organization, one that manifests itself at various structural levels.[37] At the level of the theme, the sense of formal circularity can be realized when the melodic-motivic material of the opening basic idea, rather than being liquidated, returns to provide the melodic content of the cadential idea itself. Whereas this technique has some precedents in the classical style, it is more frequently encountered in Romantic practice, where, in fact, it occurs in a manner that differs markedly from earlier manifestations of the technique.

Example 8.10 is a case in point. The theme starts off-tonic in C major with a two-measure basic idea that is immediately repeated to make a presentation phrase; the continuation brings one-measure fragments as expected. Rather than further liquidating the material to yield a conventionalized cadential idea, however, Schumann brings back in measures 7–8 the melodic content of the basic idea for an IAC in E-flat (♭III). A repeat of the continuation phrase then modulates further to the minor dominant, using another variant of the basic idea to create a PAC in measure 12.[38]

---

35. Mark Richards terms the resulting thematic structure a "trifold sentence" due to the three statements of the basic idea ("Viennese Classicism and the Sentential Idea: Broadening the Sentence Paradigm," 192–96).

36. In the context of a minuet form, I term this home-key authentic cadence an "early PAC" because it appears prior to where the minuet's A section more properly ends, with another PAC (m. 16); see *CF*, 221, and *ACF*, 614–15.

37. The idea of circular form in the nineteenth century has been discussed by a number of prominent scholars, including Charles Rosen, *The Romantic Generation*, 87–92; Robert P. Morgan, "Circular Form in the Tristan Prelude"; and Stephen Rodgers, *Form, Program, and Metaphor in the Music of Berlioz*. The notion of circular form, however, does not necessarily equate with formal closure, as explained by Anson-Cartwright, who notes that circularity can also involve an "open-endedness" in the ongoing development of melodic-motivic material ("Closure in Tonal Music," 7). In other words, one type of circularity involves something going round and round without any apparent end, whereas another type, a circling back home, can effect a sense of closure by returning to a starting point. This latter notion is the one I am referencing in the following discussion.

38. We find in this example another instance of the I–III–V sequential pattern underlying the entire thematic unit, as discussed earlier in note 25. Unusual, though, is the modal shift from major to minor in the course of the theme.

EXAMPLE 8.10. Schumann, Symphony No. 2 in C, Op. 61, iii, mm. 1–12.

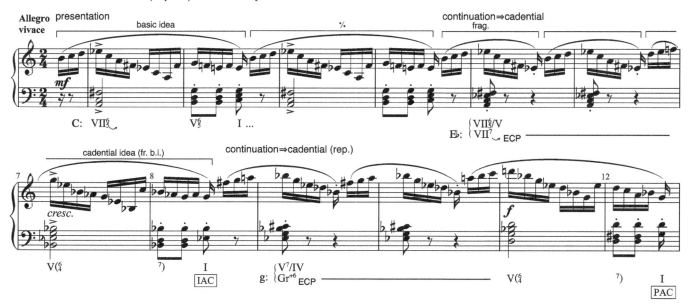

EXAMPLE 8.11. Haydn, Symphony No. 100 in G ("Military"), ii, mm. 29–36.

As mentioned before, there exist classical precedents for this cadential reuse of the opening basic idea, as seen, for instance, in the slow movement from Haydn's Symphony No. 100 (Ex. 8.11), a passage discussed by Meyer.[39] Here, the basic idea itself has a distinctly "cadential" melodic component, one that classical composers used as an ending gesture in several other works.[40] And in an obvious realization of this closing potential, Haydn brings back the idea, lightly varied, to forge the PAC at measure 36.[41] Although the compositional situation here may remind us of Schumann's theme, a significant difference lies in the nature of the melodic material used for both the basic and cadential ideas. With Haydn, the idea is intrinsically cadential, and so it is hardly surprising that he allows the idea eventually to realize its implied formal function. With Schumann, on the contrary, the melodic gesture at the opening of the theme has nothing stereotypically closing about it; in fact, it is a highly individual idea, which, even when reharmonized so as to function cadentially, retains its nonconventional quality. Operative here is the Romantic concern with originality. Whereas classical composers are content to allow their initiating melodic-motivic material to become liquidated in the course of a theme, Romantic composers are more attached to their novel melodic ideas and are thus inclined to retain them for use at the very end of the theme in a manner that promotes a circular design.[42]

---

39. Meyer, *Style and Music*, 26–30. Ex. 8.11 illustrates the A′ section of the main theme, an overall small ternary form (rounded binary version). The basic idea of this section is the same one used to begin the A section at the very opening of the movement.

40. Meyer cites the first movement of the same Haydn symphony (seen earlier in Chapter 2, Ex. 2.26, mm. 38–39), as well as Haydn's String Quartet in B-flat, Op. 64, no. 3, iii, and Mozart's Symphony No. 40 in G Minor, K. 550, iii (Trio) (*Style and Music*, 26–29).

41. Haydn uses the same idea to close the theme's A section with a dominant arrival at m. 7, and he brings the idea back again to confirm the modulation to the dominant region in the middle of the B section, m. 24.

42. The use of a "characteristic" opening gesture as a subsequent cadential idea continues to be found in later nineteenth-century repertories; the first subordinate theme from the opening movement of Tchaikovsky's Pathétique Symphony is exemplary of this practice (cf. mm. 89–91 and 95–97).

EXAMPLE 8.12. Chopin, Etude in A-flat, *Trois nouvelles études*, no. 2, mm. 1–16.

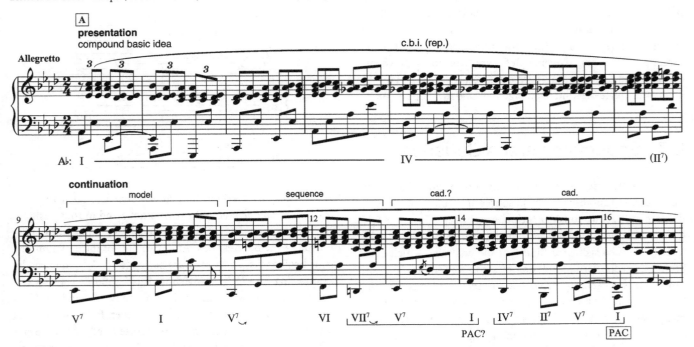

## 8.6. Symmetrical Grouping Structures

One trait typical of the Romantic style, already observed by various commentators, is the tendency within nineteenth-century music in general to emphasize grouping patterns that are uniform and symmetrical. Even more than in the classical style, Romantic compositions tend to be organized by groups that feature powers of two (i.e., 2, 4, 8, 16).[43] Four-measure units are especially prominent in nineteenth-century styles, often to such an extent that each measure can function as a single "beat" of a quadruple hypermeter.[44] Typically in such structures, the cadences closing thematic units occur in the last bar of the final four-measure unit. Indeed, we come to expect that closure will occur at these moments to such an extent that if an idea consisting of cadential material appears prior to the end of a projected four-measure group, the potential closure expressed by that idea seems premature.[45]

Example 8.12 illustrates such a situation, one that presents the kind of ambiguous cadential articulation found now and then in Romantic works. The theme begins with a four-measure compound basic idea that prolongs tonic harmony. (Although we can recognize a clear prolongation of tonic, the local harmonic rhythm, in typical Romantic fashion, reveals a change of harmony—all in root position—on each beat of the 2/4 measure.) When the unit is repeated in the following four bars, now supported by the subdominant (again, with rapidly alternating root-position harmonies), we recognize a compound presentation phrase in the making. The continuation at measure 9 establishes a two-measure model that is sequenced in the following two bars, thus fragmenting the grouping structure. At the end of the sequence in measure 12, a cadential progression begins with the pre-dominant VII$^7$/V and concludes with tonic on the downbeat of measure 14. Chopin then immediately repeats the cadential unit (though with some harmonic variants in the following two measures).[46] In the classical style, such a case of cadential repetition normally sees the initial arrival on tonic (here, m. 14) as the genuine cadence, while the repetition, in the sense of an echo, is heard as postcadential.[47] Here, however, the impression is more that the arrival on I in measure 14 is "premature" in the prevailing phrase rhythm, and that the real cadence appears at measure 16, the end of the final four-measure unit of the theme.[48]

---

43. Among the classical composers, we can even witness an increasing employment of grouping symmetry from Haydn, to Mozart, to Beethoven.

44. Cone, *Musical Form*, 79–80; Schmalfeldt, "Phrase," 325–30. See also Chapter 3, sec. 3.4.1.3.

45. We already have observed something similar in connection with Ex. 8.9, where the downbeats of mm. 7 and 15 seemed like premature conclusions within the prevailing two-measure units.

46. Indeed, we could understand the use of VII$^7$/V built on ♮④ in m. 12 as especially appropriate due to the extended prolongation of the subdominant (built on ♮④) featured in the presentation; the repeat of the progression brings back IV (now with a dissonant seventh), which then moves to a root-position II$^7$ (in Romantic fashion) before heading off to the dominant.

47. See in Chapter 2, sec. 2.8.5.

48. In a detailed study of this etude, Janet Schmalfeldt also locates the PAC at m. 16 ("Towards a Reconciliation of Schenkerian Concepts with Traditional and Recent Theories of Form," 251–53). As well, she highlights Chopin's use of the subdominant as a harmonic support for the repeated compound basic idea (mm. 5–8), which she sees functioning as a pre-dominant to V at the beginning of the continuation. She thus implies

The equivocal cadential expression here largely depends on our stylistic expectation that the theme should occupy a full sixteen bars. In the classical style, a compound sentence frequently enough compresses its continuation phrase, ending the sentence earlier than measure sixteen.[49] But I know of no cases where a classical theme then repeats such a premature cadential idea in a manner to create the kind of ambiguity found in Chopin's etude.[50]

## 8.7. Sequence versus Cadence

The Romantic practice of emphasizing root-position harmonies can give rise to another important source of harmonic and cadential ambiguity. If we consider the pattern shown in Example 8.13, we can observe that the progression can be analyzed as either a circle-of-fifths sequence (line 1 of the analysis), which could project a medial formal function of some sort (typically a continuation) or a cadential progression (line 2), which could bring formal closure.[51] Of course, a specific musical context will normally clarify which type of progression is involved: thus earlier in Example 8.5b, the progression in measures 7–8 arises in circumstances that unequivocally suggest a cadential formal function (analogous to mm. 3–4 in the antecedent phrase). In the classical style especially, composers carefully distinguish between the two progression types. A typical case arises in a passage we examined earlier in Chapter 2 (Ex. 2.6) where the continuation phrase (mm. 48–51) begins with a series of root-position harmonies organized by descending fifths. In its formal context and in its intrinsic content, the harmonies are obviously sequential, which Mozart makes clear by following the sequence with a discrete cadential progression to close the theme.

Among Romantic composers, this practice of separating sequential progressions from cadential ones is not always observed, thus giving rise to uncertainties of cadential articulation. Consider the subordinate theme from the first movement of Schubert's "Unfinished" Symphony (Ex. 8.14a), a melody so familiar to us

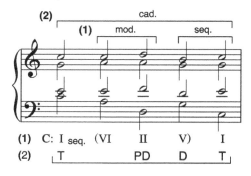

EXAMPLE 8.13. Sequential versus cadential.

that it is easy to overlook how utterly nonclassical it really is. We can first note that all of its harmonies stand in root position, which already suggests that we may encounter ambiguities in the function of the progressions. After two bars of introduction, the theme begins with a two-measure basic idea (I–V$^7$), followed by a contrasting idea (V$^7$–I). Matching this harmonic reversal is a motivic one, as shown by the analysis of motives "a" and "b." (This kind of motivic palindrome is rarely, if ever, found in classical themes.) Though it is tempting to recognize a cadence at the end of this four-measure phrase (m. 47), it is probably better to understand it as concluding without cadential closure, primarily because the harmonic pattern I–V–V–I more typically projects four bars of tonic prolongation rather than a two-measure prolongation followed by a two-measure cadential progression. Here especially, it is hard to hear the harmony in the third bar of the theme (m. 46) as a distinctly cadential dominant (one that differs from the prolongational dominant of the prior bar), all the more so given the commonality of melodic-motivic material in both measures. For these reasons, I prefer to consider this initiating phrase a compound basic idea rather than an antecedent.

At measure 48, the phrase begins to be repeated, but motive "b" of the basic idea is now sequenced up a step (supported by V$^7$/II). The "contrasting idea" (mm. 50–51) then remains a step higher than it was in the first phrase. In order to return to tonic, Schubert brings a varied sequence of the idea back down a step in measures 52–53. Though the rhythm has been modified, the sequential relationship between these two ideas could be seen clearly if Schubert had written an exact sequence, as shown in the second staff of Example 8.14b. What this rewrite also helps to illuminate is how, as shown in staff 1, the rhythmic modification of the sequence makes it sound as though it is beginning with a varied version of motive "a," whose descending fourth leap is now extended into a fifth. Finally, Schubert lets the melodic line end decisively on $\hat{1}$—decisive in that the cello melody does not directly leap down to $\hat{5}$, as earlier in measure 47 (see again Ex. 8.14a). In another sense, however, we do hear this melodic leap, since the downbeat of measure 53 brings an elided repeat of the entire theme, with its opening motive "a."[52] Indeed this elision renders especially prominent a sense of formal circularity.

---

that the entire presentation and first fragment of the continuation (mm. 9–10) is supported by an ECP, thus exemplifying the Romantic tendency to open thematic units with a cadential progression (as discussed earlier in sec. 8.4).

49. *CF*, 69, and *ACF*, 180.

50. In this connection, it is worth comparing Chopin's example to what happens in the scherzo from Beethoven's Symphony No. 7 (see earlier in Chapter 2, Ex. 2.24), in which a sixteen-measure sentence (mm. 3–18) immediately repeats its cadential idea. In this case, the initial cadence occurs in m. 18 (the sixteenth bar of the theme), and so the repetitions can more easily sound postcadential.

51. The confusion of sequence with cadence arises most often with a descending-fifth ("circle of fifths") sequence, since this type usually yields a potentially cadential V–I progression at its end. But other sequence types that can include subordinate harmonies (e.g., ascending step: V/IV–IV–V/V–V . . .) may also bring some local "V–I" progressions. See also the potential ambiguity of progression type discussed in Chapter 5 in connection with Ex. 5.37d and f, 5.69, and 5.70a.

52. The cellos then echo this motive in beats two and three of m. 53ff., but now as an accompanimental figure, not as a genuinely melodic element.

EXAMPLE 8.14A. Schubert, Symphony No. 8 in B Minor ("Unfinished"), i, mm. 42–54.

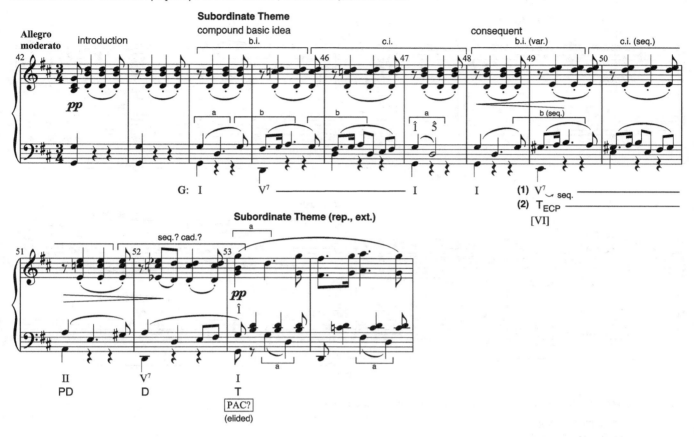

EXAMPLE 8.14B. Schubert, Symphony No. 8 in B Minor ("Unfinished"), i, comparison of sequences: staff 1, mm. 48–53; staff 2, reconstruction.

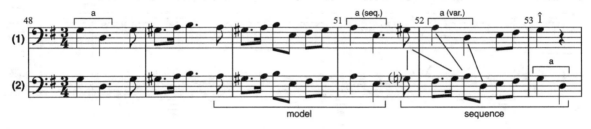

But now we must ask, has the theme actually ended with a cadence? Most listeners will probably answer yes readily enough, but we should nonetheless be sensitive to a formal ambiguity here, for what we would be construing as the cadential idea, measures 52–53, arises as a *sequential* repetition of the contrasting idea of measures 50–51. Because a sequence brings a repetition of something that is already medial in function, it should continue to project the sense of being-in-the-middle and not sound cadential. However, here it seems to do just that, namely, to bring a semblance of closure to the theme. In other words, we can hear the harmonic progression in measures 49–53 as not only sequential (shown in line 1 of the analysis) but also as cadential (line 2), with V⁷/II representing a chromatic alteration of VI, a substitute for the initial cadential tonic.

Given the harmonic and cadential ambiguities seen thus far, it is fascinating to observe some of the implications that Schubert draws from them as the movement proceeds. In the first place, the repeat of the theme in the violins (Ex. 8.14c) leads this time to a complete lack of cadential closure when the music breaks off with the general pause in measure 62. This drastic evaded cadence is unusual in that not only is a final tonic missing at the moment of expected cadential closure, but no event of any kind takes place at that location. In addition, this moment is not followed by a one-more-time repetition, as often occurs with evaded cadences.[53] Instead, an entirely new augmented version of motive "a" returns, set as a dramatic and ominous tutti *fortissimo* outburst.[54]

---

53. Not all classical evaded cadences engage the one-more-time technique, though many do. Yet almost all bring some sounding event (i.e., an "initiating harmony") in place of the cadential arrival. Schubert's evaded cadence is thus most unorthodox from a classical perspective. We will see another such evasion in a later discussion of Ex. 8.23d. For some baroque precedents, see the discussion in Chapter 6, sec. 6.1.4.2, Ex. 6.24 and 6.26.

54. Hugh Macdonald, "Schubert's Volcanic Temper."

EXAMPLE 8.14C. Schubert, Symphony No. 8 in B Minor ("Unfinished"), i, mm. 60–76.

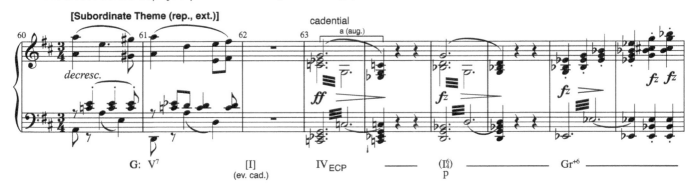

EXAMPLE 8.14D. Schubert, Symphony No. 8 in B Minor ("Unfinished"), i, mm. 274–82.

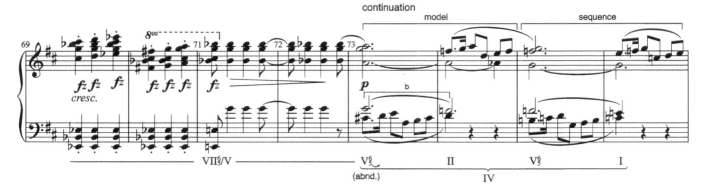

In the recapitulation, Schubert handles this passage somewhat differently (Ex. 8.14d). Here, he brings the music back from D major (the key in which the subordinate theme of the recapitulation is initially set) to the home key of B minor by more fully realizing the sequential possibilities of the contrasting idea as it appears in Example 8.14b, staff 1, and, in so doing, he significantly minimizes the contrasting idea's cadential effect. By the time we hear the general pause at measure 280 (Ex. 8.14d), we are not at all certain that a cadential evasion has even taken place; rather, the music seems more to be interrupted "mid-sequence," with little sense of any cadential function.

Returning to the exposition (Ex. 8.14c), we see that the *fortissimo* outbursts at measures 63–66 propose the beginning of an ECP by means of a prolonged pre-dominant (IV–[I$^6_4$]–Gr$^{+6}$–VII$^6_5$/V); however, the progression rhetorically runs out of steam with the syncopated chords in measures 71–72 and is effectively abandoned when, at measure 73, Schubert brings back motive "b" in an extensive call-and-answer passage, one that more fully realizes another potential for sequence in the contrasting idea, namely that proposed in Example 8.14b, staff 2. Following a decisive cadence at measure 93 (Ex. 8.14e), which ends the highly extended repeat of the subordinate theme, Schubert brings back the opening of the theme,[55] but now in a manner that resolves the ambiguity of sequence and cadence. Like the original version,

---

55. This return of opening subordinate-theme material exemplifies again the Romantic impulse for formal circularity. In the classical style, by contrast, once subordinate-theme ideas are eliminated from the theme, they rarely return, either in the context of the theme group itself or in the subsequent closing section. I will discuss another use of this technique below in connection with Ex. 8.23b, m. 78 and Ex. 8.23d, m. 117.

EXAMPLE 8.14E. Schubert, Symphony No. 8 in B Minor ("Unfinished"), i, mm. 90–100.

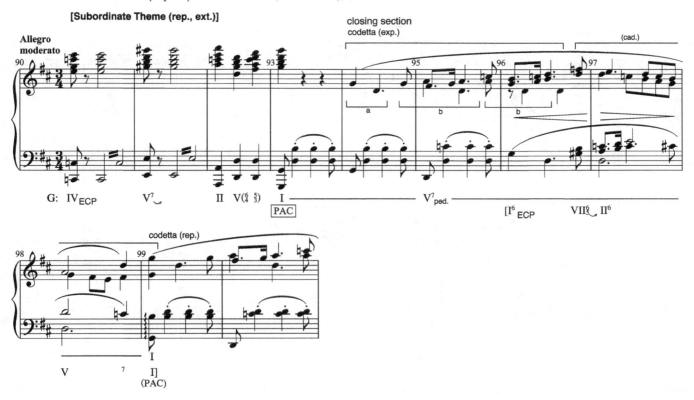

the third measure of the theme (m. 96) repeats the second half of the basic idea (motive "b"), albeit in a non-sequential manner. A completely new idea then appears (mm. 97–99), one that is more genuinely cadential in nature, with nothing sequential in the picture. The only disrupting aspect is the harmonic support, whereby the dominant reached at measure 95 is held as a pedal point until the tonic resolution at measure 99. If Schubert had supported measures 96–99 with a true cadential progression, as shown in the brackets, then we could speak of a PAC at measure 99. The retention of the dominant pedal from measure 95 on, however, blurs a sense of real cadence, thus allowing this passage to function formally more as an expanded codetta of a closing section rather than as a genuine thematic unit (i.e., another subordinate theme).

To conclude this discussion of the "Unfinished" Symphony, we can now observe that a significant source of ambiguity in the subordinate theme arises from Schubert having placed all of the harmonies in root position; as a result, the opening phrase can be heard as either prolongational or cadential, and the second phrase as either sequential or cadential. Various aspects of motivic manipulation contribute to the ambiguous effect as well.[56]

---

56. Subsequent to my published analysis of this piece in William E. Caplin, "Beyond the Classical Cadence: Thematic Closure in Early Romantic Music," 11–14, ex. 14, Steven Vande Moortele has convincingly proposed that the entire subordinate-theme area (mm. 42–104) can be viewed as a large-scale sentence, such that the "theme" in mm. 42–53 functions as an enormous "basic idea," whose repetition in mm. 53–61 forms a presentation, matched by an extensive continuation (mm. 62–93) ("The

## 8.8. Prolongational Closure

The notion of prolongational closure—the use of prolongational progressions to effect a degree of noncadential ending—has been discussed and illustrated in connection with eighteenth-century musical styles.[57] In such cases, prolongational closure normally operates at the subthematic level, not at the very end of a full thematic unit, which is closed by a genuine cadence. In the Romantic style, the use of prolongational closure increases, and some relatively rare, but striking, examples can be found in which full thematic units close noncadentially, usually by means of a bass line that descends stepwise to ①.

Schumann's "Valse noble" from *Carnaval* illustrates well how a self-contained thematic unit ends with prolongational closure (Ex. 8.15a). The movement, starting very much *in medias res*, brings two matching four-measure phrases in a manner that suggests a periodic theme type. Within the broader form of the

---

Subordinate Theme in the First Movement of Schubert's 'Unfinished' Symphony"). As such, Vande Moortele recognizes the sequential nature of the second phrase of this expansive "basic idea" (Ex. 8.14a, mm. 48–53) and thus argues against finding a genuine PAC at m. 53 (and likewise, an evaded cadence at m. 62). To be sure, at the large-scale level of form that Vande Moortele is considering, this potential cadence at m. 53 cannot represent a moment of thematic closure. Yet for those who may still want to hear a PAC at this point, it would be possible to consider it to be one of limited scope. In that way, "we can have our cadence and evade it too"!

57. See Chapter 3, sec. 3.5.1; Chapter 6, sec. 6.3.2; Chapter 7, sec. 7.1.1, 7.1.2, and 7.4.1.

EXAMPLE 8.15. Schumann, "Valse noble," *Carnaval*, Op. 9, no. 4, (a) mm. 1–8; (b) mm. 33–40.

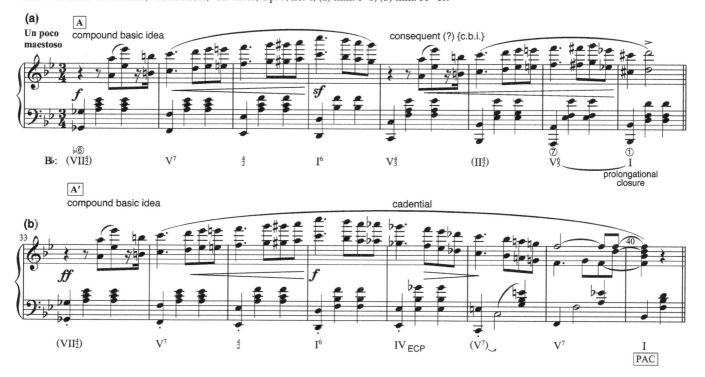

piece as a whole, these opening eight bars constitute the A section of a small ternary. In the classical style, this section would always end cadentially (with a PAC in either the home key or a subordinate key). Here, however, both phrases end prolongationally, the first with $V_2^4$–$I^6$, the second with $V_5^6$–I.[58] To be sure, the norms of the period form are referenced by the first phrase ending in a weaker manner (on an inverted tonic) than the second phrase (on a root-position tonic), yet neither mode of closure is truly cadential. Moreover, the bass line supporting the complete theme is entirely nonclassical, featuring a descending line from ♭⑥ down to ⑦, which resolves up to ① at the very end. Looking closer at the bass line and the harmonic progressions, we might want to discern a certain cadential quality to the opening phrase: the initial emphasis on dominant, which passes through a $^4_2$ to $I^6$, suggests the kind of situation that frequently obtains with an evaded or deceptive cadence.[59] If so, then we would further recognize a complete reversal of standard syntax within the theme, in that a cadential progression would precede a prolongational one, the latter being used to end the thematic unit, the very opposite of what normally occurs.

Following a contrasting middle (B section), the A′ section first brings back the material of the complete A section without any alterations. Schumann, however, obviously not satisfied in allowing the complete movement to close prolongationally, begins to sound the theme again (Ex. 8.15b), this time with a *fortissimo* dynamic. He then rewrites the harmonic support for the final phrase to make a genuine cadential progression (whose constituent harmonies, not surprisingly, are all set in root position), thus concluding the movement as a whole with a real cadence.[60] We see that, unlike classical practice, prolongational closure in the Romantic style may take place at the level of the simple theme (the eight-measure A section), but the final closure of broader formal units still requires an authentic cadence.

Every rule has its exception, of course, and we can find in Mendelssohn's very first *Songs without Words* the rare case of a complete piece, albeit a short one, ending with prolongational closure (Ex. 8.16). Built as a small ternary, the song begins with a brief thematic introduction (not shown), which prepares the way for an opening antecedent phrase of the A section. The phrase closes as expected with a regular HC (at m. 6), and the basic idea returns in measures 7–8 to propose a matching consequent, one that undergoes a pronounced extension.[61] Note that the basic idea features a relatively quick harmonic rhythm along with an internal model-sequence structure, both traits being associated with the Romantic style. Note as well that the sequence in measure 8 shifts the music into the subordinate key of B (HK: V). In the antecedent (not shown), this sequence is followed by an immediate return to the home key for the HC.

---

58. In that the first four-measure phrase is a compound basic idea, which often concludes with prolongational closure, I am not specifically annotating that mode of phrase ending.

59. Countering this argument, however, is the presence of the $VII^4_2$ at the start of the theme, a harmony that would never be part of a legitimate cadential dominant.

60. The cadence at m. 40 is a PAC because the melody, lying below the "covering tone" F, closes on B♭ (1̂).

61. Extending the consequent of a periodic formation is particularly characteristic of Mendelssohn's compositional style.

EXAMPLE 8.16. Mendelssohn, *Songs without Words*, Op. 19, no. 1, mm. 6–15.

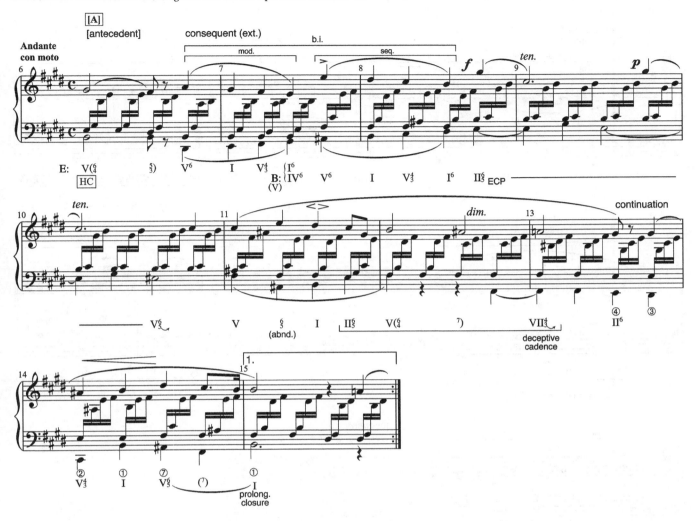

In the consequent, however, Mendelssohn keeps the music in the subordinate key and introduces in measures 9–10 cadential predominants, II⁶–V⁶₅/V, that likely signal the onset of an ECP, especially given the sudden slowing of the melodic and harmonic rhythm in these bars. The progression is abandoned, however, when the dominant at measure 11 shifts to V⁶₅. Quickly thereafter, a second cadential progression, now with a lightly expanded dominant, proposes closure for the downbeat of measure 13. Again, the promised cadence fails to be realized, this time when the leading tone moves down a half step, supported by VII⁶₅/II, thus resulting in a most unusual deceptive cadence.[62] Going forward, the music brings a new continuation, which sees the bass line push down from ④ to ⑦ (with an octave adjustment from ② to ①). The V⁷–I progression leading into measure 15 might seem like a PAC to close the A section, but the root-position dominant is immediately preceded by its inverted V⁶₅, thus rendering the dominant noncadential. Except for the II⁶ in the middle of measure 13, nothing about the subsequent harmonies leading up to this dominant implies a cadence; rather, the progression is fully prolongational, such that the root-position dominant embellishes its prior first-inversion form. The resolution to the final tonic is thus a case of prolongational closure, though the immediately preceding V in root position alludes to a genuine cadence.

Seeing as Mendelssohn strongly implied a pending PAC to complete the preceding abandonment and deception, it is important to ask why he eventually concludes the section without a genuine cadence. The answer may be found in the relation of the bass line to the melody throughout the section, where we can observe a general pattern of contrary motion and voice-exchange, as seen most obviously within the basic idea itself (mm. 7–8). Toward the end of the section, Mendelssohn emphasizes again this contrary motion, which may explain why the dominant in measure 14 appears in both second and first inversions prior to its being finally placed in root position at the end of the bar. We could also understand this reference to the contrary motion from the start of the theme as a subtle expression of formal circularity.

Following a substantial contrasting middle, the A′ section of the song returns and brings the same prolongational closure found at

---

62. The melodic situation is reminiscent of the "final" deceptive cadence we observed in J. S. Bach's first prelude of the *WTC*, where the cadential dominant resolves to V⁷/IV; see Chapter 6, sec. 6.1.4.1, and Ex. 6.19a.

EXAMPLE 8.17. Chopin, Mazurka in F-sharp Minor, Op. 6, no. 1, (a) mm. 1–16; (b) reconstruction of mm. 7–11 (from Rothstein, *Phrase Rhythm*, Ex. 2.23).

the end of the A section, but now in the home key (mm. 43–44, not shown). The work as a whole thus ends prolongationally, a practice that does not become normative until the second half of the nineteenth century, as will be discussed in the following chapter.[63]

## 8.9. Lack of Formal Closure

A more radical mode of "ending" arises when an ongoing unit fails to project any intrinsic sense of closure, yet we realize that the unit is "finished" when the onset of a subsequent unit initiates a new set of formal processes. Such situations are rare in eighteenth-century works and are hardly common in the Romantic style. Some interesting examples, however, do arise, thus revealing the breakdown of classical means of formal closure.

A casual hearing of the opening theme of Chopin's Mazurka in F-sharp Minor (Ex. 8.17a) suggests that it comprises a sixteen-measure compound period, whose compound antecedent forms an eight-measure sentence.[64] The return of the initial basic idea at measure 9 quite clearly signals the onset of the compound consequent. If we look more closely, though, we must question how the antecedent actually ends. Following classical norms, the unit would typically close with an HC in measure 8.[65] Instead, the

---

63. For more on the use of prolongational closure in Romantic repertories, see Horton, "Formal Type," 103–10, and Stephen Rodgers and Tyler Osborne, "Prolongational Closure in the Lieder of Fanny Hensel."

64. The opening four-measure unit of this sentence sees a statement of the basic idea followed by its sequential repetition up a third, the opening gesture of Chopin's "signature progression" (I–III–V–I), as Schmalfeldt describes it (see note 25).

65. Though the weak IAC might seem to be a candidate for closing a *compound* antecedent (just as it is for a simple four-measure antecedent), classical composers rarely employ such an "independent" IAC for that

harmony preceding the return of the basic idea is a pre-dominant II$_3^4$, which does not mark the conclusion of any cadence type. Not only does this formal unit not end with a cadence, but we also cannot speak of any prolongational closure at this point, since the harmony appears as a member of a broad descending-fifths sequential progression begun at measure 5,[66] one that features the kind of "slithery chromaticism" that is so characteristic of Chopin's style. Little in the intrinsic musical content projects any sense of closure whatsoever for this "antecedent."[67] We only know that it ends because the consequent so obviously begins.

Of course, what helps motivate these formal oddities is the way in which the opening basic idea is harmonized: namely with a prominent V$^7$–I prolongational progression.[68] Thus to set up the formal return at measure 9, Chopin lets the antecedent conclude on the pre-dominant II$_3^4$, which connects easily with the initiating dominant to tonic motion of the basic idea.[69] As a result, the harmonic processes of the antecedent end with the tonic of measure 10, thus overlapping with the beginning of the consequent. With this observation in mind, we can further ask whether this harmonic closure results in formal closure as well, in the sense of a cadential elision. To be sure, the root-position progression of dominant to tonic in measures 9–10, combined with the preceding pre-dominant, bring the requisite harmonic conditions for an authentic cadence. But the melodic-motivic content of these bars, with their ascending melodic motion ($\hat{1}$–$\hat{2}$–$\hat{3}$) and "characteristic" diversity of rhythmic values, has none of the elements associated with cadential closure. In other words, if we consider the theme to last from measures 1–10, it is not clear that we would hear the return of the basic idea as a functional cadence, in the sense of the formal circularity observed in the Schumann Symphony (Ex. 8.10). Another disadvantage of hearing a cadence at measure 10 would be the resulting overlap of antecedent and consequent units, a distinctly nonclassical grouping for periodic structures.[70] As well, a ten-measure antecedent matching an eight-measure consequent would yield an unusual asymmetry that is also atypical of this theme type. In the end, it is more productive to speak of a harmonic sequence (descending-fifths) reaching its conclusion at measure 10, than to invoke any form of cadential closure at that same moment.

At this point, we might consider an option advanced by William Rothstein, who wants to hear an HC ending the antecedent on the downbeat of measure 9.[71] His recomposed version, shown in Example 8.17b (with my analytical annotations), eliminates the formal overlap of Chopin's original. Presumably to make the dominant closing the antecedent more effective as a goal, Rothstein even rewrites this harmony as a consonant triad. Though this interpretation has merit, we should observe that the final dominant still emerges out of an ongoing sequential process, as supported all the more by the melodic line, which continues the same motivic content of the sequence. In other words, no distinct cadential idea is specifically associated with this proposed HC.

Rothstein, though, perhaps overlooks one detail that points to the pre-dominant of measure 8 as the real "ending" of the phrase, namely, the rhythmic alteration on the second beat of that bar from an expected dotted figure to even eighth notes. This subtle change to what is otherwise a sequential repetition helps differentiate measure 8 as a possible ending, even if it is one that cannot be construed as either cadential or prolongational. This rhythmic alteration not only serves the specific formal purpose just described, but also helps prepare for the double-eighth-note configuration that appears in the returning basic idea on the second beat of measure 9. Moreover, the use of two eighth notes in place of a dotted eighth and sixteenth (as in the prior sequential measures) effects a slight sense of rhythmic deceleration that further helps project measure 8 as a potential ending moment. Indeed, a performance by Arthur Rubenstein highlights the formal arrival there by effecting a noticeable *ritardando* within the bar.[72]

Before leaving this example, let us consider the harmonic and formal organization of the compound consequent (see again Ex. 8.17a). Following a restatement of the opening "presentation" phrase, Chopin writes a completely different continuation (mm. 13–16), one that still tonicizes the III region (achieved in the sequence of the basic idea) via an added-sixth neighboring harmony (IV$^{a6}$). The one-bar fragment in measure 13 is repeated in the following bar and then seemingly repeated again in measure 15; but this third appearance of the fragment brings a subtle, yet significant, change, one that has an effect on the sense of cadence. In measures 13–14, the subdominant harmony (of III) is made minor through the F♮ in the alto voice. At measure 15, though, the F♯ is restored in that voice, thus changing the harmonic interpretation from IV$^{a6}$/III to the pre-dominant II$_3^4$ for the final

---

formal purpose (see Chapter 3, sec. 3.2.2.3); neither have I encountered an unequivocal case in the nineteenth-century repertory.

66. More precisely, we could speak of the sequential progression as actually beginning in mm. 3–4 with the roots E and A and then continuing into the opening of the consequent with the roots D♯ and G♯. For the purposes of this discussion, however, I am focusing specifically on the sequential segment supporting the antecedent's continuation phrase (mm. 5–8) and the opening of the compound consequent (mm. 9–10).

67. Schmalfeldt also observes the lack of any cadential ending for this unit (*Process of Becoming*, 198).

68. We might be tempted to recognize an off-tonic opening here, but in fact, the melodic F♯ on the upbeat to measure 1 implies a tonic setting, one that may be easily overlooked given the lack of full chordal texture. Schmalfeldt's analysis, for example, does not indicate tonic harmony at the upbeat of the theme, in that she begins her detailed harmonic analysis only with the V$^7$ on the downbeat of m. 1.

69. In this harmonic context, the upbeat F♯ now assimilates to the pre-dominant as its seventh. As we will see in the following chapter, "ending" a formal unit with pre-dominant harmony becomes a more ready option in later nineteenth-century practice, where we can even speak of a *pre-dominant arrival* (akin to a dominant arrival); see sec. 9.2. A sense of ending of any kind, however, is barely expressed in the present example.

70. See *CF*, 51, and *ACF*, 86–87.

71. Rothstein, *Phrase Rhythm*, 46–48, Ex. 2.23.

72. RCA Red Seal 09026 63050-2, compact disk.

EXAMPLE 8.18. Chopin, Mazurka in G Minor, Op. 67, no. 2, mm. 1–16.

cadential progression. This shift from F♮ to F♯ not only affects the harmony, but also the formal meaning, since the third statement of the fragment now sounds sufficiently "different" to function, along with the material of measure 16, as the cadential idea closing the consequent (and the theme as a whole). Finally, we might be tempted to look for an initial tonic (stage 1) of the cadential progression and consider that the III harmony prolonged in measures 12–14 is a functional substitute for a more normative $I^6$.

Let us now consider another Chopin mazurka (Ex. 8.18) and compare its modes of closure, or non-closure as the case may be, to what we have just seen in the previous mazurka. Like that one, we easily recognize an overall compound period, a sentential structure for the constituent antecedent and consequent units, and an ascending-third sequence of the basic idea. Also like the foregoing piece, the opening basic idea is supported by $V^7$–I. So it is not surprising to find the antecedent ending with IV as a predominant to $V^6_5$, which supports the basic idea's return. An HC to end the antecedent, however, is nowhere in sight (nor is there any trace of an IAC, an even less likely option; see note 65).

With these similarities to the prior mazurka in mind, we can turn to some interesting differences in harmony, motive, and formal function exhibited by the G-Minor Mazurka. In the first place, the music following the "presentation" does not immediately bring any continuational characteristics (fragmentation, harmonic acceleration, etc.). Instead, a varied version of the basic idea returns in measures 5–6 (in the sense of a consequent phrase), supported, as originally, with a $V^7$–I progression.[73]

In light of their root positions, we might wonder whether these harmonies create an IAC, whose quick melodic descent from $\hat{3}$ to $\hat{1}$ produces an overhang. Sounding the material of the basic idea a third time, however, renders this idea insufficiently different to function cadentially. Moreover, the grouping norms of this dance genre generate implications for closure at the end of four-measure groups, so a cadence on the downbeat of measure 6 would seem premature. Instead, the appearance of IV on the last beat of measure 6 could have led to a cadential dominant in measure 7 to effect an independent IAC in the following bar.

The subdominant, however, returns to tonic, a move that raises the prospect of a plagal cadence to end the antecedent. From a classical perspective, such a view would normally be rejected out of hand. But for the Romantic style, the option has some validity.[74] If we were to recognize a plagal cadence, presumably it would occur in connection with the first IV–I progression at measure 7; after all, what follows in the next bar is an exact repetition. If the context were one of an authentic cadence, we would normally think that the second iteration of the cadential idea was functioning postcadentially. Yet the idea of perceiving a cadence in measure 7 contravenes the general norms of grouping structure that we already have discussed. Some other reasons, moreover, lead us to be skeptical of hearing a cadence to close the antecedent. Note that in relation to the threefold statements of the basic idea, measures 7–8 effect fragmentation into one-measure units and a harmonic acceleration that would normally occur directly following the presentation (thus justifying the label "cointinuation" for mm. 5–8). In addition, the harmonic and accompanimental syncopations are destabilizing elements that inhibit a sense of closure. In short,

---

73. The absence of a bass articulation on the downbeat of m. 5 is a wonderful touch but not easily explainable. Perhaps this rhythmic gap helps to prepare the upcoming metrical disruption by weakening the downbeat of m. 5 in anticipation of the even weaker articulations on the downbeats of mm. 7 and 8.

74. The following chapter on music in the mid- to late nineteenth century addresses the issue of plagal cadence, and some examples from the Romantic era are also brought forward at that time.

the music offers little reason to believe that any kind of cadence is operative here, let alone a plagal cadence. Like the earlier mazurka in Example 8.17, the compound antecedent "ends" without any concluding formal function.

Is there any other way of understanding the prominent IV–I progressions at the end of the antecedent? Here, Schmalfeldt points the way when she observes that in measures 5–6, "the composer simply cycles back to his opening idea and extends its tonic with a repeated plagal progression whose effect is postcadential."[75] In other words, she is asking us to accept the idea that measures 5–6 express something cadential (even if not providing a genuine cadence) such that subsequent codetta-like ideas arise from the plagal moves of IV to I.

Let us now turn to the consequent of this compound period and compare it to the antecedent. We have already noted that the opening dominant in measure 9 is inverted; as a result, measures 9–10 cannot project cadential function, and so we cannot recognize a formal overlap of the kind that Rothstein identified for the previous mazurka. A more significant change involves the manner in which the consequent ends. For unlike the antecedent, the subdominant on the third beat of measure 14 leads not to plagal motions, but rather serves as the pre-dominant of an authentic cadential progression (the rolled chord and *forte* dynamic obviously help to signal this harmony's change in function). In the ensuing cadence, the melodic line ends with the same $\hat{3}$–$\hat{1}$ descent that we observe in the "cadence-like" idea of measures 5–6, thus reinforcing our sense that it had cadential possibilities all along. Indeed, Chopin alters the similar idea in measure 14 by letting $\hat{3}$ leap down to $\hat{1}$, thus "saving" the scalar descent for the final cadence.

This detailed discussion of the G-Minor Mazurka has revealed that its opening theme, despite its external similarities to a classical compound period, is structured in ways that significantly depart from classical norms. We have discussed the potential for the third restatement of the basic idea to suggest cadential function and the implications of that suggestion for what emerges thereafter. We have also seen that the antecedent, though suggesting the possibility of closing with a plagal cadence, is better understood to end without any formal closure whatsoever.

## 8.10. Cadential Deviations

The four basic types of cadential deviation—deceptive, evaded, and abandoned for the authentic cadence, along with dominant arrival for the half cadence—normally operate in the Romantic era in the same way that they do in the classical style. Now and then, however, we encounter deviations that have little precedent in the earlier practice. The following discussion will treat some nonclassical deceptive and evaded cadences along with some dominant arrivals. I have not yet uncovered cases in the Romantic style of abandoned cadences (or abandoned progressions) that work differently from their classical predecessors.[76]

### 8.10.1. Deceptive Cadence

Two songs by Robert Schumann feature prominent deceptive cadences that, rather than behaving as way stations, as is usually the case, seem instead to be the markers of ultimate formal closure.[77]

#### 8.10.1.1. "Mondnacht"

The first song, "Mondnacht," from *Liederkreis*, Op. 39 (Ex. 8.19), has generated significant analytical discussion, especially by Schmalfeldt (who cites other studies as well), and I largely concur with her harmonic and formal analysis.[78] In the final chapter of her *Process of Becoming*, which she titles "Coming Home," she recognizes that at the end of "Mondnacht," the unit sounding in measures 56–59, which twice earlier in the song had closed with dominant harmony, now proposes to end with a PAC on the words "nach Haus" ("[to] home").[79] But the cadential progression breaks from the root-position dominant when the bass pushes down for a $V^4_2$, which resolves to $V^6_5/IV$, as a substitute for $I^6$.[80] Since that final harmony supports what is clearly the melodic goal ($\hat{1}$), we can speak of a deceptive cadence here.[81] Such a deviation typically functions as a way station, followed then by a matching PAC, which would bring full closure to the ongoing thematic unit (in this case, the complete song). But after resolving the secondary dominant, Schumann lets the subdominant of measure 60 move directly to tonic in the following bar. No further moment in the song fulfills a sense of authentic cadential closure, for the two-measure idea in measures 61–62 is readily heard as a codetta, part of a longer closing section, which lasts to the final bar of the song (not shown).

How, then, does the song formally end? A number of perspectives present themselves. The first (annotated as option 1) attends to the vocal part reaching its textual and melodic goal at measure 59. Here, the deceptive cadence functions

---

75. Schmalfeldt, *Process of Becoming*, 200.

76. On the role of extensive cadential deviations in Schumann's Violin Sonata in A Minor, Op. 105, see Smith, "Cadential Content," 42–47.

77. On way-station deceptive cadences, see Chapter 4, sec. 4.1.2.1.

78. Schmalfeldt, *Process of Becoming*, 230–36, Ex. 9.1.

79. Her translation of the final line "Als flöge sie nach Haus" as "as if it were flying home" does not include the preposition "nach" ("to"), which is unnecessary in English.

80. Just where the cadential progression starts is not entirely clear. Perhaps the simplest view, shown in my analysis, finds the progression beginning on the second beat of m. 58 with a cadential six-four. Alternatively, we could see that harmony appearing already at the upbeat to that measure, but this reading would endorse an odd syncopation of the harmony across the bar line.

81. Schmalfeldt recognizes an "evaded cadence," presumably of the "deceptive type," as she termed it in an earlier study ("Cadential Processes," 14, and Table 1).

EXAMPLE 8.19. Schumann, "Mondnacht," *Liederkreis*, Op. 39, no. 5, mm. 56–63.

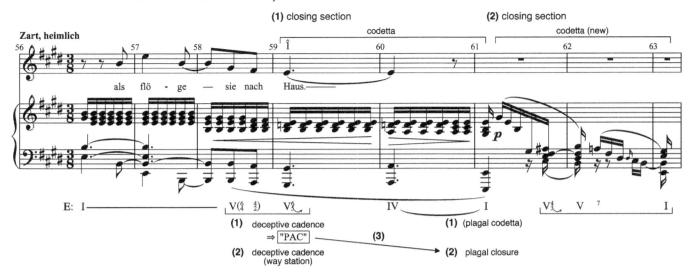

not as a way station, but rather (and retrospectively) as a "final" deceptive cadence, one that stands in for a PAC. This deceptive cadence⇒"PAC" thus emerges as the only authentic cadence of the song. The music then moves directly into a postcadential area, consisting at first of a plagal progression (IV–I) using the prevailing accompanimental pattern. As a result, it would make sense to speak here of a "plagal codetta" (and not a plagal cadence). What follows is a new codetta (mm. 61–62) with a change of texture.[82] The situation is thus strikingly similar to procedures used by both J. S. Bach and Beethoven, in which an anticipated final cadence fails to be realized, typically by replacing the expected tonic with V⁷/IV, after which no subsequent cadence appears.[83]

A second perspective (annotated as option 2) places greater structural weight on the plagal progression leading into measure 61. Here, the deceptive cadence is, in fact, heard as a way station. When a genuine authentic cadence fails to appear, we may be tempted to recognize in its place a "plagal cadence." In this view, the music of measures 59–61 is not postcadential but is rather a genuine part of the song's thematic structure, and so this view sees the closing section arising first at measure 61. To speak of a "cadence" at this measure, however, is problematic, as I have discussed on earlier occasions in this study.[84] Indeed, I develop in the following chapter (sec. 9.3) the idea that such a plagal articulation is not a genuine cadence type in its own right, but rather is a species of prolongational closure. I thus advocate using the term *plagal closure* in reference to cases where a plagal progression appears to function as the principal mode of ending a given thematic unit (hence my use of this term in the annotations at m. 61 as option 2).[85]

A third perspective recognizes that the vocal line and the accompanimental piano part diverge at the close of the song to project two, quasi-independent, modes of ending: the "final deceptive cadence" for the voice and plagal closure for the accompaniment (see the arrow, indicated as option 3). Such a view is consonant with what happens in many other songs by Schumann, in which the vocal goal and accompanimental goal occur at separate moments in time. What is attractive in this interpretation, of course, is that it allows us to assert as valid aspects of both the first and second options of closure without having to choose between the two.[86]

Finally, as a fourth perspective, we could reject the previous three viewpoints and hold that neither the deceptive cadence at measure 59 nor the plagal progression at measure 61 creates genuine thematic closure, thus leaving the song formally incomplete. By denying any formal conclusion for the work, this perspective aligns with the aesthetic category of the "Romantic fragment," a prevalent view of Schumann's miniatures promoted by Charles Rosen and many others.[87]

---

82. The music of this "new "codetta is a version of the song's thematic introduction, which itself is then used as a postcadential standing on the dominant following the HCs of strophes 1 and 2. Thus by the time we hear the version in mm. 61–62, we are fully primed to understand it as a framing, "after-the-end" function.

83. For cases by Bach, see Chapter 6, sec. 6.1.4.1, and Ex. 6.19–6.22; for Beethoven, see Chapter 3 and the discussion of Ex. 3.174.

84. See Chapter 2, sec. 2.3.1.3; Chapter 3, sec. 3.5.2; and Chapter 6, sec. 6.3.3.

85. The slur connecting the IV and I of mm. 60–61 indicates that the plagal closure is a subcategory of prolongational closure.

86. In a study on cadence and closure in the classical style, Richards introduces the idea of a "separated" cadence, one where the bass and melody reach their goals at different points in time ("Closure in Classical Themes," 35–42). Richards develops his idea in connection with classical works (most esp. with Beethoven's "Tempest" sonata), and in a response to his article, I was skeptical whether the idea was all that applicable in these cases ("William Caplin Responds," 72). In light of the modes of closure associated with the dec. cad.⇒PAC seen in Bach and Schumann (as well as one case in Beethoven, Ex. 3.174), the notion of multiple time points of cadential arrival (under conditions of retrospective reinterpretation) perhaps has a greater application than I originally thought.

87. Rosen, *Romantic Generation*, chap. 2. For additional references to the idea, see Martin, "Schumann's Fragment," 85, note 2.

At this point, it is worth speculating on how the foregoing analyses of the purely musical forces within the song might relate to various hermeneutic readings of the music in relation to the text. Schmalfeldt's interpretation, for one, is actually quite subtle. On the one hand, her analytical annotations of the passage identify only one moment of "cadential" articulation for the end of the song, the deceptive cadence at measure 59 (recalling that she calls it an evaded cadence); moreover, she speaks of the following IV–I motion as a "plagal progression," not a plagal "cadence" and omits any symbol for cadence on the downbeat of measure 61.[88] On the other hand, she focuses her understanding of "nach Haus," not in connection with the failed cadence at measure 59, but rather in relation to the harmonic processes that achieve the actual *tonic* at measure 61, thus suggesting that only there is the attainment of "home" fully accomplished:

> There is something about moving *beyond* the goal of the home tonic [proposed at m. 59], only then to settle upon it [at m. 61], that seems to make this arrival all the more powerful, satisfying, and transcendental. Schumann's coda confirms that, even if this is just a dream, the soul has arrived at the very place toward which it strove.[89]

Her view perhaps falls within the third perspective offered above, namely that both measure 59 and measure 61 are markers of closure. But rather than framing this perspective as vocal closure versus accompanimental closure, she seems to position her views in relation to what might be called the "syntactical" closure at measure 59, as something cadential, even if failed, versus the "semantic" closure of measure 61, as reflecting her understanding of what the poem means by "coming home."

David Ferris offers an alternative interpretation (one against which Schmalfeldt reacts). He finds an "open ending" to the song, suggesting that the soul's flight is elusive, unreal, and transitory.[90] Ferris's reading seems more in line with the fourth perspective, whereby the failure to bring any real closure suggests that Schumann is responding especially to the subjunctive mode of the text "Als flöge" (*as if* flying), such that the attainment of home is illusory. And so there remains no closure, with the plagal progression functioning as a postcadential moment, an "after-the-end" to no real end, an especially ironic turn of events.

### 8.10.1.2. "Waldesgespräch"

A second song in Schumann's Op. 39 set, "Waldesgespräch," also brings a deceptive cadence associated with reaching home (*Heim*) (Ex. 8.20). Eichendorff's poem consists of four stanzas, which Schumann sets with four thematic sections, each sentential in structure. On the basis of their melodic-motivic content, the four units could be labeled X1–Y1–X2–Y2 (following Schachter's analysis of the song).[91] Such a combined letter-number scheme, however, does not clarify the formal functions of these units. In one view, we might think that X1–Y1 together constitutes the first half of the song, and the varied repeat (X2–Y2) the second half, thus yielding an overall binary structure (this being Schachter's view). Alternatively, the X1–Y1–X2 pattern might be seen as a ternary structure, with Y2 functioning as a kind of coda. In fact, Schumann's setting is probably best viewed as a small ternary (A–B–A′), but the function of the final Y2 is more complex than a coda, as an examination of the song's tonal and cadential articulations reveals.

X1 promises to close at measure 15 (Ex. 8.20a) with a PAC in the home key of E major. As Schachter observes, a deceptive cadence ensues instead, whose replacement harmony, ♭VI, elides with the opening of the second section (Y1).[92] This section begins in C major (HK: ♭VI) with a thematic introduction to a new compound basic idea (mm. 17–20), whose repetition (not shown) makes up a compound presentation; a sequential continuation leads to an HC to close the section in the home key (Ex. 8.20b, m. 32). If the first unit (X1) had concluded with a PAC, it could have well functioned as an A section of a small ternary, with Y1 being heard as a contrasting middle (B section), an interpretation that makes particular sense when the opening of X1 returns at measure 33 (as X2) to constitute the ternary reprise (A′ section). Somewhat complicating this view is the sense that the Y1 unit, with its own thematic introduction and prominent initiating function (the compound presentation), sounds like an "alternative A section." We will see the ramifications of this perspective playing out later in the song.

Within this small ternary view of the form, what then is the role of the deceptive cadence at measure 15? At first it might seem to function as a way station, but when the music carries on, leading eventually to an HC to end the B section (Ex. 8.20b), that way-station status is denied, for a matching PAC is nowhere in sight. Unlike what happens in comparable situations in the classical style, however, the music that follows the deceptive cadence brings an entirely new formal section, not something that seems to continue the thematic process interrupted by the deceptive cadence. Consequently, the A section is left without a definitive formal (or tonal) closure, a significant departure from the norms of a classical small ternary.

---

88. Schmalfeldt, *Process of Becoming*, 235, and Ex. 9.1.

89. Schmalfeldt, *Process of Becoming*, 235.

90. David Ferris, *Schumann's Eichendorff Liederkreis and the Genre of the Romantic Cycle*, 145–47.

91. Schachter, "*Che Inganno!*," 287–88. Schachter actually speaks of A1–B1–A2–B 2, but I am using X and Y so as not to interfere with my own small-ternary interpretation employing the letters A, B, and A′.

92. Schachter, "*Che Inganno!*," 287–88. The cadential progression would seem to begin with the cadential six-four of m. 14. That this harmony is preceded by V$^7$ in m. 13 is odd, but this dominant is actually the final link of a descending-fifths sequence (one that begins prior to the onset of the example). If the tenor voice in m. 13 had been placed in the bass, then the resulting V$^4_2$ (see bracketed analysis) would have led to a I$^6$ at m. 14 to initiate a more conventional cadential progression, one clearly differentiated from the preceding sequential harmonies.

EXAMPLE 8.20 A-B. Schumann, "Waldegespräch," *Liederkreis*, Op. 39, no. 3, (a) mm. 11–20; (b) mm. 30–36.

Let us now consider what happens in the rest of the song, especially the manner in which it closes. When bringing back the music of the A section in A′, Schumann no longer writes a passage that implies PAC closure; rather, he forges a completely different continuation phrase, one that ends with a phrygian HC in measures 43–44 (Ex. 8.20c). Thereafter, the music of the B section returns, now remaining in the home key. Seeing as A′ only received half cadential closure, the music that follows (Y2), set entirely in E major, no longer sounds like a contrasting middle, nor does it represent a coda (seeing as A′ has not yet closed). Rather, Y2 sounds, even more so than earlier, like an "alternative" section, in this case, an alternative A′. When this music eventually closes with a PAC at measure 64 (Ex. 8.20d), we hear how the composer has united the third and fourth units of the song (X2 and Y2) into an all-encompassing, two-part, A′ section, in a manner that is entirely different from the first and second units (X1 and Y1), which have their own distinct formal functions (as the A and B sections of the small ternary). Of course, this notion of an alternative A′ (or even an alternative A, for that matter) has no precedent in classical practice. Yet with this idea of alternative sections, we can see that Schachter's view of a binary structure re-emerges as a valid option, namely A–altA/A′–altA′, a formal plan that is also entirely nonclassical. In the end, my preference is for the ternary view, because Y1 seems sufficiently contrasting to count as a B

EXAMPLE 8.20C–D. Schumann, "Waldegespräch," *Liederkreis*, Op. 39, no. 3, (c) mm. 40–48; (d) mm. 59–65.

section (though a very unusual one) and because it ends with an HC, a cadence type inappropriate for an "alternative" A. Such a view of the overall form, however, must see the deceptive cadence functioning not as a way station, but as a "representative," a stand-in, so to speak, for a more normal PAC, which is required to end an A section. The form can therefore be schematized as follows: A (= X1), "ending" with a dec. cad; B (= Y1), ending with an HC; A′ (= X2 + Y2), ending with an HC, then with a PAC.

Before concluding this analysis, I want to comment on an additional detail. Though the song as whole ends with a PAC, this moment is preceded by another deceptive cadence at measure 61; indeed, this one has a similar morphology to the one ending "Mondnacht" (cf. Ex. 8.19, mm. 58–59). In "Waldegespräch," the bass line passes down from the cadential ⑤ through ④ ($V_2^4$) and onto $VII^6_5/II$, an unusual substitute for $I^6$).[93] This way-station cadence, unlike the deceptive cadence ending the A section (Ex. 8.20a, m. 15), is conventionally matched with a PAC three bars later.

### 8.10.2. Evaded Cadence

Evaded cadences of the type found so readily in the classical style, especially when accompanied by the one-more-time technique,

---

93. This diminished-seventh harmony, however, does not resolve to II as expected, but is reinterpreted as a common-tone diminished seventh, resolving to $V_3^4$ on the downbeat of m. 62. The final cadential progression follows in the pick-up to the next bar.

appear in Romantic compositions now and then.[94] We also encounter evaded cadences that significantly differ from classical practice. In fact, we have already examined one such case in Schubert's "Unfinished" Symphony (Ex. 8.14c, m. 62), where we observed that the evasion brings neither any semblance of the one-more-time technique nor any actual musical event in place of the potential PAC. Here, Schubert's compositional practice looks forward to techniques found in later nineteenth-century evaded cadences, as discussed in Chapter 9 (sec. 9.7.2). Later in the present chapter, we will encounter another evaded cadence by Schubert that resembles what we find in the Symphony, though manifesting even more complicated modes of cadential disruption (see ahead, Ex. 8.23d, m. 112).

### 8.10.3. Dominant Arrival

We have already discussed one of the major differences between classical and Romantic styles as regards dominant cadential endings, namely, the use of the dissonant seventh in situations that are clearly half cadential (Schmalfeldt's 19cHC). The dominant arrival, a deviation technique exploited regularly during the classical era, and especially favored by Beethoven, continues to be used by Romantic composers. We should note, however, that as soon as the 19cHC is introduced as a standard cadence type, the distinction between a regular HC and a dominant arrival can become blurred; for in the classical style, the mere inclusion of the dissonant seventh within the final cadential harmony engenders a case of dominant arrival. Thus for the nineteenth century, this deviation type must involve either an inversion of the dominant (e.g., $V^6_5$) or a sense that the dominant arrives earlier than expected, thus producing a premature dominant arrival.

In the classical style, composers normally use dominant arrivals in three formal contexts: the end of a contrasting middle (of a small ternary), the end of a transition, and the end of a developmental core. In the Romantic style, these same situations may elicit dominant arrivals, but they may also appear in some other formal locations, such as the close of an antecedent or even at the very end of a work. As a case of an antecedent concluding with a dominant arrival, consider Example 8.21a. This opening of a sonata-form main theme appears to be structured as a compound period, with a compound antecedent ending on dominant harmony (exactly where, to be discussed) followed by a matching compound consequent, beginning at measure 10 and ending on tonic in measure 18. This excerpt constitutes the A section of the complete main theme, built as a small ternary. A closer look at this A section reveals some harmonic details that significantly depart from classical norms. In the first place, the opening four-measure "antecedent" phrase ends with a PAC. Indeed, the effect of this cadence type is even reinforced by the local plagal progression that embellishes the final tonic in measure 4. Such a cadence projects the sense that the opening phrase is a consequent, a situation that raises a conflict between its intrinsic function as an ending and its contextual function as a beginning. The following phrase (mm. 5–9) offers new melodic material, presumably a continuation, though few characteristics of that function are actually present. The melodic line of this phrase clearly concludes on $\hat{2}$ in the middle of measure 7, supported by dominant harmony. But we cannot speak of an HC here, because that dominant has already appeared, very prematurely, on the second quarter-note beat of measure 6. Thus the compound antecedent ends with a dominant arrival, a situation that is extremely rare in classical practice. Moreover, the close of the melody is followed by a trill in the bass, which would seem to function postcadentially, along with a rest and a fermata, two additional features that one would be hard pressed to find within a classical period.

The compound consequent begins with the same consequent-like phrase (mm. 10–13) from the opening of the theme. What follows at measure 14 is now obviously continuational, as a two-measure model is sequenced down a step, supported by a descending-fifth progression. A very quick cadential idea then produces a PAC at measure 18. Unusual, however, is that the penultimate dominant of this cadence, which supports the beginning of the cadential idea on the upbeat to measure 18, is clearly part of a broader dominant prolongation starting at the downbeat of measure 16. Thus like the first phrase, the cadential dominant appears "too early." We cannot speak here of a premature dominant arrival, of course, because the cadence is authentic. Yet the effect is similar to that of the prior antecedent. In fact the two situations are further linked motivically: whereas the bass of the antecedent's continuation phrase leaps directly from ① to ⑤ (m. 6), the consequent's continuation fills in that gap (mm. 13–16) with stepwise motion that descends chromatically to support the sequence. In each case, the goal note of that bass motion, ⑤, arrives earlier than expected. Note, moreover, that although I have spoken of the sequential nature of the harmonies supporting this phrase, we can also see an ECP underlying the phrase as well, as shown in line 2 of the harmonic analysis.[95] And because of the dual nature of the progression—being both sequential and cadential—I have chosen the label "continuation(⇒cadential)" for this final phrase of the theme.

It is interesting to observe that the theme can be recomposed in a way that eliminates the premature appearance of the bass F (mm. 6 and 16), thus rendering the theme considerably more classical. Example 8.21b shows that if we take elements from the tenor voice and place them in the bass, then more normative cadences result.[96] In fact, the bass of the original version seems more like a pedal-point that Schubert places below a more regular bass line (as proposed in Ex. 8.21b). This emphasis on pedals makes sense given how the theme continues: a

---

94. Schmalfeldt mentions a handful of nineteenth-century cases of evaded cadence in "Cadential Processes," 3–5, 30, 42.

95. Indeed, the progression is similar to what we saw in the subordinate theme of the "Unfinished" symphony, cf., Ex. 8.14a, mm. 49–53.

96. Beyond significantly increasing the harmonic rhythm (as befits a continuation), my revision in Ex. 8.21b takes some other liberties with the harmonies compared to the original.

EXAMPLE 8.21A. Schubert, Piano Sonata in B-flat, D. 960, i, mm. 1–20.

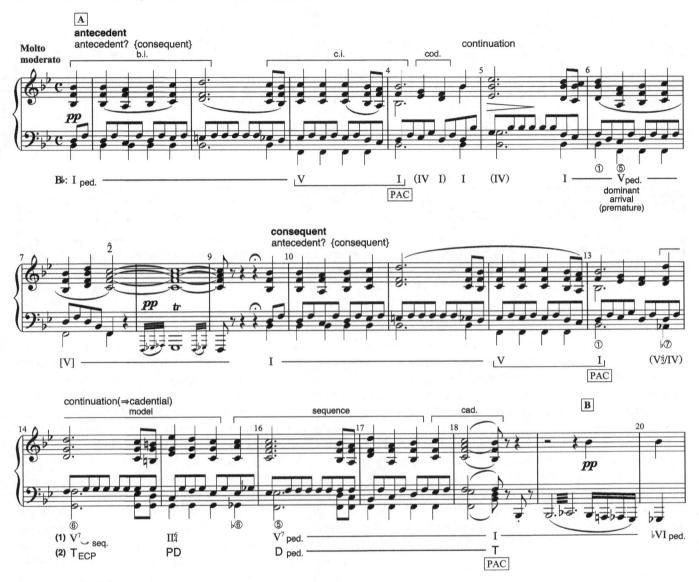

broad contrasting middle (B section) starting in measure 20 (not shown) is supported entirely by a long-held G♭ pedal. When the opening material returns at measure 36 to signal the onset of the A′ section (Ex. 8.21c), the bass G♭ steps down to F to support a cadential six-four.[97] A subsequent dominant proper at measure 38 leads to a PAC in the following bar, which concludes the highly compressed A′ section.[98] Given the prominence of pedals throughout the B and A′ sections, it is appropriate that Schubert emphasizes dominant pedals in the A section as well, for a highly active bass line, along classical lines, might have seemed out of place in the broader formal context.

Though I began the discussion of this theme within the framework of a premature dominant arrival (Ex. 8.21a, m. 6), which concludes the compound antecedent of the A section, a detailed examination has revealed a number of "premature" cadential elements within the theme as a whole: the PAC closing the first four-measure phrase of both the antecedent and consequent units; the early appearance of the cadential dominant (m. 16) closing the latter; and the A′ section beginning immediately with a cadential

---

[97]. The importance of the G♭–F motive throughout the sonata, starting as early as the trill in m. 8, continuing with the bass descent in mm. 15–16 and mm. 35–36, and culminating with the large-scale tonal design of the subordinate theme area, has been observed by many commentators; for a representative account, see Charles Fisk, *Returning Cycles: Contexts for the Interpretation of Schubert's Impromptus and Last Sonatas*, 241–53.

[98]. This PAC, of course, is the same one used to close the opening phrase of the compound antecedent and consequent in the A section. Here the phrase realizes its intrinsic closing quality by ending the entire main theme. Though A′ seems to carry on with the continuation(⇒cadential)

phrase of the compound consequent (not shown, but cf. mm. 14–18), the music ends up wandering away from the home key toward the first of two subordinate keys, thus confirming that the PAC at m. 39 effectively closes the main theme.

EXAMPLE 8.21B-C. Schubert, Piano Sonata in B-flat, D. 960, i, (b) reconstruction of continuation phrases, mm. 5–8, 14–18; (c) mm. 34–39.

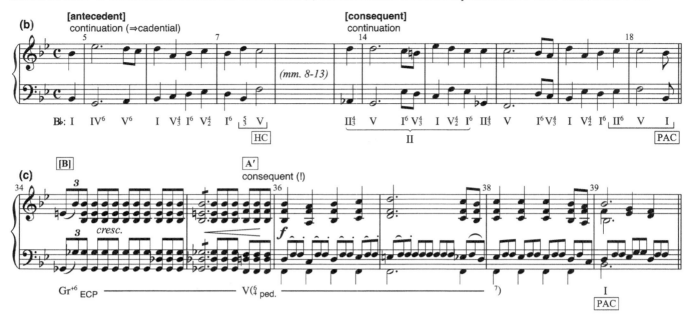

six-four. These features, along with the B section being supported exclusively by a ♭VI pedal (instead of a dominant pedal), reveal how distanced from classical norms are Schubert's compositional procedures, despite his writing this work little more than a year after Beethoven's death (and just months before Schubert's own premature demise).

A second case of nonclassical dominant arrivals arises in Schumann's song "Auf einer Burg" (Ex. 8.22a); indeed, these arrivals appear in compositional contexts in which issues of tonality, harmony, texture, and formal function present a number of analytical difficulties.[99] The song starts clearly enough in E minor, with a four-measure phrase ending with an IAC, thus suggesting a simple antecedent.[100] Noteworthy within the phrase is the polyphonic imitation of the song's basic idea, signaled prominently by an initial falling fifth (motive "x"). Already in the contrasting idea, textural complications ensue. In measure 3, the falling fifth in the bass voice, E–A, suggests that it will bring a transposed imitation of the basic idea, and the stepwise ascent to B seems to validate this hunch. But rather than completing the idea by moving up to C, the B initiates another imitation by leaping down to E, after which the idea is then fully completed in its original key. The form-functional expression of the B–E leap now becomes ambiguous: up to this point, it has signaled a formal *initiation*, namely, the start of the basic idea. In the broader context of harmony and phrase, however, the leap at measure 4 now functions to support the harmonic *close* of the antecedent, the IAC, even if beginning the full basic idea in the bass. This statement seems to *anticipate* the return of the idea in the voice part at measure 5, which begins another phrase, one that we might think will constitute a consequent. This time, however, Schumann redirects the music to C major and closes the phrase with another IAC at measure 8.[101] Thus the consequent "fails" and becomes (⇒) another antecedent.[102]

What follows next is an ascending stepwise sequence. The pattern is expressed clearly enough by the vocal line and generally supported by the harmony, which introduces a local

---

99. David Lewin summarizes various views on the tonal organization of the song, arguing that an inherent conflict between its being in either E phrygian or A minor directly relates to the different time-worlds expressed in the text (the past, projected by the statue; the present, by the bride): "the ambiguity between a minor and e-phrygian modalities enacts and is enacted by this dual nature of the ambivalent narrating persona.... *Auf einer Burg* prolongs one *Stufe* through each of its two strophes..., projecting a harmonically static v—♯ in [A] minor, or i—♯ in Phrygian" (*Studies in Music with Text*, 171). In the footnote to this comment, Lewin explicitly rejects the view of the piece as changing keys: "I rule out hearing the strophe as a 'modulation' that begins in functional e-minor and ends on a non-tonal e-Phrygian. If I am to hear the song as tonally functional, I want to hear it in a minor, not 'e minor.'" As will be immediately clear in my analysis, I do not share Lewin's view of a non-modulating strophe.

100. Given the prominence of F♯ through mm. 1–6, as well as a clear cadential confirmation of E minor by the IAC in m. 4, I find it difficult to hear E phrygian at the start of the piece. Thus as opposed to Lewin (see previous note), I view each strophe as modulating, in line with a tradition of "directional tonality" or "tonal pairing" that stems back at least to Schubert (if not earlier) and as reflected in an important collection of essays, William Kinderman and Harald Krebs, eds., *The Second Practice of Nineteenth-Century Tonality*.

101. That I regard this cadence, along with the IAC at m. 4, as having a limited scope will be explained later when considering the overall form of the strophe.

102. On the notion of a failed consequent, see *CF*, 89, and *ACF*, 246–47. Somewhat problematic in characterizing this second phrase as an antecedent is its modulating structure; normal antecedents in a classical period do not modulate, as discussed earlier in connection with the modulating antecedent of Ex. 8.5b.

EXAMPLE 8.22A. Schumann, "Auf einer Burg," *Liederkreis*, Op. 39, no. 7, mm. 1–22.

descending-fifth root motion between the pillars of the sequence, thus C–(F), D–(G), E–(A). Complicating the texture, an internal pedal C in the piano (upper voice in the right hand) creates many local dissonances within the harmonies of the sequence. A further difficulty arises from the misalignment of the harmonic pillars, which appear a half note ahead of the melody. In my annotations, I have realigned the *roots* of the sequence in order to show their implied positioning at the start of each bar.

At the end of the sequence, a quick pivot to A minor in the second half of measure 14 initiates a cadential progression in that key.[103] The subsequent misalignment of the bass in relation to the upper parts is now more palpable than ever. Thus, when the predominant German sixth resolves to dominant at the beginning of

---

103. It is not clear if this is a compact or expanded progression due to the ambiguity of cadence type that emerges toward its close.

EXAMPLE 8.22B-C. Schumann, "Auf einer Burg," *Liederkreis*, Op. 39, no. 7, (b) reconstruction of mm. 15–18; (c) mm. 36–39.

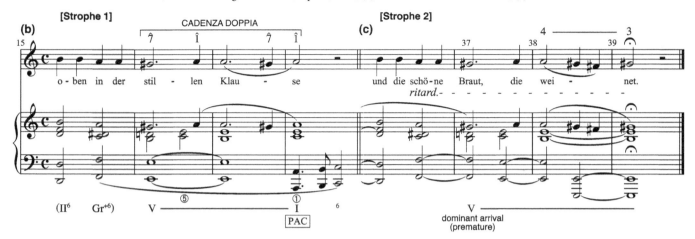

measure 16, the bass is delayed in its motion to ⑤ by half a bar. And in the following measure 17, the bass seems to move prematurely to ①, since the upper parts are still projecting dominant harmony throughout that bar. Moreover, if we are assuming the articulation of an authentic cadence (given the bass motion ⑤–①), then the upper parts do not comply, and instead continue to express dominant harmony through to the middle of measure 18. Indeed, the vocal line's leading tone on the last beat of measure 17 fails to resolve to $\hat{1}$, as required by the promise of an authentic cadence. A reconstruction of what Schumann might have done to create a PAC is shown in Example 8.22b. Here we see that by realigning the bass and resolving the leading tone, a conventional pattern emerges—the *cadenza doppia*, by now an archaic formula associated with baroque practice. Schumann's actual setting (Ex. 8.22a, mm. 16–18), however, prohibits the expression of a PAC, despite the bass motion ⑤–①, since tonic harmony is barely expressed. Thus we can more readily hear a prolongation of dominant from the beginning of measure 16 to the middle of measure 18, where the bass, sounding the basic idea of the song, moves to ③ to support I⁶. With this broader harmonic reading, we can understand that the appearance of dominant at measure 16 marks a premature arrival, since this moment not only ends up representing the final harmony of the ongoing cadential progression, but also clearly precedes the moment of literal melodic close on $\hat{7}$ (downbeat of m. 18).

If the strophe has ended with dominant harmony, what are we to make of the piano interlude, which seems to have a distinctly postcadential function? Normally, a dominant arrival is followed by a standing on the dominant. Here, however, the piano's music is emphatically oriented around tonic (of A minor), which appears most securely expressed by the I⁶ in the second half of measure 18. Tonic harmony continues to be prolonged, even when the leap of the bass ⑤–① (m. 19) brings motive "x" to initiate an additional restatement of the basic idea (following upon those in the piano's left hand in mm. 16–18 and right hand in mm. 18–19). Measure 20 contains a new harmony (VI), though one that can still be heard as a tonic substitute. A brief cadential progression begins in the second half of that measure, which is completed with the IAC in the following bar. Seeing as the strophe proper ended with the premature dominant arrival, this new IAC would seem to be limited in scope to the closing section itself. Nonetheless, this cadence finally brings an authentic cadential confirmation of A minor, just as the preceding keys of E minor and C major were confirmed with IACs in measures 4 and 8, respectively. As a result of the tonic emphasis given to this closing section, it is as though the piano is responding to the possibility that a genuine *cadenza doppia* type PAC had indeed been created, even though the voice part continues to prolong a sense of dominant ending.[104]

Looking at the strophe as a whole, we can understand that its overall organization is loosely sentential, with the two four-measure antecedent-like phrases functioning as a compound presentation,[105] upon which a continuation brings sequential organization and fragmentation into two-measure groups, leading to a dominant arrival and, paradoxically, a tonic-oriented closing section. In that view, all three IACs function exclusively within their own phrases and thus are best understood as cadences of limited scope.

Finally, let us consider the second strophe, which until its end is virtually identical to the first one. Again, a view of its ending with a dominant arrival at measure 37 emerges clearly (Ex. 8.22c), and this time it is even supported rhetorically by the *ritardando*. Unlike the first strophe, Schumann creates no ambiguity as to closure, since the bass remains fixed on the dominant, and the decorated resolution of the suspension (via F♯) throws even greater weight on G♯ as the melodic goal. Thus the harmonic complications arising at the end of the first strophe are eliminated in the second, though the song nonetheless fails to confirm its goal tonality of A minor with a PAC. Instead, the song ends

---

104. That the projection of harmony and cadence in the voice part conflicts with that of the piano part supports Lewin's reading that the voice resides in the past, while the piano at this point resides in the present (*Music with Text*, 176–77). The "ancient" *cadenza doppia*, projected most evidently by the voice part, further attests to this interpretation.

105. This type of compound presentation occurs rarely in the classical style, but appears more regularly in Romantic era; see Chapter 5, note 147.

with a dominant arrival, a situation virtually unheard of in the classical style.

## 8.11. Ultimate versus Penultimate Dominants; Dissipated Cadence

The preceding example raised the issue of the ambiguities of a dominant that can function as either the ultimate harmony of a half cadential progression or the penultimate harmony of an authentic cadential one. In the classical style, composers rarely allow this distinction to become blurred; in the Romantic era, and especially with Schubert, ambiguities about the role of the cadential dominant can give rise to problematic cadential situations. Several passages from the first movement of Schubert's Sonata in A, D. 959, will illustrate such difficulties, even allowing us to identify a new type of cadential deviation, which I term the *dissipated cadence*.[106]

We begin with the main theme, built seemingly as a small ternary, and first ask how the A section ends (Ex. 8.23a). The final bar would appear to be measure 6, because the complete change of material at measure 7 seems to mark the beginning of a new unit, namely, a standing on the dominant that comprises the whole of the B section. The A section of a small ternary normally ends with a PAC; however, here the dominant seventh in measure 6 does not resolve as expected. Instead, it gives the impression of a cadential evasion (line 1 of the harmonic analysis). Unlike normal classical practice, this evaded cadence is not a way station followed by a one-more-time technique and leading to a concluding authentic cadence. Instead, the A section seems to be left without any formal closure whatsoever.

There is, of course, an alternative interpretation; namely, that the dominant of measure 6 is ultimate, not penultimate. We would then recognize a 19cHC concluding the A section (line 2).[107] Indeed, we might look at the particular 4–3 suspension configuration found within this dominant and recall how a similar decorated resolution closes Schumann's "Auf einer Burg" (Ex. 8.22c, mm. 38–39) with an ultimate dominant.[108] Such a view also suggests that we might revise our interpretation of the immediately following measures 7–15, hearing them as a *postcadential* standing on the dominant, not as a contrasting middle (B section), and thus recognize the return of the opening material at measure 16 as the start of a potential consequent phrase, one matching an opening antecedent.[109] Several problems, though, present themselves if we believe that measure 6 is an ultimate dominant. Unlike Chopin or Schumann, Schubert does not so regularly employ the dominant seventh in half cadential situations.[110] More importantly, the A′ section leads to a similar dominant seventh at measure 21, and there, it clearly behaves as a penultimate harmony (albeit an inverted one), which resolves to tonic in the following bar, bringing prolongational closure to the small ternary form as a whole. (Just why Schubert does not place the dominant in root position to create a regular PAC at measure 22 will be addressed shortly.)[111]

Before leaving the A section and its ambiguous closure, we should consider in detail some aspects of its formal organization and melodic-motivic content. In the first place, its six-measure length means that we are dealing with either a deviation of a standard eight-measure theme or else some nonconventional type. The opening two measures could be considered a basic idea, one comprising two one-measure motives. What follows is contrasting (with strong continuational characteristics), and a cadential idea begins with the upbeat to measure 5, continuing on through measure 6, whose ambiguities we have just examined. Thus, whereas we can recognize three ideas that express the general functions of beginning, middle, and end, a conventional form does not emerge. What also seems lacking is a highly

---

106. Another work by Schubert, the first movement of his Sonata in A Minor, Op. 42, D. 845, features a number of ambiguous ultimate and penultimate dominants; Schmalfeldt discusses some of these ambiguities, especially as they affect performance decisions (*Process of Becoming*, chap. 5).

107. This half cadential articulation would then be referencing the practice of Haydn, who now and then ends an A section with an HC; see Chapter 3, note 56.

108. A similar decorated suspension arises in m. 4 of the piano introduction of Schubert's "Die Wegweiser" from *Die Winterreise*. Given that the dominant arrives in the fourth bar of what seems to be a four-measure phrase (consisting of a two-measure basic idea, and a two-measure contrasting idea), the harmony seems at first to be ultimate; however, Schubert then resolves the dominant to tonic at the beginning of the next bar in a manner that suggests its true function as penultimate within a cadential progression, one that closes a five-measure opening phrase. When the voice enters, Schubert largely repeats the phrase, but this time ends it with an HC in the fourth bar of the phrase (m. 9), as shown by Schmalfeldt, "Towards a Reconciliation," 260–64, Ex. 10. See also Carl Schachter, "Rhythm and Linear Analysis: Aspects of Meter," 38–39, and Burstein, "Slippery Events," 203–4, Ex. 1. The significance of this cadential figure (with its 4–3 suspension and decorated resolution) for the sonata movement that we are presently considering is highlighted in Julian Caskel, "Musical Causality and Schubert's Piano Sonata in A, D 959, First Movement." Caskel also cites the passage from "Die Wegweiser," just mentioned, along with two other songs from *Die Winterreise*: "Der greise Kopf" (mm. 41–42) and "Im Dorfe" (mm. 45–46). In all three songs, the cadential dominant is clearly penultimate, resolving to tonic for an authentic cadence.

109. It may not be immediately clear that mm. 16–22 reprises the opening bars; I will clarify this connection when considering the melodic-motivic material of this passage later on in the discussion.

110. Schmalfeldt does not identify any 19cHCs in connection with Schubert, only raising the topic first with her chapter on Chopin (*Process of Becoming*); see again, note 14.

111. To be sure, it is also possible to hear the dominant of m. 21 as ultimate, in conformance with a similar interpretation of m. 6 (line 2); in this case, the following tonic would have to be construed as exclusively initiating. But for reasons of voice leading and motivic processes to be discussed shortly, this interpretation seems far-fetched, and it would moreover leave the entire main theme without any degree of tonic closure. Thus the rest of the discussion will assume that the dominant of m. 21 is penultimate, even if the ambiguous status of the dominant in m. 6 is left unresolved for the time being.

EXAMPLE 8.23A. Schubert, Piano Sonata in A, D. 959, i, mm. 1–26.

profiled melodic component to these ideas. The upper-most sounding voice remains fixed on the tonic degree until the decorated resolution of the suspension in the final bar (m. 6); the bass voice also brings a tonic pedal for four measures until it finally moves up to ③ for the start of the cadential progression. The only substantial melodic impulse occurs in the two inner voices, which, bringing a modicum of motion, consist mostly of scalar patterns moving up and down from $\hat{3}$ in an alto voice and doubled a third lower by the tenor. The alto voice essentially functions as the true "upper voice" of the contrapuntal structure, with the actual soprano having a more conventional inner-voice function. If we follow the course of the parallel thirds consistently, then we would want to consider the dissonant-seventh D ($\hat{4}$) as the active melody at the end of the section, which further helps to support the idea of an evaded cadence, inasmuch as this tone strives to return to its starting point, $\hat{3}$.[112] Given the consistency of the doubled-third motion throughout the section, we might accord this texture a significant motivic function and observe its development throughout the rest of the movement.

---

112. I am regarding all of the inner-voice Es in the chord of m. 6 as doublings of the bass voice.

The $\hat{4}$, which is left hanging at the end of the A section, is transferred to the very top of the arpeggiated texture that takes over at the beginning of the contrasting middle (m. 7) and continues to sound as the principal melodic element in every bar until the liquidation in measures 14–15. As for the bass voice, it now becomes more active, rising chromatically stepwise throughout the section from ⑤ to ②, such that at the *fortissimo* climax at measure 13, the outer voices sound the doubled third pair B–D, just the same two motivic pitches from the end of the A section in measure 6. The fourth scale degree finally resolves at the beginning of the A′ section, when $\hat{3}$ is picked up again, now transferred to the tenor voice and doubled a third lower by the bass. In addition, the top voice has a new countermelody that sounds above the parallel thirds of the lower voices. Formally and harmonically, the A′ section is organized just like the A section, except that as discussed, the final dominant resolves to tonic, thus extending the unit by one bar. Just before that happens though, the F♯ in the upper line of the parallel third motion is doubled by the soprano in the second half of measure 20. That voice then continues the line with the whole-note D, while the tenor loses its melodic status and sounds the root of the dominant, E, just the note we might have expected to appear in the bass voice, which instead sustains the parallel third doubling. As a result, a wonderful reversal of texture occurs such that in measure 21 the upper and lower voices now sound the doubled third, while the inner voices take on their more appropriate function as fillers, including the decorated suspension.

We are now ready to discuss the cadential situation arising at the end of the A′ section. Following the bass line as it ascends from ① to ④ by the end of measure 20, we would normally be expecting that line to reach its goal on ⑤ to support the cadential dominant. Instead, Schubert lets the bass fall down to ②, in parallel thirds with the soprano, and then to ① for the tonic resolution. Consequently, we cannot speak here of an authentic cadence, but recognize instead prolongational closure both for the section and for the theme as a whole. As already noted, Schubert's motivation for failing to bring a genuine cadence most likely lies in the motivic work that he relentlessly pursues throughout this section, namely, the use of parallel motion as the essential contrapuntal profile of the theme.[113]

Eliding with the prolongational closure, we hear a kind of closing section (despite the lack of a genuine cadence) made up of two-measure codettas based on material from the previous B section. As the passage continues, the closing section proves to be *false*, and the codettas are reinterpreted as repeated basic ideas. These units then constitute a presentation phrase that initiates a two-part transition, whose first part closes with an HK: HC at measure 28 (not shown).

Before leaving this main theme, I want to address another formal reading that may have occurred to the reader, namely, one that focuses on the juxtaposition of two main textural blocks, namely, the homophonic material of measures 1–6 and 16–20 versus the triplet arpeggiations in measures 7–15 and 22–28. This view would see a bipartite organization to the theme: part 1, measures 1–15; part 2, measures 16–28.[114] It is not clear to me, however, just what theme type would come into play to describe this overall structure, since it does not conform to any of the classical models. If Schubert had written a PAC at measure 22, which is clearly promised, then the formal situation would have been quite evident: a small ternary main theme followed by a transition that motivically relates to the contrasting middle, a formal situation that is not without precedent in the classical style.[115]

Let us turn now to the subordinate-theme area of the exposition, where we continue to encounter cadential uncertainties similar to those discussed so far. Example 8.23b shows the first of two subordinate themes. It opens with a phrase that ends at measure 58 with an HC in the subordinate key of E major, just like an antecedent. Note the parallel thirds in the left-hand part, an obvious reference to motives from the main theme. The phrase begins to be repeated as a possible consequent, but this function "fails" when the music suddenly veers off to G major, partially confirming that key at measure 63 with the same half cadence gesture; as a result, the failed consequent "becomes" a second antecedent, which together with the prior one creates a compound presentation.[116] The continuation at measure 65 prolongs I⁶ of G, with a rocking on the tonic, which suggests that an ECP may be in the making. A simple reconstruction of the implied ECP, picking up at measure 69 (Ex. 8.23c) shows how the theme could easily have cadenced in G major. At measure 70 (Ex. 8.23b), however, the cadential progression is abandoned when the music suddenly shifts back to E major: the bass note B, which functioned as the third of the tonic of G, continues to sound (it is even emphasized by being placed an octave lower) to become the root of the dominant of E. Following a deceptive resolution to VI at measure 71, a compact cadential progression begins with the pre-dominant IV and continues in the next bar with the cadential dominant. This harmony is clearly perceived as *penultimate*, since we expect an authentic cadence to close this subordinate theme, now in the normal subordinate key of E major. The cadence is evaded,

---

113. There are perhaps additional reasons for Schubert's not having placed an E in the bass of m. 20: if the bass line of m. 20 were to continue to rise to $E_3$, the texture would be extremely thin, and thus not appropriately balanced with the texture of m. 6. Moreover, it is not possible to add the lower $E_2$ while still retaining $D_5$ in the upper voice and an octave-doubled decorated resolution in the inner parts, since two hands cannot play such a configuration of notes. Finally, the upper D ($\hat{4}$) in m. 21 would awkwardly clash against the lower E (⑤), a voice-leading situation that, if not strictly prohibited, is normally shunned in such an exposed manner.

114. This bipartite view is promoted by Julian Horton, "The First Movement of Schubert's Piano Sonata D. 959 and the Performance of Analysis," 175–77. He acknowledges the possibility of hearing a small ternary form, but finds that analysis "challenged by the parallelism between bars 7–12 and 22–27, which bolsters the sense of a two-part design" (175).

115. See, for example, Beethoven, Op. 31, no. 3, ii, mm 1–34.

116. The formal structure is the same as the opening of "Auf einer Burg" (Ex. 8.22, mm. 1–8), including the two cadences of limited scope.

EXAMPLE 8.23B. Schubert, Piano Sonata in A, D. 959, i, mm. 55–82.

EXAMPLE 8.23C. Schubert, Piano Sonata in A, D. 959, i, reconstruction of mm. 69–72.

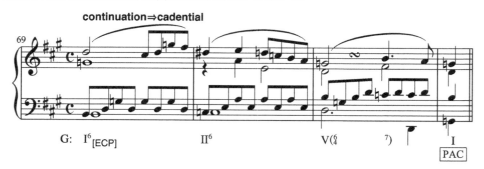

EXAMPLE 8.23D. Schubert, Piano Sonata in A, D. 959, i, mm. 95–124.

however, and the music quickly backs up to the cadential six-four for another try, one that is evaded yet again at measure 74.

At this point, something quite unusual takes place, for the music now seems to get stuck on the cadential dominant as the piano's right hand brings a new triplet figure, which gets drawn out and liquidated much like a standing on the dominant. Thus, the resolution to

tonic at measure 78 does not sound like a cadential goal but rather is exclusively heard as a *beginning* harmony, one that initiates the next phrase. What seems to have taken place is that a *penultimate* dominant (one that promises an authentic cadence) is somehow converted into an *ultimate* dominant to support a postcadential standing on the dominant, which fully removes any potential for authentic cadential closure. In association with the complete liquidation of the motivic content and a highly recessive dynamic,[117] we can have the impression that the impending authentic cadence has been entirely dissipated, thus giving rise to a new deviation technique, the *dissipated cadence*.

As just mentioned, the tonic harmony at measure 78 initiates a new phrase, one that brings back the opening basic idea from the beginning of the subordinate theme.[118] But rather than forming itself into a thematic unit, say, a consequent that finally brings cadential closure to theme, this idea is fragmented into one-measure segments all within a tonic prolongation, whose lower two voices allude to the parallel third coupling from the main theme. A sudden *forte* at measure 82 brings the start of a second subordinate theme (whose ending will be examined shortly).[119] As such, the first subordinate theme is left without any cadential closure, though, somewhat ironically, the return at measure 78 to its opening idea brings a structure that resembles a closing section (thus the annotation "cons⇒cl.sec.").

A second subordinate theme begins at measure 82 with a large-scale model-sequence plan (somewhat in the manner of a developmental core, though essentially remaining in the subordinate key).[120] At measure 95 (Ex. 8.23d), Schubert initiates an ECP, starting first in E minor but then shifting back to major two bars later. The conditions for a PAC literally appear at the downbeat of measure 101, but the sudden dropping out of the chordal texture and abrupt change back to the minor mode could also be a sign that the cadence is evaded. Both options seem available for analytical (and performative) interpretation, though for reasons of broader formal organization, I prefer hearing a cadential evasion. In any case, the passage strives forward with the same music, though now the left hand plays the running triplets, and the right hand, the slower-paced chordal blocks. The texture changes again at measure 105, and the harmonic progressions are suggestive of cadential activity. A clear cadential progression emerges at measure 110, strongly implying PAC closure for the theme. This time, though, the cadence is evaded by a general pause (recalling a similar situation in the "Unfinished" Symphony, Example 8.14c, m. 62), and when the music picks up again with the texture reduced to a single line, we understand that the dominant harmony of measure 111, which we construe to be penultimate, continues to be prolonged in a manner that resembles the end of a standing on the dominant, one that normally follows upon an ultimate dominant. The texture begins to fill out at measure 116 in preparation for a return of the opening phrase of the first subordinate theme, whose tonic at measure 117 sounds entirely initiating, not ending. In other words, we confront again a case of a dissipated cadence, whereby the subsequent standing on the dominant exhausts the potential for cadential closure to the extent that the resolution to tonic brings a new beginning, not a cadential goal, thus converting an initially perceived penultimate dominant into an ultimate one.

Up to this point, we have been assuming that the dominant achieved at measure 111 is penultimate, largely for reasons having to do with formal context: we normally expect that at this late stage of a subordinate theme, any cadential function would be aiming toward authentic cadential closure, especially when an evaded cadence (m. 101) immediately precedes it. Some details of pitch organization in measure 111, however, prompt us to entertain the idea of an ultimate dominant projecting an HC, after which the general pause creates a caesura. After all, no dissonant seventh appears there; indeed, the texture is ultimately reduced to octaves doubling the root of the harmony. Though an interpretation of HC is perhaps less likely in relation to the preceding formal context, it does make sense in light of what follows, namely, a standing on that ultimate dominant. To help elicit such a hearing, a performer would want to make the dominant of measure 111 sound like a genuine goal, which might entail a slight ritardando and diminuendo throughout the measure. Performances by Frank van de Laar and Maurizio Pollini achieve just this effect.[121] In contrast, those by Stephen Kovacevich, Artur Schnabel, and Murray Perahia increase the drive and intensity of the music throughout the complete bar, so that the effect of an interruption—a real cadential evasion—is dramatically projected.[122] In short, Schubert leaves it open for the performer to help decide such ambiguous cases.

The return of the opening of the first subordinate theme at measure 117 continues to play on the problem of ultimate versus penultimate dominant, since this time, the opening phrase ends at measure 120 with a dominant seventh and not a triad (cf. Ex. 8.23b, m. 58). As a result, it is unclear whether or not an HC is created at this point, since, as earlier discussed, Schubert does not normally employ a 19cHC. We might rather interpret the dominant as penultimate and recognize an evaded cadence, one that

---

117. On the idea of a recessive (or progressive) dynamic, see in Chapter 5, note 107.

118. This return to material from the opening of the theme is an obvious manifestation of Romantic formal circularity; see again, note 55.

119. Whether or not we should speak of a second subordinate theme is somewhat difficult to say. On the one hand, a large-scale unit of more than thirty bars is initiated at this point. On the other hand, the previous subordinate theme has not closed cadentially, and thus according to classical norms, what follows at m. 82 is best seen as the "second part" of a single, two-part subordinate theme. This view is also somewhat validated by the return of the opening idea from the "first" part of the subordinate theme (see ahead Ex. 8.23d, m. 117), in a manner that rounds off the whole.

120. For discussions of the infusion of core-like material within subordinate themes of Schubert's expositions, see Anne M. Hyland, *Schubert's String Quartets: The Teleology of Lyric Form*, 164–65, and François de Médicis, "'Heavenly Length' in Schubert's Instrumental Music," 205. The use of model-sequence activity at the start of a second subordinate theme also has clear classical precedent, since such a unit occasionally begins directly with continuation function, thus bypassing a functional initiation; see *CF*, 111–13, and *ACF*, 391.

121. Brilliant Classics 99678/2, compact disk (van de Laar); Deutsche Grammophon 4713502, vol. 6, compact disk (Pollini).

122. EMI Records, compact disk (Kovacevich); Pearl CDS 9271, compact disk (Schnabel); Sony Classical S2K 87706, compact disk (Perahia).

will motivate an authentic cadence via the one-more-time technique; in fact, a clear PAC occurs at measure 123, preceded by that same penultimate dominant. This is the cadence that finally, and unequivocally, closes the entire group of subordinate themes.

We are now in a position to step back and consider the larger formal patterns that emerge within the subordinate-theme area of this exposition. As just discussed, we can find only a single unequivocal PAC that could be considered to close a thematic unit, namely the one we just saw in measure 123.[123] Two other potential PACs were poised to appear—one at measure 74 (Ex. 8.23b), to close a first subordinate theme, and one at measure 112 (Ex. 8.23d), to close a second subordinate theme. In each case, these cadences were effectively dissipated by the conversion of their penultimate dominants into ultimate ones in the course of their standings on the dominant. If Schubert had written genuine PACs, the return of the motives from the opening of the first subordinate theme at measures 78 and 117 would have functioned as postcadential codettas. In addition, the subordinate-theme group (consisting of two complete themes) would have conformed largely to classical norms. Taking the dissipated cadences into account, however, a more complex design begins to take shape.

Consider the first subordinate theme (Ex. 8.23b). As we discussed, the section from measure 65 to measure 77 is supported by a bass note B. At first, this bass functions as the third of a $I^6$ harmony in G major, but then assumes its role as dominant of the subordinate key, E major. Broadly speaking, and appealing to the spirit of retrospective reinterpretation, we could consider this entire section functioning as a contrasting middle (B section) of a small ternary structure—an extensive "standing on the dominant" (of E). The A section would thus embrace the opening antecedent (mm. 55–59) and the failed consequent (mm. 60–64).[124] The final section of the form, however, poses difficulties. In the context of a small ternary reading, the return at measure 78 of the opening material from the A section strongly signals the start of the A′ section, most likely taking the form of a genuine consequent phrase (to make up for the failed consequent of the A section). Following the basic idea, however, the material quickly liquidates in the manner of codettas, such that the overall ternary form never receives its required PAC closure.

That the first subordinate theme remains unclosed raises the possibility of recognizing an even larger-scale ternary design by regarding this incomplete theme as a magnified A section (indicated by the larger, italicized symbol);[125] we could then regard the second subordinate theme (the latter half shown in Ex. 8.23d) as bringing together the remaining B and A′ sections (beginning at mm. 82 and 117, respectively).[126] After all, the second subordinate theme begins with extensive sequential activity in the manner of a developmental core, and thus from its start projects a powerful intrinsic medial functionality of the type that we could associate with a contrasting middle. This enormous B section would be deemed to end with the ultimate dominant that emerges from the reinterpretation of its cadential function engendered by the dissipated cadence at measure 117.[127] The large-scale A′ section is signaled by the return of the A section's opening phrase at measure 117, and the theme as a whole is closed by the PAC at measure 123. With this interpretation, the exposition would see only a single subordinate theme, one built as a huge small ternary, whose A section itself is structured as a lower-level small ternary (albeit one that does not achieve cadential closure). Given that the small ternary form is never used as the basis of a classical subordinate theme (much less a group of themes), the embedding of one small ternary within an even grander small ternary shows how far from classical norms Schubert is willing to diverge. Moreover, we see here a further expression of the formal circularity that marks a Romantic approach to form, in that we encounter two different *returns* of the opening material of the theme (mm. 78 and 117), each signaling the start of an A′ section (at two different levels of the form).

Let us come full circle and give one final consideration to the main theme of the exposition (Ex. 8.23a). In light of the two dissipated cadences that we have identified in the course of the subordinate-theme area, we can now examine again the cadential situation at measure 6 and find there the potential source of these cadential deviations. For if we take the dominant in that measure to be penultimate, an option that we gave serious consideration to in our earlier discussion, we can recognize that an evaded cadence is followed by a standing on the dominant, one that eventually dissipates any possible sense of an upcoming authentic cadence and that prepares for the return of the opening section, just the kind of situation that we encounter twice in the subordinate-theme area. When first discussing this passage, I was hesitant to introduce the notion of a dissipated cadence for the main reason that I continued to consider it a possibility that measure 6 brings an ultimate dominant to create a 19cHC. In light of what occurs throughout the rest of the exposition, however, finding here the first of three dissipated cadences (at m. 22) seems like an especially compelling interpretation.[128]

---

123. I am discounting the possible PAC at m. 101, since no coherent view of the form ensues from interpreting this as a moment of complete tonal and formal closure; instead, I recognize an evaded cadence there for the reasons cited earlier.

124. Once again (as mentioned in connection with the main theme), we would be confronting the exceptional case, seen now and then in Haydn, of an A section closing with an HC rather than a PAC.

125. The expression "large-scale small ternary" might seem odd; why not speak of a "large ternary"? The problem, of course, is that the latter is itself a distinct classical formal type, one that diverges significantly from the small ternary; see *CF*, 211–16, and *ACF*, 566–69, 574–86.

126. Horton presents the same interpretation of one small ternary, mm. 55–82, nested (as the A section) within a larger-scale ternary, mm. 55–123 ("Schubert's Piano Sonata D. 959," 178, table 9.1).

127. Or, if we believe that m. 111 brings a regular HC, shown as line 2 of the harmonic analysis, then we would not speak of a subsequent dissipated cadence.

128. A look at the coda of the movement further supports this reading. Here we find that Schubert twice brings back, in an extended form, the opening thematic unit (A or A′) and closes both with a classical PAC (mm. 340 and 349). As well, the dominant seventh of each cadence

EXAMPLE 8.24. Mendelssohn, String Quartet in E-flat, Op. 12, i, (a) mm. 18–29; (b) Romanesca-Prinner combination.

## 8.12. Prinner Cadence

As discussed in earlier chapters, the Prinner cadence (Prc), which had a ubiquitous usage throughout the galant style, receded markedly during the classical period, even while other forms of the Prinner—its prolongational and sequential versions—found continued use.[129] But this cadential formation managed to survive into the first half of the nineteenth century, with some intriguing appearances in the works of Mendelssohn and Schumann. Especially interesting to observe in these examples is how the schema not only references galant practice, but also accommodates itself to a Romantic stylistic environment.

The opening four-measure phrase of the first-movement main theme in Mendelssohn's String Quartet in E-flat, Op. 12, concludes with a PrC at measure 21 (Ex. 8.24a). From a galant perspective, we see the parallel motion between the melody and the bass, broken only by ⑤ as a metrical extension of ②. Indeed, parallel motion between the outer voices obtains right from the very beginning in a manner that suggests stages three and four of the Romanesca schema (⑥–⑤ supporting 8̂–7̂), as shown in Example 8.24b. That the PrC is a truly effective cadence (i.e., not undermined in any way) becomes clear by what follows: a new phrase that leads eventually to an HC at measure 25, in a manner that suggests the formation of a compound antecedent (mm. 18–25). Note that as regards the syntactical strength of the cadences, the PrC would appear to be weaker than the subsequent HC, similar to what we saw in connection with a theme by Haydn discussed in chapter 3 (Ex. 3.74). When the opening phrase returns in measures 26–29, our suspicion that an overall periodic organization is in the making is eventually confirmed by a PAC at measure 36 (not shown).

These galant characteristics notwithstanding, we can identify compositional features that depart from the way the Prinner is normally used in the galant or classical styles. For instance, the theme starts on an inverted tonic; moreover, except for this I⁶ and the subsequent one in the second half of measure 19, all of the harmonies appear in root position. This emphasis on root-position harmonies, along with an even greater use of leaping motion in the bass, also occurs in the embellished version of the phrase as it appears in measures 26–29; indeed, the bass actually acquires a distinctly motivic quality (see brackets). Another unusual use of the cadential Prinner concerns its relation to the formal organization of the phrase. As we saw in Chapter 7 (Ex. 7.18 and 7.20), the Prinner cadence often arises in connection with a two-measure riposte (a contrasting idea, in my terminology) that follows upon a two-measure initiating statement (a basic idea) one that projects a Romanesca schema. Mendelssohn's opening phrase can also be divided into a basic idea (framed by the I⁶ harmony and 5̂ in the melody) and a contrasting idea. Yet the

---

includes the same decorated resolution of the 4–3 suspension that we find in mm. 6 and 21, thus suggesting that these earlier moments, too, can be considered penultimate dominants.

129. See Chapter 3, sec. 3.2.1.2; Chapter 7, sec. 7.1.2.

EXAMPLE 8.25. Schumann, *Faschingsschwank aus Wien*, Op. 26, i, mm. 1–8.

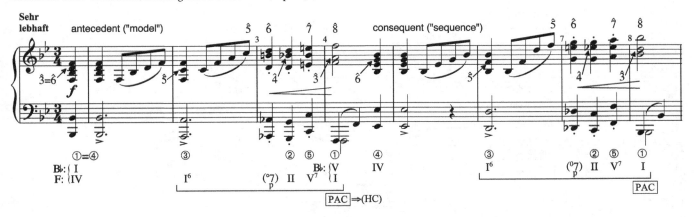

Prinner itself already begins midway through the basic idea, thus straddling the grouping structure; moreover, the basic idea, beginning on a destabilizing I⁶ and quickly employing the second half of a Romanesca, imparts a modest sense of beginning *in medias res*. In short, Mendelssohn refashions the cadential Prinner to aspects of his style that are more typical of early nineteenth-century practice than to that of the prior century.

The opening of Schumann's *Faschingsschwank aus Wien* (Ex. 8.25) contains two four-measure phrases, each of which has features of the cadential Prinner. To be sure, the Prinner melody appears only in the alto voice (see the arrows in the analysis), so the resulting cadences are actually PACs, not PrCs.[130] Otherwise, each phrase largely conforms to one of the two basic Prinner prototypes: a modulating Prinner (see Chapter 7, Ex. 7.19) for the first phrase; a standard Prinner for the second. When put together, these two Prinners result in a descending bass line that spans a full octave, thus recalling the complete Romanesca–Prinner configuration (see again Ex. 8.24b). Indeed, the opening three harmonies of a modulating Prinner (heard still in the home key) correspond to those of the Romanesca. From a galant perspective, though, Schumann's linking of two Prinners raises a problem of voice leading, since he directly follows the root-position F-major harmony of measure 4 with the root-position E♭ harmony of measure 5, thus creating consecutive octaves.

Three other anomalies from galant (and classical) practice are worth mentioning. First, the chromatic passing diminished-seventh chords, which embellish the Prinner's second stage on the downbeats of measures 3 and 7, betray an obvious Romantic touch. Second, the formal organization of the passage, in which the second phrase, a consequent, is also a complete sequential repetition of the first, an antecedent, finds little precedent in eighteenth-century practice.[131] Third, the contrapuntal relationship of the melody and bass creates a contour that differs from both the parallel descending motion of the galant Prinner cadence and the standard contrary motion of a classical authentic cadence: in fact, Schumann's cadences invert the classical contour, in that the soprano now ascends (5̂–6̂–7̂–8̂) against a largely descending bass ④–③–②–⑤–①.

A particularly exquisite PrC appears at the opening Schumann's song "Wehmut" (Ex. 8.26a). Here we see how the Romantic propensity for dense harmonic rhythms at the opening of a work permits Schumann to introduce an initiating neighbor motive (3̂–4̂–3̂) followed by a cadential Prinner riposte, all within a two-measure basic idea. Such embedding of a cadential gesture at the opening of a piece is a feature of Romantic practice that we have already discussed (see again Ex. 8.6); as such, the cadence is one of limited scope. The following contrasting idea (which is where the cadential Prinner would ordinarily have arisen in galant practice) leads to a reinterpreted HC to yield an opening antecedent phrase. Toward the end of the song (Ex. 8.26b), the emphasis on parallel voice leading within the basic idea continues to find expression, such that a new contrasting idea contains the final three stages of a prolongational Prinner. As a result, the vocal part ends with prolongational closure, and it is left to the piano postlude to bring PAC closure to conclude the song as a whole.[132]

---

130. The sense of PAC at m. 4 occurs largely in relation to the "modulating" nature of the opening measures. But when the music immediately returns to the home key, ending there with another PAC at m. 8, we can recognize retrospectively that, in the context of the entire theme, the cadence at m. 4 functions as a reinterpreted HC.

131. But see the A section of Beethoven's Piano Sonata in A-flat, Op. 26, ii, mm. 1–8 for a precursor of this technique; indeed, the opening of this scherzo resembles in a number of ways the beginning of Schumann's *Faschingsschwank*.

132. Schumann seems to have been particularly drawn to the Prinner cadence. Another prominent instance arises in the finale to his Symphony No. 2 in C, Op. 61, mm. 394–97, a direct allusion to Beethoven's song "Nimm sie hin denn," from *An die ferne Geliebte*, Op. 98, mm. 1–2. Here, Beethoven uses a regular Prinner, without the addition of a cadential ⑤; unlike galant and classical practice, however, he places the schema in an initiating position (the two-measure basic idea of the melody), as does Schumann in his symphony. In other words, Beethoven's usage looks forward to a characteristic of the Romantic style (as just mentioned in connection with Schumann's "Wehmut"), which may account, beyond the usual biographical explanations, for Schumann's attraction to this musical idea. His earlier allusion to *An die Ferne Geliebte*, in his Fantasy for Piano in C, Op. 17, i, mm. 300–301, employs a cadential variant, namely the IAC (Pr); see in Chapter 7, Ex. 7.23.

EXAMPLE 8.26. Schumann, "Wehmut," *Liederkreis*, Op. 39, no. 9, (a) mm. 1–5; (b) mm. 22–28.

## 8.13. Analytical Notes to Chopin's Preludes, Op. 28

Universally acknowledged as one of the great collections of piano miniatures, Chopin's Preludes, Op. 28, have inspired much critical and analytical commentary. The following analytical notes focus primarily on cadential closure in these small pieces, though I will comment as appropriate on issues of form, phrase structure, harmony, texture, and rhythm. Each prelude will be treated as a complete movement, since in almost all cases, the basic harmonic, melodic, and formal processes achieve a strong degree of closure, even if not always in a classical manner.

Before turning to the individual preludes, let me offer some general comments about matters of form and cadence that repeatedly arise in these miniatures. The formal plan of most of the preludes is readily discernible via the various statements and restatements of the melodic-motivic content and the general harmonic-tonal design. The form of most of the pieces can be assimilated to the classical theme types—the sentence (Nos. 2, 11, 18, and 23), the period (Nos. 1, 3–7, 14, and 16), the small ternary (Nos. 8, 9, 12, 19), and the small binary (Nos. 13, 20–22). A couple of broader formal types occur (the large ternary for No. 15, the rondo for No. 17), and a few are nonconventional in form (Nos. 10 and 24). Sentential structures tend to be somewhat loose in organization, and the period, the most commonly used form, is either balanced or features an extended consequent phrase. Unlike in the classical style, where the unequivocal expression of cadence helps to clarify potentially ambiguous or difficult formal plans, the situation is somewhat the reverse with Chopin's preludes: our relatively clear sense of the form helps us predict where cadences should arise, though complications of cadential expression may occur at, or around, those moments of presumed closure.

Typical of the genre of prelude (and in line with general Romantic practice), the texture and rhythmic patterning throughout a given piece tends to remain highly uniform, with sudden changes typically occurring at the very end, often in connection with the final cadence or with a postcadential codetta.

The nature of the textural and rhythmic changes normally lies in the direction of simplification and loss of energy. This sudden reduction at the close often gives the impression that the final cadence (or codetta) is somewhat detached from the rest of the prelude, a situation that I will call an *isolated* cadence. The purpose of this textural change seems related to a general principle of closure that we explored in the first chapter of this study, namely, the repetition/terminal-modification paradigm,[133] whereby the repetition of some structural element, in this case, a particular textural configuration or rhythmic pattern, requires a significant modification in order to help express an ending of the process. Until now, the terminal modification of a musical theme has normally been located in the harmonic and melodic content of the cadential ideas; with Chopin's preludes, textural and rhythmic processes now play a greater role.

The highly virtuosic and improvisatory style featured in many of the preludes sometimes results in the substantial ornamentation of the upper voice. For that reason, it is sometimes difficult to know whether at moments of cadential closure, the soprano has achieved its melodic goal, and if so, which pitch even represents that goal. As such, a number of authentic cadences cannot be clearly distinguished as perfect (ending on $\hat{1}$) or imperfect (on $\hat{3}$). In some cases, in fact, the structural descent to tonic only takes place in a postcadential area, following what is otherwise the final cadence of the piece.

In a number of the preludes, we find consecutive PACs of the type that we observed in works by Corelli and Scarlatti, whereby an idea that has cadential content is immediately repeated. Sometimes, the first cadential idea clearly functions to bring a sense of formal closure, and the second iteration is a postcadential reinforcement. At other times, the first cadence seems to arrive too early, often for reasons of grouping structure, so that the sense of "real" cadence only accrues to the second statement.[134] We sometimes have the impression that two cadences in a row are needed in the sense that "yes, the music is definitely closing now," as though a single articulation is somehow insufficient in itself to provide a satisfactory end.

Finally, we frequently encounter situations in the preludes where the harmonic requirements for cadence are present, but the arrival of the final harmony does not seem to project a moment of formal closure. The arrival may be premature within the prevailing grouping structure, or various other processes of melodic motion or textural continuity obscure the sense of closure.

Limitations of space prohibit reproducing the music of entire preludes (except for some very short ones), so excerpts will be used to highlight the major points of the analyses. In many cases, a given example brings together non-adjacent passages, which are separated by double bar lines. Readers are encouraged to consult the complete score in connection with the following analytical notes.

## 8.13.1. Prelude No. 1 in C

In this prelude, one that has long been associated with the first prelude of the *Well-Tempered Clavier*, the formal and cadential articulations are more clearly evident when we consider each real measure to comprise two notated measures (R = 2N), a view that seems reasonable enough given the 2/8 notated meter and the *Agitato* tempo marking. From that perspective, we can easily hear a 19cHC at measure 7 (Ex. 8.27a, beginning of real measure 4) to end an antecedent phrase. The matching consequent starting at measure 9, and highly extended, is closed by an authentic cadence at measure 25 (Ex. 8.27b). This final cadential articulation is obscured somewhat by the melodic activity; indeed, we could very well have the impression of an evaded cadence when the melodic D ($\hat{2}$) of measure 24 fails to reach its intended goal ($\hat{1}$), leaping down instead to G ($\hat{5}$) in what seems like a re-initiation of the opening bars of the prelude. (The sudden change to *piano* dynamic also helps project the grouping disjunction expressed by an evaded cadence.) We would thus expect that another cadential progression would lead, one more time, to the final cadence. Instead, the tonic harmony achieved at measure 25 is sustained to the end of the piece, and the expected melodic $\hat{1}$ only arrives at measure 29, within what is clearly a postcadential closing section.[135] The similarity of this technique to Bach's prelude is striking (see in Chapter 6, Ex. 6.19). The very final codetta (Ex. 8.27c) brings a modest reduction in texture, but one that is nonetheless significantly different from all that came before. So we might identify here an *isolated* codetta.

## 8.13.2. Prelude No. 2 in A Minor

This highly enigmatic piece presents fascinating complications in most of its constituent parameters: tonality, harmony, melody, rhythm, and texture. The prelude nonetheless projects a fairly clear cadential scheme (Ex. 8.28a). Following a thematic introduction in E minor (not shown), an opening phrase (mm. 3–7) quickly modulates to G major, as confirmed by an IAC at measure 6. This phrase functions as a model that is repeated sequentially up a fifth. Within the sequence, though, an impending IAC in D at measure 11 (Ex. 8.28b) fails due to a deceptive cadence, whose replacement harmony is highly unusual (as will be discussed shortly). A second sequence (mm. 14–19, not shown) is harmonically and tonally transposed again up a fifth. (The melody keeps its contour but is transposed by a different interval.) This time, an extension via fragmentation of the sequence (mm. 20–21) leads to a home-key PAC in A minor (Ex. 8.28c, m. 23). This PAC is an example of an isolated cadence, since its texture is distinct from its preceding material (though to be sure a reduction of rhythmic activity already occurs prior to the cadential idea proper).

---

133. See Chapter 1, sec. 1.1.

134. We have already seen this situation in Chopin's A-flat Etude (Ex. 8.12, mm. 13–14 and 15–16).

135. Agawu is explicit on this point: "In particular, my analysis notes a displacement between the global melodic resolution in m. 29 and the global harmonic one in m. 25" ("Concepts of Closure," 9, note 24). Here, we again may have a case of Richards's "separated cadence" (see note 86).

EXAMPLE 8.27. Chopin, Prelude in C, Op. 28, no. 1, (a) mm. 6–9; (b) mm. 23–29; (c) mm. 33–34.

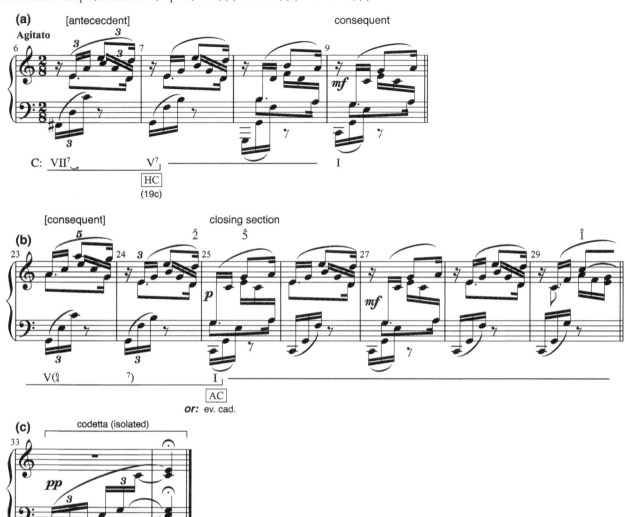

A bass-line reduction of the complete prelude (Ex. 8.28d) summarizes the main elements of its formal and tonal trajectory.[136] We see that the overall form emerges as a core-like design consisting mostly of model-sequence technique. (Not typical of a core, however, is the closing PAC, as most cores end with an HC.) In addition, the analysis highlights that the first and third phrases are supported by an ECP featuring a ⑥–⑤–① bass (the second phrase begins the same way, but ⑤ is retained (m. 11) in place of ①); thus the harmonic content of the model and its sequences consists almost exclusively of cadential progressions; the only prolongational moment arises with the neighboring V/V (m. 21, beat 4) within the dominant expansion of the final ECP. We also see that given the model-sequence technique, both the IAC and the deceptive cadence have a limited scope such that the final PAC becomes the only structural cadence for the prelude as a whole.

Finally, some remarks on the deceptive cadence in measure 11 (Ex. 8.28b). The final harmony of the progression, a half-diminished seventh (spelled in "root" position as D♯–F♯–A–C♯) is especially unusual as a replacement for the tonic in D major.[137] Yet if we allow for an enharmonic reinterpretation of D♯ to E♭, the harmony could be thought of as a VII$^6_5$/IV (A–C♯–E♭–F♯), a substitute for a dominant seventh (A–C♯–D–F♯), a harmony whose root is D. If so, then we could understand the half-diminished seventh as a "tonic" replacement in the key of D.[138] (Note that the C♯ moves to C♮ in the second half of measure 12, thus creating a fully-diminished seventh that

---

136. This bass-line analysis is inspired by a schematic harmonic plan offered by Meyer, *Emotion and Meaning*, 95; reprinted in Chopin, *Preludes, Op. 28*, 77.

137. It is not immediately obvious how to extract the harmonies of this prelude. As a rule, the pitches located on the second and sixth eighth-note beats in the lowest notes of the left hand are non-chord tones. Thus the C♯s sounding in mm. 11–14 are not members of the harmonies.

138. Meyer also considers the sonority to be an altered tonic in D major (*Emotion and Meaning*, 95).

EXAMPLE 8.28A–C. Chopin, Prelude in A Minor, Op. 28, no. 2, (a) mm. 5–6; (b) mm. 10–13; (c) mm. 21–23.

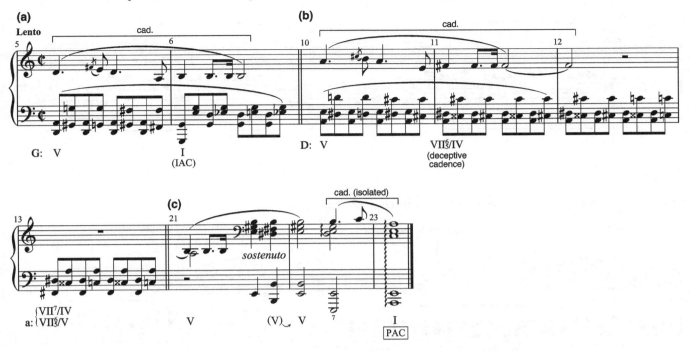

EXAMPLE 8.28D. Chopin, Prelude in A Minor, Op. 28, no. 2, bass-line reduction.

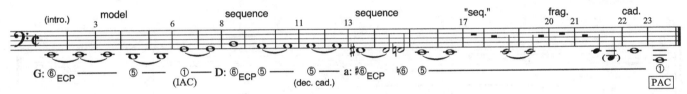

perhaps more obviously functions as a dominant-seventh substitute.) At measure 13, the diminished-seventh harmony, which is inverted so that F♯ resides in the bass, functions now as a pivot to bring the music into A minor. As such, the implied root would be B (replaced by the C♮), thus allowing the harmony to function as a conventional pre-dominant of the final cadential progression.

### 8.13.3. Prelude No. 3 in G

The form of this prelude, a compound period with extended consequent, is clear enough (ant: mm. 3–11; cons: mm. 12–26). The period is framed by a two-measure thematic introduction and a seven-measure closing section, concluded by an isolated codetta, whose chordal rolls provide a final remnant of the pervasive sixteenth-note motion of the piece. The PAC at measure 26 is completely classical, being preceded by a large ECP, whose initial harmony might be traced as far back as the $V^7/IV$ at m. 16. The half cadential articulation of the opening antecedent, however, is problematic (Ex. 8.29). In effect, we find two progressions that tonicize the dominant ($V^7/V$–V) in measures 7–8 and 9–10. If we hear the first progression as half cadential, then the sense of a genuine HC seems premature within the expected grouping structure.[139] Rather, the second progression, which now includes a seventh within the ultimate dominant, appears more to articulate a 19cHC, coming as it does at the end of the second four-measure group. Here, then, is a good example of Chopin writing consecutive cadences, the first of which appears too early, such that the second one provides a more definitive sense of closure.

### 8.13.4. Prelude No. 4 in E Minor

We encounter here another compound period, whose component antecedent (mm. 1–12) and consequent (mm. 13–25) are more balanced than in the previous prelude. A half cadential progression ($IV^6$–$V^7$) leading to the downbeat of measure 10 brings a potential phrygian 19cHC to close the antecedent (Ex. 8.30a), while

---

[139]. In the classical style, the progression $V^7/V$–V would rarely be used to articulate a simple HC, but rather would be found more typically with a reinterpreted HC; however, the Romantic emphasis on root-position harmonies (indeed, all of them in this prelude stand in this position) permits the progression to be construed as half cadential.

EXAMPLE 8.29. Chopin, Prelude in G, Op. 28, no. 3, mm. 7–10.

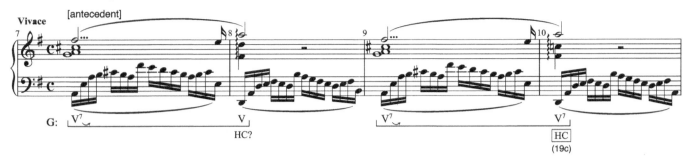

EXAMPLE 8.30. Chopin, Prelude in E Minor, Op. 28, no. 4, (a) mm. 9–14; (b) mm. 18–25.

two subsequent repetitions of the same progression support a standing on the dominant. Like the previous prelude, however, we might question whether measure 10 really marks a moment of genuine closure, because this articulation seems premature within the prevailing grouping processes. Up to this point, we have heard two four-measure phrases (mm. 1–4, 5–8); the second, a loosely sequential repetition of the first. Thus a cadential articulation only two bars later might seem too early. Yet it is not clear that any of the following dominants (downbeats of mm. 11 and 12) are necessarily more decisive. We can thus recognize a premature dominant arrival at measure 10 ending the antecedent in a decidedly nonclassical manner. Note that throughout the standing on the dominant that follows, Chopin keeps alluding to an upper-neighbor motive "x" that pervades the prelude; this time, however, what had been a stepwise neighbor (see, e.g., mm. 13–14), now becomes a leap from A to F# (thus, motive x′), which skips over $\hat{3}$ (that scale degree being recovered, however, as an accented passing tone on the downbeat of m. 12).[140]

Compared to the antecedent, the consequent initially seems to be compressed in that the "slithery chromaticism" of the melodic descent from $\hat{5}$ reaches $\hat{2}$ in seven bars (mm. 13–18), as opposed to ten bars (mm. 1–10) in the opening phrase. But Chopin then introduces two ECPs (mm. 18–21, 21–25) which restore a balance to the large-scale grouping structure of the prelude (ant. = 12 bars; cons. = 13). The penultimate dominant of the first ECP arises in the middle of measure 18 (Ex. 8.30b), at which point the dominant is expanded via the A–F# motive x′

---

140. The omission of a structural $\hat{3}$ has been commented upon by numerous analysts trying to find a complete descending *Urlinie* for this piece. For a general assessment of this issue, see Justin London and Ronald Rodman, "Musical Genre and Schenkerian Analysis," 102–11.

EXAMPLE 8.31. Chopin, Prelude in D, Op. 28, no. 5, (a) mm. 13–17; (b) mm. 29–39.

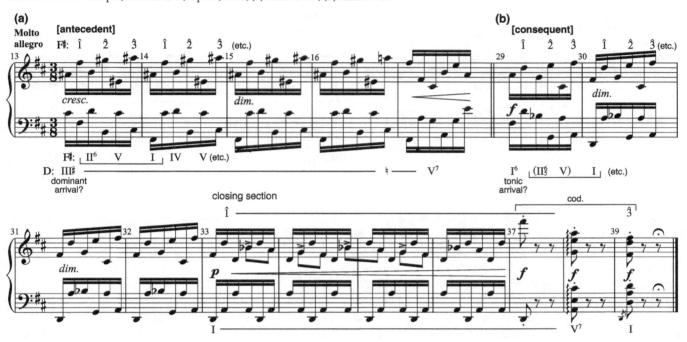

(which had earlier been associated with an ultimate dominant), only to find resolution in the deceptive cadence of measure 21. The upper-neighbor motive, now $\hat{2}$–$\hat{1}$ (x), continues through a new ECP (middle of m. 21). which prolongs stage 2 via a passing $^6_4$ to an "inverted" German sixth on the downbeat of measure 23. The final V–I completes the cadential progression with a PAC that is clearly isolated from the preceding texture. This cadence also distinguishes itself from what comes before in more subtle ways: unlike the upper-neighbor motions by which $\hat{1}$ was initially approached at measure 21 and then prolonged, the final cadence brings a contrasting lower-neighbor motion, $\hat{7}$–$\hat{1}$ (motive "x," inverted); as well, the 4-3 suspension over a dominant triad is reminiscent of a baroque cadence, as is appropriate given the prelude's prominent use of the lament topic.[141] Finally, we find a case of noncongruence between harmony and melody in the closure of this prelude, recalling Richards's notion of a "separated cadence." Unlike Prelude No. 1, where the harmony ends first and the melody reaches its goal only later, here the process is reversed: measure 21 brings full melodic closure, but the harmonic conclusion is delayed until the final bar of the piece.[142]

### 8.13.5. Prelude No. 5 in D

The form of the prelude seems periodic, with a clear return at measure 17 to the opening material. Each of the component antecedent and consequent units consists of four 4-measure phrases. The first phrase of each unit (mm. 1–4; 17–20) begins off-tonic by prolonging dominant harmony, somewhat in the sense of a thematic introduction. The second phrase (mm. 5–8; 21–24) begins with tonic harmony and brings an initial statement of material featuring a good deal of melodic-harmonic flux. The third phrase (mm. 9–12; 25–28) sequences the prior one up a step, thus beginning in II. The fourth, and final, phrase brings a renewed sense of harmonic and melodic stability. The final phrase of the antecedent (Ex. 8.31a,[143] mm. 13–16) prolongs III♯, which continues the sequential pattern established in the second and third phrases, and which features a stepwise melodic ascent $\hat{1}$–$\hat{2}$–$\hat{3}$ in F-sharp major (III♯); the shift from A♯ to A♮, at the very end of the phrase, facilitates the return to V$^7$ of the home key for the beginning of the consequent (final eighth note of m. 16). The fourth phrase of the consequent (Ex. 8.31b, mm. 29–32) is similar to the antecedent except that it prolongs the tonic of the home key, with the same $\hat{1}$–$\hat{2}$–$\hat{3}$ melodic ascent.

Though we can speak of "antecedent" and "consequent" units in general terms, determining the nature of their cadential articulations is somewhat difficult. The III♯ ending the first unit could be regarded as a dominant substitute,[144] but that

---

141. For the likely influence of J. S. Bach's "Crucifixus" (from the B-Minor Mass) on Chopin's prelude, see Nicole Biamonte, "Variations on a Scheme: Bach's 'Crucifixus' and Chopin's and Scriabin's E-Minor Preludes."

142. Carl Schachter sees the fundamental upper line move into the alto with $\hat{3}$ at m. 21; he then finds the melodic closure $\hat{2}$–$\hat{1}$ occurring in an inner voice in the final two measures of the piece, thus coordinated with the harmonic closure ("The Triad as Place and Action," 152–53).

143. To avoid clutter, I have deleted the slur mark that Chopin notates over the entire prelude.

144. See again note 16.

EXAMPLE 8.32. Chopin, Prelude in B Minor, Op. 28, no. 6, (a) mm. 6–8; (b) mm. 15–18.

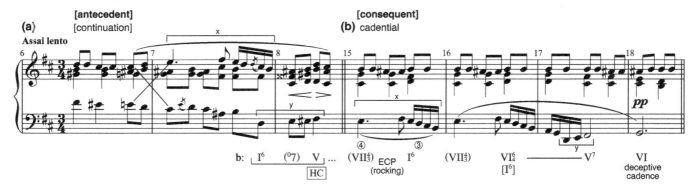

harmony is not articulated as a cadential goal; rather, it emerges as the final link in an ascending-stepwise sequence. Each subsequent appearance of III♯ (on the downbeats of mm. 14, 15, and 16) arises from a very local authentic cadential progression, but none of these creates an obvious sense of authentic cadence per se. Moreover, the stepwise ascent in the upper voice counters any tendency toward melodic closure. At best, we can probably identify a premature dominant (substitute) arrival at measure 13. The consequent ends similarly, except that the "arrival" (m. 29) is now tonic of the home key.[145] Again, we find local cadential progressions leading to the downbeats in measures 30–32, but to no real cadential effect. Thus it is not surprising that Chopin tacks on a kind of closing section in measures 33–39 (despite the absence of a clear cadence). This passage stabilizes the tonic scale degree both melodically and harmonically. The prelude ends with an isolated codetta (mm. 37–39), with $\hat{3}$ lingering on top of the texture.

### 8.13.6. Prelude No. 6 in B Minor

The "melody" of the prelude resides mostly in the left-hand part (Ex. 8.32a). Thus only certain notes of that part represent the actual bass voice. Toward the end of the opening compound antecedent, of sentential design, the melody shifts into the upper part of the right hand via the voice-exchange within the upbeat to measure 7, and the melody continues there until the HC in the following bar. When, within the following compound consequent, the melody of measure 7 (motive "x") is retained in the left hand at measures 15–16 (Ex. 8.32b), the pitches E (④) and D (③) now function as true bass notes supporting (VII$^4_3$)–I$^6$, a rocking on the tonic that initiates an ECP (VI$^6_4$ substitutes for I$^6$ in mm. 16–17). The way-station deceptive cadence at measure 18 then motivates a repetition of this cadential phrase to effect the PAC (not shown), which completes the extended consequent of this periodic form. A lovely motivic touch arises when the bass line of the half cadential progression (mm. 7–8, motive "y") is recaptured at the very bottom on the left-hand sweep in measures 16–17.[146]

### 8.13.7. Prelude No. 7 in A

The apparent simplicity of harmony and grouping structure in this prelude belies the complexity of its formal and cadential expression. (Ex. 8.33 shows the entire prelude.) Beginning off-tonic with V$^7$, all of the subsequent harmonies stand in root-position.[147] The grouping is highly symmetrical, consisting of four 4-measure phrases, each of which contains two 2-measure ideas of homogeneous motivic–textural content. Indeed, the lack of clear differentiation among the elements of the prelude is precisely what makes it difficult to determine its cadences and form.

The first four-measure phrase brings a basic idea followed by a contrasting idea (the "contrast" owing foremost to the change in melodic contour). The phrase is thus best understood as a compound basic idea because we cannot speak of a closing cadence—the single harmonic progression V$^7$–I within this phrase does not "end" any prior progression.[148] (To clarify that the harmonic progression here is prolongational, not cadential, I connect the two harmonies with a slur.) The second phrase (mm. 5–8) is not a consequent, because the opening basic idea does not return (such a restatement occurs later at m. 9). But the phrase also has no characteristics of a continuation, the other logical phrase function to follow a compound basic idea. Instead, we first encounter a varied version of the prior contrasting idea. This variant then recurs down a step (mm. 7–8) in the manner of a "response–statement" repetition. As regards the melodic scaffolding of these ideas, we

---

145. The concept of a "tonic arrival" will be explored more in the next chapter; see sec. 9.1.

146. This prelude is a good example of how the technique of invertible counterpoint can result in similar material acquiring different formal functions. The right-hand melody of m. 7 serves as a soprano voice, leading to an HC. But the same melody in the left hand of m. 15 functions as an embellished bass voice initiating an authentic ECP. For more discussion on the varying form-functional roles of invertible counterpoint, see Caplin, "*Tempest* Exposition," 103–11.

147. Alternatively, we might recognize a tonic upbeat to the first bar, in which case the opening would not technically be "off tonic."

148. Lerdahl and Jackendoff are also specific on this point (*Generative Theory*, 168–69, Ex. 7.24).

EXAMPLE 8.33. Chopin, Prelude in A, Op. 28, no. 7, mm. 1–16.

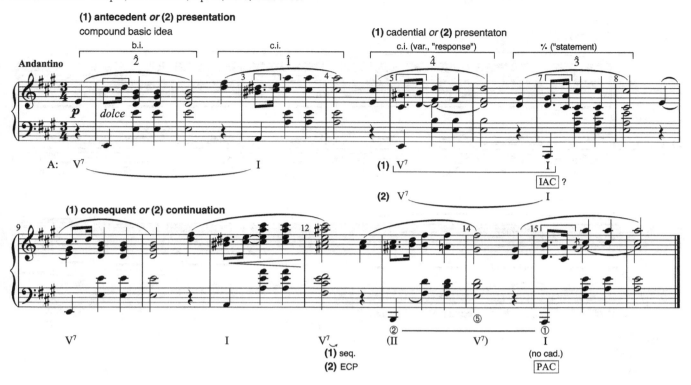

can see a clear pattern whereby $\hat{4}$–$\hat{3}$ of this second phrase matches $\hat{2}$–$\hat{1}$ in the previous compound basic idea (though the displacement of $\hat{1}$ an octave higher in mm. 3–4 somewhat obscures that connection).

The underlying harmonic progression of the second phrase, again just V⁷–I, is ambiguous. On the one hand, it could be seen as cadential (as Lerdahl and Jackendoff read it), thus closing the prevailing eight-measure unit with an IAC.[149] In this case, we could say that the second phrase serves a cadential function (option 1 in the annotation on the score). On the other hand, the progression could be seen as another tonic prolongation, a literal repeat of the prior progression. Seeing as the second two-measure idea (mm. 7–8) repeats the first idea (mm. 5–6), the lack of any distinctive "cadential idea" further dissuades us from finding a genuine cadence here. Instead, the repeated ideas raise a possible interpretation of presentation (option 2), though a compound basic idea followed by a presentation constitutes a most unconventional formal plan. Determining the overall function of the opening eight measures is also complicated. If we hear an IAC in measure 7, we could then recognize a compound antecedent (option 1). But if we hear a tonic prolongation throughout these eight bars, while also giving credence to the overall $\hat{2}$–$\hat{1}$, $\hat{4}$–$\hat{3}$ melodic framework, we could hear a compound presentation (option 2).

The return of the basic idea in measures 9–10 suggests the beginning of a compound consequent (option 1), which would

match a prior antecedent (mm. 1–8), thus lending retrospective weight to a closing IAC for that former unit. But the unexpected appearance of V⁷/II in measure 12 suddenly accelerates the harmonic rhythm and initiates a descending-fifths sequential progression (option 1 of the harmonic analysis), thus imparting a marked continuational quality to the entire unit (option 2 of the formal analysis). Seeing as all of the harmonies of this sequential progression stand in root position, the same harmonic succession can also be understood as cadential (option 2); indeed, since the final tonic of this ECP is the last harmonic event in the prelude, its cadential function emerges as genuine. Nonetheless, the inherent ambiguity of sequential and cadential harmonic expression remains palpable, such that if we take the former as decisive, then we are logically forced to deny cadential closure to the prelude (option 1).

Two additional points are worthy of mention. First, the dotted-eighth-to-sixteenth figure at the start of every odd-numbered bar is ascending in contour (see the brackets in mm. 1–7), with one exception—the PAC of measure 15, where the figure is descending. Though a minor detail, this change in contour helps to set this final idea off from all of the previous ones, and so we can recognize a terminal modification that we have discussed in connection with the more general concept of closure.[150] Second,

---

149. *Generative Theory*, 168–69, Ex. 7.24.

150. Rose Rosengard Subotnick also attends carefully to this change in melodic directionality: "The deviation from symmetry that occurs with the inversion in the melodic line at the opening of the last melodic phrase (measures 14–15) may be small, but in no way can it be discounted as transparent in effect. By setting the anacrusis G-sharp

EXAMPLE 8.34. Chopin, Prelude in F-sharp Minor, Op. 28, no. 8, (a) mm. 25–28; (b) mm. 32–34.

the bass note ② of the cadential dominant in measure 14 is placed an octave higher than most of the other bass pitches, this in order to maintain a consistent texture throughout the prelude as a whole. As a result, the final $V^7$–I progression is rendered rhetorically weaker than expected, since we may be tempted to hear a compelling registral connection from the low B (②) of measure 13 to the A (①) of m 15 (connected by a line), a melodic bass motion that is decidedly noncadential in expression.

### 8.13.8. Prelude No. 8 in F-sharp Minor

The prelude takes the form of a small ternary, whose A section is roughly periodic in design. An opening four-measure phrase ends with a 19cHC, one that emphasizes 5̂ in the upper part.[151] The matching "consequent" fails to close cadentially, ending instead on an augmented sixth of E-flat minor, the principal key of the B section.[152] The A′ section begins at measure 19 with the "consequent" of the A section, now expanded to close with an authentic cadence at measure 27 (see Ex. 8.34a). It is difficult to say just what kind of authentic cadence this is. Three options present themselves. First, we could observe that the most prominent scale

---

*below* the next melody note, B, instead of above it as in the third phrase (measures 4–5, where the anacrusis C-sharp is higher than the ensuing downbeat, A-sharp), and then by giving the dotted-eighth-to-sixteenth pattern (B to A) a *downward* direction in measure 15—this is the only time this happens—the prelude allows the dotted-eighth-note B an exceptional prominence not found on the initial first beat of any preceding phrase" (*Deconstructive Variations: Music and Reason in Western Society*), 98–99.

151. The opening one-measure idea of this initiating phrase (not shown) has embedded within it a cadential progression, a Romantic technique discussed earlier; see sec. 8.3.

152. This is a case of a "pre-dominant arrival," a technique that will be discussed in the following chapter, sec. 9.2.

degree projected by the upper voice is $\hat{5}$. So an interpretation of an IAC might be posited (option 1 in the annotations). Problematic with this reading is that most cases of an IAC occurring with $\hat{5}$ can usually be explained in some other way.[153] In this case, $\hat{5}$ seems so immobile as to resemble more an inner voice than a structural upper one. In fact, Chopin introduces a small detail in measures 25–26 found nowhere earlier in the prelude, namely, the accent marks placed above the top pitch in the left-hand part.[154] The melody outlined by these emphasized, alto-stream pitches ($\hat{3}$–$\hat{2}$–$\hat{1}$–$\hat{7}$), especially when made prominent in a performance,[155] suggests that this line might represent the structural soprano, one that is heading for a PAC (option 2). Yet this interpretation is also problematic, insofar as a resolution to $\hat{1}$ (at m. 27) is not forthcoming in any obvious way; rather, a potential closing section, eliding with the cadence, begins directly with $\hat{5}$, thus rendering a "covered" PAC with an implied resolution to $\hat{1}$. Finally, the failure to provide the melodic goal raises a third option, namely that of an evaded cadence. This view is less compelling perhaps than the other two because not only does a one-more-time technique not ensue, but also the immediately following material sounds so postcadential.

Even though melodic closure has not yet taken place, the passage from measure 27 to the end, with its characteristic plagal progressions, projects a likely closing section (mm. 29–31 are not shown in the example). A final melodic descent (though not stepwise) does occur with the isolated cadential gesture in the final two bars of the prelude (Ex. 8.34b, mm. 33–34),[156] featuring a root-position III in place of $I^6$. Is this an isolated cadence or a codetta? Both interpretations have validity: if we believe that the IAC in measure 27 represents the true formal conclusion of the piece (option 1) and that the following plagal progressions express a postcadential function, then this final gesture is a codetta ending with a PAC of limited scope; the same interpretation holds if we recognize a covered PAC (option 2). On the contrary, if we hear the IAC as a *way station* and regard the following music as part of the fundamental formal process of the prelude, then an interpretation of measure 34 as a genuine, isolated PAC makes sense; the same interpretation holds for finding an earlier evaded cadence (option 3).

## 8.13.9. Prelude No. 9 in E

The Prelude consists of three four-measure phrases, the first and third of which are sufficiently similar in design to suggest an overall ternary structure. The melody of the A section opens on $\hat{5}$ and rises stepwise to $\hat{1}$ at measure 3. The move down to $\hat{7}$, supported by a root-position V, promises to close with a PAC on the downbeat of measure 4 (Ex. 8.35a); the final tonic, however, is replaced by VI. Yet, unlike a standard deceptive cadence, the melody does not resolve to $\hat{1}$, but returns instead stepwise back to $\hat{5}$ (m. 5) from which it originated.[157] The A section thus fails to achieve cadential closure.[158] The contrasting middle modulates to III♯ (G-sharp major, notated as A-flat major), as confirmed by a rhetorically powerful IAC on the third beat of measure 8 (Ex. 8.35b).[159]

The A′ section (beginning at measure 9) sees the melody again rise stepwise from $\hat{5}$ in the context of a general ascending-step model-sequence technique. This time, however, the various modal inflections of the harmony yield chromatically flattened $\hat{6}$ and $\hat{7}$ degrees; only the final V–I leading into measure 12 resolves the leading tone to tonic in the melody. In itself, of course, this final progression qualifies as cadential, yet because it seems to emerge as the last link in a broader ascending-stepwise sequence, its cadential effect seems rather forced. Combined with the rhetorically powerful dynamic, it is as though Chopin were insisting hard that we take the final progression as cadential, even if it seems to be a part of the broader sequential process.

Although I have been speaking of the final progression as a sequential link, it actually departs from the model in a number of respects. If the harmonic plan were to continue regularly (see the arrow), the harmony on the fourth beat of measure 11 would have been C major (IV/♭III), moving then on to an A-minor triad (IV) for the downbeat of measure 12. Instead, Chopin has the bass leap a third (rather than a fourth) to support a B-major harmony, which then resolves to E as dominant to tonic. In other words, the final progression departs from the strict sequence, and in that way represents a "terminal modification" to bring closure; yet the complete homogeneity of texture and rhythm disguises these harmonic differences, thus obscuring to some extent the sense that the cadential idea contrasts with what comes before.

## 8.13.10. Prelude No. 10 in C-sharp Minor

We again confront a Prelude with a symmetrical grouping structure: four 4-measure phrases, the fourth one extended by two bars when the final cadential idea is repeated. Each group begins with

---

153. See Chapter 3, sec. 3.2.1.5.

154. In some editions these accents look more like decrescendo signs.

155. See, for example, Martha Argerich (Deutsche Grammophon, Naxos Music Library No. 00028943158428) and Rafal Bleckacz (Deutsche Grammophon, Naxos Music Library No. 00028947964438).

156. The extra emphasis on $\hat{7}$ given by the quarter-note appoggiatura in m. 34 perhaps compensates for the lack of explicit resolution of $\hat{7}$–$\hat{1}$ from the end of m. 26 to m. 27 (Ex. 8.34a).

157. This cadential deviation thus reminds us of the baroque "inverted" deceptive cadence; see Chapter 6, sec. 6.4.7. Though I am speaking here of a deceptive cadential progression, the harmonies in m. 3 could also be interpreted as a descending-fifths sequence, along the lines of Ex. 8.13, discussed earlier.

158. Although it is possible to hear prolongational closure leading to the downbeat of m. 5, I prefer to understand the preceding $V^6_5$ more as an anacrusis to the next phrase (the B section) than as a penultimate harmony closing the first phrase.

159. We might want to speak here of an "arrival six-four," a rhetorical effect described by Hatten, *Musical Meaning*, 15, 288; see also ahead in Chapter 9 (sec. 9.6) the discussion of the climax to the slow movement of Bruckner's Seventh Symphony (Ex. 9.44, m. 77, and note 122).

EXAMPLE 8.35. Chopin, Prelude in E, Op. 28, no. 9, (a) mm. 3–5; (b) mm. 8–12.

a basic idea, consisting of descending flourishes, followed by a contrasting idea of homophonic texture. In the first phrase (Ex. 8.36a), this second unit (mm. 3–4) brings no cadential closure, consisting as it does of a single dominant harmony, thus rendering a compound basic idea for the phrase as a whole. Note one oddity that plays itself out through the prelude: the melodic line of every contrasting idea ends on the third beat of the bar with a dynamic accent (in the manner of a mazurka); here, the final E ($\hat{3}$) in measure 4 suggests an unusual six-four harmony within the overall dominant.

Each of the following phrases brings varying degrees of cadential closure. Phrase two ends with an authentic cadence in the minor-dominant region (Ex. 8.36b). The third beat of measure 8 brings an accented G♯ ($\hat{1}$), which does not disrupt the harmony of the bar and clearly groups with the cadential idea. Phrase three leads to an HC in the home key at measure 12 (Ex. 8.36c), and like the first phrase, the final pitch on E ($\hat{3}$) creates the odd six-four sonority. The final phrase closes with a home-key PAC on the second beat of measure 16 (Ex. 8.36d). But now the third beat brings an even more disrupting element, ending on A ($\hat{6}$), a pitch that belongs neither to the final tonic nor to the following dominant, when the cadential idea is repeated in measures 17–18. As regards the overall form of the prelude, the cadential-tonal plan suggests a small ternary form, with the B section creating its contrast via a shift to the subdominant at measure 9 (not shown).

Finally, we need to consider the status of the final repeated cadential idea. Is it merely postcadential, or does it represent the true end of the prelude? On the one hand, the ongoing grouping structure suggests that measure 16 is a perfectly appropriate place for a cadence, seeing as the two prior phrases cadenced in their fourth bar. If so, the repetition in measures 17–18 could be seen as a supplementary codetta. On the other hand, the disruptive A ($\hat{6}$) on the third beat of measure 16 is a destabilizing moment, so we may feel that the repeated gesture brings a more decisive sense of closure and thus represents the real cadence. In either case, what may well be the reason for this two-bar extension is the lack of any "isolated" final gesture—be it a cadence or a codetta—to give special prominence to the sense of closure, as we find in so many of the preludes. Measures 17 and 18 thus provide something "different"—an extension—to help consolidate our impression that the prelude is truly complete. Additional differences include a literal ending on $\hat{1}$ followed by a quarter-note rest (thus no upward leaping, accented third beat) along with a *poco ritardando*. A terminal modification is thus palpable in the repeated idea.

### 8.13.11. Prelude No. 11 in B

The prelude contains just a single cadence, the closing PAC at measures 23–25 (Ex. 8.37). Everything preceding this moment is basically tonic prolongational, save for one descending-thirds sequence (mm. 10–13, not shown). The "stop" at measure 21 has

EXAMPLE 8.36. Chopin, Prelude in C-sharp Minor, Op. 28, no. 10, (a) mm. 1–5; (b) mm. 7–8; (c) mm. 11–12; (d) mm. 15–18.

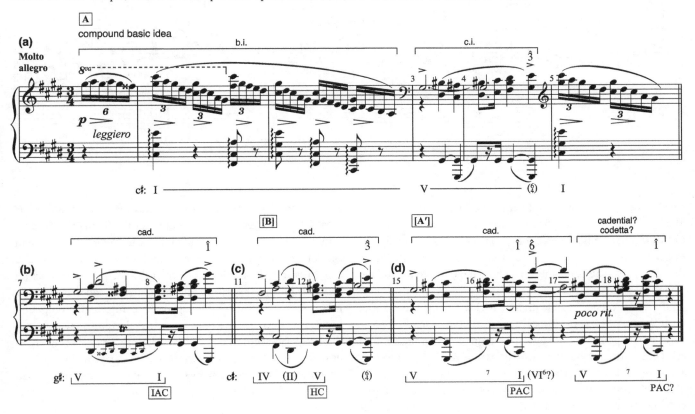

EXAMPLE 8.37. Chopin, Prelude in B, Op. 28, no. 11, (a) mm. 1–7; (b) mm. 19–27.

no cadential quality since the progression into the tonic ($V^6$–I) is exclusively prolongational; indeed, Chopin is careful to place all of the preceding dominants in first inversion. The cadential progression (m. 23) sees $V^7$/VI substituting for $I^6$. Rather than resolving deceptively to a pre-dominant IV (as discussed earlier in connection with Ex. 8.4d), the applied dominant resolves normally to VI. Paradoxically, then, both $V^7$/VI and VI function as substitutes for the initial tonic of the cadential progression,

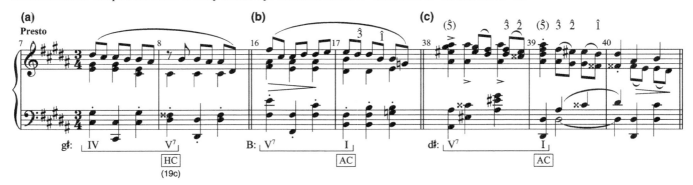

EXAMPLE 8.38. Chopin, Prelude in G-sharp Minor, Op. 28, no. 12, (a) mm. 7–8; (b) mm. 16–17; (c) mm. 38–40.

despite themselves having a dominant to tonic relationship.[160] The whiff of an ascending-third sequence can also be perceived in this last harmonic progression (V⁷/VI–VI; V⁷–I). Finally, the isolated quality of this cadence is evident, being separated from the pervasive eighth-note motion in both hands up to the sudden stop at measure 21.

If the one cadence in the prelude is clear enough, the overall form is not. After a two-measure thematic introduction (whose harmonic support is ambiguous: Is it tonic or dominant?), an eight-measure compound presentation (mm. 3–10) is followed by a four-measure continuation (mm. 11–14, not shown) consisting of model-sequence technique. Instead of moving forward into a cadential function as expected, the opening presentation returns at measure 15 (not shown), but only gets as far as measure 21. At this moment of rhythmic stop, the music seems to back up all the way to the opening thematic introduction, now unequivocally supported by tonic harmony. The cadential idea finally appears, as discussed, at the upbeat to measure 24.

As so presented, the form of the prelude consists of two, closely related, compound sentences (mm. 3–14 and 15–25), each of which is structurally incomplete in its own way. The first sentence lacks a cadential function, moving directly from a sequential continuation back to the opening presentation, which marks the beginning of the second sentence. The compound presentation of the second sentence is cut short by two bars, after which a return of the thematic introduction leads to a closing cadence. Whereas the first sentence remains unfinished in a somewhat conventional way, simply lacking its cadential function, the formal syntax of the second sentence seems at first glance to be downright bizarre: the (repeated) compound basic idea at measure 19 is cut short at measure 21 by the totally unexpected return of the thematic introduction, which then moves directly to the closing PAC.

Is there a way to make sense of the second sentence? The key is to recognize that the material content of the two-measure contrasting idea (mm. 6–7) of the constituent compound basic ideas is based directly on the content of the thematic introduction, indicated as motive "x." In both the introduction (m. 2) and the contrasting idea (m. 7), the motive functions as an extended anacrusis to the basic idea. So when the thematic introduction suddenly returns at measure 21, we can understand that it "stands in" (≈) for an implied contrasting idea to complete the compound basic idea. Since the latter has no cadential expression, and since the first sentence lacked a cadence, we are more than ready to hear the cadential idea of measures 23–24 as providing closure not only for the second sentence, but for the unconventional form of the prelude as a whole.

### 8.13.12. Prelude No. 12 in G-sharp Minor

Built as a fairly conventional small ternary, the prelude closes decisively with a PAC at measure 65 (see the full score), being preceded by an ECP, whose pre-dominant (IV⁷) is especially elongated (mm. 53–63). The periodic A section brings a 19cHC at measure 8 (Ex. 8.38a) followed by an authentic cadence in the relative major at measure 17 (Ex. 8.38b). Given the highly ornamented upper voice, it is difficult to say whether this is an IAC or PAC, hence the label "AC" in the score (see note 33). A similar problem arises in the B section with the modulation to D-sharp minor (HK: minV); see Example 8.38c. The high A♯ in measures 38–39 seems to be a covering tone, with the actual melodic descent F♯–E♯ (3̂–2̂ on the last beat of measure 38) being deflected back up to F♯, only to attain 1̂ at the very end of measure 39.

### 8.13.13. Prelude No. 13 in F-sharp

The prelude takes the form of a small binary (see full score), whose first part (mm. 1–20) is constructed as a compound period. The sentential antecedent ends with a reinterpreted HC (middle of m. 7); the consequent closes with a possible HK: PAC in 18. The cadential idea is then repeated in the following two bars. Unlike some cases where the repetition would be understood as a codetta, this one seems more like the "real" cadence, coming as it does in the final bars of a prevailing four-measure grouping structure.

---

160. One might argue that VI has pre-dominant function here. Indeed, many theorists classify this harmony as a pre-dominant. I have avoided doing so since in a cadential context VI normally progresses to a pre-dominant (IV or II⁶) before moving on to the dominant. To be sure, we find VI going directly to a cadential V often enough, even in the classical style, but in those cases the submediant usually functions as a tonic substitute, which bypasses pre-dominant.

EXAMPLE 8.39. Chopin, Prelude in F-sharp, Op. 28, no. 13, mm. 27–29.

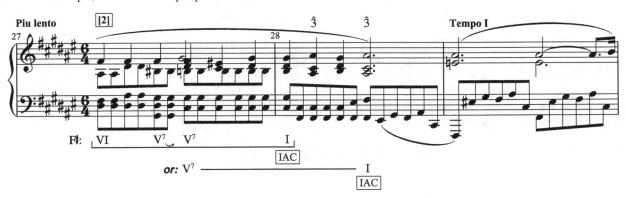

EXAMPLE 8.40. Chopin, Prelude in E-flat Minor, Op. 28, no. 14, (a) mm. 10–11; (b) harmonic reduction of mm. 10–11; (c) mm. 16–19.

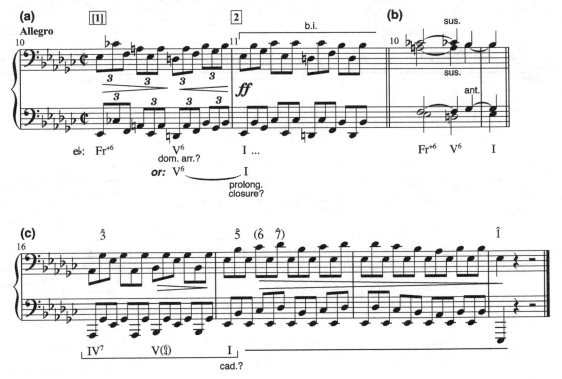

The second part of the binary (mm. 21–38) opens with contrasting material that is largely sequential in organization. Instead of ending on dominant harmony, as would be typical at this point in the form, the music pushes on in measure 28 to tonic as its harmonic goal (Ex. 8.39). We might initially want to find an IAC at the beginning of measure 28; after all, the harmonic requirements for a cadence are present. But note the odd parallel fifths in the left-hand part from the V to the I. Is Chopin asking us to hear the dominant harmony continuing on to the middle of the bar, with the low F♯ acting as a kind of anticipation? If so, the IAC would then arrive in the middle of measure 28. The second part continues on from here (not shown), leading to a pair of PACs at measures 34 and 36. Like the consecutive cadences in the first part, the first cadence seems somewhat premature due to the prevailing grouping of four bars, and so the second cadence at measure 36 seems more effective of overall closure; a two-measure codetta completes the entire form.

### 8.13.14. Prelude No. 14 in E-flat Minor

The pervasive unison texture creates difficulties for a harmonic analysis. The return of the opening material at measure 11 (Ex. 8.40a), roughly halfway through the piece, suggests some kind of bipartite structure. But neither the first part nor the second brings obvious cadences. The first "ends" on $V^6$ (m. 10), which could either be interpreted as no cadential closure at all (similar to the Mazurka in F-sharp Minor, Ex. 8.17, m. 8) or as a dominant arrival in lieu of an HC. Another possibility is to recognize a case of prolongational closure in the progression $V^6$–I on the downbeat of measure 11, though this view presumes an elision

EXAMPLE 8.41. Chopin, Prelude in D-flat, Op. 28, no. 15, (a) mm. 25–28; (b) mm. 76–89.

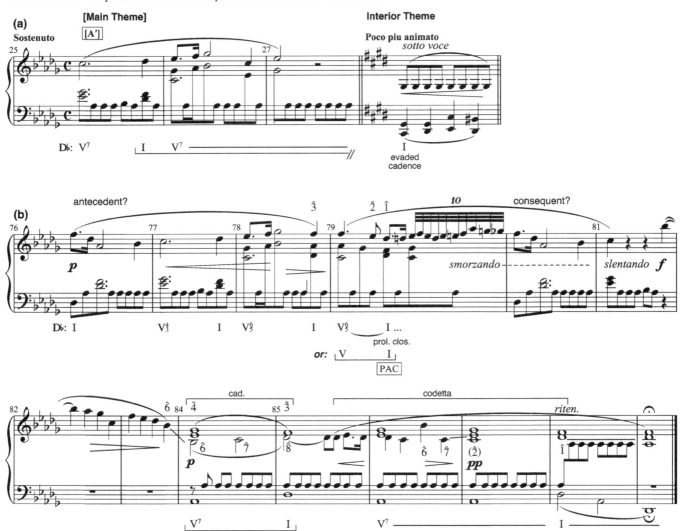

between the first and second parts, a formal situation rarely found in genuine bipartite structures (such as a period or small binary). Complicating the matter further are the non-chord tones—two suspensions and an anticipation—that occur within the V⁶ (see the harmonic reduction in Ex. 8.40b). As for the conclusion of the second part (Ex. 8.40c), we can identify an authentic cadential progression, but one that fails to bring a dominant proper following the cadential six-four. This harmonic lapse, combined with a melodic ending on $\hat{5}$ (and the odd stepping up to $\hat{6}$ and $\hat{7}$), renders the sense of genuine cadence especially obscure.[161] All of these cadential anomalies are entirely appropriate to the uncanny effect that the prelude conveys.

### 8.13.15. Prelude No. 15 in D-flat

This is the longest of the preludes (in terms of measure numbers) and the most elaborate in formal organization. The piece is structured as a *large ternary*,[162] consisting of a main theme, a *minore* interior theme, and an incomplete return of the main theme. Following classical models, the main theme is built as a small ternary, the interior theme, as a small binary.[163] In the first appearance of the main theme, the A′ section is left open (Ex. 8.41a), when, at measure 27, Chopin fails to complete the

---

161. Precedents for such an "authentic cadence" have been discussed in Chapter 5 in connection with some late symphonies by Beethoven (see the discussion of Ex. 5.74a, mm. 33–35 and note 139).

162. See *CF*, 211–16, and *ACF*, 566–69.

163. Most of the cadential articulations in the interior theme (not shown) are HCs (mm. 31, 35, 39), with the first part of the binary seeming to conclude with an IAC at m. 43. In a private communication, Schmalfeldt proposes that the "raindrop" Bs should be understood as covering tones, such that the cadence at m. 43 is a PAC, not an IAC (I concur). Following a written-out repeat of the *minore*'s first part, the second part contains only HCs (mm. 67 and 75); that the interior theme closes with dominant is typical of the large ternary form, since that closing harmony can then function to motivate the return of the main theme.

EXAMPLE 8.42. Chopin, Prelude in B-flat Minor, Op. 28, no. 16, (a) mm. 34–38; (b) mm. 45–46.

phrase and instead lets the music lead directly into the interior theme. As will be discussed momentarily, it is not clear which pitches should be chosen to represent the actual bass. But taking for the moment the repeated A♭s as the lowest voice, we might recognize an evaded cadence, seeing as a penultimate dominant is locked into place, but a final tonic does not appear.[164] Note the entirely nonclassical rhetoric associated with this evasion, as if the line had petered out, rather than dramatically breaking off. Something similar occurs in the return of the main theme (Ex. 8.41b), when at measure 81, Chopin interrupts the beginning of the consequent phrase; however, this moment is not cadential, so there can be no talk of an evasion here. Eventually, he creates final closure with an authentic cadence at measure 85 (whether this is an IAC or PAC will be discussed shortly).

Considerably obscuring the articulation of cadences in the main theme is the status of the "raindrop" pedal point (A♭/G♯) that occurs throughout most of the prelude. (To maximize efficiency in the use of examples, the following discussion will refer to the A′ section, shown in Example 8.41b, to illustrate cadential ambiguities in the main theme as a whole.) Within the opening bar of the section (m. 76), the pedal seems to function as an inner voice, with the bass D♭ lying below. But in the next number of bars, the pedal becomes the lowest sounding pitch. Thus in measures 77–78, the A♭s could be seen as the bass, supporting a root-position dominant. Then in measure 79, the harmonic closure of the phrase would require us to hear the D♭ on beat 3 as the real bass. If so, then would the C appearing on the downbeat of that bar be the bass as well? In other words, perhaps the pedal, even

when sounding as the *lowest* pitch, is still to be regarded as an inner voice, with the true bass lying above. With that interpretation, then all of the phrase-concluding tonics (such as m 79, as well as earlier, mm. 4, 8, and 23) would appear as prolongational closures ($V^6_5$–I). In order to find genuine cadences at these moments, the pedal would have to function as the bass in order to supply the root of the cadential dominants. It would be odd, however, for the opening phrase to conclude already with a PAC, as the melodic line $\hat{3}$–$\hat{2}$–$\hat{1}$ proposes. The situation, in my opinion, is left ambiguous throughout the entire main theme and its (partial) return at measure 76. Not until the very final cadential idea in measures 84–85 does Chopin resolve the ambiguity by providing a new bass line that clearly lies below the raindrop pedal. At the same time, however, he adds a new moment of confusion by introducing, below the upper voice at measure 84, a new line that seems to acquire the status of the true melody ($\hat{6}$–$\hat{7}$–$\hat{8}$), and especially so in the codetta that follows. If we take that line as the genuine soprano, then we can find a PAC at measure 85; if we still hear the literally sounding notes G♭–F ($\hat{4}$–$\hat{3}$) as the upper voice, then the prelude closes with an IAC.

### 8.13.16. Prelude No. 16 in B-flat Minor

In this periodic form (see the full score), the cadential articulations are fairly straightforward; a 19cHC closes the antecedent at measure 17 (not shown). The highly expanded consequent leads at measure 34 to the beginning of an ECP (see Ex. 8.42a), which features a rocking on the tonic. The cadential progression reaches its end in the middle of measure 37. Though the requirements for harmonic closure are achieved here, the complicated melodic organization makes it difficult to say whether the authentic cadence is perfect or imperfect. The

---

164. I will later present an alternative reading of the bass line, as shown in the comparable passage in Ex. 8.41b, mm. 77–78.

EXAMPLE 8.43. Chopin, Prelude in F Minor, Op. 28, no. 18, mm. 16–21.

ongoing melodic and rhythmic activity also blurs the impression of cadential arrival, and so it is not surprising that Chopin immediately initiates (m. 38) a second, more expansive ECP, which eventually culminates in a PAC at the very last bar of the piece (Ex. 8.42b). The sudden change to a homophonic texture in the last two beats projects this cadence as isolated from the ongoing *perpetuum mobile* style of the prelude.

### 8.13.17. Prelude No. 17 in A-flat

The cadences in this miniature five-part rondo are entirely conventional. To be sure, the final return of the main theme is supported by a tonic pedal, which obscures the cadences in this section. Having heard the rondo refrain twice already, we nonetheless know where the cadences are "supposed to be," despite the lack of genuine harmonic motion to articulate them as such.

### 8.13.18. Prelude No. 18 in F Minor

The single cadential progression closing this loosely sentential one-part form begins in the middle of measure 16 with $VI_4^6$ standing in for an initial $I^6$ (Ex. 8.43). The final resolution of the dominant to tonic (mm. 20–21), which creates an IAC emphasizing $\hat{5}$, very much isolates itself rhythmically and texturally from what precedes.[165] Unusual is the lack of leading tone in the cadential dominant; the resulting texture of empty fifths contributes to the menacing character of the prelude. An alternative harmonic analysis proposes that the dominant arrives already on the downbeat of measure 18 in the form of a cadential six-four, resolving to the dominant proper in the middle of the bar; this reading entails an implied C in the bass.

### 8.13.19. Prelude No. 19 in E-flat

Most of the cadential articulations in this small ternary form are identifiably classical. The only difficulty arises in connection with the opening antecedent phrase, which concludes at measure 8 with a 19cHC, $V^7/V-V^7$ (Ex. 8.44). Yet a similar progression, this time without the dissonant seventh in the dominant, already sounds in the two preceding bars (mm. 5–6). As we have seen on other occasions, Chopin brings a pair of cadential ideas, of which only the second seems to function to create closure, because the first one appears too early in the four-square grouping structure that we come to expect from these works.[166]

### 8.13.20. Prelude No. 20 in C Minor

Like the prelude in A major, the C-Minor prelude's apparent simplicity in texture (fully homophonic) and grouping structure (two four-measure phrases, the second of which is repeated) are at odds with some difficulties of harmonic, cadential, and formal analysis (Ex. 8.45 gives the complete piece).[167] As I will clarify later, I consider the overall form of the prelude to be a small binary.

---

165. James William Sobaskie points out that the final cadence with $\hat{5}$ reflects the fact that the piece "has no fundamental line [*Urlinie*]" ("Precursive Prolongation in the Préludes of Chopin," 52).

166. An alternative analysis may see reinterpreted HCs here, i.e., brief PACs in the key of B-flat. This view would make sense for a classical piece, but with the Romantic composers, the root-position option for a pre-dominant II or $V^7/V$ (as here) is entirely viable, as has been well established throughout this chapter.

167. To save space, I have enclosed the repeat of the second phrase within double bar lines; note that the repetition brings a change of dynamics from *piano* to *pianissimo*. In the original score, the repeat is written out.

EXAMPLE 8.44. Chopin, Prelude in E-flat, Op. 28, no. 19, mm. 4–9.

EXAMPLE 8.45. Chopin, Prelude in C Minor, Op. 28, no. 20, mm. 1–13 (R = ½N).

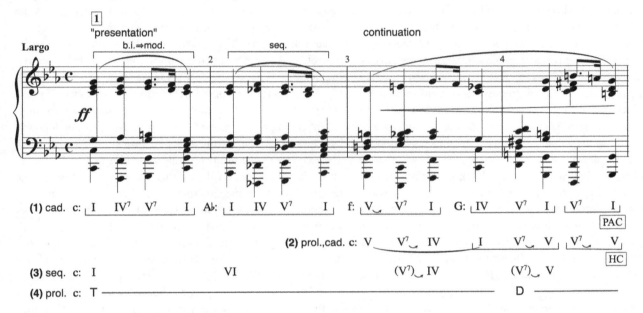

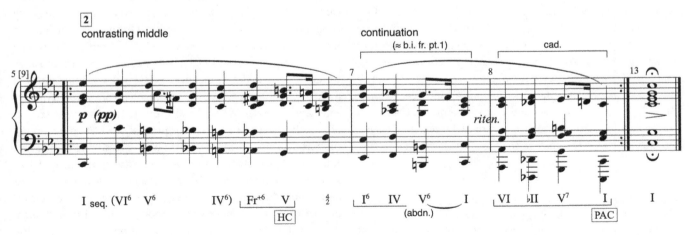

Though it is easy enough to label the individual harmonies making up the first part of the binary, it is more difficult to interpret the nature of the progressions that they form, due, in no small degree, to the fact that every chord stands in root position. The prelude begins with a Romantic-style cadential progression (line 1 of the analysis), which itself is immediately transposed down a third in the following bar. The final tonic of each progression cannot be seen to create an actual cadence, of course, since at this point in the piece, there is no prior material upon which to effect closure. We might thus consider each cadential

**490** Cadence in the Romantic Era

progression as serving, in effect, to prolong the tonic and submediant degrees respectively, thereby initiating a descending-thirds sequential progression (line 3). But we could also say that because the model-sequence technique does not continue any further, the VI of measure 2 sustains the sense of I in measure 1, thus rendering a tonic prolongation for these two bars (line 4). That the very opening measures can imply all three progression types—cadential, sequential, and prolongational—reveals well the kind of categorical blurring that can arise in Romantic works.

The following two bars are the most difficult in the prelude to interpret harmonically. The first three chords of measure 3 might seem to project a cadential progression in F minor (line 1), but the return to a C-minor sonority at the end of measure 3 suggests more the sense of a tonic prolongation, embracing a tonicization of IV (line 2). As such, we could then see this local tonic prolongation as sustaining the broader prolongation of measures 1 and 2 (line 4).[168] The final bar of part 1 briefly shifts the tonal focus to G major. What is difficult to say is whether this is a modulation to G (line 1), thus projecting two authentic cadential progressions, or else a tonicization of G within C minor (line 2), whereby we might discern a pair of half cadential progressions. In either case, the first progression of each pair is unlikely to create the impression of actual cadence, since nothing else in the music suggests beat 2 as a moment of formal arrival; indeed, the melodic trajectory obviously concludes on the fourth beat of measure 4. Whether we should regard that moment as an HC in the home key or a PAC in the new key is hard to say. On the one hand, we would normally be expecting the dominant region of a minor-mode home key to be the minor dominant, not the major one (as here), thus supporting the HK: HC interpretation. On the other hand, classical conventions call most frequently for the first part of a small binary to end with a PAC, though an HC also remains an option.[169]

In addition to the cadential analyses just discussed, the opening of measures 3–4 can be seen to project a modicum of sequential expression (line 3), inasmuch as ($V^7$/IV)–IV in measure 3 first continues the descending-thirds sequence from measures 1–2 and is then followed by an ascending stepwise sequence ($V^7$/V)–V in measure 4. Finally, we may prefer to emphasize a fully prolongational approach (as in line 4) and see measure 4 as a prolongation of the dominant (via tonicizations), thus with no cadential expression. To be sure, the foregoing analysis is perhaps excessively detailed, but the very slow tempo of the prelude permits us to speculate on the wide range of harmonic interpretations offered by this opening part of the binary.

After the complexities of the first part, the second one is rather easier to interpret, despite the greater chromaticism. The opening progression is a fairly standard variant on the lament *topos*, a descending-stepwise sequence, whose bass chromatically fills in the space from ① to ⑤. When the dominant shifts to $V^4_2$, resolving then to $I^6$ at measure 7, we might believe that a cadential progression were in the making, and the subsequent move to IV furthers this suspicion. But then comes what is perhaps the decisive harmonic moment in the entire prelude, one that rivals, if not surpasses in importance, the reinterpreted D♭ harmony in the following bar (IV/VI⇒♭II). By forcing the bass in measure 7 to leap down a tritone to B♮ to support $V^6_5$, Chopin abandons the cadential progression and creates the only unambiguous tonic prolongation in the piece. As a result, measure 8 now contains the closing cadential progression, following as it does upon the prior prolongation. Indeed, the cadential quality of this bar overrides the potential for ambiguity that comes from its also being, in true Romantic fashion, a circle-of-fifths sequence.

As regards the form of the prelude, many analysts would probably identify an overall periodic structure—a four-measure antecedent ending with dominant harmony of the home key, followed by a four-measure consequent with a stronger ending on tonic. The lack of a return of the opening basic idea to signal a consequent, however, would rule out this interpretation. Instead, the tempo of the piece suggests that we can hear each real measure as one-half of the notated measure (R = ½N). With that in mind, we might better view the prelude as taking the form of a small binary, each part of which contains, conventionally, eight real bars.[170] Part 1 takes on a sentential design, ending with a cadence of some kind (PAC or HC, as discussed). Part 2 begins with a contrasting middle ending with a home-key HC, followed by a continuation phrase concluding with a PAC. But some significant details complicate the picture, for we cannot ignore many similarities between measures 1 and 7: if the opening pitch in the melody in measure 7 had been G, and if the dominant harmony on beat three had been placed in root position, the two measures would have been almost identical (save for the opening inverted tonic). The resulting return of the initial basic idea would thus be sufficient to render the final two-measure unit as the A′ section of a small ternary design. But it is precisely that Chopin does *not* support measure 7 with the cadential progression from measure 1 that is of particular significance. For the appearance of two successive authentic cadential progressions would have created a harmonic redundancy, such that a root-position V–I progression in measure 7 would have poorly anticipated, and thus spoiled, the cadential effect of the same progression in measure 8. The sequential relation between measures 7 and 8 (as between mm. 1 and 2) would have also interfered with the sense of cadence.

---

168. Even further complicating the situation is an alternative version of the score (as suggested by a number of the original sources), which identifies a C-major harmony at the end of m. 3. This variant does not change the analysis of a broad tonic prolongation from the opening, though such a modal change within the prolongation would be odd. Yet a C-major sonority could also be construed as continuing to prolong the F-minor harmony (as its dominant).

169. An additional interpretation would find at the end of m. 4 a reinterpreted HC (i.e., SK: PAC⇒HK: HC), effectively a combination of options 1 and 2.

170. Typically, both the first and second parts of a small binary are repeated. Here, only the second part undergoes repetition.

Instead, Chopin makes measure 7 prolongational for the reasons just discussed and thus suppresses a potential ternary form.

### 8.13.21. Prelude No. 21 in B-flat

Similar to the situation we saw in connection with Schubert's String Quartet No. 8, D. 112 (Ex. 8.9), the opening eight-measure phrase of the prelude (Ex. 8.46a) seems to be supported by a single harmonic progression, one that resembles a cadential one, even if the opening tonic is in root position. As discussed in Chapter 5 (sec. 5.5), such situations pose special problems of cadential identification, though I imagine that most listeners would be prepared to find an IAC at measure 7, one that would appropriately end an antecedent.[171]

The following continuation phrase leads to a prominent dominant at measure 13 (Ex. 8.46b), which then resolves to tonic at measure 15. Two different cadential interpretations are forthcoming here. In the first, we hear the downbeat of measure 13 as an HC, seeing as this moment marks the formal goal of the ongoing cantabile melody, while what follows sees a major change in texture. The eighth-note configurations that had been exclusively accompanimental emerge to become the principal material of measures 13–16. In that measures 13–14 continue to prolong dominant harmony, these bars seem to be a standing on the dominant. Problematic, though, is that when the V resolves to I, the similar tonic-oriented material in measures 15–16, which clearly group with the standing on the dominant, no longer seem to project that postcadential function, and so these final two bars are left without any clear formal function.

These complexities suggest an alternative cadential option, namely that we hear the dominant of measure 13 as penultimate, and find an authentic cadence at measure 15. (Whether this cadence is perfect or imperfect is unclear given the considerable melodic flux throughout measures 13–16.) Yet the appearance of this tonic hardly seems like a moment of cadential arrival, seeing as the content of measures 13–14 and 15–16 project a kind of "response–statement" repetition scheme, a situation that rarely arises in connection with the dominant to tonic motion of an authentic cadence.

Despite the cadential ambiguities of the opening sixteen bars, we easily perceive a contrasting middle to begin at measure 17. After an extensive prolongation of ♭VI, measure 33 brings twelve measures of what sounds like a standing on the dominant, three bars of which are shown in measures 33–35 (Ex. 8.46c). But rather than having a postcadential quality, this passage stands alone from the prior ♭VI prolongation, such that measure 33 has little effect of being a moment of formal arrival. Still, this prolonged dominant as a whole presumably serves to end the contrasting middle; moreover, the generally recessive dynamic that occurs toward the close of this passage (Ex. 8.46d, mm. 43–45) sets up expectations for the return of the opening four-measure idea to signal the onset of an A′ section. The resolution to tonic at measure 45, however, does not recapitulate that material, and so that formal unit (A′) cannot be said to emerge. Rather, what ensues seems much like a closing section, as if the expanded dominant were the penultimate harmony of an authentic cadential progression that produced an IAC at measure 45. Indeed, the tonic prolongation that follows, which features a regular motion back and forth between V and I, combined with the neighbor motion $\hat{4}$ to $\hat{3}$, has a marked postcadential feel, even though the melody has not achieved its ultimate goal on $\hat{1}$. That degree only appears in the last three bars of the piece (mm. 57–59, Ex. 8.46e) in what the notation suggests is an inner voice, but which is actually heard as the leading line (with the $\hat{5}$ at m. 58 as a covering tone). To be sure, we could consider the final V–I progression as an isolated cadence, but just what formal unit that cadence would be ending is unclear. If the whole effect of measures 45–55 is "postcadential," then it would make more sense to speak of a final, isolated codetta in measures 58–59.

The overall form that emerges appears to be a kind of binary, but it is uncertain if an effective cadence closes either of its two parts. To be sure, each one concludes with tonic harmony (mm. 15 and 45), but the approach to, and arrival of, these tonics do not seem to represent formal goals: measure 15 appears within a change of texture that had occurred with the dominant at measure 13; and measure 45 sounds more like a beginning (of a closing section) than an end of anything. The isolated gesture in the last two bars has cadential content (with its V$^7$–I progression), but seems more like a final codetta within the closing section than a genuine cadence in its own right. In fact, the juxtaposition of the dominant prolongation in measures 13–14 and the matching tonic in measures 15–16 is reproduced later in the prelude at a higher level of form, with the large-scale "standing on the dominant" (mm. 33–44) being matched by the tonic "closing section" (mm. 45–58). Each is a self-contained harmonic block whose resolution, V to I, creates a logical syntax of harmony but a questionable syntax of cadence and form.[172]

### 8.13.22. Prelude No. 22 in G Minor

The form of the prelude is perhaps best seen as a small binary (part 1, mm. 1–16; part 2, mm. 17–41). As in the B-Minor Prelude, Chopin places the melody in the lowest voice, which, even more than with the earlier piece, complicates the cadential articulations (Ex. 8.47a). Thus measure 8 suggests an HC to

---

171. The regular harmonic rhythm projects a strong sense of hypermeter, such that we might want to identify a single four-hypermeasure phrase; this view would explain the cadence occurring at notated m. 7 (and all subsequent cadential articulations on odd-numbered measures). Indeed, we might want to recognize a situation of R = 2N, despite the textural density and complexity of material in such a real bar. Accordingly I have analyzed the opening eight-measure unit as a simple antecedent rather than a compound one.

172. Another harmonic block within the prelude is the extensive prolongation of ♭VI in mm. 17–32. Indeed, the entire second part of the binary consists of a single harmonic progression, ♭VI–V–I, a harmonic stasis that renders the identification of cadence all the more complicated.

EXAMPLE 8.46. Chopin, Prelude in B-flat, Op. 28, no. 21, (a) mm. 1–8; (b) mm. 12–17; (c) mm. 33–35 (d) mm. 43–47; (e) mm. 55–59.

close the compound antecedent (itself sentential), though the diminished-seventh VII⁷ produces instead a dominant arrival. The consequent that follows (mm. 9–16) is left without any closure whatsoever (Ex. 8.47b, m. 16).

Part 2 begins by tonicizing the Neapolitan region but quickly leads toward a home-key authentic cadence, which is evaded at the end of measure 24 (Ex. 8.47c), thus motivating a return to the beginning of the part (m. 25) in order to try for closure one more time. The cadence is again evaded at measure 33 (Ex. 8.47d), and a final attempt, this time by the cadential progression itself, leads to an abandonment, as the opening melody returns in the bass voice in measure 34. If this melody had been placed in the upper

EXAMPLE 8.47. Chopin, Prelude in G Minor, Op. 28, no. 22, (a) mm. 7–9; (b) mm. 15–17; (c) mm. 24–25; (d) mm. 32–34; (e) mm. 38–41.

voice, Chopin could have achieved a PAC to close the second part of the Prelude. Instead, the return of the opening basic idea in the lowest voice precludes cadential closure until the dramatic appearance of a pre-dominant augmented sixth at measure 39 (Ex. 8.47e), which initiates an isolated cadence to achieve final closure.[173] Even though a certain "rounded" effect is expressed by the return of the opening basic idea at measure 34, this material does not yield a substantial enough formal unit to be considered the A′ section of a small ternary form.[174]

## 8.13.23. Prelude No. 23 in F

This nonconventional one-part form is closed clearly enough by the authentic cadence at measure 17 (Ex. 8.48a), though it is difficult to know whether it is perfect or imperfect due to the continuous ornamentations in the melodic line. A closing section follows, made up of the opening material of the piece.

---

173. For a closer examination of how closure is promised and delayed throughout this prelude, see Agawu, "Concepts of Closure," 5–7. In accord with his general notions of closure, discussed in Chapter 1 (sec. 1.2.2), he emphasizes how "the phenomenon of closure is as dependent on specific closes that occur in the piece as it is on closes that do not occur" (7).

174. Additionally, if we were tempted to consider the overall form to be a small ternary, then the emphatic drive toward a home-key authentic cadence in mm. 23–24 and 31–34 would be antithetical to a contrasting middle, to which this material would have to belong.

The unusual added seventh (E♭) in measure 21 (see Ex. 8.48b) references a similar gesture in the left-hand of measure 12 (see the full score), which itself references measure 8, thus suggesting that the piece could have continued on with further statements of these ideas in the subdominant.

## 8.13.24. Prelude No. 24 in D Minor

This final prelude also takes a rather nonconventional form, though there are suggestions of a small ternary design (A, mm. 1–37; B, 38–50; A′, 51–77). The "A section" closes first with a set of two cadences (Ex. 8.49a, b shows the final V–I progression for each cadence). The first one confirms a modulation to the relative major (F major, m. 15); the second, the minor dominant (A minor, m. 19). The entire section is then sequentially repeated up a fifth (see full score), thus eventually confirming C major and E minor with a set of cadences (mm. 33 and 37).[175]

The "B section" (not shown) continues with similar material, but with a more active sequential plan, leading eventually to the dominant of the home key and a return to the initial ideas, which signals the "A′ section" at measure 51. Quickly into this section an enormous

---

175. These two sets of paired cadences, each confirming a different key, look forward to Liszt's use of what I term the *detour cadence* in the following chapter; see sec. 9.5. The main difference is that the first cadence, in F, does not seem like a detour, in that it is a regular subordinate key of the piece, not a more remote key, as in Liszt's practice.

EXAMPLE 8.48. Chopin, Prelude in F, Op. 28, no. 23, (a) mm. 16–17; (b) mm. 21–22.

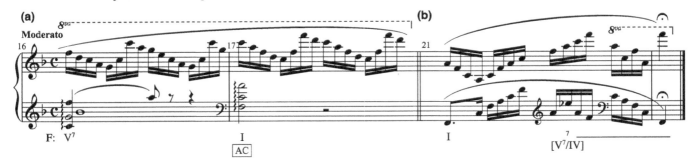

EXAMPLE 8.49. Chopin, Prelude in D Minor, Op. 28, no. 24, (a) mm. 14–15; (b) mm. 18–19; (c) mm. 56–57; (d) mm. 64–65.

ECP (mm. 54–65) begins with the pre-dominant augmented sixth (mm. 54–56) and continues with an extended dominant (mm. 57–64), closing eventually with tonic at measure 65. Example 8.49c shows the move from the German sixth into the cadential six-four (mm. 56–57), and Example 8.49d, the final V–I progression (mm. 64–65). A closing section follows. Given that this is the final prelude, it is not surprising to find here the most expanded cadential progression of the entire set (combined with the most dramatic rhetoric for a single piece), a fitting "classical" conclusion to a group of miniatures that have presented a wide array of Romantic cadential options.

# Cadence in the Mid- to Late Nineteenth Century

THIS CHAPTER CONTINUES ON FROM THE PREvious chapter by examining aspects of thematic closure as practiced by representative composers from the mid- to late nineteenth century: Liszt, Wagner, Grieg, Dvorak, Tchaikovsky, Verdi, Bruckner, Brahms, and Strauss (along with some early twentieth-century tonal excerpts by Mahler, Sibelius, Holst, and Puccini).[1] Just as in music of the second quarter of the nineteenth century, the classical cadence appears on a regular basis in later tonal repertories to effect closure of phrases and themes. But even more than for the Romantics, a greater variety of cadential modifications appear as these later tonal composers eschew the many conventionalities of classically inspired musical form, especially at middleground levels, where cadential articulation would traditionally be employed. Many of the techniques of cadence (or noncadence, as the case may be) identified for Romantic works continue to be used, but composers in the second half of the nineteenth century exploit a number of new procedures as well, and these will be the focus here. As mentioned in the previous chapter, I have deferred a detailed treatment of "plagal cadence" to the present chapter, where I will also deal with some Romantic works by Mendelssohn, Hensel, Schumann, and Chopin.

The most salient stylistic feature of mid- to late-nineteenth-century music is undoubtedly the great expansion of harmonic and tonal chromaticism in all of its forms. Curiously, however, such extensions of tonal resources seem not to have had a significant impact on how thematic areas of form achieve closure, except to the extent that the primary harmonic functions of the cadential progression (initial tonic, pre-dominant, dominant, final tonic) may be subjected to extensive chromatic alterations. Most of the techniques to be discussed in this chapter could, in principle, have taken place within exclusively diatonic contexts, and thus chromaticism per se is not necessarily responsible for the kinds of cadential manipulations witnessed in this music.[2]

---

1. The process of selecting the compositions to be examined for this chapter is described in Chapter 8, note 1.

2. One exception is the increased use of enharmonic reinterpretation, which can play an important role in the articulation of a "pre-dominant arrival," as discussed below in sec. 9.2.

Rather, what seems most responsible is the continuation of a general trend already seen in the Romantic period, one that finds further expression as the nineteenth century proceeds (and which culminates in twentieth-century repertories): a fundamental shift in emphasis away from concluding functions to initiating ones. In short, a gradual, but profound, change can be witnessed, whereby composers accord greater attention to how musical processes begin than to how they end. This change in focus gives rise to situations where the conclusion of thematic units becomes less obviously marked compared to earlier tonal styles, and the act of "ending" loses the aesthetic attraction that it had for the classical composers, whose thematic processes are powerfully teleological.

This is not to say that highly emphatic climaxes of closure are infrequently employed in the second half of the nineteenth century, for of course, they regularly appear, especially in public, orchestral genres. But the many interior moments of closure within a form are not as rigorously cadential as they are in earlier tonal styles. Often in this music an ongoing thematic process simply peters out, liquidates, without any sense of intrinsic closure, only to yield to a new unit whose marked changes in thematic content signal the onset of a new formal trajectory. At times, the effect of becoming stuck on some harmony, within which the process of formal dissolution occurs, generates a sense of a premature arrival, such that a distinct moment of closure is not well articulated. In the classical and Romantic periods, such arrivals almost always involve dominant harmony. In the second half of the nineteenth century, the two other fundamental harmonic functions—tonic and pre-dominant (subdominant)—also become associated with premature arrivals. The idea that a pre-dominant harmony can function as a formal goal relates to an increased employment throughout the century of subdominant harmony as a polar counterforce to the dominant.[3] Indeed, the final harmonic progression in many works features an emphatic plagal prolongation (I–IV–I). And the subdominant even comes to play a greater role in actual cadential articulations, either in the form of a genuine *plagal closure*—the term I prefer over "plagal cadence"—or as an interpolated harmony between the motion from V to I of an authentic cadence, a technique I call *feigned plagal closure*.

Whereas the use of clear classical cadences wanes in the mid- to late nineteenth century, thematic units continue to exploit cadential harmonic progressions; at times, in fact, the music becomes so saturated with such harmonies that it is sometimes difficult to know whether or not a given progression actually yields cadential closure. One technique, which I term the *detour cadence*, involves what seems to be a genuine cadential articulation in a somewhat distant tonal region; immediately thereafter, the music resumes its expected tonal trajectory, leading to a cadence in the "correct" key, thus effecting the expected thematic closure. The pervasive use of cadential progressions within both opening passages and continuational ones results in the bass line regularly engaging the cadential stream in initiating and medial positions within the form.

Likewise, the bass often traverses the prolongational stream in ending formal positions, thus giving rise to *prolongational closure* of the type already discussed for other tonal styles. But whereas in those earlier works, a passage that is concluded by prolongational progressions eventually yields to a final, genuine cadence, a complete thematic unit of a later nineteenth-century work, even the final one of a piece, may bring prolongational closure at its end.

Toward the close of the century and into the early years of the twentieth century, the progressive abandonment of the conventionalized classical cadence eventually gives rise to a counter-reaction, whereby nostalgic and historicist tendencies lead some post-Romantic composers to throw special light on an idealized classical cadence as a prominent formal marker. This *iconic cadence* represents an apotheosis of the cadence, emerging almost as an object in its own right, a musical *topos*, often somewhat isolated from the prevailing thematic processes. With the iconic cadence, we have come full circle, whereby the conventionalized classical cadence, having become progressively reduced in formal and aesthetic significance throughout the nineteenth century, ends up becoming a referential gesture that self-consciously, and sometimes ironically, evokes an earlier era of cadential practice.

In addition to the cadential techniques just mentioned, I will also consider here how the deviations of deceptive and evaded cadences operate in the second part of the nineteenth century, even proposing the idea of a *deceptive half cadence*. Finally, I conclude the chapter with four case studies, more extensive analyses of cadential practice in which a variety of these devices play a major role.

## 9.1. Tonic Arrival

The idea of using a premature *dominant* arrival as a noncadential mode of articulating closure arose early in the eighteenth century (some baroque and galant examples were discussed in Chapters 6 and 7) but only became a standard technique in the classical period, especially in the hands of Beethoven (Chapter 4). A comparable use of *tonic* harmony, however, seemed not to be an option in those styles, since a commitment to the genuine authentic cadence as a means of thematic closure remained secure. The possibility of ending a formal unit with an early appearance of the tonic was not normally exploited by the early Romantics as well. Only in the second half of the nineteenth century, especially in works by Brahms and Bruckner, do we encounter significant cases of premature *tonic arrival*.[4]

If tonic arrivals are rarely employed by the early Romantics, one fascinating example of the technique, which foreshadows later usage, appears in a scherzo movement by Schubert (Ex. 9.1). The

---

3. Janet Schmalfeldt, "'Nineteenth-Century' Subdominants"; Stein, "Expansion of the Subdominant."

4. For some baroque anticipations of the technique, see Chapter 6, sec. 6.3.3. Some classical cases include Haydn, String Quartet in F, Op. 77, no. 2, iii, m. 121, and Beethoven, Symphony No. 6 in F ("Pastoral"), Op. 68, i, m. 47. In a study on early Haydn, MacKay speaks of a "tonic arrival," not as an alternative to a dominant arrival, but rather more in the sense of my prolongational closure ("Declassifying the IAC," 6).

EXAMPLE 9.1. Schubert, String Quintet in C, D. 956, iii, mm. 1–56 (R = 2N).

exposition (A section) of the scherzo begins in the home key of C major and modulates to the dominant region, via a prominent tonicization of ♭VI (mm. 29–42). In many scherzos of the classical style, the home key would initially be confirmed by a PAC that ends a unit representing main-theme function. A transitional unit would then modulate to the subordinate key, as confirmed by an HC (or dominant arrival). Some semblance of subordinate-theme functionality would eventually close with a PAC in the new key.[5] These three expositional functions are readily observable in Schubert's scherzo: main theme in measures 1–28; transition in measures

---

5. See *CF*, chap. 15, and *ACF*, chap. 18.

29–44; and subordinate theme in measures 45–56. We also find the same material used for both the first and third functions (in the sense of a "monothematic" exposition). The requisite cadential articulations, however, remain elusive.[6] The beginning of the main theme emphatically articulates tonic of the home key with a pedal that lasts until measure 12 and appears again in measures 24–28, after which a sudden shift to ♭VI⁶ initiates the transition. The second entrance of the tonic pedal at measure 24, though, gives no immediate impression of being an ending moment; moreover, the preceding dominant does not necessarily belong to a distinct cadential progression. Rather, that harmony seems more initiatory, supporting a return of opening material at measure 17. So when the tonic reappears at measure 24 and then remains "stuck" on that harmony, the effect of a premature tonic arrival is palpable.

A similar situation occurs at measure 52, where, following the modulation to G major as the subordinate key, a premature tonic pedal eventually is seen to conclude the subordinate theme. The effect is one of ending by *assertion* (of the tonic), rather than the classical kind of cadential ending that is achieved through a carefully controlled *process* of simultaneous harmonic, melodic, and bass-line closure. Note that the very final measures even give the impression of being a kind of "closing section," even though it is not possible to identify a preceding PAC, upon which such a section would follow. (I return to this example in the next section of the chapter to discuss the premature *pre-dominant arrival* that ends the transition.)

A late-nineteenth-century case of a premature tonic arrival occurs at the close of the exposition in the finale to Bruckner's Sixth Symphony (Ex. 9.2).[7] Following a passage of rapid harmonic flux (involving numerous secondary dominant-to-tonic resolutions), the bass settles at measure 159 onto D, whose scale-degree function is not yet clear given the preceding instabilities of harmonic-tonal action. This D, which is sustained for two bars, initially supports a dominant-seventh-to-tonic progression (D⁷–G⁶₄) in measures 159–60. These bars then constitute a model that begins to be sequenced up a step (though only sounding an E⁴₂) in the next two measures. When the bass shifts to a B dominant seventh at measure 163, the harmony first seems like it will also participate in further sequential activity. Instead, the harmonic activity broadens out, and B⁷ is held for four bars, only to resolve to its tonic, E, at measure 167, which is sustained all the way to the end of the exposition. We thus understand that the B⁷ to E progression brings the dominant to tonic motion confirming the (second) subordinate key. Yet the V⁷–I resolution at measure 167 hardly seems like a genuine authentic cadence. In the first place, the dominant at measure 163 does not arise out of any ongoing cadential progression; rather, as already observed, it gives the initial impression of being sequential, and the preceding harmonies over the D pedal (mm. 159–62) have no cadential function at all. Moreover, the melodic line that leads into measure 167 initiates a broad ascent, one that achieves its goal only with the high E at measure 171. The repeated melodic figures, which continue to reach up to this 1̂ through measures 172–75, give the impression of being postcadential codettas, though no cadence seems to have occurred.

Listening to this passage for the first or second time, it is not immediately clear that the arrival on tonic at measure 167 articulates a cadence, and so the effect is one of a premature tonic arrival. As we become more familiar with the passage through repeated hearings, however, it is possible to perceive the tonic as a goal, though not really as a genuinely cadential one (for the reasons just discussed), and so the quality of its being premature somewhat wanes. What perhaps helps in weakening the perception of a premature arrival is Bruckner's broadening out of the harmonic rhythm from two harmonies per bar in measure 158, to one harmony per bar in measures 159–60, to a single harmony for two bars (mm. 161–62), and to four bars of dominant (mm. 163–66). So when the tonic arrives at measure 167, to initiate another group of at least four bars, that harmony does not particularly appear "too early" in the prevailing grouping structure.[8]

A more drastic case of a premature tonic arrival occurs at the end of the first movement of Bruckner's Eighth Symphony (Ex. 9.3). Prior to the onset of the passage shown in the example, a broad ascending-stepwise sequence of six-three harmonies eventually brings a diminished seventh (pre-dominant substitute) over ④ at measure 360. Pre-dominant harmony is then prolonged further by the "inverted" German sixth built over ♯④ (mm. 361–64), a passing V⁴₃/IV over ⑤ (in m. 364), and IV⁶ over ⑥ (365–68). When at measure 369 the bass gains ⑤ and we hear a long-held chord in the upper voices (a kind of agogic accent), we sense a moment of arrival on a cadential six-four, which itself is highly prolonged.[9] The effect, however, is largely one of prolonging *tonic* harmony (in six-four position). Without resolving to a clear dominant proper, the six-four reverts to a pre-dominant (over ♯④) at measure 381 for the dynamic climax of the passage. The move to what we again

---

6. The pervasive use of horn call motives, with their constant alternation of tonic and dominant along with a general lack of pre-dominant harmonies, also helps to blur the sense of cadence in this scherzo exposition.

7. Whereas the movement ends in A major, the "key" of the symphony as a whole, the exposition begins in A minor and modulates conventionally to its relative major, C, as the first of two subordinate keys. As a result, Bruckner notates the entire movement in A minor, thus with no key signature. The exposition eventually closes in E major; this second subordinate key is, of course, conventional for a major-mode movement.

8. Though mm. 159–62 contain three distinct harmonies, they are set over a pedal D; as a result, the pedal helps to project a single four-measure group, a unit size that is then matched by the following four bars of V⁷ (mm. 163–66) and the arrival of tonic at m. 167.

9. I choose m. 369 as the point of arrival not only because of the agogic accent here, but also for phrase-rhythmic reasons, as the first bar of a four-measure group, a unit size that pervades this passage (beginning with m. 361). This moment brings the bass ③, but the upper voices contain suspensions from the previous bar, which are only resolved on the downbeat of m. 370. The orchestral complexities of this passage are difficult to render in a piano reduction: note, for example, that what seems like a bass line beginning in m. 370 (second half) is actually an inner voice, still with bass support ③ (the same holds for the similar measures 374–76, etc.).

EXAMPLE 9.2. Bruckner, Symphony No. 6 in A, iv, mm. 158–76.

assume will be a cadential six-four (last beat of m. 382) once more fails to bring a dominant sonority; instead, the bass ⑤ supporting the six-four shifts to ①, played by the timpani alone in the middle of measure 386, to effect a root-position tonic.[10] (What follows, not shown, is a long-held tonic pedal, over which main-theme ideas serve as an extensive closing section.) Here, then, the prolongation of a massive cadential six-four ends up becoming a genuine *tonic* prolongation, not a dominant one. The passage thus concludes with a highly premature tonic arrival at measure 369,

initially appearing in second inversion, but re-inverting to root position toward the end. Thus a stable tonic emerges as the goal harmony for the passage, in a manner that employs authentic cadential progressions, though without a dominant sonority that could create a genuine sense of cadence. (The alternative analysis at m. 369 of "plagal closure" will be entertained later; see the end of sec. 9.3.2.1.)

Another case of tonic arrival, though with an entirely different emotional valence, arises in the first movement of Brahms's Second Symphony. Within the exposition, the subordinate theme begins with a new lyrical tune in F-sharp minor (HK: III) (see Ex. 9.4a, mm. 102–103, for the basic idea of this theme). The music, however, quickly turns toward the home key,

---

10. The timpani does not usually serve as a true bass; in this context, though, it is hard not to believe that a root-position tonic has been achieved by the end of the passage.

EXAMPLE 9.3. Bruckner, Symphony No. 8 in C Minor, i, mm. 360–92.

D major, ending there with an HC at measure 89 (not shown).[11] A new continuation resides largely in D, and, as shown, the music at measure 96 then expands the pre-dominant II⁶ in a manner suggestive of an ECP. The return to root-position tonic (of D) at measure 98 is somewhat odd, since in the prevailing harmonic context, we would more likely expect to hear this D-major sonority sounding as a cadential six-four, eventually resolving to the dominant proper, and either ending there with an HC, to yield a compound antecedent, or continuing on to tonic, as an authentic cadence (see the reconstruction in Ex. 9.4b).[12] But Brahms then uses the root-position D harmony of measure 98 (see again Ex. 9.4a) as a quick pivot back to F-sharp minor, and the music arrives on a cadential six-four in that key (m. 100). At this point, we would likely surmise this harmony to resolve to a dominant sonority to bring a half cadence, as

---

11. This returning back to the home key (D major) within the early part of the subordinate theme is reminiscent of Schubert's practice. As James Webster puts it, "In a word, Schubert hates to leave the tonic [i.e., home key]" ("Schubert's Sonata Form and Brahms's First Maturity," 24).

12. In the latter option, the resulting formal unit would no longer be an antecedent. Moreover, such a *home-key* PAC is incompatible with a subordinate theme altogether.

EXAMPLE 9.4. Brahms, Symphony No. 2 in D, Op. 73, i, (a) mm. 95–103; (b) reconstruction of mm. 95–102; (c) reconstruction of mm. 97–103.

reconstructed in Example 9.4c, thus confirming our suspicions of an ongoing compound antecedent. Instead, Brahms holds on to the F♯-minor sonority of the cadential six-four, and similar to what we saw in Bruckner's Eighth (Ex. 9.3), arpeggiates the bass down by thirds (Ex. 9.4a, mm. 100–102), such that we experience a "tonic" harmonic function being prolonged into the return of the subordinate theme's opening at measure 102. The prevailing formal unit thus ends with a tonic arrival, though it would perhaps not be unreasonable for us to hear a hint of HC, one that is relinquished by not resolving the six-four suspensions. Note that with the lack of the leading tone E♯, along with the prior emphasis on the home key, the status of F-sharp minor as a subordinate key is thrown into doubt. Indeed, as the music continues, we learn that the real subordinate key, the one confirmed by an eventual PAC, is A major, the dominant region of the home key. Thus the local technique of tonic arrival helps facilitate this broader tonal trajectory from D major to A major, via F-sharp minor.

As already mentioned, a tonic arrival often gives the impression that the tonic achieves its sense of concluding more through assertion than through process—a cadential process. The tonic thus becomes an ending after the fact, not one that we immediately perceive as such. In the slow movement of the same Brahms symphony, a sense of harmonic assertion yields a tonic arrival that is most subtle in its effect (Ex. 9.5a). The main theme is structured like a small ternary. But the cadential articulations typical of this theme type become obscured. The A section heads toward an authentic cadence at measure 5, but then is evaded when the melody leaps back up to $\hat{5}$ for another try. On the downbeat of measure 6, the melody resolves to $\hat{3}$, which with the correct harmonic context would yield an IAC. But the supporting harmony is III$^6$ (which is not clarified until the second quarter-note beat), and so we have to recognize another evasion or, depending on the performance, a deceptive cadence. In either case, measure 6 begins a new section, one that might be construed as a contrasting middle (despite the lack of closure for the A section). The I$^6$ in measure 8, moving to

EXAMPLE 9.5. Brahms, Symphony No. 2 in D, Op. 73, ii, (a) mm. 1–18; (b) reconstruction of mm. 8–12.

V$^7$/V in the following bar, proposes to resolve to the dominant (of B major, the home key), which would produce an HC to end this B section (as reconstructed in Ex. 9.5b).[13] Instead, the secondary dominant resolves deceptively to ♭III (m. 10), a D-major sonority that is then prolonged (via a dominant-functioning diminished seventh) through most of measure 12. The upbeat to measure 13 sees a return of the opening material, this time truly closed off at measure 17 with the IAC that was promised in measures 5 and 6. A repeat of the cadential idea, in the sense of a codetta, is broken off in measure 18, and as the music continues, we understand this bar to represent the beginning of the transition. Though the cadential articulation of the A section is unusual, what was promised is at least fulfilled at the end of the A′ section. But what do we make of how the B section closes? Given that A′ begins with dominant (as does A), it is perhaps not surprising that the contrasting

---

13. A reinterpreted HC is also a viable analysis; but see again in Chapter 8, note 139.

EXAMPLE 9.6. Haydn, Symphony No. 92 in G ("Oxford"), i, mm. 11–25.

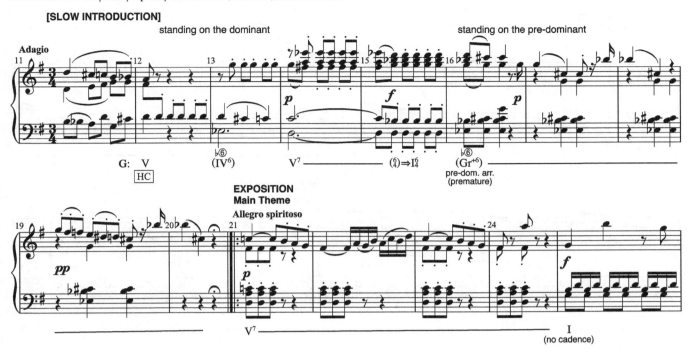

## 9.2. Pre-dominant Arrival; Subdominant Arrival

The general concept of "arrival" (as opposed to "cadence") is also applicable when the final harmony of a thematic unit is a pre-dominant. Insofar as no cadential progression concludes with that function, we must speak in these situations of a *pre-dominant arrival*. Whether or not this arrival appears as "premature" depends on the individual circumstances involved, though most often we have the impression that the music gets stuck on a pre-dominant prior to the completion of other processes.

Examples of pre-dominant arrivals already appear in some classical works by Haydn and Beethoven. In each case, the pre-dominant serves as an appropriate ultimate harmony because the subsequent thematic unit begins off-tonic (and thus does not favor the use of a preceding dominant). In the case of Haydn's "Oxford" Symphony (Ex. 9.6), the slow introduction consists of a compound sentence that closes with an HC at measure 12. The dominant is then prolonged through measure 15 with the aid of a neighboring pre-dominant IV⁶, built on ♭6̂, at measure 13. At measure 16, the harmonic motion gets stuck on a chromatically enriched pre-dominant, a German augmented sixth, which is sustained up to the fermata in measure 20. The rhythmic and textural rhetoric suggests that this moment is likely to conclude the slow introduction, a presumption that is confirmed by the change of tempo to mark the onset of the exposition. We can thus understand the pre-dominant at measure 16 as marking a premature arrival, a harmony that leads naturally into the dominant seventh that supports the opening of the exposition's main theme (m. 21).[14] With respect to the formal context in which the expanded augmented sixth functions, it is as though a standing on the dominant (mm. 12–15) gives way to a standing on the *pre-dominant* (mm. 16–21). And what facilitates what might have been a syntactically awkward move from a dominant (V⁷) to a pre-dominant (Gr⁺⁶) is the mediating six-four harmony in measure 15, which changes function from being a dominant embellishment to becoming a second-inversion tonic.

In a passage by Beethoven (Ex. 9.7), the recapitulation's main theme begins with a pre-dominant II⁶ (m. 137).[15] If the development had ended conventionally with dominant harmony, then

Earlier text (left column):

middle does not conclude on that same harmony, as would be the case had the HC shown in Example 9.5b been realized. Rather, the B section closes on a D-major sonority, which on the very foreground seems to possess the stability of a tonic, especially as it is prolonged by its own dominant. If so, then we could speak of a premature tonic arrival at measure 10, recognizing, of course, that the D sonority emerges out of a deceptive resolution of the secondary dominant (V⁷/V). In fact, if we stand back and take a broader view, we can recognize that D major (as a "tonic" substitute for the intended goal harmony of the progression, F♯ major, namely the dominant of the home key) could be seen as a kind of "dominant" arrival after all. Yet, we hardly have the impression of that harmonic function, which seems rather to assert itself as a local, concluding tonic.

---

14. The development section ends similarly—this time with a pre-dominant VII⁶/V—though without the fermata interruption; see *ACF*, Ex. 13.17.

15. At the very start of the exposition, the pre-dominant takes the form of II⁶₅ (see the discussion in Chapter 5 of Ex. 5.34b). This six-five version is recaptured at m. 139 of the recapitulation (Ex. 9.7).

EXAMPLE 9.7. Beethoven, Piano Sonata in E-flat, Op. 31, no. 3, i, mm. 125–42.

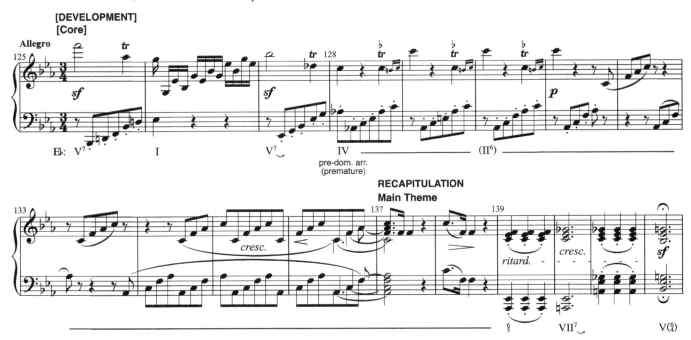

the sudden shift to a pre-dominant to begin the main theme would have been awkward. So Beethoven simply lets the development end by arriving on IV in measure 128, which is transformed and sustained, as II⁶, until the appearance of the main theme at measure 137, whereby the same harmony is simply continued on until it begins to move in the course of the main theme itself.[16]

An early Romantic example of such a pre-dominant arrival, one that, in a number of particulars, points to the way in which it tends to be used later in the nineteenth century, arises in the Schubert Quintet that we already have considered in Example 9.1. As mentioned briefly before, the transition begins at measure 29 by suddenly interrupting the tonic arrival of the main theme with a shift to A-flat major (HK: ♭VI). An eight-measure presentation is followed by a continuation (m. 37) consisting of ascending-stepwise six-three harmonies; this sequence culminates at measure 42 in a major-minor-seventh sonority built on E♭, which is sustained for almost three bars. In relation to the preceding music, this harmony can be understood as a dominant seventh of the prevailing key of A-flat. From this perspective, the transition ends, regularly enough, with a dominant arrival. But Schubert both spells the sonority, and resolves it, as a German augmented-sixth within the subordinate key of G major. As a result, we can reinterpret the ultimate harmony of the transition as projecting a pre-dominant arrival. Such a reinterpretation works because of the different enharmonic meanings associated with the major-minor-seventh sonority: as a dominant seventh or as a pre-dominant augmented sixth. Indeed, the German version of the latter harmony becomes a particularly popular pre-dominant for such arrivals later in the century, where the trace of a V⁷ sonority can hint at a more traditional dominant arrival. The use of a pre-dominant here is clearly motivated by the subsequent dominant pedal that initiates the subordinate theme.

Turning now to later nineteenth-century pre-dominant arrivals, we also encounter situations that resemble the previous Haydn and Schubert examples, where a pre-dominant is appropriate as an ending harmony because the subsequent unit begins on a dominant.[17] The rondo finale of Brahms's Violin Sonata No. 1 in G Minor is a case in point. The refrain opens on dominant, and so the return of that theme typically witnesses a pre-dominant as the arrival of the preceding couplet. As shown in Example 9.8a, the first couplet ends in measure 60 on an augmented-sixth (rather unusually with ③ in the bass). Following couplet 2 (Ex. 9.8b), which resides largely in E-flat major, the refrain is preceded again by an augmented sixth (mm. 120–23). Given the prevailing tonal context, the sonority at measure 120 sounds very much like a dominant seventh (V⁷/IV), only to become reinterpreted (as we saw in the Schubert Quintet) as an augmented sixth upon resolution to the dominant of G minor, the home key. It should be noted that just because a theme begins with dominant, it will not necessarily

---

16. Another good example of a classical pre-dominant arrival straddles the slow introduction and main theme of Beethoven's "Kreutzer" Sonata, Op. 47, i, mm. 15–19 (ACF, Ex. 16.4).

17. Graham Hunt also discusses such cases in connection with a broader study of three-key expositions ("Diverging Subordinate Themes and Internal Transitions: Assessing Internal Modulations in Three-Key Expositions," 147–51, and Ex. 2a). His analysis of the exposition of Tchaikovsky's "Hamlet Overture-Fantasy" describes an augmented-sixth ending a transition that is followed by a medial caesura, which he terms an "augmented-sixth MC [medial caesura]." The subordinate theme then begins with dominant harmony. His note 9 (p. 181) details other cases, including situations in which the subordinate theme begins directly on tonic, an issue to be discussed in more detail shortly below.

EXAMPLE 9.8A. Brahms, Violin Sonata No. 1 in G, Op. 78, iii, mm. 57–62.

EXAMPLE 9.8B. Brahms, Violin Sonata No. 1 in G, Op. 78, iii, mm. 118–25.

be preceded by its pre-dominant. In couplet 1 of the rondo (Ex. 9.8c), the opening material of a small-ternary A section begins at measure 29 on the dominant of D minor (HK: minV). Its first appearance, to be sure, is preceded by a pre-dominant VII⁷/V (m. 28). But when the material returns again (Ex. 9.8d, m. 41), now as the A′ section, the preceding B section ends at measure 39 with a *dominant* arrival, which is simply sustained for the start of A′.

EXAMPLE 9.8C-D. Brahms, Violin Sonata No. 1 in G, Op. 78, iii, (c) mm. 28–30; (d) mm. 39–42.

EXAMPLE 9.9. Brahms, Symphony No. 1 in C Minor, Op. 68, ii, mm. 63–68.

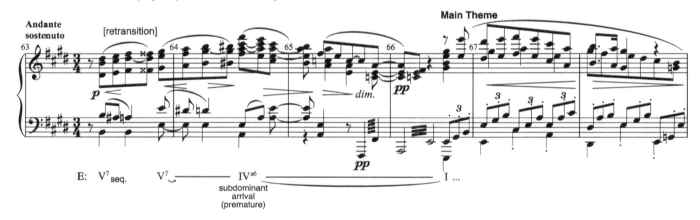

In the examples observed thus far, we are confident that the arrival is behaving as a pre-dominant because the subsequent thematic unit begins directly with dominant harmony. We also find cases, however, where what we might assume to be a pre-dominant does not actually function as such, because the following formal unit begins (as is typical) with tonic, usually in root position. Consider Example 9.9, a passage that prepares for the return of the main theme in the slow movement of Brahms's First Symphony.[18] Toward the end of a retransition restoring the home key of E major, a descending-fifths sequence (mm. 63–64) leads to a subdominant with an "added sixth" (IV$^{a6}$), which is then sustained through the first two beats of measure 66. The broadening of the harmonic rhythm and the generally recessive nature of the texture, dynamics, and contour all suggest an "arrival" in the middle of measure 64, which is confirmed when the main theme returns with root-position tonic at the upbeat to measure 67. Should we speak in these circumstances of a pre-dominant arrival in measure 64? Technically, no, since IV does not move to V as it normally does in a cadential context. Rather, the progression from IV to I is more properly understood as prolongational, as manifest especially by the common-tone—the tonic scale degree (E)—connecting the IV and I harmonies. Therefore in such cases we should preferably identify a *subdominant arrival* in measure 64, understanding the harmony to be a "lower dominant" (as initially conceived by Rameau), which represents the polar opposite of an "upper dominant," both of which dominants progress

---

18. The overall form of the movement is a sonata without development, one whose recapitulation is "truncated" (i.e., consisting only of the main theme); see *CF*, 216, and *ACF*, 595.

EXAMPLE 9.10. Bruckner, Symphony No. 6 in A, i, mm. 41–50.

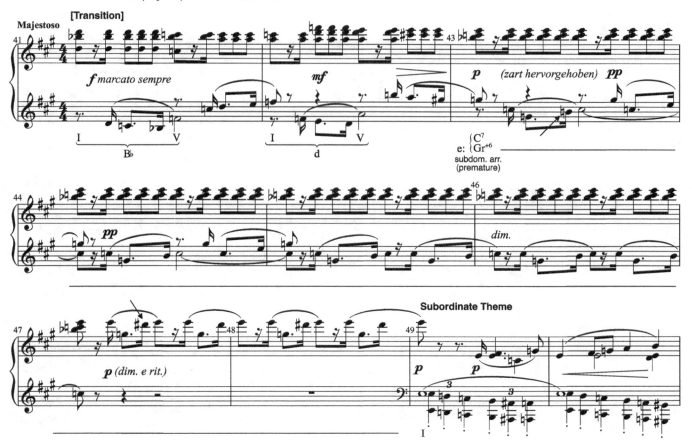

syntactically to tonic.[19] As a result, we can distinguish between a pre-dominant arrival and a subdominant arrival on the basis of which harmony initiates the subsequent thematic unit: pre-dominant, when preceding an initiating dominant, or subdominant, when preceding a tonic.

Some cases of subdominant arrival, though, are somewhat more complex. The latter part of an expositional transition by Bruckner (Ex. 9.10) features a passage of harmonic flux involving various tonic-to-dominant connections (mm. 41–42). The C⁷ sonority at measure 43 suggests that it, too, is a dominant, one that will reverse the progression by resolving to its tonic, an F harmony of some kind. Instead, the music gets stuck on this C⁷ for six bars, accompanied by a liquidation of the texture. The subordinate theme then begins on the tonic of E minor at measure 49. In retrospect, the "dominant" C⁷ ends up functioning enharmonically as a German augmented sixth, which effects a common-tone resolution to tonic at the beginning of the theme. To be sure, we normally speak of an augmented-sixth harmony as having a pre-dominant function; yet when it resolves directly to tonic, especially with that scale degree as a common tone, it behaves in the manner of a subdominant, despite not literally containing a "root" built on the fourth degree of the scale. One final point on this example: though I speak of a retrospective reinterpretation here, Bruckner already hints at the upcoming E tonality through the B♮ embellishments in the lower voice in measures 43–46 (see arrow in m. 43) and pretty much gives away the game with the D♯s in the upper voice of measures 47–48 (see arrow). Together, the B and D♯ allude to the dominant of E, the harmony of the conventional "standing on the dominant" that would normally end a transition.

A similar case of an augmented sixth resolving as a common-tone harmony to tonic arises toward the end of the small-ternary main theme of Tchaikovsky's Fourth Symphony (Ex. 9.11).[20] Following a broad model-sequence passage, measure 86 contains a diminished-seventh harmony of uncertain functional meaning, due to the prevailing harmonic-tonal instability within the ternary's B section. A half-step descent in the bass produces a major-minor-seventh sonority with a "root" G♭ (m. 87), which itself moves to D♭⁷ in the next bar. The music now prolongs this harmony for four measures, eventually resolving as an augmented sixth to the root-position tonic of the home key (F minor) at the start of the A′ section (upbeat to m. 92).[21] Much like the Bruckner

---

19. Jean-Philippe Rameau, *Nouveau système de musique théorique*, 38.

20. The contrasting middle is highly expanded due to a false return of the A section in ♭III of the home key (m. 70, not shown), eventually to be followed by the real return at the start of the A′ section seen in the example.

21. To save space, I have placed the repeat of the opening four-measure compound basic idea within double bar lines.

EXAMPLE 9.11. Tchaikovsky, Symphony No. 4 in F Minor, Op. 36, i, mm. 86–104.

example just discussed, the contrasting middle ends with a potential dominant arrival, one that is reinterpreted as a subdominant arrival when the augmented sixth effects a common-tone resolution to tonic in root position.

What follows in the A′ section is worthy of note, since the entire unit is effectively built over tonic, though the bass inverts the harmony into the six-four in measure 95 (and 99) via the chromatic motive B♮–C–D♭ (the retrograde of the opening motive "x" of the theme). Toward its end (m. 101ff.), the theme liquidates to just an alternation of the tonic and the same augmented-sixth from the end of the contrasting middle (m. 91), supporting the upper voice motive C–B♮ (x′), the final remnant of the powerful chromatic motive that informs much of the main theme. (The transition then begins with a sudden change of material at the upbeat to m. 104.) We see, therefore, that Tchaikovsky's use of a subdominant arrival at the end of the B section reflects more than just a case of late-nineteenth-century harmonic coloration, but engages motivic processes as well.

Finally, we should consider how the theme itself actually ends. Seeing as the entire A′ section is a kind of "standing on the tonic,"

EXAMPLE 9.12. Brahms, Symphony No. 3 in F, Op. 90, i, mm. 28–36.

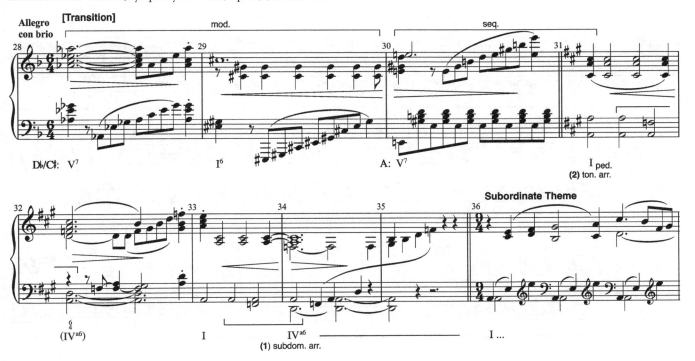

there is no harmonic progression that could potentially bring any form of cadential closure. Though we might be tempted to recognize a full-fledged tonic arrival at measure 92, this is surely stretching the concept too far. For the sense of "arrival" that we have been considering applies to a mode of *ending*, whereas the tonic here appears exclusively as a formal *beginning* (of the A′ section).[22] Nonetheless, Tchaikovsky's theme creates its effect of closure very much through a powerful sense of tonic *assertion*, much like what we observed in some genuine cases of tonic arrivals above.

Before leaving the general topic of alternatives to the standard dominant arrival—be they tonic, pre-dominant, or subdominant—let us consider two examples that somewhat blur the distinctions among these categories. The expositional transition in the opening movement of Brahms's Third Symphony literally ends with subdominant (including an added sixth); see Example 9.12, measures 34–35. Within these bars, the recessive dynamic and reduction in texture to a single voice are all signals of a subdominant arrival at measure 34 (option 1). The subordinate theme then begins with tonic of A major in measure 36. Taking a somewhat broader view, however, we can see that the arrival IV$^{a6}$ of measure 34 actually appears first in measure 32 as a neighboring harmony following the appearance of the subordinate-key tonic in measure 31. If we add the opening tonic of the subordinate theme to the mix, both of the subdominants are enclosed within a tonic prolongation.[23] We could therefore speak alternatively (option 2) of a tonic arrival at measure 31, one that continues that harmony from the end of the transition into the beginning of the subordinate theme. Note that the first appearance of tonic at measure 31 does not sound cadential, even though it is preceded by a root-position dominant, since the V$^7$–I progression in A major emerges as a harmonic sequence of the prior D♭/C♯: V$^7$–I in measures 28–29. Thus the transition seems to end *gesturally* with a subdominant arrival at measure 34; *harmonically*, however, it can also be said to end with a tonic arrival at measure 31. Both views capture legitimate aspects of closure in this transition.[24]

A second case of blurring the categories of arrival types is found near the beginning of the scherzo to Bruckner's Ninth Symphony (Ex. 9.13a). The movement opens with a long introductory passage (mm. 1–42) of "roving" harmonies (as Schoenberg might say) seemingly unrelated to D minor, the expected key of the movement (in that Bruckner normally sets his scherzos in the overall key of the symphony). Following a general pause, the upbeat to measure 43 brings a thunderous outburst of D-minor tonic in the form of a pedal, which continues on for many measures. The initial harmony of the introduction beginning with the HC and standing on the dominant (mm. 12–15) and concluding with the dominant harmony supporting the very opening of the main theme (mm. 21–24).

---

22. Likewise, we do not identify a "dominant arrival" at the very onset of a contrasting middle consisting entirely of a standing on the dominant.

23. We might see something similar in the earlier discussed Haydn symphony (Ex. 9.6), where the literal pre-dominant ending could be understood as a neighboring harmony of a larger *dominant* prolongation,

24. Further supporting an interpretation of subdominant arrival is the way in which Brahms takes the descending-thirds motive, A–F♯–D, in the tenor (mm. 31–32) and shifts it to the bass in mm. 33–34 (see the brackets in the annotations). As a result, the now root-position subdominant at m. 34 seems more like an independent harmony compared to the preceding one in m. 32, which, in its six-four position (due to the tonic pedal), assimilates more to the latter harmony.

EXAMPLE 9.13A. Bruckner, Symphony No. 9 in D Minor, ii, mm. 1–50.

EXAMPLE 9.13B–C. Bruckner, Symphony No. 9 in D Minor, ii, (b) harmonic reduction of mm. 27–34; (c) "Tristan" resolution.

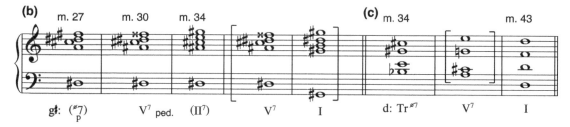

is a half-diminished-seventh sonority whose harmonic-tonal meaning is entirely unclear at this point in the piece. A variety of sonorities, most of which remain harmonically vague, ensue through an ascending-stepwise motion of the voices. A degree of harmonic focus around G-sharp minor emerges at the upbeat to m 27, where the half-diminished seventh in measures 27–30 can be heard as a common-tone passing harmony to the dominant seventh in measures 30–34, followed then by a neighboring II$^7$ (supported by a dominant pedal) in measures 34–42. Indeed, if we embed these harmonies within a broader progression (whose final two harmonies V$^7$–I are not present in the music), the sense of referencing G-sharp minor is palpable enough (Ex. 9.13b). On the musical surface, however, the very final sounding sonority of the introduction is a half-diminished seventh (in fact, the same one from the very opening of the movement). In the context of G-sharp minor, and leaving the pedal D♯/E♭ temporarily aside, this harmony can be heard as a pre-dominant II$^7$. So the idea that the introduction concludes with a pre-dominant arrival gains a degree of legitimacy.

But how are we to relate this sonority to the D-minor harmony that follows? That the emphasized harmony (being both the initial and concluding sonority of the introduction) takes the form of a *half-diminished* seventh, and given Bruckner's veneration of Wagner, it is hard not to consider some connection here to the opening progression of *Tristan und Isolde*. And indeed, a striking relationship obtains, for if we perform the "Tristan" voice leading on this half-diminished seventh,[25] we achieve the dominant of D minor, as reconstructed in Ex. 9.13c). Allowing the dominant to resolve to tonic, and then "eliding" the dominant, we arrive at the very progression that Bruckner writes from the end of the introduction to the pounding D pedal at measure 43.

As will be discussed later in the chapter, when looking more closely at Wagner's Prelude, the Tristan chord in measure 2 has been analyzed in two ways: (Ex. 9.56a) as a pre-dominant, an altered French-sixth, leading to a dominant seventh in measure 3, or (Ex. 9.56d) as an altered dominant, technically a VII$^7$ with a chromatically raised fifth (D♯), that is prolonged via voice-exchange into the dominant seventh.[26] With this situation in mind (and returning to Ex. 9.13a), we could consider that Bruckner's introduction ends with either a pre-dominant or dominant arrival, depending upon how we want to analyze the Tristan sonority at the upbeat to measure 35. One detail, however, perhaps helps to tip the balance in favor of a dominant arrival. If we consider all of the roving harmonies contained in the introduction, we see that each one includes the pitch C♯, the leading tone of D. Indeed, we might want to claim that the entire introduction prolongs the dominant of the home key, as suggested obliquely by Robert Simpson.[27] In this respect, the introduction could be seen as a prolongation not of an ending dominant, but of an *anacrusis dominant*, a before-the-beginning function that leads to a formal initiation (m. 43). Nonetheless, the idea that the introduction projects a sense of pre-dominant arrival must not be completely rejected, since that interpretation has validity for both a local G-sharp-minor context, as well as a broader D-minor one.

## 9.3. Plagal Cadence/Plagal Closure

As witnessed in the previous section, nineteenth-century repertories increasingly elevate subdominant harmony as a structural alternative to the dominant, thus producing situations in which the former can represent the *goal* of a thematic process, what I have called a subdominant arrival. We can also observe two other manifestations of this tendency: one that is purely theoretical; the other, an aspect of actual compositional practice. The first yields the idea of *harmonic dualism*, a concept of harmony in which major and minor modalities are accorded equal status and where the tonic stands in a central position surrounded by the dominant on one side and the subdominant on the other.[28] The second manifestation leads to the notion of "plagal cadence," whereby a harmonic-formal process can be completed by means of the subdominant progressing directly to tonic. Both of these ideas set the subdominant on equal footing with the dominant as polar opposites to the tonic. The following discussion focuses on the idea of plagal cadence, with occasional references to harmonic dualism where useful.

I have introduced the topic of plagal cadence already in Chapter 2 (sec. 2.3.1.3) and briefly mentioned it in Chapter 3 (sec. 3.5.2), Chapter 6 (sec. 6.3.3), and Chapter 8 (sec. 8.9). As discussed there, most cases of plagal cadence identified by theorists actually involve postcadential material. As we reach the mid-nineteenth century, we finally encounter a repertoire that prompts us to explore more deeply the idea of plagal cadence as a unique mode of harmonic and formal closure. In addition to observing some prominent cases of plagal cadence in the works of later nineteenth-century composers, I will also consider here a number of Romantic works by Fanny Hensel, her brother Felix

---

25. In Chapter 5, sec. 5.3.2.1, I discussed this voice leading in connection with Ex. 5.58 and the "DOUTH2" progression (as so-named by David Lewin); see also Chapter 5, note 89.

26. In Ex. 9.56d, the Tristan harmony is annotated as VII$^4_2$, since the seventh resides in the bass. In the Bruckner, Ex. 9.13a and c, mm. 34–42 contain a D♯/E♭ pedal, so the Tristan harmony is analyzed, by convention, as being in "root" position, thus VII$^7$. In mm. 44–48, the same harmony is set over a D♯ pedal.

27. Robert Simpson, *The Essence of Bruckner: An Essay Towards the Understanding of His Music*, 190.

28. The two most prominent proponents of harmonic dualism in the second half of the nineteenth century are Arthur J. von Oettingen, *Harmoniesystem in dualer Entwicklung: Studien zur Theorie der Musik*, and Hugo Riemann, *Harmony Simplified, or the Theory of the Tonal Functions of Chords*. Though not strictly a harmonic dualist, Moritz Hauptmann, writing earlier in the century, nonetheless conceives of dominant and subdominant as having comparable relationships to the tonic in his dialectical constructions of harmony and tonality (*Harmony and Metre*). Among recent music theorists, modern appreciations of harmonic dualism can be found in Harrison, *Harmonic Function*, and Henry Klumpenhouwer, "Harmonic Dualism as Historical and Structural Imperative."

EXAMPLE 9.14. (a) Authentic cadential progression; (b) three-stage PCP; (c) four-stage PCP.

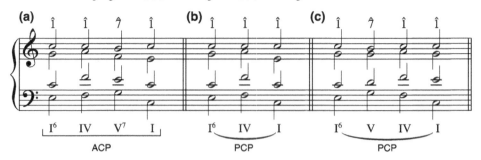

Mendelssohn, Schumann, and Chopin; these instances prepare the way for a wider use of plagal cadence in the second half of the century.[29]

### 9.3.1. Theoretical Speculations

Before looking at some concrete examples, let us pause to consider how the plagal cadence can be conceptualized within the framework of cadential closure developed over the course of this book. We will first look at the specific harmonic contexts in which a plagal cadence can be said to arise and then consider more broadly the nature of closure articulated by the motion from subdominant to tonic.

#### 9.3.1.1. Plagal Cadential Progression (PCP)

If plagal harmonic motion (i.e., IV–I) is to be accorded full legitimacy as a mode of cadential closure, as suggested by the ubiquitous references to plagal cadence in treatises on harmony, then we should presumably be able to identify a specifically *plagal cadential progression* (PCP),[30] one that differentiates itself from an authentic cadential progression (ACP).[31] What would such a PCP look like? Working backward, it would obviously conclude with a final tonic in root position, just like an ACP (see Ex. 9.14a and b).[32] The penultimate harmony of a PCP would be the subdominant, one that no longer has a pre-dominant function, but whose role is to resolve to tonic. Whether this harmony, like its dominant counterpart in an ACP, must stand in root position remains an open question; as with so much else about the plagal cadence, the lack of a broad body of repertory employing the device makes it difficult to generalize on many points of morphology and syntax. Like the other cadential progressions, we could posit a *complete* PCP to contain an initial tonic (its conventional position is also unclear), though *incomplete* versions could omit that harmony.

As proposed up to now, the PCP would be a three-stage entity: $I^{(6)}$–$IV^{(6)}$–I. If we were not speaking of these harmonies as cadential in any way, this progression would more regularly be understood as tonic prolongational. And so we might wonder whether there exists a PCP that brings all three harmonic functions working together to effect a sense of harmonic closure, as we usually find with the ACP. Such a four-stage progression would thus engage the *dominant* in some way, presumably in an antepenultimate position, as shown in Example 9.14c. And analogous to the ACP, this dominant could then be thought to function as a kind of "pre-subdominant." Of course, V–IV is normally considered be a nonsyntactical progression, one that produces a harmonic rupture, not a connection. Indeed, if theorists have traditionally had a difficult time explaining just how IV can logically progress to V in an ACP (think Rameau's *double-emploi*), the reverse progression V–IV, as something cadential, is especially difficult to justify.[33] Still, it will be instructive to keep this four-stage PCP in mind, for it will prove valuable now and then as we explore ways of understanding the plagal cadence.

At this point let us consider just how the move from IV to I, the final progression of both the three- and four-stage PCP, can be conceived as providing *syntactical* closure comparable to that effected by $V^{(7)}$–I in a standard ACP. As Meyer argues in his discussion of syntactical parameters in music,[34] such parameters

---

29. For an important, recent discussion of how a plagal cadence can be deemed "form-defining" and a genuine "agent of closure," see Hunt, "Diverging Subordinate Themes," 173–77. His examples of passages from Saint-Saëns, Brahms, and Frank complement well the examples discussed in the current section of this chapter.

30. Alternatively, "PCP" can be read as "plagal *closural* progression" in light of my proposal (to be developed shortly) to speak of plagal *closure*, rather than plagal cadence. I am reluctant to introduce yet another initialism into the discussion, yet I believe its use will facilitate our considerations of plagal cadence/plagal closure.

31. For the purposes of this discussion, the half cadential progression and deceptive cadential progression can be considered variants of the ACP.

32. Note that I indicate a PCP with a curved line embracing the harmonies of the progression. The reader may recall that in certain other contexts, I use the same annotation for prolongational progressions. Indeed, I will shortly clarify that I consider the PCP to be one particular type of harmonic prolongation. I thus reserve the square bracket for cases of ACP (including half and deceptive progressions as well).

33. I am not suggesting by this statement that we never find such progressions in actual music; we surely do, but they almost always require an explanation for why they are suitable in their specific harmonic-formal contexts. A recent study by Timothy Cutler highlights a good number of instances of dominant harmony progressing to the subdominant ("'Proper Boundaries' and the 'Incoherent' Succession $V^{(7)}$–IV"). Most of his cases arise within formal initiations; others are manifestly sequential. Only a few occur in cadential contexts, mostly in connection with a type that I call the *feigned* plagal closure (a topic to be raised in sec. 9.3.5).

34. Meyer, "Universe of Universals," 8–10; Meyer, *Style and Music*, 14–16. See Chapter 1, sec. 1.2.1.

EXAMPLE 9.15. (a) Three-stage dualist PCP; (b) four-stage dualist PCP.

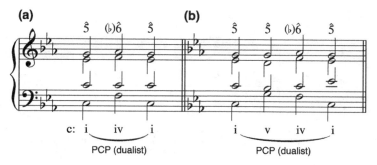

are rooted in the "functional differentiation" of its elements, a differentiation that is *implicative* in nature: a syntactical element implies its continuation to one or more specific elements. For an ACP, the parameters of melody and voice leading prompt us to recognize the leading tone as strongly implying motion to the first degree of the diatonic scale, which is also the root of the resulting tonic harmony. When the fourth degree enters the picture, as a dissonant seventh within the dominant, the intervallic tritone $\hat{7}/\hat{4}$ implies resolution to $\hat{1}/\hat{3}$, these latter two pitches being members of tonic harmony. From a purely harmonic perspective, theorists have proposed a variety of explanations for why the dominant most naturally progresses to the tonic (e.g., Rameau's idea of the dominant's fundamental bass "returning to its source").[35] We might ask, then, if the subdominant of a PCP, in its progression to tonic, has a similar syntactical force of closure. Admittedly, the $\hat{4}/\hat{6}$ degrees within IV normally lead to $\hat{3}/\hat{5}$ in I. But the fact that the two harmonies share the tonic scale degree (as fifth of the subdominant and root of the tonic) means that this common-tone relationship significantly weakens the functional differentiation needed to experience an implicative, syntactical progression. Rather, the common tone is especially indicative of a harmonic *prolongation*, rather than a syntactical succession of independent harmonies, as is clearly the case with the motion from a cadential dominant to tonic.[36] Moreover, modern accounts of tonal harmony normally speak of the subdominant as implying two kinds of harmonic succession—either to tonic (as prolongational) or to dominant (as cadential)—whereas the dominant is normally considered to have a single harmonic goal, namely to tonic alone.[37]

If the standard views of functional harmony provide scant means of recognizing the subdominant as having comparable implicative tendencies to progress to tonic, like that of the dominant, then we might wonder if some other, fundamentally different, conception of harmony might provide the answers we are looking for. And here, the *dualist* perspectives that emerged in German harmonic theory in the course of the nineteenth century might provide a theoretical context that justifies the PCP as a mechanism for syntactical closure. Harmonic dualism comes in many forms, but most approaches insist that the major/minor distinction is not simply a matter of modal variation, but rather, that these two chordal varieties represent fully independent harmonic systems, each of equal significance for tonal music. Inspired by Hauptmann, but going further than him, a number of dualist theorists see the "root" of the minor triad as being the pitch that the more standard, *monist*, harmonic view would understand as the "fifth" of the harmony: for example, the root of a nominal C-minor harmony would be the pitch G. In other words, whereas the major system of harmony is generated from bottom to top, a dualist minor harmony is generated from top to bottom. A "cadential" progression within this minor system might yield a three-stage PCP as i–iv–i (see Ex. 9.15a).[38] A four-stage version, i–v–iv–i, might look like Example 9.15b.[39] Note that the dominant harmony in this latter progression is also minor, and thus the absence of a leading-tone resolution ($\hat{7}–\hat{1}$) fails to elicit implications for an authentic cadence. In the motion from subdominant to tonic, however, we can discern an "upper leading tone" ($\flat\hat{6}$) resolving to the "root" ($\hat{5}$) of the tonic, thus imitating the kind of melodic functional differentiation demanded of a syntactical progression.

Does the theory of harmonic dualism provide a context in which most listeners hear tonal music? The answer would seem to be no, as evidenced by the vast majority of twentieth- and twenty-first-century theorists having by and large rejected, either explicitly or tacitly, such a dualist perspective on harmony, modality, and tonality. To be sure, some prominent theorists of today—Harrison and Klumpenhouwer, as cited in note 28—have embraced aspects of this viewpoint, but most modern accounts of harmony are formulated from a monist point of view. It should be obvious, of course, that my own views of harmony follow current practice.

---

35. Rameau, *Treatise on Harmony*, 143.

36. To be sure, the progression I–V⁷–I can also be construed as prolongational in certain contexts (especially initiating ones).

37. I am excluding sequential progressions from the discussion, since I consider them to be more melodic and contrapuntal in nature than functionally harmonic.

38. Unlike my usual practice, I will let lowercase roman numerals indicate minor sonorities in order to emphasize the distinction between monist and dualist perspectives.

39. For a somewhat different version of a dualist PCP, see Arthur von Oettingen's model of a "phonic" cadential progression, as shown by Harrison (*Harmonic Function*, 249, Ex. 5.5). As he notes, though, "Oettingen's dualism threatens to lose all relationship to musical art" (250).

EXAMPLE 9.16. Three-stage PCP in moment-to-moment listening context.

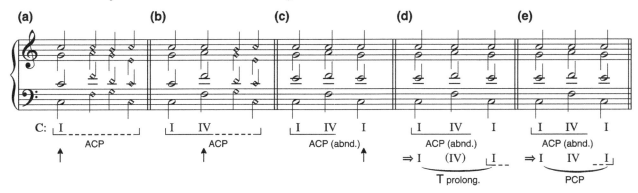

## 9.3.1.2. Plagal Cadential Progressions: Moment-to-Moment Listening Contexts

The previous accounts of both the three stage PCP (I–IV–I) and the four-stage one (I–V–IV–I) have been presented from a synoptic perspective. But how would we actually experience these harmonic successions in a moment-to-moment listening context and in a monist (i.e., nondualist) environment?[40] Let us start with the three-stage version and proceed harmony by harmony.

Toward the end of a thematic process, hence, in a context of cadential expectation, our encountering the initial tonic of a PCP could potentially evoke a sense of impending authentic cadential closure (Ex. 9.16a), though an inverted tonic (I$^6$) would more readily generate such an expectation. (Diamond-shaped note heads refer to the implied, or "protended," harmonies of the ACP.) When hearing this tonic move to a subdominant (Ex. 9.16b), we would most likely experience this second harmony as a stage-2 pre-dominant of an ACP, and we would be expecting a root-position dominant to clinch that impression. When the subdominant fails to progress to that dominant, however, and we hear a root-position tonic instead (Ex. 9.16c), we would understand that the ACP has been *abandoned*, in the sense of something having gone amiss with the dominant.[41] But now we can reinterpret the harmonic situation (Ex. 9.16d) and recognize that the IV could be understood as a neighboring harmony within a simple tonic prolongation. Here, the second tonic of the progression does not represent a formal end, something denied by the cadential abandonment, but rather groups forward with the following progression (perhaps one that is cadential or maybe again prolongational). Finally, if we experience the IV–I progression as actually achieving closure, such that the final tonic groups backward with the ongoing progression, we can alternatively interpret the harmonic situation as an actual PCP (Ex. 9.16e). The point of this exercise has been to show that perceiving a plagal progression as *uniquely cadential* is a complicated affair: the progression normally arises first in a context of authentic cadential closure, a context that is overthrown (abandoned), and reinterpreted as something plagal. Moreover, this plagal situation itself is a special case of the more general notion of tonic prolongation.

Let us now perform a similar analysis of the four-stage PCP (Ex. 9.17). Again, the formal context is one of cadential expectation. The appearance of the first tonic would be the same as that just discussed, namely as the initial harmony of an ACP (as in Ex. 9.16a). The subsequent motion to a root-position dominant (Ex. 9.17a) clinches the identity of that progression, but with the understanding that a pre-dominant has been omitted. When the dominant fails to resolve to tonic, but rather "returns" to the subdominant, we might, on the one hand, hear that the ACP has been evaded, in the sense of omitting the final tonic. The subsequent move from IV to I would then raise the same two options of creating either a tonic prolongation or a PCP (cf. Ex. 9.16d and e). On the other hand, the cadential dominant may not be heard as evaded, but rather remains implicative of a final cadential tonic. In such a case, we could recognize that the subdominant functions as an embellishment of the following tonic, either as an anticipation harmony in a weak metrical context (Ex. 9.17b) or as an appoggiatura harmony in a strong metrical context (Ex. 9.17c).[42] In these latter two cases, the dominant would retain its function as the penultimate harmony of an ACP, and the ensuing cadence would be authentic.[43]

---

40. Deborah Stein's discussion of the increased importance of subdominant harmony in nineteenth-century repertories anticipates a number of the points that follow; see especially her careful analysis of various harmonic options in connection with Wolf's "Gesang Weylas" ("Expansion of the Subdominant," 163–67). It is important to understand, however, that when speaking of "cadence"—authentic or plagal—Stein, like so many theorists, is referring more generally to harmonic *progressions*, ones that often have no particular relation to contexts of formal closure.

41. See the discussion of abandoned cadence in Chapter 4, sec. 4.3.3, where one option for abandonment sees the projected dominant failing to appear altogether.

42. For a similar distinction among possible meanings of the subdominant in plagal cadential contexts, see Stein, "Expansion of the Subdominant," 162–64, Ex. 8).

43. The harmonic situation presented by Ex. 9.17b might have a concrete manifestation in a twelve-bar blues, whereby m. 9 of the pattern is heard as a penultimate dominant of an ACP, while the subdominant in m. 10 is understood to embellishing the following tonic in m. 11, as a kind of anticipation. In sec. 9.3.5, I will show how the case of Ex. 9.17c undergirds a situation I term *feigned plagal closure*. In both of these contexts, the cadential framework is one of an authentic cadence, as defined by the penultimate dominant moving (eventually) to tonic, not a plagal cadence.

EXAMPLE 9.17. Four-stage PCP in moment-to-moment listening context.

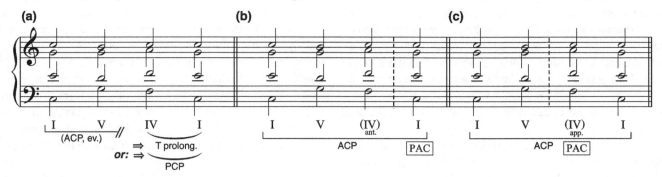

EXAMPLE 9.18. Plagal closure in sequential context.

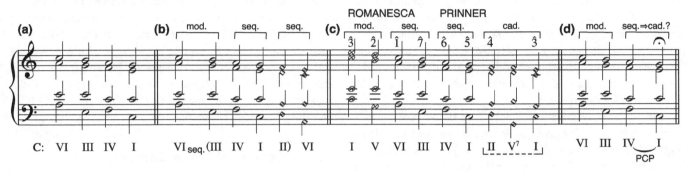

Finally, we sometimes encounter a plagal progression that initially appears in a noncadential context, but which then ends up functioning as the final progression of the passage. Consider the four harmonies in Example 9.18a.[44] The first two, VI–III, have no cadential expression; neither are they obviously prolongational. Most often we encounter them in some kind of sequential pattern. So when we then hear this harmonic pair transposed down a third, IV–I, we are reminded of a descending-thirds sequence (Ex. 9.18b). And as such, we might project ahead to hear a third link in the pattern, II–VI (as shown by the diamond noteheads).

It may have been noticed that our original four harmonies also make up part of a galant Romanesca-Prinner combination (Ex. 9.18c). In that context, our progression now appears as the third through sixth harmonies, following the conventional opening of the Romanesca, I–V (indicated by the crossed noteheads). Furthermore, we would not expect the Prinner to be completed by II–VI from the end of Example 9.17b, but rather by a progression that leads to tonic in order to support the final melodic $\hat{3}$; in this case, I have proposed a standard ACP to accomplish this task (Ex. 9.18c).

Let us say, though, that the tonic of our original progression (Ex. 9.18a) actually ends up as the true final harmony, such that an implied continuation—either as something sequential (Ex. 9.18b) or authentic cadential (Ex. 9.18c)—is not forthcoming. In this case (Ex. 9.18d), the tonic, as a genuine end (reinforced here by the fermata) could then be heard as the final member of a PCP.

This hearing, though, is certainly one that we come to very much in retrospect, such that the sequential IV–I acquires de facto a cadential quality more by its formal context than by its intrinsic harmonic expression.

In sum, the preceding discussion of how we might hear a possible PCP has revealed that it most often occurs in a context that initially implies an ACP, one that is then denied realization (evaded, abandoned) when the subdominant moves directly to a final tonic.[45] Or, the plagal progression may arise initially as something noncadential, such as a sequential context, like that discussed for Example 9.18. In other words, any theorist who advocates for a *fully autonomous* PCP has to propose a set of conditions under which the motion from subdominant to tonic is at no point in the harmonic process understood as prolongational, sequential, or authentic cadential. It is not obvious what contexts would evoke such an immediate sense—not a retrospective one—of plagal motion as *cadential* in nature.

### 9.3.1.3. Plagal Cadence; Prolongational Closure; Plagal Closure

This discussion on how to conceive of a plagal cadential progression has highlighted many difficulties attendant to that task. In the end, I remain skeptical that such a progression is truly cadential, for in principle, I hear the plagal progression IV–I as essentially *prolongational*. My views are rooted in a monist conception of

---

44. I have deliberately chosen the harmonies of this passage in relation to a real musical excerpt that I discuss ahead in Ex. 9.28.

45. Exceptionally, the situations described in Ex. 9.17b and c retain the sense of authentic cadence throughout the entirety of the progression.

harmony, whereby the only genuine mode of syntactical harmonic closure is one that engages a dominant resolving to a tonic: when both harmonies are placed in root position, some of the necessary conditions are in place for a specifically cadential sense of syntactical closure. Concomitant to such a view, I find it difficult to legitimize a genuine "plagal cadence," one that stands on par with an authentic cadence.[46] Despite the widespread use of the former term, it seems to me to be one that can sow more confusion than clarity.

We cannot ignore, however, those special cases—ones that arise infrequently in the tonal repertory—where the composer evidently uses a plagal progression to mark the harmonic-formal end of a thematic process. How should we understand such situations? The key, I believe, is to affirm the prolongational quality of the plagal progression and to consider it as having the potential to effect a form of prolongational closure. In other words, just as I do not adopt the notion of "contrapuntal *cadence*" (and the like) and thus speak of prolongational closure instead,[47] I propose that in place of "plagal cadence" we consider using the expression *plagal closure*.[48]

Having quite deliberately demoted the plagal cadence to a specific type of prolongational closure, let us now turn from purely theoretical speculations and consider passages from actual compositions, cases of formal ending that theorists might hold up as candidates for plagal cadence, and see if plagal closure might be the more suitable concept to adopt. As well, we will consider how such plagal motion functions within contexts that also project, or at least intimate, the potential for authentic cadential closure.

## 9.3.2. Analyses of Plagal Closure

In this section we will look at some specific examples of plagal closure as they arise in works by nineteenth-century composers. We will consider the harmonic and formal contexts in which such closure occurs, taking melodic matters into account where appropriate. Our first set of examples sees plagal closure having a *dependent* relation to an environment that proposes an authentic cadence, which, when failing to be realized, is replaced by plagal closure instead. A second, smaller set of examples finds plagal closure appearing *independent* of any immediate authentic cadential context. Along the way we will observe cases where it is not entirely clear if the plagal expression represents real thematic closure or, rather, arises as something postcadential. As well, we will consider some additional characteristics of melody, modality, and tonality that are often associated with plagal closure. Finally, we will often have to recognize the broader formal context in which such closure arises, for focusing exclusively on the plagal progression often fails to uncover the rich possibilities for how plagal closure achieves its effect.

As a result of pioneering work by Stephen Rodgers, we are now aware of an important source for Romantic plagal closure in songs by Fanny Hensel.[49] I will discuss a number of these songs, sometimes concurring with his analyses, at other times diverging from them. Since his work focuses extensively on such how closure is connected to the meaning of the poems, I will leave aside consideration of text-music relationships. Hensel's songs are notable not only for containing a wealth of material associated with plagal closure, but also for the variety of contexts that she finds for projecting this mode of ending.[50]

### 9.3.2.1. Dependent Plagal Closure

Most cases of plagal closure that I have encountered operate in a context in which authentic cadential closure is palpably implied. I will thus characterize such instances as exhibiting *dependent* plagal closure. The first three examples achieve their implicit sense of authentic cadence by means of a cadential six-four that fails to bring the dominant proper, yielding instead to a subdominant for the final plagal closure.

Hensel's "Wonne der Wehmut" is a case in point (Ex. 9.19). Starting in measure 22, the bass ascends steadily from ③ to ⑥, the latter degree supporting II$^4_3$ (m. 25), which ensues from the passing six-four in the prior bar. When the bass returns to ⑤ at measure 26, the second-inversion tonic now seems to function as a *cadential* six-four, one that could have resolved to a dominant proper in order to yield a standard PAC. To be sure, the six-four harmony in measures 26–27 could still be regarded as passing, in which case, the entire harmonic environment could be viewed as prolongational of the subdominant (see the *dashed* slur). At this point in the song, however, I do not find this interpretation convincing given the powerful rhetorical emphasis—both hypermetrically strong and melodically climactic—accorded the six-four at measure 26. Nonetheless, when the subdominant of

---

46. It is thus telling that Harrison, one of the strongest advocates for a renewed dualist conception of harmony, claims full legitimacy for plagal cadences ("Cadence," 563–67). Even some theorists who validate this cadence type often concede that it is not fully equivalent in effect to an authentic one. Thus Stein notes, "The basic problem in replacing the dominant [by a subdominant]…is that the plagal cadence is *weaker* than the authentic; the subdominant does not define the tonic as forcibly or precisely as the dominant" ("Expansion of the Subdominant," 164, my italics); see also similar comments cited in Chapter 2, note 75.

47. See again the discussion in Chapter 3, sec. 3.5.1.

48. I am aware, of course, that some readers will not be comfortable with the expression plagal closure in place of plagal cadence. In the discussion that follows, such readers may simply substitute cadence for closure and still be able to glean the sense of my analytical observations of specific pieces. By the way, this is not the first time that I have subsumed a particular cadential manipulation within the broader concept of prolongational closure. Earlier in Chapter 4 (sec. 4.3), I discussed how some cases of abandoned cadence also result in this type of ending.

49. Stephen Rodgers, "Plagal Cadences in Fanny Hensel's Songs." I thank Rodgers for so generously sharing his work on these songs, which has proven an invaluable resource for my own formulations of plagal cadence and closure.

50. The genre of song seems especially ripe for the use of plagal closure, most likely due to the role of the text. In addition to the work of Rodgers and Stein (already cited), see Heather Platt, "Unrequited Love and Unrealized Dominants," who considers a number of Brahms's *Lieder* by focusing on how plagal harmonies relate to the meaning of the text.

EXAMPLE 9.19. Hensel, "Wonne der Wehmut," mm. 20–32.

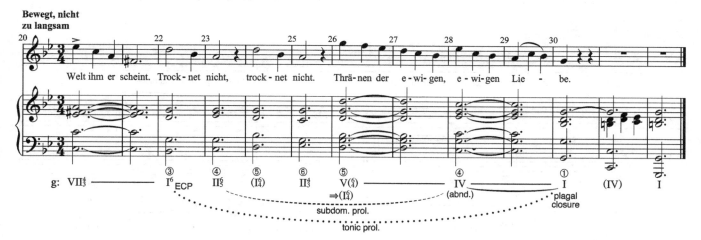

measure 28 replaces the implied dominant proper, the projected authentic cadence is abandoned, and the resulting closure at measure 30 emerges as manifestly plagal.[51] A retrospective hearing of a prolonged subdominant in measures 23–29 is thus validated. (It should be noted, however, that if we take measure 22 into account, it would not be unreasonable to hear the entire passage to the final bar as prolonging tonic harmony; see the *dotted* slur.)[52]

A similar case of dependent plagal closure arises in connection with the "Dutchman's Aria" from Wagner's *The Flying Dutchman*. The form of the aria is a fairly straightforward small ternary residing in A-flat minor (despite the three flats in the key signature). The A′ section (Ex. 9.20a) begins at measure 26 on I⁶, like the opening of the theme, moving then to II♯³ (m. 29), which is sustained for two full bars. By this point, we have surmised that an ECP is in the making, and when the bass falls to ⑤ to support an expected cadential six-four, our assumption of an authentic cadential context seems close to being confirmed. Indeed, Wagner could have easily concluded the theme with a conventional PAC, as reconstructed in Example 9.20b. Instead of leading to a dominant proper, however, the six-four returns to a pre-dominant, now IV⁶ (m. 32, in Ex. 9.20a). This harmony continues to bypass the dominant proper by shifting into root position in the second half of the bar and moving directly to the final tonic to end the theme with plagal closure. Like Hensel's "Wonne der Wehmut," our hearing the plagal closure permits us to re-evaluate the status of the six-four chord in measure 31, seeing it now as a neighboring tonic that prolongs the subdominant of the PCP.[53]

One other detail is interesting to observe with the plagal closure of the Dutchman's Aria. Comparing its final idea (Ex. 9.20a, mm. 32–33) to the end of the A section's compound antecedent (Ex. 9.20c, mm. 8–9), it is clear that the plagal closure "rhymes" melodically with the earlier HC at measure 9 (see the brackets above the vocal lines). What helps support this correspondence is the Picardy third effect of the final harmony, such that the major tonic of measure 33 can reference the major dominant of measure 9. Taking this rhyming effect into consideration, we see that the plagal progression concluding the aria also has a latent expression of half cadence in the subdominant region, D-flat minor, though this would hardly be our initial interpretation (nor our final one). As discussed later on, some cases of plagal closure raise uncertainty as to the key in which the thematic unit is closing.

Finally, it is worth reflecting a moment on the nature of the harmonic progression exhibited in both the Dutchman's Aria and Hensel's "Wonne der Wehmut" (Ex. 9.19). In both cases we might be tempted to recognize a four-stage PCP (see again, Ex. 9.14c), except, of course, that the "dominant" is represented exclusively by the cadential six-four. As such, we do not find a dominant proper progressing directly to the subdominant, a connection we have already considered to be harmonically nonsyntactical. Moreover, it would be questionable to find a four-stage PCP for another reason as well. In the experiential analyses I have been promoting, we would hear the six-four as a dominant initially in the context of an authentic cadential progression. When we retrospectively reinterpret this harmony as a *tonic* six-four moving to a subdominant, the resulting PCP would be a *three*-stage schema (as annotated with the *dotted* slur in both examples). To hear a four-stage PCP would be comparable to seeing the famous duck/rabbit optical illusion *as* a "dubbit," a situation that Lewin memorably mocks in his article on phenomenological modes of music perception.[54] I have, in fact, failed as of yet to uncover an unambiguous case of a four-stage PCP in this repertory.

---

51. In the musical examples, I annotate plagal closure with a curved line connecting the final IV–I progression of the PCP, thus emphasizing the harmonic prolongation associated with this mode of thematic ending.

52. Two other songs by Hensel, "Bitte" (mm. 15–16) and "Erwache Knab'" (mm. 20–22), exploit the same cadential strategy as "Wonne der Wehmut." For more complete analyses of them, see Rodgers, "Plagal Cadences," 135–40.

53. Such an intervening tonic six-four, however, would more typically function as a passing chord, not as a neighbor.

54. "So you see a dubbit. Who *cares* if you see a dubbit?" (Lewin, "Phenomenology," 371).

EXAMPLE 9.20. Wagner, "Dich frage ich," *The Flying Dutchman*, (a) mm. 25–34; (b) reconstruction of mm. 30–34; (c) mm. 6–9.

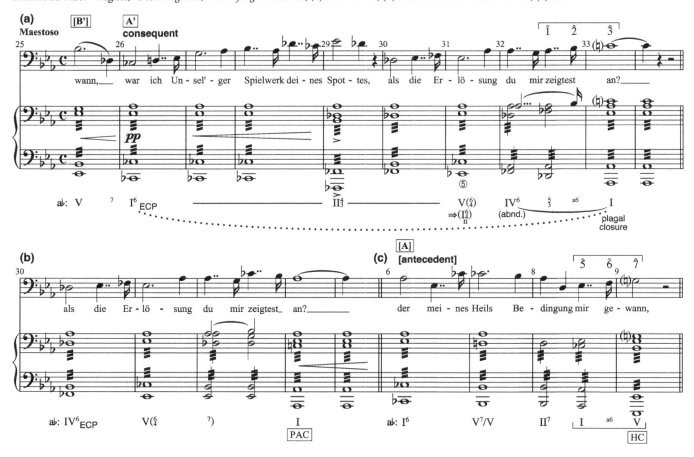

Up to now we have primarily been considering dependent plagal closure in light of an immediately preceding authentic cadential context, though with the Dutchman's Aria, we also looked back to an earlier half cadential articulation (in m. 9). But a number of works exhibiting plagal closure reveal their "dependency" when the music is obviously modeled on a prior passage that achieves an authentic cadence. An early Romantic case appears in the first movement of Mendelssohn's Octet in E-flat (Ex. 9.21a). Toward the end of a second main theme, a cadential progression, initiated at the upbeat to measure 32 by the pre-dominant VII$^7$/V, achieves a root-position dominant (embellished by several suspensions) on the downbeat of that bar. Immediately, though, the cadential dominant is undermined by V$^4_2$, resolving to I$^6$ (m. 33). At this point, an evaded cadence can be heard when the top voice $\hat{2}$ of measure 32, proposing a resolution to $\hat{1}$, leaps up to $\hat{5}$ on the downbeat of measure 33. The I$^6$ of that measure initiates a second cadential progression, leading this time to a cadential six-four (m. 34) for a second run at a PAC. Like the two previous examples by Hensel and Wagner, the six-four fails to bring the dominant proper; instead, the accented D♭ added to the harmony (in the second viola of m. 35) yields V$^4_3$/IV, a tonic substitute.[55] When this harmony resolves as promised to the subdominant (m. 36), the latter is enhanced by a shift to minor and accompanied by an added-sixth dissonance, $\hat{2}$, resolving upward to $\hat{3}$ to create plagal closure with the resolution to tonic on the downbeat of measure 37. Note, by the way, how the *diminuendo* to *piano* in measures 35–36 contributes to an effect that Rodgers so aptly characterizes as a "soft landing" onto the plagal close.[56]

The effect of this closure is clearly dependent upon the immediately prior evaded cadence, but in addition, Mendelssohn even more explicitly prepares this authentic cadential context in an earlier passage within the second main theme (Ex. 9.21b). Here, the cadential progression at the upbeat to measure 28 leads conventionally to a PAC on the downbeat of the next bar. Since the material content of measures 31–32 (see again Ex. 9.21a) is modeled on measures 27–28 (Ex. 9.21b), our hearing plagal closure in measure 37 is highly dependent on the prior authentic cadence (m. 29). In fact, this earlier PAC literally represents the structural end of the second main theme, even if the cadence is rather rhetorically understated. So the phrase leading to the second attempt at a PAC has a certain postcadential quality to it, thus further validating the composer's use of a plagal progression at the end of this repeated phrase. (Additional issues involving a plagal progression as postcadential will be discussed later in sec. 9.3.3.)

---

55. I continue to read the B♭ in mm. 34–35 as the functional bass (in Vc. 2), even if the D♭ (in Va. 2) literally lies below the bass in m. 35.

56. Rodgers, "Plagal Cadences," 133; see ahead his discussion of Hensel's "Zu deines Lagers Füßen" (Ex. 9.29).

EXAMPLE 9.21. Mendelssohn, String Octet in E-flat, Op. 20, i, (a) mm. 31–37; (b) mm. 27–29.

Another case of plagal closure that reveals its dependency on an earlier occurring passage appears in the piano miniature "Eintritt" by Schumann (Ex. 9.22a). The A section of this small ternary form opens with a four-measure phrase ending with a PAC. Note that the basic idea itself closes with a deceptive cadential progression, to which a contrasting idea responds with the PAC.[57] Following the B section (not shown), the opening phrase returns (Ex. 9.22b). This time, the contrasting idea at measure 19 ends with a genuine deceptive cadence, one that is not matched by a PAC. Instead the music continues to develop various ideas of the piece until we encounter a broad dominant pedal, the last three bars of which are shown at the start of Example 9.22c. With the second half of measure 37, the opening material occurs for a third time, and so we are particularly primed to expect a PAC to conclude the piece. Schumann, however, abandons the implied authentic cadential progression in favor of plagal closure at measure 40. The effect he achieves, though, is surely heard against a strong backdrop of a potential authentic cadence.

Plagal closure at the very end of a mazurka by Chopin (Ex. 9.23) is also highly dependent on a prior authentic cadential context, but in a manner quite different from the two previous cases already discussed.[58] In Mendelssohn's Octet and Schumann's "Eintritt," the plagal closure is built out of the same material that was formerly authentic cadential in nature. Chopin's mazurka, on the contrary, sees its plagal closure employing musical ideas not heard earlier in the piece, yet the general context that precedes the end clearly projects authentic cadential content.

In a work whose overall form is nonconventional, we can discern a main theme residing in the home key, which occurs at both the beginning and the close of the piece. In its first appearance (Ex. 9.23a), the theme brings a formal continuation in measures 17–20 that tonicizes E, the relative major. Immediately thereafter (m. 21), a Neapolitan sixth in the home key, C-sharp minor, proposes the onset of a cadential progression, one that is quickly completed in the following bar. Chopin then repeats this cadential idea three times, giving a greater rhetorical flourish to the Neapolitan at each repetition. Following the rather exaggerated "mid-cadence" fermata in the third repetition (m. 27), the final bar of the progression is fragmented, as signaled by the V–I repetitions in measures 29–30. The theme then comes to a standstill on an extended dominant in measures 31–32 (after which a new thematic section of the Mazurka takes over).

As discussed in the previous chapter, Chopin has a propensity for cadential repetition such that it can be confusing at times to know just where we are supposed to hear the closure.[59] And given the surfeit of cadential expression exhibited within this passage, it is especially difficult to determine whether any authentic cadence has actually occurred. In fact, the eventual concluding on the dominant (m. 31)—and in the form of a consonant triad no less—makes us wonder whether the theme has actually closed in some half cadential manner. Supporting this idea is the way in which Chopin quite cleverly eliminates the dissonant seventh

---

57. That the opening phrase is intrinsically a consequent, though contextually like an antecedent, is not uncommon in the Romantic style; see in Chapter 8, Ex. 8.21a, mm 1–4.

58. I thank Richard Cohn for referring this example to me.

59. See Chapter 8, sec. 8.6, and the discussion of Ex. 8.12 (the issue arises in a number of the preludes as well).

EXAMPLE 9.22. Schumann, "Eintritt," *Waldszenen*, Op. 82, no. 1, (a) mm. 1–4; (b) mm. 19–20; (c) mm. 35–44.

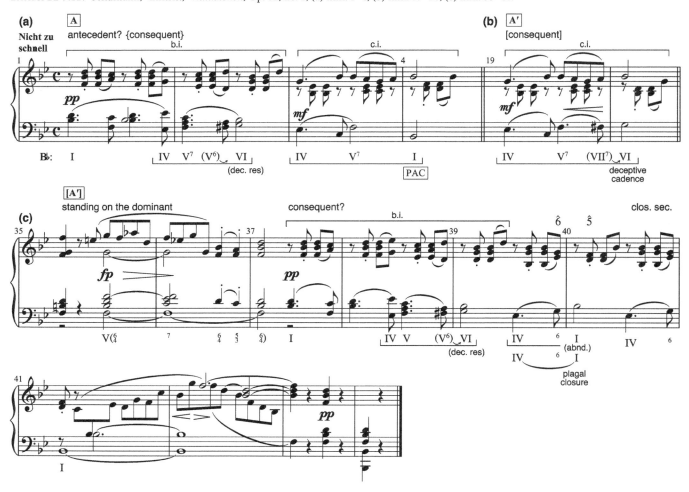

from the harmony starting at m. 29, so as to help prepare us to hear the dominant in these bars as potentially ultimate, not penultimate, as we had been assuming all along. Indeed, the tonic on the third beat in measures 29–30 seems to take on more of a neighboring role in relation to the surrounding dominant triads, rather than remaining as the final tonic of a highly compact authentic cadence. Thus despite the cadential extravagance of these bars, it is remains unclear whether, or how, cadential closure has actually taken place.[60]

The main theme returns (Ex. 9.23b) toward the end of the mazurka. This time, however, the fragmentation in measures 125–26 (corresponding to mm. 29–30) is extended for two bars (127–28). Note here a seemingly minor, but telling, harmonic change: the expected final tonic on the third beat of measure 127 is replaced by a neighboring VII$^7$/V. As a result, these bars sound more prolongational of the dominant than genuinely cadential. Indeed, they are directly analogous to measures 31–32, which featured a sustained dominant triad. So like the first time, this main theme poses the dilemma of whether or not it will actually close with an HC at measure 127 (here the effect is more of a premature dominant arrival) rather than as a clearly articulated authentic cadence.

Instead of bringing closure, however, Chopin further extends the theme with a sequential, stepwise descent of major-minor-seventh sonorities, creating his characteristic slithery chromaticism. He finally breaks the sequence (which seemed as though it could have gone on indefinitely) with a new passage that sustains II$^7$ in measures 133–38. This pre-dominant expansion generates powerful expectations that a decisive authentic cadence will finally resolve the ambiguities presented up to now and bring a clear ending to the theme, presumably a PAC. It is therefore all the more surprising, though strangely satisfying, when Chopin fails to bring a cadential dominant and rather allows the II$^7$ harmony—now more appropriately understood as a subdominant with added sixth—to resolve directly to tonic, thus producing plagal closure in the final bar of the piece.[61] Though the plagal progression is not immediately dependent upon a proximate authentic

---

60. The situation is akin to what Don Fowler describes in connection with classical (Greek and Roman) literature: "The more endings we get, the more we feel we are in the general area of The End, but also, the less confidence we feel that the 'real' end is necessarily the one for us" ("Second Thoughts on Closure," 21–22).

61. It is not entirely clear just where the II$^7$ (*qua* pre-dominant) converts to IV$^{a6}$ (*qua* subdominant). My analysis proposes that the reinterpretation occurs at the upbeat to m. 137, where the root of II$^7$ shifts from the bass to the upper part, thus allowing F♯ (upper voice in the left hand) to function as the root of the subdominant in the following two bars.

EXAMPLE 9.23. Chopin, Mazurka in C-sharp Minor, Op. 30, no. 4, (a) mm. 17–32; (b) mm. 123–39.

cadential context, the appropriateness of plagal closure here is obviously owing to the excessive degree of prior authentic cadential progressions that failed to generate a clear sense of ending to the theme. Note, as well, that whereas the two previous examples of dependent plagal closure (by Mendelssohn and Schumann) forged explicit musical connections between the prior authentic cadential context and the subsequent plagal one, the plagal dependence in the mazurka involves musical passages that are substantially different in content. The dependency relationship is thus rendered more abstract in Chopin's piece than in the previous cases.

In all of the examples of plagal dependency that we have discussed so far, the plagal closure has had the final word. In a passage from Holst's "Jupiter" (Ex. 9.24a), on the contrary, a prior plagal context sets up a final authentic cadential "confirmation" at the end of the thematic unit (though, as we shall see, a genuine PAC is evaded rather than fully realized). The passage in question is the famous hymn, which occupies a central position within the movement as a whole. The hymn is built as a small ternary, whose A section seems on the surface to be a period. But the harmonic setting creates some significant cadential deviations, motivated especially by how the theme begins. For rather than starting on

EXAMPLE 9.24. Holst, "Jupiter," *The Planets*, (a) mm. 194–202; (b) mm. 230–35; (c) reconstruction of mm. 200–201.

the tonic of E-flat, the key of the hymn, the upbeat is initially supported by III, moving directly to IV and then on to V at the end of the opening bar (m. 194), only then to revert to I⁶ at the downbeat of the following bar.⁶² As a result, this opening basic idea has a marked authentic cadential expression, with the bass line engaging the cadential stream and the supporting harmonies projecting a deceptive cadential progression (the final tonic being replaced by its first inversion). With the contrasting idea, the progression is repeated, this time with the dominant resolving to VI in measure 197, to create an independent deceptive cadence (3̂).⁶³ So even though we can recognize a basic idea followed by a contrasting one, this putative antecedent does not close with either an HC or an IAC. Both ideas, however, project a strong cadential quality, even if neither produces a genuine cadence.

When this opening phrase begins to be repeated, in the manner of a consequent, the upbeat harmony is now inverted to III⁶ so that the bass line remains focused on ⑤ of the cadential stream. The final idea of the phrase then brings a clear cadential melody 3̂–2̂–1̂ (with a neighboring 1̂ prior to the final descent). Such a melody could easily be harmonized to make a PAC (as reconstructed in Ex. 9.24c). Rather than supporting 2̂ with a cadential dominant, however, Holst inverts the pre-dominant II⁶ to its six-four position, which then moves directly to the final tonic, thus abandoning the cadential progression. Note how the bass features a most unusual upward arpeggiation ④–⑥–①. The resulting sense of closure can readily be heard as plagal, in that the whole of measure 200 is supported by a subdominant "parallel" (à la Riemann) moving to I.⁶⁴

Like the other cases of dependent plagal closure that we have already examined, this one also arises in a harmonic environment that strongly emphasizes authentic cadential progressions. But to see how Holst clinches this dependency, we must look at the very final portion of the A′ section, which largely reproduces the music of the A section (see Ex. 9.24b). Here the composer realizes in a remarkable, but only partial, way the implication that the plagal closure of the movement could more normally have been an authentic cadence. For he now harmonizes the penultimate 2̂ of the melody with V (m. 232), which, to be sure, is left dangling with a suspended fourth above the bass, to initiate a transition back to material from the opening of the movement.⁶⁵ It should go without saying, of course, that the final

---

62. In the actual score, the "upbeat" to the hymn is notated as two quarter notes in a single duple measure in the main tempo of the movement (*Allegro giocoso*). To simplify the music here, I have notated the upbeat as two eighth notes in the new tempo (*Andante maestoso*). That the harmony of this upbeat is III is not obvious from the notes that are literally sounding (which could just as well project tonic of E-flat). But the preceding music (not shown) is harmonized by a G-minor-seventh sonority, and so we can still hear the upbeat to m. 194 as projecting that harmony. Moreover, all subsequent appearances of this upbeat are explicitly harmonized as III⁶ in E-flat (see, e.g., upbeat to m. 198).

63. See the discussion of similar independent deceptive cadences in the classical style (Chapter 4, sec. 4.1.2.4, and Ex. 4.20–4.23).

64. In a subsequent arrangement of this hymn by Vaughan Williams, set to the words "I vow to thee my country" and played on many ceremonial occasions in the United Kingdom, the bass ⑥ is omitted and the sense of plagal motion ④–① is projected all the more. I thank Jon Wild for directing me to this version.

65. To avoid the potential parallel fifths that might have resulted if the dominant had followed immediately upon the pre-dominant II⁶, Holst reharmonizes the neighboring 1̂ on the second beat of m. 232 with VI, which has the additional effect of allowing him to bring in the bass ⑥ (though shifted back by a beat) that was present in the earlier plagal closures.

EXAMPLE 9.25. Hensel, "Sehnsucht," (a) mm. 17–24; (b) mm. 5–8; (c) reconstruction of mm. 20–22.

dominant, with its suspended fourth, does not create a half cadence, but clearly functions as the penultimate harmony of an authentic cadence, one that is ultimately evaded, but one that also reveals explicitly the dependent status of the prior plagal closures.

To conclude this section on dependent plagal closure, let us briefly revisit an earlier example to consider whether an interpretation of plagal closure might be an appropriate alternative to that of tonic arrival (see again Ex. 9.3). As originally presented, I considered the pre-dominant Gr+6 at measure 361 as initiating an ECP, such that the arrival of the cadential six-four at measure 369 is heard as stage 3 of an authentic cadential progression. I then discussed that this harmony becomes reinterpreted as a tonic (six-four), which is sustained (with many neighboring subdominants and a penultimate Gr+6 at m. 381) to the end of the passage, thus yielding a tonic arrival back at measure 369. In light of our discussion of dependent plagal closure, we might propose another interpretation of this passage. For once that cadential six-four is reinterpreted as having genuine tonic function, we might want to hear that tonic (again, much in retrospect) to be the goal harmony of plagal closure at measure 369. The difference between the two options probably hinges on whether we hear that bar as a moment of expected ending (thus, as plagal closure) or whether we experience that same moment as a premature arrival (of the tonic). After many hearings of the work (with a variety of conductors), I find both possibilities entirely viable.

### 9.3.2.2. Independent Plagal Closure

A second general type of plagal closure operates in a harmonic-formal context that is relatively free of any association with a prior (or future) authentic cadential expression. This type, which I term *independent* plagal closure, seems to occur with lesser frequency than the dependent type, thus attesting to the powerful hold that the authentic cadence continued to exert on tonal composers throughout the nineteenth century.[66] In the first three cases that I discuss, the harmonic progression for each is a three-stage PCP, I–IV–I. We should remember, however, that even this situation may imply an ACP (as earlier discussed in sec. 9.3.1.1). When, in the context of a potential thematic ending, we hear an initial tonic moving to the subdominant, we most naturally assume the latter harmony to function as a pre-dominant, one that will lead to dominant for an authentic cadence. When the subdominant moves directly to tonic, we understand retrospectively that independent plagal closure has occurred instead. A good illustration appears at the end of Hensel's "Sehnsucht" (Ex. 9.25a). Following a broad tonic prolongation, whose last harmonic components ($V^6_5$–I) appear in measures 17–19, the move to IV at measure 20 could signal potential authentic cadential closure, analogous to

---

66. My use of the expression "independent" in the context of plagal closure must not be confused with several other uses of this term throughout this study, such as "independent" vs. "way-station" IACs or deceptive cadences (see the earlier note 63), or the "independent" cadences of fugal theory (see Chapter 6, sec. 6.4.3).

EXAMPLE 9.26. Bruckner, Symphony No. 8 in C Minor, ii, mm. 181–90.

EXAMPLE 9.27. Hensel, "Im Hochland Bruder," mm. 8–13.

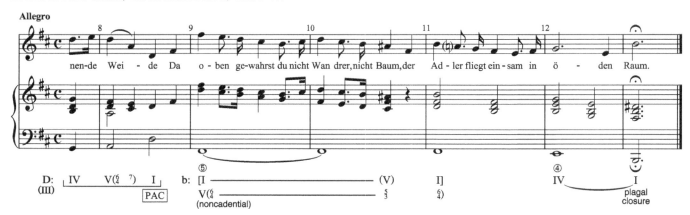

the PAC that confirms the modulation to the dominant region earlier in the song (Ex. 9.25b, m. 8); a rewritten version of the song's ending could be fashioned as in Example 9.25c. What Hensel actually writes, however, is a clear case of plagal closure when the subdominant resolves to tonic at measure 22. In the complete absence of any proximate cadential dominant, there lacks any overt expression of authentic cadence, and the strophe ends with independent plagal closure. The piano alone in measures 23–24 echoes the plagal progression as a clear postcadential gesture.

Later in the century, the scherzo from Bruckner's Eighth Symphony concludes with independent plagal closure (Ex. 9.26 shows the end of the A′ section). Following various tonal meanderings toward the latter part of the section (tonicizing A major, then D-flat major), the music settles into the home key of C minor (m. 175, not shown) with an extended elaboration of the tonic major (m. 181 of the example arises in the middle of this passage). A sudden move to the minor subdominant at measure 183 casts a menacing shadow over the proceedings, which brings back the principal motive (see bracket in the l. h.) from the opening of the scherzo. But the resolution to tonic at measure 187 brightens the mood by asserting an optimistic major modality and plagal closure for the scherzo as a whole. Though there is no reason to doubt the expression of independent plagal closure here, it is interesting to observe a detail that could easily be overlooked, namely the emphatic upper pedal G beginning at measure 183 (played by the first violins and doubled by the horns) that ominously intrudes upon the overall subdominant quality. Is this pitch an allusion to dominant harmony of a bypassed authentic cadence?[67]

Returning to Hensel, we encounter another case of independent plagal closure in her song "Im Hochland Bruder" (Ex. 9.27). Here, however, the context of this closure is somewhat more complicated than what we have seen so far. The excerpt begins with a PAC in measure 8, which ends an eight-measure hybrid theme in the key of D, the relative major of the home key,

---

67. For a similar intrusion of the leading tone within a plagal progression, see again Ex. 3.174, m. 66.

EXAMPLE 9.28. Svendsen, *Romance*, Op. 26, (a) mm. 169–79; (b) mm. 159–61.

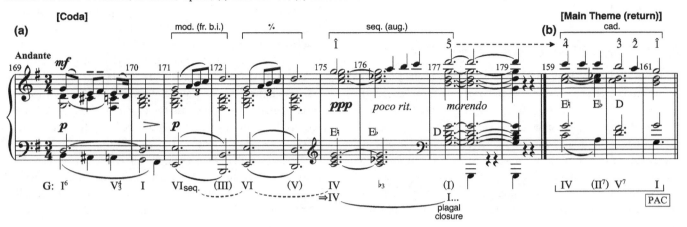

B minor. What follows in the next three bars is a dominant pedal in the home key, thus suggesting a standing on the dominant of the type we might find in a contrasting middle of a small ternary. Yet despite the pedal, the actual harmony projected by the music sounding above the bass emphasizes tonic throughout measures 9–11, except when a neighboring dominant briefly appears in the second half of measure 10. When the bass ⑤ steps down to ④ at measure 12, we hear the tonic (six-four) moving to subdominant, with a case of plagal closure arising in the final bars of the song. (The resulting form fails to realize any sense of ternary and thus remains entirely nonconventional.) Though I have analyzed measures 9–11 as largely projecting tonic harmony, the dominant in the bass might lead us to question whether the closure is fully independent. When we understand that this dominant does not in itself have any cadential function, we can be more confident that the plagal closure remains independent of any obvious authentic cadential expression.

A final example of independent plagal closure arises in a context that is largely devoid of any authentic cadential expression. Indeed, the plagal progression appears initially as a sequential link, like the situation we discussed earlier in connection with Example 9.18. The passage arises in the *Romance* for Violin and Orchestra, Op. 26 (1881), by Johann Svendsen (Ex. 9.28a). Earlier on, the large-ternary form of this movement found its structural close by means of a standard PAC (Ex. 9.28b, m. 161). Thus the passage in Example 9.28a represents the conclusion of the coda. Toward its end, a tonic prolongation in measures 169–70 leads to VI (m. 171), to support a return of the opening basic idea of the main theme (mm. 21–22, not shown). As Timothy Cutler observes, VI is further embellished by III in measure 172.[68] When the motive is repeated in the following two bars, Svendsen replaces III by V, also to be seen as an embellishment of VI (as shown by the parentheses around the roman numeral).[69] A final repetition occurs in measures 175–79, but now with two significant changes: first, the idea appears at the same pitch-class level (though an octave higher) with a marked rhythmic augmentation, thus effecting a "composed" *ritardando* (reinforced even more so by the notated *poco rit.*); second, the harmonic support is now a descending-third sequence IV–(I) of the original VI–(III). (The dashed slurs connect the main harmonies of this sequence.) It would seem, therefore, that the movement as a whole is concluding with a sequence, a medial formal function.[70] Yet the reduction in dynamic level (from *p* to *ppp*), the slower pacing of events, the harmonic shading via the minorization of IV (m. 176), and the final dying away (*morendo*) of the tonic all contribute to projecting the sense of ending a coda.[71] As such, we must reinterpret the "sequential" IV of measure 175, along with the "embellishing" I at measure 177, as forming a plagal progression, one that supports independent plagal closure. Note by the way, that it would have been syntactically possible—though unbearably corny—to have followed this ending with the identical PAC used to conclude the main theme (Ex. 9.28b). As such, the idea of seeing a sequence in measures 175–79 as a functional continuation is further validated. In fact, the odd way in which the melody closes, with its ascending melodic line from 1̂ to 5̂ (mm. 175–77) links up perfectly with the descending scale (4̂–1̂) of that PAC (see the dashed arrow). Finally, in order to assert the independence of this plagal closure, I have stressed the absence of any authentic cadential context associated with it. Yet the point I just made about how the actual ending resonates with the earlier PAC shows a lingering connection, one that is further reinforced by the inner-voice motive E–E♭–D in measures 175–77, which

---

68. Cutler, "Proper Boundaries," 62–63, Ex. 17).

69. Cutler stresses the embellishing function of this dominant, such that its connection to the following IV would not seem to be direct and thus less a violation of normal harmonic syntax.

70. To avoid confusion, recall that my identification of something as sequential is fundamentally based in the harmonic context, not the melodic one. Thus, the melody of the sequence (mm. 175–79) remains the same (except up an octave) as the melody of the model (mm. 171–72).

71. Here is an exemplary case of how statistical parameters of dynamics and tempo can help define a formal context of ending, esp. in the absence of the strong syntactical cues given by an authentic cadence; see Meyer, *Style and Music*, 303–25.

also references the same motive in stages 2 and 3 of the PAC in Example 9.28b.[72]

### 9.3.3. Plagal Closure versus Plagal Codetta

As mentioned frequently throughout this study, plagal harmonic progressions typically serve a postcadential function. Indeed, the second half of the nineteenth century sees a marked increase in the use of plagal progressions at the very end of a movement. It would seem, indeed, that the more classical V–I final codetta had largely run its course, such that a *plagal codetta*, as this formation can be termed, becomes almost de rigueur as the last utterance of a movement, especially one of a monumental or solemn character. Since such examples abound, none need be further illustrated or discussed here.

With the idea of plagal closure at hand, it should be clear that such a mode of ending should in principle be distinguished from a plagal codetta, just as we differentiate a PAC from its following "authentic" codettas (those ending V–I). Situations arise, however, where we may not be certain whether a plagal progression is closing a formal process, or whether that progression supports a postcadential codetta.[73] We have already confronted such cases that play upon this ambiguity in passages by J. S. Bach, Beethoven, and Robert Schumann, namely, where a way-station deceptive cadence, reinterpreted as a "final PAC," seems to be the real marker of thematic closure, while a subsequent plagal progression functions postcadentially.[74]

A somewhat related ambiguity concerning the functional status of a closing plagal progression arises in Hensel's "Zu deines Lagers Füßen," a song that Rodgers analyzes in detail. He uses normative reconstructions to reveal how Hensel's cadential practice is complex and highly sensitive to the meaning of the text. Unlike the position that I propose here, Rodgers is willing to recognize genuine plagal cadences, though he well understands that their use is often dependent (my expression, not his) on both a conceptual, and at times experiential, background of authentic cadential closure. His reconstruction of the opening strophe shows that it could easily have closed with a home-key PAC (Ex. 9.29a), measure 8, and that the subsequent plagal motion is obviously postcadential. What Hensel actually writes is seen in Example 9.29b. As Rodgers explains:

The piano comes to rest *after* the singer arrives on the word "Raum" ("room"): rather than a $V^7$–i progression in G minor, we hear $V^7$–I in E♭ major. We can think of this as a kind of evaded G-minor cadence, which defers a true cadence until later—yet when that cadence finally arrives, it is of course a plagal cadence (PC), not an authentic one. In fact, there's not a single authentic cadence in the song. The sense of deferral is particularly strong because the evaded G-minor PAC is itself displaced from where it might have been. In mm. 6 and 7 Hensel stretches the words "fernen" ("distant") and "fremden" ("strange") so that they each fill an entire measure rather than a half measure [cf. Ex. 9.29a, m. 7]. The music slows as it approaches what promises to be a PAC, veers unexpectedly away from that PAC, and finally makes a soft landing on a plagal cadence.[75]

Though I find convincing most of what Rodgers describes, the situation is perhaps even more complex. In particular, I believe that we can discern a prominent *sequential* context through much of the final phrase (see again Ex. 9.29b). Following a descending six-three sequence in measure 6, the $V^6$ of measure 7 resolves prolongationally to I on the downbeat of measure 8. There immediately follows a tonicization of E-flat (HK: VI) from the second beat of measure 8 into the downbeat of measure 9. This descending-third sequence then continues with the tonicization of C minor (HK: IV) in the rest of that bar, only to yield to a plagal progression into measure 10. In other words, when the voice closes on $\hat{1}$ in measure 9, it does so not in a context of *cadential* closure, but rather within a *sequential* pattern that continues on through the rest of measures 9–10. At the end of the third strophe (Ex. 9.29c), the bass line in measures 17–20 projects the sequential pattern even more strongly, though Hensel makes a crucial substitution when changing the expected VI for the downbeat of measure 19 (cf. m. 9 in Ex. 9.29b) to $V^6/IV$, which not only advances the sequential progression, but also provides a degree of "tonic" support ($V^6/IV$ being a chromatic version of $I^6$) for the final pitch in the voice.

What then is the status of the plagal progressions into measures 10 and 21? On the one hand, they clearly mark the completion of the harmonic motion up to these points in the strophes, and so an analysis of plagal closure seems justified (option 1 in the analysis). But given the prominent way in which the melodic line completes itself on $\hat{1}$ in measure 9, and even more decisively in measure 19 (due to the "tonic" support just mentioned), we might hear the plagal motion as postcadential (option 2), akin to the Bach, Beethoven, and Schuman cases discussed in earlier chapters (see note 74). Indeed, Rodgers alludes to this possibility when speaking of how "the plagal cadence now takes on conventional religious connotations," thus evoking the Amen gesture of a plagal codetta.[76] Like so many cases of ambiguous closure in tonal

---

72. For another case of plagal closure that emerges out of a strongly sequential context; see Chopin's Etude in E, Op. 10, no. 3. A cadential six-four at m. 70 proposes a possible authentic cadence, but the dominant proper in the following bar initiates a descending-thirds sequence, V–(VI)–III–(IV)–I. The tonic thus achieved at m. 73 is then prolonged by further neighboring, minor subdominants. The sequential link IV–I can thus be reinterpreted as providing plagal closure to end the piece.

73. Of course, situations involving authentic cadential closure can raise similar difficulties of interpretation, as discussed from a number of perspectives in Chapter 2, sec. 2.8.

74. See Chapter 6, the discussion of Ex. 6.19–6.22; Chapter 3, Ex. 3.174; and Chapter 8, Ex. 8.19. Some other songs by Schumann ("Die Blume der Ergebung," Op. 83, no. 2) and Hensel ("Neujahrslied") also feature a similar kind of cadential ambiguity.

75. Rodgers, "Plagal Cadences," 132–33.

76. The third option, hearing the ending as an HC in C minor, will be discussed shortly in sec. 9.3.4.3

EXAMPLE 9.29. Hensel, "Zu deines Lagers Füßen," (a) reconstruction of mm. 5–10 (from Rodgers, "Plagal Cadences," Ex. 8.1); (b) mm. 5–10 (c) mm. 15–21.

music, we should seek not necessarily to resolve the question as to whether the voice or the piano creates the moment of structural end, but rather to relish what is complicated in such music, especially in the song repertoire, where the text often prompts the composer to stretch the limits of harmonic-formal syntax.

### 9.3.4. Additional Characteristics of Plagal Closure

The discussion of plagal closure has up to now largely focused on the harmonic and formal contexts in which it is operative. But some other musical characteristics also seem associated with plagal endings.

#### 9.3.4.1. $\hat{6}$–$\hat{5}$ Melodic Closure

A number of examples of plagal closure, especially by Hensel, feature a melodic line that concludes on $\hat{5}$, normally approached from $\hat{6}$ above. We can observe this detail in Example 9.25a, measures 21–22, and Example 9.22c, measures 39–40. Although these passages place the melodic descent largely in the major modality, a number of other songs by Hensel feature the minor-mode motion $\flat\hat{6}$–$\hat{5}$, as seen in the three passages of Example 9.30.[77] It

---

77. Hensel's "Der Eichwald brauset," (Ex. 9.30c) is exceptional in that it achieves plagal closure on $\hat{1}$ at the downbeat of m. 33, but then the voice leaps down a fourth for a prominent $\hat{5}$–$\hat{6}$–$\hat{5}$ motion during the postcadential tonic prolongation.

may have already struck the reader that this emphasis on a final $\hat{5}$ approached stepwise from above is also a prominent upper-voice feature of the dualist PCPs shown in Example 9.15. Whether or not this connection is fortuitous, I make no claim that theory influenced practice (or even vice versa, which is more likely, given that the proto-dualist Hauptmann must surely have known Hensel and Schumann). Still, it is remarkable how often this particular melodic ending, one that is completely distinctive from any of the authentic cadential patterns, arises in the relatively limited set of examples examined in this chapter.[78]

### 9.3.4.2. Phrygian Modality

Another characteristic of plagal closure, one discussed by Rodgers in connection with Hensel's songs, is somewhat related to the first, namely the tendency for the melodic line to exhibit elements of the phrygian mode, specifically with its characteristic final half-step descent, be it ♭$\hat{6}$–$\hat{5}$ or ♭$\hat{2}$–$\hat{1}$.[79] An especially pronounced phrygian usage appears in the closing melody of "Zu deines Lagers Füßen" (Ex. 9.29b, mm. 6–9), which features the entire phrygian scale. A phrygian reference (though less complete) also arises at the end of Hensel's "Bitte" (Ex. 9.30a, mm. 15–16).

### 9.3.4.3. Home-Key Plagal Closure versus IV: HC

A third characteristic of plagal closure, loosely related again to the previous two, involves a certain lack of tonal clarity that some cases of plagal closure project: when a penultimate minor subdominant resolves to a final major tonic (IV♭–I♮), the effect is plagal; in some contexts, however, we may have the impression that the final major triad is a *dominant* in relation to a prior minor tonic, thus I♭–V♮. We have already encountered a situation of this type with the Dutchman's Aria (Ex. 9.20a), where the final plagal closure in A-flat minor (mm. 32–33) clearly references a previous HC in A-flat major (Ex. 9.20c, mm. 8–9). A number of Hensel's songs create a degree of tonal ambiguity as to whether the final closure is plagal or half cadential. "Zu deines Lagers Füßen" (Ex. 9.29c) ends on a G-major triad (m. 21), which in the overall tonal scheme of the song is a Picardy inflected tonic. In its more local context, however, this harmony sounds as the dominant of C minor, the final region emerging from the broader sequential pattern, as earlier discussed.[80] In "Fictenbaum und Palme" (Ex. 9.30b), an excursion to C-flat major (HK: ♭VI, notated as B major)

is completed with the tonic on the downbeat of measure 27. Though the key signature then changes to three flats, reflecting the overall E-flat major tonality of the song, the music in measures 8–9 tonizes A-flat minor (HK: IV). Thus the final harmonic progression into measure 29 sounds in its own thematic context as an HC in the tonal region of the subdominant. Only in retrospect, when this E♭ harmony is prolonged for an additional five bars (not shown), do we understand it as having effected plagal closure in the home key of E-flat.[81]

### 9.3.4.4. Subdominant with Added Sixth; $\hat{1}$–$\hat{2}$–$\hat{3}$

Most cases of Romantic plagal closure employ a subdominant *triad* as the penultimate harmony of the PCP. Mendelssohn's Octet (Ex. 9.21a) also brings at first a subdominant major triad (first half of m. 36); in the second half of that bar, however, he minorizes the harmony and includes an added sixth above the root (IV$^{a6}$). In terms of scale degree function, this pitch is $\hat{2}$, which forms a dissonance with $\hat{1}$ (the "fifth" of the subdominant). As well described by Rameau, who first drew special attention to this dissonant harmony, its resolution to tonic (his *cadence irrégulière*) sees the dissonant pitch ascend to $\hat{3}$.[82] Indeed, Mendelssohn's plagal closure highlights the ascending melodic gesture $\hat{1}$–$\hat{2}$–$\hat{3}$ in the upper voice. This constellation of features—a minor subdominant, with added sixth, resolving to a major tonic, and a melodic ascent to $\hat{3}$ in the soprano—become especially typical of plagal closure in works by mid- to late-nineteenth-century composers, as seen already in the Dutchman's Aria (Ex. 9.20a, mm. 32–33). Indeed, we will encounter additional cases by Wagner, Bruckner, and Grieg later in this chapter.

### 9.3.4.5. "Diminished" Plagal Closure

In some cases of plagal closure, Rodgers notes a harmonic variant that employs VII$^4_3$ resolving to I; he terms this a "diminished plagal cadence."[83] Normally, we would understand this diminished seventh to function as a dominant substitute (for V$^4_2$), and as such, it typically would resolve to I$^6$, whereby the progression would be deemed tonic prolongational, not plagal. When the diminished-seventh harmony resolves instead to a root-position tonic, the bass line ④–① strongly references a plagal progression; additionally, three of the pitches in the VII$^4_3$ harmony (the 3rd, 5th, and 7th) are also members of IV$^{a6}$.[84] Among the examples we have discussed so far, we can find this usage in Hensel's "Der

---

78. See also ahead Ex. 9.33, mm. 194–95. In Ex. 9.28a, mm. 177, the final melodic pitch is $\hat{5}$, though this time approached from below. A number of the songs by Brahms that Platt analyzes also conclude with an ascending approach to $\hat{5}$; "Unrequited Love and Unrealized Dominants," 30.

79. Rodgers, "Plagal Cadences," 141. Picking up on a cue from Susan Wollenberg, Rodgers suggests that Hensel's familiarity with J. S. Bach's chorale harmonizations may have influenced her use of phrygian idioms (Wollenberg, "Songs of Travel: Fanny Hensel's Wanderings," 71–72).

80. The same tonal ambiguity, though less pronounced, can be discerned in the first strophe as well (see Ex. 9.29b, m. 10).

81. See also Tyler Osborne's discussion of Hensel's "Die Äolsharfe auf dem Schlosse zu Baden" ("'You Too May Change': Tonal Pairing of the Tonic and Subdominant in Two Songs by Fanny Hensel," 122–26).

82. Rameau, *Treatise on Harmony*, book 2, chap. 7, 73–75.

83. Rodgers, "Plagal Cadences," 129, 136.

84. Harrison speaks of the same situation as a "functionally mixed cadence, plagal features predominating" ("Cadence," Fig. 27). For a broader discussion of harmonies that simultaneously express both dominant and pre-dominant (subdominant) functions, see Kevin J. Swinden, "When Functions Collide: Aspects of Plural Function in Chromatic Music," 260–72.

EXAMPLE 9.30. (a) Hensel, "Bitte," mm 14–16; (b) Hensel, "Fichtenbaum und Palme," mm. 27–29; (c) Hensel, "Der Eichwald brauset," mm. 32–35.

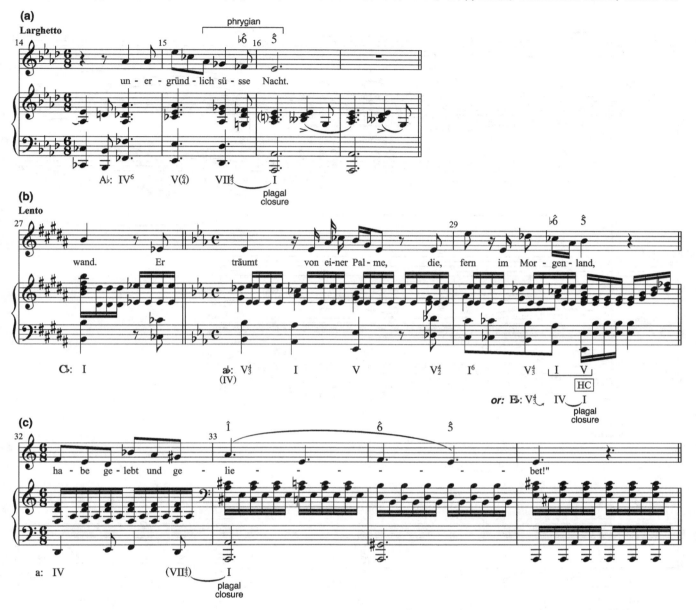

Eichwald brauset," (Ex. 9.30c, end of m. 32), where, to be sure, it is a local inflection of IV from the beginning of the bar.[85]

### 9.3.5. Feigned Plagal Closure

When the topic of nineteenth-century plagal cadences is raised among music theorists talking shop, two passages come quickly to the fore—the climactic cadence closing Wagner's "Liebestod" and the ending of Puccini's "Nessun dorma." Are these well-known pieces truly exemplary of plagal closure? Let us look first at the Wagner and then step back to consider some purely theoretical distinctions. Following a discussion of a passage from Mahler's Sixth Symphony, I conclude this section with a detailed consideration of how Puccini ends his most famous aria.

Toward the close of Wagner's "Liebestod" (Ex. 9.31), the music arrives on a dominant pedal as early as measure 54 (not shown). As this dominant is prolonged, it strongly projects being a penultimate dominant, stage 3, of an impending authentic cadence. The gradual crescendo and inexorable forward drive throughout this passage culminate at measure 61 with a *fortissimo* dynamic and a sudden change of motivic material. This moment, the obvious climax of the aria, brings subdominant harmony, which resolves to tonic in the following bar. The remainder of Isolde's text (not shown) is set to a series of IV–I repetitions, entirely in the manner of postcadential, plagal codettas.[86]

---

85. For an example by Bach of the "diminished" plagal progression in a postcadential context, see in Chapter 6, Ex. 6.21, end of m. 23.

86. Eventually a tonic pedal ensues, which prolongs this harmony until the very end of the opera, wherein the last reference to the Tristan chord and

EXAMPLE 9.31. Wagner, "Mild und Leise" ("Liebestod"), *Tristan und Isolde*, mm. 59–63.

EXAMPLE 9.32. Derivation of feigned plagal closure.

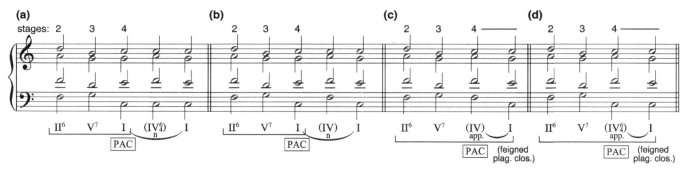

Inasmuch as the powerful subdominant-to-tonic motion in measures 61–62 represents the last two harmonies of the ongoing thematic process, listeners may well consider this moment as one of plagal closure. Yet given our impression that the preceding expanded dominant functions as the penultimate harmony (stage 3) of an authentic cadential progression (ACP), we might better understand the subdominant as *interpolated* between the dominant and tonic of an authentic cadence. And given its strong hypermetrical position (relative to the resolving tonic), this subdominant behaves as an *appoggiatura* harmony, one that belongs to stage 4 of the authentic cadence, not as the replacement of a stage-3 dominant, as would be found in cases of genuine plagal closure. To be sure, the emphasis that the subdominant projects, along with its harmonic release into tonic, gives a rhetorical impression of plagal closure; but in effect, it is one that is essentially *feigned*: the cadence is actually authentic, with an interpolated subdominant.[87]

To help clarify what I mean by *feigned plagal closure*, consider the harmonic progressions in Example 9.32. Pattern

---

its accompanying "desire" motive appears within a tonic prolongational context. These final bars will be discussed at the end of the chapter in connection with Ex. 9.56f.

[87]. Green cites this same example and identifies it as an "elaboration of the authentic cadence" due to the delaying of the final tonic, a view that entirely accords with the one that I have just presented (*Form*, 13). Cutler speaks of the subdominant in similar situations as an "inverted accented six-four chord" ("Proper Boundaries," 67–68, Ex. 21).

(a) shows a PAC whose final tonic is embellished by a neighboring subdominant six-four; in pattern (b), the subdominant is "re-inverted" to its more stable root position (a "casting out the root"). With pattern (c), the subdominant appears *in place of* the expected final tonic, thus delaying this latter harmony, which only arises when the subdominant resolves to tonic. In this context, the subdominant, now a stage-4 harmony, is still understood to embellish the final tonic. As an appoggiatura harmony, however, the former now precedes the tonic rather than follows it, as in the first two patterns. Finally, pattern (d), a variant of (c), sees the subdominant placed in second inversion, thus alluding to pattern (a).[88] As so described, all four patterns represent cases of PAC closure. Where, then, resides the semblance of plagal closure that so many listeners respond to in a passage such as the "Liebestod"? In the first two patterns, the plagal progression (I–IV–I) occupies a postcadential position relative to the PAC, thus supporting a plagal codetta. In the third and fourth patterns, the plagal motion (IV–I) is incorporated within the ACP. More specifically, the cadential arrival occurs with the appoggiatura subdominant, whereas the resolution of that harmony to tonic *feigns* a sense of plagal closure, because the appearance of the tonic no longer represents the moment of cadential end, as would be the case with genuine plagal closure (though of course the tonic still marks the purely *harmonic* end of the authentic cadential progression). With the annotations that I have provided to both Examples 9.31 and 9.32, I align the PAC symbol with the appoggiatura subdominant and then indicate the sense of feigned plagal closure where the resolving tonic appears at the end of the plagal progression.

A passage from the end of the slow movement of Mahler's Sixth Symphony shows how an emphasis on subdominant harmony manifests itself first as feigned plagal closure, followed then by genuine plagal closure. At the beginning of Example 9.33, a circle of fifths sequence in measures 177–78 continues with a pre-dominant ($V^7/V$) at measure 179. The expansion of this harmony prompts us to understand it as the start of an ECP, which continues with a penultimate dominant seventh in the next bar. This harmony is then expanded for two additional measures, setting up strong harmonic and melodic expectations that the downbeat of measure 183 will bring a PAC. The cadence is evaded, however, when the melody leaps from $\hat{7}$ up to $\hat{3}$, all the while sustaining the dominant pedal. Mahler tries for the cadence again, and at measure 186 both the melody ($\hat{1}$) and the bass (①) attain their goal. Harmonically, however, the local sonorities in measures 186–87 prolong subdominant (though still over the tonic pedal), and a complete tonic harmony does not emerge until measure 188. The effect, therefore, is related to the feigned plagal closure seen in the previous example by Wagner, except that in place of a root-position subdominant, a tonic pedal occurs at the moment of cadential arrival. The situation thus conforms to pattern (d) of Example 9.32.[89]

Even though the PAC at measure 186 fully concludes the tonal structure of the movement, Mahler starts up what seems to be another thematic unit. Indeed, the melodic content of measures 188–90 strongly references the earlier passage in measures 175–78. A look at the bass line, however, shows that after leaping down to ♯④ in the second half of measure 188, the bass ascends chromatically within the cadential stream up to ⑥, thus enacting a DCP (though with no sense of an actual cadence). The leap down to ③ (though supporting a $V^7/VI$ harmony) is suggestive of an initial cadential tonic of an ACP, such that the move up to ④, supporting a minorized subdominant, which is stretched out for three bars (becoming major along the way), gives much the impression of being a stage 2 pre-dominant. Instead of leading to dominant, however, the bottom first drops out of the texture at measure 194, with a diminished-seventh harmony arising only in the second half of that bar. This sonority, built over ①, ends up becoming the final tonic of the ongoing progression (completing itself as a sonority only on beat two of the following bar). As a result, the dominant of the cadential progression is bypassed, and the pre-dominant of the ACP is reinterpreted as the subdominant of a PCP, with the move to the final tonic, effectively, if not literally, on the second half of measure 194, creating genuine plagal closure. Note, by the way, that in measures 194–95, the penultimate melodic C ($\hat{6}$) resolves B♭ ($\hat{5}$), as we have observed in other cases of plagal closure. The remaining music of the movement plays itself entirely out over tonic harmony. Though we can speak of real, independent plagal closure here, it is important to be aware that Mahler still feels the need to create an authentic cadence to confirm the home key prior to this final plagal progression. Rarely do we find plagal closure alone bearing the full structural weight of ending a large-scale movement.

My final case of feigned plagal closure arises at the conclusion of "Nessun dorma" (Example 9.34a), a passage that presents a more complicated set of interpretations than we have seen thus far.[90] Approaching the end of the second of two strophes, the upbeat to measure 26 leads to a cadential $I^6$, whose move to $II^9$ (in m. 27 prepares for perfect authentic closure via the stage-3 dominant in the following bar. When the cadential melody resolves $\hat{2}$–($\hat{7}$)–$\hat{1}$ on the downbeat of measure 29, setting the final word of the text (*vincero*), the expected I is initially replaced by IV as

---

88. Inasmuch as this variant preserves the bass motion ⑤–①, the sense of authentic cadence is more palpable here than when the subdominant stands in root position, as in pattern (c).

89. A Romantic precursor of this type of feigned plagal closure can be found at the end of Mendelssohn's Song without Words in A, Op. 102, no. 5, mm. 60–61. Here, the composer writes a PAC whose final tonic, as in Mahler's symphony, is embellished (mm. 186–88) by a subdominant six-four. In such a case, where the subdominant six-four is *not* repositioned (i.e., remaining a six-four harmony), Cutler speaks of "embellished authentic cadences" ("Proper Boundaries," 56, 57, and Ex. 11), thus describing the essence of feigned plagal closure.

90. Cutler also speaks of this passage ("Proper Boundaries," 69).

EXAMPLE 9.33. Mahler, Symphony No. 6, iii, mm. 174–97.

EXAMPLE 9.34. Puccini, "Nessun dorma," *Turandot*, (a) mm. 25–32; (b) mm. 16–18.

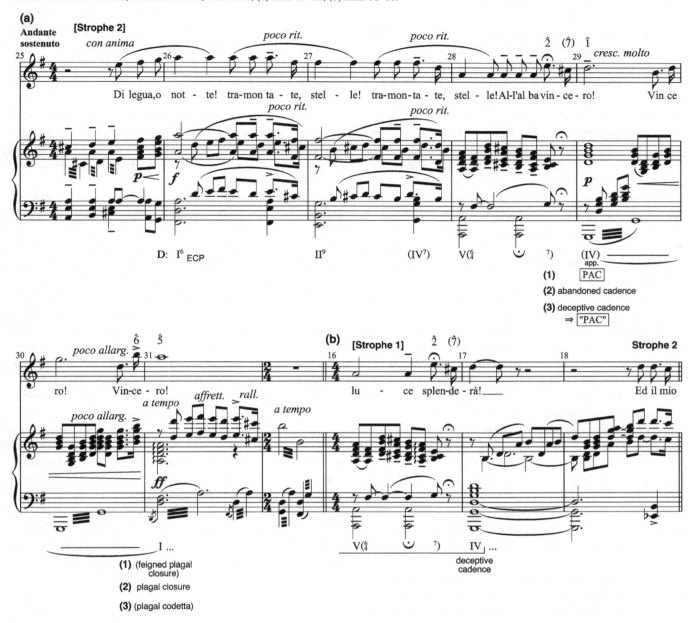

an appoggiatura harmony in measures 29–30. The final tonic eventually appears in measure 31, accompanied by the $\hat{6}$–$\hat{5}$ melodic motion that is typical of plagal closure. But is this a genuine case of such closure? It largely depends on which moment in this passage we take as the *formal* end. In option 1 of the annotations, I have proposed that place to be the downbeat of measure 29, where the penultimate dominant moves to the next harmony, where the melody achieves its normal course of completion, and where the text reaches its final syllable. If so, then we would be hearing a case of genuine PAC closure at measure 29 followed by feigned plagal closure at measure 31 (option 1).

Alternatively, we might hear the second strophe ending at the downbeat of measure 31. This interpretation puts stock in the dynamic context, whereby the *subito piano* at measure 29 initiates a broad crescendo to a *fortissimo* climax at measure 31 to articulate the true goal of the formal process. In this case, the IV–I progression would yield genuine plagal closure (option 2). But how would we, then, understand the authentic progression of measures 26–28? The idea of cadential evasion seems largely out of the question, given that the final syllable of *vincero* surely groups backward with the ongoing ECP.[91] So the possibility of an abandoned cadence seems most readily available, as we recognized schematically in Example 9.16e, along with some specific

---

91. If this were purely instrumental music, the possibility of an evaded cadence at m. 29 would be more palpable given the sudden change to *piano*, which might permit the downbeat of that bar to group forward into the plagal closure.

examples of dependent plagal closure (Ex. 9.21a, m. 35; Ex. 9.19, m. 28; and Ex. 9.20a, m. 32).[92]

We can even entertain a third interpretation, namely, hearing a deceptive cadence at measure 29, with IV as a replacement harmony (option 3). In fact, this possibility explains well what happens earlier in the aria when the same music (set to a different text) closes the first strophe (Ex. 9.34b). Again, a penultimate dominant in measure 16 leads not to I but to IV (m. 17). Here, however, the subdominant alone represents the final harmony of the first strophe, seeing as the second one starts up at the end of measure 18; consequently, no plagal progression to I complicates the harmonic-cadential situation. Returning to Example 9.34a, we now understand that the deceptive cadence at measure 29 (option 3) ends up being the real formal goal after all (like option 1, the feigned plagal cadence). As a result, this deviation represents—in retrospect—the "final" cadence of the strophe, with the subsequent plagal progression into measure 31 functioning as a postcadential codetta.

This third interpretation of "Nessun dorma" links up with a series of examples I have discussed earlier in Chapters 3, 6, and 8, whereby a "final" deceptive cadence, standing in for authentic cadential closure, is followed by a postcadential passage that emphasizes the subdominant (see again note 74). Example 9.35 summarizes the harmonic-cadential possibilities associated with this device, which can be seen to derive from a standard Quiescenza schema, shown in option (a). Here, the cadential progression leads to an unambiguous PAC, followed by a tonic prolongation that supports the postcadential Quiescenza. In option (b), the final tonic of the ACP is replaced by $V^7/IV$, thus yielding a deceptive cadential progression and a "final" deceptive cadence. The postcadential prolongation consists of the same harmonies as (a), except for the opening tonic, which has been replaced. This basic harmonic pattern can be seen at the end of Bach's first and eighth Preludes of the *WTC*, book 1 (Ex. 6.19, m. 32, and Ex. 6.20, m. 37).

The third system of Example 9.35 eliminates the $V^7$ that follows IV within the postcadential tonic prolongation. As a result, the subdominant leads directly to the final tonic. Two possible interpretations thus arise: in (c) the subdominant is heard as a neighboring harmony standing between $V^7/IV$ (a tonic replacement) and I (the literal tonic). As such, the postcadential quality following the "PAC" is emphasized, and the I–IV–I PCP yields a plagal codetta. In (d), the deceptive cadence is not heard as "final," but rather functions as a way station, with the IV–I progression effecting genuine plagal closure in place of any PAC articulation. These two patterns underlie passages previously considered in Beethoven's "Ghost" trio (Ex. 3.174) and Schumann's "Mondnacht" (Ex. 8.19). In general, it is not always clear which of these two options, (c) or (d), is most apt; it seems to depend on the analysts' intuitions as to which moment in time represents the true formal goal of the ongoing thematic unit, be it the "final" deceptive cadence (as representing a PAC) or the plagal closure.[93] In any case, a degree of ambiguity seems built into the structure.

Finally, options (e) and (f) eliminate the secondary dominant of IV, such that the cadential dominant moves directly to the subdominant.[94] In (e), the deceptive cadence, with subdominant as the replacement harmony, is heard as the "final" articulation of formal closure, with the resolution of IV to I as a strictly postcadential moment (a plagal codetta). In (f), the arrival of the subdominant does not represent a goal, but rather serves as the initiation of a plagal progression that effects thematic closure, thus abandoning the ongoing authentic cadential progression.[95] These two patterns are applicable to Puccini's aria, as shown in the analytical annotations of Example 9.34 (mm. 29 and 31). Here, analytical option (3) = schematic option (e); analytical option (2) = schematic option (f). Moreover, the possibility of a feigned plagal cadence, with which we started this investigation, must also be added into the mix, as represented by the annotations of option (1). To be sure, I have presented a complicated analysis of how Puccini ends "Nessun dorma," but it is not clear to me that a single, unambiguous interpretation can be determined. Each option affords us a particular perspective on various relationships of melody, harmony, and formal closure, aspects of compositional technique that may well contribute to the aria's undeniable appeal and enduring popularity.

\* \* \* \* \*

To conclude this study of plagal cadence/plagal closure in the nineteenth century (as applicable, to a much lesser degree, to the eighteenth century), it should be obvious that my tools for dealing with the complexity of this phenomenon are

---

92. In the case of "Nessun dorma" (Ex. 9.34a), we can speak of an abandoned "cadence" (not just an abandoned progression) because the downbeat of m. 29 is clearly available as a provisional goal (as described by option 1).

93. In the "Ghost" trio discussion at the end of Chapter 3, I argued, for simplicity's sake, for a view that accords primarily with option (c). Given the commonality of material in mm. 59–66, however, the formal goal could also be reasonably heard at m. 67, thus invoking (d). In "Mondnacht," I leaned more toward (c), since I am privileging the end of the vocal line as marking to the formal goal, whereas Schmalfeldt, taking a particular hermeneutic stance as regards the text, advocates (implicitly) for (d) (*Process of Becoming*, 235).

94. The parallel fifths potentially arising in the outer voices in (e) can be broken up by a move to $\hat{7}$ prior to the resolution to $\hat{1}$, as in (f) and in "Nessun dorma" (Ex. 9.34, mm. 16–17).

95. In principle, I can imagine a third interpretation (an option "g," so to speak). In this case, both the IV and the I are heard as legitimate moments of closure. In other words, we first hear a way-station deceptive cadence ($V^7$–IV), akin to option (d), at the arrival of the subdominant, and we then immediately hear genuine plagal closure when IV moves to I. This possibility seems problematic to me, however, in that the two moments of structural end—the deceptive cadence and the plagal closure—butt up against each other, so to speak, thus making it more difficult to separate each moment as potentially independent articulations of formal closure.

EXAMPLE 9.35. Deceptive cadence versus plagal closure.

multifarious. To be sure, it would be simpler if I accepted the standard account offered by most theorists, whereby all sorts of IV–I progressions in a diversity of formal contexts are labeled "plagal cadences." Rather, I have opted for a more nuanced, and admittedly complicated, mode of theory and analysis: where the plagal progression can be understood as prolongational and not cadential; where plagal closure can be distinguished as dependent on, or independent of, an authentic cadential context; where after-the-end, postcadential temporalities can be differentiated from genuinely ending ones; where plagal motion, as feigned plagal closure, can disguise what would otherwise be a clear PAC; and where plagal progressions can interact with deceptive and abandoned cadential progressions in a wide variety of ways. It has been my goal, not only with the particular topic of plagal closure, but with this entire study of cadence, to provide the tools necessary to explain what I believe are genuinely experiential distinctions in this rich and varied musical repertory.[96]

---

96. For an intriguing discussion of plagal cadence in film music, see Frank Lehman, "Hollywood Cadences: Music and the Structure of Cinematic Expectation." Lehman also considers a wide variety of cadential phenomena that invoke categories of half cadence and deceptive cadence (the latter, his "chromatically modulating cadential resolutions") in a tonal style that falls outside the scope of the present study.

EXAMPLE 9.36. Grieg, "Åse's Death," *Peer Gynt Suite No. 1*, Op. 46, no. 2, mm. 1–8.

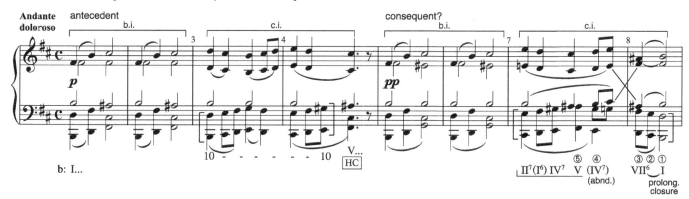

## 9.4. Prolongational Closure

As discussed on earlier occasions, eighteenth-century musical styles often employ tonic prolongational progressions (typically using the dominant as a subordinate harmony) to effect closure at the level of the phrase."[97] In the early Romantic period, such prolongational closure is used now and then to end complete thematic units (see Chapter 8, sec. 8.8). Even in those cases, however, the final thematic conclusion of a movement is normally achieved by a cadence of some sort.[98] In the second half of the nineteenth-century, prolongational progressions close thematic units even more frequently, such that a complete movement might end noncadentially.

Prolongational closure in the classical style usually sees the bass line confined to the prolongational stream, normally without engaging the cadential stream, and especially the dominant scale degree, in any significant manner. In the mid- to late nineteenth century, on the contrary, we find cases where the bass line achieves a cadential dominant, thus promising to close with a standard cadence, only then to abandon the cadential progression when the bass heads downward to fill in the gap between ⑤ and ① in a stepwise manner. The main theme of Grieg's "Åse's Death" is a case in point (Ex. 9.36). The opening four-measure phrase is straightforward enough: a basic idea (itself consisting of a repeated one-measure motive) is followed by a contrasting idea leading to an HC in measure 4. This antecedent phrase is then succeeded by what proposes to be a consequent when the basic idea returns (though chromatically enriched). The contrasting idea (mm. 7–8) seems as though it were going to effect PAC closure, but after arriving on the cadential dominant in the middle of measure 7, the bass pulls back down by a stepwise motion from ⑤ to ①, thus abandoning the cadential progression and rendering prolongational closure for this period-like theme.[99] In the two contrasting ideas (mm. 3–4, 7–8), we see that the bass acquires an entirely stepwise melodic contour. Moreover, the bass and tenor work together in parallel tenths, the result of which weakens the sense of the bass as a fully independent voice. In the classical style, a final leap from ⑤ to ① would create a harmonic interval to produce cadential closure; here, however, Grieg fills in that leap melodically in a way that is entirely nonclassical.

In the finale of Sibelius's Fifth Symphony, the penultimate thematic unit, *Un pochettino largamento*, also closes prolongationally. Its bass line's engagement with the cadential stream, however, evinces the potential for genuine cadence in a manner that is even more pronounced than in the previous case by Grieg. The theme, shown in Example 9.37, opens with a long tonic pedal. The bass line becomes more active in measure 416 and its centering around ③ in the following bar suggests the initial tonic of a cadential progression. The impression of an ECP is further reinforced when the bass moves up to ④ in measure 418, to support a predominant Neapolitan sixth. The cadential dominant appears next (m. 419), but Sibelius backs away from it, yielding an evaded cadence on the downbeat of measure 421.[100] The subsequent move from V$^6_5$/IV to IV proposes a compact cadential progression, one that is immediately abandoned by the bass line's leap down to ② and then ① in measure 422. The harmonic and melodic content of this bar, however, is not at all cadential, so little sense of thematic closure is expressed, even though the music breaks off at the end of the bar. When the bass then leaps again to ⑤ at measure 423, and is sustained for more than two bars, we strongly sense an impending cadence. At the last moment, however, the bass once more leads down stepwise to fill in the ⑤–① gap, with a similar harmonic progression found previously in measures 419–22. The theme thus closes prolongationally, even if we also sense a degree of premature tonic arrival in the second half of measure 426, seeing as the downbeat of measure 427 seems more like the real goal of the thematic process.[101] We see, therefore, that Sibelius

---

97. See Chapter 3, sec. 3.5.1; Chapter 6, sec. 6.3.2.

98. Exceptionally, Mendelssohn's first "Song without Words" (Ex. 8.16) features prolongational closure at the very end of the piece.

99. The inherently weak closure is further reinforced by the metrically weak placement of the final harmony on beat 2 of m. 8.

100. The option of a hearing an elided deceptive cadence is also valid if the dynamic crescendo into the downbeat of m. 421 helps to group that moment backward with the ongoing cadential progression.

101. The downbeat of m. 426 does not bring a sense of evaded cadence (like m. 421), yet neither does it seem to create an actual deceptive cadence. Still, the cadential progression projected from m. 423 to the downbeat of m. 426 would technically be deceptive.

EXAMPLE 9.37. Sibelius, Symphony No. 5 in E-flat, iii, mm. 407–28.

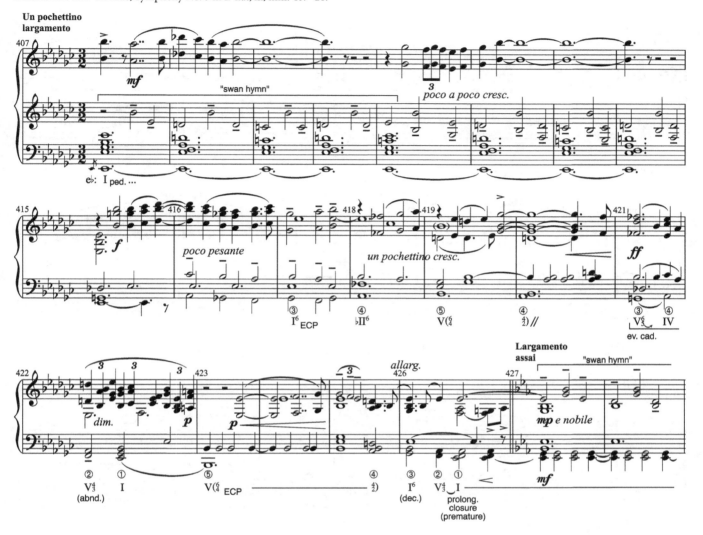

is working strongly with the conventions of classical cadential closure, but he thwarts them at every step of the way, eventually being content to let the theme close in an entirely noncadential manner. (I will return to this movement in a later discussion of the "iconic cadence" in sec. 9.6.)

The next example, from a Brahms Intermezzo, shows how a movement as a whole achieves prolongational closure in place of a genuine cadence. The piece is built as a small ternary, whose A section (Ex. 9.38a) is repeated in the manner of a rounded binary. Striking, of course, is how the movement begins by prolonging dominant for three bars, after which the bass line ascends in stepwise motion (mm. 4–6) up to ② (replacing ① with #①), thus imitating the basic idea A–B♮–(D)–C. The bass then continues in measures 6–7 by imitating the opening of the contrasting idea ⑦–#① (which itself is derived from the end of the basic idea). After a lingering around ②, the bass then imitates the second half of the contrasting idea ⑦ to ① (mm. 10–11), upon which the music quickly modulates to G minor (HK: VI), confirmed by a PAC at measure 13. Note that the cadential progression $I^6$–$V^7$–I bypasses a pre-dominant over ④ (C), probably due to the emphasis of C in the bass (② of B-flat) during measures 6–10. A closing section (of which only the first couple of bars are shown) prolongs the tonic of G minor, after which a brief retransition, ending with a subdominant arrival ($IV^6$), returns to the dominant to repeat the A section.

The contrasting middle (not shown) shifts the music to flat-side tonal regions, eventually leading to another subdominant arrival on $IV^6$ (Ex. 9.38b, mm. 31–32) to prepare for the return of the basic idea, over dominant harmony. Note that the boundary between the end of the B section and the beginning of the A′ is so smoothly crafted that the sense of "arrival" is barely perceptible, being projected only by the slight expansion of the harmonic rhythm, when $IV^6$ is syncopated into measure 32. The A′ section follows the course of the previous A section until measure 40, when the bass moves down to ①, via ♭②. At this point, there is no cadence in sight, though the subsequent leap down to ④ (m. 42), supporting $VII^4_3$ and resolving to $I^6$ at measure 43, hints at the onset of a possible cadence. Yet Brahms has the bass continue its stepwise descent all the way to the tonic goal at measure 45, the moment that corresponds to what had been a PAC in

EXAMPLE 9.38. Brahms, Intermezzo in B-flat, Op. 76, (a) no. 4, mm. 1–15; (b) mm. 31–45.

the A section (m. 13), but here in the A′ section only achieves prolongational closure. The closing section that follows remains entirely prolongational of tonic, with no cadential gesture ending the movement.

Unlike the cases of Grieg and Sibelius just discussed, Brahms does not engage ⑤ in any cadential manner in connection with the prolongational closure. This avoidance is likely explainable by the prominent emphasis that this degree has been accorded in the opening passages of the A and A′ sections. In addition, we can find a motivic rationale for why the bass behaves as it does at the end of the theme. If we look back to the cadence of the A section (mm. 11–13), we see that whereas the bass is fairly static, an inner alto voice brings a stepwise descent, in G minor, from $\hat{6}$ down to $\hat{3}$ (see circled notes). These are the same *pitches* (now interpreted in B-flat as ④ to ①) found in the bass-line descent at the close of the A′ section (mm. 42–45), though here, the line is fully chromatic.

EXAMPLE 9.39. Grieg, "First Meeting," *Two Melodies*, Op. 53, no. 2, mm. 1–26.

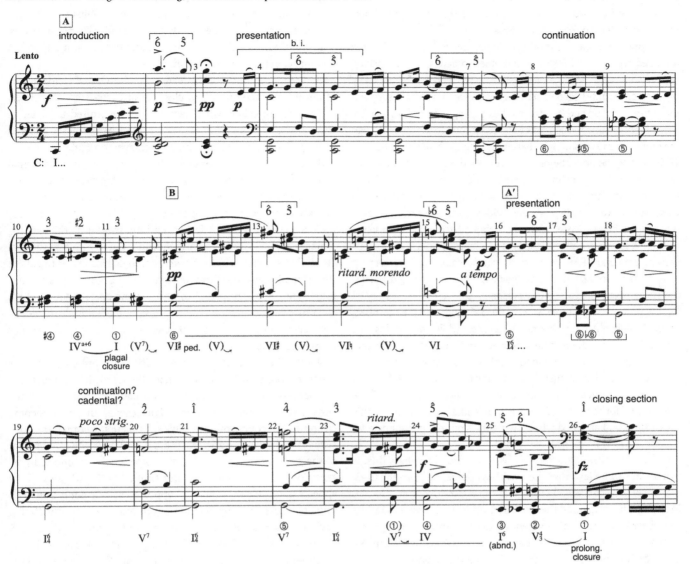

Especially prominent, since it involves the very last harmonic motion of closure, is Brahms's use of ♭② to ①, which itself refers to that same bass motion back at measures 40–41, a motive that allows the A′ section to remain in the home key rather than modulating (as in the A section).[102] We see here, as found in many late-nineteenth-century works, that the bass line participates significantly in the motivic connections established throughout the piece, a fact that most likely accounts for that line departing from classical norms in its melodic organization, especially at moments of thematic closure.

Prominent motivic work also accounts for prolongational closure at the end of Grieg's song "First Meeting," better known in its arrangement for string orchestra. The movement as a whole consists of a complete small ternary (Ex. 9.39), which is then literally repeated (save for changes in instrumentation and a small extension of the B section). Thus the prolongational closure shown at measure 26 is replicated at the end of the movement, followed then by a lengthier closing section. Returning to the beginning of the song, we see that the ternary A section opens with a thematic introduction in measures 1–3. Note the upper-voice move from $\hat{6}$ to $\hat{5}$, a motive that continues to sound within the opening presentation phrase (mm. 4–7). The motive is then shifted to the bass voice, now filled in chromatically, at the beginning of the continuation (mm. 8–9). This chromatic descent keeps going in the bass until it reaches ④, after which the leap to ① effects independent plagal closure (IV$^{a+6}$ to I) to end the A section.[103] Note that the

---

102. The C♭ is also the enharmonic equivalent of B♮, whose function as ♯$\hat{1}$ (moving to $\hat{2}$) has already been observed in both the basic and contrasting ideas.

103. We might be tempted to hear the V$^7$/VI in the second half of m. 11 as the actual harmonic goal of the A section. In the song version (*Four Songs*, Op. 21, no. 1), however, Grieg makes it clear that the tonic harmony is the true goal by bringing the final two syllables of the text in

added augmented-sixth ($^{a+6}$) within the subdominant yields a $\hat{3}$–#$\hat{2}$–$\hat{3}$ melodic closure, a variant of the $\hat{1}$–$\hat{2}$–$\hat{3}$ figure often associated with added-sixth subdominants.

Starting with the contrasting middle, the $\hat{6}$–$\hat{5}$ motive (in the tonicized region of A, HK: VI) continues to appear in the melody (mm. 13 and 15). The same motive, now in reference to the home key of C, is significantly broadened in the bass voice, such that ⑥ supports the entire B section and ⑤ supports the opening of the A′ section (m. 16), this time within the context of a tonic six-four. In the following bar, the motive sounds again in the bass, now with its chromatic inflection ♭⑥. Following the presentation (mm. 16–19), the bass continues to remain static on ⑤, supporting an alternation of a dominant seventh and tonic six-four (mm. 20–23). If the sense of continuation function in these bars is indeed quite weak, the melody nonetheless sounds like it is gearing up for a cadence. When the melodic $\hat{2}$ in measure 20 resolves to $\hat{1}$ in the next bar, however, the bass continues to hold on to ⑤, thus denying a potential PAC.[104] The melody tries again, this time reaching up to $\hat{4}$ at measure 22, but once more a possible IAC is thwarted. Finally, the melody leaps up to $\hat{5}$, and in a sweeping, rapid descent, finds its goal $\hat{1}$ at measure 26. (Note the *reversal* of the $\hat{6}$–$\hat{5}$ motive on the downbeat of m. 25, highlighted by the accented $\hat{6}$.) Meanwhile, the bass loses its grip on ⑤, and with the aid of an intermediary ① on the last eighth note of measure 23, moves down to ④ to initiate a stepwise descent to ①, thus effecting prolongational closure for the theme. Observe that even in measures 23–24, a sense of impending cadence arises when V$^7$/IV moves to IV for the onset of a possible cadential progression; but this progression is abandoned when I$^6$ continues on to a penultimate V$^4_3$ and the resulting prolongational closure.

Given the prominent motivic work accorded the bass line, it is hard not to believe that the final bass descent fills in the ④–① gap created by the plagal closure of the A section (mm. 10–11). Moreover, if we include the ⑥–⑤ motion in measures 17–18, we can observe a large-scale descent all the way from ⑥ to ①, analogous to the bass-line descent started in the A section (mm. 8–10), which only reached as far as ④. Like the previous example from Brahms, motivic play in the bass largely accounts for the mechanisms of closure employed in this work.

## 9.5. Detour Cadence

We have been largely focusing in this chapter on how standard techniques of cadential closure can be significantly modified; as a result, those places in the form, where the classical composer may have written a regular cadence, achieve their closure instead by other means. If the classical cadence is used less frequently in later nineteenth-century works than in earlier ones, this does not necessarily mean that passages of cadential content are likewise shunned. In fact, as we have seen in, say, the Sibelius symphony, a significant part of a theme may dwell upon cadential progressions, whose melodic–motivic material is cadential in nature, even if a genuine cadence is not forthcoming.

One manifestation of this cadential abundance yields a situation not normally found in classical or early-Romantic styles, but which, especially with Liszt, sees some limited use later in the century. I am referring here to cases where, toward the end of a thematic process, the music achieves a regular authentic cadence, but one that confirms the *wrong key*, given the tonal trajectory of the theme as a whole. Since this cadence does not ring true as a case of genuine thematic closure, another cadence quickly appears, now set in the expected key, and thus attains a more genuine sense of formal ending. Insofar as the first cadence represents a diversion within the journey toward the real close, the expression *detour cadence* well characterizes the effect that it makes and the function that it serves. Seeing as the detour cadence is transposed to become the correct cadence, we can observe a sequential pattern consisting of embedded cadential harmonies, a technique that we traced back to the earlier Romantic style.[105]

Liszt's "Les cloches de Genève" (Ex. 9.40) presents a detour cadence toward the close of its main theme, which is structured as a large-scale period, whose antecedent and consequent units consist of compound sentences. For reasons that will become clearer in the course of the analysis, let us first examine the consequent and start at measure 32 (Ex. 9.40a), with the exact repeat of the compound basic idea that completes the compound presentation. This four-measure unit (mm. 32–35), whose melody appears in the left-hand part, is supported by a prolongation of I$^6$, initially embellished by neighboring diminished sevenths (VII$^4_3$). Such a conventional "rocking on the tonic" with the degrees ④ and ③ reminds us of how the first stage of an ECP can be significantly enlarged.[106] In the following continuation, the bass ascends from ④ to #④ at measure 38, thus holding a stage-2b VII$^7$/V. Liszt then suddenly shifts the harmonic-tonal environment by reinterpreting this dominant-functioning harmony into a common-tone diminished seventh, so that when the bass ascends as expected to ⑤ (m. 40), it now supports I$^6$ in the key of D major (HK: ♭III). This harmony then serves as stage 1 of a compact cadential progression that completes itself (skipping over stage 2) when V$^7$ resolves to I (mm. 41–42) to create a PAC, a tonal confirmation that would normally be unexpected at this point in the form. (Though in light of what happens in the antecedent, which will be discussed shortly, this tonal digression is not a complete surprise.) But then, as if recognizing that the consequent has closed in the wrong key, Liszt immediately brings a cadential

---

the first beat of m. 11, using the secondary dominant of VI as the upbeat to the next section.

104. Problematic in speaking of potential cadences in mm. 21 or 23, however, is the lack of any real harmonic progression thus far in the A′ section.

105. See Ex. 8.6 and 8.45.

106. See in Chapter 5, sec. 5.1.1.1, "Rocking on the Tonic." That Liszt opens the piece with an ECP reflects a Romantic practice discussed in Chapter 8, sec. 8.4.

EXAMPLE 9.40A. Liszt, "Les cloches de Genève," *Années de pèlerinage I*, mm. 32–46.

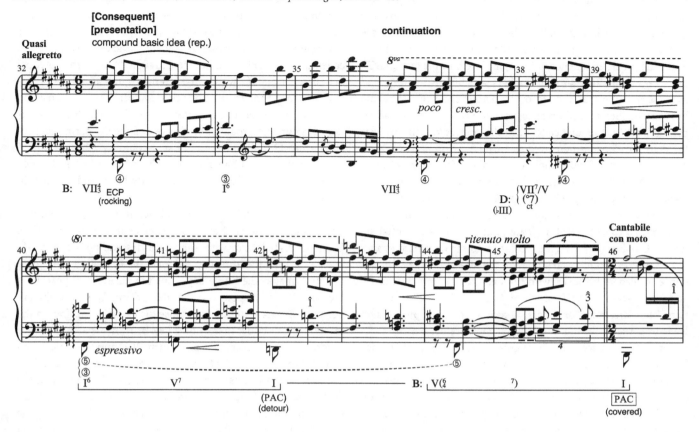

EXAMPLE 9.40B. Liszt, "Les cloches de Genève," *Années de pèlerinage I*, mm. 13–26.

six-four in the home key of B major (m. 44) and finally effects the expected cadence (a covered PAC, as it turns out) to close the periodic form.[107] In light of how the theme actually ends, we see that the first cadence, in D major, effects a detour from the true goal of a home-key cadence in B major. Note how the overall ECP breaks off at measure 40 with the bass ⑤, which is reinterpreted as ③ (supporting I⁶ in the key of the detour cadence). The same bass note is then picked up again at measure 44 (see the dashed curved line) for the final cadence in the correct key. In this way, the detour cadence is perceived as a true digression, which then gets back on track for the final cadence of the theme (m. 46).

A similar detour arises in the compound antecedent (Ex. 9.40b), which picks up with the continuation phrase at measure 13. Again, the bass moves from ④ to ♯④, but rather than continuing to ⑤, it leaps to ♭⑥ at measure 17 to support a cadential-six four in C major (HK: ♭II); the resolution to the dominant proper in measure 18 promises an authentic cadence in that key. The cadence is evaded, however, with the half-bar rest in measure 19, and a subsequent V$^4_3$/IV, which replaces the final tonic, is sustained for three additional bars. A second cadential progression leads to a 19cHC in the home key at measure 25, which marks the end of the antecedent. The digression into C major (♭II) thus brings about an *evaded* detour cadence, for the lack of a clear final tonic renders a genuine cadence unrealized (though the harmony that does appear has a C root, and the melody arrives on $\hat{1}$ in C). Of course, we know from our prior examination of the consequent that another tonal digression will occur at measures 40–42 (the same formal location as in the antecedent), this time rendered as a genuine detour cadence.

As shown in the previous example, a detour cadence may not always be completely manifest but may be evaded instead. Another case of an initially unrealized detour cadence occurs in the first movement exposition of Bruckner's Sixth Symphony. We will see, though, that when the same cadential gesture returns in the recapitulation, the cadence becomes fully realized. Rather than being a detour, however, this cadence confirms the home key, representing the true goal of the harmonic-tonal processes of the movement. Let us begin with the exposition (Ex. 9.41a). Toward its end, a broad chromatic descending-stepwise sequence (of six-five sonorities) breaks out into a German augmented sixth at the end of measure 120, which then resolves to a prominent six-four sonority over a pedal D, thus shifting the tonal focus to G major (HK: ♭VII). Seeing as the prevailing tonality has been E major, the normal subordinate key, this arrival on the dominant of G raises the possibility of its creating a detour cadence, because we are not expecting the exposition to close in that remote key, but rather to conclude in the standard subordinate key (as is Bruckner's practice). The cadential six-four is sustained for four measures, after which it resolves to the dominant proper at measure 125. The D pedal holds for another four bars, but instead of effecting the detour cadence, the ECP is abandoned, and the harmonic context shifts toward C major (mm. 127–30), moving then to an A-minor triad at measure 131. The music thus bypasses the possible detour by not confirming G major, though within that key, the C (IV) and A (II) harmonies still make sense. When a sixth is added to the A-minor harmony at measure 133 and is sustained for four bars, the resolution at measure 137 to the tonic of E major creates a case of independent plagal closure, seeing as a cadential dominant in E is nowhere in sight.[108] As for the potential detour cadence in G, we see that it remains unrealized: its cadential dominant, though initially locked in, is simply given up as the music swerves toward C. The effect is probably more like an abandoned progression than an evaded one, since the harmonic shift at measure 127 does not sound like it could have been a formal goal. But the sense of abandonment is not quite classical either, since the cadential dominant has already been held securely in place for eight bars.

In light of the failed detour cadence in the exposition, it is interesting to observe the analogous place in the recapitulation. Example 9.41b starts with the same descending stepwise sequence, leading this time (m. 304, beat three) to a pre-dominant IV$^6_5$ in A major, the home key. Thus the harmony appearing at measure 305 corresponds to the "detour" six-four from the exposition (Ex. 9.41a, m. 121). Because the cadential six-four in the recapitulation resides in the home key, Bruckner is able to resolve it normally to the dominant proper (m. 307) and to create a covered PAC at measure 309 to close the prevailing thematic unit.[109] (The coda then begins immediately.) We see, therefore, that the detour six-four of the exposition, which promised cadential closure, even if in the wrong key, returns in the recapitulation in the correct key, to realize its potential for cadence. We also see that for the final confirmation of the home key in the recapitulation, Bruckner employs an authentic cadence for this most important formal juncture, rather than the plagal closure he used to conclude the final subordinate theme in the exposition.

What is striking about the detour cadences that we have observed in both Liszt and Bruckner is the sense of a sudden, unprepared, change in harmonic color, a somewhat "darker" shade given the shift to the flat side of the tonal spectrum in all of these cases.[110] Moreover, when the journey on the path to the true tonality of the theme is resumed and the correct cadence is

---

107. I am assuming that the melodic D♯ ($\hat{3}$) in the left hand at the end of m. 45 resolves to B ($\hat{1}$) at the very end of m. 46, in the same way that the prior detour cadence resolves F♯ to D in mm. 41–42. This emphasis on a cadential $\hat{3}$ in place of $\hat{2}$ exemplifies a nineteenth-century trait, as discussed in Chapter 8, sec. 8.1.

108. Note, however, the prominence within the subdominant harmony of an embellishing leading tone (D♯) of E major in the first violins of mm. 133–36 (see arrow), which already points to a resolving E-major sonority. We also observed a similar function of this scale degree in the subdominant arrival ending the transition of this movement (see again the G♯s in Ex. 9.10, mm. 47–48).

109. This PAC at m. 309 is covered by $\hat{5}$, which initiates the main theme as it returns in the coda. The immediate leap down to $\hat{1}$, though, brings the final melodic pitch of the PAC, which continues to be emphasized in the next two bars.

110. In speaking of such color changes, I am obviously appealing to Ernst Kurth's notion of "harmonic shading" (*Selected Writings*, 103–109).

EXAMPLE 9.41A. Bruckner, Symphony No. 6 in A, i, mm. 119–37.

EXAMPLE 9.41B. Bruckner, Symphony No. 6 in A, i, mm. 303–11.

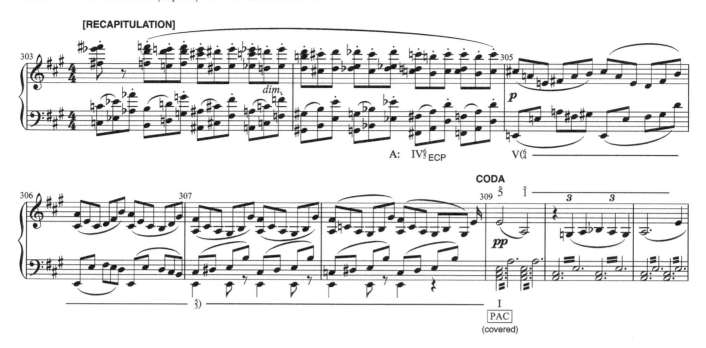

## 9.6. Iconic Cadence

achieved, we have the impression that the detour cadence had appeared like an isolated object, one that is offset from the prevailing tonal trajectory of the thematic unit. It is as though the composers were drawing attention to the specifically cadential quality of the gesture, while at the same time failing to allow that gesture to function as it should, namely to provide genuine closure to the theme. This sense of "objectification" of the cadence foreshadows the appearance of the iconic cadence toward the close of the tonal era, a topic to which we now turn.

As already noted on many occasions, the classical cadence does not simply disappear in the course of the nineteenth century: throughout the entire tonal repertoire, the cadence retains its function of creating phrase and thematic closure. But as we have seen, at many of the places where a classical composer would have routinely ended a unit with a cadence, nineteenth-century composers find other techniques for effecting such closure. Late in the century, and into the early years of the twentieth, we encounter cases where composers seem, quite self-consciously, to look back to earlier classical practice and to write passages that in the most blatant way evoke a kind of idealized classical cadence. This *iconic cadence*, as I will term it, represents an apotheosis of the cadence, a highly marked moment that is motivated by both historicist and nostalgic impulses.[111] Although it may project a normal sense of ending, the iconic cadence sometimes seems to arise, ironically, in a postcadential position, or even to announce a new beginning, rather than to conclude a formal process. Typically, the iconic cadence is rhetorically powerful, often in a most exaggerated way. Moreover, the iconic cadence often can appear somewhat *isolated* from its immediately preceding context; indeed, the isolated cadence/codetta that we identified with Chopin's preludes may be seen to anticipate the idea of an iconic cadence. Like the detour cadence, which is perhaps another forerunner, the iconic cadence often emerges as an object of attention in its own right, as a self-sufficient gesture that references the idea of cadence, even if its actual formal function may not always be cadential.

An archetypal case of an iconic cadence arises at the end of a "developmental" section in Richard Strauss's *Ein Heldenleben* (Ex. 9.42).[112] Following upon much hustle and bustle, the music at measure 628 suddenly slams on the brakes by reducing the texture to block chords and by bringing an almost schematic representation of a classical $\hat{3}$–$\hat{2}$–$\hat{1}$ cadence, one that most spectacularly calls forth a recapitulation of the main theme.[113] In its rhetorically powerful force, we easily recognize the sense of apotheosis that is a hallmark of the iconic cadence. Though this cadence seems on the surface to be quite separated texturally

---

111. Iconic cadences seem to be associated with an authentic cadence; I have not yet uncovered an iconic HC. For an iconic deceptive cadence, see the reference to Bruckner's Eighth Symphony ahead in note 120.

112. The identification of a development section assumes a loose sonata-form reading of this rather unwieldy work; for more details, see Vande Moortele, *Two-Dimensional Sonata Form*, 93–99.

113. Though this cadence so obviously references a classical cadence, elements of its harmonic content—a pre-dominant standing in root position and mildly minorized by a passing C♭ in the alto—are stylistic markers of the nineteenth century.

EXAMPLE 9.42. Strauss, *Ein Heldenleben*, mm. 618–32.

from what precedes it, we can actually discern a fairly "classical" bass line leading stepwise from ① at measure 621 up to ④ at measure 623. Even if the music hardly sounds cadential at this point, the subdominant is now expanded for five bars, such that when the bass drops to ② at the beginning of the "cadential idea" (m. 628), we can understand that an ECP had been in the making prior to the appearance of the iconic cadence proper. Finally, we should consider just what the function of this cadence actually is. We could say, of course, that it "concludes" the ongoing development, but our impression is that the gesture also serves to "announce" the recapitulation.[114] In other words, the iconic cadence may not necessarily have a normal cadential function, despite its quality of being an "idealized" cadence.[115]

Another early-twentieth-century iconic cadence appears in the very closing bars of Sibelius's Fifth Symphony (Ex. 9.43a). After a long passage of relatively uniform texture featuring the "Swan Hymn" (or "Swinging Theme"),[116] the music suddenly breaks off at measure 474, and a series of *fffz* tutti chords, followed by moments of prolonged silence, leave the listener somewhat aghast as to what will transpire. These shocking chords actually constitute a classical cadential progression, I⁶–V–I, though the melody remains up on $\hat{5}$ until the final unison leap down to $\hat{1}$. (The absence of a pre-dominant in this progression will be clarified in due course.) The iconic quality of these chords is evident in their

---

114. Recall the idea of an HC (the standard final cadence of a classical development section) having an *annunciatory* function (see Chapter 3, sec. 3.3.4.3). For a possible precursor to the specific iconic cadence by Strauss, consider a similar annunciating PAC found immediately preceding the recapitulation (by the solo piano) at the very end of the development section of Beethoven's Piano Concerto No. 4 in G, Op. 58, i, mm. 251–53.

115. To be sure, other candidates for the identification of iconic cadence can perform their normal function of formal ending; see, e.g., Strauss, *Eine Alpensinfonie*, rehearsal no. 84; Mahler, Symphony No. 3, vi, five measures after rehearsal no. 30.

116. James A. Hepokoski, *Sibelius, Symphony No. 5*, 37.

EXAMPLE 9.43A. Sibelius, Symphony No. 5 in E-flat, iii, mm. 457–82.

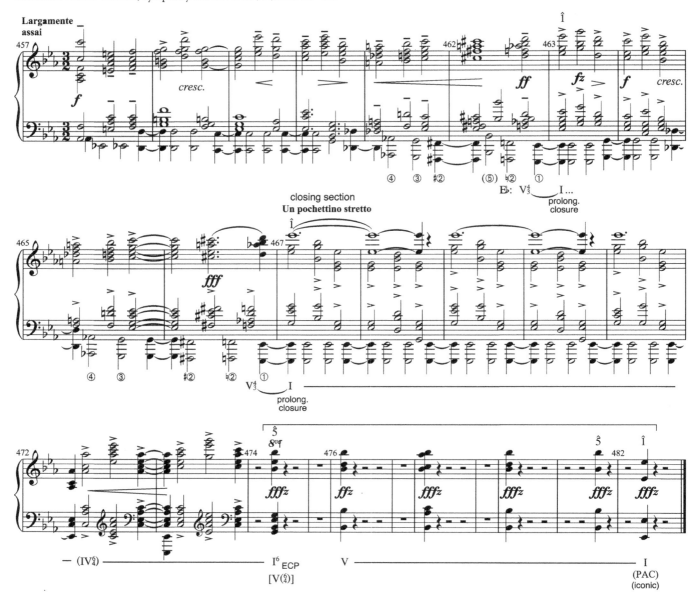

audacious rhetoric, their detachment from the ongoing textural context, and their reference to the end of many classical symphonic finales.[117]

As for its formal function, the cadence can somewhat trivially be said to "conclude" the movement, even the entire symphony. Indeed, James Hepokoski has discussed how this cadence represents the "grand *telos*" of the symphony, the true culmination of formal processes begun in the opening bars of the first movement.[118] Hepokoski's final cadence, however, embraces not only the block chords, but rather the whole passage from measure 467 to the end. He finds there a single progression consisting of the following harmonies: an initial tonic (m. 467), a pre-dominant (m. 472), a cadential six-four (m. 474), a dominant proper (m. 476), and a final tonic (m. 482). Some details of his harmonic analysis, however, are problematic. For, as he himself acknowledges, we must understand the literal I⁶ at measure 474 as "something of a substitute for the cadential $^6_4$." Moreover, the pre-dominant at measure 472 appears, most unusually, in six-four position, thus, supported still by a tonic pedal; one would be hard-pressed to find in the standard tonal literature a cadential pre-dominant taking the form of IV$^6_4$.

There is, however, a more purely *formal* reason to question whether the passage from measure 467 to the end is functioning as a genuine cadence. To gain a sharper perspective on this issue, we have to consider the large-scale thematic unit that this cadence would be ending. That unit begins forty bars earlier when the

---

117. Cf. Beethoven, Symphony No. 8 in F, Op. 93, iv, m. 482ff., for a particularly exaggerated set of tutti block-chord codettas, ones that clearly look forward to Sibelius's gestures.

118. Hepokoski, *Sibelius, Symphony No. 5*, 84.

EXAMPLE 9.43B. Sibelius, Symphony No. 5 in E-flat, iii, bass line of mm. 427–82.

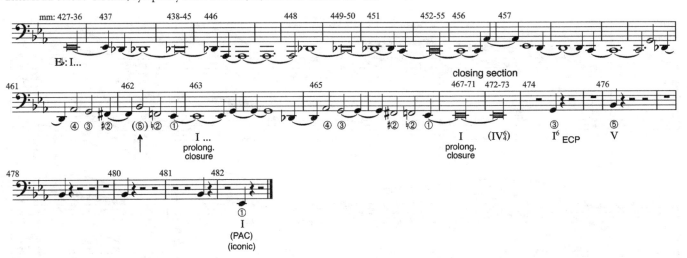

trumpets sound the "Swan Hymn" back at measure 427 (see again Ex. 9.37). Example 9.43b shows a bass-line reduction of the entire thematic unit. Note that the bass brings nothing in the way of cadential expression until the final block chords. Before then, in fact, the dominant degree appears only once (m. 462, see arrow) as an almost incidental pitch in a fully non-dominant harmonic context. Indeed prior to the block chords, only two locations project any sense of closure: at measure 463 and then again, but more rhetorically powerful, at measure 467 (see again, Ex. 9.43a). In both places, the melody and bass, in contrary stepwise motion, reach the tonic scale degree as a clear goal. Given the stepwise descent in the bass at each of these moments, we can once again, like the earlier thematic unit (in Ex. 9.37), recognize the technique of prolongational closure.

Following the second arrival at measure 467, the bass now plants itself firmly on the tonic for seven bars, and the music acquires a decidedly postcadential quality, so much so that when the local harmony moves to the subdominant at measure 472, we are fully prepared to hear a plagal "Amen" codetta to conclude the movement in the manner of so many late-nineteenth-century works. In short, I propose that we hear the subdominant at this point as postcadential, and not as a cadential pre-dominant, as Hepokoski would have it. But rather than IV moving directly back to a root-position I, as such a final codetta would normally behave, the iconic cadence ensues instead. Its cadential progression is initiated by a true I⁶ leading quickly to an expanded dominant, thus bypassing a cadential pre-dominant, a harmonic function that had been "used up" as a postcadential subdominant in the immediately preceding music (mm. 472–73).

Within the thematic context as so interpreted, the block-chord iconic cadence thus seems to have more of a postcadential function, rather than a genuinely cadential one. At the same time, since there have been no true cadential articulations throughout the entire movement, it is not unreasonable to say, in the spirit of Hepokoski's remarks, that something referentially cadential is finally being fulfilled to provide the global *telos* of both the movement and the symphony. Some troubling elements remain with this iconic cadence, however. For instance, the sudden rupture of texture and the long, irregular rhythmic gaps that confound the metrical expression make it difficult for the listener to know just what to expect from moment to moment. As well, we hear an unusual reduction in orchestral and harmonic texture as the chords progress. Thus the initial I⁶ is harmonically complete and set to a lush orchestral sound. The next three dominants are missing their chordal fifth and are scored more thinly, the timpani being conspicuously absent. And the final V–I progression further reduces the texture to doubled monophony, though the reintroduction of the timpani helps add more mass to the sound. Finally, we can include in this list the ambiguous formal function of the chords: Are they cadential or postcadential? Indeed we might best understand this ending to be an iconic *codetta*, not a genuine cadence. Thus as grand as this *telos* may be, there remains something of the "ironic" in this "iconic" cadence.

The climax of the slow movement of Bruckner's Symphony No. 7 is another candidate for the category of iconic cadence (Ex. 9.44a, mm. 176–78). This C-sharp-minor movement is written in a kind of rondo form favored by Schubert (A–B–A′–B′–A″). The passage in question arises in the final, A″ section. Toward the end of a long, progressive dynamic intensification, one of those large-scale "symphonic waves" that Ernst Kurth so vividly describes,[119] the music finds itself in B major (m. 172), developing the 1̂–2̂–3̂ motive used originally to open the second phrase of the theme (Ex. 9.44b). The music then pushes on and at measure 176 arrives on the dominant of C-sharp minor. Bruckner is thus well positioned to devise a climactic cadence of some kind to close this final section of the form in the home key. Instead, he employs one of those stock-in-trade enharmonic shifts, namely, the reinterpretation of the dominant seventh as a pre-dominant German sixth.

---

119. Kurth, *Selected Writings*, 151ff.

548　Cadence in the Mid- to Late Nineteenth Century

EXAMPLE 9.44. Bruckner, Symphony No. 7 in E, ii, (a) mm. 172–85; (b) mm. 4–6.

EXAMPLE 9.44. Continued

The resolution at measure 177 to the cadential six-four, in the brilliantly shining key of C major (leading tone of the home key), brings the rhetorical climax, as further punctuated by the infamous "cymbal crash" and triangle roll.[120] The rest of the cadential progression completes this iconic IAC with the root-position tonic of measure 178. This harmony is then further prolonged (for another five bars), with a series of aftershocks in an entirely postcadential manner.[121]

Unlike the previous cases of iconic cadence, this one is not separated texturally from its preceding material; rather, the cadence represents the culmination of the massive buildup leading to this moment of climax, signaled primarily by the cadential six-four. Yet the moment seems nonetheless to express a powerful "apotheosis of cadence," even if we have doubts about its actual cadential function, given its confirmation of a highly remote tonality (the leading tone is not normally an available region for modulation in traditional tonal practice). Indeed, at measure 183, Bruckner "corrects" the key, sliding directly up to C-sharp major (notated as D-flat) and then shifting to minor at measure 185. He continues to develop the same motivic material, now securely planted in the home key, as eventually confirmed by a PAC at measure 193 (not shown).

In addition to the ironic quality of confirming the wrong key (much like a detour cadence), Bruckner's climactic passage reveals yet another facet of the iconic cadence. The sense of *arrival*, of attaining a formal goal, is attached more to the six-four (m. 177) than to the cadential resolution in the following bar. The cadential six-four receives the cymbal crash, not the final tonic (m. 178), which seems no more marked than any other moment within the passage. And here we witness what, in the course of the nineteenth century, has become an important change in the *sign* for cadence. In the classical style, a prominent tonic in first inversion—the initial harmony of the cadential progression—typically signals impending cadential closure. This usage gradually dies out in the nineteenth century, and the cadential six-four comes to replace I⁶ as the major marker of cadential function. Robert Hatten

---

120. Despite the controversy as to whether Bruckner intended to include this cymbal crash, or whether it was pushed on him by his acolytes, most editors now believe that Bruckner eventually sanctioned its use. Also, he twice calls for the cymbal in the climax of the slow movement of the Eighth Symphony, the second time (m. 243) creating an iconic *deceptive* cadence, when the cadential progression resolves to VI.

121. A precursor to Bruckner's iconic cadence may be found in a similar enharmonic shift resolving to a climactic C-major cadential six-four in the middle of the first rondo couplet in the slow movement of Beethoven's Fifth Symphony, mm. 28–31. What distinguishes this regular classical cadence (as well as the passages cited in notes 114 and 117) from an iconic one is that the former is not referencing an earlier musical practice: Beethoven's cadences are not iconic; they are rather part and parcel of the musical language of his time.

has already identified the *arrival six-four* as an important gesture (which in certain individual cases he further characterizes as a "salvation," "elevated," or "transcendent" six-four) in the music of late Beethoven, and Michael Klein further traces the expressive qualities of the arrival six-four in works by Chopin and Liszt.[122] Indeed, from the middle of the nineteenth century on, the arrival six-four comes to play such a prominent role in announcing "here comes an important cadence," that we can speak of an *iconic six-four* despite the absence of a complete cadential progression.[123] And here, we can again witness a relationship between the iconic cadence and the detour cadence, recalling that the failure of the latter cadence in Bruckner's Sixth Symphony (Ex. 9.41a, m. 121) hinged on the lack of any resolution of the cadential six-four.

To conclude this discussion of the iconic cadence, it should be clear by now that we are dealing more with a somewhat vague "aesthetic" category rather than with a precise music-theoretical one. It is not possible to specify just what constitutes an iconic cadence in relation to the parameters of pitch, rhythm, texture, and so forth. To be sure, we can list general attributes of an iconic cadence—its isolation from its surrounding context, its referencing an earlier tonal style, its rhetoric of apotheosis, and the irony of its invoking the idea of cadence without necessarily expressing genuine cadential function. But none of these characteristics is a necessary or sufficient condition for identifying an iconic cadence. Moreover, we have to be careful not to lump every climactic passage, no matter how powerful, into the category. Rather, there additionally needs to be the sense that the cadence is being showcased in some special way. Finally, in light of how the classical cadence progressively loses its grip as the exclusive means of articulating thematic closure throughout the nineteenth century, the iconic cadence brings us full circle as composers at the end of the traditional "common-practice" period look back, with some nostalgia and irony, at the classical cadence and find there a device that they can endow with new contextual and expressive meanings.

## 9.7. Cadential Deviations

Deceptive and evaded cadences continue to be used in mid- to late-nineteenth-century music. Some important modifications to classical practice, however, are readily observable.[124] Whereas in the earlier style, these deviation types usually mark a way station on the road to eventual cadential closure, often featuring a one-more-time technique (or analogous repetition), the deceptive cadence especially, but also at times the evaded cadence, can be used in a manner in which the deviation itself fully stands for the real cadence. Thus Rothstein, building on observations by Alfred Lorenz, notes that "the Wagnerian deceptive cadence...differs fundamentally from deceptive cadences in earlier music. There, the deceptive cadence typically indicates a delay of the authentic [V–I] cadence. In Wagner, the deceptive cadence typically *replaces* the authentic cadence, which is understood to be elided."[125]

The opening of the "Tristan Prelude," of course, comes readily to mind (see ahead, Ex. 9.56a), where the initial sentential structure closes with the deceptive cadence in A minor at measure 17, after which a new thematic unit begins.[126] Similar cases abound in Wagner's writing, and we find examples of the technique in Dvorak, Bruckner, and Brahms.[127]

### 9.7.1. A Deceptive Half Cadence?

Throughout this study, I have defined a single type of half cadential deviation, namely, a dominant arrival. A short, seemingly simple, piano piece by Tchaikovsky, however, raises the possibility of identifying a *deceptive half cadence* (see Ex. 9.45).[128] The opening phrase consists of a basic idea followed by a contrasting idea, thus proposing an antecedent. Indeed, if the final progression of the phrase had been II⁶–V, then an HC would have clinched this formal interpretation. But the II⁶ of measure 3

---

122. Hatten, *Musical Meaning*, 15, 288; Michael L. Klein, *Intertextuality in Western Art Music*, 63–74. See also David Temperley's ideas on the cadential six-four as "structural cue" (and especially his colloquially termed "big cadential $^6_4$") ("The Six-Four as Tonic Harmony, Tonal Emissary, and Structural Cue," 11–16). The meaning of *arrival* in the expression "arrival six-four" must be distinguished from the idea of a dominant, pre-dominant, or tonic arrival. The latter represents an actual formal goal; the former precedes, and thus signals, a pending formal goal. The analytical context normally makes clear this semantic distinction.

123. Hatten specifically notes that an arrival six-four can still make its rhetorical effect even if the remaining cadential harmonies fail to materialize (*Musical Meaning*, 15, 288).

124. Abandoned cadential progressions and actual situations of abandoned cadence also arise, especially, in the context of plagal closure as earlier discussed. Normally cadential abandonment in this repertory works much the same as it does in earlier tonal styles, so the topic need not be further addressed here.

125. Rothstein, *Phrase Rhythm*, 254; Alfred Lorenz, *Das Geheimnis der Form bei Richard Wagner*, 66–67.

126. Though Wagner here uses VI as a replacement harmony for I, much more than in the classical style, his deceptive cadences conclude on the less stable VII⁶/V.

127. Dvorak, Serenade for Winds, Op. 44b, iii, m. 13, (ending the main theme); Bruckner, Symphony No. 8, i, m. 303 (ending the main theme in the recapitulation); Brahms, Symphony No. 2, ii, m. 6 (ending the A section of a main theme, see Ex. 9.5a, above). We observed a Romantic forerunner of this technique in connection with Ex. 8.20, m. 15. See also the cases of "final" deceptive cadences in J. S. Bach (Ex. 6.19–6.22), Beethoven (Ex. 3.174), and Schumann (Ex. 8.19).

128. I thank my colleague Nicole Biamonte for proposing the idea of a deceptive half cadence in connection with this example. Since her suggestion came at the very end of my research for this study, there may well have been other examples of the technique that eluded my sight. Thus far, I am unaware of a classical work that employs this kind of deceptive HC, nor have I encountered it in any other of the tonal styles discussed in this study. I assume that such cases must exist, but that conclusion awaits further research.

EXAMPLE 9.45. Tchaikovsky, "Morning Prayer," *Children's Album*, Op. 39, no. 1, mm. 1–16.

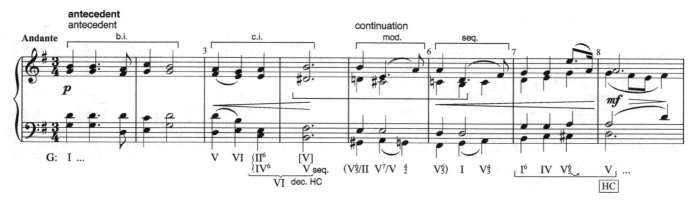

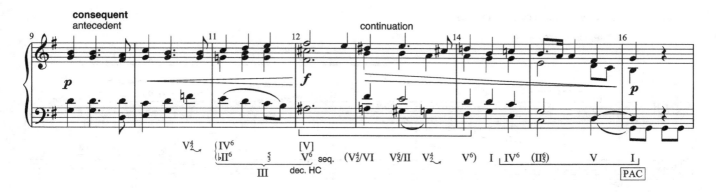

leads instead to V/VI, which produces a phrygian HC in E minor: IV⁶–V. As a result, the implied home-key half cadence is rendered deceptive by means of a "replacement" harmony for the cadential dominant.[129] To be sure, if the following phrase were a simple consequent, beginning again with a home-key tonic and leading to a PAC, the effect of a deceptive HC would be secure. Tchaikovsky, though, takes a different, more complex, path. Rather than writing a consequent, he introduces a continuation phrase, supported by a descending-fifths sequence (initiated already by the V/VI of the deceptive HC). The return to tonic (second beat of m. 6) is followed shortly thereafter by a genuine half cadential progression to conclude a *compound* antecedent at measure 8, thereby projecting a compound period structure, which in fact emerges as the overall form of the piece. Although the deceptive HC initially appears as an "independent" cadence (like the genuine HC it replaces), we might also wonder whether it could be reinterpreted as a way station en route to a final HC for the compound antecedent.

The following compound consequent brings a delightful touch, for rather than writing a regular HC in G (to conclude the simple antecedent) or even the same deceptive one from measure 4, Tchaikovsky fashions a second, different, deceptive HC, which this time employs V⁶/III as the replacement harmony

(m. 12). Here, the lightly tonicized subdominant in G (m. 11) is reinterpreted as the pre-dominant ♭II⁶ in B minor (HK: III). The continuation that follows is again sequential (though starting one link earlier in the chain of descending fifths), and the theme concludes with a regular PAC in the home key at measure 16.

Note that both of the replacement dominants used for the deceptive HCs contain the pitch F♯, the leading tone of the home key, a critical element in allowing these harmonies to act as a dominant replacement. But two chromatically altered pitches—D♯ in V/VI and A♯ in V⁶/III—are salient elements in these harmonies. They even become the starting points of two chromatic descending lines: first in the alto of measures 4–6 (as bracketed); then in the bass of measures 12–14. Though Tchaikovsky's "Morning Prayer" undoubtedly gives a general impression of simple (perhaps sentimental) innocence, it actually engages some sophisticated theoretical aspects of harmony and cadence.

### 9.7.2. Evaded Cadence

Evaded cadences continue to be exploited in the second half of the nineteenth century; unlike classical practice, however, they are not so readily associated with the one-more-time technique. Although cases of that device appear now and then (see ahead Ex. 9.55c, m. 6.90), it seems largely to have played itself out in classical and early Romantic styles. Otherwise, the evaded cadence in later tonal styles usually involves different modes of continuation. In some situations, especially in operatic genres, the evaded cadence

---

129. Note that the key of the deceptive HC is anticipated in m. 3 by the deceptive resolution V–VI that immediately precedes the pre-dominant II⁶ (pivoting to IV⁶).

EXAMPLE 9.46. Verdi, "Libiamo ne' lieti calici," *La Traviata,* mm. 17–27.

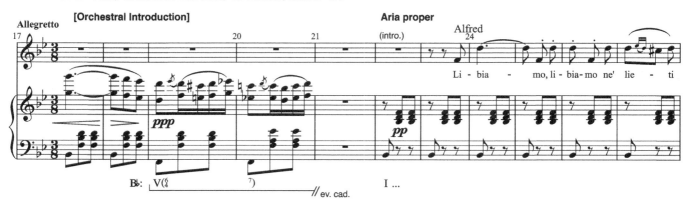

EXAMPLE 9.47. Bruckner, Symphony No. 7 in E, i, mm. 206–14.

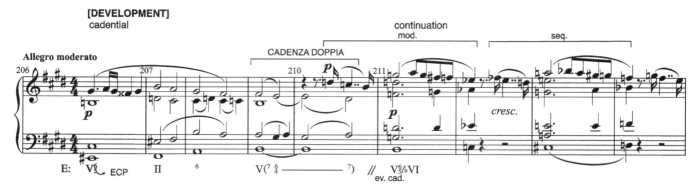

is the last part of an introductory, instrumental version of an aria's main theme, one that is abruptly halted before its obvious completion and after which the aria proper begins. Such is the case in Example 9.46, where the orchestral introduction breaks off just at the point where the cadence would be completed; a general pause of a full bar ensues instead. When the orchestra starts up again, it plays a brief thematic introduction to the aria proper.[130] Rather than sounding as an imitative "one more time," the vocal line is heard as the real thing.

At other times, an evaded cadence is followed by new continuational material. In the first-movement development section of Bruckner's Seventh Symphony (Ex. 9.47), the music approaches an expanded cadence in measures 206–10 (even referencing the by now archaic *cadenza doppia*). The failure of the dominant to resolve to tonic creates an evaded cadence on the downbeat of measure 211, which introduces a new model for sequencing, a passage that we have not yet heard within the development.

In a manner that entirely surpasses classical usage, the evaded cadence can sometimes be used to "end" a prevailing thematic unit, such that what follows represents the beginning of a completely different theme in a new tempo, style, and key. In the D-major scherzo of Mahler's Fifth Symphony (Ex. 9.48), a contrasting, slower section in B-flat major (HK: ♭VI) brings a cadential progression (mm. 171–73) that promises to close the section at the downbeat of measure 174. In place of the final tonic, a solo trumpet suddenly enters to announce the reprise of the opening section in D major. The resulting evaded cadence leads to nothing further in the slower B-flat section.[131]

A particularly emphatic use of evaded cadences to "end" a major formal unit arises at the close of the first-movement exposition in Brahms's Violin Sonata No. 2 in A (Ex. 9.49). In an obvious throwback to the classical manner, the subordinate theme arrives on a prominent I⁶ at measure 79 that initiates an authentic cadential progression. The resolution to tonic at measure 81 is a bit ambiguous: it may be heard as an IAC or, given the classical references, we might better hear an evaded cadence and one-more-time technique, with the violin of measure 81 taking on the piano's music of measure 79. In any case, what follows is definitely a series of evaded cadences (mm. 84, 85, 86, and 88) due to the omission of any final tonics. And each evasion, save for the final one, results in a one-more-time repetition. Unlike

---

130. This technique, especially common in Verdi, is even employed by Wagner; see *Die Meistersinger von Nürnberg*, Act 1, scene 3, "Zu einer Freiung." In earlier nineteenth-century Italian opera, we encounter a similar rhythmic-formal situation—the sudden breaking off of the orchestral introduction just prior to the vocal entry—though I have not yet found any cases that specifically involve an evaded cadence.

131. See also Ex. 9.24a, mm. 232–34, for a similar kind of cadential evasion.

EXAMPLE 9.48. Mahler, Symphony No. 5, iii, mm. 169–77.

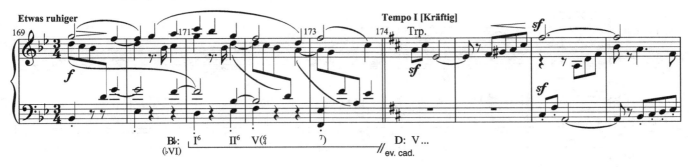

EXAMPLE 9.49. Brahms, Violin Sonata No. 2 in A, Op. 100, i, mm. 77–90.

classical practice, however, a concluding authentic cadence never materializes. Rather, in a late-nineteenth-century manner, the final evaded cadence is followed by a one-bar general pause, after which the music starts up with material from the main theme to initiate the pre-core of the development section.[132] The subordinate theme is thus left without any formal closure whatsoever. To be sure, the melodic line in the violin achieves its own ending on $\hat{1}$ at measure 86, but formal thematic closure is denied by the dominant pedal secured at measure 83 and sustained through the end of the exposition (m. 88). In fact, this emphasis on dominant harmony, along with the generally recessive dynamic, suggests a "standing on the dominant" of some kind. But such an analysis assumes that the dominant in question functions as the ultimate harmony of the cadential progression. Here, however, there has been no HC or dominant arrival; thus to speak of a standing on the dominant is not appropriate.

Another cadential technique, however, might come into consideration: the *dissipated cadence*, as discussed in the previous chapter in connection with Schubert's Piano Sonata in A (Ex. 8.23b and d). There, a presumed penultimate dominant is sustained in time, usually in the context of a recessive dynamic, such

---

132. Though I strongly hear the tonic at m. 89 as entirely initiating, it is not out of the question that a listener could hear a PAC at this moment, with the general pause perceived not as a grouping disruption, but rather as a magnified *Luftpause* that precedes the final tonic.

EXAMPLE 9.50. Bruckner, Symphony No. 8 in C Minor, iv, mm. 274–85.

## 9.8. Cadential Ambiguities

that by its end, it nevertheless gives the impression of being an ultimate dominant, after which the resolution to tonic is entirely initiating. In the case of the Brahms Sonata, however, the conversion of a penultimate dominant to an ultimate one seems not to take place: each new appearance of the dominant following the evaded cadences reaffirms its function as penultimate (especially given the cadential six-four and dominant seventh, harmonies more suggestive of an authentic cadential dominant than a half cadential one). So the category of dissipated cadence seems not to be operative here; instead, cadential evasion (with no subsequent true cadence) remains in force to the very end of the exposition. A genuine dissipated cadence will be discussed later in the chapter (see ahead Ex. 9.54a, m. 32).

We have seen throughout this study many cases where a cadential identification is rendered uncertain or ambiguous. In all tonal styles, situations appear that invoke conflicting categories to explain our perception of closure. Sometimes, the ambiguity is owing to vying musical forces that point toward alternative possibilities. At other times, we engage in retrospective reinterpretation as the passing of time gives us new information for cadential analysis. With the weakening of cadence as a means of thematic closure, music in the second half of the nineteenth century regularly presents circumstances of cadential uncertainty. Thus cases arise where it is unclear whether a dominant toward the end of a formal unit is functioning as an ultimate harmony or a penultimate one, or whether the resolving tonic represents a true formal close or a new beginning (or both). Also problematic are circumstances that lead us to doubt whether a cadence has been evaded or actually realized.

A number of stylistic traits associated with this music contribute toward making cadential identifications difficult. In the classical style, the difference between an ultimate or penultimate dominant is often associated with the specific harmonic content of that harmony. For example, the ultimate dominant of an HC must be a consonant triad, whereas the use of a cadential six-four normally signals that the dominant is penultimate. In later styles, however, the possibility that an HC may include a dissonant seventh—Schmalfeldt's 19cHC—may blur these distinctions. Another consideration involves a weakening role that *formal* expectations may implicate a particular cadence type. In earlier tonal styles, we are fairly certain that some thematic regions (e.g., subordinate themes, coda themes) will end with a PAC, whereas others will close with an HC or dominant arrival (e.g., contrasting middle, transition, developmental core). As a result, we will often resolve an ambiguous cadential situation by appealing to a particular formal convention. Thus in Chapter 4, Ex. 4.84, I prefer hearing a covered PAC at measure 9 because almost all classical main themes conclude with a genuine cadence, most typically a PAC. In later tonal styles, such conventions have broken down such that they no longer prove to be a reliable source of cadential expectation. For example, the onset of a classical sonata recapitulation is rarely signaled by a PAC ending the development section.[133] By the time of Strauss's *Ein Heldenleben* (Ex. 9.42), however, such a cadence at this formal juncture may seem like a perfectly viable option, allowing us to accept an iconic cadence arising at this point in the form (even if I also stressed the

---

133. For an exception in Beethoven, see again note 114.

cadence's role as "announcing" a formal beginning). Finally, the greater importance that secondary parameters play in the formal articulation of nineteenth-century music means that we must take strongly into account dynamic processes of progression and recession, as well as marked textural changes, when assessing cadential ambiguities.[134]

Let us begin with a couple of excerpts from Bruckner's symphonic works, which often present problems of cadential interpretation at obvious boundary demarcations. Example 9.50, arising within a development section, sees a prominent expansion of various pre-dominant harmonies of E-flat minor: II$^7$ (m. 274); Gr$^{+6}$ (m. 276); II$^6_5$ (m. 278). At this point it is unclear what kind of cadential goal we should be expecting. In the classical style, of course, we would not suppose an authentic cadence to appear within a development section. But as just discussed, such an articulation in a late-nineteenth-century work is possible enough. Given the prominent dynamic recession and wholesale motivic-textural liquidation in the second half of this harmonic expansion, we might well believe that some kind of pre-dominant arrival (occurring back at m. 274) were in the making. This interpretation, however, is negated by the appearance of V$^7$ at measure 283. At this point, if the melody were to resolve to $\hat{1}$ on the downbeat of the next bar, we would have little difficulty hearing a normal PAC. Instead, the sudden disruption of texture and melodic resolution ($\hat{7}$ leaping up to $\hat{5}$) seems to create an evaded cadence (option 1), which, as we have already discussed, need not be accompanied by a one-more-time repetition. Alternatively, we might believe that an authentic cadence is strongly enough implied to recognize a covered PAC (option 2). Finally, we should not entirely rule out the possibility of hearing the dominant at measure 283 as ultimate, thus yielding a 19cHC (option 3). In short, three different cadential interpretations are valid here, thus rendering the passage highly ambiguous as to the nature of its formal closure.

Another complicated passage, this one featuring a massive dynamic buildup, occurs at the end of a subordinate theme (Ex. 9.51). A preceding sequential passage leads at measure 101 to ♭VI of the subordinate key, followed then by a cadential six-four (m. 103). The dominant proper is consolidated in the middle of measure 104, and the rest of the passage projects a powerfully progressive dynamic, whereby a typically Brucknerian "stacking of thirds" eventually results in a dominant thirteenth sonority (m. 113). Only toward the very end of this passage does the harmony revert to a regular V$^7$ (second half of m. 122), with tonic harmony following on the downbeat of the next bar. Some suggestive tempo markings within this passage (placed in brackets in the Nowack edition and frequently performed) include *etwas belebend* ("somewhat lively") at measure 115 and *ritenuto* ("holding back") at measure 121. The resolution to tonic at measure 123 effects a clear grouping boundary due to the *subito pianissimo*, the marked change in texture, and the restoration of the original tempo.

How then are we to interpret the formal meanings of the enormously expanded dominant and the tonic to which it resolves? Again, we could consider at least three different scenarios: (1) the ♭VI at measure 101 initiates an ECP that closes eventually with a PAC at measure 123; (2) the expected cadence is evaded; and (3) the dominant is, from its inception, an ultimate harmony giving rise to a premature dominant arrival back at measure 103. Each option has its merits and demerits, and moreover, some subtle, additional interpretations can be added as well. The first scenario understands the expanded dominant as penultimate and the resolving tonic as a harmonic and melodic *goal* despite the manifest disruptions by the secondary parameters. This view is perhaps also influenced by the classical ideal that a subordinate theme should normally close with a PAC, though it is not clear that this requirement entirely holds for Bruckner's sonata forms.[135] Given the sudden change in texture and dynamics, however, the idea that the tonic of measure 123 marks a formal goal, one that groups with the preceding passage, seems problematic. And so the second scenario, that of an evaded cadence, is perhaps more convincing. The downside to this view, of course, is that the preceding unit would be left without any clear sense of closure, though as we have already seen, music in this style period seems to accept the possibility of evaded cadences (along with deceptive ones) as "replacing" a genuine cadence.

Both scenarios one and two assume the dominant to be penultimate. Indeed, the appearance of a cadential six-four helps support that view. In this particular case, however, the six-four lasts for only one and a half bars out of twenty. Many expanded penultimate dominants, especially in the classical style, see the cadential six-four taking up the majority of the expansion, with these embellishments resolving only toward the end of the prolongation.[136] But from the beginning of measure 105 on, the dominant appears as a dissonant seventh, to which Bruckner then systematically adds a ninth (m. 107), an eleventh (m. 109), and thirteenth (m. 113). At measure 120, moreover, the major thirteenth (D♯) is chromatically lowered to D♮ (see arrow), and in the second half of the bar, the major ninth (G♯) is lowered to G♮. Such an accumulation of minor dissonances could be seen to support the idea of a penultimate dominant becoming more and more unstable, thus garnering an ever-greater need for resolution to tonic. But something interesting happens toward the end of the dominant prolongation. At measure 121 the ninth (G♮) and eleventh (B) resolve down to F♯ and A♯, respectively, to double the root and third of the dominant, and in the second half of measure 122, the thirteenth (D♮) descends to C♯ to double the fifth. All of these resolutions effect a reduction in the level of dissonance such that the final utterance of the dominant is a simple major-minor

---

134. See Meyer, *Style and Music*, 303–25.

135. For example, the first subordinate theme of the Sixth Symphony (first movement) closes with either a deceptive cadence (m. 110) or with no cadence, depending upon how one hears the status of the long-held dominant prior to the resolution to VI for the onset of the second subordinate theme.

136. See Chapter 5, sec. 5.1.1.3.

EXAMPLE 9.51. Bruckner, Symphony No. 7 in E, i, mm. 101–24.

seventh. This sonority could perhaps be understood as relatively consonant in relation to the preceding dissonances and could thus be said to propose itself as an *ultimate* dominant seventh.

Thus the third scenario sees the dominant itself as the agent of closure for the ongoing thematic unit. This option is further supported by the *ritenuto* which curbs the momentum toward eventual resolution so that the dominant can emerge as the goal harmony in its own right. Problematic is that this interpretation largely focuses on the final bars of the dominant prolongation, and it is not certain that we hear an ultimate dominant articulated as far back as the cadential six-four at measure 103. So if we are persuaded that by the end of the dominant expansion, the harmony seems to be functioning as an ultimate one, we might further refine our reading and recognize a process of conversion, whereby an originally penultimate dominant "becomes" an ultimate one, precisely the situation that we find with the dissipated cadence, discussed in the previous chapter (see sec. 8.11 and Ex. 8.23b and d). The difference here is that rather than the dominant expansion bringing a dynamic *recession* (hence, the appropriateness of the term "dissipated"), the overall dynamic is one of *progression*. And given this context, we might invoke another option for how the dominant is formally behaving, namely, that of an extended upbeat, a "before-the-beginning" function. Thus rather than seeing a penultimate dominant becoming ultimate, we could recognize it becoming an *anacrusis* dominant. Of course, just where such conversions take place is difficult to pinpoint (and so I have not provided a specific annotation in the score), and that is precisely what complicates cases as ambiguous as this one. It is not at all clear that there is a definitive reading about cadence and closure that accounts for all of the competing musical forces at work in this passage.

One additional symphonic excerpt, the slow introduction to the opening movement of Brahms's First Symphony, will pull together a number of issues concerning cadential ambiguities discussed up to this point. The introduction begins with a broad tonic pedal (Ex. 9.52a) that supports highly anguished chromatic melodic lines in the upper voices. (As marked, the opening measure and a half function as a "motto" throughout the symphony.) This opening material does not form any of the standard phrase functions, so I am labeling it more generally as a functional "initiation." The tonic pedal is finally released with a powerful dominant at measure 9 to create the sense of an "expanding HC" projected when the upper voice motion $\hat{4}$–$\sharp\hat{4}$–$\hat{5}$ is supported by the progression IV$^7$–Gr$^{+6}$–V. Since the bass of measure 8 still holds the tonic pedal, the standard bass motion of that cadence type ⑥–♭⑥–⑤ cannot emerge, and so the resulting HC can be seen as a hybrid between the "simple (I–V)" and the "expanding" types.

Seeing as the material that follows this cadence is new, we sense that a first part of the slow introduction has been brought to a close by the HC. A second part leads eventually to a continuation that features sequential activity, the last portion of which is shown in Example 9.52b, measures 16–18. The following bars (19–20) contain a pre-dominant ♭II$^6$, which might well signal imminent cadential closure. Indeed, a cadential six-four appears next at measure 21 and is sustained through a dynamic buildup that brings back at measure 25 the motto, clearly referencing the very opening of the introduction (cf. mm. 1–4), though now supported by a dominant pedal. The writhing chromaticism eventually yields to a dominant triad at measure 29, which sounds very much like an arrival of some sort. Indeed, the new material that follows has the character of a postcadential standing on the dominant, whose liquidation produces a simple dominant triad in measures 36–37 (with a 4–3 suspension). The dramatic resolution of this highly prolonged dominant (since the cadential six-four back at m. 21) brings a *forte* tonic octave sounding in the lowest parts (m. 38), along with a change to *Allegro*, the tempo of the exposition proper. The motto then reappears and leads to a powerful PAC in measures 40–42. What eventually proves to be the main theme begins with the arpeggiated motive ("x") of measures 42–43 (derived from the material of the cadential six-four back at mm. 21–22).

Observing the overall harmonic and bass-line content of measures 19–37, we can identify a *single* half cadential ECP:[137] a pre-dominant Neapolitan over ④ (m. 19) leads to a cadential six-four over ⑤ (m. 21); the dominant proper appears in the second half of measure 25. This perspective (option 1 in the annotations) suggests that part 2 of the introduction closes with a cadential ♭II$^6$ leading to an HC at measure 21, whose ultimate harmony is prolonged by an enormous standing on the dominant lasting to the end of the theme. Problematic with this interpretation is not so much the length of the standing on the dominant, but rather its internal organization, which seems to be much more complex than its functional label would suggest. In particular, this view must see the "return" of the opening motto at measure 25 as absorbed, like a parenthetical expression, within the broad standing on the dominant. Moreover, this interpretation does not take into account the ways in which *dynamic-textural* forces shape a more complex formal plan.

Thus a second perspective on cadence and form in this slow introduction (see the annotations of option 2) would note that the ♭II$^6$ expansion in measures 19–20 arises at the climax of a broad crescendo that gets underway in the opening bars of Example 9.52b. The effect is clearly that of a goal, after which transpires a pronounced dynamic recession and liquidation within the expanded Neapolitan. This reading thus identifies a pre-dominant arrival at measure 19 of the sort that we discussed early in this chapter (sec. 9.2). The marked recessive dynamic within measures 19–20 would then be appropriate for this standing on a *pre-dominant*.

If measure 19 marks a formal goal, then what are we to make of the material in measures 21–24, which is supported by a cadential six-four? Here again, dynamic processes can come into play. When the pre-dominant reaches its nadir and resolves to the cadential six-four at measure 21, this harmony supports new material that spins itself out within a powerful dynamic and rhythmic intensification, culminating in the return of the motto and the

---

137. Later in the discussion, I will raise the possibility of considering these harmonies, including the tonic at m. 38, to constitute an *authentic* ECP.

EXAMPLE 9.52. Brahms, Symphony No. 1 in C Minor, Op. 68, i, (a) mm. 1–9; (b) mm. 16–43.

EXAMPLE 9.52. Continued

chromaticism of the introduction's opening. This return in the second half of measure 25 could thus represent the beginning of a third part of the slow introduction, whose prior part ends with the pre-dominant arrival at measure 19. From this perspective, we can understand the preceding four-measure phrase (mm. 21–24) as an anacrusis dominant (albeit in six-four position). As such, this extended upbeat would support a before-the-beginning, thematic introduction to this new part. Problematic, of course, is that the unit in measures 25–28 begins with a dominant seventh that is prolonged by a dominant pedal, over which the following chromatic harmonies are set. Thus, an anacrusis dominant is followed by an *initiating* dominant, an unusual harmonic-formal condition to be sure.[138]

To understand what happens next, we must temporarily ignore the dominant pedal and see that the chromatically intensified harmonies lead at the end of measure 28 to a brief

---

138. Though rare, dominant harmony sometimes begins a thematic unit, esp. a loosely organized subordinate theme, one that immediately follows upon a prior ultimate dominant ending the transition; thus an "ending" and subsequent "after-the-ending" dominant can be followed directly by an initiating dominant (see *CF*, 113–14, and *ACF*, 393–95).

cadential progression (It$^{+6}$–V$^5_3$), which formally concludes the ongoing part with an HC. Indeed, the music that follows seems much like a standing on the dominant: a new four-measure unit (29–32) begins to be repeated, but breaks down with the imitation of its opening motive (mm. 32–33, see the open-ended brackets) and an eventual dynamic recession and liquidation. A brief caesura at the end of measure 37 marks what seems to be the conclusion of the slow introduction (as indicated notationally by the double-bar lines and the change of tempo marking at m. 38). Thus our second cadential-formal perspective understands the slow introduction as a tripartite structure: the first part ending with an HC (m. 9); the second part, with a pre-dominant arrival (m. 19); and the third, with an HC (m. 29). Of course, we cannot entirely ignore the dominant pedal in measures 25–29 (which even continues on through m. 37), and for this reason I indicate the half cadence at measure 29 as one of limited scope. Indeed, the entire passage from measure 21 on prolongs dominant harmony, thus still validating the first perspective on the slow introduction (as bipartite) offered earlier on.

Looking ahead to the downbeat of measure 38, where I have posited the start of the exposition, we might wonder whether the tonic harmony at that point should be regarded as a constituent of the massive ECP identified as beginning in measure 19 and lasting through the whole of the slow introduction. In other words, is there a way to understand an *authentic cadential* progression ending, presumably, with a PAC at measure 38? To do so, we would have to regard the entire dominant prolongation as a penultimate harmony, not an ultimate one of a half cadential ECP, as assumed in the prior discussion. In fact, when we recall that the dominant begins with an expanded cadential six-four, it would not be unreasonable to consider that harmony to represent a penultimate dominant, seeing as this six-four sonority is most often associated with an authentic cadence, not an HC. Again, though, we could counter that view with an eye to the dynamic processes, for often the cadential six-four appears at a moment of climax (Hatten's arrival six-four) and rarely at the most recessive moment in the dynamic curve, as is the case at measure 21. But more importantly, it is hard to sustain an interpretation of penultimate dominant once we hear the half cadence gesture at measure 29; for by then, the dominant has certainly become ultimate, that status being reinforced by the standing on the dominant through measure 37. Further support comes from Brahms's use of a dominant triad at measures 29, 32, and 36–37, another sign of an ultimate dominant. In this light, the tonic at measure 38 should probably be heard as a beginning, not as an ending, and thus not capable of creating a genuine cadence of any kind.[139]

Before concluding this analysis, we should briefly consider what happens at the very start of the exposition, namely, the five-measure unit (mm. 38–42) that brings back the motto and then

---

139. The situation is similar to the tonic that stands between the transition and first subordinate theme in Beethoven's Piano Trio in G, Op. 1, no. 2, i, m. 99, as discussed in Chapter 2, sec. 2.11, and Ex. 2.29b.

elides with the opening of the main theme. For this phrase manifestly ends with a rhetorically powerful PAC. The formal status of this unit, however, is equivocal. It literally *begins* the exposition, yet it also seems *introductory* to the main theme proper, in the sense of an expanded thematic introduction. Seeing as the phrase stands very much on its own, strikingly separated from what precedes and follows, it does not seem to end anything other than itself. So for that reason, I regard the PAC at measure 42 as one of limited scope. Moreover, in the absence of any authentic cadential gesture in the whole of this relatively large slow introduction, the PAC seems somewhat compensatory, in the sense of making up for something that we should have been hearing at some point by now. Indeed, by bringing back the motto from the very opening of the slow introduction and then closing it down with a decisive PAC, the phrase could be seen to encapsulate the whole of that slow introduction, except for its tacking on a new cadential ending.

One final point: my admittedly complicated analysis of how Brahms begins his first symphony is belied by the directness and clarity that the music seems to project on its own. I doubt that most listeners hearing this passage would so readily experience the host of ambiguities I have uncovered here. In other words, there is somewhat of a disconnect between the sounding material itself and the attempt at explaining just what is going on. Our tools, rooted in classical compositional practice, are perhaps still too crude to deal with the nature of the cadential and formal complexities embodied in such a late-nineteenth-century work.

## 9.9. Four Case Studies

The final section of this chapter contains four case studies that feature longer passages employing a number of the cadential techniques discussed in earlier sections of this chapter.

### 9.9.1. Grieg, String Quartet in G Minor, Op. 27, Finale

The coda of the finale of Grieg's String Quartet in G Minor, Op. 27 (Ex. 9.53a), raises a number of interesting issues of how closure for this final section of a sonata form can be achieved. The recapitulation winds itself down over a tonic pedal in measures 569–94, the two last bars of which are shown at the beginning of the example. At measure 595 the coda begins with a pre-dominant German augmented-sixth (in its diminished-third position over ♯④). With a powerful crescendo, the harmony moves to another pre-dominant, IV over ♮④ (m. 599), which brings back ideas found at the end of the recapitulation. The sudden shift to *pianissimo* at measure 603 once again sees the crescendo German-sixth alternating with a *fortissimo* IV. Eventually the former wins out, and over the course of twenty bars (mm. 611–30), the persistent hammering home of this harmony creates another crescendo, leading to an impressive arrival six-four (m. 631) in the

EXAMPLE 9.53A. Grieg, String Quartet in G Minor, Op. 27, iv, mm. 593–701.

EXAMPLE 9.53A. Continued

major mode of the home key. At this point, a prominent melody from the first movement (used both in the introduction, shown in Example 9.53b, and as the subordinate theme, not shown) rings out in the first violin, accompanied by chordal texture in the other strings and supported throughout by a dominant pedal. The resolution to tonic implied for measure 647 is evaded by V⁹/IV. We can thus recognize a huge ECP (starting at m. 595) consisting of an enormously expanded pre-dominant followed by dominant. But we have to ask, is this progression ending anything such that it can be said to function cadentially? As we already noted, the recapitulation had effectively closed just prior to the first sounding of the pre-dominant Gr⁺⁶ at measure 595. So contextually, this massive ECP appears at the very *beginning* of the coda and thus cannot be said to close any prior thematic initiation. Perhaps the

reason that we anticipate a cadence for the downbeat of measure 647 is largely owing to the "first-movement tune" (as I will call this melody), which begins with the cadential six-four at measure 631. Though the tune is supported by a dominant pedal throughout, it nonetheless projects its own more local harmonization, as shown in the bracketed analysis. Thus considering the tune as a thematic unit in its own right, we could say that the expectation for cadence arises in relation to the closing of this unit, not to the prior large-scale pre-dominant to dominant progression, which, as we have just discussed, does not really end anything thematic. How, then, do we understand the preceding prolongation of pre-dominant? Given the highly charged dynamic context in which the two versions of that harmony (Gr⁺⁶ and IV) present themselves, leading ultimately to a powerful arrival six-four (m. 631),

EXAMPLE 9.53B. Grieg, String Quartet in G Minor, Op. 27, i, mm. 1–16.

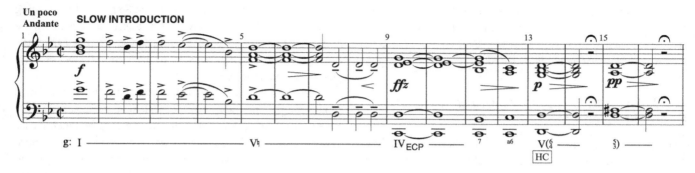

we could perhaps speak here of a huge anacrusis *pre-dominant*, one that is formally analogous to a more typical anacrusis dominant. In other words, rather than seeing the pre-dominant as the beginning of a cadential progression, it is likely more accurate to view it as a highly extended introduction to the reappearance of the first-movement new tune. But why, then, does Grieg support the tune with tonic in six-four position? Perhaps he is looking for the effect of an iconic cadence (one that is evaded at measure 647). If so, then the anacrusis harmony has to be one that will logically precede a cadential six-four: the obvious choice is a pre-dominant.

As already mentioned, the expected cadence to close the first-movement tune is evaded, after which new material (derived from the opening gesture of the third movement) leads to the tune's basic idea in diminution (mm. 651–52),[140] which itself is harmonized as another evaded cadence, one that motivates a one-more-time repetition at measure 653. (Alternatively, we might hear a very abrupt HC.) The passage that follows upon the cadential evasion at measure 659 is difficult to interpret formally. It begins with tonic harmony, which is sustained as a pedal until measure 671, after which the tonic alternates with neighboring VI chords, and a final plagal progression (mm. 678–79) completes the tonic prolongation. Though there has been no preceding cadence, this material gives much the impression of being a closing section made up of codettas, especially when the melody focuses on the high G (1̂) in measures 667–79. As a result, the concluding IV–I progression should not be thought to create plagal closure, but rather represents the final stage of the overall tonic prolongation supporting the closing section.

The end of the closing section elides with another utterance of the first-movement tune, now in a form that strongly resembles how the quartet began (see again Ex. 9.53b). There, the melodic idea, supported by tonic (in minor), moves to the minor dominant at measure 5. The subsequent IV at measure 9 proves to be a pre-dominant leading to the cadential six-four at measure 13 (which is resolved to the dominant proper at m. 15), thus creating

an HC. Toward the end of the finale (Ex. 9.53a, m. 679ff.), the situation is very similar, except that the first dominant (m. 683) is now a major sonority (matching the major tonic that precedes it), and this time the pre-dominant IV moves directly to I at measure 691, a goal tonic that is sustained until the end of the movement, supporting an obvious closing section. The cadential situation at the very end (m. 691) is somewhat problematic. Our first impression, of course, is of plagal closure, given the manifest final progression of IV to I. On second thought, though, we might observe that the subdominant stands between V and I, suggesting a feigned plagal closure. Such a view assumes that the preceding dominant (mm. 683–86) functions as the penultimate harmony of an authentic cadential progression. In the context of the theme as a whole, however, this dominant seems to group more with the opening of the tune than with the latter part, just like what we hear at the beginning of the first movement (Ex. 9.53b), where the minor dominant, in any case, cannot be heard as cadential. In other words, the sense of cadential function does not arise until the appearance of the subdominant at measure 687, and since this ending only includes the progression IV–I, our original idea of genuine, independent plagal closure can thus ultimately be validated.

Looking now to the overall form of the coda, we find that it contains two *coda themes* made up of the same melodic content: the first (m. 631ff.) is preceded by an enormous pre-dominant anacrusis and "ended" by an evaded cadence (m. 659) that, paradoxically, is followed by a closing section. The second coda theme (m. 679ff.) ends with plagal closure (m. 691). Nowhere is a standard authentic cadence realized, the last two PACs occurring earlier in the recapitulation (mm. 532 and 540, not shown), being rhetorically weak cadences that conclude a repeated subordinate theme.[141] The material of the coda, of course, is anything but rhetorically understated. Grieg even seems at times to be struggling hard to create a sense of ending in the absence of classical procedures. Indeed, we might wonder if there is a kind of inverse relationship at play, namely, that a classical

---

140. This rhythmic version of the tune's opening is heard a number of times earlier in the first movement, though not with the cadential harmonization found here.

141. These cadences might even be considered to be ones of limited scope, in that together the two statements of the subordinate theme might be seen to function as a large-scale presentation, upon which a broad continuation follows, one that does not end cadentially.

cadence can be a fairly routine matter, such that more powerful effects seem to be associated with nonclassical modes of closure, as if a greater rhetorical effort is needed to compensate for more standard cadential processes, ones that by the end of the nineteenth century may seem long outdated.

## 9.9.2. Dvorak, Symphony No. 7 in D Minor, Second Movement

Dvorak models the slow movement of his Seventh Symphony on the *large ternary* form. In the classical style, this formal type consists of three parts. First, a *main theme*, which begins and ends in the home key, is built as a complete small ternary, ending with a PAC. Second, an *interior theme*, still in the home key but with its opposite mode (i.e., a *minore* or *maggiore*), is built as an incomplete small ternary, ending with a home-key HC. Third, the main theme is reprised, usually identical in harmony and phrase structure to how it appeared in the first part. (A coda is optional to the form.)[142] Dvorak constructs his movement along these general lines, but with a number of adjustments that render the form more expansive and weighty, as appropriate for a late-nineteenth-century symphonic work. The first part, remaining entirely in the home key, is not built as a small ternary, but rather consists of two thematic units. The second part, which we will not examine, begins in the minor mode of the home key (thus alluding to a *minore* interior theme) and traverses a variety of tonal regions. The third part begins with the second thematic unit of the first part, bringing back material of the first theme only toward the close of the movement.

Let us begin with part one (Ex. 9.54a), whose first theme opens with a four-measure phrase ending with a PAC in the home key, F major.[143] Intrinsically, such a phrase expresses consequent function (basic idea, contrasting idea, strong cadential closure), though its contextual function is obviously initiating, in the sense of an antecedent.[144] In a nineteenth-century manner, the basic idea begins off-tonic, with the subdominant, though the idea ultimately regains tonic by its end. The next four-bar phrase also closes with a PAC, and its basic idea (which is new, though related to the earlier one) also begins off-tonic, this time on VI. Together, the two phrases suggest a periodic formation, except that each phrase begins with a different basic idea and ends with a PAC; so the overall form is far from a classical period in many respects.[145] The second PAC at measure 8 is then followed by what seems to be a closing section, which prolongs the cadential tonic.

The dynamic character of these two bars, however, is highly progressive, with a strong ascending contour. So rather than seeming postcadential (which normally projects a recessive dynamic), the music functions more like an introduction, an extended anacrusis leading at measure 11 to the start of the second theme, securely planted on the tonic of F.

Unlike the first theme, which, if nonconventional in form, is still fairly tight-knit (being symmetrical, tonally stable, and highly closed cadentially), the second theme proves to be much looser in organization. Following a new two-measure basic idea (whose opening motive in measure 11 has the same contour as the opening of theme 1), a contrasting idea seems like it will close with an HC at measure 14; however, the four-two position of the dominant keeps the phrase open-ended, after which a continuation leads to dominant harmony at measure 17.[146] Morphologically, the progression leading to this dominant could give rise to an HC. But as regards the grouping structure and melodic contour, this moment seems to come too early, while the melody pushes up and then falls precipitously to its goal, $E_5$, on the downbeat of measure 18. Thus the previous bar sounds more like a premature dominant arrival than a genuine HC.

There follows a standing on the dominant (mm. 18–22) featuring the alternation of a half-diminished-seventh sonority, D♭–E♮–A♭–B♭, which represents dominant harmony (D♭ and A♭ being upper-chromatic embellishments of C and G, respectively), and a neighboring II$^6_5$. Measure 23 pulls out of the dominant to bring about a new continuation, which then leads to a cadential six-four on the second beat of measure 25, thus promising to close the theme with an authentic cadence in the home key. At this point, we can look back and understand that the premature dominant arrival at measure 17 (with its standing on the dominant) is *internal* to the structure of the ongoing thematic unit, a technique we often find in a subordinate theme. The cadential six-four in measure 25, which at this point seems to function as a penultimate dominant, resolves to the dominant proper on the downbeat of measure 27 (in the form of V$^9$). The dynamic context here, however, is somewhat unusual. In the first place, a marked recession is effected throughout measure 26, such that when the six-four resolves, we would expect a quiet dominant proper to bring the authentic cadence. Strangely, though, in what seems like another standing on the dominant (mm. 27–31), the music regains energy via a rapid crescendo, and the dominant proper now proposes to resolve to tonic with a *fortissimo* cadence. Yet, this powerful momentum toward closure once again abates during the long dynamic recession of measures 29–31, and when the dominant is inverted to V$^4_3$, the cadence is effectively abandoned. The resolution to tonic at measure 32 is thus rendered noncadential. In fact, our impression throughout this

---

142. See *CF*, 211–16, and *ACF*, 566–67, 574–85.

143. Note that the III$^6$ in m. 4 (and also in m. 8) stands in for the cadential dominant; see in Chapter 8, note 12.

144. Other cases of such a "formal dissonance" include Ex. 9.22a and in Chapter 8, Ex. 8.21a.

145. Note, however, the durational lengths of the cadential progressions in the two phrases; the second is longer than the first, which in the classical style is typical of a consequent compared to an antecedent (*ACF*, 85).

---

146. Note the extensive ④ pedal in the bass in mm. 12–15, an unusual anchor to what is otherwise a fluctuating harmonic environment. This emphasis on the subdominant perhaps alludes to (and augments) the opening IV harmony of theme 1.

EXAMPLE 9.54A. Dvorak, Symphony No. 7 in D Minor, ii, mm. 1–40.

EXAMPLE 9.54A. Continued

passage is that a penultimate dominant (represented by the cadential six-four) becomes converted into an ultimate dominant, whose resolution to tonic (m. 32) represents a new beginning, not a formal goal. Here, then, is a clear *dissipated cadence*, a technique we first observed in Schubert's Piano Sonata in A in the previous chapter (Ex. 8.23) and considered, but then rejected, for the end of Brahms's Violin Sonata in A in the present chapter (Ex. 9.49).[147]

---

147. In one way, however, Dvorak's dissipated cadence differs from the earlier cases. With Schubert, the conversion from a penultimate to an ultimate dominant occurs following an evaded cadence (see Ex. 8.23b, mm. 74–78, and Ex. 8.23d, mm. 112–17); with Dvorak, the ongoing cadential progression is abandoned, as evident by the inverted dominant in m. 31.

Like Schubert's dissipated cadences, the new beginning at measure 32 (Ex. 9.54a) does not emerge as a full-fledged theme in its own right. To be sure, a new basic idea is repeated to create a presentation phrase, but there follows no significant harmonic or cadential activity; rather, the music remains stabilized on a root-position tonic. The basic idea thus functions retrospectively as a codetta within a full-fledged closing section, one that lasts through measure 39, after which the outburst in F minor initiates the second part of the large ternary.

Looking back over the course of this second thematic unit, we recognize loosening techniques associated with subordinate-theme organization, except, of course, that the theme remains entirely in the home key. Indeed, a "first-time" listener who thinks that the piece might be written in sonata form (a justifiable expectation for a symphonic slow movement) could well imagine that the opening eight bars represent a main theme, with measure 11 beginning a transition, especially given the uniform accompanimental pattern, typical of this function. The initial move to a home-key HC and standing on the dominant imply a *non-modulating* transition, after which the listener might assume that the music will modulate to a subordinate key. These expectations, however, are dashed when the music remains completely in F major. Nonetheless, the harmonic, phrase-structural, and cadential organization of this theme is reminiscent of a classical subordinate theme, except for the dissipated cadence, a nineteenth-century technique, which renders the "ending" of the theme noncadential. Moreover, the lack of any obvious beginning to a subordinate theme results in a fusion of potential transition and subordinate-theme functions.

The second part of the large ternary (not shown) is also loose in organization, bringing extensive harmonic and tonal instability in the manner of a development.[148] Toward the end of part 2, the bass line becomes fixed on the pitch E, supporting at first a variety of harmonies, but eventually settling on the dominant of A minor (HK: III). As shown at the start of Example 9.54b, this dominant resolves deceptively to VI (m. 70), which immediately is reinterpreted as tonic of the home key, leading to a simple PAC at measure 72, one that elides with the beginning of the third part of the ternary form.[149]

Here, the *second* theme of the ternary's first part enters immediately. We must ask, of course, why Dvorak bypasses the first theme (mm. 1–8). A couple of factors come to mind: first, theme 1 begins directly on subdominant harmony, which could complicate how part 2 would end and could potentially obscure the boundary between parts 2 and 3. More important might be the presence of two PACs in theme 1. At the beginning of the movement, these two cadences were unusual, but ultimately served to confirm the home tonality, especially in the absence of a PAC at the end of part 1 (due to the cadential dissipation). Here at the beginning of part 3, such a cadential emphasis would likely be inappropriate. So Dvorak opts for beginning this part with the firm tonic opening of theme 2. Of course, this decision itself generates expectations that theme 1 will reappear at some later point in the movement.

Theme 2 follows the same course as in part 1 up to the internal dominant arrival and standing on the dominant (mm. 79–82). And like what happened earlier, this dominant emphasis is succeeded at measure 83 by a new continuation (though different in content from that of part 1). The continuation ushers in a cadential pre-dominant (II) at measure 88, but rather than following with a cadential six-four as at measure 25 of part 1, the predominant leads to a simple dominant triad in the middle of measure 88, followed by a caesura. As a result, although we would be expecting a penultimate dominant of an authentic cadence, we are encouraged to hear an HC instead. Indeed, the music that immediately follows (mm. 89–90) corresponds to the standing on the dominant in part 1 (mm. 27–28) that is associated with the dissipated cadence. In part 3, however, the extension of the ultimate dominant of measure 88 leads directly to a climactic IAC at measure 91, which ends up articulating the close of the second theme. In short, we see a reversal of what happened in part 1, where a penultimate dominant (signaled by the cadential six-four in m. 25) becomes ultimate via the dissipated cadence. In part 3, on the contrary, an ultimate dominant (m. 88) becomes penultimate to effect an IAC. Thus Dvorak does not let the authentic cadence dissipate (as in the first part); rather, he allows it to be fully expressed, thus realizing (albeit with an IAC, not a PAC) the implication, aroused earlier on, for true cadential closure of this theme.

Following the cadence, a closing section, different from that in the first part, effects a dynamic recession and an eventual return of material from theme 1 at measure 95. Note that the lowest, literally sounding voice in measures 96–97 descends chromatically, thus suggesting a degree of harmonic activity. This voice, however, actually lies in the middle of the texture, under which a bass F serves as a pedal. As a result, the return of the first theme still takes place within the formal confines of the closing section, which began back at measure 91. Indeed, what appears to be plagal closure of the theme in measures 104–105 should also be understood as postcadential: what seems like a change in the bass line in measure 104 is illusory, because the left hand of the reduction is performed by the horns, which rarely function as a bass part. Thus a root-position tonic is prolonged from the beginning of this enormous closing section, one that stretches from the IAC at measure 91 to the very end of the piece.

Though Dvorak's movement may not initially give the impression of departing significantly from classical modes of phrase structure and cadential closure, a host of details in harmony, tonality, cadence, and form situate it convincingly in the latter part of the nineteenth century. Two general aspects—one tonal, the other phrase structural—are worthy of highlighting, with cadence playing an important role in both. First, we have spoken much throughout this and the previous chapter of how the classical polarity of tonic and dominant significantly breaks down in the course of the nineteenth century. Typically, the subdominant comes to replace the role of the dominant. In this piece, the subdominant receives a degree of emphasis as the opening harmony of the movement and by the ④ pedal in measures 12–15 (and mm. 73–76). But perhaps in this piece, the more notable harmonic-tonal emphasis is that accorded to the home key itself, along with its tonic. Already in the opening eight bars, we encounter two PACs confirming F major, and then the second theme remains entirely in that key. Indeed, C major—the standard subordinate key—receives no expression at any point in the movement. As discussed, even though the second theme fails to attain cadential

---

148. That the interior theme of a large ternary can resemble a development section is discussed in *ACF*, 582–84, Ex. 17.8.

149. This cadence is one of limited scope: it concludes the retransition back to the home key (mm. 70–71) rather than the entire second section, which closes with a dominant arrival of A minor earlier at m. 67 (not shown).

EXAMPLE 9.54B. Dvorak, Symphony No. 7 in D Minor, ii, mm. 68–110.

EXAMPLE 9.54B. Continued

closure, part 1 ends with an eight-measure closing section, built entirely over a tonic pedal, thus further emphasizing the home-key tonic. In part 3, the second theme receives its expected cadence, and its goal tonic is extended via a *twenty*-bar closing section supported entirely by a tonic pedal. And within this section, elements of the *first* theme finally return. In short, tonic harmony and tonality are especially emphasized throughout the movement. To be sure, dominant *harmony* plays a major role in the second theme, though in both parts it is uncertain if the dominant is functioning as penultimate or ultimate.

Second, we have seen how the phrase-structural organization of the outer parts strongly reference an exposition and recapitulation of sonata form. (Additionally, part 2 is organized much like a development section.) The first theme of part 1 can readily be considered a main theme (despite its odd cadential layout), while the second theme begins like a transition, which then fuses with the expression of subordinate-theme function. We can also think of part 3 as a kind of recapitulation, though of the "reversed" type.[150] From a formal perspective, the sense of exposition and recapitulation is strongly expressed. Problematic, of course, is the tonal organization, which belies a sonata-form interpretation. Thus some significant characteristics of sonata form are missing—the dramatic conflict of home and subordinate keys in the exposition, followed in the recapitulation by a *tonal adjustment* that resolves this conflict in favor of the home key. In a different way, though, part 3 does resolves a problem exposed in part 1, albeit a problem that is cadential, not tonal. As mentioned, the opening part ("exposition") fails to confirm the key of the second theme because of the dissipated cadence. That

---

150. *CF*, 173–74, and *ACF*, 505, 509.

task is left to part 3 ("recapitulation"), and so we might speak of a *cadential* adjustment as providing the essential functional differentiation of these sections of an incipient sonata form. To be sure, the movement is still best described as a large ternary—sufficient tonal cues point in that direction—but the referencing of sonata form clearly endows the movement with a formal gravitas well-suited to the late-nineteenth-century genre of symphony, of which Dvorak, along with Brahms, Bruckner, Tchaikovsky, and Mahler, is a true master.

### 9.9.3. Liszt, Sonata in B Minor

The highly loose subordinate-theme group from the exposition of Liszt's B-Minor Piano Sonata illustrates a host of mid-century cadential complications explored in this and the previous chapter. As we will see, the passage consists of two thematic units—the first, sentential; the second, periodic—whose initiating functions are well articulated.[151] Each unit also brings a good deal of cadential material, yet for both themes, the ongoing cadential function gets sidetracked with additional sequential activity, and genuine cadential closure never emerges. We thus see here a perfect illustration of the broader shift from an eighteenth-century emphasis on formal goals to a nineteenth-century valorization of formal openings.

The first subordinate theme begins with a presentation phrase in the standard subordinate key of D major (Ex. 9.55a).[152] There follows a continuation leading at first (mm. 111–12) to a half cadential progression in B minor (the home key). The dominant on the downbeat of measure 112 completes a regular eight-measure theme and would thus have the potential to mark an HC, except that the music presses on, reaching another possible goal on the downbeat of measure 113. This moment, too, is a potential HC, now in the dominant region (A major) of the subordinate key; yet the music still continues, expressing a third half cadential figure on the second beat of measure 114 in F-sharp minor (HK: V), a possible subordinate key. Up to now, the theme has presented three cadential ideas, none of which obviously effects closure. Yet the C# harmony achieved in measure 114 is now prolonged as a standing on the dominant, up to the second beat of measure 118.[153] As a result, the half cadential progression in measure 114 would seem to be the best candidate for projecting a genuine HC, even though it is the final one in a series of similar articulations.

Note that throughout this passage, the bass line has been falling stepwise (see the annotations of the scale degrees, all in reference to D major). Finally, the bass pushes further down to ♭$\hat{6}$ in measure 119 to support a diminished-seventh chord, a sonority that, depending upon its resolution, can assume a wide variety of harmonic-tonal meanings. Given that the preceding harmony is a B-minor triad, we might assume that this diminished seventh is functioning as a dominant of the home key. Indeed, the unison passage that follows clearly projects B minor and even brings back the main-theme's opening phrase, an odd turn of events given that we are supposedly listening to the subordinate theme. But Liszt has another surprise in store, for when the chordal texture resumes at measure 124, the leading tone A# in the bass is reinterpreted enharmonically (and is spelled) as B♭, and the music is suddenly deflected into the distant, tritone-related, key of F major. The passage that follows (using a lyrically transformed version of the main theme's opening phrase) is supported by an ECP, one that makes it as far as the penultimate dominant before proving to be deceptive, when the music (m. 133) sequences down a third into D minor, thereby regaining the subordinate key (if not its modality). The ensuing ECP then gets stuck on the pre-dominant at measure 135, which is prolonged by a variety of harmonies at least through measure 144. At this point, the cadential progression is abandoned, and an ascending-stepwise sequence takes over to provide new continuational activity. Eventually the theme leads to a dominant (m. 152) that resolves in the following bar to tonic of the subordinate key (back in the major mode), whereupon the second subordinate theme immediately begins. Though this final V–I is potentially cadential—both harmonies being in root-position—the progression does not seem to belong to anything that resembles a broader cadential process, but rather emerges as the last part of a highly chromatic set of harmonies that is not easily classifiable into any one of the three standard categories (prolongational, sequential, or cadential). As a result, the dominant in measure 152 has little in the way of cadential expression, and the ongoing thematic unit seems to conclude without a clearly expressed cadence.

Now that we see where this first thematic unit finally ends, let us step back and consider its overall formal organization. As mentioned before, its initiating function, a four-measure presentation (mm. 105–108), is obvious enough; the continuation that follows leads to a series of half cadential ideas, of which the final one (m. 114) is perhaps decisive, given the subsequent standing on its dominant. Since this music is expressing subordinate-theme function, we can assume that this HC is *internal* to the thematic structure, an assumption that proves correct when it is followed by a new continuation (though back in the home key) and a cadential phrase (first in the wrong key, F major, but then adjusted into the right key, D minor). This second cadential passage eventually goes awry, and another continuation leads to the start of the second subordinate theme without providing any satisfactory closure for the first one. Liszt is obviously modeling his theme on classical precedents—a loosely organized sentential structure—yet the various cadential units arising throughout the theme do not conform to eighteenth-century norms; rather they

---

151. Vande Moortele presents a somewhat different phrase-structural reading, finding three thematic regions within the subordinate-theme group (*Two-Dimensional Sonata Form*, 41–44).

152. Though the harmonic content of mm. 105–108 is obviously sequential (a descending-thirds pattern), the sense of tonic prolongation projected by the underlying pedal permits us to speak of a regular presentation phrase.

153. Even if the character of this theme is far too grandiose to represent the sarabande topic, the rhythmic organization of the theme regularly gives accentual weight to the second beat in the manner of that dance type, including the half cadential articulations in mm. 113–14 and the subsequent standing on the dominant.

9.9. FOUR CASE STUDIES 571

EXAMPLE 9.55A. Liszt, Piano Sonata in B Minor, mm. 105–72.

EXAMPLE 9.55A. Continued

EXAMPLE 9.55A. Continued

are refashioned in ways typical of mid-nineteenth-century practice. We especially observe the pervasive cadential "detours" for the various half cadential units (mm. 111–14) and the deceptive ECP in F major (mm. 125–33). Most importantly, the beginning of the first subordinate theme is evident enough, but its sense of ending is problematized, even if the onset of the second subordinate theme is also clear-cut.

Let us turn now to that second theme, which begins at measure 153 with a new lyrical passage based on a wholesale transformation of the sinister second phrase of the main theme, an idea that has already sounded (much like how it appeared early on) in the left-hand part of the first subordinate theme (mm. 141–42). Phrase structurally, the second theme sees a four-measure idea (mm. 153–56) repeated sequentially up a step.[154] Seeing as this eight-measure phrase stands at an initiating position, it could be seen as "presentational," yet an underlying tonic prolongation does not emerge. Instead, the sequential organization lends a certain continuational quality to the phrase.[155] A real continuation follows, with fragmentation into two-measure units, and the arrival on a cadential six-four at measure 165 potentially signals cadential function.[156] However, the return of the opening idea at this point (an entirely nonclassical procedure) sees the music drift into the remote region of C-sharp minor (HK: VII), where a cadential progression (mm. 168–169) begins to confirm that key. Not surprisingly, this turns out to be a cadential detour, and the music gets back on the tonal track by regaining the subordinate-key's dominant at the very last moment before the return of the opening idea of the theme (m. 171). As with how the first subordinate theme "ended" (m. 152), the dominant-to-tonic move into measure 171 could perhaps be seen as cadential (there being, after all, a clear II$^6_5$–V$^7$–I progression), creating either a 19cHC or an IAC. Yet given the way in which this highly compact progression emerges out of a chromatically obscure context, and especially given the *rallentando*, which inhibits the pre-dominant and dominant from reaching the progression's harmonic goal, a genuine cadential expression seems minimally expressed here. The tonic of measure 171 thus seems much more like a beginning than an ending. Indeed, the whole sentential structure gives the impression of being a kind of compound antecedent (ending, noncadentially, with dominant), whose matching consequent begins with the ornamented version of the opening idea.

This consequent follows a similar path to that of the antecedent, except that the continuation is more extended and endowed with considerable harmonic-tonal flux. A moment

---

154. This four-measure unit seems to be an expanded, simple basic idea, rather than a compound basic idea.

155. On a "presentation" that projects a sequential harmonic plan, see Chapter 8, note 26. For the classical precedent of having a second subordinate theme begin with continuation function, see *CF*, 111–13, and *ACF*, 390–91. On Liszt's penchant for sequential openings, see Vande Moortele, "Sentences, Sentence Chains," 124–30; Vande Moortele orients his study in reference to Carl Dahlhaus, "Liszts Bergsymphonie und die Idee der Symphonischen Dichtung."

---

156. Note that this is precisely the place in a classical sentence where a prominent I$^6$ would mark the onset of a cadential progression. Liszt's use of a cadential six-four at this moment illustrates well how this sonority has replaced the first-inversion tonic as a marker of impending cadence.

EXAMPLE 9.55B. Liszt, Piano Sonata in B Minor, mm. 195–214.

of stability is achieved at measure 197 (Ex. 9.55b) by an arrival six-four, which projects a distinctly pastoral topic. This passage holds out the possibility of a cadence to close the ongoing subordinate theme, especially since the six-four occurs in F-sharp major (HK: V), a potential subordinate key (though not D, the key in which the subordinate theme began). Instead of effecting closure, however, a cadenza in measure 200 leads to another pastoral six-four, sequenced down a minor third into an enharmonically notated E-flat major. Another descending-third sequence brings a new arrival six-four in C major, this one of a markedly heroic character.[157] It too is sequenced (m. 213), but only by a half-step down, thus regaining the home key. None of these detour six-fours, as we can now understand them, gets the music back on track toward an ultimate confirmation of the opening subordinate key (D major). Rather, these harmonies seem like

---

157. Klein styles this a "transcendent" arrival six-four (*Intertextuality*, 64, Ex. 3.3).

isolated events in a broader development-like impulse that emphasizes sequential repetition. Following the final six-four, in fact, we soon realize that the music has decisively moved beyond the exposition of this sonata form and into the development section, without ever achieving any sort of cadential closure of this second subordinate theme.

Before concluding this analysis, let us revisit those two moments that might seem to qualify as genuinely cadential, namely the two V–I progressions that lead into the opening of the antecedent and consequent units of the second subordinate theme (see again Ex. 9.55a, mm. 152–53 and mm. 170–71). Though they contain the minimum harmonic requirements of cadence, neither seems to function as the final utterance of an exclusively cadential process. Rather, they both act like last-second readjustments of the harmonic trajectory in order to get the music back on track for *beginning* the compound antecedent and consequent in the subordinate key. Indeed, the dominants in both cases (each of which features a forward-striving, chromatically raised chordal fifth) function more like anacrusis harmonies than genuinely penultimate ones leading to a goal tonic. It is a subtle effect, yet the formal emphasis seems to lie on each tonic as initiating, not as ending. Finally, if we know where the first subordinate theme has concluded because of where the second one begins, the latter has virtually nothing in the way of an "ending" (outside of the detour six-fours), because the development section itself does not even have an obvious point of beginning. In short, Liszt has clearly breached some essential processes of classical form, primarily in the service of new formal patterns, foremost among them being the overarching "two-dimensional sonata form" so persuasively advanced by Vande Moortele.[158]

Though Liszt clearly is distancing himself from earlier practice in the cadential areas of his two subordinate themes, he still shows his debt to the classical masters in the coda of this monumental sonata (see Ex. 9.55c). The large ECP leading up to the final return of the first subordinate theme's opening idea features an embellishment of the cadential I$^6$ via a neighboring V$^4_2$, a classical rocking on the tonic. There follows an evaded cadence (m. 690), a one-more-time repetition of the ECP, and a final elided cadence at measure 700.[159] Indeed, the passage actually sounds rather retrogressive, perhaps even nostalgic, something that Beethoven could easily have written a half-century earlier. We see here, as we have throughout these two chapters on nineteenth-century cadential practice, the powerful impact that the classical cadence continued to exert, even in the face of modifications that eventually came to demolish this cadence as a means of formal closure when the system of functional tonality eventually broke down during the opening decades of the twentieth century.

### 9.9.4. Wagner, Prelude to *Tristan und Isolde*

No chapter on harmony and cadence in the mid- to late nineteenth century can be complete without considering the most influential piece of the period—Wagner's *Tristan Prelude*. Aside from the complexities of the Tristan chord itself,[160] the prelude's harmonic content features extensive sequential progressions, especially ascending ones, with their attendant expression of emotional striving, urgency, and unfulfilled longing. Perhaps not so obvious, though, is the work's utter saturation with cadential progressions, in spite of the very few cadences actually created, including not a single genuine authentic cadence. Many of the cadential progressions themselves are embedded within the individual links of a broader sequential progression, a technique we saw used in the earlier Romantic style.[161] It has long been observed, of course, that the first thematic unit (Ex. 9.56a) consists of a broad ascending-third sequence through the first, third, and fifth scale degrees of A minor, the controlling tonality for most of the Prelude.[162] And a venerable tradition of analysis sees the first two components of this sequence projecting a half cadential progression Fr$^{+6}$–V, first in A minor, then in C minor. This analysis reads the G♯ of the Tristan chord on the downbeat of measure 2 as a non-harmonic tone resolving to A, thus completing the augmented sixth. (I will consider an alternative reading of the harmony later on.) The third link in the sequence, measures 8–11, cannot be convincingly analyzed as cadential: here the Tristan chord functions as a purely linear half-diminished-seventh sonority to the subsequent dominant seventh in E minor. The next distinct progression (mm. 16–17) is again cadential, a deceptive move from dominant to submediant in A minor, which creates a deceptive cadence to close theme 1.[163]

The following theme 2 continues to be filled with cadential progressions. The F-major harmony of measure 17 now becomes a cadential pre-dominant of C major, and this harmonic function is prolonged by secondary dominants of V through the beginning of measure 19. The root-position dominant appearing in the second half of that bar strongly implies a cadential resolution to a root-position tonic. Instead, the dominant yields to its four-two position and resolves to I$^6$, thus producing another deceptive cadential progression. Though I have spoken of this progression as beginning at measure 17 with the F-major harmony, we should also note that the previous E$^7$ sonority can also be brought into

---

158. Vande Moortele, *Two-Dimensional Sonata Form*, chap. 2.

159. For a late-nineteenth-century "rocking on the tonic," see Brahms, Piano Concerto No. 1 in D Minor, Op. 15, i, mm. 166–67.

160. For our purposes, it is not necessary to reference the many analyses devoted to the prelude, and most especially to its famous chord. Instead the reader is advised to consult the recent, comprehensive bibliography offered by Nathan John Martin ("The Tristan Chord Resolved").

161. See Chapter 8, sec. 8.3, and Ex. 8.6 and 8.45.

162. With this sequential opening, Wagner is clearly following in the footsteps of Chopin's "signature progression" (Chapter 8, note 25) and Liszt's standard mode of thematic construction (note 155 in the present chapter).

163. For a discussion of the ubiquity of deceptive cadences as thematic endings in Wagner's music, see sec. 9.7 and note 125.

EXAMPLE 9.55C. Liszt, Piano Sonata in B Minor, mm. 682–700.

the fold, thus creating a characteristically Romantic variant of stage 1.[164] Without ignoring the obvious structural division articulated by the deceptive cadence at measure 17, we can still perceive an important element of harmonic continuity forged at the end of the first theme and into the beginning of the second, thus appreciating all the more the intensity of cadential expression projected throughout these bars.

With the upbeat to measure 21, we encounter for the first time a tonic prolongational progression (VII$^7$–I), which shifts the tonal focus to D minor.[165] Immediately thereafter, the newly achieved key becomes more strongly expressed by the half cadential progression leading into the downbeat of measure 22. But then the immediate sequential repetition of this gesture into E minor throws into doubt its actual cadential function, and we once again find cadential

---

164. See Ex. 8.4d.

165. The third progression of theme 1, mm. 10–11, is also prolongational, but of dominant harmony in E minor.

EXAMPLE 9.56A. Wagner, Prelude, *Tristan und Isolde*, mm. 1–28.

progressions being embedded within a broader sequential plan. If the half cadential ideas in measures 22–23 fail to function cadentially due to their sequential setting, we might be more convinced that a real cadence is in the making as the music drives forward with greater urgency, starting with the *poco rallentando* and culminating with a *forte* A-major harmony at measure 24. Seeing as a root-position dominant resolves directly to a root-position tonic (the only time this occurs in the entire prelude), it is tempting to recognize a genuine IAC to confirm the home key. A closer look, however, reveals that the root-position V emerges from an inverted dominant ($V^6$); the overall progression is thus more accurately understood as tonic prolongational, not cadential, and thus prolongational closure becomes the operative mode of ending theme 2. For a piece that seems so systematically to shun tonic prolongations, Wagner's bringing just this progression at the one moment where a cadence might have genuinely arisen seems not only highly ironic, but appropriately expressive—at the cadential level—of the unfulfilled longing lying at the emotional core of the opera.

The four bars of music that immediately follow shift quickly to E major and bring melodic patterns suggestive of model-sequence

578  Cadence in the Mid- to Late Nineteenth Century

EXAMPLE 9.56B. Wagner, Prelude, *Tristan und Isolde*, mm. 61–74.

technique, supported by a circle-of-fifths progression, as analyzed in line 1. But measures 27–28 are not actually a transposed repetition of measures 25–26, and, moreover, the bass G♯ does not hold a III harmony, as required to make a complete sequential progression. Rather, the bass supports I⁶ (in E), which, as shown in line 2, suggests an initial cadential tonic, one that is then prolonged by the following VI harmony. The next two bars bring the cadential pre-dominant and dominant, respectively. Here we see a good case of what I described in the previous chapter (sec. 8.7) as the Romantic tendency to blur the distinction between sequential and cadential progressions.

At this point, we have considered most of the material that constitutes the prelude, because, as Morgan has convincingly demonstrated, the piece largely recycles the same content over and over again to create a unique circular form.[166] To summarize what we have observed so far, the overwhelming majority of harmonic progressions can be classified as sequential or cadential, whereby the two categories are intertwined in typically nineteenth-century ways. Moreover, only one of the cadential progressions results in an actual cadence, namely, the deceptive cadence at measure 17. Another moment of potential cadence at measure 24 achieves only prolongational closure in lieu of an IAC. Cadence and sequence are thus the most prominent harmonic categories throughout the prelude; *tonic* prolongations are scarce indeed.

---

166. Morgan, "Circular Form."

EXAMPLE 9.56C. Wagner, Prelude, *Tristan und Isolde*, mm. 98–111.

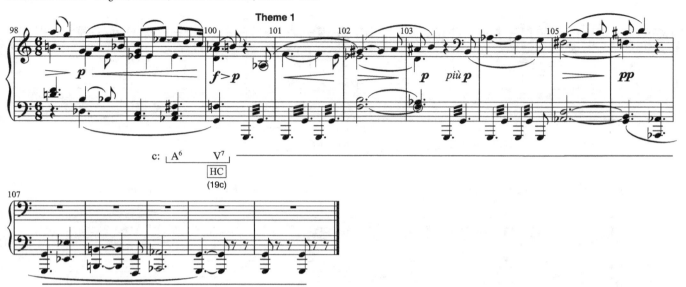

This is not to say, however, that all prolongations are shunned. For it is impossible to ignore the enormous dominant pedal that occupies a central position within the prelude (Ex. 9.56b). Following the most rhetorically powerful cadence within the piece—the HC at measure 63—Wagner writes a classical standing on the dominant.[167] Beginning in the second half of measure 66, the "desire" motive from measure 2 (Ex. 9.56a) sneaks back in as the bass moves up to F; indeed, this point marks what is essentially a wholesale recapitulation of theme 1, culminating in the deceptive cadence of measure 74. Yet the actual harmony built over the bass F in measure 66 is not the *half*-diminished-seventh Tristan chord, but rather a *fully* diminished VII$^4_2$, which well assimilates into the broader dominant prolongation. The second half of measure 70 signals the second link in the sequential chain. This time, it is not necessary to adjust the Tristan chord, since its intervallic structure can now be interpreted as a half-diminished VII$^7$, which continues to prolong the prevailing dominant of A (major). With the shift to the augmented sixth of C at the end of measure 70, the dominant prolongation of A is broken, and what follows reproduces quite literally the harmonic content of the opening theme.

The end of the prelude also features another important dominant prolongation (Ex. 9.56c), this one following the 19cHC in C minor at measure 100, the final cadential articulation in the piece. Here again, Wagner initiates another run-through of the opening material, this time supported by a pedal G. In order to assimilate these ideas into the dominant prolongation of C minor, a small number of adjustments need to be made. For example, the opening leap of a sixth into measure 101 now begins with an A♭ (see circled note) rather than A♮ (as at the opening of the piece), so as not to clash with the A♭ in the rest of measure 100.

The Tristan chord at measure 102 does not need to be changed, since it can be understood as a dominant ninth with altered fifth (E♭=D♯), the notated G♯ still being heard as A♭. But instead of the low F resolving to E at measure 103, like the opening, the F is retained (circled) in order to continue projecting the dominant ninth sonority. The Tristan chord at measure 105 also remains unaltered, and here the F♯ in the alto voice does conflict somewhat with the prevailing harmony, though not enough to override the powerful sense of the dominant prolongation, which has been ongoing since measure 100 and which is maintained to the end of the prelude.

We have now seen two passages where theme 1 returns in contexts that project two different dominant prolongations: one in the key of A, the other in C. To understand the underlying harmonic logic that helps facilitate the appearance of these prolongations, let us return to the opening of the prelude and consider some details of harmony that I passed over in my initial discussion (Ex. 9.56d). Though traditional accounts of this passage tend to emphasize the sequential or cadential nature of the harmonic organization, other commentators, inspired by the Schenkerian-oriented analysis of William Mitchell, have interpreted the Tristan chord in measure 2 not as a pre-dominant, but rather as a dominant.[168] In these readings, the G♯ is taken to be a chord tone, which enters into a voice-exchange with the G♯ in the following bar.[169] Two additional pitches of the Tristan chord—F and B—can also be seen as members of this dominant sonority. The D♯ (circled) would seem to be the conflicting element just like the F♯ in measure 105 of the previous example. The sense of

---

167. The dominant harmony of this HC is a consonant triad, another classical trait.

168. William J. Mitchell, "The Tristan Prelude: Technique and Structure, 174–76.

169. In Chapter 5, we have already noted this voice leading of the "Tristan progression" in connection with Mozart's G-Minor Symphony; see in Chapter 5, Ex. 5.58, and note 89.

EXAMPLE 9.56D. Wagner, Prelude, *Tristan und Isolde*, mm. 1–11.

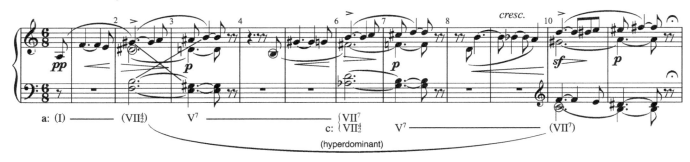

EXAMPLE 9.56E. Wagner, Prelude, *Tristan und Isolde*, harmonic prolongations, mm. 1–10 (from Morgan, "Circular Form," Ex. 5).

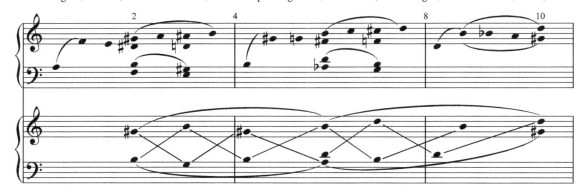

EXAMPLE 9.56F. Wagner, "Mild und Leise" ("Liebestod"), *Tristan und Isolde*, mm. 72–79.

a dominant prolongation then continues into the next link of the chain. Note that at the end of measure 4, Wagner alters the size of the ascending sixth leap by beginning it with B♮ (circled) instead of C, so as not to interfere with the dominant sonority of A that is still lingering in our imagination. The Tristan chord of measure 6 can also be easily interpreted as projecting that same dominant, the F♮ functioning as a ninth. The prolongation is then literally broken at measure 7 when G, the dominant of C, replaces the implied bass note E that has been effective at least since measure 3. But even the music that follows in measures 8–10 continues to project some of the pitches associated with the dominant of A, as a sketch by Morgan reveals (Ex. 9.56e).[170] Indeed, if we recall that a single, enharmonically equivalent, diminished-seventh sonority can function as a substitute for both the dominants of A and C, then we can recognize the prolongation of a single *hyperdominant*

---

170. Morgan, "Circular Form," 96, Ex. 5.

in measures 2–10.[171] In proposing that the opening of the prelude features a hyperdominant prolongation, I am not trying to undermine my earlier analysis, which saw cadential progressions embedded within a sequential pattern. I would hold that all three categories of harmonic progression are operative here and that their particular mode of interaction contributes to the remarkable effect that this passage has exerted on listeners since the mid-nineteenth century.

Having concluded a harmonic and cadential analysis of the prelude itself, I must nonetheless consider what happens to the Tristan chord and its attendant "desire" motive at the very end of the entire opera, the closing measures of the "Liebestod" (Ex. 9.56f, downbeat of m. 75). From the perspective developed here, it is readily apparent that the extraordinary sense of ultimate resolution and emotional discharge that some critics find here arises in part from Wagner setting the chord and its motive within an unambiguous *tonic* prolongation, just the type of harmonic progression he had so systematically shunned throughout the prelude. The wider context for this final appearance of the motive has already been discussed in connection with the feigned plagal closure occurring at measure 61 (Ex. 9.31). The rest of the music is entirely tonic prolongational to support a long postcadential closing section. At measure 75 (Ex. 9.56f), the Tristan chord appears as a chromatically altered secondary dominant of the minor subdominant, which, as a neighboring harmony, leads back to tonic. There is no hint of a forward-striving sequence nor any finality of cadential closure. The potential plagal closure is rather a plagal prolongation within a postcadential environment, a "plagal codetta," typical of so many works in this style period. The "desire and longing" associated with the motive emerges from, and dissolves back into, the stasis of harmonic prolongation, perhaps the most fitting harmonic metaphor for *Liebestod*, "love-death."

---

171. See the earlier discussion of hyperdominant prolongation in Chapter 4, sec. 4.4.3.3. Morgan's sketch (Ex. 9.56e) also suggests the idea of a single prolongation in mm. 2–10.

# Glossary of Terms

**abandoned cadence** A moment of arrival that fails to realize an implied authentic cadence due to the abandonment of its ongoing cadential progression.

**abandoned cadential progression** The failure to complete an ongoing authentic cadential progression (1) through the undermining of an already sounding root-position dominant via a change to its first inversion, (2) through the immediate appearance of an inverted dominant in place of its root-position form, or (3) through the complete absence of any cadential dominant.

**Alberti bass** A conventional accompanimental pattern consisting of arpeggiation figurations (compare **drum bass; murky bass**).

**alto melodic pattern** A cadential melody whose fundamental pitches consist of scale degrees $\hat{3}$–$\hat{2}$–$\hat{7}$–$\hat{1}$.

**anacrusis dominant** A noncadential dominant harmony that is situated in an introductory (before-the-beginning) formal context.

**annunciating function** The effect of a half cadence to shift a listener's attention forward in time to anticipate further thematic processes that will lead eventually to complete closure.

**answer (A)** A version of a fugal subject that is, more or less, transposed a fifth higher (or fourth lower).

**antecedent** An initiating phrase function consisting of a unit that closes with a weak cadence, thus implying a repetition (a consequent) to bring stronger cadential closure.

**antecedent phrase** The first phrase of the period theme type, containing a basic idea followed by a contrasting idea, which leads to a weak cadence.

**ascending melodic pattern** A cadential melody whose fundamental pitches consist of scale degrees $\hat{5}$–$\hat{6}$–$\hat{7}$–$\hat{8}$.

**authentic cadence (AC)** A cadential arrival articulated by the final tonic of an authentic cadential progression.

**authentic cadential progression (ACP)** A four-stage cadential progression whose complete form brings, in order, the harmonic functions of (1) tonic, usually in first inversion, (2) pre-dominant, (3) dominant, in root position, and (4) tonic, in root position (compare **half cadential progression; deceptive cadential progression**).

**baroque binary** A full-movement form consisting of two main parts, each of which is indicated to be repeated. The initiating material of part 1 is typically used to open part 2 but is rarely used later in the second part to mark a new beginning (in the sense of a reprise or recapitulation). The form is used as the basis of many dance-suite movements as well as some preludes.

**basic idea** An initiating function consisting of a two-measure idea that usually contains several melodic or rhythmic motives constituting the primary material of a theme.

**basic melodic pattern** Any one of four patterns—simple, soprano, alto, and tenor—that features an overall descending melodic profile (compare **varied melodic pattern**).

**basic model (bass line)** A pattern of pitches that represents the standard bass line supporting a thematic unit: ①–②–③–④–⑤–① (see also **modulating model; period model**).

**bass line** The melodic organization of the bass voice, consisting of two streams—prolongational and cadential (see also **cadential stream; prolongational stream**).

**bass melodic pattern** A cadential melody whose fundamental pitches ($\hat{3}$–$\hat{4}$–$\hat{5}$–$\hat{1}$) are associated with a standard cadential bass line.

**blurring** In fugue, the use of various textural techniques (embellishments, ongoing rhythmic continuity, overlapping subject entries) that obscure an unambiguous sense of cadential closure. It affects the rhetorical expression of a cadence, not its syntactical function.

**cadence** The general term for the most commonly employed mode of thematic closure in tonal music.

**cadential arrival** A time point marking the structural end of a thematic unit.

**cadential idea** A concluding idea function consisting of a two-measure (or shorter) unit, supported exclusively by a cadential progression, that effects (or implies) a cadence.

**cadential content** The material (e.g., harmonic, melodic, rhythmic) that normally constitutes cadential function. It may occasionally be associated with initiating phrase functions.

**cadential function** A concluding phrase function that produces the requisite conditions for thematic closure. It is supported exclusively by one or more cadential progressions.

**cadential phrase** A phrase supported exclusively by an expanded cadential progression. It does not usually exhibit continuational characteristics (compare **continuation⇒cadential phrase**).

**cadential progression** A progression that confirms a tonality and provides the harmonic support for cadential formal function (see also **authentic cadential progression, deceptive cadential progression,** and **half cadential progression**).

**cadential six-four** A second-inversion triad, built out of the pitches of a tonic harmony, that functions in a cadential context as a dominant harmony with upper-voice embellishments.

**cadential stream** A component of a bass-line melody, focused around ⑤, that traverses scale degrees ③–⑥, ascending or descending (compare **prolongational stream**).

*cadenza doppia* **(double cadence)** A baroque cadential configuration in which the stage-3 dominant is normally embellished by the figured-bass pattern $\substack{5\\3}$ $\substack{6\\4}$ $\substack{4\\2}$ $\substack{3}$. Many harmonic variants of the configuration are found, but one of the upper voices typically brings the scale-degree succession $\hat{7}$–$\hat{1}$–$\hat{7}$–$\hat{1}$ associated with an alto stream.

*cadenza simplice* **(simple cadence)** A baroque cadential configuration consisting of the harmonic progression I–V–I.

**characteristic material** Melodic and rhythmic configurations used to define a theme as unique (compare **conventional material**).

**circularity** A formal process in which a closing unit brings back the material of the initiating unit.

**clausula** An alternative term for cadence, especially in theories of medieval and Renaissance music.

**closing ritornello** The final section of concerto form. It fulfills a similar function as the subordinate-key ritornello, except that it resides entirely in the home key and is usually interrupted by a solo cadenza.

**closing section** A postcadential phrase function following a perfect authentic cadence. It consists of a group of codettas, often featuring fragmentation and a recessive dynamic.

**closure** The general process of creating a sense of ending (or closing, conclusion, completion, termination) at any level in the structural hierarchy of a musical work.

**coda** A framing section function that follows the final structural section of the complete form (e.g., a recapitulation in sonata form, a return of the main theme in large-ternary form). It contains one or more coda themes to further reinforce the home key and to serve various compensatory functions.

**coda theme** In a coda, a thematic unit that closes with a home-key perfect authentic cadence. It usually features loosening devices typical of a subordinate theme.

**codetta** A postcadential idea function constituting a closing section. It follows a perfect authentic cadence and ranges in length from a single chord to a four-measure phrase. It is supported by a tonic prolongational (occasionally a cadential) progression.

**compact cadence** A cadential function whose time span is less than four measures (or less than three measures for a half cadence); compare **expanded cadence**.

**complete cadential progression** A cadential progression that contains all of its constituent harmonic functions (compare **incomplete cadential progression**).

**compound antecedent** An initiating phrase function consisting of a simple sentence or hybrid that closes with a weak cadence, thus implying a repetition (a compound consequent) to bring stronger cadential closure.

**compound basic idea** An initiating phrase function that is a hybrid of a presentation and antecedent. It is a four-measure phrase consisting of a basic idea followed by a contrasting idea, which does not lead to cadential closure. It is supported by a tonic prolongational progression.

**compound consequent** A concluding phrase function that repeats a prior compound antecedent but ends with stronger cadential closure.

**compound melody** A melody, in one voice, that features extensive leaping motion in a manner as to project the sense of multiple voices.

**compound meter** In eighteenth-century theory, a type of meter (e.g., 4/4) that arises from the combination of two simple meters (e.g., 2/4). It typically results in the notation of R = ½N.

**compound period** A compound theme type consisting of a compound antecedent and a compound consequent.

**compound presentation** An initiating phrase function consisting of a compound basic idea and its repetition, supported by a prolongation of tonic harmony.

**compound sentence** A compound theme type consisting of a compound presentation and an eight-measure continuation, the latter often compressed.

**compound theme** A more complex version of the simple eight-measure period or sentence (rarely, a hybrid). It is normatively sixteen measures in length.

**concluding function** Any number of formal functions at various hierarchical levels that express the temporal quality of "ending" (compare **initiating function; medial function**).

**consequent** A concluding phrase function that repeats a prior antecedent but ends with stronger cadential closure.

**consequent phrase** The second phrase of the period theme type. It restates the basic idea from the antecedent, followed by a

**contrasting (or cadential) idea**, leading to strong cadential closure (usually a perfect authentic cadence).

**contextual formal function** The formal function of a unit based on its actual location (as beginning, middle, or end) within a broader formal context (compare **intrinsic formal function**).

**continuation** A medial phrase function that destabilizes the prevailing formal context by means of fragmentation, harmonic acceleration, faster surface rhythm, or harmonic sequence.

**continuation phrase** The second phrase of the sentence theme type. It fuses continuation and cadential functions.

**continuation⇒cadential phrase** A phrase supported exclusively by an expanded cadential progression. It fuses continuation and cadential functions (compare **cadential phrase**.

**contrasting idea** A concluding function consisting of a two-measure unit that follows and contrasts with (i.e., is not a repetition of) a basic idea.

**contrasting middle (B section)** A medial function that loosens the prevailing formal organization, emphasizes the home-key dominant, and generally closes with a half cadence (or dominant arrival). The second unit of the small-ternary theme type. It may also appear at the beginning of part 2 of the small binary theme type.

**conventional material** Melodic and rhythmic configurations widely used within the style and thus potentially interchangeable from piece to piece (compare **characteristic material**).

**converging half cadence** A half cadence whose bass line ascends to $\hat{5}$, typically against a melody that descends to $\hat{2}$ or $\hat{7}$ (compare **expanding half cadence**).

**core** A thematic unit of a development consisting of a relatively large model (four to eight measures), one or more sequential repetitions, fragmentation, a concluding half cadence (or dominant arrival), and a postcadential standing on the dominant.

**core substitute** A thematic unit standing in place of a regular core in a development. It may be a pseudo-core or may be organized like a transition or (modulating) subordinate theme.

**countersubject (CS)** A "counterpoint to the subject"; a recurring melodic idea that appears simultaneously with the subject (or answer).

**couplet** In rondo form, a large-scale section situated between, and contrasting with, statements of the refrain.

**covered cadence** An elided perfect authentic cadence, in which the melodic pitch that initiates the next thematic unit, usually $\hat{3}$ or $\hat{5}$, lies above the final melodic pitch of the cadence ($\hat{1}$). It thus resembles an imperfect authentic cadence but does not genuinely function as that cadence type. The situation is occasionally inverted, such that an implied imperfect authentic cadence is covered by $\hat{1}$ to initiate the next formal unit.

**Cudworth** A galant cadential schema featuring a rapidly falling scale from $\hat{7}$ down to $\hat{3}$, with a slower continuation to $\hat{1}$.

**deceptive-authentic combination** A single cadential melody whose fundamental pitches are supported together by a deceptive cadential progression and an immediately following authentic cadential progression.

**deceptive cadence** The failure to realize an implied authentic cadence by replacing the final tonic with another harmony (e.g., VI, VII⁶/V, I⁶), which nonetheless represents a provisional end of the prevailing thematic process.

**deceptive cadence ($\hat{3}$)** A deceptive cadence whose melody concludes on $\hat{3}$, thus representing a deviation of an implied IAC.

**deceptive cadential progression (DCP)** A varied form of the authentic cadential progression in which the final tonic is replaced by a related harmony (e.g., VI, VII⁶/V, I⁶) (compare **authentic cadential progression**; **half cadential progression**).

**deceptive half cadence** In a context that implies half cadential closure in the prevailing key, a sudden digression to a related tonal region to create a half cadence, whose dominant stands in place of the dominant of the expected key.

**deceptive resolution** Any case of a dominant harmony resolving to a harmony (usually VI) that substitutes for an implied tonic. The harmonic context for such a resolution may be cadential (within a DCP) or noncadential (prolongational, sequential).

**dependent plagal closure** The appearance of plagal closure in a formal context that implies authentic cadential closure (compare **independent plagal closure**).

**detour cadence** Toward the end of a thematic process, a cadence that appears as the result of a sudden digression from the prevailing key in order to confirm a more remote tonal region. It is usually paired by an immediately following cadence that closes the theme in its expected key.

**development** A medial section function standing between an exposition and a recapitulation. It may contain a pre-core, one or more cores (or core substitutes), and a retransition. It creates the loosest formal expression in the movement.

**development key (DK)** A tonal region (besides the home or subordinate keys) that is confirmed, usually in a development section, by some cadential function, though not necessarily by an actual cadence: in major-mode movements, VI, III, and II; in minor-mode ones, IV and V.

**deviations (cadential)** Devices that serve to deny the realization of an implied cadence. Authentic cadential deviations include deceptive, evaded, and abandoned cadences; half cadential deviations include various forms of dominant arrivals.

**dissipated cadence** A cadential situation in which a presumed penultimate dominant (promising an authentic cadence) is converted into an ultimate dominant to support a postcadential standing on the dominant, one that typically features wholesale liquidation and a highly recessive dynamic. The transformed dominant then resolves to a tonic harmony that is no longer cadential but rather functions exclusively as the beginning of a new thematic process.

**dominant** Various harmonies whose primary role is to progress to tonic. All dominant-functioning harmonies contain the leading tone.

**dominant arrival** A deviation of a half cadence. It arises (1) by undermining the final dominant through the addition of a dissonant seventh) or (2) through the appearance of a terminal dominant, one that arises from a prolongational or sequential progression (see also **premature dominant arrival**).

**dominant proper** Within a cadential progression, the manifestation of dominant harmony (e.g., $V^5_3$, $V^7$, $V^4_2$) that arises from the resolution of a cadential six-four.

**dominant version** A unit (typically a basic idea) whose initial harmonic support is dominant (compare **tonic version**).

*doppia* **premature dominant arrival** A type of premature dominant arrival characterized by a harmonic-contrapuntal configuration that resembles a *cadenza doppia*.

**doubled monophony** A type of texture consisting of multiple voices sounding the identical material in different octaves (compare **monophony**)

**drum bass** A conventional accompanimental pattern consisting of repeated block chords (compare **Alberti bass**; **murky bass**).

**dynamic curve** A particular pattern of progressive and regressive dynamics.

**early perfect authentic cadence** In minuet form, the appearance of a home-key perfect authentic cadence before the end of the exposition (A section).

**elided cadence** A cadential arrival that marks both the end of an ongoing formal unit and the beginning of the next unit.

**elision** Any moment of time (cadential or otherwise) that simultaneously marks the end of one formal unit and the beginning of the next unit.

**end** An articulation of formal closure (compare **stop**).

**episode** In fugue, a passage of music that does not contain the complete subject (though motives of the subject may be included within an episode); episodes are usually organized by model-sequence technique.

**episode fugue** A fugue that, following the exposition, consists largely of episodes alternating with subject entries (compare **stretto fugue**).

**evaded cadence** The failure of an implied authentic cadence to reach its goal harmony. The event appearing in place of the final tonic groups with the subsequent formal unit and (usually) represents the beginning of a repetition of a prior continuation or cadential passage.

**even-measure strong** An interpretation of hypermeter that regards the even-numbered measures of a normative eight-measure theme as metrically accented (compare **odd-numbered strong**).

**exact repetition** A unit (usually a basic idea or fragment) immediately restated in the same harmonic context (although the melody may be altered or transposed to different scale degrees).

**expanded cadence** A cadential function whose time span is four or more measures (or three or more measures for a half cadence) (compare **compact cadence**).

**expanded cadential progression (ECP)** An expansion of a cadential progression to the extent of its supporting a complete phrase (of at least four measures) or group of phrases. An expanded half cadential progression may be minimally three measures.

**expanding half cadence** A half cadence whose bass line descends to ⑤, typically against a melody that ascends to $\hat{5}$ (compare **converging half cadence**).

**expansion** An internal lengthening of the constituent members of a formal function (compare **extension**).

**exposition (A section)** An initiating function consisting of a complete thematic unit ending with a perfect authentic cadence. The first unit of the small ternary theme type.

**exposition (fugue)** The opening section of a fugue, consisting of alternating subject and answer versions. The exposition ends at that point where the final voice completes the subject (or answer). An internal episode may occur between the subject entries.

**exposition (full movement)** An initiating section function consisting of main theme (group), transition, and subordinate theme (group).

**extension** The addition of extra units (usually of similar material) in order to stretch out a formal function in time (compare **expansion**).

**failed consequent** A unit that follows an antecedent in the sense of a consequent but does not close with the expected stronger cadence.

**false closing section** A closing section that is reinterpreted retrospectively as an initiation (usually a presentation) of a subsequent thematic unit.

**false recapitulation** Near the end of a development or a rondo couplet, the appearance of main-theme material in a tonal region other than tonic of the home key.

**feigned plagal closure** An authentic cadence whose final tonic is embellished by an appoggiatura subdominant such that the resulting IV–I progression gives the pretense of plagal closure.

**final cadence** In fugue, the very last home-key authentic cadence (normally a PAC) (compare **interior cadence**).

**"final" deceptive cadence** At the close of a complete movement (or comparable formal unit), a deceptive cadence that is not followed by any further cadential activity, but rather by material whose intrinsic function is postcadential; the deceptive cadence thus retrospectively takes on the role of marking closure for the movement, yielding a situation that can be labelled dec. cad.⇒"PAC" (or "IAC").

**final dominant** In the context of a dominant arrival, the root-position dominant triad that concludes a half cadential progression (compare **terminal dominant**; **ultimate dominant**).

**final tonic** The root-position tonic that concludes an authentic cadential progression

**five-part rondo** A full-movement form in which a refrain alternates with two couplets. Couplet 1 is a subordinate-theme complex or an interior theme; couplet 2 is an interior theme or development-like unit.

**form-functional dissonance** A situation in which the intrinsic function of a formal unit conflicts with its contextual function.

**formal function** The specific way a musical passage expresses a more general temporal quality, such as beginning, being in the middle, ending, before the beginning, or after the end. Depending on the hierarchical level involved, formal functions can be further characterized as idea functions, phrase functions, thematic functions, and section functions.

**fragmentation** A reduction in the length of units in relation to the prevailing grouping structure. Fragmented units do not necessarily contain melodic-motivic material derived from the immediately preceding units.

**framing function** Any number of functions at various hierarchical levels that precede the beginning or follow the end of a formal unit.

**fusion** The combining together, or merging, of two formal functions within a single unit.

**gap-fill** A melodic process in which a leap in one direction is filled in by stepwise motion in the opposite direction, e.g., C–G (gap), F–E–D–C (fill).

**group** A general term for any self-contained "chunk" of music, embracing its complete melodic, harmonic, rhythmic, and textural content (compare **segmentation**). More specifically, it can refer to multiple units of a given formal function (e.g., subordinate theme group).

**grouping structure** The organization of discrete, perceptually significant time spans (group, unit, part, section, etc.) at any or all hierarchical levels in a movement.

**half cadence (HC)** A cadential arrival articulated by the final dominant of a half cadential progression.

**half cadential progression** A three-stage cadential progression whose complete form brings, in order, the harmonic functions of (1) tonic, (2) pre-dominant, and (3) dominant, a triad in root position (compare **authentic cadential progression**; **deceptive cadential progression**).

**harmonic acceleration** An increase in the rate of harmonic change.

**harmonic dualism** An approach to pitch organization that considers major and minor to be fully independent systems of harmony and tonality. In most such accounts, the major harmony is generated upward from a root to higher harmonic components (third, fifth) whereas the minor harmony is generated downward from a root to lower components (compare **harmonic monism**).

**harmonic function** One of three fundamental harmonies—tonic, dominant, and pre-dominant—that embrace all other harmonic formations in a key.

**harmonic monism** An approach to pitch organization that considers major and minor to be modal variants of a single system of harmony and tonality. In such an account, both major and minor harmonies are generated upward from a root to higher harmonic components (third, fifth) (compare **harmonic dualism**).

**harmonic relationship** An intervallic relationship between pitches, residing in different voices, that is established in reference to a triadic collection of pitches (compare **melodic relationship**).

**home key (HK)** The principal tonality of a movement. The key in which a movement begins and ends and to which all other keys or tonal regions ultimately relate.

**homophony** A type of texture consisting of multiple voices that exhibit a strong uniformity in musical material (compare **polyphony**).

**hybrid theme** A simple theme type combining functions associated with both the sentence and the period. Four basic patterns are: antecedent + continuation, antecedent + cadential, compound basic idea + continuation, and compound basic idea + consequent.

**hyperdominant prolongation** A prolongational progression that engages two or more dominant harmonies whose roots lie a minor third or a tritone apart. In that these individual dominants can be substituted by a single, enharmonically equivalent, diminished-seventh sonority, the effect of prolonging one, all-embracing, dominant function is thereby expressed.

**hypermeter** The perception that real measures, or groups of such measures, can be differentiated as metrically strong or weak.

**iconic cadence** In the late nineteenth century, a cadential configuration that, in a highly flamboyant, almost exaggerated, manner, references the classical cadence. Though it represents an apotheosis of cadence, it may, ironically, not function as a genuine cadence.

**idea** Minimally, a two-measure unit. A constituent member of a phrase.

**idea function** The specific formal function accorded to a given idea. It serves as a constituent function of a phrase (compare **phrase function; thematic function; section function**).

**imperfect authentic cadence (IAC)** An authentic cadence in which the soprano voice ends on the third scale degree (compare **perfect authentic cadence**).

**imperfect authentic cadence (Prinner type)** An IAC in which a Prinner melody ($\hat{6}$–$\hat{5}$–$\hat{4}$–$\hat{3}$) is supported by a standard cadential bass line (④–⑤–①).

**implication/realization (I/R)** A situation in which a compositional process of some kind (typically a melodic process, but also a harmonic, rhythmic, cadential, or formal one) arouses implications of possible continuations, of which some (or even none) are eventually realized.

**incomplete cadential progression** A cadential progression that omits either an initial tonic or a pre-dominant (or both) (compare **complete cadential progression**).

**independent cadence (fugue)** A cadence of any type that is not associated with the conclusion of the subject (or answer). It usually ends extended passages or sections of the fugue (compare **subject-ending cadence**).

**independent imperfect authentic cadence (or cadential deviation)** An IAC (or an authentic cadential deviation) that appears in a formal context that does not imply a pending PAC. It typically occurs in connection with an antecedent unit of a periodic theme (compare **way-station imperfect authentic cadence**).

**independent plagal closure** The appearance of plagal closure in a formal context that does not imply authentic cadential closure (compare **dependent plagal closure**).

**initial tonic** The tonic harmony, typically in first inversion, that begins a cadential progression.

**initiating function** Any number of formal functions at various hierarchical levels that express the temporal quality of "beginning" (compare **medial function; concluding function**).

**initiating harmony** Generally, the opening harmony of any harmonic or formal process. More specifically, the harmony that immediately follows an evaded cadence and supports the onset of the next formal unit (compare **replacement harmony**).

**interior cadence** In fugue, a cadence, of any type that occurs prior to the final cadence.

**interior theme** In large ternary or rondo forms, a medial thematic function, standing between statements of a main theme, that is modeled largely on the small ternary or small binary theme types. It resides in the contrasting modality of the main theme (*minore* or *maggiore*) or in the subdominant or submediant regions. It often is formally incomplete, concluding with dominant harmony of the home key as a half cadence or dominant arrival.

**internal episode** Within a fugal exposition, a short episode that stands between any two subject and answer entries.

**internal half cadence** A half cadence appearing within the boundaries of a subordinate theme. It can be followed by a new continuation (or cadential) passage, or it can mark the end of the first part of a two-part subordinate theme.

**interpolation** Unrelated material inserted between two logically succeeding harmonies or formal functions.

**intrinsic formal function** The formal function of a unit expressed by its musical content, irrespective of its actual location within a broader formal context (compare **contextual formal function**).

**introduction** *See* **thematic introduction; slow introduction**.

**inverted deceptive cadence** A deceptive cadence in which the leading tone in an upper voice functions as a 7–6 suspension when the bass moves from ⑤ to ①, thus creating VI$^6$ as a substitute for the final tonic.

**isolated cadence (or codetta)** In nineteenth-century genres featuring textural homogeneity (such as Chopin's preludes), a final cadence (or codetta) whose sudden simplification and loss of energy seems rhythmically and texturally detached from the preceding material.

**large ternary** A tripartite full-movement form consisting of a main theme, an interior theme, and a return of the main theme (compare **small ternary**).

**lead-in** A boundary process involving a melodic link, usually following a cadential articulation, that helps provide rhythmic continuity between two adjacent formal units.

**limited cadential scope** A cadential idea whose function is confined to the unit of form that it closes (e.g., a basic idea or a codetta), without participating in any broader sense of thematic closure.

**linking harmony** A harmony that functions both as the last harmony of one progression and the first harmony of the next progression.

**liquidation** The systematic elimination of characteristic motives, a process especially associated with cadential function.

**loose** A formal organization characterized by nonconventional thematic structures, harmonic-tonal instability (modulation, chromaticism), an asymmetrical grouping structure, phrase-structural extension and expansion, form-functional redundancy, and a diversity of melodic-motivic material (compare **tight-knit**).

**low $\hat{5}$ drop** A highly conventionalized, melodic cadential gesture, used especially to end subordinate themes in a galant or classical string quartet. It features the first violin suddenly leaping down to a low dominant scale degree ($\hat{5}$) at the beginning of a cadential stage 3a, sustaining that pitch for several beats, and then leaping back up for a cadential trill on $\hat{2}$ (stage 3b) that closes on $\hat{1}$ for the cadential arrival.

**lowered leading-tone abandonment** A form of abandoned cadence whereby an expected leading tone of the cadential dominant is chromatically lowered by a half step; this technique normally redirects the implied cadence toward a tonicization of subdominant harmony.

**maggiore** A variation or interior theme set in the major mode of a minor-mode home key (compare **minore**).

**main theme** An initiating thematic function that brings the main melodic-motivic ideas of the movement, establishes and confirms the home key, and defines a standard of tight-knit organization for the movement as a whole.

**main-theme group** Two successive main themes, each ending with a perfect authentic cadence.

**medial caesura (MC)** A prominent textural break or gap, created by a moment of silence or by a fermata on the final sonority, that occurs at the literal end of the transition in order to help highlight the entrance of the subordinate theme.

**medial function** Any number of formal functions at various hierarchical levels that express the temporal quality of "being in the middle" (compare **initiating function**; **concluding function**).

**melodic diversion** A cadential melody that implies closure on $\hat{1}$ but rises instead to $\hat{3}$ to create an imperfect authentic cadence.

**melodic pattern** An unembellished, conventional melody of a cadence. It is normally placed in the structural voice, usually the uppermost one. Each fundamental pitch of the pattern is associated with an individual stage of the cadential schema (see also **stream [cadential melody]**).

**melodic relationship** An intervallic relationship between pitches, residing in the same voice, that is established in reference to a scalar collection of pitches (compare **harmonic relationship**).

**melody and accompaniment** A multi-voiced texture in which one voice (usually an upper one) carries salient melodic material, supported by conventionalized accompanimental patterns in the other (lower) voices.

**metrical extension** A case of the Prinner cadence in which the addition of ⑤, following ②, creates an extra rhythmic beat within the third stage of the schema (compare **submetrical insertion**).

**midway cadence** An interior cadence occurring roughly half of the way through a fugue.

**mini-sentence** A four-measure antecedent (or consequent) phrase whose internal organization resembles that of a sentence.

**minore** A variation or interior theme set in the minor mode of a major-mode home key (compare *maggiore*).

**minuet** A large-scale tripartite form modeled on the small ternary theme type. It consists of an exposition (A), contrasting middle (B), and recapitulation (A′). A bipartite version is modeled on the small binary theme type.

**minuet proper** The first part of minuet/trio form. It is constructed in minuet form.

**minuet/trio** A tripartite full-movement form consisting of a minuet proper, a trio, and a da capo (of the minuet proper).

**modal borrowing (modal mixture)** The use of harmonies containing notes from the opposite modality of the prevailing mode.

**modal shift** A change of mode within the same tonality.

**model** A unit established for the purpose of sequential repetition.

**model-sequence technique** A unit (the model) that is immediately followed by a restatement transposed to a different scale degree (the sequence); the same as **sequential repetition**.

**modulating model** Variants of the basic model of bass-line organization that feature a modulation to either the dominant or mediant regions.

**modulating Prinner** A version of the Prinner schema in which the first stage begins in the prevailing key with $\hat{3}$ over ① and is then reinterpreted as $\hat{6}$ over ④ in a dominant related tonality.

**modulating transition** A transition that modulates to the subordinate key, ending on dominant harmony of that key (compare **nonmodulating transition**).

**modulation** The process of changing tonal focus such that a new tonic, confirmed as such by cadential function, is perceived to displace the previous tonic (compare **tonicization**).

**monophony** A type of texture consisting of a single voice (compare **doubled monophony**)

**monothematic exposition** An exposition whose (first) subordinate theme uses melodic-motivic content derived from the main theme's basic idea.

**motive** A collection of several notes constituting the smallest meaningful melodic or rhythmic configuration.

**murky bass** A conventional accompanimental pattern consisting of broken octaves (compare **Alberti bass**; **drum bass**).

**neighboring harmony** In a prolongational progression, a subordinate harmony situated between a prolonged harmony that retains its same position (e.g., I–$V^6$–I) (compare **passing harmony**).

**nineteenth-century half cadence (19cHC)** A half cadence in which the ultimate dominant in root position includes a dissonant minor seventh. In eighteenth-century repertories this formation would be considered a dominant arrival.

**nonmodulating transition** A transition that remains in the home key, ending on dominant harmony of that key (compare **modulating transition**).

**notated measure (N)** A unit of musical time demarcated by bar lines in the score (compare **real measure**).

**odd-measure strong** An interpretation of hypermeter that regards the odd-numbered measures of a normative eight-measure theme as metrically accented (compare **even-numbered strong**).

**one-more-time technique (OMT)** Following an evaded cadence, the repetition of the previous cadential idea or phrase.

**opening ritornello** The first section of concerto form. It is organized like an exposition but remains in the home key throughout.

**overhang** A melodic embellishment that immediately follows the final structural pitch of a cadential melody.

**part** A general term for grouping structure, often used in connection with some multi-part thematic units (e.g., the first part of a small binary or the second part of a closing ritornello). In fugue, a group of sections that yields the overall form of the fugue (e.g., bipartite, tripartite).

**passage** In fugue, a lower-level formal unit consisting of a single subject entry, an episode, or a stretto.

**passing harmony** In a prolongational progression, a subordinate harmony situated between a prolonged harmony that changes position (e.g., I–$V^4_3$–$I^6$) (compare **neighboring harmony**).

**pedal point** In a prolongational progression, the replacement of the bass voice of the subordinate harmonies by the root of the prolonged harmony.

**penultimate dominant** The dominant harmony of an authentic cadential progression (compare **ultimate dominant**).

**perfect authentic cadence (PAC)** An authentic cadence in which the soprano voice ends on the tonic scale degree (compare **imperfect authentic cadence**).

**period** A simple theme type consisting of a four-measure antecedent phrase and four-measure consequent phrase.

**period model** A variant of the basic model of bass-line organization used especially in connection with the period theme type.

**phrase** Minimally, a four-measure unit, often (though not necessarily) containing two ideas.

**phrase function** The specific formal function accorded to a given phrase. It serves as a constituent function of a theme or thematic unit (compare **idea function**; **section function**; **thematic function**).

**phrygian half cadence** A half cadence in which the bass descends a half step from ♭⑥ to ⑤.

**plagal cadential/closural progression (PCP)** A tonic prolongational progression whose penultimate harmony is a subdominant; a three-stage version brings, in order, the harmonic functions of initial tonic, subdominant, and final tonic (e.g., I–IV–I); a dualist four-stage version sees a minor dominant inserted between the initial tonic and subdominant.

**plagal closure** A type of prolongational closure supported by a plagal cadential/closural progression that concludes on a root-position tonic.

**plagal codetta** A codetta supported by a plagal cadential/closural progression.

**polyphony** A type of texture consisting of multiple voices whose pitch contour and durational profiles are individualized and clearly differentiated (compare **homophony**).

**postcadential function** One of several framing functions that express the sense of "after the end." It follows a cadence and prolongs its final harmony, usually with a recessive dynamic.

**precadential dominant expansion** The elongation of a noncadential dominant immediately prior to the onset of a compact cadential progression. It is an expansion technique used primarily in the baroque and galant styles to effect formal loosening while fostering the retention of a compact cadential formula.

**pre-core** The initial unit of a development section, preceding a core or core substitute.

**pre-dominant** Various harmonies whose primary role is to progress to a dominant. One class of pre-dominants contains the natural fourth scale degree of a key; a second class contains the raised-fourth degree.

**pre-dominant arrival** The situation in which a pre-dominant ends up representing the harmonic goal of a thematic process. The subsequent dominant, to which the pre-dominant resolves, initiates the following thematic process (compare **subdominant arrival**; **tonic arrival**).

**premature dominant arrival (PDA)** A dominant arrival, on either a final or terminal dominant, that appears before the end of the prevailing melodic-motivic and phrase-structural processes.

**presentation** An initiating phrase function consisting of a basic idea and its repetition, supported by a prolongation of tonic harmony.

**presentation phrase** The first phrase of the sentence theme type.

**Prinner** A four-stage galant schema featuring a descending melodic line $\hat{6}$–$\hat{5}$–$\hat{4}$–$\hat{3}$ supported, in parallel thirds, by the bass ④–③–②–①.

**Prinner cadence (PrC)** A cadential schema in which the modification of the Prinner sees an inserted ⑤ (at the end of stage three) supporting a root-position dominant in order to create a variant form of the imperfect authentic cadence.

**progressive dynamic** A systematic buildup of tension and excitement by various musical means, including intensity, texture, and rhythmic activity (compare **recessive dynamic**).

**prolongational closure** A noncadential mode of thematic closure supported by a tonic prolongational progression that ends typically with tonic in root position (less frequently in first inversion).

**prolongational progression** A harmonic progression that sustains the perception of an individual harmony (the prolonged harmony) through time despite the presence of an intervening, subordinate harmony of a different harmonic meaning.

**prolongational stream** A component of a bass-line melody, focused around scale degree ①, that traverses scale degrees ①–④ or ⑥–①, each ascending or descending (compare **cadential stream**).

**prolonged harmony** The harmony that is prolonged by a prolongational progression.

**Pulcinella** A galant schema built over the bass line of a deceptive cadential progression (③–④–⑤–⑥), but whose harmony is actually tonic prolongational. It typically features a sustained $\hat{1}$ (sometimes $\hat{3}$ or $\hat{5}$) in an upper or middle voice. It tends to occur in precadential formal contexts, thus leading directly to an authentic cadence.

**pulse stream** A series of discrete pulses (i.e., undifferentiated rhythmic beats) at a single level in the metrical hierarchy of a work.

**Quiescenza** A galant schema that prolongs tonic harmony built over a tonic pedal and that features an initial tonicization of subdominant harmony (e.g., I–V⁷/IV–IV–V⁷–I). Its melodic component is typically $\hat{1}$–♭$\hat{7}$–$\hat{6}$–♮$\hat{7}$–$\hat{1}$. It tends to occur in postcadential formal contexts, occasionally in initiating ones.

**R = ½N** A notational practice whereby a single real measure (R) constitutes one half of a notated measure (N) (see also **compound meter**).

**R = 2N** A notational practice whereby a single real measure (R) constitutes two notated measures (N).

**real answer** In fugue, a type of answer in which every note of the subject is transposed a fifth higher (or fourth lower) (compare **tonal answer**).

**real measure (R)** A unit of musical time corresponding to a listener's perception of a "full measure" of music (compare **notated measure**).

**recapitulation (A′ section)** A concluding function that represents a return (often adjusted and altered) of an earlier exposition. The third unit of the small ternary theme type.

**recapitulation (full movement)** A concluding section function that brings back, usually modified, an earlier exposition. It resolves tonal conflicts by adjusting all material into the home key.

**recessive dynamic** A systematic abatement of tension and excitement by various musical means, including intensity, texture, and rhythmic activity (compare **progressive dynamic**).

**refrain** The initial section of any rondo form. It functions as a main theme and is usually built as a small ternary or small binary. It regularly alternates with two or more couplets.

**reinterpreted half cadence** A local authentic cadence in the dominant region of the prevailing key that is reinterpreted retrospectively as a half cadence when the music immediately returns to the original key.

**reopened half cadence** A situation in which an authentic cadence (or a substitute deceptive cadence) is followed immediately by a root-position dominant to give the effect of an HC, typically to end an antecedent. A matching consequent follows, which is normally closed by the same authentic cadence that was promised to occur in the previous phrase.

**repetition** The immediate restatement of a unit (compare **return**).

**repetition/terminal-modification paradigm** A general mode of closure whereby a series of repeated events yields to an event that is altered such that we perceive that modified event as conclusive.

**replacement harmony** In a deceptive cadential progression, the harmony that stands in place of the final tonic (compare **initiating harmony**).

**response** *See* **dominant version** (compare **statement**).

**restatement** The reappearance of any formal unit as either a repetition or a return, with or without ornamental or structural changes.

**retransition** A formal function that effects a modulation from a subordinate key or development key to the home key, thus preparing for the return of a main theme or an A′ section. It may range in length from a single chord to a multi-phrase unit, and it frequently anticipates motives of the main theme's basic idea.

**retrospective reinterpretation** (⇒) Changing an analytical interpretation of a harmonic or formal function originally formed on the basis of one context in light of perceiving a newer context. Through this process, one function "becomes" (⇒) another function.

**return** A restatement of a unit following an intervening, contrasting unit (compare **repetition**).

**rhetorical strength** The strength (or weakness) exhibited by a cadence according to its dynamic, textural, and metrical features (compare **syntactical strength**).

**rocking on the tonic** A significant expansion of stage 1 of a cadential progression whereby the initial tonic (typically $I^6$) is prolonged by a neighboring dominant (typically $V^4_2$). It gives the impression of a "rocking back and forth" of the two harmonies of the prolongation.

**rondo** Any one of a number of full-movement forms in which a single refrain alternates with two or more couplets.

**rotation** Bringing back in a later part of the form (such as the recapitulation) the same ordering of musical events that was established in an earlier part (such as the exposition).

**rounded binary** A version of the small ternary theme type that first repeats the exposition and then repeats together the contrasting middle and recapitulation (compare **small binary**).

**schema** A formulaic melodic-contrapuntal-harmonic configuration consisting of two or more stages.

**section** A general term for grouping structure (e.g., the closing section of a subordinate theme, the development section of a sonata). In fugue, a relatively higher-level formal unit consisting of two or more passages.

**section function** The specific formal function accorded to a given large-scale section (e.g., exposition). It serves as a constituent function of a full-movement form (compare **idea function**; **phrase function**; **thematic function**).

**segmentation** the division of a succession of musical events into perceivable groups of events (compare **group**).

**sentence** A simple theme type consisting of a four-measure presentation phrase and a four-measure continuation (or continuation⇒cadential) phrase.

**sentential (sentence-like) organization** A thematic organization resembling a sentence, but often considerably looser than the standard sentence theme type.

**sentential antecedent** *See* **mini-sentence**.

**sequence** A sequentially repeated version of a model.

**sequential progression** A harmonic progression that projects a consistent intervallic pattern among the individual voices of the harmonies. It is classified in terms of the intervallic motion of its constituent roots (e.g., descending-fifth sequence, ascending-second sequence).

**sequential repetition** A unit that is followed by a restatement transposed to a different scale degree; the same as **model-sequence technique**.

**simple half cadence** A half cadence consisting of the progression I to V.

**simple melodic pattern** A cadential melody whose fundamental pitches consist of scale degrees $\hat{3}$–$\hat{2}$–$\hat{2}$–$\hat{1}$.

**simple theme** A sentence, period, or hybrid composed of eight real measures. Deviation techniques can render a simple theme more or less than eight measures (compare **compound theme**).

**simultaneously combined pattern** A cadential melody employing fundamental pitches from two or more streams at the same time (compare **successively combined pattern**; **compound melody**).

**slow introduction** A framing section function that expresses the sense of "before the beginning." It precedes a full-movement exposition (compare **thematic introduction**).

**small binary** A bipartite theme type whose parts are normally repeated. It resembles the rounded binary except that the second part contains no recapitulatory function and the first part may end with a half cadence (compare **rounded binary**).

**small ternary** A tripartite theme type consisting of an exposition (A), contrasting middle (B), and recapitulation (A′) (compare **large ternary**).

**sonata** A tripartite full-movement form containing an exposition, development, and recapitulation; a slow introduction and a coda may also be included.

**soprano melodic pattern** A cadential melody whose fundamental pitches consist of scale degrees $\hat{5}$–$\hat{4}$–$\hat{2}$–$\hat{1}$.

**soprano-tenor construct** A two-voice cadential configuration, widely used in medieval and Renaissance music, consisting of a contrapuntal progression from an imperfect consonance (a sixth or third) to a perfect consonance (an octave or unison), respectively.

**stages** The ordered components of a schema, typically defined by the scale degrees of the bass and a corresponding upper voice, usually the soprano. The stages of a cadential schema are congruent with the basic harmonies of the cadential progression.

**standing on the dominant** As a postcadential phrase function, it follows a half cadence and consists of one or more ideas supported exclusively by a dominant prolongation. As a medial phrase function, it may also follow a perfect authentic cadence at the end of a small ternary exposition to initiate a contrasting middle.

**statement** *See* **tonic version** (compare **response**).

**statement-response repetition** A tonic version of a unit (usually a basic idea) immediately restated by a dominant version.

**statistical (secondary) parameter** A parameter (e.g., dynamics, tempo, timbre) whose elements form a gradated continuum such that no individual event can express a quality of closure (compare **syntactical [primary] parameter**).

**stop** A cessation of musical activity at any point in a formal unit, not necessarily following a moment of cadential arrival (compare **end**).

**stream (bass line)** Either one of two melodic voices—prolongational or cadential—constituting a bass line (see also **prolongational stream**; **cadential stream**).

**stream (cadential melody)** A generalized melodic configuration associated with the soprano, alto, and tenor melodic patterns. Whereas a pattern occurs entirely in the structural (uppermost) voice, a stream may be placed in any literal voice. Various combinations of streams may give rise to additional patterns.

**stretto** Following a fugal exposition, a passage bringing overlapping entries of the subject.

**stretto fugue** A fugue that, following the exposition, largely consists of stretto passages (compare **episode fugue**).

**subdominant** A harmony whose root is the fourth scale degree of a key. It functions cadentially as a pre-dominant harmony when progressing to a root-position dominant. It functions prolongationally when progressing to an inverted dominant or to a tonic.

**subdominant arrival** The situation in which a subdominant harmony ends up representing the harmonic goal of a thematic process. The subsequent tonic, to which the subdominant resolves, initiates the following thematic process (compare **pre-dominant arrival**; **tonic arrival**).

**subject (S)** The principal melodic idea of a fugue (see also **answer**).

**subject-ending cadence** In fugue, an authentic cadence that occurs with the final pitches of the subject (or answer); such cadences are usually limited in scope to the subject itself, but may occasionally seem to conclude an extended passage or section of a fugue (compare **independent cadence**).

**subject entry** Following a fugal exposition, a passage of music consisting of the complete subject (or answer) in one voice; the other voices may bring one or more countersubjects or free counterpoint.

**subject transformation** In fugue, an alteration of the subject by means of transposition, inversion, augmentation, diminution, etc.

**submetrical insertion** A case of the Prinner cadence in which the addition of ⑤, following ②, takes place within the single rhythmic beat accorded to the third stage of the schema (compare **metrical extension**).

**subordinate harmony** In a prolongational progression, a harmony (typically a dominant, sometimes a subdominant) that differs from the prolonged harmony.

**subordinate key (SK)** A closely related tonal region confirmed by a perfect authentic cadence as the principal contrasting key to the home key: in major-mode movements, the dominant region of the home key, in minor-mode ones, the mediant ("relative major").

**subordinate-key ritornello** The third section of concerto form. It reinforces the confirmation of the subordinate key, is structured as a thematic unit ending with a perfect authentic cadence, and draws on material from the opening ritornello.

**subordinate theme** The third, and final, thematic function of an exposition. It confirms a subordinate key by closing with a perfect authentic cadence and loosens the formal organization in order to solidify the new key in relation to the home key.

**subordinate-theme group** Two or more successive subordinate themes, each ending with a perfect authentic cadence.

**subordinate themelike unit** A core substitute that resembles a subordinate theme in phrase-structural organization. It ends with a perfect authentic cadence in a development key (compare **transition-like unit**).

**substitute harmony** A harmony that substitutes for a more basic harmony of a given function (e.g., VI is a harmonic substitute for I).

**successively combined pattern** A cadential melody comprised of fundamental pitches from two or more streams following one after the other (compare **simultaneously combined pattern**).

**syntactical (primary) parameter** A parameter (e.g., harmony, melody, meter) in which the succession of differentiated elements (e.g., consonance/dissonance, dominant/tonic accent/unaccent) engenders an implicative mode of continuation and eventual closure (compare **statistical [secondary] parameter**).

**syntactical strength** The strength of a cadence according to its basic type as half, imperfect authentic, or perfect authentic, in order of increasing strength (compare **rhetorical strength**).

**tenor combo** A widely employed, successively combined, cadential melodic pattern featuring scale degrees $\hat{5}$–$\hat{6}$–$\hat{1}$–$\hat{2}$–$\hat{1}$, drawn in turn from the tenor, alto, and soprano streams.

**tenor melodic pattern** A cadential melody whose fundamental pitches consist of scale degrees $\hat{8}$–$\hat{6}$–$\hat{5}$–$\hat{3}$.

**terminal dominant** In the context of a dominant arrival, a dominant harmony arising out of a prolongational or sequential progression that marks the harmonic end of a formal process (compare **final dominant**, **ultimate dominant**).

**thematic function** The specific formal function accorded to a given thematic unit. It serves as a constituent function of a full-movement form or of a principal section (e.g., an exposition) of such a form (compare **idea function**; **phrase function**; **section function**).

**thematic introduction** A framing function that expresses the sense of "before the beginning" of a thematic unit. It consists of a brief passage prolonging tonic (sometimes, dominant) with a progressive dynamic. It contains minimal melodic activity so as not to suggest a basic idea (compare **slow introduction**).

**thematic unit** A theme or themelike unit.

**theme** A unit (e.g., a main theme or subordinate theme) consisting of a conventional set of initiating, medial, and ending phrase functions. It normally closes with a cadence but may in certain loose contexts lack cadential closure (compare **themelike unit**).

**theme type** A formal type associated with themes (e.g., sentence, period, small ternary), consisting of a conventionalized set of phrase functions.

**themelike unit** A unit (e.g., a transition or a core) that resembles a theme in formal organization but is usually loosely organized and is not required to close with a cadence.

**tight-knit** A formal organization characterized by conventional theme types, harmonic-tonal stability, a symmetrical grouping structure, form-functional efficiency, and unity of melodic-motivic material (compare **loose**).

**time point** An individual moment of time.

**time span** A determinate duration of time.

**tonal answer** In fugue, a type of answer in which one or more notes of the subject is transposed by an interval other than a fifth higher (or fourth lower) (compare **real answer**).

**tonic arrival** The situation in which a noncadential, root-position tonic ends up representing the harmonic goal of a thematic process (compare **pre-dominant arrival**; **subdominant arrival**).

**tonic harmonic function** The central harmony of a key, normally built on the first scale degree of a key. It is the harmony to which all others ultimately relate and derive their meaning.

**tonic version** A unit (usually a basic idea) whose initial harmonic support is tonic (compare **dominant version**).

**tonicization** A process of emphasizing a scale degree (besides the tonic) such that it is perceived as a local tonic. A tonicized region does not receive cadential confirmation (compare **modulation**).

**transition** A thematic function that destabilizes the home key and loosens the formal organization in order for a subordinate key to be established and eventually confirmed.

**transitional introduction** A passage built over dominant harmony of a new tonal region. It typically appears at the beginning of a pre-core.

**trio** The second part of minuet/trio form. It is constructed in minuet form.

**two-gapped model** A variant of the basic model of bass-line organization in which the scalar ascent to skips over ②.

**two-part subordinate theme** A subordinate theme whose first part ends with an internal half cadence (or dominant arrival) and whose second part starts with new, initiating material.

**two-part transition** A transition whose first part is nonmodulatory and closes with a home-key dominant and whose second part, often beginning with reference to main-theme ideas, modulates to the subordinate key and closes there with dominant harmony.

**ultimate dominant** The dominant of a half cadential progression (compare **penultimate dominant**; **final dominant**; **terminal dominant**).

**unison half cadence** A half cadence with monophonic (or doubled monophonic) texture.

**unit** A general term for any self-contained "chunk" of music, embracing its complete melodic, harmonic, rhythmic, and textural content.

**varied melodic pattern** The alteration of a basic melodic pattern in which the first pitch resides one step lower than the second pitch, thus creating an ascending-descending contour for the cadential melody (compare **basic melodic pattern**).

**way-station imperfect authentic cadence (or cadential deviation)** An IAC (or an authentic cadential deviation) that appears in place of an expected PAC, thus putting off complete cadential closure to a later moment in time. It typically occurs in a subordinate theme as a means of formal loosening (compare **independent imperfect authentic cadence**).

# Bibliography

Agawu, V. Kofi. "Concepts of Closure and Chopin's Opus 28." *Music Theory Spectrum* 9 (1987): 1–17.

Agawu, V. Kofi. *Playing with Signs: A Semiotic Interpretation of Classic Music*. Princeton, NJ: Princeton University Press, 1991.

Aldwell, Edward, Carl Schachter, and Allen Cadwallader. *Harmony & Voice Leading*. 5th ed. Boston: Cengage, 2019.

Anson-Cartwright, Mark. "Concepts of Closure in Tonal Music: A Critical Study." *Theory and Practice* 32 (2007): 1–17.

Anson-Cartwright, Mark. "Elision and the Embellished Final Cadence in J. S. Bach's Preludes." *Music Analysis* 26, no. 3 (October 2007): 267–88.

Bach, Johann Sebastian. *Forty-Eight Preludes and Fugues*. Edited by Donald Francis Tovey. 2 vols. London: The Associated Board of the Royal Schools of Music, 1924.

BaileyShea, Matthew. "The Wagnerian Satz: The Rhetoric of the Sentence in Wagner's Post-Lohengrin Operas." PhD dissertation, Yale University, 2003.

Bakulina, Olga Ellen. "The Loosening Role of Polyphony: Texture and Formal Functions in Mozart's "Haydn" Quartets." *Intersections* 32, nos. 1–2 (2012): 7–42.

Barthes, Roland. *S/Z*. New York: Hill and Wang, 1974.

Beach, David. "A Recurring Pattern in Mozart's Music." *Journal of Music Theory* 27, no. 1 (1983): 1–29.

Beethoven, Ludwig van. *Beethoven's "Eroica" Sketchbook: A Critical Edition*. Edited by Lewis Lockwood and Alan Gosman. Urbana: University of Illinois Press, 2013.

Benjamin, Thomas. *The Craft of Tonal Counterpoint*. 2nd ed. New York: Routledge, 2003.

Berardi, Angelo. *Documenti Armonici*. Bologna: G. Monti, 1687.

Berger, Karol. "The First-Movement Punctuation Form in Mozart's Piano Concertos." In *Mozart's Piano Concertos: Text, Context, Interpretation*, edited by Neal Zaslaw, 239–59. Ann Arbor: University of Michigan Press, 1996.

Berry, David Carson. "Hans Weisse and the Dawn of American Schenkerism." *Journal of Musicology* 20, no. 1 (2003): 104–56.

Berry, Wallace. *Structural Functions in Music*. Englewood Cliffs, NJ: Prentice-Hall, 1976.

Biamonte, Nicole. "Variations on a Scheme: Bach's 'Crucifixus' and Chopin's and Scriabin's E-Minor Preludes." *Intégral* 26 (2012): 47–89.

Bingham, W. V. "Studies in Melody." *Psychological Review: Monograph Supplement* 12 (January 1910): 1–88.

Black, Brian. "Schubert's 'Deflected-Cadence' Transitions and the Classical Style." In *Formal Functions in Perspective: Essays on*

*Musical Form from Haydn to Adorno*, edited by Steven Vande Moortele, Julie Pedneault-Deslauriers, and Nathan John Martin. Eastman Studies in Music, 165–97. Rochester: University of Rochester Press, 2015.

Blombach, Ann K. "Phrase and Cadence: A Study of Terminology and Definition." *Journal of Music Theory Pedagogy* 1, no. 2 (Fall 1987): 225–51.

Bonds, Mark Evan. *Wordless Rhetoric: Musical Form and the Metaphor of the Oration*. Cambridge, MA: Harvard University Press, 1991.

Bregman, Albert S. *Auditory Scene Analysis: The Perceptual Organization of Sound*. Cambridge, MA: MIT Press, 1990.

Brendel, Alfred. *Music Sounded Out: Essays, Lectures, Interviews, Afterthoughts*. 1st American ed. New York: Farrar Straus Giroux, 1991.

Broyles, Michael. "Beethoven's Sonata Op. 14 No. 1—Originally for Strings?" *Journal of the American Musicological Society* 23, no. 3 (Autumn 1970): 405–19.

Budday, Wolfgang. *Grundlagen musikalischer Formen der Wiener Klassik*. Kassel: Bärenreiter, 1983.

Burkhard, Remo. "Knowledge Visualization: The Use of Complementary Visual Representations for the Transfer of Knowledge; a Model, a Framework, and Four New Approaches." Sc.D. dissertation, Swiss Federal Institute of Technology Zurich, 2005.

Burstein, L. Poundie. "The Half Cadence and Other Such Slippery Events." *Music Theory Spectrum* 36, no. 2 (Fall 2014): 203–27.

Burstein, L. Poundie. "The Half Cadence and Related Analytic Fictions." In *What Is a Cadence? Theoretical and Analytical Perspectives on Cadences in the Classical Repertoire*, edited by Markus Neuwirth and Pieter Bergé, 85–116. Leuven: Leuven University Press, 2015.

Burstein, L. Poundie. *Journeys through Galant Expositions*. New York: Oxford University Press, 2020.

Burstein, L. Poundie. "Mid-Section Cadences in Haydn's Sonata-Form Movements." *Studia Musicologica* 51, nos. 1–2 (March 2010): 91–107.

Burstein, L. Poundie. "A New View of 'Tristan': Tonal Unity in the Prelude and Conclusion to Act I." *Theory and Practice* 8, no. 1 (1983): 15–41.

Burstein, L. Poundie, and Joseph Nathan Straus. *Concise Introduction to Tonal Harmony*. 2nd ed. New York: W. W. Norton, 2020.

Byros, Vasili. "'Hauptruhepuncte des Geistes': Punctuation Schemas and the Late-Eighteenth-Century Sonata." In *What Is a Cadence? Theoretical and Analytical Perspectives on Cadences in the Classical Repertoire*, edited by Markus Neuwirth and Pieter Bergé, 215–25. Leuven: Leuven University Press, 2015.

Byros, Vasili. "Prelude on a Partimento: Invention in the Compositional Pedagogy of the German States in the Time of J. S. Bach." *Music Theory Online* 21, no. 3 (2015).

Caplin, William E. "Analysis Symposium: The Andante of Mozart's Symphony No. 40 in G Minor." In *A Composition as a Problem 2: Proceedings of the Second International Estonian Music Theory Conference*, edited by Mart Humal, 155–62. Tallinn: Eesti Muusikaakadeemia, 2000.

Caplin, William E. *Analyzing Classical Form: An Approach for the Classroom*. New York: Oxford University Press, 2013.

Caplin, William E. "Beyond the Classical Cadence: Thematic Closure in Early Romantic Music." *Music Theory Spectrum* 40, no. 1 (2018): 1–26.

Caplin, William E. "Cadence in Fugue: Modes of Closure in J. S. Bach's *Well-tempered Clavier*." *Music Theory & Analysis* 7, no. 1 (April 2020): 190–249.

Caplin, William E. "The Classical Cadence: Conceptions and Misconceptions." *Journal of the American Musicological Society* 57, no. 1 (Spring 2004): 51–117.

Caplin, William E. *Classical Form: A Theory of Formal Functions for the Instrumental Music of Haydn, Mozart, and Beethoven*. New York: Oxford University Press, 1998.

Caplin, William E. "Criteria for Analysis: Perspectives on Riemann's Mature Theory of Meter." In *The Oxford Handbook of Neo-Riemannian Music Theories*, edited by Edward Gollin and Alexander Rehding, 419–39. New York: Oxford University Press, 2011.

Caplin, William E. "The 'Expanded Cadential Progression': A Category for the Analysis of Classical Form." *Journal of Musicological Research* 7, nos. 2–3 (1987): 215–57.

Caplin, William E. "Fantastical Forms: Formal Functionality in Improvisational Genres of the Classical Era." In *Musical Improvisation in the Age of Beethoven and Open Forms*, edited by Gianmario Borio and Angela Carone, 87–114. London: Ashgate, 2017.

Caplin, William E. "Funktionale Komponenten im achttaktigen Satz." *Musiktheorie* 1, no. 3 (1986): 239–60.

Caplin, William E. "Harmonic Variants of the Expanded Cadential Progression." In *A Composition as a Problem 2: Proceedings of the Second International Estonian Music Theory Conference*, edited by Mart Humal, 49–71. Tallinn: Eesti Muusikaakadeemia, 2000.

Caplin, William E. "Harmony and Cadence in Gjerdingen's 'Prinner.'" In *What Is a Cadence? Theoretical and Analytical Perspectives on Cadences in the Classical Repertoire*, edited by Markus Neuwirth and Pieter Bergé, 17–57. Leuven: Leuven University Press, 2015.

Caplin, William E. "Schoenberg's 'Second Melody', or, 'Meyer-ed' in the Bass." In *Communication in Eighteenth-Century Music*, edited by Danuta Mirka and Kofi Agawu, 160–88. Cambridge: Cambridge University Press, 2008.

Caplin, William E. "Structural Expansion in Beethoven's Symphonic Forms." In *Beethoven's Compositional Process*, edited by William Kinderman, 27–54. Lincoln: University of Nebraska Press, 1991.

Caplin, William E. "Teaching Classical Form: Strict Categories vs. Flexible Analyses." *Dutch Journal of Music Theory/Tijdschrift voor Muziektheorie* 18, no. 3 (2013): 119–35.

Caplin, William E. "The *Tempest* Exposition: A Springboard for Form-Functional Considerations." In *Beethoven's Tempest Sonata: Perspectives of Analysis and Performance*, edited by Pieter Bergé, 87–125. Leuven: Peeters, 2009.

Caplin, William E. "Theories of Musical Rhythm in the Eighteenth and Nineteenth Centuries." In *The Cambridge History of Western Music Theory*, edited by Thomas Christensen, 657–94. Cambridge: Cambridge University Press, 2002.

Caplin, William E. "What Are Formal Functions?" In William Caplin, James Hepokoski, and James Webster, *Musical Form, Forms & Formenlehre: Three Methodological Reflections*, edited by Pieter Bergé, 21–40. Leuven: Leuven University Press, 2009.

Caplin, William E. "William Caplin Responds." *Intersections: Canadian Journal of Music/Revue canadienne de musique* 31, no. 1 (2010): 67–76.

Caplin, William E., and Nathan John Martin. "The 'Continuous Exposition' and the Concept of Subordinate Theme." *Music Analysis* 35, no. 1 (2016): 4–43.

Carroll, Noël. "Narrative Closure." *Philosophical Studies* 135, no. 1 (2007): 1–15.

Caskel, Julian. "Musical Causality and Schubert's Piano Sonata in A Major, D 959, First Movement." In *Rethinking Schubert*, edited by Lorraine Byrne Bodley and Julian Horton, 207–24. New York: Oxford University Press, 2016.

Chopin. *Preludes, Op. 28*. Edited by Thomas Higgens. New York: Norton, 1973.

Clark, Suzannah. *Analyzing Schubert*. Cambridge: Cambridge University Press, 2011.

Clendinning, Jane Piper, and Elizabeth West Marvin. *The Musician's Guide to Theory and Analysis*. 3rd ed. New York: W. W. Norton, 2016.

Cohn, Richard. *Audacious Euphony: Chromaticism and the Consonant Triad's Second Nature*. New York: Oxford University Press, 2012.

Cone, Edward T. *Musical Form and Musical Performance*. New York: W. W. Norton, 1968.

Cudworth, Charles L. "Cadence Galante: The Story of a Cliché." *Monthly Musical Record* 79 (1949): 176–82.

Cutler, Timothy. "'Proper Boundaries' and the 'Incoherent' Succession V$^{(7)}$–IV." *Indiana Theory Review* 32, nos. 1–2 (2016): 41–84.

Cutler, Timothy. "On Voice Exchanges." *Journal of Music Theory* 53, no. 2 (Fall 2009): 191–226.

Dahlhaus, Carl. "Liszts Bergsymphonie und die Idee der Symphonischen Dichtung." *Jahrbuch des Staatlichen Instituts für Musikforschung Preußischer Kulturbesitz* (1976): 96–130.

Dahlhaus, Carl. *Nineteenth-Century Music*. Translated by J. Bradford Robinson. Berkeley: University of California Press, 1989.

Darcy, Warren, and James Hepokoski. "The Medial Caesura and Its Role in the Eighteenth-Century Sonata Exposition." *Music Theory Spectrum* 19, no. 2 (Fall 1997): 115–54.

de Médicis, François. "'Heavenly Length' in Schubert's Instrumental Music." In *Formal Functions in Perspective: Essays on Musical Form from Haydn to Adorno*, edited by Steven Vande Moortele, Julie Pedneault-Deslauriers, and Nathan John Martin, 198–222. Rochester, NY: University of Rochester Press, 2015.

De Souza, Jonathan. "Texture." In *The Oxford Handbook of Critical Concepts in Music Theory*, edited by Alexander Rehding and Steven Rings, 160–86. New York: Oxford University Press, 2019.

Duane, Ben. "Auditory Streaming Cues in Eighteenth- and Early Nineteenth-Century String Quartets: A Corpus-Based Study." *Music Perception* 31, no. 1 (2013): 46–58.

Duane, Ben. "Melodic Patterns and Tonal Cadences: Bayesian Learning of Cadential Categories from Contrapuntal Information." *Journal of New Music Research* 48, no. 3 (2019): 197–216.

Duane, Ben. "Thematic and Non-Thematic Textures in Schubert's Three-Key Expositions." *Music Theory Spectrum* 39, no. 1 (2017): 36–65.

Dubiel, Joseph. "Hearing, Remembering, Cold Storage, Purism, Evidence, and Attitude Adjustment." *Current Musicology*, no. 60–61 (1996): 26–50.

Duinker, Ben, and Hubert Léveillé Gauvin. "Changing Content in Flagship Music Theory Journals, 1979–2014." *Music Theory Online* 23, no. 4 (2017).

Eggebrecht, Hans Heinrich, ed. *Handwörterbuch der musikalischen Terminologie, s.v.* "Kadenz." Wiesbaden: Steiner, 1972.

Ferris, David. *Schumann's Eichendorff Liederkreis and the Genre of the Romantic Cycle*. New York: Oxford University Press, 2000.

Fischer, Wilhelm. "Zur Entwicklungsgeschichte des Wiener klassischen Stils." *Studien zur Musikwissenschaft: Beihefte der Denkmäler der Tonkunst in Österreich* 3 (1915): 24–84.

Fisk, Charles. *Returning Cycles: Contexts for the Interpretation of Schubert's Impromptus and Last Sonatas*. Berkeley: University of California Press, 2001.

Fowler, Don P. "First Thoughts on Closure: Problems and Prospects." *Materiali e discussioni per l'analisi dei testi classici* 22 (1989): 75–122.

Fowler, Don. "Second Thoughts on Closure." In *Classical Closure: Reading the End in Greek and Latin Literature*, edited by Deborah H. Roberts, Francis M. Dunn, and Don Fowler, 3–22. Princeton, NJ: Princeton University Press., 1997.

Galand, Joel. Review of *Elements of Sonata Theory: Norms, Types, and Deformations in the Late-Eighteenth-Century Sonata* by James Hepokoski and Warren Darcy. *Journal of Music Theory* 57, no. 2 (2013): 383–418.

Gauldin, Robert. "The Douth2 Relation as a Dramatic Signifier in Wagner's Music Dramas." *Music Analysis* 20, no. 2 (2001): 179–92.

Gauldin, Robert. *Harmonic Practice in Tonal Music*. 2nd ed. New York: W. W. Norton, 2004.

Gédalge, André. *Treatise on the Fugue (1901)*. Edited and translated by Ferdinand Davis. Norman: University of Oklahoma Press, 1965.

Gjerdingen, Robert O. *Music in the Galant Style*. New York: Oxford University Press, 2007.

Goetschius, Percy. *Applied Counterpoint*. New York: G. Schirmer, 1902.

Gossett, Philip. "The Overtures of Rossini." *19th-Century Music* 3, no. 1 (1979): 3–31.

Grave, Floyd K. "Freakish Variations on a 'Grand Cadence' Prototype in Haydn's String Quartets." *Journal of Musicological Research* 28, nos. 2–3 (April–September 2009): 119–45.

Grave, Floyd K. "Metrical Displacement and the Compound Measure in Eighteenth-Century Theory and Practice." *Theoria: Historical Aspects of Music Theory* 1 (1985): 25–60.

Green, Douglass M. *Form in Tonal Music: An Introduction to Analysis*. 2nd ed. New York: Holt, Rinehart & Winston, 1979.

Greenberg, Yoel. "Tinkering with Form: On W. F. Bach's Revisions to Two Keyboard Sonatas." *Music Theory and Analysis* 6, no. 2 (2019): 200–22.

Harrison, Daniel. "Cadence." In *The Oxford Handbook of Critical Concepts in Music Theory*, edited by Alexander Rehding and Steven Rings, 535–76. New York: Oxford University Press, 2019.

Harrison, Daniel. *Harmonic Function in Chromatic Music: A Renewed Dualist Theory and an Account of Its Precedents*. Chicago: University of Chicago Press, 1994.

Hatten, Robert S. "Aspects of Dramatic Closure in Beethoven: A Semiotic Perspective on Music Analysis via Strategies of Dramatic Conflict." *Semiotica* 66, nos. 1–3 (1987): 197–209.

Hatten, Robert S. *Musical Meaning in Beethoven: Markedness, Correlation, and Interpretation*. Bloomington: Indiana University Press, 1994.

Hauptmann, Moritz. *The Nature of Harmony and Metre*. Edited and translated by William Edward Heathcote. London: S. Sonnenschein, 1888.

Hepokoski, James A. *Sibelius, Symphony No. 5*. Cambridge: Cambridge University Press, 1993.

Hepokoski, James. "Sonata Theory, Secondary Themes and Continuous Exposition: Dialogues with Form-Functional Theory." *Music Analysis* 35, no. 1 (2016): 44–74.

Hepokoski, James, and Warren Darcy. *Elements of Sonata Theory: Norms, Types, and Deformations in the Late-Eighteenth-Century Sonata*. New York: Oxford University Press, 2006.

Higgs, James. *Fugue*. London: Novello, 1878.

Holtmeier, Ludwig. "Kadenz/Klausel." In *Lexikon Der Systematischen Musikwissenschaft*, edited by Helga De la Motte-Haber, Heinz von Loesch, Günther Rötter, and Christian Utz, 202–206. Laaber: Laaber Verlag, 2010.

Horton, Julian. "Criteria for a Theory of Nineteenth-Century Sonata Form." *Music Theory and Analysis (MTA)* 4, no. 2 (October 2017): 147–91.

Horton, Julian. "The First Movement of Schubert's Piano Sonata D. 959 and the Performance of Analysis." In *Schubert's Late Music: History, Theory, Style*, edited by Lorraine Byrne Bodley and Julian Horton, 171–90. Cambridge: Cambridge University Press, 2016.

Horton, Julian. "Formal Type and Formal Function in the Postclassical Piano Concerto." In *Formal Functions in Perspective: Essays on Musical Form from Haydn to Adorno*, edited by Steven Vande Moortele, Julie Pedneault-Deslauriers, and Nathan John Martin. Eastman Studies in Music, 77–122. Rochester, NY: University of Rochester Press, 2015.

Huebner, Steven. "Structural Coherence." In *The Cambridge Companion to Verdi*, edited by Scott L. Balthazar, 139–53. Cambridge: Cambridge University Press, 2011.

Hunt, Graham G. "Diverging Subordinate Themes and Internal Transitions: Assessing Internal Modulations in Three-Key Expositions." *Music Analysis* 39, no. 2 (2020): 145–89.

Huron, David Brian. *Sweet Anticipation: Music and the Psychology of Expectation*. Cambridge, MA: MIT Press, 2006.

Hutchinson, Kyle, and Mathew Poon. "Cadential Melodies: Form-Functional Taxonomy and the Role of the Upper Voice." *Music Theory Online* 28, no. 2 (2022).

Hyland, Anne M. *Schubert's String Quartets: The Teleology of Lyric Form*. Cambridge: Cambridge University Press, 2023.

Ito, John Paul. "Koch's Metrical Theory and Mozart's Music: A Corpus Study." *Music Perception* 31, no. 3 (February 2014): 205–22.

Kaiser, Ulrich. *Die Notenbücher der Mozarts als Grundlage der Analyse von W. A. Mozarts Kompositionen 1761–1767*. Kassel: Bärenreiter-Verlag, 2007.

Kellogg, Ronald Thomas. *Cognitive Psychology*. Thousand Oaks, CA: Sage Publications, 1995.

Kerman, Joseph. *The Art of Fugue: Bach Fugues for Keyboard, 1715–1750*. Berkeley: University of California Press, 2005.

Kermode, Frank. *The Sense of an Ending: Studies in the Theory of Fiction*. New York: Oxford University Press, 1967.

Kinderman, William. *Beethoven*. Berkeley: University of California Press, 2009.

Kinderman, William, and Harald Krebs, eds. *The Second Practice of Nineteenth-Century Tonality*. Lincoln: University of Nebraska Press, 1996.

Kirby, F. E. "Beethoven's Pastoral Symphony as a 'Sinfonia Caracteristica.'" In *The Creative World of Beethoven*, edited by Paul Henry Lang, 103–21. New York: W. W. Norton, 1971.

Kirnberger, Johann Phillip. *The Art of Strict Musical Composition*. Edited and translated by David W. Beach and Jürgen Thym. New Haven, CT: Yale University Press, 1982.

Kivy, Peter. *The Fine Art of Repetition: Essays in the Philosophy of Music*. Cambridge: Cambridge University Press, 1993.

Klein, Michael L. *Intertextuality in Western Art Music*. Bloomington: Indiana University Press, 2005.

Klumpenhouwer, Henry. "Harmonic Dualism as Historical and Structural Imperative." In *The Oxford Handbook of Neo-Riemannian Music Theories*, edited by Edward Gollin and Alexander Rehding, 194–217. New York: Oxford University Press, 2011.

Koch, Heinrich Christoph. *Introductory Essay on Composition: The Mechanical Rules of Melody, Sections 3 and 4*. Translated by Nancy Kovaleff Baker. New Haven, CT: Yale University Press, 1983.

Koch, Heinrich Christoph. *Versuch einer Anleitung zur Composition*. 3 vols. Vol. 1, Rudolstadt, 1782.

Kohs, Ellis B. *Musical Form: Studies in Analysis and Synthesis*. Boston: Houghton Mifflin, 1976.

Kopp, David. *Chromatic Transformations in Nineteenth-Century Music*. Cambridge: Cambridge University Press, 2002.

Kostka, Stefan M., Dorothy Payne, and Byron Almén. *Tonal Harmony: With an Introduction to Twentieth-Century Music*. 7th ed. New York: McGraw-Hill, 2013.

Kramer, Jonathan D. "Beginnings and Endings in Western Art Music." *Canadian University Music Review* 3 (1982): 1–14.

Kramer, Jonathan D. *The Time of Music: New Meanings, New Temporalities, New Listening Strategies*. New York: G. Schirmer, 1988.

Krebs, Harald. *Fantasy Pieces: Metrical Dissonance in the Music of Robert Schumann*. New York: Oxford University Press, 1999.

Kurth, Ernst. *Ernst Kurth: Selected Writings*. Edited by Lee Rothfarb. Cambridge: Cambridge University Press, 1991.

Laitz, Steven G. *The Complete Musician: An Integrated Approach to Theory, Analysis and Listening*. 3rd ed. New York: Oxford University Press, 2012.

LaRue, Jan. "Bifocal Tonality: An Explanation for Ambiguous Baroque Cadences." In *Essays on Music in Honor of Archibald Thompson Davison*, edited by Randall Thompson, 173–84. Cambridge: Department of Music, Harvard University, 1957.

Lawrence, John Y. "Toward a Predictive Theory of Theme Types." *Journal of Music Theory* 64, no. 1 (2020): 1–36.

Ledbetter, David. *Bach's Well-Tempered Clavier: The 48 Preludes and Fugues*. New Haven, CT: Yale University Press, 2002.

Lehman, Frank. "Hollywood Cadences: Music and the Structure of Cinematic Expectation." *Music Theory Online* 19, no. 4 (December 2013).

Lerdahl, Fred, and Ray Jackendoff. *A Generative Theory of Tonal Music*. Cambridge: MIT Press, 1983.

Lerdahl, Fred, and Ray Jackendoff. "Toward a Formal Theory of Tonal Music." *Journal of Music Theory* 21, no. 1 (Spring 1977): 111–71.

Lester, Joel. *Bach's Works for Solo Violin: Style, Structure, Performance*. New York: Oxford University Press, 1999.

Lester, Joel. *Compositional Theory in the Eighteenth Century*. Cambridge, MA: Harvard University Press, 1992.

Lester, Joel. *Harmony in Tonal Music*. 2 vols. New York: Alfred A. Knopf, 1982.

Levy, Janet M. "Texture as a Sign in Classic and Early Romantic Music." *Journal of the American Musicological Society* 35, no. 3 (1982): 482–531.

Lewin, David. "Cohn Functions." *Journal of Music Theory* 40, no. 2 (1996): 181–216.

Lewin, David. "Music Theory, Phenomenology, and Modes of Perception." *Music Perception* 3, no. 4 (1986): 327–92.

Lewin, David. *Studies in Music with Text*. New York: Oxford University Press, 2006.

London, Justin, and Ronald Rodman. "Musical Genre and Schenkerian Analysis." *Journal of Music Theory* 42, no. 1 (1998): 101–24.

Lorenz, Alfred. *Das Geheimnis der Form bei Richard Wagner*. 4 vols. Vol. 1, Berlin: M. Hesse, 1924.

Macdonald, Hugh. "Schubert's Volcanic Temper." *Musical Times* 119 (1978): 949–52.

MacKay, James S. "A Case for Declassifying the IAC as a Cadence Type: Cadence and Thematic Design in Selected Early- to Middle-Period Haydn Sonatas." *Ad Parnassum* 15, no. 30 (2017): 1–27.

Mann, Alfred. *The Study of Fugue*. New Brunswick, NJ: Rutgers University Press, 1958.

Margulis, Elizabeth Hellmuth. *On Repeat: How Music Plays the Mind*. New York: Oxford University Press, 2013.

Marpurg, Friedrich Wilhelm. *Abhandlung von der Fuge*. 2 vols. Vol. 1, Berlin: A. Haude & J. C. Spener, 1753.

Marshall, Robert L. "Bach the Progressive: Observations on His Later Works." *The Musical Quarterly* 62, no. 3 (1976): 313–57.

Marston, Nicholas. "Review of *Classical Form: A Theory of Formal Functions for the Instrumental Music of Haydn, Mozart, and Beethoven* by William E. Caplin." *Music Analysis* 20, no. 1 (March 2001): 143–50.

Martin, Nathan John. "Schumann's Fragment." *Indiana Theory Review* 28, nos. 1–2 (2010): 85–109.

Martin, Nathan John. "The Tristan Chord Resolved." *Intersections* 28, no. 2 (2008): 6–30.

Martin, Nathan John, and Julie Pedneault-Deslauriers. "The Mozartean Half Cadence." In *What Is a Cadence? Theoretical and Analytical Perspectives on Cadences in the Classical Repertoire*, edited by Markus Neuwirth and Pieter Bergé, 185–214. Leuven: Leuven University Press, 2015.

Marx, Adolf Bernhard. *Musical Form in the Age of Beethoven: Selected Writings on Theory and Method*. Edited and translated by Scott Burnham. Cambridge: Cambridge University Press, 1997.

Mattheson, Johann. *Johann Mattheson's Der Vollkommene Capellmeister: A Revised Translation with Critical Commentary*. Edited and translated by Ernest Harriss. Ann Arbor, MI: UMI Research Press, 1981.

McClelland, Ryan C. "Extended Upbeats in the Classical Minuet: Interactions with Hypermeter and Phrase Structure." *Music Theory Spectrum* 28, no. 1 (Spring 2006): 23–56.

McCreless, Patrick. "The Hermeneutic Sentence and Other Literary Models for Tonal Closure." *Indiana Theory Review* 12 (Spring–Fall 1991): 35–73.

Menke, Johannes. "Die Familie Der Cadenza Doppia." *Zeitschrift der Gesellschaft für Musiktheorie* 8, no. 3 (2011): 389–405.

Meyer, Leonard B. *Emotion and Meaning in Music*. Chicago: University of Chicago Press, 1956.

Meyer, Leonard B. *Explaining Music: Essays and Explorations*. Berkeley: University of California Press, 1973.

Meyer, Leonard B. *Music, the Arts, and Ideas: Patterns and Predictions in Twentieth-Century Culture*. Chicago: University of Chicago Press, 1994.

Meyer, Leonard B. *Style and Music: Theory, History and Ideology*. Philadelphia: University of Pennsylvania Press, 1989.

Meyer, Leonard B. "A Universe of Universals." *Journal of Musicology* 16, no. 1 (1998): 3–25.

Mirka, Danuta. "Absent Cadences." *Eighteenth-Century Music* 9, no. 2 (September 2012): 213–35.

Mirka, Danuta. "Metre, Phrase Structure and Manipulations of Musical Beginnings." In *Communication in Eighteenth-Century Music*, edited by Danuta Mirka and Kofi Agawu, 83–111. Cambridge: Cambridge University Press, 2008.

Mirka, Danuta. *Metric Manipulations in Haydn and Mozart: Chamber Music for Strings, 1787–1791*. Oxford: Oxford University Press, 2009.

Mirka, Danuta. "Punctuation and Sense in Late-Eighteenth-Century Music." *Journal of Music Theory* 54, no. 2 (Fall 2010): 235–82.

Mitchell, William J. "The Tristan Prelude: Technique and Structure." *Music Forum* 1 (1967): 162–203.

Morgan, Robert P. "Circular Form in the Tristan Prelude." *Journal of the American Musicological Society* 53, no. 1 (2000): 69–103.

Muffat, Georg. *An Essay on Thoroughbass (Regulae Concentuum Partiturae, 1699)*. Edited by Hellmut Federhofer. N.p.: American Institute of Musicology, 1961.

Mutch, Caleb. "Blainville's New Mode, or, How the Plagal Cadence Came to Be 'Plagal.'" *Eighteenth-Century Music* 12, no. 1 (March 2015): 69–90.

Mutch, Caleb. "Studies in the History of the Cadence." PhD dissertation, Columbia Univeristy, 2015.

Neuwirth, Markus. "*Fuggir la Cadenza*, or, the Art of Avoiding Cadential Closure: Physiognomy and Functions of Deceptive Cadences in the Classical Repertoire." In *What Is a Cadence? Theoretical and Analytical Perspectives on Cadences in the Classical Repertoire*, edited by Markus Neuwirth and Pieter Bergé, 117–55. Leuven: Leuven University Press, 2015.

Oettingen, Arthur J. von. *Harmoniesystem in dualer Entwicklung: Studien zur Theorie der Musik*. Dorpat: W. Gläser, 1866.

Osborne, Tyler. "'You Too May Change': Tonal Pairing of the Tonic and Subdominant in Two Songs by Fanny Hensel." In *The Songs of Fanny Hensel*, edited by Stephen Rodgers, 113–28. New York: Oxford University Press, 2021.

Petty, Wayne C. "Koch, Schenker, and the Development Section of Sonata Forms by C. P. E. Bach." *Music Theory Spectrum* 21, no. 2 (1999): 151–73.

Platt, Heather. "Unrequited Love and Unrealized Dominants." *Intégral* 7 (1993): 119–48.

Prout, Ebenezer. *Fugue*. 4th ed. London: Augener, 1891.

Rameau, Jean-Philippe. *Nouveau système de musique théorique*. Paris, 1726.

Rameau, Jean-Philippe. *Treatise on Harmony*. Translated by Philip Gossett. New York: Dover Publications, 1971.

Randel, Don M. "Emerging Triadic Tonality in the Fifteenth Century." *The Musical Quarterly* 57, no. 1 (January 1971): 73–86.

Ratner, Leonard G. *Classic Music: Expression, Form, and Style*. New York: G. Schirmer, 1980.

Ratz, Erwin. *Einfuhrung in die musikalische Formenlehre: Über Formprinzipien in den Inventionen und Fugen J. S. Bachs und ihre Bedeutung für die Kompositionstechnik Beethovens*. 3rd ed. Vienna: Universal Edition, 1973.

Reef, John S. "Subjects and Phrase Boundaries in Two Keyboard Fugues by J. S. Bach." *Music Theory Spectrum* 41, no. 1 (2019): 48–73.

Rice, John A. "The Bergamasca Schema in Late Haydn." In *Haydn's Last Creative Period*, edited by Federico Gon, 333–49. Speculum Musicae 42. Turnhout: Brepols, 2021.

Richards, Mark. "Closure in Classical Themes: The Role of Melody and Texture in Cadences, Closural Function, and the Separated Cadence." *Intersections: Canadian Journal of Music/Revue canadienne de musique* 31, no. 1 (2010): 25–45.

Richards, Mark. "Viennese Classicism and the Sentential Idea: Broadening the Sentence Paradigm." *Theory and Practice* 36 (2011): 179–224.

Riemann, Hugo. *Harmony Simplified, or the Theory of the Tonal Functions of Chords*. Translated by H. Bewerunge. London: Augener & Co., 1895.

Riemann, Hugo. *System der musikalischen Rhythmik und Metrik*. Leipzig: Breitkopf und Härtel, 1903.

Riemann, Hugo. *Systematische Modulationslehre als Grundlage der musikalischen Formenlehre*. Hamburg: J. F. Richter, 1887.

Rodgers, Stephen. *Form, Program, and Metaphor in the Music of Berlioz*. Cambridge: Cambridge University Press, 2009.

Rodgers, Stephen. "Plagal Cadences in Fanny Hensel's Songs." In *The Songs of Fanny Hensel*, edited by Stephen Rodgers, 129–45. New York: Oxford University Press, 2021.

Rodgers, Stephen, and Tyler Osborne. "Prolongational Closure in the Lieder of Fanny Hensel." *Music Theory Online* 26, no. 3 (2020).

Rohrmeier, Martin, and Markus Neuwirth. "Towards a Syntax of the Classical Cadence." In *What Is a Cadence? Theoretical and Analytical Perspectives on Cadences in the Classical Repertoire*, edited by Markus Neuwirth and Pieter Bergé, 287–338. Leuven: Leuven University Press, 2015.

Rosen, Charles. *The Classical Style: Haydn, Mozart, Beethoven*. New York: W. W. Norton, 1972.

Rosen, Charles. *The Romantic Generation*. Cambridge, MA: Harvard University Press, 1995.

Rosen, Charles. *Sonata Forms*. Rev. ed. New York: W. W. Norton, 1988.

Rothstein, William. "National Metrical Types in Music of the Eighteenth and Early Nineteenth Centuries." In *Communication in Eighteenth-Century Music*, edited by Danuta Mirka and Kofi Agawu, 112–59. New York: Cambridge University Press, 2008.

Rothstein, William. *Phrase Rhythm in Tonal Music*. New York: Schirmer Books, 1989.

Rothstein, William. "Transformations of Cadential Formulae in the Music of Corelli and His Successors." In *Essays from the Third International Schenker Symposium*, edited by Allen Cadwallader, Jan Miyake, and Oliver Schwab-Felisch, 245–79. Hildesheim: Georg Olms, 2006.

Salzer, Felix. *Structural Hearing: Tonal Coherence in Music*. 2 vols. New York: C. Boni, 1952.

Sanders, Ernest H. "The Sonata-Form Finale of Beethoven's Ninth Symphony." *19th-Century Music* 22, no. 1 (1998): 54–60.

Sanguinetti, Giorgio. *The Art of Partimento: History, Theory, and Practice*. New York: Oxford University Press, 2012.

Schachter, Carl. "*Che Inganno!* The Analysis of Deceptive Cadences." In *Essays from the Third International Schenker Symposium*, edited by Allen Cadwallader, Jan Miyake, and Oliver Schwab-Felisch, 279–98. Hildesheim: Georg Olms, 2006.

Schachter, Carl. "Rhythm and Linear Analysis: Aspects of Meter." *Music Forum* 6, no. 1 (1987): 1–59.

Schachter, Carl. "The Triad as Place and Action." In *Unfoldings: Essays in Schenkerian Theory and Analysis*, edited by Joseph Nathan Straus, 161–83. New York: Oxford University Press, 1999.

Schenker, Heinrich. *Free Composition*. Translated and edited by Ernst Oster. New York: Longman, 1979.

Schmalfeldt, Janet. "Cadential Processes: The Evaded Cadence and the 'One More Time' Technique." *Journal of Musicological Research* 12, nos. 1–2 (March 1992): 1–52.

Schmalfeldt, Janet. "Coming to Terms: Speaking of Phrase, Cadence, and Form." *In Theory Only* 13, nos. 1–4 (September 1997): 95–115.

Schmalfeldt, Janet. "Domenico Scarlatti, Escape Artist: Sightings of His 'Mixed Style' Towards the End of the Eighteenth Century." *Music Analysis* 38, no. 3 (2019): 253–96.

Schmalfeldt, Janet. *In the Process of Becoming: Analytic and Philosophical Perspectives on Form in Early Nineteenth-Century Music*. New York: Oxford University Press, 2011.

Schmalfeldt, Janet. "'Nineteenth-Century' Subdominants." *Music Analysis*, 41, no. 3 (2022): 349–93.

Schmalfeldt, Janet. "Phrase." In *The Oxford Handbook of Critical Concepts in Music Theory*, edited by Alexander Rehding and Steven Rings, 295–345. New York: Oxford University Press, 2019.

Schmalfeldt, Janet. "Towards a Reconciliation of Schenkerian Concepts with Traditional and Recent Theories of Form." *Music Analysis* 10, no. 3 (October 1991): 233–87.

Schmid, Manfred Hermann. "Die 'Terzkadenz' als Zäsurformel im Werk Mozarts." *Mozart-Studien* 13 (2004): 87–176.

Schoenberg, Arnold. *Fundamentals of Musical Composition*. Edited by Gerald Strang and Leonard Stein. London: Faber & Faber, 1967.

Schoenberg, Arnold. *The Musical Idea and the Logic, Technique, and Art of Its Presentation*. Translated by Patricia Carpenter and Severine Neff. New York: Columbia University Press, 1995.

Schoenberg, Arnold. *Structural Functions of Harmony*. Rev. ed. with corrections. Edited by Leonard Stein. New York: W. W. Norton, 1969.

Schoenberg, Arnold. *Theory of Harmony*. Translated by Roy E. Carter. London: Faber & Faber, 1978.

Schubert, Peter, and Christoph Neidhöfer. *Baroque Counterpoint*. Upper Saddle River, NJ: Pearson Prentice Hall, 2006.

Sears, David R. W. "The Perception of Cadential Closure." In *What Is a Cadence? Theoretical and Analytical Perspectives on Cadences in the Classical Repertoire*, edited by Markus Neuwirth and Pieter Bergé, 253–85. Leuven: Leuven University Press, 2015.

Sears, David R. W., William E. Caplin, and Stephen McAdams. "Perceiving the Classical Cadence." *Music Perception* 31, no. 5 (2014): 397–417.

Sears, David R. W., Marcus T. Pearce, William E. Caplin, and Stephen McAdams. "Simulating Melodic and Harmonic Expectations for Tonal Cadences Using Probabilistic Models." *Journal of New Music Research* 47, no. 1 (2018): 29–52.

Sears, David R. W., Jacob Spitzer, William E. Caplin, and Stephen McAdams. "Expecting the End: Continuous Expectancy Ratings for Tonal Cadences." *Psychology of Music* 48, no. 3 (2020): 358–75.

Segal, Eyal. "Closure in Detective Fiction." *Poetics* 31, no. 2 (Summer 2010): 153–215.

Sessions, Roger. *The Musical Experience of Composer, Performer, Listener*. Princeton, NJ: Princeton University Press, 1950.

Simpson, Robert. *The Essence of Bruckner: An Essay Towards the Understanding of His Music*. 2nd ed. London: V. Gollancz, 1977.

Smith, Barbara Herrnstein. *Poetic Closure: A Study of How Poems End*. Chicago: University of Chicago Press, 1968.

Smith, Peter H. "Cadential Content and Cadential Function in the First-Movement Expositions of Schumann's Violin Sonatas." *Music Theory and Analysis* 3, no. 1 (April 2016): 27–58.

Sobaskie, James William. "Precursive Prolongation in the Préludes of Chopin." *Journal of the Society for Musicology in Ireland* 3 (2007): 25–61.

Stein, Deborah. "The Expansion of the Subdominant in the Late Nineteenth Century." *Journal of Music Theory* 27, no. 2 (1983): 153–80.

Stoia, Nicholas. "Triple Counterpoint and Six-Four Chords in Bach's Sinfonia in F Minor." *Music Analysis* 34, no. 3 (2015): 305–34.

Straus, Joseph N. "Normalizing the Abnormal: Disability in Music and Music Theory." *Journal of the American Musicological Society* 59, no. 1 (2006): 113–84.

Subotnik, Rose Rosengard. *Deconstructive Variations: Music and Reason in Western Society*. Minneapolis: University of Minnesota Press, 1996.

Sulzer, Johann Georg. "Cadenz." In *Allgemeine Theorie der schönen Künste*. Berlin: Winter, 1771–74.

Sutcliffe, W. Dean. *The Keyboard Sonatas of Domenico Scarlatti and Eighteenth-Century Musical Style*. Cambridge: Cambridge University Press, 2003.

Swinden, Kevin J. "When Functions Collide: Aspects of Plural Function in Chromatic Music." *Music Theory Spectrum* 27, no. 2 (2005): 249–82.

Temperley, David. "The Six-Four as Tonic Harmony, Tonal Emissary, and Structural Cue." *Intégral* 31 (2017): 1–25.

Tovey, Donald Francis. *A Companion to Beethoven's Pianoforte Sonatas.* London: Associated Board of the Royal Schools of Music, 1931.

Tovey, Donald Francis. *The Forms of Music.* New York: Meridian Books, 1956.

Vallières, Michel, Daphne Tan, William E Caplin, and Stephen McAdams. "Perception of Intrinsic Formal Functionality: An Empirical Investigation of Mozart's Materials." *Journal of Interdisciplinary Music Studies* 3, no. 1–2 (2009): 17–43.

Van Tour, Peter. *Counterpoint and Partimento: Methods of Teaching Composition in Late Eighteenth-Century Naples.* Uppsala: Uppsala Universitet, 2015.

Vande Moortele, Steven. "In Search of Romantic Form." *Music Analysis* 32, no. 3 (2013): 404–31.

Vande Moortele, Steven. *The Romantic Overture and Musical Form from Rossini to Wagner.* Cambridge: Cambridge University Press, 2017.

Vande Moortele, Steven. "Sentences, Sentence Chains, and Sentence Replication: Intra- and Interthematic Functions in Liszt's Weimar Symphonic Poems." *Intégral* 25 (2011): 121–58.

Vande Moortele, Steven. "The Subordinate Theme in the First Movement of Schubert's 'Unfinished' Symphony." *Music Theory and Analysis* 6, no. 2 (2019): 223–29.

Vande Moortele, Steven. *Two-Dimensional Sonata Form: Form and Cycle in Single-Movement Instrumental Works by Liszt, Strauss, Schoenberg, and Zemlinsky.* Leuven: Leuven University Press, 2009.

Vivaldi, Antonio. "'The Four Seasons' and Other Violin Concertos in Full Score: Op. 8, Complete." Edited by Eleanor Selfridge-Field. New York: Dover Publications, 1995.

Waldura, Markus. *Von Rameau und Riepel zu Koch: Zum Zusammenhang zwischen theoretischem Ansatz, Kadenzlehre und Periodenbegriff in der Musiktheorie des 18. Jahrhunderts.* Hildesheim: Georg Olms, 2002.

Waltham-Smith, Naomi. "Haydn's Impropriety." *Journal of Music Theory* 62, no. 1 (April 2018): 119–44.

Waltham-Smith, Naomi. "Sequence." In *The Oxford Handbook of Critical Concepts in Music Theory,* edited by Alexander Rehding and Steven Rings, 577–601. New York: Oxford University Press, 2019.

Walther, Johann Gottfried. *Musicalisches Lexicon.* Weimar, 1732.

Walther, Johann Gottfried. *Praecepta der Musicalischen Composition (1708).* Edited by Peter Benary. Leipzig: Breitkopf & Härtel, 1955.

Webster, James. "The Analysis of Mozart's Arias." In *Mozart Studies,* edited by Cliff Eisen, 101–99. Oxford: Clarendon Press, 1991.

Webster, James. "The Form of the Finale of Beethoven's Ninth Symphony." *Beethoven Forum* 1 (1992): 25–62.

Webster, James. *Haydn's Farewell Symphony and the Idea of Classical Style: Through-Composition and Cyclic Integration in His Instrumental Music.* New York: Cambridge University Press, 1991.

Webster, James. "Schubert's Sonata Form and Brahms's First Maturity." *19th-Century Music* 2, no. 1 (1978): 18–35.

Werckmeister, Andreas. *Harmonologia Musica (1702).* Hildesheim: G. Olms, 1970.

Westergaard, Peter. *An Introduction to Tonal Theory.* New York: Norton, 1975.

Willner, Channan. "Metrical Displacement and Metrically Dissonant Hemiolas." *Journal of Music Theory* 57, no. 1 (2013): 87–118.

Winter, Robert S. "The Bifocal Close and the Evolution of the Viennese Classical Style." *Journal of the American Musicological Society* 42, no. 2 (Summer 1989): 275–337.

Wollenberg, Susan. "Songs of Travel: Fanny Hensel's Wanderings." In *The Songs of Fanny Hensel,* edited by Stephen Rodgers, 55–74. New York: Oxford University Press, 2021.

Yust, Jason. *Organized Time: Rhythm, Tonality, and Form.* New York: Oxford University Press, 2018.

Zarlino, Gioseffo. *The Art of Counterpoint: Part Three of Le Istitutioni Harmoniche, 1558.* Edited and translated by Guy A. Marco and Claude V. Palisca New Haven, CT: Yale University Press, 1968.

Zhang, Xieyi (Abby). "Apparently Imperfect: On the Analytical Issues of the IAC." *Music Theory Spectrum* 44, no. 2 (Fall 2022): 191–212.

# Index of Musical Compositions

*For the benefit of digital users, indexed terms that span two pages (e.g., 52–53) may, on occasion, appear on only one of those pages.*

**Bach, Carl Philipp Emanuel**
sonata, keyboard
  Wq. 48, no. 1, in F, i (Ex. 7.27, 7.63, 7.76a), 391, 412–13, 423–24
    iii (Ex. 7.64), 413
  Wq. 48, no. 2, in B-flat, i (Ex. 7.42), 399
  Wq. 48, no. 3, in E, i (Ex. 7.48), 402, ii (Ex. 7.72), 417–18
  Wq. 48, no. 4, in C Minor, i (Ex. 7.28, 7.62), 391, 406–8, 410–11, 419–21, 422–23
  Wq. 48, no. 5, in C, i (Ex. 7.68), 414, ii (Ex. 7.59), 406–8, iii (Ex. 7.65), 413
  Wq. 49, no. 1, in A Minor, ii (Ex. 7.38), 395, 409, 411–12
  Wq. 49, no. 6 in B Minor, i (Ex. 7.49), 402 ii, (Ex. 7.35), 394–95 iii, 424n.101
  Wq. 62, no. 1, in B-flat, iii (Ex. 7.61, 7.66), 410, 413–14
  Wq. 62, no. 5, in E, i (Ex. 7.37), 394–95, ii (Ex. 7.58), 406–8, iii (Ex. 7.55), 405
  Wq. 62, no. 6, in F Minor, ii (Ex. 7.43), 399
  Wq. 62, no. 7, in C, iii (Ex. 7.57, 7.67), 405–6, 413–14
  Wq. 62, no. 8, in F, i (Ex. 7.44), 399
  Wq. 62, no. 10, in C, i (Ex. 7.47, 7.76b), 400, 423–24
  Wq. 65, no. 13, in B Minor, i (Ex. 7.74), 409, 421–22

**Bach, Johann Christian**
Keyboard Sonata, Op. 12, no. 6, ii (Ex. 7.3e), 380–81
Toccata in B-flat Minor (Ex. 7.70), 416

**Bach, Johann Sebastian**
*Art of Fugue, The*
  Contrapunctus No. 2 349n.99, 364n.142
  Contrapunctus No. 3 (Ex. 6.84), 348–49
  Contrapunctus No. 12 (Ex. 6.82), 348
  Contrapunctus No. 13 (Ex. 6.83), 348
Brandenburg Concerto No. 1 in F, iii (Ex. 6.71), 342–43, 409
Brandenburg Concerto No. 3 in G, i (Ex. 6.45), 328–29, iii (Ex. 6.53), 307n.8, 331
"Crucifixus," Mass in B minor, 477n.141
English Suite No. 3 in G Minor, i, 321n.44
"Goldberg" Variations (Ex. 6.42), 327
Partita No. 1 in B-flat, ii (Ex. 6.55), 333, 337n.77, 339, 415n.87
Partita No. 2 in C Minor, v ("Rondeaux"), 333n.65
Sonata for Solo Violin in G Minor, i, 313n.22
Toccata in D Minor, BWV 565 (Ex. 6.22), 317, 348–49, 454n.86, 526–27, 534, 550n.127
*Well-Tempered Clavier, The*, Book 1
  fugue
    No. 1 in C (Ex. 6.89), 352n.112, 355, 356
    No. 2 in C Minor (Ex. 6.90), 26n.86, 352n.112, 353, 355–56, 371–72
    No. 3 in C-sharp (Ex. 6.100), 364
    No. 5 in D (Ex. 6.93, 6.103), 357–58, 367–70
    No. 7 in E-flat (Ex. 6.104), 370–72
    No. 8 in D-sharp Minor (Ex. 6.101), 365
    No. 9 in E (Ex. 6.92a), 358–59

*Well-Tempered Clavier, The*, Book 1 (*cont.*)
    No. 12, in F minor 352n.118
    No. 13 in F-sharp (Ex. 6.94), 358–60
    No. 14 in F-sharp Minor (Ex. 6.97), 361–63
    No. 16 in G Minor (Ex. 6.88, 6.96), 353, 362–63
    No. 18 in G-sharp Minor, (Ex. 6.105), 360, 366–67, 372–78
    No. 20 in A Minor (Ex. 6.30), 321, 328, 342, 353–54n.123, 409
    No. 21 in B-flat 352n.118
    No. 23 in B (Ex. 6.13, 6.91), 311–12, 315, 318n.38, 352n.117, 356, 364–65, 367
  prelude
    No. 1 in C (Ex. 6.19, Ex. 7.25), 307n.8, 315–16, 364–65, 385n.27, 390, 449n.62, 454n.86, 473, 526–27, 534, 550n.127
    No. 6 in D Minor (Ex. 6.77), 346
    No. 8 in E-flat Minor (Ex. 6.20), 316, 341–42, 409, 454n.86, 526–27, 534, 550n.127
    No. 9 in E (Ex. 6.11, 6.21), 310–11, 316–17, 348–49, 454n.86, 526–27, 528–29, 534, 550n.127
    No. 12 in F Minor (Ex. 6.73), 343–44, 409
    No. 14 in F-sharp Minor (Ex. 6.75), 345
    No. 21 in B-flat, 316n.34
    No. 24 in B Minor (Ex. 6.59), 316n.34, 335–36
*Well-Tempered Clavier, The*, Book 2
  fugue
    No. 2 in C Minor (Ex. 6.86), 353
    No. 6 in D Minor (Ex. 6.78, 6.99), 346–47, 363–64, 365–66
    No. 9 in E (Ex. 6.68, 6.105b), 340, 353–54, 373, 403n.64
    No. 14 in F-sharp Minor (Ex. 6.87), 353
    No. 15 in G (Ex. 6.92b), 352n.117, 356
    No. 16 in G minor, 352
    No. 17 in A-flat (Ex. 6.95, Ex. 6.98, 6.102), 359–60, 362–63, 364, 365n.145, 366–67
  prelude
    No. 5 in D (Ex. 6.12, 6.56), 310–11, 327–28, 333–34, 342, 409
    No. 6 in D-Minor, 315n.26
    No. 7 in E-flat, 334n.67
    No. 12 in F Minor (Ex. 6.65), 334n.67, 337–39, 409
    No. 14 in F-sharp Minor (Ex. 6.18), 313–15, 334n.67
    No. 15 in G (Ex. 6.27), 320
    No. 17 in A-flat, 322n.45
    No. 21 in B-flat, 352–53n.119
    No. 24 in B Minor (Ex. 6.28), 320

**Bach, Wilhelm Friedemann**
Sonata in F, Fk. 6 (Ex. 7.31), 392, 415

**Barbella, Emanuele**
Six Solos, No. 4, iii (Ex. 7.6), 380n.9, 382, 408

**Beethoven, Ludwig van**
Andante in F ("Andante favori"), WoO 57 (Ex. 3.34), 69
Bagatelle in A Minor, Op. 119, no. 9, 188–89
Bagatelle in E-flat, Op. 126, no. 3 (Ex. 3.156a, 5.62), 132, 134n.229, 258n.62, 276–77
Bagatelle in G, Op. 126, no. 1, 79n.56
Cello Sonata in A, Op. 69, i (Ex. 4.48, 4.52), 183, 189, 192n.104, iii (Ex. 4.5, 4.70), 203–4
Cello Sonata in G, Op. 5, no. 2, ii (Ex. 3.117), 108
"Nimm sie hin denn," *An die ferne Geliebte*, Op. 98, 471n.132
Piano Concerto No. 1 in C, Op. 15, i, 101n.137
Piano Concerto No. 2 in B-flat, Op. 19, iii (Ex. 3.112), 107
Piano Concerto No. 3 in C Minor, Op. 37, i (Ex. 3.115), 107–8, 131n.223
Piano Concerto No. 4 in G, Op. 58, i, 545n.114, 554n.133
Piano Trio in B-flat, Op. 11, ii (Ex. 4.46), 182–83, 186, 187n.89
Piano Trio in D ("Ghost"), Op. 70, no. 1, i (Ex. 3.174), 147–49, 157, 243n.36, 317n.37, 454n.86, 524n.67, 526–27, 534, 550n.127
Piano Trio in G, Op. 1, no. 2, i (Ex. 2.29) 23n.68, 52–54, 560n.139
quartet, string
  Op. 18, no. 1, in F, i (Ex. 4.63, 5.28, 5.46), 197–98, 225–26, 236n.27, 243–45, 246, 247n.44, 250–51, 263, 264, 265, 267
  Op. 18, no. 2, in G, i (Ex. 3.5), 17n.32, 57, 69–70 ii, 130–31n.217, iv (Ex. 3.21), 65–66
  Op. 18, no. 3, in D, i (Ex. 3.67), 83, 96n.124, iii (Ex. 3.172), 144–46
  Op. 18, no. 4, in C Minor, i (Ex. 2.23, 4.9), 42–43, 47, 154, 158–60
  Op. 59, no. 1, in F, i (Ex. 5.6), 227, 243n.37, iii (Ex. 3.123b), 110
  Op. 74 in E-flat, iv (Ex. 3.57, 3.101), 75, 104, 114n.171
  Op. 95 in F Minor, ii, 99n.134
  Op. 127 in E-flat, i (Ex. 4.45), 181–82, 183, 186, 217–18
  Op. 130 in B-flat, i, 6–7, iv (Ex. 3.156d, 4.51c), 132, 134n.229, 188–89, 192n.104
  Op. 131 in C-sharp Minor, iv (Ex. 3.53), 74
Serenade for Violin, Viola, and Cello in D, Op. 8, iv, 123n.203
String Quintet in C, Op. 29, i, 397n.51
sonata, piano
  Op. 2, no. 1, in F Minor, i, 6–7, 424–26 ii, 71n.40
  Op. 2, no. 2, in A, i (Ex. 3.145, 4.36), 122, 173, 174, 177, 211, 227, 246, 264, 274, 342n.88
  Op. 2, no. 3, in C, i (Ex. 2.5, 3.38, 3.165, 3.170), 24–25, 70, 136, 137–38, 143–44, iii (Ex. 3.2, 3.160), 57, 132–34 iv, 79n.56
  Op. 7 in E-flat, ii (Ex. 2.28, 4.11), 50, 58n.17, 154–57, 169 ii, 236n.27, iii (Ex. 5.51), 267–68, 271n.85
  Op. 10, no. 1, in C Minor, i (Ex. 3.79, 5.47), 88, 95, 265, 268, ii (Ex. 4.54, 5.38), 189–90, 257–59, 277n.95
  Op. 10, no. 2, in F, i (Ex. 4.8), 154, 160, 246, 264
  Op. 10, no. 3, in D, i (Ex. 3.106), 106, 117, ii (Ex. 5.23), 240–41, 261, 289n.120, iv (Ex. 3.129, 4.68), 104, 112, 200–2
  Op. 13 in C Minor ("Pathétique"), ii (Ex. 3.22), 65–66, 67, iii (Ex. 3.147), 123
  Op. 14, no. 1, in E, i (Ex. 4.81, 5.5), 214–16, 227, 268, ii (Ex. 3.20, 3.27, 3.135, 3.159), 65, 67, 104n.152, 114, 132, 138
  Op. 14, no. 2, in G, i (Ex. 3.102, 3.120, 3.149, 5.31), 104, 108, 116–17, 123, 210n.151, 246–47 ii, (Ex. 3.23), 57–58n.16, 66–67, 137n.234
  Op. 22 in B-flat, iii (Ex. 3.103), 104, 112, iv (Ex. 3.4c, 3.81), 57, 88–94
  Op. 26 in A-flat, i, 117n.179, 131n.222 ii, 471n.131, iv (Ex. 3.48, 3.86), 72–74, 92–93, 106n.163, 176n.66
  Op. 28 in D, ii (Ex. 3.4a), 57, 68–69, 70
  Op. 31, no. 1, in G, ii (Ex. 3.85), 92, 142
  Op. 31, no. 2, in D Minor ("Tempest"), i, 438–39n.29 iii, 294n.136
  Op. 31, no. 3, in E-flat, i (Ex. 4.26, 5.34, 9.7), 59n.21, 167–68, 237n.28, 248–50, 260, 275, 280–81, 438–39n.29, 439n.31, 503–4, ii (Ex. 3.33, 3.158, 5.9), 69, 132, 138, 223, 261, 275, 281, 465n.115
  Op. 49, no. 1, in G Minor, i (Ex. 5.54), 269, 271, 273, ii (Ex. 4.57), 22n.65, 192–93
  Op. 53 in C ("Waldstein"), i (Ex. 3.168, 5.39), 140, 258–59

Op. 57 in F minor ("Appassionata"), i,
219n.171, 219n.173
Op. 81a in E-flat ("Les Adieux"), i, 17–18
Op. 90 in E Minor, ii (Ex. 3.7), 59–60
Op. 106 in B-flat ("Hammerklavier"),
i (Ex. 5.14), 100n.135, 225–26,
231–35, 245n.41, 281, 397n.51
Op. 109 in E, ii (Ex. 5.22), 239–40,
247n.47, iii (Ex. 3.94), 99
Op. 110 in A-flat, ii (Ex. 3.90), 96–98
Op. 111 in C Minor, ii (Ex. 3.77) 86–87,
99, 106n.162
sonata, violin
Op. 12, no. 3, in E-flat, i (Ex. 4.44), 180,
182n.77, 186, 217–18, 264–65, 277
Op. 23 in A Minor, i (Ex. 4.35), 173
Op. 24 in F ("Spring"), i (Ex. 3.148),
123, iv (Ex. 3.82, 3.151), 90–91,
94, 125–27
Op. 30, no. 1, in A, i, 140n.252, ii (Ex. 3.163),
134, 138, 194, iii (Ex. 3.114), 107–8
Op. 30, no. 2, in C Minor, i (Ex. 3.110),
92–93, 106, ii (Ex. 3.55), 74–75
Op. 47 in A Minor ("Kreutzer"), i (Ex.
3.124), 110–11, 504n.16
Op. 96 in G, iii (Ex. 3.25), 66–67
symphony
No. 1 in C, Op. 21, i (Ex. 4.31, 5.67), 21,
154n.18, 170–71, 174, 177, 182–83,
238n.29, 281–82, 289n.117
No. 2 in D, Op. 36, ii (Ex. 3.41, 3.104,
5.68b), 70–71, 72n.42, 283–84, iv
(Ex. 3.150, 5.68), 125, 282–84
No. 3 in E-flat ("Eroica"), Op. 55, i (Ex.
5.70), 25n.81, 284–87, 444n.51
iv, 298
No. 4 in B-flat, Op. 60, i (Ex. 4.62),
195–97, 271n.88
No. 5 in C Minor, Op. 67, i (Ex. 3.136),
114, 131n.221, 209 ii, 549n.121, iv
(Ex. 5.71), 43n.162, 287–92, 300–2
No. 6 in F ("Pastoral"), Op. 68, i (Ex. 5.72),
209, 292–93, 496n.4 iii, 293n.130
No. 7 in A, Op. 92, i (Ex. 5.73), 294, ii
(Ex. 3.83), 91–92, 92n.109, 96–98,
294n.132, iii (Ex. 2.24), 44–45,
47n.183, 136, 405n.67, 444n.50
No. 8 in F, Op. 93, iv, 39, 297n.139,
546n.117
No. 9 in D Minor, Op. 125, i (Ex. 5.74),
294–98 iii, 99n.134, 486n.161, iv (Ex.
5.76), 289n.119, 292n.124, 298–302
Variations for Piano ("Diabelli"), Op. 120
(Ex. 3.13), 22n.64, 62
Variations for Piano ("Eroica"), Op. 35, 298
Violin Concerto in D, Op. 61, i (Ex. 5.15),
164n.42, 235–36, 276, 277

**Bellini, Vincenzo**
"Corre a valle," *I puritani* (Ex. 8.1b), 434

**Boccherini, Luigi**
String Quintet, Op. 11, no. 1,
ii (Ex. 7.3d), 380–81

**Brahms, Johannes**
Intermezzo in B-flat, Op. 76, no. 4 (Ex.
9.38), 537–39
Piano Concerto No. 1 in D Minor, Op. 15, i,
575n.159
Symphony, No. 1 in C Minor, Op. 68, i (Ex.
9.52), 557–60, ii (Ex. 9.9), 506–7
Symphony, No. 2 in D, Op. 73, i (Ex.
9.4), 499–501, ii (Ex. 9.5), 501–3,
550n.127
Symphony, No. 3 in F, Op. 90, i (Ex.
9.12), 509
Violin Sonata No. 1 in G, Op. 78, iii (Ex.
9.8), 504–5
Violin Sonata No. 2 in A, Op. 100, i (Ex.
9.49), 552–54, 564–66

**Bruckner, Anton**
symphony
No. 6 in A, i (Ex. 9.10, 9.41), 243n.36,
506–7, 542–44, 549–50, iv (Ex.
9.2), 498
No. 7 in E, i (Ex. 9.47, 9.51), 552, 555–57,
ii (Ex. 9.44), 481n.159, 547–50
No. 8 in C Minor, i (Ex. 9.3), 498–501,
523, 550n.127, ii (Ex. 9.26), 243n.36,
524 iii, 549n.120, iv (Ex. 9.50), 555
No. 9 in D Minor, ii (Ex. 9.13), 509–11

**Castrucci, Pietro**
Violin Sonata in F, Op. 2, no. 4, i (Ex. 7.10,
7.23), 382–84, 385n.26, 389–90

**Chopin, Frédéric**
Etude in E, Op. 10, no. 3, 526n.72
Etude in A-flat, *Trois nouvelles études*, no.
2 (Ex. 8.12), 46, 443–44, 471n.132,
519n.59
mazurka
Op. 6, no. 1, in F-sharp Minor (Ex. 8.17),
450–53, 485–86
Op. 30, no. 4, in C-sharp Minor (Ex.
9.23), 519–21
Op. 33, no. 1, in G-sharp Minor, 17n.26
Op. 67, no. 2, in G Minor (Ex. 8.18), 452–53
Nocturne in G Minor, Op. 15, no. 3, 436n.19
Nocturne in G Minor, Op. 37, no. 1 (Ex.
8.5), 436–37, 444, 460n.102
Preludes, Op. 28
No. 1 in C (Ex. 8.27), 473, 476–77
No. 2 in A Minor (Ex. 8.28), 473–75
No. 3 in G (Ex. 8.29), 46, 475
No. 4 in E Minor (Ex. 8.30), 475–77
No. 5 in D (Ex. 8.31), 477–78
No. 6 in B Minor (Ex. 8.32), 478
No. 7 in A (Ex. 8.33), 478–80
No. 8 in F-sharp Minor
(Ex. 8.34), 480–81
No. 9 in E (Ex. 8.35), 481
No. 10 in C-sharp Minor (Ex.
8.36), 481–82
No. 11 in B (Ex. 8.37), 482–84
No. 12 in G-sharp Minor
(Ex. 8.38), 484
No. 13 in F-sharp (Ex. 8.39), 484–85
No. 14 in E-flat Minor (Ex. 8.40), 485–86
No. 15 in D-flat (Ex. 8.41), 486–87
No. 16 in B-flat Minor (Ex. 8.42), 487–88
No. 18 in F Minor (Ex. 8.43), 488
No. 19 in E-flat (Ex. 8.44), 46, 488
No. 20 in C Minor (Ex. 8.45), 436n.19,
438n.28, 488–91, 540n.105
No. 21 in B-flat (Ex. 8.46), 491
No. 22 in G Minor (Ex. 8.47), 491–93
No. 23 in F (Ex. 8.48), 493
No. 24 in D Minor (Ex. 8.49), 493
Waltz in A Minor, Op. 34, no. 2 (Ex. 8.3),
435, 438

**Cimarosa, Domenico**
Keyboard Sonata, C 30, Allegretto
(Ex. 7.3a), 380–81
Keyboard Sonata, C 37, Andantino
(Ex. 7.4b), 381–82
Keyboard Sonata, C 78, Allegro brioso
(Ex. 7.7), 382

**Clementi, Muzio**
Keyboard Sonata, Op. 4, no. 5,
ii (Ex. 7.5), 381–82

**Corelli, Arcangelo**
concerto grosso
Op. 6, no. 1, in D, i (Ex. 6.14), 311–12,
315 , –23, 325n.53, iv (Ex. 6.24),
307n.8, 318, 445n.53
Op. 6, no. 3, in C Minor, i, 330n.59, ii (Ex.
6.64), 337, 342, 409
Op. 6, no. 4, in D, i, 312n.19, 318n.40, ii
(Ex. 6.23), 318 iv
Op. 6, no. 5, in B-flat, i (Ex. 6.25), iv, 318n.38
Op. 6, no. 7, in D, iii, (Ex. 6.49), 330, 332
v, 328n.56, 333n.65
Op. 6, no. 8, in G Minor ("Christmas"),
ii, 345n.95, v (Ex. 6.51), 330–31, vi
(Ex. 6.63), 337, 342, 409
Op. 6, no. 9, in F, iii (Ex. 7.24), 390
Op. 6, no. 11, in B-flat, i, 312n.21,
ii (Ex. 6.33), 322–23, 324n.50,
iv (Ex. 6.29), 321, 324, 325,
v (Ex. 6.32), 322

sonata, trio
    Op. 1, no. 1, in F, ii (Ex. 6.80), 347–48
    Op. 1, no. 2, in E Minor, iii (Ex. 6.8), 309–10, 325
    Op. 1, no. 3, in A, i (Ex. 6.35), 46, 324, 404n.66
    Op. 1, no. 5, in B-flat, iii (Ex. 6.81), 347–48
    Op. 1, no. 6, in B Minor, i (Ex. 6.9), 310
    Op. 1, no. 12, in D, ii, 347n.97
    Op. 2, no. 6, in G Minor, i (Ex. 6.34), 46, 320n.42, 323–24, 325, iii (Ex. 6.62), 336–37
    Op. 2, no. 9, in F-sharp Minor, i, 330n.59 iii, 337n.75
    Op. 4, no. 5, in A Minor, iii (Ex. 6.10), 310
sonata, violin
    Op. 5, no. 2, in B-flat, i, 46, 322n.45, ii (Ex. 6.37), 325, iii (Ex. 6.36), 324–25
    Op. 5, no. 3, in C, ii (Ex. 6.74), 344–45, 346
    Op. 5, no. 4, in F, ii (Ex. 6.15), 142n.257, 307n.8, 312, 315, 323
    Op. 5, no. 5, in G Minor, ii (Ex. 6.72), 342n.89, 343, 409 iii, 337n.75
    Op. 5, no. 6, in A, iv (Ex. 6.76), 345–46
    Op. 5, no. 8, in E Minor, i (Ex. 6.44), 328, ii (Ex. 6.48), 329–30 iii, (Ex. 6.58), 335
    Op. 5, no. 11, in E, ii (Ex. 6.47), 329–30, iv (Ex. 6.52), 331
    Op. 5, no. 12, in D Minor ("Follia"), i, 333n.65

**Donizetti, Gaetano**
"Una furtiva lagrima," *L'elisir d'amore* (Ex. 8.1a), 434

**Dvorak, Antonin**
Serenade for Winds, Op. 44b, iii, 550n.127
Symphony No. 7 in D Minor, ii (Ex. 9.54), 52n.216, 180n.75, 434n.12, 564–70

**Ferrari, Domenico**
Violin Sonata in A, Op. 1, no. 3, i (Ex. 7.16b), 385

**Gallo, Domenico**
Trio Sonata in G, i (Ex. 7.18), 385, 387, 388–89, 389n.33, 390n.34, 470–71

**Galuppi, Baldassare**
Concerto a quattro in B-flat, i (Ex. 7.12), 384
*Diavolessa, La* (Ex. 7.15a), 385

Keyboard Sonata in B-flat, I. 40, i (Ex. 7.21), 387–88, 394–95
Keyboard Sonata in D, I. 39, ii (Ex. 7.36), 394–95
Keyboard Sonata in E, I. 41, i (Ex. 7.69), 415, 416

**Gaviniès, Pierre**
Violin Sonata in A, Op. 3, no. 1, i (Ex. 7.16a), 385
Violin Sonata in B-flat, Op. 3, no. 5, ii (Ex. 7.3b), 380–81

**Graun, Carl Heinrich**
Trio Sonata (Ex. 7.15b), 385, 389–90

**Grieg, Edvard**
"Åse's Death," *Peer Gynt Suite No. 1*, Op. 46, no. 2 (Ex. 9.36), 180n.75, 536–37
"First Meeting," *Four Songs*, Op. 21, 1, 539–40n.103
"First Meeting," *Two Melodies*, Op. 53, no. 2 (Ex. 9.39), 539–40
String Quartet in G Minor, Op. 27, iv (Ex. 9.53), 560–64

**Handel, George Frideric**
concerto grosso
    Op. 6, no. 1, in G Minor, i (Ex. 6.67), ii, 313n.22, 339 iii 336n.73
    Op. 6, no. 2, in F, ii, 325, 328n.57, iv (Ex. 6.38)
    Op. 6, no. 3, in E Minor, iv (Ex. 6.16), 313, 321n.44, 325
    Op. 6, no. 4, in A Minor, iv (Ex. 6.46), 328–29
    Op. 6, no. 5, in D, iii (Ex. 6.79), 347
    Op. 6, no. 6, in G Minor, i (Ex. 6.26, 6.60), 336, 445n.53, iv (Ex. 6.17), 313, 318–20, 328–29
    Op. 6, no. 7, in B-flat, iii and, iv (Ex. 6.61), 336, iv (Ex. 6.39), 318n.40, 325–26
    Op. 6, no. 8, in C Minor, i, iv, 333n.65
    Op. 6, no. 9, in F, ii (Ex. 6.50), 318n.40, 330–31
    Op. 6, no. 11, in A, ii, 323n.47
    Op. 6, no. 12, in B Minor, ii (Ex. 6.54), 332

**Haydn, Joseph**
quartet, string
    Op. 17, no. 1, in E, iv (Ex. 4.55), 190–91, 204, 279
    Op. 17, no. 4, in C Minor, i (Ex. 4.4), 153–54, 169, 172–73
    Op. 17, no. 5, in G, ii (Ex. 3.99), 22n.64, 102, 192n.104
    Op. 20, no. 2, in C, iii, (Ex. 4.64), 198
    Op. 20, no. 3, in G Minor, iv (Ex. 4.58), 193
    Op. 20, no. 6, in A, i (Ex. 3.65), 80, 143, 144–46, iii (Ex. 3.96), 100
    Op. 33, no. 2, in E-flat, i (Ex. 4.43), 179, 180–81, 182n.77, 186, 217–18
    Op. 42 in D Minor, iv (Ex. 2.21), 38–39, 42, 43–44, 47
    Op. 50, no. 1, in B-flat, i (Ex. 4.6), 154, 160, 161n.35, ii (Ex. 3.166), 136, 144
    Op. 50, no. 2, in C, iii (Ex. 3.132), 113
    Op. 50, no. 3, in E-flat, i, 154n.16
    Op. 50, no. 5, in F, i (Ex. 2.25, 5.4), 45–46, 51n.212, 226–27
    Op. 50, no. 6, in D, i (Ex. 4.77), 211, iii (Ex. 3.84), 92, 280
    Op. 54, no. 1 in G, iii (Ex. 3.36, 4.13), 69–70, 157, 160, iv (Ex. 4.51b), 188–89, 192n.104
    Op. 54, no. 3, in E, ii, 247n.47
    Op. 55, no. 1, in A, i (Ex. 3.154), 128–29
    Op. 55, no. 3, in B-flat, ii, 118n.184
    Op. 64, no. 1, in C, i (Ex. 4.23), 165–66, 522n.63
    Op. 64, no. 2, in B Minor, i (Ex. 4.39), 174, 177, 185, 186, 208, 209, 239n.31, iii (Ex. 5.26), 241–43
    Op. 64, no. 3, in B-flat, iii, 442n.40
    Op. 64, no. 4, in G, i, 123n.203, 137n.234, ii (Ex. 5.43), 262
    Op. 71, no. 2, in D, ii (Ex. 4.75), 207, iii (Ex. 4.85), 220–22
    Op. 74, no. 1, in C, i, 96n.124
    Op. 74, no. 2, in F, ii (Ex. 3.60, 3.113), 76, 107
    Op. 74, no. 3, in G Minor ("Horseman"), i (Ex. 3.95), 99–100, iv (Ex. 5.55), 269–70, 272, 273
    Op. 76, no. 2, in D Minor, ii (Ex. 3.58), 75
    Op. 76, no. 3, in C ("Emperor"), i (Ex. 3.93), 99, iv (Ex. 3.37), 69–70, 142, 214
    Op. 76, no. 4, in B-flat, ii (Ex. 3.169), 140
    Op. 76, no. 6, in E-flat, i, 118n.184
    Op. 77, no. 1, in G, ii (Ex. 3.39), 70
    Op. 77, no. 2, in F, i (Ex. 5.8), 228, iii (Ex. 3.49, 5.2), 74, 225, 237n.28, 496n.4
sonata, piano
    H. 9 in F, iii, 129n.210
    H. 20 in C Minor, ii, 98n.128
    H. 21 in C, ii (Ex. 4.21, 4.83), 154n.15, 165, 217–18, 522n.63, iii (Ex. 3.97), 100
    H. 24 in D, i, 98n.128
    H. 25 in E-flat, i (Ex. 5.1), 224–25
    H. 26 in A, i (Ex. 5.18), 237–38, 264
    H. 28 in E-flat, ii (Ex. 3.30), 68, 107, 261n.68

H. 29 in F, ii (Ex. 3.63), 76–78, 153n.13, 154, 160, 161n.35, iii (Ex. 3.128), 99n.133, 111–12
H. 31 in E, i (Ex. 3.78), 87–88, 93–94, 95, 212n.156, 395–96
H. 32 in B Minor, ii (Ex. 3.61), 76, 266
H. 33 in D, i (Ex. 3.69), 83, 225–26, 267–68, iii (Ex. 3.26), 67
H. 35 in C, i (Ex. 4.29), 169–70, 174, iii (Ex. 3.130), 112–13, 122, 309n.13
H. 36 in C-sharp Minor, i, 40–41n.150
H. 37 in D, i (Ex. 4.37), 40–41n.150, 173–74, 175, 177, 179–80, 209–10, 213–14 iii, 222n.9
H. 38 in E-flat, iii (Ex. 3.52, 3.127), 74, 111
H. 39 in G, ii (Ex. 3.11), 61–62, 74
H. 40 in G, ii (Ex. 3.133, 4.25), 114, 167
H. 41 in B-flat, i (Ex. 3.47), 72–74
H. 48 in C, i (Ex. 4.5), 153–54
H. 49 in E-flat, i (Ex. 3.118, 4.56, 4.67, 5.25), 108, 191–92, 199–200, 202, 204, 241, 246, 265, iii (Ex. 3.126b), 110–11
H. 52 in E-flat, i (Ex. 5.16), 236, 263
symphony
    No. 8 in G ("Le soir"), i (Ex. 4.18), 162–63
    No. 42 in D, ii (Ex. 3.74), 51n.213, 85–86, 117, 470
    No. 45 in F-sharp Minor ("Farewell"), i (Ex. 5.13), 230–31, v (Ex. 2.17), 32–33, 34, 275–76
    No. 61 in D, ii, 125n.206
    No. 67 in F, i (Ex. 4.20), 164–65, ii (Ex. 5.19), 238–39, 281, 284n.108, 522n.63
    No. 87 in A, iii (Ex. 2.4, 5.42), 24, 261
    No. 89 in F, ii (Ex. 4.17), 162
    No. 92 in G ("Oxford"), i (Ex. 2.20, 9.6), 36–37, 99n.133, 503, 509n.23
    No. 93 in D, i (Ex. 3.111, 5.48), 107, 266, 268–69
    No. 95 in C Minor, iii (Ex. 5.50), 267–69
    No. 97 in C, i (Ex. 5.29), 245–46, 263, iv (Ex. 5.66), 280
    No. 98 in B-flat, iv, 225n.8, 225n.9
    No. 100 in G ("Military"), i (Ex. 2.26), 47–48, 442n.40, ii (Ex. 8.11), 79n.56, 442, iv (Ex. 3.155), 130–31
    No. 101 in D, ii (Ex. 3.28), 67–68, iii (Ex. 5.7), 227, 263
    No. 104 in D ("London"), i, 210n.151, 211n.155, ii (Ex. 4.74), 205–7, iv (Ex. 4.34, 5.33), 172–73, 174, 175, 177, 248, 261, 282n.105
trio, piano
    H. 6 in F, ii (Ex. 3.44), 72, 88n.100, 263n.73
    H. 7 in D, iii (Ex. 3.19, 3.54), 65, 74
    H. 12 in E Minor, iii (Ex. 5.65), 279
    H. 13 in C Minor, i (Ex. 3.45), 72
    H. 14 in A-flat, ii (Ex. 3.35), 69
    H. 16 in D, iii (Ex. 3.1), 57, 66–67
    H. 18 in A, iii, 118n.184
    H. 21 in C, i (Ex. 4.53, 5.21), 189–90, 239, 246, 265
    H. 22 in E-flat, iii (Ex. 3.116), 108
    H. 24 in D, i (Ex. 5.56, 5.59), 271, 273
    H. 27 in C, iii (Ex. 3.100, 4.15), 104, 117, 158, 176n.66
    H. 28 in E, i (Ex. 3.29, 4.19), 68, 108–10, 131, 163–64, 169, 208
    H. 31 in E-flat Minor, i (Ex. 4.69), 202–3
Variations for Piano in F Minor, H. XVII: 6 (Ex. 3.9, 3.167, 5.75), 61, 139, 182, 212n.156, 258n.63, 296, 297–98

**Hensel, Fanny**
"Äolsharfe auf dem Schlosse zu Baden, Die," 528n.81
"Bitte" (Ex. 9.30a), 243n.36, 517n.52, 527–28
"Eichwald brauset, Der" (Ex. 9.30c), 527–29
"Erwache Knab'," 517n.52
"Fichtenbaum und Palme" (Ex. 9.30b), 527–28
"Im Hochland Bruder" (Ex. 9.27), 524–25
"Neujahrslied," 526n.74
"Sehnsucht" (Ex. 9.25), 523–24, 527–28
"Wonne der Wehmut" (Ex. 9.19), 180n.75, 516–18, 533–34
"Zu deines Lagers Füßen" (Ex. 9.29), 526–27, 528

**Holst, Gustav**
"Jupiter," *The Planets* (Ex. 9.24), 521–23, 552n.131

**Jommelli, Niccolò**
*Demofoonte*, Act 2, scene 10 (Ex. 7.11), 382–84

**Liszt, Franz**
"Les cloches de Genève," *Années de pèlerinage I* (Ex. 9.40), 540–44
Piano Sonata in B Minor (Ex. 9.55), 551–52, 570–75

**Mahler, Gustav**
Symphony No. 3, vi, 545n.115
Symphony No. 5, iii (Ex. 9.48), 552
Symphony No. 6, iii (Ex. 9.33), 528n.78, 529, 531

**Marcello, Benedetto**
Keyboard Sonata in F, Op. 1, no. 1, i (Ex. 7.20), 385n.26, 387, 388–89, 470–71

**Mendelssohn, Felix**
*Songs without Words*, Op. 19, no. 1 (Ex. 8.16), 448–50, 536n.98
*Songs without Words*, Op. 102, no. 5, 531n.89
String Octet in E-flat, Op. 20, i (Ex. 9.21), 180n.75, 518, 519, 528, 533–34
String Quartet in E-flat, Op. 12, i (Ex. 8.24), 470–71

**Mozart, Wolfgang Amadeus**
"Ach, ich fühl's," *Die Zauberflöte*, K. 620, 206n.134
Allegro and Andante in F Minor for Organ, K. 608 (Ex. 3.70), 83, 96
Clarinet Quintet in A, K. 581, i (Ex. 5.44), 178n.71, 225n.8, 241n.35, 262, iv (Ex. 3.161), 57, 106n.161, 132–34, 136–37
Clarinet Trio in E-flat, K. 498, i (Ex. 4.14, 4.65), 158–60, 198–99, 275
concerto, piano
    K. 450 in B-flat, i (Ex. 3.88), 96, ii (Ex. 3.107), 70n.39, 106
    K. 453 in G, i (Ex. 4.16), 160, 164, 167n.51, 169, 211n.154, iii (Ex. 4.40), 176
    K. 459 in F, i (Ex. 3.131), 113, ii (Ex. 3.142), 115
    K. 466 in D Minor, ii (Ex. 3.89), 96, 132
    K. 467 in C, i, 247
    K. 482 in E-flat, i (Ex. 4.30, 5.41), 170, 174, 177, 212n.156, 260–61, 275
    K. 488 in A, i (Ex. 3.3), 57, 65, ii (Ex. 5.20), 239, 246, 264
    K. 491 in C Minor, iii (Ex. 5.24), 241, 246, 246n.43, 261
*Eine kleine Nachtmusik*, K. 525, ii (Ex. 3.51), 74
Fantasia in C Minor, K. 475 (Ex. 4.71), 204–5
"Fuggi, crudele, fuggi," *Don Giovanni*, K. 527, 40
Horn Quintet in E-flat, K. 407, ii (Ex. 3.40), 70
Piano Quartet in E-flat, K. 493 i (Ex. 5.64), 277–79, 282–83, 342n.88
Piano Trio in B-flat, K. 502, ii (Ex. 2.14, 3.80), 29, 88, 89–90, 121–22, 144n.268
Piano Trio in G, K. 496, ii (Ex. 4.24), 167
Piano Trio in G, K. 564, ii (Ex. 3.43, 3.64), 71–72, 78, 88n.100, 153n.13, 169
quartet, string
    K. 421 in D Minor, iii (Ex. 4.12), 157, 169, 203–4, 210n.148 iv, 123n.204
    K. 428 in E-flat, iv (Ex. 3.156c), 132, 134n.229
    K. 458 in B-flat ("Hunt"), i (Ex. 3.152, 5.27), 127, 243, 263 iv, 99n.133

quartet, string (*cont.*)
  K. 464 in A, i (Ex. 3.98), 100–1, iv (Ex. 4.60), 117n.179, 194
  K. 465 in C ("Dissonance"), iii, Trio (Ex. 3.173), 146, iv (Ex. 5.17), 236–37
  K. 499 in D, iv (Ex. 4.61), 195
  K. 575, in D, ii, 210n.151
  K. 589 in B-flat, iii (Ex. 3.32), 69
Rondo for Piano in A Minor, K. 511 (Ex. 4.7), 154, 160–62
Rondo for Piano in D, K. 485, 70n.39
Rondo for Piano in F, K. 494 (Ex. 5.11), 229, 263n.72
sonata, piano
  K. 279 in C, i (Ex. 2.19), 36, ii (Ex. 4.33), 171, 174, 175, 222
  K. 280 in F, i (Ex. 4.32), 171, 174, 175, iii (Ex. 4.82), 120n.196, 176n.64, 217
  K. 281 in B-flat, i (Ex. 3.157, 4.41), 132, 176, 177, 211–12, 392n.43, iii (Ex. 2.15, 3.141), 29–30, 31–32, 104, 115, 271, 273, 276–77
  K. 282 in E-flat, i (Ex. 3.91, 4.73), 98, 205, 208 ii, 167n.51
  K. 283 in G, i (Ex. 3.139, 4.42), 176–77, 211, ii (Ex. 3.143, 4.49), 103n.145, 115–16, 183–86, 183n.81
  K. 284 in D, ii (Ex. 3.164), 110n.166, 134, iii (Ex. 3.50, 3.108, 3.137, 3.126a), 74, 104, 106, 110–11, 114
  K. 309 in C, i (Ex. 3.140), 114–15, ii (Ex. 3.125), 110–11, iii (Ex. 4.38), 174, 175, 212
  K. 310 in A Minor, i (Ex. 4.79, 4.84), 212, 213, 218–20, 554–55, ii (Ex. 3.122), 108–10 iii, 137n.234
  K. 311 in D, ii, 137n.234, iii (Ex. 3.123a), 110
  K. 330 in C, i (Ex. 3.71), 85, 86 ii, 70n.39, iii (Ex. 3.42, 5.45), 70–71, 72n.42, 264
  K. 331 in A, i (Ex. 3.24, 3.87), 66–67, 94, 95–96, ii (Ex. 3.146), 123, 132
  K. 332 in F, i (Ex. 3.75, 4.59, 4.66, 5.53), 57n.12, 86, 93–94, 117n.177, 132n.225, 194, 199, 202, 209, 270–71, 273, ii (Ex. 3.105), 104–5, 106, 131n.221, iii (Ex. 3.46, 3.134, 4.22), 72, 114, 165, 522n.63
  K. 333 in B-flat, i (Ex. 2.16, 5.57), 23n.68, 31–32, 33–34, 271, 272, 280, ii (Ex. 3.62, 3.121, 4.28, 4.50), 76, 108–10, 169, 186–87, 309n.13
  K. 457 in C Minor, i (Ex. 4.2) 152–53, 158, 297n.140 ii, 40–41n.150
  K. 545 in C, i (Ex. 3.66, 5.30, 7.9), 80–81, 85–86, 144, 246, 382–84, 390, 415n.88, ii (Ex. 5.12), 70n.39, 229–30, 263
  K. 570 in B-flat, i (Ex. 5.61), 276, 277–78, iii (Ex. 3.10), 61, 68–69, 70, 258n.63
  K. 576 in D, i (Ex. 3.4b, 3.119, 5.32), 57, 108, 116–17, 247–48, 264, ii (Ex. 3.6b), 58–59, 110n.166, iii (Ex. 3.138, 3.162, 4.76), 114–15, 134, 177, 210–11, 261, 274
sonata, violin
  K. 296 in C, ii (Ex. 4.51a), 188–89, 192n.104
  K. 304 in E Minor, i (Ex. 2.22, 3.59, 3.72, 5.60), 38, 39, 76, 85, 114–15, 123–24, 274
  K. 380 in E-flat, i (Ex. 5.63), 277
  K. 454 in B-flat, i (Ex. 4.3, 5.52), 153–54, 158, 160, 161n.35, 268, ii (Ex. 3.68, 4.78, 4.80), 83, 117n.177, 211, 213–14, 236n.26, 263–64, 274, iii (Ex. 3.12, 3.144), 61–62, 75, 122
  K. 481 in E-flat, i, 96n.124, ii (Ex. 3.76), 86–87, 93–94, 95, 96, 212n.156
  K. 547a in F, ii (Ex. 4.10), 154, 167, 170–71, 179–80, 182–83
String Quintet in C, K. 515, i (Ex. 3.153), 40, 127–28
String Quintet in C Minor, K. 406, i, 40–41n.150
String Quintet in E-flat, K. 614, i, 32
symphony
  No. 14 in A, K. 114, i, 103n.145
  No. 35 in D ("Haffner"), K. 385, i, 52n.217, iii (Ex. 3.109), 106, 246n.43
  No. 36 in C, K. 425, i (Ex. 5.10), 229, 260, 264
  No. 38 in D ("Prague"), K. 504, i (Ex. 3.92, 5.36), 98–99, 142, 209, 240n.33, 251–53
  No. 39 in E-flat, K. 543, i (Ex. 5.3, 5.35), 52n.217, 225–26, 243n.37, 251, 275 iii, 146n.271
  No. 40 in G Minor, K. 550, i (Ex. 2.6, 5.37, 5.58), 25, 31–32, 117n.176, 253–57, 265, 271–72, 321n.43, 435n.15, 444, 444n.51, 511n.25, 579n.169, iii (Trio), 442n.40
  No. 41 in C ("Jupiter"), K. 551, iii (Ex. 2.18), 34–36, 101n.137 iv, 268
"Un'aura amorosa," *Così fan tutte*, K. 588, 20n.49
Violin Concerto in A, K. 219, i (Ex. 5.40), 247n.48, 260
Violin Concerto in B-flat, K. 207, i (Ex. 5.49), 266, 267n.80, 268–69
*Zauberflöte, Die*, K. 620, Act 1, nos. 1, 3, and 4, 153n.12

**Nardini, Pietro**
Violin Sonata in D, Op. 5, 4, iii (Ex. 7.60), 408–9

**Pachelbel, Johann**
Canon in D, 385n.26

**Peroti, Padre Fulgentius**
Keyboard Sonata in B-flat, iii (Ex. 7.26), 390

**Puccini, Giacomo**
"Nessun dorma," *Turandot* (Ex. 9.34), 529, 531–34

**Quantz, Johann Joachim**
Trio Sonata in G Minor, iii (Ex. 7.13), 380n.9

**Rossini, Gioachino**
*L'inganno felice*, 294n.134

**Rutini, Giovanni Marco**
Keyboard Sonata in F, Op. 8, no. 1, i (Ex. 7.71), 416–17

**Scarlatti, Domenico**
sonata, keyboard
  K. 26 in A (Ex. 7.77), 409, 424–26
  K. 115 in C Minor (Ex. 7.75), 422–23
  K. 141 in D Minor (Ex. 7.50, 7.52), 46, 402–3, 404, 424
  K. 159 in C (Ex. 7.73), 418–19
  K. 169 in G (Ex. 7.78), 391–92, 427–29
  K. 308 in C (Ex. 7.41), 398, 405, 418–19
  K. 309 in C (Ex. 7.29, 7.40), 391, 398, 405, 418–19
  K. 366 in F, 398n.57
  K. 394 in E Minor, 398n.57
  K. 402 in E Minor (Ex. 7.45, 7.51, 7.56), 391–92, 399, 402–3, 405, 410, 415n.85
  K. 403 in E, 398n.57
  K. 421 in C, 403n.64
  K. 450 in G Minor (Ex. 7.54), 405, 424
  K. 481 in F Minor (Ex. 7.46), 399–400, 403n.64, 405
  K. 492 in D, 397n.50
  K. 525 in F (Ex. 7.53), 404, 417n.93
  K. 545 in B-flat, (Ex. 7.39), 397–98, 405, 418–19
  K. 587 in C (Ex. 7.30), 391–92

**Schobert, Johann**
Keyboard Sonata, Op. 6, no. 1, i (Ex. 7.3c), 380–81

**Schubert, Franz**
Ländler, Op. 17, 1, no. 3 (Ex. 8.8), 280–81, 439–40
Piano Sonata in A, D. 959, i (Ex. 8.23), 318n.39, 445n.53, 446n.55, 457–58, 463–69, 553–54, 564–66

Piano Sonata in A Minor, Op. 42, D. 845, i, 463n.106
Piano Sonata in B-flat, D. 960, i (Ex. 8.21), 458–60, 519n.57, 564n.144
String Quartet No. 8 in E-flat, D. 812, iii (Ex. 8.9), 280–81, 440–41, 491
String Quintet in C, D. 956, iii (Ex. 9.1), 496–98, 504–5
Symphony No. 8 in B Minor ("Unfinished"), i (Ex. 8.14), 318n.39, 444–47, 457–58, 458n.95, 468
*Winterreise, Die,* D. 911
"Die Krähe," (Ex. 3.171), 144
"Die Wegweiser," 103n.145, 463n.108
"Der greise Kopf," 463n.108
"Im Dorfe," 463n.108

**Schumann, Robert**
"Am Kamin," *Kinderszenen,* Op. 15, no. 8 (Ex. 8.2a), 434
"Auf einer Burg," *Liederkreis,* Op. 39, no. 7 (Ex. 8.22a), 460–63, 465n.116
"Blume der Ergebung, Die" Op. 83, no. 2, 526n.74
*Davidsbündlertänze,* Op. 6, no. 5 (Ex. 8.7), 280–81, 438–39
*Davidsbündlertänze,* Op. 6, no. 8 (Ex. 8.6), 437–38, 471, 540n.105
"Eintritt," *Waldszenen,* Op. 82, no. 1 (Ex. 9.22), 519, 527–28, 564n.144
Fantasy for Piano in C, Op. 17, i, 471n.132
*Faschingsschwank aus Wien,* Op. 26, i (Ex. 8.25), 471
"Mondnacht," *Liederkreis,* Op. 39, no. 5 (Ex. 8.19), 317n.37, 453–55, 526–27, 534, 550n.127
Symphony No. 2 in C, Op. 61, iii (Ex. 8.10), 441–42 iv, 471n.132
"Valse noble," *Carnaval,* Op. 9, no. 4 (Ex. 8.15), 447–48
Violin Sonata in A minor, Op. 105, i, 453n.76

"Volksliedchen," *Album for the Young,* Op. 68, no. 14 (Ex. 8.2b-c), 434
"Waldegespräch," *Liederkreis,* Op. 39, no. 3 (Ex. 8.20), 455–57
"Wehmut," *Liederkreis,* Op. 39, no. 9 (Ex. 8.26), 471

**Sibelius, Jean**
Symphony No. 5 in E-flat, iii (Ex. 9.37, 9.43), 180n.75, 536–37, 540, 545–47

**Stamitz, Johann**
Flute Concerto in D, i (Ex. 7.22b), 388

**Strauss, Richard**
*Eine Alpensinfonie,* Op. 64, 545n.115
*Ein Heldenleben,* Op. 40 (Ex. 9.42), 544–45, 554–55

**Svendsen, Johan**
*Romance,* Op. 26 (Ex. 9.28), 515n.44, 525–26, 528n.78

**Tartini, Giuseppe**
Violin Sonata, Op. 6, no. 4, i (Ex. 7.4a), 381–82

**Tchaikovsky, Pyotr Ilyich**
*Hamlet* Overture-Fantasy, Op. 67, 504n.17
"Morning Prayer," *Children's Album,* Op. 39, no. 1 (Ex. 9.45), 187n.90, 550–51
Symphony No. 4 in F Minor, Op. 36, i (Ex. 9.11), 507–9
Symphony No. 6 in B Minor ("Pathétique"), Op. 74, i, 442n.42

**Verdi, Giuseppe**
"Libiamo ne' lieti calici," *La Traviata* (Ex. 9.46), 318n.39, 551–52

**Vivaldi, Antonio**
concerto, violin
Op. 3, no. 12, in E, iii (Ex. 6.69), 340, 342, 409, 415
Op. 8, no. 1, in E ("Spring"), i (Ex. 6.3), 307, 381n.11
Op. 8, no. 2, in G Minor ("Summer"), i (Ex. 6.4, 6.66), 339, 381n.11, iii (Ex. 6.40), 307, 327, 328
Op. 8, no. 3, in F ("Autumn"), i, 335n.72 iii, 333n.65
Op. 8, no. 5, in E-flat ("La Tempesta di Mare"), iii (Ex. 6.41), 327
Op. 8, no. 6, in C ("Il Piacere"), iii (Ex. 6.31), 321–22
Op. 8, no. 7, in D Minor, iii (Ex. 6.57, 6.70), 334–35, 340, 342, 409
Op. 8, no. 8, in G Minor, i, 335n.72
Op. 8, no. 11, in D, i, 318n.40, iii (Ex. 6.85), 350
Op. 8, no. 12, in C, i (Ex. 6.43), 327–28

**Wagner, Richard**
"Dich frage ich," *The Flying Dutchman* (Ex. 9.20), 180n.75, 533–34
"Mild und Leise" ("Liebestod"), *Tristan und Isolde* (Ex. 9.31, 9.56f), 529–31, 581
Prelude, *Tristan und Isolde* (Ex. 9.56), 243n.36, 271–72n.89, 433n.10, 511, 550, 575–81
"Zu einer Freiung," *Die Meistersinger von Nürnberg,* Act 1, scene 3, 552n.130

**Wolf, Hugo**
"Gesang Weylas," *Mörike Lieder,* 46, 514n.40

# General Index

*For the benefit of digital users, indexed terms that span two pages (e.g., 52-53) may, on occasion, appear on only one of those pages.*

abandoned cadence, 140, 160, 178, 180, 181–82
   annotation of, 182n.77
   vs. deceptive, 184n.82, 217–18, 400–1n.62
   effects prolongational closure, 178–79
   followed by new material, 178–79, 277
   formal functions of, 178–79
   in galant, 400
   lowered leadingtone, 364–66, 376
   nineteenth-century variant (includes dominant), 533–34
   repeats immediately preceding material, 178–79
   as way station, 181
abandoned cadential progression, 23, 150–51, 178, 286–87, 362n.139
   annotation of, 182n.77, 182n.79
   in baroque, 320–23
   dominant replaced by $V^4_2$, 182–83, 276, 277, 322
   dominant replaced by $V^6_5$, 182, 183, 321–22
   dominant replaced by $VII^6_5$, 296
   dominant replaced by nondominant harmony, 183–85, 275–76, 279, 323–24
   dominant undermined by first inversion ($V^6_5$), 179–82, 276–77, 321
   with ECP, 230, 236, 255, 257–58, 275–79, 321, 328, 341–42, 409n.72
   facilitates uniform harmonic rhythm, 437–38
   in fugue, 364
   in galant, 402
   harmonic expansion, role of, 186, 275
   vs. harmonic reduction, 186–87
   nineteenth-century variant (includes dominant), 534, 536, 542
   in place of abandoned cadence, 178, 182
   with plagal cadential progression, 514, 516–17, 521–22
   preceded by rocking on the tonic, 275–76
   with Prinner cadence, 387
   unusual cases of, 289, 294n.133, 402
abrupt cadence, 132n.227, 392, 413–14, 415, 419–20, 563
after-the-end, 21–22, 39. *See also* postcadential function
Agawu, Kofi, 6, 8–9, 40, 50–51, 151, 493n.173
agogic accent, 498–99
Alberti bass, 139, 189
allusion to dominant harmony. *See under* subdominant arrival; plagal cadential/ closural progression
alto cadence (*clausula altizans*), 380, 382–84
alto melodic pattern. *See* basic alto pattern; varied alto pattern
ambiguity. *See* cadential ambiguity; harmonic progression types, ambiguity of
Amen cadence/codetta, 146–47, 526–27, 547
anacrusis
   dominant, 410, 557–59, 575
   extended, 220–21, 222, 250, 421, 484, 564
   pre-dominant, 560–63
annunciatory function, 120–353, 544–45
Anson-Cartwright, Mark, 8–9, 315, 317n.35, 317n.36, 441n.37
answer (in fugue), 344–45, 351–52, 370–71, 372–73
antecedent
   ends with independent deceptive cadence, 521–22
   ends with Prinner cadence, 385–87
   ends with simple (I–V) HC, 104
   ends with reinterpreted HC, 121–23
   failed, 167
   modulating, 437, 460n.102, 465–67
   overlaps with consequent, 451, 453
   *See also* compound antecedent

antecedent-consequent relation, 95, 158–62, 438–39, 471
anticipation harmony, 514
anti-period. *See* reversed period
appoggiatura harmony, 514, 530–33
Aristotle, 2
arrival six-four, 262n.70, 481n.159, 549–50, 560–63, 573–75
artistic economy, law of, 250, 279, 302
A section
  alternative section, 455
  closes exceptionally with HC, 79n.56, 118, 463
  lacks cadential closure, 79n.56, 455, 463, 481, 501–3
  nonconventional form, 463–64
A′ section, 79n.56, 456–57, 508–9
ascending melodic pattern, 46, 75, 265
assertion, of closure, 498, 501–3, 508–9
asymmetrical grouping structure, 103
atemporality, 2, 5, 7, 8–9
augmented-sixth harmony, 104, 507
authentic cadence. *See* cadence; imperfect authentic cadence; perfect authentic cadence
authentic cadential progression. *See* cadential progression (authentic)
auxiliary cadence, 21

Bach, Carl Philipp Emanuel, 391, 399, 399n.58, 406–8, 422, 423–24
Bach, Johann Sebastian
  chorales, 307, 436n.17
  final deceptive cadence (⇒PAC), 315, 453–54
  galant style in, 334n.67, 361n.137
  preludes of *WTC* 2, 333–34
  Prinner cadence, 390
  systematic tonal plan, 307, 311–12
baroque binary form, 335–36
baroque style
  *Affektenlehre*, 437n.24
  classical forms, incipient, 333
  compact cadences, pervasive use of, 322–23
  harmonic deceleration, avoidance of, 313, 321–22
  motoric rhythms, 317–18
  periodic forms, infrequent use of, 333
  rhythmic continuity, emphasis on, 313, 321–22
  retaining cadential formula, 307
  Romantic style, influence on, 437
  subdominant region, emphasis on, 376–77
  uniformity of parameters, 326–27
Barthes, Roland, 7, 8, 20n.50, 20n.51
basic alto pattern, 64, 67–68
  with cadential six-four, 68, 261
  in *cadenza doppia*, 307–8
  in converging HC, 108–10
  with ECP, 273
  in IAC, 87–88
basic idea
  with cadential content, 35, 437–38, 442, 471, 480n.151, 489–90
  embracing two metrical downbeats, 47–48n.184
  expanded, 573n.154
  Prinner cadence, within, 471
  as repeated one-measure motive, 463–64
  repeated twice, 439
  with sequential content, 448–49
basic melodic pattern, 63–69
basic model (bass line), 27–30
basic simple pattern, 63, 64, 65, 260
  with cadential six-four, 65, 260
  in converging HC, 107
  ECP, rare in, 260
  in IAC, 86
  in simple HC, 106
basic soprano pattern, 64, 65–67, 260
  with cadential six-four, 66–67, 260–61
  in converging HC, 107–8
  in IAC, 86–87
basic tenor pattern, 64, 68–69, 261, 414
  in converging HC, 110
  ECP, frequent usage in, 261
  in IAC, 83–85, 90–91, 267–68
bass line, 25–31
  ♯④ to ♮④, 50n.200
  basic model, 27–28, 29–30, 432, 437
  cadential, nonclassical, 437
  classical, 544–45
  closure, 27–28
  complexities in multiple ECPs, 251–53
  modulating model, 28–29
  period model, 28–30
  potentially two-fold, rendered as one, 225–26, 251–52, 253
  in Romantic, 27–28
  two-gapped model, 28–30
  *See also* cadential bass line, classical; descending bass line
bass melodic pattern, 76, 265
  ascending/descending bass patterns, 265, 290–91
  embellishments to stage 3b, 76, 265
  in IAC, 88, 268
bass voice
  motivic quality, 470–71, 538–40
  registral shift signaling cadential progression, 28, 139
  as two-voiced structure, 26–27
*basse fundamental*, 26
*basso continuo*, 26
Beethoven, Ludwig van, 549–50, 575
  equal division of the octave, 201–2
  final deceptive cadence (⇒PAC), 453–54
  iconic cadence, precursors of, 545n.114, 546n.117, 549n.121
  individualized material for cadence, 33–34, 307
  late style anticipates Romantic practice, 79n.56
before-the-beginning, 22n.62, 57–58n.16, *See also* anacrusis
beginning-middle-end (paradigm), 2, 16, 20
Benjamin, Thomas, 352–53n.119, 367n.149
Berardi, Angelo, 365n.145, 365n.147
Bergé, Pieter, 140n.250
Berger, Karol, 41n.152, 47, 48–49, 50–51, 129–30n.211
Berlioz, Hector, 431n.1
Berry, Wallace, 283n.107
Biamonte, Nicole, 477n.141, 550n.128
bifocal close, 336n.74
binary sonata form, 424
Blombach, Ann, 14–15, 39–40, 46–47, 48–49
blues, twelve-bar, 514n.43
blurring, cadential, 364–67, 373–75, 377–78, 487–88
boundaries of cadential progression, 31–32, 108, 223–24, 240–41
Brahms, Johannes, 496
Bruckner, Anton, 496, 555
B section, 35–36, 118, 123, 501–3
Burstein, Poundie, 436n.16, 463n.108
  cadential ambiguities, multiple, 218–20, 221–22
  dominant arrival, critique of, 207–8
  galant form, 379n.5
  on half cadence (and/or dominant arrival), 101, 102, 187n.92, 188n.95, 198–99
  transition closing with PAC, 82n.75
Burstein, Poundie, and Joseph Straus, 142n.257, 146n.271

cadence
  abrupt. *See* abrupt cadence
  blurring, 364–67, 373–75, 377–78
  classical. *See* classical cadence
  vs. codetta, 35, 39
  emerges out of sequence, 112–13, 351, 437–38, 451, 481, 509
  etymology of, 14, 33–34, 63
  as "falling" motion, 14, 33–34, 46, 63
  as harmony, 20–25
  hierarchical conditions of, 34
  and higher-level units, 17–20, 33
  logic of, 45
  and phrase, 16–17
  as schema, 56, 151, 379–80
  as tonal confirmation, 21, 352
  "too early"/premature, 46, 47–48, 134, 443n.44, 452–53, 473, 475, 498
  traditional notions of, 14–15
  "undoing," 45
  *See also* cadential function; half cadence; imperfect authentic cadence; perfect authentic cadence

cadenced group, 16, 18–19
*cadence galante*. See Cudworth (schema)
*cadence parfait* (perfect cadence), 14, 20–21
cadence phrase/theme, 32–33
*cadence rompue* (broken cadence), 20–21
cadential abundance, 540
cadential ambiguity, 209–22, 554–60
    abandoned vs. deceptive, 184n.82, 217–18, 400–1n.62
    deceptive. vs. HC, 152
    deceptive vs. IAC, 94n.117
    evaded vs. covered, 214–16, 555
    evaded vs. deceptive (elided), 170–71, 172–73, 209–11, 320, 501–3
    evaded vs. HC/dominant arrival, 217, 232
    evaded vs. IAC (elided), 213–14, 552–53
    evaded vs. PAC (elided), 211–13, 554
    grouping structure, role of, 209
    HK: HC vs. HK: PAC, 491
    HK: HC vs. SK: PAC, 490
    multiple ambiguities, 218–22, 480–81, 485–86, 555–57
    PAC vs. IAC, 140–42, 267, 438–39, 472–73, 484, 486n.163, 487–88, 491, 493
    prolongational closure vs. PAC, 487
    *See also* cadential vs. prolongational; cadential vs. sequential; progression type, ambiguity of
cadential arrival, 13–14, 23, 31–33, 38, 39, 40, 41
cadential bass line, classical (③–④–⑤–①), 76, 307, 308–9, 311–12, 372, 380–81, 544–45
cadential closure, lack of, 17n.28, 454, 463, 570. *See also under* A section; A′ section; B section; cadence, exposition (fugue); main theme; noncadential closure; subordinate theme
cadential closure vs. noncadential closure, 143, 432
cadential content, 34
    abundance of, 405, 413, 424–28, 540, 570, 575–76
    with cadential bass line, 346
    vs. cadential function, 33–36, 39, 52, 157, 344–46, 366–67, 437–38
    main theme filled with, 413, 414
cadential conundrum, 101–2, 190–91, 280–81, 439
cadential deferral, 94, 151, 157, 208, 325, 328, 332, 340, 399–400, 419.
    *See also* cadential play
cadential dominant, 59–60
    emerges out of sequence, 477–78
    followed by dissonant seventh, 22–23, 23n.70
    followed by inversion, 23n.70
    vs. precadential dominant, 342–44
    root-position requirement, 22–23, 29–31, 59, 102, 179–80, 207, 432–33
    root-position requirement, exception to, 154, 179–80
    third inversion ($V^4_2$) representing root-position, 60, 154, 182
    triadic requirement, 22–23, 102, 205, 207
    as ultimate, 102
    undermined by inversion, 60, 179–82
    *See also* penultimate dominant; ultimate dominant
cadential function
    boundaries defined by cadential progression, 31–32
    vs. cadential arrival, 31–33
    vs. cadential content, 33–36, 39, 52, 157, 344–46, 366–67, 437–38
    compact, 31–32
    expanded, 31–32
    vs. postcadential, 32–33, 35, 38–46, 47, 146–47, 439, 440–41
    vs sequential (*see* cadential vs. sequential)
    *See also* continuation⇒cadential
cadential idea, 116–17, 373–74, 377–78
cadential phrase. *See* cadence phrase; cadential function
cadential play, 419–23
cadential progression (authentic), 22–24
    annotation style, 22–23
    boundaries of, 31–32, 53, 60–62, 67–68, 229–30, 241, 258–59, 261, 453n.80, 461n.103 (*see also* initial tonic)
    bypasses dominant proper (stage 3b), 296–97, 485–86, 498–501, 517
    bypasses pre-dominant, 112, 514, 537, 540–42, 547
    classical prototype, 307, 308–9
    in codetta, 38
    complete vs. incomplete, 60
    embedded within sequence, 437–38, 489–90, 540, 575, 576–77
    in ending contexts, 21–22
    evaded, 514
    in framing contexts, 22n.62
    Romantic variants of, 435–36
    as tonal confirmation, 22–23, 30–31
    *See also* abandoned cadential progression; deceptive cadential progression; expanded cadential progression; half cadential progression; plagal cadential/closural progressions
cadential six-four, 22–23, 59
    in baroque, infrequent usage, 307
    in dependent plagal closure, 516–18, 523
    in ECP, 247
    first-inversion tonic, substituting for, 186, 289, 546
    length, compared to dominant proper, 247, 555–57
    "re-inverted," 292, 300–2, 307–8
    signals cadential closure, in nineteenth-century, 549–50, 573
    supports new initiation, as $I^6_4$, 289, 291–92
    as tonic arrival, 498–501
    *See also* arrival six-four; stage 3
cadential stream. *See* stream (bass line)
cadential strength/weight, 32–33, 41, 51, 53–54
cadential tonic, 22–23. *See also* initial tonic; final tonic
cadential trill, 20, 164, 167, 173–74
cadential vs. cadential function, 31–33
cadential vs. prolongational, 24–25, 129n.210, 143, 185–86, 208, 388–89, 436, 444
cadential vs. sequential, 25, 256–57, 282–83, 284–85, 286–87, 310, 321, 343, 368–69, 436, 437n.23, 444–47, 458, 479, 481, 481n.157, 490, 526, 577–78
    avoided in classical style, 25, 35, 282–83, 369n.150, 444
*cadenza composta* (compound cadence), 380–81
*cadenza doppia* (double cadence), 106, 205, 307–8, 340, 343–44, 376, 377–78, 380, 461–62, 552
    with abandoned cadential progression, 311–12
    boundaries of melodic schema vs. boundaries of cadential progression, 310, 313, 328–29, 343–44
    compact, 327–29, 330
    in consecutive cadences, 324
    with covering tone, to make IAC, 312
    with deceptive cadence, 313, 317
    with evaded cadence, 318–20
    and harmonic expansion, 313, 321
    with lowered leading-tone abandonment, 366–67
    melody of, 344–45
    opening harmonized with pre-dominant ($II^6$), 330–31
    and slower tempo, 325–26
*cadenza simplice* (simple cadence), 307, 310, 362–63, 380–81
caesura. *See* stop
Caskel, Julian, 463n.108
casting out root, 112–13, 122, 279, 230, 388, 530–31
characteristic material, 33–34, 441, 442
Chopin, Frédéric, 431–32
    allusion to chorale style, 436–37
    arrival six-four, 549–50
    consecutive cadences in, 46, 443–44, 473, 519–20 (*see also* consecutive cadences: in Chopin's Preludes)
    first cadence as "too early"/premature, 46
    signature progression (I–III–V), 437n.25, 450n.64, 575n.163
    slithery chromaticism, 450–51, 476–77, 520–21
circularity. *See* formal circularity

classical bass line, 544–45
classical cadence, 15, 56, 143, 305, 380, 431–33, 575
   decline of, in nineteenth century, 432
   elimination of, 432
   idealized, 496, 544–45
   as model for stylistic comparison, 433
   in nineteenth century, ubiquitous use of, 431–32, 433, 495
clausula, 14, 105–6, 306, 380–81, 384. *See also* alto cadence; soprano cadence; tenor cadence
Clausula Vera (schema), 384
closing section, 38
   absence of, in Scarlatti, 397–98
   with cadential content, 41
   melodic descent to $\hat{1}$, within, 473
   problematic case of, 146
   without preceding cadence, 462, 465, 468, 477–78, 491, 498, 563–64
   between subordinate themes, 424n.106
   *See also* codetta; false closing section
closing theme, 38n.135, 39. *See also* closing section
closure
   atemporal/spatial, 2, 5, 7, 9
   dramatic, 6
   everyday sense of, 1
   lack of, 450–53
   law of, 2
   linguistic dilemmas, 43–44
   literary, 2–4, 7
   narrative, 2, 7
   psychological, 2
   rhetorical, 7
   syntactical, 6–7, 8
   temporal, 2, 5, 7, 8, 9
   thwarts expectation for continuation, 33–34, 56, 79
   *See also* formal closure; musical closure
coda, 119–20, 197–98, 289, 369
coda theme, 298–99, 300
coda theme vs. cadence, 39
codetta, 35, 38, 41, 405. *See also* closing section
Cohen, David, 45n.170
Cohn, Richard, 432n.3, 519n.58
color (harmonic), 300–2
combined melodic patterns, 70–75
   in converging HC, 110–11
   in IAC, 88–90
   simultaneously, 72–75
   successively, 70–72
Comma (schema), 382–84
common practice period, 433, 550
compact cadence, 224–26, 253–54, 281–82, 302
   in baroque, 223, 313, 321–23, 326–28
   embedded within ECP, 248, 281–82, 292
   in galant, 223, 409

in mid- to late nineteenth century, 540–42
   in Romantic, 437–38, 440–41
   *See also* retaining cadential formula; formula (cadential)
complete cadential progression, 23–24, 60
Complete (schema), 380, 385
compound antecedent, 96, 121–23
compound basic idea, 24n.78, 192n.104
   vs. presentation, 50n.200, 203n.129
compound melody, 26n.86, 264, 327
compound meter, 44n.165, 95, 98, 130, 131–32, 136, 185n.84, 204–5, 224–25, 394–95, 419–20, 428. *See also* R = ½N
compound period, 117, 128
compound presentation, 299–300, 462, 465–67
compound sentence, 37, 116–17, 484
compound theme vs. simple theme, 136–37
Cone, Edward, 17–18, 39, 51n.204, 138n.235, 443n.44
consecutive/repeated cadences, 44–46, 128–29, 165n.45, 165n.46, 570
   in baroque, 46, 323–25
   and cadential ambiguity, 215–16, 325
   in Chopin's Preludes, 473, 475, 482, 484–85
   content differs, 324–25
   first cadence as "too early"/premature, 46, 473, 475, 484, 488
   first perspective on, 45, 324, 404
   in galant, 46, 404–5, 413
   register, role of, 404
   in Romantic, 46, 443–44
   second cadence expanded, 324
   second perspective on, 45–46, 324–25, 405
   third perspective on, 45
consequent, 32–33, 118–19, 165–66, 219, 337–39, 471
contextual formal function, 34, 129n.209, 165, 221, 280–81, 438–39, 441, 458, 519n.57, 564. *See also* form-functional dissonance
continuation⇒cadential, 87n.97, 158, 276
continuation (function), 61n.23, 231–32, 287–89
   beginning with, 165, 244–45, 248–49, 281–82, 398, 424
continuation phrase, 17, 61–62, 251–52
continuous exposition, 337–39, 416. *See also* fusion: transition and subordinate theme
contrapuntal cadence, 102, 142–43, 346–47, 516. *See also* prolongational closure
conventional material, 33–34, 78–79, 441
conventional thematic length, 47
converging half cadence, 58n.18, 106–12
   durational emphasis of stage 2, 106–7
   with ECP, 273
   ensues from sequential progression, 108

extensive melodic embellishment in stage 2, 108–10
   melodic patterns, 106–12
   omits stage 1, 106–7, 108
   vs. simple HC, 111–12
   simultaneous melodic combinations, 108–10
   uses standard cadential bass line, 106–7
Converging (schema), 382
Cooper, Barry, 287n.113
core, 119, 474
Corelli, Arcangelo
   change in tempo marking, 325–26
   consecutive cadences, in, 46, 311–12, 323–25, 404
   melodic idea ($\hat{2}$–$\hat{5}$–$\hat{3}$) in IAC, 312
   "primitive" standing on the dominant, 336–37
   Prinner cadence, 390
   saturation of cadences, 307, 344–45
counter-exposition, 351–52, 355–56, 371–72
countersubject, 351–52
covered cadence, 140–42, 214–16, 234n.22, 292n.128, 294, 312, 320
   vs. evaded, 214–16, 555
Cudworth, Charles, 76, 381–82
Cudworth melodic pattern, 76, 88, 108–11, 266, 323–24, 406–8
Cudworth (schema), 76, 379–80, 381–82, 385
Cutler, Timothy, 186–87, 292n.127, 512n.33, 525–26, 530n.87, 531n.89, 531n.90
cymbal crash, 547–49

Darcy, Warren, and James Hepokoski. *See* Hepokoski, James, and Warren Darcy
deceleration harmonic/bassline, 322–23, 324
deceleration of rhythm, 322–23, 324–25, 326–27
   harmonic, 313, 321–23, 324, 325, 437–38
deceptive-authentic combination, 405
   in baroque, 329–32
   bass line, in connection with, 251
   with ECP, 275
   melodic line, in connection with, 76–78, 160, 167–68, 275
   within model and sequence, 346
   as noncadential, 167–69
deceptive cadence, 152, 153–54
   vs. abandoned, 184n.82, 217–18, 400–1n.62
   aesthetic effect of, 399–400
   in baroque, 313–17, 332
   as clausula altizans, 383n.15
   vs. deceptive resolution, 157
   denied, 157
   with ECP, 275
   elided, 152, 160, 169
   ends antecedent, 521–22
   ends A′ section (minuet), 157
   ends on $\hat{5}$, 153n.12

ends main theme, 157
ends subordinate theme, 157
vs. evaded cadence, 169, 170–71, 172–73, 209–11, 320, 501–3
followed by new material, 160
in fugue, 364
in galant, 399–400
vs. HC, 152
vs. IAC, 94n.117
independent, 157, 158–62, 164–67, 521–22
inverted, 356n.131, 364–65, 481n.157
for modulation, 162–63
⇒reinterpreted dominant arrival, 203–4
repeated, 176n.66, 399–400
replaces PAC (ending on $\hat{1}$), 158–60
replaces IAC (ending on $\hat{3}$), 160–62
theoretical literature on, 151n.9
unusual case of, 448–49
as way station, 157, 158–60, 453, 454, 457
See also final deceptive cadence; way-station cadence
deceptive cadential progression, 22–23, 60, 151–52, 322–23, 531
bass line of, 153–57, 182–83
with ECP, 328, 409n.72
noncadential use of, 167–69, 328
passing tone ④ in bass, 153–54, 313, 521–22
passing tone #⑤ in bass, 153–54
vs. Pulcinella, 332
See also replacement harmony
deceptive half cadence, 187n.90, 496
deceptive resolution, 157, 167, 169, 279
deferral/postponement. See cadential deferral
density (textural), uniformity of, 437–38, 471
dependent plagal closure. See under plagal closure/cadence
descending bass line, 570
in baroque and galant, 27–28, 98
in half cadence, 103–4 (see also expanding HC)
in minor-mode contexts, 103–4, 251, 290–91
in Prinner schema, 98, 471
in prolongational closure, 447–48
design, See structure vs. design
De Souza, Jonathan, 139n.242
detour cadence, 493, 496, 540–44, 549–50
abandoned, 542
evaded, 542
in six-four position, 542, 575
development key, 82, 189–90, 423
development section, 82, 119, 120, 423–24
PAC closure in, 82, 189–90, 239, 423–24, 555
deviations, cadential
ambiguities with, 150–51, 294, 320

blurring in, 367
combinations of, 208–9
exceptional ordering of, 209
with expansions, 151n.6, 223n.2, 273–74
in fugue, 364–66
loose phrase structure, 151
pejorative associations with, 151
positive role of, 151
preferred ordering of, 208–9
as surprise, 151, 154, 163n.39
diminished-seventh pre-dominant, 58–59, 240–41, 296–97, 321
dissonance (form-functional), 34, 129n.209, 377, 564n.144
dissonance practice (Romantic), 433, 434–35, 542n.107, 564n.143
dissipated cadence, 52n.216, 118–19, 463, 467–68, 469, 553–54, 557, 564–67
dissolved consequent, 118–19, 120, 219
diversion. See melodic diversion
dominant
as antepenultimate/pre-subdominant, 512
cadential vs. prolongational, 36–37, 59–60, 100–1, 102
intrinsically unstable, 207
sequential, 276, 498
"stuck on," 193–94, 197–98, 200–1
substituted by III, 434, 564n.143
theme begins on, 503, 504–5, 537
See also cadential dominant; penultimate dominant; ultimate dominant
dominant arrival, 55–56n.2, 68–69, 150–51, 187, 190–91, 204, 434–35, 509n.22
in baroque, 339–40
with descending bass (♭⑥–⑤), 189–90, 191
emerges out of sequence, 189–90, 333n.66, 340
ends complete work, 458, 462–63
fermata, role of, 187, 191, 192–93, 198–99
on final dominant, 188–92, 279, 315–16, 339
final dominant vs. terminal dominant, 198–99
in galant, 402–3
vs. HC, 187n.92, 191–92, 203n.128, 333n.66, 334–35n.70, 458
internal, 45–46, 176–77, 198n.113, 239–40, 337
of limited scope, 202–3
vs. pre-dominant arrival, 511
reinterpreted, 203–4
reopened, 204–5
in Romantic, 458–63
on terminal dominant, 192–93, 339
See also premature dominant arrival
dominant proper, 22–23, 83
bypassed, 296–97, 485–86, 498–501, 517
doppia half cadence, 106, 202, 205–6, 207, 340n.85
doppia premature dominant arrival, 205–7
Do-Re-Mi (schema), 385

Do-Si-Do (schema), 380–81
doubled monophony. See textural types
double leading tone cadence, 306
DOUTH2 relation. See Tristan resolution
drum bass, 47, 139, 189, 216
dualism, 511, 513
"dubbit," 517
Dvorak, Antonin, 431n.1
dynamic process/curve, 6, 282–83, 557, 559–60. See also progressive dynamic; recessive dynamic
dynamics (intensity), 216, 239–40, 525–26, 529, 533–34, 560–63

early perfect authentic cadence, 82, 441n.36
echo effect, 323–24
Edemarian, Naomi, 340n.87
elided authentic cadence, 140–42, 211–14, 218, 219–20. See also under deceptive cadence
end, 15. See also cadential function; closure; concluding function; musical closure
end vs. stop, 46–48, 351, 482–84
in nonmusical contexts, 3, 6, 8, 9, 46–47
ending on $\hat{5}$ (IAC), 90–93, 93n.113
enharmonic reinterpretation, 199–202, 239–40, 289, 474–75, 495n.2, 504, 507, 547–49
episode, 351–52
episode fugue, 352n.112
essential dissonance, 388–89
essential expositional closure. See under Hepokoski, James, and Warren Darcy
essential sonata closure. See under Hepokoski, James, and Warren Darcy
evaded cadence
aesthetic effect of, 399–400
annotation of, 170
in baroque, 317–20, 364
in closing section, 397–98, 399–400
vs. covered cadence, 214–16, 555
vs. deceptive cadence (elided), 169, 170–71, 172–73, 209–11, 320, 501–3
with detour cadence, 542
ends orchestral introduction of opera aria, 551–52
ends a thematic unit, 473, 552–53, 555, 563–64
followed by new material, 177, 275, 552
following evasion, no event, 318, 445, 457–58, 468, 552–53
follows genuine cadence, 318
formal functions of, 175–77
in galant, 397–99
grouping structure with, 152, 169, 170–71, 172–73
harmonic content of, 170–74
vs. HC/dominant arrival, 103, 217, 232
vs. IAC (elided), 142, 213–14, 552–53
independent, 222

evaded cadence (*cont.*)
  leap up to $\hat{5}$, 174
  limited scope, in closing section, 397–98, 399–400
  melodic content of, 174
  melodic resolution to $\hat{1}$, 174
  in mid- to late nineteenth century, 551–54
  vs. PAC (elided), 176, 211–13, 554
  rhetoric, nonclassical, 486–87
  for Rameau, 20–21
  replaces IAC, 170
  with root-position tonic, 173, 174, 176–77
  signaled by $V^4_2$, 170–71, 211, 281
  as way station, 175
  *See also* one-more-time technique
evaded cadential progression, 328, 404
  even-measure strong (hypermeter), 137–38
  expanded cadence, 223
  expanded cadential progression
  ambiguous onset of, 257–59, 272, 281, 282–83
  in baroque, 326–29
  bass-line complexities in, 251–53
  beginning a theme, 250, 280–81, 413, 438–41, 491, 540–42, 560–63
  begins with stage 2a, 250, 254, 261, 269–70, 272, 279, 281, 297, 298–99
  begins with stage 2b, 245, 246–47, 282–83
  boundary difficulties, 240–41, 246–47
  bypasses dominant proper, 296–97
  bypasses stage 2, 248–50, 271
  bypasses stage 2a, 243–46, 547
  compact cadence, embedded within, 248, 281–82, 292
  and concerto style, 281n.100, 327
  with deviations, 223n.2, 273–74, 313
  diversity of harmonic/melodic content, 224, 232, 250–57, 291–92, 300–2
  dominant emphasis, 239–40, 247–48, 262, 265, 328–29, 484
  fails to achieve PAC, 406–8
  in galant, 405–8
  Grand Cadence, 381–82
  initial tonic emphasized, 328–29
  latent, in baroque, 321–22
  longest, 294
  minimum length of, 223–24, 257, 268–71, 274
  in model and sequence, 474
  Neapolitan, 239, 246
  one harmony/stage per measure, 224–25, 269, 326–27
  pre-dominant emphasis, 237–40, 244–45, 250, 254, 274, 328–29
  with *Pulcinella*, 382
  root-position harmonies, exclusively, 292
  root-position tonic in, 271, 294
  sentential structure, embedded within, 228–29, 232, 281

  stage 3b longer than 3a, 247
  tonic six-four ($I^6_4$) as initial tonic, 297–98
  unusual case, 300–2
  *See also under* abandoned cadential progression; deceptive cadential progression; half cadential progression; rocking on the tonic
expanding half cadence, 58n.18, 557
  bass stream in inner voice, 113, 114
  with ECP, 273
  ensues from sequential progression, 112–13, 114
  half-step approach in bass, 114
  leaping motion in upper voice, 114
  in major-mode contexts, 112
  in minor-mode contexts, 114
  melodic patterns, 112–14
  omits stage 1, 112
  resembles reinterpreted HC, 122
  vs. simple HC, 557
  two half-step approach, 114
  whole-step approach, 112–13
expansion, 20, 325. *See also* expanded cadential progression
expectations
  of closure, 3–4, 25, 79, 94, 150, 158, 164–65, 191–92, 209, 340, 341–42, 443–44
  contradictory, 79, 94–95
  of half cadence, 342
  of harmony, 24, 151, 514
  HC vs. PAC, 120–21
  of form, 118–19, 151, 202–3, 554–55, 566–67
exposition (fugue), 351–52
  cadential closure of, 340, 355
  end of, 351–52
  ends with subject-ending cadence, 357–60, 365–66, 372–73
  extension of, 353–54
  noncadential closure of, 353–55, 365–66, 370–71
  voice entries, order of, 357–59, 370–71, 372–73
exposition (small ternary). *See* A section
extended anacrusis. *See under* anacrusis
extension, 380

failed consequent, 165–66, 219, 232, 465–67, 469
false closing section, 100n.135, 465
false recapitulation, 162–63, 200–2
fantasia, 204–5
feigned plagal closure, 512n.33, 514n.43, 530–34, 563, 581
feminine cadence vs. masculine cadence, 50–51, 129–30
feminine ending, 392–93
Fenaroli (schema), 385
fermata. *See under* dominant arrival
Ferris, David, 455

final cadence (fugue), 352, 369
final deceptive cadence ($\Rightarrow$PAC) 316, 455, 456–57, 550, 555, 575
  followed by plagal codetta, 147–48, 157, 315, 316–17, 449n.62, 453–54, 526, 534
final dominant, 188–89, 199
  vs. terminal dominant, 187, 198–99, 208
final tonic, 23–24, 60
first part. *See under* small binary
"first-time" hearing, 247–48, 287, 566–67.
  *See also* retrospective reinterpretation
Fischer, Wilhelm, 334–35
Fonte (schema), 385
formal circularity, 4–5, 7, 9, 377
  in nineteenth century, 441–42, 444, 446n.55, 449, 451, 468n.118, 578
formal closure, cadence as, 15–20. *See also* closure; musical closure
formal closure, logic of, 16, 18, 21, 45, 280
form-functional dissonance, 34, 129n.209, 377, 564n.144
formula (cadential), 14–15, 19–21, 33–34, 56, 62–63, 78–79, 406–8, 432
  in baroque, 307, 310, 321–22, 327, 328
  *See also* retaining cadential formula
Forte, Allen, 207–8
*Fortspinnung*, 334–35
*Fortspinnungstypus*, 334–35
Fowler, Don, 520n.60
framing functions, 21–22. *See also* coda; codetta; closing section; post-cadential function; standing on the dominant
fugal theory, 351
  cadence inhibiting rhythmic continuity, 351, 364, 367
fugue
  analysis of, 350–51
  cadence signals subject entry, 353
  compositional implications, actualizing, 355–56
  exposition, noncadential closure of, 353
  as form, genre, or compositional procedure, 351
  formal nonconventionality, 353
  invertible, 348
  subordinate key, reduced significance of, 352, 367
  terminology for, 351–52
  tonal functions in, 352
fundamental melodic pitches, 64–65, 68, 70
*Funktionstheorie* (theory of functions), 21
fusion
  continuation and cadential, 61n.23, 251–53, 257
  main theme and transition, 81, 165n.46, 415–16
  main theme, transition, and subordinate theme, 99–100, 418–19
  role of fragmentation in, 416
  solo recapitulation and closing ritornello, 164

transition and subordinate theme, 81–82, 119, 277n.96, 337–39, 416–19, 566–67, 569–70
Fux, Johann Joseph, 364n.140, 365n.143, 365n.145, 365n.147, 367n.149

galant cadence. *See* Cudworth (schema)
gap, 5
gap-fill, 26, 28, 296n.138, 458, 540
Gauldin, Robert, 21n.56, 146n.271, 271–72n.89
Gédalge, André, 351n.108, 353n.120, 355n.127
Gestalt psychology, 2, 4–5
Gjerdingen, Robert, 67n.35, 207–8, 379n.6
    cadence as schema, 56
    *cadenza doppia*, 307n.10
    Clausula Vera, 384
    Comma, 382–84
    Complete, 380
    Converging, 106–7, 382
    Cudworth, 76, 381–82
    Do-Re-Mi, 385
    Do-Si-Do, 380–81
    Fenaroli, 385
    Fonte, 385
    galant schemata, 380–84
    Grand Cadence, 224n.3, 266, 381–82
    half cadence, 101–2
    Indugio, 382
    Jommelli, 382–84
    Long Cadence, 57n.12, 382
    Long Comma, 382–84
    Mi-Re-Do, 380–81
    Monte, 385
    Passo Indietro, 384
    Prinner, 81n.72, 85–86, 372n.152, 384–85, 385n.25, 390n.35
    Pulcenella, 330–31, 332n.63, 382
    Romanesca, 98n.129
    Quiescenza, 147–48, 315
    stages of schema, 56
Goetschius, Percy, 351n.109, 353–54n.123, 355n.126
Gossett, Philip, 294n.134
Grand Cadence (schema), 381–82
Grave, Floyd, 266–67
Green, Douglass, 47, 50–51, 146n.271, 530n.87
Greenberg, Yoel, 392, 413–14, 415
group, 2
grouping structure
    ambiguous, 108, 251–52
    blurring boundaries, 189, 240–41
    and cadential melody, 67–68
    deceptive cadence, 152
    half cadence, criterion for, 102–3
    ECP, onset of, 257, 258
    and premature dominant arrival, 194
    strong boundary, 246–47
    symmetrical, 443–44, 478, 481–82
    symmetrical vs. asymmetrical, 103

half cadence
    annunciatory function of, 120, 353
    in baroque, 333–39
    with Clausula Vera, 384
    confirming development key, 119, 199
    conundrum, 101–2, 190–91
    converging, 58n.18, 106–12
    converging-expanding/expanding-converging, 115–16, 273
    grouping structure as criterion for, 102–3
    deceptive, 550–51
    vs. deceptive cadence, 152
    vs. dominant arrival, 187n.92, 191–92, 203n.128, 333n.66, 334–35n.70, 458
    early in coda, 119–20
    ends A section, 79n.56, 118, 463
    ends B section, 118
    ends complete movement, in baroque, 336
    ends compound antecedent, 117
    ends core, 119
    ends main theme, 118–19
    ends on $\hat{5}$, 92–93
    ends part 1 (baroque binary), 335
    ends part 1 (small binary), 118
    ends retransition, 118, 119
    ends sentential forms, 116–17
    ends simple antecedent, 117
    ends slow movement, 307
    ends transition, 119
    ends *Vordersatz* (of *Fortspinnungstypus*), 334–35
    vs. evaded, 103, 217, 232
    expanding, 58n.18
    followed by new initiating material, 120
    followed by new medial or closing material, 120
    followed by return of earlier initiating material, 120
    follows IAC, 117
    follows PAC, 117–18, 335–36
    follows Prinner, 385
    functional generalizations of, 120–21, 191–92
    general conditions for, 102–3
    as "incomplete" authentic cadence, 101–2, 103–4
    independent, 116–17, 128, 550–51
    Indugio, 382
    internal, to subordinate theme, 119, 337
    limited cadential scope, 334–36
    in minor-mode contexts, 118
    passing seventh with, 191–92
    in part 2 (small binary), 118
    in periodic forms, 117–18
    and phrase rhythm, 103
    phrygian, 104, 114, 335, 336–37, 391–92, 428–29, 456–57, 475–76, 550–51
    in pre-core, transition-like unit, 119
    prepares for recapitulation, in baroque, 333–34
    as postcadential, 336
    vs. premature dominant arrival, 194
    prominence of stage 2b, 104, 112, 119
    reinterpreted, 121–24
    reopened, 121, 124–29
    signaled by augmented-sixth harmonies, 104
    simple, 104, 106
    simple vs. converging, 111–12
    in small ternary, 118
    in subordinate theme, 119
    unison, 114–15
    variant, with Scarlatti, 391–92
    as way station, 550–51
    *See also* internal half cadence; reinterpreted half cadence; reopened half cadence
half cadential progression, 22–23
    cadential six-four, minimal use of, 104–5
    descending bass, 103–4
    durational emphasis on stage 2, 104, 106–7, 405–6
    with ECP, 223–24, 268–71, 405–6
    root-position tonic, prevalence of, 104
    stage 1, 104
    stage 2, 104
    stage 3, 104–5
    stages of, 103–4
Handel, George Frederic, 307, 325–26
harmonic color, 542–44
harmonic dualism. 511, 513
harmonic expansion, noncadential, 282–84
harmonic functions, 241–43, 253–57
harmonic monism, 513, 514, 515–16
harmonic progression, types of, 21–24. *See also* progression types, ambiguity of
harmonic reduction, 186–87
harmonic relationship, 26–27, 30–31
harmonic rhythm, 437–38, 443–44, 448–49, 498
Harrison, Daniel, 14–15, 14n.3, 14n.4
    cadential closure vs. noncadential closure, 143n.263
    end vs. stop, 46–47
    half cadence as incomplete authentic cadence, 101–2
    harmonic dualism, 511n.28, 513, 513n.39
    plagal cadence, 146n.271, 516n.46, 528n.84
Hatten, Robert, 6–7, 262n.70, 481n.159, 549–50, 560
Hauptmann, Moritz
    harmonic dualism, 511n.28, 513, 527–28
    meter and cadence, 129–30n.211

Haydn, Joseph
  asymmetrical grouping structure, 47–48
  ends A section with HC, 79n.56, 118, 463n.107
  mid-phrase pause, 241, 244–46
  monothematic exposition, 120, 163–64, 191–92
  wit, 239n.30
hemiola, 309–10, 311–12, 325
Hensel, Fanny, 516, 527–28
Hepokoski, James, 43–44, 410n.76, 546, 547
Hepokoski, James, and Warren Darcy
  attenuated cadence, 139–40n.247
  cadence at high structural levels, 17–18
  cadential function, 32
  cadential modules, 32–33
  cadential vs. postcadential, 39–40, 41–43
  continuous exposition, 82n.75, 337–39, 416
  dominant lock, 41
  essential expositional closure, 17–18, 41, 79n.59, 82n.79, 139–40n.247
  essential sonata closure, 17–18, 41n.153, 79n.59, 82n.79, 139–40n.247
  failed exposition, 287n.114
  grand antecedent, 219
  medial caesura, 41, 42–43, 52, 81–82, 415, 419n.96
  norms and deformation, 433n.8
  punctuation, 48–49
  rotation, 355n.129
  subordinate theme, cadential closure of, 82n.78
  syntactical vs. rhetorical strength, 50–51, 52
  type 2 sonata, 424n.102
  undoing a cadence, 45n.168
hermeneutic sentence, 7, 8, 20n.50
Higgs, James, 351n.107
higher-level formal units and cadence, 14
historicist music theory, 207–8
home key, 352, 365–66, 369–70, 372–73, 567–69
homophony. *See under* textural types
horn fifths/call, 227, 498n.6
Horton, Julian, 356n.130, 432n.3, 450n.63, 465n.114, 469n.126
Huebner, Steven, 20n.52
Hunt, Graham, 504n.17, 512n.29
Huron, David, 151
hyperdominant prolongation, 202, 433, 579–81
hypermeter, 20, 103, 137–38, 191n.99, 433

iconic cadence, 496, 544–50
  annunciatory function, 544–45
  codetta, 547
  deceptive, 549n.120
  evaded, 560–63
  as postcadential, 547
  precursors of, 544, 545n.114, 546n.117, 549n.121
  six-four, 549–50
idealized classical cadence, 496, 544–45
imperfect authentic cadence
  basic alto melodic pattern, 87–88
  basic simple melodic pattern, 86
  basic soprano melodic pattern, 86–87, 267–68
  basic tenor melodic pattern, 83–85, 90–91, 267–68
  bass melodic pattern, 88
  blurred, 412–13
  combined melodic patterns, 88–90
  Cudworth, 88
  vs. deceptive cadence, 94n.117
  deviations, combined with, 208
  dominant proper as triad, 83, 267–68
  with ECP, 267–68
  ends A section (or part 1), 96–98
  ends antecedent, 93–94
  ends complete movement, 311–12, 315
  ends compound antecedent, 96, 450–51n.65
  ends consequent, 92, 96, 99
  ends fugue, 352n.117, 356n.133
  ends main theme, 98–99, 412
  ends on 5̂, 90–93, 480–81, 488
  ends subordinate theme, 99–100, 234n.22, 294
  ends thematic unit, in baroque, 310–11
  vs. evaded, 213–14, 552–53
  "expressive" effect, 99
  implied by basic tenor pattern, 68–69
  with incomplete cadential progressions, 83, 85, 267
  independent, 93–94, 96, 98, 117, 175, 450–51n.65
  limited cadential scope, 100–1
  melodic diversion, 86–88, 96, 267–68
  vs. PAC, 140–42, 267, 393–96, 438–39, 472–73, 484, 486n.163, 487–88, 491, 493
  as PAC replacement, 312
  Prinner cadence, 85–86, 98–99
  Prinner type, 389–90
  questionable case of, 100–1
  small ternary/binary, not employed in, 79n.57
  "sweetening" effect, 312, 313n.23
  tenor combo, 88–90
  as way station, 94–96, 310–11
  vs. way station cadence, 94, 158–60, 523n.66
imperfect cadence, 20–21
implication-realization
  in bass-line melody, 28–30
  harmonic-cadential, 284, 442, 459n.98, 542
  melodic closure, 363–64
  of sequencing, 446–47
  of subject-ending cadence, 355–56, 371–72
implications, 512–13
incomplete cadential progression, 23–24, 60, 128–29, 232
  begins with stage 2, 62, 245, 246–47
  begins with stage 3, 62
  deceptive cadence, 164–67
  in deceptive cadential progression, 160
  evaded cadence, 222
  half cadence, 116–17
  and melodic analysis, 64–65
  use in IAC, 83, 85, 267
  imperfect authentic cadence, 93–94, 164–65
independent cadence (fugue), 353–54, 372, 376, 523n.66
  articulates major structural boundaries, 361
  as midway cadence, 368, 369–70, 374, 377–78
  semblance of, 356
independent deceptive cadence, 157, 158–62, 164–67, 521–22
independent evaded cadence, 222
independent half cadence, 116–17, 128, 550–51
independent imperfect authentic cadence, 93–94, 96, 98, 117, 175, 450–51n.65
  ends compound antecedent, 96
  as Prinner, 117
  vs. way station, 94
independent plagal closure. *See under* plagal closure/cadence
Indugio (schema), 382, 385
initial tonic, 23–24
  first inversion (I$^6$) signals cadential onset, 23–24, 52, 104, 108, 271, 573n.156
  unusual substitute for, 255, 300–2, 482–84, 488
  *See also* stage 1
initiating function, 19–20, 50n.199, 251–52, 292
  emphasized in nineteenth century, 432, 495–96, 570
initiating harmony (evaded cadence), 169, 170, 171–74
intrathematic functions, 79n.54
in-time listening perspective, 2, 4, 5, 7, 8–9, 315
interior cadence (fugue), 352, 353
internal episode, 371n.151
internal half cadence/dominant arrival, 45–46, 119, 197–98, 564–66
  in baroque, 337
  combined with other deviations, 208
  followed by cadential function, 120, 208, 337, 409
  followed by new continuation, 119, 120, 298–99, 337–39, 409, 411–12, 416–17, 420–21, 428–29, 564–66, 567, 570–73

followed by standing on the dominant, 119
in galant, 409
vs. precadential dominant expansion, 342–43, 344, 411–12
repeated, 411, 419–21
vs. way station, 119
interpolated episode, 160
interpolated subdominant, 530
interpolation, 241, 279, 297
interthematic functions, 79n.54
intrinsic formal function, 34, 96–98, 129n.209, 165, 176, 198n.110, 221, 280–81, 287–89, 438–39, 441, 442, 458, 519n.57, 564. *See also* form-functional dissonance
inverted deceptive cadence, 364–65, 368, 481n.157
inverted recapitulation, 569–70
invertible counterpoint, 356n.130, 478n.146
irregular cadence, 20–21
isolated cadence/codetta, 472–73, 476–77, 482–84, 487–88, 492–93, 544
    cadence vs. codetta, 481, 482
    codetta, 473, 475, 477–78, 491
Italian opera, nineteenth-century, 434
Ito, John Paul, 129–30n.211, 136

*Kadenzlehre/Klausellehre*, 14, 306, 380
Kaiser, Ulrich, 71n.40, 76, 379n.5, 390n.35
Kerman, Joseph, 352–53n.119, 353n.120, 367n.149
Kermode, Frank, 2, 8
Kirby, Frank, 293
Kirnberger, Johann Phillip, 14, 48n.188, 157n.20, 207, 307n.7, 388–89
Klein, Michael, 549–50, 574n.157
Klorman, Edward, 90n.103, 313n.22
Klumpenhouwer, Henry, 511n.28, 513
Koch, Heinrich Christoph, 14, 21n.54, 92n.108, 207, 221–22, 379–80
    basic phrase, 412
    closing phrase, 393–94
    concept of *Cadenz*, 49
    galant phrase structure, 412
    internal phrase, 393–94
    masculine vs. feminine cadence, 130n.212
    overhang, 31, 358–59, 392–95, 413n.79
    resting point (of the spirit), 48n.188, 49
    syntax, 49n.197
Kohs, Ellis, 143–44
Kovacevich, Stephen, 468
Kramer, Jonathan, 33–34, 138n.236
Krebs, Harald, 34
Kurth, Ernst, 542n.110, 547–49

Laitz, Steven, 144, 146n.271
lament (topic), 476–77, 490
law of return, 4–5

lead-in, 413, 423–24
Ledbetter, David, 352–53n.119
Lehman, Frank, 535n.96
Lerdahl, Fred, and Ray Jackendoff, 16, 17–20, 32, 39, 478n.148, 479
Lester, Joel, 20–21, 21n.54, 28n.90, 46–47
Lewin, David, 121–22, 207–8, 271–72n.89, 460nn.99–100, 462n.104, 511n.25, 517
limited cadential scope, 36–37, 39, 100–1, 471
    in baroque, 324, 334–36, 344–46
    in closing section, 39, 345
    dominant arrival, 202–3
    with formal initiation, 344–45, 447n.56
    in galant, 398, 399–400, 427–28
    half cadence, 334–36
    model and sequence, 345–46
    retransition, 567n.149
    subject-ending cadence, 355–56, 365–66, 371–72
linking harmony, 57, 61–62, 67, 106, 108, 258–59
liquidation, 33–34, 42–43, 56, 187, 258–59, 369, 424, 441, 555, 557, 559–60
Liszt, Franz, 431n.1, 549–50, 573n.155
Long Cadence (schema), 57n.12, 382
Long Comma (schema), 382–84
loose organization, 46, 151, 157, 208, 223, 269
low $\hat{5}$ drop, 66–67, 266, 267, 381–82
lowered leading-tone abandonment, 364–66, 368, 376

MacKay, James, 33n.108, 86n.94, 94n.117, 143n.265, 496n.4
main theme
    in A section, scherzo, 496–98
    cadential closure, lack of, 80–81, 142, 181–82, 412, 413–14
    cadential content, filled with, 413, 414
    cadential requirement of, 80
    ECP, supported by, 250
    fusion, with non-modulating transition, 416
    galant structure of, 412–15
    group, 165
    initiating unit, consists of, 415
    nonconventional form, 195n.109, 412–13
    Prinner cadence, ending with, 385–87
Margulis, Elizabeth, 45n.170
Marpurg, Friedrich Wilhelm, 207, 351n.106, 355n.127, 364n.140, 365n.145
Marston, Nicholas, 209
Martin, Nathan John, 82n.75, 436n.16, 439n.30, 454n.87, 575n.160
Martin, Nathan John, and Julie Pedneault-Deslauriers, 104, 105–7, 115, 115n.173, 202, 205–6, 207, 271n.86, 340n.85
Marx, Adolph Bernhard, 118–19, 219, 337–39

masculine cadence vs. feminine cadence, 50–51, 129–30
Mattheson, Johann, 14, 351n.105
McClelland, Ryan, 221n.180, 222n.185
McCreless, Patrick, 7, 8, 20n.50, 20n.51
medial caesura, 333n.66, 415. *See also under* Hepokoski, James, and Warren Darcy
melodic diversion, 86–88, 96, 267–68, 368–69
melodic-motivic material, 18–19, 33–34
melodic pattern, 62–63
melodic stream vs. melodic pattern, 64
melody and accompaniment. *See* textural types
Mendelssohn, Felix, 431–32, 448n.61, 527–28
meter, 130–32
metrical position of cadence
    antecedent, weaker than consequent, 132, 134
    in compound period, 131
    in compound sentence, 131, 134–36
    consequent, weaker than antecedent, 132, 134
    criterion for cadential identification, 138
    dance types, influence of, 129–30
    harmonic syncopation, problem of, 132
    hypermeter, 137–38
    masculine cadence vs. feminine cadence, 129–30
    notation, problem of, 130, 132
    real vs. notated meter, 130, 136–37
    reopened HC, 137
    simple vs. compound themes, 136–37
    simple period, 131, 132–34
    simple sentence, 131, 134–36
    strong metrical positions, 130, 131–32
    syntactical vs. rhetorical, 138
    traditional views, 129–30
    weaker than the norm, 132–36, 437–38, 536
Meyer, Leonard, 4–6, 5n.19, 15n.15, 56n.5, 474n.136
    cadence at higher levels, 17–18
    end vs. stop, 46–47
    formal circularity, 442
    hierarchy, continuous vs. discontinuous, 20n.50, 21
    implication-realization, 28n.93
    meter, 138n.240
    repetition, 17n.30
    statistical/secondary parameter, 5–6, 47n.177, 138n.240, 139, 283n.107, 525n.71
    syntactical/primary parameter, 6, 512–13
    syntactical vs. rhetorical strengh, 31n.102
mid-century style period, 379n.1
mid-phrase pause, 241–43, 244–46, 263

mid- to late nineteenth-century style
  bass voice as motivic, 538–40
  cadential six-four, as sign for closure, 549–50, 573
  chromaticism, increased, 495–96
  classical cadence, continued us of, 495
  detour cadence, 496, 540–44
  feigned plagal closure, 496, 529–35
  formal initiation, emphasis on, 495–96
  functional tonality, breakdown of, 575
  iconic cadence, 496
  plagal closure/cadence, 496
  premature arrivals, tonic and predominant/subdominant/, 496
  subdominant as alternative pole to tonic, 496, 511
  tonic-dominant polarity, decline of, 432
  See also Romantic style
midway cadence (fugue), 352, 353, 356, 368, 369–70, 371–72, 374, 377–78
Mi-Re-Do (schema), 380–81
Mirka, Danuta, 45n.168, 92n.108, 102n.139, 127–28, 129–30n.211, 136, 150n.1
Mitchell, William, 579–81
modal shift, 300–2, 423–24
model-sequence technique, 25
modulating model (bass line), 28–29
monism, 513, 514, 515–16
monophony. See textural types
monothematic exposition, 120, 163–64, 191–92, 496–98
Monte (schema), 385
Morgan, Robert, 578
motoric rhythms, 317–18
Mozart, Wolfgang Amadeus, 28–29, 70, 76, 82, 139, 164, 199, 205–6, 307, 443n.43
murder mystery, 20
murky bass, 139
musical closure, 4–9
  bass line, 27–28
  melodic, 26
  noncadential, 15, 19, 33
  tonal, 6, 8, 15
  two registers of, 43–44

narrativity, 7
naturalize (a prior chromaticism), 199, 236
Neapolitan, 239–40, 241, 246, 294–96, 557
negative analytical perspective, 433
neo-Riemannian theory, 432, 433
Neuwirth, Markus, 56n.7, 86n.95, 94n.117, 158n.28
  abandoned vs. deceptive, 217–18
  deceptive cadence, 151n.9, 154n.15, 157n.20, 162–63, 174n.62
  deceptive vs. evaded, 209–10
  deviations, 150n.2
  IAC vs. deceptive cadence, 157n.23
  lowered leading-tone abandonment, 365n.145

new material, 42–43, 45n.167, 117, 119–20, 162, 173
  definition of, 160n.31
  following abandoned cadence, 178–79
  following deceptive cadence, 158, 160
  following evaded cadence, 176, 177, 275, 552, 563
  following internal HC, 119
  following way-station cadence, 94, 95–96, 160
  in small binary, 118
nineteenth-century cadence, 433
nineteenth-century half cadence, 188n.93, 432–33, 434–35, 458, 468–69, 542, 554–55, 573, 579
  in Chopin's Preludes, 473, 475, 480–81, 484, 487–88
noncadential closure, 9, 24, 79n.56, 143, 339, 432. See also cadential closure; prolongational closure
non-essential dissonance, 388–89

odd-measure strong (hypermeter), 137–38
Oettingen, Arthur von, 511n.28, 513n.39
off-tonic opening, 438–40, 451n.68, 477, 478, 503–4, 564
one-more-time technique, 90–91, 158, 169–70, 176–77, 492–93
  cadential ambiguities, resolving, 176–77, 210–11
  in closing section, 397–98
  consecutive cadences, akin to, 45
  with ECP, 274
  with internal HCs, alluded to, 419–20
  in mid- to late nineteenth century, 551–53
  opening material, returns to, 176, 219n.173, 289n.122, 492–93
  repeated, 176, 274
  vs. repeated material (of IAC or deceptive cadence), 158n.26
  See also evaded cadence
opening ritornello, 275
ordering of cadential goals, 119
originality, aesthetics of, 442
overhang, 31, 358–59, 388n.29, 392–96, 412
  ascending, 413n.79
  in classical style, 395–96
  as codetta, 394–95
  with HC, 393–94
  IAC vs. PAC, 393–96

parallel/consecutive fifths, 219–20, 385n.24, 485, 534n.94
parallel/consecutive octaves, 297–98, 299n.148, 437, 471
part (fugue), 351–52
partimento, 379–81
passage (fugue), 351–52

passing harmony, 21, 22, 104, 115
pastoral (topic), 573–75
pause. See stop
pedal-point, as prolongational, 22
Pedneault-Deslauriers, Julie. See Martin, Nathan John, and Julie Pedneault-Deslauriers
penultimate dominant, 22–23
  appears "too early"/premature, 458
  expanded, prior to compact PAC, 342, 409
  vs. ultimate dominant, 52, 78n.51, 101–4, 187n.91, 217, 315–16, 463, 468–69, 519–20, 554–55, 560
  ⇒ultimate, 467–68, 469
Perahia, Murray, 468
perfect authentic cadence
  confirms all keys in a movement, 307
  in development section, 82
  early, 82
  ends core, 82
  ends part 1, baroque binary, 335–36
  ends subordinate theme, required to, 82
  ends transition, 81–82
  vs. evaded, 211–13, 554
  home-key, saved for final cadence, 347
  vs. IAC, 140–42, 267, 393–96, 438–39, 472–73, 484, 486n.163, 487–88, 491, 493
  vs. prolongational closure, 487
perfect cadence (Renaissance), 305–6
performer, influence of, 45, 112n.168, 209, 220, 320, 468, 501–3
period, 104, 117–18, 438–39, 447–48, 450–51, 453. See also compound period; reversed period
periodic functions. See antecedent-consequent functionality
period model (bass line), 28–30, 276–77
Petty, Wayne, 423n.100
phenomenological space-times, 121–22
phrase and cadence, 16–17
phrase function, 79n.54
phrase rhythm, 103, 104
phrygian half cadence, 104, 114, 335, 336–37, 391–92, 428–29, 456–57, 475–76, 550–51
pivot note/harmony, 27–28
plagal cadential/closural progression, 24, 147–48, 453–54, 512–13
  allusion to dominant in, 148–49, 524, 542n.108
  in authentic cadential contexts, 514–15
  complete vs. incomplete, 512
  dualist, 513, 527–28
  four-stage version, 512, 513, 514, 517
  functional differential, 512–13
  initially noncadential, 515
  listening contexts, moment by moment, 514–15
  as postcadential, 523–24, 526–27, 530–31

in sequential context, 526
as sequential link, 525–26
as syntactical, 512–13
three-stage version, 512, 513, 514, 517
as tonic prolongational, 146–47, 454n.85, 512–13, 512n.32, 514, 515–17, 563
plagal closure/cadence, 24, 142, 452–53, 454, 496, 511–12, 515–16
  $\hat{1}$–$\hat{2}$–$\hat{3}$ melody, 528, 539–40
  $\hat{6}$–$\hat{5}$ melodic closure, 527–28, 531–33
  added sixth, with subdominant, 147n.275, 518, 528–29, 539–40
  in baroque, 146–49, 317, 348–50
  dependent, 516–23, 526–27
  diminished plagal cadence, 528–29
  emerges out of sequence, 525–26
  vs. half cadence, in minor subdominant region, 528
  half cadence, latent in, 517
  independent, 516, 523–26, 531, 539–40, 542, 563–64
  minorization, 518, 524, 525–26, 527–28
  phrygian modality, 528
  vs. postcadential, 511–12, 516, 518, 526–27, 563, 567
  vs. tonic arrival, 523
  *See also* feigned plagal closure
plagal codetta, 147–48, 316–17, 453–54, 526–27, 529, 534, 547, 567, 581
Platt, Heather, 516n.50, 528n.78
Pollini, Maurizio, 468
polyphony. *See* textural types
Posen, Thomas, 287n.113
postcadential function, 16, 24, 38, 224n.4
  vs. cadential function, 32–33, 35, 38–46, 47, 146–47, 439, 440–41
  as cadential confirmation, 40–41
  with final deceptive (⇒PAC), 315
  optional to the form, 43
  as plagal, 24, 146–48, 316–17, 348–49, 453–54, 455, 481, 511–12, 523–24, 526–27, 530–31
  second cadence, in consecutive cadences, 45, 324
  *See also* closing section; standing on the dominant
post-Romantic, 431n.2
*Prägnanz*, 2, 4–5
precadential dominant expansion, 340–44, 362n.139
  in classical style, 342n.88, 410
  vs. deviations, 342, 343, 344
  in fugue, 361–62, 376–77
  in galant, 409, 410–12
  vs. internal HC/dominant arrival, 342–43, 344, 411–12
  vs. premature dominant arrival, 340–41
precadential dominant vs. cadential dominant, 342–44
precadential pitches, from melodic pattern, 64–65, 67, 106–8, 261, 273

pre-classical style period, 379n.1
pre-core, 119
pre-dominant, 23–24, 58–59
  diminished seventh, 58–59, 240–41
  ends slow introduction, 503, 504n.16
  in ECP, prominent expansion, 237–40, 244–45, 250, 254, 274, 328–29
  two classes of, 58
  unusual cases in ECP, 241–43, 254, 300–2
  *See also* stage 2
pre-dominant arrival, 451n.69, 480n.152, 503–5, 555, 557–60
  with augmented-sixth harmony, 503, 504–5
  in classical, 503
  vs. dominant arrival, 511
  enharmonic shift, from dominant to pre-dominant, 504
  hints at dominant arrival, 504–5
premature dominant arrival, 188, 193–202, 204–5, 458, 475–76, 520
  in baroque, 340, 348–49
  via enharmonic reinterpretation, 199–202
  on final dominant, 194–95, 316
  fragmentation process, 194, 195
  in galant, 402–3
  vs. HC, 194
  via hyperdominant prolongation, 202
  on inverted dominant, 198–99
  on major mediant (III♯), 477–78
  vs. precadential dominant expansion, 340–41
  via prolongational progression, 198–99
  and sequential progressions, 189–90, 195–97
  on terminal dominant, 195–202
  terminal dominant as sequential link, 195–98, 200–2
  *See also* dominant arrival
presentation
  vs. compound basic idea, 50n.200, 203n.129
  ⇒continuation, 279
  large-scale, 182n.78
  no cadence in, 17, 37
  repeated, 231–32
  sequential "presentation," 437–38, 450n.64, 451–52, 573
  vs. standing on the dominant, 333n.66
Prinner cadence, 85–86, 98–99, 181–82, 384–90
  in baroque, 390
  within basic idea, 471
  cadential status, ambiguity of, 388–89
  cadential syntax, violation of, 117, 470
  in classical style, 390
  closing section emphasizes $\hat{1}$, 98–99, 387–88
  with continuation phrase, 387–88
  as IAC, 85–86, 98–99
  IAC (Prinner type), 389–90

limited scope, 471
  in main theme, 385–87
  metrical extension, 387, 470
  prolongational and sequential Prinner, vestiges of, 389–90
  with reinterpreted HC, 122
  in Romantic, 470–71
  with subordinate theme, 385–87
  as way station, 385–87
Prinner (schema), 85–86, 181–82, 203n.129, 372n.152, 379–80, 383n.17, 384–85
  ambiguity of harmony over ②, 388–89, 390n.34
  cadential vs. prolongational, 388–89
  in classical style, 390
  with continuation phrase, 387–88
  followed by HC, 385, 388
  formal functions of, 385–87
  melody in inner voice, 98–99, 471
  metrical extension, 385, 470
  modulating, 385, 471
  noncadential, 85–86
  prolongational, 385–88, 390n.35, 471
  relation to tenor melodic pattern, 86
  riposte, 385
  Romanesca-Prinner configuration, 98, 385n.26, 387, 470–71, 575
  in Romantic, 390
  sequential, 385–87
  stages of, 85–86, 385
  straddles grouping structure, 470–71
  submetrical insertion. 385, 389–90
  transition, initiating, 385
progression types, ambiguity of, 24–25, 489–90
  avoided in classical style, 25, 35, 282–83, 369n.150, 444
  *See also* cadential vs. prolongational; cadential vs. sequential; harmonic progression, types of
progressive dynamic, 529, 554–55, 557–59, 564–66
prolongational closure, 59–60, 143–46, 280n.98, 306
  in baroque, 346–48
  with Clausula Vera, 384
  ends complete movement, 347–48, 449–50, 536, 537, 539–40
  ends complete thematic process, 144–46, 447–48
  ends continuation phrase, 144
  ends fugal exposition, 370–71
  ends initiating phrase, 144
  ends main theme, 80, 412, 413–14
  ends sequential model, 143–44
  ends transition, 419n.95
  with galant schemata, 382–84
  in mid- to late nineteenth century, 496, 536–40, 546–47
  morphology of, 144, 146
  vs. PAC, 487

plagal cadence/closure, 147, 516
    with Prinner, 385
    in Romantic, 447–50
prolongational progression, 21, 22
    in codetta, 38
    in initiating contexts, 21–22
    plagal progression, as, 24
    proposes/implies a tonal center, 22–23, 143
    tonic vs. dominant, 192–93, 254, 524–25
prolongational reduction, 18–20
prolongational stream. See stream (bass line)
prolongational tonic, 60–62
prolongational vs. cadential. See cadential vs. prolongational
prolonged harmony, 22
protend/"hear ahead," 33, 185n.84, 279, 514
Prout, Ebenezer, 365n.145, 365n.147
*Pulcinella* (ballet), 385
Pulcinella (schema), 330–32, 379–80, 382
pulse stream, 130n.215, 325
punctuation, 14–15, 48–50
    and syntax, 49–50

Quiescenza (schema), 147–48, 315, 379–80, 534
Quintillian, 7

R = ½N, 44n.165, 123n.203, 130, 131–34, 136–37, 183–85, 204–5, 224–25, 394–95, 415–16, 419–20, 428, 490–91. See *also* compound meter
R = 2N, 44n.165, 130, 131–34, 136–37, 138n.235, 473, 491n.171
Rameau, Jean-Philippe, 14–15, 20–21, 26, 365n.143, 506–7, 512–13, 528
Randel, Don, 306
Ratner, Leonard, 32, 34–36, 39, 40, 50–51
Ratz, Erwin, 16, 38n.136, 163–64, 250, 279, 302
recapitulation, 399–400, 424–30
recessive dynamic, 282–83, 467–68, 491, 506–7, 525–26, 553–55, 557, 559–60, 564–66, 567
recurrence, 4–5, 7
reinterpretation. See retrospective reinterpretation
reinterpreted dominant arrival, 203–4
reinterpreted half cadence, 99, 121–24, 203–4, 502n.13
    with ascending melody ($\hat{6}$–$\hat{7}$–$\hat{8}$), 122, 123
    ends B section, 123
    ends compound antecedent, 121–23
    ends simple antecedent, 123, 231–32
    function of, 122–24
    morphology, of IAC, 122
    morphology, of PAC, 121, 122
    with Prinner cadence, 471n.130
expanding HC, resembles, 122
    with root-position II, 122, 123, 475n.139, 488n.166
    in subordinate theme, 123–24, 231–32
    tonicized half cadence, 121n.198
re-inversion, harmonic, 292, 300–2, 307–8, 530–31
reiteration, 4–5, 7
reopened dominant arrival, 204–5
reopened half cadence, 121, 124–29, 204–5
rational for, 125–27
    with deceptive cadence (on $I^6$), 127–28
    harmonic rational for, 127
    metrical irregularity in, 125
    motivic reinforced by caesura, 125
repeated material, after IAC or deviation, 94, 95, 158–60, 164–65, 274–75, 277. See *also* one-more-time technique
repetition, 3, 4–5, 17n.30, 24–25
repetition/terminal-modification paradigm, 3–4, 5, 6, 9, 24–25, 76n.46, 472–73. See *also* terminal modification
replacement harmony (deceptive cadence), 151–52
    in baroque, 313
    for deceptive HC, 550–51
    groups backwards, 152
    represents final event, 152
    secondary dominant of the dominant ($VII^6/V$), 153–54, 217–18, 550n.126
    secondary dominant of the subdominant ($V^7/IV$), 153, 157, 203–4, 210n.148, 313, 374, 449n.62
    submediant (VI), 60, 151, 153–54
    tonic in first inversion ($I^6$), 153, 313
    unusual case of, 457, 473, 474–75
response-statement repetition, 478–79, 491
rest. See stop
resting point, 48–49
retaining cadential formula, 223, 248n.50
    in baroque, 307, 326–28, 340
    in galant, 380, 405, 406–8, 412
retransition, 118, 119, 120, 199
retrospective reinterpretation, 29n.96, 52, 118–19, 182, 366–67, 375, 469, 515, 523–24, 528, 554
return, 4–5, 7
reversed period, 32–33, 36–37, 117–18
reversed recapitulation, 569–70
reversion vs. resolution (harmonic), 154–57
rhetoric, 7
rhetorical emphasis/strength/weight, 20, 128–29, 544–45, 560, 563–64, 578
    vs. syntactical, 46, 50–54, 79n.59, 208, 335–36, 367
rhyme, 125, 127, 352–53n.119, 517
Richards, Mark, 143n.265, 441n.35, 454, 476–77
Riemann, Hugo, 14, 15n.15, 21n.55, 21n.56, 58n.19, 129–30n.211, 138n.236, 511n.28, 521–22
Riepel, Joseph, 14
rocking on the tonic, 227, 236, 248, 254–55, 294, 429, 487–88, 540–42, 575
    with abandoned cadential progression, 275–76, 277–79, 289
    continuational, potentially, 238–39, 258–59, 272, 276, 279
    embedded continuation(⇒cadential) function, 228, 229
    with fragmentation, 228–29
    with HC, 271, 275–76
    includes root-position tonic, 238–39, 281, 299n.148
    longest, 294
    neighboring IV (④), 227, 229, 279
    neighboring $V^4_3$ (②), 231–32
    neighboring $V^4_2$ (④), 227
    neighboring $VII^6_5$ (②), 231
    neighboring common-tone diminished seventh, 235, 236n.25
    neighboring harmony, metrically stressed, 227
    neighboring root-position dominant, 230–31
    with Passo Indietro, 384
    preceding Cudworth, 266
    on the pre-dominant (IV, $II^6$), 252n.57, 281
    rocking on the Neapolitan, 239–40, 246
    with single neighbor, 229–30
    stage 1b in, 236
rococo style period, 379n.1
Rodgers, Stephen, 441n.37, 450n.63, 516, 518, 525–27, 528–29
Romanesca-Prinner configuration, 98, 385n.26, 387, 470–71, 515
Romanesca (schema), 382–84, 385n.26, 428
Romantic form, 432n.3
Romantic style
    baroque, influence of, 437
    cadence emerges from sequence, 437–38
    cadential progression embedded within sequence, 437–38
    cadential progression in basic idea, 437–38
    cadential vs. sequential, 25, 444–47
    character piece, 437–38
    chromaticism, increased, 432, 433
    dance genres, 437
    density/texture, uniformity of, 437–38, 472–73
    dissonance, increased, 433, 434–35
    ECP as formal opening, 438–41
    formal circularity, 432, 441–42
    formal closure, lack of, 450–53
    formal initiation, emphasis on, 432
    harmonic rhythm, rapid, 437–38, 443–44, 448–49
    harmonic rhythm, uniformity of, 437–38
    IAC vs. PAC, 438–39
    individualized "character," portrayal of, 437n.24

off-tonic opening, 438–40
opening with model-sequence technique, 448–49
originality, aesthetics of, 432
root-position harmonies, emphasis on, 432
sequential "presentation" 437–38, 452
symmetrical grouping structures, 443–44
See also mid- to late nineteenth century style
root-position harmonies, in Romantic, 432, 435–38, 443–44, 448, 470–71, 478
Rosen, Charles, 17–18, 32, 39, 146n.272, 154n.16, 441n.37, 454
Rossini, Giacomo, 294n.134
rotation, 355–56, 371–72
Rothstein, William, 17–18, 17n.26, 451, 453, 550
   cadence theme, 32–33
   cadential six-four, "re-inverting," 292n.127
   cadenza doppia, 309–10
   casting out of the root, 112–13, 186n.85, 309–10
   Corelli, cadence in, 308–10, 324, 328
   meter and cadence, 129–30n.211, 138n.236
Rubenstein, Arthur, 451
rule of the octave, 27
running race, 2n.6, 43

Sanguinetti, Giorgio, 27n.88, 307n.9, 307n.10, 379n.4
sarabande (topic), 570n.153
Scarlatti, Domenico
   closing section, absence of, 397–98
   consecutive cadences in, 46, 404, 424
   dominant arrival, 402–3
   ECP, uncommon in, 405
   evaded cadence, 396–98, 405
   exposition vs. recapitulation, 399–400
   guitar-strumming effect, 424
   HC variant, 391–92
   nonclassical elements, 429–30
   recapitulation clarifies cadential goals, 424–30
   repeated deceptive cadences, 399, 402
   style period designation, 379–80
Schachter, Carl, 21n.56, 90n.103, 463n.108, 477n.142
   contrapuntal cadence, 142n.257
   DCP-ACP combinations, 168–69
   deviations, 150n.2
   plagal cadence, 146n.271
   Schumann, "Waldesgespräch," 455, 456–57
   tonicized half cadence, 121n.198
   way station, deceptive cadence, 158n.28, 160n.30
   way station, denied, 164

schema theory, 379–80
Schenker, Heinrich, 6–7, 8, 19–20
   auxiliary cadence, 21
   on bass voice, 26–27, 28n.89
   casting out of the root, 60, 112–13, 186n.85, 309–10
   on continuous hierarchy, 20n.50
   covering tone, 140–42
   hypermeter, 138n.236
Schenkerian theory, 6, 8, 19–20, 33, 64, 168–69, 207–8, 579–81
scherzo, consecutive cadences in, 45n.167
Schluß (close), 38–39
Schmalfeldt, Janet, 14n.3, 17n.27, 398n.55, 418–19n.94, 424n.106, 424n.108, 428n.112, 463n.106, 463n.108, 486n.163
   Chopin, Mazurkas, 451nn.67–68, 453
   Chopin's "signature progression" (I–III–V), 437n.25
   deceptive cadence, 150n.2, 153n.12
   ECP initiates theme, 443–44n.48
   evaded cadence, 396, 458n.94
   evaded vs. authentic, 211n.155
   evaded vs. deceptive, 209n.145, 400n.60
   half cadence, 206
   hypermeter, 443n.44
   nineteenth-century HC, 188n.93, 432–33, 434–35, 458, 463n.110, 554–55
   one-more-time technique, 45, 94n.118, 158, 169, 176, 210–11, 274, 275, 318n.40, 397–98, 398n.54
   retrospective reinterpretation, 29
   Schumann, "Mondnacht," 453, 455, 534n.93
   subdominant, in nineteenth century, 443–44n.48
Schmid, Manfred, 83n.85, 385n.25
Schnabel, Artur, 468
Schoenberg, Arnold, 16, 17–18, 21, 24, 33–34, 207–8, 441, 509–11
Schubert, Franz, 431–32, 500n.11, 547–49
   ECP, beginning theme with, 280–81
   equal division of the octave, 201–2, 432, 433
   evaded cadence, 445, 457–58
   tonic arrival, 496–98
   transition ends with SK: PAC, 119
Schubert, Peter, and Christoph Neidhöfer, 355n.127, 355n.129, 364n.140, 367n.149
Schumann, Robert, 280–81, 431–32, 438–39, 454n.87, 471n.132, 527–28
Sears, David, 56
Sechter, Simon, 21
secondary parameter. See statistical parameter
section (fugue), 351–52
segment, 2
semantics, 6

sentence, 116–17, 354n.124, 441n.35, 447n.56
sentential hybrids, ends with HC, 116–17
sequence, 25
sequential dominant, 276, 498
sequential progression, 21, 22, 575
   beginning a theme, 573 (see also signature progression)
   classified by root motion, 22
   essentially melodic-contrapuntal, 21n.55, 513n.37
   in medial contexts, 21–22
   modelled by neo-Riemannian theory, 433
sequential repetition, 25
sequential tonic, 60–62
sequential vs. cadential. See cadential vs. sequential
Shakespeare, William, 3–4, 6
signature progression (I–III–V), 437n.25, 441n.38, 450n.64, 575n.163
simple (I–V) half cadence, 104, 106
   vs. converging HC, 111–12
   vs. expanding HC, 557
   with ECP, 271, 273
simple cadence. See cadenza simplice
simple melodic pattern. See basic simple pattern, varied simple pattern
simple theme vs. compound theme, 136–37
simultaneously combined pattern, 72–75, 108–11, 264–65
slowing tempo, 325–26
small binary, 72n.41, 118, 491–92
small ternary, 118, 469
Smith, Barbara Herrnstein, 3–5, 6, 7, 56n.5
   on repetition, 17n.30, 24–25
   on terminal modification, 5, 33–34, 324–25, 361n.136, 436n.18
sonata form, derived from baroque binary, 419
soprano cadence (clausula cantizans), 306, 380, 382–84
soprano melodic pattern. See basic soprano pattern; varied soprano pattern
soprano-tenor construct, 305–6, 380
spatial closure. See atemporality
stage 1, 57
   as augmented triad (with $\sharp\hat{5}$), 226–27
   in ECP, harmonic variants of, 225–27, 281–82
   embellished by V/IV, 57, 225–26, 289
   embellished by V/II, 57, 225–26, 289
   embellished/replaced by VI, 57, 225–26, 343–44, 482–84
   in first inversion ($I^6$), 57, 224, 271
   in half cadential ECP, 271–72
   preceded by $V^4_2$, 57, 229–30
   Romantic variant ($V^7$/VI), 57, 482–84, 575–76
   in root position, in classical, 57, 104, 224–25, 244–45, 248–50, 271
   in root position, in baroque, 307

stage 1 (cont.)
    as a single harmony, 227
    stage 1b, as intensification, 236
    tonic six-four ($I_4^6$), as stand-in
        for, 297–98
    See also initial tonic; rocking on the tonic
stage 2, 58–59
    in baroque, greater use of $IV^7$, 307
    bass ascends to dominant, 58
    bass descends to dominant, 58, 103–4
    diversity of harmonies in, 236, 250–57
    with ECP, 272
    in ECP, greater use of IV, 236–37
    in ECP, extensive expansion, 237–39,
        244–45
    half-diminished seventh over #④, 391
    melodic embellishments in, 67–68, 70–
        71, 108–10, 261, 263
    root-position II, 122
    stage 2b widely used with HC, 271
    stage 2b in ECP, 243
    stage 2b precedes 2a, 50n.200, 58n.17,
        236n.27
    substages, determinate order of, 58, 236
    two classes of, 58, 236
    unusual cases in ECP, 241–43, 289, 300–2
    See also pre-dominant
stage 3, 59–60
    in ECP, 247–50, 272–73, 281n.100
    embellishing harmonies in, 247–48
    harmonic constraints in, 247, 250
    substage 3a, 59, 247
    substage 3b, 22–23, 83
    See also cadential dominant
stage 4, 23–24, 60
stages of cadence schema, 56–57
standing on the dominant, 38, 552–53
    after antecedent, rare, 116–17, 337n.82,
        416
    as B section, 118
    in baroque, 336–37
    complexity of internal organization, 557
    in continuation (middle) of a theme,
        296–97
    vs. presentation, 333n.66
    repeated, 409
standing on the hyperdominant, 202
standing on the pre-dominant, 557
standing on the tonic, 508–9
statistical/secondary parameter, 5–6,
    138n.240, 139, 525n.71, 554–55
Stein, Deborah, 514n.40, 514n.42, 516n.46
stop, 14–15, 48–49, 139, 189, 406–8, 482–84,
    567. See also mid-phrase pause
stop vs. end. See end vs. stop
Straus, Joseph, 151n.4, See also Burstein, L.
    Poundie, and Joseph Straus
Stravinsky, Igor, 385
stream (bass line), 26–28, 29–31, 182–83,
    432–96, 536–37
stream (cadential melody), 63, 64, 65, 70

stretto, 351–52
stretto fugue, 352n.112
structure vs. design, 8
*Stufentheorie* (theory of steps), 21
style, 4–5, 8
subdominant
    as anticipation harmony, 514
    as appoggiatura harmony, 514, 530–33
    essentially prolongational, 24
    fugue, emphasized toward end of, 376–78
    interpolated between dominant and
        tonic, 530
    in lowered leading-tone abandonment,
        shifted to, 365–66
    as polar opposite to dominant, 506–7,
        511, 567–69
    in postcadential context, emphasized,
        147–49
    prolongation, 516–17
    in nineteenth century, increasing use of,
        58n.19
subdominant arrival, 506–9, 511, 537–38,
    542n.108
    allusion to dominant, 507, 542n.108
    with augmented-sixth harmony, 507–8
    enharmonic shift, 507–8
    vs. tonic arrival, 509
subject-ending cadence, 355–56, 367–68,
    370–71, 372–75, 377–78
    blurring, 367
    deceptive, 364
    embraces prior episode and/or subject
        entry, 367
    emphasis in exposition, 369–70
    ends complete fugue, 361–64
    ends exposition, 357–60, 372
    feigns independence, 361, 373n.153
    fewer, in *Well-Tempered Clavier*, book 2,
        356n.134
    as formal/tonal potentiality, 355–56
    structurally weaker than independent
        cadences, 361
    subject amenable to, but unrealized, 356
subject entry, 351–52, 367, 374
subject (fugue), 344–45, 351–52
    and cadence of limited scope, 355–56,
        357–58
    ends with cadential bass line, 372
    ends with cadential material, 344–45
    as initiating function, 353–54, 355, 361
    modulating, 370–71, 372
    not amenable as subject-ending, 356
submetrical insertion, in bass of Prinner,
    385
subordinate harmony, 22, 30–31
subordinate theme
    in A section (scherzo), 496–98
    authentic cadential content, abundance
        of, 427–28
    begins with continuation, 244–45, 248–
        49, 281–82, 398, 424

begins with standing on the dominant,
    424
cadential requirement of, 82
ends with IAC, 82, 119n.190
final cadence of, 17–18
in galant, 419–23
incipient baroque case of, 333
lacks cadential closure, 43, 82, 119n.190,
    287–89, 468, 468n.119, 552–53, 573–75
in recapitulation, 18–19
reinterpreted HC in, 123
reminiscent of, 566–67
return to home key in, 500n.11
in rondo, 82, 119n.190
two-part, 119, 428–29
subordinate-theme function, 33
Subotnik, Rose Rosengard, 479–80n.150
substage, 56–57
substitute harmony, 22, 119
successively combined pattern, 70–72, 261
    alto and soprano, 70, 261, 264, 265
    alto and tenor, 70, 264, 265
    in converging HC, 110–11
    with IAC, 268
    tenor and simple, 273
    tenor and soprano (and/or alto), 70–71,
        263–64
    See also tenor combo
Sulzer, Johann Georg, 157n.20, 209–10
surprise, 151, 154, 163n.39
Sutcliffe, Dean, 316n.33, 379n.2
symmetrical grouping structure, 103, 443–
    44, 478, 481–82
synoptic perspective, 7, 8–9, 247–48, 514
syntactical emphasis/strength/weight, 51
    with HC, 117–18
    incomplete vs. complete cadential
        progression, 60
    vs. rhetorical, 46, 50–54, 79n.59, 208,
        335–36, 367
syntactical/primary parameter, 5, 6
syntax
    apparent violation of, 117–18, 447–48,
        470, 484, 525n.69
    of cadence types, 32–33
    and closure, 5, 6–7
    of form, 491, 526
    of harmony, 439, 491, 512, 517, 526
    of narrativity, 7

tempo marking, change in, 325–26
temporality, 5, 7, 8, 9
tenor cadence (*clausula tenorizans*), 306,
    380, 382–84
tenor combo, 46, 71–72, 78, 88–90,
    187, 263
    in the manner of, 110–11
    variants of, 263
tenor melodic pattern. See basic tenor
    pattern; varied tenor pattern

terminal dominant
  characteristics of, 187
  dominant arrival on, 192–93, 333n.66
  vs. final dominant, 187, 198–99, 208
  formal function of, 192–93
  as sequential link, 195–98, 200–2
terminal modification, 3–4, 33–34, 324–25, 361n.136, 436n.18, 481, 482. *See also* repetition/terminal modification paradigm
textural anomaly, 225n.7
textural types, 139
  accompaniment "without" melody, 198
  doubled monophony, 76, 114–15, 139, 144, 197–98, 245, 265, 547
  drum bass, 47, 139, 189, 216
  homophony/chordal/block-like, 139, 140
  melody and accompaniment, 76, 139
  polyphony, 139
  unison/monophony, 114–15, 139
texture
  associated with final dominant, 188–89
  bass voice, identification of, 140, 144
  and cadential ambiguities, 212, 554–55, 557
  and cadential syntax, 139
  continuous, obscures grouping boundary, 188–89
  as criterion for rhetorical strength, 139
  prolongational closure, 146
  reduction in, 547
  rhythmic stop/caesura, 139
  registral shift signals cadential progression, 28, 139, 258–59
  soprano voice, identification of, 140
thematic function, 79n.54
thematic process, 42–43n.160
theme, 16
theme and variations, 298, 327
themelike unit, 16
theme type, 16
tight-knit organization, 45, 269
time point, 8, 19n.44, 31, 32
time span, 8–9, 31–32
time-span reduction, 18–19
timpani, as bass voice, 499n.10
tonic arrival, 349–50, 477–78, 496–503, 536–37
  vs. plagal closure, 523
  vs. subdominant arrival, 509

tonic six-four, 297–98, 307–8. *See also,* cadential six-four; stage 3
"too early"/premature. *See under* cadence; Chopin; consecutive/repeated cadences; penultimate dominant;
Tovey, Donald Francis, 32–33, 38–39, 316
transition
  in A section (scherzo), 496–98
  beginning of, 412–13
  concluding function, lack of, 43
  ends with PAC, 81–82
  ends with prolongational closure, 419n.95
  ends on tonic, 52
  in galant, 415
  incipient baroque case of, 333
  reinterpreted HC in, 123–24
  rhythmic and textural continuity, 50n.199
  ⇒second main theme, 182
transitional introduction, 198n.111, 199n.118
transition-like core substitute, 198–99
trill. *See* cadential trill
trio, truncated, 198
Tristan harmony, 511, 575, 579–81
Tristan resolution, 271–72n.89, 511
two-gapped model (bass line), 28–30
two-part subordinate theme, 119


ultimate dominant, 22–23, 152, 468
  vs. penultimate dominant, 52, 78n.51, 101–4, 187n.91, 217, 315–16, 463, 468–69, 519–20, 554–55, 560
  ⇒penultimate, 567
unison half cadence, 114–15
*Ursatz*, 6, 7, 8, 19–20


van de Laar, Frank, 468
Vande Moortele, Steven, 140–42, 182n.78, 299n.147, 432n.3, 433n.8, 437n.26, 447n.56, 544n.112, 570.151, 573n.155, 575
varied alto pattern, 69–70, 263
varied simple pattern, 69, 261
  ascending chromaticism in ECP, 262
  in converging HC, 107
  in simple HC, 106, 273

varied soprano pattern, 69, 263
varied tenor pattern, 70, 263, 389n.32
*Vordersatz* (of *Fortspinnungstypus*), 334–35


Wagner, Richard, 151, 511, 550
Walther, Johann Gottfried, 365n.145, 380
way-station cadence
  deceptive cadence, replacing PAC, 157, 158–60
  deceptive cadence, replacing IAC, 157, 160–62
  denied, 162–64, 175
  evaded cadence, 175
  followed (rarely) by initiating material, 94, 158, 217, 287–89
  followed by other provisional cadences or deviations, 94, 158
  followed by new material, 94, 160
  followed (never) by standing on the dominant, 119
  vs. IAC, 94, 158–60, 523n.66
  imperfect authentic cadence, 93–94
  vs. independent cadence, 94, 96
  vs. internal HC, 119
  as loosening device, 94–95
  with main theme, 95–96, 158
  with period, 158
  repeats preceding material, 158–60
  with subordinate theme, 94–95
Webster, James, 34, 39, 51n.205, 298n.141, 500n.11
  anti-period, 33n.108, 36–37, 117n.182
  cadence phrase, 32–33
  form of Beethoven's Ninth-Symphony finale, 298n.143
Weise, Hans, 8
Westergaard, Peter, 17n.27, 21n.56
Wild, Jon, 522–23
Wyatt, Thomas, 4


Yust, Jason, 48n.186, 138n.238


Zarlino, Gioseffo, 150
Zhang, Xieyi (Abby), 86n.95, 94n.117, 117n.181, 142n.254, 280n.98